D1370593

# North Carolina:
# People and Environments
Second Edition

For more information contact:
The Authors at Appalachian State University
Department of Geography and Planning
Boone, North Carolina 28608
www.geo.appstate.edu


Library of Congress Cataloging-in-Publication Data

Gade, Ole.
    North Carolina : people and environments / Ole Gade, Arthur B. Rex, James E. Young ;
    with L. Baker Perry.—2nd ed.
        p. cm.
    Includes bibliographical references (p.) and index.
    ISBN 1-887905-63-4 – ISBN 1-887905-64-2 (pbk.)
        1. North Carolina—Description and travel. 2. North Carolina—Geography. 3. North
    Carolina—Pictorial works. I. Rex, Art. II. Young, James E. III. Title.

    F254 .G33 2002
    917.56—dc 21                                   2002025265

About the Cover:

1) This old, renovated mill site in a traditional rural setting in Randolph County might soon feel
   the pressures of exurban development.

2) This fall scene, showing the rugged terrain of Grandfather Mountain, is a mixture of spruce-
   fir and deciduous forests. This photo is located just off of the Linn Cove Viaduct in Avery
   County. (photo by Mike Mayfield)

3) Townhouses, close to Charlotte in Mecklenburg County, are overshadowed by the Bank of
   America building in the backgound.

4) The Currituck lighthouse is one of eight along North Carolina's coast that serve to protect
   ocean vessels from dangerous off shore currents.

5) This winter scene in the western North Carolina mountains is the dream of every winter
   sport enthusiast. A cross country skier prepares for a refreshing trek along the trails of
   Moses Cone Park, part of the Blue Ridge Parkway in Watauga County.

Front Cover Photographs

Back Cover Photograph

Layout and Cover Design by Arthur B. Rex

# North Carolina: People and Environments

Second Edition

Ole Gade

Arthur B. Rex

James E. Young

with L. Baker Perry

2002

Parkway Publishers, Inc.
Boone, North Carolina

*This book is dedicated in memory of*

## Robert (Bob) E. Reiman, Ph.D.

"Studying regional geography is much like studying the contents of a garbage can. Everything in there derives in some way from the physical environment, but has been fashioned by people existing in a certain cultural context, and in a particular time and place. And you never quite know what you will get when you reach into the can to pick up an object, nor will you immediately be aware of the many items to which it is attached. Some objects reflect the great contribution they have made to mankind, and others the incredible waste of earth environments generated in their manufacture and use." Garbage Can Geography? Students loved Robert Ellis Reiman's evocative approach to the complex mysteries of people and land in regions ranging from their own neighborhood, to the state, the nation, and the world at large. Bob Reiman's altruistic and holistic world view derived from the ability of always seeing the positive and constructive in the rich experiences of his own life. A Pennsylvania childhood, training as a baker's apprentice, World War II action as Air Force Intelligence Officer and pilot with retirement in the rank of Major in 1957, and attaining a Ph.D. in geography education at Florida State University, prepared him for a teaching career at Appalachian State University. Working initially as the University Coordinator of Long Range Planning and serving as Dean of University Research Services, Bob returned to the Department of Geography and Planning as the full time coordinator of the undergraduate planning program. As a result he influenced the professional training and demeanor of a very large number of planners and city managers now working in North Carolina. Following his appointment as Professor Emeritus at Appalachian State University, Bob expanded his late life career working as a professor of geography at Pembroke State University and St Andrews Presbyterian College. He continued to serve his professional capacities as geography educator with years of contributions to the World Geography Bowl, and as community and regional planner, doing strategic plan consultancy for rural counties and work for the North Carolina Chapter of the American Planning Association. In his leisure time (?) he was an active researcher of problems of land and life in economically marginal regions in North Carolina, and contributed his findings to an international university consortium on planning in marginal areas. Death found the indefatigable Bob Reiman in his late seventies at work as the first full time zoning administrator for Scotland County, having earlier completed and directed that county's Geographic Information System. Those of us privileged to fly with him to far reaches of the world, literally or metaphorically, dedicate this volume to the memory of Robert Ellis Reiman, long term teacher, advisor and friend to countless students and colleagues of planning and geography in North Carolina and the world.

iv

# Preface

## FIRST EDITION

Throughout its long history, the science of geography has developed and grown with humanity's expanding need to understand, respond to and interact with, perhaps even to dominate and control the local, regional and world environments. In the process, geography has moved in many directions and taken a variety of definitions. Its dominant task as a science, however, derives from the problems associated with the interaction of people, place, and environment.

In *North Carolina: People and Environments* we are assessing the contemporary geography of the state and projecting its future prospects. Wherever possible, we attempt to convey our findings through a variety of illustrations, with the hope of allowing the reader to develop a more intimate sense of place and environment.

As a state in the Sunbelt, North Carolina is witnessing a considerable immigration of people. Many counties throughout the state are experiencing economic growth verging on "boom" conditions. We are finding that accelerating shifts in patterns of land use, from predominantly rural to urban, industrial and leisure use activities, are causing considerable stress on the state's natural resources.

This is occurring while North Carolinians continue to take pleasure from the state's image as essentially rural. At present close to 50 percent of the people live in nonmetropolitan areas. However, the tentacles of urban North Carolina are now reaching deep into the rural areas to influence changes that rural and small town communities are ill equipped to handle. Many of these communities are feeling the evolution of an either/or situation. They are either facing a lack of employment opportunities, outmigration of the labor force, economic decay, and serious tears in the traditional family and social fabric; or they are facing, unprepared, the onslaught of suburban and exurban expansion. This change brings accelerating demand on community services and all-too-frequent disruptive and negative impacts on regional environmental resources and local ecological systems.

A basic laissez faire public attitude produces major problems for the state's physical environment, significantly affecting the quality of life. For example, the aesthetics of mountain and seashore vistas are negatively affected by the penchant of some commercial interests to capitalize on the scenery. A Ridge Law and a Coastal Areas Management Act may be only temporary holding actions, though they do reflect the existence of a deeper public concern about the future of the land. In contrast with the gluttonous consumerism (of land) and unplanned growth in selected parts of the state, we do find large portions of North Carolina to be relatively unaffected by growth, but for how long?

North Carolina retains a great potential for marshaling its diversity of human resources toward an improved quality of life, while protecting its sensitive environments for future generations. The key is for people to understand the character and problems of the environment, life, and livelihood.

So we speak in this volume to schoolteachers. May they aid our state's new generation to learn well the geographic character and problems of their home state. We speak to college students, the leaders and providers of the state's future. We speak to the leaders in business and professional occupations, as well as to public servants, of the problems of a state in the throes of change, that they may move positively and swiftly to identify and correct ills, and to plan wisely for the future. Most of all, we speak to all North Carolinians whom we hope will take a nurturing pride in their state. Our hope is that North Carolina will evolve into a land where quality of life considerations are fed by a conscious demand for a harmonious relationship between people and their local and regional environments.

## SECOND EDITION

The above statements constitute selected passages from the Preface of the first edition of this work. How many of these comments and admonitions need changing some fifteen years later? North Carolina continues to be in the throes of changes that dramatically affect natural environments and inhabited neighborhoods, and not necessarily in a positive direction. Urbanization is on a rampage, with sprawl eating up rural and open space lands to the speculators' profit and many citizens' despair. Although socio-economic conditions have generally improved, a widening gap is developing between wealthy and poor North Carolinians. These and a myriad of aspects of life, livelihood, and nature are explored in this second edition, using the most recent statistical data, including 2000 Census information provided up to November, 2001. We present these aspects using top of the line cartographic and geographic information systems technologies. The results of much of this are seen here for the first time in a general text on the state.

A general reader will find this volume to have more than doubled in size; this was necessary to better provide the details of information from the local to the state level. Visualizing state environments on all geographic levels has been facilitated by the extensive use of maps, charts, aerial and ground photography, and statistical tables. The total illustration count is 861 items, including 257 maps (31 in full color), 379 photos (234 in full color, and 225 other illustrations. So much information is provided that interested readers should be able find the details and analysis needed to write and illustrate a regional geography of their own locality or county. Alexander County, for example, is specifically referred to/analyzed in the text fifteen times, while aspects of its human and natural conditions are illustrated in about 200 maps, photos, and other illustrations. Parenthetically, we should note that all color photos have indicated source, but also that black and white photos have all been taken by Ole Gade, unless otherwise shown. Ease of access to the complex of information in this text is facilitated by four indexes provided at the end, plus a very comprehensive bibliography that is referenced profusely in the body of the text.

While structuring the text to provide critical information for understanding aspects of land, life, and livelihood at the onset of the 3rd millennium, our objective was also to provide an analytic framework that allows citizens of the state to see where current public policy needs fine tuning, if not changing, to enhance quality of life conditions across the state, for the entire population, as well as for the state's fragile natural environments. Three major sections in the text define the holistic nature of the state's contemporary geography: I. Physical environments – Chapters 1-3; II. Human environments – Chapters 4-7, with Chapter 8 providing the critical linkage between the two major environments by assessing how we humans are impacted by the natural environment, and how we in turn influence change in its essential character; and III. Regional environments – Chapters 9-13, where Chapter 9 establishes the need to move from a state level of analyzing conditions to the major regions, and finally to individual counties; the purpose being to bring a more detailed focus on the character and problems of nature and human existence. Discerning school teachers and students of the state's complex physical and social geography will be able to easily navigate the chapters for information on the Five Themes of Geography, as included in the K-12 requirements of the North Carolina State Department of Public Instruction. They will find a progression of information sequentially focusing on the natural environment (three chapters), the human environment (five chapters), and the state's regional environments (five chapters). The authors have devised a hierarchical system of regions from the state level, to four primary state regions, thirteen state geographic regions, counties and municipalities, and finally, to communities and neighborhoods. Many readers will find reasons to object to our boundary definitions. We hope to hear from you both in positive and critical terms, on these, and on other aspects that you feel need an airing to the authors of the text.

We have high expectations of the readers of this volume. On the one hand, we wish to enable readers to be able to see themselves as functioning members of their home communities, from where they have the knowledge to critically assess the varying human and physical environmental conditions across the state. On the other hand, we wish for the readers to understand the conditions of life and environments within the different regions of the state well enough to see their linkage to their own communities and impact on their own lives. Our North Carolina world is comprised of a web of interrelationships, where individual behaviors aggregate to influence the lives of others and of all natural environments, and where public and private decision making, no matter the level of government or region at which it is made, will eventually spread its impact to surrounding lands and communities. For example, a federal decision to interfere with natural processes operating on the outer banks by hardening the shoreline, by relocating masses of sand, by diverting inlets, or by dredging ship channels, will definitively affect the lives of people living in mountain communities or center city neighborhoods. While involvement in the public decision making process at the local level seems to be catching on, it is much less clear that this transfers to a commitment for personal involvement at a higher level. And politicians are notably impoverished in their ability to clearly identify state level problems in the context of their locality implications. A new definition of sustainable communities is called for. A definition that, while energized to reflect the intimacy of the North Carolina human-natural environment interface, also recognizes the life supporting attributes of community and regional inter-dependencies, and appreciates the societal framework that unites us while setting us apart. (O. G..)

# Acknowledgments

For a work of this nature and scale, many people from all walks of life have made significant contributions. As authors of the second edition of a work first published in 1986, we are grateful for the groundwork contributed by initial co-author, H. Daniel Stillwell, and we welcome Jim Young (cartographer and editor) and Baker Perry (Chapter 2) to the new edition team. The initial edition reflected the state of the art of geography. Comparing the two editions is a revelation of the incredible expansion this discipline has experienced in cartographic representation and remote sensing of the environment. This is a literal "coming of age" in geographic information systems technology. Note, for example, the use of satellite imagery in the compilation of the North Carolina Land Cover Map (Figure 1.14), whose digital files were developed by the North Carolina Center for Geographic Information and Analysis; we owe thanks especially to former director Karen Siderelis and her crew of GIS experts. These files were subsequently mapped in Appalachian State University's GIS and Image Processing Laboratory under the skillful guidance of Art Rex, and used to develop the 13 regional land cover maps found in Chapters 10-13. Our appreciation goes foremost to the chairs of Appalachian's Department of Geography and Planning, Drs. Neal Lineback and Michael Mayfield, who have encouraged and supported this effort with assistantships, released time and departmental resources. We thank Appalachian Voices and the Project for Appalachian Community and Environment for contributing their splendid map of Appalachian environmental encroachment (Color Plate 13.15).

A long list of graduate and undergraduate students who were helpful in generating maps and other illustrations include: Kevin Benge, Rebecca Bryzski, April Candler, Steve Candler, Steve Carpenter, Steve Dettbarn, Elise Fisher, Bill Fredenberg, Steven Gause, Travis Hamrick, Bert Hatchell, Rebecca Hobson, Danny Kiser, David Lambert, Heather Mann, Angela Merryman, Keith Miller, Paul Mitchell, Andrew Osherow, Kevin Pearson, Melissa Reynolds, Lee Sandridge, George Shirey, Joshua Taylor, and John Yeager. Particular contributions include those of Scott Cecchi, whose research and maps on North Carolina's Green Heart are used in Chapter 12, and Justin Dupre, Ron Hancock, Chris Larson, Shannon Mann, and Eric Schmidt for their work in the Department's GIS & Image Processing Laboratory. Eric Neel provided much needed support in the initial layout of the volume, with the help of the staff of Minor's Printing Company in Boone.

Istvan Egresi, who provided the massive database of the four detailed indexes, and helped provide their final structure, has contributed stellar work.

We are indebted to many excellent photographers, including, Mary Burroughs, James Cook, Istvan Egresi, Dan Harris, Maria Mayerhofer, Michael Mayfield, Neal Lineback, John Luxton, Ehren Meister, Hugh Morton, Tom Ross, Dan Stillwell, Chris Walton, Chris Wilson, Kirk Wilson, and aviator extraordinaire, Bob Reiman. Equally we appreciate the contributions of the East Carolina University Media Office, North Carolina Department of Commerce (Division of Tourism), North Carolina Department of Environment and Natural Resources, Nucor Steel, Volvo-GM Truck Division, and the United States Geological Survey. We are thankful to artist Anne Runyon for her natural environment drawings that grace a number of pages in the regional chapters.

In the process of compiling information for so complex a project, many individuals and organizations have proven helpful. As will become obvious to the reader perusing the volume, the organizations include state, regional, and local government agencies, non-governmental organizations including many newspaper editors and journalists, business firms, and individuals far too many to mention. Our thanks and apologies go to those throughout the state who do not see their own contribution specifically acknowledged. Particular thanks go to Ane and Bjørn Gade, and many student assistants for the many weeks spent collecting, organizing, and filing background information.

The many chapters of the book received criticism and recommendations from a slate of reviewers, selected by the editors for their particular interest and expertise. Although we hold ourselves responsible for whatever commission of errors or neglect contained in the book we sincerely appreciate the time and effort given to the evaluation of chapters by Garry Cooper, Kathleen Schroeder, Rich Crepeau, Mike Mayfield, Neal Lineback, Tom Ross, D. Gordon Bennett, Ron Mitchelson, Robert Shepard, and Doug Wilms.

Those who suffer the greatest hardship during the preparation of a work that takes close to four years to complete are the authors' families. So we owe a very special debt of gratitude to our wives, Ane Gade, Jane Rex, and Carol Marchel, and to our children, Karen, Bo, Ashley, Cassie, and Jennings, now to hopefully gain more of our attention.

# Contents

# 12. PIEDMONT REGION

# 13. MOUNTAIN REGION

# List of Figures

xiv

# List of Tables

# List of Boxes

# About the Authors

Pictured (left to right) Ole Gade, Art Rex, and Jim Young.

Ole Gade is Professor of Geography and Planning and former Chair of the Department at Appalachian State University, where he has taught since 1970. He received his Ph.D. in Geography from Michigan State University, his Masters in Geography and a Bachelors in Economics from Florida State University. He has published extensively in the areas of human migration and regional and community development, emphasizing North Carolina and Nordic conditions and issues. In 1992 he was the founding editor of the North Carolina Geographer, a journal he edited for five years.

Art Rex is Lecturer of Geography and Planning with the Department at Appalachian State University since 1981. He received his Masters degree in Geography from Appalachian and his Bachelors from Slippery Rock University in Pennsylvania. His expertise areas are physical geography, Geographic Information Systems and Image Processing. Mr. Rex has received several awards for map publications utilizing computer technologies.

James E. Young is an Associate Professor and Chair, beginning fall of 2002, in the Department of Geography and Planning at Appalachian State University. He has been on the faculty at Appalachian since 1993, teaching classes in cartography, world regional geography, United States and Canada, remote sensing, and research themes and methods. He earned a Ph.D. and Masters in geography at the University of Minnesota, as well as Masters of Education and Bachelors in psychology at the University of Wisconsin-LaCrosse. Dr. Young serves as Co-coordinator of the North Carolina Geographic Alliance, working with teachers across the state to improve geographic instruction in the schools. His interests include map design and production, children's use of maps, history of cartography, and geographic education.

# 1

# Physical Environments

## INTRODUCTION

### Physical Geography

North Carolina's physical environment varies over the state. In part, it is this diversity that makes the state's geography interesting. To understand North Carolina's people and environments a geographic appraisal of its physical environments is necessary. What then is physical geography and what is meant by a geographic appraisal? Geography is comprised of three branches, physical, cultural, and regional. Within each of these branches are many component parts. In physical geography these parts include water (hydrology, oceanography), animal and plant life (zoogeography, biogeography), soils (soil science), rocks (geology), landforms (geomorphology), and weather and climate (meteorology, climatology). Physical geography is not just the study of these individual elements of the physical environment. It is the interaction of each with one another and with people. Physical geography helps to specify these relationships, and it emphasizes the "spatial" aspects of the relationships. This spatial component allows us to view and comprehend the patterns that comprise the earth's surface. Geographers create and use maps as the 'tool' to achieve this (through the art and science of cartography). Throughout this book there is extensive use of maps and graphics to help in viewing and analyzing the geographic perspectives of North Carolina. The science of geography provides understandings of the cause and effect of these elements and the processes that create the spatial patterns. The physical section (Chapters 1, 2 and 3) introduces the important elements of North Carolina's physical geography.

### Environmental Systems

Consideration of the physical setting requires discussion of the systems involved. Here is illustrated the three parts of our environment that involve and impact people (Figure 1.1). These parts of the physical setting are atmosphere, bio-hydrosphere, and lithosphere. We will look in some detail at how each contributes to the total physical environment, we will assess their implications for the people who live in the bio-hydrosphere, and we will define the impacts on the atmosphere and lithosphere across the state.

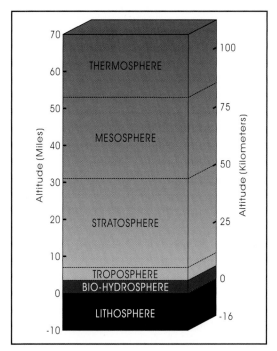

**Figure 1.1:** Physical Setting - Vertical Sections.

### Atmosphere

The atmosphere includes the "life-supporting" layer of air; its lowest level to about ten miles is known as the troposphere. It is within this zone that weather conditions occur. The atmosphere, particularly the troposphere, provides a most important natural resource: climate and its short-term character, weather. Most of North Carolina is situated in the climate region known as Humid Subtropical, although there are many variations of this throughout the state. Moisture is adequate throughout the year and is capable of supporting dense forests as well as a great variety of agricultural crops with only limited or localized irrigation or drainage needs. Temperatures are moderate with long summers and brief winters. Snow does occur throughout the state, but the mountains receive the steadiest supply throughout the winter months. Air masses accounting for this climate (Figure 1.2) are controlled by a variety of phenomena such as latitude, elevation, mountains, land cover characteristics, land and water surface differences, and more recently the possible impacts of 'el nino' and 'la nina'.

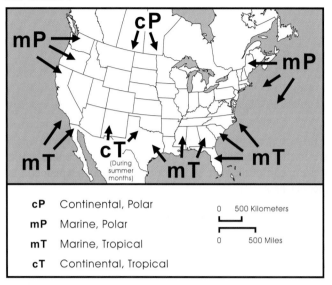

**Figure 1.2:** Air Mass Origins and General Circulation Patterns.

*Bio-hydrosphere*

The bio-hydrosphere is the thin layer where living organisms and water co-exist on the earth's surface. This includes the life layer of plants and animals as well as the surface waters that support this life and also modify the landscape. North Carolina's most dominant landscape characteristic is forest cover (Figure 1.3). The mountain and coastal regions include 26 counties having greater than 65% or more of their land in trees, while the Piedmont region has been modified heavily by human activities. A wide variety of human activity, in the Coastal Plains and Piedmont, has modified much of the vegetative cover through the management of pine forests for their commercial value. One thing is certain; this state exhibits great diversity from the western reaches of a Smoky Mountain valley to the eastern most edge of an exposed sand dune of a barrier island. Water resources in the

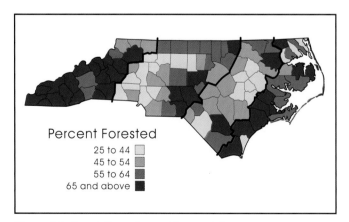

**Figure 1.3:** Forest Cover (percent by county).
**Source:** North Carolina Statistical Abstract 1994.

state are also an essential component of the physical environment. While the state receives an average annual precipitation of 122 centimeters (48 inches), precipitation ranges from 97 (38 inches) to just over 154 centimeters (100 inches). It is also important to note these variations and diversity throughout the state also characterize the systems that carry and deliver this water. These systems are discussed later in this chapter, as well as in Chapter 2.

*Lithosphere*

The lithosphere consists of surface materials and their formations downward to about 40 to 80 kilometers below the earth's surface. It is generally thought of as comprising not just the minerals and rocks but also the land surface, soils, and groundwater. Resources provided in the lithosphere are the foundation for vegetative growth, natural and managed, and some economic activities such as mining and energy production. Soils also take on new functions as areas are settled or urbanized. Soils not only produce trees and food, but also handle waste and construction, with their properties becoming increasingly important considerations. Soils are a complex mix of minerals derived from parent rock, organic matter from plant and animal life, water, and air. As a consequence, soils vary greatly according to rock type, climate, natural vegetation, location, elevation, degree of slope, solar orientation, and age. The coupling of these characteristics configure the land surface. Land surface is a product of the rock types and their associated tectonics or movement, as well as the erosional and depositional processes acting on them. Analyzing land surface form includes consideration of slope, local relief or changes in elevation, and profile type in addition to prominent ridgelines and summits, escarpments, water features, and sandy areas.

## PHYSICAL SETTING

### World and Regional Context

*Spatial Expanse*

The location of North Carolina on the earth has impacts on its physical environment. It is in the Western Hemisphere on the North American continent, and it is within the political jurisdiction of the United States of America. Within this context it has an East Coast setting that is centrally located between the states of Maine and Florida. North Carolina's norther- most border is 36°30' North Latitude while its southern-most extent is around 33°50' North Latitude. Its eastern-most edge is situated about the 75°20' West Longitude and the western extent reaches 84°25' West Longitude.

Comparatively speaking the state has a vast east to west expanse, as it is over 805 km (500 mi) wide. Its north to south expanse is not nearly as great, varying from 322 km (200 mi) in the eastern parts to 161 km (100 mi) in the west-central section to less than 40 km (25 mi) in the western most part. North Carolina has approximately 137,269 square kilometers (53,000 sq mi) of land area. CP1.1 illustrates the setting in the world and southeastern United States and shows the state's regions and counties. It is bordered to the north by Virginia, to the west by Tennessee, to the south by Georgia and South Carolina and to the east by the Atlantic Ocean. North Carolina is easily recognized by its long narrow form and the outer banks or barrier islands off the coast. This spatial expanse also helps explain some of the physical differences in the state.

## Geologic Activity

The theory of plate tectonics describes the earth's plates and their past and present interactions or movements and has influenced many aspects of geology. Tectonic activity is directly related to location on a plate. Around the edges of the plates is where the most violent activity occurs. North Carolina is centrally located on the North American plate. This does not mean that there is no tectonic activity. On the contrary, there are fault lines and earthquakes although currently there is little or no activity with critical impacts. However, we do know that there have been major geologic events that have affected this slice of the earth, such as the creation of the Appalachian Mountains and the uplifting of the Carolina coastal area. Box 1A illustrates recent geologic activity in the Carolinas.

The state is bordered by the Appalachian Mountains to the west and by the Atlantic Ocean to the east. Its elevation varies from sea level on the eastern most edges of the state to 2037 meters (6,684 ft) at the peak of Mount Mitchell in Mitchell County (CP 1.2), highest peak in the eastern United States.

## Weather and Climate

In this section we set the stage for understanding the basic elements of climate and weather. Weather and climate, critical aspects of our physical environment, are treated in detail in Chapter 2.

### Sun Angles

Earth-sun relationships are a key component in creating the varied environments of our planet, generating both daily (rotation) and seasonal (revolution) characteristics. The angle at which solar energy strikes the earth's surface varies with degree of latitude and with time of year. Resulting daily and seasonal rhythms in turn act as fundamental controls of air temperatures, winds, ocean circulation, precipitation, and storms – all of which taken together make up the earth's varied climates (Strahler 1987).

The earth's axis is tilted at 23.5 degrees from perpendicular. This means that the most direct rays, hence the strongest, of solar radiation are between 23.5 degrees north and south of the equator. Since North Carolina lies between 34 and 36.5 degrees north latitude, the strongest rays strike on June 21 (also known as the summer solstice). The weakest sun angle occurs on December 22 during the winter solstice. Figure 1.4 illustrates the sun's noon angle at the equator, a mid-latitude location (35.5 degrees north latitude, which is representative of North Carolina's

average latitudinal location), and a high latitude location. At each of these locations note the total land area that the sun's rays are concentrated on. The angle at which the sun's rays strike the surface is referred to as the angle of incidence. At North Carolina's average latitudinal location the noon angle of incidence varies from about 78 degrees for summer to 31 degrees for winter, and causes marked seasonal differences in the amount and intensity of solar energy received and thus the average air temperature.

In addition to the solar angle, the length of daylight also influences air temperature. Hours of daylight received at the latitude of North Carolina vary from a maximum of 14.5 during summer to a minimum of 9.5 during winter. Temperature differences are further complicated by the mountain environments in the western part of the state (this particular aspect is explained further in Chapter 2).

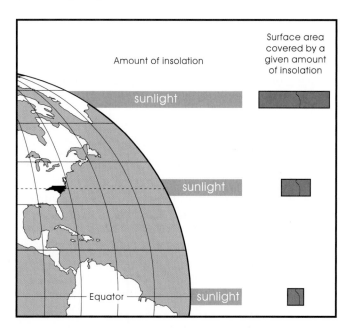

**Figure 1.4:** Sun's Noon Angles. Varying mid-day insolation intensity is illustrated for three distinct latitudinal environments: equator, mid-latitude, and high latitude.
**Source:** Modified from McKnight, 1997.

### Atmospheric Heating and Air Masses

Solar radiation is the only important source of energy reaching the earth's surface and atmosphere. Incoming solar radiation is referred to as insolation. Insolation has daily, as well as seasonal, variations. Additionally, the heating and cooling of different surfaces also varies greatly. Variation of surface conditions causes differential heating and cooling. In other words, the properties of different surfaces will dictate the rate at which surfaces heat and cool. For example, if the same amount of insolation is received by land and water surfaces, land will heat more rapidly than water, and land will also reach a higher temperature than water. However, land also loses heat rapidly while water will maintain a more stable temperature. Surface differentials in turn helps

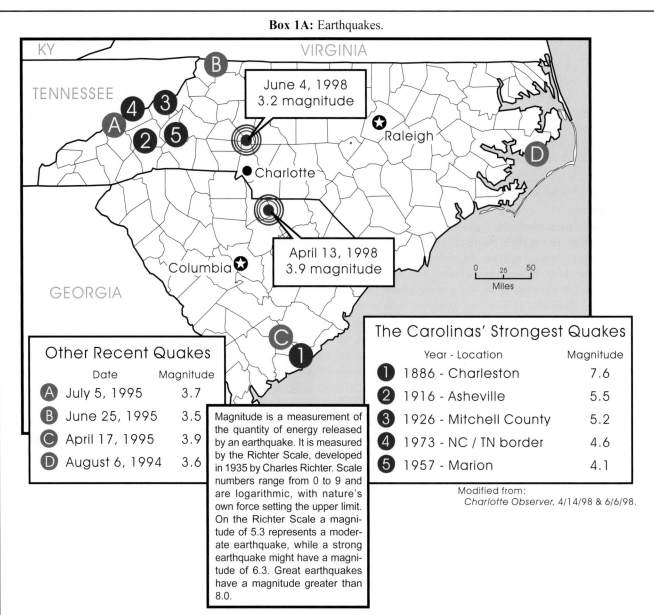

**Box 1A:** Earthquakes.

June 4, 1998
3.2 magnitude

April 13, 1998
3.9 magnitude

0   25   50
Miles

## Other Recent Quakes

| | Date | Magnitude |
|---|---|---|
| A | July 5, 1995 | 3.7 |
| B | June 25, 1995 | 3.5 |
| C | April 17, 1995 | 3.9 |
| D | August 6, 1994 | 3.6 |

Magnitude is a measurement of the quantity of energy released by an earthquake. It is measured by the Richter Scale, developed in 1935 by Charles Richter. Scale numbers range from 0 to 9 and are logarithmic, with nature's own force setting the upper limit. On the Richter Scale a magnitude of 5.3 represents a moderate earthquake, while a strong earthquake might have a magnitude of 6.3. Great earthquakes have a magnitude greater than 8.0.

## The Carolinas' Strongest Quakes

| | Year - Location | Magnitude |
|---|---|---|
| 1 | 1886 - Charleston | 7.6 |
| 2 | 1916 - Asheville | 5.5 |
| 3 | 1926 - Mitchell County | 5.2 |
| 4 | 1973 - NC / TN border | 4.6 |
| 5 | 1957 - Marion | 4.1 |

Modified from:
*Charlotte Observer,* 4/14/98 & 6/6/98.

On April 13, 1998, an earthquake that measured 3.9 in magnitude shook the Piedmont. Its epicenter was 25 miles north-northeast of Camden, South Carolina. Almost two months later on June 4; another quake occurred had a magnitude of 3.2. Its epicenter was 10 miles northwest of Kannapolis, near Mooresville, and between 10 to 15 miles under ground. We are not in California, but we are still susceptible to geologic activity. Faults, which are deep underground in the Carolinas, can produce these 'minor' quakes. Pressure builds up and after decades of silence is released rapidly by the earth's movement; this movement is known as an earthquake. The figure above illustrates recent quake activity. Predicting quakes within a specified time period is difficult to impossible, but selecting locations of the most likely area of occurrence is more realistic. Quakes can create a lot of panic and fear because people in the Carolinas are just not accustomed to dealing with them. There were no reports of injuries or significant damage for the June 4 quake, but for a few seconds, it shook buildings, rattled windows, and scared a lot of residents near Lake Norman (Charlotte Observer 1998). Although it appears that we are not in any present danger, scientists warn that there may be a future quake with a magnitude of 6.0 or better on the East Coast. The most likely epicenters, Charleston, South Carolina and eastern Tennessee, are not in the state. However, they are close enough that considerable damage could occur. Safety precautions have been taken in the construction of Duke Energy Corporation's two nuclear facilities, McGuire Nuclear Station near Lake Norman and the Catawba Nuclear Station, to withstand such a quake.

to generate the characteristics of the atmosphere above a particular surface or region. Air above a large water body will maintain its temperature and will also contain moisture placed into the atmosphere through evaporation. Conversely, air above a landmass will have little moisture present in it. Air masses are then circulated or moved across the earth's surface. North Carolina is affected by maritime tropical (warm and moist) air masses formed over the Gulf of Mexico and the Atlantic Ocean. In addition, the state is impacted by continental polar air mass (dry and cool in winter, but quite warm in summer) formed over the continental interior region. Air masses, their origins, and global circulation pattern help to generate our daily weather (Figure 1.2).

The atmosphere, especially in the lower level of the troposphere, defines a most important natural resource, climate, and its short-term character, weather. North Carolina lies within a general climate region known as Humid Subtropical. Through our lifetime we don't expect climate conditions to vary greatly, but all of us are impacted daily by weather. As mentioned earlier, air masses accounting for climate are controlled by a variety of phenomena that impact global circulation patterns. All of these phenomena make us aware that climate is an important resource, and we are also fully aware of the devastating effects it may have in influencing the weather of our daily lives. It influences the way in which we dress for the day, the way we build our homes, where we choose to live in the state, and many other facets. In most cases, we have adapted well to the limits of our physical environment. But, no matter how well we do this, nature reminds us periodically to respect its power. Localized and widespread effects of hurricanes, tornadoes, floods, power outages, and frost damage to crops are some of the problems directly relating to the atmosphere which have implications on human activities. More subtle problems involve the degradation of air and water quality, long-term effects of vegetation modification, land surface changes, and hazardous waste disposal. All of these are reminders of nature's force.

## Primary Regions

The flat surface of the coast contrasts greatly with the mountains of the west. As noted earlier, North Carolina is a state with diverse physical and cultural characteristics from the eastern most reaches of Cape Hatteras (CP 1.3) to its western most border south of the Great Smoky Mountains (CP 1.4). Elevations range from sea level to peaks exceeding 1,829 meters (6,000 ft).

Such a varied landscape makes it difficult to categorize and characterize the state without considering the regional context and its spatial variability.

Geographers recognize four primary regions within North Carolina (Chapter 9). These are the Mountains, Piedmont, Coastal Plain, and Tidewater regions (see CP 1.1). The number of counties associated with each region, amount of area (both land and water) covered by each and the percent of the state each region covers are illustrated in Table 1.1. Each primary region is endowed with suitable physical and cultural similarities to clearly distinguish it from the others. Mapping data to discover the spatial patterns that emerge within the state is a common tool in gaining a geographer's view or "geographic perspective." Comparing mapped variations within and between regions can often help define areas of high or low concentrations or the setting of a particular activity and the placing of it within the state's spatial context. Throughout this text maps allow the reader to note coincidences between and among different variables and to place these within a regional context. Our four primary regions are used extensively and an understanding of each of their component parts is needed.

Changes in the physical landscape are apparent as one moves through the state. While they may not be as pronounced from south to north as they are from east to west, these variations do impact people and their activities. Geographers are interested in why things occur where they do, and often answers affecting people and their livelihood are found in the physical geography of the state.

### Lay of the Land

Among the important components that help create the physical landscape are land cover (vegetation), elevation, slope, aspect or direction of slope, soils, and geology. People and their cultural activities have over the centuries modified these components, and thus shaped the complexities of the landscape mosaic that exists in North Carolina today.

#### Geology

Emerald was designated as the state's precious stone in 1973 and granite, in 1979, was named as the state rock. Geographers ask what caused these to be abundant and important resources of the state. Where do these resources exist, what is their spatial extent, and are they coupled with other resources or

| Regions | Number of Counties | Land Area (km. sq.) | Land Area (mi. sq.) | Percent of Total |
|---|---|---|---|---|
| Mountain | 24 | 26,367 | 10,180 | 20.9 |
| Piedmont | 35 | 42,535 | 16,423 | 33.7 |
| Coastal Plain | 22 | 34,543 | 13,337 | 27.4 |
| Tidewater | 19 | 22,735 | 8,778 | 18.0 |
| **State Totals** | **100** | **126,180** | **48,817** | **100.0** |

**Table 1.1:** The State's Primary Regions.

economic activity within the state? The earth formed four and one-half billion years ago. North Carolina, as we know it today, is relatively young when thinking of it in the context of the age of the earth. Three major classes of rock types common in the state are igneous, metamorphic, and sedimentary. Figure 1.5 illustrates the generalized geologic structure with major fault lines and the varying major classes of rock types. This begins our basic understanding of the state's geology.

North Carolina has a long and complex geologic history. Periods of uplifting and subsidence, along with accompanying erosion and deposition of materials have helped provide our current geologic setting. Sea floor spreading has caused the North American continental plate to shift westward from an original position adjacent to North Africa and Western Europe. The many parallel fault lines throughout the state mark places where stress has been relieved. Pressure build up has caused a change or metamorphism of some rock such as the belts of metasedimentary rock, gneiss, schist, and Carolina slate in the Piedmont.

*Geologic Belts*

Understanding the state's spatial and temporal geologic relationships is essential. Areas of similar rock type and age, as well as geologic history, provide a description of the states geologic belts. Figure 1.5 illustrates an increasing age and complexity of rock types from east to west. Figure 1.6 shows the spatial characteristics of the state's 10 major geologic belts, and descriptions and examples of each belt follows.

The *Coastal Plain* is comprised of marine sedimentary rocks that gradually thicken toward the coast. It is the largest geologic belt, covering about 45 percent of the state's land area. Sand and clay are the most common sediment types in this belt, with a significant amount of limestone occurring in the southern part of the Coastal Plain. Well drilling information provides a valuable source of data of the depth and the spatial extent of this belt. Near Aurora, in Beaufort County, phosphate mining is the state's most important mineral resource in terms of dollar value (Photo 1.1). Phosphate is an important component in fertilizer. Additionally, mining of industrial sand (for producing container and flat glass) and ferrosilicon (which is used for filtration and sand-blasting) can be found in the Sand Hills (CP 1.5) (North Carolina Geologic Survey, 1991).

The *Eastern Slate Belt* contains slightly metamorphosed volcanic and sedimentary rocks similar to those of the Carolina slate belt. Rocks are poorly exposed and partially covered by Coastal Plain sediments. Metamorphic rocks, 500-600 millions years old, are intruded by younger, 300 million years old, granitic bodies. Gold was once mined in the area, while crushed stone, clay, sand, and gravel are still mined today (North Carolina Geologic Survey 1991).

Granite, gneiss, and schist comprise the geology of the *Raleigh Belt*. Earlier this century a number of small building stone quarries existed, but today crushed stone for construction and road aggregate support the extraction industry of this belt (North Carolina Geologic Survey 1991).

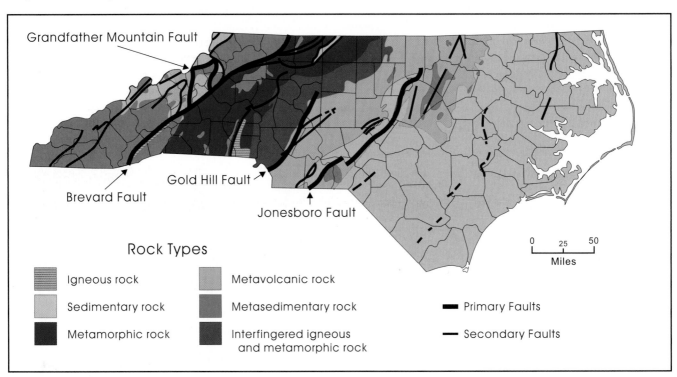

**Figure 1.5:** Rock Types and Faults.
**Source:** Modified from North Carolina Center of Geographic Information and Analysis, 1998.

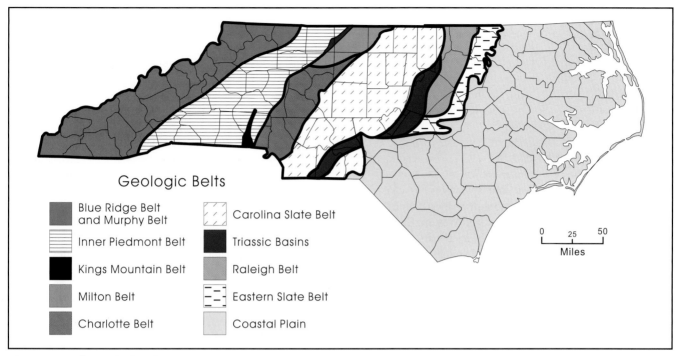

**Figure 1.6:** Major Geologic Belts.
**Source:** Modified from North Carolina Geologic Survey, 1991.

Geologic Belts

- Blue Ridge Belt and Murphy Belt
- Inner Piedmont Belt
- Kings Mountain Belt
- Milton Belt
- Charlotte Belt
- Carolina Slate Belt
- Triassic Basins
- Raleigh Belt
- Eastern Slate Belt
- Coastal Plain

*Triassic Basins* are filled with sedimentary rocks that formed about 100-190 million years ago. Streams carried mud, silt, sand, and gravel from nearby highlands into rift valleys (similar to those of Africa today). As can be seen in Figure 1.6, there are three locations of these basins within the state. Two are located in the eastern section, while the other is in the northwestern Piedmont region. Mudstones are mined and processed to make brick, sewer pipe, and structural and drain tile (North Carolina Geologic Survey 1991).

The *Carolina Slate Belt* consists of heated and deformed volcanic and sedimentary rocks. It was the site of a series of oceanic volcanic islands about 550-650 million years ago. Numerous abandoned gold mines dot the area, which reminds us that North Carolina led the nation in gold production prior to the 1849 California Gold Rush. Because companies are still showing interest, gold mining continues to be a minor extractive industry in this belt. Mineral production includes crushed stone for road aggregate and pyrophyllite for refractories, ceramics, filler, paint and insecticide carriers (North Carolina Geologic Survey 1991).

**Photo 1.1:** Near Aurora in Beaufort County is the largest phosphate mine in the state. An important component in fertilizer, phosphate is mined close to and sometimes extracted from under the Pamlico Sound. Phosphate is the state's most important resource in terms of dollar value.

**Photo 1.2:** Mining wastes are piled high above adjacent residential area, along NC 274 north of Bessemer City in Gaston County.

Further west lies the *Charlotte Belt* in the south and central sections with the *Milton Belt* to the north. Mostly igneous rocks from 300-500 million years old, such as granite (CP 1.6), diorite, and gabbro, comprise the Charlotte Belt (Photo 1.2). Gneiss, schist and other metamorphosed intrusive rocks make up the Milton Belt. Both of these belts provide good sources of crushed stone for road aggregate and some cut for building purposes (North Carolina Geologic Survey 1991).

The *Kings Mountain Belt*, the smallest belt in the state, consists of moderately deformed and metamorphosed volcanic and sedimentary rocks which are about 400-500 million years old. Lithium deposits here provide raw materials for chemical compounds, ceramics, glass, greases, batteries, and television glass (Photo 1.3) (North Carolina Geologic Survey 1991).

In the western most section of the Piedmont region, the *Inner Piedmont Belt* is the most intensely deformed and metamorphosed segment. Metamorphic rocks range from 500-750 million years in age. Younger granitic rocks have intruded areas of gneiss and schist (Photo 1.4). CP 1.7 shows the Stone Mountain State Park monadnock that is popular for recreational activities like hiking and climbing in Wilkes County. Forming the boundary between the Blue Ridge and the Inner Piedmont Belt is the northeast trending Brevard fault zone. Although this zone of strongly deformed rocks is one of the major structural features in the southern Appalachians, its origin is poorly understood. Crushed stone for road aggregate and building construction is the principal commodity extracted and produced. Photo 1.5 shows the largest open-face granite quarry in the world, located at Mount Airy (North Carolina Geologic Survey 1991).

**Photo 1.3:** Crowders Mountain, located just a few miles southwest of Gastonia in Gaston County and part of the Kings Mountain Belt, is composed of metamorposed volcanic-sedimentary rocks and is world-famous for its lithium deposits.

**Photo 1.4:** Some 25 miles north of Winston-salem in Surry County, this rural setting depicts the rolling terrain of the Inner Piedmont Belt and of the Piedmont region. The familiar silhouette of Pilot Mountain, one of the Piedmont granitic monadnocks, is in the background.

To the west is the mountainous region of the *Blue Ridge Belt.* It is composed of rocks from over one billion to about one-half billion years old and has a complex mixture of igneous, sedimentary, and metamorphic rock that have been repeatedly squeezed, fractured, faulted and twisted into folds (CP 1.8). Deposits of feldspar, mica, and quartz are basic materials used in the ceramic, paint, and electronic industries. Olivine is mined for use as refractory material and foundry molding sand. Precious stones of garnet, moonstone, ruby, saphire, aquamarine, amethyst, hiddenite, rutile, quartz, and emerald are found in this belt. The largest single emerald crystal found in North America was mined at the Rist Mine at Hiddenite in 1969 and weighed 1,438 carats. A 13.14 carat emerald cut gem, the Carolina Emerald, was also found at this mine (North Carolina Geologic Survey 1991).

North Carolina leads the nation with important mineral deposits including feldspar, lithium, scrap mica, olivine, and pyrophyllite. Additionally, the State ranks second in phosphate rock production and ranks in the top five in clay and crushed granite production. Figures 1.7a, b, and c show the spatial characteristics of mineral producing areas, mine earnings, and mining employment, respectively. It is important to note the role that geologic processes have and will continue to play in the relevant aspects of rocks and minerals, land surface, soils and groundwater potential (North Carolina Geologic Survey 1991).

Figure 1.8 illustrates the state's geologic time scale including the major geologic events. When comparing this table with the Generalized Geologic Map (CP 1.9) we see the spatial component of the geologic time scale as it exists today.

*Land Surface and Topography*

Elevation or topography varies across the state with the most marked difference in an east-west direction (CP 1.10). While this graphic does well to give us an idea of what the generalities of elevation are, a shaded relief map (CP 1.11) shows a more detailed and intricate design of the land surface within the state. A shaded relief depiction of the state allows us to better visualize the state's subtle relief changes. Relief is the local or regional change in elevation between high and low points of land surface.

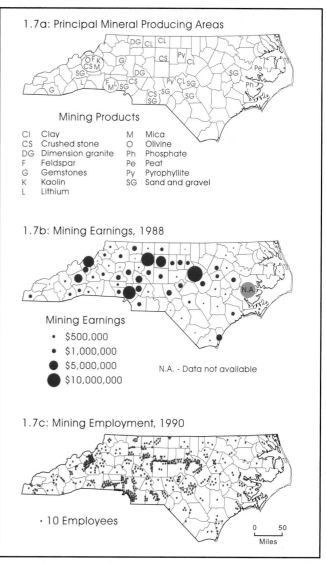

**Figure 1.7:** Mining Activity.
**Source:** Modified from North Carolina Geologic Survey, 1991.

9

| EON | ERA | PERIOD | EPOCH | | GEOLOGIC EVENTS IN NORTH CAROLINA | AGE* |
|---|---|---|---|---|---|---|
| Phanerozoic | Cenozoic | Quaternary | Recent | | Deposition of sediments in the Coastal Plain and Tidewater. Erosion of Piedmont and Appalachian Mountains to their present rugged features. | |
| | | | Pleistocene | | | 1.7 |
| | | Tertiary | Pliocene | | | 5 |
| | | | Miocene | | Phosphate deposited in eastern North Carolina (Beaufort and Pamlico counties). | 24 |
| | | | Oligocene | | Limestone deposited in the Coastal Plain and Tidewater. Weathering and erosion continue in Piedmont and Mountains. | 66 |
| | | | Eocene | | | |
| | | | Paleocene | | | |
| | Mesozoic | Cretaceous | Late | | Deposition of estuarine and marine sediments in the Coastal Plain and Tidewater. Continued erosion of the Piedmont and Mountains. | |
| | | | Early | | Sediments deposited in northern half of the Coastal Plain and Tidewater. Cape Fear Arch begins to develop. Piedmont and Mountains eroded. | 138 |
| | | Jurassic | Late | | Marine sediments deposited on outer continental shelf. Piedmont and mountains eroded. | |
| | | | Middle | | Weathering and erosion of the Blue Ridge and Piedmont areas. Emplacement of diabase dikes and sheets. | |
| | | | Early | | | 205 |
| | | Triassic | Late | | Faulting and rifting create Deep River, Dan River, and Davie County basins. Basins fill with continental clastic sediments known as "red beds". | |
| | | | Middle | | Formation of the Atlantic Ocean as North America and Africa drifted apart. Weathering and erosion of Piedmont and Mountains. | |
| | | | Early | | | 240 |
| | Paleozoic | Permian | | | Final collision of North America and Africa. Thrust faulting in west; deformation in eastern Piedmont. | 290 |
| | | Pennsylvanian | | Emplacement of igneous intrusions. | Time of uplift and erosion. | 330 |
| | | Mississippian | | | Time of uplift and erosion. | 360 |
| | | Devonian | | | Emplacement of lithium, mica, and feldspar-rich pegmatites, primarily in the Kings Mountain and Spruce Pine areas. Metamorphism of Carolina slate belt. Period of erosion. | 410 |
| | | Silurian | | | Time of uplift and erosion. | 435 |
| | | Ordovician | | | Continental collision and beginning of mountain building process - faulting, folding, and metamorphism of pre-existing rocks. | 500 |
| | | Cambrian | | | Sandstone, shale, and limestone deposited in Mountains. Continued deposition of Carolina slate belt rocks and gold deposits in the slate belt. | 570 |
| Proterozoic | Late | | | | Sedimentary and volcanic rocks deposited in the Mountains and Piedmont. Local Intrusions of igneous rocks. | 900 |
| | Middle | | | | Sedimentary and volcanic rocks formed in the Blue Ridge and metamorphosed to gneisses and schists. | 1,600 |
| | Early | | | | Oldest dated rock in North Carolina is 1,800 million years old. | 2,500 |

*Estimated age in millions of years.

**Figure 1.8:** Geologic Time Scale.
**Source:** Modified from North Carolina Geologic Survey, 1991.

**Photo 1.5:** At the Mt. Airy Granite Mining Company, Precambrian granite is being "peeled off" in one of the largest open-face granite quarry operation.

The eastern-most portion of the state begins at sea level with the outer banks (CP 1.12), a series of barrier islands separating the Atlantic Ocean and the sounds (Photo 1.6). These features are a result of sediments being moved by offshore currents as the coast slowly emerges (Box 1B). Poorly drained areas, sand flats, bays, and sounds characterize the Tidewater region (Photo 1.7). Westward across the Coastal Plain there is another noticeable change in elevation when one reaches the Fall Zone. Here elevation gradually increases to over 91 meters (300 ft) above sea level. As we approach this zone the land surface becomes gently rolling with the prominent Sand Hills on the southwest margin.

Further westward the Piedmont area consists of irregular rolling plains with a local relief of 30 to 91 meters (100 to 300 ft). Elevations reach 457 meters (1,500 ft) some 322 kilometers (200 mi) west of the Fall Zone. About 45 percent of the state is occupied by the Piedmont. From between one-half to three-quarters of its surface profile is in gentle slopes (up to 8%) on the upland surface. The term plateau is sometimes used in describing the Piedmont area. Remnants of more resistant rock, known as monadnocks, form high hills and crests. Often called mountains by the early settlers of the region, these include the Brushy Mountains in Alexander, Caldwell, and Wilkes Counties; Kings Mountain in Cleveland and Gaston Counties, Sauratown Mountains in Stokes County; South Mountains in Burke, Cleveland, and Rutherford counties; and the Uwharrie Mountains in Davidson, Montgomery, and Randolph counties (CP 1.13). Located close to the large population centers of the Piedmont Crescent the mountains provide recreational activities, camping, hiking, and fishing in the state and national forests, and game lands are popular leisure activities. The local terrain also proves to be easily formed into artificial lakes and reservoirs. These are used as water supplies for nearby cities, for flood control, and as open space for recreation.

**Photo 1.6:** Hatteras Island, where Sea Island Wildlife Refuge meets a small village with a considerable number of vacation homes. Note the low vegetation that helps stabilize these island dunes.

11

**Box 1B:** Barrier Island Formation.

Coastal barriers stretch in an irregular chain from Maine to Texas. These elongated, narrow landforms are composed of sand and other loose sediments transported by waves, currents, and wind. The term "barrier" identifies the structure as one that protects other features. North Carolina's barrier islands protect its mainland from the destructive effects of powerful storms (refer to Chapter 2) and their resulting waves. Barrier islands are dynamic landforms, and as such they are constantly changing. Popularity of these islands as vacation destinations has placed ever-increasing development pressures on these shifting landforms. This protection is vital to the productivity of estuary and lagoon habitats. Natural or human disturbances to these barrier islands will have an impact on this productivity (refer to Chapter 8 for Hurricane Floyd's impact) (Leatherman 1988).

Barrier islands can originate and develop in a number of different ways. However there are three main theories of barrier island genesis (Hoyt, Leatherman, and Dolan and Lins):

A) spit growth and later segmentation by inlets (a);

B) mainland beach ridge submergence (b); and

C) up-building of submarine bars

North Carolina's Outer Banks is best explained by Hoyt's model (b). These probably were once the dunes of ancient beaches formed when sea level was much lower. During the past 15,000 years rising seas breached the dune line, creating the shallow sounds behind them and leaving the dune islands high and dry (Figure 1.8) (Early 1993). Conversely, the Carolina capes may have evolved from Pleistocene-age river deltas formed when sea level was (91 m/300 ft) lower than present (a). As sea level rose these large deltaic sand bodies were reworked by waves and currents and pushed landward. In the process, sand spits could have grown off these eroding deltaic headlands, forming the barriers that eventually bridge the capes (Leatherman 1988).

Whatever the origin of these islands may be there is no question that they are attracting more and more people every year. With the instability of these islands for urban infrastructure and dangers from severe storms, loss of life is not uncommon. Understanding the natural dynamics of barrier islands is the key to recognizing and estimating the short and long term hazards of living on them (Dolan and Lins 1986).

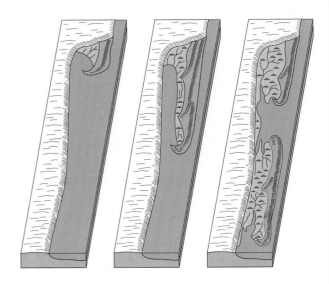

**a:** Barrier island formation by spit accretion and inlet breaching.

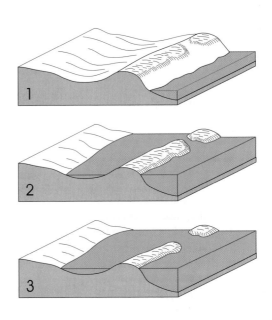

**b:** Hoyt's theory of barrier island formation by drowning of a mainland dune ridge.

**Source:** Leatherman, Barrier Island Handbook, 1988.

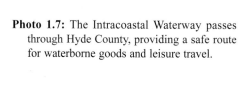

**Photo 1.7:** The Intracoastal Waterway passes through Hyde County, providing a safe route for waterborne goods and leisure travel.

The Mountain Region rises abruptly from the Piedmont along an escarpment known as the Brevard Fault. Along the eastern part of this region is the Blue Ridge Mountains with elevations to about 1,219 meters (4,000 ft) and a few peaks to almost 1,829 meters (6,000 ft). Here we have a class of open, low mountains with a profile type of over three-quarters in gentle slopes.

Within the state, 43 peaks exceed 1,829 meters (6,000 ft) in elevation and 82 peaks are between 1,524 to 1,829 meters (5,000 to 6,000 ft). Varying from 24 to 80 kilometers (15 to 50 mi) wide, the Great Smoky and the Unaka Mountains form the western part of this region. They are low mountains with some elevations exceeding 1,829 meters (6,000 ft). Mount Mitchell, the highest peak in the eastern North America, reaches 2,037 meters (6,684 ft) and is part of the Black Mountains, a cross ridge between the Blue Ridge and Smoky Mountains (North Carolina Geologic Survey 1991).

### Land Cover and Use

Differences in geologic structure create differences in land surface and topography, which in turn influence differences in the land use and cover. Land cover includes natural and cultivated vegetation, lending itself to classification and to the mapping of resulting features. Land use, on the other hand, refers to how people utilize the land. Mapping of land cover is often accomplished through the use of remotely sensed imagery acquired from satellites (CP 1.14). A detailed description of acquisition, classification and mapping is included in Box 1C. Differing uses of the land in each of the state's primary regions reflect some of the impacts of geologic processes. Several patterns readily emerge. Notice the vast amount of cultivated land in the Coastal and Tidewater regions in contrast to the urbanization of the Piedmont. A crescent of urban centers emerges in the south central part of the state from Charlotte, northward to Winston-Salem, High Point, and Greensboro, then eastward through Burlington, Durham, and Raleigh. Also, there is observable urban activity in the Coastal Plain Region in the Fayetteville and Jacksonville areas. In the Tidewater, Wilmington as well as the long narrow

corridors of coastal developments along the outer banks are apparent. Barrier Islands are popular for beach vacations and the resort areas of Kitty Hawk, Nags Head, Hatteras, Ocracoke, Atlantic Beach, Long Beach, Holden Beach, and Sunset Beach appear on the map. On the opposite end of the state, we see the urban centers of Asheville, Hickory, and the many smaller mountain communities like Jefferson, Boone, Spruce Pine, Brevard, Cullowee, and Murphy, nestled on the valley floors. Note also the easily identifiable escarpment of the Brevard Fault which can be seen as land cover changes from grassland and pastures mixed with forests in the Piedmont to the heavily forested Mountain region. In the southern part of the Coastal Plain Region appears, in stark contrast, an area spotted with elliptical lakes and wetlands, with some of them cultivated. Known as the Carolina Bays, these wetlands are of disputed origin (Box 1C). The patterns of land cover and use that are present in CP 1.14 are fascinating and merit reference throughout the use of this book. Percent Land Cover (Figure 1.9) illustrates the distribution among the major

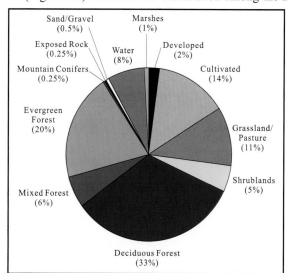

**Figure 1.9:** Percent Land Cover.
**Source:** Modified from North Carolina Center of Geographic Information and Analysis, 1998.

land cover types found in the state. Forest cover dominates the state, broadleaf deciduous forest covering over 40 percent and needle bearing evergreen forest covering over 19 percent of land area.

## WATER RESOURCES

### Introduction

Water is an essential component of the physical environment. While the value of our water resources is great, the pressure of human use is considerable and in some places excessive and detrimental to the local quality of life. A growing population has placed increasing demands on water for use in recreation, power generation, industry, agriculture, and domestic activities (Table 1.2). While these are coupled with many opportunities, if this resource is not cared for the problems of pollution, flooding, misuse, and overuse are the result. An understanding of water as a resource, and the ways it impacts our lives is, therefore, critical to an appreciation of land and life in North Carolina.

### Hydrologic Cycle

The system of movement, exchange, and storage of the earth's water in the forms of a gas, liquid or solid is known as the *hydrologic cycle* (Figure 1.10). While this demonstrates how natural systems move water through our environment, North Carolinians are well aware that people have modified these systems in different ways and in doing so have changed the environment in which we live. People dam, drain, pump, divert, and consume water. All these actions impact our landscape and place demands on the precious resource, water.

### Distribution of Earth's Water

Oceans hold 97.2 percent of the water on earth. This portion is, of course, salt or brackish water. Another 2.15 percent is held in ice sheets and glaciers, and 0.62 percent is held in ground water supplies. The remaining amount, 0.03 percent, is water in stream channels, fresh water lakes, soil water, saline lakes and inland seas, or in the atmosphere. A truly small amount of the earth's water resource, about two-thirds of one percent, is available to a water-hungry, industrializing and urbanizing expanding earth population.

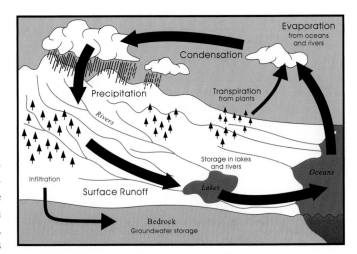

**Figure 1.10:** Hydrologic Cycle.
**Source:** Modified from North Carolina Water, 1994.

### Surface Water

An average annual precipitation of 122 centimeters (48 in) over the state amounts to some 159 trillion liters (42 trillion gl) of water with two-thirds of this returning to the atmosphere through evapotranspiration. Evapotranspiration is the water loss to the atmosphere by evaporation from the soil and other surfaces plus transpiration from vegetation. The remaining one-third finds its way as land surface or underground water, to eventually reach the sea. About 88 percent of our surface land area of 136,197 square kilometers (52,586 sq mi) drains 42 trillion liters (11 trillion gl) into the Atlantic Ocean, and 11 trillion liters (3 trillion gl) drain from the remaining 12 percent into the Gulf of Mexico.

### Major River Systems and Drainage Basins

Figure 1.11 illustrates the major surface drainage patterns with the Eastern Divide, commonly referred to as the Eastern Continental Divide. Seventeen major river systems comprise the states drainage basins or watersheds. Table 1.3 lists these watershed areas and stream lengths.

The Blue Ridge Mountains form the Eastern Divide that separates surface drainage flow east and west. Impeding surface flow are almost 50,000 lakes and reservoirs. All of those in the Mountains and Piedmont are artificial. The two largest are Fontana Lake on the Little Tennessee River and Lake Norman on the Catawba River (CP 1.15).

| Type of Use | Liters (millions) | Gallons (millions) | Percent |
|---|---|---|---|
| Domestic and Commercial | 2,983 | 788 | 9 |
| Thermoelectric | 27,520 | 7,270 | 83 |
| Industrial and Mining | 1,991 | 526 | 6 |
| Agriculture | 662 | 175 | 2 |
| **Total Water Used per Day** | **33,156** | **8,760** | **100** |

**Table 1.2** Water Use by Sector.
**Source:** Modified from North Carolina Water, 1994.

| Watershed Name | Square Kilometers | Square Miles | Stream Kilometers | Stream Miles |
|---|---|---|---|---|
| Broad River | 3,919 | 1,513 | 2,334 | 1,450 |
| Cape Fear River | 24,144 | 9,322 | 9,984 | 6,204 |
| Catawba River | 8,508 | 3,285 | 4,896 | 3,042 |
| Chowan River | 3,569 | 1,378 | 1,259 | 782 |
| French Broad River | 7,327 | 2,829 | 6,619 | 4,113 |
| Hiawassee River | 1,665 | 643 | 1,587 | 986 |
| Little Tennessee River | 4,652 | 1,796 | 4,339 | 2,696 |
| Lumber River | 8,638 | 3,335 | 3,674 | 2,283 |
| Neuse River | 16,149 | 6,235 | 4,828 | 3,000 |
| New River | 1,950 | 753 | 1,336 | 830 |
| Pasquotank River | 9,415 | 3,635 | 747 | 464 |
| Roanoke River | 9,068 | 3,501 | 3,885 | 2,414 |
| Savannah River | 443 | 171 | 336 | 209 |
| Tar-Pamlico River | 14,429 | 5,571 | 3,885 | 2,414 |
| Watauga River | 531 | 205 | 455 | 283 |
| White Oak River | 3,274 | 1,264 | 446 | 277 |
| Yadkin-Pee Dee River | 18,702 | 7,221 | 9,423 | 5,855 |

**Table 1.3** North Carolina Watershed Areas and Stream Lengths.
**Source:** North Carolina State University Cooperative Extension Service, 1997.

**Box 1C:** State Wide Land Cover – A Comprehensive Mapping Project.

The North Carolina Geographic Information Coordinating Council (GICC), established by Governor Hunt through Executive Order Number 16, directs a statewide data coordination initiative. This initiative is detailed in the "Strategic Plan for Geographic Information Coordination in North Carolina," adopted in 1994 by the Council. The Center for Geographic Information and Analysis (CGIA) provides staff support to the Council and its five standing committees: State Mapping Advisory Committee (SMAC), Geographic Information Systems (GIS) Technical Advisory Committee, State Government GIS Users Committee, the Affiliated GIS Users Group, and the Federal Interagency Committee. Additionally, CGIA manages and distributes much of the State's digital geographic data. The individual data sets, created by many government agencies, form a growing resource that is used by all public agencies, lead regional organizations, universities, community colleges, utilities, and the private sector.

A full service agency, CGIA works with clients on the generation, analysis, and distribution of geographic information. Services include system analysis and needs assessment, system setup assistance, programming, training, data layer creation and digitization, geographic data analysis, custom hard copy maps and overlays, plotting services, report generation, and digital data distribution. All work is performed on a cost recovery basis.

This land cover mapping project was developed and expedited by CGIA and is a new addition to the North Carolina Corporate Geographic Database. The data layer is a combined effort on the part of both federal and state agencies, as well as other entities.

The land cover data is a result of a combination of twenty-two multi-temporal Landsat Thematic Mapper (TM) satellite data scenes. One TM satellite scene covers an area of approximately 185 by 185 km (115 mi). This data is a raster or grid data structure, with each raster representing a 30 by 30 m ground grid cell size. Consequently, objects of this size or smaller will not be included in a data set with this spatial dimension. While satellite imagery at this spatial resolution can give enough detail to be useful at the state or county level, it may not be appropriate for use by small communities, towns, and cities. This seamless data covers the State. EarthSat classified the data through digital image processing techniques into 23 original land cover categories, based on the 1994 CGIA publication "A Standard Classification System for the Mapping of Land Use and Land Cover." The final product as seen on CP 1.14 is a combined version of the original data as the detail of such a file is too great to show at this scale.

For more information about CGIA and available digital data about North Carolina visit their home page on the World Wide Web: http://www.cgia.state.nc.us.

Natural lakes are only found in the Coastal Plain and the Tidewater regions occupying depressions in flat, peaty areas such as Lake Mattamuskeet, the largest lake in the state with a surface area of almost 43,000 acres, and smaller elliptical 'Carolina Bays.' Carolina Bays are a unique land surface (CP 1.16a and b), which still causes much discussion on just how they were formed (Box 1D). The bays vary in size from less than 20 meters to over 3 kilometers, with the more notable bays including Lake Waccamaw and White Lake.

Stream flow or runoff varies greatly with location, and daily and seasonal fluctuations. This affects water quality and use as well as the propensity for flooding. Physical and cultural environmental factors control stream flow. These include type, amount and intensity of precipitation, summer air temperature, evapotranspiration rates, size of drainage basin, topography, soils, surficial geology, groundwater discharge, and land cover. Human activity also affects stream flow through different types of land use, amount of impervious materials (rooftops, asphalt, and concrete), as well as impoundment structures (sedimentation ponds). Average runoff is greatest in the headwaters of the French Broad River in Jackson and Transylvania Counties, amounting to over 2.5 million gallons per square mile. Some of the highest amounts of rainfall are located in this area of the state and environmental conditions provide high runoff amounts. In contrast, the northern Piedmont has the lowest runoff with less than 0.6 million gallons per square mile.

Surface Geology and geologic processes are controlling factors of the drainage pattern development created through the erosion process. A dendritic or tree-like pattern characterizes drainage in the Piedmont, with most rivers flowing toward the southeast. Rivers in this region often appear muddy as tiny clay particles from adjacent soils are suspended in the water.

In the Coastal Plain streams tend to parallel each other and then either meander in broad flood plains or become braided near the coast. This is because they are carrying a much greater silt load than the water volume can handle (CP 1.17).

The western drainage has a more rectangular pattern often dictated by differences in rock type or geology. Most of the streams in the Mountain Region have little or no flood plains because erosion is still carving the area, forming many V-shaped valleys (CP 1.18), and often contain numerous waterfalls and rapids as elevation changes occur rapidly (CP 1.19 and Photo 1.8). However, the New River Basin, the third largest of this region, tells a different story. Years ago, an ancient mountain range was eroded almost to sea level before today's Appalachian Mountains rose and lifted the basin. Rejuvenated and revitalized, the river's erosion continued with more vigor. Presently, the course being carved by this river meanders through the landscape, and the path traveled resembles that of one in the Coastal Plain. It is rare that rivers in mountainous regions have these characteristics, but that is why this river is often called the 'Old' New River. Watauga County is the source of the New River, (Photo 1.9 and 1.10).

North Carolina State University Cooperative Extension Service described each of the seventeen basins in the map publication "North Carolina Watersheds" (Figure 1.11). The decriptions give insight into more than the rivers as just a source of water, by providing valuable information on the individual character and importance of each basin, and are summarized here with.

Located in the southwestern part of the state is the Broad River basin. It flows through Hickory Nut Gorge, with its scenic boulder gardens in the Rocky Broad, down to Lake Lure. Lake Lure is a popular recreation and tourism destination and was also the site for the movie "Dirty Dancing."

The Cape Fear River Basin is entirely within the state's borders and comprises its largest watershed. Tributaries of this basin include the Haw and Deep Rivers which drain much of the Triangle and Triad urban areas and flow in a southeasterly direction, as do all of the basins that begin in the Piedmont or Coastal Plain regions except for the Roanoke Basin. Its upper reaches are drained by Town Fork Creek, and then by the northeast flowing Dan River. The latter joins the Roanoke River in Virginia.

**Photo 1.8:** Pearson Falls in Polk County is one of the many waterfalls that characterize the area as surface water drains the Mountain-Piedmont region border.

**Photo 1.9:** South Fork of the New River, a Wild and Scenic River, was designated a national Heritage River in 1998. The river flows north through Ashe County prior to entering Virginia.

During the summer, Jordan Lake (in the upper Cape Fear Basin) is home to more American Bald Eagles than anywhere in the United States. The lower Cape Fear Basin is native habitat for the rare and indigenous Venus Flytrap plant and the Red-cockaded Woodpecker.

Headwaters of the Catawba River originate in the rugged terrain of the of the Blue Ridge, where the Linville River has carved a spectacular gorge more than 610 meters (2,000 ft). These headwater streams are classified as Trout Waters, and this is one of four rivers designated as a State Scenic River. The main channel of the Catawba River has seven hydropower reservoirs in North Carolina beginning with Lake James and continuing to Lake Wylie at the South Carolina border. These reservoirs provide electrical power, water supplies, and recreation for the most densely populated watershed of the state. They also receive treated wastewater, as well as overflows of sewage from private and public septic systems.

The Chowan River basin is part of the Albemarle-Pamlico estuarine system and is one of the smaller basins in the State. All of the streams and rivers in this system are free flowing or tidal freshwater. Most of the surface water in this basin originates as groundwater from the adjacent swamps rather than runoff from the surrounding land. This illustrates the important role that wetlands play in parts of our State's freshwater supply.

Mountainous topography characterizes the French Broad River basin, which contains Mount Mitchell. Whitewater rafting, canoeing, kayaking, and trout fishing enthusiasts find this basin a favorite recreational destination.

The Lumber River is a unique blackwater river. It is flanked by ancient forests of Bald Cypress trees, some of which are more than 1,000 years old. Flowing south to join the Pee Dee River in South Carolina, much of the river corridor has been designated as a State Natural and Scenic River .

**Photo 1.10:** It is hoped that the recently bestowed 'Heritage River' designation will help provide protection against further development along the banks of the New River.

Photograph Courtesy of Tom Ross.

An aerial view of Robeson, Columbus, and most of the surrounding counties of the southern Coastal Plain reveal a strange series of elliptical or oval pattern, whose long axis is oriented northwest to southeast, that dot the landscape. Features like these are shallow depressions and are sometimes filled with water and are known as "Carolina Bays". Tom Ross, a geographer at UNC-Pembroke, has investigated this unique and interesting landscape. He notes that while the theories of origin abound from the extraterrestrial to more recent and earthly theories that combine terrestrial factors, it is important to note the spatial extent and uses of the "Bays".

Carolina Bays are found mainly in North Carolina and South Carolina, although their area of occurrence extends from southeastern New Jersey to northeastern Florida. Recent studies indicate that there are some 500,000 bays, but regardless of the total number, these bays give the Coastal Plain a unique character. Most bays consist of darker soils than the surrounding landscape and are partially surrounded by a low broad sand rim. Bays are barely visible to the untrained eye at ground level, but from the air even inexperienced observers can detect their presence.

Carolina Bays are ancient lakebeds, most of which have dried up during the past several thousand years. However, in periods of heavy precipitation, most bays collect runoff water, which is held for several hours or days above the zone of saturation. A few bays have a natural, constant source of water, the two largest being Lake Waccamaw and Bay Tree Lake. A dozen or so other bays are permanently ponded, but most are swampy or wetland areas that contain water only during wet periods. The term Carolina Bay is derived from the numerous sweet, red and loblolly bay trees growing in and around the Bays, not because they are maritime bodies. Carolina Bay vegetation is not restricted to bay trees, however. It is common to find vegetated lakes, grass-sedge prairies and cypress-gum swamps in Bays. Other Bays support pond and loblolly pine, and in drier portions, scrub oaks (Figure 11.6).

Human activity is impacting Carolina Bays. Pressures of development, recreation, and agriculture are changing the ecology of the Bays. Bulldozing, ditching, draining, and pumping may hide or even destroy all evidence that the Bays ever existed.

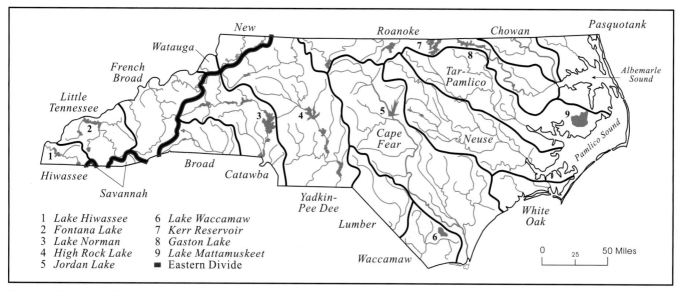

**Figure 1.11:** Surface Waters and River Basins.
**Source:** Modified from North Carolina Center of Geographic Information and Analysis, 1998.

Emptying into the Pamlico Sound, the mouth of the Neuse River flows approximately 322 kilometers (200 miles) from its headwaters in the Triangle urban area. As this river flows towards the southeast, it crosses the Fall Zone (see Chapter 3), with this elevation change increasing the velocity and providing the power for the river to carve out cliffs and canyons more than 30 meters (100 feet) deep.

The New River originates on the western slopes of the Blue Ridge and flows northward through Virginia and West Virginia, draining into the Kanawha, Ohio and Mississippi rivers before reaching the Gulf of Mexico. This river is designated as a national Wild and Scenic River as well as being bestowed the recent distinction of a Heritage River by former President Clinton (Photos 1.9 and 1.10). It is also a favorite river for canoeing, tubing, and trout fishing.

Most of the water resources in the Pasquotank River basin are contained in estuaries and wetlands, along with 3,513 square kilometers (1,356 square miles) of saltwater. The waters of the Pasquotank are also black waters, stained by the naturally occurring acidic tannins that leach from the organic soils of the surrounding land.

**Photo 1.11:** The Boone Reservoir in Watauga County is an artificial Blue Ridge lake that is fed by a small mountain watershed at the headwaters of the New River. Topography, or local relief, handicaps development of large-scale reservoirs as those along the river courses of the Piedmont Region.

The Roanoke River basin extends from the north-central portion of the state to the Albemarle Sound. Trout populations are supported in the western section of the watershed while the eastern section includes one of the largest intact and least disturbed bottomland hardwood forests in the mid-Atlantic region, with forest canopies that tower more than 30 meters (100 feet) above the river. The primary sources of water in the watershed are from twelve artificial lakes on the Roanoke and its tributaries in this state and in Virginia.

Headwaters of the Savanna River watershed originate in southwestern North Carolina and then flow through South Carolina and Georgia and into the Atlantic Ocean. Portions are designated as a state Natural and Scenic River and other portions are included in the Nationwide Rivers Inventory. More than 203 centimeters (80 inches) of rainfall per year fall in this basin, highest in eastern North America, and it is known for some of the most spectaular waterfalls of the east coast.

The Tar-Pamlico watershed includes the largest natural lake of the state. Lake Mattamuskeet, winter home for dozens of songbird and waterfowl species, also supports an unusual freshwater population of Blue Crab and the state's largest breeding population of Ospreys. Included in the watershed are the Swanquarter and Pocosin Lakes National Wildlife Refuges.

Draining westward into Tennessee is the mountainous terrain of the Watauga River watershed. This small watershed has an excellent reputation for its trout fishing and beautiful scenery. The Watauga River Gorge is one of the deepest in the State and has exceptional whitewater paddling. Over 15% of the waters in this basin are classified as High Quality Waters or Outstanding Resource Waters.

Most of the surface water of the White Oak River basin is saltwater with only 446 kilometers (277 miles) of freshwater streams. This river is habitat for many endangered or threatened coastal species, including the Leatherback and Hawksbill Turtles and the Croatan Crayfish. Its waters are also home for alligators and many delicious seafood favorites including shrimp, clams, oysters, and crabs. Unique for a coastal river, the banks of the White Oak are lined with steep cliffs, which are remnants of acient ocean dunes.

Rising on the slopes of the Blue Ridge escarpment, the Yadkin-Pee Dee River system flows across the Mountain, Piedmont, and part of the Coastal Plain regions before entering South Carolina. This watershed includes the Uwharrie mountains, which are among the oldest mountains in the United States and the site of the country's first gold rush in 1799.

### Wetlands

An important surface water resource in North Carolina is wetlands. Defining a wetland has become an important topic in the United States during the past several years. Citizens concerned with their own property rights have taken an active role in helping to define what is and what is not a wetland. The United States' first truly broad set of water-quality laws, known as the Clean Water Act, was passed in 1972. The 1995 revision to the Clean Water Act introduced the topic of seasonal and temporary wetlands. These areas are vulnerable to potential development (Audubon 1996). Whatever the definition of wetlands is, we know that they provide a valuable resource for wildlife habitat, whether they are permanent or temporary. Figure 1.12 illustrates a cross section of a typical wetland. Wetlands purify our drinking water, protect us from floods, and help support fish, waterfowl, and other wildlife. Refer to CP 1.14 to visualize the spatial extent of the wetlands within North Carolina.

### Surface Water Use

Surface water use in North Carolina varies with location and purpose. The largest use of water in North Carolina is for generating hydroelectricity. The Catawba River is heavily developed for this function. To generate electricity water flows through a turbine, which turns a generator that produces electricity, and then water returns to the river. Although hydro generation is a clean system for the generation of energy, it does require that the river be 'controlled' to avoid major fluctuations in water quantity and assure a constant production level of hydroelectricity. Many industrial applications also require water that is used as a coolant and then returned to the river (see Chapter 12).

Production of electricity in nuclear power generation facilities is a good example of such a use. This does not affect the structure of the water, but it does impact its temperature. Agriculture is another major use of water in the State. Water used to irrigate crops may become part of the plant. While some of this is transpired back to the atmosphere, some of the water used in irrigation is absorbed by the soil, some will flow back as surface runoff, and some may become part of the groundwater supply. Domestic and commercial uses also place demands on the quantity and quality of the water available. Our everyday activities of doing laundry, washing the car, filling swimming pools, watering the lawn, and the like all place high demands on the water supply. Table 1.2 details total water use and use by sector per day.

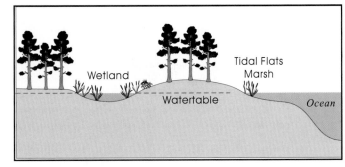

**Figure 1.12:** Wetland

Our Primary problem is whether there is enough water in a local system to provide for uses. Areas that are experiencing rapid growth and development may be prime shortage areas. Another concern is the quality of water as it is used for various functions. It may become so contaminated with various pollutants that it becomes unusable for human consumption, cooking and drinking, as well as in irrigation. Today, even some of the industrial uses require drinking quality water (North Carolina Water, 1994).

### Surface Water Pollution (point versus non-point sources)

People have modified the surface drainage patterns, through changes in the water flow, and have contaminated our surface waters with large amounts of wastes. Surface water pollution occurs in many ways and can be classified into two broad categories or sources, point and non-point.

Point pollution sources are where direct contamination occurs through the dumping of piped wastes or other systems of discharge. Such was the case in western North Carolina with this kind of pollution of the Pigeon River from the Champion International plant contamination (CP 1.20).

Non-point sources cover large areas that create a cumulative impact on the quality of water. This often occurs through varied agricultural practices, development, or recreational areas such as golf courses. This is often a result of fertilizers, high animal wastes, or large amounts of sediment finding their way to surface water flow. This type of pollution occurs throughout the state at varying scales but perhaps is concentrated in the Coastal Plains and Piedmont regions where agriculture is a dominant activity. As by its definition it is difficult to assess exactly where this pollution begins.

### Ground Water

Ground water refers to all subsurface water. Figure 1.10, Hydrologic Cycle, illustrates how water moves through the environment. Note that there are several factors that affect ground water vulnerability. These are yearly rainfall, depth to water, aquifer type, soil type, and elevation. Ground water infiltrates subsurface materials through cracks and pores, and supplies about 70 percent of domestic water used. Natural springs act as a discharge source, however, most of the groundwater is accessed through drilled wells to support human activity such as domestic uses or farming. Rates of flow and total storage amounts vary greatly according to the subsurface materials. The level of the groundwater will also vary with the intensity of recharge (rainfall) and discharge (water usage) into the water-bearing layer of rock, or aquifer.

### Acquifers and the Ground Water Table

An aquifer is a rock mass or layer of both high porosity and high permeability that readily transmits and holds ground water. Ground water is subsurface water occupying the saturated zone and moving under the force of gravity. Figure 1.13 illustrates a cross sectional view of subsurface materials that produce various aquifer situations. This geologic structure is crucial to the subsurface areas that will or will not have productive aquifer regions.

Productive aquifers are abundant in the Coastal Plains. The geologic situation consisting of deep layers of porous unconsolidated sediments, or sedimentary rock, presents a setting for high yields of groundwater. A combination of limestone and sand forms the best aquifer with wells yielding over 1,000 gallons per minute. Comparison of the Geologic Structure (Figure 1.5) with the Productive Aquifers (Figure 1.14) map, and the Ground Water Yields (Figure 1.15) map, illustrates a positive correlation between these data sets. Those areas possessing underlying sedimentary rock are the most productive aquifers, while areas consisting of metamorphic or igneous rock types have much lower aquifer productivity.

Groundwater in the Mountains and Piedmont is generally of low yield due to the predominance of hard crystalline rock. A limited amount of water may be held in the upper layer of weathered bedrock, or porous saprolite. Water moves through the joints and fractures serving as pipelines to drilled or dug wells. Occa-

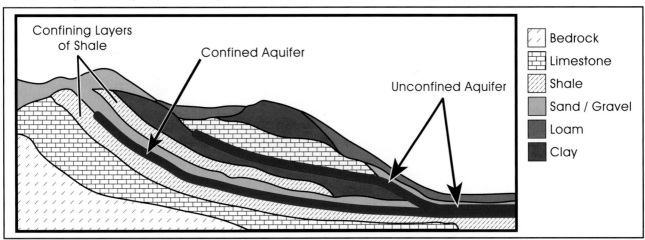

**Figure 1.13:** Aquifers.
**Source:** Modified from North Carolina Geologic Surevy, 1991 and the North Carolina Atlas, 1985.

sionally an artesian spring will discharge along the base of a slope where the water table reaches the surface. The best yields in these regions coincide with areas having thick layers of saprolite and a large, low basin area for recharge.

### Ground Water Use in North Carolina

Management of our water is a critical issue, not just the amount but the quality. Human activity can adversely effect groundwater supplies. The clearing of forest areas and the draining of wetland for farming have reduced the recharge of groundwater. Discharge has been increased through the drilling of more wells to service development of resort areas, especially along the coast. In some cases this has resulted in saltwater intrusion and contamination of groundwater supplies. Dredging of channels for navigation and the straightening of streams to improve surface drainage have likewise disturbed the natural balance of the groundwater system.

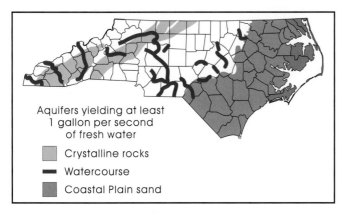

**Figure 1.14:** Productive Aquifers.
**Source:** United States Department of Agriculture, A Forest Atlas of the South, 1969.

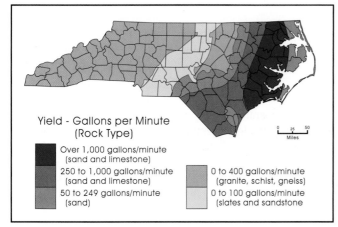

**Figure 1.15:** Ground Water Yield.
**Source:** Modified from the North Carolina Atlas,1975.

### Threats to Ground Water

#### Saltwater Intrusion

Saltwater intrusion is a problem found in most coastal areas, and North Carolina is no exception. Extensive development of the areas adjacent to saltwater has created a need for additional fresh water. As fresh water is pumped out of the ground, surrounding fresh water flows into the aquifer to replace the water that has been pumped out. If fresh water is pumped out faster than it can be replaced, then water from other sources will flow into the aquifer. In the Tidewater region this water may come from sounds, marshes, ponds, channels, and estuaries.

#### Pollution

Ground water contamination is just as possible as surface water contamination. As the use of ground water continues to increase, so does the possibility of contamination. The major focus simply stated is the contamination of the aquifer. It occurs much like saltwater intrusion, except that the seepage are contaminants from other sources. Commercial, industrial, institutional, and residential land uses are all potential pollution sources. When space is made in the aquifer through increased pumping and use of ground water, then the source of the recharge becomes the dominant factor. The water may be seeping from an already contaminated surface or another ground water source. Increasing concern in the State has been placed on underground industrial gasoline and domestic fuel oil tanks buried during the 1940's, 50's, and 60's that are failing and creating potential groundwater pollution.

The Clean Water Act of 1972 and its 1995 revision coupled with the more recent Safe Water Drinking Act may still fall short to protect and reflect our current situation. This is tough, partly because the conditions of water are difficult to capture in the kind of unambiguous statistics lawmakers like, and partly because it has become increasingly apparent that the sources of pollution are not just industrial and municipal institutions that can be controlled by specific laws. The burden of pollution belongs to all of us.

Chapter 8 and the regional chapters (10-13) illustrate these environmental concerns as they impact our need for both the quality and quantity of our fresh water supply.

# Weather and Climate

## INTRODUCTION

Weather and climate are topics that stir the interests of most North Carolinians, particularly those who have outdoor interests or those who have lived through tornadoes, hurricanes, blizzards, and floods. The earth's atmosphere is constantly in a state of change—warm air interacting with cold air, storms moving across the continents, mountain barriers forcing air to rise and descend. All of these complex processes occur in the atmosphere and cause variations of temperature, humidity, cloudiness, precipitation, pressure, winds, and storms, and together they form weather. Therefore, weather can be defined as the atmospheric conditions in a specific place at a specific time.

Even though the weather varies from day to day, month to month, and even year to year, it is possible to discuss the composite of day-to-day weather conditions over the long term. Such average conditions are known as climate. An accurate description of an area's climate requires at least thirty years of weather records, and preferably more. Climate must not be viewed as a static element. Although it is difficult to ascertain if annual variations in weather are indications of a changing climate, deviations from observed climatic conditions over longer periods of time, such as decades or centuries, can be the result of a changing climate. In the last 500 years, the earth has witnessed significant variations in climate, North Carolina included. The Little Ice Age, extremely well documented in Europe, was a prolonged period of colder temperatures on a global scale that spanned three centuries from 1550 to 1850 (Barry 1992; Grove 1998).

Weather is short-term atmospheric conditions in a specific place, whereas climate is the long-term averages of these atmospheric conditions. As the saying goes, "climate is what you expect; weather is what you get" (McKnight 1996). The cold and snowy climate of the state's northern mountains may bring skiers in hopes of great skiing, but the warm, rainy weather on a particular winter day most likely will cause them to leave.

## CONTROLS AND INFLUENCES OF WEATHER AND CLIMATE

Weather and climate are products of a combination of factors that are divided and discussed in the following manner: 1) controls, 2) synoptic (sub-continental) influences, and 3) local and regional influences. Each of these is fundamental in determining specific weather and climate characteristics for a particular region.

### Controls of Weather and Climate

Many factors control weather and climate processes in North Carolina. The most important of these controls are latitude, elevation, the distribution of land and water, and topographic barriers. Depending on the specifics of location, all of these controls have varying degrees of influence on the weather and the climate.

Latitude (degrees north or south of the equator) is the main factor in determining the amount and intensity of incoming solar radiation, or insolation. Those areas that receive the sun's noontime rays at the greatest angle are exposed to the most concentrated insolation and therefore experience higher temperatures (Figure 1.4). Highest insolation intensity occurs over the tropics, while it is lowest in the polar regions.

Solar insolation has important implications for explaining seasonal weather and climate variations. As the earth revolves around the sun, the sun's vertical rays migrate north and south of the equator and seasons occur. In December and January, the sun's vertical rays are in the Southern Hemisphere. So, maximum insolation intensity and maximum heating are found in areas south of the equator. Simultaneously, the sun's rays strike North Carolina at comparatively low angles, providing considerably less heat energy and lower temperatures. In June and July, the sun's vertical rays are now in the Northern Hemisphere and North Carolina receives more intense insolation and more daylight, leading to higher temperatures. In Raleigh, for example, the noon solar elevation is 78° on June 21, whereas it is only 31° on December 21 (Figure 2.1).

Since the tropics receive higher levels and intensities of insolation than the polar regions on an annual basis, a latitudinal energy imbalance develops. Thus, weather is essentially an attempt to redistribute the latitudinal imbalances of heat energy—both horizontally and vertically—in the atmosphere.

Elevation is a second fundamental control on weather and climate. As a general rule, temperatures decrease 6.4°C per 1,000 meters (3.5°F per 1,000 feet) increase in elevation, whereas precipitation, relative humidity, cloud cover, and wind speed typically increase with elevation. Therefore, all other factors being equal, temperatures on the highest peaks of the Smoky, Balsam, and Black mountains of western North Carolina can be expected to be around 11.7°C (21°F) colder than places just above sea level at the same latitude. The higher elevations of the mountains also receive greater amounts of rain and snow, experience higher relative humidity, and have greater cloud cover and wind speed.

Large bodies of water, such as the Atlantic Ocean, have a very important influence on weather and climate patterns. Water both heats up and cools down much more slowly than land, leading to a general moderating influence on the local and regional climate known as the maritime effect. Therefore, temperatures in the Tidewater and Coastal Plain regions, particularly within a few miles of the coast and on the Outer Banks, are generally warmer than readings in interior locations during the winter and slightly cooler during the summer. The maritime effect helps to explain why the average January temperature is 2.6°C (36.7°F) in Greensboro, whereas it is a much warmer 7.0°C (44.6°F) at Cape Hatteras. The Atlantic Ocean is also an important source of moisture. This is demonstrated with the higher average annual precipitation along the Coastal Plain and Tidewater regions, as compared with Piedmont locations.

Topographic barriers, in this case the southern Appalachians, constitute a final major influence on weather and climate in North Carolina. These highest mountain ranges east of the Mississippi River, modify and change weather systems and air masses as they move from west to east across North America, leading to differences in the weather and climate in locations such as Chattanooga, Tennessee, and Charlotte. The southern Appalachians often serve as a hedge against cold, Canadian air masses that routinely invade the eastern United States. Consequently, temperatures east of the mountains can be slightly milder in winter than one would otherwise expect. In addition, the mountains force air to rise, resulting in orographic lifting and increased precipitation totals over the higher elevations (Box 2A).

*Synoptic Influences*

Weather and climate are not only products of the physical landscape of a given area (its latitude, elevation, and relative location in relation to bodies of water and topographic barriers), but also ultimately of atmospheric processes. The controls discussed in the preceding section affect the atmospheric processes, but they do not produce them. It is the clash of different air masses and the work of upper-level rivers of air, known as jet streams, that conspire to produce most of the weather systems affecting North Carolina. Therefore, it is important to introduce some of the sub-continental, or synoptic, influences: air masses and source regions, types of precipitation mechanisms, and the location of the polar front jet stream.

Air mass characteristics are very important in determining what the weather conditions for a particular day may be, or in describing the winter climate of the mountains. Thermal and moisture properties of an individual air mass are directly related to its

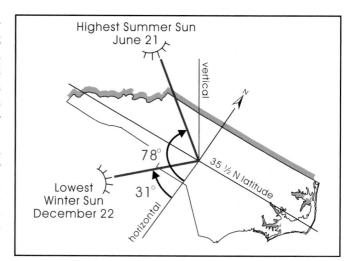

**Figure 2.1:** Noon Sun Angles.

source area. An air mass that originates over warm ocean waters will display warm temperatures and high moisture content, whereas an air mass originating in the Klondike region of Canada will be cold and dry. Based on these thermal and moisture characteristics, it is possible to identify four different types of air masses that affect us in North Carolina (Figure 1.2). Maritime tropical (mT) air masses originate over the warm waters of the Gulf of Mexico and Atlantic Ocean. Maritime polar (mP) air masses that sometimes affect our state have their source over the Labrador Current, just off the Newfoundland and Nova Scotia coast. Continental tropical (cT) air masses form mainly in the summer months over the southwestern United States and occasionally influence our weather. The continental polar (cP) air masses are those that bring the cool, refreshing air during the summer months, or the bone-chilling cold of January. They generally originate in interior sections of northern Canada, far from moisture sources (Ahrens 1991).

Maritime tropical (mT) and continental polar (cP) air masses are the dominant players in our weather and climate. In the summer months, maritime tropical (mT) air is in firm control, allowing hot and humid conditions to prevail. As we move to the fall and winter, however, continental polar (cP) air masses tend to be more dominant. During the winter and spring months, in particular, when the thermal contrast of air masses is greatest, strong jet streams develop and spawn powerful winter storms with very pronounced divisions between cold and warm air masses.

The type of air mass or the interaction of different air masses directly influences precipitation. Maritime tropical (mT) air masses, dominating our summer weather and climate, favor convectional precipitation, and are synonymous with scattered afternoon and evening thunderstorms. As the land heats during the daytime hours, temperatures rise, creating great thermal contrasts in the lowest levels of the atmosphere. Convection allows the hot air to rise, causing condensation and cloud formation. The end result is the formation of towering cumulonimbus clouds, or thunderheads, and the potential for brief, hard rainshowers and possibly hail.

In fall, winter, and spring, however, precipitation mechanisms are a bit more complex. Most of our precipitation during this period comes from cyclonic and frontal activity, in direct association with the jet stream and contrasting air masses. Mid-latitude wave cyclones, or areas of low pressure—also referred to as storms, develop along these jet streams and their counter-clockwise circulation helps to draw warm air to the north on the storm's southeastern edge and cold air to the south on the western side (Figure 2.2). As these warm and cold fronts interact with dissimilar air masses, air is forced to rise, clouds form, and precipitation results (Figure 2.3). Often, a strong cold front trailing behind a well-developed mid-latitude wave cyclone will sweep across the state, bringing with it a strong line of thunderstorms as the warmer, less dense air ahead of the front is forced to rise by the colder, denser air behind the front (Photo 2.1). Warm fronts also cause air to rise and produce precipitation, although precipitation is usually less intense, yet of longer duration, than with a cold front (Photo 2.2) (Ahrens 1992).

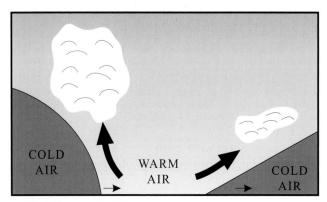

**Figure 2.3:** Frontal Lifting.

The type of precipitation, intensity, winds, and many other factors are directly related to the path, or track, of the mid-latitude wave cyclones (Figure 2.2). In the winter months, storm tracks generally fall into three categories across the eastern United States. First there are the storm tracks that follow a general west-east route, but well to our north (1). When these dominate, North Carolina can expect generally mild conditions, due to the dominant south and southwesterly flow south and east of the storm track. A second major storm track moves from the lower Mississippi Valley northeastward, paralleling the Appalachian Mountains to the west (2). Since North Carolina, particularly its western sections, is closer to the storm track, precipitation is of longer duration and greater, although temperatures remain relatively mild due to the warm sector on the eastern side of the storm. The third major storm track comes out of the Gulf of Mexico and follows the eastern seaboard, often directly over the warm waters of the Gulf Stream (3). It is this storm track that brings the most intense winter weather. As these storms (known as nor'easters as they move into the northeastern United States) pass through North Carolina, the majority of the state is in the western—or cold—section of the storm, producing heavy snowfalls in the mountains and occasionally in Piedmont and Coastal locations as well (Zishka 1980). The great Blizzard of March 1993 was of this type; it brought up to 1.3 meters (4 feet) of snow to the North Carolina mountains.

In mountain locations, orographic lifting helps to enhance precipitation throughout the year (Figure 2.4). As air is forced up

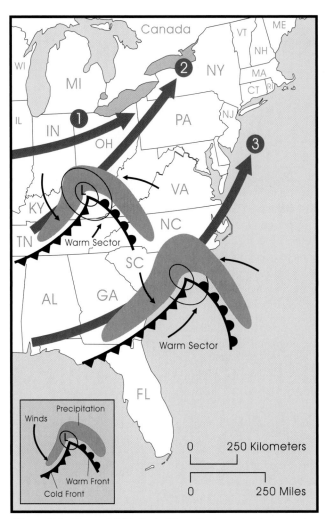

**Figure 2.2:** Mature Mid-latitude Wave Cyclone and Associated Storm Tracks.
**Source:** Modified from Meteorology Today, 1991 and Sierra Club Guide, 1980.

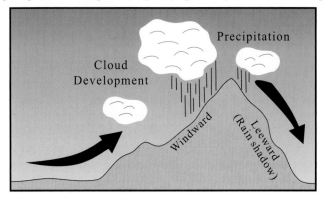

**Figure 2.4:** Orographic Lifting.

25

and over mountains, it cools, and as air cools the amount of water vapor (moisture) it can hold decreases. Clouds and precipitation often form as the water vapor condenses while the air is rising up the mountain slopes (Photo 2.3). Orographic lifting, therefore, is very effective in squeezing moisture out of the atmosphere and is an important lifting mechanism for precipitation formation in the western part of the state. Box 2B further details orographic lifting and the associated variability of precipitation totals in the mountains.

The location of the polar front jet stream is a fundamental influence on weather and climate in the mid-latitudes. This middle and upper level zone of high winds is the result of contrasting air masses; consequently, areas south of the polar front jet stream can usually expect much milder conditions than those areas to the north, or on the other side. Strongest in winter, the polar front jet stream varies widely, sometimes carving out pronounced ridges and troughs in the long-wave pattern, known as a meridional flow, or maintaining a rather uneventful zonal flow. The coldest temperatures of the year almost always coincide with a deep trough in the polar front jet stream, which allows cold continental polar air to dominate our weather. In this particular instance, we are north of the polar front jet stream. Conversely, our warmest weather in the winter is usually associated with a pronounced ridge in the upper level pattern, at which time we find ourselves south of the polar front jet stream.

*Local and Regional Influences*

In addition to the synoptic influences on our weather and climate, there are numerous regional and even local influences. Local residents and even the occasional tourist recognize that a nice breeze usually develops on hot summer afternoons along the coast, or that the valley bottoms are the coldest places on clear, calm nights. Urban heat islands, valley and mountain breezes, and rainshadow effects are also direct influences. Such regional and localized phenomena help give North Carolina's weather and climate a special flavor. This makes the job of weather forecasting in North Carolina a challenge.

A sea breeze developing in the afternoon hours along the coast brings a welcome relief to the searing summer heat. Although actual temperatures may only be slightly cooler than farther inland, the apparent temperature is much cooler, as the differential heating of land and water fuels a strong sea breeze, blowing from sea to land. On hot summer afternoons, air temperatures on land can be as much as 9°C (25°F) greater than air temperatures directly over the sea just a few miles offshore. Warm air over the land rises, creating a localized area of low pressure at the surface (Figure 2.5). A localized area of high pressure immediately develops over the relatively cool water and a pressure gradient, the fundamental force behind wind, is established. As the sea breeze kicks in, a return flow develops in the upper levels, completing the cycle. In the early morning hours, just the opposite occurs. Temperatures on land are cooler than the nearby ocean and a land breeze develops (McKnight 1996).

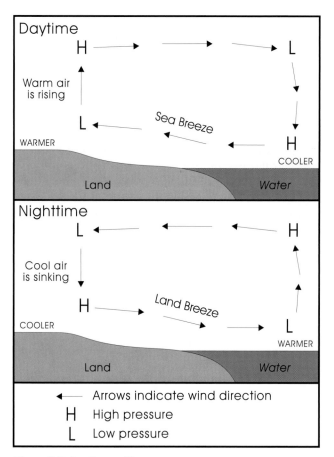

**Figure 2.5:** Sea Breeze Phenomenon.

Due to the topographic irregularities in the mountains, complex variations in temperature and precipitation occur over very short distances. Yet, some aspects of these mountain conditions are quite common and can be predicted with reasonable certainty. The formation of valley and mountain breezes is a general characteristic common to all mountain areas around the world. As Figure 2.6 illustrates, daytime heating causes the rising of air up the mountain slopes, leading to the formation of a valley breeze. At night, this process reverses, and the colder, denser air from the peaks and ridges begins to slide down the slopes and drains to the lowest level in the landscape (Figure 2.7). Thus a mountain breeze is air moving from the mountaintop to the valley bottom. During periods of clear, stable weather, cold air drainage helps to produce relatively consistent breezes on the slopes of a mountain, with a result of much colder temperatures at the bottom of the valley, as opposed to several hundred feet up the slope. These higher slope thermal belts are where those crops sensitive to late or early-season freezing temperatures, such as apples, are found. Temperature inversions are synonymous with these events, indicating that temperatures are warming with an increase in elevation, rather than cooling—as normally would be expected (Barry 1992). Topographic enclosures in close proximity to high mountains, such as the Banner Elk area of Avery County, or the Oconoluftee area of Swain County, demonstrate impressive cold air drainage throughout the year and consistently register the coldest minimum temperatures in the state.

Orographic lifting helps to produce complex variations in precipitation over short distances in mountain environments. As air rises over a mountain barrier, it cools and condenses, forming clouds and quite often precipitation. This side is referred to as the windward side. As long as air keeps rising over the topographic barrier, the lifting mechanism is present and precipitation is often the result, depending on water vapor content and temperature. However, once the air has reached the peak or ridge, it begins to descend—warming and drying out along the way. Consequently, this leeward side is much drier and warmer than the windward side. Most high peaks and mountain ranges, including our mountains, have pronounced rainshadows on their leeward sides. Box 2B highlights these precipitation variations across the southern mountains.

## ELEMENTS OF NORTH CAROLINA'S CLIMATE

Temperature, precipitation, wind, sunshine, and relative humidity are all important elements defining our state's climate. Among these, temperature and precipitation are perhaps the most obvious and easiest to observe, but the other, more subtle elements are important and have significant influences on our daily lives.

### Temperature

Temperature varies considerably across the state, depending on location, elevation, time of day, and season. Even though average temperatures follow a fairly predictable pattern during the course of the year, reaching maximum readings in the summer months and minimum readings in the winter months, summer frosts and snowfalls have been observed in the mountains and coastal locations have baked even in the middle of winter. Nonetheless, average annual temperature is a very useful descriptor and highlights important variation within North Carolina. Average annual temperature readings range from a low of 5° Celsius (40° Fahrenheit) in many higher elevation areas of the mountains to around 16° Celsius (60° Fahrenheit) in coastal locations (Figure 2.8). January is generally the coldest month of the year, with average temperatures for the month again showing great variability—ranging from -4° Celsius (20° Fahrenheit) on the highest peaks to the 7° Celsius (40° Fahrenheit) in some coastal locations (Figure 2.9). Temperatures are a bit more uniform, particularly across the eastern third of the state, during July, the warmest month of the year. The higher elevation areas of the mountains remain much cooler than the rest of the state, with average temperatures close to 15.5°Celsius (60°Fahrenheit). Most of the Piedmont, Coastal Plain, and Tidewater, however, have average temperatures between 24° Celsius (75°Fahrenheit) and 27° Celsius (80° Fahrenheit) (Figure 2.10).

The mountains have the greatest variation in temperature. Figure 2.11 highlights these variations by providing a more detailed view of the average July temperatures across the western part of the state. In spite of these complex variations, clear patterns do exist. Average temperature in the mountains is basically

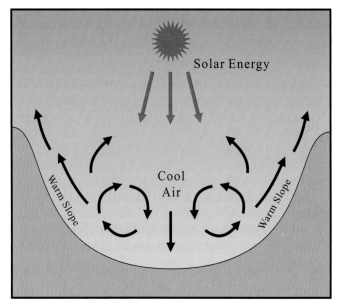

**Figure 2.6:** Valley Breezes.
**Source:** Sierra Club Guide, 1980.

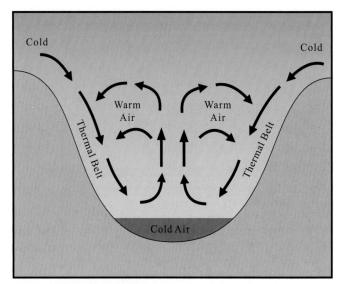

**Figure 2.7:** Mountain Breezes and Cold Air Drainage.
**Source:** Sierra Club Guide, 1980.

a product of elevation. Therefore, the highest elevations of the Great Smoky Mountains, Balsam Mountains, Pisgah Range, Black Mountains, Roan Mountain area, Grandfather Mountain area, and the Snake Mountain area experience the coolest temperatures. Conversely, the lowest elevations, the river basins of the Hiwassee, Little Tennessee, Pigeon, French Broad, Toe, and the Watauga—in addition to the Foothills counties—experience the warmest readings.

**Box 2A:** Orographic Lifting and Rainshadow Effects.

Precipitation varies greatly across the mountains—even across relatively short distances. Steep and considerable rises in the land cause orographic lifting to occur throughout the year, greatly enhancing precipitation amounts across higher elevations and windward slopes. In addition, leeward slopes with their associated rainshadow effects help to explain why some places, most notably the Asheville Basin, are the driest in the state. Orographic lifting also contributes greatly to the high snowfall totals parts of the mountains observe, whereas snowshadow effects impact annual snowfall amounts as well. Average annual precipitation variation is perhaps best represented and understood through a journey beginning in Lake Toxaway, in Transylvania County, to downtown Asheville, in Buncombe County. Lake Toxaway, at 939 meters (3,080 feet), is situated near the top of the southern margin of the Blue Ridge escarpment. As already moist air hits the abrupt escarpment, orographic lifting maximizes precipitation totals at 2,327

millimeters (91.6 inches). Rosman, at a lower elevation (671 m/ 2,200 ft) and ten kilometers (six miles) east of Lake Toxaway (as the crow flies), is still in a favorable position, along the southern margin of the Blue Ridge escarpment, for orographic lifting. Average annual precipitation of 2,080 mm (81.9 in) is predictably less than Lake Toxaway. Continuing to the northeast, we move farther away from the escarpment, but as of yet pass no significant mountain barrier, arriving in Brevard (657 m/2,155 ft) after thirteen kilometers (eight miles). Here the average annual precipitation is 1,704 mm (67.1 in). As we journey on toward the northeast and gradually curve around to the north-north east, we move farther away from the Blue Ridge escarpment and associated orographic lifting and begin to come under the influence of the rainshadow cast by the Pisgah Range, located just to the west-southwest. Here at the Asheville Regional Airport (652 m/2,140 ft), average annual precipitation totals 1,209 mm (47.6 in), almost 508 mm (20 in)

## Average Annual Precipitation

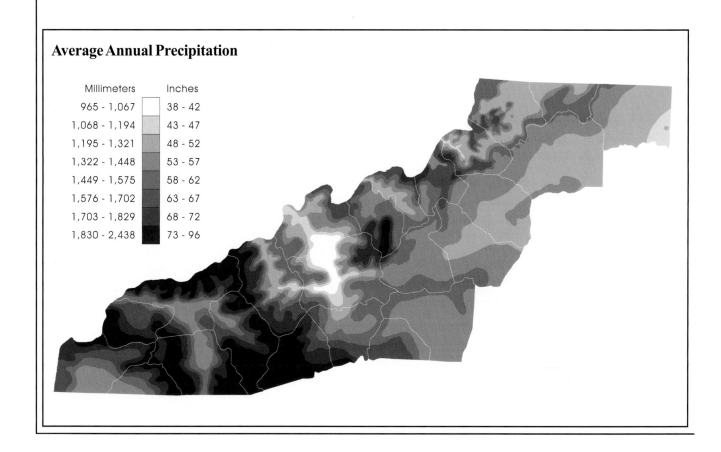

| Millimeters | Inches |
|---|---|
| 965 - 1,067 | 38 - 42 |
| 1,068 - 1,194 | 43 - 47 |
| 1,195 - 1,321 | 48 - 52 |
| 1,322 - 1,448 | 53 - 57 |
| 1,449 - 1,575 | 58 - 62 |
| 1,576 - 1,702 | 63 - 67 |
| 1,703 - 1,829 | 68 - 72 |
| 1,830 - 2,438 | 73 - 96 |

less than in Brevard, thirty-one kilometers (nineteen miles) away! Continuing north sixteen kilometers (ten miles) to downtown Asheville (683 m/2,242 ft), we actually gain some elevation but we enter a basin ringed with high mountains in all directions, except south. The rainshadow effect is dramatic here, as average annual precipitation has now dropped to 965 mm (38.0 in), less than half of the 2,327 mm (91.6 in) in Lake Toxaway, just sixty kilometers (thirty-seven miles) away. This journey from Lake Toxaway to Asheville is just one of a number that one can take to highlight the extreme variations in precipitation due to the elevation and orientation of the mountain ranges (Robinson et al. 1993).

Average annual snowfall amounts also vary considerably, depending on elevation, aspect, local relief, and regional topography. Temperature is undoubtedly the major control on snowfall, but orographic lifting is also critical in explaining the variation in snowfall amounts. Even though temperatures are cold enough for snowfall across much of the mountains quite often, it is only those favorable windward and higher elevation areas that are going to receive significant snowfall under certain circumstances. High pressure builds and provides a northwest wind with residual moisture from lake-effect snows of the Great Lakes or a backlash in association with a mid-latitude wave cyclone. Then the orographic processes serve to extract the remaining moisture. Under these circumstances, Clingman's Dome (in the Great Smoky Mountains) gets hammered with heavy snows, while Bryson City will have clear and dry conditions. North Carolina's northern mountains also tend to be affected by orographically-induced snowfall, more so than other mountain locations in the State.

As the examples in this box indicate, precipitation varies considerably on a spatial scale in the mountains. Higher elevations and more exposed windward areas exhibit the highest totals, whereas lower elevations, particularly those ringed by high mountains or in a rainshadow, receive lesser amounts.

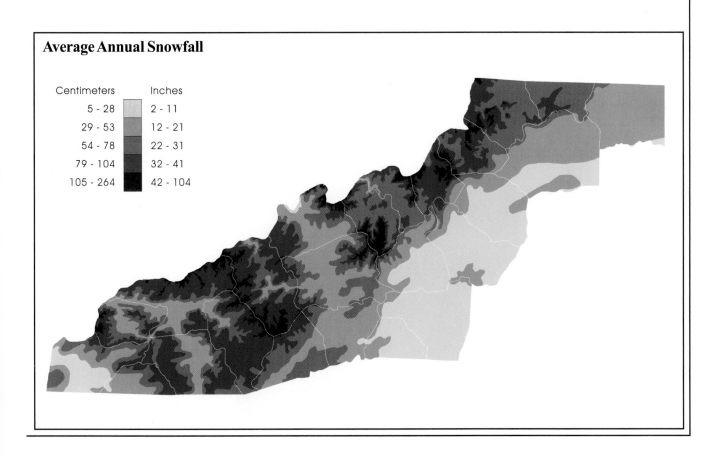

**Average Annual Snowfall**

| Centimeters | Inches |
|---|---|
| 5 - 28 | 2 - 11 |
| 29 - 53 | 12 - 21 |
| 54 - 78 | 22 - 31 |
| 79 - 104 | 32 - 41 |
| 105 - 264 | 42 - 104 |

**Photo 2.1:** Cumulonimbus clouds, or Thunderheads, often form in conjuction with cold fronts pushing through an area or through convective acitivty. Storms generated by these formations are localized, can be very severe, and may even spawn tornadoes.

Photo Courtesy of Mike Mayfield

**Photo 2.2:** Warm fronts normally produce gentle rains with several overcast days, and the stratus clouds resemble a blanket coverage in the sky. Here stratocumulus clouds, as seen from above, give testimony to this type of cloud formation.

Photo Courtesy of Mike Mayfield

**Photo 2.3:** Cloud formations, often a result of orographic uplifting, are seen here during the winter in the Mountain Region. Rapid rises in elevation force moist air over the mountain top and cause the air to be cooled and reach its dew point.

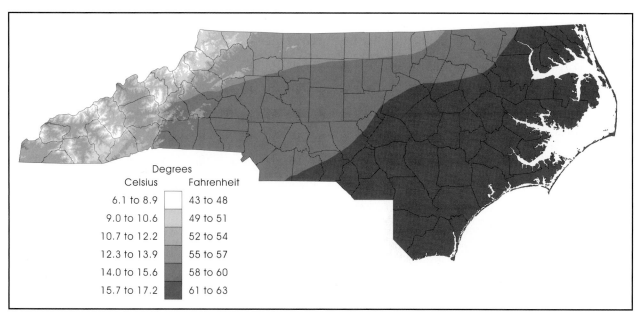

**Figure 2.8:** Average Annual Temperature.
**Source:** Monthly Station Normals of Temperature, Precipitation, and Heating and Cooling Days 1961-1990: North Carolina.

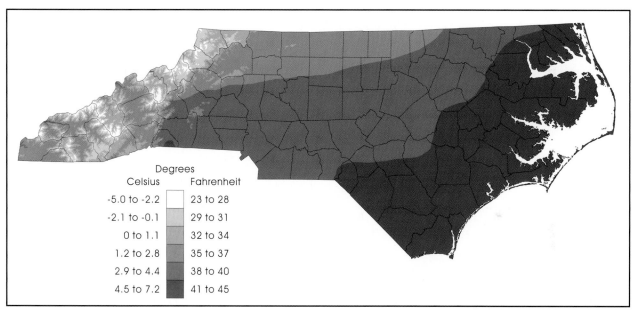

**Figure 2.9:** Average January Temperature.
**Source:** Monthly Station Normals of Temperature, Precipitation, and Heating and Cooling Days 1961-1990: North Carolina.

### *Precipitation*

Average annual precipitation also varies considerably across the state, particularly across the mountains where orographic lifting and rainshadow effects predominate. Average annual totals range from 965 millimeters (38 inches) in parts of the Asheville Basin to in excess of 2,286 millimeters (90 inches) in parts of the southern mountains, although most of the state is in the 1,092 to 1,448 millimeters (43 to 57 inch) range (Figure 2.12). It is easy to note the influence of the Atlantic Ocean on average annual precipitation. The southeastern portions of North Caro-

lina, in addition to the Outer Banks, average substantially greater amounts of precipitation than interior Coastal Plain and Piedmont locations. Here the mixing of different air masses and the greater relative impact of hurricanes provides the main rain-producing mechanisms.

Even though most of the state receives little, if any snow, during the winter months, higher elevations in the mountains can expect significant accumulations. Average annual snowfall amounts are primarily a product of elevation, although other factors such as surrounding topography, latitude, and storm tracks

31

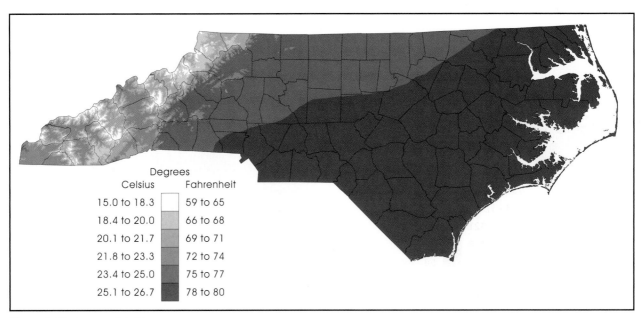

**Figure 2.10:** Average July Temperature.
**Source:** Monthly Station Normals of Temperature, Precipitation, and Heating and Cooling Days 1961-1990: North Carolina.

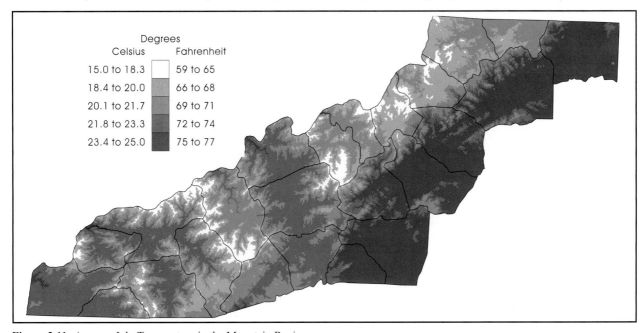

**Figure 2.11:** Average July Temperature in the Mountain Region.
**Source:** Monthly Station Normals of Temperature, Precipitation, and Heating and Cooling Days 1961-1990: North Carolina.

are very important. Snowfall totals range from 5 centimeters (2 in) across much of the Tidewater and Coastal Plain, to as much as 264 centimeters (104 in) on the summits of the highest peaks. Figure 2.13 clearly indicates that significant snowfall totals, greater than 28 centimeters (11 in), are confined to the mountains and extreme northwest Piedmont. This is not to say that Piedmont and coastal locations do not ever receive significant accumulations, but rather that heavy snowstorms are infrequent. Likewise, it is important to note that snowfall amounts are highly variable from year to year across the mountains, much more variable than the other elements of climate.

### Wind

With the exception of where strong pressure gradients are created by intense storms, winds in North Carolina are generally light, with prevailing winds out of the west. Strong winds sometimes develop in association with enhanced sea and valley breezes in coastal and mountain locations, whereas the occasional

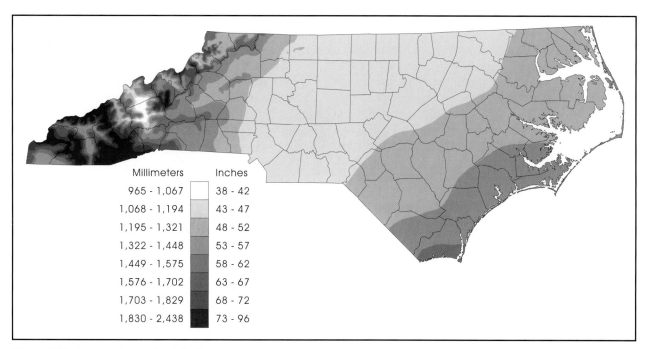

**Figure 2.12:** Average Annual Precipitation.
**Source:** Monthly Station Normals of Temperature, Precipitation, and Heating and Cooling Days 1961-1990: North Carolina.

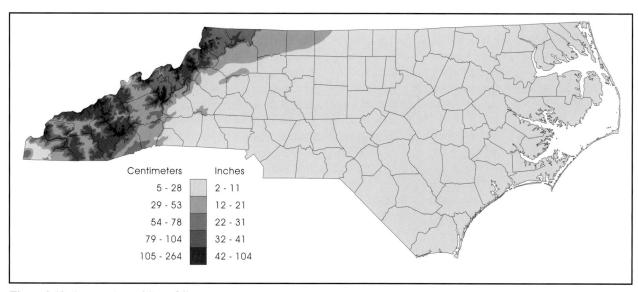

**Figure 2.13:** Average Annual Snowfall.
**Source:** Monthly Station Normals of Temperature, Precipitation, and Heating and Cooling Days 1961-1990: North Carolina.

nor'easter, hurricane, severe thunderstorm, or tornado can also pack extremely damaging winds. In fact, the highest windspeed in the state was estimated at 322+ kmph (200+ mph) on November 28, 1988 in association with a powerful tornado in Raleigh (State Climate Office 1998). Wind speeds generally increase with increasing elevation. As one moves higher in the atmosphere, the surface of the earth exerts less friction on the movement of air, allowing air to move at higher speeds. Grandfather Mountain, in Avery County, is notorious for having high winds. During the winter of 1997, observers recorded a 298 kmph (185 mph) gust, which set a new maximum speed record for that location (Box 2B).

### Sunshine and Relative Humidity

Sunshine and relative humidity vary both diurnally (daily) and seasonally. The number of hours of sunshine received at a site is dependent upon day length and cloud cover, whereas relative humidity is primarily related to air mass characteristics and time of day. Generally speaking, the highest percent of possible sunshine occurs in the summer and fall, which is also when relative humidity is lowest.

33

## CLIMATE DIVISIONS OF NORTH CAROLINA

North Carolina is officially divided into eight climate divisions, as Figure 2.14 indicates. The Coastal Plain and Piedmont are each comprised of northern, central, and southern divisions, whereas the mountains are only divided into northern and southern divisions. However, there are many more climate zones than can be officially recognized. Certainly, the Outer Banks has a distinct climate from other areas of the Coastal Plain and Clingman's Dome a strikingly different climate from Asheville. Nonetheless, for reporting purposes and divisional climatological summaries, no attempt is made by the National Climate Data Center (NCDC) to further subdivide the official climate divisions (Owenby and Ezell 1992).

To help convey the great diversity of climates across the state, Figure 2.14 also includes a sampling of climographs from across the state. A climograph is quite simply a graph of two variables plotted on a monthly basis: average temperature is denoted by a solid line and precipitation is represented by a solid bar graph. Temperature and precipitation are two of the most important elements in determining the climate of a particular location, hence the name climograph.

Banner Elk (1,143 m/3,750 ft), Avery County, is located in the Northern Mountain climate division (see Figure 2.14 for locations of stations) and represents the climate of this division fairly well. Overall, temperatures are cool and precipitation is abundant. The winter months are generally cold and snowfall is common, whereas summer is quite pleasant, with warm days and cool nights. Monthly temperatures average -0.7°C (30.7°F) in January and rise to 18.9°C (66.1°F) in July, whereas the average annual temperature is 9.7°C (49.5°F). Precipitation totals range from 81 mm (3.2 in) in December to 122 mm (4.8 in) in March, averaging 1,285 mm (50.6 in) for the year. Snowfall averages 119 cm (47 in) for the year.

Andrews (533 m/1,750 ft), Cherokee County, is in the Southern Mountain climate division. Temperatures are much milder in the Southern Mountains than in the Northern Mountains, due not only to a more southerly location, but also to lower elevations in the valleys. Average annual temperature in Andrews is 12.7°C (54.8°F), ranging from 1.6°C (34.9°F) in January to 22.5°C (72.5°F) in July. Precipitation totals are high, totaling 1,590 mm (62.6 in) for the year. Snowfall is very light, averaging only 18 cm (7 in) per year.

Clingman's Dome, the highest point in the Great Smoky Mountains (2.025 m/6,642 ft), is located in Swain County and represents the climate expected in the higher elevations of the mountains (corresponding to elevations above 1,524 m (5,000 ft) in the Southern Mountain division and above 1,372 m (4500 ft) in the Northern Mountain division). These higher elevation areas of the mountains experience climate conditions similar to southern Canada. Winters can be quite cold and snowy, while summers are cool, even chilly. Monthly average temperatures range from -3.1°C (26.5°F) in February to 15.0°C (59.0°F) in July; the average annual temperature is a chilly 5.9°C (42.7°F). Precipita-

tion is distributed fairly uniformly throughout the year, yielding an average annual total of 2,085 mm (82.1 in). Snowfall is common nine months out of the year and averages 213 cm (84 in).

Reidsville (271 m/890 ft), Rockingham County, is the fourth station and it is located in the Northern Piedmont climate division. Temperatures remain fairly moderate during the winter months, averaging 2.1°C (35.8°F) for the month of January. Summers, however, are quite warm, as the July average temperature is 24.6°C (76.2°F). The average annual temperature is 13.9°C (57.0°F). The Northern Piedmont is fairly dry in comparison to most places in the state. Rainfall averages 1,125 mm (44.3 in) for the year in Reidsville, and snowfall is 30 cm (12 in).

Monroe (177 m/580 ft), Union County, is a station representative of the Southern Piedmont climate division. Temperatures average 4.9°C (40.8°F) during the month of January, warming to 25.7°C (78.3°F) in July; the annual average temperature is 15.8°C (60.5°F). Precipitation averages 1,219 mm (48.0 in), with snowfall averaging only 10 cm (4 in).

Elizabeth City (2.5 m/8 ft), Pasquotank County, is located in the extreme northeastern corner of the state, in the Northern Coastal Plain climate division. Average temperatures range from 5.1°C (41.2°F) in January to 26.0°C (78.8°F) in July and are influenced by the maritime effect. The annual average temperature is 15.9°C (60.7°F). Precipitation averages 1,232 mm (48.5 in) and snowfall only 15 cm (6 in).

Southport (6 m/20 ft), in the Southern Coastal Plain climate division, experiences a mild climate and is influenced by the maritime effect. Winters are short and mild, whereas summers are long and hot. Monthly average temperatures range from 6.3°C (43.4°F) in January to a very warm 26.4°C (79.5°F) in July. The average annual temperature is 16.7°C (62.1°F). The maritime influence also signals an abundant moisture source, leading to 1,448 mm (57.0 in) of average annual rainfall. Snowfall is rare in this part of North Carolina, averaging only 8 cm (3 cm) a year. The 8 cm (3 in) annual snowfall average is, in fact, deceptive. It is primarily a product of a few major storms that have hit during the 30-year period, as most winters see no measurable snowfall.

Our last station is Cape Hatteras (3 m/11 ft), located in the Northern Coastal Plain climate division, but in fact almost completely surrounded by water on the Outer Banks. Hence, the maritime effect is quite strong in this vicinity, particularly in winter. Due to this strong maritime effect, January temperatures are among the mildest in the state, averaging 7.0°C (44.6°F)—a full 10°C (18°F) warmer than Clingman's Dome. The July monthly average temperature is 25.7°C (78.3°F) and the average annual temperature is 16.7°C (62.0°F). Precipitation is abundant throughout the year, averaging 1,425 mm (56.1 in), whereas snowfall is rare.

Based on the sampling of climographs just discussed, it is possible to classify North Carolina's climate within the widely accepted Modified Köppen Scheme. Within this Modified Köppen Scheme, average temperature and precipitation serve as the only data necessary for classification purposes. Divisions among cli-

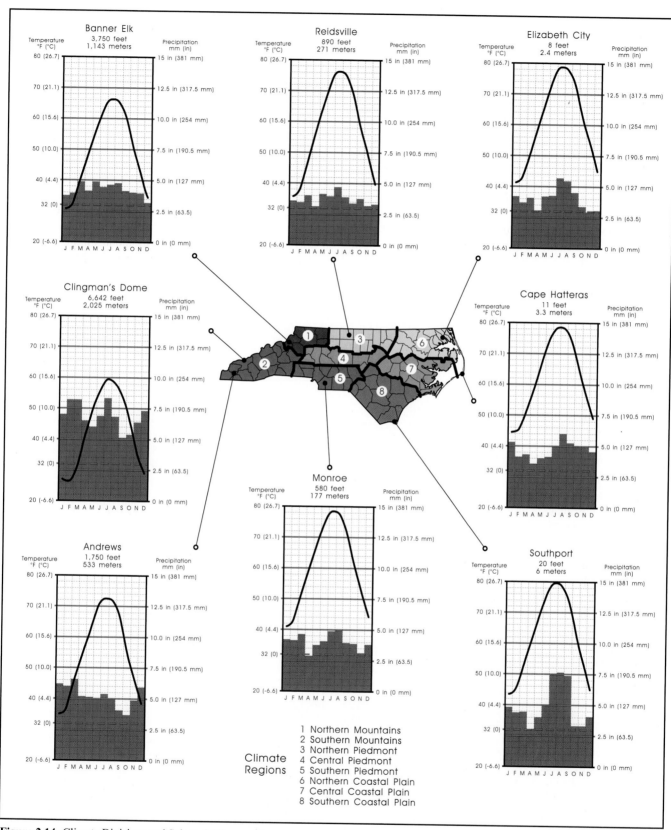

**Figure 2.14:** Climate Divisions and Selected Climographs.
**Source:** Monthly Station Normals of Temperature, Precipitation, and Heating and Cooling Days 1961-1990: North Carolina.

mate zones correspond quite well to actual vegetation patterns, which illustrate the application of such a scheme in describing global climates. The majority of the state, including the Tidewater, Coastal Plain, Piedmont, and lower elevations of the Mountain Region, falls within the Humid Subtropical (Cfa) designation. These areas all have hot summers and mild winters, with an abundance of precipitation distributed fairly equally throughout the year, as indicated by the climographs in Figure 2.14.

As elevation increases in the mountains climate moves toward a Marine West Coast (Cfb) designation. Obviously, our mountain locations are not on the west coast of a continent. However, the moist flow from the Gulf of Mexico and the Atlantic Ocean—combined with orographic lifting—leads to climate conditions very similar to the Pacific Northwest or Western Europe. Summers are generally warm, whereas winters are fairly short and mild. Precipitation is distributed fairly evenly throughout the year and most of the precipitation that falls in the winter is in the form of rain. Fog is also common any month during the year.

At the highest elevations in the mountains, generally above 1524 meters (5,000 ft), a Humid Continental (Dfb) designation is encountered. Here summers are cool and winters can be quite severe with extreme cold, deep snow, and high winds. This climate is similar to northern New England and southern Canada.

North Carolina is characterized as having the greatest climate diversity of any state east of the Rocky Mountains—and rightfully so. Even though the majority of the state is located within the Humid Subtropical zone, it is important to realize that other climate zones exist as elevations increase in the mountains. In addition, topography and the maritime effect lead to important local and regional differences within the Humid Subtropical classification.

## SEVERE WEATHER IN NORTH CAROLINA

Tornadoes, hurricanes, nor'easters, snow and ice storms, severe thunderstorms, and floods all impact the state at various times and intensities throughout the year. Our location in the middle latitudes helps to explain why we experience such active weather—particularly during the spring months. North Carolina is a battleground over which contrasting air masses struggle to equalize thermal contrasts, which are most pronounced during spring. The warm waters of the Florida Current off our coast and the Bermuda High help to keep the hurricane threat high during the late summer and early fall, whereas deep troughs in the jet stream and the same warm waters of the Florida Current can give rise to strong winter storms. Frontal and convectional activity can also lead to severe thunderstorms at any time during the year, with the associated hazards of lightning and hail. Floods and flash floods can result from a combination of circumstances at any time throughout the year.

### Tornadoes

Tornadoes are the most violent form of severe weather, packing winds up to 483 kmph (300 mph) and leaving a path of widespread devastation. Often spawned by severe thunderstorms associated with frontal activity in the spring, tornadoes are intense areas of low pressure flanked by rapidly rotating winds. Tornado intensity is classified by the Fujita Scale and ranges

| Scale | Category | Winds (kmph) | Winds (mph) | Expected Damage |
|---|---|---|---|---|
| F0 | Weak | 64 - 116 | 40 - 72 | light: tree branches broken, sign boards damaged |
| F1 | Weak | 117 - 180 | 73 - 112 | moderate: trees snapped, windows broken |
| F2 | Strong | 181 - 256 | 113 - 157 | considerable: large trees uprooted, weak structures destroyed |
| F3 | Strong | 257 - 332 | 158 - 206 | severe: trees leveled, cars overturned, walls removed from buildings |
| F4 | Violent | 333 - 418 | 207 - 260 | devastating: frame houses destroyed |
| F5 | Violent | 419 - 512 | 261 - 318 | incredible: structures the size of autos moved over 100 meters (328 ft), steel reinforced structures highly damaged |

**Table 2.1:** Fujita Scale of Tornado Intensity.
**Source:** Meteorology Today, 1991.

from F0 to F5 (Table 2.1), depending upon wind speed and damage (Ahrens 1991; Eagleman 1990). Table 2.1 further details the Fujita Scale. Tornadoes are a threat across the state, although topographic irregularities render them much less common in the mountains. Figure 2.15 highlights the paths of the most destructive tornadoes to hit the state since 1900. Memorable tornado outbreaks include March 28, 1984, when a strong low pressure system produced 22 tornadoes across North and South Carolina during a six-hour period, some of which were classified at F4 intensity (Cheney and Morrison 1985) (see also Figure 11.4).

| Category | Winds (kmph) | Winds (mph) |
|---|---|---|
| 1 | 119-153 | 74-95 |
| 2 | 154-177 | 96-110 |
| 3 | 178-209 | 111-130 |
| 4 | 210-250 | 131-155 |
| 5 | 250+ | 155+ |

**Table 2.2:** Saffir-Simpson Hurricane Classification System.
**Source:** Meteorology Today: An Introduction to Weather, Climate, and the Environment, 1991.

### Hurricanes

Tropical cyclones, known as hurricanes in the tropical Atlantic and eastern Pacific when sustained winds exceed 119 kmph (74 mph), are well-organized and strong storms that elicit much attention—particularly when they threaten coastal locations. Initially forming as tropical waves, or areas of low pressure off the coast of West Africa, they can quickly reach tropical storm and hurricane strength when upper level conditions are favorable. Table 2.2 details the Saffir-Simpson hurricane classification system, while Figure 2.15 shows the tracks of those hurricanes that have affected North Carolina since 1900. Due to North Carolina's protruding coastline, hurricanes that curve northward after tracking towards the west-northwest constitute a serious threat to the state. Cape Hatteras and Cape Lookout are particularly vulnerable to hurricane strikes. Box 2C highlights some recent hurricanes which all caused extensive damage across the state.

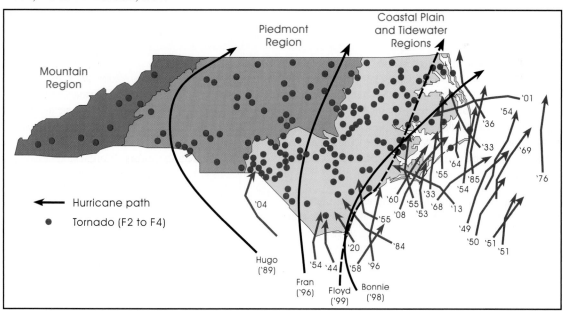

**Figure 2.15:** Major Hurricanes and Tornadoes Since 1900.
**Source:** Modified from Soule, P.T., 1993, 65-68.

37

**Box 2C:** Hurricanes Hugo, Fran, and Bonnie.

Due to our subtropical location and warm offshore waters, Tidewater and Coastal Plain locations are particularly susceptible to tropical storms and hurricanes. Even Piedmont and mountain areas are not immune to the occasional landfalling hurricane that moves inland, dumping large amounts of rainfall and spawning high winds. Three hurricanes that recently affected the state, Hugo, Fran, and Bonnie, had major impacts in all regions and continue to be entrenched our minds.

Hurricane Hugo made landfall a few minutes after midnight in the Charleston, SC, area on September 22, 1989, as a Category 4 hurricane, packing winds of 221kmph (137 mph) (National Research Council 1994). After pummeling large sections of South Carolina, Hugo entered North Carolina in the vicinity of Charlotte later that day and continued north roughly paralleling I-77 (NOAA 1989). Even though Hugo had weakened considerably by the time it reached Charlotte, sustained winds were still on the order of 113kmph (70 mph), with peak gusts of 140 kmph (87 mph). Extremely heavy rainfall associated with Hugo also caused widespread flooding in portions of the northern mountains. At the time Hugo struck, it was the strongest hurricane to hit the Atlantic Coast north of Florida in the 20th century. According to experts at the National Hurricane Center in Coral Gables, FL, Hugo represented a one in 200-year event for the Charlotte area (Garloch and Horan 1989). Hugo will be remembered for the damage to property and for bringing hurricane conditions to inland areas such as Charlotte.

Hurricane Fran also impacted areas far inland during the period of September 5-6 in 1996, most notably portions of the eastern Piedmont and the Triangle area of Raleigh, Durham, and Chapel Hill. Sustained winds approaching hurricane force (119 kmph/74 mph) pounded the Triangle area for several hours, while heavy rains also contributed to the problems. Some areas reported up to 254 mm (10 in) of rainfall, which fell on already saturated soils. Fran left more than a million homes and businesses without power for an extended period of time and claimed 14 lives in the state (Raleigh News and Observer 1996a; 1996b).

Worldwide 1998 proved to be a very active and deadly hurricane season. In a span of 35 days, August 19 through September 23, ten named tropical cyclones formed, while four of these made landfall in the United States. One of these Hurricanes, Bonnie, developed as a tropical storm over the tropical Atlantic on August 19, 1998, and moved in a west-north-west direction. On August 26, Bonnie neared the coast of North Carolina just to the west of Cape Fear and Wilmington, then turned north moving slowly over the Tidewater region towards Kitty Hawk early on August 28. Winds were recorded as high as 185 kmph (115 mph), which made it a Class 3 hurricane. Once Bonnie struck shore it quickly weakened; still it managed to damage the Outer Banks area and ocean-front developments. In addition to the physical damages three deaths were associated with Bonnie (NOAA 1998).

These three hurricanes clearly illustrate nature's force and the impact on people and environments in North Carolina. The environmental impacts of Hurricane Floyd are detailed in Chapter 8; whereas settlement and economic impacts are discussed in Chapter 11.

Photo courtesy of NOAA.

### Nor'easters

Nor'easters are mid-latitude wave cyclones that intensify substantially off the east coast of the United States. Those that intensify in and near the Cape Hatteras areas are referred to as "Hatteras lows" and are renowned for their destructive nature. Although some nor'easters have winds well over hurricane strength, these storms are not classified as hurricanes because of their extratropical characteristics: well-defined frontal boundaries, association with upper level troughs in the jet streams, and absence of a warm core (Barnes 1998). The name "nor'easter," of course, stems from the fact that winds are consistently north-easterly as the storm moves across coastal locations. Nor'easters can bring extremely high wind velocities, high waves and storm surges, heavy rain or snow, severe weather, and even blizzard conditions and extreme cold to affected areas (Hidore 1993). In fact, the Blizzard of '93 (Box 2D) was just such an example, bringing high wind, rain, and severe weather to eastern portions of the state and blizzard conditions to western portions. Nor'easters occur much more frequently than hurricanes; consequently, the impact of these storms on the Outer Banks is substantial. During a 42-year period, Hidore (1993) identified 1,300 nor'easters, or an average of 31 per year.

### Snow and Ice Storms

Snow and ice storms occur quite frequently in the mountains, but are less common as we move from northwest to southeast across the state. Our mountains are in a very favorable position for heavy snow when all the ingredients come together—namely moisture from the Gulf of Mexico and the Atlantic, a deep trough in the upper level jet stream, and cold air from Canada. Box 2D highlights two memorable months—March 1960 and March 1993—when major winter storms affected much of the state.

Occasionally, atmospheric inversions signify increasing temperatures at higher elevations. As a major storm arrives, temperatures will be below freezing at the surface, but above freezing in the lower to middle levels of the atmosphere, or some combination of the two. Freezing rain and sleet then become the dominant forms of precipitation, creating a thick coating of ice on the ground, trees, and powerlines (Ahrens 1991).

### Severe Thunderstorms

Severe thunderstorms and the associated hazards are a threat across the state throughout the year. The most violent of these thunderstorms often occur during the spring months in association with frontal activity, as contrasting air masses use the state as a battleground. However, strong cold fronts can spawn severe thunderstorms at any time during the year, and summer convectional activity often leads to their formation. These thunderstorms can pack extremely high winds in the form of microbursts (strong and localized downward-moving winds), which can cause an airplane to actually fall out of the sky and crash. Lightning and hail are other hazards associated with severe thunderstorms. Lightning strikes are a significant hazard across the state, but particularly on golf courses and on high peaks and ridges. Likewise, hail can do serious damage to property, autos for example, if the hailstones are large enough.

### Floods and Flash Floods

Floods are a threat any time of the year, under a variety of circumstances. Intense winter mid-latitude cyclones that bring large amounts of warm, moist air from both the Gulf of Mexico and the Atlantic, when combined with orographic lifting, can produce sustained periods of heavy rain in mountain locations. In addition, a snowpack can add to the runoff and potential for flooding. The occasional hurricane that tracks inland can mean very heavy rainfall, leading to high probabilities of flooding. Hurricanes Hugo and Fran both caused extensive flood damage across the state when they moved inland (Box 2C). However, they did not match the flooding of Hurricanes Dennis and Floyd's one-two punch, as they arrived one week apart (Chapters 8 and 11). Flash floods are much more unpredictable and localized. Usually the result of severe thunderstorms with extremely heavy rainfall over short periods of time, flash floods are a dangerous hazard in mountain valleys and low lying areas.

North Carolina certainly has its share of severe weather. Tornadoes, hurricanes, nor'easters, winter storms, severe thunderstorms, and floods wreak havoc across the state each and every year. It is essential that we, as citizens of this state, learn to recognize the conditions under which severe weather may develop and take the necessary precautions.

### El Niño (ENSO) and La Niña.

These conditions of the earth's surface are often the focal point of cause when severe weather occurs, and Box 2E details this phenomena.

## APPLIED CLIMATOLOGY

Certain climate indicators can be very useful to predict energy needs and agricultural potential in an area. Degree days and the average annual frost-free period are great examples of how different measures of thermal characteristics have wide-ranging applications.

### Degree Days

Degree days can be differentiated between heating degree days (HDDs) and cooling degree days (CDDs) and are simply a measure of thermal stress on the heating and cooling needs of a home or building. The base temperature for both HDDs and CDDs is 65°F. HDDs occur at any time during the year when the average daily temperature is below 65°F. For example, if Boone recorded an average daily temperature of 20°F on a given day, then 45 HDDs would be tallied, as 65 minus 20 equals 45. Seasonal and annual HDDs are totaled, providing a general description of the severity or duration of cold. Figure 2.16 shows average annual HDDs across the state. HDDs range from 2,470 along coastal locations, to over 8,000 along the highest elevations in the mountains.

Cooling degree days (CDDs), on the other hand, refer to how many degrees the average daily temperature is above the 65°F base. Seasonal and annual totals are also tallied. Figure 2.17 indicates that the higher elevations of the Mountains experience the lowest CDDs (in fact, the highest elevations average 0 CDDs!), whereas southern and eastern sections range up to 1,926 CDDs.

### Growing Season

Climate indicators are important in determining the agricultural capabilities of a given area. One of the most useful indicators is the average length of the growing season, defined as the number of days (or weeks) between the last spring freeze and first fall freeze. Peaches, for example, need a relatively long growing season and are very sensitive to spring freezes. Figure 2.18 displays the average date of the last spring freeze across the state, ranging from March 3 on the Outer Banks to late May and early June in some of the coldest mountain locations. It is worth noting that the mountain slopes' (that is, those locations that are neither ridge nor valley) average date of last spring freeze is significantly earlier than the lower elevation valleys; as Figure 2.18 attempts to portray. This is associated with the cold air drainage and thermal belt concept discussed earlier in this chapter.

**Box 2D:** Memorable March Storms.

Major snowstorms and blizzards, though infrequent across most of the state, are certainly not unprecedented. Perhaps two of the most memorable periods for heavy snow, wind, and cold came during the month of March, in 1960 and 1993. North Carolina residents of all ages will no doubt be talking about these two events for years to come.

### March 1960

March 1960 broke all temperature and snowfall records on a monthly basis for most locations across the state. Cold, high pressure dominated the weather in the interior of the United States, whereas stormy low pressure persisted across the Gulf Coast and Southeastern Coast (Hardie 1960). Therefore, the state was under the alternating influence of both of these patterns the entire month. The first major storm came on March 2, a Wednesday, and was followed by other storms on the 9th and the 16th, also Wednesdays (Winston-Salem Journal 1960). Heavy snow also fell on the coast on the 12th. The 18 to 23 centimeters (7 to 9 in) that fell on the Outer Banks was ten times the sum of all previous March snowfalls at Cape Hatteras (Hardie 1960)!

In the mountains, snow was almost a daily occurrence and wreaked havoc, particularly in the northern mountain areas of Watauga and Ashe counties, where the Red Cross and National Guard were called on to airlift food and other supplies into the region (Hardie 1960; Minor 1960; Watauga Democrat 1960). The 145 centimeters (57 in) of snow that fell in Boone, Watauga County, during the month still stands as the state record. Most Piedmont locations saw between 25 and 51 centimeters (10 and 20 in) of snow, with snow covering the ground for over two weeks.

### Blizzard of '93

Thirty-three years later, western portions of the state experienced the most intense winter storm of memory. The Blizzard of '93, as it was crowned, paralyzed all of the moun-

tains and portions of the Piedmont with heavy snow, high winds, and bitter cold.

Developing along a stationary front in the Gulf of Mexico on Thursday, March 12, the storm deepened rapidly and tracked northeastward, spreading snow into the western mountains by Friday afternoon and across the rest of the mountains during the evening and night. By Saturday morning, most valley locations in the mountains had already received 30 to 61 centimeters (12 to 24 in), with even more at higher elevations (Goodge and Hammer 1993).

As the storm continued to track towards the northeast Saturday morning, winds abruptly shifted to the northwest and increased in strength. There were even some reports that this wind shift was accompanied by thunder. By Saturday afternoon, temperatures had plummeted into the teens in valley locations and the snow continued to pile up. In addition, high winds, gusting up to 80 kmph (50 mph) in valley locations, created whiteout conditions and made for much drifting of the newly fallen snow. Consequently, all roads remained impassable except to special emergency vehicles. Even the snowplows were getting stuck! Most, if not all, towns and counties in the mountains imposed curfews and martial law as conditions continued to deteriorate throughout Saturday afternoon and evening (Goodge and Hammer 1993; The Blowing Rocket 1993).

One measure of the storm's intensity, the minimum central pressure, broke records across the Southeast, including 969 millibars (28.60 in) in Raleigh and 978 millibars (28.89 in) in Asheville. Snowfall totals were extreme; mountain areas saw between two and three feet, with higher elevations reporting up to six feet. Snowdrifts reached epic proportions; roads and cars were buried in up to 6 meters (20 ft) of snow. The extreme cold that followed the storm also set records. In fact, Waynesville, Haywood County, reported a low of -22°C (-8°F) on Monday morning, March 15, which was the coldest reading in the lower 48 states.

During periods of clear weather with good radiational cooling, cold air drains down mountain slopes to collect in the lowest topographic features. Consequently, the coldest areas, and those most susceptible to late and early-season frosts, are the valley bottoms.

Figure 2.19 shows the average date of first fall freeze across the state. Once again, there is great temporal variability ranging from mid-September in some mountain locations to early December along the Outer Banks, thanks to the maritime effect. The thermal belts, once again, show up fairly clearly in the mountains.

On the basis of the average dates of the last spring freeze and first fall freeze, it is possible to calculate the average length of the growing season. Figure 2.20 indicates that the growing season averages a relatively short 100 to 144 days across the northern mountains and the normally colder valleys of the southern mountains. The thermal belts and the Asheville Basin in the mountains experience much longer growing seasons, however, reaching upwards of 197 days in the immediate vicinity of Asheville. The average length of the growing season ranges up to 282 days at Cape Hatteras on the Outer Banks.

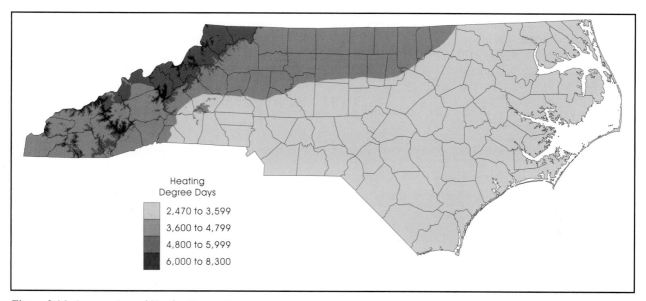

**Figure 2.16:** Average Annual Heating Degree Days.
**Source:** Monthly Station Normals of Temperature, Precipitation, and Heating and Cooling Days 1961-1990: North Carolina.

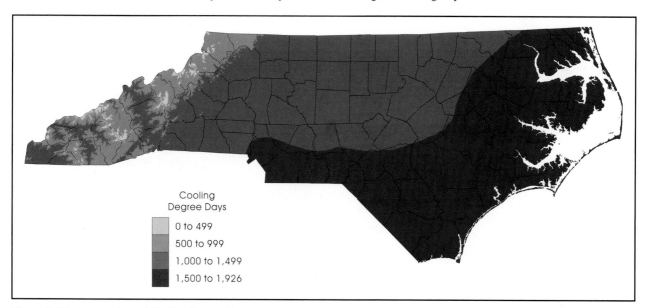

**Figure 2.17:** Average Annual Cooling Degree Days.
**Source:** Monthly Station Normals of Temperature, Precipitation, and Heating and Cooling Days 1961-1990: North Carolina.

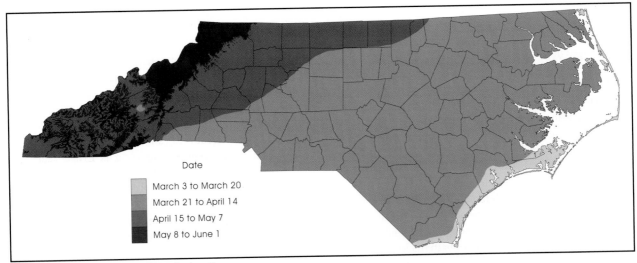

**Figure 2.18:** Average Date of Last Spring Freeze.
**Source:** Monthly Station Normals of Temperature, Precipitation, and Heating and Cooling Days 1961-1990: North Carolina.

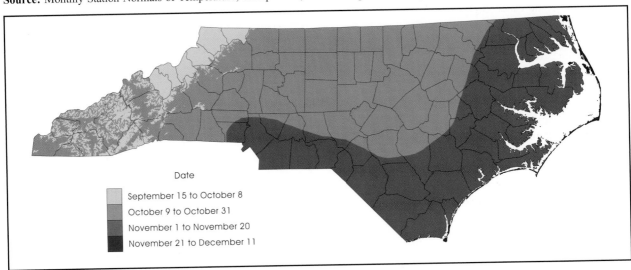

**Figure 2.19:** Average Date of First Fall Freeze.
**Source:** Monthly Station Normals of Temperature, Precipitation, and Heating and Cooling Days 1961-1990: North Carolina.

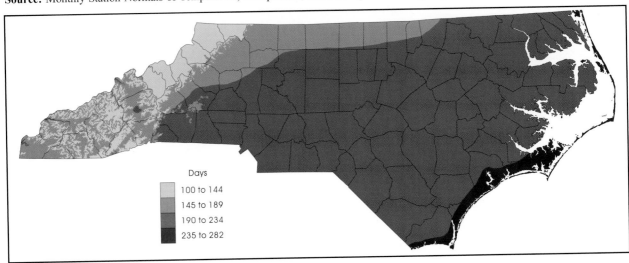

**Figure 2.20:** Average Length of Growing Season.
**Source:** Monthly Station Normals of Temperature, Precipitation, and Heating and Cooling Days 1961-1990: North Carolina.

**Box 2E:** El Niño (ENSO) and La Niña.

Changes in sea surface temperatures (SSTs) in the eastern South Pacific have major impacts on weather patterns around the globe, even in our state. El Niño, Spanish for "the child," in reference to the "Christ Child," refers to the periodic warming of ocean waters around Christmas off the west coast of South America, in the vicinity of Peru. This is most often accompanied by a flip-flop of pressure cells in the South Pacific, known as the Southern Oscillation; hence the term ENSO, or El Niño-Southern Oscillation (Trenberth 1991). La Niña is just the opposite; at irregular intervals, SSTs are below normal in large portions of the eastern South Pacific. Each of these perturbations in the oceanic/atmospheric system has strikingly different influences on weather patterns in North Carolina (Philander 1990).

ENSO is perhaps the event we are most familiar with, particularly after the exceedingly wet winter and spring of 1998—an ENSO year. Precipitation for the four-month period, January through April, was above normal across the entire state, with some areas reporting in excess of 200 percent of normal values. The mountains and portions of the Piedmont saw the greatest departure from normal, whereas northeastern sections, particularly the Outer Banks, were just slightly above normal. Above 1,372 meters (4,500 ft), a lot of the precipitation fell in the form of snow. Mount Mitchell reported 330 centimeters (130 in) during the four-month period, approximately 200 percent of normal values. As a footnote, the highest peak east of the Mississippi reported a seasonal total of 452 centimeters (178 in), approximately 171 percent of normal. Temperatures, on the other hand, were generally slightly above normal for the period (State Climate Office 1998).

So why can we expect above normal precipitation during the winter months in association with ENSO? It all is related to the upper level jet streams. During ENSO years, the subtropical jet stream is generally much more active and brings storm after storm into California. These more frequent and more intense storms eventually move across the country and have a tendency to redevelop and strengthen even further in the Gulf of Mexico, eventually affecting us. ENSO years also see a drastic reduction in the number of hurricanes forming in the Atlantic and Caribbean basins, presumably due to the stronger than normal upper-level westerly winds in association with the subtropical jet stream. The resulting vertical wind shear prevents the tropical waves from developing further (Gray and Sheaffer 1991).

La Niña events have historically led to warmer and slightly drier conditions across North Carolina, although hurricane formation is enhanced by little to no westerly vertical wind shear in the Atlantic and Caribbean basins (NOAA 1998). Consequently, we are much more vulnerable to flooding rains and high winds in association with a land-falling hurricane during La Niña years. The La Niña event of 1998 resulted in a very active Atlantic hurricane season. In fact, there were four hurricanes in the Atlantic basin at the same time, presumably for the first time in over a century (New York Times 1998).

ENSO and La Niña events have major impacts on the oceanic and atmospheric circulation on a global scale. These phenomena influence weather patterns in our state and serve as a great example of the teleconnections that exist not only between the ocean and atmosphere, but also among different geographic regions of the world. Therefore, what occurs off the west coast of Peru does indeed impact our lives, as do many other physical and human processes around the world.

# Soils, Natural Vegetation, and Wildlife

## INTRODUCTION

Combinations of physical processes, which are often modified through culture, create our 'natural' environment. Our environment consists of differing characteristics from the Tidewater
to the Mountain Region. Daily, as well as seasonal, variations in
weather help create an interesting, diverse, and ever changing
landscape. This chapter presents the soil, natural habitat and
vegetation, and wildlife distributions occurring throughout the
state. These component parts of the physical environment play
an important role in understanding a geographic perspective of
our state.

## SOILS

Geographers are intrigued with the spatial component of
soils and their capabilities. Soils are the center of the land's life
layer. Where they exist and how they were formed are important
considerations when studying this resource. Soils vary from place
to place, with controlling factors such as climate and parent material influencing their characteristics. These dictate which physical and chemical processes help create our soils. Additionally
interaction with plant and animal life play an important role in
determining the soil's properties. These properties have evolved
through millenia as organic processes interact with the physical
and chemical soil forming processes.

### Soil Formation Processes

Physical, chemical, and organic processes are continuously
active in the creation of soils. Figure 3.1 illustrates these and their
interactions. Over time wind and water erosion facilitate the physical weathering process. Severe weather events can accelerate
this process and create a vehicle for the transport or movement
of large amounts of soil through overland flow. In the cooler
mountain climates, frost heaving also can be important. While
this process is much slower, it does generate soil through water
seeping into cracks in rock forming minerals, then freezing, expanding, and breaking apart the rock. Chemical weathering is
created mainly through the interactions of atmospheric components and water. Oxidation, hydrolysis, carbonic acid reactions,
and direct solution are involved here. These processes then work

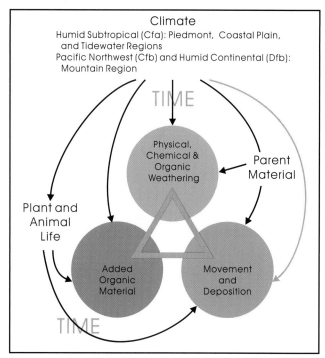

**Figure 3.1:** Soil Forming Factors.
**Source:** Modified from Bradshaw and Weaver, 1995.

on parent material made available through physical weathering
to create soil. Organic processes synthesize organic compounds,
which are eventually added to the body of the soil. Plants then
use the mineral nutrients to build complex organic molecules and
release these nutrients back to the soils, where they are reused
by living plants. Soil development processes depend on this
nutrient cycle of plants. All of these complex interactions coupled
with time have created the soils on our land today (Strahler 1997,
McKnight 1996).

### Soil Properties

One of the most obvious and identifiable properties of soil
is color. This derives from the soil forming processes and some-

times is inherited from the parent material. Soils of the Tidewater and Coastal Plain are a mix of color, from the tans of sands to a rich, dark color provided by high organic content, or humus, in some cases containing a black layer of peat (Photo 3.1). Piedmont soil colors vary, but one is dominant: red clay (CP 3.1). A form of iron, hematite, provides the red hue that has stained many children's clothes through the years. The oxidation process of iron or aluminum in parent rock material generates this color. The Mountains provide a wide mixture of colors as physical weathering processes are vigorously at work. Valley floors contain the deepest soils and most have a dark brown color. The shallower soils that occupy the slopes and the ridges are similar in color, but without the same profile.

Soils also are classified or described by their particle size or texture. Texture classes are based on the proportions of sand, silt, and clay (expressed as percentages). Figure 3.2 is a Ternary diagram representation of the three components of soil used by the U.S. Department of Agriculture, allowing all soil to be classified. Texture is an important soil property as it determines water retention and transmission rates. For instance, sandy soils allow water to pass through rapidly, while clay soils have very small particles that do not allow water to pass through easily. Texture, as well as the organic content of the soil, can then be said to control soil moisture storage capacity, which is its ability to hold water against the pull of gravity. This in turn determines what plant life a soil might sustain or what might be an appropriate use of the land.

Mineral properties also are important characteristics of the soil's personality. Soils in the state tend to be acidic due to the prevalence of granitic or gneissic parent material, the warm moist climate of the region, and the predominance of needle leaf forest vegetation. Most soils need heavy liming for agricultural productivity or for having a lush green lawn. In addition, soils may

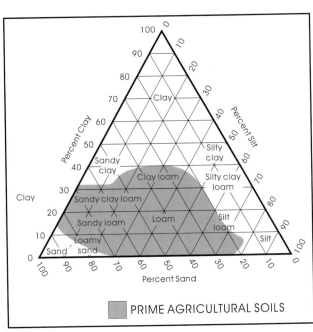

Figure 3.2: Soil Texture Classes.

suffer from leaching of mineral nutrients, particularly nitrogen, phosphorus, potassium, calcium and magnesium, as a result of excessive rainfall and warm temperatures. Preparation for agriculture through the application of fertilizers is necessary throughout the state.

While most of us normally see only its top layer, a soil profile is a valuable tool in understanding the total soil structure, including its depth. A profile, that allows for the inspection of what lies beneath the surface, can be viewed readily by visiting

Photo 3.1: An area of the Pamlico Peninsula in Tyrrell County has been cleared and drainage ditches excavated. Soils are dark and rich in humus and sometimes contain a layer of peat, which can also be used as a fuel source.

new road cuts or construction sites. Each layer is a soil horizon, which is a distinctive layer of soil set apart from other layers by differences in physical or chemical composition, organic content, structure, or a combination of those properties. We see the color transitions from one horizon to the next. Figure 3.3 illustrates a generalized soil profile. Figure 3.4 describes a soil profile from the Mountain region. Often these soils of complex terrain have thin horizons (5 cm/2 in) and overall soil depth is minimal. Topography and local relief additionally impact the soil development process, as shown in Figure 3.5.

### Spatial Extent and Distribution of Soils

CP 3.2 shows the spatial extent and distribution of the state's soils. As with other physical features of the state, the east to west variation from the Tidewater to the Mountain regions continues.

The Tidewater coastline consists of wide cusps or arcs in the southern half and a series of barrier islands in the northern half. Landscape features like these are a result of sediments being moved by offshore currents as the coast slowly emerges (Box 1B). Poorly drained areas, sand flats, bays, and sounds dominate the surface land features. Soils of this region are relatively young, generally deep, over 91 cm (36 in), and of medium to fine texture. Differences in age and thickness are a result of various periods of erosion and deposition. Wet lowlands or upland bogs (pocosins) are poorly drained with dark colored soils from decomposed vegetation. These soils belong to the soil order Histosol meaning "tissue soil", from decayed plant remains.

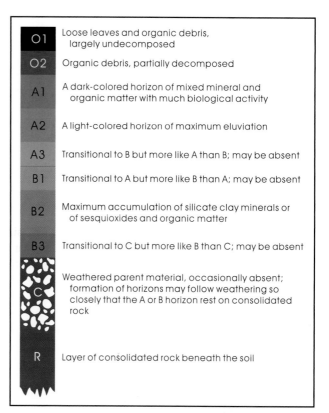

**Figure 3.4:** Designations of Horizons.
**Source:** Modified from Bradshaw and Weaver, 1995.

In the Coastal Plain Region, elevation gradually increases inland to 91 meters (300 ft) above sea level. Here land surface is characterized as gently rolling with prominent sand hills on the southwest margin. Most soils of the Coastal Plain are deep and coarse or sandy in texture with heavier sandy clay subsoil, hence the "Sandhills." These and most of the Piedmont soils belong to the order Ultisols, which are very acidic, highly leached, and weathered.

Westward, the Piedmont consists of irregular rolling plains with local relief of 30 to 91 meters (100 to 300 ft). Elevations reach to 457 meters (1,500 ft) east of the Brevard Fault. As discussed earlier, the region is interrupted by erosional remnants and includes the Uwharrie, Sauratown, Kings, Brushy, and South mountains. Piedmont soils are generally over 91 cm (36 in) deep and have heavy, red or yellow clay sub-soils. They are relatively young due to recent erosion. Differences of soil depend mainly on the type of parent material. The Central Piedmont has considerable alfisol areas, a slightly acid soil derived from more basic rock.

Topographic complexity of the Mountain Region creates many 'micro' environments in which plant and animal species can thrive. This region rises abruptly from the Piedmont along the Brevard Fault escarpment. The Blue Ridge Mountains comprise the eastern part of this region. Mountain soils tend to be young due to recent erosion and mass wasting on steep slopes caused by precipitation events. They tend to be shallower here than in the Piedmont as a result of cooler temperatures that re-

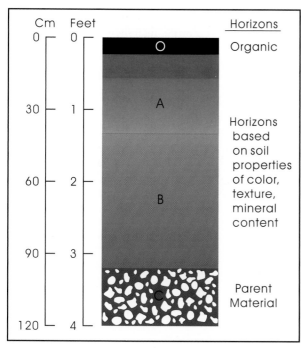

**Figure 3.3:** Soil Profile and Horizons.
**Source:** Modified from Bradshaw and Weaver, 1995.

duce the rate of parent material weathering. Sub-soils tend to have less heavy clay than the Piedmont soils. In broad valleys and basins, soils are more fertile and less leached; where a broad-leaf forest dominates, humus is less acidic than in needle leaf forest. Steep ridges and higher mountain areas, especially on south facing slopes, have thin, acidic soils of the Inceptisol order. Figure 3.5 illustrates typical mountain soil characteristics and landform types.

### Agricultural Soils

While the state's future may lie in high tech industries, its tradition is agriculture. The majority of agricultural lands are lo-

cated within the Coastal Plain (CP 1.14). What makes the Coastal Plain well suited for agriculture? Certainly there is a complex interaction of many factors. The gentle slopes and the soil and its capacity to support plant life are dominant factors. A mixture of the right proportions of sand, silt, and clay coupled with the organic content of the soil, provides the foundation for prime agricultural lands. This type of agricultural soil is generally referred to as loam (Figure 3.2), whose distribution dictate the most suitable agricultural areas of the state (CP 3.2); refer to CP 1.14 and note the coincidence of loamy soils to the areas currently in agricultural use. Additionally, climate (Figure 2.14), growing season (Figure 2.20), and availability of ground water (Figure 1.15) add to the formula of agricultural success. Photos 3.2, 3.3, 3.4, and 3.5 give testament to the wide variety of agricultural activity in North Carolina, much of which is due to soil resources.

As mentioned earlier, the use of soil for agriculture often requires input of fertilizer, particularly phosphorus and potassium. Application practices vary throughout the state and care should be taken to protect the surface and ground water supplies from the overuse of fertilizers; pollution readily occurs through runoff and infiltration processes.

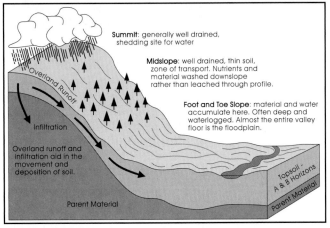

**Figure 3.5:** Mountain Soils and Topographic Influences.
**Source:** Modified from Bradshaw and Weaver, 1995.

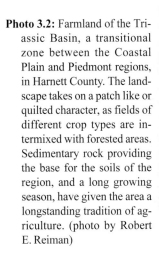

**Photo 3.2:** Farmland of the Triassic Basin, a transitional zone between the Coastal Plain and Piedmont regions, in Harnett County. The landscape takes on a patch like or quilted character, as fields of different crop types are intermixed with forested areas. Sedimentary rock providing the base for the soils of the region, and a long growing season, have given the area a longstanding tradition of agriculture. (photo by Robert E. Reiman)

48

**Photo 3.3:** Strawberry fields are found nestled in the broad valleys of the Inner Piedmont Geologic Belt where soils are generally deeper and often more fertile. This field is located in the South Mountains (Cleveland County) of the western Piedmont Region. Note the peach orchard on the back edge of the field.

**Photo 3.4:** Apple orchards are common place in the Brushy Mountains of Wilkes and Alexander Counties. Mountain soils and climate factors make the region a productive area for apple growth. This area recognizes the importance of the crop by hosting the Apple Festival each fall.

**Photo 3.5:** Soils of the Mountain Region vary within the complex terrain. Here an area near the Old Buffalo Trail (Watauga County) is being prepared for planting. Note the predominance of forest cover still surrounding this farm and the small size of the fields when compared to those of the Coastal Plain and Piedmont regions.

# NATURAL HABITATS AND VEGETATION

As seen in Chapter One, forests provide the most widespread environmental feature of the state. However, North Carolina supports a great diversity of natural vegetation. This is due in part to the variety of climatic and topographic conditions or "habitats", ranging from the moist, shaded coves of the Smokies to the exposed sand dunes of the barrier islands. Figure 3.6 displays the major vegetation types that are possible in the absence of human impact. Inevitably, people have played an important role in modifying or introducing vegetation (Box 3A), most noticeably in managing the pine forests of the Piedmont, Coastal Plain, and some of the Tidewater region. Pines are generally intolerant of shade and would be replaced by broadleaf trees as the climax vegetation in a natural succession. However, foresters have maintained pine for its commercial value by controlling broadleaf species and by planting or encouraging natural seeding of desired pine species. In the following discussion of vegetation by regions, only the common plant names are used and readers who are interested should refer to Appendix B for their scientific name equivalents.

## Tidewater Habitats

Along the easternmost edge of North Carolina are the barrier islands and outer banks, a thin chain of sandy beaches and marshes. The barrier islands are situated between the pounding of the Atlantic Ocean to the east and the sounds of Currituck, Albemarle, Pamlico, Core, and Bogue (Photo 3.6) to the west. These are popular vacation destinations for millions of people who enjoy the sea air, gentle waves, and warm weather. Colder ocean currents from the north meet the warmer southern currents at Cape Hatteras and have made ocean travel treacherous in this area for centuries (Early 1993).

Forming a series of graceful arcs, these barrier islands protect the mainland from the destructive effects of powerful storms and their resulting waves (CP 3.3). Several theories regarding the formation of these islands are presented in Box 1B.

Important wildlife habitats are found on the barrier islands and in nearby waters. Behind the dunes lie the maritime forests while on the western sides of the islands, fringing the sounds, salt marshes nurture countless numbers of fish, shellfish and wildlife. Out on the shallow continental shelf not far from the islands, are underwater habitats known as "hardbottoms", diverse communities of plants and animals. Rocky ledges provide shelter for fish and invertebrates whose only other homes are in the tropical coral reefs or on ship wrecks (Early 1993).

## Tidewater Vegetation

Strong winds, salt spray, shifting sands, extreme heat, desiccation, and flooding create an inhospitable environment for vegetation adjacent to the coast (Photo 3.7). Only the hardiest plants can survive. Sea oats and American beach grass have been used extensively in an attempt to stabilize sand dunes. Increasing pressures from development have further complicated this environmentally sensitive area, and attempts to protect ocean front property have become a priority (Chapter 10). Other plants found on dunes include croton and dune elder. Broomsedge, spurge, and primrose are found in protected areas behind dunes;

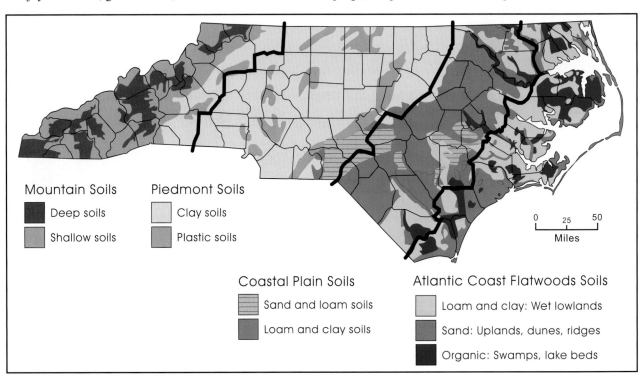

**Figure 3.6:** Natural Vegetation.

all are plants less tolerant of salt spray. A maritime thicket of yaupon, red cedar and wax myrtle often develops as an asymmetric mass to the lee of ocean winds along the inner dunes. Behind this thicket is a maritime forest dominated by live oak and, in the northern part, by beech and other broadleaf trees, holdovers from earlier periods when sea level was lower (CP 3.4). Development has caused the loss of the majority of North Carolina's maritime forests. Occasionally, an active dune will migrate and completely cover part of this forest. Where the dune moves on it leaves a stark reminder of previous life. Gnarled and wind swept branches are reminiscent of high mountain or arctic growth conditions (Photo 10.1).

Along the sounds (protected by barrier islands) and in coastal bays are found vast areas of salt marsh characterized by cordgrass and needlerush. Freshwater marshes that are flushed by large coastal rivers, such as the Cape Fear, support bulrush, cattail, and sawgrass.

### Coastal Plain Habitat

This low, flat region extends from the fall line toward the Atlantic Ocean; near the fall line elevations reach 152 meters (500 feet) above sea level. With so little slope and with little hard rock to flow through, the rivers entering the Coastal Plain form the rocky Piedmont meander in broad, graceful loops through the soft layers of sand (Early 1993).

The sandy soils make it clear that the Coastal Plain was once wholly under water. Over the last two million years, the sea has inundated it many times, leaving a series of terraces across

**Photo 3.6:** Bogue Sound in Carteret County, one of the smaller sounds, is protected by the barrier islands. Saltwater marshes thrive in the center of the narrow sound.

**Photo 3.7:** As sediments reach the sounds they no longer can be carried by the rivers that brought them there and are deposited at the mouths of these rivers. Deposition creates a braided net of shallow waters and marsh vegetation. Here the Shalotte Inlet, in Brunswick County between Ocean Isle and Holden Beaches, drains into Long Bay. Note the development on the bottom right of the photo. (Photo by Robert E. Reiman)

**Box 3A: Creeping, Climbing Kudzu.**

You are warned not to nap beside a southern roadside in summertime, or you might be covered in kudzu when you awake. There is a house in Chatam County obscured by the leafy vine, as well as a gas station in Dunn (Raleigh News and Observer 1997). Farm machinery and earth moving equipment are quickly covered by kudzu if left unattended.

The U.S. Congress' Office of Technology Assistance recently published a 390-page report on 4,500 species of exotic plants and animals that have been introduced into this country. The Associated Press quoted the project director as saying, "The economic and environmental impacts (of these exotic species) are snowballing..." Exotic species are those which have been relocated to a new environment. Many are transported accidentally, such as the tiger mosquito, which carries a virulent form of malaria. Others are brought purposefully for research, but are released accidentally, such as the African bee (killer bee). Often these exotic species are useful, but many become nuisances.

One such plant species, kudzu, has been spreading across the southeastern U.S. for nearly 100 years, creating problems for farmers, foresters, telephone and power companies, and highway maintenance crews. It now covers more than two million acres and extends as far north as Illinois, Indiana, Ohio, Pennsylvania and New Jersey, and is still going. Its potential geographic range is as far north as Michigan, Wisconsin and the states of New England.

Several kudzu vines typically sprout from a single deep-rooted stem, which may reach two to four meters (six to twelve feet) underground. The vines have wide, three-pronged leaves and short-lived purple flowers during the summer. As the vines creep across the landscape, roots may enter the soil anywhere the stem touches the ground. Additionally, wherever the vines contact trees, they will attach with root-like appendages and begin to climb. Because of the stem's ability to "take root," highway-mowing operations often help spread this plant to new sites by dragging pieces of vines into new areas.

The plant evolved in the Orient, probably in China. Kudzu has been cultivated in China, Korea and Japan for 1,000 or more years because of its hardiness and its usefulness as food, fibers and medicines. It was initially brought to the U.S. in the late 1800s as a decorative ornamental for porches and walls. Advertised as livestock feed well into the 1930s and '40s, kudzu was often promoted by the leading land grant universities and agriculture schools in the Southeast.

During the Depression, highway departments across the Southeast used kudzu to control erosion along road cuts or where roads were cut into hillsides. Today, across the Southeast, the largest and oldest expanses of kudzu follow the roads that were built during this period.

Kudzu does have some positive qualities, though they are limited. As a land cover, particularly where soil is poor and erosion prone, kudzu quickly covers the raw earth. Furthermore, the roots of kudzu nurture nitrogen-fixing bacteria that remove nitrogen from the air and place it in the soil. Although livestock will graze on the young leaves of kudzu in the spring, most will eat almost any other plant in preference. Only goats and hogs seem to truly thrive on kudzu foliage.

The negative qualities of kudzu greatly overshadow the positive ones. Perhaps the most troublesome trait is the speed of the plant's growth. Growth rates of six to twelve inches per 24-hour period are common. The plant's rapid growth and canopy of foliage make it extremely competitive with virtually all other natural plant species; it even climbs, and kills, fully grown trees, particularly pines.

Strong herbicides are not very effective in killing a mature kudzu plant. Since many roots enter the ground from various points along the stem, spraying of herbicides is seldom totally effective. Researchers at North Carolina State University are working to engineer some type of kudzu-eating bugs that they can safely introduce into the environment. It might be a bio-engineered soybean looper, a small hairless caterpillar, with an appetite enhanced for devouring kudzu (Raleigh News and Observer, 1997).

Although kudzu is used to produce fibers, medicines, and foods in the Orient, few such aspects of the plant are utilized in the U.S. Most North Carolinians consider it a weed of the most terrible variety and treat it accordingly. Perhaps the best one can say about kudzu is that it has been the subject of numerous good jokes. One disenchanted former promoter of kudzu, in comparing the vine to his favorite dog, wrote, "It was like discovering Ole Blue was a chicken killer."

Modified from Geography in the News #261, Neal G. Lineback, Appalachian State University, October 22, 1993. Photos by Ole Gade.

the landscape to mark its advances. As recently as 18,000 years ago, the shoreline would have been many kilometers east of where it is today (Figure 1.8).

Great natural diversity exists within the Coastal Plain. Most of the states wetlands - bald cypress swamps, deep peat bogs, freshwater marshes and the mysterious Carolina bays - occur in the Coastal Plain and Tidewater regions. Historically, the uplands of the Coastal Plain were covered in longleaf pines and scrubby oaks (Photo 3.8). Altered by natural and frequent fires through the centuries, Coastal Plain habitats have a rich diversity of plant and animal communities adapted to fire. Sandhills longleaf pine forest is most notable in this respect. So common was fire that plants and animals developed many adaptations to resist, avoid, or even take advantage of it. Bottomland hardwood forests, longleaf pine savanna, pocosin, and the unique Carolina Bays (Box 1D and Figure 11.6) cover other parts of the Coastal Plain (Early 1993).

### Coastal Plain Vegetation

The vegetation of this region also shows the impact of human activity. Early settlement resulted in wide spread clearing for agriculture that produced a fine mosaic of land cover. In recent decades many holdings have been consolidated, with additional land being cleared and drained for large scale farming operations, while other areas show extensive reforestation of pine for pulp and paper production. Of particular interest are the vast deposits of peat which underlie the Pamlico Peninsula, "fossil" swamp vegetation from eight to nine thousand years ago that may have great promise as an alternative source of energy. Its use, however, would have great environmental consequences.

The physical setting of the Coastal Plains is generally favorable for vegetative growth, as a long frost-free season, ample moisture, good soils, and flat terrain characterize the region. Plant diversity is encouraged by differences in drainage conditions, depth to water table, soil types, and frequency of fire. Well-drained but moist sites of the Inner Coastal Plain have finely textured soils and are generally covered with an oak-hickory and loblolly pine forest similar to that in the adjacent Piedmont. However, coarsely textured soils of the Sandhills area as well as the extreme southeast coast have open stands of longleaf pine, an understory of scrub oaks, and a ground cover of wire grass. Longleaf pines develop deep taproots during the first three years of growth, while a grass-like cluster of needles at ground level withstands the frequent fires. Then a rapid growth of its stem places needles and branches high enough to avoid fire damage. If fire were controlled, an oak hickory forest would soon replace the pines. Although fire destroys valuable timber, particularly in the southern Coastal plain, it can also be an important tool in managing the forest.

Floodplains along the river courses support two types of swamp forest. First, is a gum-cypress forest with high organic peaty soil that is almost continually under water. The second forest type is a broadleaf mixture of water oak, willow oak, sweet gum, ash, elm, sycamore, and river birch where soils usually dry out in summer months. An unusual wetland vegetation, restricted to the North Carolina lower Coastal Plain, is known as "pocosin" from the Indian description "swamp on a hill" (Figure 10.6). The pocosin evolved from the tidal sound environment as the coast was rising or as the sea receded. First, a swamp forest of cypress and gum developed; later, as thick deposits of organic matter accumulated, soils became highly acid and deficient in nutrients. Fires occurred frequently until only a sparse growth of pond pine and dense shrubs was left. Similar vegetation dominates the Carolina Bays, elliptical depressions of the southern Coastal Plain (Box 1D).

Occupying the flat areas between river courses in the southern Coastal Plain is savanna vegetation of pine flat woods. Coarser soils nurture a scattering of longleaf pine, a continuous ground cover of grasses, and a wide variety of wild flowers. Finer soils that are poorly drained support stands of pond pine as well as the endemic Venus flytrap, found only in southeastern North Carolina! Again we find that frequent fires perpetuate this savanna area; otherwise shrubs and trees would naturally succeed.

**Photo 3.8:** The Cape Fear River, as it flows through Harnett County in the Coastal Plain Region's far western edge, has a mix of land uses. The river bank is still forested, but encroachment of homes near a golf course communtiy is beginning. Note the gentle rapids on the southern section of the river. (photo by Robert E. Reiman)

### Piedmont Habitat

Early settlers used the term "Piedmont", meaning "foot of the mountain", to refer to this region west of the fall line and east of the Blue Ridge Mountains, because its softly rolling hills reminded them of their foothills homes in Europe. As rivers and streams flow across the fall line, it is the resistant crystalline rocks that form the rapids and small waterfalls (as the river erode the less resistant sedimentary materials below) (Early 1993).

Of all the regions in the state, the Piedmont has been most densely settled. Although the clay soils disappointed early settlers, the fast flowing rivers provided power for grist and textile mills and industry grew rapidly. Most of the state's urban centers and population are located in the Piedmont, and it is the most important economic region of the state (Early 1993).

Much less is left of the Piedmont's natural communities than those of any other region in the state because the original mixed pine and hardwood forests were cut and the land was farmed by the Europeans and by the native Americans before them. Topsoil has been denuded by decades of poor farming practices. As the farms became less productive, they often were abandoned and succeeded by forests (CP 3.5, 3.6, 3.7) (Early 1993).

### Piedmont Vegetation

A fine mosaic of forest and cultivated land indicates the impact that people have had on vegetation in the Piedmont. Early settlers found a continuous oak-hickory forest on well-drained uplands and a mixture of broadleaf species on the floodplains. As land was cleared for agriculture and subsequently abandoned, the growth of pines was favored. Pines dominate early stages of natural succession, requiring much light and developing as an even-aged stand. However, they will eventually be replaced by broadleaf species if left unmanaged. The need for lumber and pulpwood has enabled pines to dominate much of the Piedmont through forestry practices.

Virginia pine occupies the western and northern sections of the Piedmont, short leaf pines the central section, and loblolly pine the eastern section of the Piedmont (CP 3.8). Soil and topographic differences account for the variety of hardwood species. Fertile, upland sites favor southern red oak, white oak, and mockernut hickory. A colorful under-story of dogwood and sourwood is common. Dry sites with thin soils support post oak, scarlet oak, and shagbark hickory. Sycamore, sweet gum, tulip poplar, willow oak, river birch, elm, and ash are common to floodplain areas. Some remnants of the mountain flora such as hemlock, white pine, and rhododendron occur in cool or elevated parts of the Piedmont, as is the case with Hanging Rock in Stokes County.

### Mountain Habitat

The region of lofty mountains from the Blue Ridge to the Tennessee border has the highest peaks and the greatest concentration of high elevations in the Southern Appalachians. National Forests cover vast expanses of the region and include the Pisgah and Nantahala. Great Smoky National Park also adds to these forest reserves. It is a region of spectacular waterfalls and gorges, with varying amounts of precipitation in the form of rain, mist, and snow (see Chapter 2). Trickling down from higher elevations are innumerable cold-water streams sheltering trout and other aquatic life (Early 1993).

The Mountain Region has a rich diversity of habitats, from rare bogs, to cove forests, to spruce-fir forests on the higher mountaintops. There are nearly 1,400 species of flowering plants in the region, including 85 native tree species (Early 1993).

### Mountain Vegetation

The Mountain Region displays two major types of vegetation, a broadleaf deciduous forest (CP 3.9, 3.10), at elevations up to 1,524 meters (5,000 feet), and a needle leaf evergreen forest or spruce-fir forest above that elevation (CP 3.11, 3.12, 3.13). Also referred to as a boreal (northern) coniferous (cone-bearing) forest, this latter type resembles the vegetation of central Canada or the spruce-fir forests of New England with red spruce and Fraser fir as dominant species. Fir is found on the highest exposed ridges and often develops a banner or "krumholz" (twisted tree) form caused by the exposure to the prevailing winds and to ice breakage. Extensive logging, fires and wind-throw have allowed growth of mountain ash, fire cherry and yellow birch. While the spruce-fir forest has declined dramatically in recent decades due to environmental changes that are poorly understood.

On steep, south-facing gaps, a deciduous forest of beech, yellow birch, and sugar maple known as "northern hardwoods" often replaces the spruce-fir forest that is more sensitive to wind-throw. However, the deciduous forest is best developed at lower elevations where conditions are ideal for large and dense growth. Cove forests contain a great variety of species including tulip poplar, yellow buckeye, cucumber tree, hemlock, white pine, beech, birch and maple. Rosebay rhododendron reaches tree size in some areas. On drier, exposed south-facing slopes, oaks dominate the forest, replacing the original American chestnut which covered up to eighty percent of the area before a blight was introduced in the mid-1920s. Various species of oak have different environmental needs and migrate towards elevation zones. Northern red oak dominates from 1,524 to 1,220 meters (5,000 to 4,000 ft), chestnut oak from 1,220 to 915 meters (4,000 to 3,000 ft), and white oak below 915 meters (3,000 ft). On most steep south or southwest-facing slopes and on dry open ridges pines and black locust are dominant, with mountain laurel and blueberry providing a dense scrub layer. Fires and thin soils encourage this community to develop.

The entire Mountain Region is not characterized by forest cover; in some places treeless "balds" have developed. A thick growth of mountain laurel and rhododendron or a cover of mountain oat grass dominate balds. How the balds are caused is not completely understood. Most likely they are due to a combination of fire, windfall, and landslides, along with human activities such as hunting and grazing of cattle. For many years in the early part of this century, it was a common practice to bring in cattle from the Tennessee valley to the west, fatten them on high mountain pastures during the summer, and then send them to the Piedmont for slaughter in the fall. It is said that the community and township of Meat Camp in Watauga County derived its name from that practice.

## WILDLIFE

A variety of mammals, birds, and fish live within our landscape. Given the state's varying habitats, one finds an abundance of wildlife present throughout the state. As our landscape is modified by spreading urbanization, reservoir construction and other environment altering activities, our wildlife must adapt to survive or migrate to more appropriate habitats. However, not all wildlife adapts easily so while one species may flourish, others may suffer. Outdoor recreational pursuits include hunting, fishing, and boating. Protection of wildlife habitat from the marshes of the Tidewater to the forests of the Mountain Region is critical.

### *Mammals*

Our state mammal is the gray squirrel. Squirrels seem abundant, as they appear plentiful in any city park on a spring day. However, the population of gray squirrel has been dwindling as hardwood forests, the best squirrel habitat, has been slowly converted through the years into pine forests. Squirrels adapt to many habitats, but do not always thrive in them. Adaptation is crucial. Rabbit numbers are also down as farmers eliminate brush piles and wooded lots for crops. Pesticide and herbicide uses that cause pollution are another factor effecting squirrel and rabbit populations.

In 1910 deer populations numbered 10,000, in 1970 they numbered 300,000 and it has since more than tripled to 900,000 in 1997 (Charlotte Observer 1999). What is the cause of the increase? Figure 3.7 illustrates the deer population and distribution. Simply stated, deer are very adaptable creatures. North Carolina's checkerboard landscape of forests, pastures, farms, developments, marshes, and water create a habitat in which deer can survive and thrive. Edge environments are critical to deer habitat. Great diversity of land cover provides this edge environment and is better for deer. Yet, it is clear from 3.7 that deer habitats gradually improve from west to east.

Black bear, on the other hand, require large expanses of swamp or forests to survive (Figure 3.8). Compare the distribution of the bear populations with the pattern of land cover (CP 1.14). Note that the largest concentrations of black bear are found in the Coastal Plain and Mountain regions. Development, such as vacation homes, golf courses, and roads are diminishing the bear's habitat. While changing landscape may provide useful habitat to one mammal, others may suffer or approach extinction.

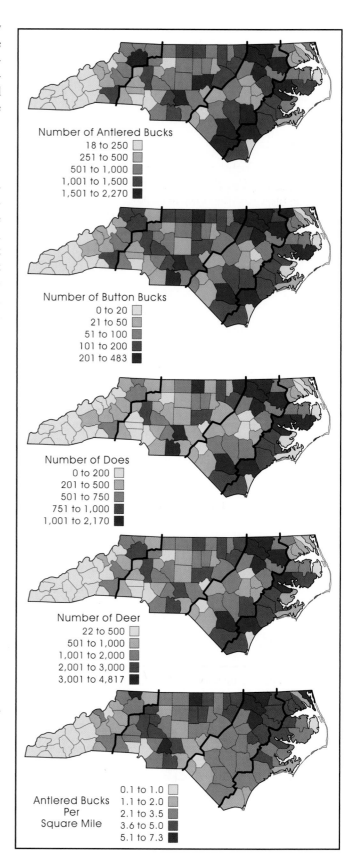

**Figure 3.7:** White-Tailed Deer Harvest, 1998-99.
**Source:** North Carolina Wildlife Resources Commission, 1999.

56

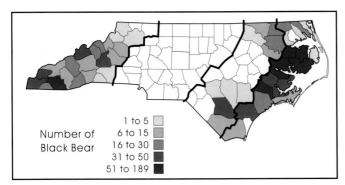

**Figure 3.8:** Black Bear Kill, 1998-99.
**Source:** North Carolina Wildlife Resources Commission, 1999.

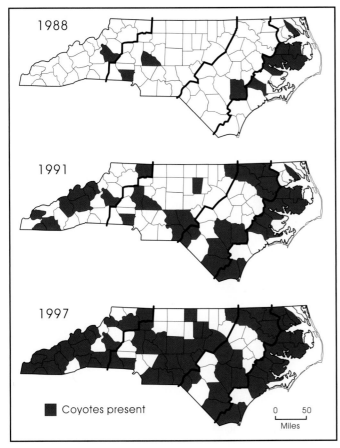

**Figure 3.9:** Coyote Diffussion, 1988-1997.
**Source:** Modified from the Charlotte Observer, 1999.

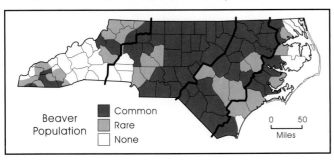

**Figure 3.10:** Beaver Distribution, 1999.
**Source:** North Carolina Wildlife Resources Commission, 1999.

Coyotes have been sighted in our state, from the Tidewater to the Mountain regions. Figure 3.9 illustrates the spread or diffusion of coyotes throughout North Carolina. If this trend continues, coyotes will soon be present in every county.

Beaver were abundant in the earlier years of settlement, were eradicated, were reintroduced in the 1940s, and today beaver are common in much of the state (Figure 3.10). It is not uncommon to see a beaver dam in the small northwestern mountain community of Beaverdam in Watauga County.

Other recent reintroduction programs for mammals have been accomplished. These efforts have included the red wolf, which has been successfully reintroduced in the Tidewater region (Figure 3.11), while attempts to stabilize a population in the Smoky Mountains have failed. Road densities and road pattern seem to have a direct impact on the success of this reintroduction program. Roads create edge habitats that are a crucial source of food for the red wolf. The otter has been reintroduced to the western part of the state after they were forced to the eastern Piedmont and Coastal Plain regions, because of diminishing expanses of quality habitat.

Wild boar were introduced to North Carolina in 1912, as 14 European wild boars were released in a game preserve on Hooper's bald in Graham County. After escaping from the preserve the wild boar established occupied ranges in some mountain counties (Figure 3.12). The first open hunting season was in 1936, and in 1979 the North Carolina Legislature designated the status of game animal to the wild boar. Figure 3.13 reflects the number and location of wild boar harvested during the 1998-99 hunting season (North Carolina Wildlife Resources Commission 1999).

Wild horses of the Outer Banks have been allowed to roam the range of a remote Carteret County island for decades and they have thrived there. In 1995, an estimated 225 horses grazed the eight-mile long Shackleford Banks (part of the Cape Lookout National Seashore). Their populations have increased since sheep, goats, and cattle were removed in the mid-1980s, when the Park Service took over the land for the national seashore. Concern for the horses has heightened as their increasing population has placed great stress on the habitat. Grasses that once grew to knee height are now eaten close to the ground level. Officials fear that food supplies will continue to dwindle and horses may starve and die off as they have on Carrot Island near Beaufort.

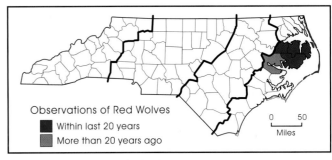

**Figure 3.11:** Red Wolf Distribution.
**Source:** United States Fish and Wildlife Service, 1999.

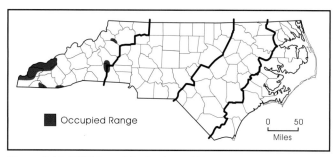

**Figure 3.12:** Wild Boar Distribution, 1999.
**Source:** North Carolina Wildlife Resources Commission, 1999.

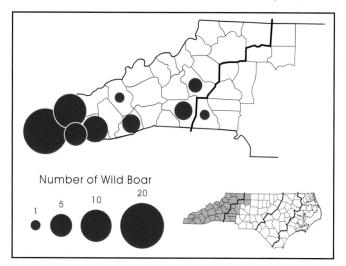

**Figure 3.13:** Wild Boar Harvest, 1998-99.
**Source:** North Carolina Wildlife Resources Commission, 1999.

### Birds

A multitude of song birds find habitat in our state, and the cardinal is designated as our state bird. However, as the large forested areas dwindle, so do the populations of the birds that need this habitat to thrive. Over the past 25 years, nearly 20 species of bird populations have declined. The loggerhead shrike, a forest dwelling bird, is down 95 percent, while meadowlarks, mockingbirds, and blue jays are down 53, 45, and 38 percent respectively. At the same time, bluebirds have increased 369 percent; cowbirds, 301 percent; and robins, 75 percent; these birds favor forest edges, which are created or enhanced with road cuts and construction (Charlotte Observer 1990).

Wild turkeys, with populations dwindling, were reintroduced through an active (3,565 birds since 1970) and somewhat costly restocking program (about $500 per restoration bird). Now the turkeys are flourishing. Populations have experienced dramatic increases since this program began. Only 2,500 birds existed in North Carolina in the early 1960s. Numbers increased to 7,500 in 1980, then to 28,000 in 1990, and in 1996 turkeys numbered more than 86,000 (Charlotte Observer 1996). Herds of over 100 birds have been seen in Watauga and Ashe Counties (CP 5.19). In North Carolina 95 of the 100 counties have wild turkey populations (Figure 3.14). Wild turkeys provide a popular game bird during the fall season, as hunters work their distinctive calls

of gobbling in hopes of attracting a bird. As will be seen in Chapter 5, the domesticated cousin of this bird has also contributed to the state economy. North Carolina is the number one turkey producer in the nation. Hunters also find the morning dove a popular game bird, though this bird along with grouse and quail have experienced declines.

Bald eagles have made a comeback since the banning of DDT. Only one nesting site was known in the state in 1972; in 1995, there were 12 known sites and in early 1999 there are over 20 sites. Seven breeding pairs were in the northeastern part of the state, nesting in Pasquotank, Chowan, Washington, Hyde, Beaufort, Tyrrell, and Dare counties (Raleigh News & Observer 1995). North Carolina, South Carolina, and Virginia have made intensive efforts to increase the population of our nation's symbol; unless people interfere again, the eagles are back to stay.

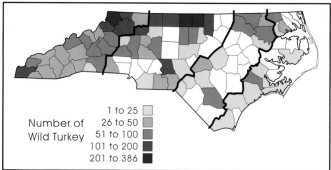

**Figure 3.14:** Wild Turkey Harvest, 1998.
**Source:** North Carolina Wildlife Resources Commission, 1999.

Not as lucky as the eagle is the red-cockaded woodpecker, a bird heading toward possible extinction. In 1989, Hurricane Hugo ripped through the nations second largest population in the Francis Marion National Forest in South Carolina. About 450 birds died and most of the rest were left without viable habitat. Now work is continuing to restablish a viable habitat in the Sandhills (see Chapter 11). Natural disasters can have a dramatic impact on habitat quality: hurricanes devastate large areas while the tornadoes impact a much smaller area (Chapter 2).

### Fish and Turtles

Fresh and saltwater fish provide a valuable economic and recreational resource for our state. Our shores are blessed with barrier islands, hundreds of miles of inland shoreline, sounds and estuaries, all providing habitat for a diverse saltwater fish population. Inland, the surface waters of our state provide many excellent recreational opportunities as well (see Chapter 10).

Over-fishing and dams have reduced the striped bass fisheries in the Coastal Plain region. However, in mountain rivers reintroduced muskies have made a comeback since the removal of some dams (Charlotte Observer 1990).

Trout, which are abundant in many of the state's rivers, suffer because of increasing development near their habitat. Development activities may release sediment that flows into streams;

this process of sedimentation can kill trout. Road, resort, and golf course development, if done improperly, devastates trout stream quality. Additionally, the clearing of forest which once shaded the waters and kept them cold are no longer there to protect the water from warming by the sun. Increasing the temperature of the water decreases the trout population. Agricultural introduction of fertilizering compounds in streams through runoff will also decrease water quality.

Loggerhead turtles find the shores most suitable for nesting from May through August. These turtles have found it increasingly difficult to thrive in the rapidly developing coastal areas. Representatives at Brunswick County's Turtle Watch Program estimate that only about 100 turtles reach adulthood for every 7,000 eggs laid. Newborn turtles are attracted to the brightest lights; years ago that light was moonlight, which lead them to the ocean. However, lights from nearby modern development attract the newborn turtles inland to their demise. Predators such as raccoons, snakes, and ants also find the turtle's eggs a tasty food source.

North Carolina's Place in the World

North Carolina's Place in the United States

Physiographic Regions and Counties of North Carolina

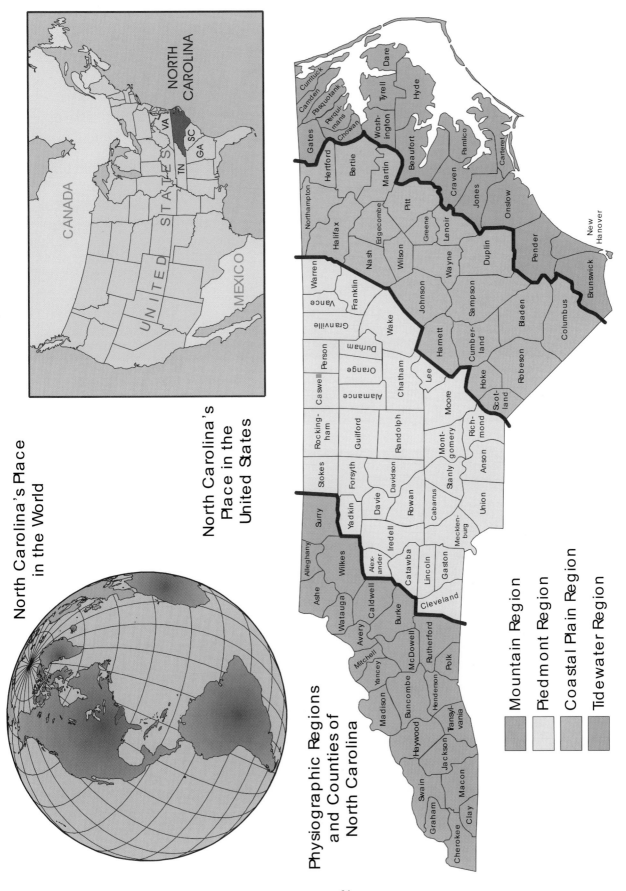

Mountain Region

Piedmont Region

Coastal Plain Region

Tidewater Region

**Color Plate 1.1:** North Carolina's World, Regional, and Local Settings.

61

*Photo by James Cook.*

**Color Plate 1.2:** Mount Mitchell (in the background of the photo) is in the Black Mountains, the highest range of the Blue Ridge. With an elevation of 2,307 meters (6,684 ft.), Mount Mitchell is the highest peak in eastern North America. Eleven other peaks in the Black Mountains exceed 1,829 meters (6,000 feet).

*Photo by Neal Lineback.*

**Color Plate 1.3:** Cape Hatteras lighthouse, tallest in the nation at 63 meters (208 feet), has helped keep maritime travel safe since it was built in 1870. Fear of destruction by natural forces caused Congress to pass a 9.8 million dollar appropriation for the National Park Service to move the lighthouse. During the summer of 1999, crews moved the lighthouse further inland some 488 meters (1,600 feet) from its original location. Cape Hatteras lighthouse is now restored, along with the lighthouse keeper's house and storage building where oil for the lantern was stored.

**Color Plate 1.4:** A panoramic view of the Blue Ridge in Watauga and Avery counties. Geologically, most of the scene falls within the "Grandfather Window," comprised of mostly Precambrian rock. In the distance, the famous "face" of Grandfather Mountain can be seen. Foscoe Valley, part of the Watauga River drainage basin, is in the center, with the Seven Devils range to the right. The Blue Ridge Mountains are just one of many ranges that comprise the Appalachian Mountains, which transect the eastern United States from New York to Alabama.

**Color Plate 1.5:** An aerial view of mining in the Sandhills illustrates the spatial expanse of such operations. All the vegetation is removed in order to expose and extract sand for industrial use.

**Color Plate 1.6:** Granite for building facing is mined near Granite Quarry in Rowan County. The granite outcrop is a monadnock outlier of the Uwharrie Mountains of the Central Piedmont.

**Color Plate 1.7:** A popular spot for outdoor enthusiasts is Stone Mountain State Park located in rural Wilkes County. This monadnock consists of a resistant granitic rock that has had the surrounding rock eroded away through time. The rounded surface fractures result from the gradual erosive effects of exfoliation.

**Color Plate 1.8:** A winter scene helps illustrate the highest elevations and the rugged terrain of the Black Mountains in Mitchell County. This east-west trending range has many peaks with elevations exceeding 1,829 meters (6,000 feet).

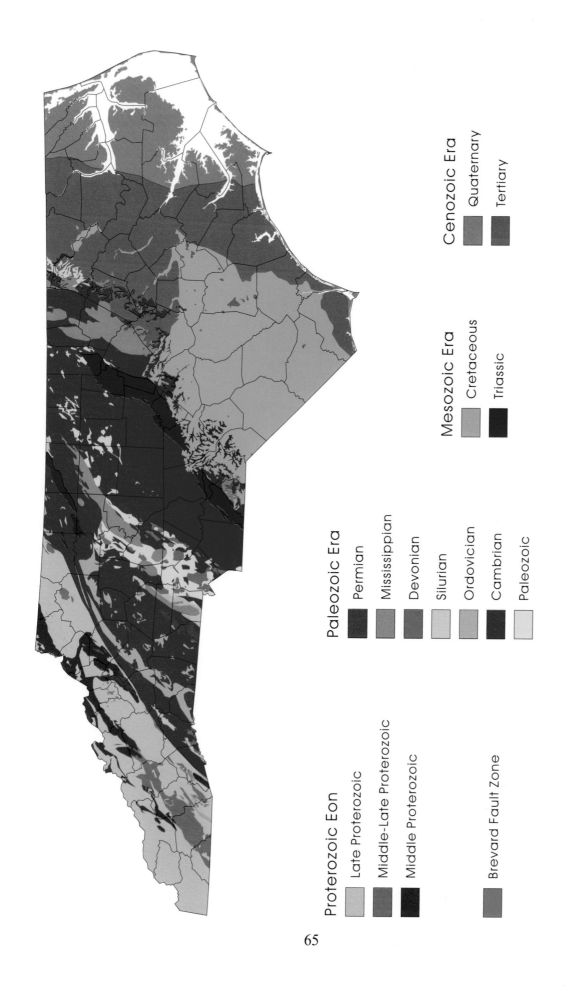

## Proterozoic Eon

Late Proterozoic

Middle-Late Proterozoic

Middle Proterozoic

Brevard Fault Zone

## Paleozoic Era

Permian

Mississippian

Devonian

Silurian

Ordovician

Cambrian

Paleozoic

## Mesozoic Era

Cretaceous

Triassic

## Cenozoic Era

Quaternary

Tertiary

**Color Plate 1.9:** Generalized Geology of North Carolina.
**Source:** Modified from the North Carolina Geologic Survey, 1991.

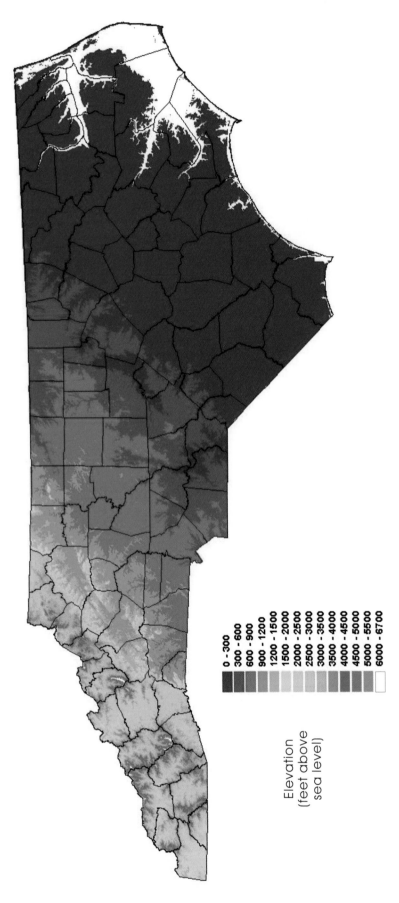

Elevation
(feet above
sea level)

| | |
|---|---|
| ■ | 0 - 300 |
| ■ | 300 - 600 |
| ■ | 600 - 900 |
| ■ | 900 - 1200 |
| ■ | 1200 - 1500 |
| ■ | 1500 - 2000 |
| ■ | 2000 - 2500 |
| ■ | 2500 - 3000 |
| ■ | 3000 - 3500 |
| ■ | 3500 - 4000 |
| ■ | 4000 - 4500 |
| ■ | 4500 - 5000 |
| ■ | 5000 - 5500 |
| ■ | 5500 - 6000 |
| □ | 6000 - 6700 |

**Color Plate 1.10:** Elevation.
**Source:** Derived from U.S.G.S. 1:250,000 Digital Elevation Models.

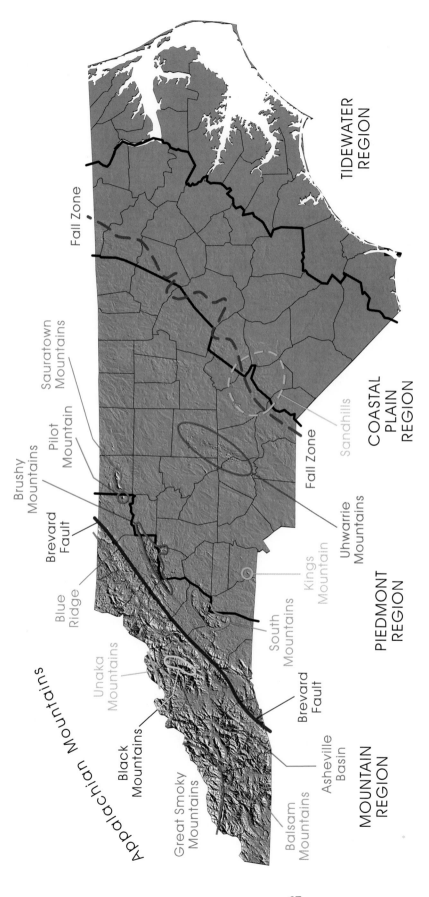

**Color Plate 1.11:** Selected Physical Features.
**Source:** Derived from U.S.G.S. 1:250,000 Digital Elevation Models.

67

*Photo by Ole Gade.*

**Color Plate 1.12:** The Outer Banks include the barrier islands that extend from the Virginia state line to Cape Lookout, near Morehead City. This late 1970s scene, looking northward from the Cape Hatteras lighthouse in Dare County, illustrates the narrow width of these barrier islands. Barrier islands are a popular destination for swimming, fishing, surfing, seashell hunting, or simply enjoying the sun and sand.

**Color Plate 1.13:** The Uwharrie Mountains (here in Randolph County), relatively low mountains or high hills composed of resistant rock, are monadnocks. Similar ranges are found elsewhere in the Piedmont and include the Brushy, Kings, Sauratown, and South mountains.

68

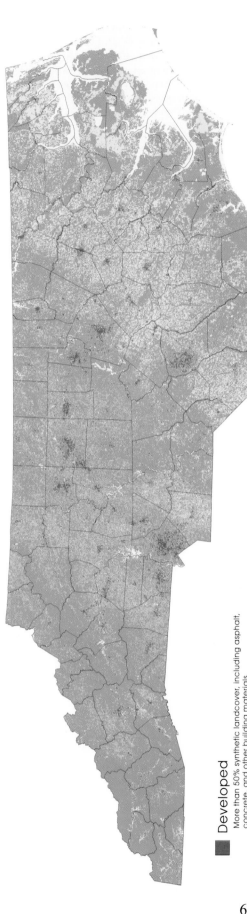

**Developed**
More than 50% synthetic landcover, including asphalt, concrete, and other building materials.

**Cultivated**
More than 50% coverage by seasonally harvested row and root crops, as well as barren or non-vegetated land that represents fallow fields that are generally cultivated.

**Grasslands/Pasture**
Land that is not classified as either Developed, Cultivated, Water, or Barren, with vegetation dominated by herbaceous species, and closure by either forest or shrub cover not to exceed 25% of either.

**Exposed Rock**
Any area where bedrock is exposed at the surface or where a layer of soil exists that is not thick enough to support significant vegetation.

**Sand/Gravel**
Sandy or silty abutting tidal areas, and inland lakes and upland sand areas that have little or no established vegetation.

**Shrublands**
Land that is not classified as either Developed, Cultivated, Forest, Water, or Barren, with more than 25% closure by a mix of evergreen and deciduous shrub species.

**Deciduous Forests**
Forested area covered predominantly by broadleaf deciduous trees that lose their leaves at the end of the growing season.

**Mixed Forests**
Forested land with an intermixture of at least 25% deciduous and evergreen species.

**Evergreen Forests**
Forest land with more than 75% stocking by needleleaf evergreen species.

**Mountain Conifers**
Forest land with more than 75% stocking by mountain species such as white pine, hemlock, and spruce-fir.

**Marshes**
Herbaceous cover in salt, brackish, and freshwater marshes in riverine and estuarine environments.

**Water**
More that 50% surface water with no or minimal emergent vegetation.

**Color Plate 1.14:** Land Cover in North Carolina.
**Source:** Modified from the North Carolina Center for Geographic Information and Analysis, 1998.

**Color Plate 1.15:** Lake Norman is the largest artificial lakes in North Carolina. An aerial view of the lake in Iredell County illustrates part of the waterfront development that is occurring along most of the lakeshore. On the east side of the bridge carrying NC 15 (right side of photo) is Crescent Resources' Pinnacle Shores, an exclusive shoreline development with 180 homes.

*Photo by Ole Gade.*

**C.P. 1.16a:** Encroachment of farmland and highways pose a threat to these naturally vegetated Carolina Bays. Most of the Bays are seasonal wetlands that harbor unique and rare species of animal life.

*Photo by Robert E. Reiman.*

**C.P. 1.16b:** In many areas, Carolina Bays are being converted for a variety of uses, including agriculture. Note the vegetated "rim" around the Bay that maintains the signature oval shape.

*Photo by Robert E. Reiman.*

**Color Plate 1.16:** Carolina Bays.

Photo by Robert E. Reiman.

**Color Plate 1.17:** Clay particles are suspended in the water of the Pee Dee River, turning the water brown as the river flows beyond Blewett Falls Lake and dam to the South Carolina border (Anson and Richmond counties).

**Color Plate 1.18:** The clear, clean waters of the Nantahala River flow through Swain County. Clean water is characteristic of most rivers found in the Mountain Region. These rivers are popular for white water rafting and fly fishing.

Photo by Ole Gade.

**Color Plate 1.19:** Waterfalls abound in the Mountain Region; the southernmost ridges are places with some of the largest annual rainfall in the continental United States. More than 200 named waterfalls are located in the region, including this waterfall on the Horsepasture River. The river formed the Jocassee Gorge (Transylvania County near Brevard), which recently has become part of the public domain through the combined efforts of the former owner, Duke Power, state agencies, and land trusts.

**Color Plate 1.20:** The Blue Ridge Paper Products plant in Canton (Haywood County) is an example of a former point pollution source along the Pigeon River. The pollution generated considerable controversy. Today the plant is meeting regulatory standards, although discoloration of the river water continues to be an eyesore.

**Color Plate 3.1:** A cleared area in Moore County shows the distinctive color of red clay, which is a trademark of the Piedmont's most prevalent soil type. Clearing all vegetative cover, a common practice in the construction process of roads and structures, exposes the soil to erosive elements of local weather. Often this is the source for some of the brown colored rivers of the region following heavy rains.

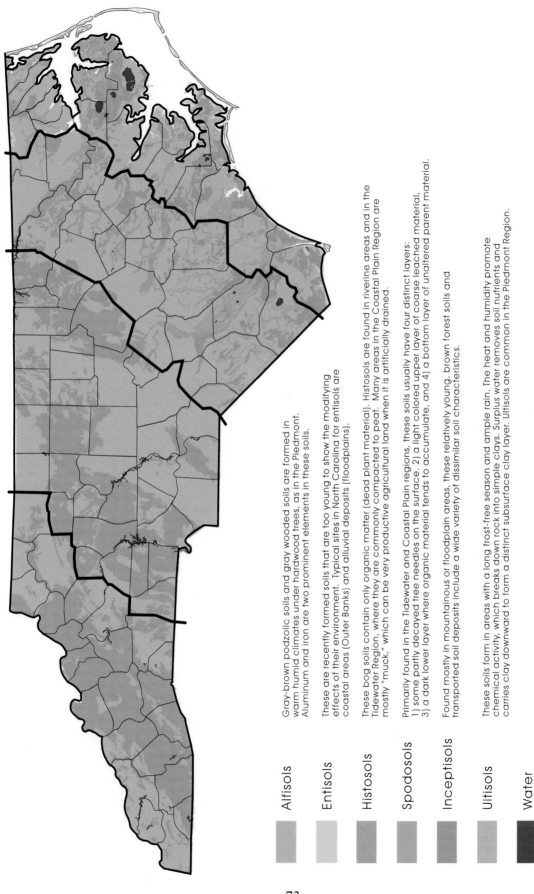

**Color Plate 3.2:** General Soils of North Carolina.
**Source:** Modified from the U.S. Department of Agriculture Soil Conservation Service State Soil Geographic Database, 2000. Descriptions modified from P.J. Gersmehl (1990) and T.L. McKnight (1996).

Alfisols — Gray-brown podzolic soils and gray wooded soils are formed in warm humid climates under hardwood trees, as in the Piedmont. Aluminum and iron are two prominent elements in these soils.

Entisols — These are recently formed soils that are too young to show the modifying effects of their environment. Typical sites in North Carolina for entisols are coastal areas (Outer Banks) and alluvial deposits (floodplains).

Histosols — These bog soils contain only organic matter (dead plant material). Histosols are found in riverine areas and in the Tidewater Region, where they are commonly compacted to peat. Many areas in the Coastal Plain Region are mostly "muck," which can be very productive agricultural land when it is artificially drained.

Spodosols — Primarily found in the Tidewater and Coastal Plain regions, these soils usually have four distinct layers: 1) some partly decayed tree needles on the surface, 2) a light colored upper layer of coarse leached material, 3) a dark lower layer where organic material tends to accumulate, and 4) a bottom layer of unaltered parent material.

Inceptisols — Found mostly in mountainous or floodplain areas, these relatively young, brown forest soils and transported soil deposits include a wide variety of dissimilar soil characteristics.

Ultisols — These soils form in areas with a long frost-free season and ample rain. The heat and humidity promote chemical activity, which breaks down rock into simple clays. Surplus water removes soil nutrients and carries clay downward to form a distinct subsurface clay layer. Ultisols are common in the Piedmont Region.

Water

**Color Plate 3.3:** Hatteras Inlet in Hyde County provides a passageway from the Atlantic Ocean to Pamlico Sound. Note the sea oats in the foreground.

*Photo by Ole Gade.*

*Photo by Mike Mayfield.*

**Color Plate 3.4:** Inland from the coast lie the coastal flatwoods (Pender County). This area is a transition zone between the Coastal Plain and Tidewater regions.

**Color Plate 3.5:** Shrub vegetation occurs throughout North Carolina, particularly after timber cutting or other landscape disturbances. Here an area cut for timber is in the early stages of ecological succession.

*Photo by Mike Mayfield.*

*Photo by Ole Gade.*

**Color Plate 3.6:** The development of the Piedmont Region is represented by the fast growing Research Triangle Park area (Durham County). The Research Triangle Park is recognized nationwide as a high technology area.

**Color Plate 3.7:** Rowan County provides natural resources for a granite quarry. This operation yields stone for the construction industry.

*Photo by Ole Gade.*

*Photo by Ole Gade.*

**Color Plate 3.8:** Weymouth experimental forest in Moore County shows the under-story of a southern yellow pine forest. Note how straight the trees are; this is an important factor in the extraction of trees for timber, chip, and pulpwood.

**Color Plate 3.9:** An autumn scene depicts the deciduous forest of the Mountain Region (Watauga County). Tourists travel from all over to view the spectacular colors.

*Photo by Mike Mayfield.*

**Color Plate 3.10:** Highway 194 is a designated state scenic highway. Along the road near Todd (Watauga County) is a mixture of deciduous forest, pasture, and agricultural lands. Much of the region has been logged in the past 60 to 80 years.

**Color Plate 3.11:** As elevation increases a transition occurs between deciduous and spruce-fir vegetation. A section of Grandfather Mountain near the Blue Ridge Parkway viaduct (Avery County) displays this mixture; the deciduous trees change color, but the evergreen forest maintains its dark green needles.

**Color Plate 3.12:** The cool damp floor of the spruce-fir forest in the Great Smoky Mountains National Park (Swain County) is covered with moss and fallen trees.

**Color Plate 3.13:** Atop Grandfather Mountain (Avery County), the spruce-fir forest is silhouetted against a blanket of clouds covering the valleys below.

# A Changing Mosaic of People

## INTRODUCTION

What is more important to a state than its people? Subsequent chapters of this text will characterize our population's attributes in a great many ways, from economic activities and development to social and political behavior; and from daily life in our communities to involvement in globalizing our economy. In so many ways we will find that North Carolina distinguishes itself in the character and quality of its population, but in some ways we see that the quality of our lives, as it compares to people living elsewhere, can be significantly improved. To assess the great variety of conditions in our state it is important to first look in a detailed manner at our demographic essentials. That is the charge of this chapter; quality of life conditions are left to Chapter 7. From this chapter the reader should come away with knowledge of the considerable variations existing from the coast to the mountains in how we have settled our land; in how we now distribute ourselves by age, gender, race, and ethnicity; and in how these differences impact local and regional economies and social conditions. In sum, here will be the basis for understanding future needs and changes. As will be seen for many of the following chapters, it is necessary to provide a historic context for understanding current changes. Newcomers to our state will find that public and private decisions affecting the welfare of communities are shaped as much by their roots in a past critically different from the present, as they are shaped by our perception of current needs, and our hopes for the future. The very fact that the state has experienced recent revolutionary changes in its basic demography contributes to an apparent reluctance to come to grips with deeply imbedded, and regionally defined, social and economic problems.

## A POPULATION REVERSAL

It was a three decades ago that a new population epoch dawned on North Carolina. The 20th Century's milestone decade was the 1970s. Prior to 1970, the state was a notable contributor to the Northeast, the Midwest, and the West, of many of its most dynamic, best educated and youthful people. In this massive flight of well educated and productive migrants to the more industrialized and urban regions of the country, North Carolina was merely representative of a predominately rural South, where employment opportunities and socio-cultural amenities were lagging. How this highly selective net outmigration process, this "brain drain", impacted the state's human resources and economy, and what could or should be done about it, were questions investigated and heatedly debated during mid-century decades.

Human migration flows have varied through time and over space, with rural areas carrying the major burden of the outflow of people. For a state which has long taken pride in being essentially rural, this process of change, tearing at the traditional fabric of social structure and culture, was viewed with increasing alarm. Of course, from the early decades of the 20th century some parts of the state (especially in the Piedmont) were industrializing and urbanizing, and thereby gaining considerably in their population base. Many rural areas were prevented from large scale depopulation by having a consistently high birth rate, while others saw themselves gradually change from a rural condition through encroaching suburbanization and exurbanization. Furthermore, changes affecting the structure of the population varied by race. Relatively small, though spatially highly concentrated, the American Indian population has not experienced the high rate of interregional mobility of whites and African Americans. On the other hand, the experience of the latter two races varied greatly. Whites initiated large-scale net outmigration during World War I and gradually increased in their excess of outmigrants. For the decade of the 1950s this total was close to 130,000. Blacks were slower to participate, but by the 1940s they exceeded in total numbers their white counterparts. During the 1950s over 165,000 more blacks left than entered the state. For the white population a complete turnaround in this migration pattern began during the early 1960s, but for the blacks this did not occur until a decade later. In this way, the 1970s provide a prism for the essential understanding of the present character of North Carolina's population, as well as for predicting changes apt to occur well into the 21st century.

So, the 1970s was a decade of demographic surprises, whose basic impacts extended into the 80s with some aspects further amplified in the 90s, where they have been joined by a new slate of demographic surprises. Birth rates have dropped dramatically, while death rates are remaining fairly constant in spite of considerable increase in life expectancy at birth. People's locational preferences have shifted. Non-metropolitan areas saw a rebirth because many perceived a rural environment with less congestion, pollution, and crime as superior to the urban environment; urban sprawl and extended commuting distances resulted from this. Others have flocked in relatively greater numbers to those same urban centers that are now clearly outgaining population growth in the rural areas. And yet, almost all parts of the state have seen a burgeoning Hispanic population flooding in to take advantage of opportunities in a booming economy's construction industry and low wage manufacturing and agricultural industries. Hispanics have more than quadrupled their numbers according to the 2000 Census, but are still suspected of having been seriously undercounted. More African Americans, and Asiatics populate North Carolina cities than ever before. Oriental restaurants, ubiquitous in urban places of all sizes throughout the state, are increasingly complemented by Mexican or other Hispanic eateries. Yet, it must be recognized that the state is but a microcosm of rather universal conditions of change in the United States. Technological revolution, family structure changes, warfare and political unrest beyond our borders, economic restructuring and globalization, spatial inequality of socio-economic opportunities, labor and retirement migration, environmental change and decay, shifts in the popular perception of just what constitutes a favorable living environment, and a host of lesser factors characterize service societies entering the 21st Century; and they all have combined to significantly affect North Carolina, its regions, and its communities.

The objective of this chapter then is to present the conditions of North Carolina's population. How did it get to be this way? How is it changing in its demographic components of births, deaths, migration, age and gender composition, and racial and ethnic character? How do all of these aspects vary from rural to urban areas, from region to region, from county to county, and even within counties? North Carolina, it will be found, is far from being a representative sample of the American melting pot ideal. Rather, its population comprise a grand mosaic, in its diversity of race, ethnicity, culture, and socio-economic status, as well as in its distinctive patterns of settlement and locational shifts.

## An Expanding State Population

With a population of 8.04 million as of April 1, 2000, North Carolina has for the fourth decade in a row continued to outpace the United States in its rate of population growth. During the 1990s, the state's population was expanding at a rate of about 2.14 percent per year (US = 1.1%), a notable increase over the 1980s rate of 1.27 percent per year (US = .98%). While the 1980s had suggested a return to the 'normalcy' in state population growth attained during most recent decades, with 11.6 percent for the 1960s, 12.2 percent for the 1950s, and 13.7 percent for the 1940s, the 1990s exceeds even the pace offered by the ebullient 1970s, when the rate of increase was 15.7 percent (Table 4.1 and Figure 4.1). Note also, that due to the increasing size of the population base the same rate of growth will produce over time a larger and larger numeric increase. Thus the 15.7 percent increase of the 1970s added a net of 798,000 to the state's inhabitants, or 50,828 for each percentage point of increase, while the 1980s rate of 12.7 percent added 749,000, or 58,976 for each percentage point of increase. For the 1990s, the percentage increase of 21.4 represented an increase of 66,209 persons per percent, the resulting 1,416,864 person expansion during the 1990s is thus more than twice the increase of the preceding decade. It should be noted here that final census figures are not announced until two to three years following the actual census. Reasons include the possible needs to re-census following local accuracy complaints, and to conduct a comprehensive assessment of undercounts for given areas and given populations. The 2000 Census undercount for North Carolina was estimated in March of 2001 to be 95,292, so some may prefer to use the unofficial total of 8,144,605 as the state's more accurate population for 2000. This include university student populations that appear to have been missed is several enumeration districts. (Population data used throughout this text comes from the preliminary United States 2000 Census

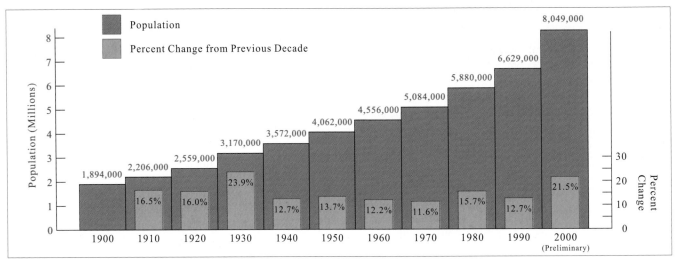

**Figure 4.1:** Population and Percent Change from Preceding Census: 1900-2000.
**Source:** U. S. Bureau of the Census, 1990; author's estimate for 2000.

| | The State | | | | Urban | | | Rural | | | % of Total Population | |
|---|---|---|---|---|---|---|---|---|---|---|---|---|
| | Total Population | Change from Preceding Census | | Places of 2,500 or More | Population | Change from Preceding Census | | Population | Change from Preceding Census | | Urban | Rural |
| | | Number | Percent | | | Number | Percent | | Number | Percent | | |
| Current urban definition | | | | | | | | | | | | |
| 2000 (Apr. 1) | 8,049,313 | 1,420,676 | 21.5 | N/A | N/A | N/A | N/A | N/A | N/A | N/A | N/A | N/A |
| 1990 (Apr. 1) | 6,628,637 | 748,542 | 12.7 | 156 | 3,337,778 | 514,926 | 18.2 | 3,290,859 | 231,945 | 7.6 | 50.4 | 49.6 |
| 1980 (Apr. 1) | 5,880,095 | 795,684 | 15.6 | 141 | 2,822,852 | 512,471 | 22.2 | 3,058,914 | 287,236 | 10.4 | 48.0 | 52.0 |
| 1970 (Apr. 1) | 5,084,411 | 528,256 | 11.6 | 138 | 2,310,381 | 508,460 | 28.2 | 2,771,678 | 17,444 | 0.6 | 45.5 | 54.5 |
| 1960 (Apr. 1) | 4,556,155 | 494,226 | 12.2 | 125 | 1,801,921 | 433,820 | 31.7 | 2,754,234 | 60,406 | 2.2 | 39.5 | 60.5 |
| 1950 (Apr. 1) | 4,061,929 | 490,306 | 13.7 | 107 | 1,368,101 | N/A | N/A | 2,693,828 | N/A | N/A | 33.7 | 66.3 |
| Previous urban definition | | | | | | | | | | | | |
| 1960 (Apr. 1) | 4,556,155 | 494,226 | 12.2 | 106 | 1,647,085 | 408,892 | 33.0 | 2,909,070 | 85,334 | 3.0 | 36.2 | 63.8 |
| 1950 (Apr. 1) | 4,061,929 | 490,306 | 13.7 | 88 | 1,238,193 | 264,018 | 27.1 | 2,823,736 | 226,288 | 8.7 | 30.5 | 69.5 |
| 1940 (Apr. 1) | 3,571,623 | 401,347 | 12.7 | 76 | 974,175 | 164,328 | 20.3 | 2,597,448 | 237,019 | 10.0 | 27.3 | 72.7 |
| 1930 (Apr. 1) | 3,170,276 | 611,153 | 23.9 | 68 | 809,847 | 319,477 | 65.2 | 2,360,429 | 291,676 | 14.1 | 25.5 | 74.5 |
| 1920 (Jan. 1) | 2,559,123 | 352,836 | 16.0 | 55 | 490,370 | 171,896 | 54.0 | 2,068,753 | 180,940 | 9.6 | 19.2 | 80.8 |
| 1910 (Apr. 15) | 2,206,287 | 312,477 | 16.5 | 40 | 318,474 | 131,684 | 70.5 | 1,887,813 | 180,793 | 10.6 | 14.4 | 85.6 |
| 1900 (June 1) | 1,893,810 | 275,861 | 17.1 | 28 | 186,790 | 71,031 | 61.4 | 1,707,020 | 204,830 | 13.6 | 9.9 | 90.1 |
| 1890 (June 1) | 1,617,949 | 218,199 | 15.6 | 18 | 115,759 | 60,643 | 110.0 | 1,502,190 | 157,556 | 11.7 | 7.2 | 92.8 |
| 1880 (June 1) | 1,399,750 | 328,389 | 30.7 | 9 | 55,116 | 18,898 | 52.2 | 1,344,634 | 309,491 | 29.9 | 3.9 | 96.1 |
| 1870 (June 1) | 1,071,361 | 78,739 | 7.9 | 5 | 36,218 | 11,664 | 47.5 | 1,035,143 | 67,075 | 6.9 | 3.4 | 96.6 |
| 1860 (June 1) | 992,622 | 123,583 | 14.2 | 4 | 24,554 | 3,445 | 16.3 | 968,068 | 120,138 | 14.2 | 2.5 | 97.5 |
| 1850 (June 1) | 869,039 | 115,620 | 15.3 | 4 | 21,109 | 7,799 | 58.6 | 847,930 | 107,821 | 14.6 | 2.4 | 97.6 |
| 1840 (June 1) | 753,419 | 15,432 | 2.1 | 3 | 13,310 | 2,855 | 27.3 | 740,109 | 12,577 | 1.7 | 1.8 | 98.2 |
| 1830 (June 1) | 737,987 | 99,158 | 15.5 | 3 | 10,455 | − 2,047 | − 16.4 | 727,532 | 101,205 | 16.2 | 1.4 | 98.6 |
| 1820 (Aug. 7) | 638,829 | 83,329 | 15.0 | 4 | 12,502 | 12,502 | N/A | 626,327 | 70,827 | 12.8 | 2.0 | 98.0 |
| 1810 (Aug. 6) | 555,500 | 77,397 | 16.2 | N/A | N/A | N/A | N/A | 555,500 | 77,397 | 16.2 | N/A | 100.0 |
| 1800 (Aug. 4) | 478,103 | 84,352 | 21.4 | N/A | N/A | N/A | N/A | 478,103 | 84,352 | 21.4 | N/A | 100.0 |
| 1790 (Aug. 2) | 393,751 | N/A | 100.0 | N/A | N/A | N/A | N/A | N/A | N/A | N/A | N/A | N/A |

**Table 4.1:** Population of the State: Earliest Census to 2000.
**Source:** U. S. Bureau of the Census, 1990 Census of Population, and 2000 Preliminary.

released in February of 2001, and from the North Carolina Office of State Planning's actual and projected statistics on municipal and county populations; these data are available online and can be checked periodically for final and certified 2000 Census results).

Of considerable significance is the fact that the character of growth in the 1970s, 1980s and 1990s is different from that of earlier decades. For the last three decades of the 20th Century more than one-half of the increase of the nearly three million is due to net immigration, more people moving into the state than leaving. On the other hand, up to the mid-1960s the state's growth was due entirely to natural increase, an excess of births over deaths. In fact, the "baby boom" of the 1950s and early 1960s more than sustained population growth. For the 15 years of the "baby boom", the state experienced a net outflow of 475,000 migrants, while still managing to grow. With the "baby bust" of the late 1960s and the 1970s the dramatic decrease in births was more than compensated for by what had become a turnaround in migration. This remarkable change in the census reflected the increasing popularization of the "Sunbelt" or the "New South" as a place to live. So now, at the start of the new millennium, it appears that the state continues to benefit from this positive image, drawing to it many more thousands of people each year than choose to leave. And with the return of a higher rate of natural increase, the state will need to prepare for even higher rates of growth into the 21st Century, even as the boisterous economic growth of the 1990s is abating.

While North Carolina's current population growth rate exceeds that of the United States, it is less than several other states in the Sunbelt. For example, Nevada expanded an astonishing 66.3 percent during the 1990s, while Arizona, Colorado, Utah and Idaho all exceeded 30 percent. On the other hand, the state is much closer to the pattern established by its regional neighbors: Georgia led with 26.4 percent, Florida gained 23.6 percent, Tennessee 16.7 percent, South Carolina 15.1 percent, and Virginia 14.4 percent. It is appropriate to note that state leaders can no longer boast of the state being the tenth most populous in the country. In car racing terms, Georgia blew around North Carolina in the early 1990s, and is now set to lap the state. North Carolina ranks thirteenth among the fifty states in rate of population growth, but with an annual net increase of about 140,000 people its numeric growth is exceeded only by California, Texas, Florida, Georgia, and Arizona. One important conclusion to draw from these comparisons is that North Carolina is as likely to suffer from the stresses of too rapid a population growth as is being experienced elsewhere in the Sunbelt. Further, the state is unaccustomed to having its population increase sustained by net immigration rather than natural increase. It is now on the receiving end of some other state's brain drain. A predominately youthful, better educated, higher skilled, opportunistic, and entrepreneurial population is entering the state with much of its cost of education and vocational training provided elsewhere. This population is complemented in numbers and diversity by newcomers with the interest and skills in supplanting the state's labor needs at the lower end of the pay scale, as well. Evolving in other parts of the country and the world has also been these immigrant populations' sociocultural attitudes and expectations of the present and future quality of life. This is an exciting and potentially highly rewarding change of conditions that portends well for continued improvement in the state's social and economic situation. At the same time it offers new challenges and continuing opportunities for expanding the basic service system needed to accommodate our new residents.

### Urban-Rural Contrasts

"Where we are" is as important a question to explore in a state's population geography as "how many we are." Previous chapters discuss the considerable variation in physical environments that exists across this 500 mile wide state. In the density and distribution of people and places we see demonstrated an equally varied condition. Among the state's four primary regions, and in all aspects of people and economy the highly urbanized Piedmont predominates. Mountain, Coastal Plain, and Tidewater regions have lower densities of population, with fewer and generally smaller urban centers. A close look will yield even greater understanding of existing disparities, not only among, but also within these four regions. While this chapter considers population conditions for the entire state, more detailed aspects are magnified in the regional chapters (see Chapters 9 to 13) defined by the four state primary regions, where individual counties are then evaluated within their respective state geographic regions.

It bears noting that the delimitation of the state's regions varies somewhat with a change from an essentially physical environmental definition for the primary regions to one of socio-economic characteristics for the 13 state primary regions. In the latter case we are dependent upon the counties' administrative boundaries, which only rarely conform to physical features. The reader should note the discussion of regionalization in Chapter 9.

### Metropolitan Counties and Their Cities

Each of the North Carolina Metropolitan Statistical Areas (MSA) has one or more central counties containing its main population concentration in an urban built-up area of at least 50,000 inhabitants. An MSA may also include adjacent, more rural counties which have close economic and social relations with the central counties. To attain this designation, these adjacent counties must have a specified level of commuting to employment locations in the central counties, and must also meet certain standards regarding metropolitan character. These include size of urban population, population density, and population growth. For the purpose of additional clarification it is notable that the inhabitants of MSAs are divided into two groups, those living inside a central city (incorporated city), and those living outside. As defined by the United States Bureau of the Census all designated MSA counties are metropolitan; other counties are considered nonmetropolitan.

North Carolina contains 100 counties, a statistical, if not an administratively, convenient number. Of these, 35 counties,

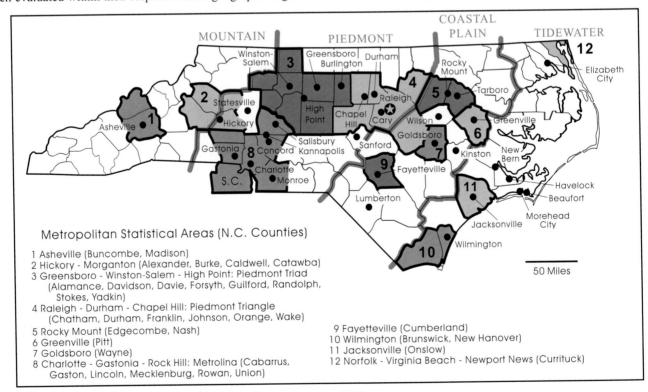

**Metropolitan Statistical Areas (N.C. Counties)**

1 Asheville (Buncombe, Madison)
2 Hickory - Morganton (Alexander, Burke, Caldwell, Catawba)
3 Greensboro - Winston-Salem - High Point: Piedmont Triad (Alamance, Davidson, Davie, Forsyth, Guilford, Randolph, Stokes, Yadkin)
4 Raleigh - Durham - Chapel Hill: Piedmont Triangle (Chatham, Durham, Franklin, Johnson, Orange, Wake)
5 Rocky Mount (Edgecombe, Nash)
6 Greenville (Pitt)
7 Goldsboro (Wayne)
8 Charlotte - Gastonia - Rock Hill: Metrolina (Cabarrus, Gaston, Lincoln, Mecklenburg, Rowan, Union)

9 Fayetteville (Cumberland)
10 Wilmington (Brunswick, New Hanover)
11 Jacksonville (Onslow)
12 Norfolk - Virginia Beach - Newport News (Currituck)

**Figure 4.2**: Metropolitan Statistical Areas and Selected Urban Places, 1995.
**Source:** North Carolina Office of State Planning, 1997.

and therefore 35 per cent, belong to a defined MSA. Over the past two decades the state has seen an increase in designated MSAs from eight to twelve, and from 25 to 35 metropolitan counties. Figure 4.2 illustrates the location of the MSAs and the counties designated metropolitan. Although only four MSAs are found in the Piedmont these include 21 of the metro counties and approaches three-quarters (73.5%) of the state's total estimated 2000 metropolitan population of 5,377,320. Three of the Piedmont MSAs are the clear leaders in total population and in numeric growth: Charlotte-Gastonia-Rock Hill with 1,334,679 persons (not including York County, South Carolina); Greensboro-Winston Salem-High Point with 1,203,060; and Raleigh-Durham-Chapel Hill with 1,187,941. While Charlotte's MSA population passed Greensboro's in the 1990s, Raleigh's is expected to not only pass Greensboro's over the next decade, but Charlotte's as well. For the details on why this is so the reader should consult Chapters 6 and 12.

Clearly the Piedmont does not compare in urban scale with the large metropolitan areas of the Northeast and Midwest, but the existence in this region of 21 contiguous metro counties makes this a highly significant metropolitan region not only on the state level, but also in the Southeast. In both area and population this, the Piedmont Urban Crescent, hereafter called simply the Urban Crescent, is larger in both area and population than the Atlanta metropolitan region, but it does not have a similar one urban node concentration of people. This pattern of settlement is what makes this a particularly striking urban area. Certainly one that is unique in an otherwise largely rural state. Outside the Urban Crescent there are fourteen metro counties belonging to nine MSAs. These exhibit varying degrees of urban character. Hickory-Morganton is a small urban agglomeration of the central western Piedmont that is gradually linking spatially to the Urban Crescent; Fayetteville and Jacksonville derive most of their raison d'etre from military installations; Goldsboro does this to a lesser extent. Asheville MSA provides the only significant urban focus in the Mountain Region, while the Wilmington MSA does the same for the Tidewater Region. Rocky Mount and Greenville are recently designated MSAs of the northern Coastal Plain, and Currituck County finds itself the southern rural extension of the Norfolk-Virginia Beach-Newport News MSA.

Thus the Urban Crescent is unique in the absence of a single, very large, and dominant city. Geographically it is best characterized as a multinucleated urban agglomeration, with the contiguous MSAs, from Gaston to Franklin and Johnston counties, containing nearly four million people, or about half of the state's population. Five central cities within this urban continuum have 2000 Census populations over 100,000: Charlotte, Winston-Salem, Greensboro, Durham, and the capital city of Raleigh. Charlotte, with 540,828 people, is the largest and it also is more than twice the physical size of any of the others. Charlotte is the central city in an urban area frequently referred to as Metrolina. Other Metrolina cities are much smaller, like Gastonia (66,277), the sister cities of Concord (55,977) and Kannapolis (36,910), and Salisbury (26,462). Raleigh (276,093), Durham (187,035), Cary

(94,536) and Chapel Hill (48,715) are the central cities of the Piedmont Triangle urban area. Greensboro (223,891), Winston-Salem (185,776), High Point (85,839), and Burlington (44,917) comprise the Piedmont Triad, the urban node of the Piedmont Dispersed City (Hayes 1976), which also includes the smaller towns of Asheboro, Lexington, and Thomasville. Finally, we have the option of including the much smaller MSA of Hickory, as a western outlier of the Urban Crescent. Hickory, its central city in a four county region, has 37,222 inhabitants.

The Urban Crescent is a metropolitan region of great internal diversity. It has an emerging urban land use continuity that may eventually merit calling it a megalopolis (that is, an interconnected string of urban places), but it is not likely to ever approach the scale of other existing megalopolises like Boston-Washington (Bos-Wash) or Milwaukee-Cleveland (Great Lakes Megalopolis). Even so, the almost continuous urbanization through the Piedmont, the effects of its transportation linkages, and the resulting pattern of industrial, commercial, and residential investment, allows us to consider the Urban Crescent's functional character as North Carolina's "Main Street" (Chapters 6 and 12). And though the Urban Crescent has reached 50 percent of the state's population, at least one-third of its MSA population live outside the central cities. As will be explored in greater detail in the following regional chapters, there are also major relocations of people within the cities proper.

Maps illustrating urban development, population size, and population density show the prominence of the Piedmont Region. Illustrations of total population by county (Figure 4.3), population density (Figure 4.4), and population settlement size (Figures 4.5; 4.5a), illustrate not only Piedmont predominance, but also the variation in population concentration within it. Metropolitan counties containing the larger central cities are clearly differentiated. Those counties having a year 2000 population over 150,000 include: Mecklenburg (695,454 people, with the city of Charlotte); Wake (627,846; Raleigh); Guilford (421,922; Greensboro and High Point); Cumberland (302,963 with Fayetteville (121,015)); Forsyth (306,067; Winston-Salem); Durham (223,314; Durham); Buncombe (206,330 with Asheville (68,889)); Gaston (190,365; Gastonia); Onslow (150,355, with Jacksonville (66,715)); and New Hanover (160,307 with Wilmington (75,838)). Among these Cumberland, Buncombe, Onslow, and New Hanover counties are found outside the Urban Crescent. Among the three major MSAs there is a continuing competition for dominance. Each has its own complex of economic base advantages, as discussed in detail in Chapter 12.

It is obvious that MSA designations provide an organizing framework for looking statistically at urban growth and change. So it is relevant to note that current usage is likely to be replaced by 2003. At that point in time the U.S. Bureau of the Census is moving to replace the current system by one that favors the concept of core populations. A Core Based Statistical Area (CBSA) "is a statistical geographic entity associated with at least one core of 10,000 or more population, plus adjacent territory having a high degree of social and economic integration

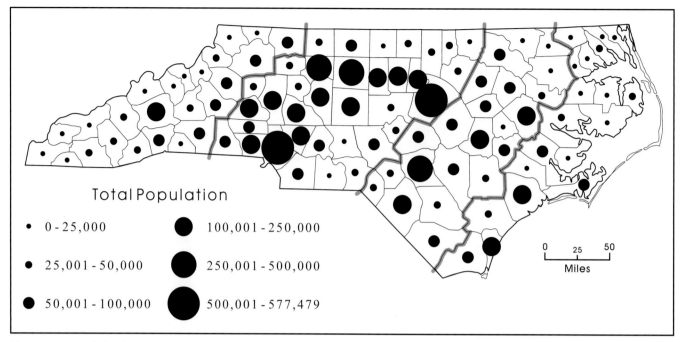

**Figure 4.3:** Population by County, 1995.
**Source:** North Carolina, Office of State Planning, North Carolina Municipal Population, 1996.

with the core as measured by commuting ties" (Kasdorf 2000). Three main areas are to be designated: Metropolitan CBSA, Micropolitan CBSA, and Other Core Based Statistical Areas. As previously, Metropolitan is defined as having an urbanized areas of at least 50,000 people. Micropolitan areas must have an urban cluster of 10,000 to 49,999 people. In addition, distinctions are drawn between 'central' CBSA and 'outside' CBSA counties, with the term 'rural' pointedly avoided. Complexities in statistical area definition are thus increasing, one result being the splitting up of many of the current major MSA designated areas. Durham and Orange County, for example, may emerge as a designated CBSA separate from a new Raleigh CBSA. It is important to local leaders and image builders to have their cities clearly identified in key federal statistical references. For High Point promoters it is harrowing to contemplate the virtual disappearance of the town's name from federal listings, as well as those of these listings many

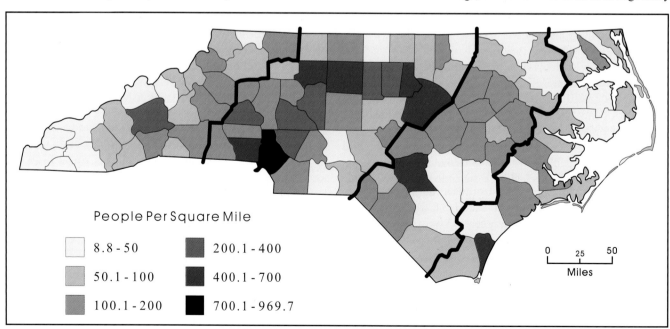

**Figure 4.4:** Population Density by County, 1995.
**Source:** North Carolina Office of State Planning, 1997.

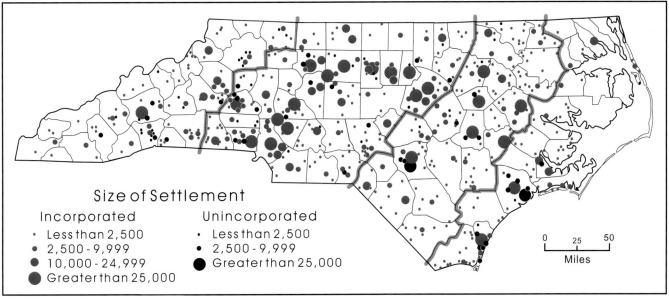

**Figure 4.5:** Settlement Patterns, 1990.
**Source:** U. S. Bureau of the Census, 1990 Census of Population, North Carolina.

users. The Greensboro-Winston-Salem-High Point MSA is slated to become a stand alone Winston-Salem CBSA, while High Point will find itself lumped with Burlington and Eden into a Greensboro CBSA (Hopkins 2000).

*Rural Counties*

A number of counties, though constituent members of MSAs, are not heavily populated. In the Urban Crescent there are rural metropolitan counties which are now being impacted by residents moving from, though still employed in, adjacent central city counties. Some of these suburbanizing counties still have small populations and, at the present, are overwhelmingly rural. Yet they are MSA counties, and they are characterized by very rapid growth. For the Piedmont Triad MSA they include Forsyth County's northern neighbor, Stokes, with a population of 44,711 (2% yearly average increase, 1990-2000); its western neighbor of Yadkin, with only 36,348 residents (1.9%); and Guilford County's southern neighbor of Randolph with 130,454 persons (2.2%). For Metrolina MSA, Union County has 123,677 residents (4.7%), and Lincoln has 63,780 (2.7%). And for the Piedmont Triangle MSA, there is Johnston County (121,965 persons), with a 50 percent increase the state's fastest growing during the 1990s. And there is Franklin County with 47,260 (3.0%), a county with five small municipalities. Its county seat of Louisburg, a scant 20 miles from Raleigh, is exemplary of small towns in the urban shadow soon to be caught in suburban expansion. The town with 3,228 people in 1980, had dropped to 3,037 in 1990; and with 3111 in 2000 it is still waiting to be discovered by the commuters. Then there is Chatham County with 49,329 people and a 2.7% annual rate of increase. Contiguous to and east of the Urban Crescent there are seven medium-sized counties in the north central portion of the Coastal Plain. Here the towns of Rocky

Mount, Wilson, Goldsboro, Kinston, Greenville and Tarboro contribute centralized populations to counties ranging in size from 60,000 to 133,000, exist in a pattern of urban development that permits us to refer to this as "Ring City", as developed in Chapter 11. In the western Piedmont a string of medium-sized counties extends from the Virginia border to the South Carolina border.

These different patterns are further amplified on the map of population density (Figure 4.4). The cartographic pattern chosen to display this information enhances visually the locational distinctiveness of the Urban Crescent. What also comes across is the existence of three large areas of relatively low population numbers and thinly distributed people. First among these is the state's largest predominately rural area, a northeastern Coastal Plain and Tidewater area with 14 counties, none of which exceed a population of 30,000, and with six counties having less than 20,000. Second, there is a tier of 15 mountain counties which have joint borders with the adjacent states of Virginia, Tennessee, Georgia, and South Carolina, all with less than 55,000 people including nine having less than 20,000 people. Third, there are two clusters of rural counties, the southern Coastal Plain and Tidewater with areally quite large counties, ranging in population from 10,000 to 60,000; and the south central Piedmont with seven predominantly rural counties. This pattern of rural, thinly populated counties distributed in large clusters through the state aids in giving North Carolina the visual, if not the statistical, impression of being a largely rural state.

North Carolina's settlements, the location of urban communities of all sizes, are presented in Figure 4.5. It is obvious from this map that the state is endowed with a rather large number of smaller cities and towns, in addition to its larger central cities. It is also clear that the pattern of urban places portrayed here varies considerably from region to region, and within some regions, from county to county. The processes influencing the evolution of this pattern of central places are fairly complex and are constantly shifting in pace and character. In describing these processes of change we will begin with a brief overview of the history of North Carolina settlement

## FOUR HUNDRED YEARS OF SETTLEMENT

North Carolina has had three distinct settlement periods in the past four hundred years. These periods are tied largely to changing economic and population mobility conditions, and include: 1) pre-industrial, to about 1850; 2) industrial, 1850 to 1960; and 3) post industrial, from 1960. More details on the character and impact of change during these periods as they have affected particular North Carolina regions are dealt with in the appropriate state primary region chapters of this text, Chapters 11-13.

### Pre-Industrial Settlement Period

During the pre-industrial period the earliest central places began as colonial villages adjacent to tidewater access to the Atlantic Ocean. Bath (Beaufort County), a French Huguenot village, became the first incorporated town in 1706. Livelihood depended increasingly on the growing of agricultural export commodities. As settlers moved into the state from the north and the northwest, as well as from the coast, the need for agricultural service centers influenced the development of a fairly even distribution of varied sized urban places throughout the Coastal Plain and Piedmont regions. The lack of an adequate land-based transportation system prevented the emergence of early dominant cities. That no significant port city developed on the scale of Boston, or the early queen city of the Carolinas, Charleston, South Carolina, is in part due to the distance of the state's coastal colonial settlements from the more prominent colonies of New England and the Mid-Atlantic area. In part it may also be due to the largely inhospitable nature of North Carolina's Outer Banks, which extend from Virginia two-thirds of the distance to South Carolina. Also the state did not become an important debarkation area for the subsequent waves of European settlers who continued to nourish the growth of large cities on the Atlantic Seaboard.

As for land-based transportation, it was not until 1789 that the first stage line was established, much later than was the case for other coastal states. The first Post Road connected coastal settlements from New England to Charleston. Subsequent roads were then gradually completed to the interior, as well as extended into the Piedmont from adjacent states. By the 1850 United States Census only four small urban places had developed: Wilmington with 7,264 inhabitants, New Bern with 4,681, Fayetteville with 4,646, and Raleigh with 4,518. While Wilmington and New Bern derived significant momentum from their coastal and tidewater locations and functioned largely as port towns, Raleigh and Fayetteville were both located along the physiographic area of discontinuity, the so-called Fall Line, separating the Piedmont's rolling land surface from the lower elevated and more subdued land surface of the Coastal Plain. River transportation and proximity to extensive areas of agricultural production were factors important in their site and situation. Raleigh also was platted as the state capital in 1792.

### Industrial Growth and the Expansion of Settlement

Construction of heavy duty plank roads began in 1849 but significant expansion in both size and number of urban places awaited the building of railroads. And though this great transportation venture began as early as 1852, the Civil War and the subsequent period of reconstruction slowed considerably any large scale urban development. Even so, built and owned by the state, the North Carolina Railroad opened the Piedmont to development and engendered in the process a major shift in economic dominance from eastern agriculture and trade interests to the emerging industrial power of the Piedmont. It was rail that ushered in the industrial period in the state's economic history. As stated in Brad Stuart's, *Making North Carolina Prosper*:

Where the railroads went, towns and cities grew. From its western terminus at Charlotte, the line extends to Salisbury, Greensboro, Burlington, Durham, Raleigh, and finally Goldsboro, the terminus of another state-owned railroad extending from the port of Morehead City. With the completion of the railroad, the long isolated Piedmont was connected to the ports and cottonlands of the East. More importantly the Piedmont itself was tied together and connected to the cities of the Deep South and to the great markets and manufacturing districts of the North. The portion of the railroad from Charlotte to Greensboro was called the 'golden link' because it completed a system of rail lines extending from Boston to New Orleans (1979, 10-11).

The New England connection became very important during the first half of the 20th century as the towns and cities of the Piedmont began receiving manufacturing industries relocating from the Northeast where costs of plant expansion, land, and labor were becoming less competitive.

Other factors influenced the emergence of an industrial and urban Piedmont. The railroad bisected the hardwood forests of the western Piedmont, and connected most parts of the commercial agricultural areas with their emphasis on cotton and tobacco. With energy demands initially satisfied by harnessing the rushing waters of Piedmont rivers, the stage was set for the evolution of the ubiquitous mill town favoring the production of textiles, apparel, furniture and food products. In this way the development of a central place system in the Piedmont varied considerably from that experienced in the Coastal Plain, where a dependence on agriculture and a uniformity of rural settling brought about a more orderly and consistent spatial pattern. The path of the North Carolina Railroad has since been paralleled by superhighways, and as these exemplified a shift in the major mode of transporting goods and people so also began a new age in the character and fortunes of urban settlement.

### Post-Industrial Changes and Regional Settlement Patterns

Over the past several decades transportation service facilities, such as trucking terminals and warehousing, have moved to the periphery of central cities, especially where facilitated by Interstate freeway connectors and beltways. Similarly, much manufacturing industry, forever in search of lower costs of location, production and operation, has relocated. This exurban location trend was further aided by the decentralization of offices and retail businesses from their former concentration in the Central Business District of the central cities. Rural areas have in the process become increasingly crowded with urban functions like industrial parks, office parks, and shopping strips and malls. Suburbanization of residences has continued with the expansion of personalized transportation and with the relocation of employment opportunities and places to shop (see further on the sprawling of North Carolina in Chapter 12). Many single industry towns have seen and are seeing their existence threatened by plant closings or layoffs of a large segment of their labor force. Towns in the Piedmont have been especially affected. Elsewhere a new focus on providing services for those in search of leisure and recreation activities or of areas favorable for retirement have enhanced the stability, or the expansion, of many small towns in the Mountain and Tidewater regions. Again the processes of urban development have shifted in intensity and direction, with significant differences in regional impact. So it is relevant to consider changes as they have affected the state's four primary regions during this most recent period of urbanization.

### Tidewater Region

In the Tidewater Region, the Barrier Islands and the coastline to the south exhibit a distribution of small towns and communities like beads on a string. Only the Cape Hatteras National Seashore provides a break in this pattern of settlements. All of these settlements are affected by seashore related leisure activities and have experienced dramatic recent growth. Riverine settlements, many dating from colonial times, dominate the remainder of the Tidewater. Their fortunes are tied to fishing, port functions, small scale manufacturing (especially of forest products), and local administration. Robbed of their agricultural hinterland in their early stages of development, their potential for growth has long been in jeopardy. Even so, it appears that this absence of growth impulses have left many of these small towns with much of their traditional architecture and visible artifacts. In towns like Edenton and New Bern this has contributed to historic preservation efforts that have been further encouraged by a growing interest in retirement migration to such places. A few, like Morehead City, Jacksonville, and Wilmington, have recently benefited from extra-regional investment in port expansion, military installations, and public services, and now finally by their proximity to the coastal leisure boom (see Chapter 11).

### Coastal Plain Region

In the Coastal Plain, where agriculture and dispersed rural settlement have persisted for several centuries, a more even distribution of urban places exists, dominated by small towns and a few medium sized cities. However, emerging in the north central part there is a clear geographically defined "donut" like urban region, with Rocky Mount, Tarboro, Greenville, Kinston, Goldsboro and Wilson encircling a very rural Greene County. An interesting resemblance exists between this evolving urban ring surrounding an essentially urban free open green space, given mostly to agricultural land usage, and the Dutch urban region called the Randstad, where a conscious planning effort for decades has been to preserve the rural integrity of its "Greenheart". Some further thoughts on this "Ring City" structure are explored in greater detail in the Coastal Plain Region chapter. A lessening in the density of urban places occurs from this region toward the south and the west, while unique clustering occurs where military bases influence development, as in the case with Fort Bragg and Pope Air Base in Cumberland County (Fayetteville), and Seymour Johnson Air Base in Wayne County (Goldsboro). The gradual evolution of a land-based transportation system appears to have contributed a degree of alignment in the pattern of urban places. For example, the Atlantic Seaboard rail linkage is paralleled by highway U.S. 117 and the recently completed Interstate 40 from Wilmington north to Goldsboro and Raleigh. Other such transportation artery alignments exist less definitively. In general, the spacing and sizing of central places in the Coastal Plain comes closer to replicating the conditions and spatial patterns promulgated by geographic settlement theory (Berry and Parr 1988). Functioning predominately as agricultural and local administrative service centers, many of these towns have experienced growth difficulties since World War II; though this is hardly the case for the military influenced towns and the new medical center attached to the Medical School of East Carolina University in Greenville.

### Piedmont Region

A very rural southeastern and central part of the Piedmont resembles that of the Coastal Plain, in both urban functional character and in settlement pattern. However, most of the Piedmont is dominated by the Urban Crescent's central cities and their satellite neighbors, plus a large number of small manufacturing towns interspersed here and there in the northern and western parts of the region. Rapidly expanding industrial and office parks, shopping centers and residential communities in the few remaining open areas within the Urban Crescent and along North Carolina's new "Main Street" (Interstates 40 and 85), are contributing to its emerging megalopolitan character. Elsewhere in the Piedmont much of the settlement pattern is transportation artery aligned. A strong urban place alignment occurs with U.S. 70 from west of Asheville, east to Hickory and Statesville. This is similarly the case with highway U.S. 74, paralleling an older Seaboard Railroad line, from Hamlet in Richmond County across the southeastern tier of rural counties to Mecklenburg County and thence west to Gaston and Cleveland counties. There are some interesting contrasts in the pattern of urban places in the western Piedmont. Compare, for example, the large concentration of rural and medium-sized incorporated and census designated places, towns and cities in Gaston County with the almost even distribution in adjacent Cleveland County. In addition to differences in spatial distribution there are also significant differences in size. In Gaston County, 13 of the 19 urban places range from 1,000 to 5,000 people, while in Cleveland County eleven places out of a total of 14 have fewer than 1,000 inhabitants. Gaston's proximity and ease of access by rail to a rapidly expanding Charlotte apparently heightened entrepreneurial activity along the main transportation corridor during the early period of industrialization. Cleveland County is farther removed from the Urban Crescent and was also slower in receiving a rail connection; thus an early pattern of single industry towns located adjacent to water power resources has persisted, as have their much smaller size.

*Mountain Region*

In the Mountain Region two distinct patterns of central places exist. One, in the eastern portion, is simply an extension of the western Piedmont pattern. A considerable number of medium- and small-sized predominately manufacturing towns are found in the foothills, in a strong transportation artery alignment. A notable extension of this pattern is into the Asheville Basin, where Buncombe and Haywood counties have seen a good deal of industrial development. The remainder of the mountain counties are dominated by relatively small central places, principally retail service centers and county seats. Several of these have been affected by large scale recreational and resort development, for example, as concentrated in Watauga and Avery counties in the northwestern mountains, which folks there like to refer to as the "High Country", and as dispersed through the southwestern mountains from Henderson and Buncombe in the east to the Great Smoky Mountains National Park on the Tennessee boundary. Many counties in this part of the state complain bitterly that economic and urban development has been severely retarded due to the high incidence of federal land ownership. Federal lands comprise about one-third of the total land area in 13 southern Mountain Region counties. Graham County with 60 percent of its land in the Nantahala National Forest is the leading case in point.

## BUT ARE THEY TOWNS?

Just what constitutes an urban place? In some European countries great care is taken in defining urban places, as for example having no more than several hundred feet between residences, but in this country we tend to define urban as being simply that which is incorporated as administratively urban. Thus a lot of contiguous urban land use is classed as rural, when clearly it is not. There are some real difficulties with this, especially when the interest is in measuring changes in land use, and in the accurate allocating of the population to rural or urban habitation. This also leaves open the issue of functionality. Generally we distinguish rural people as being those in the pursuit of rural based functions (e.g. the predominant use of the land in agriculture and forestry); others are urban by virtue of their employment in centralized urban activities (e.g. commuting to jobs in manufacturing industry, private business, and public service). The issue is complicated where people living in rural areas are beginning to favor doing business out of their own home, so-called cottage industry, ranging from arts and crafts to the "electronic cottage". In our state a large percentage of the population lives outside incorporated urban places, while working there, and thus may be counted rural while being functionally urban.

### *Census Designated Places and the Annexation Dilemma*

Since 1950, the U.S. Bureau of the Census has delineated boundaries for closely settled population concentrations that are outside the corporate limits of municipalities. Such concentrations are referred to as Census Designated Places (CDP). Two conditions contribute to their delimitation: either they are found within an already urbanized area that contains a city of 50,000 or more, in which case they must have a minimum population of 5,000, or where there is no city of that size in the vicinity, then the minimum CDP population drops to 1000. For North Carolina in 2000, the Census counted 296,105 people living in 115 designated CDPs, a rather significant addition to those declared urban only by virtue of their residence in an administratively defined municipality. Though the number of CDPs have steadily increased (they totaled 63 in 1980 and 107 in 1990), their population numbers have varied (1908: 274,322; 1990: 347,087) as they are newly identified with expanding suburbanization, or as they are annexed by growing municipalities.

For North Carolina, several generalizations can be made about the geographic occurrence of CDPs and their implication for urban development. Most are concentrated in the western part of the Piedmont and Mountain regions where persistent population growth happened over the past three decades (Figure 4.5a). Here towns and small cities predominate and these appear more reluctant to take advantage of the otherwise quite liberal state laws which permit them to annex urbanizing areas in

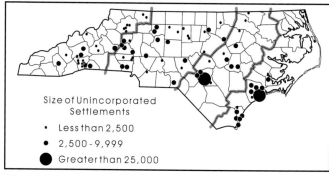

**Figure 4.5a:** Census Designated Places, 1990.
**Source:** 1990 Census of Population, North Carolina.

their proximity. Note, for example, the incidence of CDPs in the vicinity of Mt. Airy in Surry County, Wilkesboro in Wilkes County, and in mountainous Buncombe and Henderson counties. For example, in Wilkes County the population agglomeration is on the order of 20,000, Wilkesboro (3,149) and North Wilkesboro (4,116) are incorporated cheek to cheek, and Mulberry (2,269), Fairplains (2,051), Crickett (2,053), Milers Creek (2,071), Hays (1,731), Pleasant Hill (1,109), and Moravian Falls (1,440) are adjacent CDPs. Even so, the population concentration in the Wilkesboro area is close to 68 percent nonurban. The Wilkesboros and their CDPs exemplify a situation apparently caused by an impasse in the annexation process where two small municipalities are within close proximity and in historic competition for space and prominence, while being in a region where community pressure against any kind of administrative urban expansion remains strong. Another special case is Henderson County where many small rural communities have recently experienced significant population increases as many retirees moved into the county. The fear of being dominated by 'foreigners' may have been a factor in these communities' reluctance to incorporate. So they remain CDPs.

In the remainder of the Piedmont, especially in the counties with large central cities, few CDPs are found. Though rural land here is rapidly suburbanizing, the larger cities are not as reluctant to annex adjacent territory. For example, Charlotte with 17 annexations during the period of 1970-1977 added 50 square miles (130 sq km) to its territory. This expansion is as much as the total area of Boston or San Francisco. Further annexations during the 1980s (36 sq. miles) and the first half of the 1990s (38 sq. miles) has moved Charlotte to 211.9 square miles, leaving the city well over three times the area size of Washington, DC, as well as twice that of the size of the second most populated city in the state, Raleigh. The opportunity to expand city limits is enhanced by statewide annexation laws which discourage the independent incorporation of built-up areas within a certain distance of an existing city. Beyond this distance there appears to be a greater tendency to incorporate new or enlarged settlements in the Urban Crescent than elsewhere in the state. Most of the 34 new towns incorporated during the 1970s were within this metropolitan region. On the other hand the 44 additional incorporations of the 1980-1995 period were spread among 25 counties, leisure and retirement communities of the Mountain and Tidewater regions' gaining close to half of these newly incorporated towns and villages. Most of the new municipalities derived from earlier designated CDPs, though not all places having been granted legislative approval to incorporate have chosen to actually pursue this option. Nonetheless, the present rate of incorporation sustains the image of North Carolina as a state of predominately rural space and small towns.

With the option of incorporating variously as villages, towns, or cities, generally in terms of population numbers, the state's twenty villages (average population of 2,011) range from Grandfather (Avery County) with 73 persons to Clemmons (Forsyth County) with 13,827. Clemmons, as an "edge city" in the shadow of Winston-Salem, wants to be seen as a village, in spite of its size and its 13 percent annual growth rate. Our 442 towns (average population of 2,523) range from Beargrass (Martin County) with 53 residents, to Cary (Wake County), a formidable "edge city" of Raleigh, with 94,536 inhabitants, and a 1990s growth rate of 115 percent. Some smaller urban places in more rural surroundings seem pleased at calling themselves cities, but the town label apparently suits most of the larger urban places in the Piedmont Triad, including Cary, Chapel Hill, Garner, and Carboro. Our 76 urban places (average population of 37,426) incorporated as cities exhibit an even greater range in population from the small Mooresboro (Cleveland County) with 314, to Charlotte with its 540,828 residents. But where 51 percent of the municipalities in the United States as a whole have less than 1,000 inhabitants, the corresponding figure for North Carolina is only 43 percent, or 233 out of 540 municipalities. As an aside, it is easy enough to become confused by the labels that urban places bestow upon themselves. Siler City is officially a town, as is Surf City, Morehead City, Bryson City, and others,, while Silver City is not even incorporated.

The incidence of Census Designated Places in the Coastal Plain and Tidewater regions is largely limited to counties with large military, and thus more footloose, populations, such as Wayne, Onslow and Cumberland counties. In addition, within New Hanover County, territorially the second smallest in the state with less than 200 square miles, there are ten CDPs (total population approaching 45,000) crowded in with the city of Wilmington (75,838) and three other incorporate municipalities. In spite of the county being the ninth fastest growing in the state during the 1990s, there appears to be a strong reluctance of this urban center to incorporate suburbanizing communities. There is also much urbanization going on along the coast in Brunswick County, south of Wilmington, and to the north in Pender County, contributing to these counties being among the top six in percentage growth in the 1990s.

The number, size, and locational character of North Carolina's CPDs raise serious questions concerning the adequate and economically rational provision of urban services, community socio-economic differentiation, and the existence of critical variations in the quality of life. Note, for example, the comments made on declining environmental conditions in the urban shadow in Chapter 13. That many North Carolina cities are still 'underbounded', meaning that the functional spatial reach of the city lies far beyond its political definition, is a critical quality of life aspect of urban development. It may even be suggested that in North Carolina we have a specialized urban population, larger in size than Greensboro's, that live off the fat of the land by having employment, transportation, cultural and recreational benefits of the central cities without paying the taxes, and therefore are a heavier burden for the residents of the city. In strong contrast there is the example of Fayetteville whose 2000 population of 121,000 represents a growth of 45,000 during the 1990s. This expansion was sustained almost entirely through the annexation of adjacent areas containing 44,200 people.

In summary, the state exhibits considerable variation in the sizing and spacing of its central places. These variations exist between the state's major regions as well as within them. Due to the great number of small central places within the urban shadow of large municipalities, North Carolina is functionally less of a state of small towns than many believe it to be. Is it then also less rural?

### An Urban-Rural Continuum

In North Carolina much pride has been taken in the belief that the state is essentially rural. Augmenting this belief have been the census results which decade after decade continued to support it. Indeed, it was extraordinary that the nation's tenth most populated state persisted in being more rural than urban, particularly when the country for many decades has been at least 70 percent urban. It is here important to note that the traditional census definition includes only incorporated places with at least 2,500 persons. So by the Bureau of Census definition, North Carolina in 1980 had 52 percent of its population classified rural (Table 4.1). However, conditions have been changing steadily in favor of the urban proportion. While the urban population increased 31.7 percent during the 1950s, it grew by 28.2 percent during the 1960s, slipped to 22.2 percent for the 1970s, and to 18.2 percent for the 1980s. In the 1990s it skyrocketed by 30.9 percent. Meanwhile the rural population increased only by 2.2 percent in the 1950s, 0.6 percent in the 1960s, but then jumped to a ten percent increase for the 1970s, a 7.4 percent for the 1980s, and then moved to finalize the millennium with an 11.8 percent increase for the 1990s.

The notion that North Carolina is a predominately rural state is at an end. It was arguable that in 1990 the state had over 50 percent urban population, but only if one added the CDP population to the total of the municipalities. In 2000, however, the data is clear. Incorporated urban places total 4,074,636 or 50.6 percent. Should we then add the CDPs the total will reach 54.3 percent urban population. With the above urban definition in place only three counties, Camden, Currituck, and Hyde, remain 100 percent rural.

On the other hand, with a state which shows so great a variation in settlement patterns, a significant percentage of its people in small towns and unincorporated communities, a high degree of commuting from rural residence to urban centers and from urban places to rural located manufacturing plants, and with much open space within municipal boundaries as they incorporate in anticipation of development (as in Charlotte), an argument against any rigid statistical definition or urban/rural population composition can certainly be made. Rurality, or urbanity, is, in the state of North Carolina, largely a state of mind.

### Five Decades of Population Change

Rather large shifts in population from region to region, and even from county to county, have occurred over the past five decades. Changes have, however, not been persistent, though it is clear that a certain regionality seems to influence their direction. Maps of decennial percentage changes by county indicate North Carolina's changing population (Figures 4.6a-e).

#### The 1950s-A Brain Drain State

At the time of the 1950 census, people born in North Carolina, but now making their home in another state equaled 20.5 percent of the state's resident population. No less than 41 percent of the counties lost population in the 1950s. This was the result of a decade of migration of North Carolina natives to industrial and other centers of employment in the Northeast, the Midwest, and West Coast. The stream of outmigrants included a significant percentage of poor and relatively unskilled people from the Coastal Plain and Mountain regions, where the dependence on primary economic activities, especially agriculture, did not provide an adequate livelihood. Another large group of outmigrants included college graduates and others with specialized skills who were attracted to better employment opportunities outside the state. According to Herbert and Johnson (1979, 3), this outmigration of the untrained/underutilized labor force, and of those with advanced skills and education, represented a loss of tragic dimensions in North Carolina's most important asset - its human resources.

During the 1950s North Carolina was a state of heavy net outmigration not able to sustain a condition of population growth except through its large natural increase. There were significant regional and county differences in the impact of these population changes as is obvious from a glance at the map of 1950-1960 population change (Figure 4.6a). Forty-one counties actually saw a decrease in their population. One-third of these were located in the Mountain Region where all of the border counties, except for Transylvania and Henderson, lost people. About 50 percent of Coastal Plain counties and a few of the Tidewater counties also experienced decreases. Some northeastern rural counties had begun a process of a depopulation that has wavered little to this day. Those that realized the largest percent increase were principally the larger, rapidly expanding counties of the Piedmont Urban Crescent. Those with large military installations also grew notably during these Cold War years. Substantial increase also was registered in a cluster of counties in the east central Mountain and adjacent west central Piedmont regions, where foothills manufacturing communities were in various stages of take off for rapid growth.

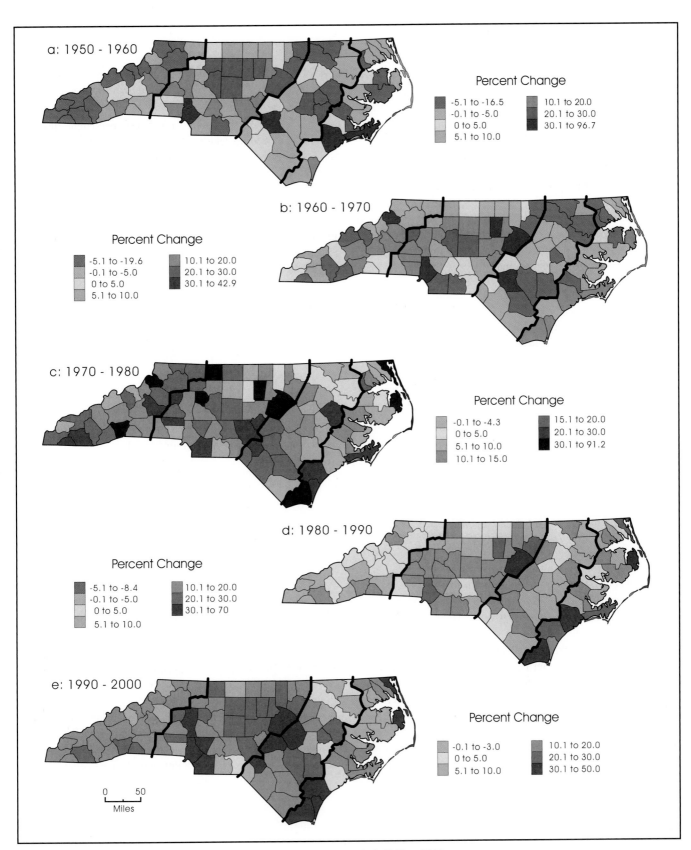

**Figures 4.6a-4.6e:** Percent Change of County Population, by Census Period, 1950 to 2000.
**Sources:** United States Bureau of the Census; North Carolina Office of State Planning.

*The 1960s-Piedmont Expansion at Expense of the Remainder*

The 1960s saw a continuation of the trends established during earlier decades (Figure 4.6b); some differences, however, are noteworthy. While the mountain border counties experienced a decrease in population loss, the Coastal Plain saw an intensification. Of the 36 counties that lost people in the state during the 1960s, 28 were in the Coastal Plain and Tidewater regions. The number of counties in these regions that decreased by at least 7.5 percent went from five to 12. Again it was the central region of the state that posted the greatest gains, but there were differences in scale. More and larger increases were seen in the western Piedmont, where the same cluster of manufacturing counties continued at the pace set during the 1950s, with additional growth spreading to neighboring counties. Military counties, with the exception of Cumberland, no longer expanded as in the prior decade. Expansion of public institutions, together with investment in open space recreation and leisure resort facilities, contributed to the beginning of a turnaround in many of the Mountain counties and rescued some Tidewater counties from a worsening of their population situation.

*The 1970s-A Princess in the Sunbelt*

In the 1970s, the big population turnaround occurred for the nation as well as for North Carolina. What had begun as a trickle of inmigration during the latter part of the 1960s turned into a flood. Further augmenting this unexpected reversal in regional migration patterns was the dramatic shift in rural-urban net migration. Counties that continued to lose population decreased to a mere three, Northampton, Hertford and Jones, all located in the Coastal Plain (Figure 4.6c). Counties experiencing dramatic increases, up to 91 percent in the case of Currituck, were spread throughout the state, though more were located in the Tidewater and Mountain regions than in the remainder. These counties derived their large percentage increases in part due to their initial small population base.

The most interesting reversal of earlier trends occurred in the Coastal Plain. Here there were still eleven counties which had an excess of migrants, but the rate of net outmigration had dwindled to the point to where the rate of natural increase, itself reduced significantly by a rapidly falling birth rate, was high enough to cause a net increase in population. In the Piedmont, the rate of increase for the more urban counties decreased markedly while more rural counties gained more than before due to their suburban proximity (compare Figure 4.5 with Figures 4.6a and b).

*The 1980s-A Cooling Off Decade*

With the recession of the early 1980s fears that the growth boom of the 1970s was over ran rampant through the state. At the end of the decade it was obvious that the 80s fell somewhere between the 60s and the 70s in its population change characteristics (Figure 4.6d). Where growth continued it was a much subdued rate, and the Coastal Plain seemed to have reignited the depopulation tendency. Here were located eleven of the eighteen counties that lost population. Three counties, Tyrrell, Hyde and Washington are on the economically poorly endowed Pamlico Peninsula in the Tidewater Region. On the other hand, population continued to boom in the coastal resort counties of the Tidewater and in parts of the central Piedmont. In the latter, major increases continued to elude the core counties of the Piedmont Triad, with their larger dependency on primary and secondary industries, while the Piedmont Triangle and Metrolina, and many of the suburbanizing counties along "Main Street" continued an expansion initiated decades earlier. Growth impacted by elderly retirement was making its appearance, as indicated by the higher rates in the coastal like Brunswick, as well as in the Mountain Region counties of Henderson, Polk, and Macon.

A more fascinating story about population loss is that experienced by the state's smaller municipalities. No less than 210 (40%) of the 527 incorporated places in the state in the 1980s saw a decrease in their population! Among the larger losers there were Kannapolis (21,902 in 1980; 21,241 in 1990; but then increasing to 26,759 (!) for its 1997 estimated population), Edenton (5,357, 5,268, and 5,354), King's Mountain (8,430, 8,007, and 9,136), Shelby (15,310, 14,669, and 19,565), Whiteville (5,565, 5,078, and 5,592), and Williamston (6,159, 5,503, and 5,857). Comparing population totals for these municipalities for 1980, 1990, and 1997 demonstrates on the one hand their tenuous situation during the 1980s, and on the other the strong comeback of some of them during the 1990s. Other chapters provide the information needed to understand why some municipalities continue to stagnate, and others enter a new flowering period.

The general malaise of the small farming community in the Coastal Plain is indicated by the example of Nash County which, while increasing its 1980s population from 67,153 to 76,677, saw seven of its eleven municipalities lose population. Meanwhile its largest town, Rocky Mount, pearl of the northern Coastal Plain "Ring City", increased by 14 percent to 32,475 (and to 39,705 by 1997). Similarly, the small manufacturing industry dependent places of the Piedmont suffered declines during this period. In Rockingham County four of the five municipalities saw a decrease in their population. This was true also for Cleveland County, where nine of fifteen municipalities experienced loses. Both of these latter counties gained people during the decade. So the 1980s appeared to be a decade of contraction with more small towns losing people to the cities and suburbs of the metropolises, and of the periphery losing to the center.

*The 1990s-Three Dynamic Growth Arcs*

For most of the 1990s, county population expansion resembled that of the ebullient 1970s. Some metropolitan centers showed renewed energy, especially in the Piedmont Triangle and Metrolina, but in both MSAs it was the suburban counties that led the way (Figure 4.6e). The Raleigh-Chapel Hill-Durham MSA ranked eighth among all United States MSAs in net inmigration for the 1990-95 period, and the Charlotte-Gastonia-Rock Hill MSA ranked 13th. Joining these in almost explosive growth was the Wilmington metro area, the tightly congested urban New Hanover County (33.3%) as well as its two principal suburban extensions into Pender and Brunswick counties, both of which have benefited as well from their coastal position in attracting retirees. Brunswick County also illustrates the impact of its proximity to the resort and tourism mecca of Myrtle Beach to the south. Except for the military reduction declines impacting Onslow County, and perhaps its neighbor Jones County, there is a coastal arc of dynamic growth evident on the map. Five of the 13 counties growing at 30 percent or over during the 1990s are coastal counties.

A second arc of dynamic growth extends from Hoke County, impacted by its proximity to Fayetteville, north through the Sandhills' golf emporium of Moore County, to the northern suburbs of Raleigh, Durham and the Research Triangle. Of twelve counties comprising this growth arc, three are the state's leading gainers (Johnston with 50%, Wake with 47.3%, and Hoke with 47.2%), and four others gained in excess of 30 percent, in toto representing more than 425,000 persons increase for the decade! This eastern Piedmont growth arc defines the state's current population boom.

A third arc of dynamic growth includes six counties extending from the South Carolina border to the heart of the Piedmont Triad metro in the western Piedmont. The four leading counties here are Union (46.9%), Mecklenburg (36.0%), Cabarrus (32.5%), and Iredell (31.6%), these are largely "Main Street" and its overflow suburbanizing counties where high percentage growth for the 1990s has increased their total population by an estimated one quarter million. In the aggregate these three emerging arcs of more concentrated growth in the 1990s affirm the state's major settlement trends:

1) the Piedmont urbanization process dramatizing the megalopolitanization of the Urban Crescent with its connective "Main Street" feature, even to the point of suggesting that the Crescent is gradually evolving into an Urban Horseshoe;

2) the continuing statewide spatial population concentration process (identified in Figure 4.10); and

3) the continuing importance of the leading leisure, recreation and retirement zones of the state, specifically the coast, the Sandhills and the mountains, with the latter experiencing considerable population expansion along the South Carolina and Georgia borders from Polk to Cherokee counties. An estimated 58% of the state's population increase for the decade has occurred in the 25 counties that constitute the three population growth arcs identified above.

What then for the changing fortunes of the state's smaller towns? The early nineties saw two-thirds of the municipalities that lost population during the 1980s turnaround and increase in their numbers (see previous section). In most cases, municipalities adjusted to economic restructuring, they hit their low point in the late 1980s, and are now mostly in recovery. This turn around in fortune may signify a return to the smaller places by people who are disenchanted with large-city life and/or are now within commuting distance of urban employment, given the persistent expansion of the state's highway system. Towns that continue to be overly dependent on declining agriculture, or on textile and apparel industries threatened by abrupt plant closures, are faced with a more challenging future.

### Summing the Recent Past

Capstone summaries of nearly half a century of countywide population changes can be gleaned from the patterns displayed on the map of 1950-1995 population change (Figure 4.7). This holds no surprises. It is the Piedmont Crescent counties that dominate in population increases, and Coastal Plain counties that dominate in population decreases, especially the economically plagued northeastern quadrant. Including three mountain counties and one in the southern Piedmont, thirteen counties had more people in 1950 than they do at present. The more recent turnaround, however, is best exemplified by comparing the migration changes of a recent one and a half decades (Figures 4.8a and b). Here it must be noted that people migrating (i.e. relocating their primary residence) are likely to be the most powerful indicator of the changing fortunes of places in terms of decline and growth. For the 1980s and the initial six years of the 1990s, North Carolina has experienced shifts similar to those of the nation at large. Most of the larger increases in net migration occurred in the MSA counties, though the intensity has varied among the counties. In addition, the continued attraction of counties identified with recreation, tourism, and the relocating of retirees is noticeable. Major gains are experienced by the tier of counties closest to the coast, the Sandhills, and a few counties in the southern mountains. Reversals from a declining 1980s population to an increase in the 1990s are seen in the southern Coastal Plain, especially in counties where heavy investments are made in the hog industry. Note, for example, the small gains made in Sampson and Duplin counties. Noticeable also is the evolving "Ring City" of the north central part of the Coastal Plain, where even its "green center" of Greene County, is now seeing the first major increase in population since the 1950s. Undoubtedly this is influenced by an exurban overflow from the university-medical center of Greenville.

## MORE PEOPLE ON LESS LAND

In spite of its image as a predominately rural state North Carolina continues to see a larger and larger share of its population concentrated in the same percentage of urban counties. The previous discussion on recent population change suggests that this process is indeed occurring, but proof positive is provided by the population concentration curves of Figure 4.9. The intent

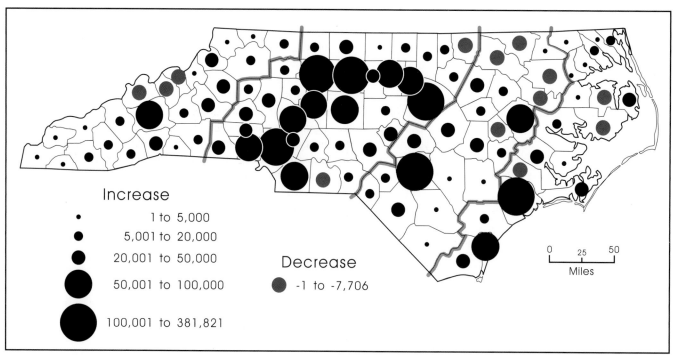

**Figure 4.7:** Population Change by County, 1950-1995.
**Source:** U. S Bureau of the Census, 1996.

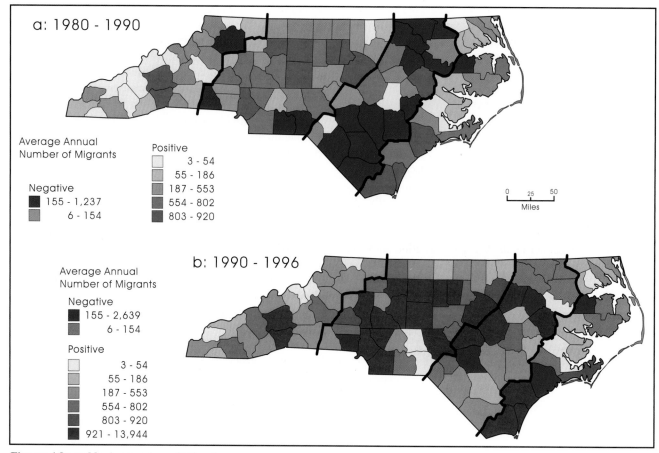

**Figures 4.8a and b:** Average Annual Migration.
**Source:** North Carolina Office of State Planning, 1996.

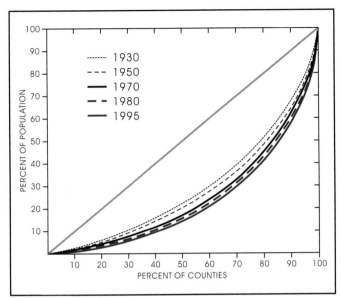

**Figure 4.9:** Increasing Population Concentration.
**Source:** U. S Bureau of the Census, 1930-1990;
North Carolina Office of State Planning, 1996.

of a Lorenz Curve is to demonstrate the degree to which a distribution varies from an even or uniform condition. In this case, the percent of population by county is measured against the percent of counties. Thus a uniform distribution of people by county throughout the state will result in a diagonal Lorenz Curve, ten percent of the counties would contain ten percent of the population, and so on. Because the historic process of population settlement never allowed an even diffusion of people through the state, the diagonal was never attained. Here the concern is with demonstrating the more recent character of population concentration, so data for 1930, 1950, 1970, 1990 and 1995 have been plotted. Initially it can be seen that North Carolina's population is very unevenly distributed. It is, in fact, quite concentrated with a significant statistical distance separating the plotted curves from the diagonal that represents a uniform statewide distribution. In addition, the plotted curves show a gradual increase in population concentration from the earliest year to the present. This increase is largest during the bidecennial period of 1950 to

1970, due, of course, to the considerable outmigration of people from Coastal Plain and Mountain counties combined with the high rate of urbanization experienced in the Urban Crescent and the scattered military impacted counties. Finally, with the very close coincidence of the 1970 and 1990 curves, it appears that the population concentration process, when measured as here on the county scale, has slowed considerably. Another way of seeing the increasing concentration is to note that it took the 18 most populated counties to exceed 50 percent of the state's population in 1980. In 2000 it took only the top 16. The gradually intensification of population pressures in the most populated counties is in part at the expense of rural counties, 27 of which achieved their highest population total some years ago. Ten of these have not increased a population size reached in 1940, and seven not since a total reached in 1950. Figure 4.10 illustrates what by now is becoming a familiar pattern in the Coastal Plain and the state's more peripheral counties.

For North Carolina, our unique patterns of urbanization suggest that we need not get unduly exercised about the prospects of urban decentralization, precisely due to the absence of large central cities to begin with, plus the fact that urban spread always has been a feature of the state's urbanization process. Urban decentralization has been affecting the fortunes of urban centers elsewhere in the country, and though it may locally intensify in North Carolina, the problem of urbanization and land use in our state it still mostly one of unregulated spread, or sprawl, frequently in association with anticipated or recently completed Interstate highways and urban loops (see Chapter 12). On the county scale, evidence indicates that population growth has attained some consistency in the sense that most counties experiencing above average rates of expansion are stimulated by socioeconomic changes that are apt to continue for a while, as is the case for the counties lagging or seeing a negative growth. In the sense that regional growth differences may be becoming more predictable, one outcome could be to simplify state policy for local and regional development.

## SPATIAL DYNAMICS OF VITAL EVENTS

Vital events statistics refers to data characterizing the changing conditions of an area's population. Here are included matters of births, deaths and migration since these are the vital elements of change in any given population. Migration was considered in the previous section and will receive less attention here. There will be some discussion about the impact of vital events on the structure of the population in terms of age, gender, and race. From a geographic perspective, the interest is largely in uncovering the spatial dynamics of these events leading to an understanding of alternative futures. That is, what differences are seen to exist in vital events within the state, from one location to another, and in their past, present and potential impact on the locality's people? These are rather critical issues in economic development and in community and environmental planning for the state and its varied regions. Just how these demographic rates are derived is illustrated in Appendix C.

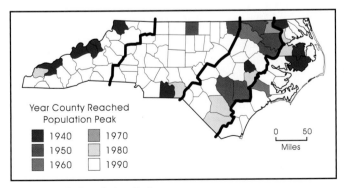

**Figure 4.10:** Population Peak.
**Source:** U. S. Bureau of the Census, 1950-1990.

**Box 4A:** United States Population Cohorts Over Four Decades.

1960

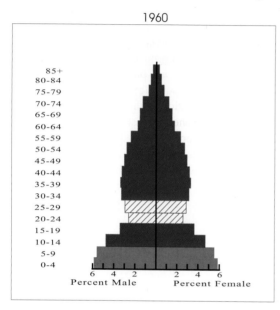

1970

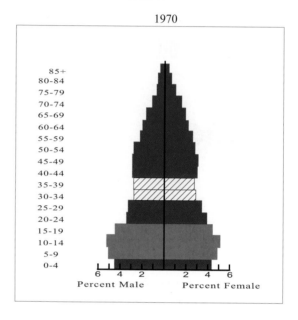

1980

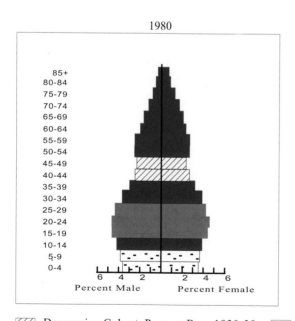

1990

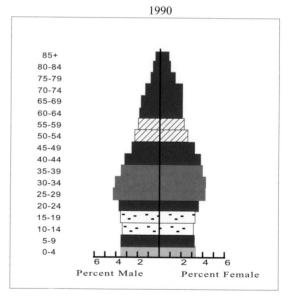

| | |
|---|---|
| ▨ Depression Cohort: Persons Born 1930-39 | ⌐▪⌐ Baby Bust Cohort: Persons Born 1970-79 |
| ■ Baby Boom Cohort: Persons Born 1950-64 | ▨ Baby Boom Shadow Cohort: Persons Born After 1985 |

**Note:** See box 9A for interpretation of cohort subsets (page 317).
**Source**: U. S. Census of Population, 1960-1990.

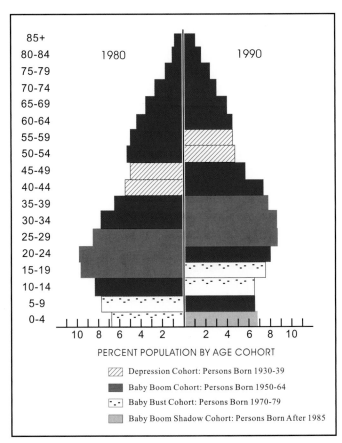

**Figure 4.11:** North Carolina Age Distribution by Ten Year Population Cohorts.
**Source:** U. S. Bureau of the Census, 1980, 1990.

### Age and Gender Composition and Population Cohorts

It is appropriate first to evaluate briefly the extraordinary character of our nation's changing population profile, the periodic rhythms of birth rates, and related size of cohorts (groups of people born during a specified time period) (Figure 9.12). Such evaluation illuminates the changing character of socio-economic needs and wants, and therefore the shifting pressures brought to bear on services provided by states and local administrations, as well as the opportunities awaiting the private business sector. The population profile for the United States demonstrates the changing conditions (Box 4A). Four diagrams show the different shares allotted to each five year cohort. Allowing for migration changes and age specific death rates, each cohort passes through its life cycle impacting the national economy as a function of its relative size. Notable cohorts appearing in the 1960 diagram include the "depression cohort", the group of persons born during the 1930s, when tight economic times resulted in a decreased birth rate. For sixty years this "baby bust" cohort was smaller than its predecessors, meaning there was a smaller labor force available to replace the larger preceding one; for example, more seats being available in public institutions, and fewer consumers for the same productive effort. In short, this particular generation

has less competition for jobs and other opportunities, and in very general terms it has improved prospects for income generation and enhanced life styles. No wonder that "baby bust" generations have traditionally been referred to as "good times" cohorts.

That being said, the apparent opposite set of conditions hold for another notable cohort making its appearance in the 1960 diagram. This, the "baby boom" generation, emerged from the late forties to the mid-sixties. Note on the 1970, 1980, and 1990 diagrams the shifting position of this cohort as it advances through its life cycle, and ponder its impacts. We built maternity wards, expanded schools from kindergarten through higher education, saw congestion on the job market and economic restructuring, all conditioned, at least in part, by the overwhelming numbers the "baby boom" generation brought to the table at different periods in its life cycle. We now are concerned about the enormous weight this cohort will place on limited resources available for the care of the elderly in the near future. Social security, medical facilities for the elderly, mobile libraries, "meals on wheels", home nursing care, as well as the availability of burial grounds, become critical issues.

The significant decrease in the state's average birth rate since the 1960s shows that North Carolina has been affected by the passage of the "baby boom" (compare Box 4A with Figure 4.11). Resulting from an unexpected increase in the number of births per woman shortly following World War II, the "baby boom" peaked in the late 50s to early 60s. Subsequently, the decrease in births that began toward the late 1960s and continued into the 1970s was equally unexpected, so much so that the 1970s have become known as the "baby bust" decade. In these ups and downs of the birth rate North Carolina's experience simply replicates that of the country at large. What is important for both nation and state is the impact of a shifting birth rate on different aspects of society. Where maternity wards in hospitals were rushed to completion in the 1950s to accommodate the boom in births, they stood relatively empty to the early 1980s. Public schools have gone through a similar boom and bust period, as has the demand for teachers. By the mid-80s, institutions of higher education, be they vocational schools, junior colleges or senior universities, were left standing with an oversupply of classroom buildings and dormitories. Now, at the turn of the century, educational institutions are steeling themselves against another major flow of incoming students, the result of the "baby boom shadow" (or "echo"), the larger number of children born to a very large "baby boom" cohort, albeit with a lower fertility rate, and on average at a later point in life for the mothers.

As the "baby boom" cohort continues aging, they are followed by a much thinner rank of the "baby bust" cohort; good times may come from this. We are already experiencing significant decreases in juvenile delinquency, crime and unemployment rates, as teenagers and young adults entering the labor force dwindle the ranks of the cohorts most prone to criminal activities. At the same time they can expect to find the labor market much more accommodating with wages and work envi-

95

ronments. On the other hand, when the baby boomers reach their retirement age, beginning about 2015, there will be dramatically fewer people available to pay for their social and medical security benefits. Additionally there is the question, are we appropriately concerned with the future impact of a much smaller labor force on an economy that has grown used to increased participation of dual earner families and an increasing share of the labor force in a part time condition?

For a state that has seen a turnaround in migration precisely during those years that birth rates have fallen so precipitously, the net effect is not as potentially devastating. As noted, the migration process tends to be highly selective with predominately young, better educated, and entrepreneurial individuals and families involved in the move to the state. Though their fertility rate is apt to hold to U.S. norms, their youthfulness and greater number in the state's population will result in proportionately more births, and insure a smoother transition.

It is important to note that significant variation in birth rates exists among the different races in the state (Table 4.2). Though the recent drop in birth rates has been experienced by white as well as by nonwhite, the latter continues with a rate about 60 percent higher. When the much more recent turnaround in African American migration to the state is taken into account, this will mean a considerably faster increase in this component of the state's population. Perhaps it would not be that noteworthy a condition if the nonwhite proportion of the total population was evenly distributed across the state. As will be seen, this is not the case. Indeed the stage is being set for future socio-economic and political difficulties (e.g. central city development, revenue sharing, school bussing, annexation).

| | White | Non-White | Total |
|---|---|---|---|
| A: Crude Birth Rate (Per 1,000 Population) | | | |
| 1960 | 22.1 | 29.8 | **24.1** |
| 1965 | 18.3 | 26.2 | **20.3** |
| 1970 | 17.9 | 24.2 | **19.4** |
| 1980 | 12.9 | 19.1 | **14.4** |
| 1991-1995 | 13.3 | 19.1 | **14.7** |
| B: Crude Death Rate (Per 1,000 Population) | | | |
| 1960 | 7.8 | 10.2 | **8.4** |
| 1965 | 8.2 | 10 | **8.7** |
| 1970 | 8.3 | 10.3 | **8.8** |
| 1980 | 8.1 | 8.6 | **8.2** |
| 1991-1995 | 8.9 | 9 | **8.9** |
| C: Rate of Natural Increase (Per 1,000 Population) | | | |
| 1960 | 14.3 | 19.6 | **15.7** |
| 1965 | 10.1 | 16.2 | **11.6** |
| 1970 | 9.6 | 13.9 | **10.6** |
| 1980 | 4.7 | 10.5 | **6.1** |
| 1991-1995 | 4.4 | 10.1 | **5.8** |

**Table 4.2:** Components of Natural Increase.
**Source:** North Carolina Vital Statistics, 1960 through 1995.

A changing age composition is a factor of great importance in planning for the state's future. In addition, it is important to consider that as age composition varies over time, so does it vary through space. For decision makers the complexities are compounded. Striking variations exist within the state's regions, metropolitan areas, and counties. Some counties have as little as ten percent of their population in the 65 years and over cohort, as in the case of Robeson, which finds itself in this situation due to its comparatively high birth rate and youthful population structure. Watauga County, on the other hand, is in the same situation due to the population imbalance caused by Appalachian State University students. Some counties have a very high percent of elderly in their population. For example, Warren County, which is heavily impacted by brain drain and a resulting relative increase of its older population (17.9% are 65 years + in 1990), is experiencing the so-called "aging-in-place" condition. On the other hand, Henderson and Polk counties are affected by high rates of inmigrating retirees that are influencing a higher percentage of elderly (21.9% are 65 years + in the case of Henderson). Smaller municipalities that have been losing people in recent decades are even more affected by the age imbalances.

### Birth Rates

North Carolina's average annual birth rate for 1991-1995 was 14.7 resident births per 1,000 population (US=12.6/1,000 in 1996). This places the state in about the middle of the range defining the limits of birth rates within the country, from Utah's 18.1/1,000 to Maine's 9.1/1,000. As indicated in Table 4.2 this is a decrease of some 40 percent since 1960, when the rate was 24.1, but a slight increase over the 1980 rate of 14.1/1,000, owing mostly to the net inmigration of younger people to the state. Average birth rates vary over space as much as they vary over time. In fact, the difference among counties in North Carolina is extraordinary (Figure 4.12). Compared to the 1991-1995 state average of 14.7/1,000, birth rates ranged from a low of 9.1/1,000 population/ year in Watauga County to a high of 21.8/1,000/year in Onslow County. From the map we see an interesting general west-east parallel orientation of birth rate classes by county. The Tidewater and the Mountain generally have the lowest birth rates, while the east central Piedmont and the Coastal Plain counties have the highest, though with a greater concentration of higher birth rates adjacent to the South Carolina boundary. Areas of comparatively low birth rates include those counties that, due to a recent past of selective outmigration, have been left with an aging-in-place population; so they have relatively few people in the reproductive age groups. Some of these counties, particularly in the mountains and along the outer coast, have had their age balance offset by the inmigration of retirees. Further complicating this picture is the fact that some of these same counties have disproportionately large college student populations, who are apt to exhibit extremely low birth rates for their age group. So it comes as no surprise that Watauga, a mountain county with Appalachian State University's students comprising one third of its population, has the state's lowest birth rate. So it is also with

Jackson County with Western Carolina University at 10.9/1000. Other mountain counties with a dominance of older people and therefore low birth rates include Clay (9.3/1,000), Alleghany (9.6), Ashe (10.0), Macon (10.2), and Polk at 10.5/1,000. In the Tidewater Region the lowest birth rates are reached by Pamlico with 10.2/1,000 and Camden with 11.1/1,000. In the Urban Crescent, where the tendency for low fertility rates among women in rapidly growing urban areas functions as a depressant on the rates. Orange County, with its very large University of North Carolina at Chapel Hill student population, stands out as having the Urban Crescent's lowest average annual birth rates in the nineties with 11.3/1,000.

Counties that saw a considerable net outmigration during the 1950s and 1960s, especially in the Coastal Plain and the southeastern-most portion of the Piedmont, have not experienced their anticipated lower birth rates due to the much higher fertility rates of their rural (particularly non-white) women (see Table 4.2 and compare Figure 4.12 with 4.6a and b). Here counties that have continued with relatively high birth rates are dominated by young families in association with military bases (e.g. Onslow with an incredible 21.8/1,000), Cumberland with 19.8/1,000), and Craven with 18.3/1,000), or they have a high percentage non-white population, notably American Indian, like Robeson (17.7/1,000, Scotland (16.4/1,000) and Hoke (18.1/1,000). Similarly, Swain County with its predominant Cherokee Indian population is quite high with 14.7/1,000. On the national scale, the American Indian population has a projected birth rate of 17.8/1,000 for the year 2000 (Edmondson p. 15).

## Death Rates

Persistently low death rates have been an important feature of vital events over the past five decades in North Carolina. Of course, the United States had experienced generally declining death rates since the beginning of the industrial revolution. Only recently, with its aging population, is this rate bottoming out. From 1900 to 1954, for example, the rate for the country decreased from 17.2 deaths per 1,000 population to 9.2, then for the following fifteen years it merely oscillated with no significant change. In 1968, the US decline resumed at a slow pace so that by 1990 the rate was 8.7 per 1,000. In the case of North Carolina, recent changes have not seemed dramatic, though the slight decrease occurring from 1960 to 1980 now appears to have been reversed (Table 4.2). For 1991-1995, the average death rate for the state was 8.9/1000 population. As the state's median age continues to rise we can reasonably expect the age specific death rate to take its toll and we will see a continued ever so slight increase in the total death rate into the 21st Century.

What is more notable is the closing of the gap between the state's white and non-white populations. In 1960, the death rate for whites was 7.8/1,000 while for non-whites it was 10.2/1,000, with a resulting gap of 2.4/1,000. By 1995 the gap had practically disappeared, with a non-white decrease to 9.0, while, with a more rapidly aging population, white death rates have moved up to 8.9, highest since 1960.

Within the state there was considerable variation on the county scale with differences as great as those measured earlier in the chapter for the counties' birth rates (compare Figures 4.13

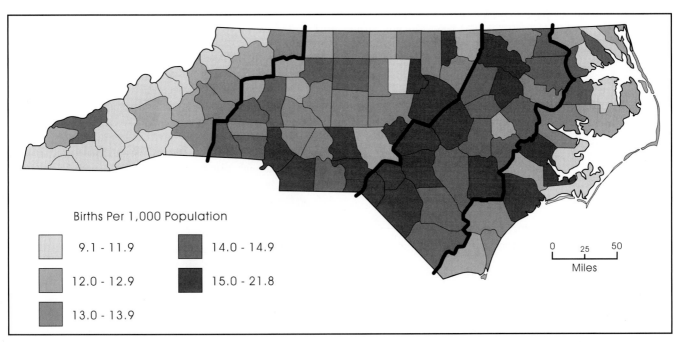

**Figure 4.12:** Birth Rates by County, 1991-1995, Yearly Average.
**Source:** North Carolina Vital Statistics, 1996.

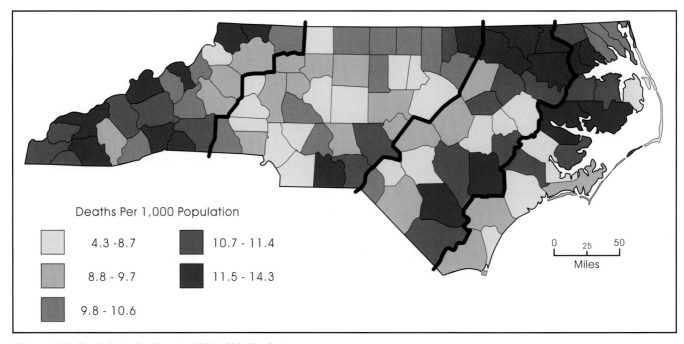

**Figure 4.13:** Death Rates by County, 1991-1995, Yearly Average.
**Source:** North Carolina Vital Statistics, 1996.

and 4.12). For the 1991-95 period the state average annual death rate ranged from a low of 4.3 for Onslow County to a high of 14.3 for Polk County. A vast majority of the counties had rates close to the state average.

The ten counties which attained rates of less than 8.1/1,000 were those having the most youthful populations, i.e., those with a disproportionately large military (Onslow, Cumberland and Craven) or college (Orange and Watauga) populations. Also, they include those that have continued urbanizing at a fairly rapid pace (Wake, Mecklenburg, and Union), or have seen a more senior population attracted to recreational resources (Dare). At the other extreme are the ten counties with rates of more than 12.1 per 1,000 population. These are counties with a fairly rapidly aging population structure. On the one hand, this is an aging-in-place phenomenon resulting from a recent history of youth dominated outmigration, as in the Coastal Plain and Tidewater counties of Northampton, Hyde, Chowan, and Perquimans, and the Mountain counties of Alleghany, Swain, and Mitchell. On the

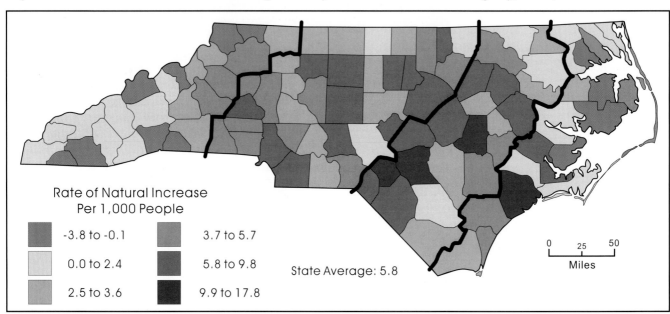

**Figure 4.14:** Rates of Natural Increase by County, 1991-1995, Yearly Average.
**Source:** North Carolina Vital Statistics, 1996.

other hand, it may be due to a relative aging of the county's population resulting from inmigrating retirees, as in the Mountain counties of Henderson and Polk.

### *Rates of Natural Increase*

Subtracting death rates from birth rates yields a most important vital statistic, the rate of natural increase. Twelve counties had an average negative rate during the 1991-95 period (Figure 4.14). For an additional 21 counties the rate was less than 2.4 per 1,000 per year, as compared to the state average of 5.8/1,000/year. Interestingly, with only three exceptions, all of these low rates are obtained in counties located either in the mountains or in the northeastern part of the state. Four counties significantly exceeded the state average, with their rate of natural increase higher than 10.0/1,000. All are either military dominated counties with very high birth rates, or their suburban extension (e.g. Hoke as the overflow county of Cumberland). It is instructive to compare and contrast the different variables contributing to overall population change. So the reader may note how the county wide distributions of birth rates (Figure 4.12), death rates (Figure 4.13), and the resulting rates of natural increase (Figure 4.14) compare with net migration (Figure 4.8b) to arrive at percent population change (Figure 4.6e). One should bear in mind that the population change equation results from adjusting the natural rate of change (birth rate minus death rate) by the net rate of migration. There should now be a fuller understanding of just what makes the state tick demographically, and what this may mean for the state's regions and counties, a critically important foundation for gauging present needs and future prospects.

## MINORITY POPULATIONS

Appropriately there is considerable sensitivity among demographers and census takers concerning the issue of race and ethnicity. For this volume on state geography it is important to highlight and explore variations in settlement patterns that reflect critical differences in these population characteristics. We do this not simply as matter of statistical thoroughness, but in recognition of the fact that for many North Carolinians their race/ethnicity is treasured as part of their very being and deeply rooted in how they perceive themselves, their communities, and their culture. Here we will follow a recent United States Office of Management and Budget (OMB) determination of race/ethnicity categories, in part a matter of necessity because this is how available data are organized and presented in census reports. Alert to objections raised within various groups, especially among people who consider themselves multiracial, the OMB is presently conducting an extensive review of the existing definitions with a view toward developing categories more reflective of conditions and attitudes of the 21st Century. In 1993, for example, twelve percent of all marriages involving a black person were interracial; this was almost double the number in 1980. As noted by Evinger (1996, 38) the OMB is doing its review jointly with the Interagency Committee for the Review of Racial and Ethnic Standards, a committee made of people representing thirty federal agencies, and with public input through congressional hearings. Categories of interest to this text include:

1) non-Hispanic White, hereafter simply referred to as 'white'
'a person having origins in any of the original peoples of Europe, North Africa, or the Middle East' (thus including people of Arab background);

2) Black (Afro-American)
'a person having origins in any of the black racial groups of Africa' (including individuals recently migrating from the Caribbean and speaking French, or a Creole patois)

3) American Indian and Native Alaskan (Native American)
'a person having origins in any of the original peoples of North America, and who maintains cultural identification through tribal affiliations or community recognition'

4) Hispanic (Latino)
'a person of Mexican, Puerto Rican, Cuban, Central or South American, or other Spanish culture or origin, regardless of race'

In this categorization, as in our more comprehensive analysis, we are leaving out detailed consideration of Hawaiian/Pacific Islanders as a special group, simply because this population is relatively small in this state with only 3,984 tallied in the 2000 Census. Small as this population is, it is still notable that it is concentrated in the very large cities, in college student populations, and in the armed forces.

The 2000 Census amplified the OBM categories by adding two racial categories, other and multi-racial, and by including Hispanic as a separate ethnic category. Thus Hispanic individuals who see themselves as white or black or multi-racial were able to claim both racial and ethnic identity on the census form. In the end this expansion of racial/ethnic determination resulted in 69 potential choices, where individuals could mark more than one response if desired. For the state, and the ten fastest growing and five slowest growing counties the 2000 Census results are shown in Table 4.3. Counties displayed in this table serve to demonstrate some of the data ranges found in this census. All counties are treated in the appropriate detail in chapters 10 to 13.

The nation as a whole is presently experiencing the largest immigration wave seen in seven decades. In 1995, 750,000 persons legally migrated to the United States; in 1996 this increased to about one million. Illegal immigrants are thought to contribute additional large numbers. With the newcomers coming predominantly from Mexico, the Philippines, China, Cuba, and India credence is lent to current population projections which indicate

2000 Census

| | Total Population | Race | | | | | | | | Hispanic or Latino (of any race) | 1990-2000 Percent Population Change |
|---|---|---|---|---|---|---|---|---|---|---|---|
| | | Total | One Race | | | | | | | | |
| | | | White | Black or African American | American Indian and Alaska Native | Asian | Native Hawaiian and Other Pacific Islander | Some Other Race | Two or More Races | | |
| **Ten Fastest Growing Counties** | | | | | | | | | | | |
| Johnston | 121,965 | 120,762 | 95,237 | 19,090 | 494 | 368 | 43 | 5,530 | 1,203 | 9,440 | 50.0 |
| Wake | 627,846 | 617,525 | 454,544 | 123,820 | 2,152 | 21,249 | 212 | 15,548 | 10,321 | 33,985 | 47.3 |
| Hoke | 33,646 | 32,928 | 14,982 | 12,664 | 3,852 | 278 | 52 | 1,100 | 718 | 2,415 | 47.2 |
| Union | 123,677 | 122,410 | 102,441 | 15,480 | 475 | 720 | 30 | 3,264 | 1,267 | 7,637 | 46.9 |
| Brunswick | 73,143 | 72,405 | 60,200 | 10,516 | 494 | 198 | 32 | 965 | 738 | 1,960 | 43.5 |
| Pender | 41,082 | 40,694 | 29,882 | 9,689 | 201 | 74 | 14 | 834 | 388 | 1,496 | 42.4 |
| Mecklenburg | 695,454 | 684,709 | 445,250 | 193,838 | 2,439 | 21,889 | 339 | 20,954 | 10,745 | 44,871 | 36.0 |
| Harnett | 91,025 | 89,595 | 64,744 | 20,481 | 794 | 591 | 61 | 2,924 | 1,430 | 5,336 | 34.2 |
| New Hanover | 160,307 | 158,623 | 128,098 | 27,203 | 627 | 1,333 | 96 | 1,266 | 1,684 | 3,276 | 33.3 |
| Cabarrus | 131,063 | 129,770 | 109,127 | 15,961 | 443 | 1,190 | 32 | 3,017 | 1,293 | 6,620 | 32.5 |
| **Five Slowest Growing Counties** | | | | | | | | | | | |
| Bertie | 19,773 | 19,678 | 7,178 | 12,326 | 87 | 21 | 1 | 65 | 95 | 195 | -3.0 |
| Washington | 13,723 | 13,627 | 6,626 | 6,716 | 7 | 44 | 6 | 228 | 96 | 311 | -2.0 |
| Edgecombe | 55,606 | 55,283 | 22,278 | 31,949 | 109 | 70 | 7 | 870 | 323 | 1,554 | 0.7 |
| Onslow | 150,355 | 145,507 | 108,351 | 27,790 | 1,108 | 2,526 | 283 | 5,449 | 4,848 | 10,896 | 0.3 |
| Hertford | 22,601 | 22,415 | 8,464 | 13,459 | 269 | 71 | 5 | 147 | 186 | 354 | 1.3 |
| **State** | **8,049,313** | **7,946,053** | **5,804,656** | **1,737,545** | **99,551** | **113,689** | **3,983** | **186,629** | **103,260** | **378,963** | **21.4** |

**Table 4.3:** Population by Race and Hispanic or Latino Origin for State and Selected Counties.
**Source:** U.S. Bureau of the Census, 2000.

100

that whites will become a United States minority by the year 2050 (Edmondson 1996, p. 17). For North Carolina the percentage white population declined from 75 in 1990 to 70.2 in 2000. The fact of the matter is that "minorities" already are "majorities" in the states of Hawaii, California, and New Mexico. And in spite of the sense that the term minority has to some people become pejorative, demeaning and dehumanizing, it evolved out of the civil rights movement and has become politicized by minority groups themselves as a term of individual identity and group empowerment. With the increase in immigration, especially of Hispanics and Asians, has come a certain degree of immigrant bashing. In North Carolina, for example, it appears that for some folks immigrants are beginning to supplant Yankees as least desired people. So it bears reflection that in the United States in 1920 foreign born persons made up 15 percent of the population, but in 1990 they were only eight percent.

### A Large Black Population

A legacy of the pre-Civil War economy, tied in large measure to the institution of slavery, is the continuing existence in the state of a large African American minority population. By 2000 this population had reached 1,737,545 persons, an 18.9 percent increase over 1990. Where the United States' population in 2000 was 12.6 percent black (12.1% in 1990 and 11.7% in 1980), the black population share in North Carolina was 21.6 percent (22.0 in 1990 and 22.4% in 1980), and thus gradually declining from being twice the national average. As indicated also, this proportion has been decreasing. In 1960 there were 1,116,021 blacks comprising 24.5 percent of the state's people, and though 621,524 were added over the subsequent four decades this was not nearly at the rate of increase by the non-black population. Here again it must be noted that respondents to the 2000 Census had the option of checking more than one box for race. For North Carolina 103,260 people declared themselves to be of two or more races. Of this number, 38,738 people indicated black as one of the more than one race checked on the census form.

What is particularly striking about the black population is not the change in their number but rather their extraordinary locational shifts within the state. As a point of departure for a closer look at this phenomenon let us consider the present patterns of black population settlement. As a proportion of the state's population on the county scale it is obvious that African Americans continue to exist in large concentrations in the Coastal Plain (Figure 4.15a). Traditionally tied by economics to the land, blacks became an essential human resource in those counties where large scale plantation style agricultural enterprises flourished in the early post-colonial years. Subsequently their numbers dominated tenancy farming. Black people also joined the flow of the rural-urban migratory movement by the mid-20th century, but later than their white counterparts. Adding the factor of a traditionally higher fertility rate among African American women, some 30 percent higher than for white women in recent decades, and the result became a relatively higher proportion of blacks remaining in most of the rural Coastal Plain and several Tidewater coun-

ties. Here a majority of the counties are over 25 percent black, though in a tight cluster of northern Coastal Plain counties, six have over 50 percent. Bertie County had the largest proportion of blacks with 62.3 percent. Counties in this cluster are predominately rural with low densities of population (compare Figure 4.15a with Figures. 4.3 and 4.4).

As elsewhere in the state, larger towns have a disproportionate share of the counties' black population. Kinston, for example, has 62.6 percent black population (57.8% in 1990) while its county of Lenoir has only 40.4 percent. Goldsboro has 52.2 percent blacks (47.4% in 1990) while Wayne County has 33.0 percent. From this it follows that the county has a much smaller proportion of blacks when its leading town is discounted. For Wayne County without Goldsboro this means 22.9 percent, or less than half the proportion found in the town, and for Lenoir County without Kinston it is 25.8 percent. Even in the more rural parts of the state we tend to find African Americans to be much more represented in towns and cities than in rural areas. Looking at the smaller civil division of the township (of which the state has 1,039), only 99 of these in 1990 had a majority black population. But at this scale, the concentrations are much greater, up to 95 percent (as, for example, in Indian Woods Township in Bertie County). A few urban townships show up with quite high concentrations, as well, as seen in the Rocky Mount Township of Edgecombe County, with a 75 percent black population, whereas the City of Rocky Mount itself has 49.6 percent. Such data have important implications for segregation of the races in the public schools, especially where local schools systems are still divided into county vs. city systems.

The Piedmont is in some ways quite different. In only a few counties adjacent to either the Virginia boundary to the north or the South Carolina boundary to the south, and thus the more rural portions, have African Americans traditionally comprised a large percentage of the population. For most Piedmont counties, blacks are decidedly urban dwellers, especially concentrated in the central cities. With 22.0 percent of the state's total population in 1990, the percentage of blacks in urban areas was 26.4, but for central cities it was 32.5, or close to one-third of the total. Note that the use of the term central city is, in this context, synonymous with municipality. But even here there are striking differences. In the larger central cities for 2000, the black population has been increasing its share to where it is in all cases larger than their state share of 21.6. Raleigh has a black population of 27.8 percent, while its county (Wake) has only 19.7 percent. For the Piedmont, this is the least attained by a major central city, but the difference between Raleigh and the suburban/exurban communities and towns in Wake County are obvious. Cary, one of the state's most rapidly expanding towns has only 6.1 percent African Americans among its 94,536 (2000) population. Elsewhere in the large Piedmont central cities these are the tallies for the black population, with the 1990 data in parenthesis: Guilford County has 29.3 percent (26.4) African American, while its cities of High Point has 31.8 percent (30.2) and Greensboro has 37.4 percent (34); Forsyth County has 25.6 percent (24.9) while Winston-Salem has (39.3); Mecklenburg County has 27.9 (26.3) while Charlotte has 32.7 percent (31.8); and Durham County has 39.5 (37) while Durham leads the state's large municipalities in percent black with 43.8 percent (45.7). Further dramatizing the concentration of blacks in the central city is the fact that Durham County's share of blacks, outside of the city of Durham is only 17 percent. And so it is for the remainder of the Piedmont.

That this condition reflects recent changes in African American migration patterns becomes apparent with a examination of black population change over the 1960 to 1990 (Figure 4.17b). Some general observations can be made from these comparisons. In total numbers, the rural counties of the Northeast and of the southern Coastal Plain have seen a net decrease of 4,765 in their black population over this period. Halifax, for example, saw a reduction from 31,926 in 1960 to 26,053 in 1980, but then this was followed by an increase to 27,616 during the 1980s. Other eastern counties were similarly affected. On the other hand significant increases were seen by the urban counties of the Piedmont. Mecklenburg led with a gain of 67,767, thereby doubling its black population over the three decades. In the process blacks netted an increase in their share of the population from 24

to 26.3%. Other large increases occurred in Cumberland, Guilford, Wake, Durham, Forsyth, and Onslow counties.

Aiding in the explanation of these changes is the significant expansion in the black share of the armed services population, indicated here by the inclusion of Cumberland and Onslow counties, but in more general terms the previously listed counties comprise the heart of the Urban Crescent. Probably the most important conclusion to be drawn from the maps is that of the immense strength of the rural-urban relocation of African Americans. This is extraordinary because it is happening precisely at the time when more and more people in general are shifting their domicile from urban to suburban and exurban locations, and especially so in the Piedmont. On the other hand, perhaps it is not so extraordinary given the wide range of discriminatory practices pursued historically by real estate agents, lending institutions, and white communities in general, in discouraging black relocation to suburban and exurban locations in metropolitan areas dominated by white populations (Turner et al 1991).

Extending the discussion to include the 2000 Census results, then for the 1960 to 2000 period, Charlotte increased its share of blacks from 27 to 33 percent, Winston-Salem from 7 to 37

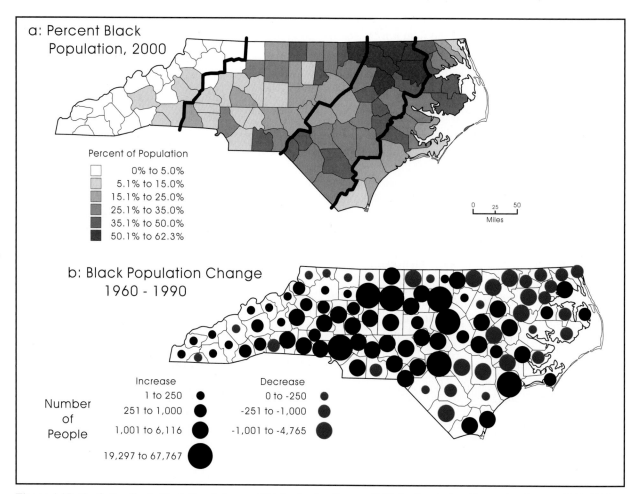

**Figure 4.15:** North Carolina's Black Population. **a:** Distribution by County, 2000. **b:** Population Change by County, 1960-1990. **Source:** U. S. Bureau of the Census, 1960-2000.

102

percent, Greensboro from 26 to 37 percent, Durham from 36 to 44 percent, Raleigh from 23 to 28 percent, and Fayetteville 35 to 42 percent. With an expected continued flow of African Americans to North Carolina's large central cities, and a continued relocation of other folks to urban fringe areas, the potential is certainly here for a majority black population in several of the state's largest cities. Durham and Fayetteville are the most likely candidates.

For all of the cities, one additional fact needs to be mentioned. Whereas the black population is shifting its weight generally from a rural to an urban location, within the cities the distinction between black and non-black concentrations can be even more clearly drawn. A sharp spatial separation between the races is one of the most readily defined residential land use contrasts in the cities. In Charlotte, for example, there is a core in its northwestern portion which contains ten census enumeration districts each with nearly 100% black persons. Similar spatial patterns of racial separation between black and white residents occur in all cities, and in so far as the proportion of blacks is increasing, solidly black neighborhoods are apt to continue to expand. One important implication of this racially segregated pattern of neighborhoods derives from the recent pressure to change public policy from the busing of school children, as one approach to deal positively with racial discrimination in educational service delivery, to an emphasis on neighborhood schools. As these changes are pressed into public practice we may expect even greater segregation of race and class in the public schools (see discussion on this issue in Chapter 7). Whether this will lead to further discrimination in the allocation of educational resources and in the location of experienced, well trained teachers remains to be seen.

As earlier mentioned, the movement of African Americans from rural to urban places in the state is given further emphasis by the turn-around in multi-state regional migration. Whereas the state lost a net of 213,663 black migrants during the 1960s, most of these were from eastern counties. During the 1970s the state gained an estimated net of 107,962 black migrants. Recent investigations have shown that the black migrant stream comprises three general categories of people. For one, these are people who are returning to the state of their birth, though not necessarily to their home county. By the late 1980s, North Carolina showed itself as the leading state in the country in return black migration, with a net gain of 17,217 return migrants during 1985-1990 (Newbold 1997, 6). Secondly, these are the underemployed or unemployed in search of better opportunities. And finally, they are the highly educated and better paid who, like people of all races, are able to take advantage of job expansions in one of the more rapidly expanding economies in the nation (Cromartie and Stack 1989). In addition to the increase obtained by return migrants, the black population gained a net of 14,811 from the latter two groups (Newbold 1997). United States Census population projections to 2025 indicate that the black north to south migration will continue at a high level. Greatest gains by state for the 1995-2025 projection period is Texas with 584,039 blacks expected to move into the state. North Carolina follows Georgia and Virginia as number four in the country; its expected gain for the period is 252,858 (Leland 1999). In the main, returning blacks are finding important and positive changes in racial attitudes and opportunities in North Carolina cities. Particularly in the larger urban centers have conditions improved over the past two decades. In the areas of housing and employment, membership in professional associations and civic clubs, and elected public officials, all contain numerous examples underscoring an improved racial climate. And yet, Martin Luther King's speech commemorating the overturning of school segregation laws in the late 1950s which ended with the ringing words of 'free at last, free at last, thank God, we are free at last' still has a hollow ring to it for many blacks, especially those concentrated in poor neighborhoods and poor counties. And we are now closing in on half of a century since these, perhaps not so prophetic, words were uttered.

## A Rapidly Expanding Hispanic Population

In the 1990s it is estimated that about 350,000 Hispanics immigrants arrived in the United States each year. In 1997 a leading demographer (Edmondson 1997, 17) predicted that they and their children might increase the Hispanic population from 26 million in 1996 to 32 million in 2001. Three years later the 2000 Census recorded a Hispanic population of 35.3 million! How many of these people make it to North Carolina, where we traditionally have seen Hispanics mostly as migrant labor moving temporarily to the state during the harvest season for vegetables, apples, Christmas trees, and other crops? Not an easy question to answer until the results of the 2000 census became available, and these are nothing short of astonishing. While the official North Carolina Hispanic population stood at 56,093 in 1980, and 69,020 in 1990, it more than quadrupled to 378,693 in 2000. Table 4.4 compares the racial breakdown of the North Carolina population with Hispanics included and without Hispanics included. Note first, that the Hispanic population is not considered a race, but rather an ethnicity attached to more than one particular race, including multi-race. So it is also of interest to note that Hispanics apparently have not understood this Census questionnaire distinction, as 177,614 marked the 'Some other race' box, even as they have also marked the Hispanic ethnic group category! This comprises 95.2 percent of this Census category. Thus about 47 percent of the Hispanic population sees itself as a race as well as an ethnicity. What is also revealing about this population is its youthfulness. While the white population has 22 percent aged 17 and younger, the Hispanic percentage is 32.7.

Though we are considering here a mere 4.7 percent of North Carolina's total population, Johnson-Webb and Johnson (1997) suggest that even such a small percentage of the total population is critical, especially since this is a culturally distinct population with a different language and with expectations of life that emerge from a background at variance from that of other populations in this state. Further, they show that the Hispanic population is a major component of where demographers are arguing that the United States' population is headed over the next half century.

| Subject | All Ages Number | All Ages Percent | 17 years or less Percent |
|---|---|---|---|
| RACE | | | |
| One Race | 7,946,053 | 98.7 | 24.1 |
| White | 5,804,656 | 72.1 | 22.0 |
| Black or African American | 1,737,545 | 21.6 | 29.9 |
| American Indian and Alaska Native | 99,551 | 1.2 | 30.2 |
| Asian | 113,689 | 1.4 | 27.3 |
| Native Hawaiian and Other Pacific Islander | 3,983 | 0.0 | 27.1 |
| Some other Race | 186,629 | 2.3 | 32.0 |
| Two or More Races | 103,260 | 1.3 | 44.1 |
| HISPANIC OR LATINO AND RACE | | | |
| Hispanic or Latino (of any race) | 378,963 | 4.7 | 32.7 |
| White | 157,501 | | |
| Black or African American | 14,244 | | |
| American Indian and Alaska Native | 4,218 | | |
| Asian | 1,273 | | |
| Native Hawaiian and Other Pacific Islander | 818 | | |
| Some other Race | 177,614 | | |
| Two or More Races | 23,295 | | |
| **Total Population** | **8,049,313** | **100.0** | **24.4** |

**Table 4.4:** Population by Race and Hispanic or Latino Origin, and Age 17 Years or Less.

**Source:** U.S. Bureau of the Census, 2000.

This, the "browning of America" argument, suggests that the non-Hispanic white population will be a minority in this country by the year 2050. Certainly there are implications in this for North Carolina. Far removed from ports of traditional entry of not only Hispanic populations, but other immigrant streams, we may doubt that this state will bear the brunt of such dramatic demographic change. Still, a healthy economy and low unemployment will attract migrants from other states regardless of race/ethnicity, and Hispanics are showing themselves to be very responsive to job opportunities and quite willing to relocate, especially to where a Hispanic community already exists. A few cases demonstrate the rapidity of recent changes. In Chatham County, where the Hispanic population reached 596 by the 1990 census, by April 1st, 2000, 4,743 live in the county and 2,740 live in Siler City alone, attracted by low paying jobs in the chicken processing industry. For Siler City Hispanics now comprise close to 40 percent of its total population. Similar is the situation in Burke County, where recruiting teams were sent out from the Morganton Case Farms Inc. chicken processing plant to attract Guatemalans from Florida, Texas, and elsewhere. Of Case Farms' 550 workers, over 90 percent are Latinos, and the overwhelming majority of these are Guatemalans (Raleigh News & Observer, 11/30/96). By 2000 there were about 2,000 Hispanics in Morganton.

In Greensboro, many new Latino dance clubs, small grocery stores, and specialty restaurants have opened during the mid-90s; and social welfare agencies, police departments, medical clinics, banks, schools, and other public or private service institutions throughout the state are hiring Spanish speaking translators (Greensboro News and Record 7/4/95). In February of 1995, Thomasville Furniture Industries, Inc. started an English as Second Language course, taught by Davidson Community College, in its plant outside of Lexington; and in Wilkesboro, Tyson Foods has expanded its education-incentive program to include Hispanics, who can get a bonus if they will learn English (Winston-Salem Journal 4/24/95). In the state's larger cities there are thriving and quite large Hispanic communities. Charlotte in 2000 led with 39,800, making Hispanic Charlotte the equivalent of the state's 20th largest city, larger than Kannapolis or Hickory. Raleigh follows with 19,000, while Durham and Winston-Salem each have 16,000. In the booming economy of the late 1990s it was largely the construction industry that captured these large numbers of Hispanics for the central cities.

Johnson-Webb and Johnson (1997) found that Hispanics have been settling in two types of communities, the Urban Crescent counties linked to the I-85 corridor, and the military complexes of Cumberland and Onslow counties, where Hispanics comprise their nationally expected proportion of members of the armed forces. Figure 4.16, which shows intercounty and interstate migration from 1985-1990, is particularly revealing since it identifies the Hispanic population as being much more mobile than the population at large. While a significant percentage is represented by military personnel, disproportionately large numbers have been moving into other counties as well. It appears that Hispanics are just now finding opportunities in this state to their liking, and are in the early stages of changing from a presence largely as migrant farm labor, and construction workers to permanent residents; initially as young men in temporary jobs with much of their salary going to parents and family at their home of record overseas, and then subsequently finding that the local environment is conducive for permanently relocating their families. Where Hispanics were located in the state in 1995 is shown in Figure 4.17. In this initial process of gradually settling in as North Carolinians, they are apt to change their address more frequently in response to improved job conditions. Figures 4.18a-c shows county by county percent distribution and how this is changing as this population exploded in the 1990s. With the economy slowing in the early 2000 decade it may be expected that the inflow of Hispanics, representing a migrating labor process strongly linked to the economic good fortunes of the state during the 1990s, will slow down as well.

### Yet Another Exploding Population: North Carolina's Asians

For the United States many minority populations have recently been growing faster than that of the Asian, which stood at 4.1 percent of the total U.S. population in 2000. Not so for North Carolina. Here the Asian and Partially Asian population reached 136,212. While this was only 1.7 percent of the state's population it represented an increase of 173 percent over the 1990 total of 49,970. It is likely that the state's universities, medicine, and technology industries are drawing in most of these Asian people, particularly from countries such as the Philippines, China, Vietnam, and India, though the positive welcome provided refugee populations has also been very important. In addition, Asiatics are increasingly moving away from the traditional gateway states of California and Washington, looking for employment opportunities. Main Street North Carolina appears especially welcoming to them, as shown on Figure 4.19. Here we see the apparent keying in of the Asiatic population to county population size. Though there are a few surprises here the Asian proportion seems to vary much less across the state than is the case for other minority populations. So the counties that lead in 2000 are Mecklenburg with an Asian community of 21,889, Wake has 21,249, Guilford has 10,294, and Durham has 7,350. These larger centers range from having 2.4 to 3.4 percent Asian population. Orange County's 4,845 (4.1% of its population) relates probably to UNC Chapel Hill and its medical facilities, while Burke County's 3,106 Asians (3.5%) may be more difficult to explain. High tech towns like Cary and Morrisville appear very attractive to Asians as they now comprise 8.1 and 9.1 percent of their total populations, respectively.

### *A Highly Concentrated American Indian Population*

Sharp contrasts exist between the changing spatial character of the North Carolina's other minority population and its American Indians, who in 2000 totaled 131,736. Though this suggests an increase of 64 percent over the 1990 population of 80,826, it must be noted that for this race, as for others, double counting was possible. Thus the 2000 Census permitted the declaration of more than one race, while the 1990 Census did not. In this way, with 36,661 of the 131,736 being counted as Partial American Indian, the state's American Indian population increased its share of the state's total population from 1.2 percent to 1.6 percent. With the United States American Indian/Alaskan Native population at 1.4 percent, North Carolina is just above the average for the country.

Due to their cultural distinctiveness, to their spatial concentration in just a few counties, and to their renewed eagerness for self-identification, American Indians are a highly visible minority. As is true in the country as a whole, they also comprise the ethnic group in the state that is expanding most rapidly solely on the power of natural increase (Shumway and Jackson 1995). In Robeson, a county of over 123,000 persons, the current demographic dynamics is gradually evolving an American Indian majority.

An additionally important factor in American Indian numeric expansion is the factor of self-identification. In Ross' (1999) recent and very comprehensive volume, *American Indians in North Carolina: A Geographic Interpretation,* he notes the virtual absence of an Indian population in the state in the 1900 Census of Population. A combination of factors account for this 'absence'. In the 1830s, by Act of Congress American Indians were classed with 'free' African Americans, as "free coloreds", with severe limited political freedom and social mobility imposed on them. Most land in Indian ownership was held in severalty, and could therefore, without an available individual patent (deed)

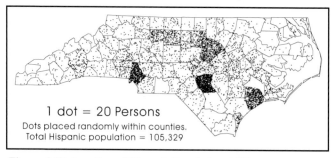

**Figure 4.17:** Location of Hispanic Population, 1995.
**Source:** Johnson-Webb and Johnson, 1997, 27.

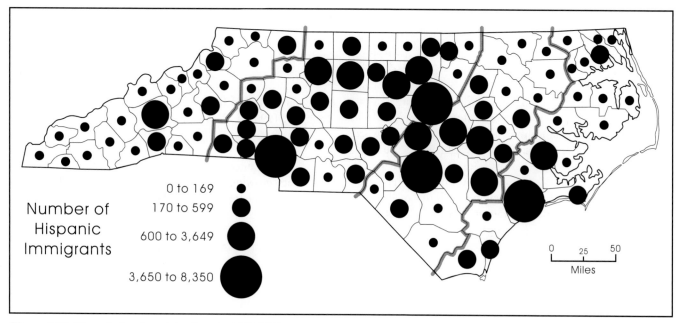

**Figure 4.16:** Hispanic Immigrants by County, 1985-1990.
**Source:** Johnson-Webb and Johnson, 1997, 29.

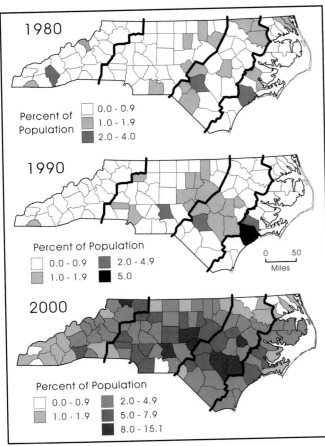

**Figure 4.18a-c:** Percent Hispanic Population by County, 1980, 1990, 2000.
**Source:** Johnson-Webb and Johnson, 1997, 28 and U. S. Bureau of the Census, 2000.

to the land, be more easily dislodged through the court system. In addition, it was not to their advantage to declare themselves Indian since this might force their removal to western territories (Ross 1999). Into the 20th Century, the economic, social, and political constraints on self identity were gradually lifted, and by 1990 there had occurred an American Indian renaissance in self- and group identity. Today there is much more pride taken in being recognized as the member of a particular tribe, so that individuals who before had qualms about being recognized as a native American, now are pleased to mark the census questionnaire as such. An example of this is the recently strenuous effort being made by the Occaneechi Band of the Saponi Nation to gain formal recognition, though the group was so widely dispersed several hundred years ago, if not in part absorbed by other tribes, that self-identity was thought to be impossible (Burnham 1996). Perhaps the problem of gaining official recognition by the North Carolina Commission of Indian Affairs of the Occaneechi Indians is further complicated by the fact that many Band members share African heritage. Where members of the Band are primarily concentrated, in the Pleasant Community of northern Orange County, the predominance of a darker hued population has led this small area from early in the 20th century to be called "little Texas", a reference to the local popular misperception of a Mexican ethnicity.

Although American Indians are found in all of the 100 counties, 77.3 percent reside in just twelve counties, with Robeson County having 47 percent of the total. Interestingly this compares with a 1990 distribution of 81.5 percent for the twelve counties having the most American Indians, suggesting a gradual decentralization of this minority population. Still close to one half of North Carolina counties have fewer than 200 Native Americans. In a U.S. American Indian/Alaskan Native and Partial Ameri-

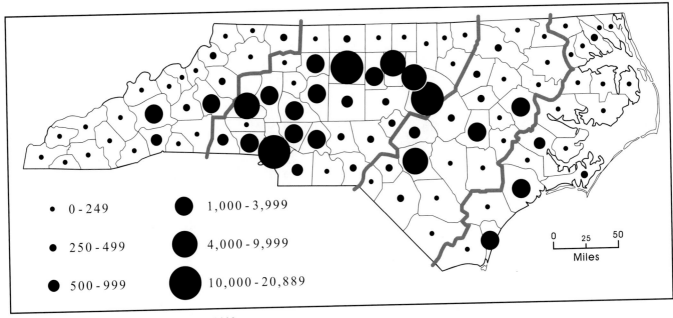

**Figure 4.19:** Asian Population by County, 2000.
**Source:** U. S. Bureau of the Census, 2000.

can Indian/Alaskan Native population of 4,119,301 in 2000 North Carolina's comprises only 3.2 percent, but in total numbers it still ranks seventh in the country (behind Oklahoma, California, Arizona, New Mexico, Alaska, and Washington).

Archeologists have found evidence of Native Americans inhabiting the lands that are now part of eastern North Carolina for over 10,000 years, and when white settlers first came to these shores there were an estimated 35,000 Natives dispersed among some 30 tribes. Continued clashes between white settlers and American Indians influenced a reduction of the indigenous to about 5,000 by 1710. The Tuscarora wars (1711-13) were particularly decimating. In the western part of the state the Indian Removal Bill of 1830, signed by (in)famous "Indian fighter" and North Carolina native son, President Andrew Jackson, forced the relocation to the Oklahoma Territory of three quarters of the Cherokee Nation. Large numbers died along this "Trail of Tears" to the western territories. Descendants of the remnants from the group now form the Eastern Band of the Cherokee. Other North Carolina officially recognized tribes include Coharie (Sampson, Harnett, Wayne, and Duplin counties), Waccamaw-Siouan (Bladen and Columbus), Haliwa-Saponi (Halifax and Warren), and Meherrin (Hertford and Bertie). Notable concentrations of Native Americans live in a few of the larger urban centers of the Piedmont (Figure 4.20).

In the southeastern corner of the state (Robeson, Hoke, and Scotland counties) live more than 40,000 Lumbee Indians. Accepted as an Indian entity by the United States Congress in 1956, the Lumbees have nevertheless been denied the large array of federal services generally available to federally recognized and supported Indian reservations. Still, an offshoot group, involving people calling themselves Tuscaroras, has defined the

25 acre (10 ha) Drowning Creek Reservation in the pine covered flatlands of western Robeson county (see Starr 1996).

Federally recognized, however, are the Cherokees, a smaller group of American Indians, almost all of whom are living in the southwestern mountain counties of Swain, Jackson, Graham, and Cherokee. The Eastern Band of Cherokee Indian Land, some 56,500 acres (22,874 ha), is divided into numerous community tracts with most of these forming the Cherokee Indian Reservation on the eastern slopes of the Great Smoky Mountains. A significant difference existed between the claim, made in 1975 by the tribal government, of a total Cherokee population of 8,381 and the official 1980 census returns, which count only 5,405 American Indians in the four counties. In 2000 the population of those four counties included 7,961 American Indians (single race counted only), an increase that may have been influenced by individuals more desirous of the designation due to the riches now being produced, and distributed in part to tribe members, by the new gambling casino in the community of Cherokee, on the Swain-Jackson counties boundary.

OTHER POPULATIONS

In the tight labor market enjoyed by the North Carolina economy in the mid- to late 1990s foreign workers provide important relief for businesses with jobs that otherwise go begging. Industries have sent recruiters throughout Central America and the Caribbean for qualified labor willing to work in lower rung jobs paying traditional low wages. Even in these jobs Latinos can make as much money in the Research Triangle's booming economy in a single hour as they might at home over three days to a week. Illegal aliens, who are able upon arrival quickly to

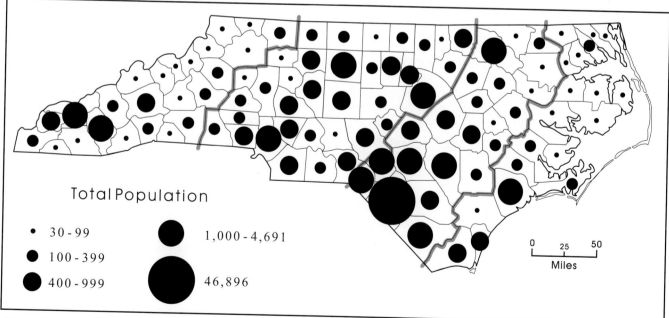

**Figure 4.20:** American Indian Population by County, 2000.
**Source:** U. S. Bureau of the Census, 2000.

obtain fake documents have become an increasingly prominent part of this labor pool. In some construction firms in the Piedmont Triangle, two thirds of the labor force is Hispanic. It was suggested in a recent journalistic investigation of labor linkages between the Triangle and Latin America that over 50 percent of the Hispanic labor force in the state is here illegally (Glascock and Whitlock 1998). If true, this will add another 375,000 to the counted 2000 Hispanic population in the state. These people suffer the disadvantages of not having any enforceable workplace rights, whether this involves underpayment, denial of workers compensation, or other breaches of labor law. On the other hand, a few years of continuous paychecks will enable the purchase of a lot and house in their home community in Central America, or perhaps complete costs of children's education, certainly these are the potential rewards that stimulates the illegal labor migration.

Two additional groups of residents are present in rather significant numbers, at least in a space specific context. Because both groups are seasonal in their residence, their characteristics will be taken up in more applicable regional chapters. So in subsequent chapters of this text we will deal with the plight of migrant farm workers, and with the economic and environmental impact of vacation home residents, especially retired populations who appear have a very focused geography.

Finally, an additional word about "missing people", or the continuing saga of census undercounting. Ensuring that everyone living in the country is appropriately tallied every decade is the constitutionally required task of the United States Bureau of the Census. But with each census it seemed that more and more people, especially the poor, the illegal aliens, and those without a permanent address, are being missed. A post-1990 Census analysis estimated that some 124,538 residents in North Carolina were not counted, the equivalent of 1.84% of the total population. Perhaps this is not so problematic, if not for the fact that the "missing people" have very particular characteristics. While only 1.38% of the white population was missed, the percentage increased to 2.86% for Asian, 3.33% for the African American, and 6.44% for the Hispanic populations (Sample 1998). For the 2000 Census it has been estimated that the undercount has been cut to 1.14 percent of the total, or 92,292 (apparently not including the illegal Hispanics). The vast majority of the missing are central city dwellers, thus their absence disenfranchises cities of some of their political power and resource base allocated by federal and state agencies based on population totals.

## DEMOGRAPHY AND PUBLIC POLICY

It is critical for decisionmakers, whether public or private, whether state, regional or local, to be fully cognizant of present and predicted future changes in the intricate mosaic of the state's population geography (Laws 1994; Outterbourg and McLaughlin 1993). Public education designed to understand and appreciate the complexities of the population mosaic will then encourage and aid decisionmakers to implement policies to better serve North

Carolina's varied humanity. The state has been impacted by nationwide changes in social and economic conditions that dramatically affect our population condition. Recent trends include a decreasing household size (reflecting fewer children per family), and more single person households, especially those headed by a woman. It includes the so-called erosion of the traditional nuclear family, and a redirection in the character and composition of migration streams that alter existing ethnic and racial balances; and it affects changes in community age and gender structure. Migration patterns, plus changes in birth and death rates affect longevity resulting in the present national passionate concerns with the caring for an increasingly aging population. Dual income households have become the norm with recent shifts in economic conditions, especially economic restructuring. As indicated in these pages, with some aspects further detailed in other chapters, it happens that these far reaching aspects of demographically altering life conditions diffuse gradually through the state, and they network through a sieve of varying local socioeconomic forces of attraction or rejection. Some communities become more dominated by certain demographies (as, for example, elderly, younger, racial minority, blue color labor, middle class suburban, seasonally retired or other unique populations), and therefore merit planning and policy attention for one particular factor alone. In other words, serious issues in the planning and implementation of policy are raised where a region, county, municipality or locality differ from the norm in its vital events, selective migration patterns, household size and racial/ethnic composition, and age/gender structure, when scant attention otherwise is paid to these realities.

Of particular concern are the following demographically related issues:

### Predictable shifts in labor demographics

1) it is clear from the foregoing that the state will lose a rather significant percentage of its labor force simply through the natural progression of existing population cohorts through their life cycle; this means that an economy conditioned by a labor force enlarged by the "baby boomers" must adjust to a much smaller labor force defined by the more recent decades of "baby bust" conditions; the only way that the labor force can be exactly replaced will be through added inmigration, probably achievable only by accepting an even greater number of people from overseas, i.e. Hispanics and Asiatics;

2) the overarching problem for American decision makers, public and private, is the fact that the window of opportunity for extracting from the "baby boom" generation the resources needed for its passage into expectedly comfortable retirement is only a couple of decades; the economic good times favoring the United States as we move into the 21st Cen-

108

tury are not being adequately tapped for future financial stability; perhaps this has to do with the general condition that those who are to be the primary beneficiaries, the "baby boomers", are also those currently in political and economic power.

## Population redistribution

1) there is an ongoing concentration of people in the Urban Crescent/Horseshoe; a serious question here is the timely planning for an expanding population's needs of public education facilities, adequate access (prospectively by public transportation) to places of employment, open space and leisure area preservation, community water and sewer connections and appropriate disposal of their wastes, as well as other aspects of their health and safety; critically important is the fact that though this issue is frequently experienced locally it extends its tentacles far into the counties and regions beyond; administration boundaries frequently act as invisible mental barriers to enhancing the conditions of life for everyone;

2) the state is affected by a highly selective migration process that attracts better educated, higher skilled, more youthful, and dynamically innovative professionals and labor to the larger cities of the Piedmont; often missed in the excitement of persistent economic growth in certain areas are the implications of the human "sieve effect", an increasing leaving behind, in the rural and more peripheral counties, of those individuals who are less competitive on the diversified urban job market; the process results in concerns for bridging community competency and basic quality of life gaps, from county to county.

## An aging population

1) some rural and peripherally located countries and their municipalities find their resources challenged by the aging-in-place process which leaves an increasingly larger percentage of older citizens behind as youth migrates out and birth rates diminish;

2) other counties are proving particularly attractive to retirees who are increasingly becoming permanent residents of communities where they have invested in vacation homes; these counties are more distant from medical centers specializing in the needs of older people, and being peripheral and rural, with small populations they have difficulty in meeting the specialized service need;

3) health care costs may be expected to continue to soar as increasing costs of high tech medicine combine with an increasing share of the population expecting it;

## Special populations

1) many communities in our state are favored by the concentration of special populations that impact in very particular ways the local economy and social life while simultaneously providing local government with unique challenges in planning and resource allocation; in addition to the concentrations of elderly, as discussed above, such special populations include,

2) college students in places like Greenville, Chapel Hill, Buies Creek, Cullowhee, Banner Elk, and Boone, where in varying degree they numerically overwhelm the local population, and set the socio-economic-cultural amenity 'needs' agenda;

3) military personnel in Fayetteville, Goldsboro, and Jacksonville (as above);

4) unique concentrations of minority populations in central cities and some rural area communities;

5) "shadow populations", not counted by the census due to their lack of North Carolina resident status: these include seasonal vacation home owners in Tidewater and Mountains locations, as well as in favored parts of the Sandhills and reservoir sites, but also itinerant tourists and business travelers; these are populations that are unevenly and seasonally concentrated over the state, yet all have their legitimate expectations of public and private services and amenities;

6) illegal populations, favored by certain elements of the state's economy, but with individuals threatened by discovery and deportation they are incredibly vulnerable to exploitation; this is clearly an 'at risk' population that needs much more attention.

# Primary Activities:
# Agriculture, Fishing, and Forestry

## INTRODUCTION

With the escalating shifts in employment patterns toward urban centered jobs, is North Carolina still considered an agricultural state? Yes, indeed, but as one that is considerably different from the one still portrayed in many books on southern economic development and in the minds of many of our citizens. Traditional dependencies on labor intensive, row crop agriculture pursued largely on small diversified family farms have given way to large scale, specialized agribusiness. Important implications of this shift reach to general conditions of economic growth and change, to the state's labor force, to the regions formerly dependent on traditional agriculture, and to the conditions of the natural environment (Photos 5.1-5.3). From the old image of tobacco, corn, and cotton, there has emerged a vigorous, combatant, and world competitive agricultural industry known better for mass produced broilers, turkeys, and especially hogs, an animal that now outnumbers people in this, the "goodliest land under the cope of heaven." It is the task of this chapter to relate these changes by first providing a foundation for understanding the structure of economic activities, and then by considering how the state, with its varied natural environments and cultural his-

tory, has provided a unique place for the position of the primary activities of agriculture, fishing, and forestry.

## THE STRUCTURE OF ECONOMIC ACTIVITY

Typically, economic geographers classify the act of deriving an income into three main classes:

1. *Primary*, which involves the activity of extracting goods from nature, such as agriculture, forestry, fishing, and mining;

2. *Secondary*, which involves producing higher value goods from primary resources through the manufacturing process; and

3. *Tertiary*, which are all of the employment activities engaged in while providing a service to someone else, frequently through some institution like public education.

**Photo 5.1**: In downtown Greensboro these architectural contrasts dramatize the shift from an agricultural to a service economy.

**Photo 5.2:** In central Wilkes County near the Wilkesboro Tyson chicken processing plant, a rural community focused on the small church appears overwhelmed by encroaching exurban housing and a new broiler contract farm.

## AGRICULTURE

For North Carolina, we find that the value of some primary products has escalated considerably in recent decades, while the number of people involved in producing them has been greatly reduced. To a lesser extent, and varying by industry, this has been the case in secondary production, as well. It is the service industries that have generally experienced an across-the-board steady growth in value generated, as well as in employment.

The reader may observe the changing relationships between these three major employment activities and their current concentrations in the state's counties on Color Plates 5.1-5.2 and Figures 6.1-6.2. Note first the gradual changes in North Carolina's employment patterns during the 20th century (CP 5.1). From an initial dependence on primary activities, largely agriculture (about two-thirds of the labor force during the early decades of the century), a complete shift has occurred to where the similar degree of dependence at the end of the century is on employment in service activities. Secondary activities, or employment in manufacturing industries, have moved from an initial low of eleven percent in 1900 to a high of about 40 percent in 1970, but have since declined to less than one-third of the labor force at the end of the century. Mid-century, especially the early years of World War II, provided the watershed period when there was about an equal dependence on employment in each activity sector. The future appears to be one of ever increasing employment in the tertiary activities, with the continued gradual decreases in manufacturing, and the relative disappearance of employment in primary activities. Here it should be noted that more detailed breakdowns of economic activity frequently add two more activity classes: quartenary, to separate out government employees, and quinary, to accommodate the increasing importance of managerial activities. These activities will be dealt with in the section on the tertiary economy in the following chapter.

### More Agribusiness, Fewer Farms and Farmers

The National Agricultural Lands Study (NALS) in its final report published January, 1981, declared that, "The United States has been converting agricultural land to nonagricultural uses at the rate of about three million acres per year" (Brewer p. 3). From 1985 to 1995, this reduction in farmland accelerated to 4.2 million acres per year. Most of the land lost to farming is now in highways, suburbs/exurbs, shopping malls and other urban uses, or in reservoirs and open space recreation areas. A considerable percentage has been purchased by land speculators who hold it in anticipation of future urban related expansion, a process of land use change that leaves large areas of former farm land in a state of disuse on the fringe of major urban concentrations. Geographers refer to this rather unsightly transition from rural to urban land usage as the urban shadow.

How does North Carolina compare? A look at Table 5.1 shows that the state is experiencing decreases in its number of farms and in its farmland at a rate that is considerably greater than for the United States as a whole. Over the past three decades, 1965-1996, the number of farms in North Carolina has been reduced by exactly two-thirds, from 175,000 to 58,000 (U.S.=38.2% decrease), though a change in the definition of a farm accounts for part of this downward shift. Over the same period there has been a decrease of 45 percent (U.S.=14.2%) in the acreage committed to agriculture, leaving a total of 9.2 million farm acres in 1996. On the other hand, there has been a considerable increase in the average size of a farm, from 93 to 159 acres (N.C., +71% vs. U.S., +38%), although part of this is also due to change in the nation's definition of what constitutes a farm. This increase is close to twice the rate of that of the country, but still North Carolina's farms are only one-third the size of the national average (Table 5.1). Presently the U.S. Census of Agriculture defines

**Photo 5.3**: Fields of beef cattle in the Central Piedmont near the Uwharries Mountains are increasingly hemmed in by exurban settlers wishing to spread out on larger lots in open and visually enticing environments; but for how long will these be available?

a farm as an operation that sells $1,000 or more in agricultural products. So farms in the state range from very small operations with few assets and incomes that cannot support a family, to very large scale, multi-million dollar entities that can control 1,000's of acres. Hog, chicken, and turkey farms resemble primary manufacturing plants, with scores of full-time employees and subcontractual relations with individual farms, while other specialized agricultural enterprises rely on seasonal migrant labor. General farming, the traditional, self supporting family farm producing a variety of crops and animal products, is becoming a relic of the past. It is giving way to the competitive need for the large scale capitalization of specialized agriculture that is fueled by globalizing markets and by economies of scale. Farms that survive on the economic margin are frequently owned by an older couple, or are in transition with an increasing share of land being leased to larger adjacent enterprises, while owners are largely dependent on nonfarm jobs and incomes.

To be sure, agricultural specialization does not necessarily require a large land base, though new innovative approaches may be helpful. For example, in Chatham County, the pressure on farmland is extreme as people leave the increasing residential crowding of Wake, Durham, and Orange counties for new suburban and exurban communities in the rural, aesthetic, and quiet surroundings of adjacent Chatham County. Many fleeing their highly congested environments are able to buy small farms or

simply very large lots, but then they wonder what to do with the land beyond that which is used for the home itself. In answer to this predicament and to the evolution of a large niche market for vegetables in the rapidly growing and wealthy Piedmont Triangle, Chatham County extension service has hired an expert to advise these new land owners on the art of sustainable agriculture and organic gardening. This new service is believed to be a first for the southeastern states (Raleigh News and Observer 1997).

Meanwhile, the greenhouse and nursery industry is presently the state's most rapidly expanding agricultural enterprise, reaching fourth place in 1995 in total cash receipts, behind hogs, broilers, and tobacco. Nurseries are mostly small enterprises serving the needs of local urban and leisure home markets. Even so, there is now an example of one nursery in the Charlotte area attaining 700 acres in size while serving an expanding national market. Vineyards also are seeing an increase in popularity with the demise of tobacco as a cash crop. This is a highly specialized crop where the producers are mostly involved in vertically integrated agricultural production from the planting of the vines to the selling of the bottled wine (Photo 5.4).

There are those who see an increasing scale of agricultural operations and further statewide agricultural diversification as keys to long term success. For the very large scale entrepreneurs, whether individually diversified or highly specialized, what

| Farms | Number of Farms and Land in Farms, 1960-1996 | | | | | | | |
|---|---|---|---|---|---|---|---|---|
| | 1960 | | 1970 | | 1980 | | 1996 | |
| | U.S. | N.C. | U.S. | N.C. | U.S. | N.C. | U.S. | N.C. |
| Number of Farms | 3,956,000 | 212,000 | 2,949,000 | 150,000 | 2,428,000 | 93,000 | 2,063,000 | 58,000 |
| Land in Farms (acres) | 1,171,411,000 | 17,800,000 | 1,098,759,000 | 15,200,000 | 1,042,245,000 | 11,700,000 | 968,048,000 | 9,200,000 |
| Average Size (acres) | 296 | 84 | 373 | 101 | 429 | 126 | 469 | 159 |

**Table 5.1**: Farm Characteristics, 1960-1996.
**Source**: North Carolina Agricultural Statistics, Various Years to 1996.

**Photo 5.4**: Duplin Wine Cellars in Rose Hill, Duplin County, dominates the production of fine wine favoring North Carolina species, especially scuppernong; in the western part of the state a number of wineries, like Biltmore in Buncombe County and Westbend in Forsyth County, favor French vinefera species and are becoming quite quality competitive with Virginia producers.

was farming is now agribusiness. In shear growth of agricultural activities, state figures bear out this shift in scale and production style. From 1974 to 1994, the state moved from sixth in the nation in net farm income to third, exceeding $7 billion by 1996. In fact, the North Carolina Agribusiness Council considers the value of this primary economic activity to be the front end of a $33 billion consumer goods industry for the state (Charlotte Observer 1996). It is noteworthy that income from government payments (price supports, etc.) is an insignificant percentage (0.6%) of this total, with the state ranking 32nd in the country. Compare this with an Iowa dependence of 6.7 percent on government payments. Perhaps the question could be raised as to whether a greater sense of self reliance on the part of the small North Carolina farmers has reduced their share of federal support and thereby contributed to their marginalization and greater reduction in numbers. Another aspect to be considered is that African American farmers have for decades suffered acute discriminatory practices in federal loans, grants, and other support schemes administered or advised by the U. S. Department of Agriculture through its county agricultural agents. Being pursued through the court system, the federal government agreed in January of 1999 to the charges of past discrimination and agreed to pay black farmers hundred of millions of dollars in restitution (Malveaux 1999). Since the U.S. Department of Agriculture has only recently begun receiving settlements claims, up to $50,000 per farmer, the data needed for understanding the impact of these practices on North Carolina farmers is not yet available, but likely it is that Coastal Plain farms have suffered the most.

It is evident from the increasing business acumen of some operators that farming is becoming agribusiness. Realizing that relatively more value is added and more income is generated by further processing of the primary product, these entrepreneurs are increasingly cutting out the middle man. For example, the grower of bell peppers might now be washing, grading, and pack-

ing directly for the market, rather than selling to an independent food processor. That same grower may also have greatly expanded his acreage and diversified his operation to arrive at a competitive position for his agribusiness. For example, Tull Hill Farms Inc. of Kinston, Lenoir County, emerged from a traditional Coastal Plain family farm. The corporation now employs up to 150 persons, depending on the season, and harvests 3,500 acres of tobacco, sweetpotatoes, Irish potatoes, cucumbers, cotton, corn, soybeans, asparagus, as well as bell peppers (Towle 1994, 50).

Demise of the family farm and the growth of specialized and large scale industrial agricultural technology, management practices, and production has resulted in drastic reductions of agricultural employment. Family workers have seen their numbers decrease by over two-thirds between 1965 and 1995, while hired workers have decreased by more than 50 percent. During this period the total number of people employed in agriculture declined from 418,000 to about 100,000, a reduction of 76 percent! And the 1995 figure is inflated by including 56,000 extra workers hired during the peak summer season (N. C. Agricultural Statistics 1996). Additionally, facing increased judicial vigilance against illegal immigrants, many working as migrant farm workers, producers are turning to a new state recruiting program that provides Mexican workers at premium wages ($6.40/hr in 1999), plus medical benefits and free housing. This, the H-2A temporary foreign agricultural worker visa program ushered in at least 10,000 Latino farm laborers to North Carolina in 1999. Immigrant workers are also more available as agricultural production moves to confined livestock, which provides year round employment, a critical aspect influencing these workers to consider becoming state residents with their families eventually joining them.

So the agricultural scene in North Carolina is changing in a revolutionary way, much more so than is the case for the United States as a whole. It is perhaps an inevitable outcome, with the

114

high rate of mechanization and increasing yields reducing the demand for worker and land alike. Expansion of educational and employment opportunities in booming cities of the 1990s are providing further impetus for labor to relocate from rural areas. Farm land is continuing its high rate of conversion to other uses where the rapidly expanding tentacles of urban growth reach deep into the rural hinterlands, especially in the Piedmont. In addition, specialized agricultural industries are insisting on their own unique roles in the economy and are influencing a shift in state government agricultural related priorities, especially with regard to environmental and community impacts. As a result of all of these changes, voices are increasingly raised, questioning whether North Carolinians in the future can afford to watch impassively as their agricultural lands and traditional rural communities are put at risk.

At the national scale, the dire prediction of the NALS study is being challenged by highly regarded critics. Emery Castle, the President of Resources for the Future, an esteemed Washington, D.C. based, non-profit think tank, has remarked that the United States is in no danger of running out of food due to disappearing farm land. Castle's argument is that more than two-thirds of the land converted to urban and other nonagricultural uses is in fact not farm land to begin with. As he further points out: "Even in the unlikely event that [the rate of farmland loss] were to continue, by 2005 we will have suffered an accumulated loss of less than four percent of the potential U.S. cropland base of 540 million acres" (Castle 1981, 23). This, he argues, is of no consequence even with a projected increase in national consumption and international demand for American food products.

For North Carolina, a state that ranks among the top ten in the country in the production of 27 important agricultural products, this argument may have less validity (Table 5.2). Whether it does depends on the nature of the leading agricultural products and on where in the state they are being produced. It is largely in the Piedmont that urban areas are voracious in their consumption of rural land. For example in Orange County, a predominantly rural county sandwiched into the Urban Crescent, population has increased from 34,435 in 1950 to 94,775 in 1990, while land in farms has decreased from 179,073 to 67,491 acres. On the other hand it is in the Coastal Plain, with only one major urban county (Cumberland) out of 23, that agriculture predominates. In the mountains, with its surplus of marginal agricultural land, there is at the same time a disproportionately large loss. In the 17 westernmost counties, cropland decreased by 69 percent from 1949 to 1978, a figure three times that of the state average.

A look at Color Plate 5.2 confirms the importance of agriculture to the eastern part of the state. Here are concentrated seventeen of the twenty counties that derive over ten percent of their total income from agriculture. As will become apparent in following sections, these high income levels are in large measure controlled by highly specialized agricultural operations. In cash receipts from agriculture in 1994, the leading counties were Sampson with $468 million and Duplin with $447 million. Then much behind these two agricultural giants follow Union and

Wayne, each with $267 million, Johnston ($194 million), Wilkes ($163 million), Randolph ($152 million), Robeson ($152 million), Moore ($149 million) and Pitt (the tenth largest in the state with $147 million). Ranked at the very bottom is Dare County with a mere $586,000 in cash receipts from agricultural production.

### Agricultural Products and Regions

What are the important commodities and where in the state do they predominate? It takes the four major products (hogs, broilers, tobacco, and greenhouse nursery) to reach 62 percent of total cash receipts, but no less than fourteen commodities to reach about 94 percent of the total (Table 5.3), and these vary considerably in their production concentration. In its distribution across the state, agricultural production is influenced by the varied physical environments, by tradition, by access to markets, and by special incentives offered corporate agribusiness.

Field crops are especially evident in the Coastal Plain (Figure 5.1). This region maintains its traditional large scale production of tobacco, corn for grain, soybeans, peanuts, and seed potatoes. Many of these crops have important extensions both east and west. The Tidewater Region contributes meaningfully to the production of soybeans and corn, and is the leading producer of Irish potatoes. The Piedmont, while sovereign in barley, share in the production of wheat and oats; its northern counties are also leading tobacco producers. Hay and corn for silage, both contributing to the favorite mountain agricultural activity of animal husbandry, dominate in the Mountain Region. Here also apples and ornamentals, including Christmas trees, are important cash crops.

Cash receipts derived from the marketing of livestock, dairy products, and poultry products indicate a much greater clustering tendency (Figure 5.2). This is shown by the dominance of hogs in the central Coastal Plain and northern Tidewater, and poultry, cattle, and dairying in the central and western Piedmont and Mountain regions. Fueled by the recent boom in hog and turkey production, Sampson and Duplin counties in the south central Coastal Plain are now approaching $500 million in yearly cash receipts from livestock operations. Exemplifying this increasing importance of livestock operations, Sampson has now reached a 5:1 livestock to crop ratio in the respective value of cash receipts. Wayne County provides something of a transition with a lesser emphasis on livestock, but still with over $250 million in yearly income. Johnston County represents the opposite emphasis in the northern Coastal Plain with a 1:5 livestock to crop ratio. Here, of course, tobacco is the leading cash crop, as is also the case in Robeson, the very large county on the South Carolina border. Elsewhere in the state, only the poultry industry dominated counties of Wilkes, Union, and Randolph rank very high on the list of agricultural income.

### Field Crops

Tobacco. An unruly handmaiden to Virginia for over a century during the colonial period, North Carolina's production of tobacco was decidedly small scale. Though the plant was culti-

## How North Carolina Agriculture Compares with Other States, 1996 Production

| Rank | Item | Production | Units | More Production than North Carolina |
|---|---|---|---|---|
| 1 | Total Tobacco | 586 | (Mil Lbs) | None |
| | Flue-Cured Tobacco | 573 | (Mil Lbs) | None |
| | Sweetpotatoes | 4,340 | (000 Cwt) | None |
| | Turkeys Raised | 59.5 | (Mil Hd) | None |
| 2 | Number of Hogs on Farms (3-1-97) | 9.5 | (Mil Hd) | Iowa |
| | Hogs Cash Reciepts | $1,749 | (Mil $) | Iowa |
| | Cucumbers for Pickles | 60 | (000 Tons) | Mich |
| | Trout Sold | 5,266 | (000 Lbs) | Idaho |
| | Net Farm Income | $2,880 | (Mil $) | Calif |
| 3 | Poultry and Egg Products Cash Reciepts (1995) | $2,056 | (Mil $) | Ark, Ga |
| | Greenhouse and Nursery Reciepts | $889 | (Mil $) | Calif, Fla |
| 4 | Commercial Broilers | 681 | (Mil Hd) | Ark. Ga, Ala |
| | Peanuts | 367.5 | (Mil Lbs) | Ga, Tex, Ala |
| | Strawberries | 161 | (000 Cwt) | Calif, Fla, Ore |
| | Blueberries | 12,000 | (000 Lbs) | Mich, NJ, Ore |
| 5 | Burley Tobacco | 13.0 | (Mil Lbs) | Ky, Tenn, Va |
| 6 | Rye | 500 | (000 Bu) | Ga, S Dak, Okla |
| 7 | Catfish Sold | 2,590 | (000 Lbs) | Miss, Ark, Ala |
| | Watermelons | 1,450 | (000 Cwt) | Tex, Ga, Calif |
| | Cotton | 1,002 | (000 Bales) | Tex, Calif, Ga |
| | Apples | 200 | (Mil Lbs) | Wash, NY, Calif |
| | Cash Reciepts from Livestock, Dairy, and Poultry (1995) | $3,735 | (Mil $) | Tex, Nebr, Calif |
| 8 | Cash Reciepts from All Commodities (1995) | $6,987 | (Mil $) | Calif, Tex, Iowa |
| 9 | Eggs | 2,988 | (Mil Eggs) | Calif, Ohio, Ind |
| | Chickens (12-1-96), (Excludes Broilers) | 16.7 | (Mil Hd) | Ohio, Calif, Ga |
| | Cash Reciepts from Crops (1995) | $3,251 | (Mil $) | Calif, Ill, Iowa |
| 12 | Grapes | 1,200 | (Tons) | Calif, NY, Wash |
| | Sweet Corn | 630 | (000 Cwt) | Fla, Calif, Ga |
| 13 | Pecans | 800 | (000 Lbs) | Ga, Tex, N Mex |
| | Export Shares (1995) | $1,358 | (Mil $) | Calif, Tex, Ill |
| 14 | Number of Farms | 58 | (000's) | Tex, Mo, Iowa |
| | Tomatoes | 224 | (000 Cwt) | Fla, Calif, Ga |
| 16 | Soybeans | 34.8 | (Mil Bu) | Iowa, Ill, Minn |
| | Sorghum Grain | 570 | (000 Bu) | Kans, Tex, Nebr |
| | Corn for Grain | 85.5 | (Mil Bu) | Iowa, Ill, Nebr |
| 17 | All Potatoes | 3,338 | (000 Cwt) | Idaho, Wash, Col |
| 18 | Winter Wheat | 26.0 | (Mil Bu) | Kans, Wash, Okl |
| 19 | Barley | 1.3 | (Mil Bu) | N Dak, Idaho, Mo |
| 23 | Peaches | 1.9 | (Mil Bu) | Calif, NJ, Pa |
| 26 | Oats | 1.2 | (Mil Bu) | S Dak, N Dak, Wash |
| 31 | Milk | 1,288 | (Mil Lbs) | Wisc, Calif, NY |
| | Number of Cattle on Farms (1-1-97) | 1,190 | (000 Hd) | Tex, Kans, Nebr |
| 35 | Hay | 1,145 | (000 Tons) | S Dak, Calif, Tex |

**Table 5.2**: How North Carolina Agriculture Compares with Other States.
**Source**: North Carolina Agricultural Statistics, 1996; North Carolina Department of Agriculture
 (http://www.agr.state.nc.us/stats/), 1997.

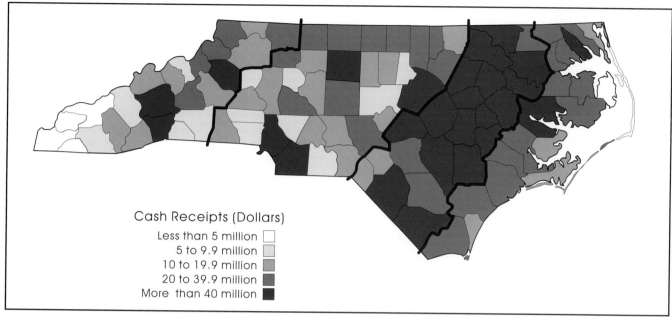

**Figure 5.1**: Cash Reciepts from Crop Production, by County, 1995.
**Source**: North Carolina Department of Agriculture (http://www.agr.state.nc.us/stats/), 1997.

vated throughout the eastern and central portion of the state, the Albemarle Sound region and the counties adjacent to the Virginia border dominated early production efforts. It was not until the hybridizing of Bright Leaf tobacco, the development of the flue curing process, and the invention of cigarette rolling machines in the tobacco factories of Durham at the turn of the 20th century, that North Carolina became the nation's leading tobacco grower and manufacturer. By the late 1940s and early '50s tobacco contributed nearly 60 percent to the state's farm income (Hart and Chestang 1996). In 1996, 13,000 N. C. farmers grew 485

million pounds of tobacco (over one third of the U.S. total, but a 20 percent reduction from the banner year of 1993), while earning $1.05 billion, or about 15 percent of all farm income in the state. However, does the present attempt to reduce tobacco smoking for health reasons spell the beginning of the end of 'Big Tobacco' in the state? Perhaps not for the immediate future, as extraordinary growth in foreign demand for the North Carolina product is apt to offset domestic demand declines for a while. Still, another future may be suggested by the example of R J. Reynolds' 1987 act of relocating its tobacco administrative world

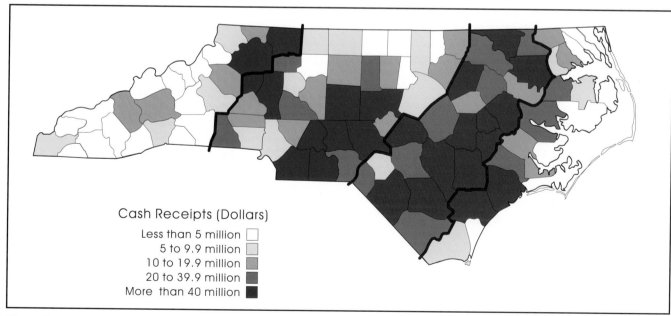

**Figure 5.2**: Cash Receipts from Livestock Production, by County, 1995.
**Source**: North Carolina Department of Agriculture (http://www.agr.state.nc.us/stats/), 1997.

| Ranking of Major North Carolina Farm Commodities, 1996 | | |
|---|---|---|
| Rank | Item | 1996 Cash Receipts Million Dollars |
| 1 | Hogs | 1,749 |
| 2 | Broilers | 1,310 |
| 3 | Tobacco | 1,021 |
| 4 | Greenhouse/Nursery | 889 |
| 5 | Turkeys | 612 |
| 6 | Cotton | 343 |
| 7 | Corn | 242 |
| 8 | Chicken Eggs | 218 |
| 9 | Soybeans | 217 |
| 10 | Dairy Products | 212 |
| 11 | Cattle and Calves | 154 |
| 12 | Wheat | 123 |
| 13 | Peanuts | 96 |
| 14 | Sweetpotatoes | 53 |
| 15 | Apples | 24 |

**Table 5.3**: Ranking of Major Farm Commodities, 1996.
**Source**: North Carolina Department of Agriculture
(http:// www.agr.state.nc.us/stats/), 1997.

headquarters from Winston-Salem to Atlanta, in 1997 to Switzerland, to then finally divesting its overseas division in 1999. Tobacco as an export product will be dealt with in a later chapter, but it is relevant to note here that the United States has not been keeping its share of the world-wide tobacco market, as its total production has declined 23 percent from the peak year of 1992 to 1995.

A comparatively high value for tobacco keeps farmers interested in continuing its cultivation, even though the process is fairly complicated. Stephen Kelly (1982), a Charlotte Observer correspondent, presented well some of these conditions in this condensed and slightly modified version written in the early eighties:

"Fifty years ago it wasn't easy to be a tobacco farmer. In addition to the usual tribulations, the farmer grew a crop on small plots that required huge amounts of labor. The crop was graded in secret by a handful of buying companies with the result that, prices being so unfair and low, the planting of next year's crop was in jeopardy. So farmers were ready for change when the Agricultural Adjustment Act of 1938 was enacted to insure supply and price stability. Now, more than 40 years later and following an extensive series of quotas and allotments, prices are stable and tobacco is graded in the open by professional inspectors. The program operates this way: Each year the Department of Agriculture decides how much tobacco can be grown while maintaining a certain price floor. The quota decided is then applied to

each farm with a tobacco allotment. These restrict the growing rights to the owners of farms to which allotments were granted in the 1930s. Quotas then establish how many acres and how much tobacco the farmer can grow and sell."

When farmers are ready to sell, they bring their already graded tobacco to a warehouse for auctioning. Should a tobacco company not be interested in paying more than the "support price" determined each year for each grade based on cost of production the farmers can sell at the support price to a cooperative that may use its own resources or government loans for the purchase. North Carolina's Flue-Cured Tobacco Cooperative Stabilization Corporation is the country's leading cooperative. Located in Raleigh, it works with assets in excess of $200 million to insure that its 40,000 members (not all are North Carolinians) will be able to sell their tobacco at expected high prices (The News and Observer, Feb. 26, 1995).

As members of Congress from tobacco states frequently point out, this agricultural support program has made small tobacco operations profitable at a time when small farmers were being squeezed out of other commodities. Note that the average allotment is still only three acres. Critics of the program, on the other hand, say that it is virtually impossible for a newcomer to grow tobacco. This is because allotments are tied to a specific piece of land, and unless a farmer owns or leases that land or its allotment, no tobacco can be raised. In 1999 about 98,000 individuals and companies own government-issued allotments in the state, but two-thirds of these do not grow tobacco, rather they lease their allotment to the farmer. Many allotment owners are retirees who depend on the little income their leased-out allotments will bring them each year as a supplement to their social security. Other ownerships have fallen into the hands of institutions such as Carolina Power and Light Company, Duke University, and Pitt County government, institutions that are essentially disinterested in raising tobacco. Allotment owners have been reeling from several years of federal government quota cuts. In 1999 the quota was 37 percent less than the average for the 1990s, and in December of that year the government announced an additional 18.5 percent cut for 2000. Traditionally nongrowers may lease their allotments for 35 to 55 cents per pound of crop raised on them. The grower is then likely to be paid $1.70/lb by the purchasing cooperative, thus yielding the farmer a net of about $1.25 per pound. With the cut in quotas the rent is apt to escalate to an average of 70 cents/lb, at the present time, this is about what the market will carry for the farmer to retain his minimum profit. Even so, the end result is a much larger income per acre for tobacco than can be gained for growing any other crop.

The artificiality of the quota and price support system has made U.S. tobacco so expensive that it is losing its share of both foreign and domestic markets. So it is of particular interest to point out that acreage allotments, commodity price supports, and the institutions derived to facilitate these aspects of tobacco production are now threatened by new efforts at decreasing federal agricultural support programs. While a new Farm Bill (1996) called for the gradual elimination of all agricultural crop stabilization programs, in 1999 tobacco farmers were awaiting the distribution conditions of the multibillion dollar court judgment against the tobacco industry, while their production for the year was the lowest in overall volume and quality since 1987. But then the 1999 tobacco season will be remembered not only for low prices and law suits, but also for droughts and flooding. Meanwhile, the legislature has debated where the state share is to go: how much, for example, in cash payments to individual farmers, to tobacco quota owners like Duke Power Company, to tobacco health related research and medical programs, to support prevention of smoking advertising, or to be placed in the care of a Foundation for future distribution.

Today's tobacco farmer operates in a society that increasingly questions a crop with a known health risk. And there are those (e.g., North Carolina Land Trustees, a Durham based group) who feel that this is the opportune time to encourage a shift from tobacco growing to other crops (Evers and Faust 1982, 19). As an example of this, the Northern Piedmont Wine Producers Association began in the early 1980s to market dinner and aperitif wines made from the produce of vineyards in lands recently converted from tobacco (Photo 5.4). Or for something much more exotic, consider the current attempt to raise French Perigord truffles as a substitute for tobacco. Truffles are intensely flavorful 'black diamond' mushrooms most frequently stimulated into rare abundance by the root system of hazelnut trees, and harvested by ground sniffing pigs or dogs. Their rarity and popularity in gourmet cooking has elevated their price to $300 per pound. In Orange County, one farmer has received a federal grant to explore the possibility for initiating truffle cultivation. Franklin Garland planted 500 hazelnut trees on former tobacco lands twenty years ago, but did not find the first truffle until twelve years later. By 1998 he was harvesting about 50 pounds yearly, at an estimated value of $14,000 per acre, considerably more than what could be gotten from tobacco (Chase 1998).

For the small farmer, the most viable alternative is probably a switch to greenhouse/nursery products, or to vegetables/small fruit production, where marketing cooperatives and organized Farmers' Markets at least promise partial security of a market (CP 5.8). The latter seems to be an even more competitive choice when the vegetables are organically grown. So, is the crop that paved North Carolina roads, built colleges, and shaped the state's economy for a century now destined for an ignominious future? Even Duke Medical Center, built with American Tobacco Company money, has banned smoking. However, the author's 1998 visit to Kinston, in the heart of tobacco country, revealed an absence of no-smoking hotel rooms.

Other states approach the known health risk by increasing taxes on tobacco products. Michigan, for example, tripled its excise tax on cigarettes in 1994 to 75¢, making a pack of twenty about 40 percent more expensive in Michigan than in North Carolina, where the tax remains at 5¢/pack. After several years it is interesting to note that this move had seemingly no effect on the

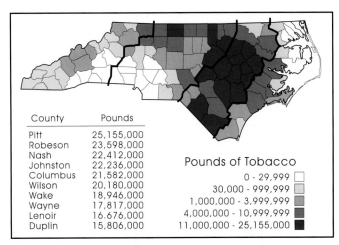

**Figure 5.3**: Tobacco Production, by County, 1995.
**Source**: North Carolina Agricultural Statistics, 1996.

consuming public since the percent of cigarette smokers in Michigan increased from 25 to 26. On the other hand, in North Carolina, where smoking decreased from 28 to 26 percent from 1994 to 1995, sales of taxed cigarettes rose 21 percent! Obviously, there is a causative relationship hidden in this math. The increase in cost for a package of cigarettes in Michigan was enough to initiate a flourishing black market in cigarettes from North Carolina. It is estimated that nearly 30 percent of the $1 billion Michigan market is contraband and that it is increasingly controlled by organized crime with elaborate transportation and distribution systems. North Carolina has made conditions more lucrative for the smugglers by ceasing to provide a tax stamp for cigarettes manufactured and bought in the state. This makes it extremely difficult for authorities in Michigan to catch the culprits, most especially since Michigan itself persists in neglecting to pass a tax stamp law. In 1996, the state estimated a loss of $150 million in tax revenue on illegal traffic in cigarettes (Williams 1997).

Figure 5.3 demonstrates the major importance of tobacco to the Coastal Plain farmer. Except for Wake, all of the ten leading counties are found here. Although the Department of Agriculture has divided the state into four districts, three of these (Old Belt, Eastern Belt and Border Belt) produce Bright flue-cured, now more appropriately referred to as bulk-cured (Hart 1996), "golden leaf" on about 250,000 acres, accounting for 96.6 percent of state tobacco production. Air-cured burley tobacco is grown on about 9,300 acres in the fourth district (Burley Belt), largely confined to the western mountain counties. Burley in North Carolina does not approach the production totals achieved in Kentucky, and appears much more vulnerable to the vagaries of weather than is Bright leaf. Yields in 1995, for example, were generally 35 percent below those of 1994 because of fall floods, and the associated occurrence of blue mold, a highly destructive tobacco disease that thrives in cool, wet weather. Even so, tobacco in the mountain counties provide a critical cash income for farmers otherwise engaged in other pursuits. Color Plates 5.4a-d show some of aspects of the tobacco landscape.

Katie Algoe (1997) relates the interesting history of Madison County's experience with tobacco production. Encouraged by its favorable site along a major east-west road over the Southern Appalachians and a rolling hilly terrain with an adequate supply of productive bottomlands, Madison farmers were early to develop a cash crop economy. Initial production of flue-cured bright leaf tobacco was fueled by increasing demand following the Civil War and was supported by an increasingly efficient transportation network. Reconstruction era rail allowed the shipment of hogsheads of tobacco to auction houses in Virginia and facilitated the movement of tobacco down the Mississippi to New Orleans. Also important was the improved market access ensured by the new Asheville tobacco market (1879). Flue-cured tobacco declined rapidly with the national fiscal crisis of the 1890s and the gradual domination of tobacco production throughout the country by the American Tobacco Company. It was the latter's near monopoly that drove prices at the farm so low that the cost of shipping tobacco to Piedmont factories exceeded its actual market value. With the breakup of the American Tobacco Company in 1911, tobacco returned to Madison County, but this time the more mountain compatible air-cured burley variety gradually beat out the Bright Leaf. Stability for the small mountain tobacco farmer was guaranteed with the federal tobacco support program of 1933. From then on the traditional grower received a yearly guaranteed cash income from the same small plot, maintaining a status quo in production acreage that has lasted to this day. While other kinds of agricultural production have virtually disappeared from the Madison landscape (like dairying and poultry), tobacco maintains its visibility. In 1993, there were 1,409 Madison County tobacco producers who generated almost $10 million from their crop (Algoe 1997, 58).

Greenhouse and Nursery Industry. In this category is classed the most rapidly growing crop production in North Carolina, with sales increasing from about $125 million in 1985 to $858 million in 1995. The 1995 sales is equivalent to 8.2 percent of the nation's production value. Coincidentally with the reaching of their mid-century years, the baby boomers have embraced gardening as a favorite hobby. Keeping up with the Jones' fancy new shrubbery and flower garden is becoming a passion. Perhaps equally important is the impact of continued urbanization on landscaping for corporate office parks, new stadiums, downtown beautification, and residential suburbs. Community colleges in the state report an all-time high interest in horticulture and landscaping curricula, and are themselves providing newly sprouting model gardens. North Carolina's homegrown major nationwide home center and discount store chains, Lowe's (of North Wilkesboro), reports that as recently as 1993 it was not including lawn-and-garden and greenhouses in all of their new stores. Now it does, with the result of a tripling of its garden sales from $329 million in 1991 to over $1 billion in 1995. It should be noted that these sales include related lawn and garden equipment, tools and supplies (Charlotte Observer, Sept. 8, 1996). For this agricultural industry, the problems of seasonality, a paucity of plant varieties, and a scale of operation too small to insure year round cash flow and profits are largely concerns of the past.

Greenhouse/nursery locations are strongly tied to the urban markets, with an almost direct relationship in scale to metropolitan counties. The one exception, Henderson County, has seen the development of nurseries to suit the new seasonal and retiree homeowners in the southern mountains and has emerged as the state's second largest county in sales, following the expected first place position of Mecklenburg County. Other mountain towns similarly have benefited from the concentration of seasonal homes and new open space resort facilities (Photo 5.5). Greenhouse farming also extends to organically grown vegetables. In Belvidere, Perquimans County, one farmer has organized a

Photo 5.5: Lakeview Nursery and Garden Center of Spruce Pine is typical of the many large nurseries increasingly found in small mountain towns to serve an expanding leisure resort and seasonal vacation population.

loosely defined cooperative, the Misty Morning Farm, for raising and selling tomatoes, green peppers, and cucumbers in greenhouses. The vegetables go to fresh markets as far away as Washington, D.C. Here and elsewhere a small niche market has developed for organically raised crops, as a small percentage of consumers is demonstrating an aversion to chemically treated fresh foods. Concerns that crops are indeed organically grown resulted in a 1990 federal bill calling for a nationwide organic certification program. In the state, the predominantly small organic farm, one to two acres in size, is certified and assisted by the Carolina Farm Stewardship Association of Carrboro (Moose 1993).

Nationwide, the organic food industry had reached a $4 billion production value in 1998, when the federal government released its criteria for 'organic' food and fueled a storm of criticism. Though offering a much needed standardized certification process, organic farm purists view the federal response as extremely permissive by not clearly disallowing a sundry assortment of technological processes in the raising of crops, including the use of biosolids (wastes from sewage treatment plants), ionizing radiation, and GEOs (genetically engineered organisms). In the case of GEOs, it is feared that genetically altered crops might spawn resistant strains of crop predators, such as boll weevils and corn borers. Similarly, the organic label may be attached to products having been exposed to antibiotics, hormones, or confinement operations in meat production. And farmers could apply pesticides and other chemicals, as long as the final product tested below a certain level of pesticide residue (Yarger 1998, 15). Indeed, the all too typical approach of the U.S. Department of Agriculture to meeting the mass production needs and objectives of corporate agriculture is diligently met in these standards. It is feared that if federal regulations are not revised to meet traditional organic food production standards at the local level, the small farmer, who previously has contributed the lion's share of marketable organic food, will not long survive.

Sales per acre of greenhouse/nursery production easily outperforms tobacco and is high enough to sustain investments in expensive urban lands. Within individual businesses, sales can be both retail and wholesale, as well as by direct consumer sales from plant beds, by continuous contract through landscaping services, and by mail order. Increasing specialization in rare species or new hybrids is leading to niche export markets. Not all plants are cultivated. A case in point is Wilcox Natural Products of Boone, now owned by Zuellig NA Inc., headquartered in Switzerland. Wilcox has buying stations scattered over four states: North Carolina, Kentucky, Florida, and Missouri. Here a great variety of plants, especially of medicinal, cosmetic and health food value, are collected from people who gather these in the wild. Ginseng root, valued in 1998 at about $300/lb, witch hazel leaves ($1.25/lb), sassafras leaves ($1/lb), or saw palmetto berries, deer tongue herb, goldenseal root, passion flower, aloe, and the bark of slippery elm or cherry, are among the many plant products collected, cleaned, packaged, and shipped to a botanical herb world market, 40 percent (!) of which is controlled by Wilcox (Hensley 1995). Aside from the example provided by Wilcox,

it is noteworthy that greenhouse/nursery agriculture does not appear to lend itself to corporate style management. It is a highly fragmented business, dominated by families and small owners, and characterized by an intense personal commitment. Of course, the industry is still in its early nurturing years. Continued expansion is apt to bring in the larger investors, gain the interest of the corporations, and change the style of management.

Cotton. In North Carolina, cotton had become the king of field crops by the early part of the 20th century, and as the number one cash crop, it helped draw the textile industry to the state. Production peaked in 1936, but then languished due to the boll weevil and changing fashions. Synthetics fibers controlled the U. S. market in the 1970s. Cotton contributed a mere 34 percent of a clothing industry infatuated with polyester and nylon. By the mid-1970s cotton was planted to only 50,000 acres per year in the state. The late 1980s saw the return to cotton as the major fiber for the clothing industry. People now wanted looser, cool, comfortable, and casual clothes, and cotton soared to 57 percent of the fiber market. Coincidentally, conditions were far from perfect in the soybean, wheat, and corn markets, and farmers sought optional crops. As Chestang (1996) pointed out, farmers find it inexpensive to shift to cotton because much of their existing row crop cultivating machinery lends itself very well to cotton cultivation. Mechanical harvesting is usually contracted out.

The explosion in demand coincided with ill times for foreign growers who were afflicted by an unusual combination of drought, pests, and floods, thus bringing further incentive for farmers to make the switch (Wilmington Morning Star, May 13, 1995). In 1994, a new record of acreage planted to cotton was reached with 484,000 acres, yielding a production of 829,000 bales and a value of $289.3 million, twice that of the previous year (CP 5.6). With a fabulous yield of 820 pounds of lint per acre and top prices, farmers rushed to purchase new harvesting equipment and to convert even more land to cotton the following year, increasing the acreage to over 800,000, or nineteen percent of the state's cultivated land. Then horrible weather conditions, including the wettest June ever in the Southeast, reduced the average 1995 yields to a mere 479 lbs of lint per acre, and a total production of 798,000 bales. Even higher prices guaranteed a reasonably successful year with an income of $304 million, enough to ensure continued acreage expansion, though marginally so, for 1996. Cotton was protected against imports until the 1990 farm legislation, which eased import restrictions, as prices increased. When 1995 prices soared, a release option was triggered allowing American mills to import 400,000 bales of overseas cotton (Hopkins 1996c). If King Cotton has indeed returned to North Carolina, it is on a roller coaster defined locally by weather and the competition for agricultural land and globally by international production, markets and price trends.

The Coastal Plain, especially the northern portion, is clearly the dominant cotton region in the state (Figure 5.4). Extensive areas of farm land in Halifax, Northampton, Bertie, and Edgecombe counties, formerly dominated by tenancy (see Chapter 11), are given over to cotton. Toward the west a gradual decrease is experienced through the Piedmont with very little, if any, production in the Mountain counties. Cotton has not yet developed the infrastructure of support necessary to ensure a more likely success. New cotton gins, which remove the seeds and clean the lint, are barely keeping up with increasing production (Wilmington Star, Feb. 25, 1995), though 48 mostly new gins are now serving the growers (Lord 1996). There is an additional need for a major oil mill to process the seeds; so far these are shipped in their hulls out of state for cattle fodder (Chestang 1996).

Other Field Crops. In eastern North Carolina, it has become tradition to emphasize a triad production of corn, soybean, and tobacco, with cotton now pressing to substitute for one of the three. Figures 5.5, 5.6, and 5.7 illustrate the county production of corn and soybeans. It is important to note that corn for grain goes to flour, grits, and other kinds of human food products, while corn for silage is food for animals. Annual production fluctuates widely with the vagaries of weather and the amount of corn planted. Years that experience some extreme in temperature and/or precipitation may see corn for grain production drop below 75 million bushels, as was true in 1995. Such variation of production influences prices when state conditions reflect those for the country at large. For example, from 1979 to 1980 corn production slipped 19 percent, but its total value increased by four percent. For the farmer it becomes something of a boom or bust situation, where in one year less than $2.50/bushel is received, while costs are in the vicinity of $2.90, and in another year the average return is $3.75/bushel at the same cost of production. In 1993, the farm receipts for corn were $139 million, but in 1996 receipts were $242 million! This was derived from plantings on 900,000 acres, one-third the acreage taken by the crop one hundred years ago.

Low income years for the farmer could mean subsequent good news at the grocery store for the consumer, since about 85 percent of the corn raised is used to feed hogs, dairy cattle and poultry. Figures 5.5 and 5.6 show dramatic differences in the production of corn for the two different usages. Corn for grain production is clearly concentrated in the Coastal Plain and Tidewater regions, although in these better agricultural regions production is threatened by crops that yield higher returns. Corn for silage is concentrated in the Piedmont, and in some Mountain counties. Here the influencing factor is mostly the symbiotic existence of beef and dairy cattle in the Piedmont. Even so, state production is not sufficient for local livestock producers, who normally have to import feed from adjacent states and the Midwest. This condition especially influences the feed needs of the new and rapidly expanding hog industry.

Most independent farmers respond to these fluctuations in income by further diversifying their agricultural production, committing additional land to soybeans, wheat, barley, oats, and other crops. A good year for one crop may thus balance a poor year for another, avoiding the situation of 1982 when a prolonged drought brought devastating results for most of the crops in the state. The abrupt shift in the prospects for a good harvest was dramatized by contrasting headlines in the Charlotte Observer,

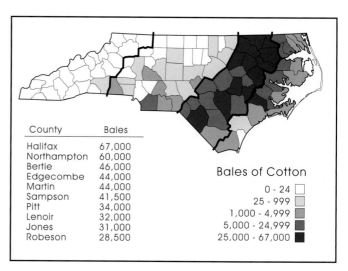

| County | Bales |
|---|---|
| Halifax | 67,000 |
| Northampton | 60,000 |
| Bertie | 46,000 |
| Edgecombe | 44,000 |
| Martin | 44,000 |
| Sampson | 41,500 |
| Pitt | 34,000 |
| Lenoir | 32,000 |
| Jones | 31,000 |
| Robeson | 28,500 |

Bales of Cotton

| | |
|---|---|
| 0 - 24 | |
| 25 - 999 | |
| 1,000 - 4,999 | |
| 5,000 - 24,999 | |
| 25,000 - 67,000 | |

**Figure 5.4**: Cotton Production, by County, 1995.
**Source**: North Carolina Agricultural Statistics, 1996.

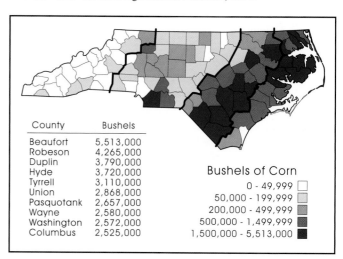

| County | Bushels |
|---|---|
| Beaufort | 5,513,000 |
| Robeson | 4,265,000 |
| Duplin | 3,790,000 |
| Hyde | 3,720,000 |
| Tyrrell | 3,110,000 |
| Union | 2,868,000 |
| Pasquotank | 2,657,000 |
| Wayne | 2,580,000 |
| Washington | 2,572,000 |
| Columbus | 2,525,000 |

Bushels of Corn

| | |
|---|---|
| 0 - 49,999 | |
| 50,000 - 199,999 | |
| 200,000 - 499,999 | |
| 500,000 - 1,499,999 | |
| 1,500,000 - 5,513,000 | |

**Figure 5.5**: Corn for Grain Production, by County, 1995.
**Source**: North Carolina Agricultural Statistics, 1996.

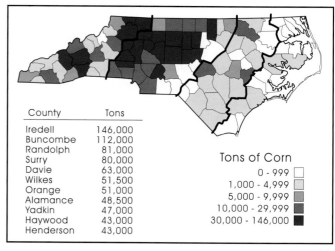

| County | Tons |
|---|---|
| Iredell | 146,000 |
| Buncombe | 112,000 |
| Randolph | 81,000 |
| Surry | 80,000 |
| Davie | 63,000 |
| Wilkes | 51,500 |
| Orange | 51,000 |
| Alamance | 48,500 |
| Yadkin | 47,000 |
| Haywood | 43,000 |
| Henderson | 43,000 |

Tons of Corn

| | |
|---|---|
| 0 - 999 | |
| 1,000 - 4,999 | |
| 5,000 - 9,999 | |
| 10,000 - 29,999 | |
| 30,000 - 146,000 | |

**Figure 5.6**: Corn for Silage Production, by County, 1995.
**Source**: North Carolina Agricultural Statistics, 1996.

which on September 19th declared: "Carolina's Rich in Soybeans - Sort of - Expected Bumper Crop Depresses Prices"; but on September 28th recanted with: "Carolina's Soybeans Withered in Drought." The latter article predicted a crop loss topping $400 million, with $105 million in soybeans alone. From the peak growing year of 1982 with 2.1 million acres were planted to this crop, acreage was reduced to 1.25 million by 1996. For that year soybean production was estimated at 35 million bushels and a value of $233 million.

It is market prices that pretty much determine the popularity of growing soybeans. In the early 1980s, the price peaked at $8 per bushel, then dropped to the $5 to $6 range for the remainder of the decade (Lord 1996, 101). In 1996 prices topped $7.00, and farmers are returning to the crop. The rapid changes from crop to crop are aided by the April, 1996, "Freedom to Farm" legislation, which removed most of the federal New Deal controls over farmers. Considerable variation may occur from one part of this rather large state to another (Figure 5.7). Soybean is a typical Coastal Plain and Tidewater crop that gradually decreases in its production per county west into the Piedmont.

Additional field crops, important within counties where their production is concentrated, but much less so as a statewide condition, are depicted in Figures 5.8 through 5.12. About twice as much acreage is devoted to sweetpotatoes as to Irish potatoes. The former, of which North Carolina is the leading producer, is concentrated in the central Coastal Plain, while the latter is more generally distributed through the Tidewater and Coastal Plain (Figure 5.8), but also found in the Mountain region (Figure 5.9). It bears noting, that the sweetpotato is the leading candidate for the honor of being the state-designated vegetable, though the cucumber appears close behind (Rhee 1995). A discerning reader will note that here the word sweetpotato is not two words. The reason is that this is not a potato. In fact, the sweetpotato is a tropical plant in the morning glory family producing purplish flowers and a large edible root.

Wheat is the fourth leading field crop in the state with 590,000 harvested acres in 1996 and a production of 26 million bushels (Figure 5.10). With double cropping (harvesting two different crops from the same field in one year), an increasing reality on the Coastal Plain since 1980, wheat has been on the upswing since the low acreage (165,000) year of 1996. Without serious competition wheat is by far the most important cash crop in the majority of the northern and central Tidewater counties (CP 5.3f). Other grain crops grown in the state include oats, barley and sorghum. These, as well as the large production of hay (Figure 5.11), are grown mostly for animal feed.

North Carolina peanuts, claimed to be the finest grown in this country, have also had a speckled production history. Presently ranked fourth in total peanut production, the state actually ranks first in producing the large kernel Virginia-style cocktail peanut. So perhaps it comes as no surprise that production is concentrated on the Virginia-Coastal Plain border, although production also takes place in the southern Coastal Plain (Photos 5.6a-b). Looking at the listing of the top county producers in

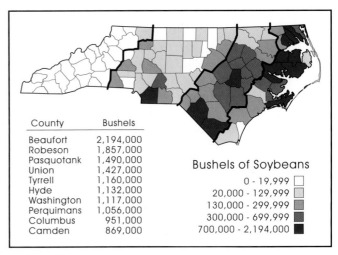

| County | Bushels |
| --- | --- |
| Beaufort | 2,194,000 |
| Robeson | 1,857,000 |
| Pasquotank | 1,490,000 |
| Union | 1,427,000 |
| Tyrrell | 1,160,000 |
| Hyde | 1,132,000 |
| Washington | 1,117,000 |
| Perquimans | 1,056,000 |
| Columbus | 951,000 |
| Camden | 869,000 |

Bushels of Soybeans

| | |
| --- | --- |
| 0 - 19,999 | |
| 20,000 - 129,999 | |
| 130,000 - 299,999 | |
| 300,000 - 699,999 | |
| 700,000 - 2,194,000 | |

**Figure 5.7**: Soybean Production, by County, 1995.
**Source**: North Carolina Agricultural Statistics, 1996.

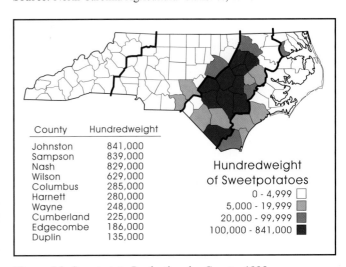

| County | Hundredweight |
| --- | --- |
| Johnston | 841,000 |
| Sampson | 839,000 |
| Nash | 829,000 |
| Wilson | 629,000 |
| Columbus | 285,000 |
| Harnett | 280,000 |
| Wayne | 248,000 |
| Cumberland | 225,000 |
| Edgecombe | 186,000 |
| Duplin | 135,000 |

Hundredweight of Sweetpotatoes

| | |
| --- | --- |
| 0 - 4,999 | |
| 5,000 - 19,999 | |
| 20,000 - 99,999 | |
| 100,000 - 841,000 | |

**Figure 5.8**: Sweetpotato Production, by County, 1995.
**Source**: North Carolina Agricultural Statistics, 1996.

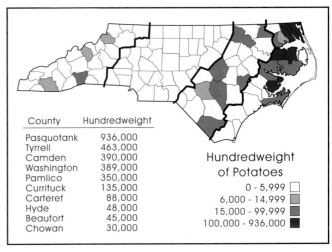

| County | Hundredweight |
| --- | --- |
| Pasquotank | 936,000 |
| Tyrrell | 463,000 |
| Camden | 390,000 |
| Washington | 389,000 |
| Pamlico | 350,000 |
| Currituck | 135,000 |
| Carteret | 88,000 |
| Hyde | 48,000 |
| Beaufort | 45,000 |
| Chowan | 30,000 |

Hundredweight of Potatoes

| | |
| --- | --- |
| 0 - 5,999 | |
| 6,000 - 14,999 | |
| 15,000 - 99,999 | |
| 100,000 - 936,000 | |

**Figure 5.9**: Irish Potato Production, by County, 1995.
**Source**: North Carolina Agricultural Statistics, 1996.

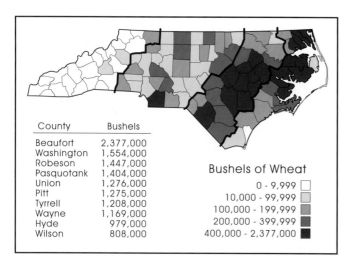

**Figure 5.10**: Wheat Production, by County, 1995.
**Source**: North Carolina Agricultural Statistics, 1996.

| County | Bushels |
|---|---|
| Beaufort | 2,377,000 |
| Washington | 1,554,000 |
| Robeson | 1,447,000 |
| Pasquotank | 1,404,000 |
| Union | 1,276,000 |
| Pitt | 1,275,000 |
| Tyrrell | 1,208,000 |
| Wayne | 1,169,000 |
| Hyde | 979,000 |
| Wilson | 808,000 |

Bushels of Wheat
0 - 9,999
10,000 - 99,999
100,000 - 199,999
200,000 - 399,999
400,000 - 2,377,000

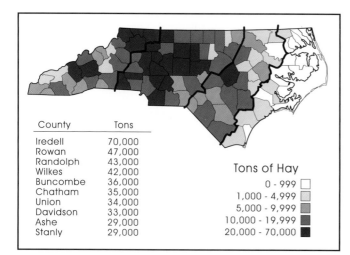

**Figure 5.11**: All Hay Production, by County, 1995.
**Source**: North Carolina Agricultural Statistics, 1996.

| County | Tons |
|---|---|
| Iredell | 70,000 |
| Rowan | 47,000 |
| Randolph | 43,000 |
| Wilkes | 42,000 |
| Buncombe | 36,000 |
| Chatham | 35,000 |
| Union | 34,000 |
| Davidson | 33,000 |
| Ashe | 29,000 |
| Stanly | 29,000 |

Tons of Hay
0 - 999
1,000 - 4,999
5,000 - 9,999
10,000 - 19,999
20,000 - 70,000

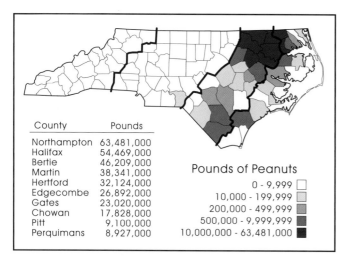

**Figure 5.12**: Peanut Production, by County, 1995.
**Source**: North Carolina Agricultural Statistics, 1996.

| County | Pounds |
|---|---|
| Northampton | 63,481,000 |
| Halifax | 54,469,000 |
| Bertie | 46,209,000 |
| Martin | 38,341,000 |
| Hertford | 32,124,000 |
| Edgecombe | 26,892,000 |
| Gates | 23,020,000 |
| Chowan | 17,828,000 |
| Pitt | 9,100,000 |
| Perquimans | 8,927,000 |

Pounds of Peanuts
0 - 9,999
10,000 - 199,999
200,000 - 499,999
500,000 - 9,999,999
10,000,000 - 63,481,000

Figure 5.12, it is clear that this is one of the most geographically focused field crops in the state.

Orchards. The commercial production of apples was up in 1995 to 270 million pounds, eight percent over the previous year. This was still a far cry from the banner years of the 1970s when 16,000 acres were in apple orchards and 1983 when 415 million pounds were produced. Apple production is concentrated in the hilly region around Hendersonville and in the Brushy Mountain area of Alexander and Wilkes counties (CP 5.3c). The reliance on migrant labor in the picking season, formidable competition from apple growing states like Washington, increasing consumer concerns about chemical sprays, and a faltering Asian market create an uncertain future for apple production in the state. In 1998, many growers let their apples rot in the orchards because it was not profitable to process them. Their choice for 1999 is to either bulldoze their orchards, which was done to the tune of 2,000 acres in 1998, or to find an alternative use, such as baby foods. Only 5,500 acres of apple orchards were left in 1999.

And so it is for peach production, where North Carolina recently ranked eighth in the nation. Weather, disease, and disinterested younger farmers appear to be major factors in declining peach production in recent years. Near total crop failures during four years of the early to mid-1990s resulted from late spring frosts. Typically, the state produces 40 million pounds of peaches on about 5,000 acres, most of which are located in the Sand Hills of Montgomery and Lee counties, especially in areas where good air drainage and southern oriented slopes combine with loose, friable sandy soils that facilitate quick water drainage (Burgin 1992).

### Livestock Production

In recent years, North Carolina has shown impressive increases in most kinds of animal production. In 1995, for example, record highs were reached for the number of hogs, broilers, turkeys, and beef cattle; in all but beef cattle, the state is a leading producer in the country (see Table 5.2). Within the state, the leading fifteen commodities account for over 95% of total cash receipts, and hogs and broilers clearly passed tobacco as the leading commodities by 1996 (Table 5.3). Important points to be made are: 1) the state has a very diversified and therefore reasonably stable agriculture; and 2) livestock production, now at close to 60 percent of total agricultural cash receipts, is moving rapidly ahead of crop production.

Hogs. Pushing the rapidly expanding livestock production is the hog industry, now at over 10 million head in the state. Figure 5.13 shows the extraordinary growth of hog inventories in the state, especially compared to the other major producing states in the country. In just six years North Carolina has tripled its inventory while other states have languished behind, and the leading state of Iowa actually shows a considerable overall decrease. Why is North Carolina the major recipient of hog industry investments? Apparently the answer is found in the state's very probusiness attitude and resulting proactive industry recruitment policies. Hog raising is no longer the province of small

124

Photos 5.6a and b: Peanuts is a traditional row crop of the Coastal Plain. In Tar Heel, Bladen County, one of the state's largest peanut factories (Houston's) collects the harvest from the growers, packages the finished product, and sells it direct to wholesalers or in their outlet store.

a) Houston's Peanut Factory Outlet with a delivery truck waiting its time to unload.

b) While the delivery truck is unloading peanuts at the Houston's Peanut Factory, a conveyor belt deposits the waste shells into a waiting truck trailer.

scale general farming. Rather it is large scale industry, with heavy up-front investments needed to establish a vertically integrated structure from the initial raising of the swine, to slaughter and packaging, and to worldwide marketing. As such, this industry is a large scale local generator of employment that influences the development of a significant service system from short-term construction to long term feed suppliers and financial support. Thus, local economic impacts are considerable. Tie this to the aspiration of the industry to locate in one of the state's more economically depressed regions, the central and southern Coastal Plain, and it is easier to understand why state recruitment efforts aided in providing favorable conditions for the location of this new type of industrial venture. The industry was already meeting opposition to its concentration in other states (especially Virginia), due to its more noxious attributes, particularly odors and waste spillage. In North Carolina the hog industry found a more open attitude toward its environmental impacts, at least initially.

In 1970, 1.6 million hogs were raised throughout North Carolina on about 60,000 small general farms; the hogs spent their short life rooting about in a pig sty and cooling themselves in mud wallows. By 1997, over 90 percent of the ten million hogs were concentrated on about 8,000 farms, where they spend their six month life in a confined, nearly sterile barn environment that is electrically heated and cooled, with automated louvered slats for air flow. Feed is released on schedule into feeding troughs for each of the eight square foot pens, with resulting wastes passed through the webbed or slatted footing and periodically flushed and cleaned out through pipes leading to outside waste lagoons. A sow is bred on a 150-day schedule in a gestation barn where the average litter of 8.9 piglets stay about 21 days, until they are weaned. At present the conditions are so favorable for maximizing litter production to twelve piglets, that an increasing percentage of sows are nearing this larger litter as a normal condition. With more than twelve piglets there are not enough nipples avail-

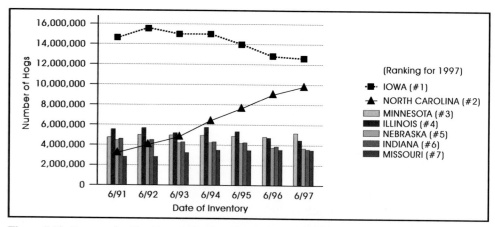

**Figure 5.13**: Comparative Hog Inventories, Leading States, 1991-1997.
**Source**: North Carolina Department of Agriculture (http://www.agr.state.nc.us/stats/), 1997.

able, a potential predicament since nipples are not shared and excess piglets will die of hunger. Innovative research is therefore pursued in the crossbreeding of American with a Japanese variety that has 18 nipples per sow. Following weaning piglets are transferred to a nursery barn where they stay until they have reached about 50 pounds. From there the hogs are moved to another location where 'finishing' barns bring them to a slaughtering weight of 230 to 250 pounds. Hogs ready for slaughter are finally shipped by trucks to a nearby meat processing facility. Color Plates 5.5a-d show some of the landscape impacts of hog production.

A most important aspect of world market expectations, and of recent changing U. S. meat consumption habits is the increasing importance of lean meat. No doubt that the three-site production process, farrowing at one site, nursing and weaning at another, and finishing at a third, has been influenced by the need for much greater health and feed control demanded by lean meat production. So feeders have responded in their efforts at 'building a better pig' by adopting lean-meat approaches like artificial insemination, early weaning, customized feedstuffs and specialized feeding regimes by sex and age. In addition they incorporate into the feeding cycle new additives (amino acids, enzymes, vitamins, disease preventive medicines) from pharmaceutical firms and veterinary suppliers (Ukes 1995). Arriving at a world competitive recognizable and standardized product is a leading characteristic of the hog meat complex of the southern North Carolina Coastal Plain, and one that insures continued economic vitality.

High levels of productivity are guaranteed by an industry that is very large scale, vertically integrated, and extremely sensitive to world market changes and developments. Having an understanding of world market fluctuations and access to those markets is critical, because total domestic consumption of pork has remained relatively unchanged over the past three decades. In the meantime, the demand for beef has declined, and poultry consumption has doubled. Any significant increase in pork production must come at the expense of other domestic meat producers, and from an expanding overseas market.

North Carolina has some of the largest hog producers in the country, including: Murphy Family Farms, which has administrative headquarters in Rose Hill (Duplin County); Carroll's Foods in Warsaw (Sampson); Prestage Farms and Coharie Hog Farm in Clinton (Sampson); and Goldsboro Farms in Goldsboro (Wayne). Murphy, Carroll's and Prestage are closely connected through suppply contracts, joint ventures, and board memberships to Smithfield Foods of Smithfield, Virginia. All four producers are in a joint venture called Circle Four Farms. Though each of these is vertically integrated, owning its operation from the "breeding" and "finishing" barns to the processing facilities and marketing network; all also depend to a considerable degree on contract farmers. Smithfield Foods, for example, ensures a steady flow of hogs into their enormous processing plant through contracts with five of the larger producers. These producers then subcontract with individual farmers. It should be of interest to note that Circle Four Farms is now building the nation's largest vertically integrated hog operation in Utah, planning to process 2.5 million hogs per annum by the year 2000, with 120 hog barns, feed mill, and slaughterhouse. Also there is the new Seaboard Farms, Inc. half a billion dollar pork production complex in the Panhandle of Oklahoma based on a networking arrangement including hundreds of contract farmers. Its plant in Guymon, Oklahoma, processes four million hogs per year. Does this mean that North Carolina's share of the total national production will soon decrease, or that the state will even see an actual decline, as more welcoming states encourage a shift in production location? With a recent legislative moratorium on capacity increases and with new rules of engagement relating to environmental pollution, the industrial hog operations may follow the textile/apparel industry exit from the state. National hog producers are known to have plans ready for building production facilities in Mexico (Hart and Mayda 1998, 76).

Generally speaking the contract system is tightly controlled by the large producers. One year contracts are generally let to farmers, who may already have mortgaged their home and land for the $200,000 to $1 million it takes to build and outfit a hog raising facility. A decent income can be made once the mortgage

126

is paid off, but a hog barn has a lifetime of only fifteen years and the equipment about half of that, so capital investments must be continued. The tendency is to increase the scale of the operation to insure efficiency and reasonable profits, but the nagging problem is that contracts have an exit clause which allows either party to discontinue after 30 days notice. Thus it appears that risk is shifted largely to the contract farmer who must pay for the essential hog raising facilities, who has the risk of environmental damage (see Chapter 8), and who has the uncertainty of contract renewal or termination (Warrick and Stith 1995, 6A). In 1994, 82 percent of all hogs were raised on contract farms, and this figure is increasing.

It is the vertically integrated contract system, adapted from its successful evolution a decade earlier in the broiler industry, that has caused the explosive growth in hogs (Hopkins 1996). This form of agribusiness has a major impact on traditional agriculture. A general farmer making independent decisions has been replaced by a contract farmer. He favors a location close to the processor and is dependent on initial large scale bank loans and continued linkage to the hog corporation, which has in large measure followed the model of the poultry industry in avoiding direct management and ownership of the meat raising end of the industry. Now the hog industry finds itself so tightly compacted into just a few counties that the media has taken to calling this "Swine Alley." Furuseth (1997) speaks of the simultaneous explosion and implosion of today's hog industry, which expands in production while it contracts in location. So we have the concentration of large hog producing contract operations in rural areas of the central and southern part of the Coastal Plain, mostly focused on Duplin, Sampson, and Bladen counties (Figure 5.14). Here we also have the feed mills and the new food processing plants, such as Lundy Packing Co. of Clinton in Sampson County. In Tar Heel, Bladen County, is the recently completed Carolina Food Processors, a division of Smithfield Foods Inc. This slaughter and meat processing plant is currently the world's largest with its daily capacity of 24,000 hogs (Photo 5.7). An area of the state that for decades has suffered from regionally high unemployment rates, net outmigration of its labor force, declining small towns, and a general apathy about future prospects, is now seeing new life pumped into its communities. In addition to the new processing plants, feed mills are built to aid in the assembly, processing, and redistribution of animal feed from as far away as Iowa. New firms like Hog Slats of Sampson County are established in response to the specialized construction boom (note Hog Slats' name on the facilities in CP 5.5c). A rapidly expanding Hispanic work force is making its impact in construction, and in milling, packing and processing plants. Workers also provide a new cultural flavor and dynamism in residential areas, churches, and the central business district of small towns. Per capita income figures have increased correspondingly, and unemployment rates have fallen to some of the lowest levels in the state. New gated residential communities are making their appearance and providing evidence of a growing wealth of the few on the landscape.

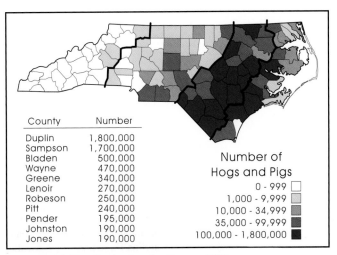

| County | Number |
|---|---|
| Duplin | 1,800,000 |
| Sampson | 1,700,000 |
| Bladen | 500,000 |
| Wayne | 470,000 |
| Greene | 340,000 |
| Lenoir | 270,000 |
| Robeson | 250,000 |
| Pitt | 240,000 |
| Pender | 195,000 |
| Johnston | 190,000 |
| Jones | 190,000 |

Number of
Hogs and Pigs

| | |
|---|---|
| 0 - 999 | |
| 1,000 - 9,999 | |
| 10,000 - 34,999 | |
| 35,000 - 99,999 | |
| 100,000 - 1,800,000 | |

**Figure 5.14**: Hog Production, by County, 1995.
**Source**: North Carolina Agricultural Statistics, 1996.

Yet not all is positive for land and life in the pork country. There are new environmental threats resulting from hog waste lagoon spillage into groundwater, rivers, and sounds. Hog barns and waste lagoons produce distinctive odor concentrations from emitted noxious gasses, which, to the anguish of hog farm neighbors, some producers simply see as the 'smell of money.' Neighbors complain about the prospects for a negative change in residential and land values. Indeed, recent research has shown these values to decrease the closer the property is to a large scale, intensive hog operation (Palmquist et al 1997). Proposed large scale hog contract farms and processing plants have recently been protested and rejected in Chatham and Harnett counties. Even within the hog belt there are active protests against new hog facilities (Photo 5.8). Hog farms planned for the Vanceboro (Craven County) area, and designed to be twice the size of the largest existing hog operations in the county, brought out people protesting the prospects of smells and Neuse River pollution, in January of 1997. The protests are being heard in Raleigh, where the legislature in 1997 passed a two year moratorium on new contract farms. However, this has not stopped the interest in expanding processing facilities. Carolina Food Processors at Tar Heel has requested state permits to increase its capacity from 24,000 to 36,000 daily hog slaughter. Running at full capacity the plant will be able to process over 13 million hogs per year. The plant has accumulated 20 citations for water quality violations, involving excess pollutants contained in the approximately three million gallons of waste the plant discharges daily into the Cape Fear River. Carolina Foods Processors' parent company, Smithfield Foods Inc., was fined $12.6 million in the 1980s for polluting the Pagan River in Virginia, the largest fine ever for a violation of the federal Water Quality Act. These environmental matters are taken up in detail in this volume's Chapter 8; also discussed are the problems generated by living in a state where corporate agriculture remains covered by laws designed to protect family farms.

Many recently developing conditions suggest that the hog agribusiness is likely to level off in North Carolina. These include

**Photo 5.7**: Carroll's Foods new hog processing plant at Tar Heel in Bladen County is one of the world's largest.

**Photo 5.8**: Not far from the new Carroll's Foods plant is roadside evidence of protests against hog production.

uncertainties about global markets for hog meat, a tightening of the meat plant and hog contractor farm inspection process, and a continuing moratorium on new large scale farms in the state, if not the implementation of new environmental regulations that will increase the cost of production. The willingness of other states, like Oklahoma and Utah, to embrace the industry's penchant for investing in outsized operations further suggest a capping of production in this state. And Mexico waits in the wings.

Poultry. In its varied forms of production, including eggs, turkeys, broilers, roasters, quail, and ostriches, poultry comprises the largest agricultural production value in North Carolina, while it is the fourth largest in the United States (Table 5.2). Its success hinged on an early pioneering adoption of large scale vertical integration and contract livestock farming. From President F. D. Roosevelt's promise of 'a chicken in every pot' during the 1930s

depression years, household consumption of poultry has grown steadily, fed in part by the seasonal tradition of turkey dinners, by the gradual shift in meat preference from red to white over recent decades, and by the continued low prices provided by the economically efficient poultry operations. Successfully keeping prices low has involved continuous changes in management practices.

The basics of the contract system involve processors like Perdue, Tyson Foods or Holly Farms, so-called integrators, who provide the contracted farmer with day-old pullets and feed, and then return to pick up the broilers at their desired weight for processing and packaging at their plants. Contract farmers borrow money to build broiler barns and are responsible for utilities, labor, and insurance against fire, wind, or flood damage. Integrators exercise complete management control (Hart and Chestang

128

1996, 183). Over the years, efficiency has improved by tightening the contract farm service area; that is, the region within which an integrator is willing to carry and service contracts. For example, to reduce transportation costs in the late 1980s Tyson Foods, which had bought out Holly Farms of Wilkesboro in Wilkes County, the leading broiler producing county in the state, gave all of their contract farmers in adjacent mountainous Watauga County a three-month contract termination notice. Dozens of farmers saw their many years of contract production come to a sudden halt, and the county is now littered with unused and deteriorating chicken houses. Such draconian measures have been applied throughout the state as a result of integrators' desire to increase the spatial concentration of the industry, as well as in response to shift in the competitive environment, market demand, and outbreak of animal diseases.

Figure 5.15 indicates a degree of clustering in the concentration of the broiler production in three main areas in the state. The northwestern Mountain region (with the largest producing county of Wilkes) and the central and southern Piedmont (where the next four largest producing counties, Union, Randolph, Moore and Chatham, are found), are complemented by a fairly even distribution throughout the Coastal Plain. In an earlier day almost all of the state's 100 counties were broiler producers, but now a contract farmer who used to provide facilities to accommodate 10,000 birds or less, is being pushed by the economics of the industry to house many times this number (Photo 5.2). It became a matter of either investing in buildings for housing larger flocks or ceasing production. Most farmers are now contracting to sell over 100,000 broilers at a time. Typically, these are accommodated in 20,000-bird houses that, constructed of metal and measuring 32 by 400 feet, are vented and heated automatically, and are supported by automated feeding from adjacent metal feed bins. Altogether, this is an operation that requires little manual labor (Hart and Chestang 1996). While facilities construction costs are high, other technological improvements have helped maintain low production costs. Selective breeding and improved feed mixes are bringing broilers to market weight one-third faster than in 1940 on 40 percent less feed, while carrying a greater proportion of the white meat favored by most Americans (Winsberg 1997, 203). As an aside, it should be noted that the excess dark meat is finding ready overseas markets, and producers are now very active in international trade. In 1994, 10,000 tons of frozen poultry was shipped out of Morehead City, primarily to Central and Eastern Europe markets (Towle 1994).

There are important ripple effects in localities where integrators have their primary (slaughtering, cleaning, deboning, and cutting) processing plants. Perdue Inc., which had 700 farmers on contract in 1994 and plants in Lewiston (Bertie County), Robersonville (Martin), Rockingham (Richmond), and Robbins (Moore), is a relevant example. The plants employed 5,314 "associates" (workers), with a considerable impact on these towns where only Rockingham has more than a population of 2,000. A 1995 buy-out of Shovill Farms left Perdue with a primary processing plant in Concord. Here, the 400 workers, largely Hispanic,

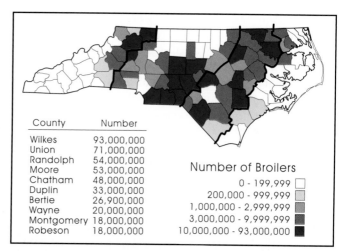

**Figure 5.15**: Chicken Broiler Production, by County, 1995.
**Source**: North Carolina Agricultural Statistics, 1996.

lost their jobs in October, 1997 when Purdue decided to change the plant operations to make prepared foods. Perdue prides itself on buying locally. In 1993, it bought $75 million worth of corn and soybeans to feed the chickens, and spent an additional $20 million for other local services (Towle 1994). Integrators provide important local markets in regions on the state's economic periphery, and are actively involved in attracting foreign labor, especially Hispanic, to these communities. Siler City (Chatham County) exemplifies the many small towns whose central business districts are increasingly dominated by Hispanic enterprises. Other impacts are less expected, as, for example, the strike for improved working conditions by Guatemalan and Mexican workers at a poultry plant in Morganton in 1996.

The turkey industry is a more recently developed large scale poultry producer in the state, and now the largest in the country (Table 5.2). In its vertical integration and confinement production process it has become an even more geographically concentrated industry (Figure 5.16). Duplin, Sampson, Wayne,

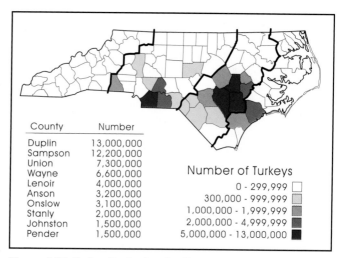

**Figure 5.16**: Turkey Production, by County, 1995.
**Source**: North Carolina Agricultural Statistics, 1996.

129

and Lenoir counties dominate turkey production in the central Coastal Plain, while Union and Anson counties do so in the southern Piedmont. A major challenge for this industry has been to decrease the relative importance of seasonality in the production process, no longer letting the popularity of the family turkey at Thanksgiving and Christmas control the demand. New ways of marketing the meat have in large measure accomplished this. In a state dominated by pork production, year-round turkey production is aided by increasing sales of turkey ham and turkey bacon, in addition to turkey veal and coldcuts. Turkey has become a leading low fat substitution meat.

Periodically, there are concerns with the prospects of overproduction. From 1995 to 1997, the price per pound of fresh turkey breast dropped from $2.07 to $1.45, a loss of 30 percent, the likely result of a flat market demand. At the same time, the cost for feed, especially soybeans, has increased. For producers, it has been a difficult time, a 10 percent decrease in overall North Carolina production in 1997 compared to the 62 million birds produced in 1992, the highest level reached in the state (Hopkins 1997c).

Prestage Farms of Clinton (Sampson County) exemplifies the large scale turkey integrator, though the family owned business also is heavily vested in hog production (Photo 5.9). Rocco Turkey, a meat processing company in Robeson County receives about 250 million pounds of turkeys from the Prestage contractors per year (Towle 1994, 61). Meanwhile, the place to sample the unique turkey flavors coming from the processor is at the annual Turkey Festival, held mid-September in Raeford, Scotland County (CP 5.7). Here, one can taste turkey nuggets, turkey pizza, and turkey sausage while watching a fashion show of customed birds dressed by area children (Whitfield 1993). On the other hand, vendors at the yearly Turkey Day in the town of Turkey (Sampson County), serve only the traditional Eastern North Carolina slow-cooked barbecue pork with tangy, vinegar

sauce, after having little success in serving turkey to the participants in an earlier year (Patterson 1996).

The inherent vulnerability of the livestock industry was demonstrated in the Fall of 1997. In Union and adjacent counties 48 contractors saw suspension of their contracts with Wampler Longacre of Marshville (a division of WLR Foods Inc., Broadway, Virginia) due to the spread of poultry enteritis and mortality syndrome (commonly referred to as spiking mortality), among their flocks. Encountered first in Union County in 1991, the disease, not harmful to humans, has presently no known cure (Hopkins 1997). WLR's approach to dealing with the problem by cutting off the supply of pullet turkeys may provide the solution, but turkey contractors are left with no income to pay for their production equipment and facilities. If the industry is going to recover in Union County, it will be several years in coming while scientists pursue new avenues in disease detection and cure. Here, as in most matters dealing with the state's agricultural industry, it is North Carolina State University's veterinary and agricultural productivity research laboratories that provide the major effort.

On the other hand, it is clear that a brand new poultry business has benefited considerably by the occurrence of disease elsewhere. Oro Verde Farms, located near Knightdale in Wake County, claims to be the first marketer of packaged ostrich meat in the United States. Its production was much helped by the "mad cow" disease (bovine spongiform encephalopathy) that caused a precipitous drop in beef sales in Europe in 1995, primarily because of its direct linkage to human health. Oro Verde raises its own ostriches, but also buys from a network reaching several states. With the only license to sell the lean red packaged ostrich meat in England in 1996, the firm expected to see sales of up to 100,000 pounds per month (Purvis, 1996). Elsewhere in the state, the novelty of raising ostriches is etched in the names of businesses like Birdbrain Ostrich Ranch (where ostrich jerky,

**Photo 5.9**: Prestage Farms turkey hatchery in Sampson County is the largest in the country. Opened in 1993, the facility is capable of delivering 450,000 pullets per week to its contract turkey farmers. The company transports the young turkeys using its own fleet of 50 18-wheel trucks.

skin wallets and decorated eggs are part of the production effort) and Longneck Ranch. Both of these firms are located in Mecklenburg County, but an additional 200 ostrich farms now dot the North Carolina agricultural landscape, and ostrich burgers are available in restaurants from Boone to Wilmington, as the market gradually overcomes consumer's reluctance to eat "zoo meat." Venture investors have shown interest in this seemingly off-beat livestock industry. In 1995, the South Piedmont Ostrich Group approached the Kannapolis City Council with a proposal to rent 556 acres of unused city land in the Millbridge Community of Rowan County for the purpose of starting as many as 30 ostrich contract farms that would support an integrated egg-to-meat-to-market operation (Young 1996).

Beef and Dairy Cattle. Both beef cattle and dairy cow livestock operations have changed relatively little over the past couple of decades, in productivity as well as in their concentration in the state. Go back a few decades to the 1950s and there were many more dairy farms than there are today. In fact, the decrease has been drastic. In 1945, North Carolina had 183,000 farms with at least one commercially producing milking cow (qualifying it to receive the dairy farm label). This had dropped to 1,300 in 1996. Even so, total milk production has decreased only minutely, due to extraordinary increases in the per cow milk yield. More important perhaps is the fact that now there are only 571 licensed dairies in the state (Hopkins 1996b). Counties such as Orange, traditionally favored for milk production because they are in the center of the milk shed of a large metropolitan region, have seen a remarkable decrease in dairy farms. In the case of Orange County this has been a reduction from 121 in 1966 to 26 in 1997. Pressures of development and associated escalating land prices have taken their toll, in addition to an unfavorable land evaluation system which assesses agricultural land at residential values for taxation purposes when a farmer wishes to sell, even when the sale is to another farmer. Also, dairying is a labor intensive activity, including the necessity of milking cows twice daily, 365 days per year. Few young people are willing to accept such a challenge, even if they are intrigued by a career in agriculture. Thus the decrease in dairy farms is frequently due to retirement of the farmer. Until recently dairy farmers were the recipients of the nation's largest agricultural support payments. This began to change in the mid-eighties when overproduction and low prices at the supermarkets caused the government to begin a $2 billion buy-out plan to reduce dairy cattle throughout the country. In addition, phasing out of the federal price support system began in April of 1966.

The dairy business differs markedly from the vertically integrated, confinement livestock industries. Individual farmers buy, breed, raise, and milk cows, frequently fed by self-grown feed. Most farmers belong to dairy cooperatives which sell the milk under conditions otherwise favorable to large scale operations. Some farmers also belong to marketing cooperatives, which provide even greater pricing power.

Producers convert milk to a variety of dairy products, including various fat level milk, ice cream, butter, and cheese. There are cooperative, independent, and grocer managed processing and marketing operations. All in all, quite a more complex and different production system from that of large scale hog, broiler, and turkey agribusiness. In North Carolina, almost all milk is sold as Grade I, which gain the highest price level due to its use as fresh, and therefore perishable, drinking milk needing quick market delivery. Only a very small percentage goes to other grades, like the Grade III that is used to process cheese at the only cheese factory in the state, the tiny Ashe County Cheese Company (Hopkins 1996b).

Cash receipts from beef cattle and calves amounting to $154 million was less than ten percent of that of hogs in 1995, while milk products with $212 million exceeded this only slightly. Although prices of beef cattle are not faring as well due to the lessening consumer desire for red and fatter meat, North Carolina producers are participating in the trend toward more exotic beef cattle, like Simmental, Polled Hereford, Saler, Santa Gertrudis, and Gelbvieh (Photo 5.3). A major objective is to raise herds that grow faster and leaner. Figure 5.17 illustrates the 1995 distribution of the 1,130,000 cattle in the state, clearly an industry concentrated in the west central Piedmont and northwestern Mountain regions. Concentrations of both beef and dairy cattle are quite similar, though there are many fewer dairy cattle (1,045,000 vs. 82,000).

Other Livestock. North Carolina also raises limited number of sheep and goats. In 1995 there were 13,000 sheep and a negligible number of goats. Raising sheep seems to be more of a recreational activity for the people involved. Herds are small, generating fleece for the region's spinners and weavers, and lamb or mutton for local restaurants, friends, and family. Sheep and goat 'farmers' are commonly exurbanites with full-time urban employment.

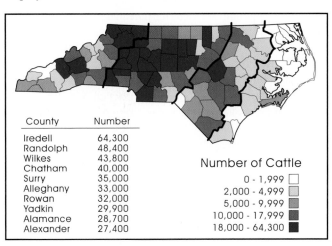

| County | Number |
|--------|--------|
| Iredell | 64,300 |
| Randolph | 48,400 |
| Wilkes | 43,800 |
| Chatham | 40,000 |
| Surry | 35,000 |
| Alleghany | 33,000 |
| Rowan | 32,000 |
| Yadkin | 29,900 |
| Alamance | 28,700 |
| Alexander | 27,400 |

Number of Cattle

| | |
|--------|--------|
| 0 - 1,999 | |
| 2,000 - 4,999 | |
| 5,000 - 9,999 | |
| 10,000 - 17,999 | |
| 18,000 - 64,300 | |

**Figure 5.17**: Dairy and Beef Cattle Production, by County, 1995. **Source**: North Carolina Agricultural Statistics, 1996.

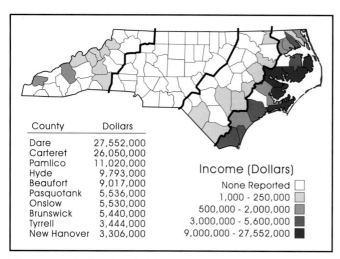

**Figure 5.18**: Cash Sales of Fish Products, by County, 1995.
**Source**: North Carolina Department of Natural Resources, Division of Marine Fisheries, 1997.

| County | Dollars |
|---|---|
| Dare | 27,552,000 |
| Carteret | 26,050,000 |
| Pamlico | 11,020,000 |
| Hyde | 9,793,000 |
| Beaufort | 9,017,000 |
| Pasquotank | 5,536,000 |
| Onslow | 5,530,000 |
| Brunswick | 5,440,000 |
| Tyrrell | 3,444,000 |
| New Hanover | 3,306,000 |

Income (Dollars)
- None Reported
- 1,000 - 250,000
- 500,000 - 2,000,000
- 3,000,000 - 5,600,000
- 9,000,000 - 27,552,000

## FISHING

Traditionally, one of the nation's top ten seafood producers, North Carolina boasts of having 6,600 km (4,000 miles) of shoreline plus about 2.5 million acres of marine and estuarine waters for salt water fishing (CP 5.9-5.12). Peculiarities of its physical geography offers the state a great variety of fish habitats, with its very large and shallow sounds and embayments, and the offshore convergence of the southward flowing cold Labrador Current and the warm northward flowing Florida Current, a coastal finger of the Gulf Stream. Also, a varied environment across the state offers opportunities for different kinds of aquaculture, in part to support increasing consumer demand for fish products, and in part for stocking the many square miles of its lakes and streams with fish for recreational fishing (CP 5.11). A positive environment for marine and inland fishing, for finfish as well as shellfish, brings onto the scene the potential for overexploitation and for conflicts of interest by a variety of user groups that see the resource from different perspectives. Figure 5.18 shows the 1995 county concentrations of sales value of commercial fish, totaling more than $100 million for non-confined seafood and close to $10 million for aquaculture production. With their access to the marine and estuarine waters, the coastal and tidewater counties dominate, led by Dare and Carteret counties, each of which accrue over $25 million annually from commercial fishing.

### *Commercial Fisheries*

North Carolina's salt water fisheries resemble the "tragedy of the commons" that has beset the global fishing industry. Oceans are generally viewed as a commons whose resources are available to all, but are then overexploited without regard to the conservation of its limited fish resources. Sustainability was never a global objective. Increased world demand for fish as a meat substitute has pushed improvements in fishing technology, which have brought increased catch and increased profits, the result of

which has been gradual overcapitalization and overfishing. So now there are far too many fishing boats and fishermen for the dramatically reduced resource. Table 5.4 compares sound and ocean fishing statistics for the relevant North Carolina counties over a twenty-year period. For 1973, at the beginning of the upswing in commercial fishing, the industry landed 138 million pounds from about 15,000 commercial fishing boats. In 1981, North Carolina experienced the peak year in its fishing history with a catch of 432 million pounds, a 215 percent increase over 1973. This peaking also shows an increase in commercial fishing vessel licenses to 25,428. A lesser increase of only 70 percent in licenses indicates the much higher average catch per fishing vessel. Soon thereafter came crashes in the catch of particular commercial species, and at both national and state levels restrictions began to be imposed on various aspects of the industry to allow species recovery. By 1993, the total catch of 171 million pounds was approaching that of 1973, and the number of licensed vessels had decreased to 18,693. Carteret, Dare, Hyde, and Pamlico have been the leading counties in commercial fish catch, though Pamlico has slipped considerably in recent years (Figure 5.19 and Photo 5.10). It is noteworthy that among owners of licensed vessels only about one third are considered full-time commercial fishermen.

Shellfish comprised close to 60 percent of a total catch for 1996 valued at $105 million. Blue crab led the way with a value of $40 million, by far the most valuable seafood caught in North

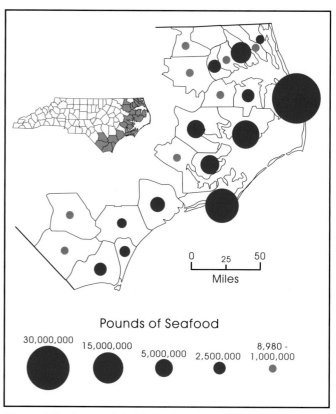

**Figure 5.19**: Commercial Fish Landings, by County, 1993.
**Source**: North Carolina Marine Fisheries Commission, 1993.

Pounds of Seafood
- 30,000,000
- 15,000,000
- 5,000,000
- 2,500,000
- 8,980 - 1,000,000

132

| Preliminary North Carolina Coastal Counties Seafood Landings and Vessel Licenses, 1973, 1981, and 1993 | | | | | | |
|---|---|---|---|---|---|---|
| | **1993** | | **1981** | | **1973** | |
| **County** | Pounds | Commercial Vessel Licenses | Pounds | Commercial Vessel Licenses | Pounds | Commercial Vessel Licenses |
| Beaufort | 4,918,238 | 1,008 | 6,895,157 | 1,098 | 2,971,600 | 752 |
| Bertie | 170,614 | 109 | 1,239,711 | 168 | 1,998,600 | 79 |
| Bladen | 40,200 | 126 | N/A | N/A | N/A | N/A |
| Brunswick | 2,396,479 | 1,677 | 2,618,704 | 1,991 | 1,718,400 | 1,318 |
| Camden | 90,788 | 70 | N/A | N/A | N/A | N/A |
| Carteret | 18,680,154 | 2,798 | 29,918,674 | 3,927 | 30,535,400 | 2,654 |
| Chowan | 2,247,131 | 149 | 3,875,757 | 233 | 7,555,700 | 215 |
| Columbus | 11,300 | 425 | N/A | N/A | N/A | N/A |
| Craven | 581,342 | 840 | 115,960 | 1,552 | 28,200 | 1,274 |
| Currituck | 1,284,353 | 303 | 1,178,710 | 355 | 87,500 | 214 |
| Dare | 33,665,695 | 1,364 | 39,421,902 | 1,209 | 11,699,000 | 738 |
| Hertford | 8,980 | 83 | 730,038 | 68 | N/A | 28 |
| Hyde | 12,174,371 | 419 | 10,251,802 | 429 | 2,224,900 | 392 |
| Martin | N/A | N/A | 131,124 | 265 | 85,200 | 142 |
| New Hanover | 1,948,802 | 1,746 | 2,416,735 | 2,649 | 558,200 | 1,528 |
| Onslow | 3,488,163 | 1,454 | 2,377,552 | 1,952 | 1,535,800 | 1,011 |
| Pamlico | 5,691,198 | 642 | 17,329,190 | 876 | 4,439,500 | 661 |
| Pasquotank | 6,759,214 | 168 | N/A | 197 | 186,500 | 168 |
| Pender | 1,480,107 | 702 | 684,544 | 891 | 180,300 | 434 |
| Perquimans | 8,996 | 121 | N/A | 128 | N/A | 78 |
| Tyrrel | 2,860,199 | 151 | 1,466,183 | 126 | 1,130,600 | 105 |
| Washington | 248,023 | 140 | 824,698 | 263 | 269,600 | 176 |
| **County Subtotal** | **98,754,347** | **14,495** | **122,591,173** | **18,377** | **67,205,000** | **11,967** |
| *Industrial Landings | 71,943,129 | | 309,414,710 | | 70,664,210 | |
| **State Total** | **170,697,476** | **18,693** | **432,005,883** | **25,428** | **137,869,210** | **14,941** |

\* Landings of menhaden and thread herring are grouped under industrial landings. These landings, which may be primarily in Brunswick, Carteret, Craven, New Hanover, Onslow, and Pender counties, are not included in the County landings.

**Table 5.4**: Commercial Fish Landings by County, 1973, 1981, and 1993.
**Source**: North Carolina Marine Fisheries Commission, 1995.

Carolina. Other crab species contributing an additional $3 million. For many years North Carolina fishermen have favored blue crab, in part due to the devastating depletion of the hard shell crab stocks in the Chesapeake Bay. Catches of other crustaceans have also fared well. The shrimp catch amounted to $13 million, with clams at $4.5 million, and oysters and scallops each contributed about $800,000. Compare these figures with the finfish catches, where flounder led with $14 million, and Menhaden, an industrial fish, had a value of $4.8 million. Atlantic croaker ($3.6 million), gray trout ($2.3 million), sharks ($3 million) and the various tunas ($2.1 million) were other valuable finfish. In 1997, the value of fish caught exceeded $160 million, and people might be deluded into thinking that the crisis is over. Not so, maintains the fisheries specialist of the North Carolina Coastal Conservation Association, "The classic signs of a collapsing fisheries is harvests going through the roof, (as) fishermen direct more effort, more people and more gear until it collapses," (as quoted in Powell 1999, 6). Closely related to this sign of impending disaster is the changing age distribution of fish caught. Marine biologists are very concerned that increasingly the catch is younger and

**Photo 5.10**: Wanchese Harbor. Sited on the south end of Roanoke Island, this fishing community was supported in the late 1970's by major state grants for the building of fish processing industries. More recently these processing industries have suffered because access to the harbor is silted in and larger boats can no longer land their catch.

younger, meaning that the fishing stock is decreasing in its average age with the older and more mature breeding fish having been overfished. The negative impact on replacement has resulted in a classification system reflecting the degree of stock depletion for a particular species.

Of the most valuable fish species, six have become depressed, meaning a species being caught and dying faster than it can replace itself. These include Atlantic croaker, black sea bass, gray trout, red drum (the state designated salt water fish), river herring, and summer flounder. An additional eight species are considered stressed, showing initial signs of serious population sustainability problems. These include, bluefish, catfish, groupers/snappers, American shad, hickory shad, sharks, spot, and striped bass (Horan 1994). Fish conservation and replenishment programs implemented by federal and regional maritime authorities have shown themselves capable of restoring some of these species to sound reproductive conditions and carefully monitored harvesting levels.

It should be noted that overfishing is not the only process reducing species numbers. Destruction of fish habitats, especially marshes and wetlands, and increasing water pollution and eutrophication that stimulates the spread of toxins and organisms deadly to fish life, are also factors of considerable importance. The most striking example of toxic river pollution occurred

with the massive hog waste spillage into the Neuse River in the Fall of 1995. An estimated ten million fish were killed by this event. One result of the devastating Neuse River fish kill was the initiation of an environmental pollution study of the Pamlico and Albemarle sounds. Completed in 1998, the study found an alarming concentration of toxic materials in extensive areas of the sounds, where, in fact, nothing was left alive (see Chapter 10). Into the year 2000 the state's population is holding its collective breath awaiting the eventual sound sedimentation and pollution outcome of the devastating flooding that resulted from the three hurricane punch of 1999.

Chemicals in the sewage are thought to stimulate the growth of the tiny dinoflagellates, especially the single celled *Pfiesteria piscicida*, which is extremely toxic to finfish, as well as to humans who come into physical contact with it. Though it apparently poses no danger to those who eat fish infected with it, recent serious outbreaks of *pfiesteria* have resulted in an outpouring of funding for its study (Henderson 1997a). Not so much attention is paid to the increasing incidence of the more deadly *Vibrio vulnificus*, a bacterium especially prevalent in the warmer waters of the Gulf and passed to humans through infected fish, especially raw oysters. It kills 75 percent of people infected, normally within days (Henderson 1997b). Two deaths in North Carolina have been attributed to *vibrio* over the past couple of years.

Periodically, the threat of red tide also emerges. Though this toxic algae, which blooms off the coast of southern Florida, is rarely seen in waters as cool as those off the North Carolina coast, it does happen. And when it happens, it can be devastating, as in 1987 when the ocean catch decreased by more than 40 percent from the previous year. It has been noted, that while North Carolina's unique coastal environment of offshore barrier islands and immense sound areas provide the foundation for rich fisheries, that same natural environment contributes to the fish kill. The very large sounds have only the few, very narrow, inlets of Oregon, Hatteras, and Ocracoke, which keep nutrients and pollutants within the sounds, allowing them to concentrate to an ultimately devastating degree (Dill 1995).

For North Carolina, the problem of fish stress and production decline is compounded by its own reluctance to ban the fishing of the overfished species, while adjacent states have done so. Thus, fishermen from these states, especially Florida and Georgia, continue fishing but land their catch without penalty in North Carolina harbors. Not that the state has remained completely idle. Table 5.5 provides a listing of preventive measures taken by the North Carolina Marine Fisheries Commission, which has authority over interior brackish water and ocean waters out to the three mile limit. Rules set by the Marine Fisheries Commission are enforced by the Division of Marine Fisheries in Morehead City.

Restrictions derive from factors other than species depletion. Our coasts are frequented by over one million seasonal sports fishers whose interests often conflict with those of the commercial fishing industry. In addition, a regional income, considerably larger than that derived from fishing, comes from tourism. Commercial fishing, in some places along the coast, is incompatible with tourism, and so at times must yield. A particular case in point is the fishing for menhaden, an oily, small, but abundant, fish used as chicken and hog feed, or as a base for margarine in Europe. Menhaden is caught by large factory ships offshore, but close to the beaches where the tourist industry fears the potential for a net rupture that would result in thousands of dead fish washing up on the beaches. So the Marine Fisheries Commission banned Menhaden boats from coming within 1 1/2 mile of the coastline.

In an act that seems to finally focus attention on persistently declining fisheries and the continuing conflict between the commercial fishing industry and the sport fishing interests, the state imposed a moratorium on new licenses in 1994. The state set up the Moratorium Steering Committee to assess what went wrong and to recommend corrective measures. Comprehensive studies and state-wide hearings by the Committee resulted in recommendations that quickly got entangled in the political whirlwind of conflicting interests. A simplified and much compromised fisheries reform bill emerged in the legislature, and

| Restrictions on Commercial Fishing, 1976-1994. | |
|---|---|
| 1977 | * Banned trawling in primary nursery areas to avoid destroying juvenile fish. |
| 1985 | * Increased minimum size of striped bass for commercial and sports catches from 12 to 14 inches; action was not adequate to restore the striped bass population so the limit was increased to 18 inches in 1991. |
| 1987 | * Closed Albemarle sound to trawling to prevent its encroachment on areas traditionally fished with stationary gear like gill nets. * Required wider 5 1/2 inch wide net mesh on the bags of trawlers that catch summer flounder to let more small fish escape. |
| 1992 | * Required fish excluders on all shrimp trawl nets to reduce the killing of millions of small finfish; the excluders are holes in the nets that let fish escape. |
| 1993 | * Banned Menhaden boats from fishing within 1 1/2 miles of Nags Head as a precaution against dead fish washing ashore and driving away tourists. * Banned commercial netting within 750 feet of fishing piers to prevent conflict with sports fishermen who complained the nets snared too many fish. * Banned commercial netting along 5 1/2 miles of Nags Head beaches * To avert conflict with sports fishermen casting for bluefish in fall. |
| 1994 | * Banned fishing with fly nets for gray trout in ocean south of Cape Hatteras. eliminated Saturday fishing for gray trout in ocean with gill nets to help meet federally required 25 percent reduction in gray trout catch. |

**Table 5.5:** North Carolina Marine Fisheries Commission    .
**Source:** Horan, 1994, 14A.

was passed in the spring of 1997. As summarized by Powell (1999 11) its essentials are as follows:

1) a new standard commercial fishing license at an annual cost of $200 for residents and $800 for non-residents, allowing the license holder to harvest shellfish as well as finfish;

2) an Endorsement to Sell is required of all holding the commercial license, with a cap placed on the number of Endorsements available, an estimated 7,500 as of July 1, 1999;

3) a new recreational commercial gear license for sportsfishers wishing to use commercial gear to catch seafood for own consumption; with an annual cost of $35 for residents, and $250 for non-residents, the license does not permit selling of the catch;

4) the Marine Fisheries Commission decreased its membership from seventeen to nine, all appointed by the governor and serving staggered terms; and

5) beginning July 1, 1999, the Commission must begin implementing plans for controlled and sustainable harvesting of individual species, with plan review taking place every three years.

### Aquaculture

North Carolina is emerging as a leading state in the nation in fish farming. As aquaculture, this is being referred to also as "The Blue Revolution" by advocates who deem its development essential for providing a fish food substitute for declining marine stocks. Between September, 1994, and August, 1995, 56 commercial trout growers sold 5.1 million pounds of trout valued at $6.5 million; and 43 commercial catfish growers had sales of $2 million during 1995. For the following year, the number of trout producers increased to 72, with a sales of just over $7 million. There are some notable differences between the two kinds of fish farming. While trout production is mostly a Mountain region phenomenon, catfish growers are primarily found in the Coastal Plain region (CP 5.11). Both contribute only a small percentage of their production directly to restaurants and retail sales, with more than 80 percent sold to food processors, but trout is more valuable at $1.18/lb than is catfish at $.79/lb (N. C. Agricultural Statistics 1996). In addition to these two types of fish farms, there are minor aquacultural productions of bass and shellfish. Invariably, aquaculture is promoted by its industry leaders and advocates as providing an option for 'sustainability' in the rural economy (Stonich 1998).

Although not close in production scale to the favorable trout raising environment of the Snake River Valley of Idaho (where the fish net $70 million per year in sales), the southern Appalachian mountain environment nevertheless is quite suitable, placing North Carolina second in the nation in trout production. However, this is not an easy endeavor. One of the larger trout producers is near the town of Brevard (Jackson County), located on a 300-acres spread dominated by fish ponds. Here the producer finds that, like the dairy farmer, the trout farmer must be on the job 24 hours a day, 365 days a year.

Catfish is farmed in much higher quantities elsewhere, Mississippi, Alabama, and Arkansas being the largest producers. Catfish used to be regarded as being very low on the scale of desirable food fish. Its traditional image was that of an overly bony, mudsucking scavenger fish of dubious taste. Now it is grain fed in clean ponds and merits consideration as the chicken of fish, lending itself to poaching, broiling, frying, or blackening. In actuality, it is a versatile and delightful food. National consumption trends confirm this observation, as they have increased from 19 million pounds of catfish sold in 1976 to 457 million pounds in 1992 (Ashcraft 1994).

For the benefit of inland sports fishing, North Carolina's Wildlife Resources Commission manages five fish hatcheries for warm-water, cool-water, and cold-water species (CP 5.12). Watha Hatchery, located just north of Wilmington, is the only warm-water fish hatchery. Here the focus is on striped bass, a saltwater fish, that like salmon must find its way to a fresh water river to spawn. The role of this operation is to provide striped bass for inland lakes and reservoirs where the fish would otherwise be absent. Lake Norman, for example, received 162,000 stripers in 1995, while High Rock Lake got 79,000, and Badin Lake, 30,000 (Barringer, 1995).

## FORESTRY

As we enter the 21st century, we are also entering North Carolina's "fourth forest" period. At the time of European settlement the original, or first, forest reflected conditions of the undisturbed natural environment, and extended almost without a break from the coast to beyond what is now the Tennessee boundary. This forest was harvested during the logging boom by the early 1910s. The "second forest" supplied wood from the 1930s to the 1970s for the furniture industry and the rapidly growing pulp and paper industry. It has been mostly cut, except for areas provided National Forest or Park protection. We are now in the process of cutting the "third forest." In a way of speaking this is one of the state's more important agricultural crops, perhaps becoming the most important with the gradual demise of tobacco. The process of forest use and regeneration should lead us to understand that we as citizens can determine just what form the "fourth forest" can take. Our options can range from complete land clearance through chip mill operations, to declaring all forested lands state game lands and national forest wilderness. Most likely some combination of use characteristics and intensity will result. A comprehensive survey of forest resources in the late 1980s suggested that the use characteristics of the "third forest" gives cause for great concern to all of the various interest groups, from wood-using industries to recreationists, environmentalists and species preservationists. After rising for decades, the survey indicated, the net annual timber growth began to decline. An increasing rate of softwood timber removal exceeded annual growth. It is becoming difficult for forests to recover, especially with the recent boom in the wood chip industry, which employs a total clearance approach, without much concern to age and quality of the timber resource. The answer to the forest industry is increased control and management of a qualitatively impaired and quantitatively reduced natural resource. For the environmentalists, the answer is to place a moratorium on logging and road construction, and otherwise leave our forests to recover from a century of human onslaught. Citizens are in general showing greater concerns about having forest management whose programs are sustainable for commercial needs and protect against despoilation and overuse. More tangible benefits, like logging and hunting, must be balanced with less tangible gains, like soil protection, clean water, enhancing endangered species habitats, and aesthetics.

### Using Our Forest

In colonial times, our "first forest" provided timber, fashioned by hand and with use of water-powered mills, for home building. The forest provided a rich habitat for game animals, and once cleared, a place to graze animals and plant crops. Fuel wood for cooking and heating was readily available. Barrels and casks could be fashioned for transporting agricultural goods from the region, naval stores provided turpentine and resin for the ship building and maintenance industry, and soft and hard woods were used in ship construction. The "tar" in Tar Heel, a state nickname, comes from the pine tar used in ship building. These activities dominated the economic exploitation of the forests, with agriculture increasing to cover close to 50 percent of the land by the late 19th century. Industrialization and urbanization fueled a northern demand for southern lumber, and the North Carolina furniture industry was beginning to make its needs felt. Simultaneously, two technological innovations made important contributions to the exploitation of southern forests: 1) the sawmill with its steam powered band saws; and 2) the rapid expansion of the rail net, to which feeder lines from the core of old growth timber areas were built. Mountain North Carolina experienced a logging boom lasting several decades. The timber industry had significant local impacts on land use, including the building of company towns, stores, schools, medical facilities, and churches, as well as rail access to the world beyond (CP 5.13 and 5.14).

### Clearcutting and the Beginning of Forestry

Efficient and total clearcutting caused frequent relocation of the logging industry and abandonment of the company towns with their now deserted mills. In many forested and hilly areas of the country, clearcutting by lumber companies, as well as by mountain farmers, had denuded the slopes and caused severe soil erosion and stream sedimentation. These conditions, plus the increasing problem of forest fires, contributed to the enactment of the Weeks Law of 1911, which allowed the federal government to provide matching funds for fire protection and for federal acquisition of despoiled lands located in the watersheds of navigable streams. For the southwestern counties of North Carolina, the shift toward federal land management was especially notable, with several counties seeing a conversion of up to 60 percent of their land into national forests (CP 5.15)

North Carolina became a leader in forestry management, with the first statewide organization in the country formed here in 1888 under the leadership of the geologist J. A. Holmes. Soon thereafter, in 1892, the first American-born forester, Gifford Pinchot, was hired by George Vanderbilt to manage the forests of his Biltmore estate near Asheville. Highly regarded for his management of the 120,000 acre estate, and with excellent national connections, Pinchot became Chief of the Division of Forestry within the Department of the Interior in 1898, and the first Director of the National Forest Service when it was located within the Department of Agriculture in 1905. Meantime, he had brought in as his successor at Biltmore the German forester C. A. Schenck in 1895. In 1898, Schenck started the Biltmore Forest School. This, the first school of forestry in the country, graduated some 300 foresters by 1913 when it was discontinued, suffering in competition against new schools developing at Yale University, Duke University, and North Carolina State University (Frome 1962). Near the town of Brevard in Transylvania County, the Biltmore Forest School is now recreated as The Cradle of Forestry (CP 5.16).

In the mid-1980s, forested lands in the state amounted to 18.36 million acres, or 58.8 per cent of its total land area. This compares to cropland (21.4 percent), pasture (6.3 percent), and other land cover including built up and recreational space (13.4 percent). North Carolina is close to the remainder of the southeast United States in lands covered by forest. However, there is a wide divergence by the state's primary regions, and within these, by land ownership. In the Mountain Region, the vast majority of the land is in forests, and almost all is federal, whether in national forests (Pisgah and Nantahalah) or in parklands (Great Smokey National Park and the Blue Ridge Parkway). The Southwest Mountains State Geographic Region has well over 60 percent of its lands in federal ownership. In the Piedmont, where close to two-thirds of the land was in agriculture in the 1920s, this is now almost reversed with about 60 percent in forest, and most of this is in private ownership (CP 5.17). The state owns significant acreage in state forest and parks, and Uwharrie National Forest and Fort Bragg cover considerable forested territory in the Piedmont. Agricultural land use continue to dominate in the Coastal Plain Region although corporate development and management of plantation pine forests is increasing, especially in the southern portion. In the Tidewater Region, considerable forest land exists (much of it in wetlands) in designated wilderness or in the Croatan National Forest. Paper companies hold and manage many acres of forest in this region. In 1990, the forest industry owned 12.9 percent of the forested lands of the state. Other private interests owned 76.4 percent, while 10.7 percent was in public ownership, slightly over one-half of this in federal forests. Details of forested lands are shown in the state geographic region land cover maps available in chapters ten through thirteen of this text, but see also Figure 3.7. Forest species are dominated by pine, short needle and loblolly, in the eastern and central part of the state, grading into a dominance by mixed hardwoods as the mountains are encountered. Upland hardwoods of primarily oak, hickory, and yellow poplar, constitute over one-third of the timberlands in the state. In all, the forests provide habitats for very diverse populations of plant and animal species.

A change in national forest management practices occurred in the early 1990s. A storm of protest was unleashed with the publishing of the 1987 Nantahala and Pisgah National Forests Land and Resource Management Plan. The Plan envisioned clearcutting 4,500 acres of forest per year for its initial seven years of operation. Clearcutting, the method to be used for 64 percent of wood removal, thus became the principal mode of logging the land. Perhaps the greater perceived danger to the forest environment was the 775 miles of logging roads that had to be restored, if not newly constructed, to provide access to lands slated for logging. Logging roads tend to fragment the large areas of wilderness required for adequate black bear and other species. Roads are often built in very steep terrain where there is the likelihood of sediment deposition in adjacent streams with negative impact on fish life. Public anguish focused on likely impacts on scenic vistas, animal habitats, water and soil quality, plant species diversity, and on quality of stands. A major irony was the fact that the Plan clearly provided a major federal subsidy to companies contracted to log the national forest. Taxpayers in 1987 paid for the $1 billion in losses that the Forest Service sustained on its North Carolina timber program. Initially, the Forest Service responded by saying that this method increases the quality of hardwoods and allows a diversity of ages among stands in the forest. It is economically efficient and will, in twenty year's time, have lost its look of desolation (CP 5.18).

The 1987 Plan was appealed by a coalition of conservation and environmental groups, including the North Carolina Chapter of the Sierra Club, the Wilderness Society, and the Audubon Council of North Carolina. From Asheville, the Western North Carolina Alliance began its "Cut the Clearcutting" campaign, which featured bumper stickers, petition drives, and an "ugliest clearcut" photo contest (Henderson 1989). A 1990 amendment to the Plan was appealed, but this time also by the timber industry that now saw its allocation of logging lands diminished. Having been instructed to pay attention to its critics, the National Forest Service (NFS) produced a dramatically refocused amendment in 1994, the so-called Amendment 5 (see review of this in Bean, 1994). Clearcutting was reduced to no more than 240 acres yearly (from 4,500!). Instead, the NFS was to emphasize two-aged management, leaving enough uncut in a particular harvested stand to allow two ages to grow there, and select harvest methods, which permits only an average of one acre to be clearcut. These approaches allow continuing wildlife habitats, and they soften the visual impacts of the logging. Within the two Mountain Region national forests, the NFS identified 320,000 acres that were visible from venues popular to the tourists, such as the Appalachian Trail, the Blue Ridge Parkway, an assortment of recreation areas, and residential communities. These "viewsheds" provide scenery protection (CP 5.18). In addition, the new concept of semi-primitive non-motorized areas (SPNM) was introduced. These are defined to be over 2,000 acres in size and removed from an open road by at least half of a mile. Shape and accessibility constraints limit forest management, and 185,100 of the 214,600 SPNM acreage was placed off bounds for timber harvest and road development. This acreage was considerably less than that advocated by the Wilderness Society in its 1992 booklet entitled *North Carolina Mountain Treasures*.

In a rejoinder to what otherwise seemed to be NFS' acceptance and implementation of major conservation goals, critics noted that only six percent more acreage had been moved to management areas that would not permit timber harvest or road building. Even so, Amendment 5 called for a graduated reduction in the Allowable Sale Quantity from the 72 million board feet/year specified in the 1987 Plan to 34 million board feet/year. To gain a better understanding of the complexities of NFS planning and how this sorts out on the ground, the reader should consult Box 5A.

Every ten years the forest plans are subjected to a major review, so the planning process began again in 1997. In 1998, a moratorium was placed on the building of service roads within designated "roadless" areas. This was extended in February, 1999 for an additional 18 months. Affected are 750,000 acres of southern forest, including the Pisgah and Nantahala National Forests.

It is interesting to note that the many decades of clearcutting have brought substantial benefits to some sports groups. Some species, such as deer, ruffed grouse, and turkey, flourish in lands that have been clearcut, so there are groups that favor continued managed clearcutting (CP 5.19). On the other hand, there are conservationists who are concerned about protecting old growth forest and the species that depend on large tracts of undisturbed lands, including bear and neotropical migrating song birds. Controversy concerning appropriate forest management pits the logging industry, the recreationists, and the environmentalists against each other. In addition, the objectives of each of these groups provide the seeds of internal discord.

### Global Impacts on Forest Use

Logging the "first forest" was heavily influenced by extraregional development and investment, although the furniture industry in the state contributed to the process. The "second forest," especially on private and corporate land holdings, was cut in greater degree to suit the needs of the developing pulp and paper companies. Major investments in land and plants were made by companies such as Weyerhauser, Federal Paperboard, Champion International, Willamette, and Abitibi. Their great need for water in the production process and the need for proximity to rivers for waste disposal and transportation placed the

**BOX 5A:** How We Allocate Land: Admendment 5.

Amendment 5 to the 1987 Nantahala and Pisgah National Forests Land and Resource Management Plan outlines what part of the forest will fall into each of the different management areas. Each management area is associated with a different mix of multiple-uses and management directions. Some management areas are intensively used and managed, while others receive relatively little use and change occurs naturally. For a discussion on the application and management decisions to the area covered by the map see page 524.

The plan amendment deals only with Management Areas 1-5. Below is a brief statement about each management area; as exemplified by a tract of land in south west North Carolina:

1B... Manage for a sustainable supply of timber and provide motorized access into the forest for traditional uses.

2A... Manage to provide pleasant scenery along roads or lakeshores for people driving or boating for pleasure. Design timber management activities to maintain pleasant scenery.

2C... Same as above, but without timber management.

3B... Manage for a sustainable supply of timber with limited motorized access. Provide habitat preferred by wild turkey, small mammals, and other compatible species. Offer recreation opportunities, such as hiking and hunting.

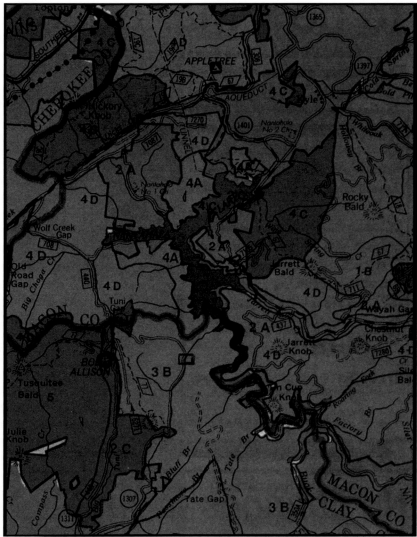

4A... Provide a remote forest setting mostly closed to motor vehicles. Manage for high-quality scenery. Design timber management activities for these conditions.

4C... Provide a remote forest setting mostly closed to motor vehicles. No timber management.

4D... Provide a remote forest setting mostly closed to motor vehicles. Manage for high-quality wildlife habitat, such as preferred habitat for black bear. Design timber management activities for these conditions.

5... Provide large blocks of forest backcountry with little evidence of human activities. No timber management.

pulp and paper industry in large measure in the Tidewater Region (Box 5B). In this region there were more opportunities for the development of silviculture, the planting, field management, and harvesting of a tree crop on a rotational basis in organized plantations (CP 5.20a, b and c). Forest management on private and corporate lands throughout the state developed a more specialized character, with the emphasis on raising large acreage of single stand trees for productive use, though many of these areas continue to serve some recreational, especially hunting, interests. Toward the end of the "second forest" period, about the mid-1970s, forests accounted for nearly two-thirds of North Carolina lands, a doubling of the forest coverage existing at the end of the "first period" in the 1920s. In the mid-1990s, there were 18 million acres of timberlands in the state.

Our "third forest" period is marked by a serious decline in state forest resources. Several local, national, and international conditions of change appear important in influencing this decline: 1) Due mostly to the threat of logging on the natural habitat of the endangered spotted owl, the Northwest Pacific national forest region has experienced a major federally required cut-back in timbering, from about 13 billion board feet in 1987 to 1.3 billion in 1994. Southeastern pine woods are now replacing the lost supply of Douglas fir. 2) Between 1964 and 1990, more than 1.2 million acres of forest gave way to urban sprawl, especially in close proximity to the North Carolina's Main Street, from Charlotte to Raleigh. 3) Home construction in the state has experienced boom times since about 1993, with escalating local demands for lumber. 4) More environmentally devastating, at least in the short run, is the forestry practice associated with the increasing global demand for chip wood; clearing all wood in the designated plot, even scraps; these are piranha-like in their complete denudation of forested areas. Responding to the demand, forest owners in the state have increased production rather dramatically (Table 5.6). They have been well rewarded; a 30-50 percent price increase over this six year (1989-1994) period has prodded onto the market even the smaller wood lot owners.

### Growth and Problems of Wood Chip Production

An outcome of the increasing world demand for paper products and the decline in wood production in the Pacific Northwest has been the explosive growth of the forest industries of the South. Here the climate is more congenial for tree growth and the terrain more accommodating for management and harvesting of the tree crop. The South is expected to increase its production of hardwoods alone by 59 percent from 1989 to 2010 and is looked upon as the world's leading wood producing region. One outcome has been the divorcing of chipping operations from pulp and paper plants. Chip mills have become free standing and quite mobile in their ability to be relocated once the local wood resource has been exhausted. Although the mills still may ship their product to the pulp and paper factories, the majority of the chip wood goes overseas, particularly to Japan and other Asian countries. An example is provided by the Willamette Industries chip mill in Union Mills, Rutherford County. Built in the spring of 1998, the mill is fully automated, and even with a capacity of 300,000 tons of chips per year it requires only six people to operate. "Nestled among hills crowned by autumn's yellow, red, and orange, the mill rumbles and thumps like a giant bowling alley, consuming up to fifty truckloads of logs every day" (Shiffer 1998, 16A). In May of 1999, a protesting crowd of 80 people gathered at the Willamette site, some anchored to trees and cranes. Though removed by police, with ten jailed, the incident marks the strong environmentalist objection to chip mills.

As is its nature in encouraging the development of new industries, state government and the General Assembly worked hard at attracting the chip mills. State government supported a growing export industry that provided the raw material primarily for chemical pulp for the Japanese paper industry, but also for fiber board, strand board, rayon, and press board siding (Manuel 1998). Companies like Weyerhauser, Canal Chip, and Jordan Lumber, exporting raw wood chips, were given $10 million in tax credit. In addition, $11.5 million in revenue bonds were issued in 1995-1996 to build chip handling facilities at the state ports in Wilmington and Morehead City (CP 5.21). With an estimated 147,740 forested acres logged by the chip industry in 1995, exports are mushrooming. In 1990, 194,902 tons of wood chip was shipped out of Morehead City; in 1997, this had increased to 877,937 tons.

By 1997, there were nineteen so-called satellite chip mills operating in the state, most of them in the Piedmont region (Box 5C and CP 5.22, 5.23). By that time the public rumbling over the potential damage caused by this industry had grown to force the interest of the state. Governor Hunt ordered a study by a blue ribbon committee to look at the growth of the chip mills and the

| Year | Sawtimber | | Pulpwood | | Total Softwood | Total Hardwood |
| | Softwood | Hardwood | Softwood | Hardwood | | |
|---|---|---|---|---|---|---|
| 1989 | 192,418 | 88,575 | 196,091 | 114,005 | **388,509** | **202,580** |
| 1990 | 216,389 | 100,525 | 207,822 | 140,402 | **424,211** | **240,927** |
| 1991 | 217,110 | 86,714 | 220,760 | 148,935 | **437,870** | **235,649** |
| 1992 | 239,892 | 90,828 | 215,562 | 153,519 | **455,454** | **244,347** |
| 1993 | 274,747 | 105,316 | 198,373 | 150,354 | **473,120** | **255,670** |
| 1994 | 276,478 | 93,137 | 205,143 | 144,898 | **481,621** | **238,035** |

**Table 5.6:** North Carolina Timber Production.
**Source:** Holmes, 1995.

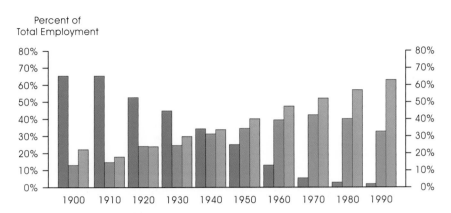

Percent of
Total Employment

## Economic Activity

■ Primary (Farming, Fishing,
Forestry, Mining)

■ Secondary (Manufacturing,
Construction)

■ Tertiary (Services)

Raising pumpkins and other
agricultural crops is a traditional
primary activity (Moore County).
Growing tobacco is a primary sector
activity, while manufacturing
cigarettes is a secondary sector
activity (abandoned plants in
Winston-Salem). Sellers of
furniture are engaged in providing
tertiary sector services (here during
High Point's International Home
Furnishings Market).

*Photos by Ole Gade.*

**Color Plate 5.1**: A Century of Employment Change.
**Source**: N.C. Department of Commerce, 1993.

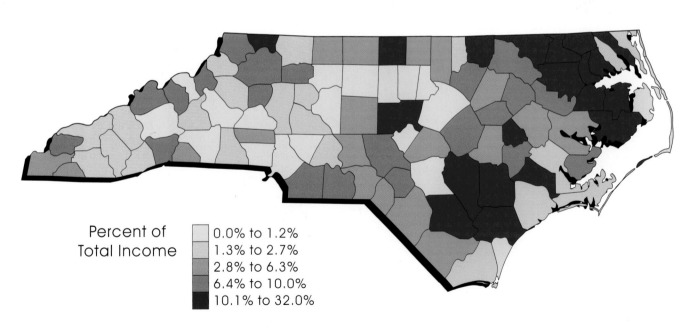

Percent of
Total Income

0.0% to 1.2%
1.3% to 2.7%
2.8% to 6.3%
6.4% to 10.0%
10.1% to 32.0%

**Color Plate 5.2**: Percent Income from Agriculture, by County, 1990.
**Source**: U.S. Department of Agriculture, 1993.

*Photo by Ole Gade.*

**C.P. 5.3a:** General farming occupies the flood plain of the valley of the Little Tennessee River and creeps up the slope of the Cowee Mountains in Mason County.

**C.P. 5.3b:** The terrain of the Blue Ridge plateau does not lend itself to row cropping, and finds itself in a transition to leisure land pursuits such as horse farming or the raising of Christmas trees. The photo is taken from the old "Buffalo Trail," used successively by herds of buffalo, Indians, "Long Knives" (early white hunters), and pioneer wagons; Ridge Mountain and Tater Hill form the background.

*Photo by Ole Gade.*

**Color Plate 5.3 (a, b)**: North Carolina Agricultural Scenes.

*Photo by Ole Gade.*

**C.P. 5.3c:** The hilly terrain of the western Piedmont, here the Brushy Mountains of Wilkes and Alexander counties, provides the needed air drainage for apple orchards.

**C.P. 5.3d:** The rolling landscape of the Piedmont varies considerably in its use for primary economic activities; an aerial photo from Harnett County shows this mix of uses with a large turkey farm in the midst of cultivated fields and forest, parts of which indicate logging activities.

*Photo by Robert E. Reiman.*

**Color Plate 5.3 (c, d):** North Carolina Agricultural Scenes.

**C.P. 5.3e:** A Coastal Plain general livestock and row crop farm lies in Camden County's mostly flat landscape. The light sandy loam soils are easy to cultivate, but need heavy applications of chemical fertilizers to achieve desired crop yields.

**C.P. 5.3f:** Tidewater sand and muck lands provide high yields until the humus layer is exhausted. Periodic rises in the water level, always close to the surface in this area with elevations less than ten feet above sea level, require the use of artificial drainage systems. A wheat crop in Tyrrell County is shown in the photo.

**Color Plate 5.3 (e, f)**: North Carolina Agricultural Scenes.

**C.P. 5.4b:** A work crew of five people is needed to help with the placement of the tobacco transplants; increasingly more sophisticated planting machinery is replacing human labor in this process.

**C.P. 5.4a:** In Bertie County, late spring tobacco work includes the careful selection of "Bright" leaf plants for transplanting to crop rows.

**C.P. 5.4c:** Older styles of tobacco curing sheds are becoming relics in the tobacco landscape.

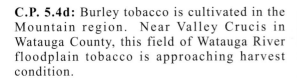

**C.P. 5.4d:** Burley tobacco is cultivated in the Mountain region. Near Valley Crucis in Watauga County, this field of Watauga River floodplain tobacco is approaching harvest condition.

**Color Plate 5.4**: Tobacco Farming.

*Photo by Robert E. Reiman.*

**C.P. 5.5a:** A large contract hog farm spreads out over the western Coastal Plain landscape. The shiny aluminum feed bins, elongated hog raising barns, large waste lagoon, and fields used for spraying waste water clearly identify the nature of this operation.

**C.P. 5.5b:** In hog country, here near Delway in Sampson County, signs showing the contract firm and the name and number of the contractor facilitate delivery of feed and the transportation of livestock.

*Photo by Dan Harris.*

*Photo by Dan Harris.*

**C.P. 5.5c:** This large Delway farm shows some of the automated aspects of the modern hog industry, with feed bins and air conditioning systems connected to the hog barns.

**C.P. 5.5d:** At the other end of the hog barns is the waste lagoon. This lagoon is fed by wastes from five units. Odors and gasses pass through the vents in the barns.

**Color Plate 5.5**: Hog Farming.

*Photo by Dan Harris.*

146

**Color Plate 5.6:** A rebirth of a traditional crop. New cottonfields face a traditional cotton plantation home in the Coastal Plain.

*Photo by Ole Gade.*

*Photo by Robert E. Reiman.*

**Color Plate 5.7:** Turkey Day in Raeford exemplifies the strong identity that specialized agriculture develops in small towns and communities throughout the state.

**Color Plate 5.8:** With strong state support, regional farmer's markets have been developed on the perimeter of the large urban centers. The photo shows an interior view of the Asheville Farmers' Market with its locally grown and prepared fresh vegetables, apples, and canned goods.

*Photo by Ole Gade.*

147

**Color Plate 5.9:** On the offshore islands, sheltered sites provided opportunities for the early fishing industry. In places like Ocracoke, the fishing industry has increasingly given way to recreational boating.

**Color Plate 5.10:** The Beaufort County harbor of Belhaven, set on the Pungo River off Pamlico Sound, is more typical in its dominance of the year-round fishing industry. Shrimpers await the daily call to the fishing grounds.

**Color Plate 5.11:** A Richmond County fish hatchery demonstrates the recent expansion of aquaculture in the southern Piedmont and Coastal Plain.

**Color Plate 5.12:** Hatcheries provide fingerlings for the many reservoirs and other lakes used extensively for sport fishing. This scene is from Lake Lure in Rutherford County.

**Color Plate 5.13:** At the turn of the 20th century, logging was done with steam engines. This facilitated almost total denudation of mountain forests over a period of four decades (1890s - 1920s). The removal of old growth wood (note size of the oak tree in the photo) led to the federal government stepping in to purchase overcut lands and establishing national forests.

*Photo by Ole Gade.*

**Color Plate 5.14:** The "second forest" is flourishing in Todd on the Ashe/Watauga counties boundary. Logging of the "first forest" continued into the 1920s, aided by a railroad linkage to Virginia and the saw mills. The railroad was discontinued when the land had no more trees to give. The train depot eventually turned into a post office for a community now in recovery because it is within commuting reach of Boone and Appalachian State University.

**Color Plate 5.15:** Expanses of the Nantahala National Forest reach beyond the horizon in this photo taken along a nature trail near Highlands (Macon County). The whiteness of exfoliated granite rock surfaces can be seen throughout the upper portions of the Cullasaja Valley; Scaly Mountain (4,800 feet) is in the upper left of the photo.

*Photo by Ole Gade.*

**Color Plate 5.16:** The Cradle of Forestry is an open air museum dedicated to the first forestry school in the country. Founded by C. A. Schenck in 1895, the school was located on the immense estate of George Vanderbilt, now mostly in the hands of the Pisgah National Forest. The museum is located off of U.S. Highway 276, a few miles north of Brevard (Transylvania County).

*Photo by Ole Gade.*

*Photo by Ole Gade.*

**Color Plate 5.17:** Large areas of forest exist in the heart of the Piedmont Crescent. Here a large saw mill exploits this resource north of Snow Camp in Alamance County.

*Photo by Ole Gade.*

**Color Plate 5.18:** A view over Brush Creek Valley in Macon County, with human encroachment of seasonal homes, agriculture, and forest clearcutting. The cut, seen in the upper left of the photo, appears to cover more than 40 acres; it is several years into regrowth. Greater concern over the protection of "viewsheds," like this one, may prevent further clearcutting in this valley.

**Color Plate 5.19:** Many game animals flourish in areas overcut or having open fields with some tree protection. These wild turkeys are part of a larger flock on the "Buffalo Trail" in the thinly populated and lightly forested northern portion of Watauga County.

**C.P. 5.20a:** A section ready for controlled burning.

**C.P. 5.20b:** A section recently subjected to controlled burning.

*Photos by Ole Gade.*

**C.P. 5.20c:** Self-planted pine seedlings dot the forest floor following controlled burning.

**Color Plate 5.20:** In Weymouth Woods State Nature Preserve, near Southern Pines, experimental forest management includes the practice of controlled burning. The objective is to reduce the potential for forest fires that are a particular threat to the pine stands of southeastern North Carolina. Clearing the decaying debris and vegetative growth from the forest floor through periodic, carefully controlled burning also provides improved conditions for pine seedlings.

**Color Plate 5.21:**
The North Carolina
State Port facilities
at Wilmington can
handle state and
national products. A
huge mound of wood
chips and stacks of
logs await shipment
to Japan and other
Asian markets.

**Color Plate 5.22:** The Blue Ridge Paper Products mill in Haywood County. Now owned jointly by its workers and an out-of-state firm, the mill has been threatened by closure. A plan to gradually decrease the pollution causing discoloration of the Pigeon River is now being implemented.

**Color Plate 5.23:** Forestry production dominates many smaller mountain communities. Here yellow poplar is trucked through Murphy (Cherokee County) en route to the saw mill. The county's magnificent courthouse rises in the distance.

*Photo by Ole Gade.*

*Photo by Ole Gade.*

**Color Plate 5.24:** Joyce Kilmer Memorial Forest (Graham County) is one of the few remaining tracts of virgin hardwood forest in the Appalachians. It is an outstanding example of a cove hardwood forest. The area around Little Santeetiah Creek was saved by the great "crash of 1929"; logging was halted due to the dramatic drop in log prices. Some trees here are as old as 400 years, over 20 feet in circumference, and over 100 feet in height. Access to the Forest has improved with the completion of the Cherohala Skyway, a joint Tennessee-North Carolina limited access highway operated much like the Blue Ridge Parkway. The Forest itself is managed in its primitive and natural state, with only two trails allowing pedestrian access.

**Color Plate 5.25:** The Sims Pond trail is off the Blue Ridge Parkway and is maintained by the National Park Service as a part of the Julian Price Memorial Park near Blowing Rock (Watauga County). Towering old growth cedar forest dominate a small and relatively inaccessible creek bed near the pond. With a walking trail cut through the forest, the Parkway motorist is but a few minutes from standing in the middle of a splendid example of old growth forest.

*Photo by Ole Gade.*

154

Value Added (Billions of Dollars)

- 0.8 to 10.0
- 10.1 to 20.0
- 20.1 to 30.0
- 30.1 to 50.0
- 50.1 to 86.3
- 158.2

North Carolina: $65.446 billion

400 Miles

**Color Plate 6.1**: Value Added by Manufacturing, 1992.
**Source**: Statistical Abstract of the United States, 1996.

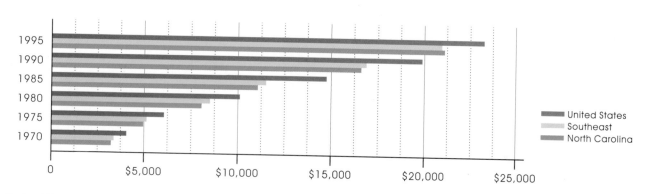

United States
Southeast
North Carolina

**Color Plate 6.2**: Per Capita Personal Income Estimates for North Carolina, the Southeast, and the United States, 1970-1995.
**Source**: N.C. State Data Center (http://www.ospl.state.nc.us/demog/), September, 1997.

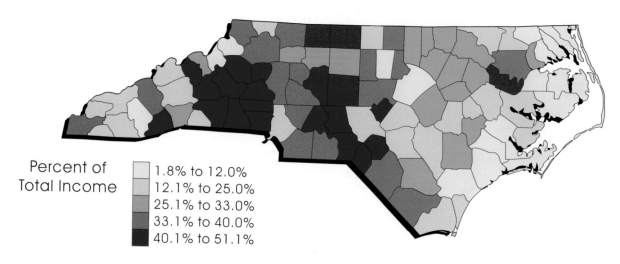

Percent of Total Income

- 1.8% to 12.0%
- 12.1% to 25.0%
- 25.1% to 33.0%
- 33.1% to 40.0%
- 40.1% to 51.1%

**Color Plate 6.3**: Percent Earnings from Secondary Activities, by County, 1990.
**Source**: N.C. Department of Commerce, 1993; U.S. Department of Commerce, 1990.

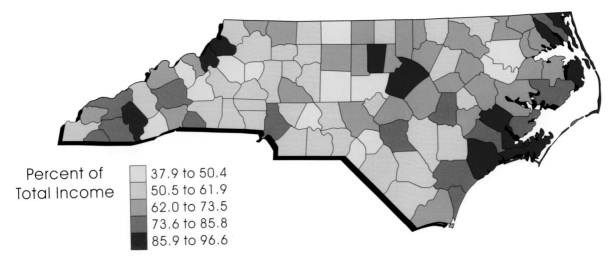

Percent of
Total Income

| | |
|---|---|
| | 37.9 to 50.4 |
| | 50.5 to 61.9 |
| | 62.0 to 73.5 |
| | 73.6 to 85.8 |
| | 85.9 to 96.6 |

**Color Plate 6.4**: Percent Earnings from Service Activities, by County, 1990.
**Source**: N.C. Department of Commerce, 1993; U.S. Department of Commerce, 1990.

*Photo by Ole Gade.*

**Color Plate 6.5:** A Haw River diversion canal in Bynum. The "mill race" initially was used to water drive a grist mill in the early 1800s. The grist mill was converted in the 1870s to a wooden structure housing the first cotton mill in Chatham County. Rebuilt in red brick, the mill first prospered and then gradually declined in production until it became a small scale lamp and lampshade factory. The factory closed and was boarded-up in the mid-1980s. Bynum now benefits from being within the commuting umbrella of the Piedmont Triangle.

**BOX 5B:** Weyerhauser Company Pulp and Paper Plant.

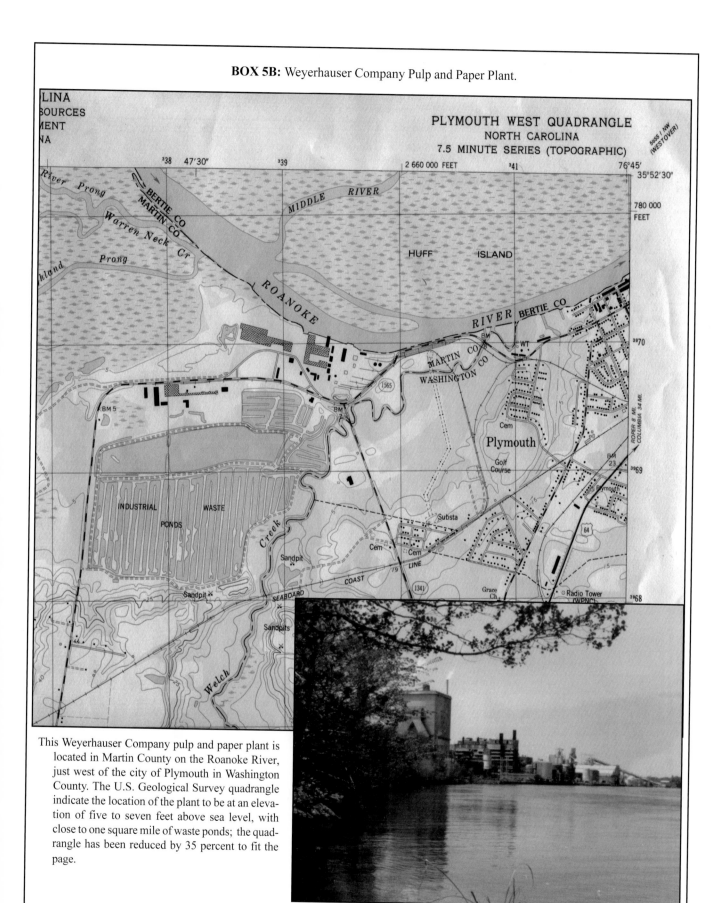

This Weyerhauser Company pulp and paper plant is located in Martin County on the Roanoke River, just west of the city of Plymouth in Washington County. The U.S. Geological Survey quadrangle indicate the location of the plant to be at an elevation of five to seven feet above sea level, with close to one square mile of waste ponds; the quadrangle has been reduced by 35 percent to fit the page.

**BOX 5C:** North Carolina Chip Mill Industry.

| Southeastern Chip Production (cords) 1994 | |
|---|---|
| Georgia | 3,128,700 |
| Louisiana | 2,411,500 |
| Texas | 2,410,500 |
| Mississippi | 2,327,700 |
| Alabama | 2,297,200 |
| North Carolina | 2,040,700 |
| Arkansas | 1,746,500 |
| South Carolina | 1,221,800 |
| Virginia | 1,070,700 |
| Florida | 880,400 |
| Kentucky | 432,500 |
| Oklahoma | 419,900 |
| Tennessee | 302,600 |

**Source:** U.S. Forest Service, 1995.

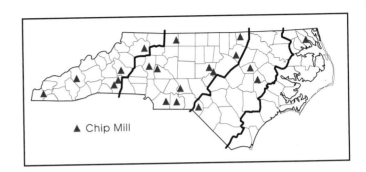

▲ Chip Mill

ABTCO's wood chip operation at Roaring River in Wilkes County. Capable of churning out 450,000 tons of chips per year the mill feeds about half on wood residue from the company's large paperboard factory in the vicinity, with the remainder coming from a 100 mile radius of clearcut acreage. Trucks unload their wood scrap and logs next to the chipper. Note the enormous stack in front of the mill, with the chips then being loaded onto trains that carry the cargo to Charleston for shipment to Japan.

| Product | Volume (million cubic feet) | Percent of Total |
|---|---|---|
| Sawlogs | 398.5 | 47.0 |
| Pulpwood (including chips) | 331.9 | 39.1 |
| Veneer Logs | 66.4 | 7.8 |
| Composite Panels | 33.9 | 4.0 |
| Chip Exports | 14.8 | 1.7 |
| Other Products | 2.4 | 0.3 |

How North Carolina Wood is Used in 1994
**Source:** N.C. Division of Forest Resources, 1995.

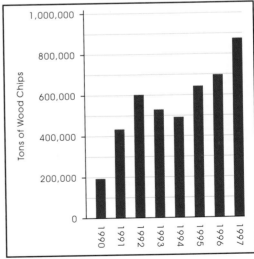

North Carolina Wood Chip Exports.
(in tons from Morehead City)
**Source:** The Charlotte Observer. Henderson, 1997.

rapid expansion of the wood chip export business, as well as the longer term implications for the environment and forest growth. The only regulatory vehicle available to the state is the general storm water permit required by the state Division of Water Quality. In 1997, this was strengthened by requiring an individual permit instead of a general permit of the Godfrey Lumber Company, about to build a chip mill in Stokes County. In effect, this upgrading of requirements has placed a moratorium on the building of new chip mills in the state.

Recent and closer state oversight of the wood chip business suggests that the political leadership has learned from its belated entry into the environmental/ economic development fray of the hog industry. Even so, it is likely that a very large number of the state's population prefer their forests pristine, much like the "old growth" of Joyce Kilmer Memorial Forest in Graham County (CP 5.24), saved from logging by its isolation and sheer difficulty of access, and the much smaller strips of "old growth" scattered through the Mountain Region (CP 5.25).

# 6

# Secondary and Tertiary Activities: Manufacturing and Services

## INTRODUCTION

How do most North Carolinians earn their keep? A lot of changes have occurred since the state, in its recent past, was dependent largely on agriculture and low skill, low wage, labor intensive industries. Many mill towns of yesterday are being renovated and becoming today's suburbs and retirement villages, while the family farm is taken over by agribusiness, and the state's employment in service and trade occupations is soaring. Indeed, North Carolina mirrors the changes in economic life affecting most Americans. As was true for most southern states, North Carolina remained in its dependency on a primary or extractive economy based on agriculture for a longer period that was true for other states in the country. Similarly, its subsequent transition from a manufacturing economy to the present tertiary or service society moved at a slower pace than for the country as a whole (CP 5.1). Now, however, the state is evolving as a national leader in a great many economic activities beyond specialized agriculture. Many corporations have found the state to be a heaven for their national or regional headquarters as well as research centers in places like the Research Triangle, University City, and the Triad "Greenheart." Associated foreign industrial investments have spurred export growth, as well as a keener public understanding of the global economy. A major new land use phenomenon, influenced directly by these changes, is taking shape in the Piedmont Urban Crescent. Between Raleigh and Charlotte a mix of manufacturing, service, retail, and residential usage is aligning along the connecting freeways to create North Carolina's new Main Street. In the process it appears the specialized economic identities attained by the three major urban regions, Metrolina with its finance and distribution emphasis, the Piedmont Triad with its traditional manufacturing industry, and the Piedmont Triangle with its government and research focus, are gradually fusing. Discrete distinctions between these three regions are becoming less notable as the predicted filling in of the Main Street economic development pattern proceeds along a more integrated path.

This chapter will deal with the locationally relevant details of production and employment, as seen in the changing character and fortunes of secondary and tertiary economic activities of the last quarter of the 20th century. Subsequent chapters will probe public and private approaches to economic development and their implications for the state's counties, cities, and communities, as well as implications for North Carolinians' quality of life conditions.

## THE 20TH CENTURY ECONOMIC ACTIVITIES SHIFT

### The National Scale

North Carolina has experienced more than its share of industrial restructuring, downsizing, and relocation, with business interests arriving at improved economies of scale by reducing their work force or by shifting operations to foreign locations with lower wage rates. One result has been the closing of traditional manufacturing plants, especially of apparel and cotton goods. Some former single industry towns are approaching a ghost town appearance. Younger workers seek employment opportunities elsewhere leaving behind the problems of a vastly reduced tax base to an aging population. Yet other industries are attracted to the state. These tend to be more capital intensive and reflective of new and expanding technologies on the global scale. In part they are attracted by a vigorous public policy of industrial development, in part by the prior location of industrial investments within the state, and in part by an entrepreneurial sense of new opportunities increasingly supported by venture capital. They contribute in a major way toward lessening the state's dependence on labor intensive, low wage, and low skill industries, while maintaining North Carolina as one of the nation's leading concentrations in manufacturing employment. On the other hand, they also tend to reflect a current trend in the new industrial spatial organization emerging in the 21st century, reagglomeration. Feeding an already well established North Carolina Main Street, there are important and possibly negative implications of this trend for the state's rural regions.

Nationally the state ranked eighth in 1987 with $47 billion in value added from manufacturing production. But the strength of traditional manufacturing and the rush of new industries into the state moved it to $65 billion in value added in 1992, while advancing rapidly on its nearest competitors, Pennsylvania and Michigan (CP 6.1). Across the categories of manufacturing, how-

161

ever, North Carolina shows considerable variation in national importance depending on the particular category. The state corners the market in tobacco products with $13.25 billion, close to 50 percent of the total U. S. production of $27 billion, and an increase of 45 percent since 1987. It leads in textile mill products with $8.37 billion in 1992 (U. S.=$30 billion), far ahead of Georgia, the nearest competitor with $5.33 billion; and in furniture and fixtures with $2.77 billion (U. S.=$22.8 billion). In other products important to the state, it ranks third in the nation in apparel with $2.36 billion in value added in 1992 (U. S.=$36.4 billion), fourth in lumber and wood products with $1.37 billion (U. S.=$33.15 billion), and fourth in chemicals and allied products with $9.6 billion (U. S.=$164.3 billion). Other manufacturing groups contribute significant value added, though the state ranks farther down the national scale with them. They include electronics and related equipment ($5.7 billion, 7th), industrial machinery and equipment ($4.1 billion, 10th), food and kindred products ($3.69 billion, 17th), rubber and miscellaneous plastics ($2.7 billion, 6th), fabricated metal products ($l.86 billion, 16th), paper and allied products ($1.81 billion, 13th), printing and publishing ($1.67 billion, 23rd), transportation equipment ($1.6 billion, 21st), and stone, clay and glass products ($1.5 billion, 6th).

Fortuitous combinations of its middle Atlantic coastal location, well developed transportation systems, desirable mid-scale metropolitan environments, supportive state entrepreneurial policies, but most especially a concentration of future focused, self-propelled and dynamic entrepreneurs and business leaders, have led the state to national leadership in a number of potent service industries. Among them are medical services, communications technology, transportation and goods redistribution, but more particularly financial services, with four of the country's largest banks (Bank of America, First Union, Wachovia and the Branch Banking and Trust Corporation) headquartered in the Piedmont Urban Crescent. Important also has been the growth of the travel and tourism industries. Most communities seem to be involved in the act of self-discovery with the objective of becoming more attractive for vacationists and leisure travelers. Advantages in economic growth for the state have persisted for decades, as, for example, a traditional 'probusiness' regulatory environment, relatively low taxation, siting, and employment costs. Other advantages are more recent. For example, the concentration of the automotive industry in Tennessee, Alabama, and South Carolina, resulted in the additional proximous location of auto component subcontractors. New suppliers appear particularly attracted to recently developed centers of growth, as in the case along North Carolina's Main Street. A comparative national assessment of state economic success by the Washington-based think tank, the Corporation for Enterprise Development, gave North Carolina high marks (in 1995) for business vitality, ranking the state 9th in the nation in economic diversity and 11th in employment gain. But negatives included relatively low pay scales, a high poverty rate, a spatial maldistribution of wealth and educational competence, and shortcomings in infrastructure, especially road access, bridges, and mass transit.

Economic restructuring of manufacturing, the attractiveness of the state for certain expanding and new industries, and the development of specialized tertiary activities on a large scale, has contributed to a relative improvement in the per capita personal income (PCPI) of its citizens. As compared to the Southeast and the nation, North Carolina has made significant strides (CP 6.2). In 1970 a PCPI of $3,259 ranked North Carolina 40th in the country at 79.9 percent of the U.S. average of $4,077, and slightly below the average for the southeast. In the late 1970s the state had slipped to 47th of the 50 states plus the District of Columbia. However, the 1980s and the 1990s were decades of persistent economic growth where the state gained measurably on the remainder of the country. By 1995 the state had improved its relative position in the nation to rank 33rd with its PCPI of $20,994, or 91 percent of the US average of $23,063, and it is above the Southeast average of $20,817.

### Revolution in North Carolina's Economic Activities

We discussed earlier the division of economic activity into three main classes: *Primary*, including agriculture, forestry, and fishing (Chapter 5); *Secondary*, which involves producing higher value goods from primary resources through the manufacturing process; and *Tertiary*, which comprise all of the employment activities which provide a service to someone else. Table 6.1 notes the twenty year, 1977-1997, increase in statewide non-agricultural jobs of nearly 1.2 million, and shows the changes that have occurred in the categories of industry most critical to the state. An inspection of these data reveals the extraordinary economic shift that is occurring as we move into the 21st century. In 1977, the core industries of tobacco, textiles and apparel had 370,000 workers, or 47 percent of manufacturing employment; manufacturing included 36 percent of the non-agricultural wage and salary employed. Twenty years later these core industries were reduced to 243,800 workers, now equal to 29 percent of manufacturing employment. Although total manufacturing employment decreased by only 53,000 workers, it represented only 22.8 percent of the non-agricultural wage earners, further evidence of the dramatically reduced influence of manufacturing. In these data we see the impacts on the North Carolina labor force of: 1) a critical shift in manufacturing industry from the more labor intensive and lower paid occupations, like textiles and apparel, to higher skill and higher wage paying industries, like machinery, metals, rubber, chemicals and printing; and 2) the evolution of the service society, where tertiary occupations have an even greater wage scale range than does manufacturing. While secondary activities are becoming more capital intensive and experiencing gradually decreasing employment, impressive gains are made in service occupations. Tertiary activities added over one and one-third million workers in just two decades, with a resulting increase in its employment dominance from 60 to 71.6 percent of non-agricultural employment. Within the services the three categories of retail and wholesale trade; finance, insurance and real estate (FIRE); and professional services, that are truly taking off. Professional services registered a two decade gain of

162

189%, while the others advanced 98%. Currently FIRE and the trades categories each have more workers than does all of manufacturing industry. Government employment made significant gains, but saw its share of total employment decrease from 17% to 15.7%. Table 6.1 also reveals the significance of the construction industry which, reflecting the booming times of the mid and late 1990s, has doubled its employment.

These dramatic changes are reflected in the mix of businesses that now dominate North Carolina's employment. A few decades ago the largest firms were mostly manufacturing, and labor intensive ones at that. A December, 1998 ranking of the 300 largest non-public employers in the state, all of them with over one thousand employees, found two of the top ten to be manufacturers: IBM ranked third and Sara Lee Corp (Hanes hosiery and underwear, etc.) ranked fifth. Retail enterprises dominated with five firms: Food Lion Inc (1st), Wal-Mart Stores, Inc. (2nd), K-Mart Corp. (6th), Winn Dixie (7th), and Lowes Inc. (9th). Duke University (including its medical center) was 4th as a services classed industry, and two, transportation, communications, and public utilities businesses, US Airways and Duke Power, round out the top ten as 8th and 10th, respectively. And more to the point, across the board manufacturing is giving way. In 1998, among the top 300 firms, each with over 1,000 employees, were 140 in manufacturing; 62 in retail trade; 61 in services; 20 in transportation, communications, and utilities; 19 in finance, insurance and real estate; five in wholesale trade; and three in other categories, including one in agriculture (Employment Security Commission 1998). This leaves our categories of primary, secondary, and ter-

| | 1997 | 1997% Employ | 1977 | 1977% Employ | 1977-97 % Change |
|---|---|---|---|---|---|
| Goods Producing Industries | 1,041,500 | 28.4 | 892,400 | 41.2 | 16.7 |
| Manufacturing | 833,700 | 22.8 | 780,900 | 36 | 6.7 |
| Food | 55,800 | 1.5 | 42,200 | 1.9 | 32.2 |
| Tobacco | 15,500 | 0.4 | 26,900 | 1.2 | -73.5 |
| Textiles | 177,200 | 4.8 | 257,800 | 11.9 | -31.3 |
| Apparel | 51,100 | 1.4 | 85,300 | 3.9 | -40.1 |
| Lumber and Wood | 43,000 | 1.2 | 33,700 | 1.6 | 27.6 |
| Furniture | 75,700 | 2.1 | 77,000 | 3.6 | -1.7 |
| Paper | 24,700 | 0.7 | 20,900 | 1 | 18.2 |
| Printing | 33,000 | 0.9 | 18,200 | 0.8 | 81.3 |
| Chemicals | 49,000 | 1.3 | 37,200 | 1.7 | 70.7 |
| Rubber | 41,200 | 1.1 | 22,700 | 1 | 81.5 |
| Stone, Clay, and Glass | 23,200 | 0.6 | ** | ** | ** |
| Primary Metals | 17,100 | 0.5 | ** | ** | ** |
| Fabricated Metals | 36,400 | 0.9 | 23,700 | 1.1 | 53.6 |
| Nonelectrical Machinery | 67,000 | 1.8 | 36,700 | 1.7 | 82.6 |
| Electrical Machinery | 63,100 | 1.7 | 44,600 | 2.1 | 41.5 |
| Transportation Equipment | 33,900 | 0.9 | ** | ** | ** |
| Other Manufacturing | 26,800 | 0.7 | 54,000 | 2.5 | ** |
| Mining | 4,000 | 0.1 | 4,700 | 0.2 | -14.9 |
| Construction | 203,800 | 6.3 | 106,800 | 4.9 | 90.8 |
| | | | | | |
| Service Producing Employment | 2,621,700 | 71.6 | 1,278,000 | 60 | 105.1 |
| Transport/Communic/Utilities | 170,300 | 4.6 | 103,400 | 4.8 | 64.7 |
| Retail and Wholesale Trade | 838,700 | 22.9 | 421,900 | 19.5 | 98.8 |
| Finance, Insurance, Real Estate | 167,300 | 4.6 | 84,500 | 3.9 | 98 |
| Professional Services | 869,000 | 23.7 | 300,600 | 13.9 | 189 |
| Government | 576,300 | 15.7 | 367,600 | 17 | 56.8 |
| NonAgricultural Wage and Salary | 3,663,200 | 100 | 2,166,800 | 100 | 69.1 |
| | | | | | |
| Total Employed | 3,704,900 | | 2,527,000 | | 46.6 |
| Unemployment | 139,200 | 3.6 | 159,000 | 4.5 | |
| Civilian Labor Force | 3,844,100 | | 2,686,000 | | 43.1 |

**Table 6.1:** Industrial Employment by Place of Work, 1977-1997.
**Source:** Civilian Labor Force Estimates for North Carolina, 1987 and 1997.

tiary with <1%, 47%, and 53%, respectively. Like the information provided in Table 6.1, this does not include public employees, nor the self-employed, like farmers and fishermen, artisans, or professionals. Obviously, though, the secondary economic activity group continues to be important in the state, though its strength is decreasing when measured by its number of employees.

Turning our attention to variations in the spatial distribution of employment in these major classes we deal first with income and employment concentration in secondary activities (CP 6.3 and Figure 6.1). There appears to be two distinct regions in the state where over 40 percent of county income, and over one third of total employment, derives from manufacturing. The Western Piedmont Manufacturing (WPMR) is defined spatially in part by the Unifour Council of Governments (Hickory, Alexander, Caldwell, and Burke counties) and economically by a concentration of traditional furniture plants and a recent emphasis on fiber optics. The WPMR extends south to include the traditional textile/apparel counties of Rutherford, Cleveland, and Gaston. On the other hand, the Central Piedmont Manufacturing Region include many of the Urban Crescent counties that are not also metro centers, such as Cabarrus, Rowan, Iredell, and Alamance. In these latter counties the growth of population and the pressure of urbanization is such that urban related service activities are reducing the manufacturing share of income to between 33 and 40 percent. A number of counties located along the Virginia border and in the Coastal Plain also have high values of income and employment from manufacturing. In most cases this results from the location of a few large industrial plants that dominate in counties with low populations.

Tertiary activities are expectedly most influential in the large urban counties, so the Urban Crescent counties are in part defined by their high commitment to services (CP 6.4 and Figure 6.2). So there are the expected concentrations of service activities in some of the leading Main Street counties, like Mecklenburg with its large FIRE and distributive trade employment, Wake with its government workers, and Orange and Durham with their concentration of higher education and health services. Other counties dependent to a greater degree on employment in higher education, like Watauga and Jackson, stand out as well. Tertiary activities are also highly concentrated in counties where tourism, open space recreation, and seasonal residences dominate. Included here are most of the coastal counties, plus a large number of mountain counties. Finally, military dominated counties rank high in tertiary activities because of their government employment. As noted in Chapter 5, and demonstrated in CP 5.1, employment in the three economic activity classes have changed over time, with tertiary activities now in the ascendancy and clearly dominating employment in the state. Concentrations in both primary and secondary activities are figured to continue to give way to tertiary. In the aggregate, these changes are pushing a positive overall economic growth for the state. Boding less well for the more rural locations is the fact that here is the greater proportion of declining manufacturing industries, especially ill-

fated branch plants, and that here job losses are not offset by new capital intensive industry and related manufacturing and service employment. These seek the economic agglomerative benefits, comprehensive services, and cultural environments of metro regions for their location.

## MANUFACTURING INDUSTRIES

In this section we provide highlights of the traditional major manufacturing industries in North Carolina, emphasizing textiles/apparel, furniture, and tobacco. Shorter sections treat aspects of other industries, including some now providing new industrial leadership, like electronics, chemicals, and pharmaceuticals.

### Textiles: *Mill Villages, Clothing Towns, and Fabric Cities*

The onset of the eighteenth and nineteenth centuries' industrial revolution was led by textiles. Here was a diversified product in strong demand that lent itself to the application of relatively simple technologies while requiring massive input of low skill labor. A ready base was provided by centuries of skills acquired in hand spinning, weaving and sewing (Dicken 1992). For North Carolina the early introduction of this industry was favored by the readily available raw material of cotton, together with large pools of excess rural labor from the small farms of the Piedmont. It was in large measure the location of milling industries along the swiftly flowing streams of the Piedmont that influenced the evolution of the state's dispersed settlement pattern of small urban places. While the Civil War devastated much of North Carolina's land and economy, it is argued that some of the early textile millers were able to quickly recapture the moment and continue their expansion, as in the case of the Holt family with their plants along the Haw and Deep rivers (Glass 1992, 23). Even so, the state had considerable difficulties with post-war reconstruction and continued to languish economically into the late 1870s. From this pit of desperation grew a movement for industrial development that had as its slogan: "Bring the mills to the cotton and to the rural labor force!" The Cotton Mill Campaign started in 1880, and 50 years later S. H. Hobbs would write in *North Carolina: Economic and Social* that from the east to the west in the Piedmont "almost every little town in this area has one or more small cotton mills." In fact, within 100 miles of Charlotte, there were close to 300 mills by 1903. Richard Manschal wrote in the Charlotte Observer on October 2, 1983:

This time of year is cotton time. Or at least it once was. In Mecklenburg and surrounding counties, the cotton would be ripe. With cooler nights, the green balls would turn brown and open, revealing a fist-size ball of fluffy lint, and field after field would look white as snow.

Soon pickers would pass through the fields, trailing burlap sacks between rows under the hot sun. The cotton would be piled in sheets, the sheets

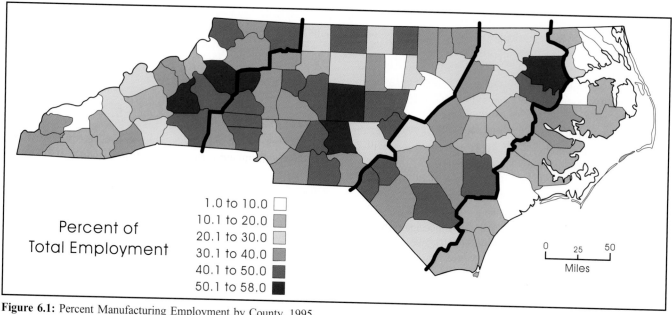

**Figure 6.1:** Percent Manufacturing Employment by County, 1995.
**Source:** Civilian Labor Force Estimates for North Carolina, 1995.

tied and loaded in a wagon and the wagons driven to the gins. Every country crossroads has a gin, where the seeds would be separated from the lint, and farmers and hands, as they waited in line, would break their solitary labor with talks of prices and yields.

Before Thanksgiving, wagons piled with bales would head for Charlotte, Monroe and Shelby. In Charlotte, the wagons would line South College Street. Cotton cutters with sharp knives would run at the wagons, vying to cut the bales. A buyer would inspect the section the cutters had removed, check it for color and leaf content, and by pulling the fibers apart, for length.

After he and the farmer settled on price, the cotton would move to the city cotton platform, an expanse surrounded by warehouses, where it was weighed, tagged and stored. Compressed and bound with six metal straps, the bales would move by train to mills in Fort Mills, S.C., and Gastonia. At the mills, it would be woven into textiles, the last wisps of cotton blowing around noisy machines.

And so it was. This cycle dominated through the 1950s, but now is broken. Cotton was raised, bought, sold, redistributed, warehoused, processed and manufactured in North Carolina. It made fortunes, founded banks and other enterprises, and

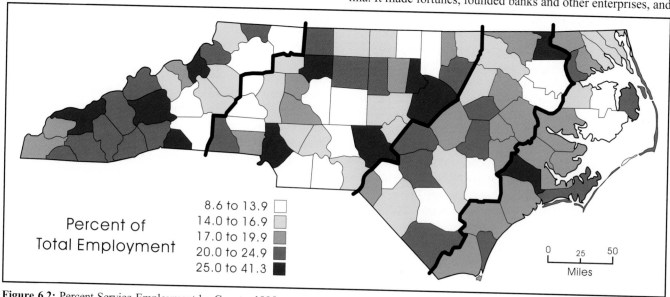

**Figure 6.2:** Percent Service Employment by County, 1995.
**Source:** Civilian Labor Force Estimates for North Carolina, 1995.

in the process contributed to the evolution of mill towns, cities, and even suburbs. Dilworth, Charlotte's first streetcar suburb, for example, was built by the cotton and textile king, Edward Dilworth. Actually, Charlotte never really became a mill town and did not emerge as a textile dominated city; few vestiges of its significance as a center of the cotton trade are now found. This was not so elsewhere in the Piedmont, where along many of the rivers, especially the Haw, Deep, and Catawba rivers, mills were established and villages built to house rural families who expected more from life than their meager survival on small Piedmont farms. They became part of what was by rural folk in the mid-19th century considered "public work" (Glass 1992). Many of the smaller mill towns gradually emerged as textile and apparel manufacturing centers, while others were too removed from the evolving transportation system and subsequently languished. Examples of this process of change are provided in Color Plates 6.5 - 6.9.

Kannapolis was until recently one of the country's largest single company towns. In the early 1980s, the Cannon family finally divested their almost total ownership of property in this "polis" of over 30,000. Initially founded as a mill village to take advantage of water power, the entrepreneurial Cannon family gradually built a textile empire featuring towels and other bath and bedroom goods, with nine separate mills and a company owned town that included a central retail core and housing for an excess of 10,000 workers. While the factories were build along architectural lines defined in New England, house styles evolved largely from southern regional forms and rural living patterns. Characteristically a mill village included rows of small individual or duplex units with a garden plot (CP 6.8a). As D. A. Tompkins (1889, p. 145) explained in *Cotton Mill: Commercial Features*:

> The whole matter of providing attractive and comfortable habitations for cotton operatives may be summarized in the statement that they are essentially a rural people. They have been accustomed to farm life where there is plenty of room. While their condition is in most cases decidedly bettered by going to the factory, the old instincts cling to them.

Thus mill villages reflect paternalism of owners in the context of traditional living expectations of a rural people recently transplanted to an industrial work setting. Though village patterns and house style may differ among the villages, for each a persistent style tends to govern the assemblage. We see this in the small textile community of Landis, a few miles north of Kannapolis, with its 19th century village ambiance still well intact. Retail activities continue to dominate the century old buildings separated from the major mill. The mill cottages were laid out in the traditional L or T plan, and were traversed by a main street in the middle of which passes a double track railroad. Here also is located the small rail station and a tiny post office (CP 6.8a-b).

The Kannapolis textile empire grew in size and manufacturer's wealth to where the luxury of a Williamsburg (Vir-

ginia) style design was implemented for the small downtown by Charles and Ruth Coltrane Cannon in the 1940s and 50s (Bishir 1990) (CP 6.9c). Following the buyout of former Cannon holdings from David Murdoch by Fieldcrest (subsequently Fieldcrest Cannon) in 1986, a number of mills were closed with a loss of 10,000 mill workers. This major corporate restructuring left about 6,000 workers in the Kannapolis mills, but the saga of firm buy-out and divestiture was not over. The mills were taken over by the Texas based Pillowtex in late 1997, and the former head offices of Fieldcrest Cannon lost some 300 managerial staff and white collar workers. Inspite of a late year 2000 Pillowtex declaration of bankruptcy leaving the firm protected by the court under chapter 11 provisions, at this writing it appears that the existing blue collar work force will remain about intact. Whether tourist focused downtown Kannapolis, now wholly owned by Pillowtex and retreaded into a furniture outlet market, will continue to be seen as a viable cognate economic center, remains to be seen.

It is now relevant to make clear the difference between textiles and apparel industries. Textile production involves yarn preparation, of which North Carolina produces 60 percent of the national total, as well as the manufacture of fabric of all sorts, including those made from chemicals based fibers (Figure 6.3). Textiles then provide the raw materials for the apparel industries which include clothing, household goods, and industrial goods manufacturers. From managerial and locational perspectives it is notable that textiles tend to be controlled by fewer and larger firms, which tend to operate out of fairly large plants frequently located in the larger urban centers. Apparel industries are more inclined to be smaller operations, frequently family owned, spread through the countryside or in smaller towns (Figures 6.4 and 6.5). Of the over 7,000 manufacturing plants listed in the 1992-93 *Directory of North Carolina Manufacturing Firms*, more than 1,400, or about 20 percent, are either textile (862 plants with 197,600 workers in 1995) or apparel (569 plants with 64,100 workers). Plant employment averages 230 workers in textiles and 113 in apparel. Textile plants are densely distributed in counties like Catawba (101 plants), Gaston (72), Alamance (64), Guilford (50), and Randolph (44), and otherwise tend to concentrate in the western and central Piedmont. On the other hand, the maximum number of apparel plants reached in a county is 23 (in both Nash and Randolph counties); the remainder are more evenly distributed throughout the state, with the Piedmont and northern Coastal Plain regions appearing to dominate. The apparel or clothing industry is dominated by the production of small piece work or finishing operations that rely on cut materials prepared in textile mills. With this comes smaller scale and family ownership; lesser use of sophisticated technologies; more labor intensivity; and lower wages. As a result, these smaller companies are more vulnerable to current restructuring trends in manufacturing industries, absorption by larger companies, relocation of production facilities in search of cheaper labor, or closure due to consumer fashion whims, costs of modernizing, or overseas competition. Textile mills are generally of a larger scale and therefore concentrate more jobs in their traditional locale, the Piedmont, but espe-

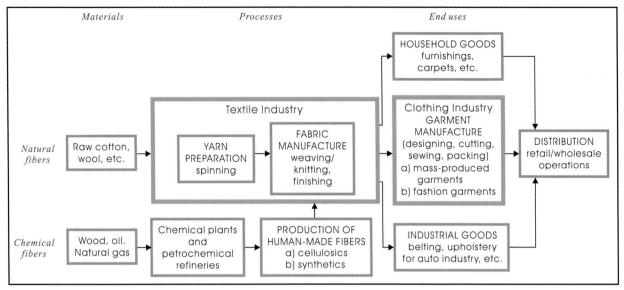

**Figure 6.3:** The Textile-Apparel Production System.
**Source:** Modified from Dicken, 1992, 234.

cially in the textile capital of North Carolina - Greensboro (see Table 6.2). They also lend themselves more readily to automation and other labor saving procedures. About 30 percent of textiles are earmarked for home furnishings such as draperies, rugs, sheets, and towels, while 25 percent or more goes to carpeting for automobiles. The bulk of the textile production in the state, about 45 percent, goes to clothing manufacturing. Here then is a vertically defined industrial production process, from the raw materials of cotton, wool, and other fibers, to manufactured yarn and fabric, and then to clothing or other consumer/industrial final goods, which is not controlled by single firms, at least not yet. Figure 6.3 illustrates the complexities and interrelatedness of these industries, and also suggests the reason for the existence in the state of a growing chemicals industry. Though for a while, from the late 1970s into the 1980s, synthetic fashions were clearly losing out, they now appear to be making a comeback.

During the 1990s gains in industrial productivity and profits, complemented by the stock market explosion, textiles remained one of the industries in the country with the lowest productivity improvement. Reasons for this include the dominance of relatively smaller companies where research and development is almost nonexistent. For the industry as a whole, only 0.5 percent of profits are traditionally reinvested in research and development, considerably less than the 3-4 percent expended annually by the chemical and electronic industries. A direct result of this is growing dependence on foreign technology, which now provides much of the new large scale machinery. A dearth of industrial research has left the development of textile related robotics to Japan and West Germany. One important result has been an increasing reliance of the U.S. consumer on imported textile and apparel products. Just take a stroll to your nearest Belk or Penney's department store and check the 'made in . . .' labels in men's shirts! An

| Company (Headquarters) | Carolina Employees | %Returns | Sales ($million) |
|---|---|---|---|
| Burlington Industries (Greensboro) | 11,000 | 4.55 | 2,180 |
| Collins & Aikman (Charlotte) | 5,400 | 8.75 | 1,060 |
| Cone Mills (Greensboro) | 6,160 | -49.58 | 746 |
| Culp (High Point) | 2,100 | 327.95 | 399 |
| Fieldcrest Cannon (Kannapolis) | 6,475 | 13.92 | 1,100 |
| Galey & Lord (Greensboro) | 2,300 | 56.98 | 412 |
| Guilford Mills (Greensboro) | 3,025 | 47.58 | 830 |
| Texfi (Raleigh) | 1,575 | -43.55 | 192 |
| Worldtex (Hickory) | 600 | 13.28 | 208 |
| Dow Jones Industrial Average | | 175.73 | |

Note: Returns and sales cover the five year period, 8/1/92 - 7/31/97; a small percentage of some firms have employees in South Carolina plants.

**Table 6.2:** Industrial Employment by Place of Work, 1977-1997.
**Source:** Charlotte Observer, August 3, 1997.

167

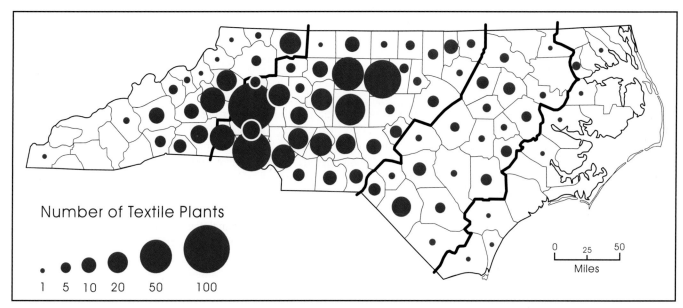

**Figure 6.4:** Employment in Textiles, by County, 1995.
**Source:** Civilian Labor Force Estimates for North Carolina, 1995.

evaluation of Table 6.2 may allow a better grasp of the North Carolina textile industry's lagging performance:

It should be noted that although a company is headquartered in a particular city, this does not mean that its productive energy is concentrated there. For example, Cone Mills, the world's largest producer of denim fabrics and the United States' largest apparel exporter, employs 6,700 workers in seven plants distributed through the Piedmont. Also, this table does not include some important apparel and yarn industries. For example, Sara Lee (Chicago headquartered with regional offices in Winston-Salem), which produces apparel, especially L'eggs hosiery and Hanes underwear, has an estimated 21,700 Carolina workers. Unifi Inc.(of Greensboro), one of the world's leading synthetic fiber producers (specializing in polyester and nylon-texturing) has 6,500 Carolina workers in 20 plants and sales in excess of $1.6 billion in 1995. In addition there is Parkdale Mills Inc. (Gastonia), the world's largest yarn maker. Recently Parkdale and Unifi joined in a creating a new yarn company, Parkdale America, giving Unifi improved access to cotton yarns, Parkdale's specialty.

Other changes are afoot. The North American Free Trade Agreement (NAFTA) has encouraged further apparel production investments in Mexico, where sewing labor costs are significantly below those in the United States. In 1996, the average hourly wage in the U. S. apparel industry was $9.56, as compared to the much higher wages of Germany ($18.43) and Denmark ($20.78). Considering then the extraordinary low hourly wages in

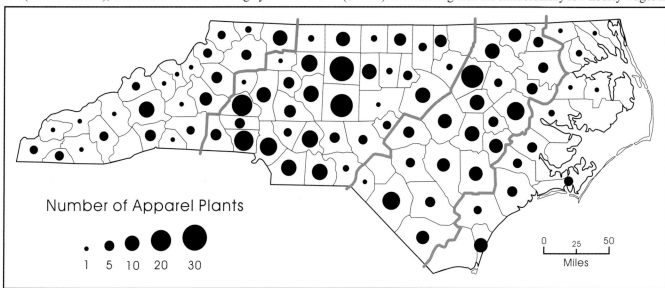

**Figure 6.5:** Employment in Apparel, by County, 1995.
**Source:** Civilian Labor Force Estimates for North Carolina, 1995.

countries like Poland ($2.10), Honduras ($1.31), Mexico ($1.08), Haiti (49¢), Bangladesh (31¢), Chinese People's Republic (28¢), and Pakistan (26¢), it is not difficult to understand the attractiveness of the pull to relocate offshore a labor intensive industry. Additional trade advantages deriving from the NAFTA agreement influenced an increase in Mexican apparel imports to the U.S. from four percent in 1993, the year before the trade agreement took effect, to eleven percent of total imports in 1996. For example, Galey and Lord, one of several large textile firms headquartered in Greensboro, bought out five Mexican sewing plants in 1996. This allows the company to expand its control over the vertical production process, while remaining internationally competitive with the price of the finished garments.

Guilford Mills, also headquartered in Greensboro, is contributing to the development of a 52 acre industrial park with eleven buildings exclusively committed to sewing operations for 4,000 workers. The park is located in Morelos, south central Mexico, the first "textile city" in a larger scheme to finance the development of a series of "textile cities" in Mexico. This initial park was founded by NuStart, Guilford Mills' Mexican venture company. Guilford Mills is convinced that the investment will help the United States textile industry because overseas American owned mills will now be supplying fabric that recently had been bought from Asian suppliers. Already an important shift has occurred in the direction of imports. Whereas Asian countries contributed 66 percent of American apparel imports in 1993 and Mexico/Caribbean contributed 22 percent, by 1996 Asia's share had declined to 35 percent and the Mexico/Caribbean share increased to 38 percent (Hopkins 1998). A more tangible statistic is provided by the shift in the import of men's dress shirts. From 1993 to 1997 the United States' imported shirts from China declined from 1.26 billion to .57 billion, while imports from Mexico increased from 192 to 930 million! These data reflect a critical NAFTA influenced redirection of international trade in apparel products, with major benefits to American producers who have been handed a vastly increased spatial platform for making their production location decisions. What is the impact of this trend on North Carolina communities?

A very direct effect of the international shift to Mexico, and Central America in general, in the low wage end of apparel and textile production is the closure of many small plants in traditional textile dominated parts of the state. A number of examples will illustrate this process. In June of 1996, Rocky Mount Mills, the oldest textile operation in the South closed its doors to 230 workers after 178 continuous years of yarn production. Elk Yarn Mills Inc., the last of the spinning empire mills of Cumberland County closed in early 1992 with a loss of 150 jobs; it was the last operating plant in the state's first mill village of Hope Mills (Cumberland County). Over the past five years, Champion Products of Winston-Salem, a holding of Sara Lee Corp., has been divesting its plants throughout the state with a total decrease in its work force of 1,400. Most recently a Clayton (Johnston County) sewing operation was shifted to a new plant in Chihuahua, Mexico.

However, it is not only cheap offshore labor costs that are closing down operations. Presently there is a considerable reduction in the appeal of polyester fiber for clothing. Thus Trevira, a Hoechst ERG subsidiary, announced in 1997 the elimination of 400 of its 5,000 Carolina jobs tied to research, sales, administration, and production in the polyester business. Subsequently, the Hoechst polyester business has been acquired by the KoSa Corporation, formed in 1998 with 4,500 of its 10,000 worldwide workers in North Carolina. Similarly, the demand for corduroy has decreased to where 3,000 jobs were lost over the 1982-1991 period due to the closure of plants producing this material. In the state, perhaps no county has been hit as hard as predominately rural Stanly where 2,000 textile job have been lost over the past few years, with minimal new in-county job options available to the unemployed. Decades earlier Stanly County was considered a textile employment success story. Now the course of economic survival for its wage earners is either to relocate, or to join the fattening commuting streams to the heart of Metrolina, Charlotte.

Persistent relative decreases in the value of textile stocks, especially occurring in recessionary periods, have made textile firms vulnerable to takeover bids by investment companies or competitors. One of the more notable changes was the purchase of the Kannapolis based Cannon Mills by Los Angeles financier David Murdoch. The cost of the firm in March 1982 was a mere $413 million; while the Pillowtex buyout of an expanded Fieldcrest Cannon in late 1997 was at a cost of $700 million, in the process creating the nation's largest home furnishings company. It is notable that Pillowtex is considering investing up to $300 million to upgrade its outmoded Kannapolis mills as part of the process of reorganizing the production lines. Pillowtex had been consolidating its interest in home furnishings, especially blankets, by purchasing the nation's largest blanket manufacturer, Manetta Mills in Monroe (Union County) in 1993; Beacon Manufacturing, in Swannanoa (Buncombe County) in 1993; and Fieldcrests' two blanket plants in Eden in 1996. The Eden plants comprised the nation's third largest blanket producer with some 750 workers. Pillowtex closed these plants almost immediately, causing considerable consternation in that small Rockingham County town that had emerged 50 years earlier when Marshall Fields of Chicago decided to initiate here the building of his Fieldcrest textile empire.

Many apparel plants have been closed, their operations having lost out to the competition, to rational consolidation, or to relocation overseas. Over decades of restructuring the industry has lost much of its darker side: the stranglehold on workers through company housing and stores, poorly paid jobs, deafeningly loud work environments that were filled with debilitating dust resulting all too frequently in "brown lung" disease and an early, painful death. The resulting negative image of the industry had kept people from choosing textiles as a career, a condition which Andy Warlick, the president of Parkdale Mills, has been quoted as calling 'the ghosts of yesterday.. .., I have spent my career slaying those dragons' (Hopkins 1997b).

Causing further problems was a longer term worsening of the import-export situation which left the United States with a negative international trade balance in textiles of $2 billion by 1989, and a negative trade balance in apparel exceeding $22 billion. Now, goaded on by the national government and a state government reluctant to see its largest industry unable to effectively compete on world markets, the textile industry is staging something of a comeback. The state took a major step in 1982 when it provided an initial $500,000 to upgrade and accelerate research into new textile and apparel technology. Exemplifying a new trend in plant investment, Burlington, the nation's largest textile firm with about five percent of total U.S. textile sales, is moving strongly to replace outmoded plants with new automated facilities.

At Cordova, in Richmond County, a $40 million, 800 employee plant was opened in 1980; the Clinchfield plant near Marion in McDowell County, operating since 1915, was replaced in 1982 by a new $35 million, 300 employee corduroy weaving plant featuring safer, quieter, and much faster equipment; and a new $55 million weaving plant has been built in the Erwin community in Harnett County. WestPoint, which bought out the Bibb terry cloth plant in Roanoke Rapids (Halifax County), has announced a $555 million plant renovation plan to include the modernizing of this mammoth operation. With the air jet looms and other new automation equipment, workers now process an average of 7.58 pounds (3.44 kg) of fiber per hour, approximately double the productivity in 1960. The result includes higher quality yarn and fabric with less waste. What is also uniform about these new plants is their siting in rural and small town locales, peripheral to the large urban centers.

Innovative testing is being done in the North Carolina textile industry on a team production approach with smaller lots. "Just-in-time" design, production, and delivery combined with a reduction in the cost of carrying a huge fabric inventory is the desired objective. Of course, the larger expectation is the improvement of the global competitive position. Predictions on 21st century state of production technology include the reality of consumers having full body scans available on ready access computers to producers who will be able to respond immediately to an individual's fashion whim (Hopkins 1996). Shopping for clothing will be but a computer screen away. New approaches to innovative marketing may also benefit the hosiery plants, many thought to be far too small to remain competitively strong in a market increasingly dominated by retail conglomerates looking for huge low cost lots, or to afford needed investments in costly new technologies. As is, the number of men's sock and women's hosiery plants in the state have dropped from 800 mills in 1976 to about 350 two decades later. Now a move is afoot to adopt a variant of the "Third Italy" success story, which emphasize industry alliances among small manufacturers intent on cooperating their way to an improved market position without sacrificing their artisan nature, and essential independence (Nelson 1996).

Responding to a record $31.5 billion trade deficit in textiles and apparel in 1993, 90 percent accounted for by labor intensive apparel products, the United States moved to establish the American Textiles Partnership. AMTEX is jointly funded by the national government and the textile industry, and is a consortium of eleven national laboratories, including Department of Energy labs. Lab projects aim to improve the international competitive position of the industry (Bass 1994).

In 1995, textiles accounted for 23 percent of North Carolina's manufacturing employment, a loss of five percentage points over the decade, while tallying 5.4 percent of total state employment. In spite of a weakening position, textiles and apparel will continue as major industries in North Carolina in the foreseeable future, with their mills contributing significant employment opportunities to rural areas and small towns in most parts of the state, as well as to some of the larger urban concentrations. Even so, it is equally expected that the industries will continue to consolidate, reduce their labor force, close plants, and thereby impact labor force mobility patterns and the economic health of North Carolina communities.

### Furniture: A Piedmont Industrial Empire

Early concentrations of American household furniture production formed in Massachusetts (Boston area) and then in Michigan (Grand Rapids). It was not until the turn of the 20th century that the Piedmont region of Virginia and North Carolina gained national attention as a major source of furniture. This came about because of proximity to the hardwood forests of the Piedmont and the adjacent Blue Ridge Mountains. Especially critical was easy access to large volumes of oak, cherry, and hickory. More importantly, since colonial days this region had a well developed affinity for making hand crafted furniture. Independent and traditional furniture makers continue to passionately pursue this highly honed and individualized craft aspect of the industry. Consider the plight of the president of a large Hickory firm who recently pondered the difficulty of running an operation that one week had his best foreman on the job and the next week had this same individual operate next door as a major independent competitor (Shuford 1995). A feature of this industry is therefore its very specialized nature contributing to the persistence of a large number of relatively small plants clustered in the western Piedmont. In fact, early in this century there emerged a tight triangle of three major furniture plant concentrations in the Piedmont. The Virginia node focuses on Martinsville, some 60 miles north of High Point, North Carolina, the center of the second Piedmont node. The third node in the triangle is anchored by Hickory (Figure 6.6). Corporate restructuring taking place in other industries that evolved into very large, horizontally integrated, and highly automated plant operations with assembly line labor requirements, did not occur in the furniture industry. Rather, individual plants continue to specialize in some component part of the process, such as wood milling, cabinetry, glueing or upholstering, or they emphasized low production flows of complete but individually crafted pieces. Thus, the tendency toward a highly flexible and uniquely skilled labor force developed at an early stage.

170

The Western Furniture Region, comprising the counties of Alexander, Burke, Caldwell, and Catawba, and including the furniture centers of Lenoir and Hickory (Figure 6.6), had reached a total industry employment of 32,700 by 1995 (Table 6.3). Lenoir, a town of some 14,000 people, calls itself "The Furniture Center of the South." And why not? Caldwell County, which contains Lenoir, had 10,050 furniture workers, or 30 per cent of the salaried jobs in the county, in 1995. In addition, there were 1,500 others sawing wood, and making glue, finishes, packing crates, cushions, and springs for furniture (Photo 6.1). On the negative side, this places the town and the county in a particularly vulnerable position when recession hits, because housing construction and furniture purchasing become early victims of reduced consumption. By 1987, Catawba County had the state's largest concentration of furniture plants, with 140 of the state's 759 plants, though some had less than ten employees.

The Central Furniture Region, comprising the counties of Davidson, Davie, Forsyth, Guilford and Randolph, have several hundred plants concentrated in the High Point/Thomasville/Lexington arch. Here employment reached 25,120 in 1995. All in all, 60 percent of the nation's furniture is produced within 200 miles of High Point. As show on Figure 6.6, most counties in the state have one or more furniture plants. Outside the two delineated furniture regions, however, only in the larger metro core counties are there over a handful. These particular plants are generally very small, with about one-third having less than ten employees, they are highly specialized, and they have a local market orientation

As may be gleaned from Table 6.3, employment in the industry experienced a considerable boom (126%) from the late fifties to the mid-eighties. But there has been much cyclical move-

|  | 1958 | 1982 | 1987 | 1992 | 1995 | 1997 |
|---|---|---|---|---|---|---|
| State Totals | 39,615 | 78,900 | 89,600 | 77,800 | 80,300 | 75,100 |
| Western Region | NA | 31,830 | 36,550 | 32,570 | 32,700 | NA |
| Central Region | NA | 24,380 | 28,710 | 24,920 | 25,120 | NA |

Notes: Industry statistics are for Standard Industrial Classification #251 - Household Furniture. North Carolina is the country's leading producer of Wood Household Furniture (SIC 2511) and Upholstered Furniture (SIC 2512). Membership in the Western Region include the counties of Alexander, Burke, Caldwell, and Catawba. In the Central Region counties include Davidson, Davie, Forsyth, Guilford, and Randolph.

**Table 6.3:** North Carolina Household Furniture Employment.
**Source:** Civilian Labor Force Estimates for North Carolina, 1977 - 1995; Hopkins, 1997a.

ment over this period as a result of the impact of recessions. The past decade reflects the business cycle impact, with a severe drop in employment from the peak of 89,600 reached in 1987 to the 75,100 in 1997 (Hopkins, 1997a).

*Marketing Furniture*

The first Southern Furniture Market (SFM) was held in High Point in 1903. To that point, sales were largely confined to the display rooms of the several hundred furniture manufacturing plants scattered through the state. In 1989, following decades of steadily increasing national attention and movement toward an equal influence on the international scene, the SFM changed its name to the International Home Furnishings Market (IHFM). By Spring, 1994, the IHFM had reached 7,000,000 square feet (about 160 acres) of exhibit space in 150 separate buildings in High Point and Thomasville, with close to 70,000 trade people from the 50 states and 85 foreign countries attracted to the exhibits of 2,200 individual furniture manufacturers. Here, the interna-

**Photo 6.1:** In Lenoir this large Broyhill Furniture Company complex provides millwork, chemical treatment, and other initial wood preparation prior to sending materials to finishing plants.

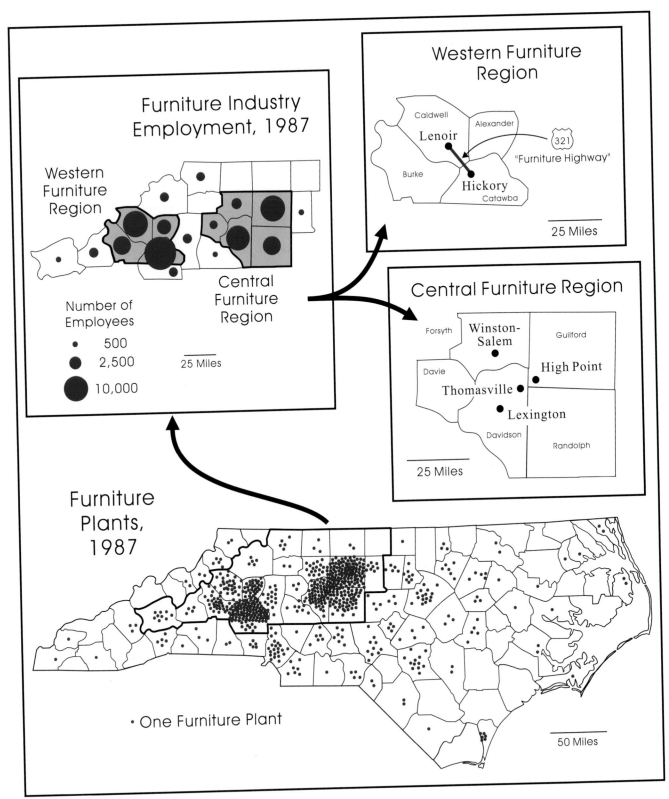

**Figure 6.6:** Furniture Plants and Districts, 1987.
**Source:** Civilian Labor Force Estimates for North Carolina, 1977-1995.

172

tional dimension was further enhanced with 7,800 foreign participants and over 200 foreign exhibitors (CP 6.10a, b, & c). This makes the IHFM by far the largest home furnishings market in the world, but also the only major furnishings market with access restricted to manufacturers/exhibitors, sales representatives, home furnishings buyers, designers and decorators, architects, exhibitor support personnel, suppliers, and news media (Barrentine 1995). Though the periodic market bars the general public, there are a number of large showrooms permanently staffed and available for public scrutiny throughout the year. In addition, the town's specialty is supported by a notable furniture library, the Bernice Bienenstock Furniture Library, with volumes dating to 1640, including complete original collections of the 18th century furniture masters, Chippendale, Sheraton and Hepplewhite. High Point recently has seen the development of the Furniture Discovery Center, a museum of furniture manufacturing that also provides consumer education. There is no question of the enormous local impact of over 70,000 individuals descending for up to two weeks, twice a year, on the Central Furniture Region. The High Point Chamber of Commerce estimated that the Spring, 1994, show had a local impact of $227 million. How the downtowns of High Point and Thomasville survive the rest of the year, with acres of downtown exhibit space standing relatively empty and without much of a flow of revenue, is quite another story (CP 6.11).

An effort of the Broyhill family of Lenoir to establish a competitive market in Hickory was apparently too late in coming. Some of the leading Western Furniture Region manufacturers, Bernhardt, Lane and Century Furniture among them, have closed their Hickory region showrooms for a permanent location in or near High Point. Even so, the Hickory Furniture Mart now accommodates over 100 individual showrooms, galleries and factory outlets, where the buying public is more than welcome any time of the year. This impressive mart has recently expanded to one million square feet of show space, and now also includes the Catawba Valley Furniture Museum, a large antique center, and a 120-room Holiday Inn Express. Perhaps of equal interest to the traveller is the nearby landscape dominated by bargain basement furniture outlets and showrooms, and dubbed the "20-Mile Furniture Highway". It is located on the new U.S. 321 connector between Hickory and Lenoir. Returning to Hickory on the old U.S. 321 will allow a view of the very traditional furniture and related wood and upholstery preparation plants lying cheek by jowl through the towns of Whitnel, Hudson, Sawmills, Granite Falls, Rhodhiss, and Longview (Photos 6.2 and 6.3).

Shipment of residential furniture within the United States increased from $13.6 billion in 1986 to a projected $20.8 billion in 1995 (Charlotte Observer 1994). Subsequently, sales have not been keeping pace with general consumer expenditures. There is a trend to spend less and less on household furniture, as indicated in the graduated decrease from 1.27 percent of disposable income spent on home furnishings in 1970 to 0.7 percent in 1990. Furniture sales also reflect the cycle of housing construction to which they are inextricably tied. North Carolina manufacturers are more vulnerable than most due to their greater dependency on household goods. Perhaps the larger concern should focus on the fact that the 77 million baby boomers, who fueled the boom of the 1980s, appear to have depleted their furniture budgets and are now preparing for retirement, whereas the so-called X-generation comprises only 45 million people (see Chapter 4), and they appear to be placing much more of their disposable income in big screen TVs, VCRs, and home computers (Whittington 1993). Potentially an improved future for the industry will arrive with the subsequent generation, the 18 year old and less, who comprise some 72 million persons. Generational shifts, representing predictable critical purchasing power variations over time, become important assessment tools for production planning in furniture, as well as in many other manufacturing industries.

The 1990-92 recession brought production in most factories to a standstill for a period of several months to over a year. This followed a period of remarkable growth in the late 1980s during which time total production, employment and company profits were at the highest level ever attained. Following the recession production energies were refueled on the one hand by the arrival of better times in 1993, and on the other by a new opportunity caused in part by the recession itself, the ready-to-assemble (RTA) production lines. RTA shipments grew by an annual average of twelve to fifteen percent during 1991-94, reaching a sales volume of $1.6 billion in 1994 (Furniture Today 1995). Even so, by 1997 the shake-out of factories was picking up speed. Examples of factory closings included, Singer closed its Caldwell County factories in April of 1997 with a loss of 720 workers (Photo 6.3), Bassett closed its Impact Division in Burke County in July of 1997, with a wipe-out of 400 jobs, and Cochrane Furniture closed its Newton plant a couple of months later, this with a loss of 125 jobs.

*International Trade*

Though furniture production ranks among the top value-added manufacturing in North Carolina, it ranks but 15th in value of exports from the state with $3.5 million, compared to apparel the industry export leader, with its $101.6 million. Traditionally, the furniture industry was isolated from international markets by high transportation costs for bulky (low value to weight ratio products) and fragile wooden goods, as well as by a generally poor knowledge of foreign style and design expectations and distribution systems (Smith and West 1994). Furniture leaders now believe that these costs are in the decline. A number of factors appear to contribute to this: 1) increased ease of transporting the product as containerized cargo; 2) new innovations like knock-down and RTA designs that permit assembly at the destination and thus facilitate shipping; 3) recently expanded international participation in the High Point International Home Furnishings Market; and 4) improvements in international marketing facilitated by the North Carolina Department of Commerce with the establishment of the Furniture Export Office in High Point. In addition, some of the larger firms are also now hiring

**Photo 6.2:** Sawmills and furniture plants dot U.S. 321 from Lenoir to Hickory like beads on a string. With larger towns pressing its territory, the Sawmills community incorporated in the1980s, including not only a sawmill, but major furniture plants, as well. One of Hammary Furniture Company's many plants is in the background.

*The Merger Immunity?*

their own international trade liaison people (Shuford 1995). Still, North Carolina furniture manufacturers lag considerably behind their colleagues in other states since the total household furniture exports of the United States amounted to $2.9 billion in 1993, leaving the state with a paltry 5.6 percent of the total (Furniture Today 1994), while it contributes about 25 percent to the United States annual production of $16 billion. Parenthetically, it should be noted that furniture imports to the United States for 1994 were expected to reach $5 billion.

An important characteristic of the furniture industry is its dependence in the manufacturing process on the workmanship of artisans, a production condition influencing the evolution of a multiplicity of mostly small, highly-specialized operations which do not readily lend themselves to the kind of corporate takeovers characterizing the 1980s. Even so, a number of buyouts led to the emergence of some high powered furniture corporations during that decade. Notable among these were: Interco of St. Louis, which bought out the Broyhill family holdings, mostly plants located in the Lenoir area; Ladd Furniture, whose holdings ex-

**Photo 6.3:** Not all is well along North Carolina's leading furniture manufacturing highway, U.S. 321. Here the very large Singer plant is being sold at auction in 1998.

174

panded to include American Drew, Lea Industries, Clayton-Marcus, and Pennsylvania House; and the giant Masco, whose holdings included Henredon, Drexel-Heritage, Lexington, Lineage, Hickory Craft, and Frederick-Edward. Interco has since reconstituted itself and evolved the conglomerate, Furniture Brands International, and Masco has sold out to LifeStyle Furnishings International. It is perhaps noteworthy that of the ten largest furniture makers only three are headquartered in North Carolina (Table 6.4). The firms at this scale are all publicly traded, and 80 percent of North Carolina's manufacturers, most of which are quite small, do not find their way to this table.

The feeling persists that the industry does not lend itself readily to downsizing its labor force due to the artisan nature dominating much of the production process (Lail 1995). In addition the majority of the production is direct-order dependent. That is, most furniture is not built in anticipation of demand, rather its construction and finishing await orders expected to flow in from buyers, mostly wholesalers and retailers, following the advertising and "showing" of new designs. Thus the extraordinary success of the International Home Furnishings Market in High Point. It follows that the industry is dominated by a flexibility in its production system that appears tightened only when recessionary periods force an increase in the RTA share. All these are factors that could intimidate the merger urge.

*Environmental Problems*

A characteristic physical feature of furniture plants is the extensive roof air circulation ducts and filtration systems. These exist where a plant provides the initial furniture component manufacturing (like particle boards) that involves a potential for severe air concentrations of wood dust or finishing glue, varnish or paint fumes. The potential of injurious chemical concentrations create special demands for the installation of air purification devices (Photo 6.2). Such hazardous materials are difficult to deal with effectively. An incident of a wood dust explosion and subsequent fire that killed two employees in a Broyhill particle board plant in Lenoir, November 20, 1994, provided an example of the constant need for vigilance in the work place. It should be noted that Broyhill in 1982 installed a state-of-the-art infrared sensor fire suppression system that douse sparks in less than a second. In the end, the considerable local agitation for improvement in work place safety, as well as related production cost factors, may

influence the relocation of the environmentally troubled end of the furniture industry to places that are less environmental impact restrictive.

Environmental problems are not exclusively those of the work place. Adjacent communities may also be negatively affected, especially with respect to air pollution. In Caldwell County, where many residents can smell chemicals from the furniture industry in their own front yards, over five million pounds of toxic pollutants were released in 1989. These included 1.2 million pounds of toluene and .5 million pounds of methyl ethyl kerotene. The Environmental Protection Agency estimated that 80 million pounds of toxins were released by furniture manufacturing plants in 1989 (Lenoir News-Topic, January 5, 1991). In response to the Clean Air Act signed into law by President Bush in 1990, the American Furniture Manufacturers Association, jointly with the National Paint and Coatings Association, launched a major study to show the negative economic impact of the Act on the economy of the furniture industry.

In sum, the North Carolina furniture industry comprises a highly concentrated regional medley of predominately small, highly specialized plants, with flexible artisan labor force requirements. The industry is quite responsive to market shifts, though with some difficult built-in problems for taking advantage of global market opportunities. One important factor that supports the persistence of furniture production success in North Carolina is the industry's statewide vertical self-sufficiency. Most inputs, including hardwood raw materials, fabrics, and petrochemical components, derive from in-state sources. Convenient access to the largest national/international market, High Point International Home Furnishings Market, continues to make felt its positive contribution.

### Tobacco: From Economic Engine to Uncertain Future

Many of the recent, and mostly very dramatic, changes taking place in North Carolina's tobacco manufacturing industry derive from grandiose corporate restructuring. In a matter of just two decades, what was the state's leading economic tiger, an anchor of economic stability and high wage employment firmly tied to particular urban centers, is now swerving the economic boat into directions difficult to predict. The five main players, RJR Tobacco, Philip Morris, Brown & Williamson, Liggett-Myers, and Lorrilard, have shifted in their commitment to manufacturing

| Furniture Company | Headquarters | NC Employment | 1996 Sales ($million) |
|---|---|---|---|
| LifeStyle Furnishings, Intl. | Thomasville, NC | 18,000 | 17,330 |
| Furniture Brands Intl. | St. Louis, MO | 3,535 | 6,697 |
| La-Z-Boy Chair | Monroe, MI | 250 | 985 |
| Klaussner Furniture Inc. | Asheboro, NC | 3,000 | 657 |
| Ladd | High Point, NC | 2,150 | 498 |
| Sauder Woodworking | Archbold, OH | 0 | 475 |
| Bassett Furniture Inc. | Bassett, VA | 1,500 | 450 |
| Ethan Allen | Lamar, MO | 0 | 301 |

**Table 6.4:** Nation's Largest Furniture Makers, 1996.
**Source:** Charlotte Observer, August 17, 1997.

in the state, and herewith has come employment trauma and hardship for some communities, and a healthy local economy for others.

American Tobacco Company (ATC), the leading cigarette maker in the 1940s and 1950s, due especially to the popular brands of Lucky Strike and Pall Mall, was established in Reidsville (Rockingham County) in 1911 with the antitrust break-up of the Duke family tobacco monopoly based in Durham. It brought to its new hometown identity, prestige, and good wages by building here its company headquarters and flagship plant. Decades later ATC was bought out by American Brands, a collector and disposer of manufacturing industries. Shortly thereafter, in 1986, American Brands divested the firm as an independently operating subsidiary, at which time ATC also announced the closing of its 100 year old facilities in Durham, with the loss of 1,000 jobs, 260 of which were shifted to the Reidsville plant (CP 6.12). ATC was purchased in 1995 by B.A.T. Industries, a British conglomerate, to be managed by its American tobacco subsidiary, Brown & Williamson Tobacco. The result was a dramatic decision to close down all facilities in Reidsville, and to relocate to Macon, Georgia! About 1,000 jobs in the town of about 12,000 and county of 86,000 were directly and negatively impacted, with the rippling effect on the locality's economy continuing into the 21st century. A company so firmly imbedded and so dominant in the local economy causes a significant void with its leaving. In Reidsville, ATC was responsible for $45 million in direct annual wages, with its hourly wage rate between $18 and $25, as compared to the regional average of $8-11; it paid $2 million, or one quarter, of the town's property tax revenue, and it was the major local philanthropic contributor. Reidsville's merchants suffered with the abrupt decline in local consumer purchasing power (Lounsbury 1995). Its population for a number of years was stagnating, with 12,183 counted in 1990 and 12,445 in 1996 - though annexation brought the town total to 14,485 in 2000.

Reidsville's economic recovery program could take lessons from the earlier demise of tobacco industries in the larger towns of Durham and Winston-Salem. Not only has American Tobacco abandoned Durham, so has Liggett-Meyers. This producer, notable for breaking the dam in tobacco litigation in 1996 by agreeing to help repay Medicaid bills for treatment of smokers, is a subsidiary of the conglomerate Brooke Group. Liggett-Myers owns the one remaining tobacco plant in Durham. In 1990, the plant had 1,700 employees, but by 1996 this had fallen to 600, a victim of corporate strategies that left it without the necessary upgrading of equipment and facilities. In Durham, community efforts to resuscitate the town focused on changing its image from "Bull Durham" (and thus tobacco) to the "City of Medicine" appears to have been successful. It is perhaps ironic that Duke University Medical Center is in a major way the legacy of the Duke family's good fortune in the tobacco industry in the city of Durham.

In recent decades it has become difficult to feret out precisely who owns what in the tobacco industry, except it is increasingly clear that decisions affecting the lives of employees and the economic security of their communities are no longer locally made. R. J. Reynolds (RJR) Tobacco Company also bought into the prevailing 1970s corporate strategy of product diversification, by joining with Nabisco Foods. The closing down of all production facilities downtown Winston-Salem was already underway, when a super modern cigarette factory in Tobaccoville, in Forsyth County about 15 miles northeast of the city, had its opening in 1987.

In 1875, the first RJR tobacco plant was built in what grew to become a sprawling complex of four to five story red brick manufacturing buildings which, for over a century has helped define the urban structure, identity, and growth of Winston-Salem (CP 6.13). In 1990, the last of these closed, with some workers transferred to the still operating Shorefair or Whitaker plants on the outskirts of Winston-Salem, or to Tobaccoville (CP 6.14). In 1987, F. Ross Johnson, then chief executive of RJR Nabisco, donated the recently constructed twenty-acre office space headquarters building to Wake Forest University, an institution itself relocated to Winston-Salem through the efforts of the Reynolds family in the early 1950s, when he decided to relocate RJR Nabisco headquarters functions and personnel to Atlanta (CP 6.15). Kohlberg Kravis Roberts & Co., a New York investment firm, bought out RJR Nabisco in 1989 for $30 billion. For the city the final blow came six years later with the relocation of the RJR tobacco world headquarters to Switzerland, a testimony to the ongoing major shift in tobacco manufacturing and markets overseas. RJR, coincidentally, owned or leased no less than twenty foreign tobacco plants, located in countries from the People's Republic of China to Poland, until its foreign division was bought out by Japan Tobacco in 1998. A late nineties divestiture of Nabisco Foods has once again left R. J. Reynolds independent, though much smaller in scale, and once again isolated to Forsyth County. With this return to its roots, RJR is refreshed, debt free, and still has 6,000 Forsyth County employees. Undoubtedly, some of these impacts would have occurred with time as the firm became more efficient with its new plants and the negative public pressure on the tobacco industry grew, but here the streamlining and office relocating resulted from the machinations of international corporate buyout strategies and the whims of executive decision makers.

Philip Morris (PM), headquartered in New York City, is the largest American tobacco company, controlling close to 50 percent of the domestic cigarette market. PM became the largest consumer products firm in the world by gradually acquiring Kraft General Foods, Miller Breweries, Jacob's Sutured, and others. Rather than divesting in North Carolina, PM built a very large and highly efficient cigarette factory in Concord (Cabarrus County) in 1983. Built on 1,200 rolling acres the plant is now seeing a $400 million addition expected to increase the production to 165 million cigarettes daily. In addition, PM owns or leases 47 plants abroad, and sells annually 230 billion cigarettes domestically, and 660 billion overseas (Stencil 1997). Interestingly, the Concord plant addition was encouraged by an increase in overseas sales, especially to Asian countries. In late 1997, 24 percent of the plant's production was being exported. Its regional economic impact is considerable, with comparatively high wages for some 2,400 workers, who commute to the plant from 16 Piedmont counties.

Lorrilard, the nation's fourth largest tobacco producer with annual sales of about $2 billion, made an unexpected move in a direction opposite that of the other major firms in the field. It announced in 1996 that it would move its headquarters from New York City to Greensboro, where it has its only tobacco plant. Here it employs 1,850 workers.

Location of the facilities of the major tobacco producers in North Carolina is decidedly a Piedmont affair, with the sole exception of a small Brown & Williamson processing plant in Wilson. Most plant divestiture has taken place in the traditional tobacco manufacturing belt of the state, from Durham in the east to Winston-Salem in the west. The Cabarrus County location of Philip Morris is relatively new. In 1994, the earnings from tobacco manufacturing for the four leading counties were as follows: Forsyth - $615.4 million; Cabarrus - $126.4 million; Guilford - $106.8 million; Rockingham - $75.8 million; and Durham - $40.9 million (Morrill and Mellnik 1996). Rockingham left this group two years later. In spite of administrative shuffling and production relocating, RJ Reynolds is still the state's leading manufacturer of tobacco by a two to one ratio over the total effort of the remainder.

### Other Manufacturing

Having dealt with the traditional top three manufacturing groups, we turn our attention in a more limited way to the rest of the manufacturing picture, some of which appears especially bright for North Carolina's future.

#### Food and Kindred Products

In 1997, the state had 55,800 workers in food production, an increase of over 13,000 (23.7%) over the past two decades. Actually, the technical definition of this category, Food and Kindred Products, includes a rather considerable diversity of manufactured goods. They vary across a spectrum from packaged meats, fresh and frozen baked goods, dairy products, canned fruit and vegetables, animal feed, confectionery, soybean and other cooking oils, to wine, beer, and Coca-Cola. Employment in this industry is dominated by two key characteristics. Meat processing and packing plants are concentrated where the majority of poultry and swine is raised, as, for example, in the Coastal Plain counties of Bertie, Bladen and Robeson, in the Piedmont county of Union, and in Wilkes County in the Mountain Region. Detailed accounting of this concentration is provided in the agricultural section of Chapter 5, with several photos illustrating some of the central aspects included there, as well (see also Figure 6.7). General food processing, on the other hand, is associated with larger urban areas, with Mecklenburg County far ahead in employment with over 5,700 workers. Here the proximity to a large food consuming market provides the impetus for a great variety of small manufacturers, like specialty bakeries, vinegar makers, and gourmet chocolatiers, but there are larger producers

also. For example, the state's largest producer of chips, crackers, and cookies, Lance, Inc. employs over 1,000 and is located in Charlotte, as is the second largest producer, Frito-Lay. Further expansion of this industry hinges on two major factors, the continuing viability and growth of global markets for North Carolina food products, and the increasing growth of the state's population. In large measure this industry ebbs and flows with the local market.

#### Lumber and Wood Products

North Carolina is blessed with considerable commercially usable forest cover, and thus has a large potential for using wood in a great variety of manufacturing. Earlier we discussed the critical importance of Mountain and Piedmont hardwoods for the furniture industry, and the overseas markets for chip wood (Chapter 5). Wood is also important in allied products such as structural lumber, flooring, paneling, cabinets, and other wood products important in the building of on-site homes, prefab housing, and mobile homes. The state had 43,000 workers in this industry in 1997, an increase of 27.6 percent since 1977. From Figure 6.8 the strong association with the furniture production is clearly indicated, with nearly 50 percent of this industry's employment in the Western and Central Furniture Regions.

#### Paper and Allied Products

Production facilities in this group are dominated by large paper and pulp mills. Largest among these is Etta Packaging, Inc., a division of The Laird Group, PLC, with over 2,500 employees in its paper box plant at Marion (McDowell County). The western part of the state, with its heavier concentration of hardwood trees, has the most pulp and paper plants (Figure 6.9). Here we find Champion International Corp. with plants in Canton and Waynesville (Haywood County), a company with an unenviable history of river pollution as discussed in Chapter 8, and the Ecusta plant of P.H. Glatfelter Co., producing printing paper and paper for the tobacco industry, in Pisgah Forest (Transylvania County). Paper and packaging for the tobacco industry is also produced in a Winston-Salem plant, with over 1,000 R. J. Reynolds workers.

Fewer of the paper and paperboard plants are located in the east. One example is the Champion plant at Roanoke Rapids (CP 6.16). On the other hand, in the east are the larger pulp mills, like the Riegelwood Operations of Federal Paperboard Co. Inc., in Columbus County, and Weyerhauser Co. at New Bern in Craven County (Box 5B). Statewide employment in this industry has increased only slightly, from 22,300 to 24,600 workers, over the past decade. However, production of one of the industry's newest and most highly contested products, chipwood, is escalating rapidly throughout the state. See Chapter 5, especially Box 5C, for detailed information about wood chips as an aspect of North Carolina forestry.

#### Chemicals and Allied Industries

Included in this class of industry are some of the most rapidly expanding industries and largest employers in the state.

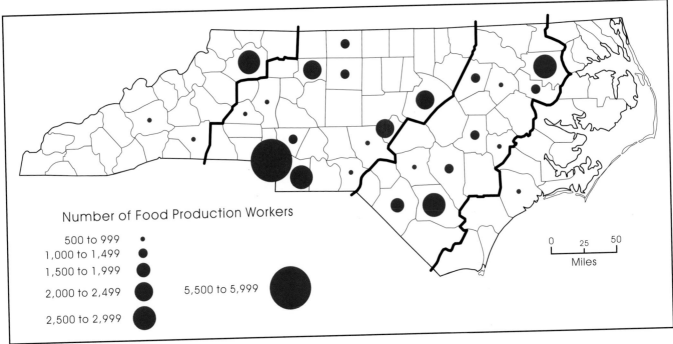

**Figure 6.7:** Food and Kindred Products Industry Employment, 1995.
**Source:** Civilian Labor Force Estimates for North Carolina, 1995.

As indicated in Table 6.1, this industry class experienced growth from 37,200 workers in 1977 to 49,000 in 1997, a 31.7 percent increase. Included here are the several polyester and other fibers plants of KoSa, led in size by its giant polyester plant east of Salisbury (Rowan County) with over 2,500 workers (CP 6.17), and smaller plants at Shelby (Cleveland County) and Wilmington. KoSa, a firm created by the 1998 merger of Koch Industries of Wichita, Kansas and the Mexican industrialist Isaac Saba, bought out the Hoechts-Celanese polyester business, now has its U. S. headquarters in Charlotte.

Included in the DuPont Corporations' statewide payroll in 1990 of 6,288, were 1,000 workers at its "Dacron" plant in Wilmington. Other fiber plants include the Enka (Haywood County) operation of the BASF Corp. These and many smaller fiber plants scattered through the state owe their existence to the large textile and apparel industry, and are therefore affected by the same market forces. In addition, the chemical and allied industries class includes the manufacturing of industrial cleaners (as exemplified by the Sutherlands Products plant at Mayodan in Rockingham County), the production of agricultural fertilizers

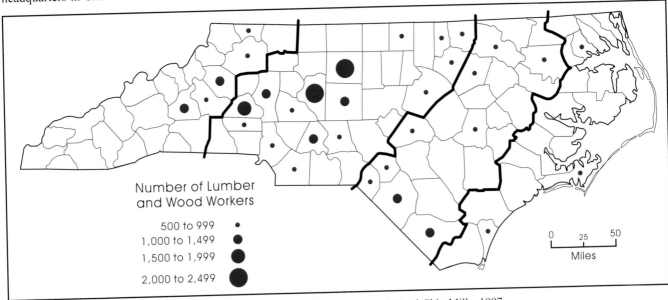

**Figure 6.8:** Lumber and Wood Products Industry Employment, 1995. Location of Wood Chip Mills, 1997.
**Source:** Civilian Labor Force Estimates for North Carolina, 1995; Henderson, Charlotte Observer, August 27, 1997.

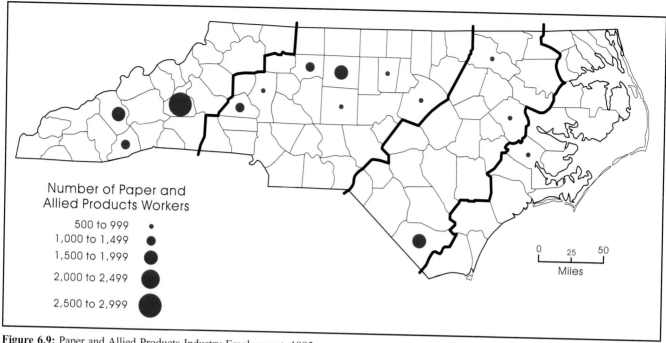

**Figure 6.9:** Paper and Allied Products Industry Employment, 1995.
**Source:** Civilian Labor Force Estimates for North Carolina, 1995.

(e.g. phosphates at Aurora in Beaufort County; discussed in Chapter 11), and pesticides (e.g. Rhone-Poulenc, Inc., and the Zema Corporation facilities in Durham County's Research Triangle Park). Many smaller plants produce industrial chemical gasses and liquids, paints, wood gums, detergents, explosives, and many forms of plastics, as well as ink, perfumes, and cosmetics. Exemplifying the latter is Coty Inc., which with seasonal production fluctuations employs 880 to 1,600 workers in its Sanford (Lee County) plant (Martin 1996). It should be noted that these industries tend to cause more than their share of problems with air and water pollution, as discussed in Chapter 8.

Among the firms in this class are also the producers of medicinal botanicals and chemicals, as well as another of the state's increasingly important producer groups, the pharmaceuticals. Especially noteworthy are the North Carolina locational impacts of four behemoth pharmaceutical companies, that emerged came out as the fist and second largest in the world through recent mergers. Glaxo Inc., the American subsidiary of British based Glaxo PLC had its headquarters in the Research Triangle Park (RTP) with 3,000 employees, and its sole U.S. production facility in Zebulon (Wake County) with 700 workers. In 1994, Glaxo bought out another British pharmaceutical firm, Welcome PLC, also with American headquarters (Burroughs-Welcome) in the RTP with 2,100 workers, and its primary production facility in Greenville (Pitt County) with 1,900 workers. Mergers at this scale are invariably pursued in the expectation of increased profits, frequently at the expense of a reduced work force. For Glaxo-Welcome, redundancies existed in the large Research Triangle headquarters and research laboratories. Subsequently employment was reduced to 4,000, a decrease of about 20 percent since the merger. Due to periodic expiration of patent protection for popular drugs, and the resulting production of low cost generic substitutes, there must be a continuing search for new drugs. So it is axiomatic that employment in such firms is heavily vested in research, one-sixth of Glaxo-Welcome's 53,500 workers worldwide are in research.

The merger of Ceiba-Geiga Ltd. and Sandoz Ltd., both Swiss based corporations, resulted in the world's second largest drug producer, behind Glaxo-Welcome. Novartis, as the firm is now called, had 1,310 workers in North Carolina at the time of the merger in May, 1996. Most of these employees are in Greensboro, where Novartis maintains its North American regional headquarters. It is relevant to note that firms of this size do tend to be fairly diversified. So Novartis' annual sales derive from health care products (59%), agricultural chemicals (27%), and nutrition products (14%).

Figure 6.10 identifies the unique concentrations of employment in the chemicals and allied products industry. Pharmaceuticals and agricultural chemicals are focused in the Piedmont Triangle, though extending to Guilford County, while the synthetic fiber plants are more numerous in the central and western Piedmont from Guilford to Mecklenburg, Cleveland, and Burke counties. Showing the concentrations of industry employment exceeding 500 workers omits the information that the chemicals industry has over 450 medium and smaller plants that are distributed through the state, with no particular geographic concentration. A number of these smaller plants have evolved recently as spin-offs from the large pharmaceutical firms and specialize in various aspects of bioscience, a new growth industry that is contributing to the developing image of the Research Triangle area as a globally recognized high tech center. We treat this phenomenon in greater detail in Chapter 14.

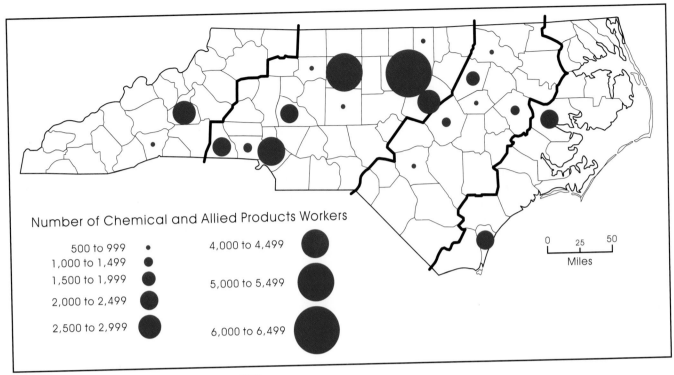

**Figure 6.10:** Chemicals Industry Employment, 1995.
**Source:** Civilian Labor Force Estimates for North Carolina, 1995.

*Transportation Products Industries*

Whereas textile mills could be referred to as the "industry of industries" during the early part of the 19th century, it is the manufacture of automotive transport that rightly has been referred to as the "industry of industries" of the first half of the 20th Century (Dicken 1992, 268). From the early 20th century, automotive and allied products manufacturing was pretty much confined to the upper Midwest, where it dominated the American industrial explosion. Corporations like Ford, General Motors, and Chrysler became gigantic in scale extending around the world in markets and investments. The industry had immense spin-off effects on suppliers and distributors; effects that reached to the furniture and textile industries of North Carolina fairly early in the century. However, the major upheavals in automotive production location since the 1960s have had much greater impact on the state's economy.

Many factors have influenced these dramatic manufacturing relocations. They include: 1) a very large increase in world demand (from 13 million automotive units produced in 1960 to 35.5 million in 1989); 2) leadership in world market penetration by European and especially Japanese manufacturers, with American bulky, gasguzzling autos not competing well overseas; 3) gradual replacement of the American invented "fordist" assembly line, a large volume assembly line production method, by the Japanese flexible production method, which relies on smaller production volumes of simpler engineered autos utilizing labor having a diversity of skills; and 4) most importantly, the building of European and Japanese automotive plants in the United States by firms not hampered by traditional automotive industry location factors

Changing production methods, and the necessity of United States firms to compete even in their home market, combined to cause the weakening of the Midwest automotive power center. Within a few years Honda was building a plant in Ohio; and there was Toyota and Ford in Kentucky; Nissan and GM Saturn in Tennessee; Mercedes-Benz in Alabama; Ford, GM, and Toyota in Georgia; and Ford and Volvo-GM in Virginia. With Freightliner/Mercedes-Benz in North Carolina, and BMW in South Carolina, the late 20th century shift of automotive industrial investment that visited Mid-America from Illinois to Alabama since the 1970s has been extended to the Carolinas. Accompanying this revolution is the magic of tailgating plant investment that brings in a variety of suppliers for the new automotive assembly plants, whether Honda in Ohio or Freightliner in Cleveland, North Carolina.

Recent decisions by the Freightliner Corporation illustrate well how the territorial logic of development appears to favor the further concentration of automotive manufacturing in North Carolina. Freightliner, the nation's number one truck maker, and a member of the Mercedes-Benz AG group, has its corporate headquarters in Portland, Oregon, and two-thirds of its production facilities in the Carolinas. In early March, 1998, the company announced plans to increase its workforce in the Carolinas to 6,700. Freightliner's largest plant, in the small Rowan County town of Cleveland, now has over 2,500 workers. Other plants are in Mount Holly (Gaston County) and in Gaffney, South Carolina. In 1999, Mercedes-Benz AG acquired Thomasbuilt Bus Company of High Point, the nation's leading school bus manufacturer, and placed in under Freightliner management. All plants are in Main Street communities, and so have easy access to I-85 or I-40, and they pay an average wage of nearly $20 per hour; high wages, indeed, by North Carolina manufacturing standards (Hopkins and Williams 1998).

It is instructive to look at what has happened recently in North Carolina in terms of the rippling effects of such large scale vehicle production investments (CP 6.18). The following individual plant investments are a sample of new ancillary industries: tires by Goodyear, General Tire, or Bridgestone/Firestone; anti-lock brakes by ITT; batteries by Douglas Battery; starters by Bepco; hydraulic pumps by Frisby; carburetors and pistons by Edmunds Manufacturing; steering and suspension systems by TRW; transmissions by Zeller Piedmont; electronics and wiring harnesses by AMP; carpeting by Collins & Aikman; motors for air conditioners and power seats by Automotive Motors; rubber window seals by Standard Products; and headliners by Guilford Mills (Whittington 1995, 18-19). For example, ITT Automotive with 1,000 workers builds anti-lock brakes for BMW and others, and Volvo Equipment has 500 employees making earth moving equipment in Asheville. To complement a growing automotive component manufacturing center in Buncombe County, in nearby Fletcher, there is Rockwell International with 625 workers making drive and steering axes for heavy trucks (Whittington 1995). Smaller scale enterprises flourish in different places: Labonte Racing Inc. in Trinity, Roush Racing in Liberty, Petty Enterprises Inc. in Randleman, and Ashley Emergency Vehicles in Ashe County (Whittington 1995).

This very large array of automotive industry suppliers identifies yet another essential characteristic of late 20th century manufacturing processes, the "just-in-time" element. Critical to success in building a competitive product for a worlds market has been the ability of the manufacturer to network with highly specialized suppliers capable of speedy delivery, and rapid turn-around in reengineered components. These are all capital intensive industries, favoring robotics and high skilled adaptable labor, and therefore yield much higher wages than those traditionally identified with apparel and textiles. Industries supporting the automotive manufacturing process now number 253 in North Carolina with over 63,000 workers. Cry your heart out Detroit! A further compelling statistic used by industrial recruiters is that, as of 1995, 84 percent of all cars and 88 percent of all trucks built in the United States are assembled within 700 miles of North Carolina (Whittington 1995, p. 18).

The foregoing suggests the difficulty of identifying in Table 6.1 just where employment of this dynamically growing manufacturing industry is classed. Certainly the new identification of employment in the transportation industry, with its 33,900 workers in 1997, is a big help (Figure 6.11). Workers in ancillary industries are more problematic to class. Some contribute to increases in the metals and machinery industries (Figure 6.12), while others comprise a major percentage of employees in the rubber industry (Figure 6.13). In all, the recent and likely continued growth of the automotive/truck complex of industries emphasize the major changes in North Carolina's manufacturing industry; increasing degree of complexity with built-in hopes for improved stability; more capital intensive and higher skills demanding jobs with much improved wage rates; and a centralization of industrial location on North Carolina's Main Street.

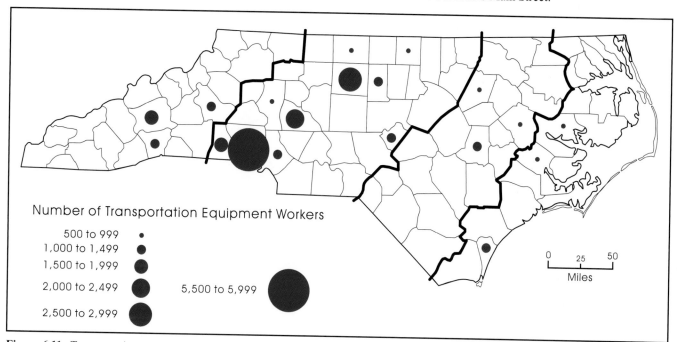

**Figure 6.11:** Transportation Equipment Industry Employment, 1995.
**Source:** Civilian Labor Force Estimates for North Carolina, 1995.

181

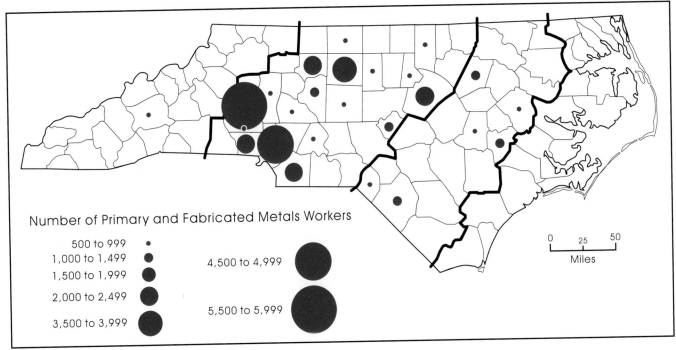

**Figure 6.12:** Primary and Fabricated Metals Employment, 1995.
**Source:** Civilian Labor Force Estimates for North Carolina, 1995.

*Nonelectrical and Electrical Machinery*

These two categories experienced the greatest numeric growth among manufacturing industries from 1977 to 1997 (Table 6.1). Many of their component industries, especially the manufacturing of computers and office equipment (20,406 workers in 1996), electrical components (8,175), and telecommunications equipment (16,486), are often referred to as high-tech industries.

For North Carolina they are, with their expectations of higher skills and resulting higher pay, looked upon as very desirable substitutions for traditional and downsizing industries. As indicated in Figures 6.14 and 6.15, employment in these industries is concentrated along Main Street and its western Piedmont outlier, with the only major exception being the concentrations in Buncombe County. It is relevant to note two more specialized con-

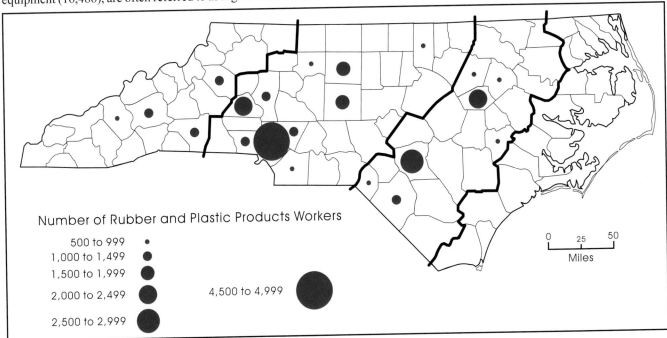

**Figure 6.13:** Rubber and Plastics Industry Employment, 1995.
**Source:** Civilian Labor Force Estimates for North Carolina, 1995.

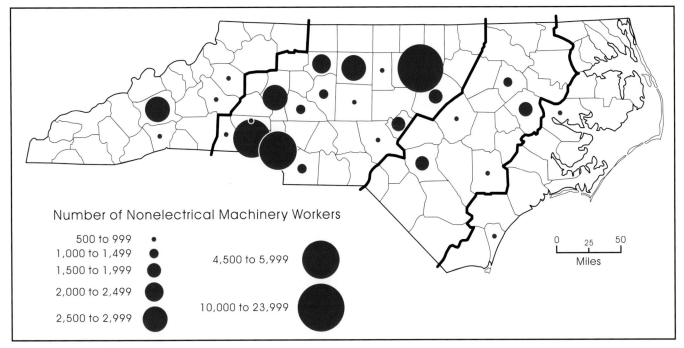

**Figure 6.14:** Nonelectrical Machinery Industry Employment, 1995.
**Source:** Civilian Labor Force Estimates for North Carolina, 1995.

centrations, textile machinery manufacturing in Gaston Country (Figure 6.14), and telecommunications (Siecor and Alcatel) in Catawba County (Figure 6.15). As for the latter, Corning Inc. is the world's leading producer of optical fiber. The fiber is sold to cable makers such as the Siecor Corporation of Hickory, acquired by Corning in a joint venture with the German company, Siemens. Having completed in 1997 a $250 million addition to its Wilmington

facility, making it the world's largest producer of fiber optics, Corning considered this the limit to that plant's capacity, and made plans to build a second North Carolina plant in Midland (Cabarrus County). With a present employment of 300 the Midland plant was completed in 1999, though 700 may be working there when fully operational in 2000. State incentives for Corning to locate in Cabarrus is nearly $19 million, but then about 70

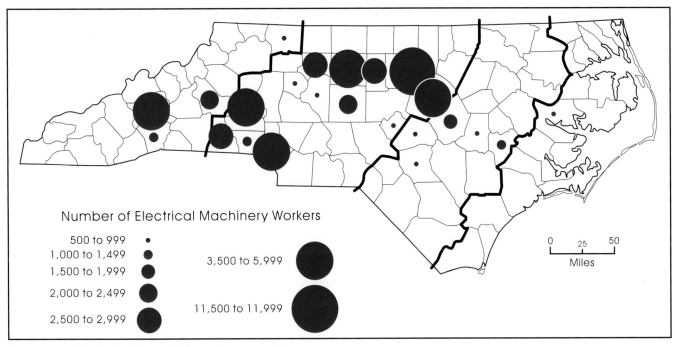

**Figure 6.15:** Electrical Machinery Industry Employment, 1995.
**Source:** Civilian Labor Force Estimates for North Carolina, 1995.

183

percent of the labor force is expected to be locally hired and with salaries several times the minimum wage. (The reader may wish to refer to the discussion of state industrial location incentives in Chapter 9.) In addition to major Hickory plant investments and employment in communications cable by Siecor and Alcatel, Cabarrus County also is seeing major expansion by CommScope, the world's number one producer of coaxial cable. CommScope is establishing its research and engineering operations in its Cable Technology Center in Newton, while expanding production in its Claremont and Catawba communities plants, with an expected 3,000 workers within a few years. There is now talk of the emergence of a fiber optic/coaxial cable manufacturing belt extending from Wilmington, over Winston-Salem and Hickory to Cabarrus County, an industrial entity that in 1999 produced circa 40 percent of the world's fiber optic cable, and an even greater percentage of optical fiber (Boraks 1999).

Much detail on the character and location of the high tech industries is provided in the sections on the Research Triangle, the Piedmont Triad "Greenheart", and the University Park, in Chapter 12. Having over 1,000 firms, with at least 35,000 workers, focusing on computer software, is characteristic of a state becoming known as a leading high tech production center on a global scale.

## SERVICE INDUSTRIES

Most people in North Carolina, like elsewhere in the country, are employed in the tertiary sector, that is, in providing services to other people or to institutions. As discussed in the early section of this chapter, and presented in Table 6.1 this is the explosive sector of the state's economy. And yet, this sector of economic activities is not all that easy to grasp. In fact, as pointed out by Warf and Grimes (1997) in their thorough assessment of service occupations in the Southern economy, service is a particularly slippery term. In this text we use the term tertiary as an all encompassing term for those occupations that are neither extractive (primary), nor manufacturing (secondary). In this broad context "service" workers include data processors, dieticians, ditch diggers, doctors, and druggists. Definitional problems abound. It is difficult to measure output of various services, due to the more intangible character of their product; it is not frequently measurable like ears of corn or tons of steel. Consider the variation in output in media, clerical work, telecommunications, and managerial decision making. Consider the work experiences of people collecting and processing information, money, food, trash, students, patients, travelers, and prisoners. The difficulties encountered in measuring their mostly intangible productivity has caused some problems in the public's perception of their contribution to the economy, and a reluctance among planners and decisionmakers to give proper due to their role in economic development and change.

One way to understand the contribution of tertiary activities, services in their widest sense, is to see them through the lens of their consumers, their market. Educational services, for example, enable their served public to compete in a complex world of incessantly growing expectations of knowledge and specialized skills. Thus, increasingly we understand that the persistent economic growth of the late 20$^{th}$ century is empowered by a "knowledge society", a more specialized and higher form of the "service society" that replaced our "industrial society" at midcentury. In North Carolina recent administrations recognize this critical foundation for economic competitiveness on a global scale, and have made major efforts to improve the educational infrastructure (see Chapter 7). Manufacturing industry now is deriving most of its productivity increases through improvements and innovations in a variety of service sectors. As noted by Wood (1990, 67), "service expertise is as likely to create profits, and initiate economic restructuring, as is manufacturing industry" (see also Hansen 1994, and Johnson 1997).

For many reasons it becomes important to disaggregate the broad tertiary economic activity sector into its most critical components. From the geographic perspective the reasons focus on distributional characteristics, which tend to demonstrate considerable spatial variations in the different service classes. Thus we have university towns, banking cities, cities of medicine, and resort counties. Still, many basic services exist as a function of consumer demand measured in population thresholds. For example, employment in retail services is largely a function of the number of people living within a given distance from where the service is offered. More people mean more retail businesses, which means more workers. Basic retail offering low order and frequently desired goods, like gasoline, food and cigarettes, is found throughout the urban and rural landscape in proportion to population density. Higher order retail, that includes more sophisticated, expensive, and less frequently bought goods, is sold in centers of shopping like central business districts, highway commercial strips, or shopping malls. The larger the population in the service area, the larger, or more frequently appearing, the shopping center.

It is much less predictable where telecommunications will concentrate its workers. When you hear a clear Irish lilt to the voice urging you to consider switching long distance telephone server, it is likely that the voice belongs to a person calling you not from within the state, but rather from one of the world's largest calling center localities, Dublin, Ireland! In North Carolina new calling centers are developing with the expansion of the banking industry, but Bank of American chose to locate 3,000 of its 'call persons' in a business park in High Point, not in Charlotte. Functionally speaking, if you can find the workers, this center could be placed in Hertford County. So it is necessary in a geographic evaluation of land and life to look at tertiary activities in their more specialized character. What follows is a commonly held categorization that includes most conceivable service occupations (modified from Warf and Grimes 1997, 252-253):

1. Finance, Insurance, and Real Estate – commercial and investment banking, security and commodity brokers, insurance carriers and agents, real estate

agents, managers, and land subdividers and developers

2. Business Services – legal services, advertising, engineering and architectural public relations, accounting, computer and data processing, building maintenance and security, research and development, and consulting. Producer service providers like attorneys are also included here

3. Transportation and Communications – trucking, warehousing and shipping, rail roads, airlines, local transportation, travel agents, telephone communications, radio and television, cable services

4. Retail and Wholesale Trade – all goods, durable (e.g., automotive, machinery, hardware, electrical, toys), and non-durable (e.g., groceries, pharmaceuticals, paper, petroleum, flowers), eating places, personal services (e.g., laundry and dry cleaning, beauty and barber shops, photo studio and shoe repair)

5. Entertainment and Leisure – motion picture production and theaters, video tape rental, physical fitness and commercial sports, hotels, bed and breakfast places, amusement and recreation services

6. Public Services – vast majority is governmental, but also includes private employment in health, education, child care, museums

7. Membership Organizations – religious, civic, business, social, labor, and political associations.

For most of these categories, employment and its changes over the last decades of the 20th century may be easily read from Table 6.1. The geographic distribution of the importance of tertiary sector in the economy for the state's 100 counties is displayed in Figure 6.2, and is discussed at the beginning of this chapter. In the following sections most of the individual categories will be considered in the context of their relative employment contribution, measured as a percent of the total non-agricultural wage and salary workers.

### Retail and Wholesale Trade

Workers in trade occupations are more numerous than those in manufacturing industry. In evaluating their distribution through the state (Figure 6.16), two aspects should be borne in mind: 1) two different categories are totaled in these data, retail trade and wholesale trade, each having a distinctive geographic pattern; and 2) percentage distributions reflect proportionality in employment, and not total workers. The objective with a percent distribution is to emphasize the dependency within a county on the particular economic activity.

Wholesale trade is of a much more concentrated nature than is retail trade. Large cities deriving benefits from a key location on the regional and national transportation system may evolve a high emphasis on the redistributive trades, focusing on the warehousing of consumer and specialized industry goods. Charlotte is one of the nation's leading redistribution centers with its favored midway location on intersecting freeways connecting the Midwest and Northeast with rapidly expanding population centers and markets of the southeast in Florida and the Atlanta area. Additional intersecting rail and air connections provide the foundations for a transportation and distribution center. As a result, Mecklenburg County had over 40,000 jobs in close to 2,500 companies involved in wholesale trade in 1996, with a land

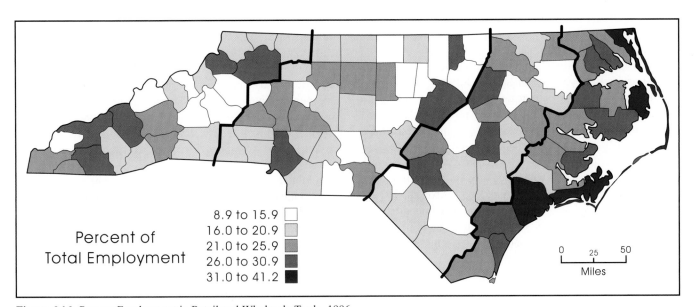

**Figure 6.16:** Percent Employment in Retail and Wholesale Trade, 1996.
**Source:** County Business Patterns, U. S. Bureau of the Census, 1997.

185

**Photo 6.4a & b:** The general store was the center of small communities. Here you could buy most of your daily needs, including food, clothing, fuel, tools, seed and fertilizers; here you could get your mail, and pass the time gossiping over soft drinks and crackers with other locals. As the social and economic center of hamlets and village only a few general stores remain, most in areas of tourism and seasonal vacationers, as in the case of Johnson's Gro. Market and Grill in Saluda, Polk County.

use impact of extensive warehousing sited in business parks at key interstate and local highway intersections, frequently in association with truck parks. This is the nation's sixth's largest distribution center (Anderson 1991). The ratio of wholesale to retail employment for Mecklenburg is 5:7, as compared with Wake County's ratio of 1:3. Similarly, Statesville's location on the more recently completed north-south I-77 at its intersection with east-west I-40 has assured Iredell County a much improved competitive position with regard to locating new wholesale businesses along the booming "Main Street." Having a fortuitous location along key transportation routes, and being able to satisfy the need for wholesale business support for agricultural production, has supported the location of wholesale businesses in smaller counties in the eastern part of the state. Thus counties like Hyde, Jones, Northampton, and Perquimans each have higher wholesale employment percentages than does Mecklenburg.

Although retail trade reflects total population numbers to a remarkable degree, there are local circumstances that inflate its employment. Counties dominated by military installations and large universities tend to have a disproportionate share of retail, especially in eating and drinking places, but also in smaller shops that cater to the needs of these particular populations. Counties dominated by resort and leisure activities similarly have a much greater dependency on retail employment, though it may have a strong seasonal flavor. Parenthetically, it should be noted that employment data published yearly by the U.S. Bureau of the Census through its County Business Patterns reports, is calculated during the month of March of each year. This has some bearing on data for resort counties that do not really gear up for the summer vacation boom until May. Even so, for a state where 20 percent of the employed labor force is in retail trade, it is the Tidewater Region counties of Dare, with 42 percent, Currituck (39%), Pasquotank (37%), Perquimans (37%), Pamlico (33%), Carteret (33%), Gates (32%), Hyde (31%), and Tyrrell (31%), that are the leaders. Compare these data with the mountain resort counties of Watauga (35%), where Appalachian State University aids in providing year-round stability in the retail sector, Macon (31%), Haywood (29%), and Jackson (29%) (Photos 6.4a & b). Although mountain resort counties are not as dominated by retail as are the Tidewater counties, the basic relationship holds quite well, and the implications for local economies are important. These are weakened in some degree by the seasonality factor, but also by the fact that such a large share of local employment opportunities are found in the lowest paid jobs (Photo 6.5).

**Photo 6.5:** J&K Foods of Taylorsville (Alexander County) exemplifies the retail business replacement of the traditional general store. Ubiquitously distributed, the stores emphasize fuel, foods and general needs of the travelling public, and are frequently open 24 hours a day, seven days a week.

For the urbanizing Piedmont, changes in the locational strategies of the retail industry is having important implications for the location of jobs. A few decades ago a major relocation of commercial enterprises from the central business districts (CBD) in the heart of the cities (Photos 6.6 to 6.8) to shopping strips, and eventually to high density concentration in rapidly growing and comparatively wealthy residential suburbs, was the hallmark of urban restructuring. The first edition of this book (Gade, Stillwell, and Rex 1986) discussed the "Malling of North Carolina" as a critical dimension in the urbanizing landscape. Disappearing retail from the CBD's accompanied "white flight" (Chapter 4) and relocating manufacturing jobs to the suburbs and beltways, adding to the pressures on rural land (Photo 6.9). The process had devastating effects on the central city, some of which continue to have recovery difficulties (Photos 6.10 to 6.12 and Chapter 12). The old locational theme of placing retail concentrations with least cost access to large consumer markets is being replayed in new clothing. So-called outlet malls, dominated by chain merchandisers, offering department-store brands at discounted prices, and factory outlet stores have been located along freeways to take advantage not only of regional markets, but of motorists passing by on some of the nation's busiest interstate highways. Similarly located are "power centers." These are dominated by big box (frequently 200,000 square feet of merchandisable space or more) versions of individual category-dominant stores, like Toy's "R" Us, K-Mart, Wal-Mart, Best Buy, Lowe's, Home Depot, Sam's, and Borders. Typical of contemporary retail functions, these warehouse-sized operations reflect the 1990s trend of value retail by clustering very much like fast food places along the shopping strip. Enormous acreage is taken by a collection of these behemoth stores; they also concentrate a significant number of retail employees. The limited space issue for many metro-centered counties along North Carolina's "Main Street", in combination with new location opportunities offered by the expanding highway system, and the continuing urban residential expansion into the rural hinterlands, are now pushing these overblown retail constellation space gobblers into adjacent, more rural counties, where very mixed feelings on the part of local residents await their arrival. This process helps us understand the gradual shift in retail to counties where the resident population will not, at least for the moment, provide the necessary market. Space is a critical issue here. In 1965, retail businesses provided an average of four square feet of shopping space per person in the average county. By the late 1990s, this had increased fivefold to 20 square feet per person!

There has been a real slow down in the state, as for the entire country, in the construction of new general consumer based super regional malls (in excess of one million square feet of gross leasable area (GLA)), anchored by two or more well known department stores. On the other hand, there is now a move toward creating super regional value-oriented megamalls that enhance the shopping experience with thematic décor, restaurants, megaplexes (movie theaters with 15 plus screens), and regularly scheduled community events. Located in southern Cabarrus County on the Mecklenburg line is Concord Mills, a 1.4 million square feet "shoppertainment" complex, as the Mills Corp. prefer to have it called. The megamall favors integration of entertainment with the shopping experience, having found in earlier studies that this combination will keep the average shopper in the mall for an average of two and a half hours, as compared to the average one hour stay per visit to the normal super regional mall (Postman 1999). People may come less frequently to Concord Mills, but will spend more while there.

Retail firms headquartered in North Carolina cities contribute their office employees to the retail sector count. This helps explain the higher concentration in Vance County where Rose's Department Stores has been located for over 80 years. This chain operation has typically operated independently in strip shopping or as an anchor in malls. It has suffered the expected competitive problems of the traditional value focused department store faced with rapidly expanding super stores like K-Mart and Wal-Mart. Rose's reached 18,000 employees in 1993 when the

**Photo 6.6:** The central business district of Forrest City (Rutherford County) is appealing with its broad main avenue lined with a great diversity of shops. A green, well planted median replaced the old two track railroad. Not having a threatening commercial strip or mall in the vicinity aids in explaining the continuing survival of the retailers.

**Photo 6.7:** Mount Airy's CBD is struggling to maintain its traditional small town functionality and ambience in the face of a new mall and nearby commercial strips. Mount Airy is the birth home of actor Andy Griffith and features 'Mayberry's' Snappy Lunch and Floyd's Barbershop on its Main Street.

**Photo 6.8:** Wilmington's CBD is flourishing, as a comprehensive downtown retail and entertainment life is encouraged by the proximity of historic residential districts and its riverfront location. A mixture of vintage architecture, aesthetic street and open space design, and shopping and eating opportunities provided within retrofitted old commercial buildings and wharf warehouses, like the Cotton Exchange, bring in the locals as well as the tourists.

188

**Photo 6.9:** Valley Hills Mall is a regional mall of some 650,000 square feet of gross leasable area. Though not a large mall, it effectively contributed to the retail demise of Hickory's CBD, now taken over largely by government functions and professional services. It is anchored by the two major department stores in the state, J. C. Penney and Belk.

bottom fell out, and a restructuring and refocusing process was initiated. The result was a reduction of 102 stores and 40 percent of its labor force. In Vance County, the organization's headquarters and distribution center, employment was reduced from 1,400 to 900. In 1996, the company sold out to Memphis (TN)-based Fred's Inc. On the other hand, Lowe's Hardware, headquartered in North Wilkesboro in Wilkes County, has been in a perpetual expansion mode during most of the 1990s. Lowe's objective is to reach 600 stores by 2000, while increasing the prototype store to 115,000 square feet, and in the process be an effective competitor to its big box competitor, Home Depot. Food Lion, a grocer and North Carolina's largest private employer, is headquartered in Salisbury in Rowan County (CP 6.19). It has a network of over 1,000 food stores dotting the landscape of 14 southeastern and Mid-Atlantic states. Other notable and locally influential retail company headquarters include Harris Teeter in Matthews (Mecklenburg County); Hardee's Food Systems in Rocky Mount (Nash County), bought out by the Canadian Company Imasco and now threatened by further sale, as well as the relocation of its administration and distribution center; and the recently bankrupted Brendle's in the town of Elkin (Surry County). While Charlotte has continued to benefit from the expansion of the Belk Stores, in Greensboro the Sears Mail Order Catalog Plant, opening in 1947, was closed in 1993 with the loss of 1,100 workers, a victim of changing consumer preferences in retail purchasing.

Crabtree Valley (Raleigh), Four Seasons (Greensboro), Hanes (Winston-Salem), and South Park (Charlotte) are all close-in, large (1.2 million square feet and over GLA), up scale, suburban regional malls that seem to be surviving the onslaught of the new retail strategies. Not so the smaller malls, especially those attached to smaller towns and within easy striking distance of the new value focused retail emporiums. Where a small mall outside of the Wilkesboros sapped the two downtowns of their retail energy in the 1980s, the mall has not survived the subsequent growth of the U.S. 421 "power strip" during the late 1990s. Similarly affected are small malls throughout the state. Domi-nated by the franchise stores whose mall related growth contributed to the demise of the traditional family owned retail enterprises of the former central business districts, they have not been able to compete with the value ladened super stores. The hidden costs of super stores continue to be the hemorrhaging of downtown retail, declining commercial strips and malls, and the further decline of locally grown retail companies, in all cases with serious negative implications for dependent residential communities.

### Finance, Insurance, and Real Estate

Employment in finance, insurance and real estate (FIRE) is by definition quite varied in occupation, as it ranges from workers manning the rapidly expanding calling centers in the finance industry, to brokers and lenders, insurance sales people, and workers hawking land deals and home buys from coast to mountains. In percentage distribution, the counties that depend most on FIRE services include the expected Urban Crescent concentration, but also a selection of resort counties along the coast and in the mountains (Figure 6.17) .One of the most extraordinary economic developments over recent decades has been the emergence of the financial stronghold of North Carolina's Main Street. Since national and regional banking laws began loosening their stranglehold on out-of-state bank acquisitions, North Carolina banks, have been busy foraging regional and national countrysides and buying out financial institutions as if they were on fire sale. Certainly some have turned out to be very expensive purchases. State laws have for a time been permissive in the extension of state-wide branch banking networks. This led to the emergence of a few highly competitive banking powerhouses, NationsBank and First Union headquartered in Charlotte and Wachovia in Winston-Salem. When North Carolina permitted interstate banking in 1981 and none of the three leaders had accumulated as much as $8 billion in assets, the largest, NationsBank, ranked 26th in the country. Lord (1987, 11) noted the conditions of change:

Photo 6.10: Fayetteville has expended large public sums to renovate its decaying CBD. With Market House (1832) as its centerpiece and commercial avenues radiating to the four corners, the physical layout is appealing, but private investment in the many retail options seems largely confined to a few antique stores. CBD redevelopment problems derive from the city's economic dependence on the nearby Fort Bragg army base, with intervening commercial strips and malls serving basic consumer retail needs.

Photo 6.11: Downtown Goldsboro seems to have been hit especially hard by suburbanization processes that has dislocated almost all of its retail functions. Given the historic architecture and soundness of structures, the potential is there for a reinvigorated downtown. At the moment, it is dominated by empty store fronts or by a dozen or more store front churches, paying low rents and no taxes.

Photo 6.12: Downtown Durham is an anachronism. Virtually dead of traditional retail activity, its streets, not impacted by the clearance effects of urban renewal or large corporate investments in commercial skyscrapers, evoke a sense of the more intimate, human scaled, retail shopping environment of the past. Easy walking distance from Duke University and medical centers might influence a more prosperous future.

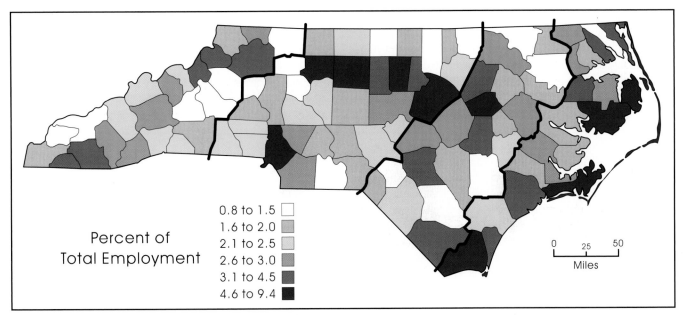

**Figure 6.17:** Percent Employment in Finance, Insurance and Real Estate, 1996.
**Source:** County Business Patterns, U. S. Bureau of the Census, 1997.

The geography of interstate banking acquisitions and the relocation of economic control points (corporate headquarters) have been influenced by the patterns, form, and timing of interstate legislation, by market and financial institution characteristics, and by bank management attitudes. The magnitude of the interstate and interurban relocation of corporate control is best measured in terms of the volume of assets exchanged.

By 1986, banks in the state were leading the country in new acquisitions, but the concentration of holdings were still overwhelmingly in New York City (with assets of $596 billion), San Francisco ($160b), and Los Angeles ($112b). However, among the 15 largest metropolitan areas in 1986, Charlotte had in a matter of two years moved from 14th to 9th place, while Atlanta had progressed to 12th place.

By the late 1990s, the fight was almost over. Metrolina, Queen City, newly crowned "Wall Street" of the South (Newman 1995), far exceeded Atlanta as a center of finance and banking. Branches of the two major banks, NationsBank and First Union covered the country like kudzu, from New Jersey and Pennsylvania south to Florida, and west to Texas and Oklahoma. In 1998, NationsBank merged with BankAmerica in a $60 billion deal, to become the nation's largest bank, with its headquarters in Charlotte, and a new name, Bank of America.

Critical to understanding the emergence of Charlotte as a banking capital is probably not so much the fact that the city was the initial gold rush center of the country, and a resultant early recipient of a regional U. S. Mint. Rather, it was the influence of entrepreneurial bankers who have determinedly carried their world view of the finance industry within a permissive legislative environment to the point where their respective banking organizations now are industry leaders. In 1994, President Clinton signed

| Rank | Bank | 1985 Market Cap | Bank | 1998 (February) Market Cap | Bank | 2000 (December) Total Assets ($ billions) |
|---|---|---|---|---|---|---|
| 1 | Citicorp | 6.4 | NationsBank | 60.5 | Citigroup | 902 |
| 2 | J. P. Morgan | 5.6 | Citicorp | 57.5 | J.P. Morgan Chase | 714 |
| 3 | Chase Manhattan | 2.8 | BankAmerica | 51.6 | Bank of America | 642 |
| 4 | Bankers Trust | 2.5 | Chase Manhattan | 48.8 | Wachovia | 324 |
| 5 | BankAmerica | 2.4 | First Union | 47.1 | Wells Fargo | 272 |
| 6 | First Interstate | 2.3 | Banc One | 38.3 | Bank One | 269 |
| 7 | Chemical Bank | 2.2 | Norwest | 29.8 | | |
| 8 | Sun Trust | 1.9 | Wells Fargo | 28.9 | | |
| 9 | Wachovia | 1.8 | U.S. Bancorp | 27.9 | | |
| 10 | First Union | 1.8 | First Chicago NBD | 23.1 | | |

**Table 6.5:** Top Banking Companies by Market Cap, 1985 and 1998; and Total Assets in 2000.
**Source:** Moore 1998, p. 11: Williams and Veverka 2001.

into law a new interstate banking bill, doing away (by 1997) with the requirement that banks operate separate subsidiaries in each state, under the umbrella of a banking holding company. Table 6.5 shows the shifts from 1985 to 1998 in the size of the leading banks, as defined by the value of their publicly held stock, referred to in the trade as "Market Cap". By this measure the Bank of America 1998 merger at a cost of $60 billion resulted in the creation of the nation's largest bank, which to the great relief and joy of Charlotteans was headquartered in the Queen City. At the turn of the Millennium it appeared that the merger fever had subsided. Banks and their public were gradually adjusting to the closing of branches, to worker layoffs, and to consumer anxieties. But another shock awaited North Carolinians. In early 2001, following a year of stock crashes and fears of a national recession, First Union and Wachovia announced their intended merger. The new bank, taking Wachovia as its name, is to have its national headquarters in Charlotte, with its North Carolina operations run out of existing facilities in Winston-Salem. It is not yet clear just how the merger impact will shake out for North Carolina communities, and for the employees of First Union and the old Wachovia. For the nation's financial giants the ordering again changes (Table 6.5). In total assets, now also including several additional large-scale mergers, six behemoth firms remain; and Charlotte, as the nations second finance city, is stronger than ever.

Community impacts of bank mergers are decidedly mixed. Whereas North Carolina can smell success in the many jobs provided and in gleaming new skylines, especially in Charlotte and Winston-Salem, states where financial institutions are bought are apt to lose considerably, in closed branches and in consolidated or relocated operations. First Union went on a buying spree in 1997-98 with its buy-outs of: the CoreStates Financial Corp. of Philadelphia; a home equity and small business finance company (The Money Store); and a major brokerage and an investment bank, all at a cost of $22.52 billion. With an excess of offices and employees, and with earnings under pressure to the point of serious slippage in the stock market, the hammer fell in March of 1999 with the announced system-wide reduction of seven percent in the work force of 79,000. Proportionately, the largest cuts are affecting operations and branches in Pennsylvania, New Jersey, and Delaware, as well as in Sacramento, California, the major employee base of The Money Store. In Mecklenburg County, First Union employment had doubled from 8,100 in 1995; so a six percent loss here, from 16,615 employees seemed less problematic. Similarly NationsBank, announced the likely cut of 6,000 position in Florida with its purchase of the Barnett Bank of Jacksonville in 1997 (at a cost of $15.5 billion). 8,000 is an early estimate on the job loss count for the NationsBank-BankAmerica merger. But consider that the new Bank of America is emerging into the 21st century with a system wide employment of 180,000! As William Jackson III, a professor of finance at the Kenan Flagler School of Business, has noted: "in terms of banking it simply does not get bigger than this" (Martin 1999, 21).

Charlotte's premier financial institutions have an incredible local employment impact. First Union's University Park campus on the northern outskirts of Charlotte had over 50 percent of the bank's local employment in mid-1999. These 8,000 workers are providing customer service via phone and computer screen; in the parlance of the day, they are providing "calling center" services. Eventually, the new service technology will begin to replace branch bank personnel as consumers shift to their home or office computers for their banking needs. First Union is providing leadership in the industry as they remake their branches on a "future bank" concept. This frees employees to sell mutual funds, make loans, and provide investment services. Traditional tasks of verifying account balances, withdrawing funds, etc. are handled by ATMs and phones, through which all queries are directed to the bank's University Park calling center. The core of the bank's employees are in Charlotte's uptown. Here they join more than 10,000 Bank of America's employees, an equal sized work force in other financial institutions, and over 10,000 employees in insurance carriers, to form the nation's second largest employment concentration in the finance, insurance, and real estate group of service activities. The official census estimate of this labor force was 53,427 for Mecklenburg County in 1996.

North Carolina's midsize banks might not survive the assertiveness of their larger cousins. Even so, they have been busy consolidating and expanding into adjacent states. While NationsBank, First Union, and Wachovia have focused largely on out of state buy-outs, smaller banks tend to the local turf. These consolidations appear to have harmed small communities and helped, once again, Main Street. In 1995, BB&T FinancialCorp. of Wilson and Southern National of Lumberton combined into an 8,000 employee operation with assets of $18.8 billion, the 35th largest bank holding company in the country. The new scale of operation apparently required a new and more imposing headquarters location, so Winston-Salem was selected. In 1997, the new Southern National Corp. bought United Carolina Bancshares Corp. of Whiteville and moved to the lead position in banking within the Carolinas, just surpassing Wachovia. Points to be made from these changes? Continued consolidation favors "Main Street" at the expense of the outlying cities, where banking operations and employment lose out. The ongoing gradual transition to electronic banking is likely to speed up this centralization process.

### Government Employment

Government employment includes federal, state, and local government, and it ranges from occupations in forestry, wildlife management, social welfare services, military bases, public schools and universities, state agencies, and local tax office and sewage plants. All counties have a minimum share of government workers through the ubiquitous local government offices, and where the county population is small the employees of these offices tend to become a fairly large percentage of total employment (Photos 6.13 to 6.15). Note in Figure 6.18 the importance of public employment in some Tidewater Region counties, and in

192

**Photo 6.13:** These three photos demonstrate the range of government political authority through its different levels. Shown here is the pride and joy of the municipal government of Maxton (Robeson County), which in 1997 moved into its historically renovated flat iron building from the latter part of the 19th century.

**Photo 6.14:** Sampson County courthouse in Clinton.

**Photo 6.15:** North Carolina's legislative building in Raleigh.

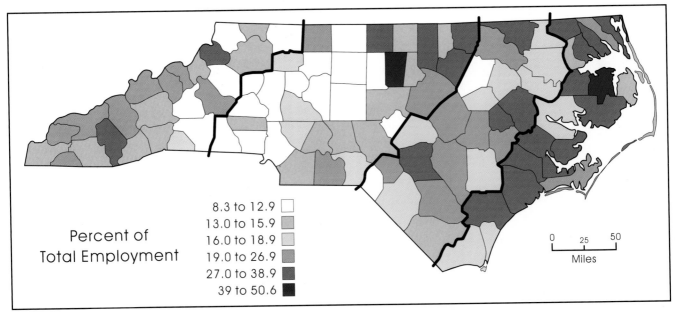

**Figure 6.18:** Percent Employment in Government, 1996.
**Source:** County Business Patterns, U. S. Bureau of the Census, 1997.

the south-central counties of the Mountain Region. Some counties may have large federal institution, like the military bases of Onslow, Cumberland, and Craven counties, while others have state institutions, like universities (Pasqoutank, Pitt, Orange, Watauga, and Jackson counties) or mental health (Burke County). State government and its agencies spill over from Wake County into adjacent counties. Federal and state governments provide services in rural, economically lagging counties, and often will push government employment to an excess of one-third of total wage earners. Although the University of North Carolina at Chapel Hill and its medical and other specialty centers provide the state's highest public payroll in Orange County (46% of total employment), Tyrrell County on the Pamlico Peninsula is second with 43 percent. Other predominantly rural and less wealthy counties with over one-third of employment on a public payroll include Gates, Granville, Greene, Hyde, Perquimans, and Washington. Though public employment in the state increased by 56.8 percent (367,600 to 576,300) from 1977 to 1997, its share of total wage earners actually decreased from 17 to 15.7 percent.

### Other Service Industries

Other services figure prominently in North Carolina's employment shift and growth. The dimensions and regional/local implication of transportation/communications/ utilities (TCU), health, and leisure services receive more detailed treatment in Chapter 7, but we will touch briefly on the distributional characteristics of employment in these service areas. Slightly less than five percent of the state's employed labor force is in TCU, with no remarkable increase for the twenty year comparison period (Table 6.1). Some counties have larger percentages of employment in this category, though for different reasons (Figure 6.19). Mecklenburg County, with one of its major economic emphases on wholesale and distribution, logically has a large number of

truck parks along its intersecting freeways. In 1996, almost 16,000 people worked in trucking and warehousing activities in Mecklenburg County. By comparison, these activities involved less than 6,000 persons in each of the next ranked counties of Wake, Guilford, and Forsyth. Air transportation employment is also a highly localized phenomenon. The existence of a U. S. Airways hub in Mecklenburg County, and its contribution to the 1996 work force of 8,500 in air transportation services (N.C.=17,500), lends further credence to the claim of Charlotte as an emerging national transportation and distribution center. Charlotte also is the headquarters of the nation's largest investor owned electrical utility. Duke Energy serves 1.8 million customers located mostly in the central and western Piedmont Region. A leader in innovative energy resource delivery, the company owns three nuclear power generating plants, eight coal-fired plants, 27 hydro-electric plants, and is moving toward becoming one of the earliest nationally large-scale integrated energy suppliers with the $10 billion purchase in 1997 of Pan Energy of Houston, a major natural gas producer with 37,000 miles of gas pipelines. This added about 5,000 workers to the 17,000 already working for the company in the Carolinas. Duke Energy's forays into other parts of this country, and onto the international scene, are not being copied by its major North Carolina rival, Carolina Power & Light Company of Raleigh, a company that serves 1.2 million customers with about 6,500 workers. Smaller counties look strong in this service sector when they are the home base for major trucking firms (Henderson, Surry), major phone service centers (as located in Person, Jones, and Edgecombe counties), or major power plants, as in the case of Carolina Power & Light Company's Brunswick Nuclear Power Plant.

Health services has been one of the most rapidly expanding employment arenas of the last quarter century; in 1996, 280,000 employees accounted for 9.2 percent of wage earners in the state,

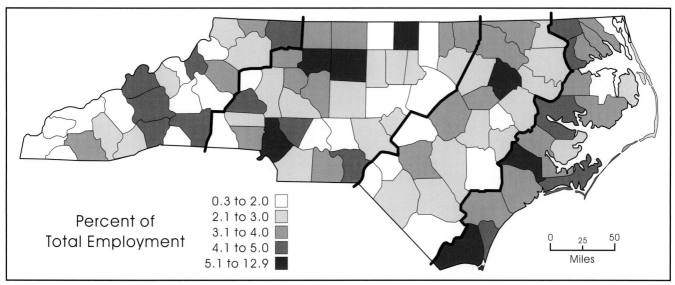

**Figure 6.19:** Percent Employment in Transportation, Communication and Public Utilities, 1996.
**Source:** County Business Patterns, U. S. Bureau of the Census, 1997.

about twice the number of people working in TUC. A break down of this working population reveals a few surprises. Expectedly, hospital employment leads the list, with about 130,000 workers or 46 percent of the total. Medical and dental clinics are next with close to 70,000 workers. The unexpected was the high employment of 72,000 in nursing and personal care facilities and home health care services. Demographics (especially the aging of the population), increased federal and state support (improving access to medical services), and improvements in specialized medical technology and health education are all factors contributing to the rapid expansion of employment in this service sector. These factors aid in understanding the relative importance of health services for the counties (Figure 6.20). In the larger counties, regional hospital complexes tend to drive employment. In Durham County, for example, Duke Hospitals, Durham Regional Hospital,

and the Veterans Hospital contribute 9,000 of the close to 15,000 jobs in the county's health industry. Placed in the overall state employment perspective, this still leaves the county only marginally above the state average in health service employment. Obviously, it is Duke Hospitals' world wide fame rather than a preponderance of health support people that allows Durham to see itself as the "City of Medicine." Hospital employment in the larger cities seems to be merely proportional to the total population. That way, Orange County with a much smaller employment base stands out because of its University of North Carolina Medical Center. Asheville, once called "Sanitarium City" due to its former significance as a treatment center for respiratory illnesses, has grown as a Mountain Region medical mecca, with two major regional hospitals, St. Joseph's and Memorial, in addition to the VA Hospital and Thoms Rehabilitation Hospital. Simi-

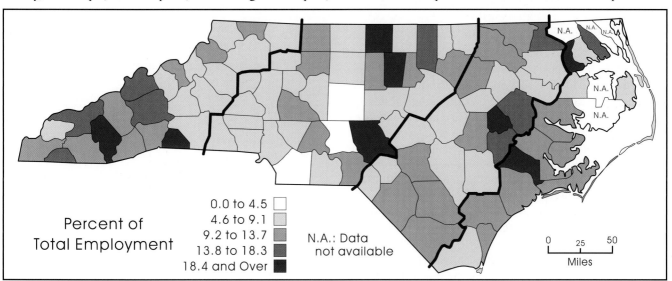

**Figure 6.20:** Percent Employment in Health Services, 1996.
**Source:** County Business Patterns, U. S. Bureau of the Census, 1997.

195

larly, smaller counties, that have regional hospitals with service regions that extend much beyond their county's boundary, will have larger than normal hospital employment. Examples include Moore, Jackson, and Chowan counties.

For North Carolina and its communities there are many implications of the ongoing shift in employment characteristics and the spatial reconcentration of economic activities. Many impacts are glossed over by reference to the reality of economic restructuring in the face of national and global competition for markets. But for individual communities impacted by these changes the reality is sometimes stark and uninviting with recurring loss of jobs, and ultimately loss of identity. The movement of labor out of the primary economic activities is now complemented by worker reductions in secondary activities, while employment in the tertiary sector is booming. Rural areas tend to lose out in this process, especially those farther removed from Main Street. Those in closer proximity and impacted by the suburbanization of economic activity may gain job opportunities, but lose their treasured open space, while central cities dwellers are now spatially disenfranchised from jobs that have relocated to the urban periphery. The central issue for the state and its decision makers is: will the manufacturing shift toward more capital intensive, higher skill demanding, and better paying, industries, complemented by the inexorably increasing dominance of service industries, improve employment opportunities and quality of life conditions for all parts of the state; will, indeed, a rising sea lift all boats, or are some too firmly anchored to the bottom? Peripheral and lagging regions and communities seem increasingly distant in the prospects for economic development and in their hope for the future, in part because of the full employment and booming times that are experienced so obviously in most of our counties.

## GLOBALIZING THE ECONOMY

### From Agricultural Surplus to Metropolitan Incubators

As discussed in Chapter 5, beyond North Carolina the state has long been known for its agricultural products. In some degree this is still the case with animal products having replaced cotton and tobacco as leading in production values (Tables 5.3 and 5.4), though tobacco continues to figure prominently in export trade. The economic shifts discussed in this chapter highlight the arrival of electronics, truck and automotive parts manufacturing, pharmaceuticals, and many other specialized products. These have arrived in the state due in part to its increasingly enhanced status as a major player in globalizing markets, as a recipient of direct foreign investment and of in-migrating skilled and unskilled labor. Other homegrown industries of major national and international importance include the giants of finance, such as Bank of America and Wachovia Bank (in its new First Union clothing), medicine (Duke University Hospitals), and consumer energy (Duke Energy).

*Exports*

One common measure of a state and region's developing integration into the world economy, the globalization process, is the record of how much of the goods and services produced locally are sold to overseas markets. In 1988, the value of North Carolina's exports was $5.4 billion, or 2.27 percent of total U.S. exports. In 2000, exports had more than tripled in value to over $19 billion, or about 2.8 percent of the U.S. total. In the meantime North Carolina moved from a 14th to a 10th position among states in the country. As indicated in Table 6.6 computers and other electronics are the leaders followed by chemicals (mostly pharmaceuticals) and industrial machinery. Leading positions, while a previous export leader, tobacco, has been steadily falling during the past decade. Textiles and apparel are on the rebound from the 1998 downturn resulting from the Asian financial disaster. In the aggregate agricultural products are on a serious downslide in recent years.

North Carolina's international trade partners are mapped by their relative importance in Figure 6.21, information that is complemented in Table 6.7. The two North America Free Trade Agreement partners of Canada and Mexico are both showing substantial recent increases in the receipt of North Carolina exports. Combined they accounted for 38.2 percent in 2000. Otherwise the major world regions come close to equally sharing the remainder of the state's exports. The 15 member nations of the European Union share 22 percent, as do the counties of Latin America (not including Mexico). Asian countries, which share about 20 percent, are still playing catch up with Hong Kong and the Peoples Republic of China increasing quite well. Japan, which for long was state export's second most important destination, has been sliding downward steeply for the past few years.

| Exporting Industry | Dollars (millions) | | Percent Change |
|---|---|---|---|
| | 2000 | 1998 | |
| Computers and Electronics | 3,468 | 2,925 | 18.6 |
| Chemicals (Ind. Pharmaciuticals) | 2,387 | 2,120 | 12.6 |
| Machinery | 1,778 | 1,568 | 13.4 |
| Textiles | 1,363 | 1,038 | 31.3 |
| Apparel | 1,278 | 1,125 | 13.6 |
| Primary Metals | 1,208 | 597 | 102.3 |
| Transportation Equipment | 1,114 | 1,075 | 1.7 |
| Tobacco and Beverages | 824 | 1,171 | -21.1 |
| Crops and Food Products | 805 | 1,124 | -28.4 |
| Plastics and Rubber | 804 | 520 | 54.6 |
| Paper | 698 | 575 | 21.4 |
| Electrical Equipment | 578 | 492 | 17.5 |
| Fabricated Metals | 483 | 468 | 3.2 |
| Miscellaneous Manufactured | 406 | 373 | 8.8 |
| Other | 1,825 | 2,044 | -10.7 |
| **Totals** | **19,119** | **17,215** | **11.1** |

**Table 6.6:** Leading Export Commodities, 1999 and 2000.
**Source:** Wachovia World Trade Index.

| Country | Dollars (millions) | Percent Change from 1998 |
|---|---|---|
| Canada | 5177 | 19.3 |
| Mexico | 2133 | 63.1 |
| Japan | 1611 | -3.6 |
| United Kingdom | 1244 | 27.7 |
| Germany | 797 | -1.4 |
| Korea | 513 | NA |
| Netherlands | 464 | -4.3 |
| France | 449 | 11.1 |
| Hong Kong | 406 | 24.9 |
| Belgium | 390 | -50.1 |
| China | 376 | 16.7 |
| Honduras | 319 | NA |
| Costa Rica | 316 | NA |
| Brazil | 305 | 4.4 |
| Taiwan | 296 | 4.2 |
| Others | 4323 | NA |
| **Total** | **19119** | **11.1** |

**Table 6.7:** North Carolina Leading Export Destinations, 2000.
**Source:** Wachovia World Trade Index.

*Foreign Direct Investment*

A leading measure of globalization of the state's economy is the degree to which businesses of other countries invest in economic development. Comprehensive and complete foreign direct investment (FDI) data has been available since 1987, so it is possible to provide here a 13 year record. Lowest years of FDI, i.e., between $630 and $700 million were 1987, and the recession years of 1991 and 1992. Highest FDI, in excess of $1 billion per year was achieved in 1990, 1997, and 1999. Total FDI in the state for the period amounted to $11.4 billion. The N.C. Department of Commerce estimates that the investment created over 5,000 jobs per year, on the average, which translates into about $175,000 invested per job created. Companies from Japan, Germany, and the United Kingdom are the leaders in seeing the promise of making money in North Carolina, from each country has flowed in excess of $2 billion in investment capital over the 13 year period. Investing between $100 million and $1 billion have been Canada, Denmark, France, the Netherlands, Sweden and Switzerland (Figure 6.22). In 1999 the N.C. Department of Commerce

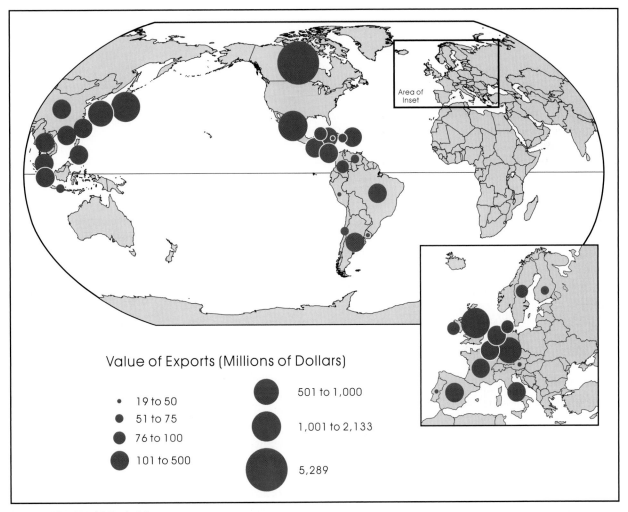

**Figure 6.21:** World Trade Map.
**Source:** Wachovia World Trade Index.

197

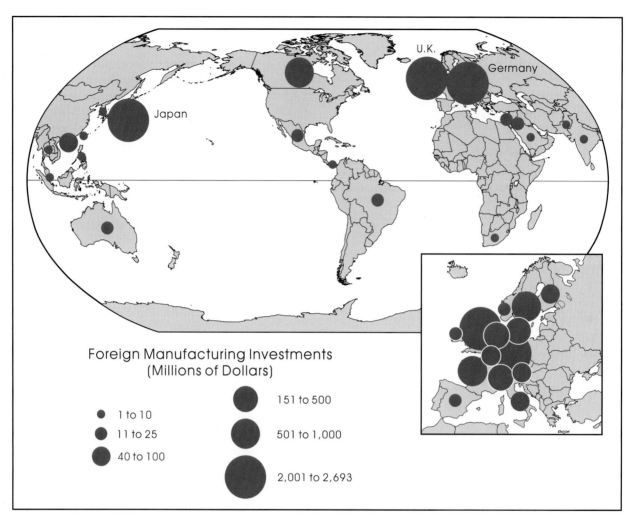

**Foreign Manufacturing Investments**
**(Millions of Dollars)**

- 1 to 10
- 11 to 25
- 40 to 100
- 151 to 500
- 501 to 1,000
- 2,001 to 2,693

**Figure 6.22:** Source Countries of Foreign Direct Investment, 1987-1999.
**Source:** N. C. Department of Commerce.

provided a listing of 792 foreign forms and subsidiaries in the state. By country their distribution is not very different from the amount of FDI invested. Japan, Germany and the United Kingdom are the clear leaders with 162, 159, and 146 firms, respectively. Down the ladder comes Canada with 64, Switzerland with 60, followed by France (38 firms), and the Netherlands and Sweden, both with 26 firms. Companies from 32 countries are represented. Where these foreign owned firms are located is another matter, certainly they are not spread evenly across the state. It is predominantly the leading metro areas and lesser places along Main Street that show the impact of new plants or the expansion of existing foreign owned facilities (Figure 6.23). Especially favored in the location of foreign owned firms and subsidiaries is Mecklenburg County with over one third of the total in 1998, making this county a very special case in the country, let alone the state. Charlotte is emerging as a center of foreign firms whose locational interest in the U. S. is to be close to others sharing a similar business culture. For North Carolina, Charlotte also benefits by having more direct air linkages to foreign locales, especially Europe with several daily direct flights to London, Paris,

and Frankfurt. This makes the city the primary Gateway for the estimated annual 700,000 foreign visitors to the state.

From the state traditional manufacturing industries, especially textiles and apparel, are relocating much of their productive capacity to places outside the country, where some of the factors of production, especially labor costs, are seen as more competitive for their particular markets and profit margins, as detailed earlier in this chapter. Even manufacturers who appeared to be relatively invulnerable to the attractions of overseas labor markets are now responding. In February, 2001, Universal Furniture announced it was relocating its production facilities from Marion, McDowell County, to the People's Republic of China; and Furniture Brands, the St Louis-based proprietor of Thomasville Furniture, Broyhill Furniture and Hickory Chair, announced that in the future it will build no more U.S. factories, rather any increased market will be met by buying and rebranding furniture from overseas manufacturers (Hempel and Cannon 2001).

The critical difference between the outflow and inflow of FDI is the impact on the North Carolina job market. Low wage industries are leaving and relatively higher skill demanded and wage paying industries are moving in or are expanding. For a state in the process of divesting itself of labor intensive, low wage industries this is a very positive direction.

Some of the 1990s economic restructuring influences on North Carolina productive efforts were spurious or difficult to gauge, as exemplified by R. J. Reynolds' Tobacco world headquarters games (e.g, Winston-Salem to Atlanta to Switzerland). The recent consolidation of large pharmaceutical companies, like Glaxo-SmithKline, may cause similar uncertainty. Some international incidents are having at least a limited impact on the state's economy, as shown by the temporary boost in poultry exports to Eastern Europe with the breakup of the Soviet Empire, and a similar boost in shipment of white meats to European countries following the mad-cow disease scare of the mid-1990s. Then there is the foot and mouth disease plaguing many European countries at the beginning of the 21$^{st}$ century, which North Carolina is able to take advantage by moving into the vacuum left by the European traditional control of the world pork market. Exotic meats are being impacted, as well. While the popularity of Ostrich and Emu farms dwindled rapidly in the mid-1990s when farmers found that they had to be able to sell the meat to the American market to survive in the business, now a foreign market is ready to accept much more than can be produced by the remaining farmers. Membership in the N. C. Ostrich Breeders Association had 200 or so members in 1996; this had fallen to 20 in 2001 (Choe 2001). What is true for all state ties to matters international, they are incredibly vulnerable in times of world recession and instability, as exemplified by the decline of North Carolina exports in 1998 with

a crashed Russian rubble and an economic disaster in Asia. After a recovery in 2000, problems were again in the offing with the recession and international terrorism of late 2001.

On the more positive side, and of lasting impact for the foreseeable future: the Metro areas in the state are now among the leading commercial and technological incubators in the nation, with influences that reach the world over. Much of this is shown in yet another index of state outreach, business and vacation travel (Figure 6.24). The outcome of these different measures is powerful evidence of a state critically tied to global conditions of markets (including financial), investments, and the mobility of people, goods, and services.

## SUMMARY

For North Carolina and its communities there are many implications of the ongoing shift in employment characteristics and the spatial reconcentration of economic activities. Many impacts are glossed over by reference to the reality of economic restructuring in the face of national and global competition for markets. But for individual communities impacted by these changes the reality is sometimes stark and uninviting with recurring loss of jobs, and ultimately loss of identity. The movement of labor out of the primary economic activities is now complemented by worker reductions in secondary activities, while employment in the tertiary sector is booming. Rural areas tend to lose out in this process, especially those farther removed from Main Street. Those in closer proximity and impacted by the

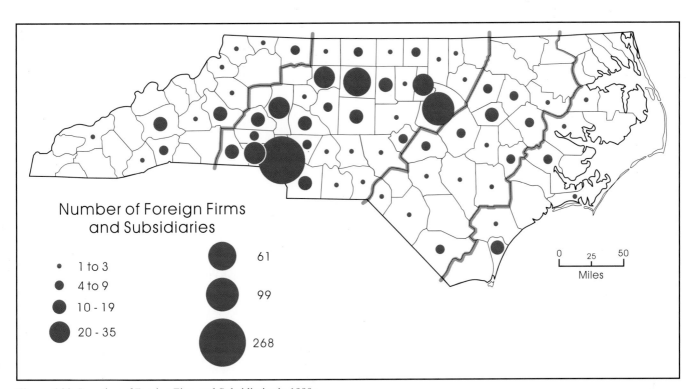

**Figure 6.23:** Location of Foreign Firm and Subsidiaries in 1999.
**Source:** 1999 North Carolina International Firms Directory.

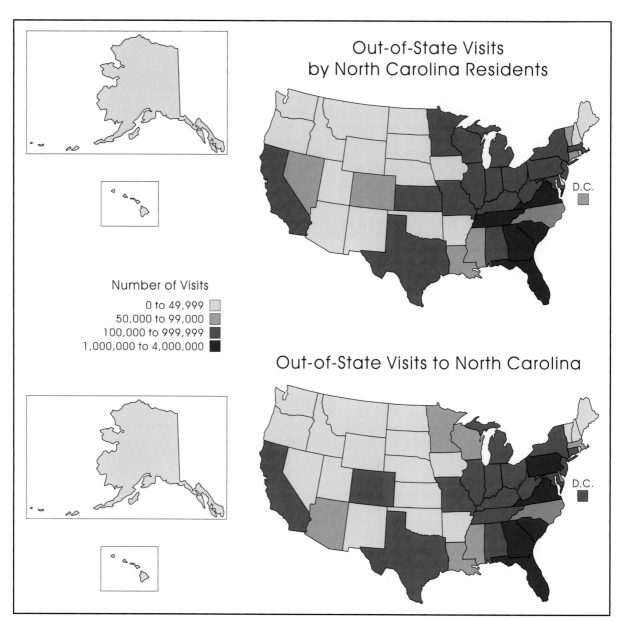

**Figure 6.24:** Business and Vacation Travel, 2000.
**Source:** N. C. Department of Commerce, Division of Tourism.

suburbanization of economic activity may gain job opportunities, but lose their treasured open space, while central cities dwellers are now spatially disenfranchised from jobs that have relocated to the urban periphery. The central issue for the state and its decision makers is: will the manufacturing shift toward more capital intensive, higher skill demanding, and better paying, industries, complemented by the inexorably increasing dominance of service industries, improve employment opportunities and quality of life conditions for all parts of the state; will, indeed, a rising sea lift all boats, or are some too firmly anchored to the bottom? Peripheral and lagging regions and communities seem increasingly distant in the prospects for economic development and in their hope for the future, in part because of the full employment and booming times that were experienced so obviously in most of our counties during the 1990s. In fact, it is even less likely that the fortunes of marginal areas will improve with the recession initiated during the early part of the new millennium.

Notes
(1)    This chapter includes materials from Gade (1996), by permission of the Association of American Geographers.

# Social Capital: Earning Power, Health, Education, and Civic Justice

## INTRODUCTION

Three fundamental attributes contribute to the composite of a state's human geography: demography, economy, and social capacity. Infinitely intertwined these three provide the foundation for growth and change. To this point, we have found diversity and multiculturalism to be critical in understanding North Carolina's changing population, while increasing diversification in production and services appears to be the key element in securing a more promising economic future. We now turn our attention to the complexity of elements that characterize and govern our social condition. These elements include individual and community aspirations for access to appropriate and facilitating systems of employment, education, health, housing, transportation, leisure environments, and public safety. These social elements reflect our personal behaviors such as: individual and family economic independence, aspirations for ownership of property, participation in cultural and leisure time activities, voting and political affiliation, civic engagement, and labor union membership. Also they reflect our tendencies for having health problems as well as our proclivity toward criminal activity. Social characteristics, norms of behavior, and popular aspirations find expression in a community will that has provided systems of public education, health, welfare, and civic justice. We refer to the aggregate of these elements as the state's social capital. In this way we may compare social capital with economic capital, such as the prevailing nature and productivity of economic activities, business investment and market forces shaping economic development, and government intercession in the location of business activity and growth. Conditions of economic capital are covered in chapters 5 and 6, with aspects of state involvement in business location and economic growth dealt with in Chapter 9.

We deal in this chapter with the realities of income differentials, public education, political parties, changing social welfare patterns, caring for the ill, the infirm and the elderly, providing public parks, and incarcerating the mentally impaired and the criminals. In a nutshell, we will identify the basic needs of North Carolinians, and establish how the private and public sectors are responding to these needs and beyond. Most especially, we are concerned about defining base lines in the quality of these responses. From the particular perspective of geography, the reader may come to better appreciate that critical differences existing in the distribution of various elements of social capital across the state. In most instances these differences are amplified along the urban-rural continuum, within metropolitan spaces, and among the state's geographic regions. This chapter's many maps, charts and tables, displaying indices of social capital, may be evaluated in greater detail by further reference to individual state geographic region evaluations and the county data tables presented by state geographic region in chapters 10 through 13.

## EMPLOYMENT AND ECONOMIC WELFARE

### Income Moves Toward the National Average and Divergence

At mid-20th century, North Carolina was in the backwash of national economic development, its people responding by massively fleeing the state for livelihoods elsewhere (Chapter 4). In 1950, a family of four in the state attained, on the average, an income amounting to about 45 percent of that of the average for the nation. Though this improved strikingly during the subsequent two decades with a major reversal of the migration stream back to the state, salaries and incomes were still far below national averages in 1970. In response to persistent comparatively gloomy economic conditions, the North Carolina Council on State Goals and Policy, in its 1973 Second Annual Report, articulated the central goal for economic development:

1) The goal for economic development for the State shall be to establish and maintain a position of leadership in the Southeast in per capita personal income, and, in so doing, to continue to close the gap in per capita personal income which exists between North Carolina and the Nation;

2) In accomplishing this goal, it will be the policy of the State that all parts of the State be given the opportunity to share equitably in the economic development which must take place;

3) The economic development required to attain the per capita personal income is to take place with no detrimental effect upon the environment of the State, with equal opportunity for all citizens, and with improvement rather than detriment in the quality of life available in North Carolina.

Many of the measures subsequently taken by the state to implement the overall goal of economic development are considered in detail in Chapter 9. We note there how initially federalism provided an impetus for an approach to enhance economic development equitably across the state, and then how federal revenue sharing's subsequent demise brought into being a larger role played by market forces, organized regionally. Here our concern is with characterizing the actual status of the economic condition of our population and its direction of change over the past three decades.

North Carolina's per capita income of $3,259 in 1970 was 79.9 percent of the national average ($4,077), ranking it 38th among the 50 states (CP 6.2). As elaborated in chapters 5 and 6 the most important reason for this low status was the state's extraordinary dependence on low skill, low wage, and labor intensive manufacturing industries. At that point in time, employment in manufacturing industry numbered 733,000 workers, or 33.6 percent of total employment (CP 5.1). Production workers were paid wages that on the average ranked 49th in the nation. This disparity found itself exacerbated within the state, as shown on Figure 7.1. The lowest average income county of $1,668 was just 40.6 percent of the average income of $4,144 in the highest county. Counties are mapped by their quintile ranking. Patterns of income inequality is pretty much as expected, with the bottom ranked counties generally found on the periphery of the state, especially in the Mountain and Coastal Plain regions. The Piedmont had entered its boom period by 1970, with people flocking in to take advantage of a new wealth in job opportunities and

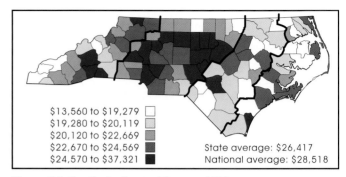

**Figure 7.2:** Per Capita Personal Income, 1999.
**Source:** U.S. Bureau of Economic Analysis, June, 2001..

diversity, but note that the highest income county still but barely exceeded the national average (Gade 1989).

By 1999, the state had gained considerably with its per capita income at 92.6 percent of the national average. In addition, it is noteworthy that the state's lowest ranked county was at 47.5 percent of the national average, as compared to 41 percent three decades earlier (see CP 6.2 and related discussion in Chapter 6). However, within the state, the condition of geographic inequality by county had worsened. The Piedmont counties so outgained the remainder of the state that the lowest per capita income county ($13,560) was only 36 percent of the highest ($37,321). With the highest county now exceeding the national average by 30.9 percent there is apt evidence of the increasing gap between the most and the least wealthy counties. Clearly these differences are evident as rural-urban contrasts, with Main Street counties appearing increasingly distinguishable as units in a regionally defined bastion of high income. As seen in Figure 7.2 this nucleation of high income in the state is complemented by islands of high income primarily associated with leisure resorts, second home development, and tourism in the Mountain and Tidewater regions. Yet changes over the three decade period are more subtle than a comparison of the extreme conditions suggests. Note particularly the narrowing of the per capita income differentials among counties occupying the middle three classes in Figures 7.1 and 7.2, the middle 60 per cent in income counties. In this group, the difference between the highest and the lowest county amounted to 47.1 per cent in 1970 but only 27.4 percent in 1999, a strong tightening of incomes at the mid-level. Note also that this occurred while the wealthiest county increased its position over the poorest from 148.4 percent in 1970 to 175.2 in 1999.

What we have here is simply evidence of North Carolina catching up not only to the national income average, but also, less positively, to national norms in income divergence. A 1996 U. S. Bureau of the Census report, "A Brief Look at Postwar U. S. Income Inequality", assessed household income distributions from 1968 to 1994. It determined that within each of the five economic indicators of household income there occurred a pronounced increase in the gap between the incomes of the well-to-do and those of the poor and lower middle income households (Holmes 1996). Over these nearly three decades, the average income for the top 20 percent of the households increased from

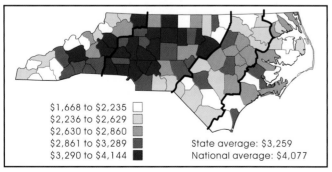

**Figure 7.1:** Per Capita Personal Income, 1970.
**Source:** U.S. Bureau of the Census.

$73,754 to $105,945, an increase of 44 percent after inflation adjustment. Meanwhile, the bottom 20 percent of income households experienced a constant dollars increase of only seven percent, from $7,202 to $7,762. A few years later, the Federal Reserve Board released a family wealth study based on 1995-1998 data that suggested a further amplification of the economic well-being gap. While the Fed report indicated that the average American's net worth increased from $60,900 to $71,600 during these boom years, it also noted that not all households did equally well. Families earning less than $10,000 actually saw their net worth decline by 25 percent to $3,600, while families earning between $10,000 and $25,000 saw a 20 percent decrease in their net worth. At the other end of earnings continuum, families earning over $100,000 experienced an explosion in their average net worth over the three year period from $1.41 million to $1.75 million, a gain of 22.5 percent. North Carolina ranked 17th in the nation in income inequality in 1998 according to the Center for Budget and Policy Priorities, a Washington DC think tank (Waggoner, 2000).

Evidence of the wealth gap is readily observable in the North Carolina cultural landscape. Note, for example, the dramatic differences in the landscapes of poverty and wealth exemplified in Color Plates 7.1 and 7.3. However, differences in per capita income are not defined exclusively by urban-rural contrasts. Extraordinary wealth differences exists within cities and metropolitan areas, as well. Note, for example, the visible evidence provided by photographed scenes in the regional chapters (for example CP 11.8 and CP 12.29), and by their accompanying discussion.

### The New Economy and a Living Wage

The general improvement in per capita incomes have been fuelled by a raise in wages fed more by the restructuring and shifts in economic activities than by an elevation of the minimum wage, although the frequent attainment of full employment has helped push upward the lowest wages in areas of labor shortages. We dealt with the recent patterns of economic restructuring and shifts in the importance of different employment types in previous chapters. Complementary to this analysis is Bill Finger's "Making the Transition to a Mixed Economy" (1996). Finger points to the three major economic shifts in North Carolina that in our estimation have improved wage levels, but also have compounded the problem of the income gap:

1) a shift within the manufacturing sector from labor intensive to capital intensive industries–from mill hands to machine operators;

2) a shift from the manufacturing sector to trade, service, and government jobs–from blue collar to white collar jobs; and

3) a shift within the agricultural sector from small farms relying intensively on tobacco income to larger farms diversifying into many commodities–including crops but also

livestock, dairy, and poultry–often run by corporations or under contract.

Our interest here is to show that not only have rising wages impacted Main Street counties, but also that urban-rural, center-periphery locations contribute their own influences to differentiating wages across the state, making more pronounced the disparity between the haves and the have-nots. Consider first the general shifts in the three main economic activities, as identified on CP 6.2: primary, secondary , and tertiary. Note then, in Table 7.1 and 7.2, how employment and wages play out for primary industries (agriculture, fishing and forestry, Standard Industrial Classification (SIC) codes 1-13), secondary industries (manufacturing, SIC codes 14-39), and for tertiary industries (service producing, SIC codes 41-99). Several observations are warranted. In evaluating both manufacturing and service industries the variations in employment totals for individual types are striking, as are wage differences. It is far from given that moving away from a greater share of employment in low wage manufacturing has lead to higher average wages. Not only are service wages not especially higher, they have a much greater divergence by SIC code than does manufacturing. The reader may wish to compare the employment leaders in manufacturing and service industries in terms of their average weekly wage. For example, wages for workers in eating and drinking places are less than one half of those in the lowest wage manufacturing industry. Workers in many types of retail and some types of business and government service (i.e. janitorial and secretarial) fare little better. Though it is true that the industries paying the lowest wages, (apparel and textiles) are also seeing major job losses, it is the service industries paying far lower wages that are expanding the fastest.

Figure 7.3 shows how average annual wages were distributed by county in 1999. Clearly influencing this distribution of higher wages in the Main Street counties are its concentration of the higher wage industries (see industry location maps in chapters 5 and 6). Average wages on the Pamlico Peninsula are dependent to a great degree on agriculture and other primary industries, as opposed to the concentration of high paying electronic and knowledge industries in the Piedmont Triad.

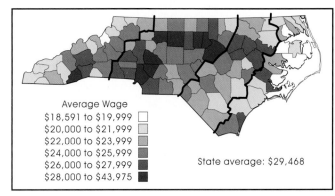

**Figure 7.3:** Average Annual Wage for Salaried Workers, 1999.
**Source:** Civilian Labor Force Estimates, Employment Security Commission of North Carolina, 2001.

203

| SIC Codes 1-39 | Industry | Number of Employers | Employment | Average Weekly Wage |
|---|---|---|---|---|
| 1 | Agricultural Production-crops | 1,233 | 15,384 | 293.57 |
| 2 | Agricultural Production-livestock | 608 | 11,040 | 481.7 |
| 7 | Agricultural Services | 4,030 | 30,424 | 390.52 |
| 8 | Forestry | 208 | 1,141 | 491.45 |
| 9 | Fishing, Hunting, And Trapping | 22 | 162 | 285.48 |
| 10 | Metal Mining | 1 | 1 | 538 |
| 12 | Coal Mining | 1 | 1 | 1,865.00 |
| 13 | Oil And Gas Extraction | 19 | 83 | 555.06 |
| 14 | Nonmetallic Minerals, Except Fuels | 181 | 3,849 | 835.72 |
| 15 | General Building Contractors | 9,439 | 58,270 | 624.8 |
| 16 | Heavy Construction, Ex. Building | 1,788 | 34,315 | 604.53 |
| 17 | Special Trade Contractors | 17,331 | 143,018 | 544.82 |
| 20 | Food And Kindred Products | 504 | 53,742 | 538.06 |
| 21 | Tobacco Products | 32 | 14,100 | 1,076.90 |
| 22 | Textile Mill Products | 1,200 | 142,673 | 519.51 |
| 23 | Apparel And Other Textile Products | 626 | 35,403 | 413.07 |
| 24 | Lumber And Wood Products, Except Furniture | 1,862 | 41,210 | 492.85 |
| 25 | Furniture And Fixtures | 778 | 75,849 | 484.06 |
| 26 | Paper And Allied Products | 273 | 23,998 | 792.47 |
| 27 | Printing And Publishing | 1,559 | 34,347 | 613.49 |
| 28 | Chemicals And Allied Products | 457 | 48,865 | 1,063.07 |
| 29 | Petroleum And Coal Products | 34 | 1,125 | 687.69 |
| 30 | Rubber And Misc. Plastics Products | 505 | 41,624 | 658.95 |
| 31 | Leather And Leather Products | 52 | 2,425 | 474.43 |
| 32 | Stone, Clay, And Glass Products | 622 | 21,945 | 680.04 |
| 33 | Primary Metal Industries | 170 | 18,966 | 755.79 |
| 34 | Fabricated Metal Products | 882 | 37,510 | 641.83 |
| 35 | Industrial Machinery And Equipment | 1,628 | 68,343 | 933.45 |
| 36 | Electronic & Other Electric Equipment | 484 | 60,622 | 926.38 |
| 37 | Transportation Equipment | 362 | 36,290 | 743.54 |
| 38 | Instruments And Related Products | 272 | 15,784 | 1,520.84 |
| 39 | Miscellaneous Manufacturing Industries | 413 | 8,451 | 529.53 |

**Table 7.1:** Employers, Employees, and Weekly Wages in Goods Producing Industries, 2000.
**Source:** N. C. Employment Security Commission.

However, to account for the extremes in wages across the state, and show how rural areas appear to suffer discriminately, we must look at examples of wage differentials within the same industry type (Figures 7.4 and 7.5). One of the most rapidly expanding service industries, most labor intensive, and lowest wage paying, is SIC 58, Eating and Drinking Places (restaurants, fast food places, ice cream and soft drink parlors, and sports bars, among others). While the average annual wage in this employment type is $11,087, there is an extraordinary variation in salaries from one county to another for essentially the same work. Wait staff and bar tenders receive only half the wages for the same work in 14 counties as those who work in the highest pay county. While it might be argued that these jobs are frequently entry level, or not requiring particular skills and experience, and therefore lowly paid, this does not answer the question of the extraordinary spatial differences. Such differences also hold for the normally more stable jobs to be had in the food service industry, where the average annual wage is $29,468 (Figure 7.5). Here there are butchers, bakers, green grocers, cashiers, aisle checkers, and an assortment of other specialists who, in lower pay counties, receive on the average wages that are also close to fifty percent of those working the same jobs in the highest pay county. One answer to this question of disparity is found in cost of living variations, but likely more relevant is the keener competition for an urban work force in scant supply and with a greater diversity of employment options and opportunities. What is obvious though is the resulting urban-rural differentiation in wages that has the effect of dissipating gradually from highs achieved in the

**Color Plate 6.6:** Company store and post office of the Saxapahaw mill village (Alamance County), on the Haw River 15 miles upstream from Bynum. The cotton goods mill was sold by Sellers Manufacturing Company in 1978; the 33 company houses also were divested. Dixie Yarns bought the property and closed the mill in 1994.

**Color Plate 6.7:**
Saxapahaw housing and some land was sold to the Jordan family, which is experiencing little difficulty in developing the village and adjacent areas due to the nearness of Chapel Hill.

**C.P. 6.8a:** Landis village center.

**C.P. 6.8b:** Co-author Jim Young is assessing the former mill housing landscape.

**Color Plate 6.8:** The classic case of a still operating large textile mill, its company housing, and small town center focusing on the rail station and post office, at Landis in southern Rowan County. As an example of restructuring in the yarn business, the mill in 6.8a is one of three Landis yarn operations sold to Parkdale Mills (Gaston) in 1996.

**C.P. 6.9a:** A lake in the heart of the mill town.

**C.P. 6.9b:** Fieldcrest Cannon corporate headquarters, now being threatened with closing due to the recent purchase of the business by Pillowtex, which prefers to keep a new combined head office in Texas.

**C.P. 6.9c:** A Williamsburg (Virginia) style village center and its specialty stores has enhanced the draw on bus tourism.

**Color Plate 6.9:** Kannapolis (Cabarrus County) mill town scenes.

*Photo by Ole Gade.*

**C.P. 6.10a:** At the height of the nine-day long biannual International Home Furnishings Market, High Point's downtown is thronged with 70,000 makers, sellers, and buyers of furniture and its accessories. Participants are hurrying from showroom to showroom.

**C.P. 6.10b:** This showroom, one of over 1,000 distributed over seven million square feet of display space, is demonstrating rattan based pieces from the Philippines.

*Photo by Ole Gade.*

*Photo by Ole Gade.*

**C.P. 6.10c:** Preceding and following the biannual furniture market, the streets of High Point reflect the feverish activity relating to stocking and clearing out display spaces.

**Color Plate 6.10:** High Point (Guilford County) scenes from the International Home Furnishings Market.

208

**Color Plate 6.11:** Thomasville is an important cog in the Central Furniture District. Its "Chair" is the symbol of a town where the Thomasville Chair Company early established its major plants.

*Photo by Ole Gade.*

*Photo by Ole Gade.*

**Color Plate 6.12:** American Tobacco abandoned large acreage of tobacco plants over the past several decades. Some of these have been retrofitted, as is the case with Brightleaf Square, a downtown Durham shopping/office center.

*Photo by Ole Gade.*

**Color Plate 6.13:** Downtown Winston-Salem was even more devastated by the loss of the tobacco manufacturing plants. Some of the closed century-old factory buildings are now being modernized and retrofitted to suit other businesses or they are being replaced. The light grey of the new county jail can be seen in the center of the photo.

**Color Plate 6.14:** Several R.J. Reynolds plants remain in Forsyth County; the Whitaker Park plant is one of them.

*Photo by Ole Gade.*

*Photo by Ole Gade.*

**Color Plate 6.15:** R.J. Reynolds post-modernistic architectural jewel, its World Headquarters, was built during the 1970s peak of R.J.R. It was donated to the College of Business at Wake Forest University in 1987. A decade later, the "Glass Menagerie," as it had become known as locally, was placed on the market because it did not really lend itself to university use.

**Color Plate 6.16:** The Champion International plant in Roanoke Rapids (Halifax County). Pulp, paper, and paperboard plants tend to be very large, use great quantities of water, and have localities concerned about their propensity to pollute air and water. They also tend to be located in smaller communities where they provide a major part of the employment and economic base.

**Color Plate 6.17:**
This Kosa polyester plant, a huge industrial enterprise located in western rural Rowan County, benefits from direct rail connections, from easy access to its major markets along "Main Street," and from the willingness of labor to commute from a thirteen county region.

211

*Photo by Ole Gade.*

**Color Plate 6.18:** The Volvo-GM Truck Division has its North American Headquarters in Greensboro, located on "Main Street," in the center of the Piedmont Triangle "Greenheart," and a few miles from the Triad International Airport.

**Color Plate 6.19:** Food Lion, the largest private employer in North Carolina, provides its grocery stores with goods from its own warehouses and distribution centers; this one is in northern rural Harnett County, close to highly urbanized Wake County.

*Photo by Ole Gade.*

*Photo by Ole Gade.*

**C.P. 7.1a:** "Up the hollow" is still an expression encountered in the mountains. Not infrequently it refers to a residential community that is located in tight topographic surroundings to where a marginal agricultural society found itself pushed in the latter parts of the 19th century. At present, these Ashe County homes are served by well water, outhouses, and electricity.

**C.P. 7.1b:** Gated communities provide stark contrasts in shaping a mountainous environment to the perceived needs of the wealthy, most often seasonal, residents. These "needs" include golf courses (often a massive engineering task given the terrain), sumptuous single family homes and condos, and club house and activity areas, as well as the sense of exclusivity and security that money can buy. This particular location is in Macon County.

*Photo by Ole Gade.*

**Color Plate 7.1:** These two scenes are apt testimony to some of the contrasts of poverty and wealth that exist in North Carolina's cultural landscape. Although both scenes are from the Mountain Region, similar contrasts exist throughout the state, at times in very close proximity.

213

*Photo by Ole Gade.*

**C.P. 7.2a:** Among the elite public institutions is North Carolina State University, the state's 19th century land grant university. A valuable asset of NCSU is available land for expansion in the booming Raleigh metropolitan area. NCSU has been in the process of building its multi-billion dollar, 1,000 acre Centennial Campus over the past decade. The photo shows a portion of the new engineering and joint venture public/private research complexes, constructed to preserve the natural landscape of Walnut Creek in West Raleigh.

**C.P. 7.2b:** Prestigious private institutions include Duke University, Davidson College, and, shown in this photo, Wake Forest University (in Winston-Salem, Forsyth County). Wake Forest University was relocated from the town of Wake Forest (Wake County) with the financial support of the Reynolds family. Tobacco money has been critical in the growth of the two leading private institutions of higher learning in the state.

*Photo by Ole Gade.*

**Color Plate 7.2:** North Carolina is endowed with rich contrasts in educational opportunities and offers some of the most affordable access to higher education in the United States.

*Photo by Ole Gade.*

**C. P. 7.2c:** Historically Black Colleges and Universities (HBCUs) have been important as higher education options in the state. The five public HBCUs are now seeing considerable efforts in the upgrading and expansion of their facilities. Typical locations in or near downtowns contribute to the development of professional schools that thrive on night and weekend programs in areas with high population densities and ease of access. At North Carolina Central University (located in southeast Durham), the Law School has proven attractive to a diverse population since 1940; Mike Easley, the present governor, graduated from the NCCU Law School.

**C.P. 7.2d:** With 58 community colleges, the two-year system of higher education supports continuing adult education, worker training, and pre-professional programs in North Carolina. Spread across the state, the colleges vary in size (based on their rural or urban locations) and in some of their specialized programs. Tri-County Community College in Murphy is an example of how a variety of programs attracts students of all ages.

*Photo by Ole Gade.*

**Color Plate 7.2:** North Carolina educational opportunities.

Photo by Ole Gade.

**C.P. 7.3a:** Rural areas have escalating demands for basic, low cost homes for individuals and families with few resources. A common solution has been the use of prefab units capable of being moved over roads. Manufactured home parks, with their own particular community ambience, dot the countryside. This scene is located in Cleveland County.

Photo by Ole Gade.

**C.P. 7.3b:** Covering a similar ground space, but priced at values at least 25 times higher, are houses in this single family cluster housing in Charlotte. This residential neighborhood exemplifies the in-fill approach to increasing center city housing densities.

**Color Plate 7.3:** Population growth and competition for housing are becoming increasingly intense, with rural and urban areas showing responses that, in part, vary by affordability.

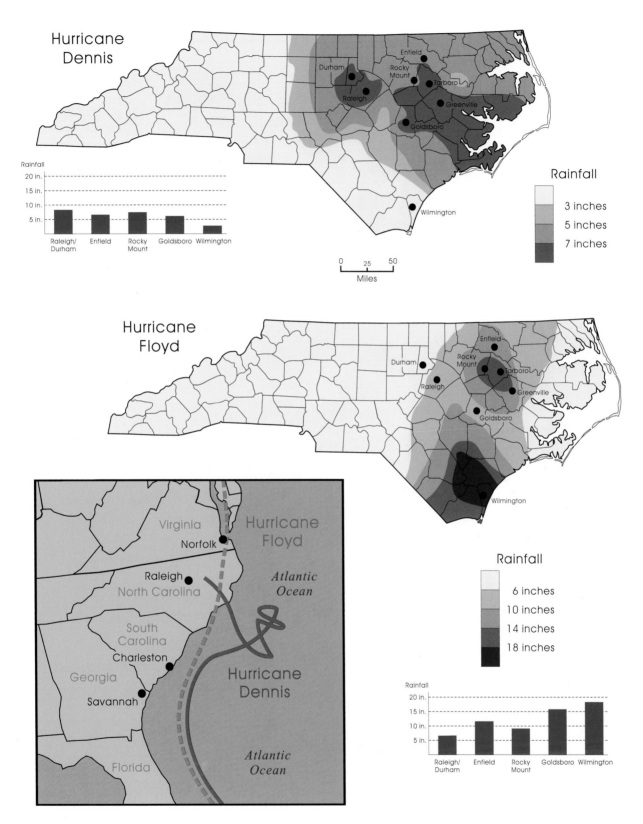

**Color Plate 8.1:** Track and Precipitation Amounts of Hurricane Dennis and Hurricane Floyd.
**Source:** Modified from *Raleigh News and Observer*, November 7, 1999.

217

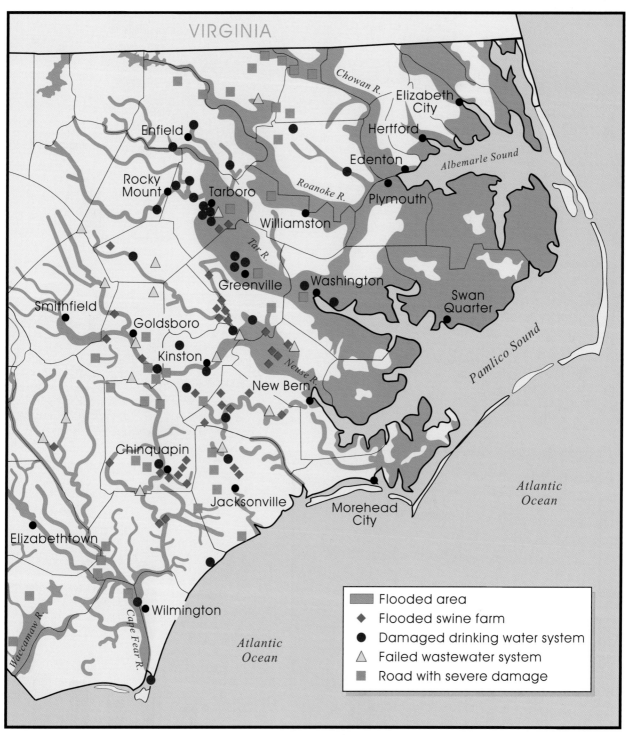

**Color Plate 8.2:** Flood Damage from Hurricane Dennis and Hurricane Floyd.
**Source:** Modified from *Raleigh News and Observer*, November 7, 1999.

**Color Plate 8.3:** The Neuse River swelled beyond its capacity and inundated the surrounding countryside in Wayne County. Note the power line cut through the center of the photo. Flooding made repair and maintenance a difficult task. Many areas were without electric, phone, and cable service for weeks after the flood.

**Color Plate 8.4:** Areas surrounding Greenville (Pitt County) were hard hit by flooding. Here a new housing development was damaged by high waters, while the apartments, on slightly higher ground, were left untouched.

**Color Plate 8.5:** The Edgecombe County towns of Tarboro and Princeville were extremely vulnerable to the one-two punch of Hurricanes Dennis and Floyd (CP 11.4). The path of the Tar River (top of photo) is difficult to discern as the entire town of Princeville was covered with twelve feet of water. Afterwards, the community leaders of Princeville considered rebuilding the town at a new, higher elevation location, but rejected that idea and have since begun rebuilding at the old site.

*All photos courtesy of the U.S. Geological Survey.*

**Color Plate 8.6:** Low lying transportation arteries were flooded and became temporary rivers filled with brown, silt laden waters. The flooding denied access to many areas of the Coastal Plain and Tidewater regions for weeks. Shown is the intersection of U.S. Highway 64 and Tanner Road in Rocky Mount.

**Color Plate 8.7:** Outside of Goldsboro (Wayne County), this sewage lagoon was breached and flooded. The wastewater (green colored water in the photo) was carried into nearby surface and ground water supplies. This type of contamination was wide-spread and caused a serious health threat.

**Color Plate 8.8:** Often the devastation was not visible until the floodwaters had subsided. East of State Road 1585 in Pitt County, a farm sewage lagoon ruptured and emptied its contents into the local freshwater system.

*All photos courtesy of the U.S. Geological Survey.*

| SIC Codes 41-99 | Industry | Number of Employers | Employment | Average Weekly Wage |
|---|---|---|---|---|
| 41 | Local And Interurban Passenger Transit | 405 | 5,356 | 379.1 |
| 42 | Trucking And Warehousing | 4,619 | 66,776 | 599.69 |
| 44 | Water Transportation | 177 | 1,524 | 463.61 |
| 45 | Transportation By Air | 339 | 34,134 | 751.45 |
| 46 | Pipelines, Except Natural Gas | 7 | 107 | 1,023.80 |
| 47 | Transportation Services | 1,046 | 8,973 | 815.8 |
| 48 | Communications | 1,405 | 41,345 | 922.9 |
| 49 | Electric, Gas, And Sanitary Services | 582 | 23,558 | 1,000.90 |
| 50 | Wholesale Trade-durable Goods | 12,576 | 119,952 | 789.67 |
| 51 | Wholesale Trade-nondurable Goods | 7,667 | 82,029 | 703.11 |
| 52 | Building Materials & Garden Supplies | 2,557 | 39,221 | 500.73 |
| 53 | General Merchandise Stores | 1,716 | 83,733 | 311.63 |
| 54 | Food Stores | 5,854 | 110,671 | 303.55 |
| 55 | Automotive Dealers & Service Stations | 6,232 | 70,476 | 581.74 |
| 56 | Apparel And Accessory Stores | 3,088 | 31,663 | 272.19 |
| 57 | Furniture And Homefurnishings Stores | 4,354 | 36,711 | 559.17 |
| 58 | Eating And Drinking Places | 12,963 | 243,290 | 224 |
| 59 | Miscellaneous Retail | 9,460 | 76,582 | 373.97 |
| 60 | Depository Institutions | 2,871 | 70,556 | 757.55 |
| 61 | Nondepository Institutions | 2,210 | 17,941 | 925.77 |
| 62 | Security And Commodity Brokers | 1,291 | 10,233 | 1,817.16 |
| 63 | Insurance Carriers | 1,314 | 29,597 | 892.97 |
| 64 | Insurance Agents, Brokers, & Service | 3,421 | 15,715 | 722 |
| 65 | Real Estate | 6,629 | 35,394 | 542.63 |
| 67 | Holding And Other Investment Offices | 370 | 4,706 | 2,083.20 |
| 70 | Hotels And Other Lodging Places | 1,897 | 42,086 | 293.26 |
| 72 | Personal Services | 4,890 | 31,511 | 352.28 |
| 73 | Business Services | 16,536 | 271,011 | 528.37 |
| 75 | Auto Repair, Services, And Parking | 5,380 | 30,788 | 481.24 |
| 76 | Miscellaneous Repair Services | 2,040 | 9,714 | 512.76 |
| 78 | Motion Pictures | 1,083 | 10,469 | 228.2 |
| 79 | Amusement & Recreation Services | 2,923 | 47,366 | 372.91 |
| 80 | Health Services | 11,011 | 251,699 | 666.79 |
| 81 | Legal Services | 3,519 | 20,839 | 790 |
| 82 | Educational Services | 998 | 37,550 | 640.11 |
| 83 | Social Services | 5,203 | 79,387 | 318.22 |
| 84 | Museums, Botanical, Zoological Gardens | 94 | 2,177 | 406.57 |
| 86 | Membership Organizations | 1,648 | 20,584 | 349.72 |
| 87 | Engineering & Management Services | 9,789 | 78,474 | 893.85 |
| 88 | Private Households | 6,255 | 7,668 | 265 |
| 89 | Services | 222 | 951 | 716 |
| 99 | Nonclassifiable Establishments | 1 | 6 | 651 |

**Table 7.2:** Employers, Employees, and Weekly Wages in Service Producing Industries, 2000.
**Source:** N. C. Employment Security Commission.

urban Piedmont to the lows of the peripheral counties of the state. Is it not surprising that people tend to seek opportunities in the higher wage areas of the state, regardless of their skill and level of education, and if they are out of commuting distance will relocate their household. In both of the SIC cases exemplified, here it should be noted that a few counties benefit in the alloca-tion of salaries of workers who are employed in headquarters and distribution facilities of some of the corporations specializing in fast foods and groceries.

Additional information relevant to understanding the ex-tent of the shift toward a mixed economy is provided in Figures 7.6 and 7.7. The pie charts in Figure 7.6 indicate changes in the per-

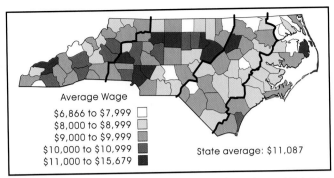

**Figure 7.4:** Average Annual Wage for Workers in Eating and Drinking Places, 1999.
**Source:** Civilian Labor Force Estimates, Employment Security Commission of North Carolina, 2001.

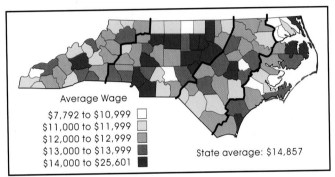

**Figure 7.5:** Average Annual Wage for Workers in Food Stores, 1999.
**Source:** Civilian Labor Force Estimates, Employment Security Commission of North Carolina, 2001.

centage share of employment in different industry sectors over the 1975-1995 period; the bar graphs of Figure 7.7 show the actual three decade employment changes by sectors. Notable is the decrease in textile and apparel employment share and the increases in services, retail and government. Table 7.3 ranks North Carolina's wage earners in the United States.

While the state is moving emphatically toward a new economy, with greater diversification and opportunities for some, it is certain that for many others the potential for earning a reasonable middle income wage is deteriorating. This new mixed economy has clear dualistic characteristics indicated by a gap in wages defined not only by sectors of employment, but also by location. This latter situation is ameliorated, in part, by income derived from sources other than wages. In fact, unearned income from retirement portfolios and other investment income, social security, unemployment benefits, Medicaid, and other government income maintenance may amplify quality of life in a considerable degree. For the state, these sources of income have gradually increased from about 17 percent in the late 1960s to nearly 32 percent in the late 1990s (Orr and Stuart 2000, 138). On the national level, unearned income has remained at about five percent higher than that for North Carolina. Overall the major reason for the persistent increase in recent decades has been economic good times with families able to increase their proportion of an-

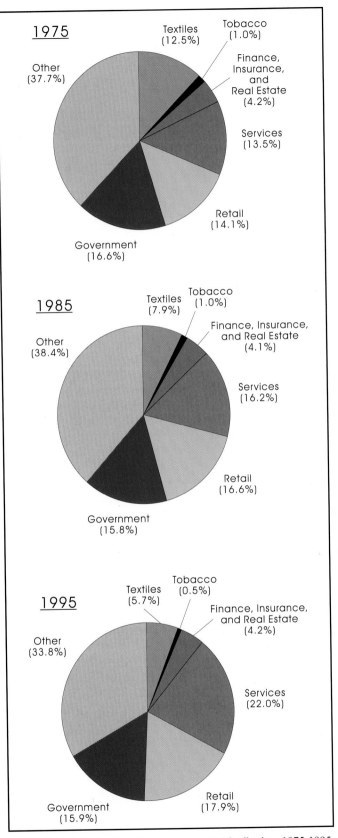

**Figure 7.6:** The New Work Force in Percent Distribution, 1975-1995.
**Source:** The Raleigh News and Observer, July 21, 1996.

222

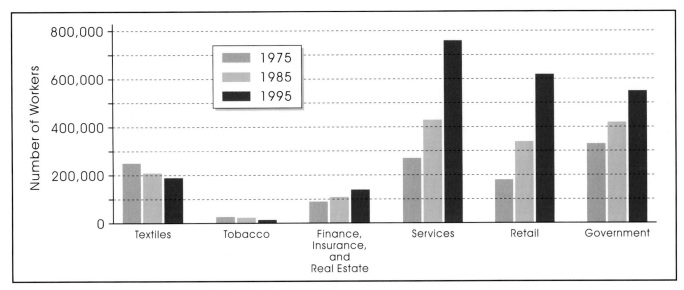

**Figure 7.7:** The New Work Force in Numeric Distribution, 1975-1995.
**Source:** The Raleigh News and Observer, July 21, 1996.

nual income from their investments, and with an increasing percentage of individuals retiring in places where their retirement portfolio and social security payment then contribute a disproportionate share of average county family income. For some North Carolina counties, the inflow of non-wage income is substantial, and a major factor in reducing otherwise abject poverty conditions. A very definitive spatial pattern emerges when these county differences are mapped (Figure 7.8). Counties that have seen a large influx of retirees are especially impacted by unearned income. The southwestern mountain counties of Swain, Graham,

Cherokee, Clay, Macon, Transylvania, Henderson, and Polk are seeing unearned income approaching or, in the case of Polk County, exceeding 50 percent of their total annual income. Moore County in the Sandhills also finds itself in that same condition, and not far behind are some of the coastal counties. Government maintenance payments play a much larger role in the northeastern part of the state, where Hyde, Tyrrell, Pamlico, Chowan, and Perquimans counties accrue high percentages of unearned income. The picture here is complicated by the mix of unearned income that in varying scale influences the counties, such as

| Item | Value | Rank |
|---|---|---|
| State minimum wage in 2000 | $5.15 | 12 |
| Average annual pay in 1998 for: | | |
|   Manufacturing | $32,378 | 40 |
|   Retail | $15,970 | 25 |
|   Service | $26,266 | 24 |
|   Private Industry | $27,953 | 27 |
|   Government | $28,944 | 28 |
| Increase in average annual pay, 1997-98 | 5.40% | 19 |
| Companies offering health insurance in 1993 | 51.90% | 25 |
| Per-capita personal income in 1998 | $24,122 | 31 |
| Median household income in 1998 | $36,407 | 27 |
| Increase in jobs, 1998-99 | 1.80% | 31 |
| Unemployment rate in 1999 | 3.20% | 11 |
| Fatality rate per 100,000 workers in all industries in 1998 | 6 | 34 |
| Nonfatal injury/illness rate per 100 private industry workers in 1998 | 6.1 | 12 |
| Average weekly unemployment benefits in 1999 | $204 | 17 |
| Total workers unionized in 1999 | 3.30% | 50 |

**Table 7.3:** Ranking North Carolina Wage Earners in the United States.
**Source:** Jones and Collins 2000.

223

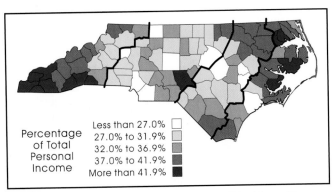

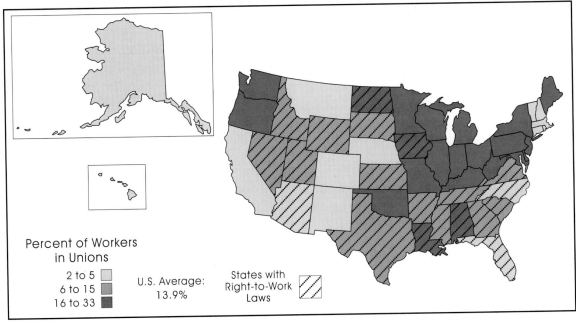

**Figure 7.8:** Unearned Income as a Percentage of Total Annual Income, 1995.
**Source:** Orr and Stuart, 2000, 138.

Medicaid, unemployment insurance, and agricultural price support payments, as well as social security. Some counties would rank much higher should all unearned income actually be accounted for. For example, the millions of dollars that annually flow to college students from parents and scholarships do not enter in any way the income accounting stream, and counties like Watauga, Orange, and Pitt remain undervalued as a result.

This appears to be the major characteristics of the "new economy": rapid productivity increase, nearly full employment, and moderate inflation, resulting from advances especially in the knowledge and technology industries. Does the new economy then initiate a 'rising tide that lifts all boats'? Unhappily, for North Carolina, our evidence points to the contrary. It suggests that shifts in economic structure, employment, and wages occasioned by technological change is also a leading cause of the increase in earnings inequality, a conclusion also supported in recent research by economists (Dadres and Ginther, 2001).

## Labor Unions and "Right to Work"

It has been argued that the absence of labor unions has been a major depressant on wage levels in North Carolina. This is a "Right to Work" state, meaning that within any plant where workers have organized, and a union contract has been negotiated and signed, other workers are still free to not join the union even though they are equally entitled to union benefits. North Carolina is the least unionized in the country (Figure 7.9), with only 3.3 percent of its workforce carrying a union membership. This condition derives from the nature of the manufacturing industries that grew to dominate in North Carolina and their early record of paternalism and community control in small single industry communities; it is fueled by a general strong southern work ethic co-existing with a lamentable complacency about work conditions. Organizing the North Carolina textile and apparel industries proved a formidable, and in the end an unsuccessful, objective for the unions. Early defeats came with violence and bloodshed during the depression years of the 1930s, as exemplified by the Luray Mill confrontation in Gaston County (CP 12.35). Years of combating J. P. Stevens, a textile firm that moved to new plants in Roanoke Rapids (Halifax County) in the 1920s to escape the unions and higher wages in the North, succeeded in 1976 with a union victory, though it took an additional four years of demoralizing court appeals for a negotiated contract to finally be settled (see discussion in Chapter 11). The power bastion of anti-unionism, Cannon Mills, fell to the union movement in the late 1990s, but not until the Mills had changed ownership several times over, and had become but a shadow of its former size and local influence (Chapter 6). When Philip Morris considered building its state-of-the-art plant for 3,000 unionized workers in Concord, local businesses, especially the non-union Cannon Mills, voiced their opposition strongly enough to persuade the Cham-

**Figure 7.9:** United States Percent Unionized Labor Force, 1998.

ber of Commerce to withdraw its earlier endorsement of the plant. The fear of many North Carolina communities was that the higher paying companies with union contracts would negatively affect existing industry, causing their wage costs to increase and counter attempts to retain their own lower paid workers. So it was with Brockway Glass, which was not welcome in Roxboro (Person County) by the local industrialists, and located instead in Danville, Virginia. And so it was with Miller Brewing Company, which was requested to go elsewhere by the Raleigh Chamber of Commerce when state officials informed chamber officials that it was likely to be a union plant (Betts 1996). Though a more subdued approach reigns at present in the state directed industrial recruitment effort, it was but a few years ago that low wages and non-union attitudes were a major component of the sales pitch. In many North Carolina communities there is now a changing attitude toward unions because new companies attracted from outside the state are carrying with them a history of management – union relations that will continue in spite of the relocation.

### A Persistence of Poverty

An advocacy group in the forefront of investigating issues of family poverty in the state issued a report in January 2001 claiming that more than one million North Carolina households do not make enough money to meet the costs of their essential needs. This is equal to over one-third of the households filing tax returns, and well in excess of the percentage deemed to fall below federal poverty levels. Reasons for the difference in establishing comparable poverty levels are the federal government's indifference in assessing rural-urban variations in cost of living, and its failure to consider increasing child care, health care, and housing expenses; so argues the study of the North Carolina Justice and Community Development Center and NC Equity (Schmidt and Gerlach 2001). In 2000 urban North Carolina, the

average minimum monthly costs of living for a two-parent, two-child household include: housing–$602, food–$466, child care–$771, health care–$266, transportation–$214, taxes–$296, and miscellaneous essentials–$228. Those monthly bills aggregate to $34,000 per year. For rural areas the essentials are reduced to an annual cost of $30,000 (Goldberg 2001). These figures for urban and rural basic living costs are referred to by Schmidt and Gerlach as the Living Income Standard (LIS). For the state, the average number of families earning less than the LIS was 35.8 percent in 1997. Within the state, the counties ranged from 22.9 percent in the case of Camden to 53.8 percent in the case of Edgecombe.

An earlier study of Wake County that focused on the impact of the boom of the 1990s also pointed out that not everyone had prospered equally (Perez 2000). In fact, a clear racial division existed among those reporting an inability to pay for the necessities of life. For whites 21 percent fell below the poverty threshold, for Hispanics 49 percent fell below, while for blacks 61 percent fell below. This is remarkable, because of the recency of the study and because it was conducted in Wake County, one of the wealthiest in the state. Still, it reflects the racial divide in wealth on the national level. The earlier cited Federal Reserve Board study found that the median net dollar worth of Hispanic, African America, Asian and other minority families was $16,400 in 1998, while the net worth of white families was $94,900, or 500 percent higher.

The standard approach to assess variation in poverty is that used by the U. S. Bureau of the Census, the so-called Federal Poverty Level (FPL). In 1990, North Carolina's average percent of families living below the FPL was 9.9 (Figure 7.10). On the county level this ranged from 4.8 to 23.8 percent, therefore presenting a rather substantial variation in standards of living across the state. The usual list of suspects appear as the more poverty

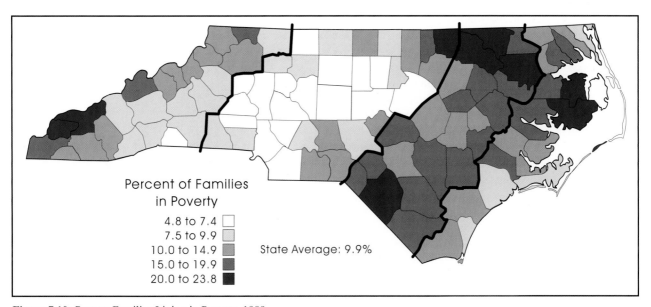

Percent of Families in Poverty

4.8 to 7.4
7.5 to 9.9
10.0 to 14.9
15.0 to 19.9
20.0 to 23.8

State Average: 9.9%

**Figure 7.10:** Percent Families Living in Poverty, 1989.
**Source:** U.S. Bureau of the Census, 1990.

prone counties: the northeastern state geographic regions of Pamlico and Roanoke (see Chapter 9 on the defining and labeling of state geographic regions), portions of the Cape Fear and Sandhills regions, and the Southwest Mountains. In fact, outside of the Main Street core counties only the resort counties of Polk and Dare fall into the lowest poverty category

Schmidt and Gerlach, in *Working Hard Is Not Enough* maintain that the FPL is inadequate and obsolete. Specifically they note that the FPL, when defined in the 1960s, was derived from basic food costs being an average one third of a family's total budget, leaving the present FPL defined as the cost of a basic "thrifty food plan" times three (2001, p. 3). For a family of two, the FPL in 1999 was $10,869; for a family of four it was $17,029. Since the average family now spends only 13.5 percent of their budget on food, equating the "thrifty food plan" to 13.5 percent and multiplying the total derived by three to arrive at a the Federal Poverty Level will account for only 40.5 percent of today's cost of basic needs. A complementary point is that a person on minimum wage for a year of forty-hour work weeks will earn $10,712 per year, less than the official FPL for a family of two, and only 35 percent of the more realistically defined Living Income Standard. Aside from the inadequacy of its basic definition, the universality of the FPL (not allowing for cost of living differences across the country and from urban to rural areas) is a major problem, as is also the changing composition of the family/household.

North Carolina political and business leaders must consider new realities in basic living costs in formulating welfare policies and minimum wage standards. For a family of one adult and a preschooler to attain the LIS will require an hourly pay rate of $8.50 in rural and $11.00 in urban North Carolina. A family comprising two working adults and two young children will require $7.12/hour for each adult in rural areas and $8.12 in urban areas. Federal standards on the minimum wage, heatedly debated on a recurring basis in Congress, is currently $5.15. This is the North Carolina standard in 2001, as well. Eleven other states have increased the minimum wage for their states, up to $6.75 in the case of Massachusetts, and "living wage" proposals for municipal workers have been approved by city councils the country over. In North Carolina, the city of Durham passed its Living Wage Ordinance in 1998, providing a wage floor of $7.75/hr for municipal workers and requiring contractors for the city to pay at least this amount as a minimum wage. Meanwhile, the Greensboro City Council voted six to two against a Living Wage Ordinance, and the city of Charlotte turned down a request from city employees for a "living wage standard," with the mayor citing the proposal as a socialist ploy (!). The reader may reflect on Marie Antoinette's attitude to the Parisian public plea for greater government support since many families could no longer afford the very basic necessities, like bread; "Well, let them eat cake!" she retorted. Attitudes on poverty and approaches to its alleviation in our state may change slowly, but their purveyors are not likely to suffer the fate of Marie Antoinette, who was sentenced by the French Revolutionary Council and guillotined in October of 1793.

Increasingly attention has focused on children (under 18 years of age) as the key element in poverty assessment. Data released through the North Carolina Department of Health and Human Resources considerably broadens the range of the poverty measure in the state by evaluating the poverty conditions of children. Results from 1995 data (Figure 7.11), show the poverty range from 9.7 to 40 percent, as compared to the earlier noted FPL county range of 4.8 to 23.8 (Figure 7.10). Aside from providing evidence of deeper poverty and stronger contrasts across the state in the condition of poverty, these data are spatially little different from the 1990 U. S. Census in the ranking of counties.

Other means of establishing conditions of poverty include data enumerating births to mothers who benefit from the federally sponsored Aid to Women, Infants and Children (WIC) program (1998 state average of 41.1%) and persons eligible for Medicaid (1998 state average of 16.1%). These more recent data further dramatizes conditions of low income. In the case of WIC mothers, the range of 16.7 percent (Dare County) to 73.3 percent (Bertie County) indicate the higher threshold for government support, as well as the greater attention paid to the health and well-being of children at the earliest stage (Figure 7.12). Lowest levels of federal support are given in the Piedmont Triangle, Metrolina, and Albemarle state geographic regions, and the highest in the northeastern quadrant of the state (excepting the Albemarle counties), southeastern counties bordering South Carolina, and the Southwestern Mountain region. The spatial patterns reflected

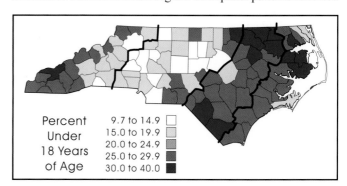

**Figure 7.11:** Children Living in Poverty, 1995.
**Source:** N.C. Department of Health and Human Services, Health Data Sheet, 2000.

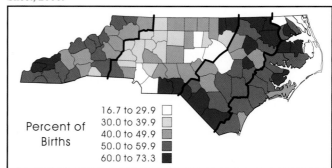

**Figure 7.12:** Percent Births to Low Income Mothers (WIC Program) 1998.
**Source:** N. C. Department of Health and Human Services, Health Data Sheet, 2000.

in Figure 7.13, concentration of Medicaid payments, are not much at variance with the WIC data, except for a diminishing of the poverty condition in the southwest and an overall reduction of the percentages affected. WIC and Medicaid are so-called means-tested federal antipoverty programs. They fund nutritional and medical assistance to low income elderly, blind, and disabled individuals, to members of poor families with children under the age of 18, and to some other pregnant women and other children. It can be noted here that means-tested programs also include the following cash transfer programs (Scholz and Levine 2000):

1) Supplemental Security Income (SSI), focused on the needs of the disabled;

2) Aid to Families With Dependent Children (AFDC), the central safety net for poor families from 1936 to 1996 when it was discontinue by the welfare reforms;

3) Temporary Assistance for Needy Families (TANF), a program that replaced AFDC in 1996; and

4) the Earned Income Tax Credit (EITC), begun in 1975 to encourage low skilled workers to enter the labor market – this is currently the fastest growing antipoverty program, aided by the 1990s economic expansion, longest economic growth period in U.S. history.

In addition, means-tested programs include the following in-kind transfers:

1) food stamps, an entitlement program for people with low income and assets that has faced a steep decline since 1994;

2) housing assistance, a program to support housing needs of families that are homeless, living in substandard housing, displaced involuntarily, or paying more than 50 percent of their income for housing;

3) school breakfast and lunch programs, entitlement programs based on family income; and

4) Head Start, a non-entitlement program that provides a range of services to children under five, and their families.

In April of 1997, all social insurance programs (the universal programs of social security, Medicare, unemployment insurance, and workmen's compensation) plus all means-tested benefits totaled nationally $59 billion in federal expenditures. Of this amount, about one quarter went to alleviating poverty. Between 1971 and 1998, total federal spending on means-tested programs, excluding Medicaid, ranged between 1.3 and 1.9 percent of the Gross Domestic Product. This narrow a range of antipoverty funding indicates a stability that has been worrisome to many

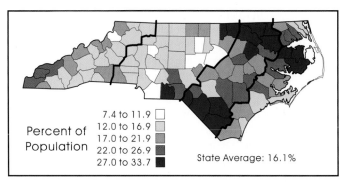

**Figure 7.13:** Percent Population Eligible for Medicaid, 1999.
**Source:** N.C. Department of Health and Human Services, Health Data Sheet, 2000.

who study the persistence of poverty (Scholz and Levine 2000, 15). In North Carolina, the Census 2000 Supplementary Survey was released in late July, 2001. It found that the state's poverty rate, as measured by the Federal Poverty Level, is about the same as it was a decade earlier, 13 percent, or about one million persons, an increase of 195,000 since 1990. The greater problem here lies with a rate of poverty for children, which far exceeds that of adults. About 20 percent of North Carolina's children (366,000) are poverty stricken. As we will discuss in the following section, this lack of improvement in poverty conditions during a period of economic prosperity coincides with the reduction, by 70 percent, of households receiving social welfare support (Dodd 2001).

### The Social Welfare Devolution

Throughout the world, communities and governments combine efforts in varying ways to help those who cannot help themselves, or experience temporary difficulties in their socio-economic or physical condition. So-called social welfare states represent a greater commitment on the part of the state to insure that a comprehensive social safety net exists from birth to death for all of its citizens. In the Scandinavian countries of Norway, Sweden and Denmark, for example, citizens have for 70 years gone to the polls to ensure the continuance of the social welfare state, in spite of its incredible cost to themselves as taxpayers. Such a commitment by the citizenry continues to provide a quality of life whose high bottom line for all residents persists in spite of the recent inflow of migrant workers and refugees from the world over. In the United States, much more is expected of the individual, and the government does not step in as readily and willingly to support individual inability or infirmity. One result has been the growth of church affiliated and other non-governmental organizations (NGOs) to define measures and support systems for the indigent. Hastening the involvement of the NGOs has been the implementation of the New Federalism in social welfare during the 1990s.

New Federalism is a term coined during President Reagan's Administration in the 1980s. Its avowed purpose was to transfer from the federal government to the states both money and the responsibilities for managing assistance to low income populations. This process of "devolution" is expected to pass federal responsibility ultimately to the local level of counties and/or municipalities. In Chapter 9 we consider the impact of "devolution" on the evolution of mid-level public decision making regions in North Carolina, especially as it relates to industrial recruitment and job creation; here we look only at the federal government's diminishing role as the standard bearer of the social safety net, a position it strongly claimed and developed during the 1930s depression years and subsequently strengthened during the Great Society programs of the 1960s.

A number of guiding principles and concerns seem to dominate the many welfare reform bills considered in Congress during the 1980s and early 1990s. For one, the focus was value-driven. Heavy emphasis was placed on the value of work, on the value of delaying the birth of a child until resources permitted it, and on the value of setting personal responsibility conditions as a quid pro quo for benefits (meaning time limits, work requirements, school attendance, and so on). The idea of "entitlement", the center piece in previous federal welfare legislation, was relegated to the trash can. Lawmakers now expressed a concern about reducing costs of welfare. From the federal perspective, this was to be accomplished by the gradual transfer of such responsibilities to the states. In opposition to this were concerns that continuing deficit reductions and mounting costs of social security and Medicare programs, too politically powerful to be slated for discontinuance, were harming programs supporting the least well-off in society, especially poor children (Blum 1996). Some lawmakers also expressed concern that federal policy deregulation and decentralization might lead to a state by state competitive 'rush to the bottom,' suggesting that no state wants to become widely known as being more generous in their welfare support, and thus attract poor families in from states that are less generous (Corbett 1996). This concern extends especially to where devolution is carried beyond the state to the local government level. A number of other concerns were voiced about the impact of welfare devolution. These included: 1) the likelihood that new state mounted social welfare approaches would wind up so differentiated from state to state, and among localities, that no longer would it be possible to fairly compare and judge their success; and 2) the interactive nature of welfare reform changes affect health, housing, employment, and child care in so great a diversity of ways, depending upon family structure, local support environments, and funding capabilities, as to make it difficult, if not impossible, to measure probable outcomes. Regardless of a multitude of concerns and issues, in 1995 President Clinton signed into law the new federal welfare legislation, the Personal Responsibility and Work Opportunity Reconciliation Act, gradually reducing the funding made available through the Aid to Families with Dependent Children (AFDC) and the Temporary Assistance to Needy Families (TANF) programs. Simultaneously, their management were turned over to the states.

States stepped in quickly to reduce their welfare rolls. Some were ahead of the game with significant reductions already in hand at the time of the new legislation. Between September, 1996, when the federal law was implemented, and April, 1997, Wyoming lead the reductions with 47 percent and Massachusetts followed with 45 percent. North Carolina's neighbors Tennessee and South Carolina achieved reductions of 26 and 22 percent, respectively, while North Carolina itself attained a seven percent decrease (Pugh 1997). Nationally, in that one half year, over one million people left welfare rolls (that one year earlier included eleven million). Likely the haste was conditioned by the new federal requirement that states which did not decrease their welfare rolls by at least one half by 2002 will see a reduction in their federal benefits. As in other states, the North Carolina federal share can be shown as a contribution to the annual state budget. Figure 7.43 indicates the increasing share of federal contributions to the North Carolina state budget during the 1990s. In 1990-91 the federal contribution to the total state budget was 20.2 percent, while in 2000-01 it had increased to 25.9 percent.

In North Carolina, Governor James Hunt signed his administration's major welfare reform bill, Work First, into law in June, 1995. Much General Assembly discussion had preceded the enactment of the reforms. Welfare recipient numbers reaching a high of 120,000 families in 1993, double that of 1986, no doubt influenced the urgency of taking action. In the end, the Assembly favored reweaving the social safety net through a "tough love" approach, as Pheon Beal, director of the new North Carolina Work First Program, would have it (Stancil 1996). At this time, the composition of welfare families included a racial break down of 63 percent black, 31% white, 2% Hispanic, 2% American Indian, and 2% other races (Box 7A); single parent families constituted 65 percent of the total, child only–27%, teen parent–6%, and two parents–2%. By age, 40 percent were adults and 60 percent were children. Families qualified for welfare when their monthly income did not exceed $472 for a two member family, $544 (3 members), $594 (4 members), and $648 (5 members). Qualifying families could receive up to $236 if they had two members, $272 (3 members), $294 (4 members), and $324 (5 members). Beal's "tough love" provisions refer in part to the limit of two years that any family is permitted to be on the program. To that point in time (1996) more than 36 percent of recipients had been on welfare for over two years, 15.7 percent for over five years. "Tough love" also involved a series of penalties imposed where recipients fail to observe some of the personal responsibility conditions. For the initial six months after being put in place in July 1996, penalties were imposed on 2,907 families for failure to satisfy the work requirement and on 1,154 families for failure to cooperate with child-support enforcement officials. Lesser numbers were penalized for failure to keep a child in school and for failure to get a child immunized. In 1997 welfare recipients were concentrated in the poorer parts of the state (the northeast, the southeast and parts of the southwestern mountains), ranging from 1.1 percent of the population in Dare County to 9.3 percent in Halifax County (Box 7A).

In 2000, the North Carolina Department of Health and Human Services began issuing its yearly Work First report cards demonstrating the degree to which individual counties were meeting goals defined by the program. The second annual report card covering July 1999-July 2000 achievements was issued at year's end. Goal attainments were as follows:

1) Decrease in the number of people on welfare by 40 percent – with the welfare rolls decreasing 46.6 percent, 72 counties earned an A by achieving 110 percent or more of their 40 percent goal; 20 counties fall below the A level; but worst off are eight counties that attained less than 32 percent of the 40 percent goal, they will need to develop and implement corrective action plans; (Figure 7.14a);

2) Help 20,105 Work First recipients move from welfare to work – 79 counties exceeded their goal by at least ten percent; three counties need to develop and implement corrective action plans (Figure 7.14b);

3) 85 percent of former Work First participants stay off welfare – since Work First began in 1995, 93 percent of those who left for work have remained off welfare; all counties attained at least 90 of their goal;

4) collect ten percent more child support – statewide the increase was twelve percent, with no county reaching less than 90 percent of their goal.

Moving from "entitlement" to "tough love" constitutes a revolutionary change in social welfare policy. For those who have been able to take advantage of regular welfare cash payments for two years and more, requires a change in their culture of poverty. No longer can a single mom spend most of the day caring for and protecting her children in project housing, and taking part-time job training courses. She now has to arrange for day care and find a way to access a job not likely to be found within walking distance of her home. The kind of jobs that a poorly educated and inexperienced welfare recipient might qualify for are apt to be retail, food service, hotel maid service, hospital and nursing care aides, and other "caring professions" that offer low wages, no employer health insurance or other traditional benefits like vacation time and sick leave, and limited upward mobility. These jobs also tend to be located along commercial strips on the periphery of the city and in suburban shopping centers, typically far from public transportation. They are jobs also taken traditionally by women, and for the same skills provide wages that are 81 percent those of males having similar job skills (Boushey 2001). While a job may insure a steady cash flow into the family, this may also now be encumbered by child care costs (considering that in 1997 there were over 7,000 children waiting in line for subsidized child care in the state), by having to

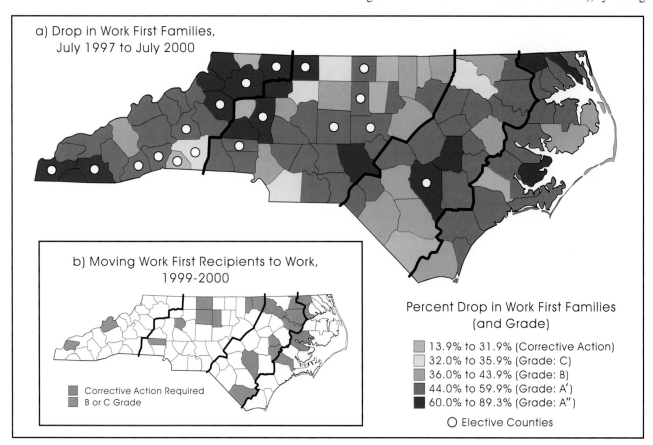

**Figure 7.14 a and b:** a. Decrease in Work First Families, July 1997 to July, 2000.
**Source:** N.C. Department of Health and Human Services, 2000.
b. Moving Work First Recipients to Work, 1999-2000.
**Source:** N.C. Department of Health and Human Services, 2000.

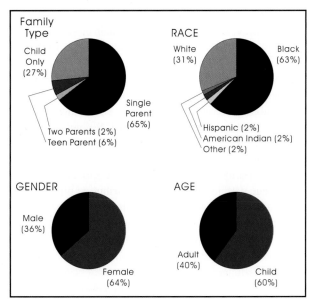

Family Type

Child Only (27%)

Two Parents (2%)
Teen Parent (6%)

Single Parent (65%)

RACE

White (31%)

Black (63%)

Hispanic (2%)
American Indian (2%)
Other (2%)

GENDER

Male (36%)

Female (64%)

AGE

Adult (40%)

Child (60%)

Who is on Welfare?

Amount of Income Limits.

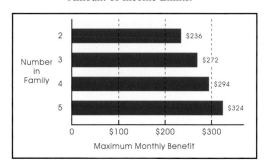

Amount of Welfare Payments.

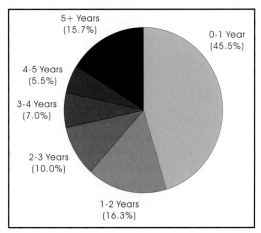

Time Spent on Welfare.

Number of Families on Welfare.

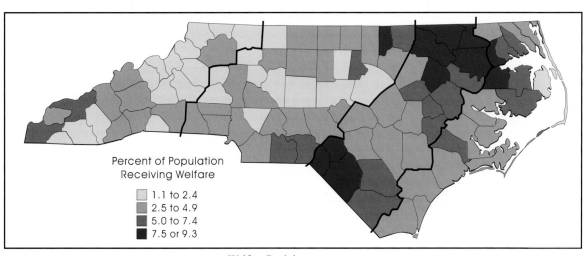

Percent of Population Receiving Welfare

☐ 1.1 to 2.4
☐ 2.5 to 4.9
☐ 5.0 to 7.4
☐ 7.5 or 9.3

Welfare Recipients.

**Source:** Wagner and Shiffer (1997).

offset the cost of Medicaid (free health insurance available to welfare recipients), and by the potential loss of food stamps. In recognition of the difficulty of providing health insurance for families no longer eligible for Medicaid the federal government made available a matching program to support the purchase of health insurance for children of the working poor. North Carolina was able to receive $80 million in 1998. This combined with a $28 million state match provided for 71,000 uninsured kids. By January, 2001 there were about 101,000 children eligible for the N. C. Health Choice program, leading the state to freeze applications at 71,600 rather than increase the match (Wilson 2000).

For social service agencies, imposing penalties on their clients, the welfare family, is difficult to do. Social service directors, even the new county Work First supervisors, do not like slapping cash penalties on uncooperative recipients out of concern for their children. In Durham and in other counties it is claimed that this reluctance has a rough correlation with the failure to lower the welfare rolls. Social service departments also are finding that a significant percentage of their funds now go toward providing commuting services for the recipients; but when the latter have made the transition, this free transportation is lost.

Durham County welfare families exemplify the nature of the problem inherent in the new welfare philosophy of getting recipients into jobs as quickly as possibly. Of the 3,720 families on Work First Family Assistance in Durham County in 1997, more than 50 percent were without a high school diploma, 60 percent did not own an automobile, and 28 percent were afflicted with some kind of substance abuse (Shiffer 1997). Further, the group was overwhelmingly black (85%). Durham, however, is not one of the 18 counties that have elected and been approved by the state to take their proportion of Work First money from the state and set up their own programs (Figure 7.14a). From the initiation of welfare reform at the federal level in the mid-1990s the devolution of the process has reached the local level for these 18 counties. Are the earlier expressed concerns of Congress seeing the light of day?

Perhaps the biggest worry of people who are directing the Work First effort is a downturn in the economy. Here at the beginning of the initial decade of the 21st century we are in a downturn approaching recession proportions. Will now the decreased funding for social welfare cover the increased needs of people not finding jobs? Is a rush toward decreasing the social welfare case load, a major measure of success of the reforms, purchased at the cost of greater family distress, today or in the near future? Will there be a renaissance of the traditional social welfare philosophy, a return of the "culture of poverty"?

### Patterns of Unemployment

Unemployment thrives on national economic downturns and in regions where the economic structure is lagging in national or international competitiveness. Nationally, downturns seem to have something of a ten year incidence over the past several decades; for example, 1970-71, 1981-83; 1990-92 were all

recessionary periods. The most recent downturn was initiated in late 2000. Regions with greater dependence on those industries that are in the throes of globalizing changes with resulting plant closing and layoffs then tend to find their structural problems further exacerbated. North Carolina mirrors these conditions. As the national economy began teetering in late 2000, exhausted from an extended period of strong growth, the incredibly low unemployment rates of the late 1990s began showing an increase. North Carolina reached remarkably low unemployment monthly rates of 3.0 percent or less from the mid-1990s until the early part of 2000. State averages, of course, yield no information on regional variations. These are quite evident in the illustration (Figure 7.15) of county unemployment rates in April of 2000 when the state average was 3.0 percent. This distribution reflects times of almost full employment and yet indicate that such conditions were not equally shared across the state. Circumstances like these simplify the task of identifying critical differences in the ability of the 100 counties to foster near full employment. Clearly the Piedmont and a number of adjacent counties have benefited the most from the 'good times,' at least through the assessment of this indicator. Orange County, with its emphasis on knowledge and health industry employment, ranks invariably at the lowest level of unemployment at one percent in April of 2000. Others, counties with disproportionately high dependency on higher education, such as Watauga and Transylvania, were at 1.4 and 1.7 percent, respectively. Counties benefiting from their proximity to

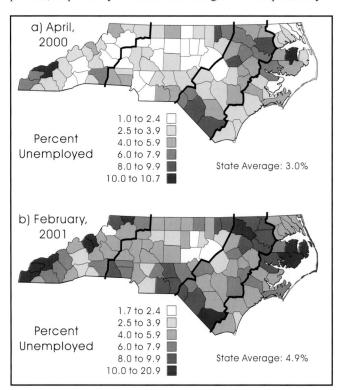

**Figure 7.15:** Comparative Unemployment Percentages, April 2000 and February 2001.

**Source:** Employment Security Commission of North Carolina, 2000 and 2001.

231

metropolitan growth centers, such as Union, Chatham, Johnston and Alexander, also came in at 2.0 percent or less. Those counties that have been able to take advantage of the new economy in employment, for example Wake and Durham, expectedly stand out, while the western manufacturing counties of Catawba and Caldwell are more surprising. Also, at the low end of the spectrum are most of the Asheville and Albemarle regions. In the northern Albemarle counties of Gates, Camden and Currituck, their proximity to the growth engine of southeastern Virginia encouraged full employment.

Yet there are many counties, that even during the best of times, still suffered comparatively large unemployment rates. These include counties that tend to be singularly dependent on a primary extractive economy, such as those where traditional agriculture continues to dominate the local economy. Approaching or exceeding three times the state average were Vance, Wilson, Bertie and Tyrrell counties in the northeast, and Columbus and Robeson counties in the southeast. Counties with a greater dependence on seasonal activities that had not yet geared up for the year also were in considerable distress. Note the southwestern concentration of relatively high unemployment that included Swain, Graham, and Cherokee counties. State policy makers should take note of counties in relative distress during 'good times,' since these are apt to be the state's chronic trouble counties.

The economic downturn at the inception of the Third Millennium began toward the end of 2000. In North Carolina the negative impacts were felt by early 2001, as indicated by the state average unemployment reaching 4.8 percent by February. Comparing these two months further highlights the differences across the state in economic fortunes (Figure 7.15). There are really few surprises, but it should be noted that the February data further encumbers counties dependent on seasonal tourism, so that some coastal and mountain counties fare even more poorly. The worsening economic conditions have further stretched the range from low to high unemployment rates, again with Orange County having the lowest rate (1.7%), but now with the highest rate nearly double that of just a few months earlier reached, in both cases, by Swain County (from 10.6 to 20.9%). In this county it appears that the newly introduced gambling industry poses particular problems during times of economic trauma, though the month of February is likely not the most attractive in any year.

### The Urban-Rural Divide

#### Defining Rural Spaces

This text already has considered in detail some of the geographies of changing rural-urban conditions in the state. In Chapter 4 we looked at the continuing growth and centralization of our urban population and how some of this was occurring at the expense of more rural areas. For example, Figure 4.2 shows the location of the 64 counties not yet included within a particular Metropolitan Statistical Area (MSA); not infrequently this definition is used in providing the administrative boundary between urban and rural counties. Figures 4.3, on the other hand,

suggests the degree of rurality that exists in terms of actual population size. Here we find 28 counties having a total population of less than 25,000 people and there are 23 counties with a population ranging from 25,000 to 50,000. Both Figure 4.4 and 4.5 demonstrate some aspect of relating population totals to the size of territory occupied by this population (i. e., population density). Careful examination of Figure 4.5 will reveal the existence of 63 counties having no municipality with over 10,000 people. However, it is Figure 4.4 that takes on particular significance in public policy relating to rural development in the state. Here the counties are displayed by categories of their population density, with those under 200 people per square mile officially designated rural by the North Carolina Rural Economic Development Center, Inc., the leading rural issues think tank in the state (Matthews 1999). This definition was recently used in the Bowles Report, a comprehensive examination of rural issues and problems, and suggested strategies for their solution generated by the Rural Prosperity Task Force (2000).

A more generally accepted approach to the delimitation of rural counties, focusing on critical urban differences, is that used by the U.S. Department of Agriculture, Economic Research Service (Garcia 1991). Table 7.4 indicates three ranges of non-metropolitan counties, each range further defined by their adjacency to an MSA county. This scheme permits us to locate counties defined as urbanized, less urbanized, and rural, in relation to metropolitan core areas. According to the Economic Research Service (ERS) definition, to be truly rural there has to be less than 2,500 persons living in municipalities within the county. Based on 2000 Census data, Figure 7.16 illustrates the North Carolina application of the ERS definition of non-metropolitan and metropolitan counties, with the further identification of metro counties that have over 200 persons per square mile. The general image of the state is again one of urban counties concentrating in the center with rural counties on the periphery.

#### An Emerging Urban-Rural Divide?

In Chapter 5 we looked at changes shaping the rural economy emphasizing agriculture, forestry, and fishing. Overwhelmingly, traditional forms of rural economic activity has lost out to urban centered activities (CP 5.1). In spite of a traditional Jeffersonian attitude of farms and rural communities constituting the building blocks of democracy, and a correspondingly pervasive public policy support of the agricultural economy throughout American history, rural America has been transformed. Probably the most notable feature of this transformation has been the virtual disappearance of the family farm. One result was the gradual dependency of rural communities on outsiders, with the concomitant individual, family, and community loss of self reliance. Most rural economies prospered through the 1960s and 1970s; declines in family farms were offset by the expansion of corporate agriculture and by rural industrialization, itself led by low tech and low wage industries dominated by branch plants of non-local corporations. Rural prosperity generally came to and end at the close of the 1970s. Rising energy prices, increased

|  | Size of Urban Population | | |
| --- | --- | --- | --- |
|  | Less than 2,500 | 2,500-20,000 | More than 20,000 |
| Adjacent to metro county….. | rural adjacent | less urbanized adjacent | urbanized adjacent |
| Not Adjacent to metro county….. | rural nonadjacent | less urbanized nonadjacent | urbanized nonadjacent |

**Table 7.4:** Economic Research Service Classification of Non-metropolitan Counties. **Source:** Garcia, 1991, 38.

foreign agricultural product competition, and relocating low wage industries to overseas locations provided most of the negative impetus. Nationally, rural unemployment increased from 5.7 percent in 1979 to 10.1 percent in 1982. By 1987, rural exceeded urban unemployment by 40 percent (Garcia 1991, 41). The stage was set for a developing rural-urban divide.

In North Carolina the rural transformation mirrored that of the nation, except that for some counties the impact was devastating. Columbus County is one case in point. All of this county's textile industry has relocated to Mexico, with the loss of close to 3,000 manufacturing jobs. At the same time dwindling tobacco allotments have produced a loss of $80 million in annual tobacco revenues. With tobacco and textiles comprising the twin pillars of the Columbus County economy, how does it recover? By retraining its former textile workers? These are mostly women in their fifties who have been working as seamstresses, for example, and who will find it very difficult to upgrade their skills to the needed high-tech level. In the meantime, they are finding work as service personnel in the coastal tourism industry, at about $6.00 an hour, with at least two hours of commuting by van per day (Hall 2001). Box 7B provides some dimensionality to the emerging urban-rural development gap. Income derived from different

economic activities clearly favor urban locations; in some cases, average incomes for the same job generates $10,000 less per year in the rural setting. The manufacturing jobs remaining in rural areas are still dominated by the traditional low wage, labor intensive industries. Differences in average annual incomes across the state are dependent largely on the degree of rurality.

### A Spatially Defined Socioeconomic Development Continuum

If now we look at combining the spatial realities of county land use as defined by the Economic Research Service (i.e., metropolitan, urbanizing, less urbanizing and peripheral), with the functional attributes that results in differences in quality of life conditions (i.e., the urban-rural development divide), then it is possible to conceive of a socio-economic landscape where differences in development are related to distance from metro cores. In this landscape it is also suggested that land use change is more or less continuous across space. One does not fall into a socioeconomic abyss upon leaving the metropolitan core counties, as suggested by a too stringent definition of the urban-rural divide; rather there is a more gradual transition defined by the travel distance from metro centers. Geographers and regional scientists refer to this space change phenomenon as a distance

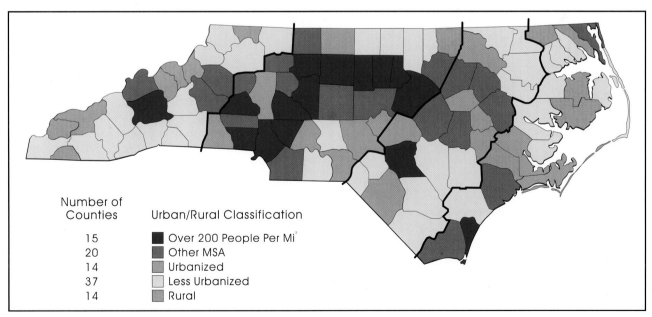

| Number of Counties | Urban/Rural Classification |
| --- | --- |
| 15 | Over 200 People Per Mi² |
| 20 | Other MSA |
| 14 | Urbanized |
| 37 | Less Urbanized |
| 14 | Rural |

**Figure 7.16:** U. S. Department of Agriculture Economic Research Service Land Use Classification System Applied to North Carolina. **Source:** Garcia, 1991, 38.

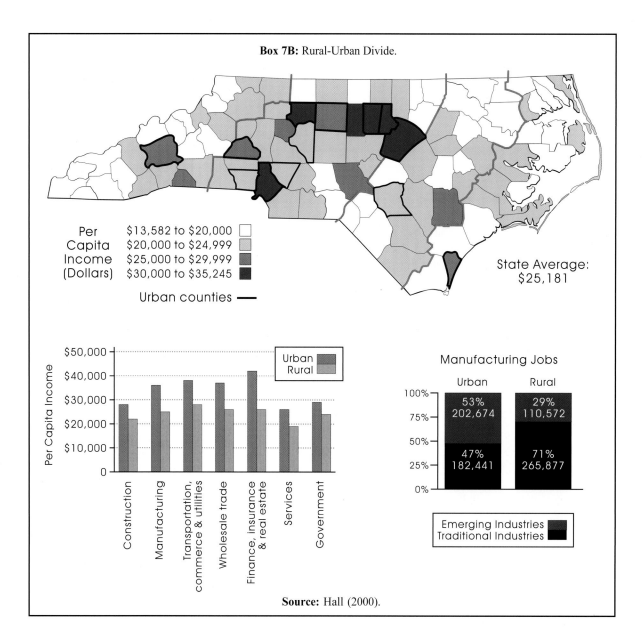

**Box 7B:** Rural-Urban Divide.

Per Capita Income (Dollars)
- $13,582 to $20,000
- $20,000 to $24,999
- $25,000 to $29,999
- $30,000 to $35,245

Urban counties —

State Average: $25,181

Manufacturing Jobs

Urban | Rural
53% 202,674 | 29% 110,572
47% 182,441 | 71% 265,877

Emerging Industries
Traditional Industries

**Source:** Hall (2000).

decay function. Figure 7.17 demonstrates the hypothetical existence of a quality of life gradient (Line A-B), which gradually decreases in value from the metropolitan core to the outer periphery, as a function of distance (Gade 1991; Persson and Wiberg 1995). Here we define quality of life as an average result of a statistical analysis of a number of critical social capital conditions discussed in this chapter. Line A–B represents a continuum of decreasing quality of life from metro core to rural periphery, while the lighter blue line suggests some of the variation likely to exist along this landscape traverse. Key terms (like central city, suburbia, etc.) indicate the locational influences on the quality of life gradient. Applying actual North Carolina county data and statistical analysis to this hypothetical landscape results in Figure 7.18. This analysis attempts to answer the question: is a low quality of life in rural North Carolina an evolution of community quality of life differences that can be defined along a continuum

from most urban to most rural? We find that the so-called emerging urban–rural divide has a clear spatial dimension to it, where a lower quality of life is a function of increasing distance from the opportunities and amenities of urban centers. Statistical data representing the following social capital variables were used in arriving at Figure 7.18: commuting to and from individual counties, retail sales, access to physicians, high school graduation rates, serious crime rates, unemployment rates, population change, youth dependency, elderly dependency, unemployment, migration, population below poverty level, non-manufacturing employment change, and housing quality. The resulting classification earmarks counties in the state in terms of their average quality of life conditions, with counties ranked from high to low: Metropolitan Growth Core, Urban Centered, Intermediate Urban-Rural, Rural Periphery A, and Rural Periphery B. This continuum of quality of life conditions suggests the important need for de-

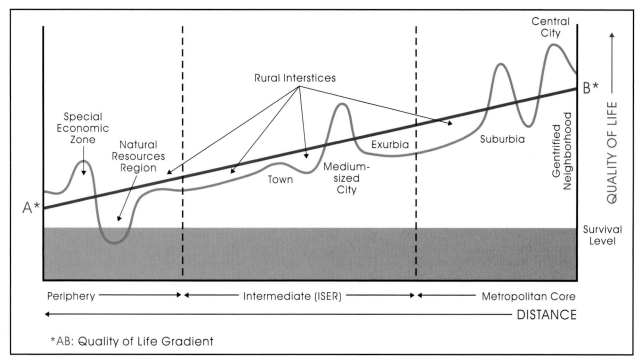

**Figure 7.17:** The Socioeconomic Development Continuum.
**Source:** Gade, 1991, 21; Persson and Wiberg, 1995, 3.

veloping a public strategy of rural renaissance that focuses more specifically on the lower quality of life conditions actually existing in the peripheral counties, especially in Rural Periphery B counties.

Clearly, dealing effectively with the problems of rural development requires an understanding of the multiplicity of factors that encourage a lower quality of life in rural settings. The persistence of these tightly woven problems, and their seemingly insoluble nature, indicate a deepening of the gap between the wealthiest urban and poorest rural counties in the state. The growing gap has pushed the governor's office and the state legislature time and again to study the issue and to call for corrective action. In July 1999, when announcing the N. C. Rural Prosperity Task Force, Governor Hunt articulated the situation this way, "We're on the verge of becoming two North Carolinas. One is urban and thriving; the other is rural and struggling" (Rural Prosperity... 2000, 9). Chaired by a prominent businessman, Erskine Bowles of Charlotte, and including a diverse and bipartisan membership of 25 equally prominent North Carolinians, the Task Force outlined its guiding principles to include (p. 10):

1) Rural North Carolina is facing significant–and irreversible–long term challenges leaving rural communities devastated; these include recent natural disasters, plant closings and job layoffs, decline of tobacco, world agricultural products competition, continuous decreases in the farm population;

2) Rural North Carolinians living near urban centers face a different set of challenges than those in more remote locations; in addition wetland communities are challenged differently from mountain communities; the result of this diversity is to focus on community capacity building which emphasizes the uniqueness of place and people in development strategies;

3) Education–at every stage of life–is the key to success;

4) Taking a regional approach to economic development is hard. And it works. In a rapidly globalizing world that impacts rural as well as urban areas, competition is likely to be worldwide with community collaboration essential for survival and eventual prosperity;

5) Rural North Carolina is critical to the entire state.

The Task Force issued six major proposals, with over 70 highly specific recommendations, including: the creation of a rural redevelopment authority to provide grants and loans for rural projects; expansion of internet access (a key problem since some rural counties face a ten fold higher access cost than do urban places); approve a major water and sewer infrastructure bond issue; move more rapidly in building already planned rural roads; develop new crop planting programs; and open new markets (Betts 2000). With an estimated state cost of $677 million plus over $1 billion in federal matching funds, over a five-year planning period, funding was expected to be a problem, espe-

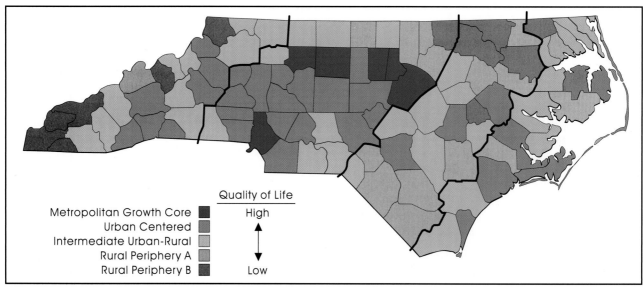

**Figure 7.18:** Socioeconomic Development Regions in North Carolina.
**Source:** Chang, Gade, and Jones, 1991, 159.

cially given the negative situation the state budget was in during 2000-01 (Griffin 2000). Perhaps the very real efforts of the North Carolina Rural Economic Development Center, Inc, and the tangible recommendations flowing from the Rural Prosperity Task Force failed to gain their apparent public and political relevance by casting too wide a net in their inclusion of the kind of counties labeled rural. On the one hand, including 85 percent of the counties, with over 50 percent of the state's population likely reflects the felt need to embrace as large a political base as possible, and thereby the suspected greater likelihood of General Assembly support of rural development objectives. On the other hand, sympathy for extra-ordinary government efforts to support rural development is equally likely to be hampered by a public insensitive to so-called rural problems, because the problems are not as readily apparent in the majority of those 85 counties. Data presented, in this and other chapters of this text, makes it clear that it is in counties classed as peripheral (Figure 7.18) where embedded structural poverty continues to exist in a pervasive and so far unconquerable degree. From this data, there are 29 counties with a total population of 810,000, about ten percent of the state's population in 2000, that fall into the peripheral region categories, and thus may be characterized as socio-economically marginal. These are counties that are so clearly on the margins of "the goodliest land under the cope of heaven," that they merit special attention in socioeconomic upgrading efforts. They do not merit inclusion in rural development initiatives so spatially broadly defined that their unique human needs remain relatively untouched, if not essentially unrecognized. It should be pointed out that the socioeconomic development classification (Figure 7.18) is based in data about a decade old, thus a few counties (Franklin, Granville, and Madison) may have bootstrapped themselves out of the peripheral category. Other counties, however, may have lagged sufficiently in their 1990s development that they are now classed at the peripheral level, such as Anson,

Montgomery, Richmond, Mitchell, and Washington counties. Much more detail on peripheral and near peripheral counties is provided in the relevant regional chapters and related State Geographic Region discussions. On the various ways of establishing what is rural in the state see McLaughlin and Skinner (1997). A discussion of state regional policy and the urban-rural paradox is provided in Chapter 9.

## A STATE OF GOOD HEALTH?

### *Introduction*

In a critical review of North Carolina's health conditions in the 1990s Ken Outterbourg quotes an early observer of life in the Carolinas (1996, 529):

> The only business here is of raising hogs, which is mang'd with the least Trouble, and affords the Diet they are most fond of. The Truth of it is, the Inhabitants of N Carolina devour so much swine's flesh, that it fills them full of gross Humours. For want of a constant Supply of Salt, they are commonly obliged to eat it Fresh, and that begets the highest taint of Scurvy. . .

William Byrd's pithy comment in 1728 is not without a contemporary corollary. Some aspects of life have a long history in the Tar Heel state, now the second largest producer of hogs in the country, with a people who are avid connoisseurs of hog meat. Consider that Bob Melton of Rocky Mount opened the state's first sit-down barbeque restaurant in 1924. In various forms of smoked pork, with special sauces that bring out a keen regional competitive spirit, hog meat ranks as high as an attribute of Carolina culture as does college basketball. However, the production of hog meat, with its attendant environmental problems

(Chapters 5 and 8) has changed as dramatically as has the character and environments of the public's health. Rarely do we hear of scurvy as a contemporary health problem. Generally speaking, the people of North Carolina are the healthiest ever, and it is one state in a country that is the healthiest ever. Yet, the United States health care system, frequently claimed to be the finest anywhere in the world, is not producing the expected result. In this country, a far greater proportion of the gross domestic product is spent on health care than in any other developed nation. Yet the U.S. ranks 21st in infant mortality and 17th in life expectancy for women (worse for men). In comparing North Carolina's health conditions to those elsewhere in the country, it is clear that we are not as healthy as we should be. Herein is found another of the many paradoxes that keeps turning up as the details of the state unfolds in this text. It is well appreciated the world over that North Carolina shines in medical research and innovative approaches to treating illness and infirmity. As a leading example of this, Duke University persistently ranks among the top five in the nation for its medical degree programs, and its hospital is among the world's most esteemed. Other exceptional medical centers exist in Winston-Salem, Charlotte, and Asheville. Yet, the state leads the nation in indices that suggest a worst case scenario of health conditions in a developed country. Consider, for example, the persistently high infant mortality rates, the chasms in health care occupied by the mentally ill and the elderly of the state, and the continuing problems of automobile and work place accidents. Overall the state ranked 32nd in the nation in a 1991 survey of state health statistics, although well ahead of many other southeastern states. Some argue that being a very low 44th in the country in state per capita expenditures for health care, but a more respectable 32nd in achieved health is a fair accomplishment (Outterbourg 1996). For North Carolinians, the major barriers to attaining universal good health continues to be education, access, and cost. Therefore, differences in health across the state is defined by urban-rural, as well as income/ wealth and racial parameters.

### *Mortality and Its Determinants*

#### *The Relevance of Age Adjusted Mortality Rates*

One of the most widely used sources of information for establishing the health status of a particular area is the mortality for different segments of its population, and records of why and at what rate people die from different causes. It is relevant through this discussion for the reader to refer to materials provided on the state's demographic characteristics in Chapter 4. Critical differences in arriving at different data sets should be understood. For example, the data providing the map in Figure 4.14 is the unadjusted crude death rate, a good measure of the overall magnitude of mortality in a given population. For counties with an average older population, such as Polk, a high crude death rate can be expected and is a useful indicator for the planning of elder care facilities. Age adjusted death rates, used in this section, take on a greater significance in the context of health assessments. A

detailed and comprehendible explanation of differences between adjusted and unadjusted death rates is provided by Paul Buscher (1998). Here it is sufficient to note that age adjusted death rates make clearer the incidence of age specific mortality, and thus the varying significance of infant deaths, motor vehicle accidents, sexually transmitted diseases, various forms of cancer, and other causes of death, in a given county's population. Hertford County, for example, has an age specific death rate in the 0-4 age group of 3.68 per 1,000 population, in that age group among the highest in the state. Not until the 45-54 age group is reached is the age specific death rate higher in this county. Cumulatively Hertford County winds up with a lower unadjusted death rate than that of the adjusted death rate (8.7/1,000 vs. 11.9/1,000), due in part to a smaller proportion of older people. For the state this is equally the case (7.4/1,000 vs. 8.9/1,000). Figures 7.19a and b allow comparison of the annual average adjusted death rates (ADR) by county for the period of 1979-1983 with the period of 1994-1998. Note that the ADR for the state as a whole had fallen from 10.2 to 9.4/1,000, and also that the number of counties in the highest category of 11.4 to 12.1/1,000 decreased from 16 to six. Among these six high incidence counties, four (Bertie, Edgecombe, Jones, and Vance) experienced increases in their adjusted death rates! It is notable that the lowest adjusted death rates are observed in the mountain counties from the early to the latter period of observation. The highest adjusted death rates remain concentrated in the Coastal Plain Region, though here also significant decreases are seen. Counties that have a higher remnant blue color labor force and American Indian populations continue to be at higher rates than average for the state (for example Gaston, Cleveland and Rutherford counties with their traditional manufacturing emphases, and Swain, Robeson, and Scotland counties with their large American Indian populations). On the other hand, counties dominated by retirement and university populations have low adjusted death rates. Note, for example Polk, Henderson, Macon, and Moore counties, probably soon to be joined by the coastal counties, of Brunswick, Pender, Carteret, and Dare. For college counties, Jackson, Watauga, and Orange all have very low age adjusted death rates.

#### *A Caution About Use of Rates*

Data on death rates present particular problems in statistical evaluation and mapping. For counties of small populations there tends to be a greater variability from year to year in the frequency of deaths due to certain causes. For this reason, data records for several consecutive years are combined to assure improved accuracy of persistent conditions, and more reliable comparisons of changes over time. In addition, where there are diseases with low frequency of occurrence, there is likely to be substantial random variation over time, a condition that statisticians refer to as a large standard error. Typically, where the number of deaths total less than 20 as the numerator in any given death rate, particular care should be taken in making comparisons or assessing trends. Unusually high or low rates may be due to small numbers.

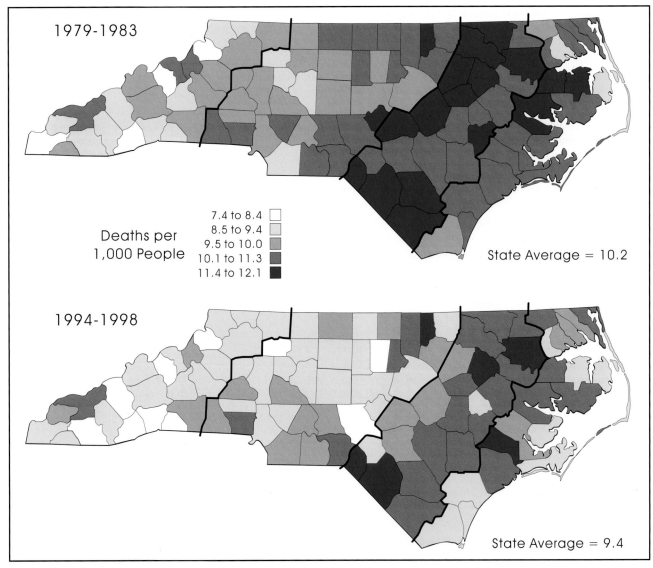

**Figure 7.19:** Comparative Age-Adjusted Mortality Rates per 1,000 Population: Annual Averages, 1979-83 and 1994-1998.
**Sources:** N. C. Department of Health and Human Services, North Carolina Vital Statistics, March, 2000.

*Major Causes of Mortality*

As noted in *North Carolina Leading Causes of Death* (2000, 3), the main reference for this section of analysis, mortality arises from causes imbedded in the social fabric, and medical care is only one aspect of the general condition of health. Accordingly, death is hastened by negative environmental factors (such as atmospheric and water pollution, toxic waste deposition, occupational exposure to hazardous substances), with the disabled, the very young and the very old populations especially vulnerable. Unemployment and poverty provide its own hazards, because having fewer resources and experiencing higher stress make people more vulnerable to infectious agents and hazards at home and at work. Rural populations, likewise, are troubled due to their lack of ready access to medical care, and their lesser tendency to have medical insurance. A health adverse lifestyle also contributes to an early death. What makes a person live longer is influenced by being physically active, not indulging in narcotics and drugs, getting enough sleep, and maintaining an appropriate body weight. Lifestyles habits are influenced by age, sex, and race characteristics. Men are more likely to smoke and drink excessively. Blacks tend to be more sedentary, with black women more likely to be substantially overweight. Being white, young, and less educated is more generally a smoker's handle. Biological factors add a further dimension to determinants of mortality. Age is especially important, as personal health is invariably tied to the life cycle. Men are more readily diseased, while women live longer, on the average. Many diseases are genetic in origin, with some being racially selective. The public health and medical care system is also a determinant of mortality in the sense of prolonging life; factors include vaccinations, diagnosis and drug prescriptions, expert life cycle medical practice, advances in disease and health problems research, new technology in emergency and surgical facilities, equipment, and improved professional expertise. Mistakes and risk taking in medical practice may reduce the positive nature of the health support dimension.

While the previously discussed factors all are defined as determinants of mortality, the health risks that people take also are critical determinants of health; each individual can take charge of their own behaviors and modify them to reduce their own chance of illness and an early death. For example, two of the more important factors contributing to mortality from various diseases are high blood pressure and cigarette smoking. Hypertension is a stealthy killer, as only ten million Americans of the 42 million estimated to suffer from high blood pressure are successfully treating it. Others are ignoring this condition and not modifying personal behaviors appropriately (i.e., weight control, physical exercise, special diets, and medicine regimen), or they are not being aggressively treated by their physicians, claims a study published by the *New England Journal of Medicine* in August, 2001. Hypertension is associated with death from all cardiovascular diseases, diabetes mellitus, cirrhosis of the liver, and renal failure. Use of tobacco products similarly contributes to a large number of diseases and death. Although lung cancer is the most notable, 30 percent of all cancer deaths are attributable to cigarette smoking.

Over recent decades there have been significant breakthroughs in medicine, and society has passed through a number of socioeconomic and demographic transitions that have changed health behaviors. The impacts of these changes on the leading causes of death in North Carolina for 1938, 1958, and 1998 are shown in Figure 7.20. The most notable increases have been experienced by heart disease and cerebrovascular disease. These have moved from 26 percent of causes in 1938 to 51 percent in 1998. We will look briefly at the details of the more significant of these diseases as they affect the state and its 100 counties.

*Heart Disease*

As the leading disease in the state, heart disease accounted for 19,441 (29%) of all deaths in 1998. This translates into an overall mortality rate of 257.6 per 100,000 residents. Among counties in the state, the age adjusted death rate due to heart disease varied from a high of 421/100,000 in Hyde County to a low of 216.7/100,000 in Polk County, a nearly two to one ratio. High rate counties tend to be minority dominated and in relatively poor socioeconomic circumstances (Figure 7.21). Differences in the mortality rate by sex and race were significant. Male death rates were 59 percent higher than female rates, and minorities experienced a rate that was 26 percent higher than for whites (Figure 7.22). In recent decades, improved early identification for at-risk populations, improvements in medical regime, and an increase in personal behavior modifications, have combined to reduce coronary heart failure. The gains have come primarily among white males. Cigarette smoking is the most critical of the known modifiable risk factors for heart disease, and yet North Carolinians

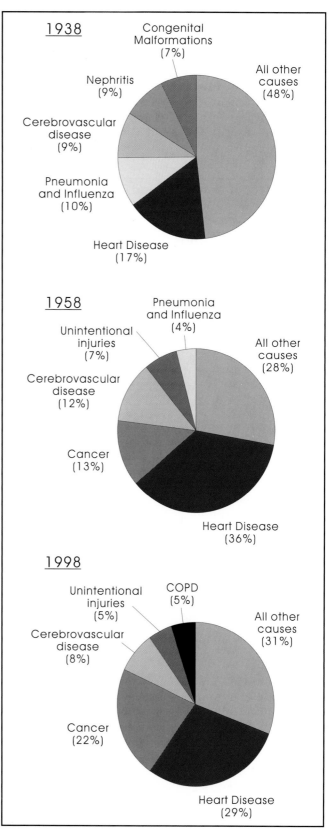

**Figure 7.20:** Causes of Death, 1938, 1958, and 1998.
**Source:** N. C. Department of Health and Human Services, North Carolina Vital Statistics, Volume 2, March, 2000.

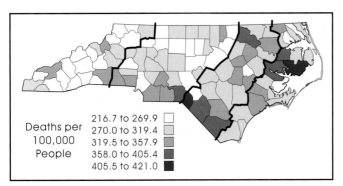

**Figure 7.21:** Heart Disease, Death Rates per 100,000 People, Age-Adjusted, 1998.
**Source:** N. C. Department of Health and Human Services, North Carolina Vital Statistics, Volume 2, March, 2000.

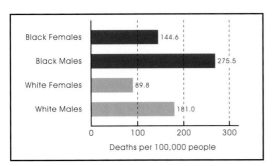

**Figure 7.22:** Heart Disease Death Rates by Race and Gender, 1996.
**Source:** North Carolina Minority Health Facts.

persist in having a percentage of smokers 11th highest among states in the nation. Physical inactivity is also an important modifiable risk factor, and yet North Carolinians have the eighth lowest physical activity participation in the country. A third important modifiable risk factor is poor diet. In spite of the vast recent increases in vegetable and organic agricultural production, North Carolinians generally consume a high-fat, low-fiber diet, and the proportion of the population that is overweight is increasing.

*Cerebrovascular Disease*

Cerebrovascular disease (strokes) ranks third in the state in mortality, with a rate of 72/100,000 population, or 5,434 persons, in 1998. Like heart disease, deaths due to strokes have been steadily declining in recent decades. Even so, North Carolina has the nation's fourth highest mortality rate of cerebrovascular disease. In part, this is due to the location of the state in the so-called "stroke belt," a tier of counties in the Coastal Plain Region of eight to ten states where death rates due to strokes are 1.3 to 2.0 times higher than the national average. Thus mortality rates are much higher in certain Coastal Plain counties like Jones (highest with 121.5/100,000), Bladen, Sampson, Duplin, and Edgecombe (Figure 7.23). On the other hand, strokes are much less significant to the residents of the southwestern and some other mountain counties, with Avery County having the lowest death rate (44.7/100,000) due to cerebrovascular disease. Risk factors are quite similar to those for heart disease, and the rates

for minority populations are markedly higher than for whites (Figure 7.24). It is relevant to point out that no research has indicated a racial linkage to higher cerebrovascular disease rates. Higher minority rates are a function of being disadvantaged, rather than being non-white. To some degree, access to health care facilities for trauma cases is also a more important factor for stroke victims.

*Diabetes Mellitus*

The fourth leading cause of death in the United States, and a contributing factor to kidney failure, cerebrovascular and heart diseases, diabetes appears to be increasing at epidemic proportions in recent years. Two types of diabetes exist. Type 1 is insulin dependent and affects five to ten percent of the diabetes population. It occurs mostly during childhood and adolescent years. Type 2 is non-insulin dependent. For the country as a whole it is estimated that no les than six percent of the population have the disease. In North Carolina, diabetes is the sixth leading killer disease, with 1,900 deaths in 1998. Minorities fare worse by this disease than any other, aside from AIDS. Minority males reached an age-adjusted death rate 2.2 times that of white males, while the minority female rate was three times that of the white female rate (Figure 7.25).

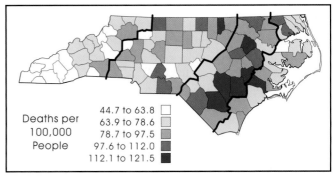

**Figure 7.23:** Cerebrovascular Disease (Stroke) Death Rates per 100,000 People, Age-Adjusted, 1998.
**Source:** N. C. Department of Health and Human Services, North Carolina Vital Statistics, Volume 2, March, 2000.

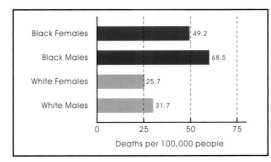

**Figure 7.24:** Cerebrovascular Disease (Stroke) Death Rates by Race and Gender, 1996.
**Source:** North Carolina Minority Health Facts.

240

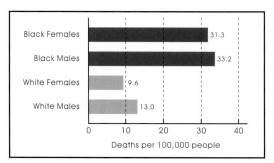

**Figure 7.25:** Diabetes Death Rates by Race and Gender, 1996.
**Source:** North Carolina Minority Health Facts.

## Cancer Deaths

Cancer is a group of different diseases dominated by the uncontrollable growth of abnormal cells. External (toxic chemicals, radiation, and viruses) and internal (hormones, immune conditions, and inherited mutations) factors cause cancer. Frequently, an extended period ensues between onset and detection and death due to cancer. In North Carolina, cancer is the second most prevalent cause of death, with 20 percent of deaths (15,327 individuals) due to cancer in 1998. Unlike heart disease, which has been on a steady decrease over the past three decades, cancer rates are holding steady and can be expected to comprise an increasing share of deaths in the future. A particular onerous disease, with less than a 14 percent 5-year survival rate, is lung cancer. In part, this is due to the difficulties of early detection because symptoms generally do not appear until the disease is in an advanced stage. This is the leading cause of cancer death in the United States, and in North Carolina, where lung cancer accounted for 30.6 percent of all cancer deaths in 1998.

Northeastern North Carolina contains a cluster of high rate cancer counties, led by Camden County with 298.7 deaths/100,000 persons in 1998 (Figure 7.26). Mountain counties again lead the lower death rates in the state, with Yancey County the lowest (163.2/100,000). Being a number of different diseases, cancer risk factors vary by type. Affliction also varies by race. African American males are more than twice as likely to die of prostate cancer than are their white counterparts (Figure 7.27). Black men also are more likely to die from colon, rectum, lung and bronchus cancers. African American women are more likely than their white counterparts to die of colon, rectum, breast and cervical cancers (Figure 7.28).

## Sexually Transmitted Diseases

Known euphemistically not so long ago as "social diseases," sexually transmitted diseases (STD) include gonorrhea, syphilis, chlamydia, and acquired immune deficiency syndrome (AIDS). This coterie of infectious diseases have been particularly problematic for North Carolina, where the incidence of their more virulent types (syphilis and AIDS) experienced dramatic increases in the 1980s. Between 1980 and 1990, syphilis cases increased from 908 to 3494. In 1999, Wake County recorded 105 cases. That year the federal Centers for Disease Control and

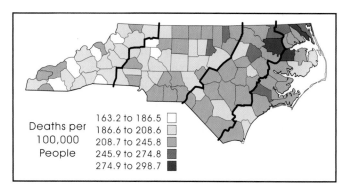

**Figure 7.26:** Cancer Death Rates per 100,000 People, Age-Adjusted, 1998.
**Source:** N. C. Department of Health and Human Services, North Carolina Vital Statistics, Volume 2, March, 2000.

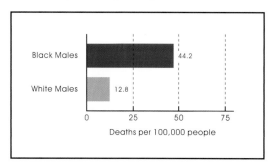

**Figure 7.27:** Prostate Cancer Death Rates by Race, 1996.
**Source:** North Carolina Minority Health Facts.

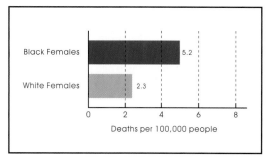

**Figure 7.28:** Cervical Cancer Death Rates by Race, 1996.
**Source:** North Carolina Minority Health Facts.

Prevention (CDC) found that five counties in North Carolina (Wake among them), were included among the 28 worst case counties, accounting for 50 percent of the syphilis in the country. Forsyth County's rate dropped from 117.9 cases for every 100,000 people in 1994, the peak year for syphilis in Forsyth, to 29.2 in 1998 (85 total cases). When realizing that the epidemic proportions reached by the disease in the mid-nineties were beyond the resources and staff of the Forsyth Public Health Department, a community partnership evolved to deal more effectively with the prevention of its further diffusion. Workers and volunteers visited high drug traffic neighborhoods, handing out condoms, offering a screening for syphilis at no cost, and providing information on disease treatment available at the county health department. Impressed with the Forsyth County results the federal government decided to use the county as one of the models for a national campaign. Syphilis is readily cured with antibiotics, but left untreated the disease can linger in the body for years, and then lead to lesions and fevers, and finally to heart disease, dementia, and death. The worst aspect of this increase is the concomitant growth of congenital syphilis, where a mother passes on the disease to her child. Where this occurs children are likely to suffer deafness, seizures, developmental delays, and bone deformation. Such instances were not known in the state (i.e., no reported cases), until 1986, but by 1990 there were 30 cases. What amounted to a national epidemic in the 1990s has been fought effectively by the CDC, which lead a successful campaign to cut the congenital syphilitic rate by half by 2000. In the Carolinas, the rate persisted above 40.0 per 100,000 births, while the national rate had been reduced to 13.4/100,000 births. Syphilis has struck especially hard in the African-American community. For every white person with this disease there are 35 black persons who have it (Rochman 2000a and b). In toto, sexually transmitted diseases affected an average of 48.7/100,000 people in the state in 1998. Few cases existed in the mountains or in the western Piedmont regions, except for the larger urban counties (Figure 7.29). STD remains largely concentrated in the Coastal Plain region, with a lesser incidence recorded toward the east into the Tidewater counties, and west into the eastern Piedmont.

*Acquired Immune Deficiency Syndrome*

Among the sexually transmitted diseases, HIV/AIDS is the most threatening to life. This is a very recently recorded disease in the country. Apparently it was first noticed with a strange outbreak of a disease in Los Angeles in June of 1981. Five men had come down with a rare form of pneumonia, one that was known to occur with the breakdown of a person's immunity system. The clue that all five were homosexuals led to the belief that the disease was sexually transmitted. By mid-2001, the world wide estimate of AIDS deaths exceeded 22 million people, but now the disease is being effectively fought with early screening tests and continuous advances in control medicines. Theoretically, the antiviral drugs now in use can extend longevity by 30-35 years, if not for the occasional drug toxicity case. Although

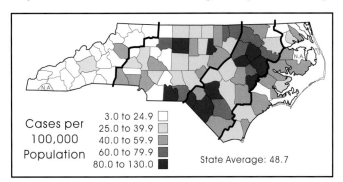

**Figure 7.29:** Sexually Transmitted Diseases per 100,000 People, Age-Adjusted, 1998.
**Source:** N. C. Department of Health and Human Services, North Carolina Vital Statistics, Volume 2, March, 2000.

the AIDS vaccine has yet to be invented, getting the disease is no longer a death sentence, but it is still a chronic illness. For the United States, the mid-to late-1980s saw 100,000 to 150,000 people getting infected each year. 1995 was the peak year in deaths from AIDS, with nearly 50,000 dying from the disease. The number of people infected now is about 40,000 annually, with about 10,000 people dying in 1999. It is estimated that 800,000 to 900,000 people presently carry the disease, with one-third of this total not knowing that they are carriers (Haney 2001).

In North Carolina, AIDS accounted for 432 deaths in 1998, equal to 5.7 deaths per 100,000 people. Improved treatment and education about the disease resulted in a dramatic drop in the death rate from the high attained in 1995 of 15/100,000. Since 1998, there has been a slowing of the decline. From a geographic perspective, AIDS shows very distinctive concentrations in the state (Box 7C). For 1994-1998, the county age-adjusted mortality rates due to AIDS ranged from 0 to 23.6/100,000 (Box 7Ca), with a clear concentration in rural Coastal Plain counties and in the large metropolitan counties. These basic settlement morphology characteristics are illustrated in diagram (Box 7Cb). Here a conceptual model of AIDS diffusion through the North Carolina landscape, with source regions in the poverty neighborhood of the urban Piedmont and "newer frontiers" for the disease in poor, rural areas in the Coastal Plain (Pyle and Furuseth 1992, 9). It follows that AIDS is closely associated with concentrations of the state's black population (Elmore 2000). This aspect is further highlighted in Box 7Cc and e where an incredible ratio of black to non-black AIDS deaths of 5:1 was reached in 1995. Clearly also this a predominantly a male disease as indicated in both Box 7Cd and e.

*Unintentional Injuries*

Mortality from injuries fall into two categories. Unintentional injuries include automotive vehicle accidents, falls, poisoning, fires, drowning, and suffocation. Deaths from intentional injuries include murder and suicide. Unintentional injuries, frequently simply referred to as accidents, are the nation's fifth most common cause of death; more notably, for individuals aged 1-44, they are the most common cause. In 1998, 92,200 people died from accidents (two people are killed every ten minutes), and yet this represents a dramatic decrease in significance of accidents as a cause of death. In 1912, the national rate was 82.5 deaths/100,000; by 1995 it has reached a low of 34.0/100,000. The latest figure of 34.1 for 1998 suggests that perhaps a leveling off has occurred. People are more accident prone in western states, with Wyoming having the highest rate of 57.2, followed by New Mexico's 53.9 and Alaska's 53.5; lowest in the country is New York state with 18.7, followed by Massachusetts' 20.6 and Rhode Island's 23.1 (The New York Times Almanac 2000, 377). North Carolina came in slightly over the national average with a rate of 42.6 deaths/100,000.

Accidents come in many guises. Most significant is death from unintentional motor vehicle injury. In North Carolina, 1,632 died from such injury, in 1998, considerably higher than the na-

**Box 7C:** AIDS.

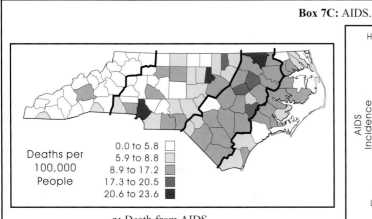

**a:** Death from AIDS.

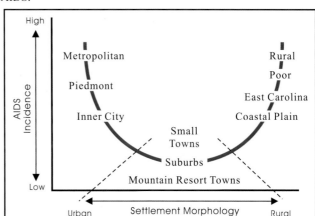

**b:** Aids Incidence and Settlement.

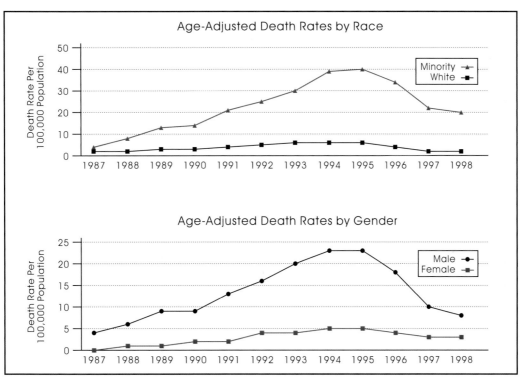

**c and d:** AIDS Deaths by Race and Gender.

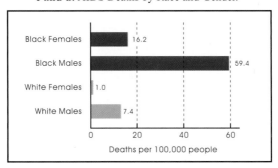

**e:** Death Rates - AIDS, 1996.

**Sources:** North Carolina Leading Causes of Death, 2000; Pyle and Furuseth (1992).

tional average. As shown in Figure 7.30, this is more of a rural problem, due perhaps to less police vigilance on rural highways that also are more readily used as raceways by young speeders (Outterbourg 1996, 537). However, a factor of greater influence is alcohol related accidents, with 44 percent of all road fatalities related to intoxicated drivers. A decade earlier the Safe Roads Act of 1983 was passed to address this issue. However, it is difficult to assess the direct influence of this act because other conditions have been changing simultaneously. For example, roadways and signage have been generally improved, although speeds have been increased, as well. Automobiles have become heavier and presumably safer in an accident, though also more destructive to smaller vehicles. Use of seatbelts have become law, with special provisions for children to the age of twelve for both back and front seat restraint, but their use declined from a high of 78 percent statewide to 60 percent over the decade following the imposition of the adult seat belt law in 1987. An interesting comparison can be made between actual traffic tickets issued by police and state troopers in 1996-97 (Figure 7.31) with 1998 traffic fatalities illustrated in Figure 7.30. It appears that patrol vigilance is especially favored in counties leading to coastal resorts. Craven County, for example, leads by far in tickets issued, with a rate nearly double that of the next county, Tyrrell; Tyrrell County has almost twice the rate of tickets issued than the next three counties of Chowan, Perquimans, and Bladen. All of these counties are either on the coast or are one county removed (Diamant 1998). What the motivating factor is for issuing a high rate of traffic tickets in counties like Watauga and Stokes, with the lowest fatality rates in the state, is not as immediately apparent as is the positive result.

All other injuries accounted for 1,586 deaths in 1998. The spatial pattern emerging from a map of these deaths reveals a tendency toward the more rural counties to have a higher incidence (Figure 7.32). Possibly, a distance decay function is operative here. With the much greater need for immediate emergency care, in the case of life threatening injury, access to a hospital with appropriate emergency care facilities becomes critical, and time is of the essence. In assessing this data, it is important to recognize the influence of small data values, both as county

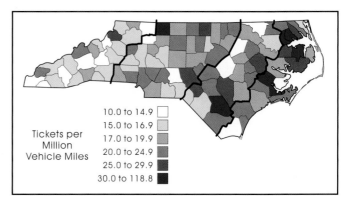

**Figure 7.31:** Traffic Tickets Issued per Million Vehicle Miles, 1996-1997.
**Source:** Charlotte Observer, February 8, 1999.

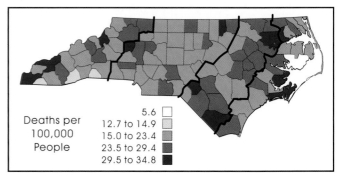

**Figure 7.32:** All Other Injuries Death Rate per 100,000, Age-Adjusted, 1998.
**Source:** N. C. Department of Health and Human Services, North Carolina Vital Statistics, Volume 2, March, 2000.

populations and as incidence of injury deaths. Camden County provides a good example of this. Whereas the state age-adjusted death rates for all other injuries have been on a consistent decline from 1979-1983 (28.4) to 1994-1998 (21.5), Camden County has varied from 68.7 to 18.6, with a decrease of only four occurrences accounting for the decline in the rate.

*Intentional Injuries*

North Carolina apparently ranks close to the average in the country in the rate of self-inflicted injury resulting in death, suicide. In 1998, 846 residents committed suicide, thus accounting for a death rate of 11.2/100,000. Men are about four times as suicidal as are women, One of the most senior of the age cohorts, the 75-84 age group, leads the other age groups with a suicide death rate of 19.7; but the next highest rate was among the 35-44 age cohort (16.5). Whites committed suicide at about twice the rate of nonwhites. The more rural counties were also at the higher end of the suicide rates. Across the state there were some remarkable differences (Figure 7.33). The highest age-adjusted suicide death rates are recorded in the Mountain Region. It would appear that the combination of white predominance, an older population, and rural people come together to influence rates that reach 24.7 in Avery, 20.4 in Ashe, and 20.3 in Alleghany.

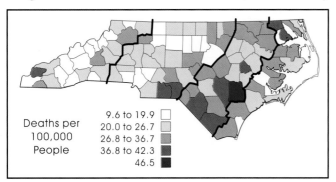

**Figure 7.30:** Motor Vehicle Accidents Death Rate per 100,000 People, Age-Adjusted, 1998.
**Source:** N. C. Department of Health and Human Services, North Carolina Vital Statistics, Volume 2, March, 2000.

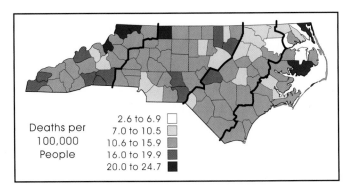

**Figure 7.33:** Death by Suicide per 100,000 Population, 1998.
**Source:** N. C. Department of Health and Human Services, North Carolina Vital Statistics, Volume 2, March, 2000.

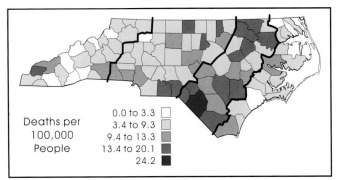

**Figure 7.34:** Death by Homicide per 100,000 Population, 1998.
**Source:** N. C. Department of Health and Human Services, North Carolina Vital Statistics, Volume 2, March, 2000.

Some coastal rural counties also attain very high rates, as for example, Hyde with 22.1 and Currituck with 20.1.

Homicide occurred in the state at a rate significantly less than that of suicide, although still at a rate about 28 percent higher than the national average. In 1998, there were 664 murders in North Carolina, accounting for about one percent of total deaths. Though hardly a leading cause of death, homicide assumes greater significance when age, race, and sex categories are evaluated separately. For the age cohort 15-24, homicide was the second leading cause of death (motor vehicles being the first). Among American Indians, homicide accounted for 3.9 percent of their total deaths during the year, while for African Americans that percentage was 2.4. The highest homicide rate, an astonishing 74.7/100,000, for any particular group was that of minority males aged 15-24 years, while minority males aged 25-34 had an only slightly lower rate of 71.9. Over the past several decades it appears that the rate of homicide has been tied to the general status of the economy. During good years the rate is lower, ranging from a state-wide 8.5 to 9.1 in the mid-to late-1980s, while a high of 12.5 was reached during the recession and high unemployment year of 1991. Higher unadjusted and age-adjusted homicide rates occur in the northeastern and south central portions of the state, with the highest rates reached in a band of counties from Anson (19.4/100,000), to Richmond (20.1), Scotland (19.7), and Robeson with the highest in the state of 24.2/100,000 (Figure 7.34). Among the 58 largest metropolitan areas in the country, Charlotte's murder rate ranked eleventh in 1998 with 9.7/100,000; however, this is much lower than the record year of 1991, when 115 people were killed in the city. At this time of newly introduced crack cocaine, cheap and highly addictive, with high profits for dealers scrambling for territory, the city's death rate due to homicide was 27.5/100,000, this compared to Durham's rate of 23.2, Hickory's 17.6, Gastonia's 16.4, and Raleigh's 12.5 (Urban 1992). Nearly three quarters of the murders in Charlotte were of young black people. It is then of interest to note where the newly adopted concealed gun law has had its greatest impact. One might logically assume that where the threat of homicide is the greatest there would be the largest demand for the personal protection offered by a legally concealed defensive

weapon. Well, not so. A comparative glance at Figure 7.34 and Figure 7.35 will indicate that very little direct overlapping county correlation exists between the actual incidence of homicide and the applications for concealed weapons permits. On the other hand the pattern of applications suggest a linkage that those in the shadow of the central metro counties are more apt to seek this kind of protection. Cabarrus County, for example, had 5.1 concealed gun permits per 1,000 residents in 1996, more than any other in the state. This was twice the number per/1,000 than adjacent Mecklenburg County, itself ranked 49th in spite of having the state's highest crime rate (Dyer 1996). By 1999, there were 37,143 permits issued in the state (about one half of one percent of the population), with Iredell County leading with nearly ten per 1,000 residents (Dyer 1999). The psychology behind the individually expressed need for carrying a concealed weapon, as indicated by going to the county sheriff's office and completing the permit application process, is very complex. Fear factors, fostered in part by media reporting, especially exaggerated TV News reporting, are likely to rule, but the nature of their origin is not shown on the application, so readers are left to their own devices in reasoning the answer to this question.

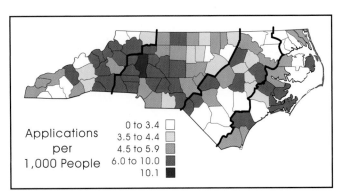

**Figure 7.35:** Applications to Carry a Concealed Weapon per 1,000 People, 1996.
**Source:** Charlotte Observer.

## Health and Special Populations

### Children

What more special population do we have than our children? And, very unhappily, this is a population we have been abjectly failing. A 1994 State Center for Health and Environmental Statistics study found that an increasing number of young children were dying from physical abuse, while poor newborns weigh too little and then become too overweight as they grow. On the state level there were 59,907 reports of abuse and neglect involving 95,811 children, an 82 percent increase from just four years earlier. In general, the study found a bleak picture of poverty, poor nutrition, and inadequate health care to be the main contributing factors. Births classified as low weight reached 8.7 percent in 1993, the highest since 1975. Twice as many black mothers gave birth to low weight babies (5.5 pounds or less), than did white mothers. By 1997, the state average had increased to 8.8 percent, with counties ranging from 3.2 percent to 14.1 percent. There is a higher incidence of low weight births in rural and disproportionately poor counties with a higher percentage of minority populations (Figure 7.36). Low weight is the leading contributing cause of infant deaths. Children of poor circumstances are troubled with common problems, including incomplete immunizations, elevated blood lead levels, development disabilities, untreated dental defects, and a low incidence of breast feeding. Much of this is spurred on by the greater frequency of out-of-wedlock births. Nearly one-third of the state's mothers in 1993 were unwed. From the state health policy and tax payer cost perspective, it is worth noting that the hospital cost of delivering a full term average weight baby is less than five percent that of the cost of intensive care for an infant born twelve weeks prematurely and of low birth weight. Investing in prenatal care is clearly the answer.

State officials, having assessed a surprising slight increase in the infant mortality rate (IMR) in 1983, found this increase to be not alarming (Hammersly 1983). Perhaps the reason for this was conditioned by the persistent drop in the IMR, defined as children dying before the age of one year, from the very high rates of the early 1970s. 1970 began with an IMR of 24.1, which

then declined over the next two decades (Figure 7.37a). Then the IMR spiked again in the late 1980s, exceeding 12.0/1,000, giving North Carolina the highest infant death rate in the nation (which had an average of 9.9/1,000). For developed countries, the United States has a higher than average IMRs, typically ranking behind 20 or so other nations. In response to the high IMR, there was a major national effort in the 1970s, echoed on the state level, to improve conditions for low income mothers and their babies with better access to medical care and better nutrition. In North Carolina, heavy use of support services during the 1980s caused waiting lists at public health clinics for women during their most critical early weeks of pregnancy, with particular dire consequences for minority women. As indicated in Figure 7.37b, the problem for black mothers has not improved significantly, with their IMR falling only slightly during much of the 1990s, only to increase again in 1998. The increasing gap between white and black IMRs is symptomatic in a state where poverty and race have not assumed legislative attention in proportion to the socio-economic impact of these factors. For every child that dies, many more will survive, but lack proper nutrition, health care, and those other necessities of life that encourage the development of individuals capable of competing on a level playing field for the rest of their lives. From the racial perspective there is a generally acknowledged perinatal paradox (Figure 7.37c). Black women, regardless of income level, bear children with higher IMR than do white or other minority women (Wilson 2000a). Still, North Carolina's IMRs do not compare favorably with other states for any race. For whites, the IMR is exceeded by only seven states.

Notably, in 1999 the state also had the nation's highest incidence of neural tube defects such as spina bifida. South Carolina had an equally high rate of this birth defect some years ago, but was able to cut the rate in half through a vigorous statewide education program promoting increased use of folic acid, and costing $900,000 yearly. In 1999, the North Carolina legislature reluctantly funded a one shot $150,000 educational campaign (Saving Our Babies 2000). All of the negatives come into play when trying to account for the distribution of infant deaths in North Carolina counties, averaged over the 1994-1998 period (Figure 7.38). Rural counties with higher concentrations of blacks, who also have higher birth rates, are the counties exhibiting the highest infant death rates. With the very highest rates exceeding 16.0/1,000 in counties like Tyrrell, Camden, Pasquotank, Perquimans, and Northampton, it would appear that difficulty of access to medical facilities is an additional cause.

### The Aged

About 40,000 elderly people live in North Carolina's 400 nursing homes, at an average patient cost, in 1998, of $36,000 per year (Zaldivar 1998). One half of the total cost is borne by Medicaid. Many more elderly reside in rest homes and assisted living facilities, where, in most cases, the care is not as intensive nor is it as medically focused. This is an area of health that is of growing concern to state policy makers, especially as more and more

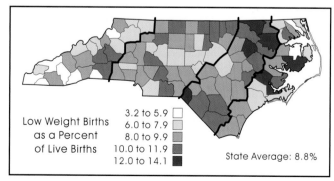

**Figure 7.36:** Percent Low Birth Weight, 1998.
**Source:** N. C. Department of Health and Human Services, North Carolina Vital Statistics, Volume 2, March, 2000.

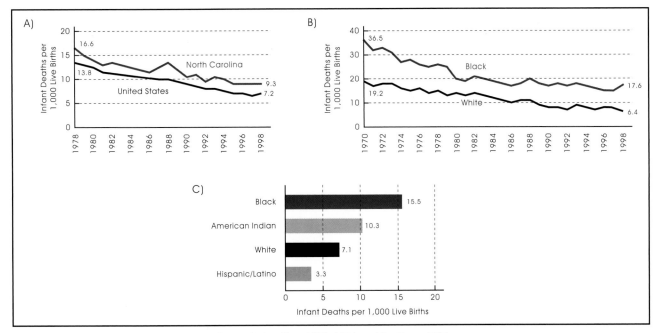

**Figure 7.37 a, b and c:** Infant Death Rates in North Carolina, 1970-1996, and by Race, 1996.
**Source:** North Carolina Minority Health Facts.

people are living into their 80s and 90s. In a few decades pressures for nursing home space will become acute as the bulk of the baby boom generation reach this age. Persistent complaints by residents of nursing homes, rest homes, and assisted care facilities, and by their families, focus on adequacy of care, training and skill levels of care givers, problems of abuse, lack of appropriate attention to people with special needs like Alzheimer patients, and general quality of life conditions. Federal quality standards are enforced by a system of state inspection, but at times the system fails due to inadequate staff funding and accountability. Major studies have been conducted by research groups like the North Carolina Center for Public Policy Research (Outterbourg 1996; McLaughlin 1996; Lambrew and Betts 1996; Yeager and Betts 1996; and Sharer 1999) and leading newspapers (Alexander and Kelly 2001; and Wilson 2000b). New rules of nursing and rest home operations were enacted by the state legislature in 2000, and entrepreneurs are rushing in to take ad-

vantage of financial opportunities. The latter is exemplified by the mid-90s rush to build assisted living facilities for wealthier residents. A transitional problem resulted as these facilities were drawing wealthier residents from rest homes, thus increasing these other homes' reliance on the poor and causing problems of financial survival. While the cost of assisted living care exceeded $2,000 per resident per month in 1998, the state paid $915 per month to rest homes for each indigent resident. In 1997, the state placed a building moratorium on rest homes and assisted living quarters to arrest a rise in vacancies, but succeeded only in causing a boom in construction because developers wanted to get facilities on line prior to the beginning of the moratorium date. An excess of space have caused even the more costly assisted living facilities to face problems of staffing, turnover, and quality of care.

*Workers and Occupational Health*

Workplace safety used to be a concern largely of manufacturing plants (see Chapter 6). However, in white color jobs increasing focus is on injuries caused by repetitive motion, carpal tunnel syndrome, and tendonitis. In part this reflects changes taking place in manufacturing industries, i.e., the closing of plants in industries more prone to occupational injury and the increasing substitution of automated equipment for hands on work. It reflects also the recent industrial restructuring that has seen the dramatic emergence of service industries as the major source of employment. On the job injuries have experienced a steady decline from 167,518 in 1994-95 to 142,869 in 1998-99 (Bivins 2000). Injuries range in severity from sprains to chemical burns and amputations. Work fatalities have been slowly declining over the past decade with 197 people dying from injuries in 1997 (Buggs

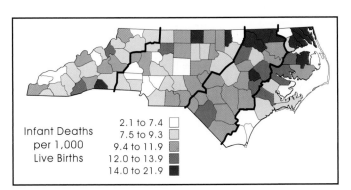

**Figure 7.38:** Infant Death Rates, 1994-1997 Annual Average.
**Source:** N. C. Office of Vital Statistics, 2000.

247

1998), but some industries persist in high rates of work related injuries, as exemplified by construction, forestry, and food processing. Work safety laws are monitored by the Department of Labor through its Division of Occupational Safety and Health inspectors. Fines are levied against companies, especially where they are repeat offenders. A fine of $808,150, the largest ever, was levied against Imperial Food Products of Hamlet (Richmond County) in 1991, following a fire that caused 25 deaths and 56 injured, one of the worst industrial accidents in U. S. history (Speizer 2000). The fire was started by the rupturing of a hydraulic line on a deep-fat fryer. Ninety on-site workers scrambled for a way out of the greasy smoke fire, but found that key exits, including specified fire exists, had been padlocked from the outside by a management wanting to keep workers from sneaking outside to take a break. During the 1990s, with the federal Occupational Safety and Health Administration (OSHA) playing a much more active role, other large fines have been levied. Stick Proof Co., was fined $508,800 in 1998 for not appropriately educating their workers on the hazards of cleaning medical scalpels, needles, and other medical equipment, and thereby exposing workers to infectious materials and blood borne diseases (Rhee 1998).

The North Carolina Insurance Commission requires workers' compensation insurance for individual firms with over ten employees. Over the years, all states, except for Texas, have required companies to pay insurance against work related illness and injury. In essence, this is a compromise where benefits are paid regardless of who is to blame for the mishap, thus the employer will not have to admit liability and the employee receives benefits without having to sue. Companies with workplace safety programs in place and a solid safety performance can bargain for lower rates, but in general, insurance rates have increased. In fiscal year 1998-99, employers paid $603 million in workers' comp premiums, while 68,000 workers filed for benefits and received $304 million for medical costs and lost wages. For some firms self-insurance is becoming a viable alternative. The bottom line is that workplace safety is now a top priority for employers (Bivins 2000). A main concern lies with the increasingly costly repetitive motion injuries deriving especially from work in financial services and information technology. The field of ergonomics, the science of designing procedures for workers to do their jobs safely and efficiently, has blossomed with the growth of those particular industries. Ergonomic standards are favored by labor organizations because they protect workers from musculoskeletal problems, such as carpal tunnel syndrome. In January, 2000, OSHA was ready to implement new rules that required companies to educate workers about ways to avoid potentially nerve damaging injuries from job related repetitive movements. Jobs focused on typists, chicken processors, apparel workers, and store clerks who use swipe scanners. A new federal administration placed a hold on the implementation of the new OSHA ergonomic rules immediately upon taking control in January, 2001. A similar set of occupational health rules in North Carolina was rescinded by the new State Labor Commissioner when she came into her position in January of 2001. Businesses tend to oppose such rules due their impact on workplace costs. While health and medical professionals generally are strong supporters of ergonomic rules, the rules are strongly opposed by organizations like the National Coalition of Ergonomics, a group of more than 200 companies formed to slow government imposed ergonomic standards in the workplace (Franklin 1999).

### The Mentally Ill

If it appears to the reader that state policies relating to health care issues may be characterized as too little and too late, this goes double for the state response to the crisis in mental health care. For decades, the state has responded to the growing crisis by enacting ambitious plans that never get funded and implemented. Problems include outdated hospitals, severely short-changed community mental health agencies, nursing shortages, and a demand much beyond the current capacity of support services and facilities (Clabby and Bonner 2000).

North Carolina was early among states to engage the problem of mental health. The oldest of the state's psychiatric hospitals, Dorothea Dix, was built in Raleigh in 1856. Its main building, McBryde Hall, dates to 1910 and is typical of many of the facilities of the four public psychiatric hospitals. In general, the hospitals at Butner (John Umstead), Goldsboro (Cherry), and Morganton (Broughton), as well as Dix, all suffer the inadequacies of design suitable to an earlier age, with long, dark wards and little space for therapeutic support (Clabby 2000). In fact, their care has been characterized as being more custodial (as in criminal detention), than therapeutic (as in hospital rehabilitation wards). These hospitals, overcrowded as they are, have been discharging 90 percent of their mentally ill patients since 1960 in the expectation that antipsychotic drugs can maintain treatment without supervision. One result is a growing population of homeless people that are mentally ill. One estimate suggests that 50 percent of street people are mentally ill (Fullwood 2000). Many more patients have been sent to area mental health authorities, 40 of these in the state, where they live in rest homes and receive little mental health treatment. As the social services director of Cleveland County has said, "These places (rest homes) were designed for the elderly. (For the state) they became a cheap and easy place to place somebody in a hurry" (Cenziper 2000). Communities and neighborhoods have taken on greater responsibilities for the mentally ill. While Asheville has come far enough in the development of group homes to serve as a model for the rest of the state, other communities exhibit deplorable NIMBY (not in by back yard) responses. With the deinstitutionalization of the mentally ill as state policy, and the devolving of major responsibilities for their care to the localities, community groups are finding that neighborhoods frequently are not willing to accept a group home in their midst. Zoning ordinances usually provide the means for neighborhood success in denying access. Even so, small scale mental health and adult care homes have increased from fewer than 3,000 in 1994 to over 4,000 in 1998, following the state's Mental Health Study Commission recommendation to move the mentally and physically disabled into smaller residential settings (Jones 1998). Will success in placing more and more of the afflicted in these setting dramatically improve the mental health situation, or will we continue to hear of the plight exemplified by one Chapel Hill student? As a suicidal depression patient, this 26 year old, who had been bounced in and out of psychiatric hospitals and rest homes without sensing much interest and time committed to medical treatment of his illness, noted, "I don't believe psychiatric patients are any less deserving that victims of Hurricane Floyd, one suffers as much as the other" (Clabby and Bonner 2000).

The state-wide system of mental health administered by the Division of Mental Health, Developmental Disabilities, and Substance Abuse (DMHDDSA) is supported by an annual budget of nearly $1.2 billion, much of which is federal support from Medicaid. A top official in the Division has suggested that to provide adequate support for everyone in need will take an additional $2.5 billion annually. Official reports vary in their estimate of the number of North Carolinians who at any one time suffer from some form of mental illness, varying from severe depression to the fear of wide open spaces; estimates have ranged from 900,000 to 1.2 million. Severe cases (people needing continuous confined care), constitute about 1.76 percent of the state's population, with another 1.15 percent needing treatment for schizophrenia (Otterbourg 1996).

### Determinants of Health

Strategies for promoting good health are increasingly encased in a holistic view of health as a critical component in a well functioning society. The preceding extensive discussions identify many factors that influence incidence of mortality and disease, factors such as age, genetics, nutrition, economic and social status, and spatial characteristics. The following discussion is intended to provide the reader with the holistic context of health and personal well-being. As discussed by Ratzan, Filerman, and Lesar (2000), good health practices begin with the individual and extends through the community to the larger world. A hierarchical sequence of increasing intensity of intervention appropriate to secure and maintain good health goes like this (p. 11):

1) How do we keep ourselves well? (primary prevention)

2) If we are getting sick, how can we detect these conditions early? (secondary prevention).

3) If we are sick, how do we get the best care? (tertiary prevention).

Figure 7.39 is a health field model, adapted from the work of Robert Evans and G. Stoddart (Ratzan et al 2000, 12-13), that displays the relationships among important determinants of health. In addition to demonstrating the role of the individual in making decisions about personal health and well-being, the model shows the position of global factors that structure the environments within which these decisions can be made. At this larger, structural level, the individual's influence varies. Community and social environment factors include social status and networking, as well as government policies and their effective implementation. In North Carolina, all these aspects need greater attention.

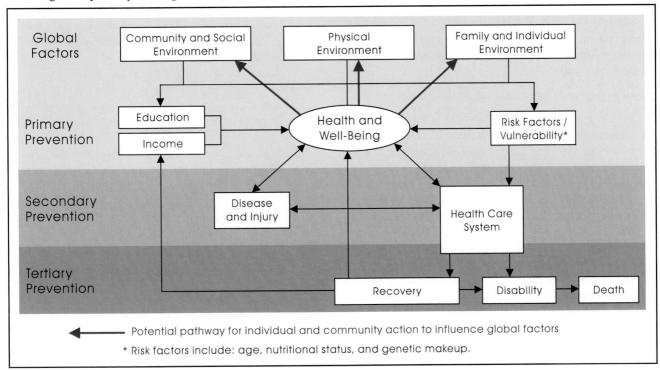

**Figure 7.39:** Determinants of Health: A Field Model.
**Source:** Ratzan, S. C., et al (2000).

249

Governments and institutions from state to local levels need to develop a greater sensitivity and determination to effectively combat existing problems of inequities and discrimination in health service delivery. Conditions of the physical environment include not only the more general factors of temperature and moisture variations, as well as the potential for natural disaster the state over, but also, and more critically, the negative conditions of the atmosphere, water and soils imposed by polluting industries and personal behaviors. In addition, this class of global factors include environmental hazards, such as chemical and biological agents, as may occur in the home, the workplace and the community. Here the individual has potentially greater latitude for influencing negative attributes, although standing in the way are several inhibiting aspects: 1) the cost of environmental improvements frequently need to be borne by recalcitrant industries; 2) government agencies are at times unable or reluctant to enforce existing environmental protection laws; and 3) elected officials are not adequately representing the health interests of the indigent. The role of the individual in improving conditions for personal health and well-being reigns supreme in the family and individual environment, the global class of factors. These characterize individual behaviors and lifestyles, personal hygiene, housing conditions, family and community support systems (i.e.,. church and human welfare outreach institutions), and the individual's access to and use of medical care. In the center of the model, the circle indicates that individual health and well-being are related to all factors indicated in the model. For readers interested in pursuing greater understandings of where matters stand for individual diseases, or threatened populations, or particular neighborhoods and communities in the state, place the focus of interest in the center circle, and then work the model to arrive at holistic understandings. From there, diagnose the essential factors determining conditions of health, and isolate where remedial action is necessary.

### Support Systems and Indices of Community Health

The Sheps Center for Health Services at the University of North Carolina at Chapel Hill issued a report in 2000 that showed a steady increase in the number of doctors practicing in the state, while the number of dentists declined, over the past 20 years (Avery 2000). For medical doctors this translates into an increase from 12.4 doctors per 10,000 people in the state in 1978 to 20/10,000 in 1998. Regardless of the increase in medical practitioners, these are not moving readily to the state's rural counties, and the urban-rural gap is persisting or increasing in severity. Eighteen counties actually reported a decrease in their supply of physicians. Figure 7.40 provides some support for the contention that a serious urban-rural gap exists in the provision of doctors, here indicated as numbers of persons per doctor within each county. Particular deficiencies appear in many counties of the Coastal Plain and the Tidewater region, although some of the worst cases are of counties next to larger urban centers where doctors concentrate. Presumably, folks in adjacent suburbanizing rural counties find doctors accessible in the next-door urban

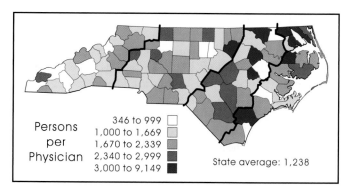

**Figure 7.40:** Persons per Physician, 1999.
**Source:** N. C. Department of Health and Human Services, Health Data Sheet, 2000.

setting, although at higher transportation costs. On the other hand, this leaves these counties' impoverished population at a distinct disadvantage. This same condition seems to be replicated by some of the suburban counties in the Piedmont. Mountain Region counties on the whole appear best off in availability of physicians. This is likely due to the emphasis placed on health care by the Appalachian Regional Commission, and the resulting greater incidence of medical clinics of higher standards in equipment and care facilities in rural mountain counties. It may also be due to the preference of new physicians, wishing to take advantage of federal support in writing off some of their medical school indebtedness, to locate in rural mountain locales as opposed to the rural Coastal Plain and Tidewater counties. Cultural factors undoubtedly have some relevance here, as well, as the vast majority of medical degrees are awarded to white physicians to whom the mountain environment and its mainly white population is more attractive.

A concomitant problem for rural counties is their absence of hospital facilities or the declining fortunes of those that remain. The worst case scenario exists for six contiguous coastal counties that now have no hospitals. Small rural hospitals simply have not been able to keep up with their urban and suburban counterparts. The latter are able to attract specialists and the best doctors, and are able to afford the cutting edge medical equipment desirable in more complicated and costly treatment processes (Lambrew and Betts 1996). As the more affluent rural families take advantage of more distant urban services, rural hospitals are left with an indigent elderly population and, thereby, a distinct cost disadvantage.

Complementing the health services provided by physicians and hospitals is the state-wide system of community health departments where a schedule of mandatory services are available. Some these are free, such as basic immunizations and the diagnosis and treatment of sexual diseases, while others are fee based (although in many cases fully paid by Medicaid). A recent study comparing health care availability and use in two rural communities in Johnston County found that travel time, whether or not people had to rely on others to drive them to medical care, individual health status, and the individual's health insurance status were most significant in successful accessing medical care (Gesler et al 1999).

Dental care suffers a significant maldistribution through the state. Urban areas have no shortages. Rural areas not only are experiencing major shortages, but are in a worsening situation. For 64 counties. there was a decrease in the number of dentists between 1989 and 1999 (Goldberg 2000). For rural counties, there were on the average three dentists per 10,000 persons, though Tyrrell, Hyde, and Jones had no dentists at all in 1999 (Figure 7.41). Urban counties had about 4.5/10,000 people. Overall the state lagged the national average of 5.8/10,000.

Social geographers and others are often at odds in deciding on the health variables that are most likely to contribute to an overall understanding of spatial variations in quality of life conditions. Infant mortality rates are a choice of many. Others favor life expectancy rates. In assessing the previous discussion on North Carolina health conditions, readers may compare and contrast the multitude of maps and other data provided in this volume, and arrive at their own conclusions. They may tilt toward life expectancy as the better of alternative indices to quality of life. After all, is not how long you live a kind of comprehensive affirmation of conditions of livability? Figure 7.42 certainly provides testimony that North Carolina's primary regions are distinguishable by their residents' average longevity. In some counties people will live on the average seven years longer than people are expected to in others. Counties with longer life expectancy are predominantly concentrated in the Mountain Region. In the Piedmont Region there is a greater mix. Rural counties positioned farther east fare less well, as do some of the western manufacturing counties. Aside from high ranked Wake County, metro counties are not as conducive to stimulating long life. Rather, it is some of the suburban counties that take the lead, as do most of the counties of the "Green Heart" (see Chapter 12). On the average, people living in Coastal Plain counties have lesser life spans. In fact, this condition alone appears near perfect in arriving at the boundaries of this primary region! In the Tidewater Region the picture is mixed, with those counties benefiting from heavier re-

tirement settlement in attaining higher average longevity. Therein lies one of the keys to understanding the superior positioning of the mountain counties. A disproportionately large retirement population heavily tilts the result toward longer average life spans, and detracts from the effectiveness in using this variable as an indicator of quality of life conditions. Perhaps the severity of community health problems at the beginning of the life cycle, as reflected by infant mortality rates, does provide the more meaningful quality of life index.

In sum, a major factor that confounds and complicates access to health care in North Carolina is the condition of rurality. Yet, this is further complicated by poverty and cultural factors, which differentiate some rural counties from others. In addition, there is the nagging issue of a state scrambling to rid itself of a past riddled with avoidance and minimization of the problems of community health. The devolution of social welfare responsibilities to the local level affects individual health and well-being, as well, bringing with it potentially significant differences in health standards and health care delivery on the county level. Continuing threats to the federal social welfare net, especially Medicaid, may leave the state with an even greater urgency to move expeditiously toward a holistic, state-wide, community focused, health care system plan that it is willing to provide adequate resources.

## EDUCATIONAL ATTAINMENT

### Introduction

North Carolina has had an enviable succession of governors who have made education the cornerstone of their administration. Alas, their success has been hampered persistently by a General Assembly existing in varying economic circumstances and with different funding priorities. Governor Robert Scott, in the early 1970s, would often comment on the difficulties of funding education and worker training, especially compared to the ease of building highways, "I have a feeling that if this state goes down the road to economic stagnation, it will be on a six-lane highway" (as quoted in Betts, 1996, 496). And although funding resources and priorities are the most critical among educational issues, it is only one set of many elements to be sorted out by educational planners and policy makers confounded by the complexities of life and livelihood of the early 21st century and their spatial ramifications.

In an article on work force preparedness, Jack Betts argues that workers of the 21st century needs an education that provides much more than proficiency in reading, (w)riting, and (a)rithmetic, the three r's. Individual success in 21st century life, also requires competence in critical thinking, communication, collaboration (team players), and computer literacy, the four c's of the emerging knowledge society (1996). This array of educational objectives are generally agreed upon by the public, the educational establishment, and policy makers, but they are evolving in a new century offering increasing complexities in arriving at their at-

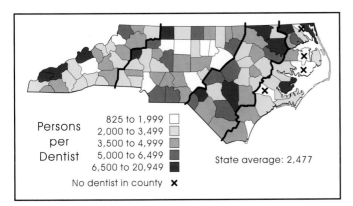

**Figure 7.41:** Persons per Dentist, 1999.
**Source:** N. C. Department of Health and Human Services, Health Data Sheet.

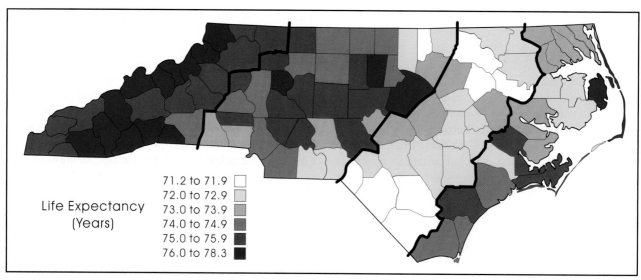

**Figure 7.42:** Life Expectancy at Birth, 1997.
**Source:** N. C. Department of Health and Human Services, Health Data Sheet, 2000.

tainment. While educational expectations are expanding, the environment of their application is changing. Demographically, these are boom times in student enrollments, although more and more kids come from households with fewer children per household. Minority populations are growing increasingly dominant in many school districts, yet, at the same time, educational attainment continues to be defined by race and income. Teacher recruitment is becoming more difficult as professional opportunities for women continue to expand, as school systems are resegregating, as turnover led by the young and the brightest among teachers is becoming more problematic, as salaries and benefits remain non-competitive while workloads increase, and as a large share of the existing teaching pool is moving toward retirement within a few years (*A Profession in Jeopardy* 1996). An image of a failing public school system is encouraging new innovations in educational delivery and funding, with magnet and charter schools offering the public school system new opportunities in student assignments and parents' new options for school choice. A legislative mandate initiated charter schools in 1996 on an experimental basis, with a cap of 100 schools for the entire state, a cap reached in 2000-01. The initial formal evaluation is due in 2002 (*Public Policy and Charter Schools* 2000). Although students in charter schools continue to lag others in state-wide tests scores, they have had impressive improvement over the early years of dismal performance (Hui and Ebbs 2001). Home schooling was the choice for parents of 33,800 children in 2000-01, an increase of 21 percent over the previous year. Fears have been expressed that these new innovations have the potential for becoming a Pandora's Box, letting lose a covey of educational ills upon an unsuspecting public. Closing-in competitively, and contributing to the unease of public school administrators, are also the private schools. Many of these have evolved out of a concern for the character of current educational reforms affecting the public schools, and from the parental judgment that their kids are, for a

number of quite varied reasons, better off in a private school environment (Averitt 1994). In addition, pressures to carry on the education equivalent of the welfare devolution are still being fought determinedly at both the federal and state levels. Even given the present situation of overall state authority over educational policy, much of the funding is still local. As such, there is wide divergence in funding capability, with resulting spatial inequalities in educational service delivery and facilities.

It is not that recent state administrations have stood idly by in the face of these challenges. Over the past several decades new teacher certification requirements have been matched by increasing salaries and scholarships to prospective teachers through the Teaching Fellows Program. Student performance has been enhanced through the panoply of the ABCs (accountability, teaching of basics, and local control), with new required student testing processes, complemented by the state-wide awarding of performance attainment grades for each individual school. New initiatives for early school entry by disadvantaged students are being implemented, as exemplified by Smart Start, which complements the federally funded Head Start Program. About 40 percent of the state's estimated 43,000 three and four year old children who are below the poverty line were served by Head Start in 1999. And some schools districts are trying out the concept of year-round schools, which some studies have found to be advantageous, especially for at-risk students, but also for locking in a more competitive teacher salary schedule. In the mid-1990s the state had the nation's third highest number of schools doing some kind of year-round schedule. In general, though, it appears that this is a movement in very slow progression. Too many parents still see it as too revolutionary (Silberman and Bradbury 1997).

North Carolina's public school system is essentially run by the General Assembly which passes laws and appropriates funding. Important input in the decision making process comes from the State Board of Education (SBE), local school boards, and citizens. While the SBE is charged with supervising and administering the public schools and the related funding, the Department of Public Instruction (DPI) implements the policies and directives issued by the SBE, and monitors the application of state and federal laws. Leading the day-to-day operations of the DPI is the elected State Superintendent of Public Instruction, who also serves as secretary to the governor appointed 13-member SBE. The DPI develops the N. C. Standard Course of Study for K-12 schools, and provides testing, reporting and other services to the local school districts. Each of the 117 school districts set student discipline guidelines, school calendars, local graduation requirements, student attendance requirements, and provide school buildings. School districts are mostly operating at the county level. Some time ago there were many more municipal school districts, but consolidation has incorporated most of these into county-wide districts. There still remain 17 municipal school districts, some in continuing conflict over consolidation. For example, tempers have been running high in Cleveland County, where the three school district consolidation court battle was producing $500,000 in legal costs when the County Commission (which was fighting consolidation) called a halt to the proceedings in August of 2001. The present Commission was elected to try to undo the success of the previous Commission. The previous Commission's proposal to consolidate the three districts of Kings Mountain, Shelby, and Cleveland County was approved by the U.S. Department of Justice, and the State Board of Education (Cimino 2001). In toto, the state has 2,024 public schools and 80 charter schools with an enrollment of approximately 1.2 million students.

### Funding Public Education

#### The Federal Level

A strong, unwavering commitment to public education in the United States goes back at least 150 years. With over 65 million students and four million teachers, staff, and administrators, the cost of this enormous enterprise came to over one half a trillion dollars in 1996-97. This factors out to about 7.3 percent of the national gross domestic product, or $6,853 per student. For the states, the revenue expended per student actually varies considerably from this average figure. Leading states are New Jersey with $10,825 per student, New York ($10,323), and Alaska ($10,078). On the bottom we find Utah with $4,499 per student, Mississippi ($4,680) and Alabama ($4,810). Among the fifty states, North Carolina ranked 39th with a public expenditure of $5,617 per student in 1996-97. By the 1998-99 school year North Carolina's position had improved to 31st, although its per student expenditure had increased just barely to $5,773 (*New York Times Almanac* 2001). Differences among states are in some degree governed by the proportion of school expenditures provided by each of the government levels, federal, state, and local. Though the federal overall contribution has increased steadily over the past century, it still accounted for only 6.8 percent of the total school budget in 1997-98 (*The World Almanac and Book of Facts* 2000). States varied in the federal share of their own public school budgets from 3.1 percent in the cases of New Jersey and New Hampshire to 12.6 percent for Alaska and 13.0 percent for Mississippi. North Carolina was close to the national average with 7.1 percent. As a percentage of the total state operating budget for North Carolina, the federal share has increased from 20.2 percent in 1990-91 to 25.9 percent in 2000-01 (Figure 7.43). The distribution of these funds vary by school district, because the federal share is program focused (i.e., support for the school lunch program for the less well-off students). So federal expenditures, ranging from $240 to $1,415 per pupil in 1999-2000, are to a greater degree concentrated in areas of greater economic and social need in North Carolina. These include Coastal Plain and Tidewater region counties and the westernmost Mountain Region counties (Figure 7.44). Where municipal school districts have a disproportionate share of the county's poor students, frequently minority dominated, there also is a greater federal contribution. Note, for

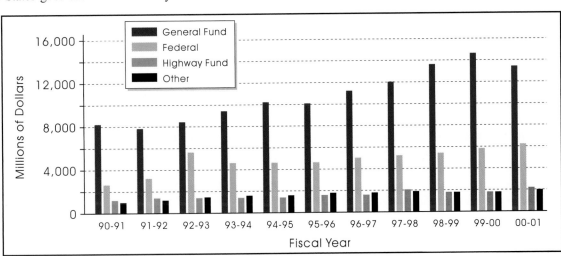

**Figure 7.43:** North Carolina Total State Budget by Source of Funds, 1990-91 through 2000-01.
**Source:** North Carolina Office of State Budget and Management.

253

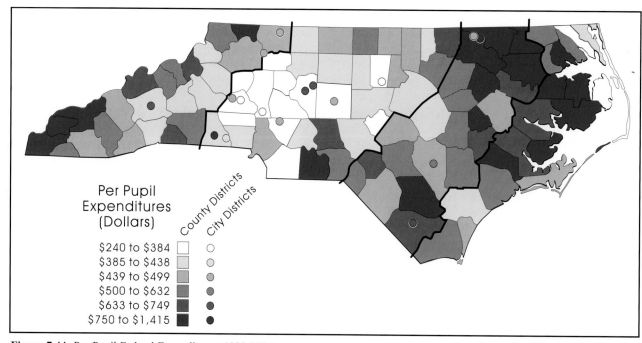

**Figure 7.44:** Per Pupil Federal Expenditures, 1999-2000.
**Source:** North Carolina Department of Public Instruction, Statistical Profile, 1999.

example, the contrasting situation of the Asheville School District in Buncombe County, and Shelby in Cleveland County, but especially the polarity existing in Davidson County. This county provides some of the more interesting contrasts in funding sources and levels when its three school district are compared and placed in their state context. Lexington City School District (37% white students) received $639/pupil in federal support, Thomasville City SD (43% white) received $729/pupil, and Davidson County SD (96% white) received $276/pupil in federal support.

*The State Level*

In some states public schools are almost entirely supported by the state government, as exemplified by the 90.3 percent provided by the state of Hawaii. Michigan similarly is quite high, with state government providing an 81.8 percent share. At the lower end is New Hampshire with 6.1 percent and Vermont with 28.0 percent. Obviously these differences are anchored in traditional views concerning state versus local responsibility for publics school costs. Whereas the average contribution of state governments accounted for 49.4 percent of the nation's public school costs, North Carolina was at the high end with 65.8 percent. This level of support represented 26 percent of the total state operating budget of $24,501 million in 2000-2001 (Figure 7.45). However, a better sense of the dimensions of the costs of education to state government may be gleaned by comparing its share relative to the State General Fund, as in Figure 7.46. The General Fund derives from revenues sources internal to the state, but the Total Education Operating Budget (TEOB) includes state and federal contributions. In 1990-91, the General Budget–TEOB ratio was 1:0.67, while in 2000-01 the ratio was 1:0.60, indicating a

relative diminishing education position. Figure 7.46 also shows the differences in the changes experienced by education's three components: public schools, university system, and community colleges. Of the TEOB, which itself expanded by 60.1 percent to $7,787 million during the 1990s, the public schools budget share increased by 67 percent to $5,563 million, the University System budget share by 48.5 percent to $1,697 million, and the community college budget share by 53.4 percent to $595 million.

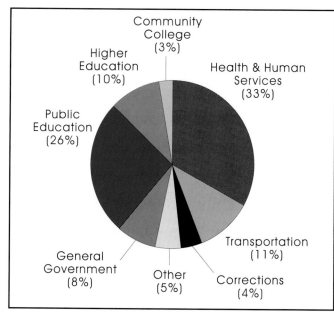

**Figure 7.45:** North Carolina Total State Operating Budget from All Sources By Department, 2000-2001.
**Source:** Office of State Budget and Management.

254

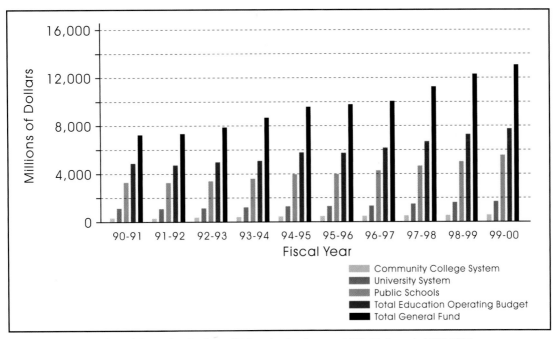

**Figure 7.46:** General Fund Operating Budget of Education by System, 1990-91 through 1999-2000.
**Source:** North Carolina Department of Public Instruction, Statistical Profile, 1999.

As indicated in Figure 7.47, there is also quite a range in state expenditures per pupil among the individual school districts. Alamance-Burlington School District received the least, with $3,979/pupil. Receiving the most in 1999-2000 was Hyde County, with $8,264/pupil. In fact, the patterns of the federal and state school expenditure figures are quite similar, reflecting the greater concern of both levels of government with supporting those school districts least able to help themselves. The contrasts existing between some municipal school districts and their county cousins exist also in the case of state allocations. From the perspective of some counties, their state allocation does not meet the needs defined by the state constitution's guarantee of a basic education.

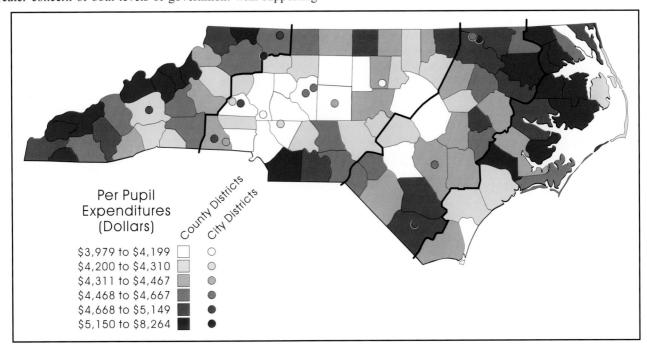

**Figure 7.47:** Per Pupil State Expenditures, 1999-2000.
**Source:** North Carolina Department of Public Instruction, Statistical Profile, 1999.

*The Local Level*

At the national level, local governments contributed 43.8 percent of total public school expenditures. As suggested above, there also are great variations among the states, with high local contributions exiting in New Hampshire (90.8%), Vermont (67.2%), and Illinois (66.3%). North Carolina ranks at the lower end, with 27.1 percent contributed by local governments; however, other states are much lower, as, for example, Michigan with 11.6 percent. For North Carolina, the local school district level comparisons reveal the strongest contrasts in per student allocations (Figure 7.48). The lowest level of local support is Swain County, with $535/pupil in 1999-2000; however, Swain County has extraordinary support from the federal government which supports completely the Cherokee Indian Reservation schools. Other low levels of support include Robeson County ($563/pupil), Hoke County ($621/pupil), Duplin County ($735/pupil), Jones County ($748/pupil), Graham County ($754/pupil), and Bertie County ($765/pupil). Others with less than $800.00/pupil local support are Whiteville City and Richmond County. These are all poverty stricken school districts, comparatively speaking. High per pupil support by local school districts exists in highly urbanized counties, and in most of the municipal districts. The highest level of local support is achieved by the Chapel Hill–Carboro School District with $3,538/pupil, followed by Asheville City at $3,294/pupil. Only five other local school districts exceed $2,000/pupil, Carteret, Dare, Durham, Mecklenburg, and Orange. It is perhaps notable that Wake County comes in at only about one half the local support per pupil of Chapel Hill–Carboro.

In the final accounting, the total allocation flow to schools in the districts results in rather large differences between districts (Figure 7.49). Hyde County, one of the state's poorest school districts, receives the highest per pupil allocation ($11,508) in 1999-2000. Hyde is the leading recipient of both federal and state funds, while ranking 15th in local support. Highly populated counties, like Mecklenburg, Forsyth, and Guilford, expectedly rank high on total expenditures per pupil. It is surprising that their neighboring suburban counties have the least total support for their school districts. School children here are much more likely to come from fairly well-to-do families, recent arrivals from out-of-state or from the adjacent metro county, and their school districts are struggling with raising money to provide new educational facilities in the face of a population explosion. Of course, some counties are traditionally loath to increase taxes in support of education; the least monies are available to the students of Randolph County School District (only $5,368/pupil). Others school districts having less than 50 percent of Hyde County's support level include: Alamance, Alexander, Cabarrus, Caldwell, Davidson, Gaston, Iredell, Lincoln, and Union counties. The military dominated counties of Onslow and Cumberland were at the low level of support, as were Robeson and Duplin counties. Again the contrasts existing between the few remaining municipal school districts and their county level school districts are worthy of note. Contrasts are clearly the strongest in Davidson County, where the county school district ranks 116th in the state, while Lexington City ranks 39th and Thomasville City ranks 29th. A more curious situation is found in Halifax County ,where Roanoke City School District (with 77 percent white students) ranks 46th in total support per pupil, and Weldon City (5.6% white) ranks 4th; the county school district (5.9% white), ranks 34th. These discrete racial profiles of the state's school districts may be explored using Figure 7.50

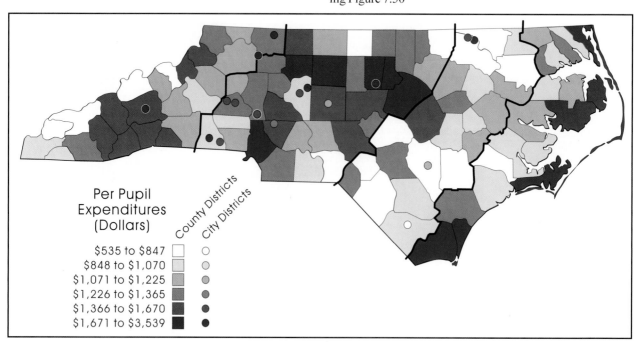

**Figure 7.48:** Per Pupil Local Expenditures, 1999-2000.
**Source:** North Carolina Department of Public Instruction, Statistical Profile, 1999.

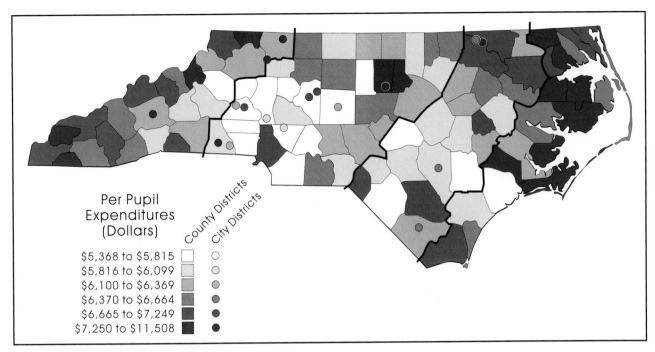

**Figure 7.49:** Per Pupil Total Expenditures, 1999-2000.
**Source:** North Carolina Department of Public Instruction, Statistical Profile, 1999.

## North Carolina's School Funding Model: Time for Change?

North Carolina's school funding model is at the heart of education issues. Funding schools through county levied property taxes was a process enacted by the General Assembly in 1839. In 1900-1904, there was a major initiative by Governor Charles Aycock to equalize funding for the poorer school districts by providing state supplements. During the depression years of the 1930s, the counties had such difficulties that the state refined the funding model. Now the state provides most of the funding needed for instruction, based on enrollment, while counties are left with providing the capital for educational facilities. In varying degrees, the counties also fund supplies, maintenance, and supplementary salaries for administrators, teachers, substitutes and

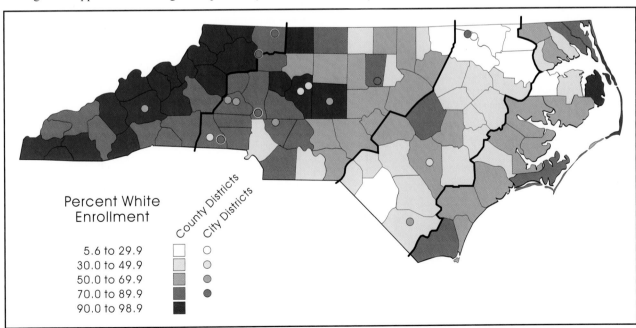

**Figure 7.50:** Percent White Students in Public School Systems, 1998-1999.
**Source:** North Carolina Department of Public Instruction, Statistical Profile, 1999.

teachers aides. Here is the source of inequities in funding, since some counties simply do not have the wherewithal to provide what is needed (Martin 2000). Figure 7.48 shows the range in local support for schools. Poor counties, like Hoke and others, can muster only 20 percent or so of the per pupil expenditures supported by the wealthiest counties, although in many cases the pressure may be eased by projected declines in enrollments (Figure 7.51). The local capacity to support schools is determined by the wealth of the local real estate. This leaves prosperous counties with a major comparative advantage in providing excellent schools. In the attempt at raising the necessary capital, poorer counties are forced to continue to increase their property tax rates. For the ten wealthiest counties in 2000 the average effective tax rate is .444, while for the poorest ten counties it is .729, a gap that has been increasing rapidly over the past years,

as seen in Figure 7.52 (Poteat and Giannusa 2000). Even allowing for this difference in greater costs for a poorer population, the plight continues, as dramatized in Figure 7.53.

The annual drop-out rate, a major annual evaluation tool of school district success, is affected (Figure 7.54), as are graduating seniors intentions about attending an institution of higher education (Figure 7.55). North Carolina continues in its unenviable low position in the rate of its population having attained a high school graduation; with 79.8 percent in 1999, the state ranked 43rd in the country.

Taxing themselves at a continuously higher rate is not preventing the poor counties from falling further behind. Successful recruitment of teachers, for example, depends frequently on the salary supplement a school district is able to provide. Wealthy districts will readily offer two to three thousand dollars more, to

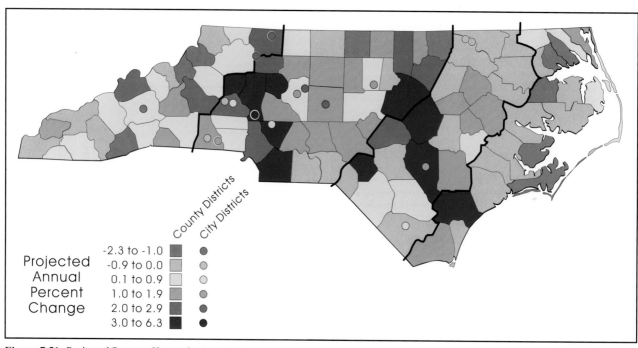

**Figure 7.51:** Projected Percent Change in Annual School Enrolment, 2000-2004.
**Source:** North Carolina Department of Public Instruction, Statistical Profile, 1999.

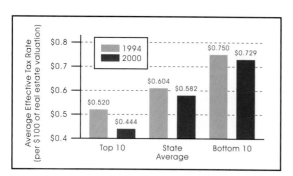

**Figure 7.52:** Average Effective Property Tax Rates, Comparing Wealthiest and Poorest Counties, 1994-2000.
**Source:** Poteat and Giannusa, 2000, 3.

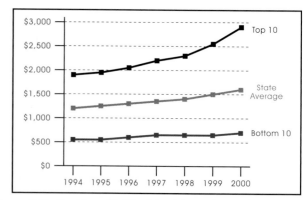

**Figure 7.53:** Total Local Public School Expenditures per Pupil, Comparing Wealthiest and Poorest Counties, 1994-2000.
**Source:** Poteat and Giannusa, 2000, 2.

258

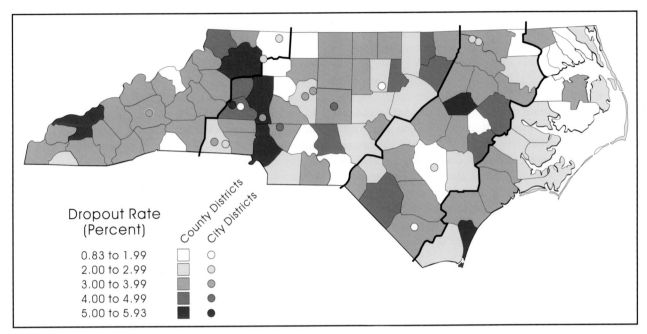

**Figure 7.54:** School District Student Drop-Out Rate, 1998-99.
**Source:** North Carolina Department of Public Instruction, Statistical Profile, 1999.

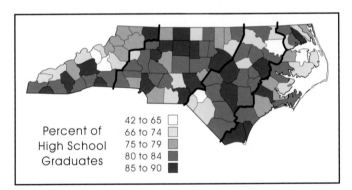

**Figure 7.55:** Graduating High School Student's Declared Higher Education Intentions, 1999.
**Source:** North Carolina Department of Public Instruction, Statistical Profile, 1999.

buttress recruitment advantages that also may include more and better teaching equipment and supplies, as well as an amenity-rich urban environment. Poorer school districts are left with a much higher proportion of the least experienced and least desired individuals on the job market. To simply survive, they wind up with an increasing share of their teaching pool being uncertified. With 20 percent of teachers in the state not certified to teach their assigned classes, this is a crisis in its own right (Silberman 2000). A comprehensive look at the disparities among school systems, and how they could lead to a logical next step of suing the state for infringement of constitutional rights, was presented by Whitman (1996). The 1994 Leandro Case suit sought to force the state to equalize funding deficiencies for poor school districts. The suit was joined by the following county school districts: Hoke, Robeson, Cumberland, Vance, and Halifax. In 1996,

the state Court of Appeals ruled against the petitioners with the argument that the state constitution requires only equal access to schools, not necessarily equal funding. In 1997, the N.C. Supreme Court overturned that ruling with the new argument that students have an equal right to a sound, basic education. A landmark decision for public education in the United States the so-called Leandro Decision defined the terms of "Sound Basic Education" (Poteat and Giannusa 2000, 2):

We conclude that Article I, Section 15 and Article IX, Section 2 of the North Carolina Constitution combine to guarantee every child of this state an opportunity to receive a "sound basic education". For purposes of our Constitution, a "sound basic education" is one that provide the student with at least:

1) sufficient ability to read, write, and speak the English language and a sufficient knowledge of history, fundamental mathematics, and physical science to enable the student to function in a complex and rapidly changing society;

2) sufficient fundamental knowledge in geography, history, and basic economic and political systems to enable the student to make informed choices with regard to issues that affect the student personally or affect the student's community, state, and nation;

3) sufficient academic and vocational skills to enable the student to successfully engage in post-secondary education or vocational training;

259

4) sufficient academic and vocational skills to enable the student to compete on an equal basis with others in formal education or gainful employment in contemporary society.

The N. C. Supreme Court ruling granted the petitioners the right to pursue their suit against the state. Following court hearings, a series of rulings began issuing from the office of Wake Superior Court Judge Howard Manning during the fall of 2000. Judge Manning agreed that existing funding arrangements were constitutional, in fact, the problem was not money. The state simply had failed to provide at-risk students, mostly minority, poor, and children of broken families, a sound, basic education (see Box 7D). He then ordered the state to create preschool programs for at-risk students, even at the expenses of existing programs such as magnet schools or special high level electives (Flono 2001). Not that Judge Manning saw Constitutional barriers to the offering of specialized programs, only that the Constitutional guarantee for a sound education for each child must first be met.

Seven years of comparatively good economic times during the 1990s afforded the state and its taxpayers an opportunity of improving its public school environment. Education programs made significant contributions to a state budget growing at a rate of eleven percent annually during the 1990s. Yearly education budget increases demonstrated the General Assembly's determination to have public school teacher salaries at least reach the national average (Figure 7.56). The Excellent Schools Act and Smart Start added $1.69 billion per year. Good times also permitted a cut in taxes of $1.4 billion annually. With the good times also came a flood of in-migrating younger families with children to the state. This, combined with the offspring of the baby boomers (Chapter 4), were adding some 20,000 to the public school enroll-

ments during the latter half of the 1990s. The peaking of public school enrollment due to the baby boom occurred in 1970 with 1.18 million students. Years of declining enrollment followed as the baby bust period took effect, but a new high was reached with 1.2 million students in 1997-98. High school enrollment alone is expected to increase by 25 percent between 1996 and 2006. In these good times, with increasing enrollments and a pressing need for new education facilities, the taxpayers' response was to pass the state's largest ever bond referendums for public schools, community colleges, and universities, with bonded indebtedness payments to reach $600 million/year by 2005. Now the squeeze is on. A few months following the end of Jim Hunt's, the 'Education Governor,' administration in 2001 a national economic slowdown was echoed in the state by a serious revenue shortfall, expected to reach $800 million by the end of 2001. Add to this evolving dilemma having to pay $1 billion in legal judgments against the state and the extraordinary flood relief expenses of $800 million resulting from Hurricane Floyd. According to *Making Strategic Choices* (2001), the budget crisis likely will extend into the years ahead, with potentially devastating results for public education in the state. The declaration of Governor Hunt, well supported initially by legislative action, that North Carolina will be First in American Education by the year 2010, will have to overcome many barriers before reaching its goal.

### Structure and Facilities of Higher Education

Included in North Carolina's state constitution, adopted soon after the state declared its independence in 1776, was the charge to promote learning in one or more universities. From this charge, the University of North Carolina system was initiated as the first public institution of higher education in the nation, with its Chapel Hill campus receiving the first students in 1795. North

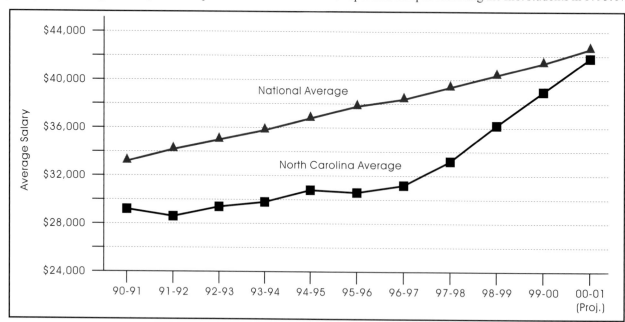

**Figure 7.56:** Average Public School Teacher's Salaries, 1990-91 Through 1998, and Projected to 2000-2001.
**Source:** North Carolina Department of Public Instruction, Statistical Profile, 1999.

Carolina communities take much pride in their community colleges, a system comprising 59 schools scattered through the state, with comparatively easy access of anyone living in the state, at very low tuition cost. In addition, there are 36 member institutions of the North Carolina Independent Colleges and Universities organization, among them some of the best known and most highly regarded private institutions in the country, such as Duke University, Wake Forest University, and Davidson College. The 16 public universities have been enjoying strong support from state government. Among 16 southern states in 1999-2000 North Carolina's expenditure per student ranks second, pay of professors ranks first, and average tuition and fees are the lowest per student.

Though the Community College System at times appears to have been treated poorly, there does not seem to be much public and political contention about overall support for public investment in higher education, as has been the case with the public schools. One result, perhaps, is the much better standing that the state has for people over 25 years of age having completed four or more years of college education. In 1999 this was 23.9 percent, ranking the state 29th in the country, as compared to its 43rd position for attaining a high school degree (data for individual counties appear in the regional chapters). The state's recent locational attractiveness for high tech industries demanding higher skills, and the relocation to the state of people with higher education credentials, undoubtedly also contribute to the higher status. Staying competitive with colleges and universities in faculty recruitment and research grants continues to be a major challenge. Another challenge will be preparing the system for the additional 80,000 students expected to crowd onto the campuses by 2008. A significant step toward meeting these challenges has been the $3.1 billion facilities construction bond passed by the voters in 2000; $600 million of this is going to the community colleges.

The infusion of such dramatic investments in construction provide major boosts to the localities where these institutions are located. In a number of cases the ordinary local economic impact of a college and university can be extraordinary, although the impact obviously is a function of the size of the institution as well as the size of its home community. Clearly, UNC-Chapel Hill, East Carolina University, and Western Carolina have a much greater impact on their communities and counties than N. C. State University, UNC-Asheville, UNC-Charlotte, or Fayetteville State University have on their much more economically diversified and larger situations. An example of this extraordinary impact is Appalachian State University. Boone is an incorporated town of 13,472 people in the County of Watauga (with 42,695 people). Appalachian students residing in the town and/or county as of the census date of April 1st, 2000 are included in these census totals. A likely two-thirds of the town's population are students, as are at least one quarter of the county's population. A recent study indicated that Appalachian State University's annual impact on Watauga County's economy amounted to $407 million (Dave, Dotson and Kirkpatrick 1999). This total includes the lo-

cal expenditures of the state paid employees (faculty and staff) of the institution and the students, a total of 17,300 persons. The university itself spend $129 million with local businesses, and $6.1 million is contributed to local charities. Conferences, concerts, athletic activities, summer institutes, and festivities and other university related attractions pull in some 392,000 people yearly to the town and county. State institutions can play an inordinate role in the more peripheral counties, .

*A Sixteen Campus Public University*

In 1971, following many decades of evolution and changes in public universities in the state, the Higher Education and Reorganization Act established the University of North Carolina. The system is led by a 32 member elected Board of Governors and a central administration. A sixteen campus system found itself with campuses distributed throughout the state, although concentrations and size favored the more populated Piedmont Region (Figure 7.57). When to the public universities are added to the private institutions the resulting geographic pattern even more clearly favors Main Street counties, with the Piedmont Horseshoe clearly identifiable. Two large regions stand out as being slighted in the distribution: Coastal Plain/Tidewater with only eight institutions in 40 counties, and the Western Manufacturing District of the Piedmont Region with three private colleges in 14 counties.

Demographically, university students reflect the changing times. Their average age is increasing as larger numbers of older people retool skills that require university training. As populations diversify, and as minority populations are more readily accessing employment opportunities competitively, campuses are showing the effects of racial integration and multiculturalism. These latter traits do tend to vary by region, with institutions like Appalachian State University in Boone and Western Carolina University in Cullowhee persistently failing in meeting minimum expectations for minority enrollment. At the same time similar difficulties are being experienced by the historically black colleges and universities in attracting a larger white student population.

The Historically Black Colleges and Universities (HBCU) were moving on their separate, but hardly equal, path before the civil right legislation of the 1950s and 60s. HBCUs include the following members of the North Carolina University System: N. C. Central University in Durham (funded by the General Assembly in 1925 as the first state supported liberal arts college for blacks in the nation); N. C. Agricultural and Technical University in Greensboro; Winston-Salem State University; Fayetteville State University; and Elizabeth City State University. Pembroke University was chartered as an American Indian institution in the support of the Lumbe Indians concentrated in Robeson and adjacent counties. Opening up the exclusive white colleges to minority populations further deepened the survival problems of the HBCUs. While still favored by many promising African American young people as more amenable to personal and cultural identity, and as having a rich history of nurturing black intellec-

**Box 7D:** Minorities and the Public Schools; Are We Resegregating?

Discussion:

Over the past several years there has been a spate of media attention directed toward what some see as the most burning issue in the North Carolina public school system. The Raleigh News and Observer published two major series, *Worlds Apart: The Racial Education Gap* (Simmons 1999) and *The New Segregation* (Simmons and Ebbs, 2001). The Winston-Salem Journal contributed a series titled, *Dividing Lines: Race Relations in Forsyth County* (Gilmor and Scheve 1998); and the Charlotte Observer chimed in with a three month series *Deciding Desegregation* (Smith, Morrill and Cenziper 1999). Editor Anders Gyllenhaal phrased it succinctly, "North Carolina's schools are gradually but steadily returning to a two-tiered system that is increasingly divided by race, class and, most notably, student performance… Resegregation is moving at a pace that is likely to accelerate in almost every part of the state…. Many low performing (black) schools are caught in a debilitating blend of inexperienced staff, turnover and educational shortcomings." (2001). The data on these pages presents some of the contrasts that reflect these sobering comments.

Some 45 years following the Brown decision, public schools are still providing inferior education to schools that are predominantly poor and black. Research conducted in the Charlotte-Mecklenburg school system showed that black and white students with comparable academic abilities were placed on separate academic tracks, with blacks placed in lower track classes that had more limited curriculum and teachers who were less qualified (Flono 2001). Lesser educational expectations of minority kids is a pervasive and troubling problem throughout the state. Coincidentally, the Charlotte-Mecklenburg Board of Education had been agreeing to match dollar for dollar the contribution to schools that PTA fundraisers were able to collect. Consider the capability and interest in PTA activities of inner city poor schools as compared to upper middle income white dominated schools of the suburbs in generating PTA dollars. And then to be twice blessed by having your money doubled by the Board of Education! Obviously, this good will to encourage parental involvement resulted in additional discriminatory funding. A few important examples of existing disparities will suffice here. In Mecklenburg County in 1999 only 30 percent of mostly black schools have their classrooms wired for networked computers, as compared to 54 percent for predominantly white schools; predominantly black schools had an average supply

money shortfall of $88 per student, versus $44 for predominantly white schools; 79 percent of mostly black schools were in need of major renovations, as compared to 14 percent for mostly white schools (Cenziper 1999). It should be noted that the 83 elementary schools in Mecklenburg County range from 98 percent to 6 percent nonwhite enrollment. To avoid busing, an anathema of both white and minority parents, neighborhood schools are pushed as the alternative. So far, research is concluding that this is one certain way to return to segregated schools and educational inequities, due to existing patterns of concentrated poverty and minority populations in particular parts of town (note examples provided in Chapter 12 and in the following section of this chapter).

---

Notable Public Schools Court Decisions:

-1896 U. S. Supreme Court decision (Plessy vs. Ferguson) allowed separate, but equal, educational facilities by race

-1954 U. S. Supreme Court decision (Brown vs. Board of Education) declared separate but equal schools unconstitutional by providing inferior education to minority students

-1969 U. S. District Court decision (Swann vs. Mecklenburg County) mandated busing to achieve goals of integrated and equal educational opportunities for all students

-1971 U. S. Supreme Court upholds the Swann decision, clearing the way for nationwide mandated school busing to achieve desegregation of public schools

-1999 U. S. District Court decision that Charlotte-Mecklenburg Schools have eliminated segregation and that future race based student assignments are unconstitutional

-2001 4th U. S. Court of Appeals upholds 7 to 5 the District Court's decision that the Charlotte-Mecklenburg school system was unitary (i.e., free of intentional segregation); on the other hand, the Court of Appeals also ruled, in a 6 to 5 decision, that the local school board was on its own cognizance in using race, income, or other factors in making school assignments and in allocating educational opportunities and funding.

---

"I think resegregation is a giant error. When people look back they will think, how could there have been this tool that actually worked fairly well and instead of trying to make it better they returned to a system that was used for 70 years that did not work at all?" Gary Orfield, Co-Director of the Civil Rights Project at Harvard University

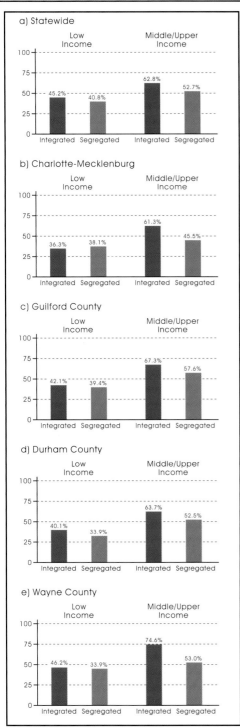

a) Statewide

Low Income — Integrated 45.2%, Segregated 40.8%; Middle/Upper Income — Integrated 62.8%, Segregated 52.7%

b) Charlotte-Mecklenburg

Low Income — Integrated 36.3%, Segregated 38.1%; Middle/Upper Income — Integrated 61.3%, Segregated 45.5%

c) Guilford County

Low Income — Integrated 42.1%, Segregated 39.4%; Middle/Upper Income — Integrated 67.3%, Segregated 57.6%

d) Durham County

Low Income — Integrated 40.1%, Segregated 33.9%; Middle/Upper Income — Integrated 63.7%, Segregated 52.5%

e) Wayne County

Low Income — Integrated 46.2%, Segregated 33.9%; Middle/Upper Income — Integrated 74.6%, Segregated 53.0%

**a.-e:** Numbers show the percentage of black students in grades three through eight who have passed their reading and math tests in 2000. The racial mix in schools, integrated versus segregated, affects performance of all black students, but those of middle and higher incomes are clearly more affected.

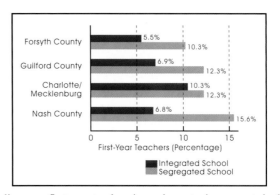

Forsyth County — Integrated 5.5%, Segregated 10.3%; Guilford County — Integrated 6.9%, Segregated 12.3%; Charlotte/Mecklenburg — Integrated 10.3%, Segregated 12.3%; Nash County — Integrated 6.8%, Segregated 15.6%

First-Year Teachers (Percentage)

Integrated School
Segregated School

**f:** Reliance on first-year teachers is much greater in segregated schools.

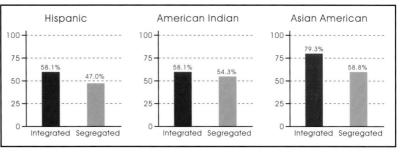

Hispanic — Integrated 58.1%, Segregated 47.0%; American Indian — Integrated 58.1%, Segregated 54.3%; Asian American — Integrated 79.3%, Segregated 58.8%

**g:** Resegregation issues tend to focus on black children, because they comprise 80 percent of the nonwhites, but other minorities also fare worse under segregated conditions.

**h:** Number of black students attending minority schools per category of segregation. More than half of North Carolina's 395,000 black children attend schools where whites are in the minority.

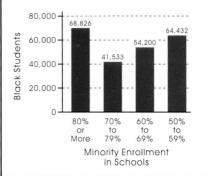

Black Students: 80% or More — 68,826; 70% to 79% — 41,533; 60% to 69% — 54,200; 50% to 59% — 64,432

Minority Enrollment in Schools

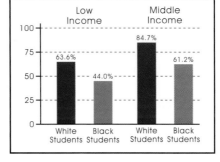

Low Income — White Students 63.6%, Black Students 44.0%; Middle Income — White Students 84.7%, Black Students 61.2%

**i:** Percentage of children at or above grade level in grades three through eight. The achievement gap exists regardless of school setting.

"When I was on the Board of Education I thought integration was the salvation of minority kids. But what we started to correct 25 years ago we still haven't fixed. You have to question whether this is as good as it gets" Vernon Malone, Wake County Commissioner, first black chair (in 1976) of the Wake County school board.

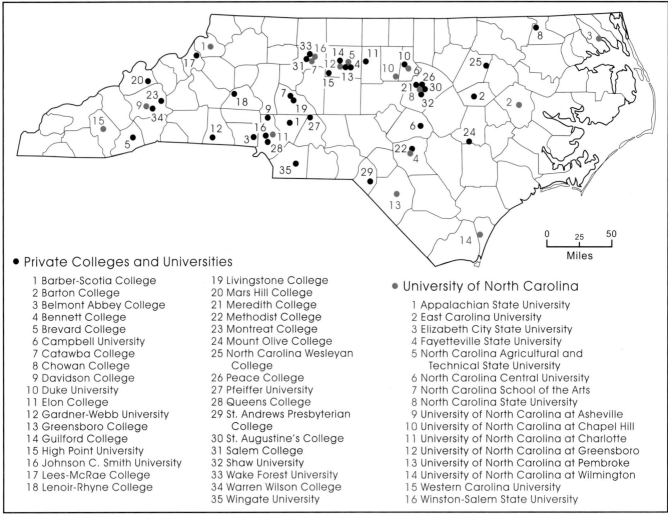

**Figure 7.57:** Distribution of Campuses of the University of North Carolina and North Carolina Independent Colleges and Universities, Inc.

● Private Colleges and Universities

1 Barber-Scotia College
2 Barton College
3 Belmont Abbey College
4 Bennett College
5 Brevard College
6 Campbell University
7 Catawba College
8 Chowan College
9 Davidson College
10 Duke University
11 Elon College
12 Gardner-Webb University
13 Greensboro College
14 Guilford College
15 High Point University
16 Johnson C. Smith University
17 Lees-McRae College
18 Lenoir-Rhyne College
19 Livingstone College
20 Mars Hill College
21 Meredith College
22 Methodist College
23 Montreat College
24 Mount Olive College
25 North Carolina Wesleyan
    College
26 Peace College
27 Pfeiffer University
28 Queens College
29 St. Andrews Presbyterian
    College
30 St. Augustine's College
31 Salem College
32 Shaw University
33 Wake Forest University
34 Warren Wilson College
35 Wingate University

● University of North Carolina

1 Appalachian State University
2 East Carolina University
3 Elizabeth City State University
4 Fayetteville State University
5 North Carolina Agricultural and
    Technical State University
6 North Carolina Central University
7 North Carolina School of the Arts
8 North Carolina State University
9 University of North Carolina at Asheville
10 University of North Carolina at Chapel Hill
11 University of North Carolina at Charlotte
12 University of North Carolina at Greensboro
13 University of North Carolina at Pembroke
14 University of North Carolina at Wilmington
15 Western Carolina University
16 Winston-Salem State University

tuals and leaders, the HBCUs were suffering serious enrollment problems. After several decades of struggling to meet federal racial and financial equity requirements, a consent degree was signed between the UNC system and federal officials that increased funding and infused new energy into the black colleges in the mid-1980s. However, money remains tight, ageing buildings are not being expeditiously renovated, and new technologies are not being provided as needed. Attracting large numbers of quality students remains difficult. Lower standards of admissions means that entering student's average SAT scores lag the corresponding UNC institutions by 150 to 200 points, and their four year graduation rate is typically under 25 percent (Simmons 2000). In a society where racism, though perhaps pushed from the surface of everyday life, still negatively influences and disenfranchises young blacks, black colleges and universities will continue to play a role in nurturing African Americans who may have struggled in high schools, but can blossom in college. Together with the six private four-year black colleges (Johnson C. Smith University, Barber-Scotia College, Livingstone College,

Bennett College, Shaw University and St. Augustine's College), North Carolina has the largest number of four-year HBCUs of any state in the country. Two demographic aspects favor their survival. While college aspirations of black youth are escalating, black students now entering the college environment are much more apt to be second generation black college attendees, with pressure to attend a parent's alma mater. Secondly, black colleges, several being relatively under-enrolled, are expected to carry a disproportionate share of the burden of providing college space for the large numbers of students the state expects to enter the system by 2008.

*One of the Nation's Largest Community College Systems*

The Post World War II generation unleashed a massive demand for higher education, not least of it in specialized vocational training. North Carolina was in the nation's vanguard in establishing community colleges. Ubiquitously distributed through the state, eventually 59 community college campuses were created (Figure 7.58). The colleges are under the aegis of local government which funds campuses and their maintenance, and which hires administrative leadership, and thereby faculty and staff. All colleges are campuses of the North Carolina Community College System, an arm of the State Board of Education, the General Assembly designated agency for curriculum and program development serving 760,000 community college students each year. In their distribution, community colleges are found in all of the large and medium sized counties, but are designed to serve up to seven counties where the population threshold does not warrant a single county college. Large territories are assigned to the College of the Albemarle and Beaufort County Community College, for example. It does appear that the northeastern quadrant of the state is less well served. However, most of the multi-county community colleges have divisions in counties where they are not headquartered. Similarly, many community colleges have division facilities in towns otherwise without an institution of higher education. In many cases, the local community college is the pride of the community. Close relations tend to exist be-tween industries, community leaders, and the college administration and curriculum planners, with faculty contributing time and expertise in resolving community issues. Frequently the campus buildings huddle around a central open green space, or they are sited in expansive and enticing natural environments.

Most community colleges were initially focused on preparing workers for technical skills demanded by new and restructuring industries. Programs were either formal two year Associate of Arts (AA) degree programs, or they were certificate programs. A lesser number of colleges were more specifically focused on the needs of students expected to transfer to senior institutions. In both cases there was a varying emphasis on adult and continuing education, including adult high school diploma classes. With the maze of special agreements that existed between community colleges and senior institutions for the transfer of college credits, and with the expected explosion in college bound students over the next ten years, all community colleges are now on line with the new standardized intercollegiate credit

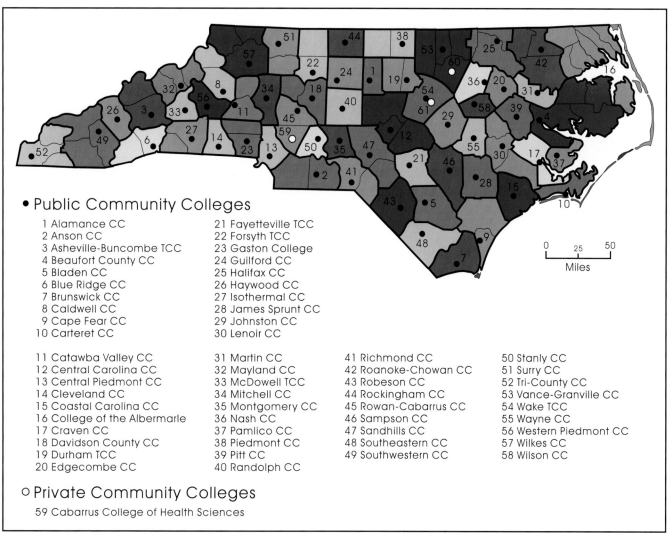

## • Public Community Colleges

| | |
|---|---|
| 1 Alamance CC | 21 Fayetteville TCC |
| 2 Anson CC | 22 Forsyth TCC |
| 3 Asheville-Buncombe TCC | 23 Gaston College |
| 4 Beaufort County CC | 24 Guilford CC |
| 5 Bladen CC | 25 Halifax CC |
| 6 Blue Ridge CC | 26 Haywood CC |
| 7 Brunswick CC | 27 Isothermal CC |
| 8 Caldwell CC | 28 James Sprunt CC |
| 9 Cape Fear CC | 29 Johnston CC |
| 10 Carteret CC | 30 Lenoir CC |

| | | | |
|---|---|---|---|
| 11 Catawba Valley CC | 31 Martin CC | 41 Richmond CC | 50 Stanly CC |
| 12 Central Carolina CC | 32 Mayland CC | 42 Roanoke-Chowan CC | 51 Surry CC |
| 13 Central Piedmont CC | 33 McDowell TCC | 43 Robeson CC | 52 Tri-County CC |
| 14 Cleveland CC | 34 Mitchell CC | 44 Rockingham CC | 53 Vance-Granville CC |
| 15 Coastal Carolina CC | 35 Montgomery CC | 45 Rowan-Cabarrus CC | 54 Wake TCC |
| 16 College of the Albermarle | 36 Nash CC | 46 Sampson CC | 55 Wayne CC |
| 17 Craven CC | 37 Pamlico CC | 47 Sandhills CC | 56 Western Piedmont CC |
| 18 Davidson County CC | 38 Piedmont CC | 48 Southeastern CC | 57 Wilkes CC |
| 19 Durham TCC | 39 Pitt CC | 49 Southwestern CC | 58 Wilson CC |
| 20 Edgecombe CC | 40 Randolph CC | | |

## ○ Private Community Colleges

59 Cabarrus College of Health Sciences

**Figure 7.58:** Distribution and Service Regions of North Carolina's Community Colleges, 2001.

transfer program, which certifies courses from the community colleges for transfer into any of the state's 16 senior public institutions. Though not everyone is comfortable with the idea, community colleges are now also preparing to take on the challenge of teacher preparation. Since teacher training has been beset by rules that have limited certification of teacher preparation programs to four year institutions, this will challenge the tradition of seeing community colleges as open-admission, low cost feeders to four-year universities.

An enduring problem for the community colleges is their difficulty in attracting a permanent and certifiable faculty due to prevailing low wages, large workloads, and tight quarters. Community college teachers received, on the average, $3,856 less than public school teachers in annual salary in 1998. In fact, their average annual salary of $33,027 is over $2,000 less than that of their colleagues in South Carolina, and ranks 48th among states in the country, a far distance from the national average of $44,798 (Crouch 2000). Quality faculty are hard to find and those on board are difficult to keep, with nearby high schools offering higher salaries for the same professional experience (Wildman 2001). Salaries for part-time instructors are even more problematic. Requirements for teaching college transfer courses, according to the certifying body, the Southern Association of Colleges and Universities, include a masters degree with 18 semester credit hours in the subject taught. For a part-time instructor a three semester hour college transfer course might yield a salary of $800 to $1,400, without benefits. A surprisingly large number of community college faculty are individuals teaching part-time at several colleges, at penurious salaries, and without benefits (i.e., retirement, insurance).

*Higher Education in North Carolina: How Good Is It?*

Comparable evaluations of state systems of higher educations are infrequent, but desirable. These evaluations may aid higher education policy makers to see their own system in a larger more objective context. For proponents of higher education improvements, comparisons may add ammunition in legislative deliberations. Such a report was recently published in late 2000 by the National Center for Public Policy and Higher Education, coincidentally chaired by North Carolina's Governor Jim Hunt (Kane and Wagner 2000). The report was in the form of a report card, grading the most critical features of affordability, college completion, student preparedness, state derived economic benefits, and participation. North Carolina's grades among the fifty states evaluated ranged from an A to a D.

Affordability received the highest grade of A. Higher education in our state is low cost, from favorable tuition and fees among the public institutions, to the omnipresence of community colleges guaranteeing a near uniformly distributed availability from one's home or work. Geographic accessibility contributes to affordability.

Student preparedness received a B. With higher education facilities universally available to all qualified citizens due to accessibility and affordability, it is the gradually evolving seamlessness of the educational experience from K-12 to the university degree that aids in gaining a comparatively high grade on student preparedness. For students least prepared to enter the university environment, only a high school diploma from any school in the state is necessary for entering a community college. Successful completion of an Associates of Arts degree guarantees acceptance by a senior institution. For an individual who dropped out of high school the diploma may be achieved through GED/equivalency classes at the local community college.

College completion received a B+. The college experience is now being viewed as less threatening. Student can see the entire educational experience as seamless, with partnering existing between community colleges and high schools, and between major universities and community colleges. Recent fusing of academic calendars have contributed, as well. These efforts ease the transition from high school to the senior institution of higher education, and they provide the student at risk a greater sense of belonging and security. At the university level major efforts are made to insure degree completion, especially through remedial courses, tutoring services, and support for handicapped students, from wheelchair access to special programs and psychological counseling.

Resident participation received a D. The major emphasis placed on higher education in the state makes it remarkable that not more of the state's residents actually participate. A longstanding image of not needing a college education was built on the state's economic dependency on agriculture and low skill manufacturing, although this condition never seem to have impeded a historically strong and pervasive support for higher education. However, there is evidence of this image being altered. The recent (2000) vote on the $3.1 billion higher education construction bond passed overwhelmingly throughout the state, with up to 70 percent in support from counties with the smallest percentages of higher education completion.

Economic benefits to the state received a D+. This more negative judgment is directly linked to the historic result of low participation, resulting in a low percentage of residents having attained a four year college degree. In an industrial recruitment context this is problematic. Community competence as defined by the educational attainment of its people is becoming an increasingly important factor in the business investment and industrial location process. Clearly though, the foundation has been placed for this condition to improve dramatically in the near future.

## HOUSING

### *Introduction*

As one of life's necessities, the roof over our head defines us in a very visible way. The homes we live in provide evidence of our status in life, our level of income and our demography. Housing quality is a major attribute of social capital. Homes, distributed individually and in groupings over space, are also a major feature of the cultural landscape. In their essential physical characteristics of space demands and relationship to natural landscape elements, infrastructure support systems, architecture and quality of construction, homes define neighborhoods and communities. As major investments during our lifetime housing, has encouraged the development of major industries, including realty and land development, construction, furniture and appliances, transportation, mortgage finance, and insurance. Housing is of critical importance in the quality of life of individuals and families. Consequently, the public domain is committed to the availability and adequacy of housing all citizens. The federal government is a very active player in the housing market. Federal urban renewal projects have eradicated entire neighborhoods and supported public or project housing. Other programs subsidize affordable housing for poor people, provide low-cost interest loan support for home purchases, and allow mortgage interest tax write-offs. State and local governments establish minimum construction standards through building codes, zoning ordinances, and other special requirements for residential location and neighborhood public safety. Public housing authorities (and there are 3,400 of these in the country), construct, own and maintain public housing facilities, mostly financed by joint federal-private market resources. At the very minimum level of human survival, local government and non-governmental institutions provide temporary shelter housing for the indigent, many of whom otherwise find shelter wherever they can.

We deal with the processes of land use change as it affects the character and distribution of housing in Chapter 12. In that chapter human occupancy of the landscape is viewed through the lens of the last few decades of metropolitan evolution. Distinct variation in age, style, and quality of housing is strongly linked to the locational attributes of communities varying along the urbanizing continuum from rural to exurban, suburban, and center city neighborhoods.

### Residential Historic Preservation

Historic homes are strongly represented in smaller towns and villages that have not experienced the tumultuous changes of the late 20th century. A special emphasis is placed on these more traditional neighborhoods and the process of historic preservation in the regional chapters (Photos 10.14, 11.8a, 12.5, and 12.28; CPs 10.3, 11.2a, c and d, 12.8e, 12.21 and 12.22). Since the 1970s and the American Bicentennial celebration there has been a major emphasis on historic preservation of individual homes and neighborhoods. Publications on residential architecture of the state or its regions are fairly plentiful, but the interested reader should consult the work of Bishir and Southern (1990 and 1996), and Bishir, Southern and Martin (1999). Most counties have catalogued their historic properties through comprehensive historic and architectural surveys, and have established historic properties commissions with the dual role of ensuring continued local support for restoration and preservation projects and of overseeing a new slate of land use and structural restrictions appropriate to preserve historic structures, sites, and situations for future generations. At the county and municipality level, much well illustrated literature is available, best exemplified by the recently published work on Wake County (Lally and Johnson 1994). One of the traditional community forms best preserved in many parts of the state is the historic mill village, as exemplified by Landis (CP 6.8b), Saxapahaw (CP 6.6), and Glencoe (CP 12.17). With traditional company housing it is more a matter simply of the survival of the housing stock without the presence of a formal historic preservation effort, as seen in Roanoke (CP 11.14b) and Gastonia (CP 12.34).

### Rural Housing

Housing in traditional, rural, agricultural North Carolina is exemplified by the family dairy farm in Camden County (CP 5.3e), and by the traditional distribution of residences and farm buildings in Harnett County (Photo 3.2). Newer agricultural residential landscapes are those influenced by contract farming, which brought in more agricultural workers (Photo 5.2). Some residences in rural areas are clearly quality impaired, as indicated in CP 11.8a and CP 7.1a. To compensate for deteriorating rural housing and its frequent absence of basic necessities like running water and toilets, investments are widely made in manufactured (mobile) homes trucked in and placed on a single lot (CP 11.8a) or in a mobile home park setting, as found in rural Cleveland County where the basic infrastructure of road access, water and community septic systems are part of the residential life package (CP 7.3a; see also Photo 8.1b). North Carolina is the nation's mobile home mecca. In the mid 1990s there were more manufactured/mobile homes shipped to dealerships in the state than to those of any other state; only Georgia manufactured more mobile homes. As frequently argued by the North Carolina Rural Economic Development Center and as recently illustrated by the Housing Assistance Council (2001), a national nonprofit organization, good quality housing promotes rural community safety, security, and economic well-being.

However, decent housing is not so easy to come by, and many rural counties lack minimum quality housing codes. Even in rapidly growing Wake County, some rural communities, like Sunset Acres, still had occupied residences without plumbing and running water in 2000; meanwhile, on land adjoining Sunset Acres, the town of Apex was busily annexing and providing city water and sewer lines to a golf subdivision with homes ranging from $200,000 to $700,000 (McDonald 2000). Note, in Figure 7.59, the distribution of dilapidated housing in 2000, especially its concentration in rural eastern North Carolina. Dilapidated means that the housing unit is essentially beyond the repairs needed to arrive at minimum standards. The 2000 Census results showed that 13,156 homes in the state were without indoor plumbing. While this amounts to only 0.43 percent of the total residences in the state (and a drop from 1.5 percent of all units in 1990), the importance of the data is found in the strong continuing concentration of outhouses and straight-piping, where sewage flows directly into an adjacent stream, in certain Mountain and Coastal Plain region counties. Several programs intended to work with

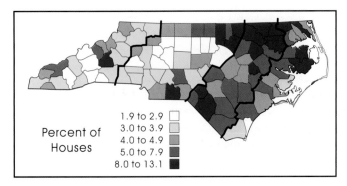

**Figure 7.59:** Percent Dilapidated Housing, 2000.
**Source:** U. S. Bureau of the Census, 2001.

residents to improve this particular situation are now being promoted by the state Department of Environment and Natural Resources (Waggoner 2001).

Nationally, over 35 percent of rural households with children present have problems with home cost, crowding, or the absence of essential infrastructure. In North Carolina, rural Coastal Plain neighborhoods compete with the metro regions' central cities for having the lowest percent of home ownership (Figure 7.60). In addition, rural housing mortgage rates are frequently significantly higher than those in metropolitan areas. In part, this is due to the large number of mobile home loans, which are often carried by subprime lenders at much higher interest rates. As a result there is less home ownership in the poorer eastern rural part of the state, a condition also influenced by the earlier agricultural tradition of sharecropping. This has left many rural families on rental property, a situation that has led to an egregious degree of owner maintenance negligence, as illustrated by the concentration of dilapidated housing in Figure 7.59.

### Housing in the Center City

Incredible differences exist in housing quality in the center cities of the state. Diffused through the state's center cities are examples like Charlotte's gentrified 4th Ward (CP 12.28), Dilworth (CP 7.3b) and South Park District (CP 12.30). These are all upscale neighborhoods, certainly more so than the new mixed income neighborhoods facilitated by the complete overhaul taking place in the 1st Ward (Earle Village), a former public housing project (CP 12.29). Urban renewal, a process discussed in detail in Chapter 12, is still going on in the center city, at times to the detriment of the residents of existing public housing.

### The Case of Halifax Court

Raleigh's Halifax Court is a public housing project of 28 barracks-like structures containing 318 residential units (Geary 1997). It was built in 1941 following urban renewal of a deteriorating single family, mostly rental, housing area in Raleigh's center city. Halifax Court was initially filled by white families within walking distance of employment centers, like Cotton Mill and Pilot Mill; bus service made downtown shopping readily available. The 1950s and 1960s was the period of "white flight" to the suburbs, of relocating manufacturing facilities to spaces beyond, and the removal of the downtown retail sector to arterial strip centers or suburban malls (see chapters 6 and 12). Halifax Court with its 318 households, was essentially abandoned by its employment base and its commercial support. Like other similarly afflicted public housing projects in central cities throughout the state, Halifax Court gradually evolved into a drug infested environment of poor people, lots of them children, but also with 85 percent of the households headed by black single mothers. Everyone were terrorized by drug gangs and their internecine warfare. In the early 1990s, the city finally acted on the problem of

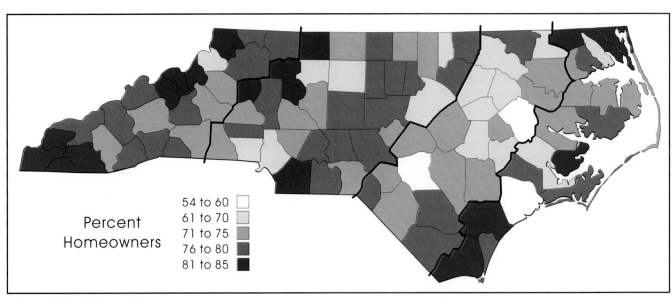

**Figure 7.60:** Percent Homeowners By County, 2000.
**Source:** Charlotte Observer, July 14, 2001.

268

crime and alienation by placing an 11-person Raleigh Police substation in the middle of the project, by improving playground facilities, and by providing improved bus service to a downtown emerging from its Rip van Winkle state.

Having emerged as a relatively stable and crime free community, Halifax Court now became embroiled in a new controversy, the results of the social welfare devolution and a new national move toward ridding center cities of project housing, and subsidized housing in general. It is a mute question as to whether this particular project, with its vastly improved identity, actually had the potential, given the appropriate capital investment, for emerging as a truly habitable urban village (Geary 1997). Halifax Court was handicapped by the nature of its resident households, with its 85 percent dependence on some kind of public welfare, the cost of its public maintenance, but especially by its critical location in a newly dynamic part of downtown Raleigh. In the late 1980s, the project was nearly surrounded by wastelands of abandoned textile mills and other deteriorated and abandoned housing blocks. This was rapidly changing in the 1990s as downtowns again became desirable for residential life. Just a few blocks away to the south, the old Cotton Mill had been successfully rehabilitated into upscale apartments. Immediately to the north of the projects was the sprawling complex of Pilot Mills. Recently added to the National Register of Historic Places, Pilot Mill is now in the process of redevelopment into residences and shops (Photo 12.11). Nearby, the CSX railroad line is the focus of plans to build commuter rail service between downtown, North Raleigh, the Research Triangle Park and Durham, with a transit station eyed on Halifax Court's doorstep. Perhaps most critically is the location of Peace College on Halifax Court's southern boundary. This is an exclusive women's institution that has recently changed from a two-year to a four-year program, and the college desperately needs land for expansion of facilities that are within shouting distance of the state's capitol center. Abandoning Halifax Court will allow its land to reach a new realistic market value and permit a 'natural' evolution of dynamic inner city land use change already set in motion. But what about the people, the residents of the project? Halifax Court, for better or worse, is an example of state-wide public housing projects caught in the new vise of urban renewal.

## Charlotte and HOPE VI Neighborhood Revitalization

In 1994, the Department of Housing and Urban Development consolidated 60 HUD programs into three performance-based funds (Grosvenor 1996). In keeping with the social welfare devolution objectives of the Clinton Administration, HUD's intent was to delegate more responsibility to state and local officials, allowing them flexibility in the development of strategies that might involve public/private partnerships to turn around troubled public housing projects. HUD retained its federally prescribed monitoring authority for insuring that fair housing, income targeting, and community-based participation were met at the local level. However, the overriding objective was to provide opportunities for public housing tenants to make the transition to economic independence and eventual home ownership. Charlotte was one of eleven winners of the initial series of HOPE VI Urban Revitalization Demonstration grants with its proposal to transform the Earle Village public housing project into an affordable transitional residential neighborhood. Over the following years, the Charlotte Housing Authority and its private partner, NationsBank Community Development Corporation received $100 million in HOPE VI funds to demolish the Earle Village, Dalton Village, and Fairview Homes public housing projects and to replace them with nicer, but less dense housing complexes (CP 12.29); the demolition displaced over 50 percent of the project households (Leonnig 1999) (CP 12.29) In fact, only twelve percent of the Earle Village residents returned to First Ward Place, the project's replacement. In reality, most project residents were provided public housing units elsewhere in parts of the city less pressured by development and land value increases, or they were given rent vouchers. It is an unhappy mark of our times that black, poor, single-parent households with children are finding it very difficult to find decent housing even when, with rent voucher in hand, they are able to afford it. Charlotte had 3,600 public housing apartments in 1999, with 3,500 households on the one-to three-year waiting list; 2,200 families received rent vouchers, with another 1,100 eligible families on a four-to five-year waiting list (Chapman and Leonnig 1999). One might surmise that city councils like the HOPE VI approach because it aids in transforming dilapidated project areas of the center city into gleaming new and affordable residential neighborhoods much in tune with increasing demands for uptown living; meanwhile, this approach displaces most of the indigent and worsens their housing malaise.

## *Affordable Housing*

A current mantra of city councils and public housing authorities is that poor households are better off scattered throughout the city so as not to suffer the negative side of the poverty ghetto (i. e., decrepit housing, drugs, crime, alienation, and despair). For any low income household, residential space in the center city is very difficult to come by, and not only for poor people stigmatized by rent vouchers. The residential land development and construction companies do not see the profits in building affordable housing, at least not as long as more upscale and profitable residences are in demand. Further, there is some confusion about the question of just what is affordable housing. A Charlotte builder contributed this definition. An "affordable" home is one that can be bought by a person making up to 80 percent of the local median income. If this amounts to $57,100 per year for a family of four, then 80 percent equals $45,680. According to current banking standards, a family making that much can spend one-third on housing, including mortgage, insurance, utilities, and taxes, or the equivalent of $1,256 per month. Assuming the prospective purchaser has an adequate credit rating and can manage the down payment, this will allow the purchase of a home at the "affordable" price of $90,000 to $100,000 (Burke 2001). In 1999, over 88,000 households in the Charlotte region paid over one-third of their gross income on housing costs alone; and even worse, 30,000 households spent more than 50 percent of their gross income on housing costs (Chapman and Leonnig 1999).

On the national level a standard of "housing wages" is being used to ascertain the degree to which the hourly wage sustains a household's ability to afford adequate living accommodations. "Housing wage" is the hourly wage needed for a worker to be able to afford adequate housing using 30 percent of income earned. As reported in a Charlotte Observer Editorial (2001, October 8), North Carolina comes in 22nd in the country in "housing wages". The National Low Income Housing Coalition's "Out of Reach" report indicated that a North Carolinian would need to earn $11.27 an hour to afford living in a two-bedroom home, by the 30 percent standard. In a ranking of counties of the United States (some 3,000), the "Out of Reach" report found that four North Carolina counties were among the ten that had experienced the highest increase in "housing wages" (i.e, increasing housing costs without accompanying increases in income). These counties were: Polk, Cleveland, Jackson, and Rutherford, all are located in the southwestern part of the state. Meanwhile, Mecklenburg County's average monthly rent for a two bedroom apartment is $693.00, unaffordable by 42 percent of county resident households. The real crisis in affordable housing appears to be clearly understood by neither the building industry nor the various city councils in the state.

Some relief for low income household housing needs is provided by non-governmental organizations (NGOs), such as Habitat for Humanity, and quasi-government nonprofit agencies, such as the Charlotte-Mecklenburg Housing Partnership. In most North Carolina cities there are organizations with an armful of success stories of providing new or renovated low income housing. One example that received national attention in the 1990s was that of Genesis Park in Charlotte, a run down neighborhood. The C-M Housing Partnership aided 90 families in renovating or building new homes, Habitat for Humanity contributed ten new homes, and the city provided improved roads, new sidewalks, and increased police monitoring (Chapman 1999). In Durham the Campaign for Decent Housing, created by the Durham Affordable Housing Coalition, has set its goal to bring the city's 4,000 substandard housing units up to code compliance by 2003 (Gomez 1999). However, it is a huge step to go from these very valuable, but highly scattered and limited, NGO efforts, to the all-out assault required to provide all North Carolina center city households in need with decent housing.

Elsewhere in the center city there is pressure to provide more residential space. In traditional and stable residential neighborhoods of the major cities, especially Raleigh, Winston-Salem and Charlotte, single family housing dominates and is becoming quite expensive. One approach to increasing population density is through in-fill projects, as illustrated in CP 7.3b. In Charlotte, this process is complemented by the large scale condominium projects being built by Bank of America. All in all, there is a general return of middle and higher income households to the center city, a major reversal of conditions only a few decades earlier, when white flight dominated the interurban migration stream (Chapter 4).

### Housing in Suburbia and Exurbia

Much is said in Chapter 12 concerning suburban and exurban residential development, especially as they are identifiable with urban sprawl and the more limited attempts to correct this expansive rural to urban shift in land use by building alternative residential communities. The traditional suburban excesses are well illustrated in Photos 8.1a, 12.4, 12.15, 12.16, 12.17 and 12.18. Approaches to smart growth are illustrated by the Fearrington and Southern Village examples in CP 12.12 and 12.13. These types of development have become more popular in recent years as subdivision developers are moving increasingly toward mixed land uses in their new planned communities.

### Leisure and Seasonal Housing

Three regions in the state (Mountains, Tidewater, and Sandhills) have had several decades of continuous home construction due to their scenic and leisure activity attractions for seasonal living,, as well as for retirement communities. In general terms these activities reflect the booming 1990s, with North Carolina sites affordable and available for retirees seeking an option to Florida and Arizona for retirement, and North Carolinians having the wherewithal to afford seasonal homes in the mountains and along river, lake, bay, and sea shores (Photo 1.10). Much retirement housing is seasonal, occupied by Floridians who spend their winters in the warmer climate. Thus the seashore retirement communities depicted in Chapter 10 are largely empty in the winter season, while those shown in Chapter 13 may show life during the skiing season.

## CRIMINAL BEHAVIOR, JUSTICE, AND INCARCERATION

North Carolina's Department of Corrections was established by the General Assembly in 1977, following a series of renaming exercises that began with the founding of a unified state run prison system in 1957. Including city and county jails, road camps, and state prisons, the system evolved into the largest in the country in term of number of prison units (Betts 1999a). Increasing rates of incarceration and subsequent overcrowding of a system with outdated and dilapidating facilities led, in the late 1980s, to a consolidation move enhanced by the building of new prisons. In 2000, there were 76 state prisons, plus seven contracted facilities operated by private non-profit or private, for-profit entities (Department of Corrections 2000). There were 31,579 inmates in prisons that ranged in capacity from 25 inmates to 937. Prison were distributed seemingly haphazardly across the state (Figure 7.61). The center of the Mountain Region has a concentration of prisons, as does a north-south trending set of counties from Granville to Harnett, and a grouping of counties in the southern Piedmont Region. In addition, there appears to be an almost

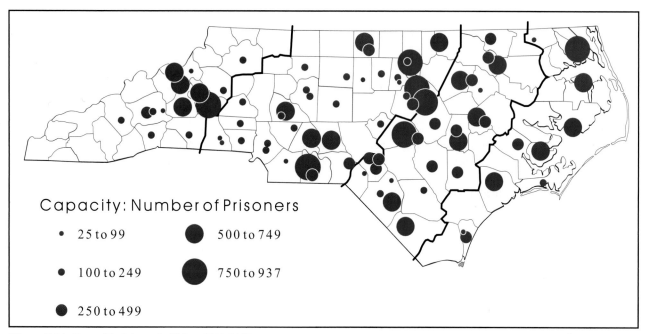

**Figure 7.61:** Statewide Prison Facilities, 1999-2000.
**Source:** Derived From N. C. Department of Correction, Annual Statistical Report, 1999-2000.

even distribution of medium sized prisons in the Coastal Plain and Tidewater Regions.

A Criminality Index (CI) has been devised to explore significant differences in the state in terms of a tendency toward crime. Using June, 2000, data from the Annual Statistical Report of the Department of Corrections, the CI is derived by adding resident prisoners to criminals supervised on parole, probation and post release, and then dividing by the total population of the individual criminal's county of conviction. As can be seen from Figure 7.62, the county criminality index varies from 0.7 criminals per 100 residents in Watauga County to a high of 3.6 per 100 in Scotland County. For Scotland County, this means that in the year 2000 there was one convicted criminal for every 28 persons, as compared to one for every 143 persons in Watauga County. On a regional basis, the lowest CIs are found in the Mountain Region, with the exception of three northwestern counties of Surry, Alleghany, and Wilkes. In fact, the latter three seem to form a starting point for an almost contiguous set of relatively high CI counties stretching across the state to New Hanover County on the coast. The node among these counties is in the Sandhills State Geographic Region (see Chapter 9). Similar concentrations are found in the Roanoke and Pamlico SGRs. A notable aspect of the CI index is its low numbers in the metro core counties. Mecklenburg is a relatively low 1.3, while Wake and Guilford are not much higher with 1.6, still below the state average. The highest criminality index values are found in mostly rural counties (compare with Figure 7.16). One weakness of the Criminality Index is its dependency on a single year of data.

North Carolina was experiencing a bevy of problems with its correctional system during the 1970s and 1980s. Part of this was reflected in the increasingly outmoded and dilapidating jails and prisons, but problems also resulted from the increasing number of people incarcerated, thus adding to the problem of over crowdedness. In fact, in 1987 a federal court was threatening to take over the state prison system if something was not immediately done to alleviate its over crowding. The state placed a cap (17,460 in 1987) on the number of prisoners to be accommodated by the existing system. In 1993, the Criminal Justice Partnership Act established community based correctional programs to further alleviate the pressure on state prisons, but the cap had to be raised to 25,500 in 1994 (Lubitz 1996). Still a surplus of prisoners had to be shipped to prisons out of state, at considerable additional expense to the taxpayers. Simultaneously, felons found themselves serving less and less of their sentence time. In 1986, felons on average served 40 percent of their sentence, while by 1993 this had been reduced to just 18 percent. Other problems derived from great variations across the state in judgments rendered for essentially similar felonious activities. Subsequently the state has moved to consolidate the prison system, closing down 20 outmoded and smaller, costly facilities and replacing them, at a cost of $423 million, with eleven larger, more economic, and modern facilities. Several prisons are in predominantly rural counties, where the related employment boost has been especially appreciated. A new approach to uniform sentencing was assured by the Structured Sentencing Act of 1993 (Lubitz 1996). For the remainder of the 1990s, the inflow of new prisoners has held fairly steady at about 25,000 per year. A drop of about 1,000, seen in 1999-2000, was due in part to the administrative transfer of the IMPACT boot camp program out of the Division of Prisons. Although the number of new prisoners has remained steady, longer sentences and fewer early releases have had the net effect of accommodating more prisoners. Inmates totaled 19,048 in 1991

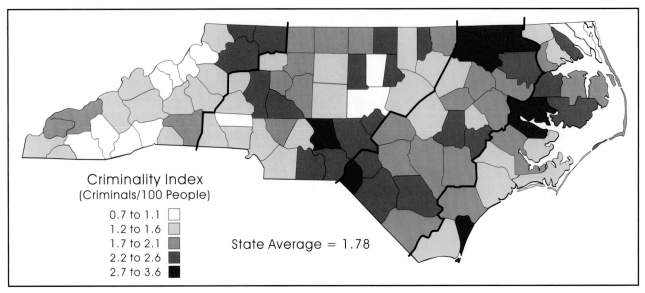

**Figure 7.62:** Criminality Index By County, 1999-2000.
**Source:** Derived From N. C. Department of Correction, Annual Statistical Report, 1999-2000.

and 31,535 in 2000, an increase over the decade of 66 percent. The projection is for 40,000 by 2010. It is expected that two or three maximum security prisons will soon join the present thirteen, prospectively to be constructed in Anson, Alexander, and Scotland counties (Wright 2001). Detailed information on the current status of prisoners in the system is provided in Box 7E.

North Carolina is now experiencing a reduction in the rate of most forms of criminal activity. Reasons certainly include sentencing reforms and a tougher line on meting out longer stays in prison, but it also needs noting that the segment of society most likely to commit criminal acts, the youthful male population, has been declining in its share of the total population over these same decades. In any case, there is now a much larger number of people in prison, with escalating costs to the taxpayer for clothing, feeding, sheltering, protecting, and perhaps rehabilitating each criminal. Funding for the Department of Corrections increased from $821 million in 1995-96 to $921 million in 1998-99. With this, and several thousand more prison beds, it appears that state has responded to the public clamor for incarcerating criminals. Less concern seems to be expressed for the funding needed to eliminate the causes of crime, and once in jail, to rehabilitate the criminal. North Carolina's incarceration rate of 345 felons/100,000 people in 1999, ranks it 30th in the nation where the average is 476/100,000. In the larger context, there continues to be a question of what might be wrong when one of the world's most prosperous nations puts people behind bars at rates six to ten times those of other industrialized nations.

## ELECTORAL PARTICIPATION AND POLITICAL PARTIES

### Who Votes and Why?

Previous sections of this chapter indicate that changes affecting life and livelihood in North Carolina is part of an emerging massive public agenda. As life increases in complexity, as people are increasingly interwoven into a web of communication that spans the world, as their lives are increasingly impacted by changes occurring in places they had never heard of, as policy and decision making is getting refocused from the federal to the state and local level, many people are getting actively involved in their community and in the affairs of state and nation. In a viable democracy, individuals register to vote, inform themselves, and then actually vote on issues of the day and for politicians who will pursue with vigor their sense of the times. In fact, the United States, the leading purveyor of democratic ideals in the world, is also the democracy with one of the lowest voter turnouts in the western world. On the national level, voting for the presidency for the 1996 and 2000 elections reached new lows with less than 50 percent of the voting age public going to the polls. The highest voter participation rate, reaching back to the time of the first Roosevelt administration in 1932, was the 62.8 percent who turned out to vote in the Kennedy-Nixon election of 1960. Since then, national voter participation has been generally decreasing. Paradoxically, one reason for the drop below the fifty percentage level has been the lowering of the age of eligible voters to 18 in 1972. Young people appear less interested in having their say in the election booth.

North Carolina has generally lagged the country's voting participation rate. The highest reached was 54.4 percent of the voting age public in 1968, and the recent low was 42.9 percent

**Box 7E:** Incarcerated Persons in North Carolina Prison System, 2000.

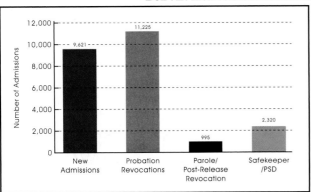

**a:** Types of Admissions.

There are four types of admissions to prison: new admissions, probation revocations, parole/post-release supervision revocations, and safekeepers/pre-sentence diagnostic inmates. It may surprise many that people entering prison due to parole violations outnumber new admissions. Source: Department of Corrections 2001, p. 5.

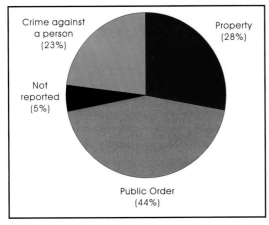

**c:** Crimes Committed by Inmates.

The most frequent type of a crime that results in a prison sentence is public order crimes. These include drug offenses (5,616), driving while impaired (2,581), traffic violations (1,027), and others, such as being a habitual felon or being a felon in the possession of a firearm (1,295). Property crimes include larceny (2,531), breaking and entering (2,219), fraud (723), forgery (563), and burglary (267). Crimes against a person include assaults (2,482), robbery (1,334), sexual offenses (9,750), and homicides (689). Source: Department of Corrections 2001, p. 7.

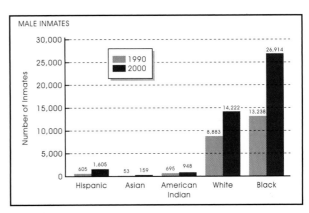

**b1:** Male Inmates.

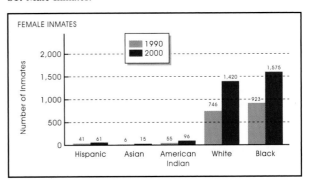

**b2:** Female Inmates.

Among inmates there is a clear racial dominance by blacks, of whom there are now almost twice as many as there are white prisoners. For 2000, this number is also double the number of blacks held in prisons ten years earlier. Even more disturbing is the fact that one out of every 30 black males in North Carolina is in prison, as compared to one out of every 200 white males. Blame for the high incarceration rate is given to alcoholism and drug addiction, high school drop-outs, and the break-up of families. What this data does not show is that there is also a disproportionate number of crime victims that are black. Women account for only about seven percent of the incarcerated population. Note that the data in Box 7E-b.includes inmates in the federal prisons in the state as well as those in the state system. Source: Wright, Frazier, and Mellnik 2001.

**d:** Cost to the State per Day for the Different Classes of Custody.

The cost to the state for the average prisoner is increasing at a rate faster than inflation, it also depends on the nature of custody, which defines the resources needed. Notably, two new private prisons, Mountain View and Pamlico Correctional facilities, with capacities of 528 and 524, respectively, are contracted to the state for $36.79 per inmate per day. Sources: McDowell 1991, p. 62; Department of Corrections 2000, p.3-4.

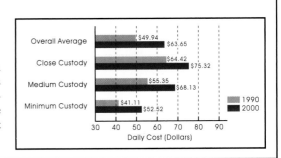

273

in 1972. In 1996, the voting age participation rate was 47.6 percent. It is important to note that the percentage participation of eligible voters is not the same as percentage participation of registered voters. Not all eligible adults register to vote in spite of major efforts to get people registered, as exemplified by the Motor Voter Registration Act of 1995. The difference can be dramatic. For example, the highest percentage of registered voters participating in a North Carolina presidential election over the past four decades occurred in the 1968 election with 76.4 percent, which represented 54.4 percent of eligible voters. This indicates a 22 percent gap between eligible voters and those registering to vote. In the 1996 presidential election 60.5 percent of the registered voters, representing 47.6 percent of those eligible, turned out at the polls. The 2000 election also brought out about 60 percent of the registered voters, with considerable variations in the participation rate across the state (Figure 7.63). Lowest in the state was Scotland County, with only 26 percent of its registered voters participating. Camden, Johnston, and Anson also were at the very low end of the spectrum. In looking at the statewide distribution, there appears to be no clear patterns. Perhaps it is notable that counties with a high proportion of university students (Watauga, Jackson, Orange, and Pitt) have low participation rates. Otherwise, both the most rural and the most urban have great variances within their groups. Compare, for example, the highs achieved by Mitchell and Graham, with the low of many other rural counties; compare also the percentages of Wake and Durham counties.

While North Carolinians have lower voter participation rates than is average for the country, and while there are significant differences within the state on a county basis, there are also significant differences by race. A Charlotte Observer analysis of voting behavior in the 2000 presidential election showed that for twelve counties in the Charlotte area, blacks generally fell significantly behind white in participation. The gap was greatest in Iredell County where 52 percent of the white voting age public went to the polls, while only 38 percent of the black voting age public participated, resulting in a percentage point difference of 14. The least point difference (5) was found in Caldwell County, but here only 36 percent of the whites went to the polls, as compared to 31 percent of the black population (Bell, Morrill and Mellnik 2001). Black participation rises at the higher end of the socioeconomic ladder, in fact, here it exceeds that of the whites. What is true, regardless of race, is that where there is a larger proportion of people in poverty, and with less education, there is also a lesser likelihood of voter participation. A tradition of being discriminated against and feeling powerless, even in a voting booth, may also keep some blacks from the polls. Of course, not all who wants to vote may do so. This is the case for the prison population, where blacks comprise 59 percent of the total.

### Congressional Election Districts

An interesting game to play at a social gathering, or in a classroom, is to ask individuals to characterize the shape of the current North Carolina congressional districts. The tortured shape of some N. C. districts have resulted in an electoral district map that *The Wall Street Journal* has branded "political pornography," and Supreme Court Justice Sandra Day O'Connor has called "bizarre" (Trevor and Morrill 1993). As Eyre points out, electoral districts are shaped around regional variations in population numbers, racial character and political affiliation (1993, 45). However, redistricting is inherently a political process used by the party in power when given the opportunity to redraw the map. Unusual geographic shapes have resulted from gerrymandering approaches to the delineation of electoral districts in a state. The term derives from the (sala)mander appearance resulting from the 1842 manipulation of a particular district in Massachusetts to suit the sitting governor (Gerry) and his political party. In the past, this device was used in North Carolina to insure the reelec-

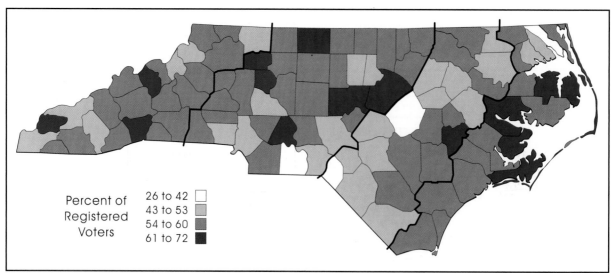

**Figure 7.63:** Voter Turnout as a Percent of Registered Voters, 2000 National Elections.
**Source:** Raleigh News and Observer, November, 2000.

tion of incumbents or to prevent Republican majorities. Further complicating the issue, the Voting Rights Act of 1965 was enacted by the United States Congress to insure minority electoral participation without state or locally imposed hindrances such as poll taxes, literacy tests, or property ownership. In 1982, the Act was amended to guarantee that redistricting of electoral districts would not be in violation of minority rights. Perhaps, inadvertently, the amendment encouraged a new form of gerrymandering. A 13 percent population growth in North Carolina during the 1980s qualified the state for an additional congressional district for the 1992 elections. A Democratic General Assembly approved a redistricting plan which left most incumbents unthreatened, and generated a Republican district, and a black district. Following challenges to the plan and a rejection by the U. S. Department of Justice, the plan was revised to include two predominantly black districts (given the state's 22 percent African-American population). Though used in subsequent elections, the 12th District has been under continuous challenge. It was finally upheld by the U. S. Supreme Court in 2001, although not without several boundary changes along the way. Figure 7.64 shows the final, court approved twelve congressional districts in the state (Johnson 2001). The Court's 5-4 vote suggests that the issue may soon be visited again, especially now that the state's continuing growth has gained it yet another seat. A new 13 district plan will be developed and proposed, by a Democratic General Assembly, and approved in some form by the 2002 congressional elections.

### Recent Elections

As the state appears to continue being swayed to the Democratic side in state politics, so it is revealing a strong conservativism that has resulted in frequent victories by Republican presidential candidates (Table 7.5). In 2000, North Carolina had a majority Republican congressional representation, with the Senate split evenly; for a while, in the 1990s there were two Republican Senators. This schizoid electoral behavior is illustrated in the map comparing presidential and gubernatorial votes by county (Figure 7.65). Twenty-three, mostly Coastal Plain, counties were "pure" Democratic in their combined victories for Democrats Gore and Easley, 37 counties were "pure" Republican with their majority votes for Bush and Vinroot, but 40 counties went

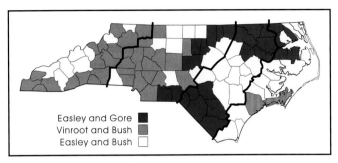

**Figure 7.65:** Presidential and Gubernatorial Results of the 2000 Election.
**Source:** Raleigh News and Observer, November, 2000.

Republic on one level and Democrat on the other. Finally, of course, Republican Bush and Democrat Easley split the state. Heppen (2000) writes that the 2000 results suggest the continuing existence of many Souths in North Carolina (Figure 7.66). First of all, the state is a microcosm of the South, while still geographically diverse. The "Deep South" remains in the predominantly rural and black populated Coastal Plain Region, where the Democratic Party still rules, with Bush showing poorly though he won the entire state. Secondly, the Republican Blue Ridge has been a fact of political life since Reconstruction, though this is weakening by in-migrating retirees and college people. Thirdly, it is the Western Piedmont that carries the "Southern Republican Paradox," strongly traditional, religiously conservative, and patriotic blue collar industry populations. Finally, metropolitan areas, as elsewhere in the South, are much more of a mix. The metro areas tend toward a more middle-of-the-road position, due to the greater concentration of blacks in the center city and newcomers (Northern moderates and liberals) in some of the suburbs; the exception was Mecklenburg County whose favorite son ran for Republic Governor, thus skewing the results.

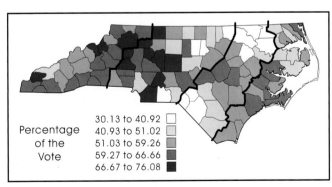

**Figure 7.66:** The Bush Vote in North Carolina Counties, 2000.
**Source:** Heppen, 2000.

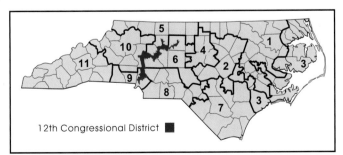

**Figure 7.64:** 1997 North Carolina Congressional Districts as Sanctioned by the U.S. Supreme Court.
**Source:** Johnson, 2001.

| Year | Total NC Voting-Age Population | Total NC Registered Voters | North Carolina Turnout | | | Party of Winner | | |
|---|---|---|---|---|---|---|---|---|
| | | | Number of Voters | Percent of Registered Population | Percent of Voting-Age Population | President | Senator | Govenor |
| 1960 | 2,585,000 | N/A | 1,368,556 | * | 52.9 | D | D | D |
| 1962 | 2,647,000 | N/A | 813,155 (senate) | * | 30.7 | * | D | * |
| 1964 | 2,723,000 | N/A | 1,424,983 | * | 52.3 | D | * | D |
| 1966 | 2,798,000 | 1,933,763 | 901,978 | 46.6 | 32.2 | * | D | * |
| 1968 | 2,921,000 | 2,077,538 | 1,587,493 | 76.4 | 54.4 | D | D | D |
| 1970 | 3,043,000 | 1,945,187 | 932,948 | 63.9 | 30.7 | * | * | * |
| 1972 | 3,541,399 | 2,357,645 | 1,518,612 | 64.4 | 42.9 | R | R | R |
| 1974 | 3,725,037 | 2,279,646 | 1,020,367 (senate) | 44.8 | 27.4 | * | D | * |
| 1976 | 3,884,477 | 2,553,717 | 1,677,906 | 65.7 | 43.2 | D | * | D |
| 1978 | 4,053,977 | 2,430,306 | 1,135,814 (senate) | 46.7 | 28.0 | * | R | * |
| 1980 | 4,222,654 | 2,774,844 | 1,855,833 | 66.9 | 43.9 | R | R | D |
| 1982 | 4,416,444 | 2,674,787 | 1,330,630 | 49.7 | 30.1 | * | * | * |
| 1984 | 4,585,788 | 3,270,933 | 2,239,051 | 68.5 | 47.4 | R | R | R |
| 1986 | 4,738,687 | 3,080,990 | 1,591,330 (senate) | 51.6 | 33.6 | * | D | * |
| 1988 | 4,887,358 | 3,432,042 | 2,134,370 | 62.2 | 43.7 | R | * | R |
| 1990 | 5,016,747 | 3,347,635 | 2,068,904 (senate) | 61.8 | 41.2 | * | R | * |
| 1992 | 5,182,321 | 3,817,380 | 2,611,850 | 68.4 | 50.4 | R | R | D |
| 1994 | 5,359,333 | 3,635,875 | 1,533,728 | 42.2 | 28.6 | * | * | * |
| 1996 | 5,499,000 | 4,330,657 | 2,618,326 | 60.5 | 47.6 | R | R | D |
| 1998 | 5,620,000 | 4,740,272 | 2,012,143 | 42.4 | 35.8 | * | D | * |
| 2000 | NA | 4,930,319 | 2,958,191 | 60.0 | * | R | * | D |

**Table 7.5:** North Carolina Voter Registration and Participation in General Elections, 1960-2000.
**Sources:** Updated from Beyle, 2000, p. 3.

## OPEN SPACE RECREATION AND LEISURE

As is evident from a review of Chapters 1 through 3 the state of North Carolina is endowed with a richness and great variety of natural environments. Their use in recreational activities by a people traditionally close to nature is elaborated in the regional chapters (10-13) of this text. Throughout this book many photographs illustrate the diversity of the state's recreation and leisure environments. What follows here is a brief, perfunctory discussion of soma attributes of the state-wide recreational geography.

North Carolina has long been known through the eastern part of the nation as a prime vacation land. The image of mountains, sandhills, and coastal areas have been especially important, and many resorts and other economic activity has resulted. Yet, for the state's own people there is a dearth of leisure space, with the state park system falling to 49th in the country in support in the early 1990s. Kentucky, alone among southern states to identify their state park system as an economic development tool, spent $14.69 per person on their system, while next-door neighbors, Tennessee and South Carolina, were able to spend $7.39 and $4.84 per capita, respectively. North Carolina languished at the bottom with an allocation of merely $1.57 per person (Krueger and McLaughlin 1996, 684-684). The recreational literature indicates that more than 50 percent of a person's open space recreational activity takes place within two miles of the home.

Having readily available leisure and recreational areas is for many residents a quality of life matter, but many counties do not well respond to this challenge. Figure 7.67 identifies the enormous differences in outdoor recreational space available to the residents of individual counties. With a state average of 2.73 persons per acre of open leisure space, the range varies from .06/ acre in Swain and Hyde counties, representing the vast spaces available in the mountain and coastal milieu, to 2,103 persons/ acre in Hoke County, representing equally well the absence of leisure space in poorer, and predominantly agricultural, counties of the eastern part of the state. These rural counties lack local pressure on the state and county to provide additional recreational resources. This is less the case in the more populous counties. Mecklenburg County, for example, has seen residential and commercial growth eat up its rural land at a pace not matched by the county and its municipalities in their preservation of open space. Concerned over their very limited open space (128 persons/acre), Mecklenburg voters passed a $200 million bond issue in 1999 for the purchase and preservation of open space lands over the following decade. An absence of implemented recreational space planning in the county caused the dwindling remaining supply of available land to escalate in price to where the bond issue will have been exhausted by 2002.

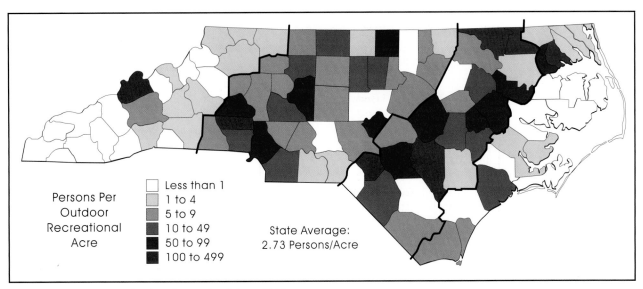

**Figure 7.67:** Persons per Outdoor Recreational Acre, 2000.
**Sources:** Statistical Abstract of North Carolina Counties, 1992; U. S. Bureau of the Census, 2001.

A state-wide concern had been expressed for several decades as per capita funding for the 58 unit state park system stayed near the bottom in the country. A 158,339 acre park system of 38 state parks, two natural areas, and four recreation areas, attracted over 13 million visitors per year (Figure 7.68). The parks struggled for years with inadequate staff levels, low pay, and haphazard management. Inconsistencies in funding persisted, with the General Assembly seeing the system as a low priority and therefore providing funding only on an irregular basis. A dedicated source of funding, whether from taxes, fees, and licenses, donations, bonds, and lotteries, was absent in North Carolina. The poor status of the parks was described in a report to Governor Jim Martin by the State Goals and Policy Board, in 1986 (Krueger and McLaughlin 1996, 682):

> North Carolina's Parks and Recreation System is in generally deplorable condition, is a burden to the full development of the state's tourism industry, and is inarguably a worst-case example of a public trust and the abdication of responsibility.

Public users, discontent with existing conditions, spearheaded a $35 million bond issue to be invested in general upgrading of facilities and land acquisition in 1993, and the General Assembly added $10 million to the same objectives in 1995. Also, in 1995, the General Assembly finally decided on a dedicated funding source utilizing the state's share of the property transfer tax. This was expected to pump in about $10 million per year into the state park system, an amount still considered marginal for the parks operation. From data showing monies allocated to land acquisition and capital improvements from 1987 to 1999, it is clear that the General Assembly is intent on improving its record in support of the state parks system (Figures 7.69 and 7.70). With

support from private donors and land trust organizations, the state was able to acquire the Jocasse Gorges site of 9,760 acres, and the 18,000 acre Buckridge Coastal Reserve in 1999.

## SUMMARY

The dramatic improvement in the status of the state park system, although not complemented by most counties in providing local recreational space, is evidence of the state's increasing willingness to deal in some positive manner with a quality of life and environment issue; in this case, a citizen's ability to conveniently access appropriately defined and managed public open space for leisure and recreation. Other social capital elements, potentially more critical, have also seen a recent increase in public interest and government treatment of their more negative characteristics. Although bottom lines are yet to be clearly or sufficiently drawn in matters of hourly wages, housing conditions, and access to quality health care, they are at least being actively investigated with a more open mind to provide means of improving them. Turning away from the welfare state ideals defined by federal government programs of the 1960s and 1970s, to a much narrower context of social support systems managed at the state and local levels, has moved the most needy in North Carolina from an "entitlement" stake in their survival prospects to taking a personal responsibility for their own and their family's welfare. From cash handouts to 'Work First' expectations has indeed removed a vast majority of families from the welfare rolls, but this positive result is due in part, perhaps even mostly, to the economic good times and conditions of full employment of the late 1990s.

Attaining basic levels of expectations in their quality of social life conditions energize people, and leave them more receptive and adaptable to changes that will affect their livelihood

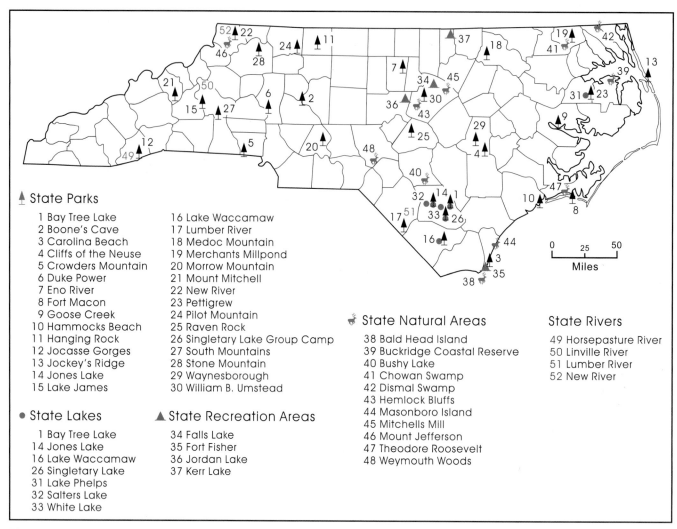

**State Parks**

| | |
|---|---|
| 1 Bay Tree Lake | 16 Lake Waccamaw |
| 2 Boone's Cave | 17 Lumber River |
| 3 Carolina Beach | 18 Medoc Mountain |
| 4 Cliffs of the Neuse | 19 Merchants Millpond |
| 5 Crowders Mountain | 20 Morrow Mountain |
| 6 Duke Power | 21 Mount Mitchell |
| 7 Eno River | 22 New River |
| 8 Fort Macon | 23 Pettigrew |
| 9 Goose Creek | 24 Pilot Mountain |
| 10 Hammocks Beach | 25 Raven Rock |
| 11 Hanging Rock | 26 Singletary Lake Group Camp |
| 12 Jocasse Gorges | 27 South Mountains |
| 13 Jockey's Ridge | 28 Stone Mountain |
| 14 Jones Lake | 29 Waynesborough |
| 15 Lake James | 30 William B. Umstead |

**State Lakes**

1 Bay Tree Lake
14 Jones Lake
16 Lake Waccamaw
26 Singletary Lake
31 Lake Phelps
32 Salters Lake
33 White Lake

**State Recreation Areas**

34 Falls Lake
35 Fort Fisher
36 Jordan Lake
37 Kerr Lake

**State Natural Areas**

38 Bald Head Island
39 Buckridge Coastal Reserve
40 Bushy Lake
41 Chowan Swamp
42 Dismal Swamp
43 Hemlock Bluffs
44 Masonboro Island
45 Mitchells Mill
46 Mount Jefferson
47 Theodore Roosevelt
48 Weymouth Woods

**State Rivers**

49 Horsepasture River
50 Linville River
51 Lumber River
52 New River

**Figure 7.68:** North Carolina State Parks System, 2000.
**Source:** Updated from Krueger and McLaughlin, 1996.

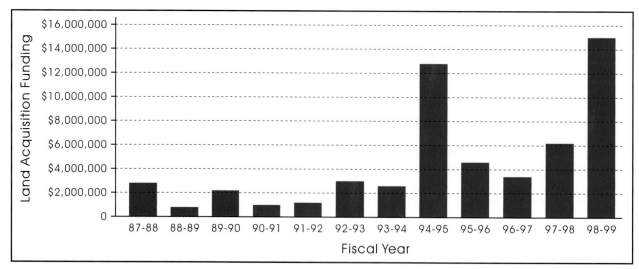

**Figure 7.69:** Capital Improvements for the State Park System, 1987-88 through 1998-99.
**Source:** N. C. Department of Natural Resources, December 1, 1999.

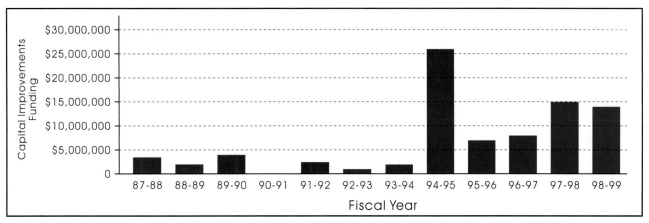

**Figure 7.70:** Land Acquisition Funding for the State Park System, 1987-88 through 1998-99.
**Source:** N. C. Department of Natural Resources, December 1, 1999.

and life styles. Propelled by the competitive fervor of globalizing processes, these changes may otherwise seem intrusive, if not terrifying, particularly to those least able to cope. It is the task of government to ensure an even playing field, and with the active participation of local communities to provide the support needed for all residents to reach these basic quality of life expectations. In the final accounting it is the quality of life conditions, as defined by the various elements of the state's social capital, by which the state is measured to have met its obligations as defined in Section 1 of Article 1 of the Constitution of North Carolina, to wit:

We hold it to be self-evident that all persons are created equal; that they are endowed by their Creator with certain inalienable rights; that among these are life, liberty, the enjoyment of the fruits of their own labor, and the pursuit of happiness.

# A Fragile Environment

## INTRODUCTION

The pressures of industry, agriculture, fishing, forestry, mining, population growth and development. From the coast of the Atlantic to the Great Smoky Mountains, North Carolinians enjoy environments rich in diversity, but also those that are fragile to excessive development (Figure 8.1).

The economy and the environment often have a cause and effect relationship. Balancing the natural systems of the environment with their human modifications to these is critical. Issues concerning our environment have two primary problem foci: 1) those that are caused by natural events and 2) those that are caused by human modification. Often they combine, as one event will accelerate or cause another; such as development often increases erosion or hurricane Floyd causing North Carolina's worst natural disaster (CP 8.1 – 8.8 and CP 11.4). The scientific axiom that for every action there is an equal and opposite reaction certainly applies to our fragile environment. This chapter focuses on geographic perspectives of environmental issues that North Carolina is presently facing.

### A History of Environmental Concern

North Carolina has a long tradition of environmental concern. In 1783, the Colonial Assembly passed an act "to prevent killing deer at unreasonable times." Many other conservation laws aimed at assuring the proper use of our natural resources followed this act. The North Carolina Geologic Survey was established in 1891 to evaluate and manage mineral resources, and by 1925 care of all natural resources was unified under the Department of Conservation and Development. This agency functioned until 1971 when twenty-five separate agencies were merged to form the Department of Natural and Economic Resources; then in 1977 a further reorganization brought into being the present Department of Natural Resources and Community Development. As this name implies there is a strong correlation between the protection and the use of our natural resources. The name was later changed to the Department of Health, Environment, and Natural Resources (DEHNR), and is now called the North Carolina Department of Environment and Natural Resources (NCDENR) as the health section was reconstituted as a separate agency.

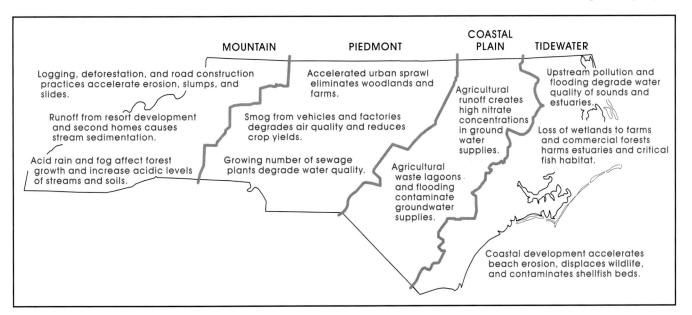

**Figure 8.1:** Regional Environmental Issues
**Source:** Modified from The Charlotte Observer, April 22, 1990.

Environmental concerns were largely expressed in volunteer actions until the 1970s, when strong legal and enforcement policies were adopted. Today there are over 500 state environmental laws aimed at controlling pollution and misuse of natural resources. Some of these laws carry out federal incentives, while others were developed in anticipation of federal directives. State laws often follow and parallel federal laws to control oil spills, dredge and fill activity, dam construction, and mining. The management of scenic rivers and roads, forests, and wildlife, including endangered species, as well as the preparing of environmental impact statements, also are included at the federal level.

The federal Clean Air and Clean Water acts of the early 1970's set basic pollution control standards that the state administers. The state also must assess the economic impacts of proposed air quality standards and all stream reclassification requests. Additionally, regulations controlling toxic substances, hazardous and solid waste, and safe drinking water are delegated to the state from the federal government. State and local programs such as coastal zone management and protection of small watersheds, have federal encouragement (Office of Regulatory Relations 1981).

North Carolina has been active in initiating some environmental programs and laws completely apart from federal interest. These actions recognize the importance of North Carolina's environment by and for its people. These include the control of stream sedimentation, oil refining, water allocation and non-discharging septic tanks.

During the past three decades there has been a strong and growing concern from public and private sectors to protect the natural environment of our state. Environmental Legislation of North Carolina (Table 8.1) illustrates some of the major actions protecting the state's environment. Land is under greater stress than ever before, with an increasing population spreading across its surface (see Chapter 4), the abandonment of manufacturing industries in some areas and the expansion of service industries elsewhere (Chapter 6), and an increased need for energy (Photo 8.1 and 8.2). Strong environmental laws and enforcement proce-

**Photo 8.1a and b:** Accomodating the increasing population of the state is witnessed through residential growth.

**a)** Suburban residential sprawl near the town of King, in the southwestern corner of Stokes County, is within a 20-minute commute to downtown Winston-Salem. Neighborhoods like this continue to change rural agricultural areas and forests into mini-urban pockets, as retail chains are quick to follow.

**b)** Located in rural surroundings the mobile home park offers singles and young families a lower cost housing alternative. Mobile home parks often have a density of three times that of a single-family home neighborhood. These parks frequently suffer from water and sewage problems when not tied into a community system.

| Year | Legislation |
|------|-------------|
| 1967 | Solid Waste Management |
| 1967 | Air Pollution Control |
| 1971 | Environmental Policy Act |
| 1971 | Mining Act |
| 1971 | Floodway Regulations |
| 1972 | Water Pollution Control Act |
| 1973 | Sedimentation Pollution Control Act |
| 1974 | Coastal Area Management Act |
| 1974 | Natural Rivers Act |
| 1979 | Plant Protection and Conservation Act |
| 1984 | Mountain Ridge Protection Act |
| 1984 | Wilderness Act |
| 1989 | Water Supply Watershed Protection Program |
| 1989 | Solid Waste Management Act |

**Table 8.1:** Environmental Legislation of North Carolina.
**Source:** Modified from Gade, Stillwell, Rex, 1986.

dures, along with increasing public awareness and interest, are positive signs for the improvement of our natural environment. Regional environmental issues in our state include are air and water pollution and the land degradation issues of development, logging and deforestation, erosion, slumps, and slides (Figure 8.1).

As presented in Chapters 1 and 2, the natural occurrences of weather and geologic events are very difficult to predict and

**Photo 8.2:** Urban sprawl and industrial development create the need for more electricity. The McGuire Nuclear Power Plant contributes to serving the demands placed on the rapidly expanding Charlotte area.

often are uncontrollable. The force, power, and unpredictability of nature demand respect. It seems that in the last decade these natural catastrophes are more severe and the frequency of occurrence has increased. Public interest, education, and awareness of the "el nino" and "la nina" phenomena created great speculation into possible driving forces behind the recent severity of our weather (Chapter 2). Natural events are often the cause of change to our landscape and to our fragile environment.

## ISSUES OF HUMAN-ENVIRONMENT INTERACTIONS

### Pollution Issues

When most North Carolinians think of air and water pollution we think of the larger and expanding urban centers, industry, coal fired power plants, exhaust from cars, or the rivers brown with sediment after a heavy shower. These are the most obvious examples of pollution but there are many other ways that air and water quality is affected on a daily basis by human activities.

Past legislative acts have provided the foundation by which North Carolinians control the quality of our water and air. However, in the face of continued development, are they effective measures? Do they provide the necessary funding for clean up (Box 8A)? Understanding the processes involved and their spatial extent requires a basic understanding of natural systems and human impact on these systems.

### Surface and Ground Water Pollution

People modify surface drainage patterns through changes in the water flow and contaminate our surface waters with large amounts of wastes. Commercial, industrial, institutional, and residential sites are all potential sources of pollution. Our fresh water resources are in the form of overland flow or surface water and water stored under the surface as ground water. The geographic characteristics of surface and ground water supplies within the state are discussed in Chapter 1.

### Point Versus Non-Point Sources

Surface water pollution can occur in many ways, but can be classified into two broad categories or sources: point and non-point. Point pollution sources (Photo 8.3 and CP1.20) are situations where direct contamination occurs by dumping wastes through a pipe or some such system of discharge. In western North Carolina, the Champion International plant (now Blue Ridge Paper) was a point pollution source on the Pigeon River. Non-point sources (Photo 8.4) cover large areas and create a cumulative impact on water quality. This often occurs through varied agricultural practices, development, or recreational areas such as golf courses. Non-point pollution can be a result of over fertilizing, concentrated discharges of animal waste, or large amounts of sediment finding; the fertilizers, waste, and sediment find their way to surface water flow. This pollution occurs throughout the state at varying scales, but perhaps is most concentrated in the Coastal Plain and Piedmont regions where agriculture is a dominant activity. A land cover map (CP 1.14) is a data set that can provide a valuable geographic insight into the possible spatial extents of non-point pollution sources.

### Surface Water Quality

North Carolina has approximately 37,600 miles of freshwater streams and rivers contained with the 17 major river basins. The varied physiography of each region creates varied potential for pollution and water quality.

Streams and rivers located in the Mountain region are generally small and swift flowing as compared to those in the Piedmont, Coastal Plain, and Tidewater regions. Water quality in the Mountain region is usually characterized as high in dissolved oxygen and low in waste loading or pollution. Exceptions to this are waters downstream from point pollution sources. Thus, water resources in this region usually are well suited for drinking water sources and recreational purposes (North Carolina Focus 1996).

The Piedmont region's streams and rivers are slower and wider, due to gentle elevation changes of lower, rolling hills. A majority of the state's population and industrial base is located here and water resources are more susceptible to waste loading than in any other of the state's regions (Box 8B). Much of this waste comes from sediment originating from agricultural, construction, and urban runoff. Controlling development along the lakeshores is a critical factor in reducing sedimentation. Setbacks and vegetative buffers are often used as effective tools in providing a minimum distance from lakeshores and a 'natural' filtration system to catch and hold sediment (Figure 8.2). Additionally, this region has the heaviest point-source waste loading due

**Box 8A:** Why North Carolina Needs an Environmental Index.

An Environmental Index is based on a careful analysis of data over time. It helps state officials and lawmakers make rational judgements about where to spend money on environmental problems and could help settle disputes about whether our environment is improving or declining.

Using existing reports and data, for example, one could cite evidence showing that:

| *The Environment is Improving* | *The Environment is being Degraded* |
|---|---|
| 1) North Carolina ranked 1st in surface water protection and 9th in overall environmental protection in a 50 state study by Renew America in 1988. | 1) North Carolina ranked 28th in water pollution problems and 23rd in overall environmental conditions in a 50 state analysis by the Institute for Southern Studies in 1991. |
| 2) North Carolina tied for 3rd in a 50 state ranking of programs for protecting drinking water in a 1989 study by Renew America. | 2) North Carolina ranked 21st in the percentage of water systems in significant noncompliance with drinking water standards in a 50 state analysis by the Institute for Southern Studies in 1991. |
| 3) Only 7 percent of North Carolina's residents lived in counties not meeting federal clean-air standards in June 1988, ranking the state 5th among the 50 states in a 1989 study by Renew America. | 3) The Raleigh and Greensboro metropolitan areas were two of only eighteen urban centers in the nation that violated federal standards for both ozone and carbon monoxide from 1987 through 1989, according to the U.S. Environmental Protection Agency (EPA). |
| 4) The volume of low-level radioactive waste shipped for disposal dropped by 52 percent in North Carolina from 1985-1990, according to the Department of Environment, Health, and Natural Resources (DEHNR). | 4) North Carolina generators shipped more low-level radioactive waste for disposal than any other state in the U.S. in 1987, according to the Institute for Southern Studies. |
| 5) North Carolina increased its annual operating expenditures for its state parks by 72 percent from fiscal year 1985-86 to fiscal year 1990-91, according to DEHNR. | 5) North Carolina spends less money per capita on its state park system than virtually any other state, ranking 49th out of 50 in 1988, according to the National Association of Park Directors. |
| 6) North Carolina has retained about three-fourths (76 percent) of the 7.8 million acres af wetlands that originally covered the state, according to DEHNR. | 6) North Carolina lost nearly half (49 percent) of the 1.1 million acres of wetlands that originally covered the state, according to the U.S. Fish and Wildlife Service. |
| | **Source:** *North Carolina Focus* 1996. |

to the large municipal and industrial wastewater treatment plants servicing the concentrated population and industrial centers (North Carolina Focus 1996).

The hydrography of the Coastal Plain and Tidewater regions is diverse and consists of streams and rivers with their origin in the western regions, tidal rivers, blackwater streams and rivers, swamps and coastal wetlands, and estuaries and sounds. Streams and rivers of these regions carry large amounts of sediment and have high nutrient loading, their drainage basins are comprised of mostly agricultural land. Population growth and tourism in the regions over the last 25 years are point source contributors (North Carolina Focus 1996).

Almost 2 million acres of the Tidewater region are estuaries and sounds, with 328 miles of ocean shoreline. Seven major river basins feed these estuaries (Cape Fear, Neuse, White Oak, Tar-Pamlico, and Pasquotank, Chowan, and the Roanoke - Figure 1.11). Continued development has contributed to a deterioration of estuarine water quality from agricultural and urban runoff, leaking septic tanks, marinas, conversions of maritime forests, and the dredge and fill of coastal wetlands. Estuarine eutrophication (a body of water abundant in plant and animal life, but lacking in oxygen at times) is mostly attributable to nutrient runoff from agricultural land upriver (North Carolina Focus 1996). Massive septic spills from municipal sewage facilities and hog farms

**Photo 8.3:** This point pollution source along the Pigeon River illustrates the devastating impact on water quality. With the Pigeon River flowing into eastern Tennessee that state has vigorously protested the pollution from the Blue Ridge Paper Plant of Canton (Haywood County). The plant has subsequently been bought out by a consortium of plant workers and private firms. The chemical pollution has been considerably reduced though periodic intense discoloration continues to plague the river on its route to Tennessee.

**Photo 8.4:** Golf courses comprise large areas and can be a non-point pollution source if improperly managed. This course is in Buncombe County. Note the Asheville skyline in the distance.

Photo Courtesy of the North Carolina Division of Tourism, Film and Sports Development.

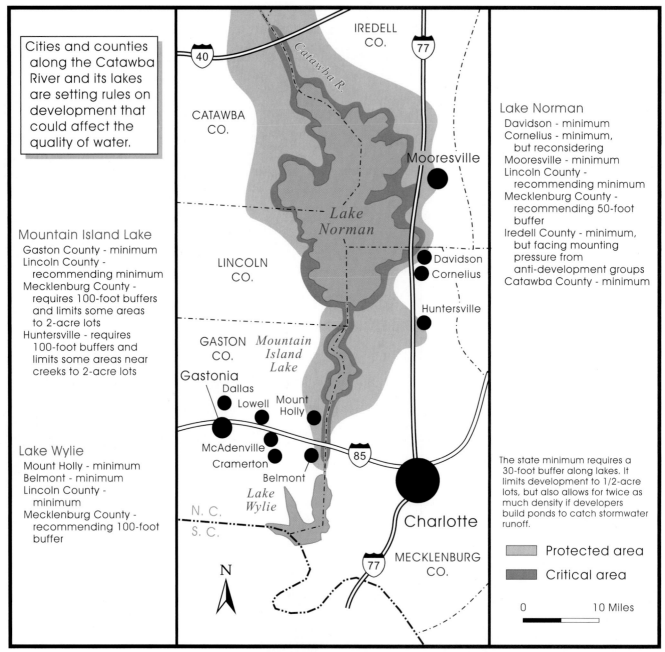

Figure 8.2: Lakeshore Buffer Regulations.
Source: Modified from *The Charlotte Observer*, February 7, 1994.

have been found to stimulate the appearance of the dinoflagellates like *Phisteria piscicida*, that are toxic to finfish (see Chapter 6 and 10).

### Ground Water Quality

Groundwater is the primary source of drinking water for approximately 43 percent of North Carolinians. The state's public water supply systems provide 50 billion gallons of groundwater annually to almost a million residents, and private water supplies provide almost 38 billion gallons of groundwater annually to approximately two million residents. Additionally, groundwater is used for public supplies as well as domestic, mining, industrial, livestock, commercial, and irrigation needs (North Carolina Focus 1996).

Most of the state's high-quality groundwater is found in the deep aquifers of the Coastal Plain and Tidewater regions. The Mountain and Piedmont regions have relatively shallow aquifers and provide a limited amount of lower-quality groundwater (North Carolina Focus 1996). As the use of ground water continues to increase, so does the possibility of contamination. The major focus is the contamination of the aquifer, the underground rock layer capable of storing water. When space is made avail-

286

**Box 8B:** Different Worlds, Same Water.

"The pin-striped Banker bends down for a quick sip from the water cooler in a richly-appointed office in Uptown Charlotte. Outside on Trade Street far below, a construction worker turns on a water hose to wash out a wheelbarrow, then brings the hose up for a drink. These two people may be worlds apart in every other way, but they have one important thing in common: They're both drinking the same water" (Tuttle 1999). This excerpt illustrates the common need for the protection of a most valuable resource – clean water.

Charlotte is supplied with water from Mountain Island Lake (Figure 8.2). Like all of the lakes in the region it is a human-made lake, one of many along the Catawba River. Duke power constructed many lakes years ago for hydroelectric production. Mountain Island Lake is to the south of Lake Norman. Uncluttered development provides Charlotte a valuable source of water.

Pressures of population growth in and around Charlotte have caused many to take interest in water quality issues. Crescent Resources, Duke Power's property development subsidiary, is feeding these pressures by selling lakefront property for residential, commercial, and recreational uses. In turn, this could ultimately contaminate a valuable resource.

The solution is one that is easy to identify, but can be difficult to implement. Charlotte and several environmental groups identified a six-mile long strip of land on the western shore to act as a buffer and a natural filter to prevent pollutants from entering. This was a great idea that lacked financial support. Where would the money come from? In the meantime, Gaston County has moved vigorously to protect the western shorelines of the Lake.

On the coast there was a similar concern. Atlantic Beach had one last undeveloped stretch of the sound, Hoop Hole Creek (see photos). Hoop Hole Creek, home of large healthy oysters, filters the water from the tidal creek into Bogue Sound and then into the Atlantic Ocean. The North Carolina Coastal Federation and local governments agreed that protecting the land was a necessity. Once again where would the money come from?

With both situations money was acquired from the Clean Water Management Trust Fund created in 1997, the fund is financed by the taxpayers of our state. To date this agency has handed out a total of 92.5 million dollars to local governments and nonprofit conservation groups all across the state (Tuttle 1999).

| Purpose of Grant | Amount Funded (Dollars) |
|---|---|
| Acquire Buffers | 40,618,700 |
| Acquire Greenways | 4,156,000 |
| Easements | 2,929,638 |
| Planning | 4,056,913 |
| Restoration | 13,150,983 |
| Stormwater | 3,460,514 |
| Wastewater | 24,180,432 |
| **Total** | **92,553,180** |

Project Categories Funded by the Clean Water Management Trust Fund as of January 1, 1999.
**Source:** Modified from the North Carolina Department of Environment and Natural Resources, 1999.

Aerial photos of Hoop Hole Creek illustrate the encroachment of resort and recreational development on this fragile environmental system. Note in the top photo the large condominium complex adjacent to the wooded area. While in the bottom photo a golf course straddles the upper reaches of the channelized creek. Protection of this endangered estuarian ecosystem is key to future populations of shellfish. (Photos by Robert E. Reiman)

able in the aquifer through increased pumping or use of ground water, or during drought conditions, then the source of the recharge becomes the dominant factor in water quality. Water may seep in from an already contaminated surface or another ground water source (North Carolina Focus 1996).

Factories, towns and farms in Eastern North Carolina's central Coastal Plain are sucking groundwater dry. To protect the Cretaceous aquifer they are drawing from, the state passed a regulation to limit unrestrained pumpings in fifteen counties (Figure 8.3). In December of 2000, the Environmental Management Commission decided unanimously to force large water users to reduce their siphoning of deep aquifers as much as 75 percent. Millions of dollars will be spent to find new water supplies to help preserve the aquifers and hopefully return them to their past levels. These aquifers were once considered inexhaustable, the Black Creek and Upper Cape Fear aquifers have dropped as much as 150 feet from years of pumping. The decline is likely to continue for some time as the regulation will take as many as 16 years to be fully implemented (Shiffer 2000).

Increasing concern in the state has been placed on underground tanks buried during the 1940s, 50s, and 60s, which are now failing and creating potential groundwater pollution sources (Figure 8.4). However, surface spills of gasoline and diesel fuel are the most common groundwater pollutants (North Carolina Focus 1996).

Increasing populations and related facilities growth create demands on present municipal and home wastewater management systems. Figure 8.5 illustrates how these systems work and describes how they might fail. Failure of these systems could contaminate both ground and surface water supplies. Figure 8.6 shows residential septic tank densities in the state. While there are concentrations in the urban crescent, note especially the spreading concentrations in the western Piedmont and the Moun-

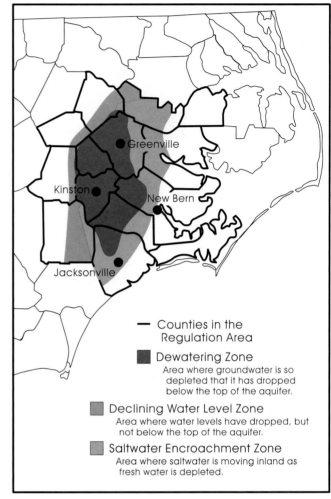

**Figure 8.3:** Depleting Groundwater Supplies.
**Source:** Modified from The Raleigh News and Observer, Shiffer, 2000.

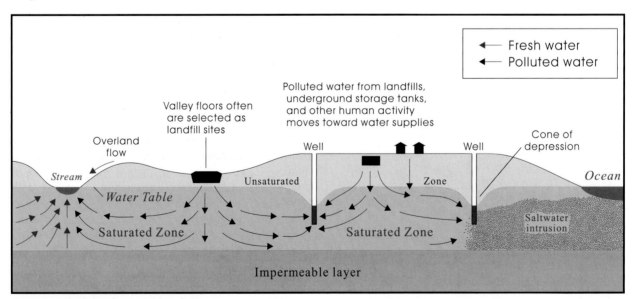

**Figure 8.4:** Ground Water Contamination.
**Source:** Modified from Strahler, 1998.

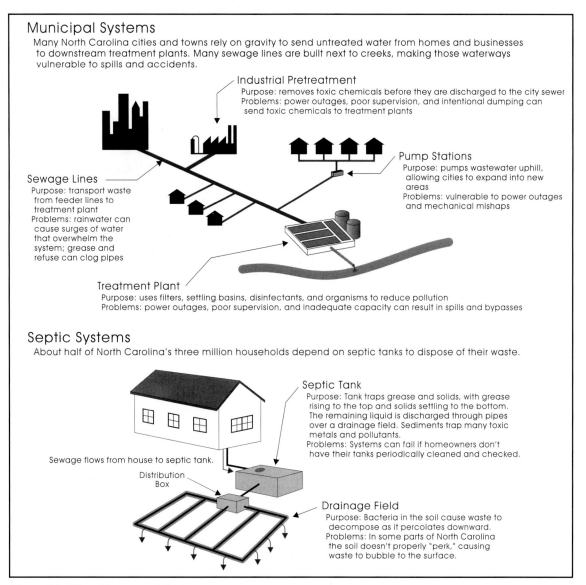

## Municipal Systems

Many North Carolina cities and towns rely on gravity to send untreated water from homes and businesses to downstream treatment plants. Many sewage lines are built next to creeks, making those waterways vulnerable to spills and accidents.

### Industrial Pretreatment
Purpose: removes toxic chemicals before they are discharged to the city sewer
Problems: power outages, poor supervision, and intentional dumping can send toxic chemicals to treatment plants

### Pump Stations
Purpose: pumps wastewater uphill, allowing cities to expand into new areas
Problems: vulnerable to power outages and mechanical mishaps

### Sewage Lines
Purpose: transport waste from feeder lines to treatment plant
Problems: rainwater can cause surges of water that overwhelm the system; grease and refuse can clog pipes

### Treatment Plant
Purpose: uses filters, settling basins, disinfectants, and organisms to reduce pollution
Problems: power outages, poor supervision, and inadequate capacity can result in spills and bypasses

## Septic Systems

About half of North Carolina's three million households depend on septic tanks to dispose of their waste.

### Septic Tank
Purpose: Tank traps grease and solids, with grease rising to the top and solids settling to the bottom. The remaining liquid is discharged through pipes over a drainage field. Sediments trap many toxic metals and pollutants.
Problems: Systems can fail if homeowners don't have their tanks periodically cleaned and checked.

Sewage flows from house to septic tank.

Distribution Box

### Drainage Field
Purpose: Bacteria in the soil cause waste to decompose as it percolates downward.
Problems: In some parts of North Carolina the soil doesn't properly "perk," causing waste to bubble to the surface.

**Figure 8.5:** Waste Management Systems.
**Source:** Modified from the Raleigh News and Observer, November 16, 1997.

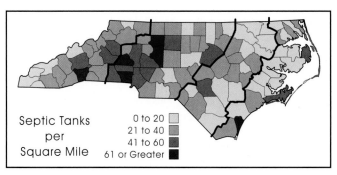

Septic Tanks per Square Mile

0 to 20
21 to 40
41 to 60
61 or Greater

**Figure 8.6:** Septic Tank Distribution.
**Source:** Modified from the Raleigh News and Observer, November 16, 1997.

tain regions. Many of these areas simply are not serviced by municipal systems. Growing populations and second home developments have generated an increasing use of septic systems in these more rural mountainous areas. County health departments are usually charged with approval and inspections of such systems. However, thirty years ago many homes may have been constructed with inadequate or no septic systems. And, as discussed in Chapter 13, relying on single home septic filtration fields on steep slopes with their thin soils is a recipe for downstream environmental disaster.

Fresh water aquifers of the Coastal Plain region are the most productive in the state, but are becoming increasingly prone to pollution. This predominately agricultural area has experienced an increase in wells with high nitrate concentrations (Figure 8.7). Farm fertilizers, livestock wastes, and septic tanks are considered prime sources of well contamination.

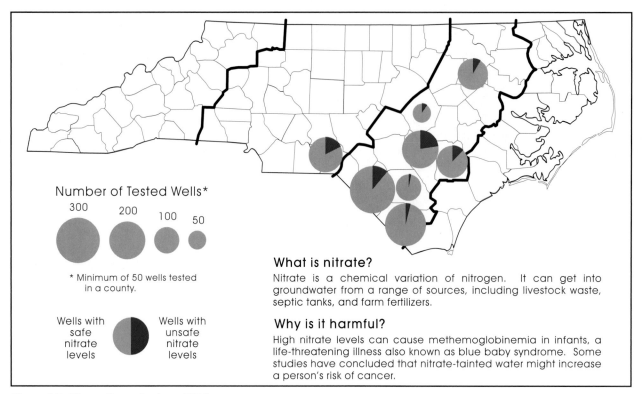

**Figure 8.7:** Nitrate Contamination of Wells.
**Source:** Modified from the *Raleigh News and Observer*, May 21, 1998.

North Carolina has 10,383 public water supply systems, of which only 320 are surface systems. However, surface systems serve 83 percent of the state's population, since they were constructed to serve towns and cities. Local governments own 68 percent of the surface systems, while private ownership accounts for 63 percent of the groundwater systems of the state (North Carolina Focus 1996).

The Clean Water Act of 1972 and its 1995 rewrite, coupled with the more recent Safe Water Drinking Act, may still fall short of protecting water quality. Partly because the state of water is difficult to capture or describe in the kind of unambiguous statistics lawmakers utilize and partly because it has become increasingly apparent that the sources of pollution are not just industrial and municipal institutions that can be controlled by specific laws. Consider, for example, the toxic chemicals that gradually filter into local streams from private home driveways that have been cleansed of their periodic auto and lawn implement spills. The burden of pollution belongs to us all.

### Saltwater Intrusion

Saltwater intrusion is a problem found in most coastal states including North Carolina. Extensive and increasing development of the areas adjacent to saltwater has created a need for additional fresh water. As fresh water is pumped out of the ground, surrounding fresh water flows into the aquifer to replace the water that has been pumped out. If fresh water is pumped out faster than it can be replaced, then water from other sources will flow into the aquifer (Figure 8.4). In the Tidewater region, this water may come from saltwater in sounds, tidal flats, marshes, ponds, channels, and estuaries. Once saltwater contaminates an aquifer the reversal of the condition is almost always impossible, and freshwater to support the needs of the area must be transported by piping from a remote location or provided by some other means. Note the discussion in Chapter 10 on this particular problem as it is increasingly affecting the barrier islands.

### Air Pollution

During the summer of 1998 air quality in North Carolina was second only to California for the number of unhealthy air days. Emissions that contribute to this phenomena come from a variety of sources and can be classed into two major groups: stationary and mobile. Stationary sources are the diverse types of industries throughout the state, while mobile sources include cars, diesel trucks, and other transport vehicles. Sad to say, North Carolina has five of the country's worst coal-fired power plants. In fact, all of the state's 14 coal-fired heating plants exceed federal smokestack nitrogen oxide and sulpher dioxide emission limits (Betts 1999). Interestingly, these plants were grandfathered with respect to the federal clean air act of the early 1970's, and have not since been pushed to meet standards. In late December of 2000 the federal government sued Duke Energy, claiming that recent modifications to eight coal-fired plants illegally increased smokestack emissions that forms ozone, acid rain and haze.

Although some amount of air pollution is produced in rural areas (mainly dust from farming, pesticide spraying from airplanes, road construction and mining), major air quality problems are concentrated in urbanized and industrialized areas of the Piedmont. Even so, it was reported that the state set a record for bad air days in the mountains in 1998 that was then exceeded in 1999 (Betts 1999). As Betts indicated, air pollution is no longer the mere problem of a hazy sky, now people are hospitalized with respiratory illnesses. Degradation of the air occurs through two main human activities: 1) burning fossil fuel for power generation (stationary source), and 2) transportation (mobile source). Coal-fired thermoelectric power plants produce most of the state's energy, but at the same time emit sulfur dioxide and particulate matter. Automobiles and trucks account for the most prevalent air pollutants in the form of carbon monoxide and ozone. Nitrous oxides are also a product of transportation and, when combined with volatile organic compounds and hydrocarbons, may produce ozone (Scott 1999).

In 1999 North Carolina ranked 5th in the country in recorded number of days in violation of Environmental Protection Agency ozone standards, following California, Texas, Tennessee, and Georgia. For metropolitan areas within the state conditions are critical. Metrolina, the Piedmont Triad and the Piedmont Triangle are experiencing some of the most days with ozone violations in the country, Metrolina was in the top ten in the country in 1998. The reduced incidence in 1999 levels is thought to be attributable to the severity of the hurricane season of that year (Dyer and Feagans 2000).

A Memorandum of Understanding (MOU), recently signed by the state in cooperation with the U.S. Department of the Interior and the U.S. Department of Agriculture's Forest Service, placed requirements that go beyond the current regulations of the Clean Air Act. The MOU is designed to protect and ultimately improve air quality. Tennessee signed a similar agreement in 1987 in hopes that other Southern Appalachian Mountain Initiative (SAMI) states would follow with a similar agreement. North Carolina followed suit, even though it may place our state at an economic disadvantage to other states vying for industrial growth. In addition, new federal regulations for acid rain, ozone, fine particulate, regional haze, and nitrogen oxide reductions will further improve air quality throughout North Carolina (Scott 1999).

In the meantime, it should be noted, vigorous efforts at reducing the compliance costs for business and industry are pursued by a coalition of business interests. In 1998, changes urged by North Carolina Citizens for Business and Industry and the Manufacturers and Chemical Industry Council in the toxic air emission program were approved by the N. C. Environmental Management Commission (EMC). North Carolina's toxic air regulations are tighter than those of the federal mandates, and thus compliance is more difficult. Industry interests argued successfully that two sets of compliance tests were one too many for individual industries, and that compliance with the federal regulations should be sufficient. Also, EMC mandated that once compliance had been secured the involved industry would be exempt for five years before testing would be again required (Scott 1998).

### Greenhouse Gases

Much attention has recently been given to the topic of global warming and, in turn, greenhouse gases. The gases that have the ability to produce global warming are known, but the environmental and human impacts of these gases are the great unknown. There are many greenhouse gases that can have an impact. The most commonly produced are water vapor ($H_2O$), carbon dioxide ($CO_2$) (Figure 8.8), methane ($CH_4$) (Figure 8.9), chlorofluorocarbons (CFCs) and other ozone depleting compounds (ODCs), and nitrous oxide ($N_2O$) (Figure 8.10). The processes that produce these gases vary from the natural to the human induced. However, there has been an increasing amount of these gases placed into the earth's environmental systems. These systems are open and balance must be achieved. How the systems react in an attempt to achieve this balance is an ongoing "experiment." Severe weather, climate changes, agricultural outputs, and in our general environment are all impacted. Some of the changes can be seen or felt (air and water pollution), while others are much more subtle (long-term climatic changes) (Box 8C).

Water vapor can be produced by human activity (fossil fuel consumption), but natural evaporative processes produce the vast majority. Water vapor content in the troposphere exhibits a large amount of spatial and temporal variability. It is the most dominant greenhouse gas and is the source of all precipitation. The amount of this gas produced by human activity is insignificant. However, the amount of water vapor that could be produced if other greenhouse gases accelerate the natural evaporative processes might produce major environmental changes.

Methane can be produced by several human activities: landfills are the most abundant sources, but agricultural methods of waste management from farm animals (swine, cattle, and chickens) are other methods. Landfills have the potential for groundwater contamination, but the threat of explosion from the buildup of low-grade methane gas has prompted a new look at the large number of closed landfills that operated with the approval of the state in the past. North Carolina has first hand experience with the danger of explosion. As with many of these sites, Charlotte has taken advantage of the large areas of level land to use for parks and recreational activities, such as golf courses. One such park experienced a minor explosion and measures were taken to assure better ventilation and dispersion of the methane produced from the underlying landfill. These environmental, and safety concerns have prompted county and state action.

### Smog and Temperature Inversions

Site and situation are important local considerations for the occurrence smog or temperature inversions. Local physical settings, coupled with human activities, are directly related to the occurrence of smog. North Carolina's topography and localized weather conditions and patterns create many favorable circumstances for smog. Meteorological conditions can concentrate air pollution. The Piedmont and Mountain regions experience a high frequency of surface temperature inversions for about half of the

**Box 8C:** Is North Carolina Heating Up?
Development of a Statewide Plan to Reduce Green House Gas Emissions.

In the summer of 1999 more North Carolinians complained about the heat than in the past. Is the earth's climate changing? How does this impact North Carolina's climate? Appalachian State University researchers are developing a state action plan to help reduce factors that affect global warming. State advisory committees are assisting Appalachian's Department of Geography and Planning in producing a plan that will provide achievable, economically efficient strategies for state and local governments, businesses and individuals to reduce levels of greenhouse gas emissions contributing to global warming.

This project is supported by a grant from the Environmental Protection Agency's State and Local Climate Change Program and North Carolina Energy Division. The plan's goal is to reduce emission levels of greenhouse gases - such as carbon dioxide, methane, nitrous oxide, chlorofluorocarbons and other ozone depleting compounds - to at least 7 percent below 1990 levels by 2012. Strategies such as fuel switching, the use of fluorescent light bulbs and renewable energies are being evaluated for feasibility and cost effectiveness.

The plan will not be legally binding, but it will be available to state legislators and agencies as a guideline for North Carolina's greenhouse gas reduction. Developing the action plan comes at a time when many regions of North Carolina are experiencing higher temperatures than in the past. January through August 1998 were the fourth warmest months on record nationally, according to the U.S. Commerce Department's National Oceanic and Atmospheric Administration.

Greenhouse gases help maintain the radiant balance of the earth by allowing sunlight to strike and warm the earth's surface. They trap some of the radiant heat and slow its return to space, causing the troposphere to warm. This natural process is necessary to sustain life on earth. However, human activities, primarily the burning of fossil fuels, raise the level of greenhouse gases and increase the rate of atmospheric warming. Raleigh experienced 20 more days reaching temperatures of at least 90 degrees Fahrenheit between May and August, 1998, than was averaged over the last 30 years. In Charlotte, 18 more 90-degree Fahrenheit days were recorded for the same period, according to information from the State Climate Office of North Carolina at North Carolina State University. For 1999 mean temperatures in Charlotte (61 degrees Fahr-

enheit) and Raleigh (50 degrees Fahrenheit) were at least one degree higher than the 30-year averages of temperatures. These patterns represent effects of a warming trend in the earth's atmosphere generally accepted throughout the scientific community. Scientists working with the Intergovernmental Panel on Climate Change (IPCC) estimate global temperatures will rise two to seven degrees Fahrenheit by the end of the next century.

If greenhouse gas emissions continue to rise, North Carolina could see a three degree Fahrenheit temperature increase and a 15 percent rise in precipitation by 2010, according to IPCC projections and the United Kingdom Hadley Centre's climate model. Such climate changes could cause sea level rises, flooding of coastal property, erosion of beaches, saltwater contamination of drinking water and coastal vulnerability to storms, EPA reports indicate. Diseases such as malaria and encephalitis could also become more common with warmer temperatures. EPA records show that a three degree Fahrenheit temperature rise in Greensboro would increase summer heat-related deaths by approximately 70 percent.

In December 1997, representatives from 160 countries met in Kyoto, Japan, to negotiate the Kyoto Protocol on Climate Change. Participating governments agreed to work toward lowering emissions rates. Industrialized nations were asked to reduce green house gas emissions to below 1990 levels by 2010. In 1997, the Clinton Administration drafted a five-year, $6.3 billion tax incentive and research and development program aimed at improving energy efficiency and renewable energy development (Lineback, Nelson, and Warmuth, 1998). In early 2001, the Bush Adminstration pulled the United States out of the Kyoto Protocol agreements.

| Emission Source Category | GWP (tons/yr) |
|---|---|
| Fossil Fuel Consumption | 122,044,351 |
| Biomass Fuel Consumption | 783,600 |
| Production Processes | 4,652,216 |
| Agriculture and Livestock Production | 9,655,734 |
| Waste Disposal, Treatment, and Recovery | 6,395,615 |
| Human Emissions | 1,139,980 |
| Land Use Changes | -9,560,229 |
| **Total Emissions** | **135,111,269** |

Global Warming Potential by Sector, 1990.
**Source:** Appalachian State University, 1996.

year. High-pressure cells from July to March, in conjunction with relatively low wind speeds, dominate these areas. These conditions foster air stagnation and the concentration of pollutants. The many valleys and basins of the Mountain and Piedmont regions produce favorable settings for temperature inversions and, depending upon regional activities, smog (Figure 8.11a, b, and c).

### Acid Rain

A subtler human induced impact on our fragile Mountain region is acid rain. A British chemist first recognized acid rain in 1872, but its complexity, causes and effects are still being studied over a century later.

Acidity is a measure of hydrogen ion (H+) concentration and is expressed as a pH value. A pH value of 7, also termed

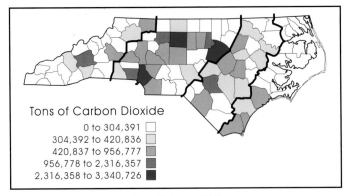

**Figure 8.8:** Carbon Dioxide Emissions, 1990.
**Source:** The North Carolina Greenhouse Gas Emissions Inventory for 1990.

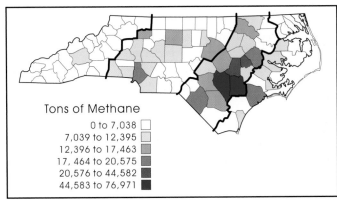

**Figure 8.9:** Methane Emissions, 1990.
**Source:** The North Carolina Greenhouse Gas Emissions Inventory for 1990.

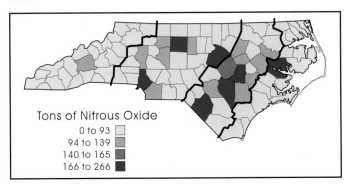

**Figure 8.10:** Nitrous Oxide Emissions, 1990.
**Source:** The North Carolina Greenhouse Gas Emissions Inventory for 1990.

neutral, represents 10-7 gram atoms of Hydrogen ions per liter. Each lower pH number represents 10 times more acidity. Normal rain has a pH of 5.6 (slightly acid from combining with carbon dioxide). Acid rain has a pH of less than 5.6 and may even reach 2.4, almost equivalent to lemon juice!

Acid rain starts as an emission of sulfur dioxide from burning of fossil fuels or nitrous oxide from vehicles. Transported aloft, these oxides combine with water and oxygen transforming them into sulfur and nitric acids, or acid rain. Falling to earth, acid rain can have profound effects on fragile ecosystems (Figure 8.12 and Box 8D).

### *Waste Incineration*

Waste incineration is another waste disposal practice that contributes to greenhouse gas emissions and air pollution. Facilities that constitute this category are:

1) large municipal solid waste and infectious waste incineration facilities
2) on-site commercial/industrial incineration
3) on-site institutional incineration (schools)
4) on-site infectious waste incineration (hospitals)
5) open burning of rural waste (land clearing, logging, agriculture)
6) open burning of yard waste (residential)

Since the 1990 Amendments to the Clean Air Act, many of the smaller on-site incinerators in North Carolina have shut down their operations. This trend will continue as technological advances and recycling efforts continue to expand (North Carolina Focus 1996).

## LAND DEGRADATION ISSUES

Clearing land for residential, commercial, and industrial growth are drastic changes to our landscape. Changing landscapes can have dramatic impacts on local, regional, and global environments.

### *Logging and Deforestation*

Forests covered the state when settlers first arrived on the North Carolina coast except where native populations modified the vegetation. Since that time the vegetation has been modified by humans. Pressures of development and the need for timber have diminished the old growth forests in North Carolina and across the United States. Today we can enjoy North Carolina's old growth forests only in the western-most reaches of the Appalachians (See Chapter 13). Forest preservation has taken a front seat nationwide and we have seen confrontations between logging industries and preservationists.

North Carolina has traditionally been one of the leading manufacturers of furniture and more recently has become involved in the chip mill industry. In the Coastal Plain and Tidewater regions the growing of timber as an agricultural crop is a thriving industry. These managed areas are similar to other cropping practices, except for the length of time for trees to reach harvesting stage. While crops such as corn, tobacco, or cabbage have a growing cycle from three to six months, timber crops may have a fifteen to 30 year growth cycle. Conversely, logging of theslower growing hardwood species of the Piedmont and Mountain regions may have growth cycles of more than fifty years. Intensive management of these areas and controlled and mandated extraction practices are necessary, especially in areas that

293

Acid rain's impacts may be starting to show in the Mountain region. As discussed in Chapter 2, the impact of elevation on precipitation amounts in this region is varied. In addition, severe air stagnation may trap pollutants brought in by prevailing winds from the industrial areas to the west (Tennessee Valley Industrial Complex) and southwest (Birmingham, Alabama, iron and steel plants). This combination can produce acid fog, which can be up to 100 times stronger than acid rain. About fifty percent of acidic conditions as evidenced in mountain vegetation and water resources are from acid rain and the rest from acid fog. After being washed from the atmosphere, these acids enter the drainage network and are most concentrated in the headwaters of major streams (Figure 8.8 and 8.12).

Researchers at Oak Ridge National Laboratory in Tennessee indicate that acid rain is the chief suspect in the slowed growth of red spruce trees on the higher peaks of the Appalachians. Acidity erodes the protective waxy coating from the trees' needles, speeding up the natural loss of nutrients. Soil acidity washes away nutrients, depleting soil of calcium and magnesium the trees need. It also releases toxic aluminum in the soil. Trees absorb aluminum, which blocks nutrient uptake and slows the tree's growth.

North Carolina's mountains have the distinction of having the highest peaks in the eastern United States. However, this distinction may also cause the demise of plant life within these fragile environments. Peaks at this high altitude support Fraser fir with its insidious insect pest, the balsam wooly aphid, and at the same time intercept air pollution from industrial activity to the west in the form of acid rain and acid fog. Mounting evidence shows the combination of insect damage and acid rain may be harming these firs. It is estimated that the highest peaks of the Smoky Mountains receive twice as much sulfur from acid rain as mountains in New York and four times as much as lowland sites in the northeast, where lakes have experienced the devastating effects of acid rain and many are considered 'dead'. Mount Mitchell, near Asheville, has thousands of dead Fraser firs at its summit and has become a vivid, yet disputed, symbol of acid rain damage.

Researchers from the federally sponsored National Acid Precipitation Assessment Program found that only one percent of the streams of the Southern Blue Ridge has more acid than normal, while across the Eastern United States it is six percent. Still, in 1980 over 500 adult rainbow trout and 35,000 fingerlings died in a fish hatchery near the Great Smoky Mountains National Park, most likely from acid rain. Buffering with lime helped save other fish. Lime neutralizes the acid in the water, by driving the pH value higher.

While many consider acid rain damage already too much for North Carolina, there are possible reasons as to why the damage has not been more severe in the Mountain region. It lies in the origin of our lakes; they are all artificial. Consequently, stream flow may flush out pollutants more readily than the natural, spring-fed lakes of the New England area that have suffered severe fish kills. Another reason lie in the mountain soils that contain higher amounts of iron and aluminum, which aid in soaking up sulfur. Soils of the Piedmont, Coastal Plain, and Tidewater have an even greater capacity to absorb sulfur. However, the capacity of the soils to continue absorbing sulfur will be used up within 40 years in some areas particularly in the thinner soils of the mountain sides and ridge tops and the result will be acid streams. If the proper implementation of the Clean Air Act is successful in continuing to lower the sulfur emissions throughout the United States then further deterioration could be limited and possibly even a slow reversal might occur.

have high erosion and sedimentation potential. Large clearing operations affect the visual quality of the Mountain region. Each year, millions of visitors flock to the Blue Ridge to take in the panoramic views and the changing seasons as they drive the scenic Blue Ridge Parkway. These visitors expect to view a natural, undisturbed landscape.

### Mining

A particularly unique land use is the strip mining of phosphatic rock, a sedimentary rock containing phosphates in commercial quantity and used for fertilizers and other products, near Aurora on the Pamlico River in Beaufort County of the Tidewater region. Recent topographic maps indicate that about fifteen square miles of surface have been disturbed thus far. There is a continuing process of stripping, sorting, storing, and shipping out the materials, as well as redistributing the waste materials on environmental reclamation sites (CP 10.21 to 10.23). The Texasgulf Corporation began excavation in 1962, but sold the property in 1995 to the Potash Corporation of Saskatchewan, Canada. Recognized by the Smithsonian Institution as one of the country's leading fossil sites, collectors line up for the weekly tour of the 110 feet deep mine pit (Photo 10.8). Shark teeth and corral are frequently found on the streets of Aurora and roads of the adjacent countryside, paved, as they are, with waste materials from the mine. With over 1,000 employees commuting from a four-county region, the mine is an important economic engine of the Pamlico area. On the other hand, the mining and refining operation is also one of the worst environmental polluters in the state of North Carolina (CP 10.23). Other mining operations in the state include sand, gravel, and clay extraction in the Coastal Plain; lithium, feldspar, granite, clay, mica, and crushed stone in the Piedmont; and granite, crushed stone, sand, gravel, olivine, mica, feldspar, and gemstones in the Mountain region (Figure 1.7a).

### Erosion, Slumps, and Slides

Human interaction with the landscape is a primary cause of mast wasting (erosion, slumps and slides). Human activities often accelerate soil erosion, slumps and slides. The most notable

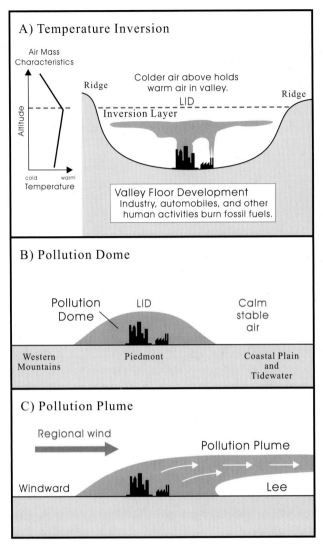

**Figure 8.11a, b, and c:** Temperature Inversions and Air Pollution. **Source:** Modified from Strahler, 1998.

slide of 1997 was the Interstate 40 slide in the western part of the state in Haywood County (Photo 8.5), and more recently a slide on the Blue Ridge Parkway in 1999. While the I-40 slide made national news, mass wasting also exists throughout the state in smaller versions.

Slumping and erosion is often associated with excavation projects, particularly in the Mountain region (Photo 8.6 - 8.7). Do people control the force and unpredictability of nature? Can people work in harmony with the environment to better manage these occurrences? The I-40 slide dramatically demonstrates the need to coordinate technology, information, economic development, and environmental factors.

### Waste Disposal

Disposal of waste is one of the most critical environmental problems of modern society. North Carolinians produce solid waste at an average of 1.02 tons per person per year. This is up from the 0.9 tons per person per year in 1984. Since the 1971

legislation was enacted, open burning dumps are being replaced with the solid waste or landfill disposal sites which we are familiar with today (Figure 8.13). The organic content in the waste, such as paper, food wastes, and yard wastes can produce methane and carbon dioxide when decomposed in landfills. Most landfills emit these greenhouse gases directly into the atmosphere.

Landfills are the largest single source of methane emissions in the United States. Perhaps with advances in technology, methane from landfill emissions will be harnessed and used to generate power.

Solid waste management is an issue of major concern to this state and the entire nation. In 1989, the state adopted an "Act to Improve the Management of Solid Waste (SB111)," and has amended the Act in subsequent sessions of the General Assembly. This state law sets goals and policies, establishes new programs, bans certain materials from landfills, and mandates planning and reporting requirements.

The federal government, through the Environmental Protection Agency (EPA), has issued regulations referred to as "Subtitle D Regulations." These federal regulations deal with the required environmental protection standards for municipal solid waste landfills. In addition, financial assurance requirements are detailed. North Carolina is approved by the EPA and has the authority to implement the federal requirements. In 1994, the ramifications of this federal legislation, Subtitle D Municipal Solid Waste Landfill Facilities, were evident. Fifty-four unlined landfills were closed in the state (Photo 8.8). Because of the closings, the need to transport increased volumes of solid waste longer distances grew at a rapid rate. As a result, twenty-five new transfer stations began operation in 1994, which shipped waste out-of-county to regional landfills. There are an increasing number of lined landfills operating throughout the state (Figure 8.13).

Since inception of the state and federal regulations, North Carolina has done an excellent job in data collection, management and implementation of these requirements. Reduction and recycling programs have made a significant impact towards reaching North Carolina's goals. By 1994, a localized approach to this effort has come about through 122 local governments implementing some type of waste reduction program, and around 580 localities implementing recycling programs (Photo 8.9). As disposal costs continue to rise, as technology changes, and as market demand for certain materials increases, programs will continue to gain in the public sector and will probably appear more within the private sector.

North Carolina has clearly taken an active role in waste disposal, treatment, and recovery. Through education, financial incentives, new technologies, and computerization of databases, coupled with increased awareness and state and federal regulations, North Carolina has become one of the nation's leaders in waste disposal, treatment, and recovery.

### Hazardous Waste (Toxic and Radioactive)

Hazardous waste is solid waste that because of its quantity or physical and chemical characteristics may: "1) cause or

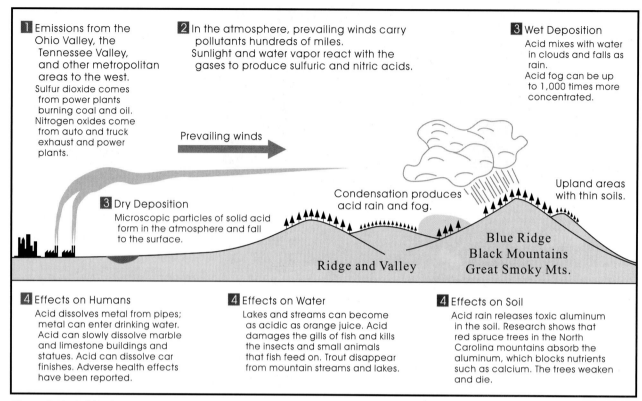

**Figure 8.12:** Acid Rain.
**Source:** Modified from The Charlotte Observer, January 21, 1990.

significantly contribute to an increase in mortality, irreversible, or incapacitating illness; or 2) pose a substantial present or potential hazard to human health or the environment when improperly treated, stored, transported or disposed of, or otherwise managed" (NC General Statutes 130A-294).

North Carolina has 11 commercial treatment, storage, and disposal facilities for hazardous waste (Figure 8.13). These facilities are located near or in Raleigh, Creedmoor, Reidsville, Greens-boro, Archdale, Charlotte, Norwood, and St. Pauls. Recycling of hazardous waste has diminished greatly, but the amount of waste processed through treatment methods is increasing; from 1989 through 1993, an increase of 1,700 percent occurred. In 1993, 11 million pounds of hazardous waste was being stored in the state (North Carolina Focus 1996). Public opposition remains firmly intact with the possible siting of future hazardous waste facilities (Photo 8.10).

**Photo 8.5:** Not even the law can stop a landslide. This photo taken on July 1, 1997 shows a state trooper hurrying his pace as sliding continues (upper right) even as clean up had begun. The I-40 landslide was a major disruption to traffic flow through Haywood County. I-40 is a crucial connection to Tennessee and other westward destinations. The size and slope of the cut along with the geologic structure were prominent factors contributing to this slide. (Photo courtesy of Kirk Wilson)

**Photo 8.6a, b, and c:** Development often accelerates landslides, slumps, and rockfalls.

a) NC 105, near Hound Ears resort in Watauga County, gives way following a heavy rain on May 28, 1973. Rock strata dips in line with the slope cut causing an unstable roadbed or landslides. Similar results have occurred on US 321 as the road was widened into four lanes.

b) North of Boone in Watauga County, an earth flow or slump occurs due to an excessive slope cut for a mobile home site. Contractors must consider slope as a limiting factor with excavation projects becoming even more common place in the Mountain region.

c) A rockfall on NC 105 near the Watauga-Avery County line. The large boulder tore loose from a steep slope in the foreground due to an excessive road-bed cut and natural weathering processes.

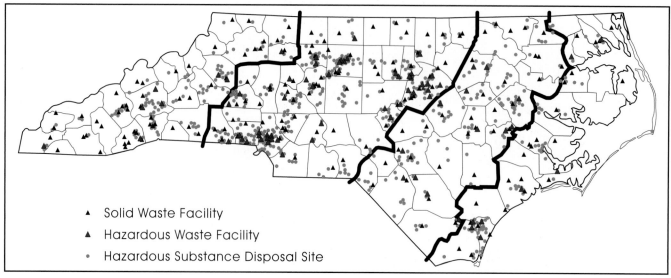

**Figure 8.13:** Hazardous and Solid Waste Facilities.
**Source:** Modified from North Carolina Center of Geographic Information and Analysis, 1999.

▲ Solid Waste Facility

▲ Hazardous Waste Facility

• Hazardous Substance Disposal Site

Government agencies, academic institutions, industrial complexes, the medical community, and utilities generate low-level radioactive waste. While the numbers of facilities generating waste has grown, the volume of waste generated has not. Waste is either handled by onsite incineration or storage, or shipped to processing facilities out of state. From 1989 through 1993 waste shipped out of state went to Nevada, Washington, and South Carolina, with 99 percent sent to Barnwell, South Carolina. In 1995, North Carolina's Low-Level Waste Management Authority originally approved the siting of a commercial processing facility on the border of Wake and Chatham counties and later rescinded that decision (North Carolina Focus 1996).

## Development Issues

The pressures of development follow population increases throughout the state. Carrying capacity is an ecological concept and relates to this situation. Our land and resources can only support so many people before outside resources are necessary. The land's carrying capacity varies from place to place and with the type of human activity. Certain environments are capable of supporting larger populations and increased human activity. Physical factors help to determine this level or capacity of the land. However, the demand placed on certain fragile environments in the state can be devastating to the environment and can have major economic impacts.

**Photo 8.7:** Extraction of renewable resources often facilitates environmental degradation. Logging practices vary, but clearcutting is most damaging to the environment particularly in areas of steep terrain. Erosion processes are accelerated as the land is striped of its vegetation and roads are cut to facilitate access for removal of logs and chipwood. Once the soil is exposed to the elements of weather it is transported and often ends up in streams affecting aquatic habitat. This scene is from the South Mountains of northern Cleveland County.

**Photo 8.8:** Landfills are quickly reaching capacity in many parts of the state. Once full, proper methods to 'cap' the affected area are necessary to insure safety from methane emissions and underground sepage of contaminants into the ground water supplies. The Watauga County landfill as seen here in the midground is a large flat grassed area within an otherwise mountainous terrain. When the area is considered safe then they are often converted for recreational purposes such as athletic fields or golf courses. (Photo courtesy of Art Rex)

Resorts and vacation or second home developments are found throughout the Mountain, Piedmont, Coastal Plain, and the Tidewater regions. North Carolina's mountains and outer banks have long been favorite vacation destinations. Recently there has been increased popularity of the piedmont and coastal plain areas, particularly along river courses or shorelines of the many reservoirs and within the Uwaharrie and South Mountains. Development has continued to fragment our forests, decreasing contiguous habitat for much of the states' wildlife.

## THE STATE'S RESPONSE

The need for action from the state is obvious, and costs associated with conservation, preservation, and clean up are growing each year. The population of the state is expanding, development of open space is increasing, critical habitat is being lost or altered, scenic quality is diminishing, and bio-diversity is decreasing. All of these issues have an economic impact on the state. Agriculture, forestry, and tourism depend on environmental quality.

Table 8.1 presented the legislative actions passed to help protect our environment, but nothing has a greater impact than the pride that North Carolinians take in keeping the state clean and green. Many initiatives have already been adopted and embraced. Efforts like Keep America Beautiful, Adopt-A-Highway, Scenic North Carolina, Keep North Carolina Clean and Beautiful, and others address environmental issues on a daily basis at a local level. The bumper sticker seen throughout the nation 'Think Globally - Act Locally' has been taken to heart by the state. While there has been progress, much work still needs to be done.

**Photo 8.9:** Small recycling drop-off facilities like this one in Watauga County have appeared across the state. Collection containers for glass, plastic, newspaper, cans, and cardboard are at these local sites and give easy access for residents to do their part in protecting the environment. (Photo courtesy of Art Rex)

**Photo 8.10:** Public sentiment towards waste disposal sites still runs high. The NIMBY (Not In My BackYard) acronym is well stated in Richmond County of the Piedmont region. (Photo courtesy of Robert E. Reiman)

## Clean NC 2000

One such initiative that reflects this sense of pride is the Clean NC 2000 program and its slogan of 'Nobody Trashes North Carolina' (Photo 8.11). The goals of Clean NC 2000 are:

1) Instill a Sense of Pride among North Carolinians in the beauty of the state and a responsibility to keep it that way.

2) Reduce the number of unsightly, unsafe, and irreparable structures from North Carolina's roadsides.

3) Remove litter and other debris from the roadsides, rivers, lakes, streams, and ponds.

4) Educate North Carolinians, including our children, on the importance of recycling and keeping NC litter free.

5) Recognize and honor the people who contribute to keeping North Carolina clean and green.

Quality of life, economic development, and travel and tourism are directly affected by the cleanliness of the state. Neither industry nor tourists are inclined to locate or visit in areas where they feel as though the residents do not have pride in themselves and their community (Clean NC 2000).

**Photo 8.11:** Former Governor Hunt practicing what he preaches during a clean up day at a dumpsite in Wake County as part of the Clean NC 2000 program.

Photo Courtesy of the North Carolina Department of Environment and Natural Resources.

## Million Acre Plan

North Carolina's economic vitality is encouraging unprecedented growth. Another 2 million people will be added to the state's current population of 8.04 million by 2020. Our state needs a green infrastructure of protected open space and farmland to complement this growth and development and to maintain our high quality of life. Therefore, Governor Hunt has challenged North Carolina to add one million acres to North Carolina's current assemblage of permanently conserved open space and farmland by the end of the year 2009 (NCDENR 2000).

Most of the lands currently preserved in North Carolina are concentrated in the mountains and coastal areas. The federal government owns the majority of the 2.8 million acres preserved (8.6 percent of the state's land area), with the remaining acreage under ownership of the state and local governments and non-profit organizations. The Million Acres Initiative would increase North Carolina's acreage of protected lands by 35 percent over a ten-year period; a total of 12 percent of the state's land area would be permanently set aside. Currently, the State of North Carolina spends over $30 million per year on permanent open space protection. Such funding is complemented by investments of the federal and local governments, including a number of recent local bond issues, as well as private stewardship and donations (NCDENR 2000).

The Million Acre initiative will focus on lands permanently protected through voluntary acquisition of fee title interest or conservation easements by federal, state, local, or private non-profit land managing organizations (NCDENR 2000).

The Million Acre Initiative provides an alternative to unfettered conversion of farmland and forests to sprawl and development. The initiative will help meet several environmental, economic, and quality of life objectives.

1) Protect the quality of streams, rivers, lakes, estuaries, sounds, and coastal waters.

2) Protect significant or sensitive natural areas, rare species, and wildlife habitat,

3) Protect wetlands and riparian buffers.

4) Protect drinking water supplies.

5) Reduce risks to people and businesses from flooding.

6) Protect forestland from conversion to non-forest uses.

7) Protect farmland, especially small family farms, from conversion to non-farming uses.

8) Provide public access to outdoor recreation including public waters.

9) Protect scenic beauty.

10) Protect significant archaeological, cultural, and historic sites.

11) Protect urban green-spaces.

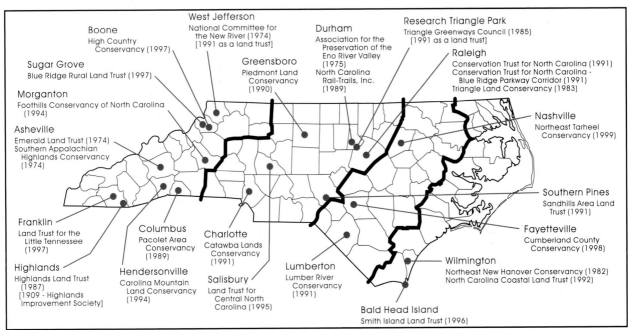

**Figure 8.14:** Conservation Trusts of North Carolina.
**Source:** www.ctnc.org, 2000.

301

As North Carolina works toward this million-acre goal, the state can conserve either a patchwork of lands or lands that are related to each other in a logical way. A statewide plan cannot be prescriptive about which objectives should be most important to a community, and thus, priorities for open space acquisition need to be set at the local or regional scale. For example, coastal communities may be most concerned about flood mitigation, piedmont communities may be most concerned about urban greenspaces, and mountain communities may be most concerned about scenic beauty. Priorities may also differ between urban and rural communities (NCDENR 2000).

Unlike other trust funds and conservation programs, the farmland preservation program is relatively undeveloped. Therefore, Governor Hunt and the NC Smart Growth Commission have afforded farmland preservation special attention. A proposal to expand the farmland preservation infrastructure for North Carolina is currently being developed by Department of Environment and Natural Resources, the Department of Agriculture and Consumer Services, and Cooperative Extension. The Farmland Preservation Trust Fund should fund the conservation of both farmland and forestland (NCDENR 2000).

### Land Trusts and Conservation Easements

Land trusts and conservation easements are the fastest growing procedures in the United States for protecting the environment and North Carolina has embraced this movement (Figure 8.14). By 1998, a Conservation Trust spokesperson stated that efforts were paying off as various land trusts already had protected 3,195 acres at 61 sites through direct ownership or arranged conservation easements (Thompson 1998).

Land Trusts are non-profit organizations that work to protect and preserve the unique natural and cultural qualities of the land. The Conservation Trust's executive director proclaimed that land trusts have had an unprecedented impact on protecting our state's natural resources and heritage. There are twenty-one land trusts in the state (Figure 8.14). During a six-month period, from January until June of 1998, the land trusts received direct grants of over six million dollars and were involved as secondary project sponsors for another fifteen million dollars in grants. Additionally, land trusts focus on promoting land stewardship through educational and outreach programs (Thompson 1998).

Conservation easements provide valuable incentives to landowners and developers. An easement is set forth as a legal document that is recorded in the county's register of deeds office. Owners designate part of their land to the easement and in return receive a tax incentive for this donation. The value of the easement is determined by an independent appraiser and is considered a charitable donation. Conservation easements are perpetually binding, with the stated restrictions recorded with the deed.

Emphasis by land trusts is often placed along riparian corridors or land adjacent to streams and rivers. Riparian corridors have a unique linear shape and as such carry a difficult task of managing the adjacent lands. Control of land in close proximity to the stream channel serves several purposes: 1) to reduce sediment in stream channel, 2) to provide a buffer from possible polluting activities, and 3) to protect visual quality. Tourism and recreational activities are a thriving economy in the Mountain region. Land trusts in this region are active in protecting the water of Wild and Scenic Rivers and National Heritage Rivers, as well as Scenic Highways and panoramic views.

### *1999 Accomplishments*

#### *Hurricane Relief*

Disaster Recovery Assistance - Employees throughout the NCDENR were reassigned to short and long-term projects aiding in Hurricane Floyd recovery efforts. Park rangers provided law enforcement in Tarboro and Bethel, environmental health specialists assisted county health departments on a full-time basis, and NCDENR employees worked in distribution centers and tearing out flooded homes.

#### *Clean Water*

Enhanced Wastewater Enforcement - Beginning July 1, 1999, enforcement decisions for municipal, industrial and other wastewater collection systems included operation and maintenance components. Evaluations include whether operators conduct routine inspections, perform regular line cleaning and right-of way maintenance, keep records of problems and repairs, maintain back-up equipment for pump stations, and implement a schedule to address ongoing problems. The policy is designed to prevent spills and overflows through early recognition of trouble spots and preventative maintenance.

Strengthened Enforcement of Sedimentation Rules - The 1999 General Assembly strengthened the Sedimentation Pollution Control Act by increasing the maximum fine for violations from $500 to $5,000 per day. The Hunt administration also wants to dramatically increase the number of inspections of construction sites. In response to Governor Hunt's request, lawmakers appropriated funds in the 1999-2000 State budget for 10 additional sedimentation inspectors to prevent water pollution from construction run-off.

Wetland Protection - To enhance wetland protection, North Carolina developed a policy for the regulation of activities such as ditching and draining. These activities degrade the ability of a wetland to provide environmental benefits. In 1999, the U.S. Environmental Protection Agency and the Army Corps of Engineers joined North Carolina regulators in seeking enforcement against illegal wetlands ditching and draining activities. Restoration orders have been issued and fines have been levied.

Wetland Restoration - To improve wetland protection coordination, the state Departments of Transportation (DOT) and NCDENR signed a landmark agreement in July, 1999, launching a partnership to protect the state's wetlands and streams. The agreement called for the Department of Transportation to pay DENR $17.5 million during the next seven years to locate wetlands and streams most in need of restoration. Also, during the next seven years, DOT's Transportation Improvement Program sets aside $175 million to protect wetlands, restore streams and preserve wildlife habitat.

1999 Clean Water Act - On July 21, Governor Hunt signed the Clean Water Act of 1999 into law. The act extended the moratorium on new or expanded large-scale hog farms, raised the maximum water pollution fine from $10,000 per day to $25,000 per day, and imposed public disclosure requirements for spills at wastewater treatment plants and from animal operations. The bill also authorizes the Environmental Management Commission to adopt temporary rules to protect water quality in the Cape Fear, Catawba, and Tar-Pamlico river basins.

Drinking Water and Wastewater Bonds - The department awarded 54 grants totaling $100 million to local government units across the state for drinking water and wastewater system improvements. The department also awarded loans totaling $9.7 million for drinking water and wastewater. The clean water bonds provide grants and loans to help local governments expand and improve water supply and wastewater collection and treatment systems, and to undertake water conservation and reuse projects.

Improved Operation of Drinking Water Systems - All applicants for new drinking water systems receiving permits after October 1, 1999, must prove they are financially, technically, and managerially capable of operating the system. This protects customers from the effects of poor maintenance, unsafe water and possible abandonment of the system.

Septic System Upgrades - As of January 1, 2000, septic tanks are required to have filters to remove solids from the wastewater and risers to allow access to the tank for maintenance. Filters at the tank outlet will keep very small solids from entering the drain field and clogging the pipes and soil, extending the life of the system and saving the homeowner on repair costs. The cleaner wastewater entering the ground better protects public health and the environment; raw sewage is less likely to pool on the ground, run into a stream or contaminate a drinking well. Access risers at the entrance and exit of the tank will make pumping, necessary every three to five years to remove solids, easier.

Sewage Notification Law - Effective October 1 polluters are required to inform local news media when more than 1,000 gallons of sewage spills; they are required to place ads in local papers in the event the spill is over 15,000 gallons. This public notification requirement will urge municipalities to move quicker to repair, upgrade or replace existing wastewater systems.

Conservation Reserve Enhancement Program - On March 1, Governor Hunt and U.S. Department of Agriculture Secretary Dan Glickman announced a new $275 million agreement to reduce pollution in several major North Carolina waterways. Under the agreement, the USDA and North Carolina will offer farmers incentives to restore up to 100,000 acres of wetlands and streamside areas and habitats through the Conservation Reserve Enhancement Program (CREP). CREP uses financial incentives to encourage farmers to enroll highly environmentally sensitive land adjacent to the Neuse, Tar-Pamlico, and Chowan river basins and the Jordan Lake watershed in 10-year to 15-year contracts. Under the contracts, farmers agree to remove the land from agricultural production and to plant and maintain hardwood trees, grass filter strips, streamside buffers, vegetation serving as habitat for wildlife and restored wetlands. The vegetation and wetlands will filter contaminants from water runoff before it enters streams and rivers.

*Clean Air*

Reduction of Vehicle Emissions - In July, 1999, the General Assembly approved legislation enacting a major portion of Gov. Hunt's Clean Air Plan for protecting public health, the environment, and jobs. The legislation will require the use of low-sulfur gasoline statewide by January, 2004, expand the motor vehicle emissions testing program from the current 9 counties to 48 counties by July, 2006, and promote the use of alternative-fuel vehicles.

Reduction of Industry Emissions - In April, 1999, North Carolina and Tennessee signed an agreement with federal land managers to ensure that new industrial emissions do not degrade air quality in the Great Smoky Mountains and other pristine natural areas. The pact establishes formal procedures for reviewing permit applications for new or expanded utilities and other industries.

Air Awareness Expansion - In May, 1999, the Division of Air Quality expanded its Air Awareness/ Ozone Action Program to a five-county region surrounding Asheville. The mountain area's "Clean Air Campaign" is the fourth regional participant in this voluntary initiative for reducing ozone. Similar programs operate in the Charlotte, Triangle and Triad metropolitan areas. Through ozone forecasts and other activities, the program educates and informs the public about air pollution, its causes and effects, and things people can do to help reduce pollution.

1st Annual Governors' Air Summit - In April, 1999, Governor Hunt hosted the first annual Governors' Summit on Mountain Air Quality in Asheville. The multi-state summit was aimed at building regional cooperation and support for solutions to ozone, haze, acid rain, and other air quality problems in the Southern Appalachian Mountain region. The state of Georgia has agreed to host a second summit in 2000.

Controlling Animal Odors - In March, 1999, North Carolina began enforcing one of the nation's first comprehensive programs for controlling odors from animal operations. The state Environmental Management Commission adopted temporary odor-control rules in February, 1999, and is now developing permanent rules.

*Coastal Protection*

Coastal Buffers - In November, 1999, the Coastal Resources Commission adopted a rule requiring structures to be built at least 30 feet from the water on coastal waterfront property. Buffers help water quality by filtering pollutants and nutrients from runoff. They also help protect houses and other structures against flooding. The rule applies to property along rivers, streams, sounds, marshes and other navigable waters in the 20 coastal counties.

25TH Anniversary of the Coastal Area Management Act (CAMA) - This landmark legislation protecting the state's coast, an important ecological and economic resource, from improper development created a partnership designed to protect coastal resources through a combination of local land use planning and state regulation. Over the past 25 years, CAMA has accomplished much, including the creation of the North Carolina Coastal Reserve Program (for the acquisition of undeveloped natural areas) and the Public Beach and Coastal Waterfront Access Program (for establishing public access to coastal waters).

*Improved Fisheries*

Marine Fisheries - The state budget, signed by Governor Hunt on June 30, 1999, included $1 million to continue data management improvement efforts in the Division of Marine Fisheries. The funds will be used to enhance permitting and licensing programs and increase access to commercial landings and habitats and fisheries management data.

Dam Removal - The NCDENR, with the help of the U.S. Marines, blew up the 71-year-old Rains Mill Dam in Johnston County in December, 1999, opening 49 more miles of Little River streams and tributaries as spawning areas for fish. It was the third dam in the Neuse River basin to be removed.

*Superfund Cleanups*

Cleanup of NC Military Superfund Sites - The Division of Waste Management's Superfund Section completed an agreement with the Department of Defense to record and track future land use restrictions associated with cleanup actions at military facilities in North Carolina. The agreement is the first of kind in the country that gives the state authority to enforce the mandated cleanup.

*Natural Resources Protection and Environmental Education*

Gorges State Park - The state purchased almost 10,000 acres in Transylvania County from Duke Energy Corporation in April, 1999, to establish North Carolina's first state park west of Asheville. The park covers almost 7,000 acres, while the Wildlife Resources Commission will manage the remaining 3,000 acres as gamelands. Placing the land in public ownership will preserve a portion of the Blue Ridge escarpment, one of the most significant scenic and biological sites in eastern North America. An elevation rise of some 2,000 feet in only three to five miles, combined with rainfall in excess of 80 inches per year, creates a temperate rain forest and supports an extensive collection of waterfalls.

Expansion of Hammocks Beach State Park - The department purchased Huggins Island, adding 210 acres to Hammocks Beach State Park in Onslow County.

25th Anniversary of the NC Zoological Park - Throughout 1999, the North Carolina Zoo celebrated its 25th Anniversary with a variety of special events. The N.C. Zoo became the nation's first state-operated zoo when it opened to the public on August 2, 1974. On that date, then Lt. Governor Hunt cut the ribbon on the Interim Zoo, a collection of temporary facilities used to ex-

hibit animals until permanent exhibits could be completed. Today, the N.C. Zoo has gained international recognition as one of the world's largest and best natural habitat zoos and remains one of only two state-owned zoos in the country.

Elephant and Red Wolf Tracking Web Sites - In January, 1999, the N.C. Zoo unveiled one of the country's most innovative educational outreach programs. Launching a new web site that enables students and teachers to communicate directly with scientists working in the field to help save the elephants of Cameroon, West Africa. "The Elephants of Cameroon" web site at www.nczooeletrack.org has had visits from students from all 50 states and users from more than 80 countries. In October, the Zoo launched a second educational Web site, www.nczooredwolf.org, based on the U.S. Fish and Wildlife Service effort to reintroduce the red wolf in eastern North Carolina.

Zoo Rankings - Two popular magazines named the North Carolina Zoo as one of their top attractions in 1999 readers' polls. *Southern Living* magazine, in its November, 1999, issue, named the N.C. Zoo as one of the top five zoos in its 1999 Readers Choice Awards. Readers of *Our State* magazine in November, 1999, named the N.C. Zoo as the "Best Spot for Children."

Customer Service Center (CSC) - In September, 1999, NCDENR established a Customer Service Center, a "one stop information" source for all of the department's environmental and natural resources programs, services, and regulations. Environmental professionals at the center assist residents with questions and concerns through a toll free help line (1-877-623-6748) or through the CSC web site. The CSC added more phone lines following the devastating effects of Hurricane Floyd to assist citizens with disaster recovery.

Adult Environmental Education through River Basin Signs- A partnership of DENR and the Department of Transportation installed 38 River Basin highway signs in the Cape Fear River Basin. A total of 102 river basin signs have now been installed in 2 of the 17 river basins.

Environmental Education Garden - The Environmental Education Garden was first planted on Earth Day, April 22, 1999, in front of the Archdale Building in Raleigh. The garden serves as a model-training site to demonstrate and promote the uses of gardens and native plants to teach students, including state employees, about the ecological relationships between plants and animals. The garden was created using grants and donations without the use of government funds.

## SUMMARY

North Carolina is blessed with many different ecosystems of varied purposes and inherent beauty. These ecosystems are "fragile." Both natural catastrophes and human modifications can interfere with these ecosystems and cause long term or irreversible damage. This chapter has described the major environmental issues concerning the state and has outlined the state's actions or response. Chapters 10, 11, 12, and 13 describe in detail the four regions of the state and subsequently deal with specific problems within each region. While the state has been active in protecting, cleaning up, and maintaining environmental quality, it must be noted that this apparently has not always been the case. Legislation is necessary because modifications to the environment can cause environmental damage. Active citizen awareness and participation has been a key to the environmental successes. Perhaps with the continued efforts on all fronts North Carolina will continue to be "clean and green."

# The Emergence and Nature of North Carolina's Regions

## INTRODUCTION

One of the current 'hot potatoes' in state politics derives from the difficulties that decision makers have with regional issues. In part this dilemma results from the increasing emphasis to encourage communities, municipalities, counties and regions to turn their interests and the resolution of their problems into a bottom-up decision making process. Traditionally, political decisions affecting conditions of human and environmental welfare were to a greater degree top-down. That is, decisions were imposed upon the localities by the legislature or by the state or federal governments. And, in part, the dilemma derives from the increasing influence that private/corporate decision making is having in the local/regional arena. For North Carolina regions questions raised include these top-down concerns: Are there regions suffering from socio-economic developmental disadvantages, and if so how may we best treat their ills? Who is best equipped to deal with regional inequalities, the private or the public sector? Which services lend themselves best for being provided through a regional delivery system (as opposed to counties and/or municipalities)? How are product or service regions to be delimited, and which territories belong 'naturally' to which region? And who is to determine this regional delimitation? From the bottom-up these questions are confronted by the reality that people have their own sense of 'their region', and tend to be concerned about the preservation of regional identity and therefore community cooperation within their region. Although at times reduced to intra-regional rivalries, such as the traditional local high school football or basketball competitive fever, these regional identities exist in the public mind. They are, however, not often used to drive the emergence of bureaucratic regions that in various ways impact and manage the lives of individuals, families, and communities. And therein lie the seeds of regional discontent that are, perhaps too frequently and unfortunately, styled as urban-rural conflicts over resource allocations and employment opportunities.

The following maps illustrate only some of the great variety of state government regional definitions that affect service delivery in North Carolina (Figures 9.1, 9.2, 9.3, and 9.4). All of these regional service systems figure prominently in the lives of North Carolinians, who may wonder at the absence of harmony

in their regional definitions. At the very least they may ponder the degree to which relevant information flows from the seven Environmental Management Regions to the fourteen Department of Transportation Highway Divisions, and conversely, when there is very little coincidence in the county boundaries of the two regional structures. Similarly, agricultural extension agents, who witness directly the problems of imbalances in agricultural labor, exist within a regional structure (Figure 9.3) that has little in bound-

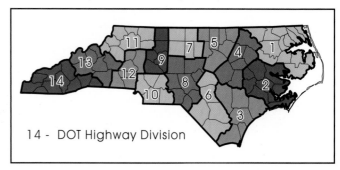

**Figure 9.1:** North Carolina Department of Transportation, Highway Divisions.
**Source:** State and Federal Service Areas in North Carolina (1995). Hickory: Geographic Information Systems, Piedmont Council of Governments.

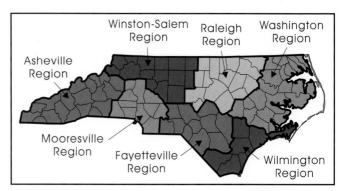

**Figure 9.2:** North Carolina Division of Environment Regions.
**Source:** State and Federal Service Areas in North Carolina (1995). Hickory: Geographic Information Systems, Piedmont Council of Governments.

307

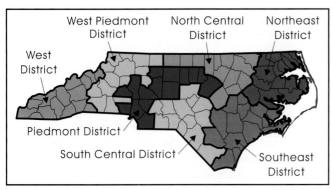

**Figure 9.3:** North Carolina Cooperative Extension Service Regions.
**Source:** State and Federal Service Areas in North Carolina (1995).
Hickory: Geographic Information Systems, Piedmont Council of Governments.

ary similarity with the folks who provide job training programs for people impacted by economic restructuring (Figure 9.4), or aid in establishing new business ventures (Figure 9.5). Thus efficiency in achieving common goals may be hampered by decision makers, with their own agendas, having little in common. The reader might also like to compare the boundaries of this sample set of regions with those that define the state's eighteen regional Councils of Governments, a mid-level regional administrative structure designed to facilitate the diffusion of federal and state mandated support to local governments (Figure 9.6).

In large measure it may be suggested that North Carolina regions serving the complex needs of the public have been defined more by political dominance, narrowly defined self-interest, hairsplitting and compromise, rather than by objective and strictly defined parameters equally applied throughout the state. The resulting regional organization of the state appears massively confusing to all but the few intimately involved in its structuring and management. It is the objective of this chapter to provide some basic understandings of the geographers' approach to dealing with regions, to carve up the state into regions that more meaningfully organize the presentation of information in this text, and, in the process, to aid the reader in gaining more detailed understandings of the workings of the state on the regional level. Superimposed on the already developed framework of four state primary regions (Tidewater, Coastal Plain, Piedmont and Mountain) we identify the existence of thirteen state geographic regions. We argue that these provide the critical level of public identity needed to fuse the state's hierarchy of regions

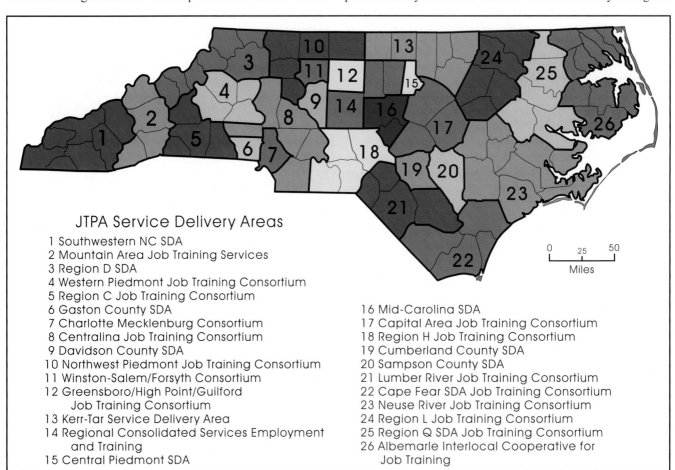

## JTPA Service Delivery Areas

1 Southwestern NC SDA
2 Mountain Area Job Training Services
3 Region D SDA
4 Western Piedmont Job Training Consortium
5 Region C Job Training Consortium
6 Gaston County SDA
7 Charlotte Mecklenburg Consortium
8 Centralina Job Training Consortium
9 Davidson County SDA
10 Northwest Piedmont Job Training Consortium
11 Winston-Salem/Forsyth Consortium
12 Greensboro/High Point/Guilford
    Job Training Consortium
13 Kerr-Tar Service Delivery Area
14 Regional Consolidated Services Employment
    and Training
15 Central Piedmont SDA

16 Mid-Carolina SDA
17 Capital Area Job Training Consortium
18 Region H Job Training Consortium
19 Cumberland County SDA
20 Sampson County SDA
21 Lumber River Job Training Consortium
22 Cape Fear SDA Job Training Consortium
23 Neuse River Job Training Consortium
24 Region L Job Training Consortium
25 Region Q SDA Job Training Consortium
26 Albemarle Interlocal Cooperative for
    Job Training

**Figure 9.4:** Job Training Service Delivery Areas.
**Source:** State and Federal Service Areas in North Carolina (1995). Hickory: Geographic Information Systems, Piedmont Council of Governments.

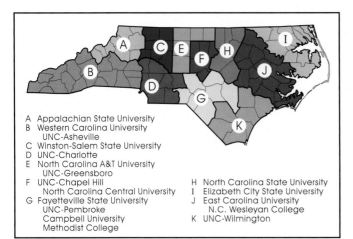

A Appalachian State University
B Western Carolina University
  UNC-Asheville
C Winston-Salem State University
D UNC-Charlotte
E North Carolina A&T University
  UNC-Greensboro
F UNC-Chapel Hill
  North Carolina Central University        H North Carolina State University
G Fayetteville State University            I Elizabeth City State University
  UNC-Pembroke                             J East Carolina University
  Campbell University                        N.C. Wesleyan College
  Methodist College                        K UNC-Wilmington

**Figure 9.5:** Small Business and Technology Centers.
**Source:** State and Federal Service Areas in North Carolina (1995). Hickory: Geographic Information Systems, Piedmont Council of Governments.

from the basic unit of community/neighborhood, through municipality/county to state geographic region, and at the apex of the hierarchy, to the state itself. In the process we arrive at a formal framework for evaluating the present use of regions in attaining a variety of federal, state and local development objectives. We exemplify this by comparing and contrasting the two major mid-level regional management systems, the Councils of Governments and the Regional Partnerships. But first, this chapter serves as an introduction to the more detailed regional geography descriptions and evaluations in the four primary region specific chapters that follow.

## WHAT KIND OF REGIONS?

To improve their ability to manage information of relevance to them, scientists of all kinds develop systems of classification. In geology, the main classification system, or taxonomy, involves a geologic time table covering more than a billion years, to which is sequenced the evolution of earth materials. For history, a time table, structured by era, ages, and periods, accommodates the written history of humankind, and facilitates analysis of important events. Biology classes all living things in a hierarchy by descending order of kingdom, phylum, class, order, family, genus, and species. The reader will already recognize one of the taxonomies used in geography, that of urban settlements, as hierarchically structured by size and function, from megalopolis, to metropolis, city, town, village, and hamlet.. However, the primary interest of the authors of this text is to evaluate conditions of land and life, and its evolution and prospective future, for the regions of our state. A taxonomy that allows a hierarchical structure of state regions from large to small is called for. This classification system is organized not temporally, as for history and geology, and not vertically, as for biology; rather it is organized

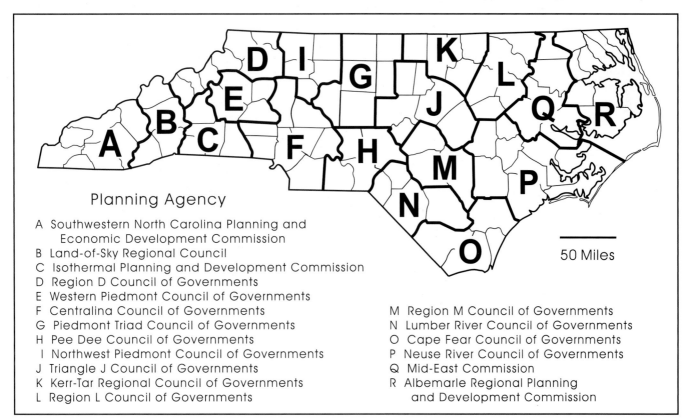

### Planning Agency

A Southwestern North Carolina Planning and
  Economic Development Commission
B Land-of-Sky Regional Council
C Isothermal Planning and Development Commission
D Region D Council of Governments
E Western Piedmont Council of Governments
F Centralina Council of Governments
G Piedmont Triad Council of Governments
H Pee Dee Council of Governments
I Northwest Piedmont Council of Governments
J Triangle J Council of Governments
K Kerr-Tar Regional Council of Governments
L Region L Council of Governments

M Region M Council of Governments
N Lumber River Council of Governments
O Cape Fear Council of Governments
P Neuse River Council of Governments
Q Mid-East Commission
R Albemarle Regional Planning
  and Development Commission

50 Miles

**Figure 9.6:** Lead Region Organization Areas.
**Source:** North Carolina Department of Administration, Division of Policy Development.

spatially, since the objective is to move from the generalizing patterns of human activity in the landscape for the larger regions, to more detailed understandings of conditions as they exist on the community level.

For our purposes we categorize five layers of regions in North Carolina, with the state itself defined at the top of the hierarchy. Then grouped by decreasing size are these categories: the four primary regions, the thirteen state geographic regions, the one hundred counties, and finally communities /localities within these. In the text we deal explicitly with all of these, except that county and community analysis is more selective. In this way, the discussion in the following four chapters, covering each of the primary regions, will initially focus on major characteristics and trends, for then to provide a more detailed view of the state geographic regions, including consideration of county population conditions.

A difficulty for geographers is that they have a need to pursue regional classification for reasons other than to provide a spatially organized hierarchical system, as described above. These needs reflect geographers' interests as being focused on the essential characteristics and mechanics of the earth's physical or cultural systems, expressed by their regionally defined spatial variations and similarities, or on the dynamics of systems change. So, throughout this volume the reader will see discussed and mapped a great variety of regionally defined geographic phenomena. Just how these are organized within the discipline of geography may be seen in Figure 9.7. An additional caveat in the treatment of regional issues is that in many cases the regions of today are not the regions of tomorrow. So though we argue that there are three distinct metropolitan focused state geographic regions within the Urban Crescent, the fact is that Main Street North Carolina is fusing these into one extensive megalopolis, while extending its tentacles of urban spread into adjacent more rural counties.

# A REGIONAL GEOGRAPHY OF NORTH CAROLINA

## Four Primary Regions

The Tarheel State has a rich diversity of physical and cultural environments in its 500 mile (800 km) east-west reach from the shores of the Atlantic Ocean to the peaks of the Appalachian Mountains. Popularly held perceptions of these regional variations are united in the simplistic image rendered by cartoonist George Breisach (1988) in the *Charlotte Observer* (Figure 9.8). Geographers formally complement this image with a set of boundaries that define the four primary state regions of Tidewater, Coastal Plain, Piedmont, and Mountain (Figure 9.9). These regions are basic to arriving at generalized understandings of critical differences in the state's physical and cultural environments. Table 9.1 illustrates some of these differences for land area, population totals, and population changes over the 1980-1996 period.

As demonstrated by this data the Piedmont dominates the state in all of these measures, in shear physical size, as well as in total population, population growth and population density. In rate of population growth the Tidewater barely beats out the Piedmont, but both regions are growing at about twice the rate of the Mountain and Coastal regions. The Piedmont, about two and a half times as crowded as any of the other three, now holds 57 percent of the state's population, a condition reflecting this region's persistent attractiveness for investment and employment opportunities. Providing basic information on these varied landscapes will set the stage for the subsequent chapters on North Carolina regions, and be our point of departure in this chapter for evaluating the state's changing socioeconomic conditions in their regional contexts. Here it must be noted that the four primary North Carolina regions are viewed as composite physical/cultural landscape regions, and thus fit into the regional classification scheme presented in Figure 9.7 as a homogenous

---

**A REGIONAL CLASSIFICATION SYSTEM**

I.  Homogenous (Formal) Region (spatial distributions of particular phenomenon)
   - A.  Physical Environments (natural regions, e.g., climate, landform, natural vegetation, see Chapters 1-3)
   - B.  Cultural Environments (cultural regions, e.g., economic, ethnic, electoral, see Chapters 4-7)
II. Functional Region (functionally integrated, often about a core, and always with flexible boundaries and tentacles of influence reaching beyond these)
   - A.  Activity Region
      1.  Economic production
         - a.  Hierarchically structured (e.g., manufacturing industry)
         - b.  Horizontally structured (e.g., industrial districts, Figure 6.6)
      2.  Service provision
         - a.  Hierarchically structured (e.g., central place system, Figure 4.5)
         - b.  Vertically structured (e.g., multicore city regions, Figure 9.10)
   - B.  Administrative Region
      1.  Hierarchically structured (e.g., administrative hierarchy, Figure 9.11)
      2.  Horizontally structured (e.g., cross boundary)

**Figure 9.7**. A Regional Classification System.

| STATE PRIMARY REGION | Counties | Land Area (sq. km.) | % State | Population 1990 | % State | Population 2000 | % State | % Pop. Change | Population Density (sq.km.) |
|---|---|---|---|---|---|---|---|---|---|
| 1. Mountain | 24 | 26,367 | 20.9 | 917,685 | 13.8 | 1,044,139 | 13 | 13.8 | 39.6 |
| 2. Piedmont | 35 | 42,535 | 33.7 | 3,639,379 | 54.9 | 4,615,593 | 57.3 | 26.8 | 108.5 |
| 3. Coastal Plain | 22 | 34,543 | 27.4 | 1,380,720 | 20.8 | 1,595,181 | 19.8 | 15.5 | 46.2 |
| 4. Tidewater | 19 | 22,735 | 18 | 694,664 | 10.5 | 794,026 | 9.9 | 14.3 | 34.9 |
| **State Totals** | **100** | **126,180** | **100** | **6,632,448** | **100** | **8,049,313** | **100** | **21.4** | **63.8** |

**Table 9.1:** State Primary Regions, Base Data, 1980-2000.
**Sources:** U.S. Bureau of the Census, 2000.

regional system. Simultaneously, each region displays greater internal homogeneity in physical and cultural environmental factors than those existing between any two of the regions defined.

### Tidewater Region

This coastal landscape has characteristics that separate it as an independent region from the larger interior region of the Coastal Plain. Characteristically underlain by geologically recent (Cenozoic) sedimentary rocks, the Tidewater is characterized by a seemingly uniform distribution of flat, low lying terrain covered mostly by pine forest or swamplands that is cut in its northern portion by sounds reaching up to 50 miles into the continent. Seaward, and capping the sounds of Albemarle, Pamlico, Core and Bogue, are the barrier islands. Without intervening major sounds, these islands then extend south and west to the South Carolina border. Along these 320 miles of offshore islands, a settlement pattern of small communities and towns is broken by the Hatteras National Seashore and the Cape Lookout National Seashore. Traditionally dependent on fishing and coastal trade, these communities are now dominated by seasonal economies related to open space recreation/leisure activities in one of the country's most fabulous ocean beach environments. Riverine settlements from colonial times dominate the remainder of the Tidewater. The fortunes of these places, anchored in the north by Elizabeth City and in the south by Wilmington, are tied to fishing, port functions, small scale manufacturing, forest and food products, public services, and local/regional administration. Medium and small cities in this region have, in recent decades, benefited from top-down regional investment in state port expansion, higher education, military installations, and public services. An absence of a major port city, like Charleston or Jack-

sonville, is notable. On the other hand, one of the highest rate of population growth for small towns in the state is being experienced by the coastal resort communities. A critical aspect of understanding this region is the sensitivity of its physical environment to the impact of people and their facilities, whether these have to do with the increasing pressure of people and their activities on the fragile nature of the barrier islands, with the occasionally occurring major landscape denudation and severe pollution of rivers and sounds by mining, forest or agricultural industries, or with the encroachment of development on wetlands. The geography of this region is presented in Chapter 10.

### Coastal Plain Region

Here an agricultural economy and its related dispersed rural settlement have persisted for several centuries. Overwhelmingly a rural region, urbanization is dominated by small agricultural service centers and a few medium sized cities, dependent until quite recently on labor intensive and low wage manufacturing industries. This emphasis on traditional primary and secondary industries has generally left this region lagging behind other regions in the economic development boom engulfing the state over the past several decades. As a result, the State Department of Commerce in its annual review of socioeconomic conditions on the county level regularly assign Coastal Plain counties a much higher proportion in the most severely economically distressed category, Tier I (see Figure 9.14). For 1998, this primary region had eight of the state's twelve counties so classified, or over a third of its total counties. From this designation comes a greater state and local government support for the location of new industry, providing a diversification of employment opportunities and higher wages.

In the mid-1980s, three counties began billing themselves as Triangle East, the eastern manufacturing entrance to the Research Triangle (Cook 1992, p. 22). The Triangle East coalition towns of Rocky Mount, Wilson, and Tarboro, however, continue to show only slight population increases. A larger urban region enters the economic growth mosaic when the concept of Triangle East is extended to the immediate east and south, to include adjacent counties, in toto comprising the earlier identified Coastal Plain "Ring City" (Figure 9.9).

With East Carolina University's recently inaugurated medical center leading the expansion, Greenville is the fastest growing urban center in the region, closely followed in size by Goldsboro with its traditional economic anchor, Johnson Seymour Air Force

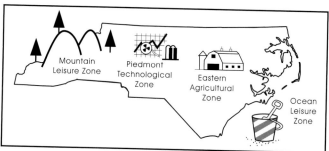

**Figure 9.8:** George's Breisach's 'Popular Image' of North Carolina.
**Source:** *The Charlotte Observer,* 1988.

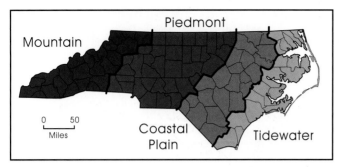

**Figure 9.9:** North Carolina's Four Primary Regions

Base. Kinston is the designated home of that newest of North Carolina's large scale public/private joint venture economic planning efforts, the Global TransPark. After nearly four decades of the success of the Research Triangle Park, state development experts point to the 21st Century as the century of air transportation. Thus, the Global TransPark is to provide an industrial complex that responds to the expanding need of linking new economic growth to international markets, just-in-time production, and multi modal transportation. With legislative support in 1991, an investment scheme to develop a 5,000 acre international air-cargo industrial complex centered by runways of 11,500 feet has been initiated, though it remains highly tentative (Kasarda 1995). Fayetteville, with its Fort Bragg military installation, provides another source of economic stability in the Coastal Plain. In most parts of the Coastal Plain, agriculture and its processing facilities, largely food and tobacco related, have provided decreasing employment opportunities, especially where a number of counties contain a majority African-American and/or Native American population. In the southern Coastal Plain, agriculture has recently turned around with the emphasis on agribusiness scaled hog production. Here Hispanic workers have been welcomed by agribusiness. The geography of this region is presented in Chapter 11.

*Piedmont Region*

This region is best described as a multi-nucleated "Urban Crescent," with its adjacent rural land increasingly given over to the residential and recreational needs of the expanding urban population. It has three distinct urban clusters: "Metrolina" with its core of Charlotte and Gastonia; the "Piedmont Triad" with Greensboro, Winston-Salem, High Point and Burlington; and the "Piedmont Triangle" with Raleigh, Durham, Chapel Hill, and the rapidly expanding edge city of Cary. These clusters are embedded within designated Metropolitan Statistical Areas. Along with the much smaller Hickory MSA, they demonstrate an almost spatially continuous urban region, aligned along North Carolina's "Main Street," an arch of urban land usage defined by the passage of the I-85/I-40 limited access highways through the Piedmont (Figure 9.10). Along "Main Street," opportunities for a diversity of investments and employment growth vary. Here the Piedmont Triangle, with its knowledge society economic base well established in major universities and research and business

parks, and further supported by its concentrations of state and federal government employment, is leading the way. The finance and distribution center of Metrolina, is close behind. Overlapping the center of "Main Street" is the Piedmont Triad, which, anchored to a more traditional manufacturing industry, is lagging in growth. These three urban clusters comprise 19 of the state's 100 counties, but contain about 45 percent of the state's population. Functionally, the Piedmont is a very complex manufacturing and service employment region with a diversity of jobs that act as important magnets for continuing growth.

A number of Piedmont counties continue to be largely rural in character, though several are affected by spill-over suburban and exurban growth. As suggested by Table 9.1 the 16 remaining counties in the Piedmont have only nine percent of the state's population, leaving these predominantly rural counties at a density resembling that of the thinly populated Tidewater Region. Concerns in the Piedmont have been expressed for decades over the continuing loss of rural land, and not only that endowed with superior agricultural values. During the 1970s, there were attempts at defining an open space no growth area between the tri-cities of Greensboro, High Point, and Winston-Salem. This "greenheart" idea, however, quickly lost out to the speculative development caused by the "Main Street" development band-wagon. So the Piedmont Triad "greenheart" is rapidly being invaded by business parks, as exemplified by the Triad Airport and the Interstate Highway related industry, business and residential developments. In addition, up-scale residential communities, with their golf courses, are pushing into the rural countryside. Now, a larger vision of the Piedmont's "greenheart," focusing on the Uwharrie Mountains and the Pee Dee River basin, is being pursued. Still, the gradual fusing of urban development, not only within the Piedmont Triad, but along the entire "Main Street," is providing a distinctive megalopolitan character for the Urban Crescent. The geography of this region is presented in Chapter 12.

*Mountain Region*

In this region there are two distinct patterns of settlement. In its eastern foothill portion there is an extension of the western Piedmont's dispersed and slow growing small manufacturing towns, depending largely on textile, apparel, and furniture production, with interstices of relatively dense rural settlement. Connected to this is the Asheville Basin, with its concentration of tourism facilities and manufacturing plants. The remainder of the Mountain Region is dominated by relatively small towns, mostly retail service centers and county seats. A scatteration of small manufacturing enterprises reflects in part the 1960s effort of a state supported rural industrial location policy. Several communities have been affected by large scale tourism and recreational resort development, as, for example, those centralized in Watauga and Avery counties in the northwest, and those dispersed through the southwestern mountains in Buncombe and Henderson counties, and along the Georgia border to the Great Smoky Mountains.

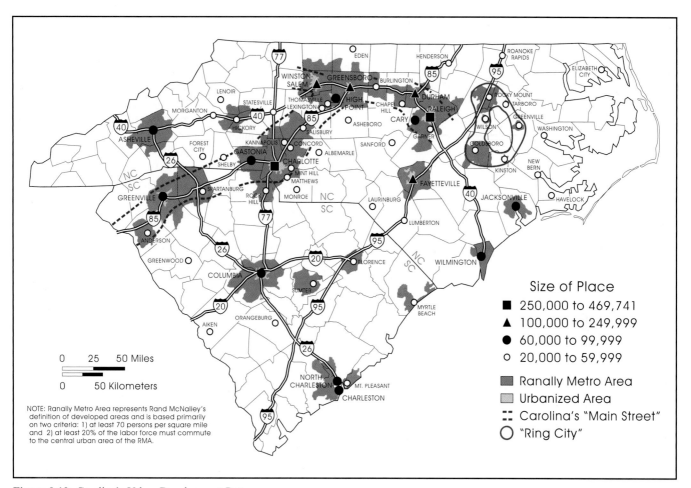

**Figure 9.10:** Carolina's Urban Development Patterns.
**Source:** Modified from Rand McNally's Commercial and Marketing Guide, 128th Ed., 1998.

Mountain agriculture continues its shift from family farms to "gentleman farming" with its emphasis on stock raising and horse stables, and to horticulture and its diversified focus on the Christmas tree business, on specialized nurseries, and on the collecting of native medicinal plants. Even so, there is in the northwestern mountains a strong commercial general agriculture economy. In the so-called "High Country" of the Blue Ridge, as well as in many other mountain counties, much land is being converted to recreational use, vacation homes, and resorts. Especially attractive to developers are, on the one hand, ridge tops with adjacent steep slopes providing fine wide-ranging vistas, and on the other hand, the more pristine river valleys, like the New River Valley. Here developers have flocked in at the very beginning of the federal and state designation of the river as "wild and scenic." Tragically, the more fragile the physical environment of our Mountain Region, the more desirable for development it seems to become, and as a result the increasing land values make it more difficult, if not impossible, to preserve this land in a natural condition for future generations. As an echo to

the environmental misfortunes resulting from the region's inappropriate development are the employment problems. Some counties are finding it very difficult to attract industrial and business investments and continue to experience high rates of unemployment, which explains, in part, a negative migration balance and an aging population. Elsewhere in the region there is nearly full employment, but jobs in perhaps too many places are dominated by seasonally defined resort, recreation, and vacation industries, which are notably on the low end of the pay scale for workers. The geography of this region is presented in Chapter 13.

### Thirteen State Geographic Regions

#### The Delineation and Naming of Regions

Describing and analyzing conditions in a state this large in area and population cannot be done in the appropriate detail at the scale of the four state primary regions. In fact, the boundaries of these traditional, essentially physical geography based regions, do not lend themselves perfectly to the task. Accordingly

313

the state has been divided into thirteen state geographic regions (Figure 9.11). These are defined more on the basis of internal economic functionalities and cultural cohesiveness, than on natural conditions, though strong relationships do exist between the physical and cultural environmental parameters. Some regions are clearly metropolitan focused, while others are as clearly rural activity and settlement dominated.

We have chosen names for the state geographic regions (SGR) that in most cases are used with some familiarity by people living in these regions. In other cases, like "Ring City", regions are labeled and bounded by their emerging characteristics. By what magic then are boundaries of these regions placed on the map? Normally geographic regions take their identity from some well known feature or combination of features. Such features may be more strongly associated with a particular portion of the region, especially its urban center, thus leaving the more peripheral portions more in doubt about their inclusion.

Take the Albemarle State Geographic Region as an example. Here the following traits have been used in defining its boundaries: counties included lie mostly within the tidewater natural region, are tied hydrologically to the Albemarle Sound, and are in the northern portions influenced by labor markets in adjacent Virginia. Agriculture and recreational opportunities complement each other in a land use that in an absence of intense regional development has afforded only the evolution of small villages and towns. With few land elevations in excess of 15 feet above sea level the swamp, riverine, sound and ocean environments provide a unifying wetlands landscape within which local culture has evolved a sense of a holistic, well integrated physical/human environment. Gates County might be viewed as a toss-up as to its inclusion in this SGR. However, its Chowan River natural boundary with Hertford County in the Roanoke State Geographic

Region, its sharing of the Dismal Swamp with other members of the Albemarle, and its Virginia labor market orientation, overshadows its distance from the Albemarle Sound.

In the Pamlico State Geographic Region, Jones County is very similar in its physical geography, economic activities, and settlement patterns to the Cape Fear State Geographic Region's interior counties, but its proximity and functional connectivity to New Bern made the decision. And so there are one or more counties in most of these regions that may seem questionable in some quarters by their inclusion. Almost a coin toss, for example, placed Montgomery County in the Sandhills State Geographic Region. Montgomery is about equidistant from the Charlotte and the Greensboro portions of "Main Street", but the county's central and northwestern half is dominated by the Uwharrie National Forest. Thus the Forest and the Pee Dee River provides something of a natural boundary with the Piedmont Triad and Metrolina SGRs . In general terms, the conditions of land use and the traditions of culture seems to tie Montgomery County more effectively to the Sandhills SGR. More details on regional definition and boundaries are provided in the regional chapters. Over future decades, depending on the dynamics and directions of change in the state, state geographic regions (SGR) may change in name and boundary. Readers are invited to do their own evaluations, and to participate in this exercise by contributing their suggestions for changes in new editions of this work.

*State Geographic Region Comparisons*

At this level of detail provided by the thirteen State Geographic Regions (SGR), striking differences in development and future prospects emerge and a larger data set is used to explore some of these (Table 9.2). This data set of thirteen variables is the same as that used in subsequent chapters for counties within

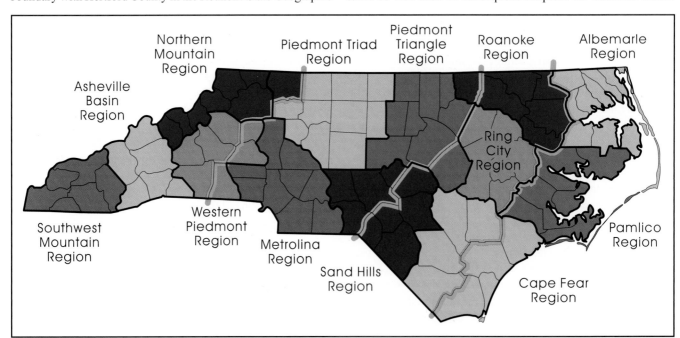

**Figure 9.11:** Thirteen State Geographic Regions.

| STATE GEOGRAPHIC REGIONS | Counties | Land Area in sq. km | Pop 1990 | Pop. sq.km. 2000 | Pop 2000 | 1990s % Pop. Change | % White 2000 | Median Age in 2000 | % Fam. Below Poverty | Annual Average Infant Mortality Rate 1994-98 | % High School Grads'90 | % Coll. Grads. 1990 | Fem. Fam. Head of Hshld'90 | NC Enterprise Tiers'97 |
|---|---|---|---|---|---|---|---|---|---|---|---|---|---|---|
| 1. Albemarle | 9 | 6,758 | 124,795 | 21.3 | 144,221 | 15.6 | 70.9 | 38.7 | 13.9 | 13.7 | 65.1 | 11 | 12.3 | 2.9 |
| 2. Asheville Basin | 6 | 6,863 | 347,983 | 60.7 | 416,829 | 19.8 | 91.7 | 43.1 | 9.6 | 8.9 | 71.4 | 17.4 | 8.8 | 4.2 |
| 3. Cape Fear | 8 | 16,227 | 515,504 | 38.3 | 621,138 | 20.5 | 71.6 | 37.2 | 14.8 | 8.3 | 66.1 | 11.1 | 13.1 | 3.3 |
| 4. Metrolina | 9 | 10,871 | 1,198,493 | 141.7 | 1,540,714 | 28.6 | 73.9 | 36.4 | 7.8 | 8.5 | 66.3 | 12.8 | 11.7 | 3.9 |
| 5. Northern Mountains | 8 | 7,897 | 234,567 | 33.6 | 265,235 | 13.1 | 97.9 | 40.2 | 12.2 | 7.9 | 58.7 | 11.8 | 8.6 | 2.5 |
| 6. Pamlico | 6 | 9,007 | 202,643 | 25 | 224,918 | 11 | 74.6 | 39.4 | 14.7 | 9.9 | 67.6 | 11.6 | 12.7 | 2.7 |
| 7. Piedmont Triad | 10 | 12,626 | 1,157,030 | 104.4 | 1,366,938 | 18.1 | 77.1 | 38.1 | 8 | 9.4 | 66 | 13.3 | 11.3 | 4.3 |
| 8. Piedmont Triangle | 9 | 12,090 | 965,929 | 108.8 | 1,315,016 | 36.1 | 68.3 | 35.8 | 9.6 | 10.3 | 69.7 | 20.1 | 12.8 | 4.3 |
| 9. Ring City | 7 | 8,511 | 485,234 | 63.8 | 542,589 | 11.8 | 57.8 | 36.2 | 14.6 | 12.2 | 64.3 | 13 | 16.3 | 3.1 |
| 10. Roanoke | 6 | 8,303 | 161,568 | 20.2 | 167,395 | 3.6 | 37.2 | 37.7 | 20.8 | 12.8 | 55.3 | 8.8 | 18.4 | 1.2 |
| 11. Sandhills | 9 | 12,507 | 672,575 | 62.7 | 784,166 | 16.6 | 62.1 | 35.3 | 13.6 | 10.8 | 64.1 | 18.6 | 15.8 | 3.1 |
| 12. Southwest Mountains | 6 | 6,468 | 96,128 | 18.1 | 116,966 | 21.7 | 89.7 | 42.4 | 16.3 | 7.5 | 62.4 | 12.2 | 9.4 | 2.3 |
| 13. Western Piedmont | 7 | 8,052 | 470,000 | 67.5 | 543,188 | 15.6 | 85.9 | 38.1 | 7.7 | 8.7 | 60.6 | 10.1 | 10.8 | 3.4 |
| **State Totals/Averages** | **100** | **126,180** | **6,632,449** | **63.8** | **8,049,313** | **21.4** | **73.1** | **36.1** | **9.9** | **9.4** | **70** | **17.4** | **12.3** | **3.2** |

**Table 9.2:** Thirteen State Geographic Regions, Base Data.
**Sources:** U. S. Bureau of the Census; North Carolina Office of State Planning, 1997-2000.

each SGR, and therefore allows for easy comparisons. For example, in their physical dimensions the SGR vary from the smallest, the Southwest Mountains of only some 40% the size of the largest, the Cape Fear (see Figure 9.11). Upon closer inspection it appears that the more peripheral SGRs (located in the northeastern and in the western parts of the state) are generally much smaller in size. This is due to the absence of larger urban centers that, as in the case of Piedmont SGRs, over a wider distance tend to fuse adjacent rural counties functionally to them. Thus the more rural and isolated the SGR the smaller it is, due largely to the historically relatively poorer communication and transportation infrastructure. Smaller urban focused SGRs like Asheville and Ring City are exceptions to this latter condition. In total population and population density these variations repeat, with the more peripheral SGRs at the lower end. With minor variations these center-peripheral contrasts seem to hold across most of the data set. The more urban SGRs, centrally located in the state, are also those with higher rates of population growth, more youthful populations, lesser poverty, lower incidence of infant mortality, and greater educational competence. A definitive west-east tilt is presented in the racial distribution data with above 90% white dominance in the west to a non-white dominance in Roanoke SGR in the east. An inverse west-east tilt is seen in the percentage of families headed by a female. One important result from differences that argue the existence of important spatial variations over the state in socio-economic welfare is the derivation by state authorities of Enterprise Tiers. Using data sets somewhat akin to those in Table 9.2 the State Department of Commerce has come up with a classification system to aid in the distribution of public resources to industries interested in locating within the state. The lower the Tier designation the greater the state support available to entice private location investments. In this way the more peripheral SGRs, with their evidence of greater needs of economic development support, achieve lower Tier designations. Note the relevant discussions in Chapter 11.

In Chapter 4 we treat in some detail the character and changes in North Carolina's demography. This discussion is supported by age-gender cohort diagrams that lie as foundation for understanding variation in population characteristics across the state (Box 4A and Figure 4.11). In looking at the extraordinary differences in conditions among the SGRs we find it now relevant to bring the cohort analysis to the county level. Since the population structure of each county, when totaled, aggregates to the result shown in the state age-gender cohort, this can be used as a kind of norm against which to compare county variations. In Figure 9.12 we show the 1990 North Carolina population data by gender and five-year age cohorts. It should be noted that the same information, though not identified by gender, is shown in Figure 4.11. In the latter it is compared to the 1980 conditions, thus enabling us to note the changes that have occurred over the decade. For Figure 9.12 the value lies in the ability to compare age-sex conditions with those indicated for the individual counties in the following four chapters. Box 9A then demonstrates different analytical potentials of demographic subsets contained within the population diagram. Analysis of these subsets allows focus on a variety of population issues and problems for individual counties and their SRGs, as follows:

> 1) the share of the total population that is of female child bearing age indicates the potential for population change; thus rapidly growing urban counties like Durham and Wake can be predicted to continue at a fairly high rate of population growth due their greater percentage of persons in this class; on the other hand that may also be said of Orange until it is realized that the vast majority of this child bearing population is comprised of students at UNC-Chapel Hill, with their very low propensity for reproduction, and with their likely from the county with their education.

2) years of formal employment and their likely percentage share of the individual cohorts are indicated on this example; as expected, males enter the work force earlier and to a greater degree than do females, who, on the other hand have a greater, though a decreasing, tendency to work at home; most urban counties appear to have a particularly favorable dominance of working age populations, given a relative absence of unemployment; see, for example, the cohorts of Forsyth and Guilford counties;

3) this indicates the age of eligibility for military service, still confined largely to males; the reader can see this on the Cumberland and Onslow counties' cohort diagrams, and less markedly on that of Wayne County;

4) youth and old age dependencies provide different issues for the counties so encumbered; old age dependency is a notable feature of both the Alleghany and Brunswick counties, though for Alleghany this is a result largely of an aging-in-place process that over the years also have resulted in a reduction in youth; for Brunswick there is clear evidence of a concentration of the retirement here of a younger retirement population that then flees the county when reaching the age of greater infirmity; here also an absence of youthful outmigration has left a normal entry of births.

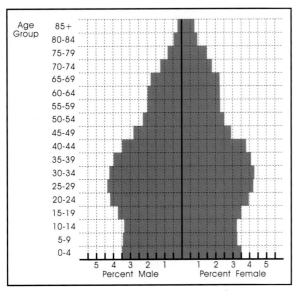

**Figure 9.12:** Age-Gender by Five Year Cohorts, 1990.
**Source:** United States Bureau of the Census, 1990.

Readers interested in deriving greater detail of knowledge about counties of interest to them are encouraged to compare the individual county population cohort profiles in subsequent chapters with that of the state, and in the context of the above analysis suggestions. It behooves decision makers and the public at large to be informed about these differences as they have important implications for public investments in particular types of infrastructure, like elderly healthcare and education facilities, and for private investments, especially in home construction and retail sales.

## ECONOMIC DEVELOPMENT REGIONS

### *A Context for Regional Development*

We have now established a hierarchy of North Carolina regions with thirteen state geography regions encased in four primary regions. These are heuristic regions, containing an inherent socio-economic functional logic that supports their eventual emergence at a uniform multi-county administrative level. In the way of such an evolution stand the existing, highly complex, and geographically overlapping politically designated service regions, as indicated in the introduction to this chapter. Among these and perhaps more directly affecting the lives of North Carolinians are the regional development regions that have emerged over recent decades. The reference here is to the emergence of the seventeen Councils of Government during the 1970s, and to the subsequent appearance, in the late 1980s, of the so-called Partnership Regions. A shift in the evolutionary forces bringing about these regions raise questions concerning the foundations for regional change and progress in the state. Are such foundations anchored more securely by focusing public support on the social welfare needs of localities, or on local economic development initiatives? Perhaps there have always been reasons to question why states find it necessary to define formal multi-county regions for dispensing public revenues in the cause of socio-economic development and community needs, especially since the implementation of such regions establishes another layer of public administration. However, the issue grows more complex when recent changes in national political philosophy have contributed to the superimposition of a new set of North Carolina regions on an already existing regional structure. For the average citizen, and for many communities, it is becoming increasingly difficult to determine just what public is being served by the different and geographically overlapping regions, and to what (or to whose) end.

How can we assess these complexities of regional determination? Let us begin by summarizing recent demographic and economic development shifts and how these have differentially affected regional change and growth for each of the state primary regions (Tidewater, Coastal Plain, Piedmont and Mountain). How then have these changes led to concerns that uneven development may continue to require direct state intervention in those counties least able to provide for their citizens? In the

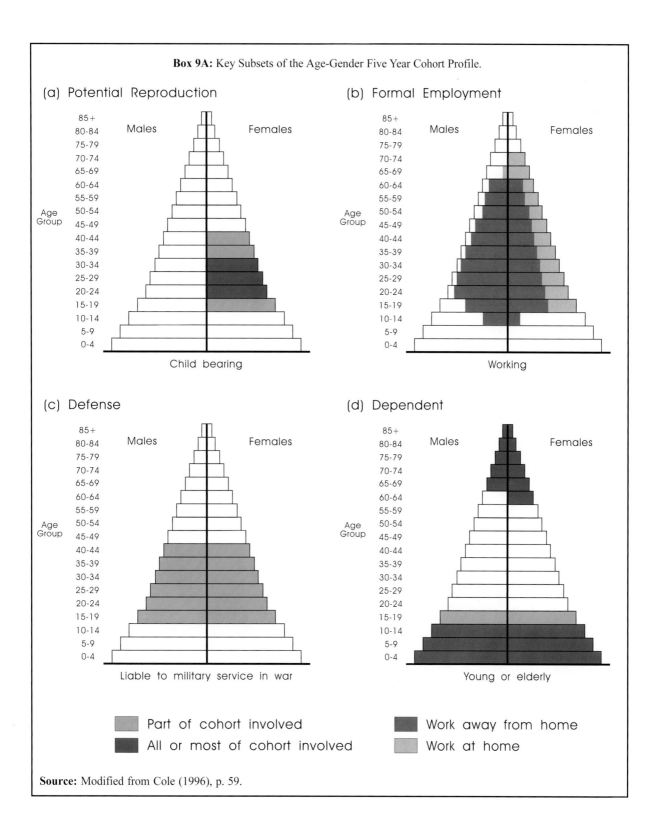

**Box 9A:** Key Subsets of the Age-Gender Five Year Cohort Profile.

(a) Potential Reproduction

Age Group: 85+, 80-84, 75-79, 70-74, 65-69, 60-64, 55-59, 50-54, 45-49, 40-44, 35-39, 30-34, 25-29, 20-24, 15-19, 10-14, 5-9, 0-4

Males    Females

Child bearing

(b) Formal Employment

Males    Females

Working

(c) Defense

Males    Females

Liable to military service in war

(d) Dependent

Males    Females

Young or elderly

Part of cohort involved

All or most of cohort involved

Work away from home

Work at home

**Source:** Modified from Cole (1996), p. 59.

317

process we will find that state regional development policy has shifted to influence a continuing concentration of economic activities and settlement patterns, away from its original intent of providing a more secure foundation for equal opportunity and welfare throughout the state.

### Four Decades of Regional Change

To lead into a discussion of the state's role in regional definition and development, let us first provide a brief on the changing regional conditions of population settlement and economic development for the most recent decades (Gade 1989; Gade 1991; Gade and Cui 1994). A similar recent history of demographic change elaborated in Chapter 4 provides supportive background.

#### 1950s

Decades of net out migration from North Carolina culminated in the 1950s. Peripheral portions of the Mountain and Coastal Plain regions approached exhaustion of their surplus labor and were becoming troubled by an aging population. Centrally positioned rural areas similarly lost population, but in their case, mostly to adjacent urban areas within the state. Growth is largely confined to the Piedmont cities and to areas with large military installations, like Fayetteville and Jacksonville.

#### 1960s

Selective out-migration from rural areas continued, but at a reduced rate. A significant turnaround in intrastate migration fueled growth in metropolitan areas. Central cities saw an increasing share of their population relocating to their fringes. In the process, they became more segregated by race, a process also influenced by the gradual increase in returning African-Americans to their home state, though not necessarily to their home county. Continued urban growth in the Piedmont saw the gradual fusing of the three major urban clusters toward a megalopolitan character. Meanwhile, Mountain and Coastal Plain counties became more economically disadvantaged, although labor intensive, low wage industries, dominated by branch plants, were localizing in rural areas, slowing the outflow of people.

#### 1970s

This was North Carolina's decade in the sun. The sun-belt migration took hold, with the state experiencing unprecedented regional change. However, positive impacts were confined largely to the rapidly growing metro regions, where stronger inter regional linkages were facilitated by an expanding interstate highway system. These influences continued the growth of suburban and exurban employment, service, and residential centers. General improvement in the quality of life and inter regional transportation also aided the growth of mountain and seashore related retirement, and vacation home and resort communities (Bennett 1992).

#### 1980s

The slowing of the sun-belt phenomenon and a lessening of inter-regional migration appeared to be offset by a willingness of more people to travel even further from their home to their place of work. An increasing percentage of metropolitan residents were vacationing and owning second homes in the state's periphery, intensifying flows and linkages between regions. However, the relative distance in per capita income levels between the wealthiest and poorest counties persisted at a rate approximating a 2:1 ratio, as has been the case since the 1950s. Piedmont counties also continued to see an increasing concentration of the state's residents (Gade 1989).

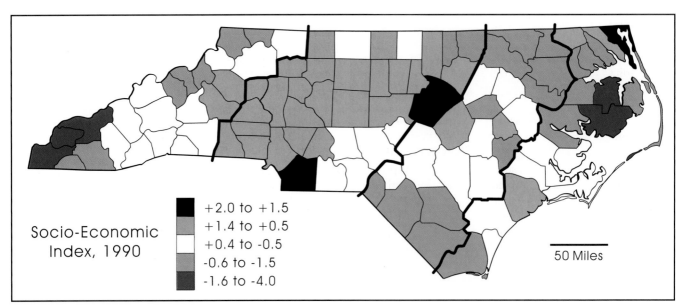

**Figure 9.13:** Socioeconomic Index.
**Source:** Gade and Cui, 1991.

Net returns of these decades of change to the 100 counties and therefore to regional development are well summed in the socio-economic index provided in Figure 9.13. This shows one set of results from a larger study evaluating three decades of change in North Carolina's counties (Gade and Cui 1994). The index was fashioned by combining different county based data sets, including: 1) unemployment rate; 2) percent persons in poverty; 3) median family income; and 4) percent aged/disabled receipts of social security income, food stamps, and AFDC aid to dependent, aged and disabled individuals. On this basis, the best conditions of life in the state (highest scores) are found, with very few exceptions, in a large set of contiguous, essentially urban, Piedmont counties. Conditions of the peripheral counties appear to worsen with increasing distance from the urban counties of the state. The reader may wish to compare socio-economic conditions as portrayed in Figure 9.13 with the North Carolina Enterprise Tiers shown in Figure 9.15.

### The State Anchors Its Economic Development Policy

Over time, what has been the state response to obvious needs in socioeconomic development and to patterns of regional disparity? It is Archibald Murphey, a lawyer and state senator from Orange County, who is generally credited with providing the initial direction for what became the persistent twin cornerstones in state planning policy: transportation systems and public education. In 1815, Murphey presented the first set of state economic development reports, wherein the problem of people fleeing the state for perceived better opportunities in the West (of the United States) was highlighted: "thousands of our poorer citizens . . . . being literally driven away by the prospects of poverty" (Escott 1991, 35). The state chartered the North Carolina Railroad in 1849 and underwrote two-thirds of the cost of construction to link Goldsboro with Charlotte via Raleigh, Hillsborough, Salisbury and Concord. Commercial agriculture flourished in the Piedmont and central Coastal Plain by the 1880s, and with it the market towns. As a result, further initiatives for rail transportation were forthcoming.

North Carolina became known as the "Good Roads State" in the early part of the 20th century. Continued investment in road building earned the state the sobriquet of "progressive" southern state, a notion further enhanced by a depression-era measure to deal more directly with the problems of local roads. In 1931 North Carolina became the first state in the union to take over responsibility for all county roads, an important transportation development move followed subsequently only by Virginia and West Virginia. Then, in the 1940s, Governor Kerr Scott's "farm to market" road program was instituted to directly affect economic development of rural areas. One of the most extensive networks of state maintained road systems in the nation evolved gradually over half a century (Escott 1991, 36), a transportation system whose future was secured in 1989 by the legislative enactment of the $9 billion Highway Trust Fund. The Highway Trust Fund provided the financial resources in support of the state's ambi-

tious policy of building four-lane roads accessible to every nook and cranny of the state. Yet, it may be that this extraordinary emphasis in support for land transportation has further encouraged the concentration of industrial and urban development in the Piedmont. Recently, this emphasis was further aided by a legislative yearly subsidy to improve passenger rail transportation between Charlotte and Raleigh, through the Urban Crescent. Although this creates the prospect of further intensifying Piedmont economic development, this can also be seen as a move to redirect the geography of economic development by initiating the Global TransPark in the eastern Coastal Plains as an important regional development effort in the traditional spirit of 'transportation improvement' for a needy rural peripheral region.

Although a persistent emphasis in state policy toward providing an excellent transportation system has aided in concentrating development in the Piedmont Crescent, it is also important to understand that, with the exceptions of a few peripheral rural locations, roads now connect all parts of the state thoroughly and efficiently. Whether this means that the statewide rural peripheral-urban center differences highlighted in Figure 9.13 would have worsened without these transportation linkages, is perhaps a moot question. The fact is that people are now able to commute further distances for the urban jobs, and are less likely to change their residence to be nearer the job location. Even so, other factors enter the rural-urban development dichotomy, as we shall see.

By contrast, the state's role in educational improvement does not have as glorious a history. North Carolina was first to have a statewide public education equalizing program, inaugurated in 1900. This was complemented by assuming, in 1931 and 1933, at the height of the depression years, the responsibility of paying the operating expenses for the constitutionally mandated school term. In addition, the state has had considerable success in establishing, some three to four decades later, a comprehensive 58-campus system of community and technical colleges, as well as a 16-campus university system. On the downside, the state lags considerably the national average in the percent of its population having completed high school. The problem is compounded by the relatively low state wages paid public school teachers, who then find the wealthier counties willing to provide a salary supplement. Considerable unevenness in the quality of public education develops as the better teachers are drawn to the wealthier counties, or to those that otherwise place a higher premium on public education and are willing to provide the tax dollars for salaries, as well as for facilities. In spite of the promise provided by the 1985 Basic Education Program, that all school systems would have equal resources available to secure an adequate education program, a number of counties found it necessary, in 1997, to sue the state in order to ensure a compliance with this goal (see Chapter 7).

## A Federal Role

It is likely that state initiatives have contributed to the centralization of economic development in the Urban Crescent, with the potential result of deepening regional disparities. This core-periphery development condition is hardly unusual in economically advanced countries, and it is a special trait of states in the United States. For North Carolina, having one hundred counties has additionally caused an unwieldy passage of top-down central government support programs, whether from national or state government levels. Complicating the flow problem was the vast increase in such programs during the 1960s. By 1968 there were eight major federal programs that required multi-jurisdictional cooperation. To insure a smoother transition the U.S. Congress passed the Intergovernmental Cooperation Act in 1968, followed shortly by Circular A-95 from the federal Office of Management and Budget. This required a regional board review of local applications for federal grants. Within a few years this led to the emergence of 670 super county/municipality regional organizations throughout the country. Seventeen were founded in North Carolina after the General Assembly's 1969 edict, that the Department of Administration work in developing "a system of multi county regional planning districts to cover the entire state" (Regionalism... 1980, p. 3). This was not to be achieved in any haphazard way, but through administrative constellations. Thus regional boundaries were defined by careful evaluation of the following factors: "the economic and social interrelationships between urban centers and surrounding areas, existing cooperative programs between counties and municipalities, and the existence of physical boundaries, such as mountain ranges or rivers, that might separate one region from another; ... no region (was) to contain less that three counties, nor fewer than 100,000 people" (Regionalism.... 1980, p. 3). This was truly a comprehensive and worthy prescription toward delineating ideal functional regions from a geographer's perspective. Local governments chose whether they supported a Council of Government (COG) or a Regional Planning and Economic Development Commission (RPEDC) form of regional organization. Only five organizations chose the latter, though it merits noting that the RPEDCs, Regions A, B, C, Q, and R, are geographic opposite extremes in the state and in the economic periphery as well (Figure 9.6). Internal schisms in Region G, the Piedmont Triad COG, led in 1978 to a division comprising the present regions G and I.

## Lead Regional Organizations

To complement its regional policy the state, in May of 1971, created the Lead Regional Organization (LRO) concept. The result was to assign all regional programs administered through the state and the federal governments to the COGs and the RPEDCs. In spite of considerable criticism, especially from metro regions who thought of LROs as administrative devices that favored rural and peripheral areas at the expense of urban development, the LROs became the vehicle for funneling federally mandated and state resources to local governments. Other critics pointed to the absence of LROs' taxing powers, the inability to condemn property, and the absence of independent power to implement their own plans. In addition, the fact that local governments can renounce membership at any time, was suggested to be a critical factor weakening the organizations (Stuart 1979). On the other hand, the LROs brought important benefits to the table. They had a strong state mandate, and developed considerable expertise in delivering federal funding to localities. They served increasingly well in articulating local needs to higher levels of government and provided mid-level support in attracting federal funds to areas in special need. In an article written by the Executive Director of the Region D Council of Governments, a coalition of seven counties and a handful of municipalities in North Carolina's northwestern corner, he listed the primary purposes of the Region 'D' COG as identified by its Executive Board:

> 1) to serve as a forum for discussion of regional problems and interests; a facilitator of good intergovernmental relations among member governments, as well as a means of resolving conflicts among member governments;
>
> 2) to function as an 'umbrella' agency to coordinate other regional public agencies of the seven county area in order to ensure that public efforts act in concert and avoid duplications of efforts; to facilitate effective communications among member governments;
>
> 3) to promote efforts to use economies of scale for member governments in such matters as providing services through sharing scarce or specialized resources;
>
> 4) to promote and exercise leadership among member governments by serving as an advocate for individual governments; and
>
> 5) to serve as a consensus voice for member governments on matters mutually impacting or affecting them (Fender 1991, p. 94).

Clearly this indicates a bottom-up functioning mid-level governmental agency. It is equally clear that to the services listed above, offered in response to local government needs, there are important services that facilitates federal and state revenue sharing of specially funded programs and review processes for the localities. However, only four of these were in 1989 uniformly administered by the eighteen regional councils (Figure 9.14).

This absence of uniformity in LRO accepted responsibilities extended to matters of economic development. Among the

| Major Regional Council Programs or Services | Lead Regional Organization | | | | | | | | | | | | | | | | | |
|---|---|---|---|---|---|---|---|---|---|---|---|---|---|---|---|---|---|---|
| | A | B | C | D | E | F | G | H | I | J | K | L | M | N | O | P | Q | R |
| Program on Aging | ◆ | ◆ | ◆ | ◆ | ◆ | ◆ | ◆ | ◆ | ◆ | ◆ | ◆ | ◆ | ◆ | ◆ | ◆ | ◆ | ◆ | ◆ |
| State Data Center Alliance | ◆ | ◆ | ◆ | ◆ | ◆ | ◆ | ◆ | ◆ | ◆ | ◆ | ◆ | ◆ | ◆ | ◆ | ◆ | ◆ | ◆ | ◆ |
| Emergency Medical Services | ◆ | ◆ | ◆ | ◆ | ◆ | ◆ | ◆ | ◆ | ◆ | ◆ | ◆ | ◆ | ◆ | ◆ | ◆ | ◆ | ◆ | ◆ |
| Grantsmanship | ◆ | ◆ | ◆ | ◆ | ◆ | | ◆ | ◆ | ◆ | | ◆ | ◆ | ◆ | ◆ | ◆ | ◆ | ◆ | ◆ |
| Intergovernmental Review | ◆ | ◆ | ◆ | ◆ | ◆ | ◆ | ◆ | ◆ | ◆ | ◆ | ◆ | ◆ | ◆ | ◆ | ◆ | ◆ | ◆ | ◆ |
| Job Training Partnership Act | ◆ | ◆ | ◆ | ◆ | ◆ | ◆ | | ◆ | ◆ | | ◆ | ◆ | ◆ | ◆ | ◆ | ◆ | ◆ | ◆ |
| Appalachian Regional Commission | ◆ | ◆ | ◆ | ◆ | ◆ | | | ◆ | | | | | | | | | | |
| Coastal Area Management Act | | | | | | | | | | | | | | | ◆ | | ◆ | ◆ |
| Community Development Block Grant | ◆ | ◆ | ◆ | ◆ | ◆ | ◆ | ◆ | | ◆ | | ◆ | ◆ | ◆ | ◆ | ◆ | ◆ | ◆ | ◆ |
| Economic Development Administration | ◆ | ◆ | | ◆ | | | | | | | | ◆ | | | | ◆ | ◆ | ◆ |
| Farmers Home Administration/Housing | | ◆ | | ◆ | | | ◆ | | | | ◆ | | | | | | | ◆ |
| Housing/Urban Development - Section 8 | | | ◆ | ◆ | | | ◆ | | | | | | | | | | | |
| Land and Water Conservation Fund | ◆ | ◆ | | ◆ | ◆ | ◆ | | | ◆ | | | | | ◆ | | | | |
| Small Business Administration 504 Certified Development Corp. | ◆ | | ◆ | ◆ | ◆ | | | ◆ | | ◆ | ◆ | ◆ | | | ◆ | ◆ | ◆ | |
| Senior Employment | | ◆ | ◆ | | | | | | | ◆ | ◆ | ◆ | | ◆ | | ◆ | ◆ | ◆ |
| Revolving Loan Fund | ◆ | | | | ◆ | | | | | | ◆ | | | | | ◆ | | ◆ |
| Child Development | | | | ◆ | ◆ | | | | | | | | | | | | | |
| Computer Services | | | | ◆ | | ◆ | | | | | | | | | | | ◆ | |

**Figure 9.14:** Programs and Services of the LROs.
**Source:** Office of Intergovernmental Relations, Department of Administration, State of North Carolina, 1989.

half a dozen or so services offered that are linked directly to aspect of economic development, none are offered across the board. It appears, in fact, that the regions that are especially in need of economic development have less of these services offered through their Councils.

*A Balanced Growth Policy*

Governor Hunt's first administration tried to ameliorate this situation when, in 1976, it initiated a balanced growth policy. The objective was to channel federal resources to disadvantaged small towns and rural areas. A rather simple formula was devised to determine degree of regional disadvantage for each of the LROs:

*% of total jobs in region/*
*% of total state working population in region*

That the formula masks other critical conditions, such as comparative growth rates, labor market and wage conditions, and unemployment differences, appeared to either be of little significance or felt to unduly complicate the model. When applied to actual conditions the model yielded a range from .75 to 1.16, with the low ranked LROs included: R (.75), A (.77), D and M (.84), and N (.87). The high ranked regions included: E (1.16), F (1.08), J (1.07), and G (1.05), thus reflecting core-periphery contrasts (Gade 1989). Aided by President Carter's belief in the virtue

of nationally balanced growth, the state policy initially was successful in obtaining federal agency agreements to steer $1.2 billion (out of a total state annual federal allocation of $7.6 billion) to the so defined disadvantaged regions. Soon, however, the initiative lost out to a new federal administration.

For rural LROs, the Executive Director of Region D COG noted, "(t)he ultimate effectiveness of the regional council in rural areas has to lie in their ability to meet locally perceived needs either through actually providing the needed services and resources or by being in a position to broker the services and resources of other governmental and private sources...., (Region D COG) has been more involved in building local capacity" (Fender 1991, p. 99). Certainly this is a much less ambitious objective for the rural disadvantaged areas than that envisaged by the Governor's Office, but perhaps more reasonable in the context of the already diminishing flow of federal dollars to the localities. Still, the focus of LRO activities has always been more social than economic development in nature.

***The Entrepreneurial Region***

New federal and state agendas of decentralized government, decreased public involvement in the affairs of individuals and their communities, and a greater expectation of local initiatives developed in the 1980s and has continued into the 1990s. This new vision of public responsibility is coupled with corporate restructuring and global investment initiatives, which seem to further the interests of those growth regions that possess the appropriate capitalopportunity structure, while providing disincentives for positive change in the lagging regions. Relating to this new vision is the not so subtle philosophic shift away from the social welfare to the economic development agenda.

The greater capacity of Piedmont counties to marshal and assert their entrepreneurial and cooperative spirit resulted in the founding of three economic development partnerships. For example, the Greater Charlotte Economic Development Corporation was the product of an early 1980s effort in joint promotion of the region's economic potential. It held a meeting in 1990 to discuss strategies for operating under its new name, the Carolina Partnership, Inc. While largely a chamber of commerce idea, it was soon broadened to include other citizen groups, but critically, it remained a private enterprise venture! So did the two other Piedmont groupings, the Piedmont Triad Partnership and the Research Triangle Partnership. These "partnerships" evolved independently, without the urging of the state and without the counsel or direct support of the COGs. Business interests, for example, fused the formerly disharmonious Regions I and G COGs. A marked policy shift from public to private sector regional economic planning initiatives mirrored the new federal philosophy of the 1980s, but especially so as it reflected regional economic development goals.

With the beginning of the second Hunt Administration in 1992 came renewed support for state involvement in regional development favoring the more disadvantaged counties. Most critically, this was to be accomplished through the Governor's Industrial Recruitment Competitive Fund (IRCF), funded with an initial appropriation of $5 million in 1993. The Fund, which provides $1,000 for each job created by a new or relocating industry, complemented other state industrial investment incentives. These include: 1) the Building Renovation Fund for counties declared economically distressed; 2) the Income Tax Credit of $2,500 for each new employee beyond nine that is hired by an industry located in a distressed county; and 3) the Department of Transportation Site Access Program for roads built to new industrial facilities. It should be noted that of the $3.5 million IRCF monies dispensed in 1993-94, about one third went to the urbanized Piedmont Crescent counties, while only about one half of the new jobs generated went to economically distressed counties. Figure 9.15 locates the counties receiving funds as white dots superimposed on the 1997 North Carolina Enterprise Tiers, a map demonstrating the degree of economic distress by the allocating of greater state support to those worse off. Developing a statistical device for state support is obviously not the same as getting industrial clients to commit to build plants in particular places. For many distressed counties, attracting any manufacturing enterprise may elude even the most skilled industrial recruiter with the most attractive public support packet! The North Carolina legislature's enthusiasm for the Fund clearly dampened as its allocation of $20 million for 1994 was scaled down to $5 million for 1995. Citizens up in arms over direct grants and other public support given to private industry, took the state to court in 1997 to contest the constitutional legality of state activity and programs in this arena. Though the state won, opinions continue to be mixed on this issue.

In 1993, a North Carolina Economic Development Board was convened to assess the state's annual $100 million economic development program. The total program was found to be quite inefficient in its delivery, an "Octopus with many tentacles" (Tuttle 1994, 4), and the Board recommended streamlin-

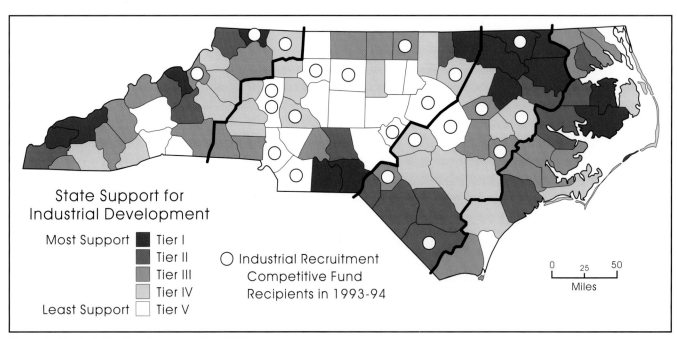

**Figure 9.15:** North Carolina Enterprise Tiers, 1997.
**Source:** Department of Commerce, State of North Carolina, n.d.

322

ing the delivery process by creating a set of regions through which economic policy could be implemented and resources re-allocated. Obviously, no thought was given to the existence of the 18 Lead Regional Organizations, that in some cases already had clear commitment to economic development planning. In 1994 the General Assembly created five new economic development commissions (EDCs), and provided a $2 million budget for their initiation to be shared with existing partnerships. It was expected that the EDCs would evolve into partnerships like the three in the Piedmont, and thereafter join the Partnership Board. After some initial juggling of a few counties for most desired alliance, seven Economic Development Commissions (Partnerships) are now in place Figure 9.16. In 1995, the North Carolina Partnership for Economic Development, chaired by the Secretary of the Department of Commerce, was founded as the state/private enterprise joint venture for planning and implementing the new state policy through the seven partnerships (Tuttle 1995, 16). Partnership boundaries are determined by local governments using the following criteria: primary economic linkages, principally through commuting patterns; existing development organizations and relationships; natural boundaries; principal economic

centers or "engines" within the region; anticipated major projects; and other bases for cooperation (*Making North Carolina....* 1994, 16). This is not a set of criteria significantly different from those earlier used in defining the existing LRO boundaries. However, there are 18 LROs and only seven Partnerships! Figure 9.17 shows the degree to which a coincidence exists between the two sets of regions. Seen here are the 14 counties that appear to have been maneuvered out of place, in the context of their continuing membership in an LRO where boundaries do not coincide with the particular county's position in a new partnership. These "overlap" counties take on a regional pattern of their own, especially in identifying a kind of intermediate region positioned between the wealthier Piedmont Crescent counties and disadvantaged eastern counties. Note also the comparison here to the location of low level socioeconomic counties in Figures 9.13 and 9.15. The vast majority of the state's more disadvantaged counties are gathered into the larger and more peripherally located Northeast Economic Region, Southeastern Economic Commission, and the Western Economic Commission. In the latter, only Cleveland County, which chose to switch out of the Western Economic Commission, exists as an "overlap" case. Otherwise, a clearly disjunct western region of 22 relatively disparate counties, stretching 250 miles from Cherokee County on the Georgia border northeast to Alleghany County on the Virginia border, comprise its own partnership.

An interesting regionalizing system has evolved where internal geographic harmony seems to come natural to only the three Piedmont Region partnerships, and possibly also to the Global TransPark Region, though the latter seems more of a top-down creation. These four partnerships clearly have their "economic engines" in place, but what about the largely non-urban peripheral partnerships? The Northeastern Economic Region is totally without a dominant central place. The influence of Asheville in the Western Economic Commission reaches not much beyond the counties adjacent to Buncombe. In the Southeastern Eco-

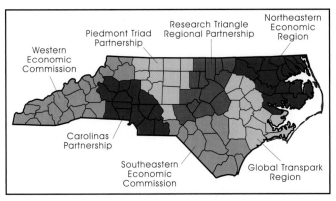

**Figure 9.16:** Economic Development Commission Regions in 1999.

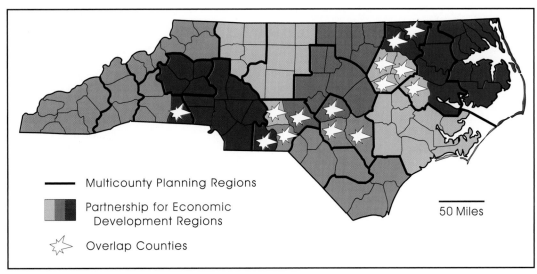

Multicounty Planning Regions

Partnership for Economic Development Regions

Overlap Counties

50 Miles

**Figure 9.17:** Regions Gone Astray?
**Source:** Gade, 1995.

nomic Commission, the two medium sized cities of Fayetteville and Wilmington may find that they have too little in common to comfortably provide the leadership needed for the Partnership.

What about the future role of the LROs? A traditional problem for the state in regional politics is the general absence of regional alignment among state agency geographical divisions. As recently as 1992, this was seen by the North Carolina General Assembly, Government Performance Audit Committee as a situation conducive to inefficiencies and lack of cooperation among agencies charged with furthering the interests of the citizens (GPAC 1992, 4.3). LROs are assigned the task of supporting local governments and of channeling, if not administering, the revenue flow of federally mandated programs to localities. In post-federal times, as governmental functions and facilities decentralize and the public purse is weakening, the LROs situation appears to have weakened considerably. At present, the worst case scenario appears to be realized by Region H, whose four counties have been absorbed into no less than four different economic development partnerships. Whose interests are being served here?

### Who is Being Served? Glocalization - North Carolina Style

The idea behind the somewhat awkward term, glocalization, is that global competition makes regional/local cooperation necessary for expanding existing internationally competitive industries and in attracting new regional investment. The avowed purpose of Governor Hunt's administration was to provide direct state support for the localization of new industrial investment in lagging regions, so the question now focuses on the extent to which the new state measures may succeed. Will the new regional delimitations for economic development help localities define their place in the world, or will it deepen their struggle for maintaining some measure of community identity? Will the place wars (Haider 1992), which deepened in North Carolina through

the 1980s diffusion of county-based economic/industrial development committees/boards, be intensified where independence of action appears to be usurped by 1) a new, powerful urban presence; or 2) the inability of a more peripheral region, without a competitive urban center, to remain business investment attractive? Some of the evolved Partnership Regions may have difficulties in identifying their "core competencies" due to their quite large, predominately rural, and culturally diffuse territories. Certainly the state is hoping that this new approach will realize a long sought North Carolina goal–providing an even playing field for its varied regions in their search for parity in socioeconomic development opportunity and cultural sustainability. For residents of the non-urban periphery, there may be less appreciation for the sentiment expressed in a *Charlotte Observer* editorial piece, "regionalism provides an avenue for communities to avoid being lost in the world, if they can overcome their fear of being lost in the region," (Bradbury 1994, 18A). The newly formalized Partnership regions of these counties, absent in 'internal economic engines' may provide for their residents a straitjacket within which they will have even less assurance of needed state support for economic development initiatives.

As discussed in this chapter, those implementing decisions affecting the lives in the state's communities operate from a profusion of overlapping regions. Our major example, contrasting the LROs with the new Partnerships, suggest some of the community difficulties that result from this confusion of regions. We suggest that a simpler approach be used to identify and derive boundaries for regions meaningful in North Carolina's evolution of settlement patterns and long term community networking context. The following four chapters, will deal with the realities of land and life throughout the state, with the information organized by the four primary regions, and within these, by the thirteen state geographic regions and their 100 counties.

# 10

# Tidewater Region

## INTRODUCTION

Coastal North Carolina presents some remarkable contrasts with a physical landscape of over 300 miles of wide beaches and barrier islands, vast tidal flats and sounds, and intricate waterways. Its cultural landscape includes small villages reminiscent of the early 1900's, territorially demanding new resort communities and booming port cities, as well as huge corporate farms. Although different in physical appearance from other North Carolina regions, this region shares common problems of land and people. What tends to unite the counties of the Tidewater Region are the commonalties in both their physical and their cultural environments. These counties are mostly comprised of low lying lands within, or in close proximity to, the tidal ranges of the Atlantic Ocean and its riverine estuaries; lands that were among the earliest settled in the state (Figure 10.1)

Many communities of the sounds and estuaries are deeply anchored in a history that continues to be written in the visible landscape of antebellum homes and street plans developed in the 18th Century. Their contemplative demeanor, persisting through a century of stable or declining economic fortunes, contrasts strongly with the pulsating drive of development about to overcome the communities of the barrier islands and coastal Cape Fear. In economic terms, Tidewater counties are mostly focused on the primary activities of forestry, agriculture and mineral extraction, or on water related resources such as fishing and recreational activities. All are members of the Coastal Resources Commission, and thus subject to the land use requirements pertaining to the Coastal Areas Management Act (CAMA). Many localities continue to reflect a powerful combination of bounteous natural environments, that periodically display their explosive character, and a quiet relaxed life style, that persists in maintaining a strong visible landscape linkage to their cultural history. These unique environments are attractive to those seeking energy and inspiration for their creative impulses, from artists to movie studios, as well as to seasonal vacationists and retirees looking for rest and renewal from the stresses of contemporary life.

In this chapter we will deal briefly with early patterns of human occupance prior to assessing the nature of a physical environment that has variously attracted and repelled settlers, but not, in many cases, without major modifications to its natural character. Then we focus on the promises and difficulties of present day economic activities, land use, and maintenance of environmental integrity. Finally, we will discuss in greater detail the localities and communities of Albemarle, Pamlico, and Cape Fear, the three state geographic regions of the Tidewater Region that are wholly or largely contained within it. The reader should know that this primary region seems to have attracted more attention from writers, be they naturalists, scientists, or travel authors, than any other region in the state. Note, for example, the recent contributions of Barefoot (1995), Bishir and Southern (1996), Frankenberg (1997), Morris (1998), Pilkey and coworkers (1998), Schoenbaum (1992), the Simpsons (1990 and 1997), and Stick (1998).

## EARLY PATTERNS OF HUMAN SETTLEMENT

### Europeans and American Indians

It is believed that the first European setting eyes on what is presently North Carolina was Giovanni da Verrazzano, an Italian exploring eastern North America in the service of the French King. In 1524, he happened upon the Outer Banks across which he spied the vast expanse of Pamlico Sound. He thought this to be the long-sought western oceanic passage to the Orient and referred to it as "the way to China, India, and Cathay" (Schoenbaum 1992, 22). Farther north he made landfall at Nags Head, where the beach, the maritime forest, and the existence of a peaceful native population led him to name this place Arcadia (from the Greek meaning a place of rural peace and simplicity). In fact, Algonkian Indians had been inhabiting these eastern coastal parts of the Carolinas at least since 1000 AD, and archeological evidence indicate that the region has been sporadically inhabited for 10,000 years. Some 3,000 years ago their ancestors moved from a primitive hunting and fishing society to a more sedentary existence living in villages and depending on agriculture and trade. According to Schoenbaum (p. 19), the Algonkian people had settled an area along the North American eastern seaboard that extended south to include almost precisely the region of estuarine North Carolina. To their immediate west were the Tuscarora, an Iroquoian people, and to the south of the Neuse River were tribes of Siouan lineage. Present day evidence of this Native American past is found in the place names of the region. For example, Chowan, Roanoke, Pocosin, Hatteras, Neuse, Pamlico, Corolla and Core (Core Banks) are all place name derivatives from earlier Indian tribes.

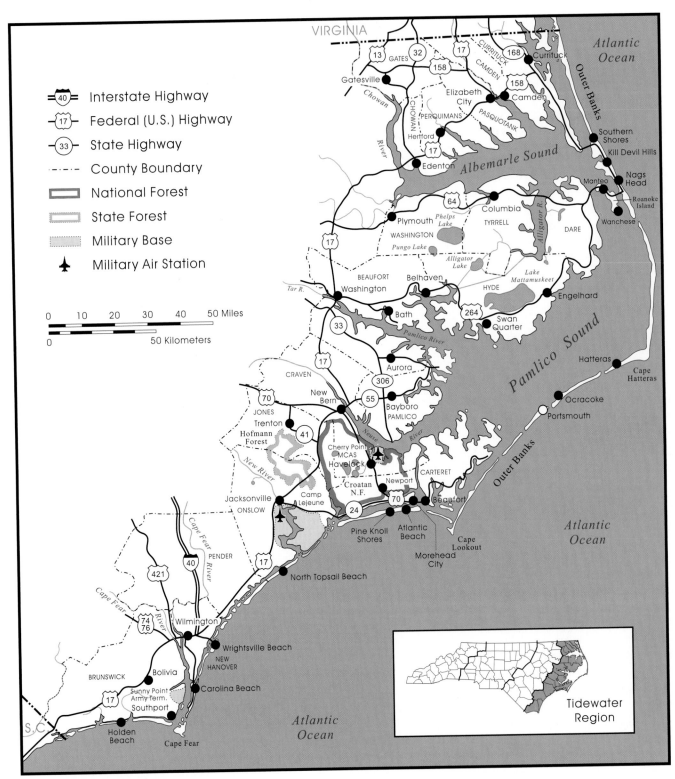

**Figure 10.1:** Tidewater General Location Map.

326

### The English and Virginians Come to the Tidewater Region

European settlement dates to 1585 and 1587, with the remnants of the earlier settlement returning to England and the latter, Sir Walter Raleigh's "Lost Colony" on Roanoke Island, leaving only scant physical evidence of their existence. In fact, it is likely that the colony's original site was inundated since sea level has risen about one meter over the ensuing 400 years. Fort Raleigh National Monument now occupies the general area (Figure 10.2). With this abortive beginning, it was not until the 1650s that fur trading posts were established to the south of the Virginia settlements of the Chesapeake, in the lands of the Albemarle. In fact, the first recorded land purchase was made by one Nathaniel Bates (Batts) who settled in what is now Perquimans County. His agreement with a local tribe was soon followed by others (Morris 1998, p. 7). This long delay in the southward expansion of the Virginians was undoubtedly influenced by the intervening broad belt of low-lying wet lands, especially the Great Dismal Swamp. However, with the eventual success of fur trappers and Indian traders came permanent settlers, to the far better drained and agriculturally much more promising interfluves of the rivers emptying into the Albemarle Sound: Chowan, Perquimans, Little, Pasqoutank, and the North. Colonial North Carolina was thus settled initially from Virginia (Watson 1987) (see Figure 10.3).

### Settling the Outer Banks

During the 18th Century, settlements flowed from the mainland to the Outer Banks, where islanders found protection from floods and high winds in the maritime forest, on the lee side of sand dunes. They eked out a sparse living raising cattle, catching fish and scavenging shipwrecks. The villages of Portsmouth and Ocracoke, and many smaller current settlements along the Outer Banks, owe their survival to those early settlers who understood and respected the environment. While they appreciated the protection offered by the sound side maritime forest environment, they also toiled with the persistent difficulties in the transport linkage from ocean to sound through the ever shifting inlets. Ocracoke Inlet, for example, had emerged as the most important access route during the early Federal Period, and considerable concern had been expressed over its natural dynamics as an impediment to trade. Witness the comments of A. D. Murphey in 1816, (as quoted in Dunbar 1958, 27):

No part of our coast seem to be subject to greater or more frequent changes than that near Ocracoke. . . . The Inlet has widened very much within the last fifty years, and the depth of water across the Bar has lessened. . . . Vessels drawing more than eight feet water, have to lighter in crossing the swash; and this circumstance, added to the other of there being no harbor, renders the Navigation through this Inlet not only inconvenient, but often extremely dangerous. To lessen this inconvenience, it has been proposed to use Camels for taking vessels across the swash; and to lessen the dangers of Navigation, it has been proposed to

sink Piers, mooring anchors and chains. The peculiar gurgling quality of the sands at this Inlet, renders it very doubtful whether any erection of piers would prove permanent.

Other inlets of that day, such as the Roanoke and Currituck, have been thought to provide opportunities for artificial improvement to secure permanent ocean access. In 1787, the Colonial Assembly authorized individuals to construct an inlet, presumably an improvement of the existing Roanoke Inlet, that would enable the "extensive, fertile country watered by the Roanoke (River) and its tributaries" to rival the concentration of productive trade that built a town the size of Norfolk (Dunbar 1958, p. 24). This effort failed, as did attempts to bypass the fickle inlets by the building of the Dismal Swamp Canal (Figure 10.3), connecting the Albemarle Sound region to the Chesapeake, as well as the Clubfoot and Harlowe's Creek Canal, that connected the Neuse River to Beaufort, thus avoiding the problems of Ocracoke. Over the next century the economic fortunes of the Outer Banks continued to decline (CP 10.1). Presently Ocracoke and many coastal villages are recovering due to tourism, but Portsmouth, with its cluster of a few original buildings maintained by the National Park Service, is now a ghost of the village that grew to 600 inhabitants (Figure 10.2).

Resort development started more formally in the 1830s with Nags Head (da Verrazzano's Arcadia) on Bodie Island as the first seaside seasonal recreation community. Soon after, in the 1850s, Morehead City was founded on the mainland of Bogue Sound and grew in importance with the completion of the rail connection to Raleigh toward the end of the century. A railroad was also built in the late 1800s from Wilmington to Wrightsville Beach to open up more beachfront for vacation homes and seaside tourism. Some early communities have not survived the rigors of coastal storms and flooding. For example, Diamond City on Shackleford Island was abandoned in 1899, and the village of Holden Beach was completely destroyed by Hurricane Hazel in 1954, only to be rebuilt with a greater density of homes than before. Since the 1940s, bulldozers have competed with hurricanes for changing the character of the coast.

### Settling the Estuarines and Inner Tidewater

Meanwhile, colonial villages and towns emerged on the estuarine shores, especially where physical sites favored a natural harbor and where their specific situations were supported by an evolving agricultural hinterland and by ease of access to navigable rivers. Having a reasonably direct route to a navigable inlet to facilitate a maritime connection aided in the expansion of a few of these early urban centers. Bath, the first incorporated town in the state, was founded in 1705 on the northern shore of the Pamlico River, in the center of a small group of farms and plantations lying on both sides of the river and sound. In spite of a decade of local rebellion and Indian strife, the town prospered, being designated Port Bath in 1715 and becoming the terminal of a post road leading to Edenton, the center of the Albemarle settle-

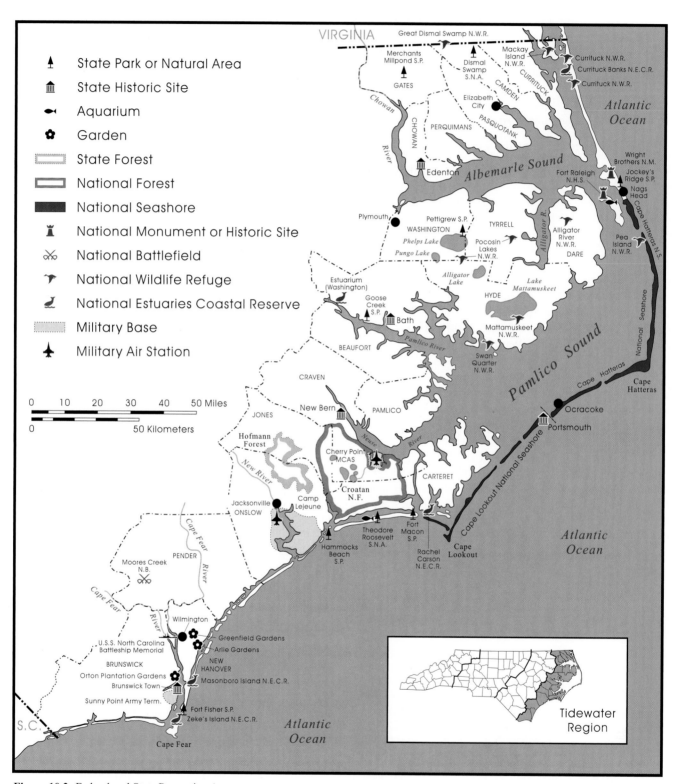

**Figure 10.2:** Federal and State Recreation Areas.

328

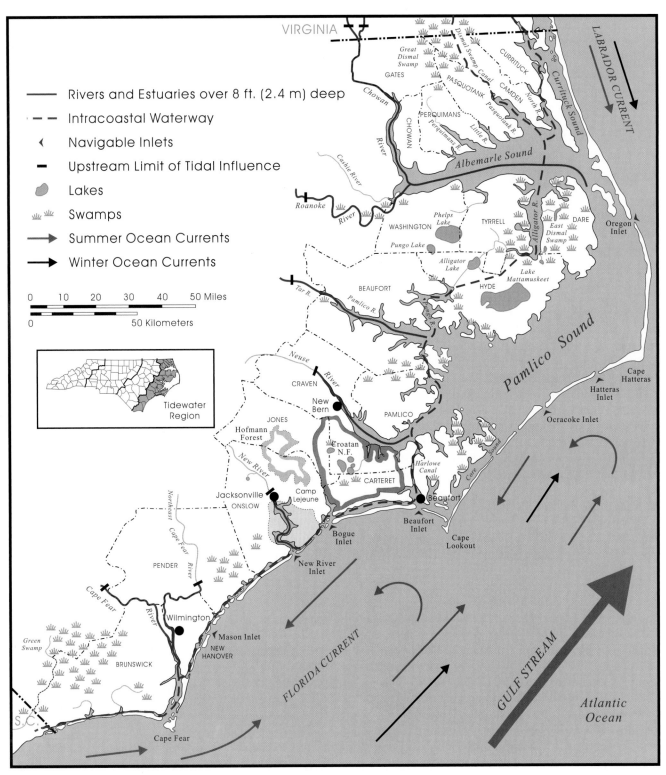

**Figure 10.3:** Water and Wetlands Features.

329

ments. Though never growing to be very large, even by standards of colonial times, Bath did gain visibility by being the home of several colonial governors, and the periodic meeting place of the Colonial Assembly until 1752. It also gained notoriety by being, beginning in 1717, the home base of Edward Teach, Blackbeard the Pirate. His 100 foot flagship, the Queen Anne's Revenge, was shipwrecked in 1718 about one and a half miles off Atlantic Beach. Rediscovered in 1997, it is now being salvaged with some of the artifacts going to the North Carolina Maritime Museum in Beaufort (Allegood 1997).

Edenton was founded in 1712, 52 years after the County of Albemarle was organized and had elected its first Assembly. Although equally slow in growth, Edenton benefited by being the major center in the Albemarle and by emerging as the unofficial capital of the North Carolina Colony in 1729, when the territory became a royal colony. However, the population grew more rapidly south of the Albemarle, and in 1746 the colonial capital was established at New Bern by Crown Law. Even so, Edenton flourished in the latter half of the eighteen century with the post road that connected Williamsburg and Philadelphia to New York. Edenton became the agricultural center of a region specializing in the commercial production of tobacco, corn, naval stores and wood products. Simultaneously it became the leading port for the waterborne trade connecting the Roanoke Inlet, then open to the Atlantic Ocean, and Roanoke Island settlements to interior locations in the Albemarle and Roanoke River upcountry. Shallow-draught coastal service boats brought rum, silk, linens, spices, and sugar. For close to a century, Edenton was North Carolina's leading entrepot and remains today exemplary of the antebellum town, retaining its 18th Century town plan and a wonderful collection of North Carolina historic architecture (CP 10.2 and CP 10.3).

Settling of the lower Neuse River basin was led in the first decade of the 18th Century by Quaker and French Huguenot families. The founding of New Bern at the juncture of the Neuse and Trent rivers had to await a group of Swiss and German Palatinate settlers who arrived in 1710, initially calling their community Neuse-Bern. The town's designation as colonial capital was implemented in 1765 when newly arrived William Tryon called the first Colonial Assembly meeting there. Subsequently, he built his 'palace' and the permanent seat of the Assembly in New Bern (CP 10.4). At the turn of the 19th Century New Bern, specializing in the export of tobacco and naval stores, prospered as the main port city accessible to Ocracoke Inlet, which for a long time was the major passage for North Carolina overseas trade. New Bern was the most populous town in North Carolina until 1840, and in spite of being ravaged by major fires a number of times over two centuries there remains a considerable stock of buildings of historic value. An area coincidental with that plotted on a 1769 map of the town was designated a "historic district" by the National Register of Historic Places in 1973. Much of the old commercial downtown and adjacent residential blocks is preserved here, including an eclectic mix of fourteen architectural styles dating back to the 1760s (Barnett 1993).

Local Indians referred to the estuary of the only North Carolina river actually emptying into the Atlantic Ocean as the Chicora. It was the early Europeans who, while exploring for places to settle along the Carolinas' coast, labeled this the Cape Fear, and it was so noted on the Molyneaux globe of 1592 (Schoenbaum 1992, 222). In his *Islands, Capes, and Sounds: The North Carolina Coast*, Schoenbaum quotes what he considers the very best description of the origin of the Cape Fear name as provided by George Davis in an article for the South Atlantic Magazine in January, 1879 (p. 223):

Looking then to the Cape for the idea and reason for its name, we find that it is the southernmost point of Smith's Island, a naked bleak elbow of sand jutting far out into the ocean. Immediately in its front are Frying Pan Shoals pushing out still farther 20 miles to sea. Together they stand for warning and woe; . . . It is the playground of billows and tempests, the kingdom of silence and awe, disturbed by no sound save the sea gull's shriek and the breaker's roar. Its whole aspect is suggestive, not of repose and beauty, but of desolation and terror. Imagination cannot adorn it. Romance cannot hallow it. Local pride cannot soften it. There it stands today, bleak and threatening and pitiless, as it stood three hundred years ago when Grenville and White came near death upon its sands. And there it will stand bleak and threatening and pitiless until the earth and sea give up their dead. And as its nature, so its name, is now, always has been, and always will be the Cape of Fear.

Land in the Cape Fear estuary was hotly contested by North Carolina and South Carolina in the early 18th Century, and into this conflict came Maurice Moore in 1727 to lay out the parameters of a new town of Brunswick on the western shore of the Cape Fear River. He did this in the hopes of gaining Crown approval for Brunswick as the center of a new colony to lie between colonial North Carolina and South Carolina. Within two years the North Carolina Assembly founded the New Hanover Precinct to extend from the White Oak River to the South Carolina border. That itself was not to be finally agreed upon until 1765. Settlement then proceeded rapidly, in part by translocated planters from South Carolina who developed large new plantations committed to growing indigo and rice with the help of large pools of slave labor. Brunswick's subsequent growth was checked by the increasing competition of the new town of Wilmington, founded in 1739 as the county seat of New Hanover County. Being farther up river also meant being further from harm's way. So it was the more exposed Brunswick that was plundered by the Spanish in 1748, and sacked by the British during the Revolutionary War. By 1830, the town was abandoned. Today, following years of archeological field work, the site is a state historic park.

Having captured the dominant position in the lower Cape Fear, Wilmington grew to become the region's only major city. It's port function is critical to its economic development, though it should be noted that Wilmington and Morehead City are very small tonnage ports by comparison to the nearest Atlantic Seaboard ports of Charleston, South Carolina, and Norfolk, Virginia.

It was the unhappy lot of the Tidewater region to move from a frontier and dominating position in North Carolina's economy to a backwater, peripheral condition over the centuries. With the emerging Piedmont as the bastion of industrial and urban development, and the declining influence of the primary activities of agriculture, forestry and fishing, there were few attempts at restarting the economic engine. One of these was the failed attempt at converting the state's largest lake, Mattamuskeet, into an agricultural empire by draining and reclaiming it. Investors bought the lake from the state in 1914 for $100,000, and began the first attempts at controlling water and drainage by canal construction. In 1925, New Holland Farms built what was thought to be the largest pumping station anywhere, and dredged miles of canals to facilitate water control. By 1932, the third set of owners had reconstructed and planted some 13,000 acres to various crops. However, the low lying nature of the terrain coupled with periodic winter storms and hurricanes, severely tested the company's engineering capability. Already the next year the venture had failed, and the lake began refilling. Two years later the property was purchased by the U.S. Government, and turned into the Mattamuskeet Migratory Bird Refuge. After the Civilian Conservation Corps had completed a spiral staircase in the smokestack of the former powerhouse converting it to an observation tower, the newly refurbished facility became the Canadian goose hunting capital of the world (Betts 1998b). Relabeled the Mattamuskeet National Wildlife Refuge, the 50,000 acre site is yearly visited by several hundred thousand migratory ducks, geese, and Tundra Swans.

## THE NATURAL LANDSCAPE

The tidewater landscape is dominated by considerable landscape variety. In essence there are three major ecosystems. On the eastern side of the Tidewater Region, facing the brunt of the Atlantic Ocean while protecting the mainland, is the barrier islands ecosystem. To the immediate west lie the sound and tidewater basins which comprise the estuary ecosystem. Finally, the upland surface ecosystem lies between the major rivers. This upland surface has a mix of poor and well drained conditions.

### Barrier Islands

The barrier islands have evolved as two distinct types. One is set close against the mainland for about 192 km (120 mi) north from the South Carolina border to Bogue Inlet. The other consists of a series of Outer Banks which extend 336 km (208 mi) north to the Virginia border. They trail out onto the continental shelf as much as 50 km (31 mi) from the mainland. Thus the North Carolina barrier island protected coastline totals 528 km, or about 328 miles. As a result of the northward moving Florida Current (a near shore finger of the Gulf Stream), the southward moving Labrador Current, and complementary longshore drifts, the islands are arranged in three major cusps, or arcs, and are separated by 22 inlets. Five of these are presently navigable depending on the size of the vessel (Figure 10.3). During the Pleistocene Ice Age, sea level was substantially lower, by as much as 132-165 meters (41-51 feet). Consequently, the shoreline was far out on the continental shelf. Sand dunes were built up along the shore by winds blowing toward the land. As the ice melted and sea level rose, between 19,000 and 5,000 years ago, these dunes became separated from the shore in places, thus forming the barrier islands. Breaching of the banks during storms caused inlets to develop and lagoons to be flooded and eventually emerge as wide, shallow sounds. Continual wave action caused the islands then to migrate toward the land, absorbing wave energy and protecting the sound. In addition, the shoreline retreated as sea level rose further (see Box 1B for further elaboration on barrier island formation theories). Today some islands are migrating landward, in effect they are rolling over, at a rate of up to 3 meters each year, while the sea level is presently rising about 30 centimeters per decade (Pilkey et al. 1978, 21).

Figure 10.4 demonstrates the natural dynamics of a typical barrier island ecosystem. Most important in understanding the difficulties of human construction here is the fact that nature is persistently at work in shifting and changing these features. In summer, the prevailing winds are from the southwest with salt sprays having a pruning effect on the woody shrubs and trees, giving these a wind form appearance. Wintry "nor'easters" have less wind driven salt effect, but are often severe, and may break through the banks to create new inlets, as was the case in 1962 when a wide inlet opened up at Buxton on Hatteras Island. As indicated in Figure 10.4, natural communities tend to parallel the shoreline with a few species dominating each narrow and elongated plant community. Nearest the ocean, herbaceous communities are dominated by beach grasses, sea oats, saltmeadow cordgrass and other salt tolerant species (Photo 1.6). Toward the more sheltered part are shrubs and low growing trees, featuring wax myrtle, yaupon, marsh elder, and stunted live oak (Photo 10.1). Farther into the landward flats of the islands a thicket woodland is dominated by red cedar, red bay, loblolly pine, live oak, and a pervasive tangle of greenbriar that contributes much to the inpenetrable nature of the thicket.

A two story maritime forest has become the most stable and the tallest plant community on the outer banks. Here we find live oak, laurel oak, red cedar, American holly, and ironwood forming the upper story, while red cedar, wild olive, red bay, flowering dogwood, willow, and wax myrtle dominate a large mix of trees, with shrubs and vines intermingling. Using aerial photography and field surveys, CAMA scientists found in 1988 that maritime forests covered about 12,000 acres, with 90 percent of this in only four major stands: the 5,000 acre northern Currituck Bank forest, the 3,000 acre Buxton Woods near the Hatteras Light House, a 1,900 acre tract near Kitty Hawk, and 755 acres at Nags

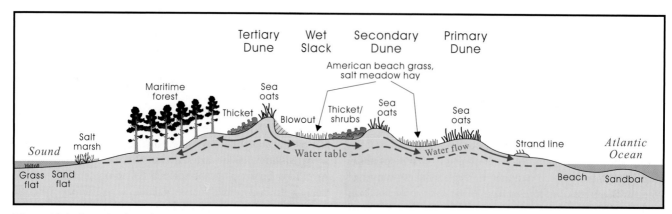

**Figure 10.4:** Cross Section of Typical Barrier Island.
**Source:** Frankenberg, 1997, 24-25 and 36-37.

Head. Even so, this acreage is but a shadow of the extensive maritime forests that covered the lee sides of the off-shore islands at the time of European colonization. They became the favorite locale for early settlements seeking shelter from weather elements and were used for construction and firewood. Today, they are again threatened and being reduced by road building and shopping centers, as well as by resort and vacation home siting (Photo 10.2). An increasing share of what remains of the maritime forest is in the North Carolina Estuarine Coastal Reserve, established in 1982 to include these and other environmentally sensitive lands as set aside for long term research, monitoring, education and compatible public uses. With the recent addition, effective April 1, 1999, of Bald Head Woods and Kitty Hawk Woods, the Estuarine Coastal Reserve now includes 12,000 acres. Included here is a 816 acre site in Buxton Woods. Much of the remainder of the Buxton Woods is gradually being developed, though in low density, fairly large home sites.

Obtaining fresh water has always been a problem for people on the outer banks. The shallow wells and cisterns of the early settlers have long since proven inadequate, and have been re- placed with deeper wells, as in the Buxton Woods; with reverse osmosis desalinization plants now located at Ocracoke, Rodanthe, Kill Devil Hills; and with water pumped from deep wells on Roanoke Island. In essence, because an island is a unitary dynamically changing ecosystem, human encroachment anywhere will impact it universally. A management plan of the human carrying capacity of the barrier islands is clearly called for.

### Tidewater Wetlands

#### Tidal Flats and Salt Water Marshes

Wide sounds and estuaries are the result of an interplay between rising sea level and eroding shorelines. North Carolina has a tidal shoreline of over 3,000 miles (4,800 km), ranking it sixth in the nation. Its estuarine zones, areas of flooded coastal rivers and sounds, total almost three million acres or 4,687 square miles (1,200,000 ha), making this the leading area of coastal water on the Atlantic Seaboard. In order of size, the Pamlico Sound is by far the largest with its 1,622 square miles. Then follows Albemarle Sound with 492 sq.mi, Currituck Sound (116 sq.mi), and Core

**Photo 10.1:** Windblown vegetation on the Outer Banks. Salt spray kills off buds on the windward side causing a 'banner' effect. Dunes are migrating over juniper trees causing their gradual demise (Photo courtesy of H.D. Stillwell).

**Photo 10.2:** While a large percentage of the shrubs of the sound side thickets have given way to roads and homes, a sufficient coverage remains to provide some shelter from excessive winds. Photo is from Topsail Island, Pender County.

Sound (88 sq.mi). Comparatively speaking North Carolina's contiguous sounds are about 84.5 per cent of the size of the Chesapeake Bay. Even so, the Albemarle and Pamlico sounds have the least waterborne commercial trade and transportation for its size in the United States. Thus, the area also has the least port activity. The primary inhibiting factor is the lack of adequate access to the Atlantic Ocean given the shallow, shifting nature of the few inlets existing north of Morehead City. It is understandable, therefore, that the small tonnage of waterborne cargo shipped on the sounds is mostly internal. Half of the waterborne cargo of about two million tons per year is mined at the phosphate mines of Aurora in Beaufort County, and barged in the form of fertilizer materials to Morehead City (Photo 10.3). In return, the phosphate company receives liquid sulphur. Some 25% of the cargo transported on the sounds is locally derived pulpwood transported to mills, such as the Weyerhouser plants at New Bern and Plymouth (Box 5.2) (Stanley 1992, 12-13). Passing through the estuaries at their coastal perimeter is the Intracoastal Waterway (Photos 1.7 and 10.4). This transportation artery provides 260 miles of protected and maintained navigation for commercial and recreational vessels (Stillwell and Leahy 1970).

Tidal flats are formed as sea level fluctuates and fine sediment and organic matter are deposited. As salt water of the ocean works its way into the sounds and mixes with the fresh water emptying from the rivers, tidal flats become the brackish wetlands of the intertidal zone. From the perspective of protecting and regulating the use of these ecologically sensitive environments there are standards that define just what they are and where they are located. Brackish or salt water marshlands, which total about 150,000 acres within the Albemarle and Pamlico sounds alone, are considered coastal wetlands. Coastal wetlands are easily identified by their plant life, especially an absence of tree growth and a predominance of ten particular plant species. Most frequently observed are the following: Salt marsh or smooth cordgrass that forms one to eight feet tall meadows spreading to the open water's edge; black needlerush, three to five feet tall grasses that predominate on the higher areas of the marsh where they are reached by only unusually high tides; spike grass; glasswort; and sea ox-eye, with its daisy like flowers in early summer (Frankenberg 1977, 61-67). Salt marshes are the major feature of the wetland environment in the areas south of Bogue Sound, where the distance between the outer banks and the mainland narrows considerably. Compare, for example, the intertidal flats shown in Photos 3.6 and 3.7, and in CP 10.5 and 10.6. Wetland areas like Currituck Banks, Rachel Carson (see CP 10.25), Masonboro Island, and Zeke's Island are included within the North Carolina National Estuarine Coastal Reserve. With more than two million acres in wetlands this is the third largest state preserved estuary system. In Washington, Beaufort County, at the mouth of the Tar River, the state has recently opened the North Carolina Estuarium, the nation's first public access center focusing on estuaries, with their melding of freshwater rivers and salt water oceans permitting critical nurseries of all manner of life.

These wetlands are favored by bird migrations along the coastal flyway. Come here during the appropriate season and be amazed at the massive over flight of ducks and geese, or visit the wintering waterfowl at Lake Mattamuskeet, Pea Island, Alligator River, Pocosin Lakes, or Mackay Island National Wildlife Refugees. The southbound migration peak occurs in December.

### Submerged Aquatic Vegetation

An area of critical environmental concern is the approximately 200,000 acre zone of submerged aquatic vegetation (SAV) inhabiting the sounds. This large biomass produces a nurturing environment by providing organic matter for food utilized by microorganisms, by species higher in the food chain like shrimp, blue crabs, hard shell clams, and bay scallops (the SAV is the only nursery grounds for the North Carolina bay scallops), and

**Photo 10.3:** Morehead City State Port is largely a heavy commodity port emphasizing the outshipment of phosphates, chipwood, and other raw materials. Here a barge is unloading phosphate mined at Aurora in Beaufort County.

**Photo 10.4:** Tugs are pulling a barge loaded with logs followed by a logging raft on the Intracoastal Waterway in Hyde County. Here the Waterway is cut through what has recently become the Pocosin Lakes Natural Wildlife Refuge. This particular scene is from an area just north of Lake Mattamuskeet where drainage ditches have been cut to allow for the eventual use of the land for cultivated crops. As can be noted in the top of the photo, tracts of land have already been converted for this purpose (Photo courtesy of NC Department of Commerce).

by larval and juvenile fish like grey trout, red drum, spotted sea trout, mullet, spot, silver perch, and summer flounder. Problems for the SAV are multiplying with the occasional outbreak of plant disease, at times encouraged by increasing development pressure (including dredging and filling, nutrient enriched run-off that encourages plankton bloom, and untreated sewage), as well as by greater use of mechanical harvesting methods. Clam-kicking, a method of harvesting hard clams utilizing a powerful propeller wash to dislodge the clams, is thought to seriously harm SAV plant communities (Steel 1991). An important outcome from the concern over the decline in SAV habitats has been the increase in state and federal laws requiring a permitting process for modification or development in SAV areas.

*Fresh Water Wetlands and Pocosins*

Fresh water wetlands occur within the outer Coastal Plain, along many streams and rivers. Where these are tidal marshlands they are easily distinguished from a distance where cattails domi-

nate (Photo 10.5). Also seen are wire grass, sawgrass, common three square sedge, white top, and a number of wild flowers, such as iris, arrowhead, and pickerel weed (Frankenberg 1997, 68). On CP 10.7, which shows the Lockwoods Folly Inlet some 23 km (15 mi) east of Cape Fear, there are fresh water marshes just beyond the Inlet and the Intracoastal Waterway. From the sea to the interior, the typical east-west traverse reveals a transition from a savanna, an open piney woodland with meadows of grasses and mature longleaf pine, to pond pine woodlands and pocosins that are supported by organic rich soils confined between sandy ridges (Figures 10.5 and 10.6). Pocosins (Algonquin Indian for "swamp on a hill") are elevated above the surrounding land, but maintain their wetland character by their foundation in poorly drained and nutrient deficient peaty soils with a very high moisture content.

The process of peat accumulation is thought to have begun some 5,000 to 7,000 years ago to the point to where high centered bogs developed with the deepest layers of peat in their

**Photo 10.5:** Fresh water swamp on the Pamlico Peninsula, here dominated by wire grass and loblolly pine. Drainage canal is in foreground (Photo courtesy of H.D. Stillwell).

middle portion. Precipitation is the only source of water for these "high centered bogs" with the result that water drains in all directions. Pocosins are thus nontidal wetlands. Due to their high organic soil content and higher elevations, in a land otherwise close to sea level, pocosins are desirable for agriculture, despite the absence of mineral nutrients. These must then be added in copious amounts as fertilizers. Note, for example, the lime bags stacked and waiting to be disbursed on newly cleared land in CP 10.8. Typically, the natural pocosins are covered by plant communities of very dense evergreen and deciduous shrub vegetation. Tall trees exist only at the margins where the pocosins meet the dry pine forests, except in those pocosins where peat accumulation is more recent and thus thinner. Here enough nutrients are retained or mineral soils are close enough to the surface to permit the growth of pond pine. It is possible, therefore, to distinguish between shrub (high centered peat bog) and tree pocosins, that are frequently referred to as "high pocosins" due to their tall vegetative growth

In the "low pocosins" (high centered peat bogs) nutrient deficiencies favor the shrubs, but also a unique plant community which derives its nitrogen from consuming insect life. North Carolina has a remarkable concentration of insectivorous plants, notably the Venus flytrap, pitcher plants, sundews, and bladderworts and butterworts. Green Swamp, a very large fresh water swamp with considerable pocosin, located just south of the Cape Fear River in Brunswick and Columbus counties, is justly famous for its concentration of this plant community (Figure 10.2).

Throughout the Tidewater Region fresh water wetlands totaled about 200,000 acres before major drainage projects converted 50,000 acres for agricultural purposes. The pocosin environment of the Pamlico Peninsula has been affected by the process of land clearance, ditching to lower the water level, peat extraction, and finally the preparation of a soil bed for agricultural production (CP 10.8 to 10.10). With the kind of resources needed for this large scale land conversion, the farms that developed on the Pamlico in the 1970s were corporate farms, with financing coming from trucking firms and French and Japanese investors. Extensive agricultural production of grains, intermixed with cattle and hogs, now dominate the flat terrain, creating a scene perhaps more reminiscent of agriculture in the Great Plains than North Carolina.

Land conversion has eaten up most of the East Dismal Swamp in Washington County, a formerly important wetlands area contributing to water flow regularities and ecosystem support for adjacent estuaries and sounds. With the conversion to agriculture came a large outflow of excess nutrients deriving from agricultural chemicals, and contributing to algal bloom and fish kills. Then in 1984, on a much more environmentally promising note, the Prudential Life Insurance Company and its agricultural subsidiary, Prudlo Farms, donated to the Department of the Interior all of its holdings in mainland Dare County. With this land transfer the Alligator River Wild Life Refuge was created, preserving for the future three-quarters of the present 150,000 acre site, the 'thumb' of the Pamlico Peninsula. A few years later the Conservation Fund acquired about 50,000 acres from First Colony Farms, the state's largest agricultural enterprise, in Tyrell County and another 11,000 acres in Washington and Hyde counties. These and other lands have now been passed to the Federal Government as the 112,000 acre Pocosin Lakes National Wildlife Refuge. Easing the transfers of these lands has been a lessening interest in using their massive peat resources for power generation. This latter idea was first considered by Peat Methanol Associates in the early 1970s, and by 1984 a peat-to-methanol plant was being built in Washington County. Then the political-economic environment changed and the plant was never brought on line. Presently, attempts are being made to restore the natural hydrology by planting pond pine, cypress and American white cedar (Hinesley 1996). Complementing the return of the vast wetlands of Hyde, Tyrrell, and Dare counties to a more natural state, has been the return of the red wolf. In the late 1980s the wolf recovery program was initiated. In the mid-1990s the program survived a legal challenge from predator-wary landowners who had been supported by a 1994 state law allowing landowners to kill wolves encroaching upon their property. The District Court ruling upheld the federal government's right to protect red wolves on private lands under the Constitution's broad definition of interstate commerce.

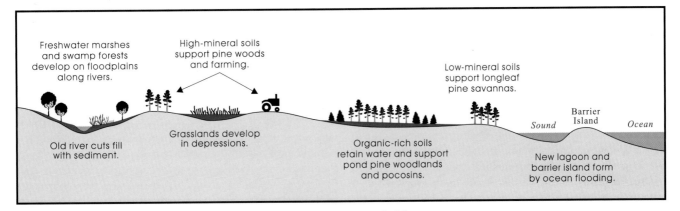

**Figure 10.5:** Fresh Water Wetlands in the Tidewater Region and Outer Coastal Plain.
**Source:** Frankenberg, 1997, 49.

335

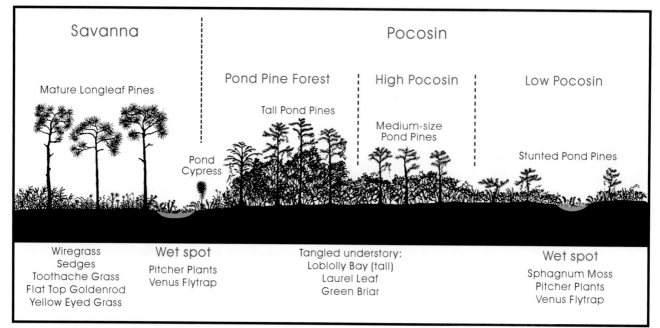

**Figure 10.6:** Savanna and Pocosin Plant Communities.
**Source:** Venters (1995); illustration by Anne Runyon, by permission.

It must be noted that on the state level there also has been an increasing conversion of land back to natural habitat conditions, though the motivation for this has a slightly different take. Traditionally, in this predominantly rural state, if a Tarheel wanted to bag wild game for dinner, he would simply set out his back door and head for the woods or the wetlands. However, with increasing urbanization, especially exurbanization, by the late 1960s this had become an activity that was very difficult to pursue. In response, the state began arranging cooperative agreements with public and private landholders for the purpose of designating "game lands," where licensed hunting for deer, bear, turkey, and other game could be permitted. Initially the arrangement focused on leasing land rather than purchasing it. With the creation of the Natural Heritage Trust Fund in 1994, it was finally possible to purchase a greater percent of land, and in 1995 the state's Wildlife Resources Commission managed over 1.7 million acres of game lands. In 1998, the Commission was able to purchase the Dawson Tract in Currituck County, and add its 1,400 acres to the outstanding bear habitat of the North River Gamelands (Manuel 1998).

It is also of interest to note that the North Carolina Environmental Defense League suggests one of the effects of the hog explosion in eastern North Carolina to be a contribution of about 135 million pounds of ammonium nitrogen escaping into the atmosphere each year, and subsequently releasing this awesome pollutant on coastal areas, including pocosins of Green Swamp and their rare plant communities. Between 1990 and 1995 scientists at the Morehead City Research Station reported a 25 percent annual increase in atmospheric ammonia (Leavenworth and Shiffer 1998). Most of the fresh water wetlands, pocosins for the most part, are protected by an array of federal and state designated areas. From north to south in the Tidewater Region these include seven national wildlife refuges, the Croatan National Forest, the Hofmann State Forest, plus a number of state parks. These are all identified on Figure 10.3.

*The Disappearing Wetlands*

There has been a wealth of research focusing on the gradual disappearance of wetlands in North Carolina. In assessing this research it is clear that at least 50 per cent of the state wetlands have disappeared since colonial times. In 1989 the United States Department of Agriculture, Soil Conservation Service, reported that 1,244 miles of canals and dikes had been completed in the state, with another 1,459 miles planned. In the summer of 1998, while hastening to beat a deadline on a state edict to halt wetland ditching, developers ditched and drained thousands of acres of soon to be protected wetlands in the Cape Fear River Basin. Claiming that it did not have the staff to draft, in a timely manner, a new set of wetland rules defined by the state's Environmental Management Council, the Division of Water Quality delayed the process of invoking the new wetlands regulations until March 1, 1999. Factors contributing to wetlands intrusion are land clearance related to agriculture, forestry and urban/recreational development, as well as mosquito and flood control in and around municipalities (Steele 1994). It is interesting to compare this recent flurry of wetland reclamation in the Cape Fear River Basin with the near halt, if not actual retreat, of land diversion on the Pamlico Peninsula. It appears that most of the recent land reclamation is intended to increase the acreage available to managed pine forests for use by the paper and chip board industry, a very particular problem for areas of the Green Swamp in Brunswick County. In 1986, nine private timber companies owned almost

**Color Plate 10.1:** A late 18th century population decline on the Outer banks was countered by Price in 1795 when he said of Ocracoke, "This healthy spot ... Is the resort of many of the inhabitants of the main" (quoted in Dunbar 1958, 38). Over 200 years later, the 600 inhabitants carefully protect Ocracoke Harbor's image, but speculators and developers are knocking on the door.

*Photo by Ole Gade.*

**Color Plate 10.2:** The Cupola House (1725) is one of many prominent homes built in Edenton (Chowan County) when the town emerged as the lead urban center in the Albemarle.

*Photo by Ole Gade.*

**Color Plate 10.3:** In Edenton, the many column, double-tiered porch of the Hays House (1814) looks across Queen Anne's Creek to the line of plantation homes festooning the shoreline.

*Photo by Ole Gade.*

Photo by Ole Gade.

**Color Plate 10.4:** New Bern's Tryon Palace (Craven County) was built on the Trent River in 1770 to accommodate not only the residence of Colonial Governor William Tryon, but also the permanent seat of the Colonial Assembly. The building, now a major tourist attraction, was rebuilt in the 1950s.

**Color Plate 10.5:** Brackish water readily infiltrates the fresh water drawn from subsurface sources near finger canal development on Sunset Beach. Septic systems, densely placed on the narrow fingers, contribute to gradual pollution of the groundwater. The high nutrient input flowing into the canals, combined with their poor circulation, contribute to fish kills and generally high pollution content. The tidal flats and salt marshes reach to the narrow length of the Intracoastal Waterway, just noticeable in the upper right of the photo. Habitation here, as along all of the Brunswick County beaches, was completely eradicated by Hurricane Hazel in 1954. Now development is at a fever pitch.

Photo by Robert E. Reiman.

Photo by Robert E. Reiman.

**Color Plate 10.6:** Newer finger development in Bogue Sound (Carteret County). Near Atlantic Beach, a contemporary finger hardened into the existing salt marsh wetlands provides another example of extremely dense settlement in a fragile area. Community water and septic facilities for over 200 condo units do not further distract from the essentially negative ecological and visual encroachment. Bogue Sound experiences a strong tidal current so pollutants do not build up.

**Color Plate 10.7:** Fresh water marshes exist in estuaries of creeks and rivers emptying into the sounds. Here the Shallotte River and the smaller Saucepan Creek (Brunswick County), with their extensive fresh water marshes and adjacent swamp forests, empty into the Intracoastal Waterway opposite Shallotte Inlet.

*Photo by Robert E. Reiman.*

*Photo by H. Daniel Stillwell.*

**Color Plate 10.8:** Land clearance, ditching, and preparation for agriculture took place on the lands of First Colony Farms (Washington County) in the early 1980s. Note the roots and logs piled up opposite the drain ditch and the bags of minerals ready for spreading on soils rich in little other than acidity.

**Color Plate 10.9:** A later stage shows cultivation of the peaty, dark soils, with the green of the initial crop appearing. Drainage ditches and artificial pumping facilitate the maintenance of the soil water level below root growth. Much of this land has now reverted to the federal government as part of the new Pocosin Lakes National Wildlife Refuge. In the distance is an untouched pocosin forest of loblolly pine.

*Photo by Ole Gade.*

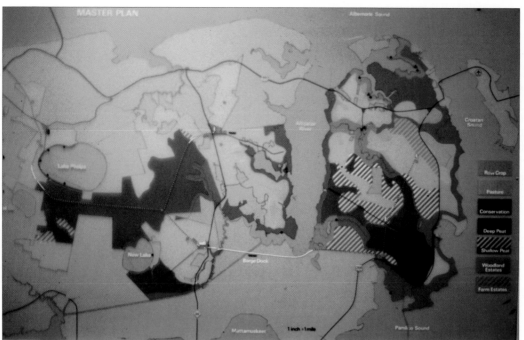

*Photo by Ole Gade.*

**Color Plate 10.10:** Land ownership and use can change rapidly. Part of the land owned by First Colony Farms was acquired by Prudential Insurance. Subsequently, it was donated to the Alligator National Wildlife Refuge. Other First Colony Farm property was acquired by the Conservation Fund, subsequently to become the Pocosin Lakes N. W. R. This 1970s land use plan indicated the direction of land exploitation prior to the demise of the peat industry.

**Color Plate 10.11:** A vacation and private home explosion is engulfing Currituck Banks (Currituck County). This area had remained fairly free of development until the North Carolina Department of Transportation assumed control over the private road that linked Sanderling with Corolla, a distance of some ten miles. The Department of Transportation made the road public, providing access for development.

*Photo by Ole Gade.*

*Photo by Robert E. Reiman.*

**Color Plate 10.12:** Harbor Island, near Wilmington, is gradually emerging from salt water marsh. A remnant of the marsh remains in the center of the artificially created island. Here are found condominiums and residential resorts with adjacent marinas.

# Albemarle Region

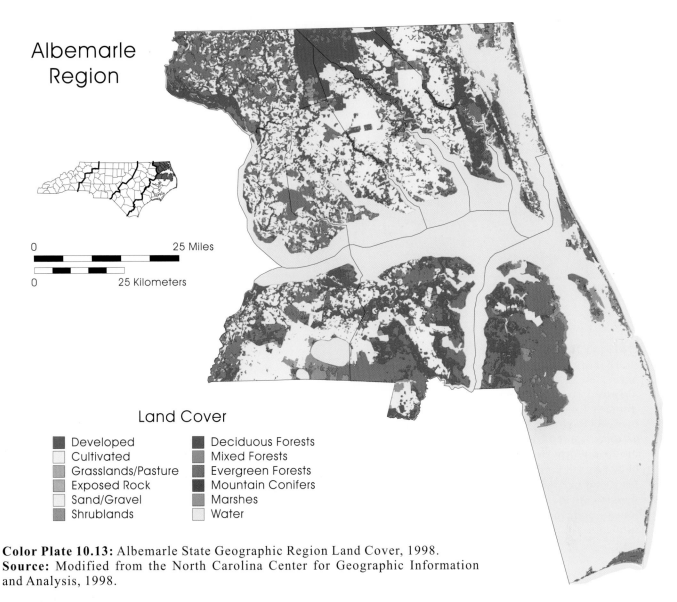

0              25 Miles

0              25 Kilometers

## Land Cover

- Developed
- Cultivated
- Grasslands/Pasture
- Exposed Rock
- Sand/Gravel
- Shrublands

- Deciduous Forests
- Mixed Forests
- Evergreen Forests
- Mountain Conifers
- Marshes
- Water

**Color Plate 10.13:** Albemarle State Geographic Region Land Cover, 1998.
**Source:** Modified from the North Carolina Center for Geographic Information and Analysis, 1998.

**Color Plate 10.14:** The ferry ride from Knott's Island to Currituck Court House on the mainland is a brisk and stimulating trip in early March, a time of the year when the major passenger loads are students traveling daily to and from the mainland. Time travel from these homes on the island is less to Virginia Beach (Virginia) than it is to Elizabeth City (North Carolina).

*Photo by Ole Gade.*

*Photo by Ole Gade.*

**Color Plate 10.15:** Merchant's Millpond is a state park in Gates County where canoeing and fishing are favorite activities. In 1811, Kincken Norfleet built the first dam here to provide power for a saw mill and a grist mill. Land donated by the Coleman family, later supplemented by The Nature Conservancy, contributed to the development of the state park in 1973. Now canoeers can leisurely paddle the dark waters of one of the most interesting water ecosystems of the Atlantic Seaboard; the area has over 160 plant species (including enormous 100 year old bald cypress and water tupelo), a richness of animal species, the mud and stick lodges of beavers, and, depending on the season, hordes of frogs.

**Color Plate 10.16:** Logs, and increasingly chipwood, are being harvested in the coastal forests and shipped to other countries. The Yamato Lumber Company, located on U.S. Highway 64 in Washington County, is sending wood products by the Hanjin Trucking Company to Morehead City State Port for shipment to Asia via the Japan Line.

*Photo by Ole Gade.*

**Color Plate 10.17:** Downtown Edenton is historically renovated and its four blocks of shopping along Broad Street have all of the basic amenities, including hardware and drug stores. The town citizens are concerned about the demise of these centrally located business functions, because development strip shopping centers are threatening the competitive edge of downtown.

*Photo by Ole Gade.*

**Color Plate 10.18:** Currituck Lighthouse recently has been renovated and is now accessible for gorgeous views of sound and ocean. Built in 1875, it is the only lighthouse along the North Carolina coast that has not yet been moved and it is the only one not painted.

*Photo by Ole Gade.*

**Color Plate 10.19:** CAMA built an access to the back swamp through a Currituck Island thicket. This is one of the few points of public access to the Currituck Sound on the island, which stretches from Sanderling some 23 miles to the Virginia border.

*Photo by Ole Gade.*

343

## Pamlico Region

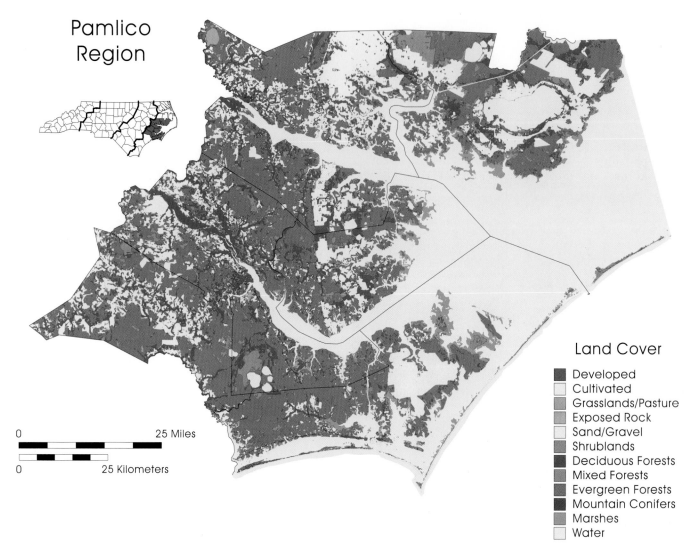

### Land Cover

- ■ Developed
- □ Cultivated
- ■ Grasslands/Pasture
- ■ Exposed Rock
- □ Sand/Gravel
- ■ Shrublands
- ■ Deciduous Forests
- ■ Mixed Forests
- ■ Evergreen Forests
- ■ Mountain Conifers
- ■ Marshes
- □ Water

0 ———— 25 Miles

0 ———— 25 Kilometers

**Color Plate 10.20:** Pamlico State Geographic Region Land Cover, 1998.
**Source:** Modified from the North Carolina Center for Geographic Information and Analysis, 1998.

**Color Plate 10.21:** The Potash Corporation of Saskatchewan runs an extensive open pit mining operation near Aurora in Beaufort County. Giant draglines clear off 100 feet of surface materials and scoop up the lower lying 35 to 40 feet of phosphate ore.

*Photo by Ole Gade.*

344

**Color Plate 10.22:** The phosphate refinery facilities at Aurora separate and process the mined materials to produce products such as granulated triple superphosphates, Diammonium phosphate, and purified phosphoric acids. Air pollution is a serious issue.

*Photo by Ole Gade.*

*Photo by Ole Gade.*

**Color Plate 10.23:** Water seeping into the mine is a problem for the operation and is dealt with by pumping the water into adjacent settlement ponds and canals. Frequent seepage into the Pamlico River has caused major problems of excessive algae growth and extensive pollution of shellfish and fin fish breeding grounds.

**Color Plate 10.24:** New Bern's waterfront redevelopment began in the late 1970s. The open space still seen in this photo, taken in 1986, gradually is giving way to commercial and taxable use.

*Photo by Robert E. Reiman.*

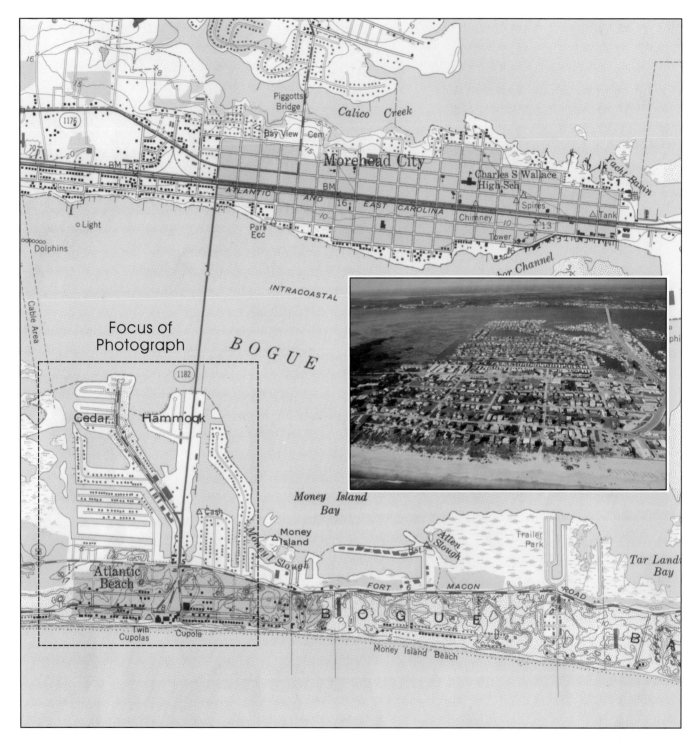

**Color Plate 10.25a:** Atlantic Beach (Carteret County) is attempting to revitalize its traditional boardwalk entertainment atmosphere by emphasizing family values. The sound side wetlands have been fully developed during the past two decades as Cedar Hammock. The bridge to Morehead City is in the upper right of the photo. Photo by Robert E. Reiman.

Map Source: U.S.G.S. Beaufort, North Carolina quadrangle.

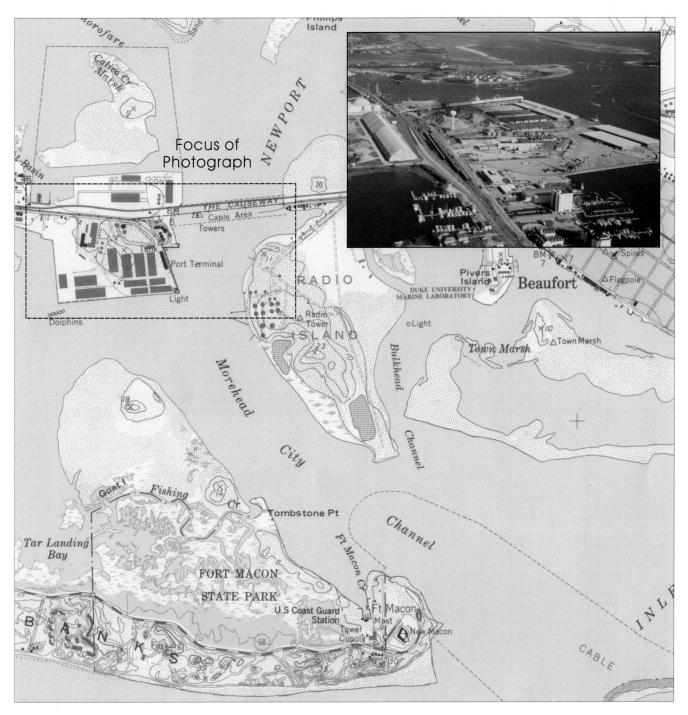

**Color Plate 10.25b:** The state port facility at Morehead City lies on an artificial island just west of Beaufort, which can be seen in the upper left of the photo. Dominating port functions is the overseas shipment of phosphates (note the elongated white storage houses and the acid tanks) and chipwood (note the enormous pile and train load of chips). Most of Radio Island in the upper center of the photo has been purchased by the State Port Authority. A tank farm for petroleum and natural gas is in evidence. Access to the Atlantic Ocean is obtained by the Beaufort Inlet (to the upper right), which separates Shackleford Banks from Bogue Banks. The green of Bogue Banks is the site of Fort Mason. The Rachel Carson National Estuarine Research Reserve is located between Shackleford Banks and Beaufort.

Photo by Robert E. Reiman.

Map Source: U.S.G.S. Beaufort, North Carolina quadrangle.

*Photo by Ole Gade.*

**Color Plate 10.26:** Beaufort provides evidence, as seen in this photo of a selection of state roadside historic markers, of being the third oldest town in North Carolina. The town has a national historic designated district, as well as a new harborscape with marinas and a remodeled quay on Front Street.

**Color Plate 10.27:** At Bogue Banks (Carteret County) just west of Fort Macon State Park, the complex land use and residential crowding onto the island is shown by individual family homes, several trailer parks, and condominiums of varying densities. This area was annexed by Atlantic Beach, under protest. Across Bogue Sound, in the distance, is Morehead City with the State Port facility to the upper right.

*Photo by Robert E. Reiman.*

*Photo by Robert E. Reiman.*

**Color Plate 10.28:** Pine Knoll Shores is a private, though incorporated, residential community located about mid-island (Bogue Banks). It varies in settlement density and form, but allows no public parking and access to the ocean. In the center right of the photo are the two buildings, swimming pool, and tennis courts of the Pine Knoll Shores development at Ocean Grove.

**Color Plate 10.29:** Ocean Grove is a beach front property with a residential cluster of eleven condo units per acre. The design maximizes natural components (note the elevated boardwalks over the front vegetation dune in CP 10.28), and yet has open space for a large lawn, swimming pool, and tennis courts. The property manager's home faces N.C. Highway 58. This is an example of environmentally sound development making aesthetic and efficient use of available space.

*Photo by Ole Gade.*

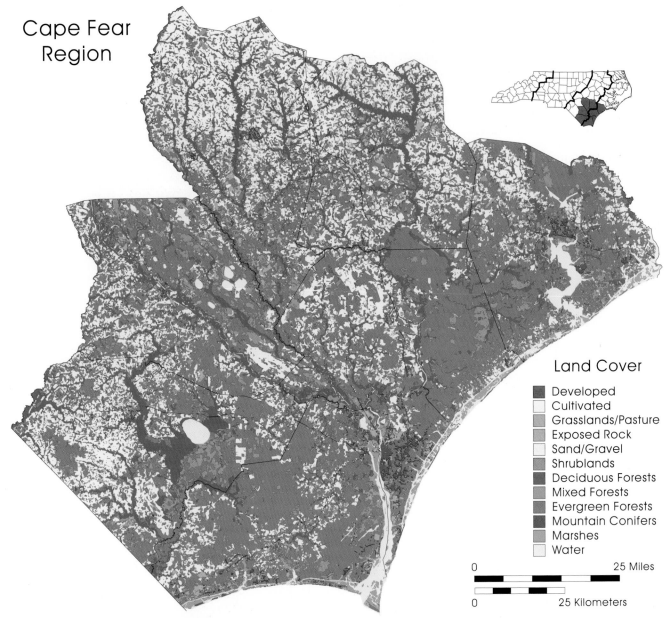

## Cape Fear Region

### Land Cover

- ■ Developed
- □ Cultivated
- ■ Grasslands/Pasture
- ■ Exposed Rock
- □ Sand/Gravel
- ■ Shrublands
- ■ Deciduous Forests
- ■ Mixed Forests
- ■ Evergreen Forests
- ■ Mountain Conifers
- ■ Marshes
- □ Water

0 ———————————— 25 Miles

0 ———————————— 25 Kilometers

**Color Plate 10.30:** Cape Fear State Geographic Region Land Cover, 1998.

**Color Plate 10.31:** Downtown Jacksonville (Onslow County) is home to local and regional government and legal offices. The town closed down the military dominated "adult district" with its bars, video stores, pawn shops, and prostitution, and is now working diligently at reactivating commercial businesses. In the photo, one of the many city blocks of empty store fronts provides an artistic vision of downtown's future.

*Photo by Ole Gade.*

**Color Plate 10.32:** North Carolina has developed financial incentives and built port facilities to allow an increased share of international trade to be conducted through North Carolina cities. Mid-1990s deepening of the Cape Fear River channel now permits wood pulp carriers an additional six inches of draft, enabling ships to carry an additional 700 to 800 tons of pulp. Pulp and wood chip, piled high on the dock in the photo, is by tonnage the largest export out of Wilmington. To stay competitive in the global market place of merchant shipping, it will be necessary to deepen the channel a further two feet.

*Photo by Robert E. Reiman.*

*Photo by Robert E. Reiman.*

**Color Plate 10.33:** Imports and exports of packaged goods have increased measurably with the completion of the container docks, shown here with the expanded storage space and with a ship in the process of loading cargo for an overseas destination.

**Color Plate 10.34:** With the retrofitting of Wilmington's "Cotton Exchange" on Front Street, access to the recently developed River Boardwalk was made difficult by the construction of an unaesthetic and ungainly parking garage stretching several blocks between the river and Front Street.

*Photo by Robert E. Reiman.*

**Color Plate 10.35:** Shell Island Resort (Wrightsville Beach) is increasingly threatened by the southward migrating Mason Inlet. Although signing off on the state warning that the site was in an extreme risk zone and that no variance for artificial hardening of the shoreline (see Figure 10.10) will be granted, the resort owners are pursuing a court decision to allow them to take measures to protect the property.

**Color Plate 10.36:** Shell Island Resort has been permitted to continue, within a given time limit, to sandbag the shoreline to protect the resort against the inlet's move. In the meanwhile, New Hanover County officials are supporting efforts to dredge the inlet to impede its progress. Evidence of damage from Hurricane Fran (1996) can be seen on the walls of the resort.

**Color Plate 10.37:** The Holiday Inn was razed following severe damage sustained during Hurricane Fran in 1996. In 1998, following a suit against the Town of Wrightsville Beach to gain approval of plans to build a nine story structure to replace the earlier four story building, the hotel is being rebuilt to seven stories. The new hotel will be at a slightly higher elevation, but will be on the same filled-in inlet. Construction of the new Holiday Inn can be seen in the center of the photo.

twenty percent of the Tidewater Region land (Moorhead 1995, p. 28). One of these, the Weyerhouser Corporation, owns over 2,246 square kilometers (565,000 acres)of North Carolina land, mostly concentrated in the Tidewater and adjacent Coastal Plain regions. This compares in size with the largest of Tidewater Region counties (see Tables 10.2-10.4).

As land is converted from natural vegetation to crops, runoff carries great amounts of soil into the estuaries and sounds. For example, the average annual transport of sediment from the Tar-Pamlico rivers basin, an area of 4,300 square miles, is over 200,000 tons. Meanwhile, the Corps of Engineers annually must dredge about 3.5 million tons of sediment to maintain navigation at Sunny Point Military Ocean Terminal, 18 miles south of Wilmington, at a cost that annually exceeds several million dollars. Dredging has brought unforeseen benefits to wildlife in the lower Cape Fear River. Sediments removed from the ship channel build up as spoil bank islands. These island are creating new nesting grounds for the once endangered Brown Pelican (Photo 10.6) and other water birds such as the Royal Tern, once sought for plumage. The open sandy space minimizes predation by raccoons and foxes.

The Fourth Annual "State of the Coast" Report of the North Carolina Coastal Federation, made public in October of 1998, describes in stark terms the negative side of the sediment flush–their contaminant load. After four years of intense examination of the many feet of sediments washed into the sounds, scientists have found that forty percent of our estuaries, and the lower courses of rivers like the Neuse and the Pamlico, are virtually devoid of the life forms critical to the maintenance of fish, shrimp and crabs. Where the bottom layer of the marine life food chain is absent, the affected sounds are dead, killed by decades of accumulating noxious metals, DDT, and other chemicals, flushed into the sounds by their feeding rivers. No wonder that the top of the food chain, mined successfully for years by local fishermen, has been in serious decline over the past decade. This is a direct and dramatic evidence of the severe stress exhibited by the sound ecosystem.

In response to deteriorating environmental conditions a set of new rules is being considered in 1999 by the Coastal Resources Commission (CRC). These rules include the twin requirement that a swath of vegetation 75 feet perpendicular to a shoreline be left free of development and that development within 200 feet of the shoreline have less non-permeable surfaces, such as driveways and rooftops. Urged on by real estate officials and home builders, Brunswick County commissioners dug in their heels against the new rules, which are intended to severely limit sediment flush and the wash-out of noxious pollutants. The political process for final definition and implementation of the rules involves public hearings in each of the 20 counties regulated by the Coastal Area Management Act and approval by the state

**Photo 10.6:** These birds were on the endangered species list, victims of an earlier widespread use of DDT. Banning the pesticide in 1972 led to a gradual recovery with the removal of the pelican from endangered status in 1985. Spoil banks created from dredged materials deriving from shipping lanes provide the appropriately isolated location for the species to flourish. This Brown Pelican nesting area is on a spoil bank in the Cape Fear River near Wilmington. (Photo courtesy of Hugh Morton)

legislature. As always, the process toward coastal environmental protection is contentious and frequently results in compromises little appreciated by any of the special interest groups.

Meanwhile, in the northeastern portions of the state a similar pace of development has brought considerable deterioration in the fragile natural resource base, leaving the five river basins draining into the Albemarle-Pamlico sounds in a serious state of disrepair. For decades river basins have been polluted by farms, industries and community sewage plants. In response to the threat of continuing destruction of natural habitats, and the associated deterioration of human community environments, a huge Comprehensive Conservation and Management Plan for the Albemarle-Pamlico Estuary was published in 1994. Its aim is a kind of middle-of-the-road approach to arriving at a compatible relationship between economic development needs and desires and the acquisition of threatened wetlands, wildlife habitat and development-free buffer zones. As noted elsewhere in this volume, the inland portions of this region are desperate for generative economic development efforts, so the proposed stiff environmental rules of behavior to cover equally all of the 36 counties in this massive watershed had to be compromised.

### Upland Surfaces of the Tidewater Region

All of the flat outer Coastal Plain evolved when the region was under the sea, as limestone and phosphate deposits verify. Here the Coastal Plain and Tidewater regions demonstrate the gradual evolution of surface landforms resulting from the layering of materials deposited in an earlier ocean expansion or eroded from the Appalachians during oceanic retreat over the past 100 million years as the continents have separated (Figure 10.7). Notable here is the existence of a number of old shorelines (terraces or scarps) marking the gradual increase in elevation of the Coastal Plain over geologic time (Figure 10.8). The most prominent terrace system, the Suffolk Scarp, has two ridges with their typical steeper east slope: Pinetown Scarp, which carries Long Ridge Road, and Chapel Scarp, on which is built NC 32. Between the scarps and upland surfaces are found extensive deposits of peat up to three meters thick and many buried cypress stumps that reveal an earlier time when dense swamp forests dominated the landscape. Mattamuskeet, Phelps, Pungo, and Alligator are large lakes occupying depressions in the Pamlico Peninsula. To the south of the Pamlico River a large system of lake filled depressions exist within the Croatan National Forest. Likely all of these have resulted from sinking after surface fires had compacted the peat, and underground solution had reduced the underlying support.

## THE NATURAL-HUMAN ENVIRONMENT INTERFACE

### Disasters in the Making

We have found the Tidewater to be a dynamic natural region reflecting the interplay of forces - wind, ocean currents, wave action, flooding and vegetative dynamics - constantly altering its shape and character. Introduce humans to this region and a host of environmental problems are apt to arise. Some of these problems have already been looked at; their cause, effects, and possible cures will be now be examined.

### Developing the Barrier Islands

About 40 percent of the barrier islands are developed for residential and recreational use. A vast array of seasonal homes, apartments, motels, and condominiums line the coast along narrow access roads in five strips, delimited by Oregon Inlet, the capes (Hatteras, Lookout, and Fear), and the two state boundaries (Figure 10.2). Poor location and construction have resulted in much storm damage. Hurricanes are part of the natural processes which continually modify the coast, but they become serious hazards to human occupancy in exposed areas. Their incidence is depicted in Figure 2.14. Note that the path of Hazel in October of 1954 barely touched the southern coastal fringe and moved almost due north. However, this caused high storm surges with easterly winds that brought widespread flooding and destruction (White et al. 1976, 244). Nineteen people were killed and $100 million worth of property destroyed. The following August, Hurricane Diane passed directly over Cape Fear, becoming the first storm in the United States to cause over $1 billion damage (Pilkey et al. 1978, 14). The 1980s had a scant four hurricanes hitting the North Carolina shores, but Bonnie in 1998 marked the eighth hurricane of the 1990s. An additional three hurricanes ravaging the coast and interior of the state in 1999 (see Chapter 11).

Particularly devastating was Fran in 1996. It killed 27 people and caused an estimated $5.4 billion in damages in North Carolina alone. Before and after Fran there were two other hurricanes that brought damages to the state in excess of $1 billion each: Bertha, just prior to Fran in 1996, and Bonnie in 1998. A decrease in the incidence of hurricanes in the future is not expected. In fact, long range weather forecasters predict that the tally of major hurricanes making landfall in North Carolina will increase by two to four times over the next several decades (see discussion on hurrincanes Floyd and Dennis in Chapter 8).

Since the major disaster from Hurricane Hazel in 1954, development in hurricane-prone areas has increased, seemingly with a total disregard of a well known environmental hazard. However, residents are now accepting building restrictions in flood-prone areas. New homes are being elevated on deep pilings protected from storm tides and are set back from the shoreline to prevent undermining by erosion. Floors are bolted to the pilings and all walls are tied with metal connectors (Baker 1982). Further stabilization technologies in housing construction followed the extensive damages of Hurricane Andrew in 1992 which caused $15 billion in insured losses, though mostly in South Florida. The Federal Government funded initial grants for environmentally conscious architecture through the National Hazard Mitigation Project. "Project Blue Sky" was one of the very positive results. It is anchored in the belief that flawed construction as well as hurricane winds destroy homes at risk. In essence the construc-

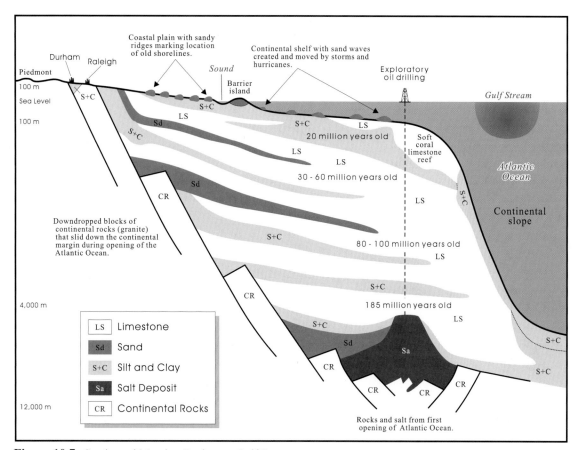

**Figure 10.7:** Continental Margins, Durham to Gulf Stream.
**Source:** Frankenberg, 1997, 6-7 and 10-13.

tion modifications include: having the roof pitch angled to a steeper 25-35 degrees; tying together all parts of the house from roof to foundation with "hurricane (metal) strips"; minimizing glass walls because of their lack of rigidity; and tucking the house more securely into embankments surrounded by tree and shrub buffers. These structural and architectural improvements may run up against the traditional building codes of many seaside communities. Southern Shores initiated "Blue Sky" with a height restriction of 30 feet, making most builders use flat roofs to maximize living space, then had to change its height restriction to 35 feet (Horan 1995). New statewide construction rules adopted by the Building Code Council to reflect the results of "Blue Sky" went into effect January 1, 1997. Condos and single family housing mushrooming in Currituck are built with the restrictions included in the "Blue Sky Project" (CP 10.11).

Structural improvements and the increasing competition for prime home locations have escalated prices for both property and home construction. From 1990 to 1997 property values have increased from thirteen percent (Carteret County) to 79 percent (Pender) and 83 percent (New Hanover). A more specific example is that of ocean front lots at Nags Head, increasing from $150,000 in 1978, to $400,000 in 1988, and then to $750,000 per lot in 1998 (Betts 1998). Holden Beach (in 1999) appears to be one of the hottest property markets in the state. County records indicate that a sandy beach lot measuring 600 by 120 feet sold for $300,000.

Compare this with the cost of a similarly sized lot in booming southeast Charlotte. This might fetch between $150,000 and $225,000. Of course, this reflects increasing coastal population pressures, but also, to use the realtor's terminology: location, location, location. While the state increased its total population twelve percent during 1990-97, the CAMA counties experienced increases from 12 to 29 percent. Only Onslow County, still adjusting to military reductions in base expenditures and manpower, fell short. Significantly, the population increase includes only permanent residents, and therefore not most owners of rapidly expanding vacation communities with their wetland impacting golf courses, swimming pools, and marinas. People in these communities, being permanent residents of perhaps Florida, perhaps New York, perhaps Ontario, constitute a kind of shadow population, paying property taxes, user fees, and benefiting local retail merchants. However, they are not counted in the census and are not privileged to vote in local elections, though their owners associations may provide formidable support for specialized lobbies acting on their behalf. Certainly they contribute to the escalating property values, and, at times, to gated communities. St. James Plantation in Brunswick County, for example, may eventually become even more exclusive and insulated from their locality by choosing to incorporate as an independent municipality.

Hurricane evacuation procedures have been formulated using computer models. Variables considered included popula-

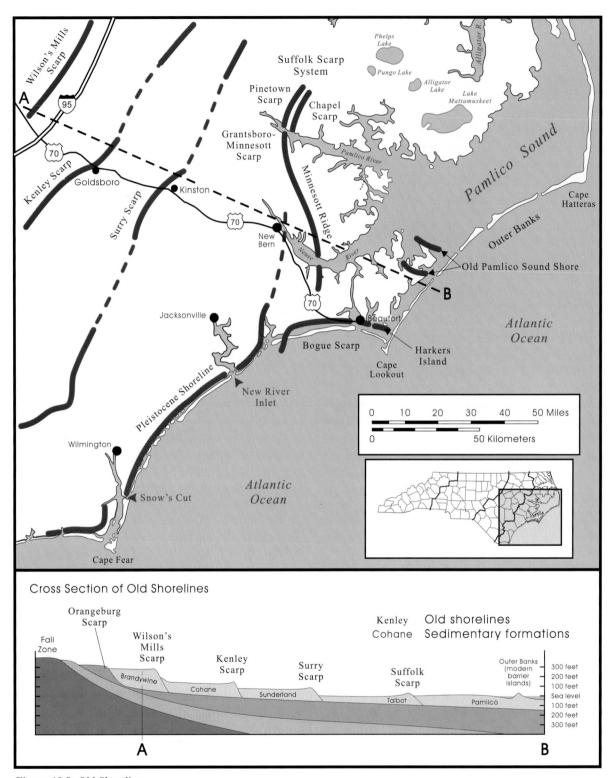

**Figure 10.8:** Old Shorelines.
**Source:** Frankenberg, 1997, 12-13.

356

tion density, coastal topography, transport system and hurricane behavior. A five-stage alert recognized the following conditions:

Condition 5 alert - general watch through the hurricane season, June to October
Condition 4 alert - hurricane advisory: plans reviewed, shelters checked
Condition 3 alert - 48 hours in advance: police, local officials and Red Cross notified
Condition 2 alert - 24 hours in advance: shelters opened, emergency equipment made ready
Condition 1 alert - 12 hours in advance: orders for evacuating beach and flood-prone areas

Preparations for recent hurricanes suggest that people in threatened areas are well conditioned to leave at initial warnings, especially when these affect the off shore islands. And well they might be, for with its coastal snout firmly implanted in the Atlantic Ocean's "Hurricane Alley" North Carolina figures prominently on the tally sheet of 20th Century hurricanes. Table 10.1 indicates the number of direct hits suffered by the leading hurricane states, with North Carolina coming in fourth in the country.

Another problem that affects all of the barrier islands, regardless of the degree of development, is longshore migration of sand. Results of this process include the closing of inlets, the development of shoals that hinder navigation, and the undermining of structures positioned in harm's way. Over time inlets come and go. Presently the most threatened is Oregon Inlet, where expensive effort are persistently pursued to keep the channel wide and deep enough for the larger fishing boats from sound harbors, like Wanchese (Photo 5.10). Various methods have been employed to reduce shoreline erosion, but results are not encouraging (Figure 10.9). Beach replenishment involves moving sand at low tide from near the water's edge to the upper beach with huge trucks and then smoothing it out with bulldozers. Sand may also be dredged from adjacent underwater areas. This results in a rapid renewal of lost sand, but is costly and must be repeated every few years depending on the erosion rate.

What frequently emerges as the solution to coastal erosion for property owners comprises a series of measures collectively referred to as "hardening of the coastline." The results from the implementation of such measures are also derisively called "Jerseyization," with reference to the degree to which the Atlantic Ocean in New Jersey meets not sandy beaches, but reinforced concrete. Various structures at right angles or parallel

| State | All Hurricanes | Category 3 or above |
|-------|----------------|---------------------|
| Florida | 57 | 24 |
| Texas | 36 | 15 |
| Louisiana | 25 | 12 |
| North Carolina | 25 | 11 |

**Table 10.1:** Direct Hurricane Hits by State.
**Source:** Raleigh News and Observer, August 28,1998.

to the shore have had mixed success in stabilizing sand movement. Breakwaters are off-shore rock walls or floating structures which reduce the force of waves. Groins built of wood pilings and heavy planks, steel, concrete, or rock effectively trap sand. Some existing structures extend as much as 61 m (200 feet) into the water. A series of groins usually results in a jagged shore which ultimately recedes. Jetties are similar to groins, but much longer and placed beside a channel to avoid sand filling in. Sea walls to keep the sea out and bulkheads to keep the land in provide the most drastic measures to save a shoreline, but they too are only temporary (Figure 10.10). Revetments are materials laid directly on the dune slope to impede wave action. They may be stone, concrete blocks or nylon bags filled with sand.

Though the Coastal Area Management Act rules forbid 'hardening' solutions, variances have been granted for certain historic properties, such as Fort Fisher at the mouth of the Cape Fear River. An exception is made for non-ocean front shorelines where about 200 miles of artificial bulkhead stabilization has been permitted over the past two decades. Along the coastline only the use of sandbags is allowed to protect certain threatened structures, and only when erosion reaches within twenty feet of the foundation. Sandbag permits are issued for one time only per structure, regardless of change in ownership, for a limit of two years for structures with less than 5,000 square feet of floor space; a five year limit exist for larger structures and for communities that are actively pursuing a policy of beach nourishment (i.e., sand replenishment).

The impact of development on the coastline can be summarized briefly: erosion is a problem only when structures are built; construction changes the shoreline; and protective measures are costly and emphatically temporary. A relentless conversion of dunes to condominiums and parking lots must eventually give way to the equally relentless natural process of beach evolution.

### The Federal Response

Of all coastal natural features, barrier islands and oceanic shorelines are perhaps the most sensitive to human activities. The response has been a series of federal level measures intended to protect against misuse. As early as 1935, over 30,000 acres on a 112 km (72 miles) length of outer banks from the Roanoke Island bridge on Bodie Island to Ocracoke Island were set aside as the Cape Hatteras National Seashore, the first of its kind in the nation. Pea Island National Wildlife Refuge was later added in the northern portion. Then, in 1966, an additional 15,000 acres on a 56 km (36 miles) stretch including Core Banks and Shackleford Banks were added as the Cape Lookout National Seashore (Figure 10.3). Five state parks were added, thus protecting a total of 46 percent of the barrier islands. Unfortunately, 'protection' is a misleading term. As early as the 1930s the Civilian Conservation Corps was active in constructing new dunes along much of the chain of barrier islands. Since the late 1940s the National Park Service has attempted to stabilize these and natural dunes by erecting barriers on the ocean side, as well as by building sand

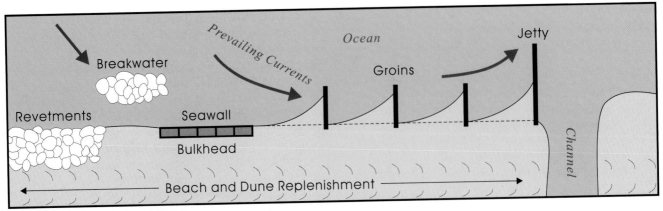

**Figure 10.9:** Methods of Stabilizing the Beach.
**Source:** Modified from Pilkey et al, 1978.

fences and planting sea oats (Figure 10.11). This was done mainly to protect roads and houses on Ocracoke and Hatteras Islands. It was then discovered that beaches were becoming narrower since normal overwash to the sound was restricted and wave energy was diverted, thus undermining the dunes (Dolan et al. 1980). Occasional heavy storms would bring major loss to road-beds and buildings, so in 1976 the National Park Service decided to abandon stabilization efforts and to let nature take its course.

A further limitation on seashore construction was imposed in 1990 when the federal government added 788,000 acres to the Coastal Barrier Resources System, first established by the Coastal Barriers Resources Act of 1982 with 450,000 acres. The Act declares this Atlantic and Gulf coast acreage ineligible for federal insurance guarantees or development support. How then to explain the federal largesse in the wake of Hurricane Fran in 1996? Fran virtually wiped out North Topsail Beach, but two years later the federal government poured $14 million into the seaside community for street repair and water and sewage installation, and $4.2 million for a sand replenishment project, including building a protective sand dune. Fran was the worst storm to hit the North Carolina coast in 30 years. It did an estimated $5.2 billion in damage all in all, and the federal government contributed $160 million in disaster aid, with almost all going to Topsail Island and Wrightsville, Carolina, and Kure beaches. Importantly, the money did not rebuild homes, but it did provide support for the infrastructure necessary for homes to exist on a continuing perilous site. Each full-time resident received an averaged $10,000 of federal tax money (Perlmutt and Rhee 1998). Two year later Hurricane Bonnie wiped out half of the newly created Topsail Beach dune. Bonnie left the rebuilt homes standing, but for how long? In early 1999, the State Insurance Commissioner approved an average of a 20 percent increase of the home insurance rates for barrier island properties. In fact, most of the coastal home owners insurance policies are written through a Beach Plan initiated by the General Assembly and financed and operated by a coalition of insurance firms. Beach Plan policy holders pay over twice the state's average rate.

The United States Army Corps of Engineers plays a major role in influencing changes along the seashore, by pursuing its dual objectives of protecting human facilities in coastal habitats and by maintaining access to harbors and the Intracoastal Waterway. Certainly the Corps has the heavy equipment and the budget to impact natural ecosystems in a major way, and it has felt obligated to use it. Further, the Corps has the authority to issue construction permits for projects seeking to alter the tidewater environment. Though defined by national and interstate interests and needs, the Corps' activities were eventually seen to be in conflict with an evolving state vision of appropriate coastal environmental management. Its activities also brought it into conflict with those who feel it more appropriate for nature to take its own course. Wetlands became a critical issue early in the complex considerations that led to the legislative enactment of the Coastal Area Management Act. The Corps had seen the limit of its jurisdiction to be the mean-high-water mark, and thus refused to deal with projects impacting the coastal wetlands, an immense ecosystem that develops and sustains itself below the high water mark. Thus marina developers and others had a free hand to get permits for their above the high water line construction that in the process might destroy acres of wetlands. Development of Smith Island at the mouth of the Cape Fear River in the mid-1970s brought matters to a head, with developers and the Corps sued by the Sierra Club and the Conservation Council of North Carolina. In the end the courts instructed the Corps to regulate any development above the high-mean-water line that might impact ecosystems lying below the high-mean-water line (i.e., oyster beds, submerged aquatic vegetation, and salt marsh), in the process ensuring that environmental impact evaluations were carried out. Concurrently, the Federal Government was heightening its concern over coastal shorelines and estuaries, and in 1972 enacted the Federal Coastal Zone Management Act. Federal monies and guidelines was now available for states to proceed toward the enactment of their own coastal zone legislation.

***The State Response***

Following several years of proposals and public meetings, the essential contrasting issues were brought into clear light. Those who favored restricting development and protecting en-

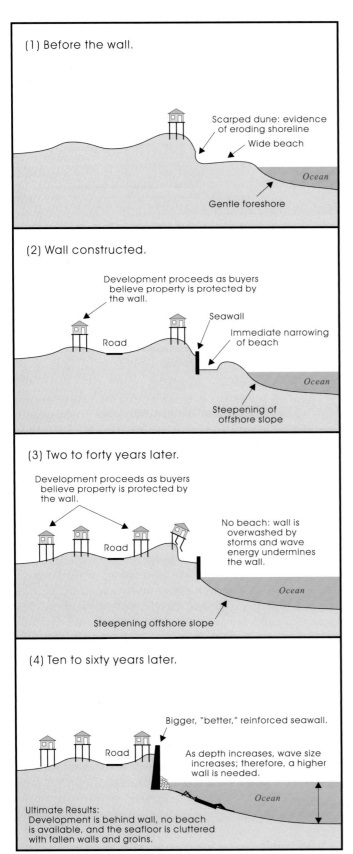

(1) Before the wall.

Scarped dune: evidence of eroding shoreline

Wide beach

*Ocean*

Gentle foreshore

(2) Wall constructed.

Development proceeds as buyers believe property is protected by the wall.

Seawall

Immediate narrowing of beach

Road

*Ocean*

Steepening of offshore slope

(3) Two to forty years later.

Development proceeds as buyers believe property is protected by the wall.

No beach: wall is overwashed by storms and wave energy undermines the wall.

Road

*Ocean*

Steepening offshore slope

(4) Ten to sixty years later.

Bigger, "better," reinforced seawall.

Road

As depth increases, wave size increases; therefore, a higher wall is needed.

*Ocean*

Ultimate Results:
Development is behind wall, no beach is available, and the seafloor is cluttered with fallen walls and groins.

**Figure 10.10:** Saga of a Seawall.
**Source:** Modified from Pilkey et al, 1978.

vironmental values initially emphasized the need to enact regulations favoring the following:

1. The designation of a specific geographic zone within which coastal regulations were to be implemented, to include all counties containing shorelines and estuarine waters as well as an outer limit defined by the state's three mile oceanic jurisdiction;
2. County governments were to have a considerable role to play, but would have to adhere to basic state imposed guidelines;
3. The state would have jurisdiction over designated natural and historic areas, and control development affecting these through a permit process;
4. Local governments would have to implement basic coastal management principles strictly defined by a state plan designed to guide the future of all coastal and estuarine development.

Opposition to these conditions were led by several factions:

1. Banking and real estate interests were concerned about the demise of the explosive growth recently initiated in the coastal portions of the Tidewater;
2. Local officials decried the removal of local authority by a "state zoning bill";
3. Owners of speculative but undeveloped property were up in arms about a "takings" issue, reducing the value of their property through land development restrictions.

So, the essential issues focused on the traditional American values of private property rights and local control over land use. After months of debate, a somewhat weakened North Carolina Coastal Area Management Act (CAMA) was passed by the legislature and signed into law by Governor Holshouser in 1974. CAMA designated 20 coastal zone counties and founded the Coastal Resources Commission (CRC), a state agency whose task it is to decide on permit applications and approve local land use plans required under the Act. The decision making membership of the CRC comprises 15 individuals, twelve of whom are appointed by the participating local governments, a selection factor critical for the subsequent successful operation of the Commission (Schoenbaum 1982). In the words of Senator Staton: "I am not a strict environmentalist. But it is the consensus of the mass of people in North Carolina that we ought to protect our delicate ecological features. . . . The people who own property on the coast do not own the Atlantic Ocean. All the people of this state have an interest in that ocean" (as quoted in Schoenbaum 1982, 266).

In summary, the basic elements of CAMA include local land use planning, regulations for development in Areas of Environmental Concern, and providing and monitoring regulations in the twenty member counties of CAMA. There are special pro-

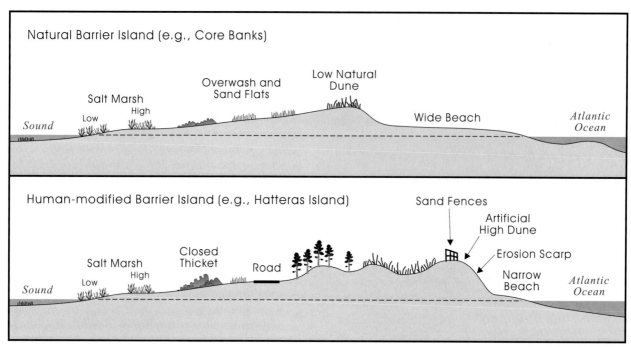

**Figure 10.11:** Comparison of Natural Versus Human Modified Barrier Island.
**Source:** Modified from Pilkey et al, 1978.

grams for beach access and estuarine sanctuaries. Policy for CAMA is set by the CRC, with advice from the Coastal Resources Advisory Council. The entire state effort is administered by the Division of Coastal Management within the Department of Environment, Health and Natural Resources. With its main office in Raleigh, there are field offices located in Elizabeth City, Washington, Morehead City, and Wilmington. By the early 1990s, twenty years after the founding of CAMA, considerable progress had been made in protecting the Tidewater Region environments from overzealous development, as may be seen in Box 10 A. In 1994, the "Year of the Coast," as designated by Governor Hunt, a Coastal Futures Committee provided recommendations for future improvements in CAMA. As indicated by Horan (1994), the more significant of these are to;

1. Require developers and sellers of coastal property to disclose known dangers, like recurring beach erosion;
2. Provide the CRC with the power to tear down or relocate structures threatened by erosion and/or in the way of public beach access;
3. Provide funds sufficient to purchase land, walkways, and restrooms for public use of beach;
4. Widen buffer zones to prevent pollution from seeping into sounds and waterways;
5. Provide further incentives for property owners to donate lands too hazardous to develop for conservation and protection;
6. Further discourage the use of bulkheads along shorelines;

7. Restore fish habitats, but particularly the submerged aquatic vegetation areas;
8. Improve and expand locally required land use plans to include consideration of long term cumulative effects of new development.

*Coastal Area Hazard Mitigation*

The Coastal Area Management Act has proven itself to be effective to some degree in reducing natural hazards and in protecting some of our natural environments from excessive human encroachment. It will not reduce the frequency and severity of hurricanes and nor'easters. Calls for further arming the government with the tools to mitigate the effects of natural hazards are issued with each major natural disaster. Following the devastating Hurricane Fran of 1996, for example, a North Carolina Disaster Recovery Task Force was given the goal of identifying needed hazard mitigation legislation and programs. Its report, *Coastal Hazards Mitigation: Public Notification, Expenditure Limitations, and Hazard Areas Acquisition* emphasized the need for state legislation specific to these areas of concern (Godschalk 1998):

1. Requiring full disclosure and hazard notification to persons acquiring property on barrier islands;
2. Restricting future state subsidies and support of development in designated high hazard areas on barrier islands; and
3. Establishing a state hazard acquisition area program.

**Box 10A:** Coastal Area Management Act, 25 Years of Achievement

*Major Achievements*

1. Banned construction of seawalls and jetties in 1985 to keep beaches natural. Seawalls and jetties, while protecting buildings from erosion, speed up erosion on adjacent beaches by blocking the flow of sand.

2. Helped reduce damage from storms to houses and other facilities with mandatory setbacks. Developers must set back buildings from the front dune to allow for beach erosion. Putting buildings farther back from the ocean's waves reduces storm damage, thus lowering taxpayer cost of cleanups.

3. Helped halt destruction of saltwater marshes. Developers used to dredge marshes to create new high ground for houses.

4. Imposed anti-pollution requirements, with some exceptions, for buildings built within 75 feet of rivers and sounds. With some exceptions, lawns and natural areas must cover at least 70% of lots to allow the ground to absorb polluted runoff.

5. Provided money to buy more than 220 areas for public beach access. Private development increasingly blocks access to beaches. The General Assembly created the Coastal Beach and Water Access Program in 1981, and in 1996 began providing an annual percentage of the Parks and Recreation Trust Fund for coastal public access.

6. Halted the practice of letting property owners put bulk heads (wooden walls) well beyond the shorelines. Property owners would dump dirt behind the bulkhead, extending their laws into publicly owned rivers and sounds.

7. Gave citizens a forum to comment on projects when developers apply for a permit from the N.C. Division of Coastal Management. The Division says it requires in 60 to 70% of permits to meet coastal rules.

8. An increasingly important facilitator of the purchase of natural areas along the coast, including rare maritime forests on the Outer Banks. With the addition of the 18,000 acre Buckridge Tract on the Alligator River in Tyrrell County, the Division of Coastal Management has worked with the N.C. Estuarine Coastal Reserve Program to purchase for public management ecologically sensitive lands along the cost and sounds.

9. Required communities to adopt land use plans to guide growth to minimize environmental damage. By the early 1990s, 20 counties and 63 localities had prepared land use plans that met the specifications of CAMA. Subsequently, having had to turn down a number of unacceptable plan amendments and revisions, the Coastal Resources Commission in November, 1998, suspended for two years the land use planning process in order to try to improve it.

*What CAMA is not authorized to do*

1. Put a limit on the height of high rise hotels and condos. Local communities set height limits.

2. Require property owners to let the public cross their property for access to sea and sound. Private property rights laws prevail.

3. Block development along beaches and shorelines of rivers and sounds. Developers can still build along the waterfront, within set limits.

**Sources:** Adapted from Horan 1994, and 1998-1999 issues of CAMAgram, North Carolina Coastal Management Program.

---

Most critically, the report called for the adoption of its recommendations as a package, reflecting their obvious integrated nature, and for immediate action by the state legislature. It is very clear that avoiding hazard prone areas today will reduce considerably the costs to taxpayers and localities by future natural disaster.

Special provisions already exist within the natural environment protection initiative of the Coastal Resources Commission to identify Areas of Environmental Concern. At the present these AECs are confined to tidal or estuarine shorelines, and do not extend to the beaches. Understanding the difference between AEC designations and natural hazard areas is therefore critical to understanding the problems of environmental protection. Areas of Environmental Concern are restricted to those ecological subsystems that are especially sensitive to economic exploitation and development, or where human encroachment will lead to environmental deterioration in their proximity or downstream. On the other hand Environmental Hazard Areas (EHAs) may be defined on their past experience with adverse weather conditions,

and thus can be classified from their degree of exposure. EHAs are more of a concern to beach property owners. Increasing knowledge of the details of barrier island exposure and historic incidence of storm impacts has led geologist Orrin H. Pilkey and his associates to compile detailed maps of hazard zones based on a risk classification scheme (Pilkey et al 1998).

### Special Problems in Land Use on the Barrier Islands

*The Setback Controversy*

Restrictions on the placement of structures along the coastline have been in effect since 1974. Further restrictions were set in 1979 requiring buildings to be placed behind the primary dune and set back 60 feet (18 m) from the first line of stable vegetation or a distance 30 times the annual erosion rate, whichever is more. This assumes that the average dwelling has a 30-year life. In the Spring of 1983, the Coastal Resources Commission, decided to raise this to 60 times the erosion rate for large structures, i.e., buildings of over 5,000 square feet or with over four dwelling units. This would require developers at Nags Head, where erosion averages 5 feet per year, to set back 300 feet (90 m) from the ocean front. Following a public hearing in the Fall of 1983, setbacks were limited to a maximum of 50 feet.

*Beach Access*

Public access to North Carolina beaches has long been considered a basic right by state residents. However, along many beaches there have been simmering feuds between private property owners and people who recreate on the sands between them and an otherwise unspoiled view of the ocean. For many densely settled beaches the issue has in part been resolved by providing state access from the road to the public beach. Note, for example, the boardwalks connecting the Sunset Beach road with the beach in CP 10.5. However, at recently developed private subdivisions the issue has grown new teeth. North of Sanderling on the Currituck Banks, members of the Whalehead Club have sued the state to prevent the public from passing across their private land. The legal challenge filed in Currituck Superior Court in June of 1997 centers on the area of sand that lies between the dunes and the strand line (Figure 10.4). Critical here is the interpretation of private land to include that which lies upsurface from the mean-high-tide line, below which the public beach is defined. For the state, the issue is not who owns these "dry sands" areas, but rather the fact that the legal maneuver, if successful, will close off an area of beach to which people traditionally have had access for travel, fishing, or sunbathing (Henderson 1997).

*Marinas and Wetlands*

During the Reagan presidency, special tax write-offs for private sports boats up to the size of large yachts fuelled a boom in the boat building industry, and in the construction of new marinas. Associated problems include pollution from sewage, wash water and fuel spills, as well as the encroachment of the marinas into public marshlands and waters (CP 10.12). In 1995 the state proposed a fee structure for easement rights covering waters to be taken up by marinas. This caused heated protest from boat owners and developers, with the result that a Submerged Lands Advisory Committee was established to deal with the issue. State officials want to follow the lead of Florida and Texas, among other coastal states, that charge for use of submerged lands. In North Carolina, at present, smaller marina operators charge monthly rentals for boat slips varying from $100 to $300, while large marinas have recently charged up to $30,000 for ownership of one slip (Nichols 1995). Though it is agreed by all parties that waters occupied by marinas are public, the owners believe that they are already subjected to heavy fees and taxes. Others suggest that whereas golf courses of the Sand Hills and ski slopes of the High Country are developed in part to attract lot/home buyers, only in the case of marinas is public property the venue for sales and profits. One very important wetland impact of marinas is on fisheries. On the national scale it is estimated that 70 percent of the nation's commercially important fisheries are supported by coastal wetlands, but by 1990 over 50

percent of these wetlands had been lost to various forms of development, and about 20,000 additional acres are lost yearly (Spaid 1991). As wetlands are developed, large volumes of fish nutrient recharge areas are removed and are replaced by a humanized landscape giving off toxins that further deplete the fish stock.

In response to the real and potential problems of wetlands encroachment, and to recommendations issuing from past task forces and study committees, the Coastal Resources Commission provided in 1998 its Shoreline Protection Initiative. Having the authority to require permits for development activities within areas designated as Areas of Environmental Concern (AEC), the CRC proposes that property owners obtain permits for developing within 200 feet (62 m) of the water's edge, or 575 feet (177 m) along waters classified as Outstanding Resource Waters, Nutrient-Sensitive Waters and Primary Nursing Areas. The areas affected are all shorelines adjacent to "public trust waters" or waters that are navigable in fact, but within the 20 CAMA counties. Proposed rules will require 75 feet (23 m) vegetated buffer zones that have special requirements for water-dependent structures, such as docks. In addition, there are provisions in the Initiative to further limit artificial structures in built-upon areas in the AEC to fifteen percent of the building lot in question, and to further limit the use of bulkheads as a shoreline stabilization measure.

*Attempts to Stabilize the Oregon Inlet*

Inlets are especially vulnerable to storms, opening and closing frequently. An aerial photographic study by Simon Baker (1982) documented changes of inlets from as early as 1949 through 1974. For example, the New River Inlet shifted about 1,220 m (4,000 feet) southward in 11 years (1949-1960); it has now closed. The north end of Oregon Inlet moved south 1,739 m (5,700 feet) between 1958 and 1974; the south end moved south 214 m (700 feet) during the same period. This reduced the inlet to one-half its former width and undermined support for the Bonner Bridge built in 1962 (Photo 10.7). With an initial span over the inlet of 2.5 miles, the inlet is now narrowed to 2,000 to 2,500 feet. The dramatic narrowing has caused a corresponding deepening to 60 feet (18 m) in much of the channel, but the latter is unreliable and could make changes in its configuration during major storms. Until the placement of rock revetment on the southern side of the inlet, the rate of southerly shift has been between 75 and 125 feet per year (Pilkey et al 1998).

In 1970, Congress authorized the construction of jetties at a cost of $11 million to keep sand from filling in the channel at Oregon Inlet, but funds were not appropriated. In 1980, a Seafood Industrial Park at Wanchese on Roanoke Island was opened at a cost of $8.1 million, mostly from state funding. This 69-acre project was to be a model for economic development of marine resources. Nature had other plans though; the channel had filled so that in places only six feet of water remained. The 60 vessel fishing fleet at Wanchese was land locked! By 1981, the Corps of Engineers proposed two jetties: 1,830 and 2,754 m (6,000 and 9,000 feet) long at a cost of almost $100 million (12 times the

**Photo 10.7a:** Bonner Bridge looking north from Hatteras Island in 1963, just before the official opening November 20th. The Atlantic Ocean is on the right in the photo and the Pamlico Sound on the left. (NC Department of Commerce) **b:** Bonner Bridge looking south with the Atlantic Ocean in the Background. By 1974 the south end of Bodie Island, left foreground, had shifted to within 400 meters (1250 feet) of the main channel. (NC Department of Commerce)

proposal of 1970). However, the National Park Service, and various conservation groups objected on the following grounds:

1. jetties might cause severe environmental damages to the National Seashore;
2. engineering may not be possible;
3. costs would be too high;
4. the Project may not provide safer navigation;
5. jetties may reduce the movement of fish and fish larvae through the inlet; and
6. jetties will increase erosion south of the inlet.

An alternate plan was proposed for yearly dredging at a cost of $500,000 compared to the estimated $7 million per year cost to maintain the jetties. Sand could be pumped to the south side preventing excess beach erosion there. In the fall of 1983 the Corps of Engineers dredged a 16 foot deep channel with a width from 275 to 375 feet. This enabled the fishing fleet to renew activity and continue as long as dredging can be maintained. Then, in 1989, the Corps began building a $16 million rock groin as a stop gap measure to stabilize the inlet and protect the bridge. Still, in 1990, a dredge knocked out five of the spans of the bridge during a storm, and the Corps' jetty proposal remains stalled.

*Black Gold*

The possibility of petroleum deposits on the coastal plains and offshore has intrigued North Carolinians since the first of over 100 wildcat wells was dug in Craven County in 1925. Petroleum is often found in sedimentary strata, particularly sandstone, where it may be contained in a dome or other trap. Thus far, drilling to as deep as 3,066 m (10,000 feet) at Cape Hatteras has been in vain, but the energy crisis of the late 1970s revived interest. A reef buried over 100 million years ago about 208 km (130 miles) east of Cape Hatteras in the Blake's Plateau may contain petroleum (Figure 10.7). Deep layers of sediments accumulated when North America split from Africa; organic matter at the lower level of these sediments may have been squeezed into the reef as gas and petroleum, then sealed off with fine-grained limestone.

The federal government has divided the offshore area from New England to Florida into five square km. tracts for oil leasing. Some 5,718 tracts lie off the North Carolina coast, as close as 19 km (12 miles) east of Cape Hatteras. If drilling occurred and oil spills resulted, it could have disastrous effects on wildlife, the fishing industry, and tourism. However, the procedure is complex. Petroleum companies would first have to obtain the approval of state and federal agencies. Then a permit is needed from the Corps of Engineers to insure non-interference with navigation. Following this the Environmental Protection Agency must check on possible effluent discharges. An exploration plan and environmental report is reviewed by the Outer Continental Shelf Task Force, followed by a six-months study of ocean currents. Then a permit to drill is obtained from the Minerals Management Service and oil spill contingency plans are filed with the U.S. Coast Guard. Finally, the company must demonstrate oil spill clean-up capability. By spring of 1984, no petroleum companies had shown interest in drilling off the North Carolina coast after four years of unsuccessful exploration off New England and New Jersey. In 1988, Mobil Oil requested permits to begin exploratory drilling at "the Point". This is located some 75 km (45 miles) northeast off Cape Hatteras where the continental shelf drops off to a depth of 1,575 m (5,170 ft) and currents collide, creating a perfect environment for fish nourishment, and therefore for sports fishing, if not commercial fishing. Mobil was subsequently sued by environmental interests and state regulators, tying the permit process up in the courts. The fishing industries, if not the onshore tourist dependent resort industries, breathed a sigh of relief. Perhaps this was premature. With the Mobil application still pending, up to bat stepped Chevron Oil in 1997 with a permit request to drill in a block just south of Mobil's planned intervention. Following low 1998 fourth-quarter earnings, and the geological finding that there is only a seven percent chance of finding oil or natural gas, and only two percent chance of this being in commercial quantity, the company put its exploratory plans on hold in February of 1999. If exploratory drilling eventually is successful and commercially viable oil or natural gas is found, it is apt to take another decade of planning and permitting before actual extraction can take place. Not that this process is heartening to the fishing and tourism industries. They fear for the worst should an energy industry sprout off the North Carolina coast.

### The Tidewater Region Into the Future

An appeal for action to save the Tidewater Region environments was made by 90 coastal and wetland scientists to Governor Hunt on February 1, 1999. In essence the appeal (Box 10B) states the case for continued and improved vigilance in protecting this treasured natural environment in the face of environmental pollution, declining shell fish habitats, disappearing fin fish, and overdeveloped and overpopulated natural hazard defined coastlines. It argues that effective protective action should cover total drainage basins, not be limited solely to the 20 CAMA counties. Further, it emphasizes the difficulties faced by CAMA in its comprehensive efforts to ensure a persistent reduction in the Tidewater threats, especially in the more rapidly growing counties where development pressures are at their most intense. The appeal also cautions against the delaying tactics of calling for an endless stream of scientific studies (note frequent references to just a few of these in this chapter), when the problems and the measures needed for their resolution are, in fact, well known.

## THREE STATE GEOGRAPHIC REGIONS

### Introduction

In this section we will have a more detailed look at the three state geographic regions (SGRs), that comprise the Tidewater Region: Albemarle, Pamlico, and Cape Fear. In fact, the southernmost region, Cape Fear, overlaps into the Coastal Plain Region, so for this SGR we will present statistical data and regional maps, and will split the description of the Coastal Plain portion between the two chapters. Table 9.2, in the previous chapter, illustrates the basic similarities and differences among the thirteen SGRs. It may be instructive for the reader to refer to the basic statistical data in Tables 9.1 and 9.2, to provide a comparative context for the individual SGRs as these are presented in the following sections.

### *Albemarle*

North Carolina's northeastern most State Geographic Region is comprised of the nine counties jutting south on Virginia/North Carolina's Albemarle Peninsula and east on the northern tier of the Pamlico Peninsula (Figure 10.12). The heart of the SGR of Albemarle is the Albemarle Sound, to which eight of the counties are closely tied by sea access, while to the west the Chowan River insures the inclusion of Gates County. To the east Currituck and Dare counties share about 100 miles of the very narrow outer banks. Most of this region's land and water territory is tidewater and riparian wetlands, whose characteristics and problems are treated in detail in an earlier section of this chapter. Color Plate 10.13 provides vivid detail of the water bound nature of the Albemarle. Critical natural environments include the major rem-

nants of the Great Dismal Swamp, which extends south from Virginia into three counties: Camden, Pasquotank, and Gates. The western edge of the Great Dismal Swamp is defined by the Suffolk Scarp, while its southern perimeter is being inexorably pushed north by wetland drainage and land reclamation. Portions of this wetland are maintained in the Dismal Swamp State Park.

Bland Simpson (1990) has provided an eloquent and highly personalized historic account of the Dismal Swamp from its earliest experience as a speculative rice cultivation venture of George Washington in the 18th century. In 1956, much of the Swamp and its richly endowed hardwoods was donated by the major owner, Union Camp Company, to the Department of Interior's Fish and Wildlife Service, with the assistance of the Nature Conservancy. At that point in time, this was the largest single land donation to the American people for wetlands and wildlife preservation. Very

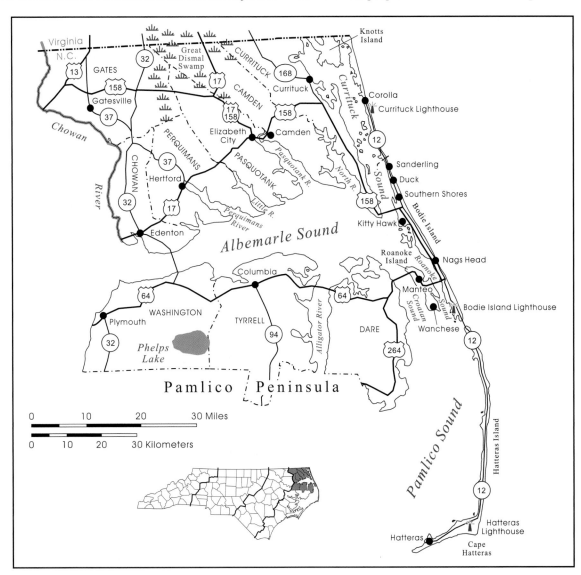

**Figure 10.12:** Albemarle State Geographic Region.

365

| ALBEMARLE | Land Area in sq. km | Pop. 1990 | Pop. sq.km. 2000 | Pop. 2000 | 1990s % Pop. Change | % White 2000 | Median Age in 2000 | % Fam. Below Poverty | Annual Average Infant Mortality Rate 1994-98 | % High School Grads'90 | % Coll. Grads. 1990 | Fem. Fam. Head of Hshld'90 | NC Enterprise Tiers'97 |
|---|---|---|---|---|---|---|---|---|---|---|---|---|---|
| Camden | 623 | 5,904 | 11.1 | 6,885 | 16.6 | 80.6 | 40.2 | 12.1 | 18.5 | 66.2 | 10.1 | 10.3 | 3 |
| Chowan | 447 | 13,506 | 32.5 | 14,526 | 7.6 | 60.5 | 39.6 | 14.5 | 8.8 | 63.3 | 12.2 | 15.0 | 3 |
| Currituck | 678 | 13,736 | 26.8 | 18,190 | 32.4 | 90.4 | 38.2 | 8.1 | 16.9 | 67.7 | 8.2 | 8.1 | 5 |
| Dare | 989 | 22,746 | 30.3 | 29,967 | 31.7 | 94.7 | 38.1 | 5.2 | 4.0 | 81.0 | 21.4 | 7.3 | 4 |
| Gates | 882 | 9,305 | 11.9 | 10,516 | 13.0 | 59.1 | 37.5 | 12.7 | 7.3 | 60.9 | 7.4 | 12.1 | 3 |
| Pasquotank | 588 | 31,298 | 59.4 | 34,897 | 11.5 | 56.9 | 35.3 | 16.6 | 17.0 | 67.4 | 14.4 | 14.8 | 3 |
| Perquimans | 640 | 10,447 | 17.8 | 11,368 | 8.8 | 70.8 | 41.8 | 17.6 | 16.0 | 61.2 | 8.8 | 11.7 | 2 |
| Tyrrell | 1,010 | 3,856 | 4.1 | 4,149 | 7.6 | 56.5 | 39.9 | 21.1 | 21.9 | 58.0 | 7.6 | 14.5 | 1 |
| Washington | 901 | 13,997 | 15.2 | 13,723 | -2.0 | 48.0 | 38.1 | 17.2 | 13.3 | 60.6 | 8.7 | 16.5 | 2 |
| **Region Totals** | **6,758** | **124,795** | **21.3** | **144,221** | **15.6** | **70.9** | **38.7** | **13.9** | **13.7** | **65.1** | **11.0** | **12.3** | **2.9** |

**Table 10.2:** Albemarle State Geographic Region, 1990-2000.
**Source:** U.S. Bureau of the Census; North Carolina State Planning Office.

little of the original swamp remains in Pasqoutank County, where the slightly elevated areas of Lynchs Corner and Tar Corner on opposite banks of the Pasquotank River have been in agricultural land use for well over a century. This area was isolated until the great land reclamation of the 1950s and 60s brought nearly 50 square miles of swamp land into controlled drainage. Early editions of the U.S. Geological Survey maps (for example, the 1941 edition of the 1:62,500 scale South Mills) provide interesting land use change evidence when compared to current maps. The Great Dismal Swamp is quite accessible. Though most visitors will drive to the western entrance near Suffolk, Virginia, or traverse by boat on the Intracoastal Waterway, the more intrepid may bike 100 miles of old logging trails or slip by canoe into the historic canal system, "a crazy-quilt pattern of lock-regulated waterways" (Turnage 1995, p. 26).

Also protected are the major wildlife refugees of Alligator River, the Pocosin Lakes in southern Tyrrell and Washington counties, and Mackay Island in Currituck County, which is within a 20 minute drive from Virginia Beach, but accessible from the remainder of North Carolina only by ferry (Figure 10.2 and CP 10.14). Within the great expanses of the Alligator River National Wildlife Refuge exist two highly contrasting uses of the land. In the dense wilderness lives the only animal declared extinct in the wild, but successfully reintroduced, *canis rufus*, the red wolf. Its numbers have increased from 14 in the 1970s to nearly 300 at present (Burgess 1999). 'Howling safaris' are led by Refuge staff from the Creek Cut Trailhead off of U.S. 64, some 25 miles west of Manteo. On the other hand, along U.S. 264 between Engelhard and Stumpy Point, visitors may have their wilderness experience interrupted by the roar of jets streaking low overhead. Air Force planes from bases along the Eastern Seaboard regularly make practice runs on the Dare County Bombing Range located in the southeastern part of the Alligator Refuge.

Note how the wetlands stand out as green and brown colored areas on the Albemarle land use map (CP 10.13). Several smaller wildlife refugees, a couple of state parks, Wright Brothers and Fort Raleigh National Monuments and, most notably, the Cape Hatteras National Seashore complement the extensive designated and protected lands of the Albemarle. Much recreational use is made of these natural areas, as exemplified by Merchant's

Millpond, a state park in Gates County (CP 10.15). This particular county is much more uneven in its wetland character, a condition that has in an earlier day yielded a number of mill ponds.

Two major arteries provide for the region's transportation needs. On the one hand, there is the natural waterway provided by the Albemarle Sound and its smaller linkages of Currituck, Roanoke, and Croatan sounds, to the Pamlico Sound and the Oregon Inlet. Through these sounds, and with the help of the region's sections of the Intracoastal Waterway, move a great variety of waterborne traffic, from all sizes of pleasure crafts to fishing trawlers and barges full of woodchips, logs, or roadbed materials.

On the other hand, land transportation is facilitated by a combination of roads that reach into the region from its surroundings, encircle the Albemarle Sound by a number of bridges, and then extend in a similar fashion to the Outer Banks. The increase in traffic to the Outer Banks was aided in 1995 by the addition of a new two lane span on the Wright Memorial Bridge across the Currituck Sound. The 4.4 km (2.8 mile) span is expected to hasten traffic flow by one hour during peak periods when the bridge carries upwards of 60,000 vehicles per hour, most of it originating in Virginia. North Carolina traffic to the Dare and Currituck beaches arrives via Roanoke Island. Though this route is not as infamous in its traffic congestion, there are serious problems during periods of hurricane evacuation. In early 1999 construction began on the state's longest bridge, a structure that will take U.S. 64 on four lanes nearly six miles across the Croatan Sound, bypassing the town of Manteo.

Highway access to and within the Albemarle is considered quite limited, with the only four lane highways being a fifteen mile stretch on US 158 and a longer distance on US 17. These connect the region from Hertford and Elizabeth City to Virginia, most of the route following the Intracoastal Waterway/Great Dismal Swamp Canal. The 1.5 million population Norfolk-Virginia Beach metropolitan area, with its concentration of jobs, shopping opportunities, and tourist markets, is but a 30 minute drive from Elizabeth City, and an hour or so from the Currituck beaches. It is no wonder that Virginians dominate the new vacation homes which increasingly crowd the dunes. Clearly, the Virginia influence on this part of the Albemarle SGR, initiated with southward flowing 17th Century agricultural settlements, is greater than that of any North Carolina metro region. One caveat associated with road building in this very low lying terrain, is the need for drainage canals to be positioned parallel to the roads. Many canals were created by providing fill for the road bed in an earlier day. Over the two decades since 1980 there have been 30 drownings of people whose autos have gone off the road and plunged into a parallel canal.

Comparatively speaking the region has an older population, more poverty, a higher infant mortality rate, and lower levels of education than the average for the state (Table 10.2). Though not the most desirable human condition, this is the norm for the more rural geographic regions in the state. However, in the Albemarle, dynamic change is occurring along the seashores where a building boom is affecting the once thinly populated beaches. Notable contrasts exists among the nine counties comprising the Albemarle Region. In population, Pasquotank County is the largest with 34,897 in 2000; about 50 percent are found in the region's largest town, Elizabeth City, home of one of the state's 16 regional university campuses. This is also about one fourth of the region's total population. With the exception of the Dare and Currituck coasts, people are spread thinly over the wetlands and the slightly elevated interfluves, concentrating only in the few small county seats. Neither Camden nor Currituck counties have incorporated county seats, with the latter's courthouse/jail standing forlorn and isolated in the northern part of the county, close to Virginia, but 35 miles from the heated development activity along the Currituck coast. Plymouth, the county seat of Washington, is the second largest town with 4,107 people in 2000. However, Plymouth and most other towns on the mainland of the Albemarle SGR have been losing population over the past decades. The average population growth of 21.4 percent for the 1990s for the state is exceeded only by Dare and Currituck counties, but with their 31.7 and 32.4 percent increases, respectively, these are also two of the most rapidly growing counties in the state. In fact, Dare County more than doubled its population over the past two decades. On the other hand, Washington and Tyrrell counties are both losing population at the turn of the millennium.

The county's age-gender diagrams portrayed in Figures 10.13a-i reflect these population contrasts. Approaches to evaluating these are provided in Chapter 9. With the state's characteristic profile (Figure 9.12) providing a standard of comparison in these diagrams (black lines) several distinguishing aspects can be pointed to. For the counties in general, the population profiles appear more ragged than the norm due to their generally small population totals. Thus small deviations assume greater influence when plotted by their five year age cohort distributions (note especially Tyrrell and Camden). Still evident is the more youthful appearance of the rapidly growing counties of Currituck and Dare, where 25 to 40 year olds dominate the recreational support economy. Here also is evidence of early retirement settlement. Elizabeth City's influence is clearly seen on Pasquotank's diagram. A young population tied to the state university and the

largest town in the Albemarle SGR has also determined the largest percentage of children. Virginia employment opportunities are influencing recent slight increases in Gates County's 20 year cohorts, especially for males. It will be interesting to see the effects on its population of the opening of the Nucor Steel plant across the Chowan River in Hertford County (see Chapter 11). An aging-in-place process explains the more top-heavy appearance of counties like Perquimans, Chowan, and to a lesser extent, Washington.

Economically, the Albemarle SGR is founded primarily on agriculture (compare CP 5.3e with CP 5.3f), some forestry (CP 10.16) and fishing (Photo 5.10), and retail and service industries. During the 1960s, agriculture increasingly came into the hands of large corporate farms that were very busy in the 1970s dredging, ditching and reclaiming wetlands, in part in anticipation of accessing the peat resources (CP 10.8 through CP 10.10). As of 1974, First Colony Farms, Inc. owned close to 375,000 acres of land in Washington, Dare, and Hyde counties. Nearby acreage was owned by Mattamuskeet Farms and Shima-American Farms. These lands are readily identified on CP 10.13 as very large contiguous cultivated areas, in fact, the largest in the state. Crops raised include corn, wheat, soybeans, peanuts, Irish potatoes, and cotton. Livestock includes primarily broilers, but also hogs and cattle. Particular problems attend the emphasis on agriculture and forestry in Tyrrell, Washington and Perquimans counties. Resultant economic weaknesses have caused the state to place these counties in its Enterprise Tiers 1 and 2 (see Chapter 9). In the three counties, double digit unemployment is not unusual in the best of times, and all three find it disconcerting to see the thousands of tourist and vacation home owners passing through their county, leaving little behind except for occasional holiday traffic jams and rutted roads.

In Tyrrell County, there has recently been a special effort to capture the public en route to the beaches. Columbia, with a population of about 850, is the county seat and a community in place for over 200 years. It is now being renovated. A boardwalk along the Scuppernong River has been built, canoe trails have been marked, and local merchants and investors are encouraged to invest in tourist facilities and services. An outgrowth of several communities in the region pursuing environmental education interests has been the Partnership for the Sounds, now headquartered in Columbia. Complementary to these developments, the state has plans to buy the 18,000 acre Buckridge Tract that link two parts of the 30,000 Alligator National Wildlife Refuge, thus allowing black bears and red wolves to roam freely. Now the objective is to encourage eco-tourism. Presently owned by French interests, the Buckridge Tract is heavily logged yet it still holds some 5,000 acres of Atlantic white cedar, the largest known concentration in North Carolina, and half of the state's remaining acreage of this species. Further, the tract will become the Coastal Management Division's first inland Estuarine Coastal Reserve. It is hoped that a special kind of tourist will plan to stop at Buckridge, while supporting individuals in the Columbia community: the artist, the tour guide, the bed and breakfast owner, the gas sta-

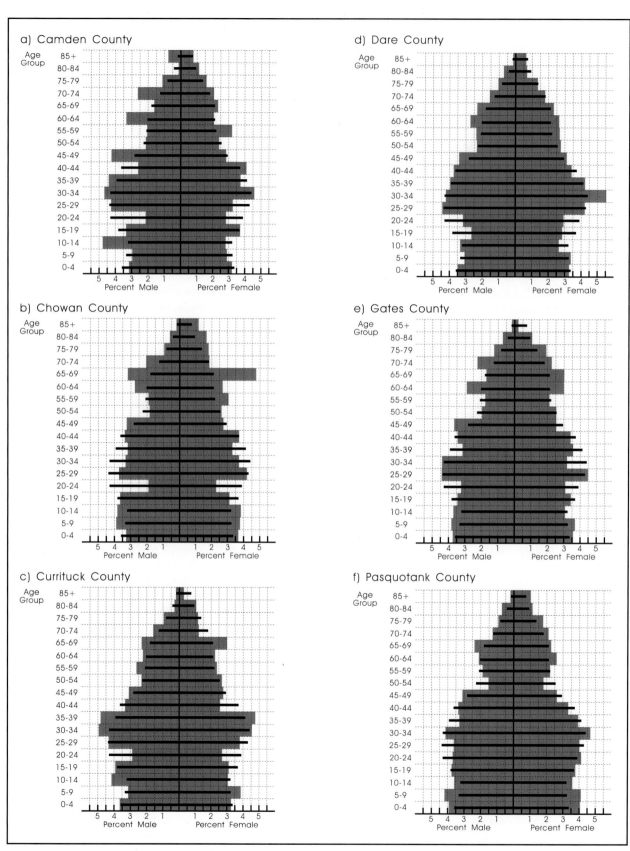

**Figure 10.13 a-f:** Albemarle Population Diagrams. Solid black lines represent state averages.
**Source:** U.S. Bureau of the Census, 1990.

368

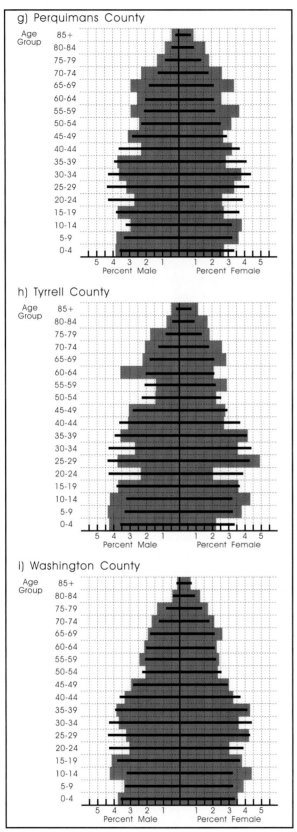

g) Perquimans County

Age Group

h) Tyrrell County

Age Group

i) Washington County

Age Group

**Figure 10.13 g-i:** Albemarle Population Diagrams.
Solid black lines represent state averages.
**Source:** U.S. Bureau of the Census, 1990.

tion attendant (Henderson 1998). The efforts at establishing Columbia as a historically renovated community attractive to the tourist is the last in the line of preservation efforts for the Albemarle communities. Among these Edenton (CP 10.2, 10.3 and 10.17) and Hertford offer outstanding examples, as does Elizabeth City. It is interested to note how the late 20th Century rush in development, that has transformed towns elsewhere in the state, by its absence here has left the region's historic architectural treasures virtually intact.

Manufacturing employment in the Albemarle is the lowest among the state geographic regions. Rather, it is in service employment that opportunities reign. Here the jobs are at the coast, and to a critical degree they are seasonal in nature, due to the seasonal ebb and flow of tourism. Also they tend to be toward the lower end of the pay scale. Even so, small retail businesses, restaurants, and tourist services, complemented by realty and construction people, are increasingly populating the beach resort communities on a year around basis.

Concerns over the fate of remaining natural areas are heightened by continuing development pressures in both Dare and Currituck counties. New developments in combination with the ravages of ocean and weather are rapidly overtaking the traditional and historic facilities, as in the case of lighthouses and coastal rescue stations. A couple of decades ago there was very little activity on the Currituck beaches, except for the Whalehead Club built by E. C. Knight in the 1920s and the Currituck Lighthouse built in 1875, the oldest on the coast and the only one never moved (CP 10.18). From the top of the lighthouse there is a splendid view of the ocean and sound environments split by the slender barrier of sand supporting the lighthouse and the rapidly growing number of resort communities to the south. Toward the north are views of a wilderness where the few remaining Outer Banks wild ponies, not now confined to the Shackleford Banks near Atlantic City in Beaufort County still roam (CP 10.19).

The Hatteras Lighthouse was in a much more precarious natural setting. In 1996, Hurricane Bertha covered NC Highway 12 under twelve feet of water just a few miles south of the lighthouse. The lighthouse stood 1,600 feet from the shoreline when built. By 1998, this distance had been reduced to 120 feet. A controversy resulted about whether to protect it where it stood by hardening the shoreline, or to relocate it. Subsequently, in 1998, and over strong local protest, Congress funded the move of the 208 foot high, 4,800 tons, 131 year old brick lighthouse, to a position 1,600 feet away from the ocean (CP 1.3). At an estimated cost exceeding $12 million, the move was successfully completed in July of 1999, in spite of the structural problems evidenced by razor thin vertical cracks running foot to top. The relocated lighthouse should be safe for another 100 years at the present rate of coastal erosion (Woodbury 1999). In the meantime, offshore ships, sailing near the "Graveyard of the Atlantic," rely on their navigational global positioning systems to stay clear of the dangerous shoals. Here, incidentally, new attempts have been made to raise the turret ironclad USS Monitor, laid to rest during a fierce storm on New Year's Eve, 1862, some 16 miles southeast of Hatteras.

369

Settlement on the Dare County beaches varies. By far the densest population is on Bodie Island in and near the villages of Southern Shores, Kitty Hawk, Kill Devil Hills, and Nags Head. In the aggregate, these villages have seen their populations grow from 9,460 in 1990 to 13,789 in 2000, and these are the permanent residents! Due to the awesome population explosion occurring during the vacation season and holidays, the area experiences many problems of the human-physical environment interface. The Cape Hatteras National Seashore, and other federal and state environmental preserves and parks, including Jockey's Ridge State Park and the Wright's Brothers Memorial (now preparing for its century celebration in 2003), combine with numerous commercial attractions to draw in masses of tourists that move at a snail's pace along the limited access routes. That the latter part of the tourist season coincides with the peak of the hurricane season only worsens the prospect of human disaster. Other, seemingly smaller problems, gnaw at human-environment relations. Jockey's Ridge is on a relentless march relocating itself at the whim of the wind. What is the answer for threatened roads, businesses, such as the miniature golf course with only the parapets of its castle visible above the sands and private homes? Do we allocate a million dollars to move parts of the largest sand dune on the Atlantic Seaboard, dump truck by dump truck, as was proposed in 1994? Or do we buy out the private property owners? The state declared the ridge an Area of Environmental Concern in 1988, an act that should leave out any options for interfering with its natural migration.

Or take the problem of the plover, a small endangered shore bird that has the unfortunate habit of nesting from April to August in areas popular with vacation fishers. The federal government controls most of this property, and therefore has the responsibility to protect the wildlife. It decided in 1995 to ban the flying of kites, off-road vehicles, fishing, fireworks, and other activities threatening the domestic tranquility of the plover, thereby releasing a storm of protest from local public officials and businesses who viewed the potential loss of cash paying tourists to be much greater that the prospective loss of another species (Photo 1.6).

*Pamlico*

The Pamlico State Geographic Region is a water and wilderness wonderland. Dominated by its three peninsulas (the southern half of the Pamlico, the Aurora Peninsula and the Carteret Peninsula) and by the Pamlico Sound, its other major water features include Lake Mattamuskeet, Pungo River, the lower courses of the Pamlico and Neuse rivers, and Core and Bogue sounds (Figure 10.14). Pocosins and wetlands cover much of the 9,007 square kilometers of land area (the reader can compare essential data in Table 10.3 with other state geographic regions in Table 9.2). Much of the land is preserved in large designated wildlife refuges (Mattamuskeet, Pocosin Lakes, Swanquarter, and Cedar Island) and other federal lands. Some holdings are large, like the Croatan National Forest, the Cape Lookout National Seashore and the Ocracoke Island part of the Cape Hatteras National Seashore. Others are small, like the Theodore Roosevelt Natural Area on Bogue Banks. State lands are also extensive, including part of the Hofmann State Forest in Jones County, designated Game Lands covering thousands of acres, and two state parks, Goose Creek in Beaufort County and Fort Macon in Carteret County. Thus, as observable on CP 10.20, land use is mostly forest, pocosin, and open savanna, with some water controlled cultivated areas, on the mainland. Then there are the slender offshore islands with dense development confined to Bogue Banks and Harker's Island, and a few larger urban places situated at favorable river sites (New Bern and Washington) or at port locations with channel access to the Atlantic Ocean (Morehead City and Beaufort).

A particularly unique land use is the strip mining of phosphatic rock, a sedimentary rock containing phosphates in commercial quantity and used for fertilizers and other products, near Aurora on the Pamlico River in Beaufort County. Recent topographic maps indicate that about fifteen square miles of surface has been disturbed thus far. There is a continuing process of stripping, sorting, storing and the shipping out of the materials, as well as redistributing the waste materials on environmental reclamation sites (CP 10.21 to 10.23). Escavation was begun in 1962 by the Texasgulf Corporation, with the property sold in 1995 to the Potash Corporation of Saskatchewan, Canada. Claimed by the Smithsonian Institution to be one of the country's leading fossil sites, collectors line up for the one day per week tour of the 110 feet deep mine pit (Photos 1.1 and 10.8). Shark teeth and

| PAMLICO | Land Area in sq. km | Pop. 1990 | Pop. sq.km. 2000 | Pop. 2000 | 1990s % Pop. Change | % White 2000 | Median Age in 2000 | % Fam. Below Poverty | Annual Average Infant Mortality Rate 1994-98 | % High School Grads'90 | % Coll. Grads. 1990 | Fem. Fam. Head of Hshld'90 | NC Enterprise Tiers'97 |
|---|---|---|---|---|---|---|---|---|---|---|---|---|---|
| Beaufort | 2,144 | 42,283 | 21.0 | 44,958 | 6.3 | 68.4 | 39.7 | 15.9 | 12.9 | 65.9 | 10.8 | 13.5 | 2 |
| Carteret | 1,376 | 52,408 | 43.2 | 59,383 | 13.3 | 90.4 | 40.2 | 9.1 | 7.8 | 75.5 | 16.2 | 9.5 | 4 |
| Craven | 1,801 | 81,812 | 50.8 | 91,436 | 11.8 | 69.9 | 33.4 | 10.5 | 7.6 | 75.9 | 15.1 | 11.9 | 3 |
| Hyde | 1,587 | 5,411 | 3.7 | 5,826 | 7.7 | 62.7 | 40.9 | 20.1 | 10.7 | 60.0 | 7.7 | 15.3 | 1 |
| Jones | 1,226 | 9,361 | 8.5 | 10,381 | 10.9 | 61.0 | 38.6 | 16.9 | 13.6 | 62.4 | 8.1 | 13.8 | 3 |
| Pamlico | 873 | 11,368 | 14.8 | 12,934 | 13.8 | 73.2 | 43.4 | 15.8 | 6.8 | 65.9 | 11.6 | 12.1 | 3 |
| **Region Totals** | **9,007** | **202,643** | **25.0** | **224,918** | **11.0** | **74.6** | **39.4** | **14.7** | **9.9** | **67.6** | **11.6** | **12.7** | **2.7** |

**Table 10.3:** Pamlico State Geographic Region, 1990-2000.
**Source:** U. S. Bureau of the Census; North Carolina State Planning Office 1997-2000.

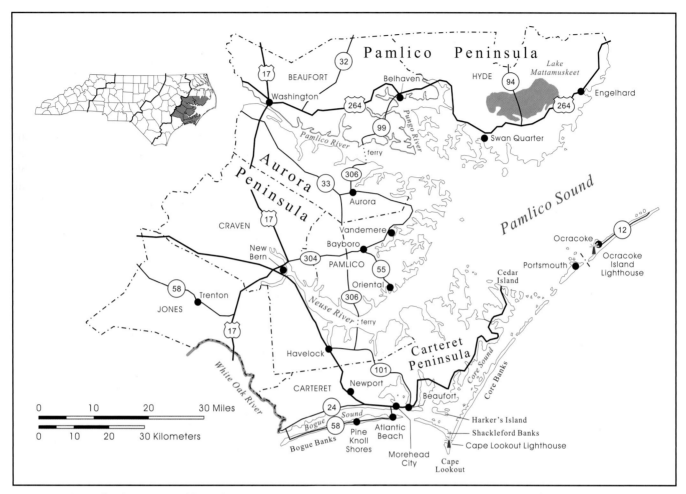

**Figure 10.14:** Pamlico State Geographic Region.

corral are frequently found on the streets of Aurora and roads of the adjacent countryside, paved, as they are, with waste materials from the mine. With over 1,000 employees commuting from a four county region, this is an important economic engine in the Pamlico Region. On the other hand, the mining and refining operation is also one of the worst environmental polluters in the state of North Carolina (CP 10.23 and Chapter 8).

Figures 10.15a-f aptly show the demographic characteristic of aging-in-place county populations that dominate all but Craven and Carteret counties in the Pamlico SRG. So in four of the region's six counties the tendency is for an above state average share of people beginning with the 50-54 cohorts; people who have grown or are growing into their retirement years by staying in their place of residence. Pamlico County is particularly striking in this condition. Though Carteret's profile resembles this same condition, its excess of elderly is conditioned greatly by retiree migrants finding a permanent home in the popular beach communities on Bogue Banks, in Beaufort and along the sounds, at least for their early years of retirement in the county (Bennett 1992). Craven, on the other hand, has a population whose decidedly youthful character is influenced by the U. S. Marines base at Havelock. Here also the large youthful component contributes

to a higher than average number of births. Interestingly it is the much higher fertility rates in Beaufort, Pamlico, and Jones counties that is keeping these counties' percentages of children higher than the norm for the state. With few opportunities for people finishing their education the age cohorts of 20-34 are left at extraordinarily low levels in the counties of Beaufort, Hyde, Pamlico, and Jones.

Table 9.2 shows the Pamlico SGR to be a comparatively slow growing region at 11 percent for the 1990s, about 50 percent of the state's population rate of increase, and much less than the Cape Fear SGR to the south. Dependent to a large extent on seasonal tourism and vacationers, the permanent population of 224,918 in 2000, is older than the state average with a higher rate of poverty. With so much land in natural areas the population tends to be highly concentrated, although no large city exists in the region. The three northern counties of Hyde, Beaufort and Pamlico have the most thinly distributed population, and are very much like the counties of the Albemarle SGR, a condition clearly evident in their county population diagrams (Figure 10.15). For these counties only Washington (9,583 people), county seat of Beaufort, provides comprehensive urban services. Villages, including Bath (the colonial settlement on the north shore of the

371

**Photo 10.8:** Phosphate mine pit on the Durham Creek leading into the Pamlico River, in Beaufort County. From this early mine, depicted here in the mid-1960s, the operation has expanded to cover fifteen square miles of land surface, as indicated in Color Plate 10.22. Here a huge dragline removes 54 Cubic meters (70 cubic yards) in each scoop. Use the pick-up truck this side of the dragline to help understand the scale of this operation. (NC Department of Commerce)

Pamlico River), Belhaven (also a popular stop-over for the "boat people" travelling the Intracoastal Waterway; Photo 5.10), Engelhard, and Ocracoke depend largely on fishing and tourism. Ocracoke Island is accessible only by ferry (CP 1.12, 5.9 and 10.1). Its more rapid and more frequent connection to Hatteras Island by a free state road ferry has made the locals feel closer to the people of Dare County than with those of their home county of Hyde. A two-hour and 15-minute private and fee based ferry journey connects Ocracoke Village to the very small and unincorporated county seat of Swan Quarter. Here one occasionally hears complaints and talk of secession from the island across the Pamlico Sound. However, the 600 plus Ocracoke islanders contribute 40 percent of the tax revenues of a county of over 5,000 people. So Hyde County is not apt to let the island go. Ocracoke is still surviving well with its intent to stay clear of major resort development in the vicinity of its sheltered cove (Photo 10.9). Hatteras National Seashore prevents private land use on the remainder of the island.

New Bern, county seat of Craven, doubled its territory by annexation during the 1990s, and had 23,128 in 2000. As noted at the beginning of this chapter, this was a colonial capital of North Carolina, and as such it is a very viable historic center attractive to tourists (CP 10.4). In the late 1970s, many of the Tidewater towns improved their attractiveness considerably by engaging in comprehensive waterfront redevelopment projects. In the case of New Bern, urban redevelopment in the 1960s opened a lot of space in the heart of the city and along the waterfront (CP 10.24). Today the town functions primarily as an important processing center for the regional lumber/pulp/paper and agricultural industries, while being the leading commercial center for the Pamlico

**Photo 10.9:** Ocracoke, looking northwest across the village on Spring Lake, the harbor site. Three centuries of shifting economic fortunes now finds the village struggling to maintain its romantic aura in the face of threatened speculative development. (NC Office of Tourism)

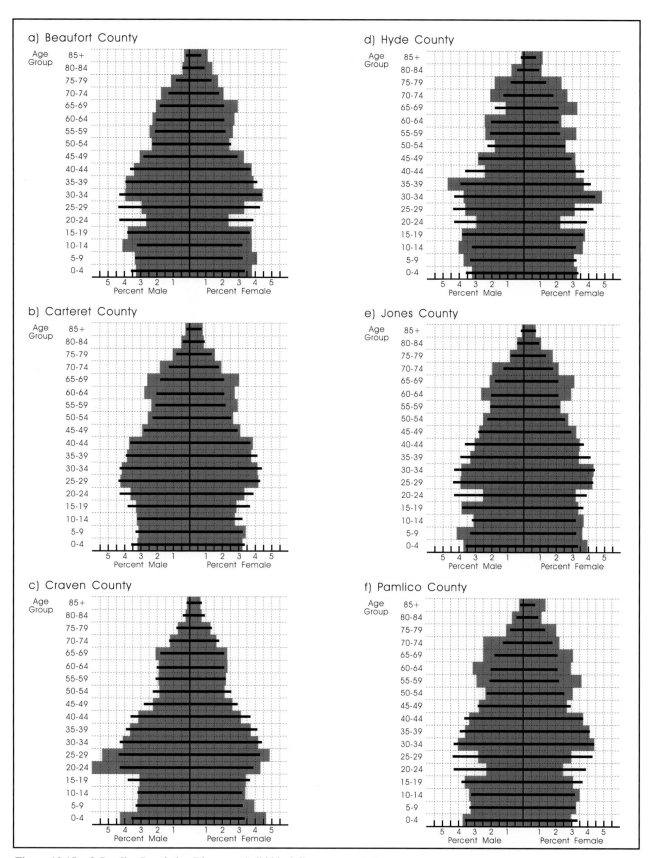

**Figure 10.15 a-f:** Pamlico Population Diagrams. Solid black lines represent state averages.
**Source:** U.S. Bureau of the Census,1990.

373

Region, particularly the nearby Cherry Point Marine Air Station. Cherry Point's concentration of Marines also impacts Craven County's population, as indicated in Figure 10.15c where two male cohorts (20-29 year olds) are each in excess of six per cent of the total population. There is also a large boat building firm (Hatteras Yachts).

New Bern connects to the Carteret County "Crystal Coast" via U.S. 70, by far the busiest stretch of highway in the Pamlico SGR. Tying together the towns of New Bern, Havelock (with its Cherry Point Base), Newport, Morehead City, Beaufort, and Atlantic Beach, the road also passes through the only national forest east of the Piedmont Region. Croatan National Forest occupies an unrelentingly flat area, typical of the Tidewater Region, with no elevation exceeding four meters (twelve feet). It has been equally affected by the sequence of settlement behavior, from the 18th century development of agriculture and water mills, to the late 19th century beginning of the "cut-and-get-out" period that saw the area riddled by logging railroads. By the 1930s the land was degraded from decades of cut-over forestry, and available at a cost reflecting its low productivity, for assembly into the Croatan National Forest (Phillips 1997). Very little of the earlier cultural imprint remains in a landscape now dominated by poorly drained swamp and pocosin, or by upland surfaces managed by the forest service for timber harvest of pine trees at a 30-35 year rotation. Croatan National Forest covers about 160,000 acres of land in Craven, Carteret, and Jones counties. Jones, the least densely populated county in the Pamlico SRG, with a persistently declining population, shares another large regulated forest, the Hofmann Forest, with Onslow County. Hofmann is North Carolina State University's experimental forest.

Carteret is the most rapidly growing county in the Pamlico (Table 10.3). Its population profile exhibits a typical young adult dominated structure, though there is also evidence of early retiree settlement (Figure 10.15f). Port facilities, fishing and boat building industries flourish in the twin cities of Morehead City and Beaufort. Seasonally conditioned recreation and tourism dominate the islands of Bogue Banks, and Harker's Island remains very much a "waterman's" island, not a playground. Morehead City (7,691 people in 2000) has one of the two state port facilities, the other and larger being in Wilmington (CP 10.25). This town also has the bridge to Bogue Banks, and thus the heavy summer traffic. The county seat of Beaufort (3,771), a seaport founded in 1710, appears more laid back and devoted to sailing sports (CP 10.26). Across Taylor Channel it may be possible to spot the herds of wild ponies. In excess of a hundred ponies are presently grazing on Shackleford Banks. The wild mustangs are the remnants of a larger herd of close to 300 that in 1997 was afflicted by a devastating disease called equine infectious anemia. Shackleford, incidentally, is being proposed as a designated wilderness area. Despite the earlier location on the Banks of two whaling villages, Diamond City on the east and Wade's Shore on the west, the island has long been abandoned, and there is now little evidence of any physical structure ever having existed here. Combined with federal management, these

are all aspects that lend support for the seven mile barrier island to be included in the wilderness system (Morris 1998).

Waterfowl brought considerable seasonal income to the vast coastal areas of Carteret County. In addition to the long since abandoned village of Portsmouth on Portsmouth Island there were a number of villages on the mainland along Core Sound (Atlantic, Stacy, and Davis among these) that provided boarding houses, hunting guides, decoy makers, lodge caretakers, and boat builders for the many sport hunters who began frequenting the area shortly following the Civil War. Core Sound Islands and the Core Banks provided locations for some of the prominent clubs, such as Hog Island Hunting Club, Harbor Island Club, the Carteret Gun and Rod Club and the Pilentary Hunting Club, which was visited by Franklin Delano Roosevelt prior to his presidency (Dudley 1993). Of longer lasting relevance were the new skills brought to a local population traditionally engaged in agriculture, forestry and fishing. The vast land purchases made by outsiders in the support of the clubs also had a long lasting impact. Holdings on this scale made it easier to move from private to federal ownership in the process of procuring the Cape Lookout National Seashore in the 1960s.

Portsmouth Island, Core Banks, and Shackleford Banks now provide North Carolina with its most extensive length of unspoiled and difficult to access, Outer Banks. But to the immediate west of Shackleford is Bogue Banks, the throbbing heart of the "Crystal Coast", and its most crowded and environmentally endangered part (Figure 10.14). The 21 miles of N.C. 58 on Bogue Banks is just about one continuous commercial and residential strip (CP10.27-CP10.29). One hundred percent development of Bogue Island is prevented by a portion of the old Roosevelt family estate being preserved as the Theodore Roosevelt Natural Area, a 265 acre maritime forest and tidal wetlands, and by the eastern point serving as Fort Macon State Park.

Spatial variations in the human landscape, and among the communities comprising the Pamlico State Geographic Region, these are, as we have seen, considerable. Counties in the region do not benefit equally from their ocean and sound proximity, and some of them exhibit major internal contrasts. They range in wealth from the Tier 1 designated Hyde, with 20% of its families below the poverty level, to the Tier 4 designated Carteret. They reflect the complexities of life opportunities, from Hyde, which gained only 7 percent population in the 1990s, to Carteret which gained 12.3 percent (Table 10.3 and Figures 10.15a-f). Some of the data, of course, is weakened in its ability to demonstrate basic social relationships due to the small size of the population for several counties.

### Cape Fear

The Cape Fear State Geographic Region is the state's largest in area (Table 9.2 and Figure 10.16). It is defined on the human spatial organization that is linked in settlement, transportation and historic economic development to the ecologic uniqueness of the lower Cape Fear River basin. An inspection of CP 10.30 supports this contention. A slender ribbon of coastal and frequently highly congested habitation gives way to a broad band of traditional Tidewater Region wetlands and forests. Providing sustenance for the natural environment in its predominately flat and close to sea level condition is the Cape Fear River and its tributaries. The central drainage arteries of this large watershed can be seen on the map to extend its green network far into the Coastal Plain Region linking the latter naturally and, over history, functionally to the Wilmington node. A boundary between tidewater and coastal plain geography is observable as the dominance of natural environmental features give way to a cultural landscape dominated by agricultural lands. These are in only two significant areas interrupted by poorly drained and thinly settled conditions. Northwest of Wilmington, upstream from the confluence of the Cape Fear and its tributaries of the Black and the South rivers, lies an area suffused with oblong shaped lakes, shrublands and forests. This is the heart of the Carolina Bays, a natural region described in greater detail in Chapter 11. While

much of this natural area is enclosed by the Bladen Lakes State Forest, to its south there is the largely privately held Green Swamp. Focused on Lake Waccamaw, and owned largely by pulp and paper companies, this, the largest remaining swamp in the state, is clearly observable as well on CP 10.30. For the remainder of the Coastal Plain Region the map shows the very clear land use contrasts between cultivated lands and the river courses.

As a metropolitan dominated state geographic region, the only one in the Tidewater, Cape Fear demonstrates a considerable diversity in its population characteristics measured by five year age cohorts in Figures 10.17 a-h. The four interior counties of Sampson, Duplin, Bladen and Columbus share an above average percentage of children in the 10-19 age cohorts, for then to see an abrupt drop to well below state averages for the 20-29 age cohorts, a condition that is duplicated less definitively by Pender County. These are rural and agriculturally dependent counties that are limited in opportunities for young people, though the

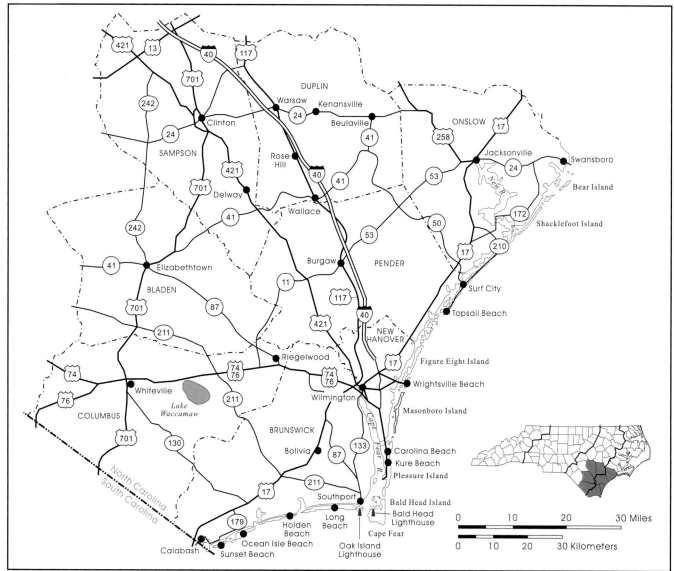

**Figure 10.16:** Cape Fear State Geographic Region.

375

predominantly female labor force demand in the recently expanded hog manufacturing industry is boding well for younger and middle aged women; already in 1990 there is a considerable difference in males and females in the 30-44 age cohorts in Bladen County. For Pender County as for Brunswick there is a considerable fattening of the population profile in the 60-74 age cohorts, clear evidence of the younger retireee population settling into these coastal counties. The absence of elderly care support systems leave a lower than norm older retiree population in these counties.

As earlier discussed it is the estuary of the Cape Fear that evolved as the critical node of settlement and economic influence in this state geographic region. Figure 10.16 shows the Wilmington location as the heart of a web of road connections. U.S. 74/76 connects the city along a southern trajectory to Whiteville (Columbus County seat) and Charlotte, with U.S. 76 dropping off to Columbia, South Carolina. U.S. 421 ties the city to the central portion of the Cape Fear SGR to Clinton in Sampson County, and beyond this to Fayetteville and then diagonally across the state to its northwestern margins. Interstate 40 now brings people of the Wilmington region within an hour and a half of the state capital and the heart of Main Street. The Tidewater Region's major transportation link, U.S. 17 connects Wilmington to Jacksonville, and points north, and to Myrtle Beach and Charleston, in South Carolina, to the south. U.S. 17 is also the major connector to the beach resorts. In sum, the functional region of Wilmington extends well into the Coastal Plain tying the counties of Columbus, Bladen, Sampson, and Duplin more effectively to this port city and cultural heart of North Carolina's southeast. Of course, another city is included within the Cape Fear State Geographic Region. Jacksonville provides a very different and economically more narrowly defined urban region. Its experience of recent explosive growth, its population more than doubling from 30,398 in 1990 to 66,715 in 2000, was fuelled almost entirely (98 percent) by annexation. Most of the residential areas adjacent to the massive Marine Corps base of Camp Lejeune became incorporated to the city that by this administrative expansion more than doubled its area. Wilmington, on the other hand, increased largely through net inmigration from 55,530 in 1990 to 75,838 in 2000. Wilmington had very limited annexations in spite of the threat of the city administration to aggressively annex territory within New Hanover County. Voters, however,

have traditionally fought annexation and, in 1995, disapproved a city-county consolidation. So Wilmington continues as the most spatially confined incorporated urban place in the state, with urbanization spilling out of the city into small communities fiercely guarding the independence of their municipalities. In New Hanover County the preference clearly favors a multiplicity of municipalities rather than an administrative simplicity and economy which might lead to farsighted integrated urban planning.

For Jacksonville and Wilmington the other side of the coin becomes visible by comparing population change for their respective counties. Here New Hanover County (Wilmington) passed Onslow (Jacksonville) during the 1990s (Table 10.4). Certainly, both counties have substantial populations, over 150,000 each in 2000, but now New Hanover, the second smallest in physical size in the state, will be four times as densely populated as Onslow. In population size their nearest competitor of Brunswick is at 73,143 in 2000, but all counties in the region have substantial populations, three times the size, on the average, of the Albemarle and Pamlico SGR counties.

There are other critical differences between the two leading urban counties. Jacksonville's dependence on Camp Lejeune, and its ancillary bases, leaves the population structure decidedly skewed toward the young and the male of the species. Its 19-34 year old cohort was 40 percent of its population in 1997, while New Hanover's was 17 percent. Notice in Table 10.4 the difference in the two counties' median age, and the reverse in the rate of attainment of high school and college diplomas. Population profiles (Figures 10.17e and f) further substantiate the critical differences in these two counties. New Hanover has a typical urban structure with a dominance of young and middle aged people, including late year teens because of the University of North Carolina at Wilmington. In contrast Onslow's population is dominated by young male Marines, who tend to rotate in and out of the base to other places during their tour of duty. With recent reductions in the Marines, and in the non-service support workers on the bases, Onslow County is barely maintaining its present population, while New Hanover continues to outpace statewide population growth due to its entrepot and recreational service functions, and to its historic/cultural significance. The military bases have an estimated direct and indirect impact on the Onslow County economy of $1.19 billion/year (Oliver and Towle

| CAPE FEAR | Land Area in sq. km | Pop. 1990 | Pop. sq.km. 2000 | Pop. 2000 | 1990s % Pop. Change | % White 2000 | Median Age in 2000 | % Fam. Below Poverty | Annual Average Infant Mortality Rate 1994-98 | % High School Grads'90 | % Coll. Grads. 1990 | Fem. Fam. Head of Hshld'90 | NC Enterprise Tiers'97 |
|---|---|---|---|---|---|---|---|---|---|---|---|---|---|
| Bladen | 2,266 | 28,663 | 14.2 | 32,278 | 12.6 | 57.2 | 39.3 | 19.4 | 10.3 | 56.4 | 7.7 | 16.4 | 2 |
| Brunswick | 2,214 | 50,985 | 33.0 | 73,143 | 43.5 | 82.3 | 41.7 | 11.9 | 5.4 | 69.2 | 10.7 | 10.1 | 3 |
| Columbus | 2,426 | 49,587 | 22.6 | 54,749 | 10.4 | 63.4 | 38.3 | 19.8 | 11.3 | 59.4 | 9.1 | 14.9 | 2 |
| Duplin | 2,116 | 39,995 | 23.2 | 49,063 | 22.7 | 58.7 | 37.7 | 16.2 | 11.0 | 56.4 | 6.6 | 14.1 | 4 |
| New Hanover | 515 | 120,284 | 311.3 | 160,307 | 33.3 | 79.9 | 37.5 | 9.9 | 6.7 | 78.1 | 21.2 | 13.3 | 5 |
| Onslow | 1,986 | 149,838 | 75.7 | 150,355 | 0.3 | 72.1 | 25.4 | 9.8 | 8.2 | 83.0 | 13.4 | 9.5 | 2 |
| Pender | 2,255 | 28,855 | 18.2 | 41,082 | 42.4 | 72.7 | 39.4 | 13.8 | 4.1 | 64.6 | 11.6 | 12.3 | 4 |
| Sampson | 2,449 | 47,297 | 24.6 | 60,161 | 27.2 | 64.0 | 38.2 | 17.4 | 9.5 | 61.3 | 8.1 | 14.4 | 4 |
| **Region Totals** | **16,227** | **515,504** | **38.3** | **621,138** | **20.5** | **71.6** | **37.2** | **14.8** | **8.3** | **66.1** | **11.1** | **13.1** | **3.3** |

**Table 10.4:** Cape Fear State Geographic Region, 1990-2000.
**Source:** U. S. Bureau of the Census; North Carolina State Planning Office 1997-2000.

376

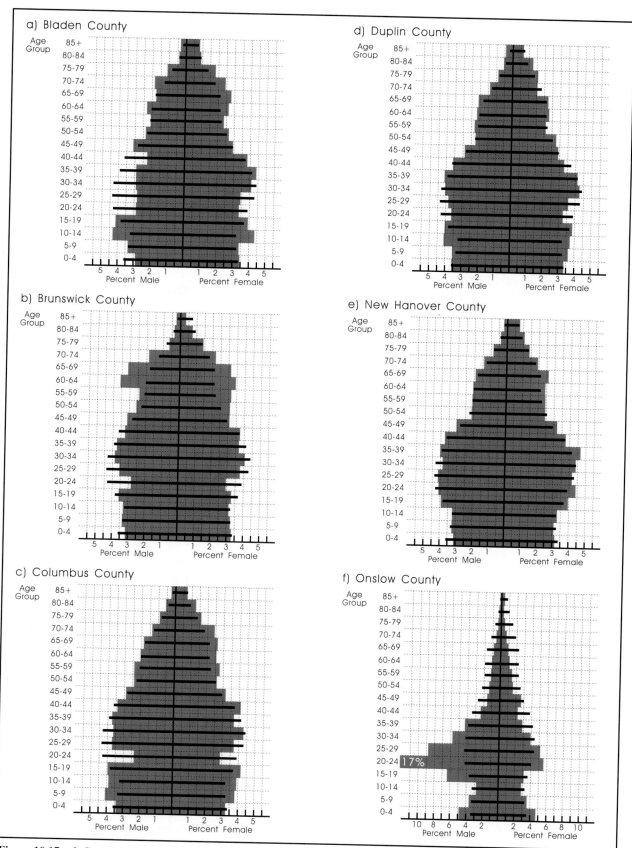

**Figure 10.17 a-f:** Cape Fear Population Diagrams. Solid black lines represent state averages.
**Source:** U.S. Bureau of the Census,1990.

377

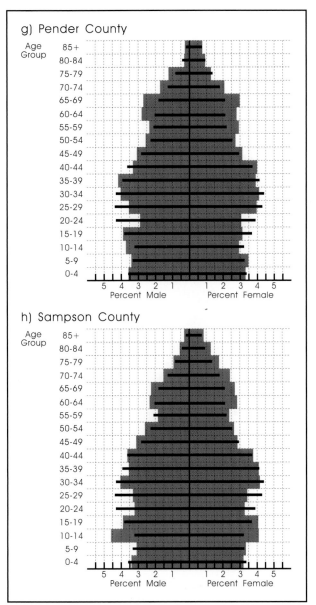

**Figure 10.17 g-h:** Cape Fear Population Diagrams.
Solid black lines represent state averages.
**Source:** U.S. Bureau of the Census,1990.

Wilmington's urban growth has been supported by a complexity of factors over the centuries. Duncan Randall (1968) identified three distinct periods of growth since early colonial times. Initially Wilmington functioned as a regional port, deriving its energy from its position as the entrepot of the Cape Fear river basin. At the turn of the 20th century the town's function as a regional trade and service center, and increasingly as a manufacturing city, emerged superior in significance to its port economy. From 1950 through the 1970s, the port function has been reestablished, notably through the establishment of the North Carolina State Port Authority and the building of the initial State Docks; manufacturing strengthened by the Riegel Paper Corporation's pulp and paper mill located some 20 miles upstream on the Cape Fear River, in Columbus County (Photo 10.10); and spillover from urban growth has caused the relocating of trade activity beyond city limits, with the resultant demise of the central business district.

At the beginning of the new millennia we see Wilmington evolving new complexities. Manufacturing has further diversified (Photo 10.11), although diminished in terms of total employment. Globalization and international trade is pushing the state port to enlarge its capacity and to facilitate access of the ever increasing size of cargo ships (CP 10.32-10.33). A historically renovated city, with a newly completed river boardwalk, has resulted in a resurgence of central city commercial activities especially focused on leisure time consumer behavior (Photos 10.12-10.14, and CP 10.34). The cultural attractiveness of Wilmington has also encouraged the investment of the motion picture industry. While referring to itself as the "Hollywood of the East," may seem a bit presumptuous, given the continuing lead role played by New York City, there are now two major studios in the city. Carolco Studios is the largest with the capability of producing five to six films on its sound stages, concurrently (Landau 1995). The image built by the film industry and the enhancement of culture and recreational commerce along the river front in the central city is also providing the city a major boost in tourist income; witness the proliferation of bed and breakfast places in nearby historic residential sections, where residents worry that newfound neighborhood ambience provided by their renovated 18th and 19th century homes will be disrupted by the increased traffic.

Wilmington urbanization is spilling over into the adjacent counties of Pender, to the north, and Brunswick, to the south. Whereas New Hanover County's population increased over 25 percent during the 1990s, both Pender and Brunswick counties increased by over 40 percent, a difficult growth transition for these two rural counties (Table 10.4). And it is clear from their population profiles (Figures 10.17b and g) that their very positive growth is assured by continuing in-migration of young retirees, as well as growth of young households locating in suburban areas adjacent to Wilmington.

However, it is not only urban overspill that is affecting change here. More important has been the continuing growth of the residential seashore. From the "Crystal Coast" to the South

1993). This includes expenditures by their supported ancillary populations of 41,000 active duty personnel, 70,000 civilian employees and dependents, and 10,000 plus military retirees (many of whom have, in fact, relocated to Core Banks in Carteret County), but does not include a multiplier effect. With the emphatic tilt in youthful and narrowly defined purchasing power, the city of Jacksonville exhibits the typical look of a "base town." A downtown with an abandoned look to it, and strip commercial development, along main highways leading to base entrances, that is dominated by second hand auto dealers, mobile home sales, and restaurant/bar concentrations, all of which reflects a military personnel presence (CP 10.31).

**Photo 10.10:** The Riegelwood Operations of Federal Paperboard Co. Inc., a pulp and paper mill with over 1,000 employees, critical to the rural employment base of Bladen and Columbus counties, and with an enormous appetite for pine logs and chip wood from the Cape Fear river basin.

**Photo 10.11:** Corning Inc. fiber plant exemplify the emergence of Wilmington as a center of the chemicals industry. Hoechst Celanese and DuPont corporations, the latter with over 2,500 workers, also located here in the late 1960s.

Carolina border, the off shore islands, with few exceptions, are humming with growth and related environmental and land use conflicts, many of which have already been dealt with. There is, in fact, a rather eclectic use of these near-shore barrier islands. Bear Island, off the coast of Pender County, is 900 acres of unspoiled habitat, with probably the most impressive dune field (30-60 feet in height) remaining along the North Carolina coast. Bear Island is now a part of Hammocks Beach State Park and accessible only by toll ferry. Shacklefoot Island is part of the Camp Lejeune Marine Corps Base and not generally accessible to visitors. Topsail, a slender island 22 miles in its northeast-southwest orientation, is shared by Pender with Onslow County. It is populated largely by single family vacation homes, all of which court disaster by their presence since the island is rated as 'most extreme risk' for any physical structure (Pilkey, et al 1998). The one-two slam of the island by hurricanes Bertha and Fran, in 1996, cleared off or damaged hundreds of homes (Photo 10.15). Two small islands, Lea and No Name lie south of Topsail; neither are populated though some 40 lots have been sold on Lea since the mid-1980s, ten of these have already gone under water from the shift in inlets. Figure Eight Island, the northernmost in New Hanover County, is privately owned and studded with expensive homes that nonetheless face natural hazards since they are even less protected than structures on Topsail Island. So far, artificial dunes are being built about as fast as they are eradicated by the elements. Figure Eight Island is accreting considerable new land as Mason Inlet is migrating in a southerly direction while eating into the northern shore of Wrightsville Beach. Here is located Shell Island Resort (CP 10.35 and 10.36), which built its ten story condominium directly in harm's way, with full knowledge of the consequences. Shell Island was joined to Wrightsville Beach by filling in the intervening inlet. A four-story Holiday Inn was placed precisely on the middle of the fill. It was the only structure on Wrightsville Beach to suffer major damage during the twin hurricanes (Bertha and Fran) of 1996 (CP 10.37). Almost completely built over, Wrightsville Beach was developed early enough to leave a continuing landscape of the old style seasonal family cottage dominated beach town. Masonboro Island is nearing complete ownership by the state, and functions as a National Estuarine Research Preserve.

Quite different is the complex of land uses found on Pleasure Island. Here, for example is Carolina Beach, a town that thrived in the 1940s and 1950s as the beach entertainment center for the Cape Fear Region, with a boardwalk, the Ocean Plaza Ballroom and eight 'juke joints', the celebrated birthplace of the 'shag' (Smith 1996). Following several decades of gradual deterioration that accompanied a crowd changing to the more boisterous and rowdy, Carolina Beach is setting an example, watched

**Photo 10.12:** In 1974, much of Wilmington's central city was listed in the National Register of Historic Places. With 200 city blocks designated this is the largest historically preserved district in the state. Eateries and other tourist attractions have flourished along Front and Water streets with the development of the River Boardwalk.

**Photo 10.13:** Cape Fear River provides important barge transport of chip wood, logs and other bulk products through several locks connecting to the inland port of Fayetteville. In the heart of Wilmington tourists can sightsee on the Henrietta II, a sternwheel riverboat, or take the river taxi to the Battleship North Carolina.

**Photo 10.14:** Wilmington's designated historic residential district covers many city blocks; here sightseers are passing a renovated early 19th century Georgian style home.

**Photo 10.15:** Ocean City Restaurant and Pier at North Topsail Beach, severely damaged by Hurricane Fran in August of 1996, was one of very few structures left standing in any shape. The federal government paid for the sand replacement that can be seen on the photo as being built up some six feet in height under the pier remnants. This new 'dune' was completely wiped out by Hurricane Bonnie in 1997. (see Box 2C and Figure 2.14)

closely by Atlantic Beach in Carteret County, of reinventing itself as a laid-back, family focused, simplistic and low cost alternative to Myrtle Beach. Pleasure Island continues with Wilmington Beach, and Kure Beach, and very little access to the sea for visitors, until Fort Fisher State Historic Site is reached. From here a ferry connection eases transit to Southport.

In Brunswick County the barrier islands veer almost due west from their beginning with the Smith Island Complex, that includes the Cape Fear promontory on Bald Head Island. On Bald Head congestion is not a problem due to private ownership and the absence of a bridge connection plus a vehicle ban, not including bikes and golf carts. Still, here and along the remainder of the islands to the South Carolina border the same litany of environmental hazards prevail; and construction of bridges and commercial buildings, as well as residential density are issues vigorously debated, and rarely resolved simply through the application of CAMA rules.

In the Cape Fear SGR there are great contrasts between the major economic activity and settlement patterns, the slender band of intense barrier island development, Wilmington's and Jacksonville's contrasting metropolitan influence, and the large interior spaces dominated by Tidewater and Coastal Plain natural environments, forestry and agriculture. Implications for the basic human condition can in part be gleaned from Table 10.4, where the upland counties of the Cape Fear Region, Duplin, Bladen, Sampson, and Columbus, distinguish themselves in various ways. These are uniformly large counties, by North Carolina standards, with low population densities distributed fairly evenly across the agricultural landscape. Population growth is below regional and state averages, while poverty levels, infant mortality rates and female heads of household rates lie well above. These are conditions well supported by the population profiles of these counties (Figures 10.17a, c, d, and h). All exhibit mature population structures that suggest little future growth. The recent boom in the hog industry is boosting the economies of

Duplin, Sampson and Bladen, resulting in their removal from the lower levels of the North Carolina Enterprise Tiers (see Chapter 9). A more detailed discussion on natural environments and economic change in the Coastal Plain portions of the Cape Fear Region is in Chapter 11.

# Coastal Plain Region

## INTRODUCTION

"Down East" is a common North Carolinian reference point for the vast plain that is bounded on the east by the inland reaches of the Tidewater and on the west by the Fall Line (Figure 11.1). The Fall Line defines the limits of a Piedmont Region with its harder crystalline rock surfaces of a higher elevation. Slightly elevated terraces, visually observed on the surface by their east facing scarps, mark the location of former floors of the Atlantic Ocean. While paralleling each other in a southerly trend, they are breached west to east by great seams of water: the Roanoke, Tar, Neuse, North East Cape Fear, South, Cape Fear, Lumber and Waccamaw rivers (Figures 10.7 and 10.8). Averaging 35 miles (120 kilometers) wide, the plain gently decreases over 200 feet in elevation from the northwest to the southeast. Well-drained dark and loamy soils of the upland surfaces provided the essential foundation for agricultural prosperity (Figure 3.6). Over the past two centuries agriculture has cycled from plantations featuring cotton to corporate and family owned farms relying on tenancy labor and prospering from tobacco, and then to a mixed crop production and animal husbandry (Photos 3.2, 5.3; CP 5.3d, CP 5.4a-c, CP 5.5, CP 5.11). While the major rivers and their tributaries drain the upland surfaces, their lower courses link to lakes and low lying swamps. Cultivated lands veined by riverine wetlands dominate the Coastal Plain. Wetlands appear more prevalent in the southeastern quadrant, with the oblong depressions of the Carolina Bays and the immense Green Swamp. It is not surprising, therefore, that commercial land use in this quadrant is governed by forestry (Figure 1.3). A land cover map for the state (CP 1.14), and in greater detail for the Cape Fear State Geographic Region (CP 10.30), the Roanoke SGR (CP 11.10), the Ring City SGR (CP 11.13), and the Sandhills SGR (CP 11.19), bring out the essential cultivated lands feature that distinguishes the Coastal Plain from other North Carolina primary regions.

With a land area of 13,337 square miles (34,543 square kilometers), the Coastal Plain covers 27.4 percent of the state, second largest of the four primary state regions. Its 22 counties rank it third in total number of counties, behind both the Piedmont and the Mountain regions, a position caused by the larger size of the average Coastal Plain county. In 2000, the population barely exceeded one and a half million, some 20 percent of the state total. Still, this left the region in second place among the four State Primary Regions in total number of inhabitants due to its physical size and to a population density that exceeded that of the Tidewater and the Mountain regions (Table 9.1). With a population much more rural in nature, Coastal Plain counties have less than one-half the density of population experienced by the much larger Piedmont region.

Mid-19th century expansion of the rail net (CP 11.1) into all potentially productive sections of the Coastal Plain only temporarily offset a major handicap of economic development, the absence of port cities for extra-regional trade. Yet, the region had been developing a powerful merchant and planter class, well sustained by large numbers of imported African slaves. In the Lower Cape Fear and Roanoke river basins, blacks outnumbered whites already at the end of the 18th century. Fairly evenly distributed agricultural production contributed to the emergence of a generally even density of rural settlement and to similar sized agricultural trade centers. A few towns, such as Halifax on the Roanoke River, Tarboro and Greenville on the Tar, and Kinston on the Neuse, benefited from the additional advantage of waterborne trade and transport. Others, such as Roanoke Rapids, Rocky Mount, Wilson, Goldsboro, and Smithfield were founded where river transport became impeded by narrows and rapids, necessitating the building of locks to bypass the hindrance, or a land transfer to further upstream or to overland transportation (Photo 11.1). As a result their economic geography labeled them as 'break-in-bulk' towns. However, the existence of vast sounds to the north and broad wetlands to the south, with no landform feature favoring a coastal port site matching those of Virginia, South Carolina or Georgia, left the Coastal Plain lagging in market access and deficient in competitive development at a critical point in its early settlement history. The Civil War and the gradual evolution of a manufacturing industry in the Piedmont Region further left the Coastal Plain economically stranded and marginalized. Its pattern of urban development became stalled in time without the emergence of an early dominant city capable of self sustained growth. No metropolis burst upon the Coastal Plain landscape.

At the turn of the 20th century, increases in rail density further stimulated commercial agriculture, and enhanced the expansion of large-scale logging and paper and pulp industries, as well

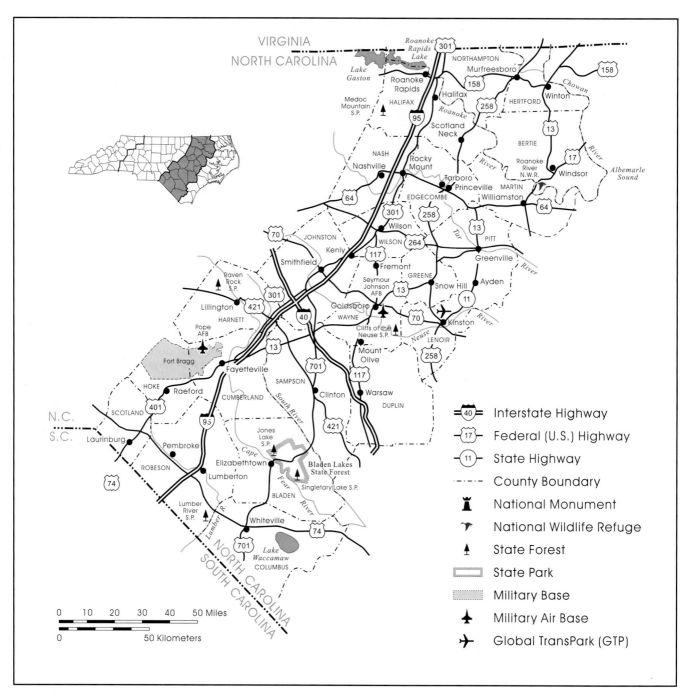

**Figure 11.1:** Coastal Plain General Location Map.

384

**Photo 11.1:** In some cases river rapids have been bypassed by the provision of locks, and places far inland have benefited by this advance in river transportation technology. Shown here is the lower Lock No. 1 of the two that have been constructed along the Cape Fear River to provide improved river access to Fayetteville, located 140 miles upstream from the Atlantic Ocean. Rapids can be seen adjacent to the lock, which raises/lowers ships ten feet.

as the growth of labor intensive manufacturing industries, especially cotton textiles. Benefiting initially as nodes in the expanded rail network were Fayetteville, Rocky Mount, Goldsboro, and Wilson (CP 11.1). However, the essential isolation from major markets continued. Without further incentives for major investments until the hayday of the military bases during and following World War II, settlement and town development peaked for most of the region's counties in the early part of the 20th century. Consequently today's cultural landscape is dominated by traditional farm assemblages and small towns where time seems to have stood still for most of the past century. For example, many of the region's larger urban places have skylines dominated by a few six to ten story "skyscrapers," built to house banks and hotels during the more ebullient decades surrounding the turn of the 20th century. In no city in the Coastal Plain has the urban renewal process of the 1960s, the bane of historic preservation in many Piedmont cities, cleared out what might now be considered to be architectural jewels of public buildings, commercial business districts, and residential neighborhoods (Photos 11.2 and 11.3; CP 11.2a-d). Dominated by human-scale and historic architecture, as well as by aesthetically designed and maintained neighborhoods, most Coastal Plain towns now exude a tranquility that belies the hectic social and economic pace at the beginning of the new millennium. Many urban places define the concept of residential aesthetics by their sweeps of Queen Annes, Painted Victorian Ladies, Greek and Tudor Revivals, Southern Colonials, and Bungalows sitting amidst towering trees and generous open green spaces.

As is the case for all of the regional chapters of this text, the information presented here is organized in the following order: (1) a survey of critical natural landscape features, (2) consideration of natural-human environmental interface characteristics that are more or less specific to the Coastal Plain, and (3) a

survey of the dominant individual state geographic regions. As indicated earlier, for some of these geographic regions there are significant overlaps with the adjacent state primary regions of the Tidewater and the Piedmont, and critical information pertaining to all of this primary state region is dispersed throughout the thematic chapters of this text for the reader's perusal. It is unfortunate that this region of North Carolina has not captured the interest of recent writers of regional geography, history, and political economy, though the more specialized topic of regional architecture is well covered by Bishir and Southern (1996). It should be noted that on the county level there are numerous county histories, though of varying detail and foci. Residents of Moore and Robeson counties are fortunate in the recent availability of very thoroughgoing and well illustrated descriptive county atlases (Ross 1994 and 1996).

## THE NATURAL LANDSCAPE

### Land Surface Development

The plain's surface evolved through a complexity of geologic change over several hundred million years. By the end of the Triassic Period, about 190 million years ago, vast sediments had been deposited, accompanied by intrusions and block faulting in the earth's crust. Following a lowering of the surface some 100 million years ago, the Cretaceous Sea covered the plain. There followed an extended period of marine deposition interbedded with sands, marls, and clays before the plain was again uplifted to form the present Coastal Plain surface. The slow process of uplift resulted in the positioning of a series of six terraces (Figure 10.8). Sea level changes during the Pleistocene Ice Age have further aided in shaping these terraces, with their escarpments facing the ocean, and with their gentle slope land-

**Photos 11.2 and 11.3:** Before the turn of the 20th century a magnificent eight story hotel was built on the corner of Walnut and Center streets in the heart of Goldsboro (Wayne County), complemented a few decades later by the Paramount Movie Theater on the opposite side of Center Street. These were symbols of the good times afforded by tobacco, an early manufacturing concentration, that also included the first large furniture plant in the state, and excellent rail connections. A double wide Center Street subsequently resulted from covering the tracks of the Atlantic Coast Line Railroad, which with Southern Railroad and the Atlantic and East Carolina Railroad, intertwined in the heart of downtown. With the 1960s and 70s outmigration of retail and residences to the suburbs downtown Goldsboro declined in attractiveness for investors and consumers, and the hotel went out of business. It and many other buildings fell into disrepair. A new perspective on the future of downtown curried by excitement over the potential success of nearby Global TransPark development has energized the historic revitalization effort. The once again splendid buildings stand as testimony to the city's vision of its future (Compare to Photo 6.11).

ward. The terraces can be identified readily where traversed by the major rivers, as for example, on the Roanoke River near Scotland Neck, on the Cape Fear River near Fayetteville, and on the Neuse River near Goldsboro. Here, for example, Cliffs of the Neuse State Park provides evidence of how the Neuse River has eroded the Black Creek Formation of Cretaceous vintage to 100 feet below the high points on the cliffs (CP 11.3). Dig deep enough and the more ancient and harder rocks of the Piedmont appear, as demonstrated by the existence of a granite quarry near the village of Fountain in Pitt County, far from the Fall Line. A more convenient place to explore the surface meeting of the crystalline rocks of the Piedmont and the sedimentary rocks of the Coastal Plain is at Medoc Mountain State Park in western Halifax County.

Medoc Mountain was named for the famous French commercial vine region, the Medoc, due to extensive vineyards founded in this part of Halifax County in the mid-19th Century by the noted farmer and wine educator, Sidney Weller. The 'Mountain' itself is a north-south trending ridge, elevated up to 160 feet (50 meters) above the plain surface, its northern and western slopes rising steeply over a distance of a quarter of a mile. Medoc Mountain is a biotite granitic outcrop of the crystalline surface of the Piedmont. Displaced but few miles east of the Fall Line, it is more resistant to erosive processes than the surrounding softer Cretaceous sand and clay strata. Although from this perspective Medoc Mountain qualifies as a monadnock (see Chapter 1), it really is a part of the more generally defined Fall Zone, demarcating the landform transition from Piedmont to Coastal Plain conditions. Raven Rock State Park on the Cape Fear River in Harnett County provides a similar example of the abrupt change in geomorphology from the Coastal Plain to the Piedmont (Photo 11.4).

The Sandhills State Geographic Region (Figure 9.11) derives its name from a physiographically distinctive area in the southwestern part of the Coastal Plain. With its more gently undulating and hilly surface configuration, the Sandhills differs from the almost uniformly flat surface features of the remainder of the Coastal Plain. The Orangeburg scarp marks a transition created by wave cuts during the Pliocene some five million years ago (Cabe and Reiman 1996). Surface materials comprising the Sandhills were deposited at an earlier time, some 90 million years ago in the case of the Middendorf Formation (Late Cretaceous Period) and 45 million years ago, in the case of the Pinehurst Formation (Eocene Epoch of the Tertiary Period; see Figure 1.8). More recent Pinehurst materials, distinctively sandy in nature and presently heavily mined, overlie the Middendorf's more consolidated clayey sands and frequently comprises the upper reaches of the hills. The transition from the soils of the Sandhills to those of the Piedmont may be observed by comparing CP 1.5 with CP 3.1 further west in Moore County. Elevations range from 270 to 600 feet generally east to west. On its western and northern edge, the Sandhills clearly differentiate from the Piedmont's more rugged appearance. Here igneous and metamorphic rock of the Carolina and Eastern slate belts control surface configurations; Figures 1.5, 1.6 and 10.8 illustrate these basic relations on this western Sandhills extension of the Coastal Plain.

Rivers pass over the plain topography at an average gradient of only 0.6 feet per mile, as compared to their traverse over the Piedmont surface, where, for example, the upper Cape Fear averages out to a gradient of two feet/mile. Such a fairly uniform, gentle slope has encouraged a parallel drainage system (Figure 11.2). The very low gradient has also resulted in extensive interior floodplains and wetland areas. Exemplifying the complexity and size of these drainage basins is school principal

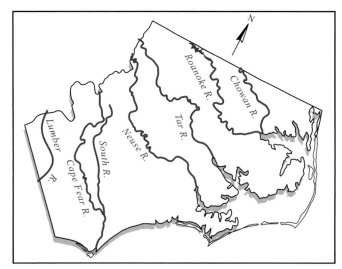

**Figure 11.2:** Generalized Drainage Pattern of Major Streams Crossing the Coastal Plain.

Needham Bryan Cobb's 1887 tally of the Roanoke tributaries, a poetic contribution designed to entice rote memorization by elementary school pupils, so including only those tributaries that empty into that great river from North Carolina:

"Wolf Island and Marrows, Town, Hogan and Show,
And Neilman and Double, two prongs of Hyco,
And Big, Mill and Moon (these names are no jokes),
From Rockingham, Caswell, Person and Stokes;
And Bearskin and Nutbush, from Granville and Vance,
Big Grassy, Big Island and Jonathan's prance
With Sassafras, Gardener's and long County Line
Kehukee, Skewarkee and old Sandy Run."
(Arthur 1995, 14)

**Photo 11.4:** Raven Rock State Park is the location of this striking quartzite and slate overhang that dramatizes the change in geomorphology from the sedimentary rock materials of the Coastal Plain to the Piedmont's mix of geologic base rocks. Here Raven Rock rises over 100 feet above the upper reaches of the Cape Fear River, hidden by the trees in the left of the photo, some 15 miles north of Lillington, Harnett County. The rock was a noted landmark for pilots of steamers plying the river from Fayetteville to Haywood in Chatham County through the system of locks and dams built by the Cape Fear and Deep River Navigation Company beginning in 1854.

Absent in other notable physical features, the Coastal Plain frequently sees its rivers provide administrative boundaries for many of its counties, as well as sites for urban places.

### Atmospheric Influences

Among the various weather extremes attained within the state, and depicted in Box 2B, only the monthly average daily maximum of 110°F, reached at Fayetteville in 1983, falls within the Coastal Plain. Generally, the plain is free from temperature and moisture extremes, a positive condition for agriculture. Spring tends to come earlier to the Sandhills due to the loose, friable, and well-drained soils that warm rapidly over a day of cloudless sky. Earliest state flowering dates of redbud and dogwood trees occur in the Sandhills (Figure 11.3). But the earlier the flowering, the greater the danger for a damaging late frost.

Occasionally weather plays morbid tricks on the region. Hurricanes can dump 15 inches or more of precipitation during a passage and cause severe flooding, a major problem for agriculture as well as for the region's towns. Hurricane Fran in 1996 caused an estimated $1 billion in damages to agricultural facilities, fields, as well as animal and crop production. In September of 1999, the drenching rains of Dennis, having been degraded to a tropical storm, were followed a couple of weeks later by the even more devastating Hurricane Floyd (note the detailed discussion and illustrations provided in CP 8.1-8.8). Eight inches of Dennis' precipitation topped off river and ground water levels; then came Floyd's fifteen inches over a 24 hour period. The Tar River exemplified the record Coastal Plain flood levels. On September 18, the river crested at 34 feet at Tarboro, fifteen above normal flood level. The lower lying town of Princeville, on the opposite bank, was by then twelve feet under the water (CP 11.4 a to c). With the very gentle gradient of the plain insuring a slow movement of flood waters toward the sounds and the ocean, the flood crest of the Neuse River at Kinston was not reached until a full week later. How physical features of the Coastal Plain contributed to making this flood the largest disaster in the state's history is well developed by Paul Gares (1999). Incredibly, Dennis and Floyd were followed on October 16 by Hurricane Irene, though this storm was by far the most benign of the three, causing measurable damage only in the Lower Cape Fear area. Re-

sults from the flood boggles the mind: 51 people dead; 43,000 damaged homes, of which 15,000 became uninhabitable; 30,000 damaged farms with 100,000s of drowned livestock, especially hogs, turkeys and chickens; burst or overflowing hog waste lagoons; 21 flooded waste water treatment plants; 241 disinterred coffins; and 70,000 people seeking recovery support (Zagier 2000, 9-10)

Tornadoes used to be thought of as being more dramatic as localized environmental hazards; certainly they can be equally traumatic. A extreme example, possibly the worst ever in the state, was the March 28, 1984 storm that spawned many tornadoes and caused destruction throughout the Coastal Plain. In North Carolina, fourteen counties were hit, 51 people died and 691 were injured, and 1,407 homes were destroyed (Figure 11.4). Figure 2.14 provides further evidence that Tornado Alley is an appropriate moniker for this stretch of Coastal Plain. Its extensive flat terrain, offering little resistance to the winds, is more frequently visited by this devastating natural hazard than is any other part of the state.

### Vegetative Cover and Wetlands

Trees dominated the natural vegetative cover of the Coastal Plain, as may be expected from the humid subtropical climate (see Chapters 2 and 3). Now only 50 to 60 percent of most of the counties are tree covered, as agriculture and urbanization have exacted their share of forest clearance (compare Photos 3.2 and 3.8). A great variety of hardwoods and Loblolly pine are sovereign on upland surfaces, except in the Sandhills State Geographic Region where longleaf pine is in preponderance, and where, in fact, the counties of Moore and Montgomery approach 80% forest cover (CP 3.8). In wetland areas, vegetative cover is more complex, and much more interesting (Figure 3.6).

#### Upland Forests

A mature upland hardwood forest, considered to be at least 50 years of uninterrupted growth, is represented mostly by members of the oak family; here there are a profusion of chestnut oaks, mixed with white, black and northern red varieties. Mockernut hickories and red maples are present, as well. A diverse understory is dominated by blueberry and huckleberry shrubs. In places where fields are no longer cultivated or grazed, pine will dominate the transition to an upland hardwood forest. Several pine species figure importantly among the earlier transition blackberry thickets and juniper. Pulp and paper companies now own extensive acreage of uplands where they manage and harvest loblolly pine plantations. Before there were loggers in the Sandhills there was an almost uniform cover of virgin longleaf pine. With the decimation of the longleaf, second growth forest became dominated by loblolly and slash pines. Both of these are now managed on private property as short-term rotated pulp and chip wood (see CP 5.20a-c).

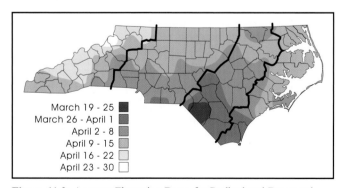

**Figure 11.3:** Average Flowering Dates for Redbud and Dogwood. **Source:** Reader, et al (1974).

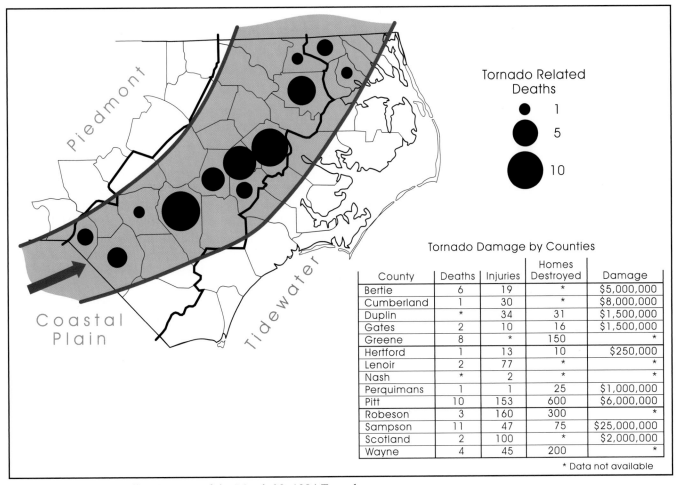

**Figure 11.4:** Tornado Alley. Passage of the March 28, 1984 Tornadoes.
Source: *Charlotte Observer*, 1 April, 1984.

Tornado Related Deaths

| | |
|---|---|
| • | 1 |
| ⬤ | 5 |
| ⬤ | 10 |

Tornado Damage by Counties

| County | Deaths | Injuries | Homes Destroyed | Damage |
|---|---|---|---|---|
| Bertie | 6 | 19 | * | $5,000,000 |
| Cumberland | 1 | 30 | * | $8,000,000 |
| Duplin | * | 34 | 31 | $1,500,000 |
| Gates | 2 | 10 | 16 | $1,500,000 |
| Greene | 8 | * | 150 | * |
| Hertford | 1 | 13 | 10 | $250,000 |
| Lenoir | 2 | 77 | * | * |
| Nash | * | 2 | * | * |
| Perquimans | 1 | 1 | 25 | $1,000,000 |
| Pitt | 10 | 153 | 600 | $6,000,000 |
| Robeson | 3 | 160 | 300 | * |
| Sampson | 11 | 47 | 75 | $25,000,000 |
| Scotland | 2 | 100 | * | $2,000,000 |
| Wayne | 4 | 45 | 200 | * |

\* Data not available

*Bottomland Hardwood Forests*

Bottomland forests or wooded wetlands is also referred to more formally as riparian/alluvial forested wetlands. They occur along all of the main rivers traversing the Coastal Plain. Much variation exists among the vegetation in these wetlands, but commonalities include a strong linear form aligned adjacent to a corridor for the transport of water and erosional materials, as well as a critical connection with upstream and downstream ecosystems (Adams et al 1994, 36-38). Bottomland forests act as important buffers between the flow of rivers and their interfluves; with their fluctuating water regime these forests have a high inherent level of productivity for aquatic species. They are especially supportive for fish spawning during overbank flooding in late winter and early spring. They are highly regarded as wildlife habitat, notably for white-tailed deer and wild turkey, and tend to have a high concentration of bird life, frequently including pileated woodpeckers, wood ducks, white breasted nuthatches, and barrel owls (Venters 1995, 20). Often these are the only remaining tracts of forest remaining in a region overcut for agriculture or development, and thereby they become important avenues for wildlife. They also provide critical services to downstream ecosystems, by slowing flow of waters during flood stage, by trapping excess sediment, and by lifting organic materials during floods and making them available for the estuarine food chain. All of this protects the salinity levels in estuary fish and shellfish spawning grounds and nurseries.

Characteristic of tree species inhabiting the wetlands forest are those that adapt well to seasonal flooding and have tolerance to anaerobic conditions. Bald cypress and water tupelo dominate in the wettest areas (Figure 11.5 ). Where the water flows more swiftly,  and where higher banks and narrower channels exist, a different vegetative complex occurs. Here there may be a greater concentration of American elm, red maple, sycamore, sweet gum, green ash, laurel oak, swamp cottonwood, water hickory, water oak, sugarberry, river birch, Shumard oak, overcup oak, cherrybark oak, and others. While black willows and river birches may overhang the stream, natural levees may see a concentration of small pawpaws and swamp chestnut oak. On the steeper banks, American beech and mountain laurel dominate.

389

Bottomland hardwood forests in the Albemarle-Pamlico river basins were in a 1990s study calculated to cover about two thirds of the state total of this kind of wetland. Conversion to other uses has been occurring at a rapid rate. Still the Albemarle-Pamlico area itself is one of the largest and least disturbed bottomlands forest ecosystem remaining along the mid-Atlantic region. Here is the summer habitat of important migratory birds, like the ruby-throated hummingbird that wings its way from across the Gulf of Mexico, the cerulean warbler that over-winters in Peru, and the prothonotary warbler that does the same in Venezuela. The birds share the ecosystem with the striped bass and the hickory shad spawning below Roanoke Rapids in Halifax County. These are anadromous fish who in their life cycle return from the ocean, from as far away as Newfoundland, to spawn close to the Fall Line. Water rushing off a series of rock ledges oxygenates the water and creates conditions favorable for egg hatching and the survival of the hatchlings. The Roanoke River is once again considered a mecca for fishing, and fishermen and environmentalists take heart from the success of the recent fifteen-year effort in restoring bass and shad to the formerly dead river. Even so, the river fails to flood as once it did. A sequence of dams impounds the river and affects stream flow. A person interested in observing the character of the bottomland forest may visit the Roanoke River National Wildlife Refuge, paralleling the Roanoke along US 13/17 north of Williamston into Bertie County.

On the Neuse River, below Smithfield in Johnston County there is an extensive bottomlands forest dominated by cypress and gum trees (clearly noticeable on Piedmont Triangle land cover map in Chapter 12) These wetlands are dominated by wide swaths in the landscape created by a meandering Neuse River, in places so bent up on itself due to the very gradual decrease in elevation that many oxbow lakes have resulted. Variously referred to as the 'Let 'Lones', a name likely derived from the area's capability of sheltering or hiding hermits and bootleggers, the Neuse

Lakes, the Marshes, or the Low Grounds, these wetlands are considered one of the most significant natural areas along the Neuse River by state biologists (Shiffer 1998).

### Seasonal Wetlands and the Carolina Bays

Forested wetland areas, where poor drainage and high water tables develop an appearance of ponded water for extended periods during the year, are referred to as nonriparian forested wetlands, a form of nonriverine swamp forest. Frequently, they occur near the edge of large peatlands, grading into pocosins toward the interior of the peatlands, as on much of the Pamlico Peninsula (Figure 10.6). More often, however, they occur in depressions that periodically collect and store excess water draining from elevated surroundings. Temporary wetlands are normally not very deep and tend to disappear during the warm season with its higher rate of evaporation. In their most peculiar form, they comprise most of the ecosystems of the Carolina bays (Figure 11.6); wetlands in this form cover most of Bladen County (see CP 1.16a and b, and Box 1D). Like all wetland communities the majority of the Carolina bays store water and release it gradually into stream and lakes, thus reducing peak flows.

Fluctuating water levels contribute to a peculiar combination of flora and fauna. While there are not many rare plant species found in seasonal wetlands, they do appear critical to the survival of a number of amphibians. Rare tiger salamanders and gopher frogs breed in these wetlands due to the absence of the amphibians' more significant predators (fish). By breeding in winter their young develop before standing water disappears in spring, but their proliferation does attract wading birds such as the great blue heron.

These wetlands are especially vulnerable to exploitation, in part due to their excellent soils. They are easily ditched and drained, providing promising lands for agriculture and forestry. Deciding what is a wetland and what is not is particularly frustrating when soils of an area are only seasonally wet. This can

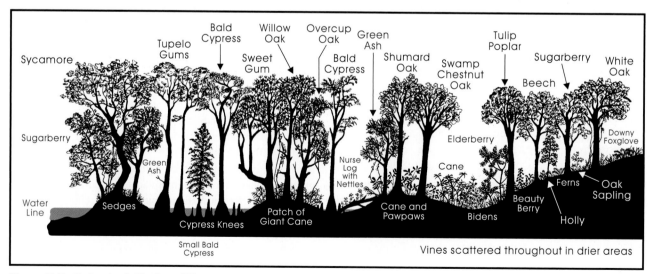

**Figure 11.5:** Bottomlands Hardwood Forest.
**Source:** Venters (1995, p. 21); illustration by Anne Runyon, by permission.

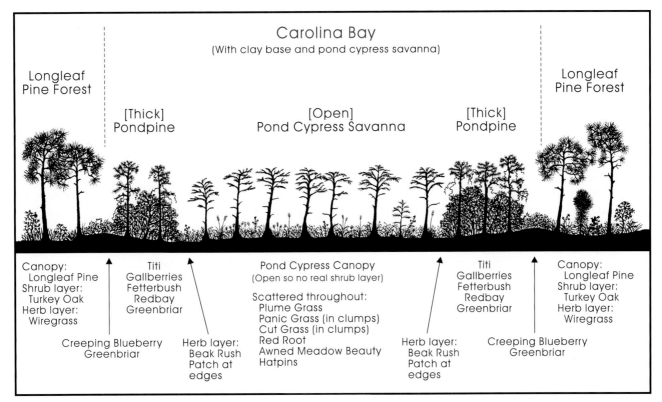

**Figure 11.6:** Seasonal Wetlands.
**Source:** Venters (1995, p. 21); illustration by Anne Runyon, by permission.

become a contentious issue in the interpretation of federal and state regulations regarding the use of wetlands, especially where these are owned by paper companies who like to manage them for loblolly pine plantations. Most seriously affected by large scale conversion to managed timberlands are the seasonal wetlands and pocosins of Green Swamp in Brunswick County (Moorhead 1995). Though the Carolina bays have seen a reduction of over half of their acreage over the years, it remains possible to inspect aspects of this ecosystem at Bladen Lakes State Forest, and at the state parks of Jones Lake and Singletary Lake, also in Bladen County. CP 10.31 well displays the Carolina Bays land surface of shrublands intermingled with forest and water in Bladen County and in the Green Swamp of Columbus County (CP 11.5).

North Carolina has empowered its Environmental Management Commission to establish wetlands rules and the Department of Environment and Natural Resources' Division of Water Quality to enforce these rules. In an earlier day, this was the responsibility of the Army Corps of Engineers. In 1996, the Commission initiated a ban on the ditching and draining of wetlands for development, when it appeared that the federal courts might strike down the wetlands rules of the Corps. This actually occurred in the summer of 1998. Unhappily, it took the state more than nine months to begin enforcement of the Commission's ban, and during this period 15,000 to 20,000 acres of wetlands were drained by developers in the southeastern part of the state, though mostly in Brunswick County. While developers are contemplat-

ing suing the Commission for reinstatement of their presumed right to drain and reclaim their lands as they see fit, Governor Hunt, in September of 1999, asked for restoration of the illegally drained and ditched wetlands.

## THE NATURAL–HUMAN ENVIRONMENT INTERFACE

### Land Use and Wetlands Environmental Management Issues

Major Coastal Plain land use issues seem to stem mostly from concerns over wetlands preservation, the drainage of low lying areas, and use of river courses for the actual or potential dumping grounds of sewage, agricultural chemicals, animal and human wastes, or other pollutant forms. Extensive areas lie within floodplains and are especially vulnerable to most forms of human use, as dramatized by the 1999 Hurricane Floyd flooding damage. Some of the land use issues have developed into serious controversies involving the private sector, local communities, special interest groups, and the state and federal governments. Conflicts over appropriate land use are also more frequently engaged where, as in the siting of the Nucor Steel plant and the proposed Wisconsin Tissue mill, the issue seems to boil down to public financial support for private industries locating in environmentally sensitive areas of counties seriously lagging state norms in economic development.

*The Water Pipeline Controversy*

Lake Kerr, Lake Gaston, and Roanoke Rapids Lake, are sequenced dammed lakes along the Roanoke River as it crosses from Virginia into North Carolina. Some 70 miles to the east lies Norfolk-Virginia Beach, Virginia's largest metropolitan area, where overdevelopment has caused a frequent municipal need to ordain severe water use restrictions. For twenty years there had been an ongoing controversy whether water, some 60 million gallons per day, could or should be pumped through a proposed 76 mile pipeline from Lake Gaston to the Virginia metropolis to aid in alleviating the perennial water shortages. Upstream users in both states contend that they should have a say in the use of Roanoke River basin water due to its economic and environmental importance. The users had been moving a case through the court system to block the pipeline. The federal government and court system continued to uphold both the Army Corps of Engineers' pipeline permit and the Federal Energy Regulatory Commission's approval of withdrawal of water from lakes created for hydroelectric power. Meanwhile, Virginia Beach completed the pipeline at a cost of $150 million, and, declaring a fait acompli, began tapping the water in November of 1997 (Allegood 1997). While the opponents will continue the challenge to the U. S. Supreme Court, it is notable that the water draw down constitutes only about one percent of average daily river flow at the point of the draw. The Roanoke carries the largest amount of water among North Carolina's great rivers. In its traverse from the Blue Ridge Mountains in the west, the river drains over 10,000 square miles of Virginia and North Carolina lands.

*A Steel Mill on the Chowan River*

Huge clusters of bald cypress line the Chowan River as its dark waters slowly ease their way from the Virginia boundary to their confluence with the Albemarle Sound. As its estuary broadens, the river forms an increasingly wide water boundary between Hertford and Bertie counties in the Coastal Plain Region and Gates and Chowan counties in the Tidewater Region. Heavy moisture-ladened air infused with the earthy sweet-sour aromas of swamps and forested wetlands hangs over a sixty mile stretch of river unbroken by human habitation except for a few surviving fish camps. Where the river once gave life to an abundance of freshwater finfish, decades of pollution and overfishing exhausted a valuable resource. In the early 1970s, gross environmental mismanagement at a fertilizer plant located at Trenton in Hertford County caused massive nutrient pollution. Chowan River eutrophication, algal blooms, and fish kills were the result of what became the state's first major warning of several decades of environmental disaster events for its rivers (see Chapter 5). Groundwater at the former site of the fertilizer plant, since declared a National Superfund site, is still contaminated. With stronger environmental controls the Chowan River now appears to be moving toward recovery.

Nucor Corporation, a leading national steel recycler, was granted state permits in early 1999 to build a $360 million steel plate manufacturing plant on a 900 acre site adjacent to the Chowan River. Expected to be the largest of its kind in the United States in tonnage of sheet steel produced, the mill is designed to eventually manufacture up to 1.5 million tons yearly (CP 11.6). The site is a few miles downstream of the former pesticide plant. Notably, in spite of the wilderness nature of the site and much to the anguish of environmental, wildlife, and fisheries groups, this was done without a comprehensive environmental impact statement. The state found itself in a bind as state Commerce Department and local industrial recruitment officials fought to bring a plum in industrial investment to the Roanoke, the poorest state geographic region. Nucor responded positively to the state's offer of $161 million in tax write-offs and other financial incentives (Henderson 1998). Some 800 workers prepared the site and built the plant, which went on line in 2001. A 300 plus person permanent labor force work there, at an average salary of $60,000, about three times the current average salary of Hertford County residents. So while the North Carolina taxpayer is, in effect, subsidizing the location of this mill at a cost of about $535,000 per job generated, we may expect considerable returns to the locality and its region.

Of course, locally most people are overjoyed at the prospects of high paying permanent jobs to be generated directly by this industry. For well-trained manufacturing workers, presently commuting 180 miles round trip to their work places in the Norfolk metro region, this offers a potential for stable at-home employment. The plant will noticeably strengthen the local tax base in a poor county where the property tax is more than 25 percent higher than in wealthy Mecklenburg County. With higher expectations of newly affordable local service, and with an ability to provide a much needed influx of investment in upscale housing, residents may experience considerable improvement in education, health, shopping, and overall community wellbeing.

Particular environmental concerns regarding the Nucor plant's location include: 1) daily transportation of scrap metal by barge through waters previously confined mostly to recreational bass fishermen; 2) expected release of some 6,800 tons of air pollutants per year, mostly in the form of sulphur dioxide, decreasing visibility and potentially harming the Swan Quarter National Wildlife Refuge 65 miles to the southeast; 3) the major need for clean water in the production process will require the plant to draw up to a million gallons of groundwater daily from an area where local wells periodically are running dry; 4) a river already overloaded with nutrients might be further troubled by the anticipated nitrogen oxide emissions; and 5) long term impacts on air and water quality, scenic areas, and wildlife in the mill's vicinity, by the mill and by other firms magnetized into their location by the Nucor facilities.

*A Paper Recycler on the Roanoke River*

Environmentalists are asking whether the Roanoke River, where fish are once again returning to spawn, is the appropriate place for a new paper recycling plant. The proposed site of a

Chesapeake Corporation's Wisconsin Tissue plant is a few miles downstream from Weldon, where it will have a daily intake of three million gallons of river water very close to the favorite spawning area for the American and hickory shad, and the striped bass. Concerns also focus on the potential for renewed river degradation with the waste water from the paper plant. This is an example of the traditional and agonizing issue of attracting new industries into environmentally vulnerable regions that qualify for extraordinary state and local location incentives due to their relatively large unemployment and poverty. As *Charlotte Observer* correspondent Jack Betts (1999) has noted, "Are jobs always the trump card when environmental questions arise?" Like Hertford County, Halifax is one of twelve North Carolina counties rated Tier 1-economically distressed (Figure 9.14). Thus it qualifies for $12,500 in tax credits for each new employee, a $1,000 tax credit for each employee receiving job training, plus a seven percent investment tax credit for new machinery. In toto, $30 million in state support may be available for the building of a $180 million mill with an anticipated 155 jobs with an average $30,000 yearly salary. When fully operational the mill might employ 800 workers. Since the plant is to be sited on Mush Island, an area that for a decade has been pushed by environmental groups for inclusion in a federally managed wildlife preserve, it is particularly notable that an environmental impact statement (EIS) has not been required by the state. An EIS would outline and document the potential adverse effects on the environment and on local communities from the siting of a facility. It evaluates the cognate and cumulative effects, looks at alternatives, and requires public hearings. However, in the Wisconsin Tissue case, as well as in the Nucor steel mill case an EIS was not initially required by the state, raising a serious concern regarding future decisions of a similar nature. Subsequently, Wisconsin Tissue has volunteered to comply with the EIS expectation, but now it is uncertain that the Chesapeake Corporation will, in fact, locate its plant here!

### The Neuse River — Surely We Can Do Better!

In Colonial days the Neuse River provided a communication and commerce artery from the Pamlico Sound to the fall line. Barges and steamboats established a Coastal Plain heart line that influenced the location of New Bern, Kinston, Goldsboro, and Smithfield. Well into the 20th Century pine logs were floated downstream to sawmills in New Bern. Then increasing development pressures began to degrade water quality. An absence of appropriate buffer zones in areas of heavy residential construction activities, especially along creeks that empty into the 230 mile river within the Piedmont Triangle Region, was contributing massive concentrations of pollutants to the Neuse. So was the runoff from logging and agriculture taking place too close to the streams of the river basin. Add to that the problem of 200 plus identified point sources of pollution, mostly treated and untreated waste water pipes that fed into the river or its tributaries. Subsequently the Neuse suffered the impact of chronic leaks and spills from the waste lagoons of a hog industry that exploded

during the 1990s without much regard to its environmental implications. An excess of nutrients, mostly nitrogen and phosphates, created a fertile brew that provided a positive environment for the flourishing of the fish killer *phisteria* (see Chapter 5). The rancid smells drove away users of the river. By the mid-1990s, the Neuse River was dying. In response to a suit brought against the state by the Neuse River Foundation, the U.S. Environmental Protection Agency (EPA) was placed in a position to compel the state to comply with a provision in the national Clean Water Act that called for a maximum total daily load of individual contaminants. With a goal of reducing pollution in the Neuse River Basin by some 30 percent, government inspectors would have to more carefully identify the sources of ammonia gas from swine waste lagoons that would return as pollution in rain through the Neuse estuary. Already stricter regulations cover the emission of sewage from municipalities and factories, and the EPA has agreed to a state imposed cap on the total daily amount of nitrogen pollution flowing from fertilizers, animal waste and every other source. Perhaps soon the new "River Keeper" of the Neuse, a position created in 1993, will be seeing the river once again populated by nature's bounty and by contented recreational fishermen (Peters 1995).

### A Success Story of River Protection — The Lumber

In the mid-1980s, residents of the Lumber River basin were alarmed to find that a site on the river was being considered for the location of a hazardous waste treatment plant that would discharge about half a million gallons of waste into the river each day. Sufficient popular protest encouraged the state legislature, in 1989, to designate a new state park covering the 115 mile stretch of the Lumber River from just above Wagram in Scotland County to the South Carolina border in Robeson County. Initially this most unusually shaped state park protected only the river course, from shore to shore, but gradually shorelands are being added. The Lumber River State Park master plan calls for the acquisition of about 6,000 acres, mostly bottomland hardwood forest, with over 2,300 acres of this having been acquired by 1997. Strong attachment to the river is shown by traditional residents of the area, the Lumbee Indians, who found that the maze of swamps and wetlands traversed by the lower course of the river offered them protection against European settlers (Shiffer 1996). In 1998, 81 miles of the Lumber River received federal designation as "wild and scenic," adding this to the state's previously designated stretches of the New, the Chattooga, and the Horsepasture rivers, all located in the Mountain Region.

### The Saga of the Red-Cockaded Woodpecker

In the entire world there are now only an estimated 4,500 groups of the red-cockaded woodpecker, representing 10,000 to 14,000 birds (Earley 1996). Inhabiting over a dozen population centers concentrated largely on piney forest lands in the southeast of the United States, the red-cockaded woodpecker had been declining rapidly due its vulnerability. For example, in a single evening Hurricane Hugo destroyed the habitat of this species in the Francis Marion National Forest in South Carolina, killing an estimated 60 percent of the birds. One estimate indicates a decline of 25 percent during the 1980s. Now the second largest concentration remains in the Sandhills, where private land owner resentment developed against the forest cutting restrictions placed by the Fish and Wildlife Service for the purpose of protecting the habitat of the red-cockaded woodpecker as an endangered species. That habitat, incidentally, improves with the kind of economic activity favored in these slightly rolling piney woods: golf courses, seasonal fires to control underbrush for ease of growing and harvesting pulpwood, and the newest fad, the collecting and baling of pine needles for vegetable mulch. Woodpeckers thrive in open pine forests, and all of these activities favor the evolution of this habitat. Unhappily, some of these activities depend on regular cutting of the forest and thus habitat destruction. At present the two major managed and well-populated woodpecker sites in the Sandhills are on the military reservation of Fort Bragg and on the North Carolina Wildlife Commission's Sandhills Game Lands and Camp Mackall, with the sites separated by a wide belt of private lands. Connecting the two bird populations and thus ensuring the maintenance of a sufficient number of colonies to guarantee survival over the long run, became a major issue. The Safe Harbor Program was the answer. This operates simply by signed agreement with private owners, encouraging them to develop habitats. Once developed, and attracting colonies, the owners are then not responsible for habitat maintenance. In a way of speaking the land owners have a "safe harbor" in the future case of destroyed habitat and endangered colonies that their action may have encouraged into being. Applying good management practices like controlled burning and providing artificial nesting sites should allow enough new colonies to become established with resulting direct linkages between the two primary nesting areas. This will permit land owners to further develop their lands for commercial purposes without any responsibility for the new populations attracted due to their management efforts, except to allow wildlife management people the opportunity to remove any nesting birds. As a trade-off for the benefits of their participation in the "safe harbor program" private landowners accept responsibility for maintaining the current level of red-cockaded woodpeckers colonies on their property. As for the public lands, Fort Bragg is very actively pursuing an improved woodpecker habitat program by shifting practice parachute jumping zones and bombing ranges (the larger of these are clearly visible on the CP 11.19 land cover map as four almost parallel occurring grassland areas just west of the sprawling Fayetteville urban region). When the Endangered Species Act was passed by the U.S. Congress and signed into law in 1973, Fort Bragg was required to have 250 breeding pairs of red-cockaded woodpeckers that produce young for a period of five consecutive years in order to ensure a recovering woodpecker population for the Sandhills region. A more detailed program involves marking trees used for nesting sites and providing a buffer zone of 200 feet around each tree, with only people on foot permitted access within the buffer (Weeks 1995).

## Land Use and Socio-Economic Issues

### Migrant Farm Workers and Their Children of Poverty

There are children who travel from farm to farm and from state to state with their parents who cultivate and harvest America's crops. They come in buses with names like "The Bird Without a Nest," "The Cold Heart", and "Bean Picker's Express." Their parents are the one quarter of a million migrant workers who gather $3 billion worth of the state's tobacco, cucumbers, cabbages, corn, potatoes, tomatoes, and apples each year. They are the children of the most educationally, culturally, and socially disadvantaged group in the United States.

Migrant farmers are like no other group of labor. They form a subculture, a living contradiction to the myth that those who work by the sweat of their brows and the strength of their backs shall be appropriately rewarded. What they typically get are substandard housing, substandard health care, substandard wages (averaging $3,500 per year in the late 1990s), substandard education, and a substandard place in society, without options for politically influencing improvements of their lot in life. For some especially unfortunate workers, within the past two decades, conditions have included actual slavery. As indicated in an earlier edition of this book, over the five year period ending in 1982, ten of the 21 federal slave convictions originated in North Carolina. Subsequently, a state legislative study commission recommended the passage of legislation that included an anti-slavery law, coverage of migrants under the Workmen's Compensation Act, more migrant encampment inspectors, and a commission to coordinate state efforts to clean up the system. Only the anti-slavery provision was finally passed by the state legislature, and only after its key provision was deleted – that farmers who knowingly hire crew leaders guilty of enslaving workers would be criminally liable. Not passed was the provision that mandatory sanitation inspection be extended to migrant labor camps housing less than ten workers. This provision would have ballooned the number of camps inspected from 175 to 3,750 in the late 1980s. The decrepit conditions of work, and total absence of political power, have stimulated many non-governmental organizations to act in the behalf of the migrant farm workers. These include the Farmworkers Legal Services of North Carolina, and many more regional organizations such as the North Carolina Farmworkers Project (NCFP). The *Raleigh News and Observer* reported on a July, 1998, visit of a team of NCFP volunteers who characterized as typical what they found at a labor camp near Benson in Johnston County (Paik 1998, 1):

22 native Floridian, Jamaican, Haitian, and Mexican farm workers live side by side in small concrete rooms, most without fans and only bare bulbs for light. Thin, filthy mattresses lay atop single bed frames, two to three to a room. In one a worker tried to add comfort with a pair of ragged curtains which hung crooked over the screened window. The rest of the room was bare except for three beds, a small tele-

vision on the floor, a roll of toilet paper, a beer can and a few images of bikini-clad women torn from magazines and taped to the walls. The air was heavy and stagnant while dragonflies buzzed throughout the room.

Some have suggested that the basic creature comforts provided by North Carolina jails for its criminals far exceed those generally made available to the migrant labor that cultivates and prepares the food we eat. These generally unsavory living conditions are further negatively complemented by another unconscionable provision that many of the migrants are forced to adhere to. When H2A guestworkers (see Chapter 5) sign the North Carolina Growers Association (NCGA) contract that allows them to work they unknowingly also sign away their right to receive visitors to their personal (labor camp) living quarters. Here it must be noted that the NCGA is required to have H2A contract provisions, including the waiver of tenancy rights, approved by the U.S. Department of Labor, raising the serious question of federal collusion in this illegal treatment provision (Klein 2000). Having otherwise limited access to transportation and to a telephone, migrant laborers are very restricted in their ability to summon professional medical assistance, legal help, or any other community service providers; and they may not be visited!

In Mount Olive, a town in Wayne County, the nation's second largest cucumber pickle company, Mt. Olive Pickle Company, began being boycotted by the Farm Labor Organizing Committee (FLOC) of the AFL-CIO in March of 1999. The objective was to compel the company to influence a labor contract that will improve the wages and work conditions of the 5,000 migrant cucumber pickers in North Carolina, where FLOC sees the conditions for such workers to be the worst in the country (FLOC 1999). Mt. Olive Pickle Company disclaims any responsibility for migrants who work for farmers contracted to the company. Its own labor force of 500, swelling to 850 during its peak production period, is made up of 17 percent Hispanic, 49 percent black, and the remainder white. There are no migrants in this work force that has among the highest average manufacturing wages in the Coastal Plain (Martin 2000). Yet, it should be noted that organizing migrant farm workers elsewhere has resulted in an improvement of their quality of life. Following a FLOC boycott of the Campbell Soup Company a few years ago, this food producer began insisting that its contractors provide improved working conditions for migrant workers. Now, in northern Ohio, migrant farm workers live in camps with indoor bathrooms, showers, hot water, heating, kitchens, and private bedrooms for parents.

Meanwhile migrant children in North Carolina continue to suffer disproportionately from diseases such as rickets, scurvy, pinworms, nutritional anemia, acute febrile tonsillitis, and dangerous protein deficiencies. A large number have dental abnormalities. Infant mortality rates among migrant workers are twice the national average. Inadequate plumbing and sanitation conditions make even routine grooming and hygiene difficult. Whole families often sleep in one room with several children per bed, should one be available for them. Lack of modern food storage, refrigeration and cooking appliances, plus the absence of basic nutritional knowledge, add up to poor diets. Whole families frequently work together, with about 40 percent of the children working in the fields.

Who then are these people? Mostly they are Hispanics, including Mexicans, Guatemalans and El Salvadorans, but they also include Jamaicans, and Haitians. Only thirty percent are born in the United States, with the remainder being immigrants; among these, the vast majority (90 percent) are Mexican (Rothenberg 1998). In North Carolina, an estimated 900 labor camps are registered with the state, but an equal number is not (Paik 1998). It is estimated that some 280,000 seasonal farm laborers inhabit these camps, with about half of these being uncounted due to their likely illegal residence status (Photos 11.5-7). Over the past three decades, African Americans, who dominated the migrant crews of the southeast, have been replaced by immigrants (CP 11.7). A recent case study of the shift from a traditional employer dependence on local women to Mexican women, brought in under the provisions of the H2A temporary workers program, illustrates this process. The case study dramatizes the impact of internationalization in the crab processing industry, while pointing to the increasing difficulty of operating seasonally defined extractive industries on existing local labor resources. In the process the small communities studied in Carteret, Pamlico, and Beaufort counties are undergoing important changes in traditional worker-employer relationships (Selby 1999).

*A Military Presence*

For reasons of good politics, favorable land deals, and an accommodating climate, North Carolina has emerged as one of the nation's largest concentrations of military personnel and activities (Tables 11.1 and 11.2). Ranked eleventh in total population, the state was fourth in military personnel, behind California, Texas, and Virginia. Although bases have closed throughout the country as the U.S. military reduced its manpower by one third during the 1990s, North Carolina bases are held sacrosanct due to their essential mission of speedy response to trouble spots around the world. Consider the fact that during the Cold War, from the end of World War II to 1990, the military responded to overseas crises a total of ten times, but from 1991 to 1997, it responded to 25 crises. These latter include major commitments to actions like Desert Storm, Somalia, and Yugoslavia. This explains why personnel of the 82nd Airborne Division, stationed at Ft. Bragg in Cumberland County, are expected to be in an aircraft ready to jump within 18 hours of being called. Pope and Seymour Johnson air bases (in Cumberland and Wayne counties, respectively), which provide the army's air support, are therefore in a similar state of preparedness. So is the 2nd Marine Division at Camp Lejeune in Onslow County, and its supportive air arm based at New River and Cherry Point in Onslow and Craven counties, respectively (Box 11A). These counties also bear the

**Photo 11.5:** The *La Mexicana* delivery truck can be seen in the many Latino communities of Sampson and Duplin counties. Based in a converted fast food store in Clinton (Sampson County) the business is owned by a Mexican-American family from Durham. It took advantage of the commercial opportunities presented by an immigrant labor force, and provides desired cultural affinity goods, a familiar language and a down-home atmosphere that eases the transition of migrants into the American scene.

**Photo 11.6:** Red Springs (Robeson County) exemplifies a small rural town where the commercial heart has been suffering the dual impacts of rural depopulation and improved transportation that facilitates consumer shopping in nearby larger centers. Here affordable and available commercial spaces have been converted to establishments serving the daily needs of a Spanish speaking population. In shops like *La Flor de Izucar*, in addition to Latino foods there is a large stock of Spanish language videos, and a bank of telephones that is jammed with international calls on weekly paydays.

**Photo 11.7:** Many cultural and social service organizations are experiencing considerable stress in serving the needs of a new migrant population. Finding and training Spanish speaking priests, and establishing and staffing churches to serve a frequently deeply religious people, has been a challenging task for the Catholic Diocese of North Carolina. Like many new Latino churches throughout the state, the *Iglesia del Cuerpo de Cristo* in Red Springs serves not only spiritual needs but also broader community activities, family gatherings, and festivals, much as is the case in the rural peasant communities that are home to the Central and South American migrants.

| Places | Payroll | Contracts | Total |
|---|---|---|---|
| Fort Bragg | 1,664,226 | 222,942 | 1,887,168 |
| Camp Lejeune | 591,471 | 98,200 | 689,671 |
| Greensboro | 19,673 | 454,728 | 474,401 |
| Cherry Point | 319,828 | 66,500 | 386,328 |
| New River | 162,982 | 19,696 | 182,678 |
| Seymour Johnson | 134,868 | 23,908 | 158,776 |
| Pope | 138,973 | 8,840 | 147,813 |
| Raleigh | 43,566 | 77,848 | 121,414 |
| Charlotte | 56,655 | 42,623 | 99,278 |
| Winston-Salem | 6,797 | 78,696 | 85,493 |

**Table 11.1:** North Carolina Top Ten in 1991 Military Revenues.
**Source:** Oliver and Towle (1993, 20).
Note: Where contracts appear by a particular base the expenditures are local, as for Fayetteville in the cases of Fort Bragg and Pope; Jacksonville, in cases of Camp Lejeune and New River; and Goldsboro, in the case of Seymour Johnson.

initial brunt of the disaster of war and terrorism against the United States. Because Camp Lejeune was their home base, Onslow County was first in line for the news of the 225 Marines who died in the explosion in Beirut, Lebanon in October of 1983.

Among the state's 100 counties, 80 are impacted by military spending. A 1991 study indicated that for direct defense contracts alone this amounted to $1.5 billion per year for the state, with Greensboro's textile industries being the clear winner, with Winston-Salem, and its tobacco industry, a distant second (Table 11.1). However, North Carolina was ranked 22nd among the states in winning Department of Defense (DOD) military contracts. The state received a mere six percent of that awarded California (Oliver and Towle 1993). What tells in the state, rather, is the impact of military payrolls, plus civilian payrolls paid by the DOD. With 96,500 military personnel and a civilian work force of 15,750, in Spring of 2000, North Carolina was outranked only by California and Texas (Table 11.2). It is to the benefit of the economically lagging part of the state that military bases, and thus their buying power and ancillary benefits, are located here. For the Coastal Plain the military means the existence of the core city in the Sandhills State Geographic Region, Fayetteville, and the survival of Goldsboro as one of the main Ring City SGR urban places. Even so, the local enormity of the military impact is perhaps best read in the economy of the

Tidewater Region's Craven County, which has the one of the nation's three remaining navy aircraft repair and maintenance depots. Here, under the leadership of a black female Marine Corps colonel (in Spring of 2000), is a $1 billion business conducting the highest level of part replacement and maintenance service on military planes. Aircraft, including helicopters, are stripped to their bare metal and reassembled piece by piece. Under her command are 3,700 civilian maintenance workers and engineers, averaging $43,000 in annual benefits, well above average for this coastal county (Hopkins 2000).

An additional stabilizing benefit of the large military bases results from the desire on the part of military retirees to continue living in an environment that offers them amenities they tie to a good quality of life: a continuing circle of friends with common experiences, a mild climate, and access to post facilities, including shopping, recreational services, and hospitals. No small plum, for example, is the new $250 million medical center recently completed on Forth Bragg military reservation. Community impacts of the state's 60,000 military retirees are significant and varied. The substantial retirement checks flowing from the federal government to the communities are important. However, they probably do not count for nearly as much as the support retirees can contribute by virtue of being still quite young, and having a multitude of skills as well as a strong sense of community. All are important labor force characteristics that make Fayetteville and Goldsboro especially attractive to industrial investment.

*Small Town Revitalization*

One of the little known benefits that came out of the nation's love affair with its Bicentennial in the 1970s was the National Trusts' Main Street Program. This was an innovative self-help approach to historic restoration through economic revitalization. The guiding philosophy was that salvaging the economy of fading small town centers could be accomplished with historic preservation as a key component. However, it also was thought that such a process would be essentially incapable of implementation without a partnership effort of local government, civic groups, and the local business community.

Among towns selected by the National Trust soon after its founding were several in the east of the state, including New Bern, Washington, and Tarboro (Photos 11.8a-c). Many others, including Sanford (Photos 11.9a-c), joined the preservation movement

| Military Base | Service | Acreage | Military Personnel | Civilian Personnel | Payroll ($1,000) |
|---|---|---|---|---|---|
| Fort Bragg | Army | 161,000 | 41,120 | 7,890 | 1,453,000 |
| Camp Lejeune | Marine Corps | 158,000 | 37,686 | 1,540 | 966,000 |
| Cherry Point | Marine Corps | 29,000 | 7,486 | 5,684 | 549,000 |
| Seymour Johnson | Air Force | 5,100 | 5,189 | 1,330 | 202,000 |
| Pope | Air Force | 2,200 | 5,033 | 512 | 179,000 |
| **Totals** | | **401,200** | **96,514** | **16,956** | **3,349,000** |

**Table 11.2:** Five Largest Military Bases in North Carolina in 2000.
**Source:** Hopkins 2000.

**Photo 11.8a, b, and c:** Tarboro's 200 year history is reflected in its two public commons and its stately old homes. Preservation-minded citizens were successful in initiation a historic revitalization program that began with a $2.7 million urban development grant and a designation of the town as one of thirty communities to participate in the National Main Street program in 1980. With 45 residential square blocks of the town now included in the National Register of Historic Places, and a $20 million renovation of the downtown the people of Tarboro have nurtured their 'sense of place' into a historic and architectural legacy.

a. The 16 acre Town Common of Tarboro (Edgecombe County) was established in 1770. It continues to provide a well maintained open green space with lawns, activity areas, and large shade trees in the heart of town.

b. Restored cotton gin, built in 1860 to press cotton using horses as draught animals, and relocated to the Tarboro Common.

c. Downtown street in Tarboro in the middle of the historic restoration period of the early 1980s.

**Photo 11.9a, b, and c:** Two decades separate these scenes of downtown Sanford (Lee County). These reveal the time conditioned changes affecting central business districts throughout the state's medium and smaller sized towns (see also Photos 6.6-6.8). The earlier photos show 1977 streets of the Central Business District with Belk and J. C. Penney's department stores on opposite sides of one street, competing with each other and with footwear, clothing, furniture and other retail stores in a hectic commercial environment where parking places are at a premium and downtown streets are heavily traffic congested by shoppers and their automobiles. Downtown decay developed as department stores and retail business relocated to strip shopping centers and a mall.

**a.** Main Street, Sanford in 1977.

**b.** Downtown hotel and movie theater, the latter already converted to retail business in 1977.

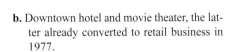

**c.** This 1997 photo show some of the effects of years of historic renovation efforts. Century old commercial buildings have been shed of their 1950s-1960s aluminum and neon lit false front panels, as well as of their concrete overhangs. A much more welcoming and aesthetically pleasing architectural environment now greet the much more occasional visitors to a CBD devoid of retail businesses, uncongested and with many empty parking places.

later. Building on a reference to North Carolina as a 'rural laboratory' by President Carter in 1978, the state's proposal for a National Main Street Center Demonstration project noted: "Downtown revitalization of small communities through the National Main Street Center captures the spirit of the Rural Lab in North Carolina." The first town in the state to be evaluated for Main Street status by the Washington base National Trust resource team was Tarboro in Edgecombe County. Incorporated in 1760, Tarboro was a tranquil community of 8,634 in 1980. Lying on the slow moving Tar River, Tarboro was dependent largely on tobacco production, warehousing, and trade. Old tobacco brick warehouses, redolent in fall with the rich smell of tobacco leaves, lined the western edge of town. A person arriving in town from the north was greeted by an aesthetic residential district of Federal, Queen Anne, and a few Victorian style homes. Then followed a downtown main street of remarkably intact commercial buildings in styles ranging from Greek Revival, to Classical Revival, to Victorian. Of notable historic interest are two town commons dating to its beginnings, along with the state's only remaining mule drawn cotton press.

Implementing the Main Street program in Tarboro provided the town an important boost in self-identity and regional recognition. Locally, people were able to translate their 'sense of place' into a lasting historic and architectural legacy, while improving the aesthetics and quality of life of their community. Important lessons for other towns in the state have been learned from Tarboro and the equally positive experiences of other North Carolina Main Street demonstration communities. Note also the discussion on the results of historic preservation and downtown revitalization in Salisbury in Chapter 12, as well as the extensive photo coverage of similar community efforts throughout the text.

## THREE STATE GEOGRAPHIC REGIONS

### Introduction

Among the three state geographic regions that we discuss in this chapter, only the Ring City State Geographic Region (SGR) is contained wholly within the Coastal Plain Primary Region (PR). The Roanoke SGR finds Warren County as part of the Piedmont PR, as are four counties of the Sandhills SGR. In Chapter 10, we considered most attributes of the Cape Fear SGR, which has four of its counties located in the Tidewater PR. Finally, the Coastal Plain PR includes Johnston County, which due to its gradually increasing functional fusion to the Piedmont Triangle now falls within this SGR which otherwise finds itself entirely within the Piedmont Primary Region (see Figure 9.11).

In this fashion, county similarities and spatial continuities and shifts in economic development and settlement patterns aid us in defining state geographic regions whose boundaries do not necessarily coincide with a Coastal Plain primary region, since the former are essentially functional regions while the latter is a natural region. Therefore, Warren County is included within the Roanoke State Geographic Region. Sharing a small portion of

the Roanoke River drainage basin might, in its own right, place this county within the Roanoke SGR, but more critical are conditions of agricultural land usage and a predominant rural black population. Thus, there are physical as well as cultural geographic homogeneities that influence the definition of the Roanoke SGR. For the Cape Fear SGR, the unifying aspects include the Cape Fear River basin, the commercial and cultural influences that extend upstream as well as into adjacent counties of the Wilmington metropolitan area, and spatial continuities that are provided by forestry and agricultural land use. For the Sandhills SGA, on the other hand, it is a predominance of certain geologic/hydrologic features and their associated soils and natural vegetation complexes that provide the essential anchors for this region's delimitation, while legitimizing its extension from the Coastal Plain to portions of the Piedmont Primary Region. In addition, the military and leisure resort/retirement uses of the land, the dominance of Native Americans in some counties, and the geographic influence of the region's leading city, Fayetteville, contributes as well to firming up the essential homogeneity of the Sandhills SGR. The third state geographic region treated in detail in this chapter is the Ring City. Here the Coastal Plain situation has fostered a loosely knit coalition of well connected medium and small sized towns, in a close enough proximity to each other to warrant their consideration as a unified urban region.

Comparative data contributing to an understanding of these three state geographic regions is contained in Table 9.2. It is clear that this data reflects the publicly held image of Coastal Plain socio-economic conditions. As a region dependent to a much greater degree on extractive production in agriculture and forestry, and on labor intensive manufacturing and low paid service industries, the Coastal Plain is still largely rural and small town in population settlement. Lacking in diversified and well paid employment opportunities, the region is suffering the effects of decades of "brain drain," with its better educated, more opportunistic, and younger population tending to leave for the better jobs and amenities of the urban Piedmont, if not out of state. The population diagrams for the counties of the Roanoke SGR demonstrate this aspect very well. Even so, there are some striking differences among and within the SGRs considered in this chapter. Ring City SGR, dominated as it is by medium sized towns, had a population in 2000 just in excess of 500,000, or about two-thirds of the Sandhills SGR, where Fayetteville's military dependence pushed this region to a much larger population. On the other hand, just about equal in physical size to Ring City, the Roanoke SGR had less than one-third of its population. Coastal Plain SGRs are dominated by counties that tend to be at the lower end of the socio-economic scale in the state, with higher female head of household percentages, higher poverty rates, slower population growth, higher infant mortality rates, and lower worker competencies as evidenced by lesser percentages graduated from high school and college.

Down East, as the Coastal Plain is frequently referred to, presents strong contrasts in people's perception and reality of life and livelihood (CP 11.8 and 11.9). Historian William Powell calls it "God's country." A "third world country" is the description of the director of the Eastern North Carolina Poverty Committee headquartered in Greenville (Pitt County), "(w)hen you drive through Eastern North Carolina, it looks quaint. But it's a national disgrace. There are horses in stables living better than people in these shacks with outhouses. Out of the poorest 100 counties in the United States, ten are in Eastern North Carolina" (Leland 1992). An opposite, perhaps equally accurate and certainly more locally popular, view is expressed by the director of the Economic Development Institute of East Carolina University, also located in Greenville:

> I can drive 30 minutes back to the farm I grew up on and I might as well be in the next continent. They are still essentially earning their living off the land, and centering their social life around the church and the school. They are still leaving their houses unlocked and notes on their doors to their neighbors about their whereabouts. They don't steal from each other. They still hold wakes for funerals. They can tell you who's buried in every graveyard. And they still celebrate family birthdays and hold traditional Christmas pageants in their churches, and say prayers in their schools. They go on as if nothing happen(s) outside their communities (as quoted by Leland 1992).

Is this not a lifestyle to be treasured? Perhaps, but along with this sense of community there is a prevailing dissonance of low incomes, higher incidence of unemployment, an absence of educational opportunities and low expectations for individual attainment, stronger contrasts in quality of life conditions between the haves and the many more have-nots, a greater dependence on the state and on outside investors and land owners, low standards for housing and environmental comforts, and a general malaise characterized by a negative sense about tomorrow.

In the mid-1990s the state-wide regional differences in the funding and quality of public education were dramatized when five county school systems sued the state for falling far short of the state's constitutional guarantee of a 'uniform' education for all of its children. Boards of Education for the counties of Cumberland, Robeson, Hoke, Halifax and Vance held that poor counties were severely disadvantaged in their capacity for supplementing the state support for educational facilities, equipment, maintenance, and especially teacher's salaries. Maps in Chapter 7 dramatize the plight of these counties. Qualitative differences result in markedly lower student attainment, and children in the poor counties, as the lawsuit noted, "have diminished prospects for higher education, for obtaining satisfying employment, and for providing well for themselves and their families; they face increasing risks of unemployment, welfare dependency, drug and alcohol addiction, violence and imprisonment" (Yeoman 1995).

Poor communities also have scant political power and are less influential in preventing environmentally noxious industries from invading their localities. This was the conclusion of a 1999 investigation which assessed the locational coincidence between 2,514 hog farms and community wealth. For 4,100 census blocks in the state, poorer and minority dominated blocks were shown to have 18 times more hog farms. These areas of least resistance to environmentally exploitative development subsequently suffer disproportionately from groundwater contamination, pungent odors, and decreasing property values, all contributing to a lowering of their quality of life. The power of wealth was demonstrated when, in 1997, the legislature adopted a hog industry reform bill that among other edicts prevented the proposed location of hog farms near the Pinehurst golf mecca (Henderson 1999). In recent decades major efforts have been pursued by the state and federal governments to provide improved foundations for socio-economic development in Coastal Plain communities. Some of the more noteworthy of these efforts include:

1) Education and health, as in the highly successful effort to elevate Greenville's East Carolina University, with its new medical school, to a secure position in the second tier of state institutions of higher education, where it will be in the company of the likes of the University of North Carolina campuses at Greensboro and Charlotte (CP 11.10 and 11.11).

2) Economic development anchors, as in the persistent effort to establish a 15,300 acre manufacturing industry and transportation hub, the Global Trans-Park, at Kinston. Also, as in supporting the location of new industries, like the steel mill and a federal prison in Hertford County, and the distribution center of QVC telemarketing in Roanoke Rapids (Edgecombe County).

3) Persistent support for large scale corporate agriculture, in spite of known environmental consequences. As a result agriculture is experiencing major shifts in production technology and market orientation from family farms and farm workers tied to tenancy and share cropping, to a major emphasis on agribusiness, contract farming, and dependency on foreign labor. Associated features include, an upgrading of the essential infrastructure, increasing per capita incomes in counties most affected by these changes, and a concomitant decrease in rural populations.

4) Transportation improvements, as in the completion of I-40 from Raleigh to Wilmington, and in providing four lanes and limited access for a number of west-east U.S. highways and their city bypasses, most notably US 74, 70, 264 and 64.

More regionally limited efforts include the city of Wilson's attempts to evolve an industrial investment image, "Triangle East," identifying the city as the preferred eastern and closely connected manufacturing industry location of the corporations operating out of the Piedmont's Research Triangle Park. In addition, there is no denying the considerable community facilities improvement resulting from massive investments and employment generation of agribusiness, especially in counties like Duplin, Sampson, and Bladen (see Chapter 5), though the impact on rural settlement patterns, given the massive influx of foreign labor, is as yet uncertain.

Whether the economic and environmental disaster relief efforts resulting from hurricanes Dennis and Floyd can be linked to an overall "Marshall Plan for Eastern North Carolina," as recommended by Governor Jim Hunt, remains to be seen. Early large scale estimates of state and federal relief packages were slow in arriving. One and a half years later $180 million in relief funds remained unclaimed.

"Down East" is now much better connected to the rest of the world. The aforementioned west-east highways connect to the market and employment rich Piedmont of the state, and to the recreational resources of the Tidewater. In north-south connections the Coastal Plain is well served by I-95 (New York to Miami) and the planned extension of I-78 to Wilmington (connecting to Chicago and the Midwest). Highways US 258 and US 13/17, traversing the central and eastern margin of the plain, await four laning and limited access/bypass improvements. The first state geographic region of the Coastal Plain to be considered,

Roanoke SGR, exemplifies some of the complexities of land, life, and livelihood of this state primary region.

### Roanoke

Vividly portrayed on the land cover map (CP 11.10) is the Roanoke River and its adjacent wetlands, the heart of a river basin that provides the central connective natural environmental tissue for the Roanoke State Geographic Region. Northeastern portions of the SGR drain into the Chowan River, while southern portions lie within the Tar River basin. Eastern and western perimeter counties of Martin and Warren seem to have a greater preponderance of shrublands, while the central counties of Halifax and Northampton show the greatest relative concentration of farmlands. With its six counties, the size of the Roanoke SGR is about in the middle of the 13 state geographic regions. On the other hand, its population of 167,355 makes it one of the least densely populated parts of the state with only 20.2 people per square kilometer (Table 9.2; Figures 9.11 and 11.7). However, when one considers the fact that this is the state geographic region with the lowest rate of population growth in the 1990s, it becomes clear that serious problems of livelihood, and perhaps land as well, exist. The six counties range in their 2000 population from 19,733 in the case of Bertie to 57,370 in the case of Halifax. All are predominately rural or small town in settlement patterns. Warren County, however, showed the largest percentage population increase with 15.7 for the decade of the 1990s, while Bertie experienced a decrease in its total population (Table 11.3). Had not Warren County, benefiting from its proximity to

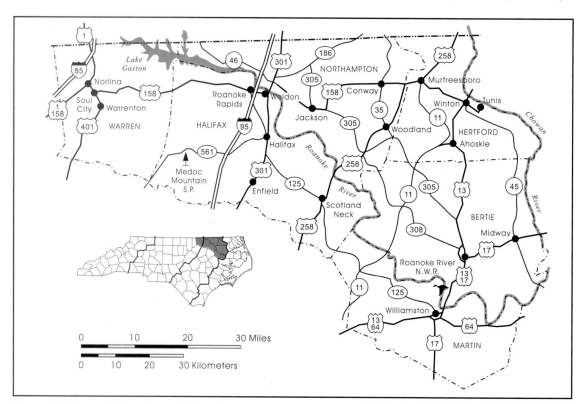

**Figure 11.7:** Roanoke State Geographic Region.

402

| ROANOKE | Land Area in sq. km | Pop. 1990 | Pop. sq.km. 2000 | .Pop. 2000 | 1990s % Pop. Change | % White 2000 | Median Age in 2000 | % Fam. Below Poverty | Annual Average Infant Mortality Rate 1994-98 | % High School Grads'90 | % Coll. Grads. 1990 | Fem. Fam. Head of Hshld'90 | NC Enterprise Tiers'97 |
|---|---|---|---|---|---|---|---|---|---|---|---|---|---|
| Bertie | 1,811 | 20,388 | 10.9 | 19,773 | -3 | 36.3 | 30.1 | 21.3 | 9.5 | 54.9 | 8.0 | 19.1 | 1 |
| Halifax | 1,879 | 55,516 | 30.5 | 57,370 | 3.3 | 42.6 | 36.6 | 21.0 | 15.5 | 53.9 | 8.6 | 19.8 | 1 |
| Hertford | 916 | 22,317 | 24.7 | 22,601 | 1.3 | 37.4 | 37.0 | 19.7 | 15.2 | 58.1 | 10.7 | 18.1 | 1 |
| Martin | 1,198 | 25,078 | 21.4 | 25,593 | 2.1 | 52.5 | 38.9 | 18.6 | 11.5 | 58.3 | 9.5 | 16.3 | 2 |
| Northampton | 1,389 | 21,004 | 15.9 | 22,086 | 5.2 | 39.1 | 41.3 | 20.5 | 17.8 | 52.8 | 8.8 | 18.9 | 1 |
| Warren | 1,110 | 17,265 | 17.9 | 19,972 | 15.7 | 38.9 | 42.1 | 23.8 | 7.0 | 53.7 | 7.1 | 17.9 | 1 |
| **Region Totals** | **8,303** | **161,568** | **20.2** | **167,395** | **3.6** | **37.2** | **37.7** | **20.8** | **12.8** | **55.3** | **8.8** | **18.4** | **1.2** |

**Table 11.3:** Roanoke State Geographic Region.
**Sources:** United States Bureau of the Census; North Carolina State Planning Office.

I-95 and US 1 and thereby to the Piedmont Triangle, showed some considerable population growth (as compared to the state growth in the 1990s of 21.4 percent), then this SGR would be the only one in the state demonstrating a near zero change in its population.

Counties, like Hertford (Figure 11.8c) with its population growth of 1.3 percent, provide limited job opportunities, and see their young people leave on a large scale (note Table 4.8a and b); happily for Hertford this condition is very likely to change soon with the completion of the Nucor Steel Mill in 2001, and the new federal prison (near Winton), designed to handle a 1,200 prisoner overflow from the District of Columbia, scheduled for completion in 2001. The population of these counties otherwise peaked in the 1940s or 1950s; only high birth rates prevent a more rapid aging of the population, though in the cases of Northampton and Warren counties this latter condition appears to be occurring (see maps provided in Chapter 4, and Figures 11.8e and f). Note that these counties' median ages are five to six years higher than the state average. This is also the only SGR in the state with a majority black population. Warren and Bertie counties each have over 60 percent African American populations. This particular racial tilt is apt to intensify for some time since all six counties are experiencing a late 1990s negative rate of population increase in their white inhabitants, without this loss being offset by a net positive migration flow, while their non-white populations continue to have more births than deaths. Population profiles of the counties reflect these changing conditions in varying degrees (Figures 11.8a-f). Especially notable is the indentation in the profiles for the 20-29 age cohorts which are absent of the young migrants who have relocated in their search of opportunities outside the region. The inflated 50+ cohorts indicate the aging-in-place process that is contributing to higher death rates than the norm for the state. Though the percentage of children do not deviate much from state norms, this condition is supported by the much higher birth rates for the younger non-white population.

It is the condition of prevailing rural poverty, coupled with decades of out-migrating young people, that has led to extraordinary socio-economic development efforts. Due to the work of Floyd McKissick, then the National Director of the Congress for Racial Equality, the Federal Government committed $14 million

in 1972 to aid in the building of a new town to be named Soul City in rural Warren County (CP 11.13). A thirty year plan called for a manufacturing based economy to support a community of some 40,000 persons of mixed income and culture to reside in neighborhoods that included single family homes, as well as town houses. Further, the plan included a center city commercial district, a large municipal park, five neighborhood parks, and a golf course. With the support of low interest government loans and grants, 5,000 acres had been purchased by 1972, and homes were built for several dozen families. But federal support ceased in the late 1970s after only one industry, a labor intensive, low wage apparel firm, had located to the site. Within a few years this firm closed its doors. The community failed to incorporate and gradually lost its growth impetus, as well as much of its land, with its residents commuting elsewhere to their jobs. With a fire station, a recreational center including swimming pool and tennis courts, 44 black families living in well kept homes and town houses along curved paved roads and cull-de-sacs, a rural health clinic, and a home for the elderly, Soul City projects a wellbeing belying its absence of local employment opportunities and its location in one of the state's poorest counties. The population, mostly in place since the mid-1970s, is nearing or beyond retirement age. A dozen or so are working at the new state prison just down the road. In 1999, however, the delayed promise of jobs was buoyed by the state tax incentive support for CVS Pharmacy to build a new regional distribution center in the community, that would in a few years add some 350 workers to its present pool of 200. CVS, the country's largest drug store chain, was to receive a $12,500 tax credit for every job located in Warren County, while staying and enlarging at its present location in Henderson, Vance County (a mere 15 miles distant), would net the company only $4,000 for each new employee due to this Vance's much better economic position. Late spring of 2000 CVS decided that the economics for the company would not favor the relocation and Soul City missed out. Having purchased the old apparel plant, the state is now moving ahead with its plans to convert it to a vocational training center for the prison population. In addition a new natural gas transmission line is being installed, so new neighborhoods are being planned, and perhaps the renewal of life will urge new leadership to incorporate and provide finally the full fledged urban environment hoped for by McKissick (Ball 1999).

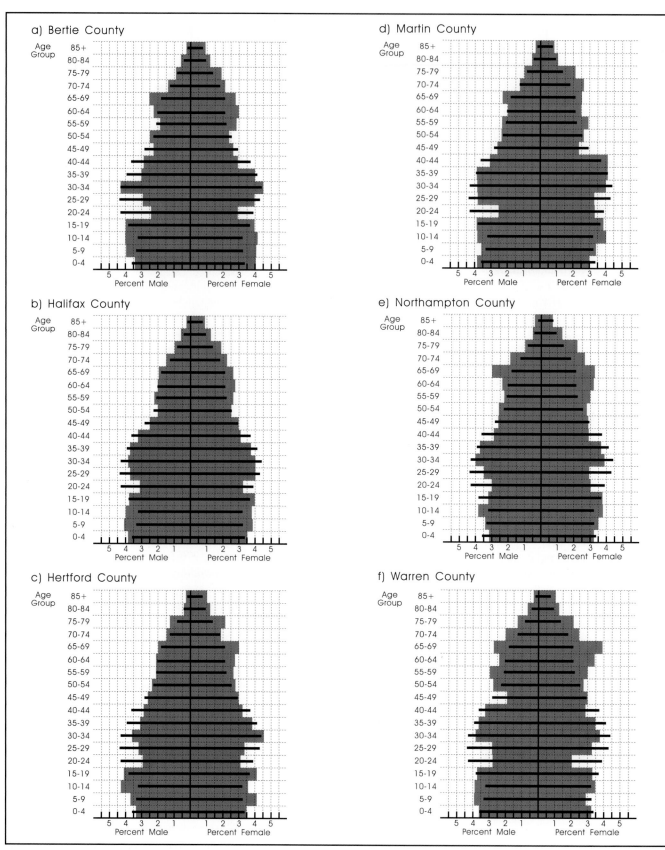

**Figure 11.8 a-f:** Roanoke Population Diagrams. Solid black lines represent state averages.
**Source:** U.S. Bureau of the Census, 1990.

With their major economic dependencies anchored in primary and low-wage secondary economic activities, Roanoke SGR counties also experience higher than average unemployment and poverty rates. In 1995, the North Carolina poverty rate of 13.1 percent was lower than the national rate (14.1%) for the first time in recent memory, yet there were 56 counties in the state with worse than national conditions. Among the latter, three Roanoke counties were close to twice the state and national poverty averages: Halifax with a poverty rate of 25.3% and Hertford and Northampton both with 24.6%. This has resulted in the Roanoke SGR having the state's highest designation of economic distress. In the entire state, only twelve of the 100 counties are designated Enterprise Tier 1; five of these twelve are in the Roanoke SGR. Only Martin County is graded at the Enterprise Tier 2 level, still some distance from the Tier 5 counties of greatest economic wealth (see Figures 9.12 and 9.14).

Epitomizing the difficulties in development is Roanoke Rapids, the region's largest city with some 16,000 people (1998 estimate), and a mill town of historic significance to the labor movement (CP 11.14a and b). This is where workers in the J. P. Stevens' seven cotton mills were finally able to win the right, in 1974, to unionize, after 14 years of trying. This was a monumental victory for organized labor in the south. J. P. Stevens, at the time the second largest textile company in the country with 85 plants and 45,000 workers, had become known as the 'nation's number one labor law violator,' and had accumulated a dozen orders from the National Labor Relations Board to cease and desist its unfair labor practices (Adler 1994). The heroic efforts of cotton mill worker Crystal Lee Sutton provided the story line for the film *Norma Rae* (1979), with the Oscar winning performance of Sally Field. Unhappily, even though salaries have doubled for the unionized workers over the subsequent 20 years, J. P. Stevens was bought out, mills were consolidated, and employment decreased from about 3,000 workers in the 1970s, to less than 1,000 in 1999. Employment in the SGR remains tilted toward labor intensive, low skill demanding, and low wage industries. Government management on both the county and municipality levels is troubled by a general absence of innovative leadership in its own ranks, as well as from among the region's leading stakeholders of business, labor, and land owners.

In the Roanoke SGR, a lag in health services development is evidenced by the region having an infant mortality rate some 45 percent higher than that of the state average, itself one of the highest in the country. Consequently, major efforts are made by the state to locate new industries within this region, in the expectation that this will aid in retaining its labor force, enhance the competency base, improve the local tax situation, and provide the needed local revenue for education, health, and other quality of life improvements. Major and persistent stumbling blocks in bringing high skills industries, with their higher salaries, include the existing critically low competence level as reflected in low college and high school graduation rates, the unusually small labor force in the all important 20-44 age cohorts, and an absence of dynamic and future focused leadership among the region's decision makers.

## Ring City

A loosely fitted rectangle of predominant urban land usage some 150 miles in circumference describes the concept of "Ring City". The Ring City State Geographic Region comprises those counties within which a set of urban places make up a 'ring of cities.' This Coastal Plain concentration of medium sized towns exist within a fairly intensively cultivated land and are within easy traveling distance of one another (Figure 11.9). Counties included in the SGR are Edgecombe, Greene, Lenoir, Nash, Pitt, Wayne, and Wilson, with their urban "Ring" nature well displayed on the land cover map (CP 11.15). Urbanization flows from the individual central places of Rocky Mount (55,893 population in 2000; +14.1% change in the 1990s), Wilson (44,405; 20.2%), Goldsboro (39,043; 12.7%), Kinston (23,688; -6.4%), Greenville (60,476; 31.3%) and Tarboro (11,138; 0.9%); the smaller towns and villages of Sharpsburg (2,421; 57.6%), Elm City (1,165; -28.3%), Black Creek (714; 16.1%), Freemont (1,463; -14.3%), Pikeville (719; 20.2%), La Grange (2,844; 1.4%), Grifton (2,073; -12.7%), Ayden (4,622; -2.5%), Winterville (4,791; 70.0%), Bethel (1,681; -8.7%), Conetoe (365; 25.0%), and Princeville (940; -43.1%); plus many more unincorporated communities, all lying along the interconnective transportation corridor made up of US 301, US 117, US 70, NC 11, US 13, and US 64. This is truly a "ring road" of highways. Even so, the urban places finding their connectivities within the Ring City are obviously not faring equally well in terms of population change. The few towns exhibiting rates of growth approaching that of the state for the 1990s (21.4%) have gained due to annexation. The only truly self-sustainable growth center is Greenville, which is also influencing the growth of a few villages within its commuting range.

As within most state geographic regions there are appreciable differences in basic attributes (Table 11.4). The total rural character of Greene County contrasts with the surrounding more urban counties, but this county's centrality in the SGR contributes to its experience of a recent population growth rate twice that of the region. Edgecombe County, on the other hand, saw a population decline in the 1990s, that in combination with a high family poverty level, low competency levels, and high single female head of household percentage, contributed to its Enterprise Tier 1 designation. Other counties fare much better, resulting in their Tier 3 or 4 ratings. Were it not for its critical location within the Ring City orbit, Edgecombe seems to reflect better the cultural, socio-economic, and land use conditions of the Roanoke SGR. The straight-line north-south boundary between Edgecombe and Nash counties, defined by the tracks of the CSX Railroad, neatly splits white and black populations of this portion of the Coastal Plain, as evidenced by Edgecombe's 56.4 percent nonwhite population and Nash County's 32.3 percent nonwhite population.

Driving along the "ring road" provides evidence of the essentially urban functional nature of Ring City. It is not just the actual linear lineup of the incorporated places that provides support for this statement. It is this combined with the existence of interlinked unincorporated stretches with closely spaced com-

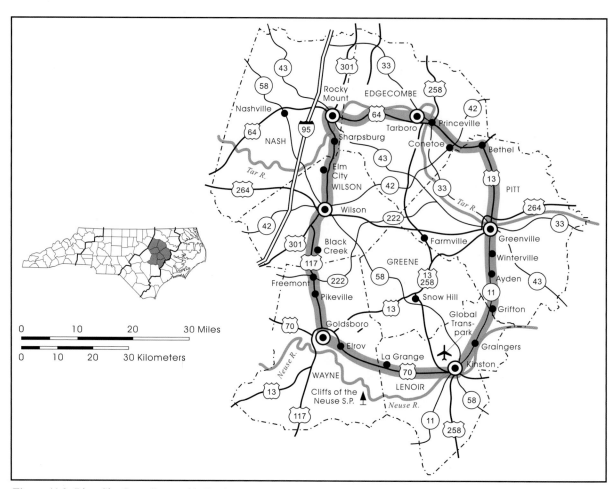

**Figure 11.9:** Ring City State Geographic Region.

mercial business and the rural homes of people who commute to the various centers of employment. The urban ring includes about 3/5ths, or 320,000 of the total Ring City SGR population of 542,589, making this a region larger in urban population size than Forsyth County (Winston-Salem) and Cumberland County (Fayetteville).

Conceptually, coalition of urban places, much like the Ring City, have been given much consideration in the geographic literature. Terms ranging from "polynucleated metropolitan region" to "oligopolis" to "dispersed city" have been proposed to de-

scribe their internal distributional and functional character. Essentially, this urban character is defined by having a set of urban nodes in close proximity to each other, separated by tracts of non-urban land use, and functioning as one large city because the distances among them are short enough in travel time to facilitate their use for different purposes, i.e., shopping, entertainment, education, and employment (Beimfohr 1953; Burton 1963; Hayes 1976). In essence, the urban outcome is a metropolis without a core. At one point in time, the Piedmont Dispersed City had a similar structure, an elaboration of which was provided by

| RING CITY | Land Area in sq. km | Pop. 1990 | Pop. sq.km. 2000 | Pop. 2000 | 1990s % Pop. Change | % White 2000 | Median Age in 2000 | % Fam. Below Poverty | Average Annual Infant Mortality Rate 1994-98 | % High School Grads'90 | % Coll. Grads. 1990 | Fem. Fam. Head of Hshld'90 | NC Enterprise Tiers'97 |
|---|---|---|---|---|---|---|---|---|---|---|---|---|---|
| Edgecombe | 1,308 | 56,692 | 42.5 | 55,606 | -1.9 | 40.1 | 35.2 | 17.6 | 9.3 | 58.5 | 8.1 | 21.1 | 1 |
| Greene | 688 | 15,384 | 27.6 | 18,974 | 23.3 | 51.8 | 39.1 | 14.2 | 14.9 | 59.2 | 8.9 | 16.2 | 4 |
| Lenoir | 1,036 | 57,274 | 57.6 | 59,648 | 4.1 | 56.5 | 38.3 | 16.5 | 12.8 | 62.9 | 11.5 | 17.3 | 3 |
| Nash | 1,399 | 76,677 | 62.5 | 87,420 | 14 | 61.9 | 37.0 | 10.7 | 13.7 | 65.1 | 13.7 | 13.7 | 4 |
| Pitt | 1,688 | 108,480 | 79.3 | 133,798 | 23.3 | 62.1 | 31.5 | 15.5 | 13.6 | 71.0 | 21.9 | 14.5 | 4 |
| Wayne | 1,431 | 104,666 | 79.2 | 113,329 | 8.3 | 61.3 | 35.2 | 11.9 | 9.7 | 71.2 | 12.7 | 14.4 | 3 |
| Wilson | 961 | 66,061 | 76.8 | 73,814 | 11.7 | 55.8 | 37.1 | 16.1 | 11.6 | 62.2 | 14.4 | 16.7 | 3 |
| **Region Totals** | **8,511** | **485,234** | **63.8** | **542,589** | **11.8** | **57.8** | **36.2** | **14.6** | **12.2** | **64.3** | **13.0** | **16.3** | **3.1** |

**Table 11.4:** Ring City State Geographic Region.
**Sources:** United States Bureau of the Census; North Carolina State Planning Office.

406

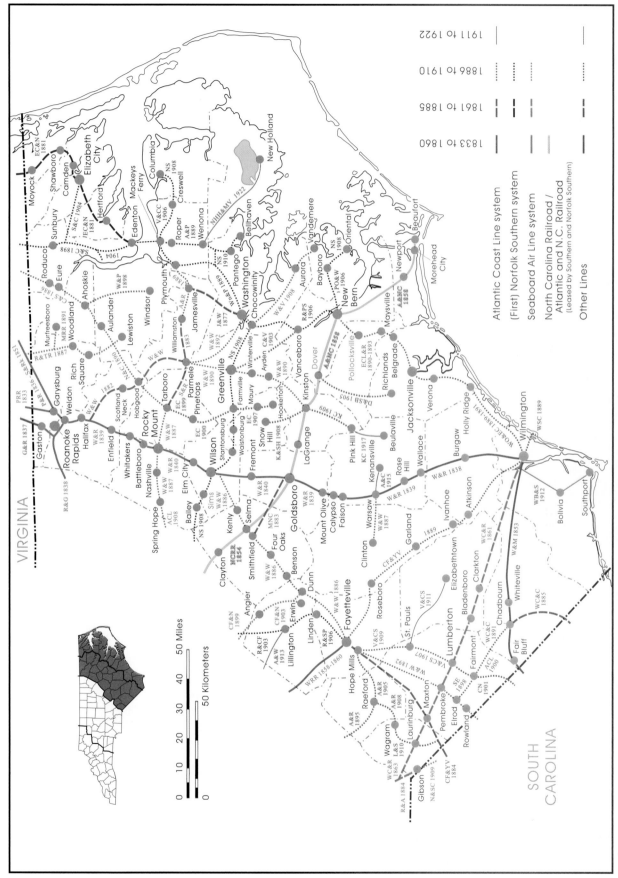

**Color Plate 11.1:** Evolution of the Coastal Rail Net from 1833 to 1922. **Source:** Modified from Bishir and Southern (1996, p. 44).

407

**C.P. 11.2a:** Historic Downtown Rockingham (Richmond County) exemplifies the energy and commitment that the citizenry in the Coastal Plain is making to revitalize downtown spaces. In 1996, the Fidelity Bank decided that it no longer needed the 1835 Leak-Wall House that had been purchased from the family in 1974 for use as a branch bank. It took 170 newfound members of the historical society one year to raise the $100,000 required to acquire the property for a permanent and publicly available addition to the Historic District.

*Photo by Ole Gade.*

*Photo by Ole Gade.*

**C.P. 11.2b:** Rocky Mount (in Nash and Edgecombe counties) has similarly embarked on a major historic renovation effort. Many commercial buildings on the Edgecombe side of downtown have been gutted, leaving remnant foundations and walls supporting the turn-of-the-20th century commercial architecture.

**C.P. 11.2c:** This colonial style historic home in Clinton (Sampson County), in a traditional residential block close to the county courthouse, is itself an historic treasure.

*Photo by Ole Gade.*

**Color Plate 11.2:** This set of photos demonstrates one of the important aesthetic attributes of the Coastal Plain Region - its richness of well-maintained and historically renovated architecture distributed generously throughout the region's villages and towns.

**C.P. 11.2d:** An 1880s traditional and well-maintained home in a residential neighborhood of Beulaville (Duplin County). Wealth flowing into the county from investments in the livestock industry has been very important in attracting people interested in maintaining and upgrading the existing historic housing stock.

**Color Plate 11.3:** Cliffs of the Neuse State Park demonstrates the erosive power of the river. In this picture, taken in September, 1964, from cliffs elevated 100 feet above the river bed, the Neuse River is at an unusually low level due to a dry summer in the Piedmont.

**C.P. 11.4a:** Here a residential street and the town hall of Princeville shows clear evidence of being submerged below the high water levels of the flooded Tar River. The flood "dirt line" (marked in red) passes across the building at high window level.

*Photo by Chris Walton.*

**C.P. 11.4b:** The flood "dirt line" is shown on a Princeville residential street.

*Photo by Chris Walton.*

**C.P. 11.4c:** A dramatic example of the flood damage shows a house floated over and onto a pickup truck. The house behind the three Appalachian State University students was almost completely submerged by the storm waters. In spite of this rather concrete evidence of nature's real and potential wrath, the town's people have decided to use relief monies to rebuild in place, rather than relocate to higher ground.

*Photo by Chris Walton.*

**Color Plate 11.4:** Hurricanes Floyd and Dennis unleashed incredible destruction on life and land in the Coastal Plain. Princeville (Edgecombe County) was founded as a black community on the northern floodplain side of the Tar River, across from Tarboro. The river thus became a symbolic, as well as a physical barrier. A dike built in the 1920s, and further improved in 1965, offered little protection against so overwhelming a flood, and the entire town was up to twelve feet under water.

Photo by Ehren Meister.

**Color Plate 11.5:** Waccamaw Lake is the largest Carolina Bay. It is adjacent to Green Swamp. Covering close to half of Columbus County and nearly one-third of Brunswick County, this is the largest remaining swamp in the state. Most of the Land is owned by private paper and pulp companies such as Federal Paperboard and Weyerhauser. Aside from forestry, human activity of the lake and pocosin swamp area is recreational, dominated by camping, boating, fishing, and hunting.

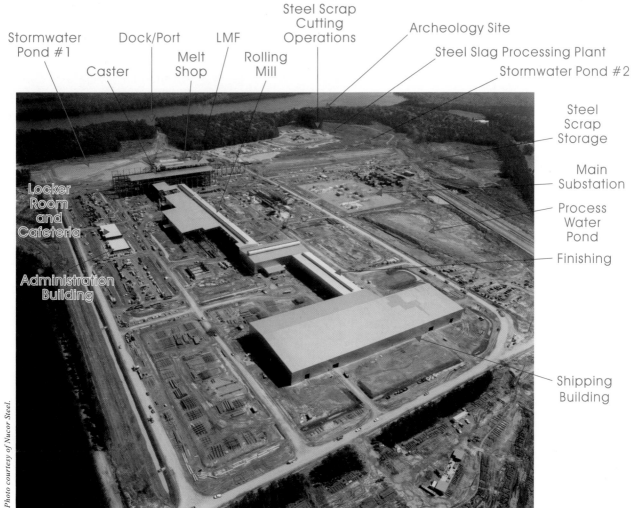

Photo courtesy of Nucor Steel.

**Color Plate 11.6:** The Nucor steel plant is expected to be in production in the spring of 2001. Located in rural Hertford County, it is expected to bring a measure of economic prosperity to one of the poorest areas in the state.

411

*Photo by H.D. Stillwell.*

**Color Plate 11.7:** The process of transplanting tobacco is labor intensive, although field equipment has been developed to reduce the toils of stoop labor. This crew was pictured in Bertie County in 1978. While the reduction in tobacco acreage and increasing mechanization are decreasing the need for migrant field hands, what jobs do remain are increasingly taken by less costly Latino labor.

**Color Plate 11.8:** Considerable contrasts in housing quality exist throughout the Coastal Plain. In poor neighborhoods there is frequent evidence of upgrading from wooden structures in dilapidated condition and without water or sewer connections, to house trailers, as seen here near Lillington (Harnett County).

*Photo by Ole Gade.*

**C.P. 11.9a:** Rowland's downtown commerce appears dominated by antique and bric-a-brac shops without the typical mix of central business district functions. The potential of attracting customers from the nearby I-95 appears an option for development.

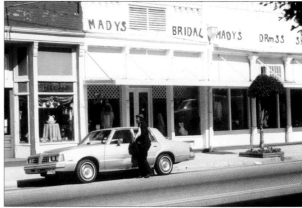

*Photo by Ole Gade.*

*Photo by Ole Gade.*

**C.P. 11.9b:** The Rowland railroad depot is now dysfunctional in its original usage, but still the building retains its historic value, as does much of the commercial building stock in town.

**Color Plate 11.9:** Some communities have never been wealthy and now suffer the shock of rural depopulation and an absence of any kind of development in agriculture, industry, or tourism. Left behind, the communities struggle to survive. Rowland (Robeson County) is a well-kept and clean town that lost the use of the rail depot. The railroad and local agricultural production were the focus of earlier economic growth. With close to 100% black population and located a few miles from the South Carolina border, the community has little political power and scant economic resources to coerce positive change into being.

412

**Color Plate 11.10:** New library of East Carolina University.

**Color Plate 11.11:** Scene of the East Carolina University Campus.

*Source: www.photos.ecu.edu.*

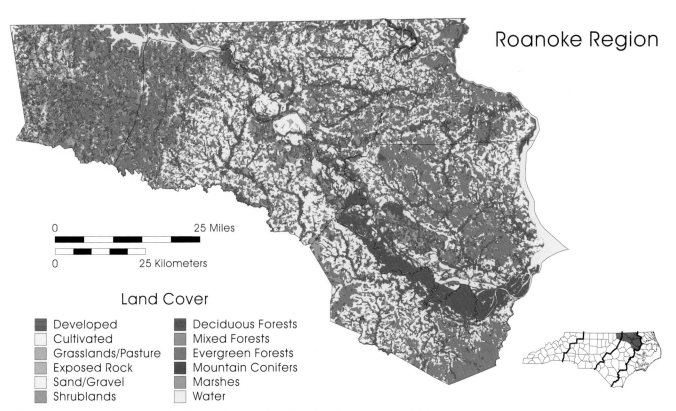

# Roanoke Region

0            25 Miles

0            25 Kilometers

## Land Cover

- Developed
- Cultivated
- Grasslands/Pasture
- Exposed Rock
- Sand/Gravel
- Shrublands
- Deciduous Forests
- Mixed Forests
- Evergreen Forests
- Mountain Conifers
- Marshes
- Water

**Color Plate 11.12:** Roanoke State Geographic Region Land Cover, 1998.
**Source:** Modified from the North Carolina Center for Geographic Information and Analysis, 1998.

**Color Plate 11.13:** Soul City (Warren County), a planned community of the 1970s, lost its economic growth and stability impetus with a change in federal administration, the decline in rural manufacturing plant location, and a failure in diversifying the community's population.

*Photo by Ole Gade.*

*Photo by E. Meister.*

**C.P. 11.14a:** One of the seven plants built by J.P. Stevens in Roanoke Rapids' heyday, this plant is on the verge of closing, having been caught in the 1990s frenzy of corporate buyouts, plant closings, and labor layoffs.

**C.P. 11.14b:** Company housing frequently was provided by the textile and apparel companies. Block after block of houses were built in the 1920s. In recent years the houses have been sold to their occupants, but continue to provide visible evidence of the traditional urban manufacturing landscape.

*Photo by E. Meister.*

**Color Plate 11.14:** Roanoke Rapids (Halifax County) exemplifies towns that blossomed during the textile boom of the early 20th century. There has been little incentive for economic diversification in Roanoke Rapids, and the town suffers to a much greater extent from the loss of textile employment.

414

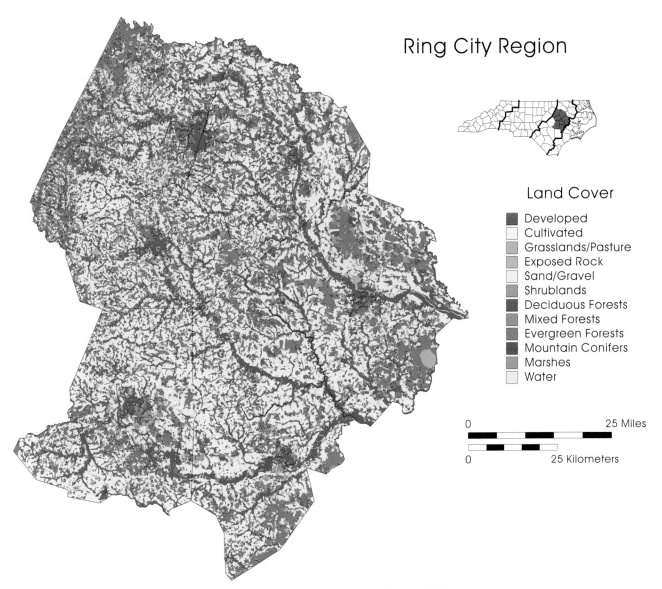

# Ring City Region

## Land Cover

- Developed
- Cultivated
- Grasslands/Pasture
- Exposed Rock
- Sand/Gravel
- Shrublands
- Deciduous Forests
- Mixed Forests
- Evergreen Forests
- Mountain Conifers
- Marshes
- Water

0           25 Miles

0           25 Kilometers

**Color Plate 11.15:** Ring City State Geographic Region Land Cover, 1998.
**Source:** Modified from the North Carolina Center for Geographic Information and Analysis, 1998.

**Color Plate 11.16:** A main street dominated by railroad tracks is the main landscape feature of downtown Rocky Mount, a key Coastal Plain transportation center from the early days of rail. As Amtrak continues to expand passenger service, this key role of Rocky Mount will grow. The tracks also serve as the boundary between Edgecombe County, on the near side, and Nash County, on the far side.

*Photo by Ole Gade.*

**Color Plate 11.17:** As tobacco fields decline in number, museums such as the Tobacco Farm Life Museum on Kenly (Johnston County) are taking on additional significance. Visitors enjoy the fragrance of hung and yellowing "golden leaf" at the museum.

*Photo by Ole Gade.*

*Photo by Ole Gade.*

**Color Plate 11.18:** Snow Hill, the largest town (1,544 people in 1998) and county seat of Greene County, gets its name from the light sand banks of Contentnea Creek, where Indians camped and referred to as "snowy hills."

416

# Sandhills Region

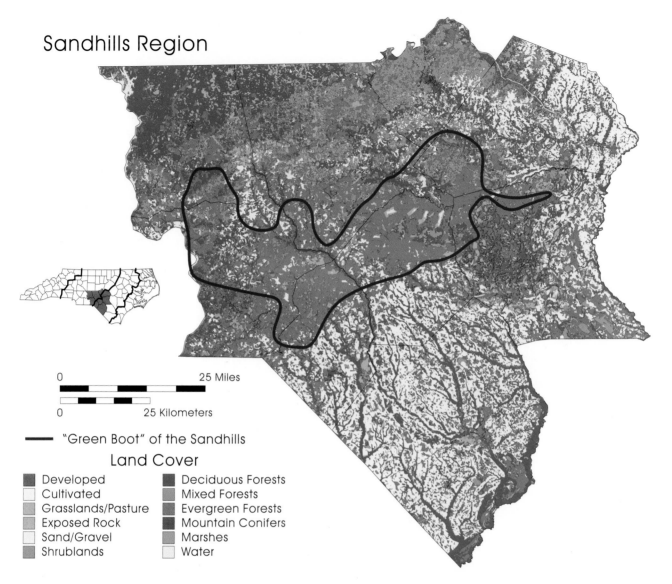

**Land Cover**

| | |
|---|---|
| ■ Developed | ■ Deciduous Forests |
| □ Cultivated | ■ Mixed Forests |
| ■ Grasslands/Pasture | ■ Evergreen Forests |
| ■ Exposed Rock | ■ Mountain Conifers |
| □ Sand/Gravel | ■ Marshes |
| ■ Shrublands | □ Water |

—— "Green Boot" of the Sandhills

0 _____ 25 Miles

0 _____ 25 Kilometers

**Color Plate 11.19:** Sandhills State Geographic Region Land Cover, 1998.
**Source:** Modified from the North Carolina Center for Geographic Information and Analysis, 1998.

**Color Plate 11.20:** The importance of turkey production as a basic industry in Hoke County is inescapable.

*Photo by Robert E. Reiman.*

417

**Color Plate 11.21:** Campbell University is a large private institution with professional schools, including a law school. The university dominates the small rural community of Buies Creek (Harnett County).

*Photo by Robert E. Reiman.*

**Color Plate 11.22:** In Southern Pines (Moore County) horse farms cover large lots especially zoned for their interest. The horse farms constitute one of the more unusual urban landscapes in the state.

*Photo by Ole Gade.*

**Color Plate 11.23:** Sandhills piney woods lend themselves to golf course development. This golf course is near Aberdeen (Moore County).

*Photo by Ole Gade.*

**Color Plate 12.1:** Greensboro's downtown (as viewed from the air in the late 1970s) captures the CBD status of this period, following massive urban renewal and commercial disinvestments. Vast acreage is turned into parking lots. Large government investments had been made in county administrative facilities, federal courts, and a central post office. The absence of private/corporate investments in high rise office buildings was largely due to the traditional manufacturing base dominating Greensboro's economy.

**Color Plate 12.2:** R.J. Reynolds' Whitaker Tobacco Plant and facilities was built in the 1970s to use newer and more automated approaches to cigarette manufacturing. The large acreage, single story facility replaced the multistory plants of the central city. Subsequently, an even larger plant was opened in Tobaccoville, in a rural area some 15 miles northeast of Winston-Salem (see CP 6.13).

**Color Plate 12.3:** Built in the 1970s, The Four Seasons Mall reflects the outmigration of retail businesses to the perimeter of the city. The importance of the automobile in the site selection process is evident in the location at the freeway intersection of I-40 and High Point Road, a few miles from downtown Greensboro, as well as in the large acreage of parking spaces. The success of the mall's location led to the building of a hotel and then the Koury Conference Center.

**Color Plate 12.4:** A nostalgic view of Salisbury's CBD (Rowan County) is shown in a wall mural painted in preparation for the 1976 National Bicentennial Celebration. While the artist took some liberties in placing the more notable downtown buildings, she captured the ambience and activity of the central city at the turn of the 20th Century. In comparing this image with CP 12.3, it is clear that a world of difference exists in the century apart location of shopping facilities.

**Color Plate 12.5:** Uptown Charlotte's Independence Square, at Tryon and Trade streets, remains the commercial high-value intersection. Four statues mark the former crossing of two Indian trails: *Commerce*, *Transportation*, *Industry*, and *Future*. Small corner parks with water fountains and the El Grande Disco provide human-scale relief from the imposing high rises surrounding the square. An Overstreet Mall connector crosses East Trade Street, a reminder of the general absence of street level retail. Within the four blocks are found the 60-story Bank of America corporate headquarters, other high rise office buildings, and two hotels. Sales of buildings in 1999 indicated a market value of $125 - $135 per square foot.

*Photo by Ole Gade.*

*Photo by Ole Gade.*

**Color Plate 12.6:** Second level pedestrian walkways connect major office buildings in downtown Winston-Salem (Forsyth County) and remove potential consumers from street level shops. From its 1960s failure with a pedestrian mall to the present, downtown Winston-Salem has experienced continuing outmigration of its retail businesses. However, available space and reasonable rents have enticed a new breed of users to the downtown, where several city blocks now have a specialization of arts and crafts studios and outlets.

*Photo by Ole Gade.*

**Color Plate 12.7:** Raleigh's Fayetteville Street Mall provides excellent pedestrian open space in four blocks of the downtown CBD, but is popular only when office workers are out during their lunch hour. Closed retail stores and the general absence of restaurants and entertainment facilities contribute to a gloomy atmosphere. The Mall is dark after office workers go home, but its future appears brighter with recent increases in downtown condos, townhouses, and apartments, and therefore permanent residents and consumers. However, the Mall might be reconverted to automotive traffic.

*Photo by Ole Gade.*

**C.P. 12.8a:** The Salisbury Railroad Corridor National Historic District includes the splendid Spanish Mission style railroad station built in 1912.

422

Charles Hayes in 1976 (see Chapter 12). Critical to the identification of Ring City as a dispersed city is the evolution among its populace of the 'idea of the city.' In the minds of people living here, there emerges a consciousness of Ring City existing as an umbrella metropolis within which their own urban place operates as a specialized cog. Fuelling this perception is ready access provided by the state-of-art interconnective transportation corridor, and by the Greene County 'green common'. Further support of the notion of Ring City emerging as a distinctive urban region was the U.S. Bureau of the Census designation in the 1990s of Rocky Mount (including Edgecombe and Nash counties), Goldsboro (Wayne County), and Greenville (Pitt County) as independent Metropolitan Statistical Areas (see Figures 4.2 and 9.10). One might anticipate a future Bureau of the Census decision to fuse these coalescing MSAs into one unit with the addition of Kinston (Lenoir County).

This SGR has an unusual occurrence of urban places that are cut by administrative boundaries. Rocky Mount has over two-thirds of its population and almost all of its white population and its wealth in Nash County; the remainder are in Edgecombe County. Sharpsburg counts its population within its incorporated limits in three counties, while Grifton does so in two counties. A further interesting aspect of Ring City SGR is a large rural, green space in its very center, occupied largely by Greene County, whose urban population is confined to three small incorporated places: Snow Hill (1,514), Hookerton (467), and Walstonburg (224) out of a county population of 18,974. Thus Ring City is further defined by the unusual situation of having a rural green heart within its ring of urban places.

Historically speaking, Ring City existed 150 years ago as the very same oblong rectangle of urban places, but then linked by rail; in this case, all connections were eventually serviced by the Atlantic Coastal Rail Line (CP 11.1). The five principal towns benefited from their location in the midst of agricultural prosperity about evenly distributed through the landscape. With their initial success assured by an equidistant position from each other, thus having equality of opportunity as service centers for their own agricultural regions, the towns attracted and subsequently thrived on the extraregional connections that the railroad provided, and grew to a near similar size in economy and population. Much later there began a specialization in economic development.

Rocky Mount, for example, emerged early as Ring City's transportation center, in part because of its regionally superior connections to northern markets and the bustling "Main Street" of the Piedmont, and in part because it housed Seaboard Coast Line's switching yards and maintenance/repair complex (CP 11.16). The town also experienced a major concentration of textile and apparel plants; and therefore the negative impact of plant closings over the past two decades (see Chapter 6). Industrial diversification and improved economic stability has been attained by the arrival of Abbott Laboratories' medical equipment plant, employing over 1,000 persons, as well as of new plants manufacturing jet engine fuel controls, automotive locks, rubber, and steel frame buildings. All of this new manufacturing industry relies on higher skills and offers better wages. The more recent construction of an interstate distribution center by the telemarketeer QVC is further testimony to Rocky Mount's image as a transportation center.

Greenville is growing more rapidly and bypassed Rocky Mount's population size over the last decade. Greenville's claim to fame is the newly invigorated East Carolina University (ECU), with its medical complex and expanded options for health care industries. Although this is Ring City's, as well as northeastern North Carolina's, city of health and higher education, Greenville also stars as a diversified manufacturing center. The downtown is gaining praise for community efforts in revitalizing it. Evans Street was the town's main commercial drag until outlying shopping strips and malls divested it of its merchants. An attempt to reinvigorate the street, located next to the burgeoning ECU campus, as a pedestrian mall with decorative planters and no-through traffic (in the style of the federally supported National Main Street programs) subsequently failed to stop the outflow of retailers. Now, a new transformation appears to be successful in economically restructuring the downtown. A joint private-public partnership has substituted the pedestrian mall for one way automotive traffic. A zoning change to allow high density residential units, thus permitting townhouse apartments in a retrofitted large former commercial building, has attracted new investments favoring professional and business services, as well as commercial and leisure/entertainment facilities. All are wrapped in a vastly improved aesthetic downtown environment and a stylish, attractive university campus (CP 11.10 and 11.11). Expectations of having to add 6,000 students to its present base of 18,000 has the institution frantic in its search for additional construction space. As it is situated in very tight quarters the university has the problem of expanding without conflict with its neighbors. Older residential neighborhoods feel particularly threatened at present.

Over the last quarter of the 20th century, Greenville has emerged from a small tobacco focused market town with a teachers college to a regional center. More than 41,000 university and medical center employees, and students, provide a range of consumer interests, purchasing power, and cosmopolitan amenities, much beyond the norm for a Coastal Plain urban center. On the town's outskirts a wealth of new suburbs and horse farms spread onto former tobacco fields in a county that is still the leading grower of tobacco in the nation.

For Goldsboro, the anchor of stability is the Seymour Johnson Air Force Base. With its 5,000 military personnel and 6,000 civilian workers, the base has a considerable cultural and economic influence on a town that also has found favor with military retirees. An estimated 27,000 highly skilled, middle aged armed forces veterans populate the area, and their presence attracts high tech industries, like the jet fighter navigational repair division of Martin Marietta. Although the city saw its population expand in the 1990s at a rate exceeding that of the state, this was mostly through the annexing of suburban residential development. Its downtown mirrors the experience of other major 'base' towns, dominated by commercial buildings either standing vacant or offering rents low enough to attract used goods entrepreneurs and a bevy of store front churches (Photo 6.11).

Kinston shares with Goldsboro the potential benefits of the Global TransPark. At issue for the future is still the question of whether the air freight facility surrounded by just-in-time manufacturers providing thousands of jobs will, in fact, ever become a reality (Walden 1992; Bascom, Carey and Zonn 1996). At present only two companies, both air transportation services, have located at the park. Without the expected jet port developments, Kinston lost population during the 1990s. During the 1980s the industrial labor force in Lenoir County, of which Kinston is the county seat, decreased 14 percent and average annual wages dropped 35 percent when measured in real dollars (Peek 1993). A dependence on textile and apparel manufacturing plants facing economic restructuring and layoffs has seriously damaged the town's economic vitality.

Wilson is almost twice the size of Kinston. It grew at close to the state average during the 1990s, but is facing employment problems. Not only are the labor intensive plants closing down, but the town is seeing the closing of one third of its twelve large tobacco warehouses, due in part to continuing quota cuts in tobacco acreage and in part to the increasing tendency for tobacco companies to contract with growers rather than to buy at auctions (CP 11.17) (Hart and Chestang 1996). Ring City's leading banking firm, Branch Banking and Trust, Inc. (BB&T), which developed in Wilson supported by the tobacco money, has recently relocated its headquarter facilities to Winston-Salem. However, it appears that a turnaround in fortune is in process. As a long standing nationally leading marketeer and producer of tobacco, a product facing imminent statewide decline, Wilson has been somewhat successful in recasting itself as "Triangle East." This promotes the economic development idea of having the Research Triangle Park keep the administrative offices and research

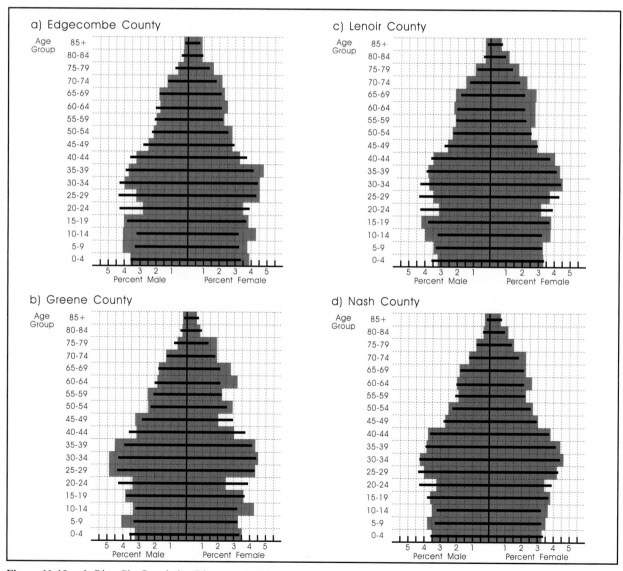

**Figure 11-10 a-d:** Ring City Population Diagrams. Solid black lines represent state averages.
**Source:** U.S. Bureau of the Census, 1990.

424

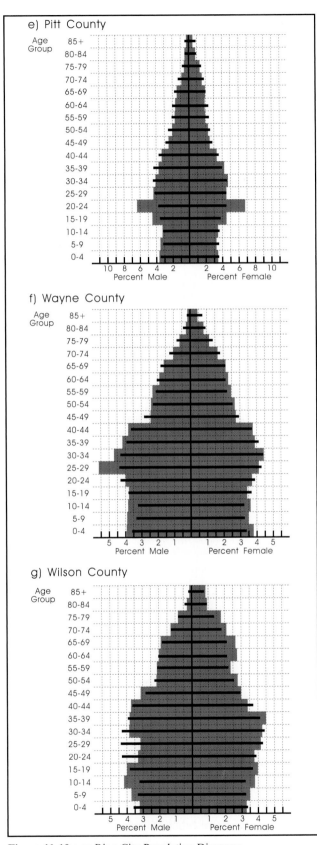

e) Pitt County

f) Wayne County

g) Wilson County

**Figure 11-10 e-g:** Ring City Population Diagrams.
Solid black lines represent state averages.
**Source:** U.S. Bureau of the Census, 1990.

labs of major corporations, but sending the manufacturing plants to Wilson. Its location just 45 miles east of Raleigh and on I-95, seems to provide Wilson with reasonable advantages. Already several pharmaceutical plants (Merck and Novopharm among them) have located there. The town also has been improving on the viability of its historic downtown, aided by a strong commitment to culture, and has been expanding its image as a center of antiques retailers and fabulous Eastern North Carolina barbeque.

Among the seven counties' population profiles four (Nash, Edgecombe, Wilson and Lenoir) are quite similar in their lower than state average in their young adult cohorts, which is a peculiarity in urban centered counties (Figures 11.10a to g). On the other hand, a general pattern of higher fertility rates through the mid-1980s in this part of the state has fuelled the larger than norm 5-19 age groups. Pitt and Wayne counties deviate from these patterns due to university and armed forces populations. Both of these show the expected large 20-29 cohorts, with males clearly dominating in Wayne County, but with Pitt's student population not providing a high fertility rate this county's child cohorts are below state norms. To accommodate the dominance of young people, attributable to East Carolina University, on Figure 11.10e it was necessary to halve the scale of its horizontal axis. Green County is demonstrating that having a boundary within eight miles of each of the towns of Kinston, Greenville, Wilson and Goldsboro is beneficial to the growth of young families, as indicated by its outsized 25-39 cohorts (Figure 11.10b and CP 11.18).

Ring City satisfies several of the expected criteria for a dispersed city. For the moment, though, the needed umbrella image has yet to develop sufficiently among the populace of the region. Perhaps the new entrepreneurial region, the Global TransPark Commission Region , which includes the seven counties of the Ring City SGR, will contribute to the emergence of this image through its large scale regional promotion efforts.

### Sandhills

The Sandhills State Geographic Region is the state's third largest SGR in physical size, and the fourth largest in total population (Table 9.2). Earlier sections of this chapter considered the physical environments of this region, noting especially the geologic and surface feature peculiarities that causes its Sandhills designation. The heart of the region is a largely unpopulated boot-like territory, with its calf defined by the four county reach of the Ft. Bragg Military Reservation, a boot strap extending toward Lillington and Dunn in Harnett County, and its foot anchored in the Sandhills Game Lands, the heel covering the northwestern quarter of Scotland County and the toe poking well into Richmond County. The "Sandhill's Green Boot" is bisected by a ten kilometer wide belt of mixed cultivated and forested land between its calf and ankle, and central portions of the foot are gradually being gnawn away by expanding urbanization of Hamlet and Rockingham. Providing a continuous green linear wetlands, the Lumber River snakes through the Sandhills at the ankle of the "Green Boot" and continues its journey to the South Carolina

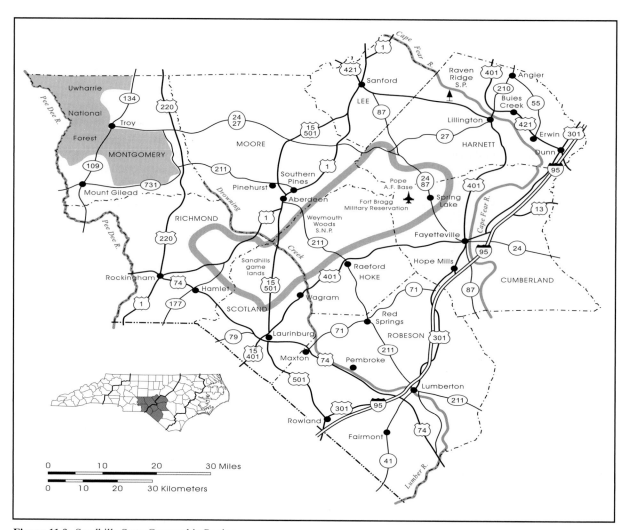

**Figure 11.9:** Sandhills State Geographic Region.

border as a federally designated "wild and scenic" river (Figure 11.11 and CP 11.19).

The Sandhills' major urban concentrations exist at the perimeter of the "Green Boot". Here, on the east in Cumberland County, we have Fayetteville, with its 2000 population of 121,015; and a 1990s growth rate of 60.0% (due largely to vigorous annexation of adjacent suburbanizing territories). Fayetteville's neighbors of Hope Mills (11,237; 37.3%) and Spring Lake (8,098; 7.6%) are now feeling the impact of their close proximity. Much of the county's land is given over to the military, leaving little space for additional development and encouraging new residential neighborhoods to flow into the adjacent counties of Harnett to the north and Hoke to the south. In both cases low cost land, an absence of zoning, and benign building rules (as, for example, permitting extensive tracts of mobile home housing) have energized development favoring young families in both of these counties. The location of many of these residential subdivisions next to the Fort Bragg and Pope Air Force Base boundaries are causing increasing concerns due to the problems attendant to military exercises, congestion and noise factors. Fayetteville's potential for future growth appears severally limited due to an eco-

nomic base founded on the military on the one hand, and labor intensive manufacturing industry on the other. While the military seems to be a continuously stable factor, Cumberland County has seen the closing of all of its textile mills over the past several decades (Box 11A). This was the leading cotton processing and manufacturing center in the state before the Civil War (Bingham 1997).

With an absence of serious corporate investments, especially in financial and insurance services which provide the impetus for high density and high rise commercial buildings in other large cities in the state, Fayetteville's downtown is left without significant change since World War II. It is also not a major employment destination. Now that Hay Street has been cleaned up of its 'Red Light District' image, even fewer people travel the streets. Outside of the working day's 8:00-5:00 hours, the downtown is largely dead (Photos 6.10 and 11.10). The absence of recent commercial development is perhaps a blessing in disguise since it has permitted the retention of large areas of historic properties. Residential neighborhoods on the National Register of Historic Places include the Haymount District, with its oldest house dating from 1817, while commercial districts include the three blocks of the Olde Fayetteville Commons and the symbol of Fayetteville, the 1832 Market House (Morris 1993).

Whereas Cumberland's population profile (Figure 11.12a) demonstrates the expected dominance of young people, especially males in the 20-29 cohorts, both Hoke's and Harnett's profiles (Figures 11.12c and b) are beginning to acquire some similar traits. In all three cases the 0-9 cohorts also exceed in size that of the state norm (Figure 9.12), with Hoke's profile reflecting the 1980s surge of young families with their children into the county from Cumberland County. Simultaneously these counties have the Sandhills' smallest percentages of people over 50 years of age. As a result we see Hoke County expanding at a rate of 47.2 percent, during the 1990s, though its county seat of Raeford (3,386) was located away from the growth zone and lost 2.4 percent (CP 5.7 and CP 11.20). To the northeast of the "Green Boot," Harnett County's cluster of small urban places, including Dunn (9,196; 10.3%), and Erwin, Coats, Buies Creek (CP 11.21), and Angier (all with less than 5,000 people), are feeling growing pains. This is resulting not only from the residential overflow from Ft. Bragg, but also from the proximity to I-95 and its intersection with east-west trending US 421, and the proximity to the booming southern portion of Wake County. Angier, for example, is within the commuting shadow of Raleigh, 20 miles to the north, and is exploding with a 1990s addition of 12,100 residents within a five mile radius of town (estimate provided by Musante 1997). Its incorporated town 2000 population total of 3,419 is thus grossly deceptive of the actual changes impacting a rural countryside, where speculative land development thrive due to comparatively low land cost. For a county in this kind of transition, Harnett is experiencing the expected pressure on its school system, as well as periodic water shortages. Perhaps not so well known are the additional conflicts resulting from the expansion of urban settlement into areas with pervasive traditional rural North Carolina values. On the northern outskirts of the "Green Boot," near Manners, there have been a recent increase of complaints of illegal deer hunting and the straying of hunting dogs onto residential property.

Sanford, county seat of Lee County, had a 2000 population of 23,220, 60.4 percent over its 1990 total. It lies to the northwest of the "Green Boot," its growth boosted by annexation and new manufacturing industries. Positioning itself as the "Gateway to the Research Triangle," Sanford has been able to greatly diversify its industrial base over the past several decades. Larger industries include cosmetics, automotive parts, electrical components, air cleaning equipment, faucets, medicines, and food processing. This has also attracted a diverse labor force, including a sizable Hispanic component (19%). The growing reality of the "Gateway" concept may succeed in Lee County being added to the existing Raleigh-Durham-Chapel Hill Piedmont Triangle Metropolitan Statistical Area by the United States Bureau of the Census following the final assessment of the 2000 Census results. In that case Sanford could emerge as a fourth anchor, with a resulting Piedmont Quadrangle MSA. One aspect of improving economic conditions is found in the rehabilitation of Sanford's downtown. A Main Street Program was begun in the early 1980s, with its success measured by the granting of historic district status in 1997, denoting particularly Sanford's role as a rail head during the late 1800s (Photo 11.9a to c). Lee County, incidentally, is the most recently (1907) formed county in North Carolina, and the state's smallest (Table 11.5). Its population profile (Figure 11.12d) reflects the importance of a middle age blue color labor force that may be expected to age-in-place.

A thin slice of land in Moore County, adjacent to Fort Bragg, has become part of the "Green Boot" through a peculiar form of rural zoning. The land is part of a larger tract, some 15 square miles, that has for many years been 'horse country.' To protect against encroachment of speculators who might subdivide the land for residential purposes, land owners petitioned the village of Southern Pines to extend its zoning powers to the east, in effect covering nearly five square miles with a 'rural estate' designation. Within this zone no horse farm may be less than ten acres, and no residential lot less than five acres (CP 11.22).

This preservation of open space complements existing land use of this part of Moore County, referred to by some as the 'Golf Capital of the United States'. Centered on Pinehurst and Southern Pines three dozen championship golf courses and many resorts dot the Sandhills' rolling countryside (CP 11.23). Leisure focused land use began in 1895 with the purchase of 5,000 acres

| SANDHILLS | Land Area in sq. km | Pop. 1990 | Pop. sq.km. 2000 | Pop. 2000 | 1990s % Pop. Change | % White 2000 | Median Age in 2000 | % Fam. Below Poverty | Annual Average Infant Mortality Rate 1994-98 | % High School Grads'90 | % Coll. Grads. 1990 | Fem. Fam. Head of Hshld'90 | NC Enterprise Tiers'97 |
|---|---|---|---|---|---|---|---|---|---|---|---|---|---|
| Cumberland | 1,692 | 274,713 | 179.1 | 302,963 | 10.3 | 55.2 | 29.4 | 12.1 | 10,4 | 80.3 | 16.6 | 14.1 | 4 |
| Harnett | 1,541 | 67,833 | 59.1 | 91,025 | 34.2 | 71.1 | 34.1 | 13.8 | 9.5 | 64.0 | 9.3 | 12.5 | 4 |
| Hoke | 1,013 | 22,856 | 33.2 | 33,646 | 47.2 | 44.5 | 32.4 | 17.5 | 11.0 | 55.7 | 8.4 | 21.7 | 3 |
| Lee | 666 | 41,370 | 73.6 | 49,040 | 18.5 | 70 | 37.6 | 11.5 | 11.3 | 72.4 | 14.3 | 13.6 | 5 |
| Montgomery | 1,272 | 23,359 | 21.1 | 26,822 | 14.8 | 69.1 | 35.9 | 10.1 | 9.3 | 55.3 | 7.8 | 13.5 | 2 |
| Moore | 1,810 | 59,000 | 41.3 | 74,769 | 26.7 | 80.2 | 43.1 | 8.2 | 11.3 | 74.3 | 19.9 | 10.4 | 5 |
| Richmond | 1,228 | 44,511 | 37.9 | 46,564 | 4.6 | 64.8 | 36.1 | 13.0 | 11.6 | 60.4 | 7.9 | 15.2 | 1 |
| Robeson | 2,458 | 105,170 | 50.2 | 123,339 | 17.3 | 32.8 | 32.8 | 20.7 | 12.0 | 57.0 | 11.0 | 20.3 | 2 |
| Scotland | 827 | 33,763 | 43.5 | 35,998 | 6.6 | 51.5 | 33.7 | 15.6 | 11.0 | 60.7 | 13.6 | 19.8 | 2 |
| **Region Totals** | **12,507** | **672,575** | **62.7** | **784,166** | **16.6** | **62.1** | **35.3** | **13.6** | **10.8** | **64.1** | **18.6** | **15.8** | **3.1** |

**Table 11.5:** Sandhills State Geographic Region.
**Source:** United States Bureau of the Census; North Carolina State Planning Office.

of pine forest by a Bostonian, James Walker Tufts. Having assessed the land prospects, Tufts brought in the Scot, Donald Ross, to lay out the area's initial golf course. Eventually the development grew into the Pinehurst Resort and Country Club. The village of Pinehurst was established simultaneously. It emphasizes a quaint New England style layout, simplicity and architecture, that in 1996 contributed to its being named as a National Historic Landmark, only the third town east of the Mississippi to be so named (the two others being Lowell, Massachusetts and Chautauqua, New York). Prestigious area courses bring national golf events each year, their accompanying publicity, and thousands of tourists. The latter are, however, also attracted to the opposite corner of the county where about 50 percent of the Seagrove Area Potteries are to be found. With an estimated 5,000 tourist industry employees, Moore County is the leading tourist county in the state outside of the coast and the mountains (Hackney 1992). However, tourists are not the only arrivals, retirees are flocking in as well. Moore County's population profile (Figure 11.12f) attests to this. Here we have the prototypical population age-gender profile for a retirement county, with its three bulges increasing in their dimensions with age.

Upscale golf developments have encouraged major investments in upscale retirement communities. Young retirees (60-74 aged cohorts), those who work in the tourism service industry and in the many labor intensive manufacturing industries in the county (primarily the 30-49 cohorts), and children of the latter group provide the three major bulges on the county population profile. The skewed dependency ratio (see Box 9A) does not upset the economic balance, because of the wealth brought into the county from the outside. Locally derived income is supplemented by government, retirement, and investment benefits. In addition, the low natural replacement rate is offset by a continual

in-flow of retirees. One aspect of population age-gender distribution not illustrated on Figure 11.12f is the major age cohort differences existing between the white and the non-white populations. As indicated by the analyses provided in Ross' detailed Moore County Atlas (1996), the county's black population is strongly youthful, concentrated in children aged 0-19 and young adults aged 25-39, while concentrations among whites are in the 60-74, and 25-44 ranges. Black populations are aging-in-place while whites are largely made up of retirees. The latter find their retirement amenities well defined in incorporated and restricted villages such as Whispering Pines, Pinebluff and Foxfire, where more than 90 percent of the 3,500 people are retirees.

The heart of the golf empire is the fused towns of Southern Pines (10,918; 19.6% population increase during the 1990s), Pinehurst (9,704; 90.2%), and Aberdeen (3,400; 25.9%). Dominated by golf courses, very little space is left between the towns for additional incorporation. Here also is set the pace for the county's rapid population expansion over the recent decade; elsewhere the county's socio-economic conditions more closely resemble those of its neighbors, Montgomery and Anson with their rural Piedmont populations fleeing for the opportunities of the urban regions. So Moore County still lags both Hoke and Harnett in population growth, and barely surpasses Lee (see Table 11.5).

To the south and southeast of the "Green Boot" three towns dominate the urban scene. Rockingham, the county seat of Richmond with a 2000 population of 9,672 and an increase of 2.9 percent for the 1990s (CP 11.2a), and Laurinburg, the county seat of Scotland (15,874; 36.3%), both represent economic conditions in slow growth counties. Laurinburg's increase is mostly through annexation. The third town, the Robeson County seat of Lumberton (20,795; 11.8%), mirrors the growth tendency of the county. Though these three counties are more youthful than the

428

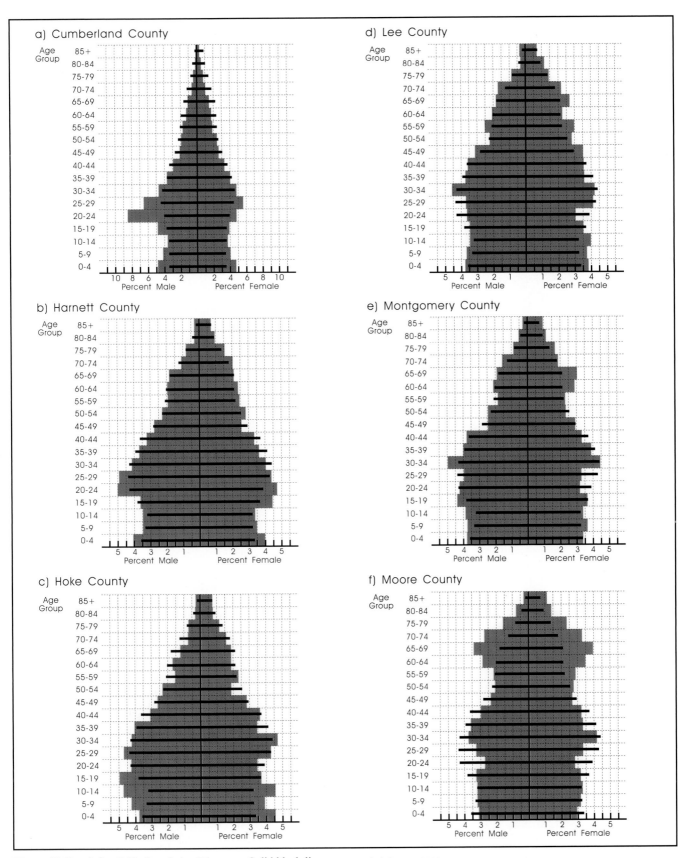

**Figure 11.12 a-f:** Sandhills Population Diagrams. Solid black lines represent state averages.
**Source:** U.S. Bureau of the Census, 1990.

429

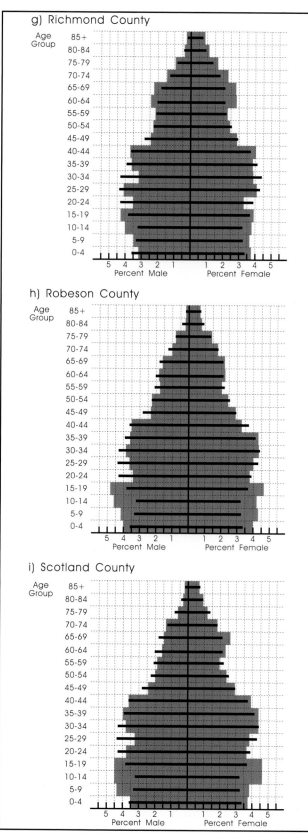

**g) Richmond County**

**h) Robeson County**

**i) Scotland County**

**Figure 11.12 g-i:** Sandhills Population Diagrams.
Solid black lines represent state averages.
**Source:** U.S. Bureau of the Census, 1990.

remainder of the Sandhills SGR (Figures 11.12h, g, and i), Robeson's is much more youth dependent, while Richmond and Scotland are showing stronger aging tendencies. The three counties are all more agricultural dependent and have difficulties in attracting manufacturing and service industry investments that allow for economic diversification and expansion of job opportunities. Absent these jobs there is a continuing 'brain drain' of the post high school generation. As a result, these counties figure prominently in the state's effort to attract extra-regional employment investments (Table 11.5). In the meantime, the counties favor agriculture. Robeson, the state's largest county, has over 25 percent of its land cultivated, with soybeans, corn, tobacco, wheat, and cotton the leading crops (Ross 1992). It leads the state in farm cash receipts and has been able to attract food processing facilities to the county (Photo 11.11). The near future will see an improvement in access as Interstate 73/74, passing through all three counties, is being completed.

Robeson is a very special case in the demographics of North Carolina counties since its population is dominated by a considerable majority of the state's 40,000 plus Lumbee Indians. For Robeson County they comprised 38 percent of the 2000 county population. Whites equaled 32.8 percent, blacks 25.1 percent, and the remaining races 4.1 percent. Due to the fact that the Lumbee tend to desire large families and to not leave the county in search of jobs and other amenities (and if they do, they are likely to return to their home eventually), their age-gender profile is strongly youth focused. Blacks have a more stable population profile, while that of the white population is decidedly aging. The long term result appears to be the evolution of a Lumbee

**Photo 11.11:** Campbell Soup Company's Maxton plant (Robeson County) is set on 1,100 acres and has been in operation since 1982. In the peak season from August through January 1,200 workers process 200 different soups. In the process the plant consumes the following (in millions of pounds/year): potatoes/42; carrots/28; flour/20; chickens/13l; celery/11; mushroom/7; pork/2; plus many other food products. Most of these raw materials are purchased from local growers with nearly $50 million being spent within the state by the plant.

430

majority within the county by 2010 (Thomas Ross, as cited in Starr 1994). As discussed in Chapter 4, this Native American group is not recognized by the federal government as is the Cherokee Nation, though the Lumbee are pushing strongly for this recognition. Yet they have made a clear imprint on the state and Robeson County, in part by insuring the development and continuing support for UNC at Pembroke, an institution that evolved from an earlier teaching college committed to the training of American Indian educators.

Removed some distance to the west from the "Green Boot," but revealing an even greater open green space is Montgomery County. In fact, a close inspection of CP 11.19 shows the southern portions of North Carolina's Green Heart to extend into Montgomery County via the Uwharrie National Forest, and into northwestern Moore County, and northern Richmond County. It is no surprise that this is one of the state's most heavily forested areas, with each county being more than 60 percent forested (Figure 1.3). As discussed in Chapter 12, this is part of a central Piedmont open, green space that is almost surrounded by "Main Street" urbanization and congestion. Four million people are in search of recreational and leisure-time open space, leaving Montgomery County with the economic promise and environmental threats of tourism. Montgomery County, a rural county in the center of the state, and almost equidistant from the major metropolitan centers of Charlotte, Greensboro, Raleigh, and Fayetteville, is very difficult to fit into a particular state geographic region. Our judgement is that its conditions of population and social characteristics, economic activities and development has it resembling Sandhills SGR conditions better than those of the SGRs representing the Piedmont urban counties.

# 12

# Piedmont Region

## INTRODUCTION

North Carolina's Piedmont is a nationally prominent example of the impacts of urban changes on natural environments, land use, and quality of life conditions. Here urban growth developing along Interstates 80 and 40 has expanded onto rural and open spaces, creating one of the country's most distinctive urban regions, the North Carolina Urban Crescent (Figure 12.1). With population expanding by 26.8 percent during the 1990s, the urbanization process is currently so rapid and extensive that the Crescent is developing into a continuous citified landscape resembling a Horseshoe, with knobs and spurs projecting from many of its parts (Figure 12.2; Photos 12.1-3). All three metropoles of the Piedmont (Metrolina, Piedmont Triad, and Piedmont Triangle) are vigorously extending their urban tentacles into adjacent rural perimeters.

On the eastern flanks of the Crescent the Piedmont Triangle's metropolis is now reaching due south into Harnett County, edging in the direction of the northern outskirts of Fayetteville. It is also extending an urbanizing link across Chatham County toward Sanford in Lee County. To the southwest, Metrolina's urban shadow is reaching deeply into South Carolina. Along feeder Interstate highways, Metrolina is expanding westward beyond Gastonia toward Shelby in Cleveland County, north toward Statesville in Iredell County, northeast toward Salisbury in Rowan County, and southeast toward Monroe in Union County.

Meanwhile, the Crescent's central metropole, the Piedmont Triad, is demonstrating evidence of renewed vigor through its expansion northwest toward Mount Airy, west toward Yadkinville in Yadkin County, southwest and south toward Statesville, Salisbury, and Asheboro in Randolph County with the newly designated and partially built I-73/74 providing additional impetus. The 'green lungs' of the Piedmont, the nine-county region largely comprised of open green spaces dominated by forests, farms and reservoirs, which we choose to refer to as the 'Green Heart' of North Carolina, is increasingly encroached upon by advancing urbanization. These dimensions of urban land use may be observed on Figure 12.2, though its real world dimensions are perhaps best seen on Color Plate 1.14. We refer to the result of this uniquely intertwined and continuous urban landscaping as North Carolina's Main Street (Figure 9.10).

Main Street's evolution plays out in a physical environment that is part of a larger Appalachian landform province extending from New Jersey to Alabama. In our state, the piedmont portion of the Appalachian Province has a maximum width of about 200 miles, being bounded on the east by the Fall Line and in the west by the Blue Ridge Front, as defined by the Brevard Fault (Color Plate 1.11). Piedmont actually means 'foot of the mountain.' The name appropriately describes the rolling plains, rounded hills, and occasional low ridges, the erosional remnants of earlier more prominent geologic features.

**Photo 12.1:** Examples of industries new to North Carolina, driving much of its newfound growth, include truck and automotive assembly plants. Here, located on Interstate 80 between Winston-Salem and Greensboro with easy access to the Piedmont Triad International Airport is Swedish owned Volvo-America Headquarters. Volvo has plants in Asheville, Greensboro, and Virginia. (Photo by Jim Stratford; by permission, Public Information Office, Volvo).

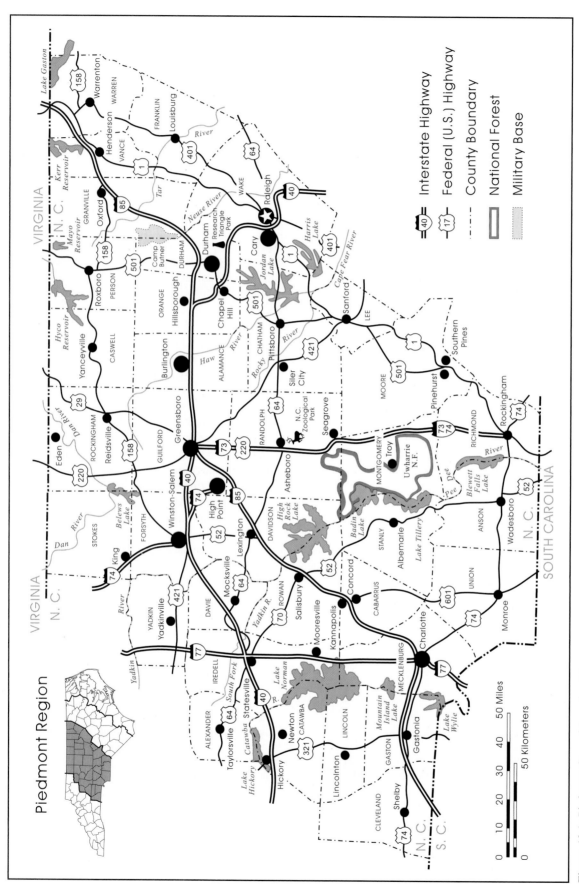

**Figure 12.1:** Piedmont General Location Map.

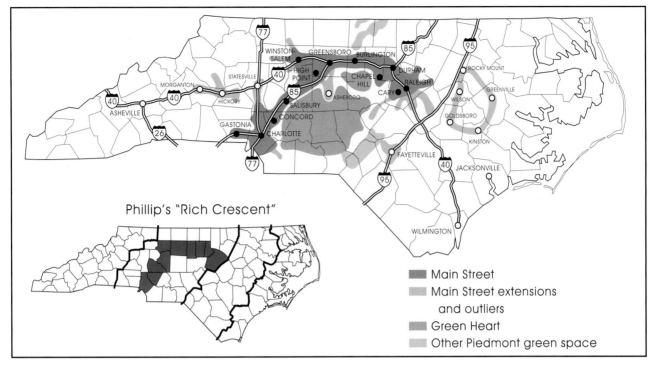

Phillip's "Rich Crescent"

■ Main Street
■ Main Street extensions
   and outliers
■ Green Heart
■ Other Piedmont green space

**Figure 12.2:** Main Street North Carolina with Its Knobs, Spurs, and Outliers; Inset Map of Coy Phillips' "Rich Crescent."
**Source:** Phillips 1955.

As one of our four state primary regions (Table 9.1), the Piedmont Region is defined administratively. Positioned within the piedmont's physical geography, this largely excludes those counties in its western portion that have hard-rock ridge remnants of the Appalachians, like the South Mountains and the Brushy Mountains. The eastern reaches of the Piedmont State Primary Region boundary is mainly defined by counties that are traversed by the snaking path of the Fall Line (compare the Piedmont's physical and state primary region boundaries in Color Plate 1.11). Though not quite covering the territory of the physical piedmont, the Piedmont State Primary Region (hereafter simply referred to as the Piedmont) includes an area of 16,419 square miles, or slightly over one third of the state's land area, distributed within 35 of the 100 counties and has an estimated population of 4.38 million in year 2000. The population of the Piedmont is well over half of the state's total population and is growing at almost twice the rate of the Tidewater, Coastal Plain or Mountain regions. Even so, there is a discernible difference in both population density and growth rates within the Piedmont Region. Four state geographic regions (SGR) are discussed in this chapter: Western Piedmont, Metrolina, Piedmont Triad, and Piedmont Triangle SGRs (Figure 9.11). As is true for all of the regional chapters, the socio-economic geography based SGRs overlap in many cases with the physical geography-based state primary regions. Only Metrolina is entirely within the boundaries of the Piedmont Region. With the state experiencing a 21.4 percent increase in population from 1990 to 2000, the Piedmont SGRs vary from Piedmont Triad's 13.9 percent to Piedmont Triangle's 36.1 percent for

**Photo 12.2:** With its 50,000 employees the Research Triangle Park is North Carolina's claim to world recognition in research and development parks. Among many leading edge facilities are IBMs largest plant, and a large concentration of telecom firms, including SISCO and NORTEL. A large share of leading companies and total employment is also held by the pharmaceutical companies, here represented by Glaxo-SmithKline's twin American headquarter base in the RTP.

435

**Photo 12.3:** University Research Park north of Charlotte also finds itself in the throes of success. The thirty five year old, 3,200 acre park has far exceeded expectations having now 40 companies with some 23,000 employees. In the center of the photo amidst its circular parking space sits the Wachovia Bank Campus (formerly First Union) a 2.1 million square feet customer information center with 10,000 workers. Adjacent, to the immediate upper right, sprawls the manufacturing facilities of IBM. Now building a regional operations/call center is TIAA-CREF, the world's largest private pension system.

the decade (Table 9.2). These differences are magnified at the county level. Rockingham County's relatively small 6.8 percent increase contrasts strongly with what is more symptomatic of Main Street, the incredible 47.3 percent growth of Wake County. This is truly an astonishing rate of growth for what is likely to become the state's most populated county by 2010.

With these contrasts come community and regional conflicts as the urbanization process continues to devour rural land at an unprecedented rate (Photo 12.4). Suburbanizing counties on the periphery of metropolitan counties swallow up of farms and forests for new subdivisions, yet these counties are overwhelmed by new residential household demands for public facilities and services, especially educational. County residents are troubled to see their treasured rural lands disappear and their inadequate road systems overloaded with commuters. Meanwhile, the traditional central cities have been deteriorating, with residential neighborhoods and commercial hearts and strips suf-

fering neglect as attention focuses on growth at the ragged edge of the city. One of the more notable traumas involves the gradual deterioration of the natural environment. On the one hand, the environment receives, supports, and accommodates the process of urbanization, while on the other hand it eventually sets the physical limits of growth. In our suburban complacency, we may feel that our human community is in harmony with our particular pocket of the natural environment. However, around us the urbanizing spread is systematically drawing down the natural environment account by "lowering the quality of air, water, and soil; introduc(ing) new and often toxic compounds, and more generally impos(ing) burdens on local ecosystems that clearly cannot be sustained over time" (Bourne 1991, 188). A brief, yet dramatic example will suffice here. When Charlotte began measuring its air pollution in 1989, it had just one day of purple warning, defined as days when the toxicity of the outdoor air we breathe requires that we stay indoors in air conditioned spaces (Chapter 8). Ten

**Photo 12.4:** Suburban development extends like the point of a dagger into the heart of some of the Piedmont's best farmland, as here in a scene from the western perimeter of Main Street.

years later, this critical pollution-warning index had increased to 59 days, or nearly two months of intolerable pollution.

What has permitted this unconscionable approach to urbanizing our landscape with such environmentally devastating results? Two factors appear to be responsible. First and most critically, we have essentially written off the cost of environmental degradation to the next and subsequent generations of residents. We have transferred this cost forward in time, with scant attempt to assess its future impact. Secondly, we have allowed the urbanization process, our Main Street "spread city," to deplete the natural environment in its more remote rural hinterland. Thus, in our travels through the countryside and long before we catch a glimpse of the fabled Main Street, we see its dark shadows enveloping the land: hazy and smoggy air; crowded highways festooned with billboards and garbage strewn ditches; sewer plants, landfills and junk yards; asphalt and power plants; gravel pits and quarries; proliferating telecommunications towers, ministorage facilities, and manufactured home sales; and empty lands growing up in wild blackberry, winged sumac, and other weeds. These lands, in the speculator's hands, await the coming of the city.

Some bright lights do intrude on urban shadows. Freeway interchanges see the flowering of large planted groupings of North Carolina native species (facilitated by buyers of vanity automotive license tags and the N. C. Department of Transportation). Off the Interstates, enlightened approaches to new urban forms are evident. Historically renovated small villages are flourishing especially where they are within the metropolitan commuting range (CP 6.5-6.7 and CP 12.17a-c; Photo 12.28). "New urbanism communities" favoring a total environmental approach to quality of place and life values and a land conservation ethic that is giving threatened natural landscapes a greater chance of being preserved appear to be emerging. As for the metropolitan areas' central cities, where the prospects for renovation and restructuring appeared dim just a few years ago, we now see renewed efforts at physically revitalizing and economically awakening the old central business and abandoned manufacturing and warehousing districts, as well as the gentrification of center city historic residential neighborhoods. Nor are traditionally neglected public housing projects of the inner city being ignored. Their proximity to new vibrant city centers are influencing investments in affordable and mixed income housing, though hardly at the pace needed for the masses of poor people still inhabiting the cities. New conceptual approaches to urban design (living in the 21st century in greater harmony with nature) are being entertained and in some cases seeing implementation. Concepts such as "spread city," "edge city," "retrofitting and adaptive re-use," "brownfields," "historic communities," "conservation easement," "transfer of development rights," "mixed-use development," "in-fill," "urban growth boundary," "smart growth," "new urbanism," and "sustainable cities" are becoming part of our daily vocabulary.

In this chapter we will deal with the contexts, characteristics, and problems of North Carolina's Main Street, its rural countryside, and its natural environments. As in other regional chapters, we consider first some aspects of the natural environment of particular concern to this region. The reader is reminded that earlier chapters treat the state's physical geography in detail and that aspects considered for the Piedmont are intricately linked to the larger environmental systems of the state. We will then have a look at the intricacies of the Main Street phenomena and subsequently identify some special issues affecting North Carolinians as the results of their land use decisions. It is equally relevant to remind the reader of the information on demographic characteristics and socio-economic development provided in chapters 4 through 7. Most of the contemporary processes elaborated in those chapters are framed and stimulated by what happens in the Piedmont. Finally, we assess conditions and changes on the larger scale through an examination of the Piedmont's state geographic regions and counties within these regions.

## THE NATURAL LANDSCAPE

Topographically, elevations in the western part of the Piedmont reach an average of about 1,476 feet, while in the eastern portion the average elevation is less than 325 feet. In the western part the local relief is often marked with steep ridges edging the landscape, as compared to the easier flow of undulating hilly stretches in the Piedmont's eastern section. This permits a general division of the Piedmont's physiography into "Uplands" and "Lowlands" sections.

### Piedmont Uplands

In the west are the headwaters of several important rivers: the Roanoke flows northeast; the Tar, Neuse and Cape Fear flow southeast; while the Yadkin-Pee Dee, Catawba, and Broad flow south. The physical dimensions and locations of these river basins or watersheds are depicted and discussed in Chapter 1 (Table 1.3 and Figure 1.11). Watershed size and orientation is controlled by a generally eastward slope of about 10 feet per mile, but is also modified by complex rock structures, a deep layer of weathered materials, and a series of northeast-southwest aligned belts representing particular rock types and tectonic episodes (Figure 1.6). From west to east are the Brevard Fault belt of Precambrian granitic rock and the Inner Piedmont Belt of gneiss and schist containing erosional remnants. These erosional remnants, known as "monadnocks," form the South Mountains of Rutherford and Burke counties (with peaks to 2,953 feet), as well as the Brushy Mountains of Alexander and Wilkes counties (with peaks to 2,674 feet). The Sauratown Mountains, with peaks to 2,595 feet at Hanging Rock, lie almost due west-east across Stokes and Surry counties.

Piedmont landscapes east of the Inner Piedmont Belt are dominated by more gentle contours, mostly irregularly rolling plains with a local relief of 330 to 660 feet. Most noticeable are the forest-covered Uwharrie Mountains (CP 1.6 and 1.13), whose more resistant rocks protrude as softly edged ridges. The highest peak, Cedar Rock Mountain, reaches 950 feet. Smaller outliers are found in southern Alamance County (the Cane Creek Mountains) and in southwestern Granville County (the Butner Hills). Granitic outcrops of this region are quarried for building stone, as is the case southeast of Salisbury (Rowan County) in the vicinity of the town of Granite Quarry (CP 3.7). Immediately south of here begins the gold bearing portions of the Carolina Slate Belt. Where slopes are steeper and the terrain is of denser rock materials, rushing waters have cut canyons into the surface. In the northern part of the Slate Belt are areas traversed by the Eno River. Steeply etched gorges and narrow flood plains, frequent outcroppings, and rocky rapids mark stretches of the river valley. Especially notable terrain of this kind is found in the Eno River State Park, lying within a larger section of land a few miles north of Chapel Hill and west of Durham, referred to locally as the Eno Wilderness. Local relief ranges to 330 feet within a couple of miles, with cliffs of up to 165 feet adjacent to the river. Local place names record the popular perception of these hilly tracts with names like Occoneechee Mountain, Poplar Ridge, and Mountain View. Facing stone used in the buildings of Duke University and elsewhere in the Piedmont has been quarried in this area. To the immediate south of Hillsborough lies Chapel Hill in the drainage basins of Morgan, Bolin, and Meeting of the Waters creeks. On the edges of the plateau occupied by central Chapel Hill, the older parts of the University of North Carolina campus, and adjacent town of Carboro, and traversed by a fairly flat Franklin Street, erosional processes have carved up to 185 feet in local relief, most dramatically exemplified by the steep valley of Stillhouse Bottom.

### Piedmont Lowlands

As described by H. Daniel Stillwell, in an earlier edition of this work (1986), the eastern section of the Piedmont includes downfaulted basins filled with younger, unaltered sedimentary rocks and displays more fully dissected surface terrain than the Piedmont Uplands. Prominent among the physiographic landscapes is the Triassic Lowland Basins, locally known as the Deep River Basin (Photo 3.2). This stretches from Wadesboro in Anson County to Durham and Oxford in Granville County (CP 1.9). Sandstone, shale, conglomerate, and even some coal give variety to this area. Near Sanford (Lee County) lies the state's only major coal deposit. The southern portion of the Deep River Basin is also noted for interbedded clays that support a major brick manufacturing industry. North Carolina leads the nation with about 15 percent of the country's total brick production. An isolated section of the Triassic Lowlands lies in the Dan River Basin in Rockingham County. Likewise an isolated section of the Carolina Slate Belt (Figure 1.9) is located east of Raleigh. This section, and the Sandhills to the south, provides a lower elevation level transition, bounded on the east by the Fall Zone and the Coastal Plain flatlands.

### Climate, Soils, and Natural Vegetation

Climate, soils, and vegetation elements of the physical environment are described in detail in chapters 2 and 3. A brief review of their interrelatedness, with some attention paid to a few locationally unique ecosystems, will suffice here. In general, the Piedmont enjoys a climate favorable for biotic activity, both natural and human. Relatively mild temperatures prevail; this in turn means a moderate need for winter heating, as well as a generous growing season. Coupled with adequate year-round precipitation and well-drained clay soils, the Piedmont supports diverse natural vegetation and agricultural production.

### Headwater Forest

Headwater Forests are wetland habitats common in the Piedmont, though they also are found in the Coastal Plain and the Mountain Region. Where they appear, they take on considerable importance in providing natural habitats for dispersed wildlife populations (such as deer, rabbits, opossums, raccoons, and songbirds) in a region pressured by the space demands of a rapidly expanding urban population. A particular issue is the apparent excess of foxes and coyotes. Excesses resulted from the illegal import of foxes to satisfy hunting interests to coyotes migrating in to favorable habitat with both species becoming increasingly confined by the pressure of urban sprawl (Chapter 3). Another issue is the state's successful attempt to restore wild turkeys. Having succeeded in increasing turkey numbers from 2,000 in 1970 to currently over 100,000, the wild turkey management program now faces the issue of stock maintenance, i.e., having to find and maintain unbroken tracts of at least the 5,000 acres needed to sustain turkey populations (Chase 2000). Headwater forests are supported by rainfall and higher water levels in lowland swales, where the topography and water resources combine to initiate stream flow. In their drier upland soils, red and white oaks, hickories, tulip trees, maples, gums, beech, holly and sourwood dominate headwater forests. In wetter areas, there is frequent appearance of river birch, privet, alder, greenbriar, elderberry, poison ivy, ferns, and canes (Figure 12.3). Situated in the upper reaches of watersheds, these habitats are critical for retaining sediments and filtering out nutrients and other pollutants before the water from streams and lakes are used for drinking water. Where residential and other development reach into headwaters habitats, regional water quality is endangered by the excess of runoff from paved surfaces and by reduced natural areas that provide the essential filtering systems.

### Freshwater Marsh

In a natural environment increasingly threatened by development, particular efforts are made to protect all wetland areas. Freshwater marshes are especially vulnerable, due to their varying size and due to their more haphazard occurrence. Often highway engineers and construction personnel have considered these marshes too small to protect. These wetlands are frequently found behind beaver dams and where streams enter larger bodies of water. Wetlands are critical upstream ecosystems that store excess storm waters and filter out pollutants, while sheltering a variety of wildlife, such as muskrats, reptiles, and amphibians. Depending on their individual size, freshwater marshes may sup-

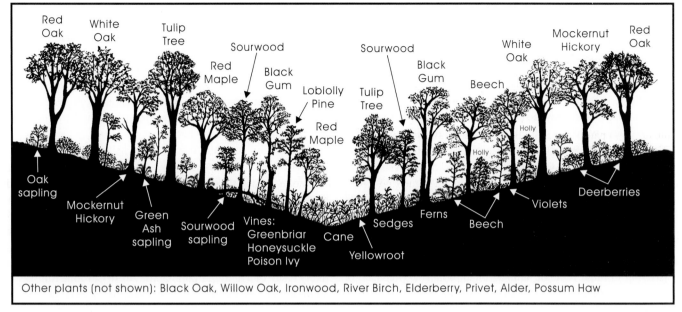

**Figure 12.3:** Headwater Forest.
**Source:** Venters (1995); illustration by Anne Runyon, by permission.

port an array of waterfowl, while their deadwood trees become the habitat of owls and woodpeckers. As indicated on Figure 12.4, some of the species that dominate the freshwater marsh ecosystem include sedges and cattails, bulrushes and water lilies, and many other flowering plants. Shrubbery and small trees favoring wetland sites may be spotted here, as well. Found throughout the state, freshwater marshes are more prevalent in the undulating terrain of the Piedmont.

*Piedmont Prairies*

Rolling uplands of the western Piedmont once supported extensive areas covered by prairie grasses, similar to the prairie of the U. S. Midwest. In the mid-1980s, botanists discovered natural prairie species like coneflowers and the endangered Schweinitz' sunflower. Historical accounts favor the notion that extensive prairie-like grasslands did cover much of the western Piedmont. Hernando de Soto, in his 1540 travels through the region, made reference to many "open savannas." German traveler John Lederer in 1670 and the Britisher John Lawson in 1701 made similar observations. Prairies are being recreated in Mecklenburg County's McDowell Park and on Latta Plantation near Mountain Island Lake, as well as in adjacent South Carolina piedmont counties (Newsom 1999).

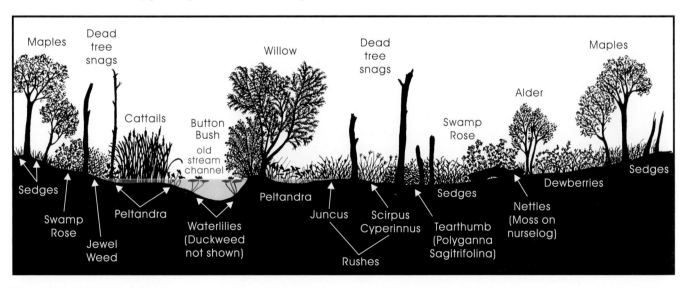

**Figure 12.4:** Freshwater Marsh.
**Source:** Venters (1995); illustration by Anne Runyon, by permission.

439

# MAIN STREET – NORTH CAROLINA'S EMERGING MEGALOPOLIS

### *Historical Considerations*

Settlement patterns of the Piedmont developed much later than those in the Coastal Plain Region. In the vast space of the Piedmont, only three towns had reached a size of 1,000 people by 1850. These were the capital city of Raleigh, Salisbury (then thought of as the western capital), and Charlotte (then booming from gold fever). The remainder of the Piedmont suffered from poor transportation. Most people engaged in subsistence farming and local market agriculture. A legislative decision to fund and build the first trans-state railroad in 1846 ended the isolation for much of the region. With the primary objective of providing the farmers a means to market their goods, within a few years the North Carolina Railroad connected Goldsboro with Charlotte (passing through Raleigh, Hillsborough, Graham, Greensboro, Lexington, Salisbury, Kannapolis, and Concord), inscribing in the process a crescent urban shape on the Piedmont. Meanwhile, the railroad linked the northern edge of the Cotton Belt, passed through the North Carolina-Virginia Old Bright Tobacco Belt, bisected the hardwood forest of the western Piedmont, and crossed upper courses of rivers and streams that provided the hydrologic potential necessary for the siting of water powered mills and their related mill towns (Chapter 6 and CP 6.5-6.8).

Communities touched by the railroad became successful purveyors of the state's three main developmental industries: cotton textiles, wood furniture, and tobacco manufacturing (Phillips 1955). Other communities languished (Photo 12.5). The Civil War and the Reconstruction Era slowed progress, but as markets for cotton, textiles, furniture, and tobacco developed in northern states, so did the Piedmont Crescent. While Durham and Winston-Salem profited from the invention of cigarette manufacturing machines in the 1880s, the Metrolina area benefited from the connections of the North Carolina Railroad to the Southern Railway System. Charlotte became the epicenter of the greatest concentration of cotton textile manufacturing in the country, as evidenced by the pattern of cotton spindles in 1925 (Figure 12.5). Over time, more sophisticated textile manufacturing plants and companies were centered in Greensboro.

Though eventually dispossessed as the major transportation mode of the Piedmont by the evolving highway and interstate freeway system, the North Carolina Railroad (NCRR) clearly began the transportation linkage, stimulating several regional and urban economic engines, and contributed to the settlement pattern that today we identify as foundational to the existence of Main Street (Photo 12.6). It is a credit to the 19th Century railroad planners that their efforts are now being reevaluated, with the likely result of a reinvigoration of the North Carolina Railway as an important transportation mode for Main Street (Figure 12.6). In 1997, the state bought out the private stockholders who owned 25 percent of the railroad. A problem for re-instituting a competitive NCRR is the degree to which development over the years has encroached upon the right-of-way. The original right-of-way has been encroached upon in 5,000 places by factories, salvage yards, roads, parking lots, and other uses, many obtained illegally (Neff 2000). To succeed once more, NCRR must oversee the removal of all encroachment in the way of replacing the existing one-track bed with a double track along its entire 317 linear miles. Otherwise, conflicts with freight trains will encumber efficiencies. In addition, all traffic inhibited crossings need removal.

Coy Phillips' concept of the 'Rich Crescent' included ten Piedmont counties (Figure 12.2), extending from Mecklenburg in the southwest to Raleigh in the east (1955). In 1950, these coun-

**Photo 12.5:** Union Mills (Rutherford County) suffered an early demise in the absence of a railroad connection to markets.

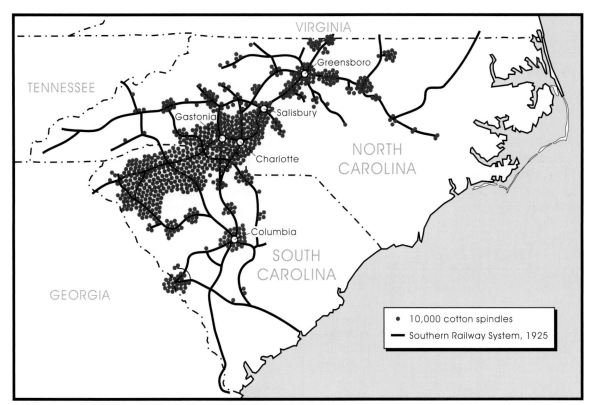

**Figure 12.5:** Setting the Stage for Main Street. Distribution of Textile Industry as Evidenced by Cotton Spindles in the Carolinas as Served by the Southern Railway System in 1925. This represents about 62 percent of the then existing 17,359,420 spindles in the cotton-growing states.
**Source:** Modified from a Southern Railway Map (1925).

ties included about 25 percent of the state's population of five million. In 1970, their share had increased to 32 percent. By the April 1st, 2000 Census, these ten core counties of North Carolina's Main Street increased their share of the state's population (8.05 million) to about 36 percent. While the process of increasing population concentrations in these few counties continues, today we see an increase to 22 in the number of the counties that are a part of Main Street development; when these counties are considered, the share of the state population increases to 52 percent (Figure 12.7).

**Photo 12.6:** Durham historic contrasts. A miniscule AMTRAK station lies adjacent to the North Carolina Railroad tracks in front of a former Liggett-Myers Tobacco Co. warehouse. The 15 story post-modern architecture styled People's Security Tower rises in the background.

441

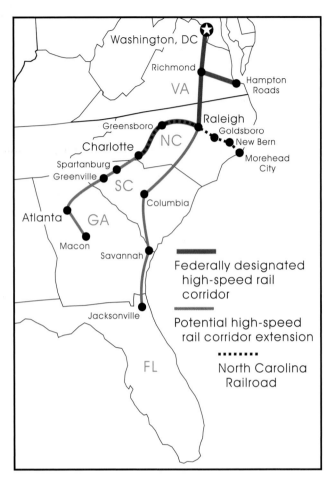

**Figure 12.6:** Proposed High Speed Train Service of the North Carolina Railroad and AMTRAK.
**Sources:** Whitacre (2001) and Neff (2000).

### *Main Street's Functional Cohesiveness*

*From "City States" to Main Street*

Urban analysts consider an urban system to include two basic attributes: structural and functional relationships among urban places within the urban system, and the evolving internal structure of the individual urban places. Conceptualizing the functional attributes of the urban system comprised by Main Street has the advantage of viewing Main Street holistically, as opposed to seeing the three different metropolitan areas as essentially independent. In Chapter 11, it was suggested that internal complementary functions were tugging at the various towns of the Coastal Plain "Ring City," with the effect of integrating this urban region as a functional whole. This idea originated with Charles Hayes' work on the functionally integrated attributes of the Piedmont Triad. Hayes (1976) argued that the Triad comprised a system of cities whose economic, social, and amenity functions were so intertwined that each of the cities had evolved specialized functions attractive to the residents of the remainder of the region. In this way the cities, though physically separate, emerged functionally as one urban center. This is not just a theo-

retical perspective. "The whole area is your city," an executive director in a furniture firm was quoted as saying to a Charlotte Observer reporter in 1984, "I live in Lexington. I'm 20 minutes from my office in High Point and 35 minutes from Greensboro. I can live in one political division and still be a citizen of the whole Piedmont." Extending this argument to the entire Main Street weakens the idea only marginally. In effect, a new geography of economic interdependence rules this urban system, pulling on each of the metro regions in various ways. Acting independently on large-scale projects in economic and infrastructural development is now a practical impossibility.

This was the reality recognized by the counties of the Unifour Region (Catawba, Alexander, Caldwell, and Burke), led by the city of Hickory. The four counties decided to join the Carolinas Partnership, operating out of Charlotte, in an effort to enhance the successes of business recruitment, rather than to go it on their own (Chapter 9). It is this reality that has pushed a number of recent administratively integrated efforts for regional solutions to pestering problems of transportation, water resource development, air pollution control, and urban sprawl. Similarly, prospective corporate relocation or new investment in any of the Main Street cities likely will be influenced in its location decision by the sheer scale, complexity, and global influence of this total economic system. Somewhere on Main Street, a prospective new business will find a successful combination of land, labor, capital availability and cost, access to raw materials, and symbiotic relationships with industries and support businesses and markets, whether these are local, regional, national, or global in scale.

Integration of telecommunication, transportation, and decision-making systems with socio-economic activities along Main Street has the further advantage of ameliorating losses by some metros through gains by others. The metros have not fared equally well in the economic upheavals of the 1980s and early 1990s. For example, economic restructuring, globalization, and relocating of

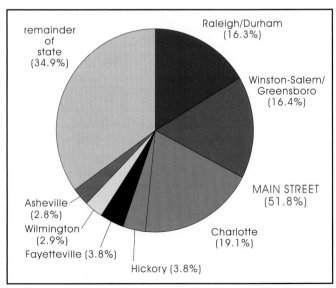

**Figure 12.7:** Main Street Metro Share of State Population in 1998.
**Source:** Brookings Institution (2000, 6).

442

critical industries, as well as corporate buy-outs have been devastating in their impacts on the Piedmont Triad. Yet, this traditional manufacturing dependent region is more capable of converting its base economy to service and information-knowledge industries due to the region's centrality on Main Street. Consider the mid-90s location in High Point's bustling new Piedmont Center of a Bank of America call center with 3,000 employees. We may conclude that one of the most important geographic realities emerging in North Carolina is the continuing integration of urban form and function along Main Street.

What was not so long ago a set of distinctive and independently functioning city regions is becoming an elongated and fused urban entity. Charlotte, for example, was considered in the *Pierce Report: Recommendations for Our Region's Future* (1995) as a "city state." This was defined by Neil Pierce and his collaborator, Curtis Johnson, as "A region consisting of one or more historic central cities surrounded by cities and towns which have a shared identification, function as a single zone for trade, commerce and communication, and are characterized by social, economic and environmental interdependence." Now, the Charlotte "city state" (referred to in this volume as Metrolina), along with the "city states" of the Piedmont Triad and the Piedmont Triangle, is developing as a lesser order functional system, subservient to a locational decision making process deriving its strength from the complexities and integrated opportunities of the total Main Street. In manufacturing, consider the recently expansive nature of the automotive/truck assembly and the fiber cable industries. In services, note that Charlotte is no longer the only important banking city; Winston-Salem has seen large recent gains, even considering the relocation of the new Wachovia Bank (merged with First Union) to Charlotte. In addition, financial institution call centers are proliferating throughout Main Street. Most notably though, it is the recent history of Main Street evolving the nation's leading "new economy" metros that persists in fuelling economic growth and population expansion. Whereas U. S. metros averaged an employment growth of 45.5 percent from 1978 to 1997, the Piedmont Triangle increased 105.3 per cent, Metrolina 72.2 percent, and the Piedmont Triad 49.9 percent (*State of the South 2000*, 41). While this indicates that the combined metro employment expansion, exceeding the national rate by 60 per cent, may be dominated by the cities at the opposite poles of Main Street, the overheated expansion of the pole metros is clearly being propelled toward the center of Main Street, where the Triad is now on the path of recovery from its losses in traditional industry employment. This defines the spatial continuity in "new economy" metros and aids in cementing, in reality and in our minds, North Carolina's Main Street.

The characteristics of North Carolina's urban system, identified first by Coy Phillips (1955) and amplified in the 1975 edition of the *North Carolina Atlas*, is its absence of a single dominant city. There is no state primate city like Atlanta, New Orleans, Detroit, or Los Angeles. In spite of the overwhelming significance of the finance-redistribution sectors of Metrolina, the traditional manufacturing sectors of the Piedmont Triad, and the research-education-medicine-government sectors of the Piedmont Triangle, none of these three "city states" have experienced the evolution into a dominant and pre-eminent urban center, controlling the economic and social affairs of the state as a primate city. Instead, it is the diversity of these metro areas' economic base that is the strength, the raison d'etre, of Main Street North Carolina. Indeed, this urban system is evolving as a new and distinctive reality among American urban landscapes, reflecting a postmodern landscape where, "fragmentation, multimodality, fluidity, plurality, and diffusion (the 21st century progression of chaotic urban change) are more in evidence than homogeneity, nodality, and hierarchy (the results of 20th century spatially ordered modernism)" (Knox 1991; see also Bourne 1991).

### The City and Its Land Uses

#### Concentric Zones

As there are important differences in the economic base of the urban centers along Main Street, so too are there differences in the ways land is used within the individual cities. With these differences come an assortment of land use conflicts. Cities have experienced tumultuous changes, from the tearing down of historic buildings in order to accommodate modern high density office towers, to the virtual disappearance of whole neighborhoods while gaining freeway access to the central city, and to the degrading of traditional commercial corridors and residential districts as suburban and exurban places gain favor in locational decisions. To provide a general framework for understanding how the various urban places along Main Street have experienced a continuity of tears in their urban fabric since the 1950s and how they have coped with the resulting problems, we will need to consider briefly the traditional land use structure of the city. Box 12A illustrates, in a simplified form, the major ideas that have been advanced concerning the internal structure and growth of a city. Though they vary in their complexity, each idea or model advances our overall understanding of the dynamics of change as it affects urban physical spaces and land use.

The fundamental processes are best expressed in Box 12A, a and d, the concentric zone theory and its related land value curve. Extrapolated from the work of the 19th century German agricultural land use geographer von Thunen, and formalized by the University of Chicago sociologist Burgess, the model suggests that urban places will evolve focused on a nucleus of commercial activities located at the point of maximum accessibility to their consumer market. Further, the model represents most clearly and simplistically the land use structure of the 'city as a container,' which prevailed through the industrializing 19th century. Essentially, the model represents land value curves for the major urban land uses of commercial, manufacturing, and residential. The land is sold or rented to the highest bidder, generally whichever group of land users can generate the most revenue from it. [These ideas are more formally presented in introductory urban and economic geography texts; see, for example Cadwallader (1996), Berry, Conkling, and Ray (1997)]. Commerce wins out at

443

**Box 12A:** Urban Growth Models and Land Values.

## a: Concentric Zone Model

## d: Traditional Land Value Profile

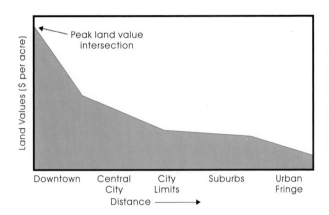

## b: Sector Model

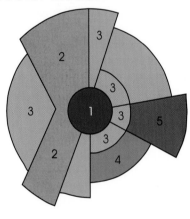

## e: Contemporary Land Value Profile

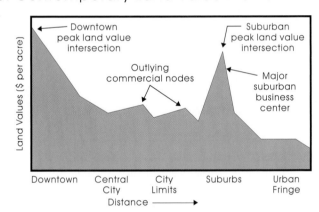

## c: Multiple Nuclei Model

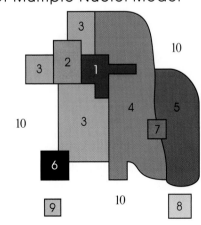

## Figures a, b, c: Area Functions

1: Central Business District (CBD)
2: Wholesale, light manufacturing
3: Low-class residential
4: Middle-class residential
5: High-class residential
6: Heavy manufacturing
7: Outlying business district
8: Residential suburb
9: Industrial suburb
10: Commuter zone

**Photo 12.7:** 1970s images of Main Street Central Business Districts:

**a.** Raleigh's Fayetteville Street Mall. Opened in 1977, as the local version of the national trend called Streets for People, the four block long pedestrian mall was intended to enliven the aging central business district. However, a suburbanizing metro area left the mall without activity and people except 8am to 5pm on weekdays. The end of Raleigh's pedestrian plaza now appears on the horizon after years of failing retail businesses and investment uncertainty. Paving over the mall is now being seriously considered.

**b.** Durham's Main Street. A dynamic economy, with tobacco and textiles remaining strong even during the depression years of the 1930s, favored the evolution of a significant and architecturally historic CBD focusing on Main Street. When, in 1976, it was declared part of a national historic district that encompassed nearly 30 blocks and 150 buildings, it was the first such in the country of mainly 20th century structures. A fine variety of building styles exist here, including excellent examples of "Neoclassical Revival" and "Art Deco". Ironically, this eclectic mix of commercial buildings has survived in part due to Durham's dwindling economic fortunes in mid-to-late 19th century, with no razing to make place for office high rises.

**c.** Charlotte's Tryon Street. The heart of North Carolina's fastest growing city has completely changed since the 1950s. Very little of historic architecture remains as entrepreneurial opportunities have translated into wholesale land clearance to make room for high rise office complexes.

445

the heart of the city (Photos 12.7a, b and c). Adjacent to this Central Business District (CBD) is a zone of wholesale trade and manufacturing establishments and beyond lies residential zones defined by their decreasing densities of population. The major contribution of this oversimplified model of urban land use is its insistence that a gradient in land value exists from high value in the center to low value on the periphery, and that public and private location decision making processes have responded positively to this distance decay principle. An economic foundation was thus laid at an early date in the American city for zoning, our prevalent system of urban land use control.

In North Carolina, along Main Street, these land use relationships are especially evident in Winston-Salem, Greensboro, High Point, and Durham. Beyond the CBD and the employment district afforded by warehousing and manufacturing lie an area of transition, roughly corresponding to fairly high density residential areas that deteriorated in quality and became blighted, eventually to have most of its structures removed during the 1960s national policy of urban renewal. Much of this space was given over to vast parking spaces and garages to accommodate one of the most important change agents of urban space usage - the automobile (CP 12.1). Outward from the transition zone, the concentric zone model postulates successive zones of decreasing residential density combined with increasing affluence of the occupants. Thus, poorer people are more likely to be living in smaller, more crowded, rental units toward the CBD and wealthier people inhabit larger propertied, self-owned dwellings toward the periphery.

It should be noted that the land use structure of all North Carolina towns and cities reflects this simplified pattern, but also that the process of CBD decay, the increasing abandonment of industrial sites in the central city and the blighting of adjacent residential areas, describes most urban places during the 1960s and 1970s. This disinvestment experience of the central city significantly altered the land value gradient. More recently, from the mid-1980s to the present, in the public and private reinvestments in CBDs and in the gentrification of deteriorated neighborhoods of historic value there has been created some semblance of the original gradient. What the concentric zone model clearly fails to do is to explain, on the one hand, the specific dimensions of residential segregation, and on the other hand, the evolution of high land values on the periphery of urban centers.

### Sectoral Divisions of Land Use

Box 12A, diagram b, depicts the wedge or sector theory, as developed by Homer Hoyt in the 1930s. He was interested in illustrating that urban development responds not only to the land value gradient, but also to the evolution of major transportation corridors and to other special locational attributes. He found that the better and more affluent residential areas tend to develop: 1) along radial axes or wedges outward from the city center near major highways; 2) toward higher ground free from the potential of flooding and other environmental hazards; and 3) toward areas being developed with retail and recreational fa-

cilities. In addition, he found that different social groups tend to find compatible housing in wedges radiating out from the core of the city. The model thus comes closer to describing the peculiarities of race and income segregation by residential districts. Once particular socio-economic neighborhoods are established, they will continue to grow outward in the same direction because this is where land for their usage is generally available (Mayer and Hayes 1983, 32). The reader can reflect on the model's accuracy in predicting residential segregation by race and income in North Carolina cities and ponder the predominant directions of suburban growth. Suburban growth appears to be directed toward the south, east, and north in Charlotte's case; southwest and northwest from Winston-Salem; mostly north and westward from Greensboro; and for Durham and Raleigh to converge upon the Research Triangle from opposing locations.

### Multiple Nodes in Urban Development

Neither the concentric zone nor the sector model account for the tendency of large urban areas to develop multiple nuclei; that is, a number of centers of retail and/or industrial/commercial activity some distance away from the core of the city and in clear competition with the core. As was the trend throughout the country, North Carolina's metropolitan areas evolved a new look following World War II. The private automobile and the trucking industry took control of urban periphery development, urged on by a variety of economic and social externalities and including post-war federal suburban residential subsidization, interstate freeway system development, white flight, persistent rural-metropolitan migration, and growth of the global corporation. Facilitated by improved transportation access, industrial parks proliferated on the city's outskirts. New business employment centers developed in suburbia, while regional shopping malls seem to sprout from the green fields of farms around the urban periphery. Universal to these changes is the evolution of endogenous subcenters peripheral to the city proper, which subsequently become major engines of urban sprawl. Most of these changes were anticipated in the multiple nuclei model (Box 12A, diagram c), first proposed by geographers Chauncy Harris and Edward Ullman in 1945. The shift in land values from the CBD to the periphery reflects these changes in land use and its site competition (Box 12A, diagram e).

The outlying subcenters seem to thrive more on their mutual competitiveness, rather than showing particular concerns of a potential threat to their continuing growth from the CBD, as has been the case between the University City (north suburban) and South Park (south suburban) commercial nuclei of Charlotte. On the other hand, it has been shown that CBDs are more successfully challenged where there exists two or more suburban nuclei. Continued growth of peripheral nuclei is now a dominant feature of metropolitan landscapes. In some cases, this may evolve with a degree of independence that propels the emerging nuclei into what appears to be a fully functional independent urban center. These "edge cities" are beginning to appear on our Main Street, marked by seemingly insatiable growth. In most cases, they have evolved from small towns that have existed for a long time on the periphery of the city proper, as is the case of Cary (southwest of Raleigh), Pineville (south of Charlotte), and Clemmons (southwest of Winston-Salem). At the turn of the 20th century, all of these small towns thrived as centers of their own small rural trade area. Subsequently, they experienced a decline due to the increasing competition from the adjacent and expanding major cities and they lost businesses and people as a result. Gaining credence and substance as suburban nuclei during the last third of the 20th century, they are now flourishing as centers capable of attracting private development investments, given their own resources and access to markets via excellent communication and transportation linkages to the various parts of Main Street.

Though not necessarily a criterion of "edge cities" on the national scale, having their own administrative jurisdiction and local government is a major benefit to the North Carolina variant. These very rapidly growing places provide critical linkages along Main Street and contribute to fusing its larger cities into an urban continuity. On a larger scale, geographers have referred to this linkage of urban centers as a megalopolis. They point to the example set by the urbanizing Eastern Seaboard from Washington, DC, to Boston. The North Carolina metropolitan centers of Charlotte, Winston-Salem, Greensboro, and Raleigh do not approach in their populations the size of Washington, Baltimore, Philadelphia, New York, and Boston; nonetheless, a similar process of land conversion to urban usage between pre-established urban centers is taking place at a very rapid pace at the beginning of the 21st century.

## Main Street and Land Use

In some considerable degree, the three models of urban land use are useful to demonstrate the nature of urban change over time, with the multiple nuclei best representing the most recent manifestation, at least for the larger cities. For smaller urban places, especially those that have experienced relatively little change over the past fifty years or so, a combination of the concentric zone and the sector models contribute well to an understanding of their land use structure. Towns of the Coastal Plain and the Mountains are well represented by these two models. In any case, what comes clear from the above discussion is that something very remarkable is happening in the process of urbanizing North Carolina's Piedmont. Not only is this process restructuring the landscape, from the hearts of cities to the joining of their extending tentacles, it is of such dimensions that our way of thinking about urban development must be restructured as well. Thinking about a system of cities, like Main Street, can no longer be separated from considering processes of land use change within the individual city. Land usages, be they commercial, residential, or manufacturing, were formerly and predictably neatly tucked into their proper city envelope. Now they are being scattered hither and yon, but stand especially revealed in that new landscape of chaos – urban sprawl.

## URBAN ENVIRONMENTS

Urban landscaping on Main Street takes on a variety of characteristics, problems, and proffered solutions. In large measure, these differences are a function of distance from the center city node (Figure 12.8). We will consider in order, the Central Business District, older manufacturing and warehousing districts, higher density residential areas with their concentration of public housing and gentrifying neighborhoods, older suburbs, newer suburban nodal developments, and finally the systems that link them.

### *The Center City*

#### *The Disinvestment Process*

Over recent decades Main Street's center cities have been making an extraordinary comeback, although the transformation has not been uniform across all the cities. Decades of disinvestments, resulting from the heated suburbanization of the 1950s through the 1970s, produced a landscape of abandonment. Downtown streets of closed and boarded shops, deteriorating residential communities dominated in places by ill-designed public housing, and extensive areas cleared of buildings and given over to concrete waste lands or asphalted parking lots were all common sights in Main Street cities (CP 12.1). The causes of this unattractive landscape included a persistent outflow of central city dwellers, predominantly white, middle class folk who anchored themselves in suburban locations, aided by generous government supported low cost mortgages with tax free interest.

Manufacturers relocated from traditional high density, labor intensive, and largely obsolescent facilities in space-confined industrial zones that inhibited expansion, and were corporate tax burdens. New facilities were built in the wide expanses of rural, inexpensive lands that accommodated the favored single story plant with its large-scale, horizontally-organized, and labor-saving production lines, as well as appropriately scaled parking surfaces (CP 12.2). Also aiding in manufacturing decentralization was the increasing availability of accommodations in peripherally located industrial parks with easier access to major transportation arteries and airports.

Commercial activities that had dominated the center city left in tandem with the most important consumer market-middle class families. Outmigration of retail functions coincided with the development of suburban malls where the chief attraction was the cluster of department stores that previously had been located in the center city's high rent district (CP 12.3 and CP 12.4). The masses of smaller scale businesses, largely family owned, were unable to survive in their center city shopping street locations and either closed or joined the anchor stores and a legion of franchise retailers in regional malls, leaving the traditional central business district virtually empty of retail businesses (Photos 12.8 and 12.9)

People remaining in the center city were predominantly poor and overwhelmingly minority. Issues of housing inadequacies had been responded to by building massive public housing projects that simply reinforced the emergence of urban ghettos. In the end,

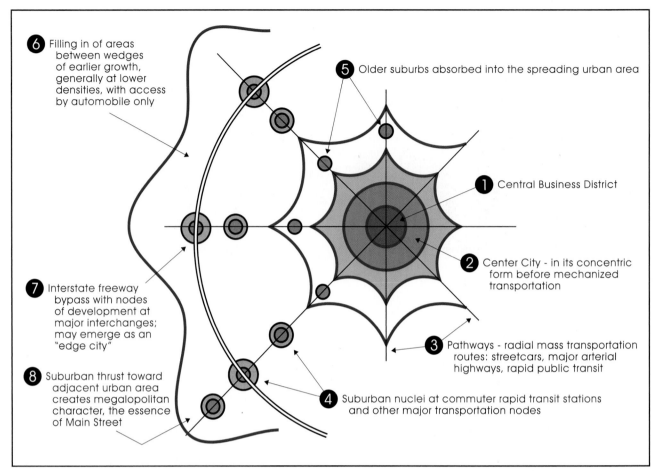

**Figure 12.8:** Metropolitan Area Development.
**Source:** Modified From Mayer (1969).

many became drug and crime ridden, devoid of any residents except those who could not afford to relocate to owner occupied or rental housing elsewhere, or who simply suffered from the absence of affordable housing in areas where they were otherwise welcome. By and large, blacks were excluded from the suburbs due to affordability, as well as to blatant racial discrimination, ranging from real estate steering practices to bank and mortgage company red lining of minority neighborhoods. Having little economic and political power, these people became, in essence, disenfranchised from the on-going geographic shifts in homes, jobs, and shops. Low-skill jobs left the center city and public transportation provided inadequate links between an available center city labor force and employment opportunities in the suburbs. Shopping opportunities for center city families have become extremely limited and disproportionately expensive. Options might include shopping at poorly stocked small groceries or convenience stores where costs for basic foods are much higher that at large competing grocery chains in the suburbs, necessitating for many a costly weekly taxi run to a distant grocery store and shopping center. Acknowledging these difficulties for poor people in the central city in 2000, the Charlotte City Council allocated over $400,000 to provide a standard one-way

$1.50 taxi fare for poor people, especially elderly poor. The sum was used up long before the year's end. Shifts in homes, jobs, and shops also characterized an associated problem for city government, the flight of its center city tax base, though this has not figured as negatively for North Carolina municipalities due to the state's liberal annexation law.

*The Reinvestment Process*

All of the cities on Main Street have suffered the stresses from this complex urban re-landscaping process in varying degrees. How have they responded to the plight of their center city? How have public and private entrepreneurial interests differentially focused on the problems and in what degree have they come together to resolve them? How have conditions improved for the people living in the center city? Heavy public investments in center city improvements, including the ill-fated urban renewal and public housing projects of the 1960s, led primarily to land clearance and ghetto formation. However, with land available largely in the hands of the public sphere, it was affordable and expedient to increase the public presence in the center city. Governmental functions have long been important, with post office, federal and county court houses and jails, city

**Photo 12.8:** Hickory's CBD exemplifies center city commercial concentration, as well as its several decades of transition. Though much effort has been put into renovations of buildings and environmental aesthetics, retail stores have largely left the CBD for commercial strips and the I-40 accessible Valley Hills Mall. Nearby, along US 65/70, big box commerce is thriving, further limited the chances of a retail recovery in the CBD. (Photo by Istvan Egresi)

hall, and fire and police stations being omnipresent features of the center city. Now public land use could be expanded by the ever increasing needs of government administration, planning, public health and welfare, law enforcement and court systems, libraries, and museums, plus those most rapidly expanding quasi-public institutions, hospitals and health care centers (CP 12.1). Government reinvestment in the center city often established in many cases the initial engine for economic restructuring, providing jobs across many skill levels, as well as enhancing public service availability and amenity options. Government also acted as a magnet in assembling a coterie of related professional services, especially law firms, bail bondsmen, real estate offices, and tax services. With their need for accessibility to public venues and their clients, these businesses have filtered into the formerly abandoned store fronts and in many places contributed to striking aesthetic streetscape improvements, the latter aided also by the federal and state supported National Main Street

Program (Chapter 11). Over the past decade and a half, public investments in the larger cities, frequently supported by joint venture arrangements with private interests, also have made a big splash with new convention centers and sports arenas. The government role in reinventing the central city is more noticeable in medium sized and smaller towns, such as Concord, Salisbury, and Burlington. These are towns that have neither the size for self-sustained growth nor the specialized dynamic economic growth base enabling them to independently attract large private investments.

Whereas government reinvestment has been a universal contributor to center city redevelopment, the direction, scale, and impact of private investment has varied markedly, depending on the size of the city and on the city's economic base. It is the size of the center city and the convenience of access to it, that in large measure defines a city's consumer market for retail goods and personal/leisure services. Until very recently, only

**Photo 12.9:** Lenoir Mall was completed in the early 1980s, effectively closing down the retail life of the downtown. The mall lasted until the U.S. 321 strip got going with its bargain retail boxes (Wal-Mart, Lowes, etc.) in the 1990s, and now stands mostly abandoned.

very limited investments have been made in retail shopping and entertainment facilities in center cities in North Carolina. The evolving tradition has been to concentrate these investments at the outskirts of the city or beyond. For Main Street, it appears that the specialized economic base of individual cities has been the critical element in the private/corporate redevelopment effort. Uptown Charlotte (CP 12.5), for example, has benefited from its incredible emergence as a financial center, as has, to a lesser degree, downtown Winston-Salem (CP 12.6), still reeling from the downsizing of its major traditional industry base. Investment in hospitals and related health research and service facilities allows Durham to consider itself the City of Medicine, much as High Point can justly lay claim to being called the City of Furniture, with its center city now dominated by some eight million square feet of space exclusively committed to furniture display and sales (Chapter 6 and CP 6.10a-c). Raleigh, meanwhile, thrives on its combination of government and education (CP 12.7). In all of these cases, center cities have been economically stimulated due to massive corporate investments, especially in their base specializations. Most of these cities are also of a size sufficient to have encouraged the development of convention facilities supporting investments in hotels, restaurants, and pubs.

The growing public and private presence in the center city has brought in thousands of commuting workers from the suburbs and the further reaches of the metropolitan area. With this has come demands for improvement in the city's infrastructure, including streets and highways, parking decks, water, sewage treatment, and waste disposal. Increasingly, people have found the center city to offer an amenable living environment; private developers are rushing to provide residential options, especially townhouses and apartment buildings that suit the more limited and costly space. Where older neighborhoods have not been converted to large public housing or other usage and where houses are of historic value, gentrification has become an important process for residential neighborhood improvement, returning middle and upper classes and the residential tax base to the city. Elsewhere, loft apartments are retrofitted from older, but still usable manufacturing buildings and whole new residential neighborhoods are being fashioned out of decaying public housing tracts. For the larger Main Street cities it now appears that a major turnaround in the fortunes of urban land use is in the making. Center city is once again the focus of public and private investment on a large scale, one clearly competitive with suburban interests.

The scars of the past, however, are not fully removed. The recent robust national economy has left behind a minority population that is relatively poorer, more isolated, and less equipped to improve its lot than at any time in the past quarter century (Hackett 1999). Some residential communities, wedges of poverty in the center city urban fabric, have hardly been impacted by the recent positive changes and continue to verge on desperation. They exhibit the continuing combination of run-down conditions, absentee land ownership, poverty, criminal activity, and minority population concentration. Thirty-six percent of the average income of the poorest fifth of U.S. families, people who occupy these center city wedges generally distant from shops and jobs, goes to transportation costs, further diminishing these people's possibility for acquiring their own home. Cars diminish wealth; homes add wealth (Pierce 2001).

The CBD streetscape is in many places no less depressing in its non-human scale dimension. Its concentration of towering shiny office towers encourage wind tunnels at street level, where the lack of shop windows present fortress-like canyons that many pedestrians find psychologically oppressive (Weber 1981). An enticing distant image of the center city, rising like a Phoenix from the ashes, may translate into something entirely different for those who have to cope daily with a largely dehumanized environment. Provisions for adequate open space and parklands amid the high-rise office buildings has rarely been on the center city planning agenda. Also, in only a few of the larger cities are there still significant historic public, commercial, or industrial buildings existing in a condition that may warrant historic preservation efforts. Charlotte, especially, is known for reckless abandonment of its visible history. On the other hand, smaller towns seem to have discovered themselves through the agency of historic preservation. Outstanding examples include Kannapolis, Concord,

**Photo 12.10:** Southern Railway began building its Spencer Shops complex in 1896 at a point roughly half way between Washington and Atlanta. In its hayday the Shops employed 2,500 people and provided the economic foundation for the town of Spencer. The decline of railroad activity following World War II reduced the need for labor at the Shops, and work ceased entirely during the 1970s. Subsequently Southern Railroad deeded the property to the state of North Carolina, which then began the development of its Transportation Museum, the Historic Spencer Shops. The 38 bay roundhouse and its companion back shop are the more prominent buildings in this late 1970s photo.

Burlington and Carrboro, but none have done as well as Salisbury (CP 12.8a-d, and Photo 12.10). Elsewhere, the problems of abandoned industrial plants, fuel depots and stations, and certain warehousing facilities continue to fester in the center city environment.

New tools have now been adapted by state and city governments to ameliorate the noxious qualities of so-called "brownfields," which are sites where past industrial usage have produced on-site contamination that threaten human health and the larger environment. Under the state's Brownfield Property Reuse Act of 1997, an extension of the federal Comprehensive Environmental Response, Compensation and Liability Act (CERCLA) of 1980 (the so-called Superfund Law), entrepreneurs can arrange with the state to clean up a brownfields site to a degree that is economically feasible, though the site may remain non-threateningly polluted (Hower 1998; IFC Consulting 1999). What is especially critical for businesses investing in the conversion of polluted sites is that they are not legally responsible for the pollution traceable to prior owners, in the event of future sale of the property. Unhappily, the state has not provided enough state officials to guide prospective developers through the paper maze, so the hope of bringing countless empty buildings and properties back on the tax rolls is far from being realized. Throughout the state, only three properties over three years have entered the process of rehabilitation, whereas five to ten per year had been expected. With a likely 1,000 sites in the state (Whisnant 1999), no less than 200 sites have been identified around Durham (Stradling 2000). In Raleigh, a "brownfields" grant is being used to identify this kind of property among the abandoned warehouses, auto-repair shops, and oil and chemicals distribution facilities on the south side of town (Photo 12.11). The state's most notable rehabilitated area was the Charlotte "brownfields" conversion to football practice fields for the Carolina Panthers. Concentrated in older parts of the cities, "brownfield" sites are precisely those needing redeveloping as a deterrent to sprawl.

## Older Suburbs and Pathways

As cities expanded at the turn of the 20th Century, transportation technology permitted the implementation of a streetcar system to facilitate access to the center city. Developers saw the opportunity to invest in so-called streetcar suburbs. In most Main Street cities, those areas continue to be primarily residential. In fact, they have become very popular with people who can afford to remodel and maintain older homes on larger lots with higher property taxes. Even the streetcars are beginning to make a comeback (Photo 12.12). In these transition areas to suburban development there is a continuing conflict over just what constitutes highest and best land use. Some residents and historic preservationists prefer community environments that continue to strongly reflect a historic past, maintaining the look and atmosphere defined by tree canopied streets, and large garden lots with 70-plus year-old homes undefiled by modernistic enlargements. Developers and planners are concerned about increasing population densities and prefer to see townhouses, apartment buildings, and other in-fill residential development. This latter situation will increase population thresholds to where local shopping centers are demanded, though this is apt to further increase street congestion and agitate local land use conflict.

It is perhaps curious, that even as revitalized older suburbs are beginning to clamor for local shopping centers, nearby older pathways connecting newer suburbs to the center city are experiencing serious problems in retail retention. These are the main transportation arteries to downtown. They initially attracted large lot auto sales businesses, easy access restaurants, and the big box discount stores. It was called strip development, the evolution of a stage in the retail concentration process that contributed to the downfall of the Central Business District. Strip development now appears slated for its own abandonment, emerging graveyards of empty stores and large parking lots. A recent count in Charlotte identified 30 vacant big box stores, formerly occupied by Kmart, Wal-Mart, Target, Giant, or other retailers

**Photo 12.11:** Environmental "hot zone" becomes a "hot" development spot. Pilot Mills a few blocks north of the Capitol in Raleigh is being retrofitted to new use through the "Brownfields" Property Reuse Act of 1997. This permits cleanup and development by new owner without liability for earlier incurred pollution and noxious contamination that may linger on the property.

Photo 12.12: Return of the trolley. Trolleys used to uptown Charlotte with its suburbs and manufacturing districts fanning out in all directions. Dilworth and the South End Manufacturing District is now being reconnected, as the initial venture into a very large scaled and financially well supported new mass transit plan for the city and its immediate hinterland. Developers are rushing to take advantage of not only improved transit but also of the reality that uptown living is once again in vogue. Old plants are being retrofitted into loft condos, restaurants, shops, and offices, an eclectic mix in land use befitting new life styles and residential habitats.

that have either been bought out or have closed these properties while chasing their wealthy consumer base even further into the newer suburbs. They have relocated to where they may have fortuitous access to a new freeway bypass intersection (Dodd 2001). The abandonment process mirrors the earlier experience of the CBDs, with smaller retailers following their anchor stores. One problem with big box stores is their insistence on a huge parking lot and an enormously scaled, generally windowless, building, normally without any redeeming aesthetic value. Typically, they are built with minimal investment, intending a short life cycle. So when they are abandoned, they are difficult to shift into another use. They may stand empty for years contributing to the "broken-window" syndrome, and from there to a self-fulfilling prophesy of neighborhood blight and declining land values (Photo 12.13 and 12.14). For local residents, their closings also means a drop in shopping options, longer distances to shop, and a resulting degradation of air quality.

A particular problem for transition areas has been the perceived need for improved access to the center city. The response to this need has been cutting limited access highways through traditional neighborhoods. Probably, in this state, no neighborhood has been as deleteriously affected by this developmental maneuver as has the black business and residential community of Hayti (hay-tie) at the southern edge of Durham's CBD (CP 12.9). Minority and poor neighborhoods, lacking the necessary political power base, have been particularly vulnerable to these urban land use change tactics. Affording access to the center city in this manner appears to be a more recent version of urban renewal.

### Suburbs and the "New Urbanism"

The ticky-tac of suburban housing developments is becoming a scene of the past. Suburbanites were, perhaps 20 to 40 years ago, content to live in single-family homes on small lots,

Photo 12.13: Wilkinson Boulevard is one of Charlotte's major connecting thoroughfares, At one time lined with shopping centers, restaurants, and service stations Wilkinson shows the negative land use side to changing times. The disinvestment process that began with center city retail has moved to the strip centers. In the process nearby communities are hurt, as big boxes stand empty they become a cause for further decay. In this shopping plaza only Heilig Myers Furniture remains, but not for long.

essentially white middle class suburban ghettos, and without sidewalks, public green spaces, or recreational areas. Suburbanites were willing to commute considerable distances for jobs, schools, shops, and recreational amenities. Except for the onerous commuting aspect, this scenario no longer is much in evidence (CP 12.12). Now planners and developers speak of "new urbanism," "mixed use development," and "sustainable communities." In the not so distant past, these concepts were rolled into the idea of "new town" development. Major efforts at seeing the building of such integrated communities in North Carolina have in fact occurred. One such community, the rural "new town" of Soul City (Warren County), was discussed in Chapter 11. Another is University City, north of Charlotte, a new town envisioned on the pattern and principles of the Swedish new town of Vällingby outside of Stockholm. In essence, the new town ideal is to design an entire new community with the needed commercial, governmental, education, health, and public amenities in the town center, high density housing within walking distance, and town houses and single family homes at a further distance (but well connected to the town center by pedestrian walkways and bikeways sheltered from automotive traffic). Manufacturing and service businesses locate within public transit distance of the labor pool afforded by the town. Natural environment components are emphasized throughout the town, with lakes, exposed streams, forested strips, and nature trails acting as green ribbons tying together the human habitation and use areas. In the United States, a leading example of this approach to integrated sustainable urban communities is probably Reston, Virginia, with its Lake Anne Center. As for University City, it is easy to see in its layout some of the critical design components, but when it was developed it was not possible to marshal all of the necessary interests and decision making powers necessary to complete the task. Predictably, the concept got entangled in the essentially uncontrolled and overly rapid development of northern Mecklenburg County, as can be seen in a comparison of CP 12.10

and 12.11. The North Carolina approach to community planning is dominated by corporate enterprise and the profit motive. Major historic failures in public planning for home and land have been punctuated by the absence of: 1) comprehensive and well integrated governmental guidelines firmly applied; 2) the provision of financial backing for the significant up front capital costs; and 3) a general public disinterest in divesting itself from automotive dependency and the stand alone single household home. The desirable upper middle class home now being presented in suburban neighborhoods is a three-garage house with a huge interior space and a large exterior apron of asphalt or concrete; a golf course and a nearby access ramp to the freeway add to the desirability of their neighborhood. Yet, this is not the end of the story.

There is something of a ground swell toward integrated "mixed development" communities taking place on Main Street, although this movement is very much tempered by developers' perception of marketability and thus far has been confined to the periphery of the major metropolitan centers. Notable examples include Ballantyne in south Charlotte and Wakefield Plantation in north Raleigh (Photo 12.15), both of which are spread city examples of vast acreage committed to upper scale single-family homes. Broad bands of highways, as in the case of Ballantyne Commons, connect residential spaces to shopping centers. In both cases, the attainable population thresholds encourage the local government to plan for schools in or near the developments, but jobs are elsewhere. Southern Village in Chapel Hill is a leading example of the ideals of socially and functionally well-integrated and environmentally designed communities (CP 12.13).

### Main Street Cities and Annexation

North Carolina provides distinctive advantages for physical growth of municipalities due to its unusually liberal voluntary and involuntary annexation codes. Note also discussion on annexation and Census Designated Places in Chapter 4. This liberal

**Photo 12.15:** Wakefield Plantation (Wake County). Here are planned 3,000 upscale single-family homes, condos and apartments, plus 400 acres of offices, shops, restaurants, and a large entertainment center. No mass transit has been planned to connect to Raleigh and the Research Triangle Park, where most of the residents are expected to be working. The eventual population will generate an anticipated 150,000 daily auto trips on nearby roads, necessitating, for example, the widening of the New Falls Road from two to seven lanes.

approach to expanding city limits contributed to the amazing municipality population increases of the last two decades of the 20th century. Among the twelve fastest growing incorporated urban places in the state, only Wilmington added less than 50 percent of its population increase through annexation (the weight of its increase was due to net in-migration and natural increase). Population growth through territorial expansion of city limits has been a key to the rapid increases in the size of Main Street cities. Cary obtained 50 percent of its 1980-1998 population increase from annexation, while Durham, Chapel Hill, and Charlotte all added 56 to 57 per cent through expanding their municipal boundaries. Fueled by an interest in controlling future land use in the vicinity of its Outer Belt (now under construction), Charlotte's City Council voted in January of 2001 to annex territory the physical size of Salisbury. It is notable that much territorial annexation in the crowded Piedmont is at the behest of developers who apparently prefer to work with city councils as opposed to county commissioners. Certainly, this is the case in Durham County where 43 annexation decisions in 1999 were requested by subdivision developers (Barrett 2001)

As shown on Figure 12.9, the Piedmont Triad urban centers are especially notable in their annexation dependency for population increase, with High Point recording a 72 percent increase due to annexation alone, Greensboro 81 percent, and Winston-Salem an incredible 92 percent. This manner of population increase somewhat dampens the enthusiasm generally shown for the recovery of the Triad in its position as the central link in Main Street. Still, the annexation process in the Piedmont expanded the municipal territory of the five largest cities by some 164 square miles during the 1990s alone, an urban land grab approaching the size of a small North Carolina county. One result is, of course, a considerable expansion of the formal urban spatial dimension of Main Street.

Land annexation improves land use planning and efficiencies in providing public services to expanding urban areas and ensures uniform governmental rules, regulations, and behaviors in the urban region, but it is not without its opponents. Communities have been known to fight tooth and nail the expansionist aims of an adjoining municipality. At times, the response has been defensive incorporation, which may in the end result in higher taxes due to inefficiencies in service delivery for the new smaller town. At other times, the conflicts result in dramatic confrontations at public meetings and in a signage protest along threatened streets (Photo 12.16). Frequently, municipalities arrive at a gentleman's agreement as to what rural share of the particular county they are apt to annex over time. However, there is keen competition among adjacent municipalities, as is the case in Wake County where Holly Springs, Apex, and Morrisville are wearily watching the territorial design of Cary, and Wake Forest continues to agonize over Raleigh's northward expansion.

A related problem to that of annexation is simplifying urban government through city-county consolidation. Already, this is taking place in the delivery of some public services, especially planning. Although frequently analyzed by some larger cities during the past several decades, the fear of the loss of identity and local control on the part of the smaller municipalities seem to turn the tide against consolidation, regardless of proffered savings by a unitary governmental entity. The issue is frequently considered in Mecklenburg County, where plans to vote on a merger were called off with the election of a new County Commission in 1994. Appearing occasionally on the County Commission agenda of Durham County, voters have twice rejected city-county merger plans since the 1960s. What is apt to drive an interest in consolidated government is a vision of the likely gridlock resulting from the continuing struggle over divergent approaches to transportation planning. Pulling in the opposite direction is the movement toward neighborhood schools that are isolated from what some see as a negative influence of the city.

In sum, a distinctive North Carolina urban trait of a clearly defined urban edge separating city development from the green

*Photo by Ole Gade.*

**C.P. 12.8b:** The station hotel (The Yadkin House, built in 1913) was renovated in the 1980s to accommodate elder care apartments.

**C.P. 12.8c:** Union army troops of General William T. Sherman destroyed the Confederate Prison (10,000 prisoners in 1864), the railroad station, and manufacturing plants, but spared city's commercial and residential sections. W. Innis Street has the Confederate Monument (1909), the former Federal Courthouse built of Italian marble in 1911, and the seven story 1913 Beaux Arts-style Wallace building, now restored and fully occupied following many years of abandonment. Downtown Salisbury has 98% user occupancy.

*Photo by Ole Gade.*

**Color Plate 12.8:** Salisbury (Rowan County), chartered in 1755, was once considered the western capital of North Carolina and the only city of significance west of Raleigh until the mid-19th century. As such, it was a major station on the North Carolina Railroad. Positioned in the triangle of three interstate highways and on Main Street, the city continues to have a much favored location for investment and development. It is fortuitous that the spirit of pride in its history propelled Salisbury's residents to restore and to preserve the city's visible urban landscapes. Eight historic districts were placed on the National register of Historic Places in 1975. They include historic districts committed to different land uses, such as transportation, commerce, and residences.

**C.P. 12.8d:** A garden spot by the 1892 Presbyterian Church Bell Tower, all that remains of the Richardsonian Romanesque church which caught fire in the 1970s (see also CP 12.4).

**C.P. 12.8e:** The West Square Residential District has a 200-year architectural record. Examples include a 1902 Queen Anne (The Rowan Oak House) and a 1906 Neo-Classical Revival with a massive neo-Palladian portico (The Cannon-Guille House).

**Color Plate 12.8**: Salisbury Historic Districts.

**Color Plate 12.9:** In the 1920s, Hayti was a prosperous and cohesive black community with a hospital, large educational institutions, a booming residential market, and a well-defined commercial heart focusing on Pettigrew and Fayetteville streets - the nation's "Black Wall Street." Unfortunately, Hayti was in the way of the 1960s urban renewal machine and the need for a freeway connection to downtown Durham from the Research Triangle. So far, limited success has been attained in reintroducing commercial activities in the area now crisscrossed by highways. Although a Fayetteville Street Historic District is being planned, the community has lost much of its earlier justification and self identity.

*Photo by Ole Gade.*

*Photo by Ole Gade.*

**Color Plate 12.10:** University City (Mecklenburg County) is a 1970s example of community design utilizing the principles of new urbanism. This air photo from the early 1970s shows the village center, offices, residential areas, and a hotel, all connected by pedestrian footpaths and wrapped around a large lake.

**Color Plate 12.11:** Today the village center is hardly noticeable in a forest of development, featuring big box retail, the University Research Park, an expanding UNC-Charlotte, and crosscutting highways lending little comfort to anyone not driving an automobile. Current land usage generates urban sprawl.

*Photo by Ole Gade.*

**Color Plate 12.12:** Fearrington Village is located in northeastern Chatham County, near B. Everett Jordan Lake and ten miles south of Chapel Hill. The Scottish-born owner of a sizeable farm decided to take advantage of the housing needs of nearby professionals in Chapel Hill and developed residential neighborhoods of varying design. The earliest neighborhood, one that found great favor with university faculty, was designed to carefully fit homes into a forested environment with minimum tree removal. The neighborhood seen here is based on a European plan with internal green and public spaces reached by footpaths from surrounding homes placed in tight quadrants. Farm buildings continue to adorn the Village, with black belted cattle grazing the fields adjacent to the village stores and restaurants. This is a remarkable example of an individual landowner's approach to smart growth.

**C.P. 12.13a:** Southern Village includes a mix of housing densities with easy pedestrian access.

**Color Plate 12.13:** Within Chapel Hill (Orange County), south of N.C. Highway 54 but within a few miles of the UNC campus, lies the very large community of Southern Village. On par with Wakefield Plantation (Photo 12.15) in population size expectations, Southern Village is different in most other aspects. Here are sidewalks, back alleys for driveways, a mix of housing densities and styles (from single-family detached to townhouses and apartment buildings), a village shopping center with post office, churches, playgrounds, pre-school facilities, an elementary school, and public transit to Chapel Hill and Carboro.

**C.P. 12.13b:** In Southern Village, townhouses provide variation in style for large homes without a garage, but with a premium on open space for private use.

**C.P. 12.13c:** In the middle of a single-family, detached homes neighborhood lies a café. It is open throughout the day and into the evening. The café is easily reached by neighborhood mothers with children in strollers for mid-morning coffee with friends, as well as by couples stopping in for a glass of wine, a snack, coffee, or ice cream at any time.

**C.P. 12.13d:** Playgrounds and pre-school facilities are scattered throughout the community.

**Color Plate 12.14:** The Lake James shoreline winds its way through the foothills of the Blue Ridge. As the first of eleven Duke Energy lakes on the Catawba River, and the farthest from major population concentrations, its shoreline is the least developed. Crescent Land Resources, Duke Energy's land developer, is now involved in developing a number of residential subdivisions on the lakeshore.

**Color Plate 12.15:** Lakes used for drinking water and fishing are especially vulnerable to surface runoff and seepage from underground pollution. These lakes merit special consideration for extended green buffer zones. This photo illustrates the problem of houses clustering too close to one of the lakes on the Catawba River system.

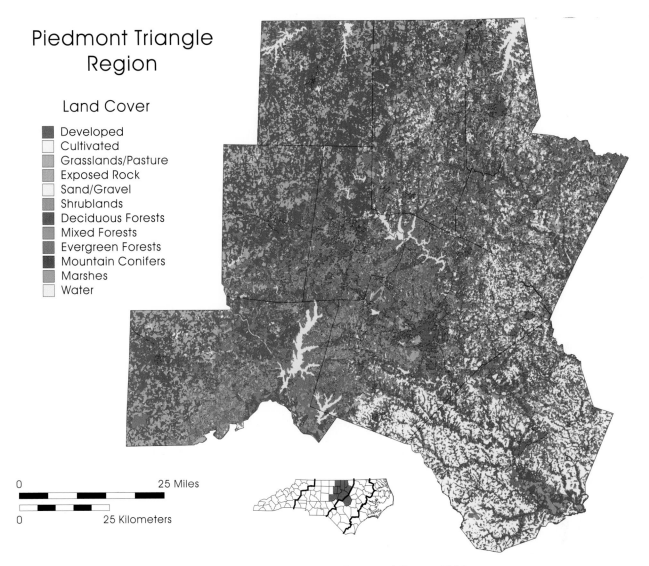

## Piedmont Triangle Region

### Land Cover

- ■ Developed
- ☐ Cultivated
- ▨ Grasslands/Pasture
- ▨ Exposed Rock
- ☐ Sand/Gravel
- ▨ Shrublands
- ■ Deciduous Forests
- ▨ Mixed Forests
- ▨ Evergreen Forests
- ■ Mountain Conifers
- ▨ Marshes
- ☐ Water

0         25 Miles

0         25 Kilometers

**Color Plate 12.16:** Piedmont Triangle State Geographic Region Land Cover, 1998.
**Source:** Modified from the North Carolina Center for Geographic Information and Analysis, 1998.

**Color Plate 12.17:** Glencoe (Alamance County) was founded as a mill village on the upper reaches of the Haw River in the late 19th century. Textile manufacturing was discontinued some decades ago, and the village was essentially abandoned. Buildings constructed by an early mill owner are now in various uses. With a housing stock considered worthy of renovating and with the potential of recapturing the historic village environment, Glencoe has been placed on the National Register of Historic Districts and is being restored through the support and promotional efforts of Preservation North Carolina. Restoration is aided by the commuting proximity of Glencoe to Burlington and Main Street development, as well as an increasing interest of newcomers in settling these kinds of restructured historic rural environments.

*Photo by Ole Gade.*

**C.P. 12.17a:** Original company houses are available for restoration in Glencoe.

461

**C.P. 12.17b:** The largest property in Glencoe is a former mill house from the 1880s.

*Photo by Ole Gade.*

**C.P. 12.17c:** Several restoration projects have been completed or are in process.

*Photo by Ole Gade.*

**Color Plate 12.17:** Glencoe (Alamance County) restoration.

**Color Plate 12.18:** Midway Business Park on N.C. 55 and I-40 has benefitted from its proximity to the Research Triangle Park. Midway Business Park is designed along the lines of RTP, but with less open space. Still, Midway provides an enticing land use mix of structure and space.

*Photo by Ole Gade.*

# Piedmont Triad Region

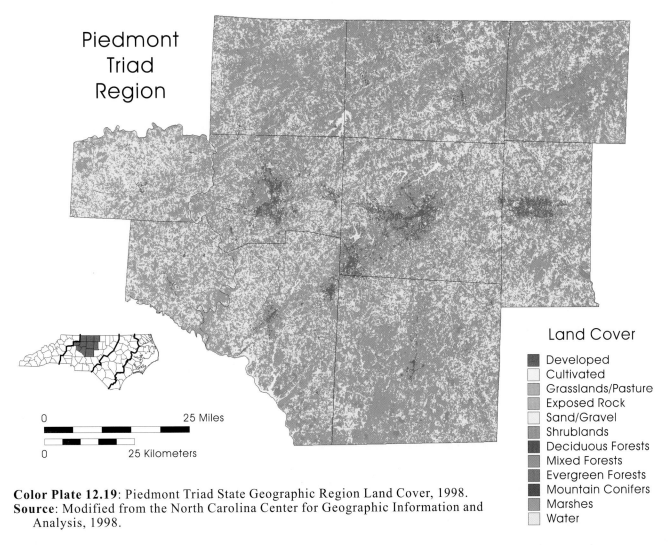

## Land Cover

- ■ Developed
- □ Cultivated
- ▨ Grasslands/Pasture
- ▨ Exposed Rock
- ▢ Sand/Gravel
- ▨ Shrublands
- ■ Deciduous Forests
- ▨ Mixed Forests
- ▨ Evergreen Forests
- ■ Mountain Conifers
- ▨ Marshes
- □ Water

0 _____ 25 Miles

0 _____ 25 Kilometers

**Color Plate 12.19**: Piedmont Triad State Geographic Region Land Cover, 1998.
**Source**: Modified from the North Carolina Center for Geographic Information and
    Analysis, 1998.

**Color Plate 12.20:** The Brookstown Inn is one of several retrofitted textile manufacturing plants in an industrial district of Winston-Salem. The renovated structure is in a district that began developing in the 1830s. The renewal effort has sparked interest in providing nearby high density housing and shops.

*Photo by Ole Gade.*

**Color Plate 12.21:** Old Salem is in the heart of Winston-Salem. This is an historically accurate restoration and reconstruction of buildings, gardens, and commons of Salem Village, founded by Moravians in 1766. Old Salem is very popular with tourists and provides low density relief in a hectic urban environment.

*Photo by Ole Gade.*

*Photo by Ole Gade.*

**Color Plate 12.22:** Reflecting the traditional house architecture of central Europe, this landscape in Old Salem was created by Moravian settlers in the 1760s. Nearby, and more rural in nature, are the preserved remnants of the Moravian settlements of Bethabara and Bethania.

**Color Plate 12.23:** South of Asheboro and the North Carolina Zoo lies one of the state's more enchanting cultural regions, its major pottery district. At the heart is Seagrove (Randolph County), with its many large potteries and the Pottery Museum.

*Photo by Ole Gade.*

**Color Plate 12.24:** The Pottery District overlaps the juncture of the Moore, Randolph, and Montgomery counties' boundaries. The Pottery District is in the central part of North Carolina's "Green Heart." An old, renovated mill site in beautiful natural surroundings demonstrates why this area is popular and in need of protection from exurban development.

*Photo by Ole Gade.*

*Photo by Ole Gade.*

**Color Plate 12.25:** In Randolph County's northeastern corner, the small town of Liberty is hanging on to its tradition with the Rand Ol' Opera House, a take-off on its big sister in Nashville, Tennessee.

**Color Plate 12.26:** While some traditions are maintained in Liberty, the town is not impervious to that major aspect of population change in the 1990s - Hispanic migrants. Throughout the Piedmont and elsewhere in the state, small stores are being converted to serve the needs of new Hispanic residents.

*Photo by Ole Gade.*

**C.P. 12.27a:** Photo of uptown in the 1980s.

*Photo by Ole Gade.*

**C.P. 12.27b:** Photo taken in 2000 with a slightly wider angle exposure to accommodate the expanding uptown.

*Photo by Ole Gade.*

**Color Plate 12.27:** Evidence of the growth in Charlotte is shown with photos separated in time by two decades, taken from the identical spot in Marshall Park.

**Color Plate 12.28:** In Charlotte, construction fever does not stop with the building of new skyscrapers. The move back to the center city was led by a gentrification movement several decades ago, highlighted by the redevelopment of the Fourth Ward. Single family homes cluster in a quiet neighborhood backed by the high rise buildings of uptown.

*Photo by Ole Gade.*

**C.P. 12.29a:** The red clays of the Piedmont are bared as construction begins to replace the 420 public housing units of Earle Village. Urban renewal projects razed hundreds of single family homes in deteriorating neighborhoods in the 1960s to make way for public housing, but the projects were able to accommodate only a fraction of the displaced population.

*Photo by Ole Gade.*

*Photo by Ole Gade.*

**C.P. 12.29b:** Two sample "shot gun" houses of the adjacent African-American cultural center contrast strongly with uptown Charlotte. The tallest building is the headquarters of Bank of America, which joined the Charlotte Housing Authority in bankrolling the community transformation.

**C.P. 12.29c:** It is perhaps ironic that the low to middle income housing that replaced Earle Village is not affordable by most of the 367 displaced families. Once again, the poor have been disenfranchised in the process of urban redevelopment.

*Photo by Ole Gade.*

**Color Plate 12.29:** Earle Village, a postwar public housing project that had become a blight in the heart of Charlotte, was razed during the mid-1990s with funds from a Department of Housing and Urban Development Hope VI Urban Revitalization Demonstration Grant. Earle Village was near the heart of the First Ward, one of the four wards comprising the center city, and was surrounded by underused or vacant land. An urban redevelopment plan incorporated all of this land and a new community has been built, supported by private investments.

**Color Plate 12.30:** Charlotte's perimeter sparkles with recent high value investments. Uptown's nearest competitor for commercial and residential development is South Park. With the state's largest mall in place, several up-scale shopping centers, a large concentration of high rise office buildings, and exclusive residential neighborhoods, South Park qualifies as Charlotte's "downtown." Phillip's Place defines the new urbanism, with its mix of stores, offices, residences and quiet, pedestrian-friendly environs.

**Color Plate 12.31:** Lowe's Motor Speedway, in the northern Mecklenburg sector generally referred to as University City, epitomizes the strength of automotive racing in North Carolina, a state of race tracks.

468

## Metrolina Region

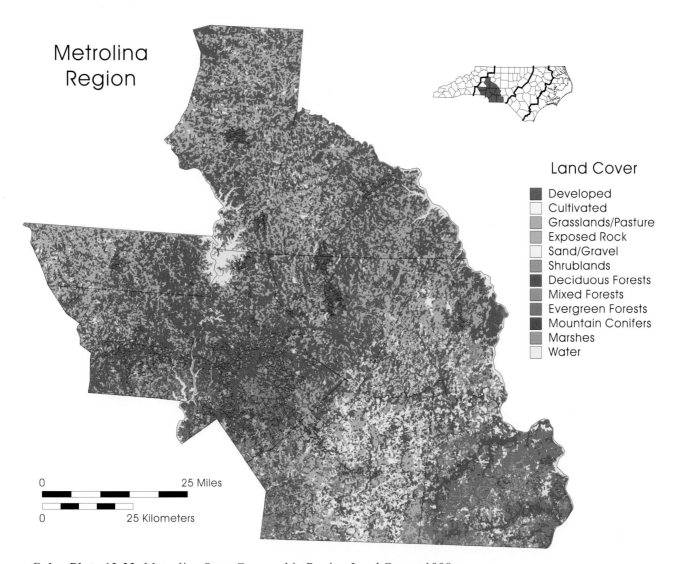

### Land Cover

- Developed
- Cultivated
- Grasslands/Pasture
- Exposed Rock
- Sand/Gravel
- Shrublands
- Deciduous Forests
- Mixed Forests
- Evergreen Forests
- Mountain Conifers
- Marshes
- Water

0              25 Miles

0              25 Kilometers

**Color Plate 12.32**: Metrolina State Geographic Region Land Cover, 1998.
**Source**: Modified from the North Carolina Center for Geographic Information and Analysis, 1998.

**Color Plate 12.33:** Much of Stanly County is within the state's Green Heart region. At Badin, employment is dominated by the Alcoa aluminum plant. The low cost energy demanded by the electrolysis process is generated at dams built along the Pee Dee River.

*Photo by Ole Gade.*

469

Photo by Ole Gade.

**Color Plate 12.34:** When Alcoa banned the display of Confederate flags, the edict fanned pent up anxieties of people who treasure the history, as they read it, of the old Confederacy and its symbols. Here, at the Alcoa administrative building on Lake Badin, demonstrators wave an assortment of flags of the Confederacy.

**Color Plate 12.35:** The Luray textile plant in Gastonia (Gaston County), long abandoned as a site of manufacturing, was once the largest plant in the South. Surrounded by former company housing, the plant is now slated for historic renovation and retrofitting into new usage.

Photo by Ole Gade.

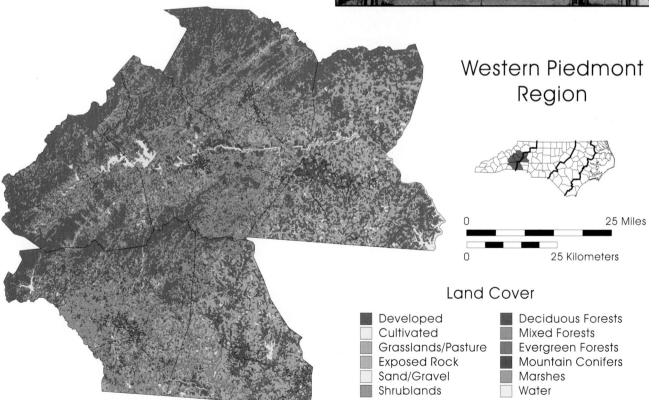

## Western Piedmont Region

0 ——————— 25 Miles

0 ——————— 25 Kilometers

### Land Cover

■ Developed
□ Cultivated
■ Grasslands/Pasture
■ Exposed Rock
□ Sand/Gravel
■ Shrublands

■ Deciduous Forests
■ Mixed Forests
■ Evergreen Forests
■ Mountain Conifers
■ Marshes
□ Water

**Color Plate 12.36**: Western Piedmont State Geographic Region Land Cover, 1998.
**Source**: Modified from the North Carolina Center for Geographic Information and Analysis, 1998.

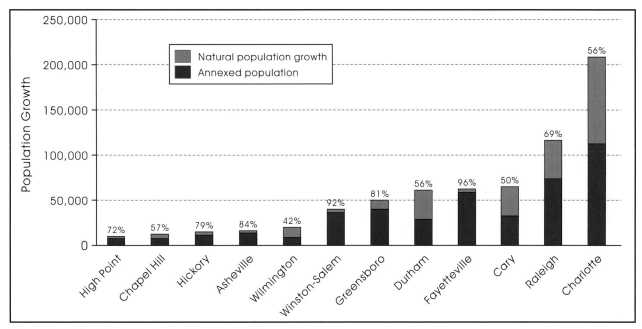

**Figure 12.9:** City Growth by Annexation, 1980-1998.
**Source:** Brookings Institution (2000, 10).

fields of agriculture and forests has changed. The revolution in automotive transportation eradicated the urban edge to where we now only dimly perceive it in the haphazard appearance of metropolitan expansion, the leapfrog patterns of suburban development, and the beltway nucleation of commercial activities and employment centers. The latter now have the potential of being defined as edge cities, should they attain the relevant functional complexity and size. Clearly defined urban edges are once again a viable planning objective, while edge cities are viewed as stimulating continued urban spread, if not sprawl.

## THE NATURAL-HUMAN ENVIRONMENT INTER-FACE

### Introduction

At the beginning of the 21st century, the challenges facing municipal and county governments are essentially beyond their individual capability of control. Land use regulation powers of local governments date to the 1920s and reflect a process of development that has long since ceased to exist. Land use issues have become multi-jurisdictional, requiring state intercession and

**Photo 12.16:** Many homeowners in suburban areas west of Winston-Salem are protesting with signs on their lawns their imminent annexation by the city.

471

local governments' cooperation in a regional context. Part of the reason is found in the changing conditions of livelihood and mode of transportation, and part is found in the recent rapidity of urban expansion. Figure 12.10 illustrates the recent changes in statewide land use. These data are further dramatized by North Carolina's ranking as the sixth fastest urbanizing state in the country. Ten years ago 10.2 percent of the state's land was developed, it is now 14.7 percent, a 45 percent increase in total land developed. This is a very troubling relationship, given the predicted continuing population growth of the Piedmont Region and the exorbitant demand for new land.

Similarly, our increasing use of other natural resources far outstrips our increasing numbers. Mecklenburg County's water use, for example, increased over 50 percent during the 1990s while its population increased by only 21 percent. We are far removed from what many now promote as desirable in land use. That is, we are not moving in the direction of sustainable development. The United Nations' Brundtland Commission (1987) stated that sustainable development involves local planning seeking to obtain a balance of environmental protection, economic profitability, and equity among its beneficiaries (people in the communities being affected by change). Without doubt, North Carolina is presently on an unsustainable urbanization path. The most alarming growth and expansion is taking place in the urbanizing Piedmont, traversed by Main Street. Leaving the issue of equity to the discussion in Chapter 7, we will focus in this section on a few examples that dramatize the inability of the Piedmont natural environment to sustain the present onslaught of development. The complex picture of environmental stresses are covered in Chapter 8; our examples here will focus on Piedmont problems of urban sprawl and associated loss of open green spaces, biodiversity, water resources depletion and quality degradation, atmospheric pollution, and waste generation and disposition. In all situations, there are vigorous efforts at dealing with the problems generated, some more successful than others.

## Urban Sprawl

Urban Sprawl is a concept that conjures up images of uncontrolled, rapacious development devouring open green country-side in great chunks, consuming a natural environment and heritage, that is forever lost to future generations. These are images hardening in the minds of many. In early 2000, the Pew Center for Civic Journalism reported that sprawl and growth issues had pushed aside crime as the major issue of concern for urban and suburban Americans. Many, many articles and editorial pages in the North Carolina's leading newspapers have recently focused on the theft, currently averaging 100,000 acres per year, of the state's natural resource base, an otherwise bounteous rural landscape of farms, woods, streams, and hills. In many communities, meetings are called to assemble the primary stakeholders (local citizens, business owners, land developers, public officials, politicians, and academics) to jointly focus on their local and regional community of the future. Increasingly, focus groups are asserting their message through the World Wide Web. Although gaining momentum, the natural land conservation and preservation train appears slowed in its progress by a welter of special interests that may benefit financially from urban sprawl. With their considerable political influence, these special interests argue against any increase in governmental encroachment on their right for profit taking. For example, realtors and home builder associations argue that increasing taxes and regulations will drive up the costs of housing and reduce choices for buyers and sellers of property. Voices of land development also benefit from the general absence of a popular interest in community welfare. By and large, North Carolinians are people motivated primarily neither by a sense of community nor a sense of commitment to place and space.

In the Piedmont Region, sprawl is the most noticeable process in the landscape (Photos 12.17 and 12.18). Just how do we measure this? Consider that The New York Times referred to Atlanta in November of 1999 as the epicenter of the nation's struggle with road congestion, air pollution, and over development. Atlanta is in effect, "choking on growth." The reason is an uncommonly low population density in Atlanta's metropolitan

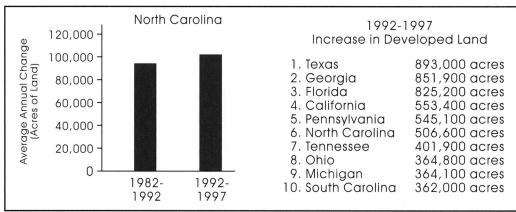

**Figure 12.10:** Average Annual Land Development, 1982-1992 and 1992-1997.
**Source:** Brookings Institution (2000, 12).

472

**Photo 12.17:** Sprawl is simply the conversion of rural land in farms, forests, and wetlands to some kind of urbanizing land use. Here Charlotte is pushing its sprawling residential subdivisions toward the east. Though this bedroom neighborhood dates to the 1970s the uniformity of the cul-de-sac street pattern without sidewalks and parks or playing fields, and middle class homes surrounded by lawns (not gardens) provides the standard drab image of a suburban ghetto.

region. In 1990, its population density was 730 people per square kilometer. This compares with 1,200 or more for more compact metro areas such as Minneapolis-St. Paul and Portland (Oregon), and with about 700 for the Piedmont Triangle! The Atlanta region now has a population two and a half times that of the Triangle, and sprawls over an area more than twice the size. In 1950, the Atlanta Region consumed less than half the present area of the Triangle for the same population currently in the Triangle. Although Atlanta's sprawl has been awesome, the Triangle's has been even worse. A 260 percent population growth has been at the expense of a 944 percent areal expansion. As noted by Geary (1999), "spreading people out so thinly chews up too much land," while it provides gross inefficiencies in public infrastructure and services, let alone the costs accruing to everyone from the extended commuting ranges.

So, is there hope for open space conservation, especially in the state's large remaining rural areas? Perhaps, but only if the investors in development will begin to see open space as a limited resource and begin to see that they can more than just meet their bottom line from promoting it this way. For those anxious to see the preservation of our remaining open green spaces, the answer appears to lie in a greater effort at cultivating the development community, arguing that mutual benefits, including financial, may accrue from a land conservation policy. In this case, it could be a policy that does not exclude profitable development, especially in pre-selected places within already designated "green areas." This argument builds on the notion that consumers place great value on clean, healthy natural environments and on natural beauty and scenic areas when planning their vacations and weekend holidays. Also, there are artisans and profes-

**Photo 12.18:** Much like a large moth eating away at nature's green coat is the traditional subdivision; here feasting on North Carolina's Green Heart. Its only difference from the 1970s variety is the doubling of private home size and the greater distance to be covered by private automobile to shops, employment, and schools.

sionals who derive their inspiration from practicing within such environments. Other special groups of people may equally see an advantage to living here. These include retirees and cottage industry workers, particularly those increasingly favoring the electronic cottage as a means to their livelihood. This approach, therefore, encourages a particular form of investment, angling toward tourism, resorts, and retirement centers, with a focus on pre-existing smaller rural communities. Within existing green spaces there are attractive communities where people see most any kind of economic stimulus as welcome to their relatively narrowly defined, if not declining, rural economy. Will their hopes and expectations be met in the context of their region's designation as a "green space" economic development zone or region? Comments by a resident raising Appaloosa horses in rural Anson County, with Metrolina's urban shadow on the horizon, underscores this dilemma: "The county I live in is not exactly a rich county. Mecklenburg has its ideas of what it wants and has the mind frame that everyone else will want what it wants. But what if they don't? We need industry too if we're going to be everyone else's green space" (Henderson 1998).

### The Central Park Concept

The value of undeveloped space is precisely the pitch delivered by promoters of the Central Park Concept, an idea floated initially in 1997 by Dr. David Jones, the Director of the North Carolina Zoo. Jones envisioned a "partnership" formed among the diversity of interests found within the Central Park Region (Figure 12.11). The reality of a need for recreational, green space for Main Street's burgeoning millions, has led to a seven-county

alternative economic development strategy. Arrived at through the cooperative efforts of all stakeholders, the purpose of the strategy is to preserve rural character, visible cultural history, and natural landscapes, while developing sustainable tourism and open space recreation opportunities and attracting a range of small and environmentally benign industries to the area (Cooper 1998). Successful implementation of such a strategy should result in the protection and preservation of the unique character and assets of the region for future generations, while attracting wealth from Main Street and providing open recreational space for its urban denizens. We will consider the principals in this project, the character of the regional environment, and the changes the region has been experiencing, and then let the reader decide whether North Carolinians are ready for this scale of structured and integrated forward planning in our rural areas.

Located almost in the epicenter of the state is the North Carolina Zoo, a state-owned facility managed under the auspices of the Department of Environment and Natural Resources. The zoo's location was planned to minimize the costs of access by the largest possible number of North Carolinians. It spreads out over a rolling 1,200 acres a few miles south of Asheboro (Randolph County), just off the center of Main Street and within a two-hour drive of 60 percent of the state's population (a critical maximum distance for school busses carrying day visitors). Being one of the best designed zoological and botanical properties in the country, the North Carolina Zoo hosts upwards of 800,000 visitors annually. However, the zoo's mission reaches beyond the display of wild animals into relevant ecological habitats and pleasant surroundings. Its goals include broader based educational

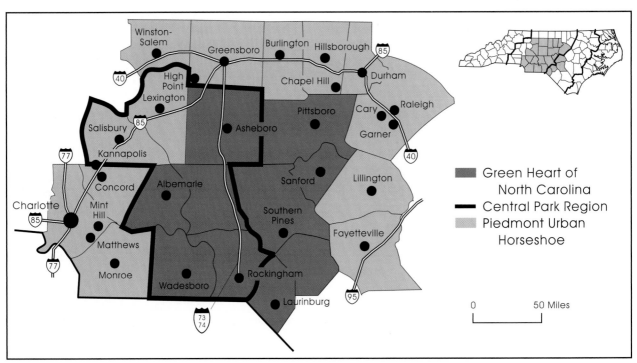

**Figure 12.11:** The Central Park Region and North Carolina's Green Heart.
**Source:** Cecchi (1999).

474

objectives focusing on conservation and management of wildlife and wild spaces, natural environment stewardship, and promotion of environmentally sound tourism. The park also is engaged in stimulating the rural quality of life through cooperative projects, "which bring together the best practices in environmental planning and stewardship together with sustainable development and wealth creation, particularly in the rural sector" (Jones 1997).

In the early 1990s, an eight county organization (Davie, Davidson, Rowan, Randolph, Stanly, Montgomery, Anson, and Richmond) was formed to help coordinate a balance between rural economic growth and environmental stewardship. Focusing on the Yadkin-PeeDee River drainage basin, the project is funded by the state legislature, local governments, and a variety of private donors. The Yadkin-PeeDee Lakes Project has funded the Land Trust for Central North Carolina, pushed for the definition and labeling of N.C. Scenic Byways and bike trails, and provides ongoing educational information and activities. Although maintaining traditional rural economic activities of agriculture and forestry is critical to the purpose of the project, so too is the search for alternative and environmentally appropriate industries, especially tourism. Success of the project is stimulated by the existence of large property owners such as the Alcoa Corporation, celebrating its 85th anniversary in 2001 as an aluminum producer on Lake Badin. The town of Badin takes its name from Adrien Badin, former president of L'Alumininium Francais, which began smelting aluminum at the site before World War I. Though condemned for earlier waste practices which befouled the lake water with high concentrations of cyanide and fluoride, Alcoa has cleaned up its environmental act, which otherwise has been dominated by an enlightened policy regarding recreational use of its water resources.

What's happening across the lake is another story. Here the 1,300 acre Uwharrie Point residential golf club development is having great success selling $35,000 interior lots to $200,000 lots fronting a denuded 17 miles of Lake Badin's shoreline (Davis 1991). While it is possible to see the tax advantages of this development for Montgomery County, a county far down the economic prosperity list in North Carolina, it is also possible to suggest that a more environmentally benign design for this gigantic residential development could have been applied in the first place. The Uwharrie Point development is owned by a partnership with its major participants in Virginia and Chapel Hill. Therefore, it is unlikely that much of the revenue stays in the local communities, a requirement for sustainable development. Apparently the absence of county defined and monitored environmentally appropriate design guidelines is an issue that Yadkin-PeeDee Lakes Project leaders will need to face as they contemplate their role in an overall management strategy for the larger Central Park Region.

The third partnership is held by the Uwharrie Capital Corporation. This is the parent body of the Bank of Stanly and other local financial institutions interested in supporting investments in sustainable business opportunities. As noted by Jones, "The Uwharrie Capital Corporation strongly believes in building on the existing rural assets by investing in ventures which will encourage people to use those assets in a sustainable way, and where the wealth generated remains within the region for the benefit of the whole community" (1997). This is certainly as powerful a statement of sustainable development purpose as we can expect to see from a business wedded to the local economy.

Success of the Central Park concept hinges on several critical factors. They include: 1) bringing in local and regional business as active participants in a natural region, resource, and community sustainable economic development effort; and 2) insuring the active participation of local communities throughout the region. It is, in fact, much easier to get support and commitment from urban interests in adjacent counties of Main Street, where the problem of decreasing open space is acute.

*North Carolina's Green Heart*

The Central Park Region is part of a larger open green space region in the center of the Main Street Horseshoe, a region we refer to in this text as The Green Heart of North Carolina. On the county level, this is portrayed in Figure 12.11, where the overlap with the Central Park Region is also identified. The Green Heart comprises natural and cultural regions in addition to those identified above (Photo 12.19). What unifies this predominantly rural, green open space is its pocket in the urban Piedmont and thus its uniform accessibility to a very large potential consumer pool. Here is found the only national forest of the Piedmont, the Uwharrie, established in 1961 as one of the nation's smallest on 43,000 acres. The Uwharrie National Forest (UNF), a hunter's haven, consists of 50 different varying-sized parcels of land scattered among private holdings in Montgomery, Randolph, and Davidson counties. "Infill" purchasing by the Forest Service increased forest acreage to 47,000 by the early 1990s (Hodge 1993). The UNF is bounded on its western side by the Uwharrie Lakes, a series of reservoirs on the Yadkin-PeeDee river system. From the north, the reservoirs include the quite large High Rock Lake (mostly in Davidson County), Lake Badin and Lake Tillery (in Stanly and Montgomery counties), and Blewett Falls Lake (in Richmond County) (CP 1.17). The PeeDee River takes over from the Yadkin at Falls Dam, a few miles south of the Badin Dam.

Other aspects of interest in the Green Heart include the Pottery District, an area with about 80 potters scattered mostly south and east of Seagrove, site of the new (1998) North Carolina Pottery Center (CP 12.23). District potters continue a tradition said to have begun in the 1700s when the British enacted a tax on colonial pottery to ensure that colonials would purchase pottery ware manufactured in Great Britain. Finding local clay amenable to their production, potters set up their trade far away from the British influence. Within a scenic rolling terrain of horse, goat, sheep, emu, and cattle farms set among fields, forests and creeks, with a renovated water mill (CP 12.24), an abandoned former county seat (Lawrenceville), and a covered bridge (Pisgah), potters have set up their studios in their own highly individualized, creative and attractive niche environments. The communities of Why Not, Westmore, Jugtown, and Erect, and adjacent areas offer a rewarding cultural tourism experience.

475

**Photo 12.19:** Along Pee Dee Valley Drive just south of Badin (Stanly County) rural residents and travelers are provided a view of Morrow Mountain rising to an elevation of 936 feet, and separated from the remainder of the Uwharrie Mountains by the Pee Dee River.

Although discussed in Chapter 11, the Sandhills are a part of the Green Heart, as is also Chatham County. Chatham is quite possibly the county experiencing the greatest local upheaval relating to encroaching urban sprawl, with growth pressure emanating south from Chapel Hill and west from Wake County communities, especially Cary. To aid in defining the rural nature of the Green Heart Region refer to Figure 12.12, which shows population per square mile for the portion of the Piedmont occupied by the Main Street Horseshoe and the Green Heart. With an average population density of about 444 people per square mile for the entire state, it is clear that the Green Heart is very thinly populated. Figure 12.13 provides a dramatic indication of where urban sprawl is most directly affecting open green spaces.

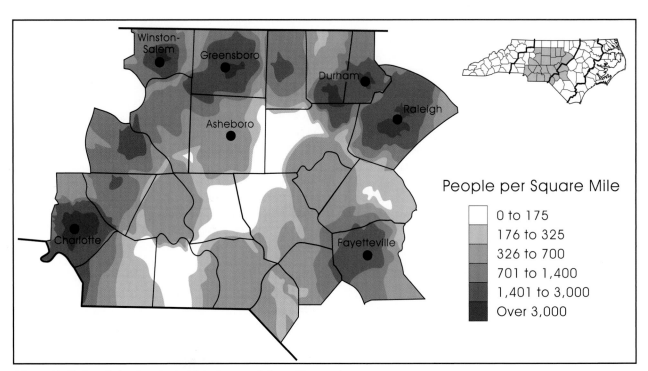

**Figure 12.12:** Population Density in Main Street and Green Heart regions.
**Source:** Cecchi (1999).

476

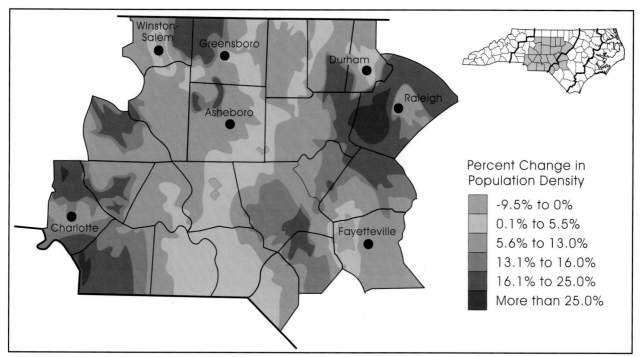

**Figure 12.13:** Population Density Change in Main Street and Green Heart regions, 1990-1997.
**Source:** Cecchi (1999).

*Sprawl*

Who Pays ?

Throughout the Piedmont, urban sprawl is pervasive, but its Green Heart is especially vulnerable. In counties, such as Union, Randolph, Chatham and Harnett, daggers of urban growth are piercing the rural perimeter. Everywhere sprawl is insidiously worming its way into green spaces beyond the urban shadow, as commuters seem to persist in demanding their rightful ownership of the last remaining acre of open space (Photos 12.17 and 12.18). Leapfrog urbanization is especially troublesome here. How can this be stopped? The simplistic answer is to cease having government subsidize urbanization so that the full costs of urban sprawl are built into public and private decisions about local land development. Subsidies for suburbia and exurbia are built into many government activities, road building being the most obvious example. Federal and state supported highways will open up new lands for urbanizing development, sprawling tract homes, and commercial strips, with 70 percent of the cost carried by all motorists paying gasoline taxes and other user fees, not just by the people who move to the new developments. The remaining 30 percent is financed by general revenues (Longman 1998). Taxpayers and motorists in Montgomery County contribute equally to paying for new outer belts in Charlotte, Winston Salem, and Raleigh. Sprawl adds other cost involving the expansion of county infrastructure, such as sewage lines, new schools, extended school bus routes, more fire stations, and other capital projects not needed if residential patterns stayed more compact. Additionally, there are the human health costs of air pollution, equally suffered by people not contributing to them, through extended commuting distances.

Are There Solutions?

Are there options available to individuals and communities? Locally, short-term moratoria on construction activity have been tried in suburbanizing counties, such as Cabarrus, Johnston, and Union. However, these tactics only slow down a process that will proceed even more vigorously when the moratoria are lifted. The north Mecklenburg towns of Cornelius, Davidson, and Huntersville, exploding in population growth, are cooperating in using growth management tools to fight sprawl, reknitting the urban fabric and giving pedestrians a fighting chance. A common view of the future as one of hectic sprawl development is pushing these towns to protect their traditional small town milieu, full of charm, intimacy, and sense of place. The towns are ready to identify future zones of focused, high-density, multiuse development, that will maintain their tradition of sidewalk cafes, neighborhood retail and restaurants, courtyard shops, and apartments above stores, all encased in an architecture and designed green space that reflects the human scale and lifts the human spirit. Such zones are logically placed along the Norfolk-Southern railway tracks that will in a few years provide mass transit to the heart of Charlotte. A 1997 N.C. General Assembly passing of the "sphere of influence" rule, granting them zoning powers within areas designated for future annexation, aided the three towns in their innovative efforts.

Local building codes and zoning regulations that traditionally favor spread-out, low density, and single-use development patterns — the essential definition of sprawl — are increasingly viewed as being in serious need of modification. Change comes very slowly, though builders and their lenders may argue that this is really where the shoe pinches. They contend that they simply follow the path of least resistance. Changes in existing government restrictions and rules, they argue, and smart growth approaches are more likely to win the land use game (Newsom 1998). Still, homebuilder associations lobby against sprawl-busting strategies, such as construction moratoria, sphere of influence zoning, and transfer of development rights.

Impact fees, making developers pay for public infrastructure needed for their home buyers and thereby transferring costs directly to the user, have not yet found firm support in North Carolina state law. Toll roads and transit taxes have little support. On the larger scale, statewide growth management plans (even when implemented as in Florida in the 1980s) have largely failed in the face of their top-down regulatory nature and stiff local opposition. Mid-level, regional management efforts may provide a potentially successful model. In Oregon, Portland's "growth boundary" has been able to contain sprawl and increase residential densities in the central city. Clearly, concerted multi-county cooperation is necessary to protect our valuable natural resources and rural communities. For example, land conservation efforts spearheaded by the Yadkin-PeeDee Lakes Project are notable and laudable, but need expansion of purpose and region served to encompass the entire Green Heart. Efforts of individual citizens are credible as well; as discussed in Chapter 8, private land trusts are fundamental to land conservation and smart growth. In the Green Heart, the Conservation Trust for North Carolina network includes: Catawba Lands Conservancy, Land Trust for Central North Carolina, Piedmont Land Conservancy, and the Eno River Association. Individuals may contribute land, monetary, and leadership support to these organizations that are at, "the forefront of local community efforts to save vital green space and natural areas" (Roe 2000). Local conservationists still recall with horror proposals pursued during the Reagan administration to sell most of the Uwharrie National Forest to private interests!

*Smart Growth Strategies*

On a practical business decision level, it is notable that the current restructuring of the state's economy is attracting major capital investments and employees into a state that has traditionally been viewed as rural and with affable environmental conditions favoring a positive quality of life. As noted above, all aspects of this view are now seriously being contested. Nurturing of the state's more traditional quality of life image by appropriate business and state development interests will be needed for out-of-state investors and prospective employees to continue to find favor with the state. In 1999, in response to a widely acknowledged deteriorating situation, the State General Assembly appointed a North Carolina Smart Growth Commission with the task of defining a smart growth toolbox — a menu of planning techniques, local land use regulations, and taxes that should be available to local governments. In essence, this is an effort to begin empowering local growth management within more broadly elaborated state directives. Representing a cross-section of interests, the Commission struggled to reconcile widely divergent ideas for toolbox content. By early 2001, broad based agreement has been reached on the following important recommendations (Stradling 2001 b):

1) Growth should be planned and local governments should be encouraged to coordinate plans with their neighbors;

2) The state should make decisions concerning roads and other state spending that are consistent with local plans;

3) More funds should be made available to protect farmland and to help build affordable housing;

4) Wetlands and beaches must be better protected;

5) In center cities, more schools should be built, older buildings should be reused, and government should favor locating its new buildings here; and

6) Communities than plan in careful anticipation of growth should be given the necessary power to enact new kinds of development restrictions and regulations and to levy taxes and fees to pay for local schools, parks, roads, alternative modes of access, and sidewalks.

Concerning point 6, it should be noted that North Carolina is a Dillon Rule state. This rule insists that local governments seek legislative approval for powers not specifically granted them under the annotated state code.

There were many other recommendations of perhaps lesser significance, or facing greater difficulties in legislative passage, especially in 2001, a year of economic retrenchment. The weight of these recommendations favored passing on to local governments the opportunity, if not the responsibility, to act decisively in dealing with development pressures and sprawl on their own terms. Thus, the Assembly is expected to act on a range of legislation enabling greater local autonomy.

On a smaller scale it is easier for landowners, developers, and communities to adopt smart growth initiatives (CP 12.12). In various parts of the Piedmont and elsewhere in the state, the following appear to be catching on in varying dimensions:

Farmland Preservation. This may involve owners of farmland to sell or grant the rights of developing their land to local governments or to provide a permanent conservation easement to a legal conservator, who then monitors the easement agreement. A number of Piedmont counties (Wake, Orange, and Durham) have adopted Farmland Preservation ordinances. However, in spite of the hefty tax benefits and cash payments to participants, there have been few takers. Likely, the reality of preservation being forever — neither present nor future owners can develop the land — is the cause for the reluctance to participate. An absence of dedicated local government funding probably contributed to this sentiment (as in the case of Mecklenburg County where voters in the 1980s approved millions in bonds, only to see their county commission under pressure by developers refuse to issue the bonds). And yet, in adjacent Alamance and Chatham counties, farmers are themselves responding to recent threats of land conversion in their midst by taking action to donate or sell easements to the Piedmont Land Conservancy of Greensboro. Five farmers in the Sutphin Community of Chatham County ensured that themselves or future owners would never develop their land held in easements. Saying that farmers are their own best neighbors, ten more farmers are now considering a similar option. It is hoped that 1,500 to 2,000 acres in the community will be preserved (Stradling 2001a). Typical easement provisions include:

1) Owners may not use the property for anything not specifically listed in the contracted easement, without the expressed permission of the conservator (county/land trust, etc.);

2) Officials may monitor property use at any time;

3) Owners with timber rights must maintain an approved forest management plan; and

4) Best management practices protecting water and air quality must be followed by owners (Barrett 2000).

In Metrolina, some landowners have opted to donate their land. An example is a 198 acre portion of a historic north Iredell County farm, the Daltonia Plantation. Including a plantation house built in 1857, and surrounded by log buildings from an earlier period, working fields and hardwood forests, the property was placed on the National Register of Historic Places in 1976 (Wrinn 1999). It now has an easement that protects it from commercial development and strictly limits residential development. The land is not being opened to public use, but may be deeded or sold to heirs. In the Triangle, planners are hoping for more landowners to initiate a process, that once begun is thought to be capable of rapidly escalating. On the other hand, northern Mecklenburg County appears en route to becoming a hornets' nest of sprawl busters. Here Cornelius, Huntersville, and Davidson's efforts at keeping sprawl at bay are supported by owners of large land parcels adjoining Ramah Creek and the new Cornelius-Davidson-Huntersville District Park. Six landowners have now signed 531 acres over to permanent conservation easements with the Catawba Lands Conservancy, limiting all future development to one house per 25 acres. Here, the land easement approach is becoming contagious, with an expected addition of up to 1,500 acres over the next two to three years and at no cost to the taxpayers (Henderson 2001b). A further wind in the sails for land preservation is the state's Farmland Preservation Trust Fund, which until 1999 was without allocated funds. With its first state assembly allocation of $1.7 million, the Trust Fund protected twelve easements totaling 1,981 acres (Brookings 2000, 19).

Transfer of Development Rights. As discussed above, farmland preservation can occur by public or private interests providing funds for farmland development rights through conservation easements. It is also possible to establish Transfer of Development Rights programs, whereby zones for agriculture and for more intensive development are delimited. Developers then may obtain permission to build in designated development areas in exchange for purchasing development rights in the agricultural zone.

New Urbanism. This provides a conceptual framework that captures a number of new smart growth approaches. Essentially the objective is to encourage subdivisions that have the look and feel of a small town. New urbanism is designed to narrow street pathways and to eliminate cul-de-sacs; to provide sidewalks, curbing, foot paths, bike trails, public open green spaces, playgrounds, and schools; to have higher densities and compact residential areas that include affordable housing; and to integrate commercial work places and other compatible uses with residential neighborhoods, so as to effectively reduce automotive dependence. In other words, mix and tighten the use of land in new developments. Eschew sprawl. Everywhere in the Piedmont developers are using some or all of these parameters in providing new and higher quality living arrangements. One of the leading examples in the state is Southern Village in Chapel Hill (CP 12.13a-d). Its design features narrow streets, public use areas (including a school, church, stores, and a movie theater), and variable housing densities that include single and multi-family housing and rental apartments. A second example is the smaller scaled Vermillion subdivision in Huntersville (Mecklenburg County), which was highlighted as one of 52 nationally best examples of smart growth by the Sierra Club in 2000. Many other smart growth design communities are in the planning stages. Some, such as Carpenter Village in Cary, focus on high-density, functionally integrated centers in preexisting downtowns. New urbanism approaches in existing urban environments can be hard-sell propositions, as residents of neighborhoods fight larger buildings, new streets, and public walkways that seem to threaten their present habitat. In Mayor Kincaid's published response to local landowners protesting Davidson's new approach to land use planning, the Mayor noted:

New urbanism is really just common sense. Combining cluster developments, open space, and a mix of uses minimizes the drawbacks of the conventional subdivision. These developments permit us to walk to more places, thereby decreasing our automobile dependence. And most importantly, new urbanism holds the promise of building community. . . . In new urbanism, open space naturally follow from cluster development. By putting all the development on one half of the land, we can leave undisturbed the creek banks, the hardwood forests and the steep slopes. Instead of cutting those treasurers into multiple private lots, we leave them for all to enjoy. Rather than devaluing property, I believe that new urbanism makes property more valuable. Many developers and consultants agree. Well-planned, walk-able communities draw more buyers, who bid up the price of the land (Kincaid 2001).

New behemoth subdivisions in the Triangle and Metrolina, such as Ballantyne (south of Charlotte) and Wakefield (north of Raleigh; Photo 12.15), qualify on some counts, but least on that which is most significant. They eliminate neither suburban sprawl nor automotive dependency. They are mixed-use, mostly high-end exclusive developments, accessible to outer beltways, and include golf courses. In shear size they qualify as independent towns, except for the absence of work places, so commuting is required. Other new large-scale developments, such as Southpoint between Durham and Chapel Hill, continue the traditional suburban pattern, in this case of building a 1.3 million square feet mega-mall, large box discount retail, offices, and apartments in an area already festooned with single family home subdivisions.

### The Catawba River Basin

The Piedmont is blessed with a generally wet climate, supplemented by waters draining the Appalachian Mountains. Extensive river basins topographically lend themselves to harnessing water power, industrial and municipal water use, and public recreation, while facilitating the dilution and degradation of sewage and industrial/municipal waste water. Nowhere are the complexities of the human-natural interface better demonstrated than in the Catawba River Basin. The Catawba River emanates from the joining of smaller creeks just west of Black Mountain (Buncombe County). Flowing northeast of Marion, the stream becomes a river as the steep slopes of the Blue Ridge Escarpment provide a catchment zone extending from Mount Mitchell to Blowing Rock. Along this journey, the Catawba is joined by the Swannanoa, North Fork Catawba, Linville, and Johns rivers, along with a multitude of creeks; these streams are famous for their rugged gorges and waterfalls, mostly confined within the Pisgah National Forest. The river traverses 440 miles from the western North Carolina Piedmont to the South Carolina coast north of Charleston. In western North Carolina, the Catawba passes through a large concentration of industries, mostly textiles and furniture, before turning due south toward Gastonia and Charlotte. While the river extends along a corridor of some 225 miles from Lake James to the South Carolina border, the tributary streams of the Catawba Basin total 3,100 miles in length. An estimated 1.7 million people inhabit the North Carolina portion of the Catawba River's 5,000 square mile drainage basin. As a result of early industrialization and energy needs, the Catawba became "the most electrified river in the United States" at the turn of the

20th century, initiating the rise of Duke Power Company as one of the country's leading energy producers. Among the eleven reservoirs created along the Catawba, seven are within North Carolina: from west to east are Lake James, Rhodhiss Lake, Lake Hickory, Lookout Shoals Lake, and then turning south, Lake Norman, Mountain Island Lake, and Lake Wylie.

The earliest dam was built on Lake Wylie in 1904, and the latest was Cowan's Ford Dam at the southern terminus of Lake Norman. No less than thirteen Duke Power dams straddle and interrupt the flow of the Catawba along the company's controlled 224 miles of the river. Almost the entire river is now contained in reservoirs (Henderson 2000a). It has been suggested that a bucket of water dropped into Lake James will now take at least a year to reach Lake Wylie. Although the dams and reservoirs were created for the purpose of hydroelectric power generation, a multitude of usages have evolved in concert with power generation. Lake Norman was constructed in 1963, to support Duke Power's earlier developments: 3,200 acre Mountain Island Lake (1923) and 12,000 acre Lake Wylie (1925). Lake Norman is 32,000 acres in size, largest in North Carolina, with a shoreline of some 520 miles. Powerboats and jet-skis compete with water skiing, swimming, sailing, fishing, and more contemplative pursuits, while the lake's waters are used by adjacent municipalities and as cooling water for Duke's McGuire Nuclear Power Station. Meanwhile, Duke Energy Company's real estate arm, Crescent Land Resources, is busily dividing the shoreline into innumerable housing tracts, mostly for expensive homes.

Exemplifying the popularity of lake living are the skyrocketing land values. Property with homes that sold for $20,000 in 1971, now sell for $100,000 and new homes will be expensive in order to sustain the high lot costs. In addition, lakeside property owners expect to be able to build boat piers. In 1998, Duke Energy permitted 1,590 new piers along its Catawba Lake shores, a 77 percent increase over the prior year. Large-scale developments on Lake Norman, such as Crescent Resources' yacht and golf course community, The Peninsula, began selling in the early nineties. Several very large scale communities are now being planned, one for 4,000 homes on Lake Wylie (Griffin 1998). In the westernmost part of the reservoir system, Lake James (of *The Last of the Mohicans* motion picture fame and relatively pristine for so long that Burke County residents have been taking the natural condition for granted) is now seeing ten Crescent Land Resources developments, ranging in size from ten to 260 lots. Of course, where entire lakes are privately owned, as in the case of Lake Tahoma upstream from Lake James, an entirely different set of parameters guide their usage (CP 12.32).

Lakeside suburbs, with their associated problems of access and amenities resulting from an irregular and strung out physical character are rapidly expanding all along the Duke (Catawba River) lakes. Buyers of land on the reservoirs should perhaps reflect on the fact that permanence of any particular hydroelectric reservoir cannot be guaranteed. Some power companies have been induced to take down older dams, as in the case of the Carolina Power and Light Company's removal of a

Neuse River dam to reestablish a flowing river and to aid seasonal fish migration (Chapter 11). The bottom of a former lake looks rather desolate to residents located along a former shoreline. Similarly, relicensing agreements have elsewhere resulted in increasing water flow between reservoirs to accommodate fish stocks and river sports, consequently decreasing lake water levels. In addition, dammed lakes have an unerring tendency to fill with sediments over time, more rapidly in areas of more steeply sloped drainage basin land. Lake Rhodhiss, for example, has lost about 40 percent of its volume to sediments.

Duke Power Company was given a comprehensive federal license to manage the water and related land resources of the Catawba River Basin in 1958, a license that is up for renewal in 2008. Conditions of these licensing agreements have changed. Now the Federal Energy Regulatory Commission (FERC) is interested in seeing the need for electricity production balanced with the impact on the environment. Specifically, Duke must show justification for diverting a public resource, the Catawba River, to usages that benefit its stockholders. Early evidence of difficulties that the corporation may have with other users of the Catawba River and lakes was shown in the initial reaction to its proposed shoreline management plan (presented to FERC in March 2001), an update of the 1994 version. Plan objectives are to guide placement of marinas, piers, and dredging operations along 1,635 miles of shoreline. Although the new plan calls for an increase from 15 to 24 percent of the shoreline in natural areas unsuitable for development, it also adds 22 percent of shoreline, formerly classed as undeveloped, to future commercial or residential development. Presently, 39 percent of the total shoreline is occupied by residential or business structures. Most lake marine commissions and environmental watchdog groups are demanding that development not exceed 50 percent of the shorelines of any of the lakes. As indicated in Table 12.1, it is clear that Duke Energy is preparing for an eventual 80 percent development of Lake Norman's shore and well over 50 percent shoreline development for the remaining lakes. Duke Energy does not appear to be responding to the sentiment voiced by the Catawba Riverkeeper support group that future shoreline usages should be confined to, "maximize the scenic, aesthetic, environmental and recreational values at the expense of developmental values, not the other way around" (Henderson 2001a, 3B). This attitude is well supported across the board by the various public interest groups, as well as by local and regional governments. Still, in December of 2000, the FERC agreed to Duke Energy's proposed balance of shoreline classifications.

Public interest groups also criticize Duke Energy for not playing a larger and more sensitive role in total river basin management, acting, as it does, within a set of limited parameters defined by its energy needs. The company is rejecting a more active role in assessing increased sewage discharges and increased sedimentation loads of streams flowing into the lakes system and in showing concern for the impacts of a built out shoreline. However, the failure to arrive at a total vision of what the entire Catawba River Basin should look like cannot be laid solely at the door of Duke Energy. There is a multiplicity of other public and private interests involved here and little success has resulted from efforts to establish some kind of joint basin authority. Smaller scale, multi-jurisdictional agreements have been reached, including Catawba and Burke counties reaching an agreement on the amount of Lake James shoreline they will permit

| Shoreline Classification | Lake Name | | | | | | |
|---|---|---|---|---|---|---|---|
| | James | Rhodhiss | Hickory | Lookout Shoals | Norman | Mountain Island | Wylie |
| Commercial/Nonresidential | 1 | 0 | 1 | 0 | 1 | 0 | 2 |
| Commercial/Residential | 3 | 0 | 2 | 3 | 4 | 1 | 1 |
| Residential | 9 | 0 | 47 | 19 | 53 | 10 | 41 |
| Business/Industrial | 0 | 0 | 1 | 0 | 0 | 0 | 1 |
| Public Recreation | 1 | 0 | 1 | 0 | 0.4 | 0 | 1 |
| Public Infrastructure | 1 | 1 | 2 | 2 | 3 | 11 | 5 |
| Project Operations | 2 | 1 | 1 | 5 | 1 | 4 | 0 |
| Future Commercial/Nonresidential | 41 | 26 | 6 | 14 | 3 | 0 | 3 |
| Future Commercial/Residential | 3 | 2 | 12 | 5 | 7 | 11 | 7 |
| Future Residential | 11 | 5 | 6 | 5 | 6 | 3 | 5 |
| Future Public Recreation | 7 | 2 | 3 | 6 | 5 | 21 | 3 |
| Impact Minimization Zones | 6 | 2 | 2 | 10 | 2 | 5 | 3 |
| Environmental Areas | 11 | 21 | 16 | 20 | 12 | 32 | 20 |
| Natural Areas | 6 | 38 | 0 | 11 | 1 | 2 | 7 |

**Notes:** Values are percentage of shoreline; these may change as plan is completed; numbers may not total 100 percent because of rounding.

**Table 12.1:** Duke Energy Company's Catawba Lakes' Shoreline Classification.
**Source:** Duke Energy, Draft Shoreline Management Plan Update (Henderson 2001a).

being developed (CP 12.14). On the other hand, 12 of the 28 municipalities/communities in the Catawba River watershed are expecting to be beyond their ability to provide adequate industrial and public water within 20 years (Henderson 2000c).

Individual municipalities often make independent decisions based on their perception of local needs. Charlotte, for example, is now doubling its municipal drinking water pumping capacity on Mountain Island Lake to 330 million gallons daily, more water than the aggregate pump capability of the rest of the communities on the eleven lakes. Yet, the city does not find it necessary to consult with its watershed neighbors on so dramatic an increase. The remarkable situation of Statesville is a further case in point. Having slashed by one quarter the amount of water the city could take from the nearly exhausted South Yadkin River in 2000, the state left the city no alternative but to look elsewhere for its drinking water. Statesville's response was to plan a water intake on Lookout Shoals Lake on the adjacent Catawba watershed, a plan that other users of water up and down the Catawba learned about by reading their morning paper! In Alexander County, which controls 24,000 acres next to Lookout Shoals Lake (while Iredell County controls only 2,100 acres), the reaction has bordered on the violent. Watershed maps that indicate limits for development and needing approval by the Alexander County Commission were denied by the Commission even though it was under threat of being fined $10,000 daily by the N. C. Division of Water Quality.

Duke Energy Company is getting a bit edgy about the persistent increase in water draw down and has requested FERC to place a cap on Charlotte's yearly intake from Mountain Island Lake. Before Charlotte's intake enlargement, Mountain Island Lake provided drinking water for 600,000 people in Gaston and Mecklenburg counties. The Catawba lakes were built for power generation, not for being drained by municipal and industrial water needs (presently 500 million gallons daily maximum) and then being filled by wastewater and treated sewage (of which 400 million gallons daily is currently permitted). However, actual daily withdrawals and discharges are much smaller than allowable. What is especially critical is the increasing amount of raw sewage accidentally spilled into the Catawba River Basin each year. In 1999, for example, nine million gallons of raw sewage overflowed from the collector system of sewage pipes and conduits in about 500 incidents. Of this total, about 3.5 million gallons flowed into feeder streams and lakes (Henderson 2000a). In this area, the center of the textile industry in the state, an additional problem is the continuing outpouring of textile dye waste. The South Fork Catawba River is called Rainbow River due to the range of water coloration from raspberry red to deep purple caused by concentrations of varying colored textile dies. For Charlotte, an even greater headache may result from its serious pollution of downstream waters. Although water quality drops steadily from Lake James to Mountain Island Lake, the quality decrease is greatest as the Catawba picks up the treated sewage and frequent spillage from Charlotte's and Gastonia's waste water treatment plants. In South Carolina, lakes are ladened with algae growth from the excess nutrients; home communities on the shores of

Lake Wateree feel victimized by Charlotte. As indicated by Henderson (2000b), persuading local governments to let go of control of their share of the Catawba River is a key to future success in sustainably allocating the river's water resources. This suggests that the most critical problem for water resources management in the Catawba Basin is the fact that no one seems to have the overall picture in view. Separate municipalities and counties regulate the use of water and the discharge of wastewater, but overall management of the lakes, which define the entire system, is by a private energy company that simultaneously is the major lake front developer.

What is needed for the Catawba River Basin is a regional/interstate compact that will allow cooperative decision making on key issues affecting the well being of the basin's people and the continuing integrity of its natural environment. A compact will allow an integrated management approach to the resolution of issues, such as how much drinking water to withdraw at specific locations, where treated sewage is to be discharged, how the water resource should be protected against runoff and sedimentation loads from construction, agricultural, and logging practices, and how much land should be allowed to be developed for various purposes along the shoreline in perpetuity. Guaranteeing local and regional governments their appropriate representation on a Catawba River Basin Commission should counter any concerns they might have of their minor loss in sovereignty needed to facilitate integrated water resources planning and management. Elsewhere in the country, water resource planning is approached in this manner, the Susquehanna River Basin Commission providing a model example. Here three states, New York, Pennsylvania, and Maryland, have formed a successful interstate compact, working in a consensual manner in water allocation, in the preparation of long range plans, and in crisis control of flooding and drought conditions. The time is opportune, not only in the context of the need to deal effectively, immediately, and in a future focused fashion with the welter of Catawba River Basin issues discussed above, but also because Duke Energy's 2008 deadline to renew its license for the eleven Catawba River hydroelectric power plants will allow citizen and local government input on the character of river management (Henderson 2001c). Perhaps the truly greater problem for this region is the persistent failure to act on the obvious need for integrated river basin management.

***Other Water Resource Issues***

*The Water Crises in Cary and Other Piedmont Cities*

Other water resource issues surface for increasingly crowded Piedmont communities. Acute water shortages are a reality through much of Main Street; in some places shortages are seasonal in nature, in others they are becoming endemic with increasing population growth and urban sprawl. Cary (Wake County) experienced the most explosive population boom of any community in North Carolina during the 1990s (Photo 12.20). As a crossroads town, it reached a population of 7,000 in 1970 (on three square miles of land); twenty years later the population stood at 43,000. Then came the peopling deluge of the final decade of the century, with the population reaching 94,536 in 2000 (now on 40 square miles of land). By the mid-90s, it was becoming clear that the town was unable to meet the basic needs of the uncontrolled expansion of residential areas. Especially problematic were the pricey new subdivisions with high expectations of urban amenities such as swimming pools and expansive lawns. In many cases, lawns of individual homes were outfitted with $3,000 irrigation systems set to automatically spray water for one hour every other day at the rate of 860 gallons per hour. In the meantime, Cary has to build two new wastewater treatment plants after spilling treated water into Lake Jordan. However, in the absence of overall careful planning, resources were rapidly being depleted without proper budgeting for new facilities (i.e., sewage plants, landfills, schools, etc).

Gradually, conservation ideas are being considered and implemented. For example, ameliorating the treated wastewater problem has been an increasing use of the so-called "reclaimed" or recycled water. Although filtered and chemically treated so that it is clear and odorless, reclaimed water is still not fit to drink because of its trace amount of coliform bacteria and other pollutants. However, it can be used very profitably to irrigate golf courses and lawns. Reclaimed water also can be used in manufacturing processes as cooling water in industrial plants, fighting fires, street cleaning, dust control at construction sites, and decorative fountains. At least ten municipalities, including Cary, are now in the process of installing pipes through which to transfer reclaimed water (Rawlins 1996). Still, in the spring of 1999, Cary was forced to impose a moratorium on new home and building permits, because no more water was available for additional hookups. Although receiving twelve million gallons of water daily

from a Jordan Lake water treatment plant jointly owned with Apex, itself in a growth spurt, Cary had to negotiate water contracts with Durham and Raleigh for an additional eight million gallons daily. When an unusually long 1999 summer dry spell hit the Triangle, the flow of drinking water from Durham and Raleigh ceased. With a 40 percent cut in what was already a severely strained system, a serious water crisis was at hand in Cary. Pro-growth leaders declined to run for reelection to the town council and proponents of slow growth management now rule the town. Stressed Piedmont municipalities increasingly consider new approaches to growth management. Growth caps and building moratoria now provide needed time for these communities to breathe and to reassess the pressure of residential expansion, assuring that new families can be adequately served by existing public facilities and resources.

Greensboro has suffered a periodic lack of drinking water much longer than has Cary. The city has been supported by Winston-Salem's abundance of water from the upper Yadkin River, but officials have worried that continued expansion of growth throughout the Piedmont Triad will make this connection tenuous and unpredictable. One result has been a request to share the waters of Lake Jordan, owned by the state and dispersed to needing communities. Part of the Neuse River drainage basin, the lake was filled in the early 1980s. Presently, a state commission has allocated about 44 percent of the lake's available drinking water. The cities and towns in the Triad have gotten accustomed to thinking of Lake Jordan as being exclusively their water resource. Not so, says the State, maintaining that this is a regional resource with Greensboro, and even downstream Fayetteville, as eligible as any other city in this larger region to receive an allocation. In late 2000, the State's Environmental Management Commission (EMC) was getting ready to allocate

Photo 12.20: A wall mural of Cary (Wake County) in an earlier day. A city of about 100,000 people Cary literally exploded during the 1990s and in the process has completely left its downtown behind, though some flicker of life is being re-ignited. Most notably a fine restoration of its railroad station, a stop on north-south Amtrak routes, and a planned commuter stop for the expected Piedmont Triangle regional rail system.

the remaining 56 percent to applicant water users, including Chatham County, Durham, Wake County, Cary, Apex, and Morrisville, in addition to Fayetteville and Greensboro. One outcome of this EMC allocation process was the controversial March, 2001, proposal to let three Wake County towns transfer eleven million gallons of drinking water daily from Lake Jordan (the Cape Fear River basin) to the Neuse River basin (Figure 1.11). Wilmington was immediately up in arms, but the city, expecting to meet its future and expanded water needs from the Cape Fear River, might well learn from the earlier Virginia Beach experience in river basin water transfer. Virginia Beach now is transferring up to 60 million gallons of water from Lake Gaston (Roanoke River basin), much to the anguish of both upstream and downstream users in North Carolina, which sued Virginia Beach and lost (Chapter 11).

Greensboro has a more promising future in attaining needed drinking water. This will come through the completion of the Randleman Dam, being built near where US 221 crosses the Deep River some ten miles south of Greensboro. Planned in the early 1970s to provide for the expected 21$^{st}$ Century drinking water needs of Piedmont Triad municipalities, Randleman Reservoir will have a shoreline of 110 miles with the Piedmont Triad Water Authority owning a 200-foot buffer width around the lake. Only those homes already existing in the area will be permitted next to the lake, if the Authority has not already bought them. No new subdivisions, piers, or shoreline restaurants will be allowed. That it is taking close to three decades to place a new reservoir on line in the Piedmont demonstrates the dilemma of acquiring the considerable acreage needed to supply drinking water to inhabitants of a region whose growth and development sprawl is simultaneously limiting that needed acreage. Such large-scale land assembly is an increasingly difficult and costly process and building dams is very expensive. Only one other recent example exists of a successful acquisition of reservoir land in the entire Piedmont. Planning also has been ongoing for about three decades for the 1,500 acre Little River Reservoir (about 1/10$^{th}$ the size of Lake Jordan) as a water source for growing eastern Wake County municipalities, including Knightdale, Wendell, and Zebulon. Initial land purchase of acreage needed, in 1995, was at a cost of $3,300/acre, well in excess of per acre funds allocated initially by the local governments to purchase all the acreage required. This case is a clear example of the effects of sprawl in driving up rural land prices and the inability of local government to adequately predict these land use changes. Additional costs will be incurred by buying buffer zones and parkland around the proposed lake, not to speak of the current estimated $40 million cost for the dam itself (Rawlins 1995).

It is perhaps odd to discuss in the same breath as water shortages caused by over-development the problem of flooding that results from the same development. As sprawl continues, the danger of flooding mounts with increasing surface coverage by impervious materials, often structural facilities, such as homes, malls, industries, or roadways. Simultaneously, natural areas, with the capability of excess water absorption and a gradual release of this excess into aquifers, streams, and lakes are being reduced.

Homes built today may well be higher in elevation than an earlier designated 100-year flood level. However, due to a proportional increase in surface impermeability in the drainage basin, a more rapid surface runoff results in a greater frequency of floods at higher elevations than thought likely. Flood zones have changed for the worse. In this way, the 100-year flood level has risen by five to ten feet in many of our peripheral urban neighborhoods.

*Green Buffer Zones*

Creeks and streams have been receiving increasing attention for: 1) their role in channeling storm water (flood control) and thus the need for bank stabilization with plant life rather than rip rap (crushed stone); 2) restoration of water quality to swimmable standards; 3) green buffer zones protecting against polluted water runoff (CP 12.15); 4) the facilitating of greenways; and 5) the even larger and costly issue of stream channel restoration. In Mecklenburg County, there are an estimated 3,000 miles of creek channels, very few of which are being managed to insure any of the listed conditions, as indeed is the case for most of the remainder of the state's streams. Most cities now incorporate greenway systems into their comprehensive plan process. Raleigh presently lists 27 designated greenway trails, with another seven on the way. Mecklenburg County's Greenway Plan expects to see the development of 185 miles of paths that meander through floodplains and along stream beds where buffer zones are most apt to be designated (Figure 12.14). These walking/biking trails connect neighborhood and city district parks, schools, and other activity areas mostly along existing streams and rivers. Many of these streams have recently been restored from a former existence in underground concrete and composite materials conduits. This opening of the green landscape in Piedmont cities is one of the most aesthetically pleasing and environmentally sound aspects of contemporary urban change.

In recent years the State has moved imaginatively and effectively to deal with these water resource problems. A Clean Water Management Trust Fund (CWMTF), created and well funded by the General Assembly in 1996, provides substantial grants every year for a variety of projects, including stream side buffers, runoff controls, and full scale restoration. (See Box 8A for a directory of CWMTF project categories.) In the Piedmont in 1998, the CWMTF committed to a six-year, $36 million program to turn strips of farmland adjacent to the Neuse and other rivers into forested buffer zones. Sadly, from a conservationist perspective, the CWMTF must have funds allocated each budget cycle, with strong protests over this use of tax money raised in the General Assembly each cycle. In 1998, it was estimated that it would cost $11 billion to bring the state's water and sewer systems into the 21$^{st}$ century. Other state agencies are getting into the act, as in the case of the Department of Transportation contribution of funds to construct bike paths on greenways. On the other hand, that same department is moving to expropriate property to four-lane NC 16 in northwestern Gaston County adjacent to Mountain Island Lake, a 20 acre slice of land which is part of a 1,200 acre section bought earlier in 1999 by Gaston and Lincoln

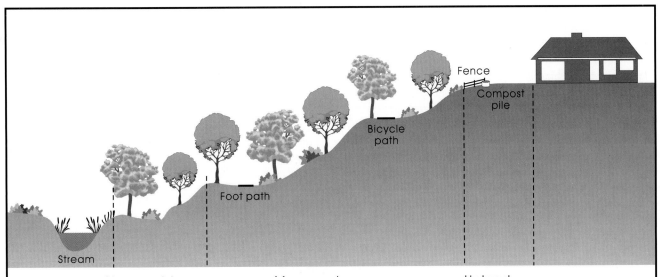

## Stream-side Zone

Protects the physical integrity of the stream
Undisturbed, mature forest; trees could be replanted if the area has been disturbed.
Very restricted use limited to flood control and bank stabilization; land disturbances not permitted except for specific uses when no practical alternative exists.

## Managed-use Zone

Provides distance between upland development and the stream-side zone.
Managed forest, with some clearing allowed.
Restricted uses limited to some recreation, greenway trails, bike paths, and storm-water control structures.

## Upland Zone

Prevents encroachment and filters backyard runoff.
Usually grass, but trees are encouraged.
Limited to lawns, gardens, paved trails, storage buildings, and stormwater control structures; no homes or commercial buildings allowed.

Stream buffers can reduce pollution from eroding soil, lawn fertilizers, motor vehicle oil, grease, and other sources.
Possible reduction of pollutants:
    Sediment - 75%
    Nitrogen - 40%
    Metals - 60%
    Hydrocarbons - 75%

### Buffer Widths

| Drainage Basin Area | Stream-side Zone | Managed-use Zone | Upland Zone | Total Buffer |
|---|---|---|---|---|
| 100 - 300 acres | 20 feet | none | 15 feet | 35 feet |
| 300 - 640 acres | 20 feet | 20 feet | 10 feet | 50 feet |
| More than 640 acres | 30 feet | 45 feet | 25 feet + 50% of flood fringe area | At least 100 feet |

**Figure 12.14:** An Exemplification of Mecklenburg County's Stream Buffer Rules.
**Source:** Adapted from Henderson (2000c).

counties from Crescent Land Resources to prevent its use for development (Dodd 1999). Conditioned by a state-placed conservation easement against future development, the 1,200 acres were acquired through a $3.6 million grant from CWMTF. Now Gaston County refuses to sell the watershed land to the DOT, leaving that department only two options: either reroute the highway (at considerable additional cost) or go to the Council of State (made up of the governor, attorney general, and other state executives) with the request to violate the conservation easement. Meanwhile, Lincoln County residents fume because their long awaited road widening project is further delayed. This con-

flict is an example of the perils that result from the absence of regionally integrated water basin planning!

### Private Wells and Public Water Systems

Surface waters, made available by public water systems, provide only 50 percent of the state's drinking water. Although one half of the state's population relies on wells, these wells are primarily concentrated in the western half of the Piedmont (Figure 8.5). Herein lies another major problem. Well tests, resulting from user complaints, demonstrate that between 25 to 30 percent of private and community well systems are contaminated to a degree that it can impair personal health. Not a small contributor to this particular problem is the more than 775 closed landfills that are spread across the state. Most of these predate environmental requirements for liners and enclosed systems that collected the water seeping through the landfill. It is this leachate that is capable of polluting local wells. (Concerned readers may wish to consult the state's database of 14,000 groundwater sites at http://gw.dehnr.state.nc.us/, for the latest update on known contaminated sites.)

Today's landfills adhere to strict regulations. They are almost odor free, are lined, and most are quite large and technologically up to date. From the 500 active landfills of the 1970s, there are now only 30 active sites in the state in 2001. However, the earlier very negative image continues to haunt plans for installing new landfills. Citizens in counties where landfills are being proposed are moving from an active NIMBY (not in my backyard) attitude to one the can be characterized as more BANANA (build absolutely nothing anywhere near anyone) in nature, a devastating problem for local governments having to deal with waste disposal. A case in point is the current problems in finding adequate new landfill sites in the Piedmont Triangle. Following the opposition to proposed installation in Harnett and Wake counties, a 200-acre proposed landfill in southeastern Chatham County was vigorously protested by a well-organized public, and then denied by the county commission in early 2001. How citizens can defend such diehard attitudes in the face of their personal annual production of household wastes totaling 2,000 tons per year is the question. Even as we are producing more trash, we become more hostile to having it disposed in our own communities. Well, the neighbors do not want it either.

In 1999, about 1,000 wells were dug in the state, many of these suffering from shoddy construction that allowed noxious materials in adjacent soils to seep into the wells (Figure 8.4). This deplorable situation caused the North Carolina Home Builders Association to recommend a licensing procedure for well diggers, a recommendation that resulted in a state mandate for licensing all well diggers beginning in January 2000. In the past, anyone wanting to start a well drilling business simply had to pay a $50 filing fee. Now, requiring well diggers to take an exam and have considerable prior experience is a major improvement in guaranteeing the construction of satisfactory wells. Lamentably, the State is not providing the inspectors needed to certify the installation process. Additionally, many wells have been placed in soils already plagued by contamination. In Gaston County, one community was discovered to have 10 to 25 times the safe level of trichloroethylene (TCE) in the ground water. This site was added by the Environmental Protection Agency to its Superfund list. Homes in the community are now being connected to the Gastonia public water system at an estimated cost of $3.8 million to the federal government.

### Cooleemee: The Day the Air Was Unfit to Breathe

An article in the *Winston-Salem Journal* on problems of air pollution by Frank Tursi (2000) began with a focus on the sad state of atmospheric conditions that occurred in the Yadkin Valley some miles south of Winston-Salem.

It was an ill wind that shifted on Aug. 13, 1999, and blew back on the little town of Cooleemee in Davie County. It had been out of the northeast the previous day, carrying car and truck exhaust and smokestack pollutants from Winston-Salem and Greensboro on by. A southwest wind the next day, though, brought it all back, along with pollution from Charlotte to the south. This noxious brew of chemicals cooked in the hot sun, which drove temperatures that day to near 100 degrees, and turned to smog that settled like a haze over the Yadkin River Valley. Little Cooleemee got slammed.

Subsequent assessment of the pollution intensity showed this to be the nation's third worst example of smog and ozone concentration during 1999, with only Houston and Atlanta having had an occurrence of higher concentrations that year. Note that this measurement was taken in Cooleemee, a town with scarcely 1,000 people and with nary a smokestack. Consider then, that the average person inhales 3,400 gallons of air per day and the issue of personal health becomes apparent. Further, the point should be made that the problem was largely the result of home grown polluting activities. At a more general level, only California and Texas exceeded the state of North Carolina in total number of instances that state and federal ozone standards were exceeded that year. Then, on June 1, 2000, Charlotte experienced the country's highest ozone level. The primary problem, it seems, is that North Carolina's 14 coal-fired power plants are emitting an average of 1,100 tons of smog-causing nitrogen oxide (NO) daily, or 44 percent of the state total. Automotive exhausts account for 30 percent of nitrogen oxide emissions, non-highway vehicles such as lawn mowers and boats provide 18 percent, and other industry about eight percent (Figures 8.9 and 12.15, and Box 8C).

Duke Energy Company's Belews Creek Steam Plant in southeastern Stokes County was completed in 1975; the most recently constructed Duke coal-fired plant. With 3,000 tons of NO emitted daily, it is the company's most polluting plant. This results from the plant burning 13,700 tons of coal daily, enough to fill 200 railroad cars and converting it to 2,200 megawatts of electricity. The EPA is up in arms, not only because of Duke and Carolina Power and Light companies' flagging response to this deficiency in pollution controls, but also because North Carolina's volatile air masses bring disaster to other states. Up to 45 percent of Virginia's ozone concentration originates in North Carolina, the EPA claims. At stake is the State's loss of federal highway money and further federally required restrictions on industrial emissions. It should be noted that the companies' coal-fired plants were essentially grandfathered out of having to meet standards when the Clean Air Act was amended in 1977. It was apparently thought that these were old plants that would be replaced in a few years by new pollution-controlled plants. Instead, Duke and CP&L simply added to the power generating capacities of the old

486

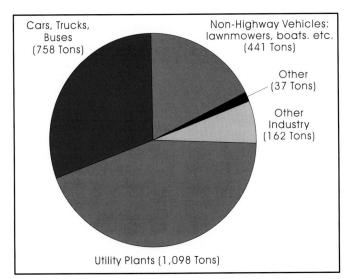

**Figure 12.15:** North Carolina Sources of Nitrogen Oxides: Average Daily Emissions.
**Source:** Tursi (2000).

plants, adding to the problem rather than resolving it. For the Belews plant, which has expanded by one-third since 1992, this was like adding 1.3 million cars and their fumes to the roads (Tursi 2000). More recent federal atmospheric acidity controls are forcing the power companies to invest in smog reducing technologies, with Duke Energy able to reduce its total production of 88,000 tons of NO during the "ozone season" (May-September) to 57,000 tons over the past five years.

Automobiles, trucks and other petroleum product-driven vehicles take over as leading polluters in large city-centered regions. In the City of Charlotte, these polluters contribute 62 percent of the emitted NO (Henderson 2000c). Environmental Protection Agency researchers at EPA's Atmospheric Research and Exposure Assessment Laboratory in the Research Triangle Park have identified over 400 chemical compounds in automobile exhaust. In different combinations, these compounds form carbon monoxide and ozone, the two major air pollution problems (Manuel 1992). In mid-2000, the State Department of Environment and Natural Resources (DENR) issued a report to the EPA that indicated that the problem was worse than ever suspected. With 60 "ozone alerts" in the state in 1999, the DENR found that 17 entire counties of the Piedmont, plus portions of an additional 23 counties in the state are non-attainment areas (Figure 12.16); that is, they are unlikely to meet new and stricter federal air quality standards (Tuttle 2000). In addition to data provided by air monitoring stations scattered throughout the state, DENR considered commuting patterns, current and projected populations, and current and projected driving distance per vehicle. Designation as a non-attainment area increases the likelihood that the EPA will block highway construction and cause the denial of new or expanding industry permits. In all, this designation is thought to negatively influence the prospects of future economic expansion, although it is equally likely to improve the quality of life conditions for residents. For some of these residents, the condi-

tions are critical and public and private decision makers are on notice. After all, we are knowingly continuing to allow the most vulnerable members of our families, the children and the elderly, to suffer needlessly the unhealthy brew of pollutants being emitted from vehicles, public utilities, and other sources. Especially vulnerable are those with existing heart and lung ailments, including asthma, chronic bronchitis, and emphysema, but everyday joggers, bicyclists, hunters, and people engaged in any outdoor activity are also affected. And nowhere are we safe. As was so vividly demonstrated by the example of Cooleemee, air pollutants are mobile. In a rural area without industry or many commuters and where residents do not normally think of polluted air, people who think their congestion is caused by pollen in the air may in fact be choking on noxious pollutants released far away.

Consider finally two additional critical warnings regularly issued on environmental health. The Toxics Release Inventory of the EPA compiles information on all chemicals injected into the air, land, and water by major industries or generated and shipped elsewhere by these industries. For 1999, the Inventory ranked North Carolina 11th in the country and highest in the Southeast, citing over 800 state industries that emitted 158 million pounds of toxic chemicals. Leaders in North Carolina were: 1) Roxboro Steam Electric Plant, Person County, a Carolina Power and Light Company plant, with 21.4 million pounds released; 2) Belews Creek Steam Station, Stokes County, with 15.4 million pounds, and 3) Marshal Steam Station, Catawba County, with 14.1 million pounds released; the last two are Duke Energy plants. Counties and metropolitan areas in the country are ranked by the American Lung Association (ALA) in terms of the severity of air quality and the number of infractions. For 2000, the ALA ranked Metrolina 8th worst in the nation, while the Piedmont Triangle was ranked 17th worst.

On a related energy production aspect the Bush Administration has recently (2001) emphasized its interest in urging a renewed emphasis on nuclear power as a major source of municipal and industrial electrical energy. Progress in this direction brings into sharper focus the issues related to an energy source that for a while had diminished in its importance throughout the country, as well as in North Carolina. The reader may wish to consult Box 12B for details on these issues.

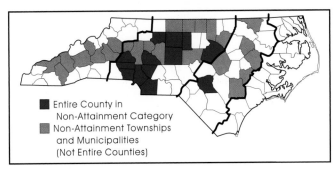

**Figure 12.16:** North Carolina's 'Non-Attainment' Areas.
**Source:** North Carolina Department of Energy and Natural Resources, 1999.

**Box 12B:** Nuclear Power.

An aerial photo of the Brunswick nuclear power plant.

The Cooling Tower of CP&L's Harris nuclear power plant rises above the landscape.

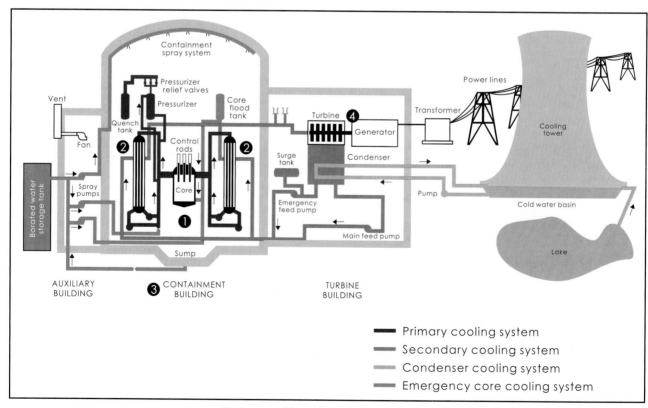

The inner workings of a nuclear power plant

A critical issue in nuclear energy development is the expected longevity of nuclear power plants. North Carolina has three of these (though plant owners Duke and CP&L have three additional plants in adjacent South Carolina and Virginia). Most of plants are closing in on the date for determining whether or not to request an extension of their initial 40 year license. In a relicensing process the U. S. Nuclear Regulatory Commission is generally concerned with detailed inspections and evaluation of the following structures (dimensions referred to here are those of the McGuire plant) and storage aspects:

**1. Reactor Vessel**. The nuclear fission process is a controlled chain reaction of splitting uranium atoms, which heats water circulating through the reactor vessel. The reactor holds the uranium fuel core in two 805-ton steel vessels, each 40 feet tall, 15 feet wide, and walled by eight inches of steel sheathing.
Problem potential:  the possibility of vessel embrittlement which may result eventually by the constant exposure to harsh chemistry conditions. Embrittlement may cause the vessel to shatter like glass. Vigilant monitoring of vessel standards is the only existing preventative measure.

**2. Steam Generator**. The steam generator is fed by 600 degrees Fahrenheit steam from the reactor. In passing through the 1000s of steam generator tubes this primary and radioactive coolant conducts its heat to a non-radioactive coolant causing this to boil and produce steam.
Problem potential: It is necessary to replace the steam generators periodically to prevent the infusion of radioactive coolant through leaking tubes.

**3. Containment Building**. Should an accident occur, it is expected that it will be contained within this steel-lined concrete building.
Problem potential: Built to withstand earthquakes and hurricanes containment buildings are considered safe for many decades of use.

**4. Electrical Generators**. Steam generated within the containment building is passed to plant where it turns turbines that generates electricity.

**5. Radioactive Waste Disposal**. Plants are increasingly storing their own spent nuclear "fuel assemblies" within secure reinforced chambers under 20+ feet of water for cooling.

Problem potential: A recent proposal by CP&L to increase its storage capacity from 3,548 to 8,265 spent nuclear assemblies for its Shearon Harris plant has resulted in a protest being filed to the Federal Atomic Safety and Licensing Board Panel by Orange County, where commissioners and other residents are concerned about living within 20 miles of what may become the nation's largest collection of high-level radioactive waste. The Nuclear Regulatory Commission agrees that spent fuel up to ten years old will ignite should the cooling pools at Shearon Harris become even partially drained exposing the nuclear waste to air (Bolton and Warren 2001).

Duke Power brought on-line the McGuire plant on Lake Norman in 1981 (Photo 8.2). At issue is the rapidly increasing population density within a potential disaster zone (see 12.Bb). Within this zone Duke Power's sister company of Crescent Resources have been selling property and constructing homes in exclusive communities (CP 1.16a and earlier section in this chapter). Though highly unlikely, a nuclear event will have serious implications for people seeking to make a fast exit since evacuation routes have not been improved with the increasing population density (Stancil 1999). (Readers may wish to draw similar zones around sites occupied by CP&L Shearon Harris nuclear power plant on Harris Lake in southwestern Wake County).

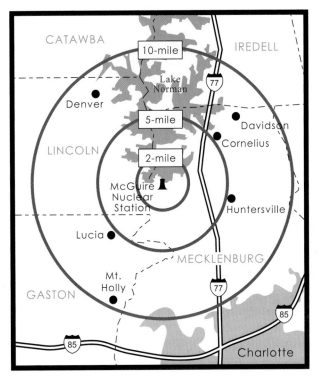

Proximity to McGuire Nuclear Station.

# FOUR STATE GEOGRAPHIC REGIONS

## Introduction

Among thirteen State Geographic Regions (SGR), four are included for discussion in this chapter on the Piedmont Primary Region. Two of these, Metrolina and the Piedmont Triad, are found totally within the Piedmont (Figure 9.11). The Piedmont Triangle SGR has one county, Johnston, in the Coastal Plain Primary Region. Only the Western Piedmont SGR seems completely out of tune, with four of its seven counties actually lying in the Mountain Primary Region. Of course, this somewhat curious result comes from our concern about keeping the functionally urban Piedmont counties and their regions together. Within the four counties of Caldwell, Burke, McDowell and Rutherford, economic activity and population concentrations are clearly Piedmont-focused and transportation-linked. From Lenoir southwest to Morganton and Marion and then south to Rutherfordton, there is an almost continuous human activity zone. While this assures these counties' inclusion in a Piedmont-based State Geographic Region, their inclusion in the Mountain Primary Region is related to their physical separation from the remainder of the Piedmont by the South Mountains, as well as by their western, very thinly populated portions being part of the Blue Ridge. Again, to remind the reader, our four primary regions are derived mostly from their physical geography characteristics, while the thirteen state geographic regions are assembled from counties that are adjacent to each other and have the most in common from a functional perspective (Chapter 9). Four counties of the Sandhills SGR, plus one county of the Roanoke SGR intrude upon the Piedmont Primary Region.

Scanning Table 9.2, which compares a selection of critical data for the thirteen SGRs, we find that three of our Piedmont SGRs are the most populous in the state, while two of these, Piedmont Triangle and Metrolina, are the fastest growing. No surprise here, as our inclusion of these four SGRs comprise nearly 60 per cent of the state's population, as of the 2000 census. At present rates of growth, the Hickory-centered Western Piedmont SGR is lagging the United States' over all average rate, while The Piedmont Triad SGR is matching it. Metrolina's growth rate is at twice the national average, while the Piedmont Triangle SGR is three times the national average. Socio-economically, these regions stand out, as well. As an average condition, here we have the best educated, healthiest, wealthiest, and youngest populations, though also the most crowded. As noted earlier, there are considerable variations from the high average results for the SGRs when we look at their county conditions. It may be of interest for the reader to compare and contrast data tables provided in the following sections with Tables 9.1 and 9.2.

## Piedmont Triangle

Nine counties make up the State Geographic Region that goes by the name of the Piedmont Triangle SGR (Figure 12.17). Comprising a triangle of urban space defined by Raleigh, Durham, and Chapel Hill and operating as the eastern terminus of North Carolina's Main Street, this is the largest concentration of people in close proximity to each other and the state's worst degree of urban sprawl, as indicated on the map of regional land use in 1998 (CP 12.16). Urged on by a very successful combination of new-line growth industries (microelectronics, telecommunications, pharmaceuticals, biomedicals), research and development enterprises, health care facilities, and government employment, the four primary urban centers of Raleigh, Durham, Cary, and Chapel Hill are gradually fusing into one continuous urban conglomeration. The result is recorded in the many human-physical environmental interface problems discussed earlier. Here there is the culmination of traffic congestion, environmental pollution, and competition over increasingly scarce water resources, discontent with central city development, and intercommunity disagreements over the placement of public facilities. Here, also, are opportunities, in employment, residential communities, and recreational and cultural activities that compare favorably with any region of the United States, as frequently cited in a variety of quality of life and business opportunity ratings conducted by leading agencies and magazines. Here also are adjacent rural counties that are gradually being pressured by urban sprawl as it diffuses from the urban core. Meanwhile these counties continue to represent opportunities for open space recreation, as well as small town historic preservation (Photos 12.21-12.24; CP 12.17a-c).

A core of four counties (Wake, Johnston, Durham and Orange) totally dominated the past decade's population growth experienced by the Piedmont Triangle SGR. In the aggregate these counties have increased by an astonishing 308,000 people, to the point where their total population exceeded one million people in the census year of 2000 (Table 12.2). In all, the Piedmont Triangle added 36.1 percent to its population, well in excess of the state's 21.4 and the nation's 13.4 percent. Only Person and Vance counties were lagging the state average in population growth, a sure sign that the Triangle urban sprawl have yet to reach their borders with any significant impact, though some exurban land use changes are clearly evident in these counties' southern perimeter. The 1990 population cohort diagrams portrayed in Figures 12.18a-i demonstrate well the kind of population apt to be found in counties that are part of an expansive metropolitan region. Wake County (Figure 12.18i) illustrates the dominance of youthful to early middle age workers found in an explosive growth county. In 1990, we are barely able to see the beginnings of the suburbanizing of the two rural counties of Franklin and Johnston to the east of Wake County (Figures 12.18c and e). But especially in Johnston is there evidence of in-migrating middle age families with children. Durham County (Figure 12.18b) is very similar to Wake. The population structure of Orange County (Figure 12.18f) is overwhelmed by the youthful constituency of the University of North Carolina at Chapel Hill. To be sure, there are large college populations also in Durham (Duke University and Medical School) and Wake (North Carolina State University), but these

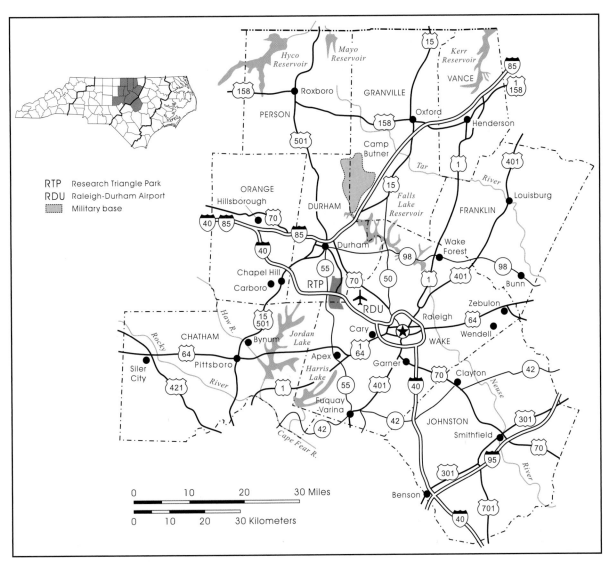

**Figure 12.17:** Piedmont Triangle State Geographic Region.

counties' much larger populations tend to hide the effects of this youthful dimension. Chatham County (Figure 12.18a) is in the beginning of a major transition phase in its population structure. Elderly and the middle aged populations are in excess of state norms, while the absence of colleges, military bases, and basic industries causes a major drain in the more youthful population. This condition intensified during the 1990s, although suburban families continued their in-migration to the county prior to an energizing of their birth rate.

Population dimensions of the three counties of the Piedmont Triangle SGR that border Virginia depend on their immediate relations with the core of the metro region. Granville County (Figure 12.16h) indicates some expansion of the early middle aged population, except that women appear to be lagging state averages. However, both Person and Vance counties (Figures 12.18g and h) exhibit their more rural nature with their higher birth rates, and thus larger childhood populations, as well as a higher percentage of older people who likely have retired in place.

As is generally true throughout the state, in the Piedmont Triangle SGR the more urban counties have higher percentages of high school and college graduates, a lower percent of families below poverty levels, and a lower percent minority populations (Table 12.2). The exception is Vance County, which might find a better fit with the Roanoke State Geographic Region, because of its minority white population. Vance, Person and Franklin counties are the only Piedmont Triad counties rated lower than the highest rating given for N. C. Enterprise Tiers. Lower ratings acknowledge deficiencies in economic development and provide special state support for new and enlarging businesses (Chapter 9). Other population aspects of these counties, including minority attributes, are dealt with in Chapter 4.

*Research Triangle Park*

Dominated during the first half of the 20th century by the economic activities offered by the largely single industry dependent towns of Raleigh (state government), Durham (tobacco in-

**Photo 12.21:** Several large reservoirs provide open space relief in a region overflowing with urban development. Limited attention has been paid to providing connections between urban centers by means other than automotive. Even in such scenic surroundings as along Jordan Lake bikes are challenged by truck and auto traffic.

**Photo 12.22:** Zebulon (Wake County), and other towns in the urban periphery, is still weighing its options in the face of approaching overspill. Events are already now overtaking its ability to carefully plan for the future.

**Photo 12.23:** Hillsborough (Orange County) is a county seat with much history dating to an early attempt at establishing the state capitol here, and with a significant stop on the state railroad during mid-19th century. A major effort has been expending in recording and preserving its visible history.

**Photo 12.24:** Even small hamlets, some distance from the urban core are seeing enough visitors to encourage restoration of historic property, and its entrepreneurial use. This is Goldston in south central Chatham County.

| PIEDMONT TRIANGLE | Land Area in sq. km | Pop. 1990 | Pop. sq.km. 2000 | Pop. 2000 | 1990s % Pop. Change | % White 2000 | Median Age in 2000 | % Fam. Below Poverty | Annual Average Infant Mortality Rate 1994-98 | % High School Grads'90 | % Coll. Grads. 1990 | Fem. Fam. Head of Hshld'90 | NC Enterprise Tiers'97 |
|---|---|---|---|---|---|---|---|---|---|---|---|---|---|
| Chatham | 1,769 | 38,979 | 27.9 | 49,329 | 26.6 | 74.9 | 40.0 | 7.4 | 10.9 | 70.0 | 19.5 | 10.5 | 5 |
| Durham | 753 | 181,844 | 296.6 | 223,314 | 22.8 | 50.9 | 33.4 | 8.7 | 10.2 | 78.9 | 33.4 | 14.3 | 4 |
| Franklin | 1,273 | 36,414 | 37.1 | 47,260 | 29.8 | 66.0 | 36.1 | 11.6 | 7.9 | 62.4 | 9.2 | 13.8 | 5 |
| Granville | 1,376 | 38,341 | 35.2 | 48,498 | 26.5 | 60.7 | 36.9 | 10.0 | 10.8 | 62.0 | 9.6 | 14.2 | 5 |
| Johnston | 2,051 | 81,306 | 59.5 | 121,965 | 50 | 78.1 | 36.7 | 11.5 | 9.0 | 64.6 | 11.1 | 11.5 | 5 |
| Orange | 1,035 | 93,662 | 114.2 | 118,227 | 26.2 | 78 | 31.9 | 6.4 | 9.3 | 83.6 | 46.1 | 9.4 | 5 |
| Person | 1,016 | 30,180 | 35.1 | 35,623 | 18 | 68.8 | 38.5 | 9.6 | 11.3 | 63.2 | 7.6 | 13.5 | 3 |
| Vance | 657 | 38,892 | 65.4 | 42,954 | 10.4 | 48.2 | 35.1 | 15.3 | 15.0 | 57.1 | 9.5 | 18.2 | 2 |
| Wake | 2,160 | 426,311 | 290.7 | 627,846 | 47.3 | 72.4 | 33.5 | 5.5 | 8.5 | 85.4 | 35.3 | 10.0 | 5 |
| **Region Totals** | **12,090** | **965,929** | **108.8** | **1,315,016** | **36.1** | **68.3** | **35.8** | **9.6** | **10.3** | **69.7** | **20.1** | **12.8** | **4.3** |

**Table 12.2:** Piedmont Triangle State Geographic Region.
**Source:** U. S. Bureau of the Census, 2000; North Carolina State Planning Office, various years.

dustries), and Chapel Hill (education), and suffering along with the remainder of the state from economic lethargy and a case of acute brain drain, the Piedmont Triangle was propelled into national and international prominence with the farsighted development of the Research Triangle Park (RTP) in the late 1950s (Box 12C). RTP facilities were sited snugly into the forests and green open spaces then found between Durham and Raleigh, and in the locational epicenter of the three research universities that gave it birth: UNC-Chapel Hill, Duke University, and North Carolina State University. RTP's success has influenced the paradigm shift in North Carolina's industrial character, from one of old-line, labor intensive, low wage industries, to one much closer to reflecting the United States' new millennium emphasis on new-line industries (Box 12Ca and b). With 70 percent of its land in Durham County and 30 percent in Wake County, the 6,900 acre Park has had an incredible impact on its surrounding communities and counties, as well as the state at large. In sheer size, the present 40,000 employees, 85 per cent of whom hold higher education degrees, also comprise the highest salaried community in the state, and as such have a major impact on local/regional/state economy, political, social, and cultural affairs. Mutually beneficial to the Park's corporate tenants and the region's universities are the existing cross-currents of relationships. Over 90 percent of the Park's employees have a formal relationship with one or more of the universities. Part of this is owed to the early founding of the Research Triangle Institute (RTI). RTI is a consortium of the region's universities that yearly receives close to $150 million in research contracts and grants. A persistent major emphasis on research and development, and the scale of production it has attained, has caused at least one leading researcher to refer to RTP as the world's largest research complex (Stackhouse 1994). Here is a community of creativity, from where ideas are transformed into products and services for the global market place.

Though emphasized as a locational mecca for research and development activities, some actual manufacturing also has located in the RTP, as exemplified by the 13,000 employee IBM facilities, its largest in the country. A listing of major occupants among the 100 or so with facilities at the RTP reads like a Who's Who of prominent leading-edge global corporations. Biotechnology firms include BASF Corporate Agricultural Products, Rhone-Poulenc Ag Company and Novartis; Environmental Sciences include the U. S. Environmental Protection Agency and Lockheed-Martin; Microelectronics and Software companies are represented by IBM, Data General and DuPont; Telecommunications and Internetworking corporations include Nortel Networks, Ericsson, Lucent Technologies and Cisco Systems; Chemicals include Rheichold and the AATCC; and Pharmaceuticals and Healthcare corporations include Glaxo-Smith/Kline; Novartis and the National Institute for Environmental Health Sciences (Photo 12.2). With its campus-like milieu of large lots where facilities, including parking spaces, may leave only small development footprints (15% of the land) in the open spaces of forests, lakes, and pedestrian pathways, the RTP is especially attractive to this kind of clientele (Box 12Cf).

In spite of its recent extension into Wake County, the Research Triangle Park is fast running out of space. As a non-profit foundation, the RTP itself has nurtured a great number of independent new company start-ups through its First Flight Venture Center, and through its corporate tenants' ability to attract leading scientists and innovators, who may subsequently split off to establish their own firms. In the vicinity of the RTP 35 new business and research parks, with over 25,000 employees, have located to cultivate symbiotic relations with Park tenants as well as to glimmer in RTP's reflected sunlight (CP 12.18). Some of these proximity centers are now being designed as new urban communities with homes, shops, and places of work within easy reach of major highways and the anticipated new mass transit system, not to mention the Triangle's location near the Raleigh-Durham International Airport. In part, this multifaceted kind of development is a response to one of the problems seen by employment is a response to one of the problems seen by employees at the Park – its complete dependence on corporate land. RTP is controlled by a private foundation, is not incorporated, and by agreements with adjacent municipalities is untouchable for annexation. Consequently, only county taxes are paid, although this is a formidable source of revenue especially for Durham County. The ex-

## Box 12C: The Research Triangle Park

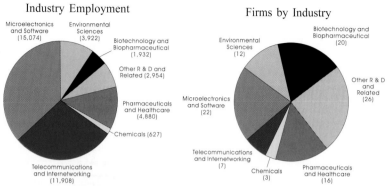

### Industry Employment

- Microelectronics and Software (15,074)
- Environmental Sciences (3,922)
- Biotechnology and Biopharmaceutical (1,932)
- Other R & D and Related (2,954)
- Pharmaceuticals and Healthcare (4,880)
- Chemicals (627)
- Telecommunications and Internetworking (11,908)

### Firms by Industry

- Biotechnology and Biopharmaceutical (20)
- Environmental Sciences (12)
- Other R & D and Related (26)
- Microelectronics and Software (22)
- Telecommunications and Internetworking (7)
- Chemicals (3)
- Pharmaceuticals and Healthcare (16)

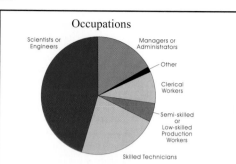

### Occupations

- Scientists or Engineers
- Managers or Administrators
- Other
- Clerical Workers
- Semi-skilled or Low-skilled Production Workers
- Skilled Technicians

| Industry | Employees | Firms |
|---|---|---|
| Biotechnology and Biopharmaceutical | 1,932 | 20 |
| Environmental Sciences | 3,922 | 12 |
| Microelectronics and Software | 15,074 | 22 |
| Chemicals | 627 | 3 |
| Pharmaceuticals and Healthcare | 4,880 | 16 |
| Telecommunications and Internetworking | 11,908 | 7 |
| Other R&D Related | 2,954 | 26 |
| **Total** | **41,297** | **106** |

**a:** RTP Companies by Industry, 2000.

| Occupation Type | Mean Percentage |
|---|---|
| Scientists or Engineers | 45.5 |
| Managers or Administrators | 16.8 |
| Skilled Technicians | 22.4 |
| Clerical Workers | 8.7 |
| Semi- or Low-Skilled Production Workers | 5.2 |
| Other | 1.4 |
| **Total** | **100** |

**b:** RTP Occupation Types, 1998.

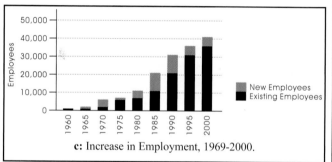

New Employees / Existing Employees

**c:** Increase in Employment, 1969-2000.

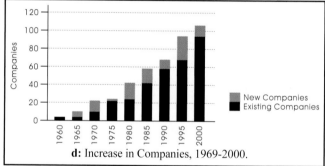

New Companies / Existing Companies

**d:** Increase in Companies, 1969-2000.

**e:** Ciba-Geigy's Biotechnology Research Facility. (now Novartis Corporation) (photo by O. Gade)

| SIC Code | SIC Description |
|---|---|
| SIC 28 | Chemicals and allied products |
| SIC 35 | Industrial machinery and equipment |
| SIC 36 | Electronic and other electrical equipment |
| SIC 37 | transportation equipment |
| SIC 38 | Instruments and related products |
| SIC 48 | Communication |
| SIC 60 | Depository institutions |
| SIC 61 | Non-depository institutions |
| SIC 62 | Security and commodity brokers |
| SIC 63 | Insurance carriers |
| SIC 64 | Insurance agents, brokers. and service |
| SIC 65 | Rael estate |
| SIC 67 | Holding and other investment offices |
| SIC 73 | Business services |
| SIC 80 | Health services |
| SIC 81 | Legal services |
| SIC 82 | Educational services |
| SIC 87 | Engineering and management services |

**f:** New-Line Industries.

**Source:** *The Research Triangle Park: The First Forty Years*, Hammer, Siler, George Associates, 1999.

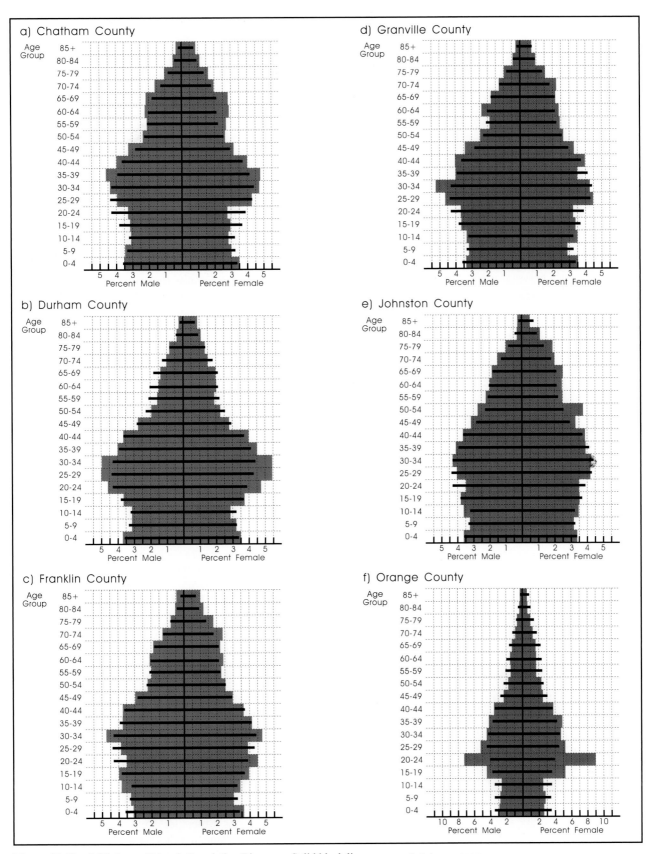

**Figure 12.18 a-f:** Piedmont Triangle Population Diagrams. Solid black lines represent state averages.
**Source:** U. S. Bureau of the Census, 1990.

495

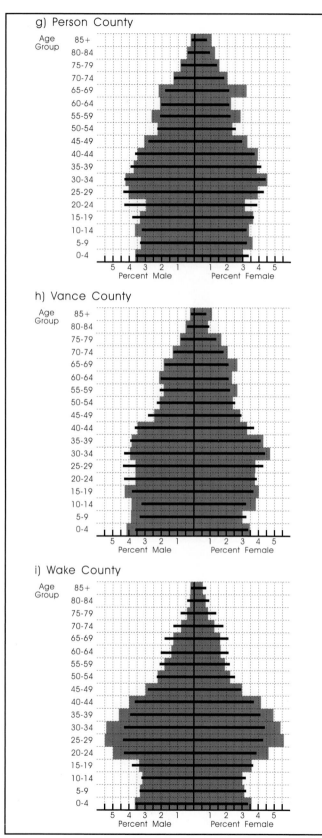

**g) Person County**

**h) Vance County**

**i) Wake County**

**Figure 12.18 g-i:** Piedmont Triangle Population Diagrams. Solid black lines represent state averages.

**Source:** U. S. Bureau of the Census, 1990.

clusivity of corporate business land usage, exempted only to allow for a small shopping center and one hotel, carries its price for employees. Commuting is required for all, even during the lunch hour.

The powerful magnetism of the Research Triangle Park and its satellites extends to the remainder of the Piedmont Triangle. An additional 100 new-line industry companies, led by technology firms, are concentrated in southwestern Wake County, especially in and around Cary, and on the northern periphery of Raleigh. Notably here is SAS Institute, a software company. With its offices and 3,500 employees sprawled over a manicured campus in Cary, its shear size and the magnetism of its founder and corporate chief, James Goodnight, strongly influences town politics and development. In general terms, the central cities of Durham and Raleigh are losing out in their competition for the location of new-line industries, which prefer to locate in or near the center of activities, in close proximity to the RTP. Councils of both cities are engaged in ongoing debates on how to pump new life into their aging, and somewhat dilapidated central business districts. Durham seem to be getting an earlier and potentially much better start with the old tobacco plants and warehouses of American Tobacco and Liggett Myers. Retrofitting of these industrial buildings for residential housing, shops and restaurants has been ongoing at a steady pace for the past two decades.

### Piedmont Triad

The Piedmont Triad is the pivot of Main Street. Centered on the cities of Greensboro, Winston-Salem and High Point, this metropolitan state geographic region tallies over 1.3 million inhabitants. In this way, the Triad SGR has the attraction of urban concentration and scale, while it is also evolving as the connecting center between Main Street's termini of the Triangle and Metrolina metropolitan areas. A look at CP 12.19 will confirm this urban continuity along Interstates 85 and 40 from Burlington to Winston-Salem and to High Point. The Piedmont Triad State Geographic Region includes ten counties containing population and socio-economic characteristics quite similar to the Triangle and Metrolina, except this SGR is much slower in its population expansion (Figure 12.19 and Table 12.3). Although the Piedmont Triad SGR has about the same population density as the Triangle and a marginally larger population, its growth over the decade of the 1990s (13.9 percent) is only about one-third that of the Triangle (36.8 percent) and much less than that of the state (21.4 percent). Metrolina passed the Triad in total population in the 1980s while the Triangle is expected to do so during the very early part of the 2000 decade.

We have earlier discussed the particular problems of economic restructuring being experienced by the Triad cities (Chapter 6), focusing on this region's greater dependence on old-line industries (CP 6.13-15). Even in the case of new-line activities Winston-Salem has difficulties. Note the possible relocation of Wachovia Bank headquarters to Charlotte, as Wachovia and First Union began their merger in 2001. It seems that Winston-Salem has, for several decades, qualified as one of America's poster

496

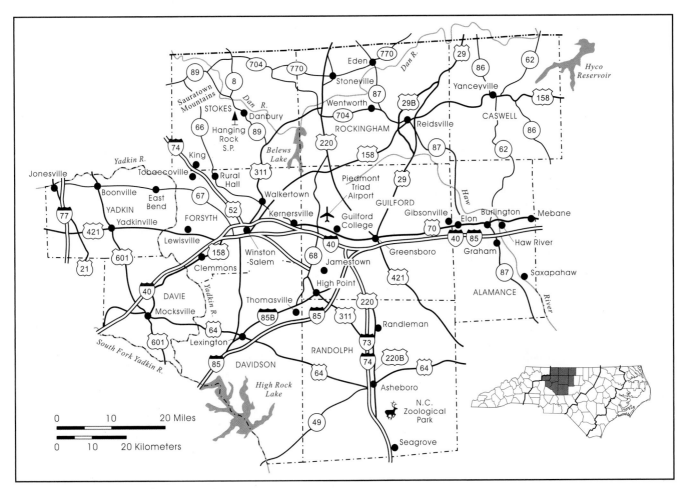

**Figure 12.19:** Piedmont Triad State Geographic Region.

children of economic despair, with industry after industry leaving or closing down major plants in the city (Piedmont Airlines, Hanes, R. J. Reynolds Tobacco, Stroh's Brewery) (Compare CP 12.20 with CP 12.2 and CP 6.13-16.). Also, as noted in Chapter 6, Greensboro's textile and apparel empire has been in the process of relocating much of the labor intensive, low wage components of its manufacturing process to Mexico. For its part, High Point has seen Thomas Built Busses absorbed by Freightliner, while its furniture industry and world market center is in one of its periodic downturns in the early years of the 2000 decade (CP 6.10-6.12). Yet, economic diversification is intensifying in the Piedmont Triad with new line industries now accounting for about 26 percent of the labor force. While textile/apparel, tobacco and furniture is in decline, industries including plastics, automotive parts, and fiber optics are in the ascendancy. So is also a variety of new age service industries, especially in health and business.

Difficulties of the economic turn-around for Triad municipalities increase with increasing distance from Greensboro–High Point–Winston-Salem. Outlying urban centers, such as Reidsville, Burlington, Asheboro, Thomasville and Lexington, continue to suffer to a greater degree the withdrawal pains of a gradually disappearing traditional industry. Marketing the Piedmont Triad

as a favorable location for new-line industry is focused on its core, at the expense of the periphery (Photos 12.24-12.28; CP 12.21-12.26). People here must be content to serve the increasingly labor impoverished core of Guilford and Forsyth counties. Already in 1990 there were over 100,000 workers commuting to the core counties from neighboring counties (Box 12D). Several interesting conclusions emerge from the conditions portrayed in Box 12E. First of all, the act of commuting confers on the core counties the role of economic providers of the region, while it also clearly defines differences in urban-rural characteristics. Secondly, the degree of suburban county dependency can be read from commuting data. For example, while Stokes County sent 8,756 daily commuters to Forsyth County in 1990, only 917 went to Guilford County. Similarly, Rockingham County sent daily 7,808 commuters to Guilford, and only 524 to Forsyth. On the other hand, Caswell County also serves as a bedroom community for Danville, Virginia. Thirdly, as indicated by the diagram, longer commuting time is a fact of life, and it increases proportionately over time as it expands across space. The reader should think of the relationships exemplified by Piedmont Triad counties as being symptomatic for all of the major core areas of Main Street and their adjacent counties. Core area influences are felt

497

**Photo 12.25:** Among the six Piedmont region counties forming the boundary with Virginia, Main Street pressures perhaps least disturb Caswell. Again historic properties benefit from this absence of developmental attention. Exemplifying not only Caswell historic values, but also one of the grandest of the 100 courthouses in North Carolina, here is the Caswell County Court House at Yanceyville.

**Photo 12.26:** Buildings of historic value have not yet received an appropriated attention in Rockingham County, but in small towns like Mayodan they flourish. Here commercial strips and malls have not yet robbed the downtown of its vitality and life.

**Photo 12.27:** On U. S. 311 outside of the town of Mayodan, and on the Dan River, lies an abandoned motel built in the 1920s. Though not easily seen on the photo, each of the rooms on the roadside comes with its own garage.

**Photo 12.28:** Bethania (Forsyth County) is a well preserved and maintained village milieu tracing its founding to 17th Century Moravian settlers.

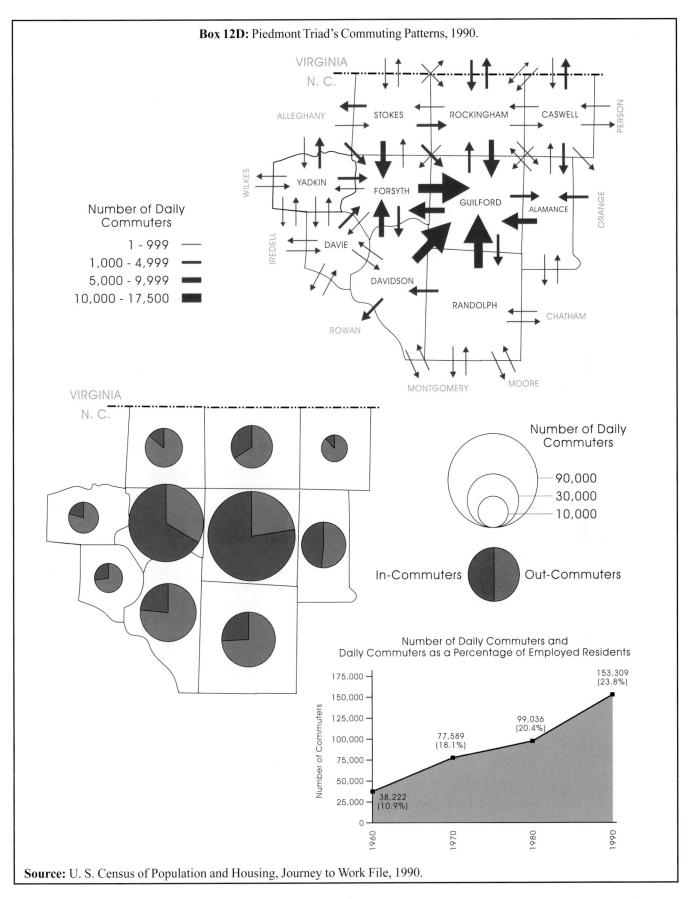

**Box 12D:** Piedmont Triad's Commuting Patterns, 1990.

Number of Daily Commuters

1 - 999
1,000 - 4,999
5,000 - 9,999
10,000 - 17,500

VIRGINIA
N. C.

ALLEGHANY    STOKES    ROCKINGHAM    CASWELL    PERSON

WILKES    YADKIN    FORSYTH    GUILFORD    ALAMANCE    ORANGE

IREDELL    DAVIE    DAVIDSON    RANDOLPH    CHATHAM

ROWAN    MONTGOMERY    MOORE

VIRGINIA
N. C.

Number of Daily Commuters

90,000
30,000
10,000

In-Commuters    Out-Commuters

Number of Daily Commuters and
Daily Commuters as a Percentage of Employed Residents

153,309
(23.8%)

99,036
(20.4%)

77,589
(18.1%)

38,222
(10.9%)

175,000
150,000
125,000
100,000
75,000
50,000
25,000
0

Number of Commuters

1960    1970    1980    1990

**Source:** U. S. Census of Population and Housing, Journey to Work File, 1990.

directly as an increasing distance decay function defined by people's increasing willingness to travel longer distances to their place of work. What we are seeing is an increasing expansion of the umbrella of urban influence depicted in Figure 12.8, and along with this, a spatial expansion of urban sprawl. Exemplary, this is seen in the explosive territorial expansion of Stokesdale (3,267 people in 2000; with a 53 percent increase during the 1990s) and Summerfield (7,018; 242 percent), incorporated towns in northeastern Guilford County that function primarily as dormitories for the Greensboro labor market. The equally vigorously growing suburbs of Winston-Salem, such as Kernersville (17,176; 58 percent population growth during the 1990s), Walkertown (4,009; 234 percent), Tobaccoville (2,209; 141 percent), Lewisville (8,826; 175 percent), and Clemmons (13,827; 130 percent), also serve as bedroom communities. It is of interest to note that Winston-Salem (185,776; 29.5 percent) itself gained 42,000 people during the 1990s, 2,000 more than its county of Forsyth, which includes all of the suburbs above. This demonstrates the power of annexation in increasing the population base.

As in the case of the Piedmont Triangle SGR, new industries in the Piedmont Triad SGR are finding especially amenable location in the heart of the region. In the 1970s there was a concerted attempt by planners and other public officials to guarantee some degree of maintaining the open space between the cities of Winston-Salem, High Point, and Greensboro. A vision of an open "greenheart" was urged by city leaders, but extensive improvements in arterial highways gradually wore down any chances of concerted action in green space preservation (Photo 12.29). The completion of the I-40 connector south of Winston-Salem and the confluence of I-40 and I-85 south of Greensboro invited much strip development, and many new industrial and business parks resulted (CP 6.18, CP 12.3). Completion of the newly designated stretches of I-73/74 will further congest development in this part of the Triad. With the anticipated addition of a Federal Express Mid-Atlantic Hub, expansion is expected of the Triad International Airport, itself fortuitously centrally located at the eastern edge of the earlier considered "greenheart". Continental Airlines developed a low fare hub here in the early 1990s, but following several years of building passenger traffic to nearly two million per year, this was cut by almost 50 percent with the demise of Continental Air Express. In the meantime, cargo shipments have continued to grow, tripling in size over the decade. It is this condition, deriving from the Triad centrality on Main Street, that determined the locational decision of Federal Express (along, of course, with the state's generosity in subsidized location support).

An example of new development in what is now the "development heart" of the Piedmont Triad is the Piedmont Centre Business Park, lying mostly within the vastly expanded city limits of High Point. In just a few years, this venture has seen the construction of facilities of firms such as Prudential Life, Bank of America (call center), and Ralph Lauren Company, adding over 6,000 jobs to the regional employment pool. Piedmont Centre is adjacent to NC 68, which is recently emerged as the major strip development between High Point and the Piedmont Triad International Airport. Further east along Main Street, on I-40/I-85 between Greensboro and Burlington, is located Piedmont Centre's nearest competitor, Rock Creek Center. This is a business park that includes tenants such as Konica USA, Shionogi Qualicaps, Dana Corp., Pass & Seymour Legrand, Focke & Co., and Medi USA, among others. It is also a business park that is moving toward multi-use development, with anticipated residential developments and consumer service facilities, due to its location on urbanizing Main Street.

Changes occurring in Piedmont Triad counties are well defined in Table 12.3. Population growth during the 1990s ranged from the high of 25 percent attained by Davie County to a low of 6.8 percent experienced by Rockingham County; only Davie and Randolph counties exceeded the state average. In population structure, the two Triad core counties of Guilford and Forsyth come closest to replicating state norms, except for a higher percentage of working households in the 30-40 cohorts (Figures 12.20f and e). Note the greater dominance of younger women in the Guilford age-sex structure, the likely influence of the preponderance of women in Greensboro's colleges and universities, as well as in the labor market of the insurance industry. Greensboro

| PIEDMONT TRIAD | Land Area in sq. km | Pop. 1990 | Pop. sq.km. 2000 | Pop. 2000 | 1990s % Pop. Change | % White 2000 | Median Age in 2000 | % Fam. Below Poverty | Annual Average Infant Mortality Rate 1994-98 | % High School Grads'90 | % Coll. Grads. 1990 | Fem. Fam. Head of Hshld'90 | NC Enterprise Tiers'97 |
|---|---|---|---|---|---|---|---|---|---|---|---|---|---|
| Alamance | 1,115 | 108,213 | 117.3 | 130,800 | 20.9 | 75.6 | 38.4 | 6.0 | 8.8 | 67.9 | 14.6 | 12.0 | 4 |
| Caswell | 1,103 | 20,662 | 21.3 | 23,501 | 13.7 | 61.1 | 40.9 | 14.5 | 15.8 | 55.0 | 6.6 | 13.7 | 3 |
| Davidson | 1,430 | 126,688 | 103 | 147,246 | 16.2 | 87.1 | 37.5 | 7.3 | 7.5 | 64.2 | 10.0 | 10.5 | 5 |
| Davie | 687 | 27,859 | 50.7 | 34,835 | 25 | 90.4 | 39.5 | 6.1 | 7.1 | 69.6 | 14.7 | 8.8 | 4 |
| Forsyth | 1,061 | 265,855 | 288.5 | 306,067 | 15.1 | 68.5 | 36.7 | 7.8 | 12.4 | 77.6 | 24.1 | 13.1 | 5 |
| Guilford | 1,684 | 347,431 | 250 | 421,048 | 21.2 | 64.5 | 36.6 | 7.3 | 9.9 | 76.1 | 24.8 | 12.8 | 5 |
| Randolph | 2,040 | 106,546 | 63.9 | 130,454 | 22.4 | 89.2 | 36.8 | 6.5 | 6.9 | 62.0 | 9.1 | 9.6 | 5 |
| Rockingham | 1,467 | 86,064 | 62.7 | 91,928 | 6.8 | 78.9 | 39.0 | 9.3 | 9.8 | 59.2 | 8.8 | 12.5 | 3 |
| Stokes | 1,170 | 37,224 | 38.2 | 44,711 | 20.1 | 93.4 | 37.5 | 7.4 | 7.8 | 62.8 | 7.3 | 9.0 | 5 |
| Yadkin | 869 | 30,488 | 41.8 | 36,348 | 19.2 | 92.5 | 39.2 | 9.7 | 7.9 | 58.9 | 7.1 | 9.3 | 4 |
| **Region Totals** | **12,626** | **1,157,030** | **104.4** | **1,366,938** | **18.1** | **77.1** | **38.1** | **8.0** | **9.4** | **66.0** | **13.3** | **11.3** | **4.3** |

**Figure 12.3:** Piedmont Triad State Geographic Region.
**Source:** U. S. Bureau of the Census, 2000; North Carolina State Planning Office, various years.

500

**Photo 12.29:** Reservoirs throughout the Piedmont provide opportunities for open space recreational activity. Here, on Belews Lake, jet-skis are enjoyed by high school students skipping classes to take advantage of an unseasonably warm late fall day.

is the headquarter city of Jefferson-Pilot Insurance Company. Alamance County (Figure 12.20a) probably reflects to the greatest degree the cohort composition of a traditional blue color labor dominated economy with its preponderance of older workers and former local workers who have retired in place. Davie, Stokes and Yadkin counties (Figures 12.20d, i., and j) exhibit the characteristic suburbanizing structure of a larger-than-norm share of middle age households, 30-54 years in age. These three counties also share with the rest of the more rural counties a shortage of young adults (20-24 cohort), due to the absence of employment opportunities, colleges, and military bases, as well as a greater prominence of older cohorts (aged 65 and over). Note especially the case of Caswell County (Figure 12.20b), the least populated, most rural, and second slowest growing county in the Piedmont Triad SGR. Rockingham County is where the ill-fated town of Reidsville (Chapter 6) has contributed to the lowest decennial population growth in the Triad, with only 6.8 percent for the 1990s. Due to restructuring affecting the textile and apparel industries in the county during the 1980s, there is also evidence of having an unusually large older population (60-79 age cohort) already by 1990 (Figure 12.20h). This can be expected to increase proportionately as workers move out of the county in search of jobs to replace those lost when Brown & Williamson closed its tobacco plants in 1996. The counties of Davidson and Randolph fall into a special category. These are counties still dependent on traditional labor intensive industries, but a location in the Main Street arch provides benefits of overflow suburbanites from Forsyth and Guilford and from new investments attributable to their key location. The benefits, for the 1990s, seem to be directed more toward Randolph County, which is stronger in the middle aged suburbanizing household (40-59 cohorts), whereas Davidson County has the edge in the proportion of older cohorts. (Compare Figure 12.20g with Figure 12.20c.)

### Metrolina

What are we to make of the continuing arguments concerning the the naming of central city of Charlotte and its metropolitan related space? Traditions, undisturbed by shifts in economics, urban expansion, and perceived dominance, have maintained the legitimacy of the Piedmont Triangle and the Piedmont Triad as the ultimate *nom de plume* of two of the three metro areas of Main Street. However, the "Queen City" of the Carolinas, Charlotte, so clearly dominates its metropolitan region that many feel it proper to have its name distinguish the metro. In this way, the name Charlotte would represent both the "Queen City" and a metropolitan region comprising nine North Carolina counties and two South Carolina counties. Certainly both the Piedmont Triad and the Piedmont Triangle are polynucleated, having more than one dominant urban node or center, while Metrolina, with its sole dominant urban center, is mononucleated. Will that condition not favor using the name of that major city as the regional moniker? Perhaps, and especially so from the perspective of the city of Charlotte's administration, its Chamber of Commerce, and an assortment of image makers and promoters. However, to some leaders of the many smaller cities and towns within the metropolitan umbrella, who are seeking to salvage some degree of self identity for their respective places, this is seen as a degree of chest pounding and self adulation that verges on being offensive. Metrolina was a name proposed for this urban region following a Chamber contest to 'name this region' (Whitmore 2000). Furthermore, the Metrolina concept was thought to reflect the dynamic evolution of a metropolitan region overlapping the boundary of the two Carolinas, and in this context was promoted by the Chamber, and was highlighted in documents, articles, and books (viz. *Metrolina Atlas* (1972), and *The Metrolina Urban Region: An Economic Atlas* (Clay et al, 1982)). In addition, the Charlotte centered metropolitan region is one of three major metropolitan nodes in the developing Carolina's Main Street which indeed traverses the two Carolinas from Greenville, South Carolina, in the southwest to Raleigh in the northeast (Figure 9.10). These were considerations in the choice of Metrolina

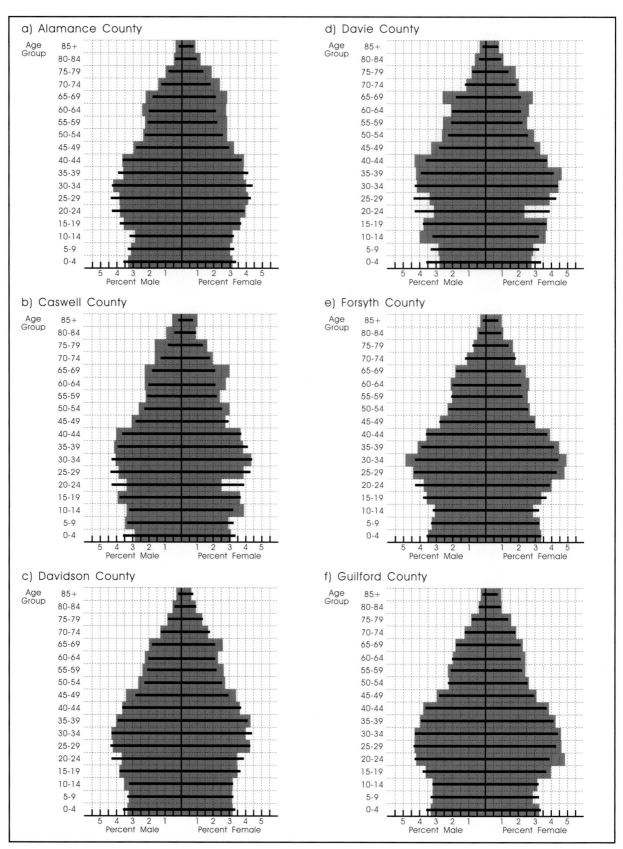

**Figure 12.20 a-f:** Piedmont Triad Population Diagrams. Solid black lines represent state averages.
**Source:** U. S. Bureau of the Census, 1990.

502

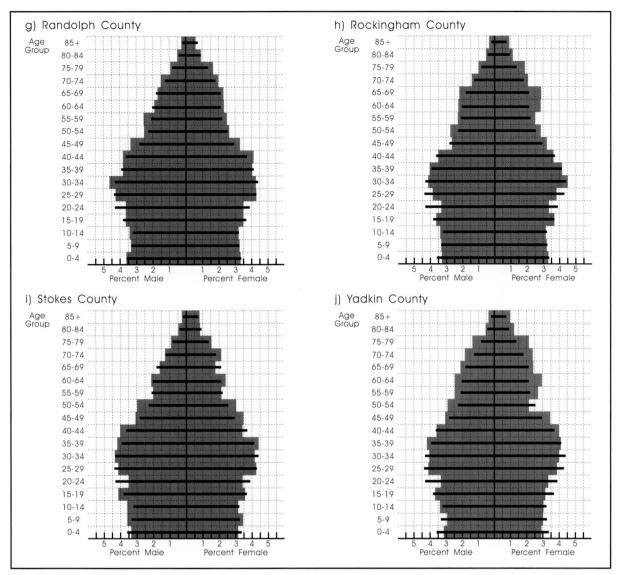

**Figure 12.20 g-j:** Piedmont Triad Population Diagrams. Solid black lines represent state averages.
**Source:** U. S. Bureau of the Census, 1990.

by the authors of the initial edition of *North Carolina: People and Environments* (1986). Arguments that the city of Charlotte is in the process of acquiring a national/international image through its finance institutions and sports teams, and is now less likely to be confused with the southern "Ch" cities (Charleston, South Carolina, Charleston, West Virginia, and Charlottesville, Virginia), not withstanding, the choice for a name of the Charlotte centered metropolitan region continues to be Metrolina (Photo 12.30). We also find this moniker more suitable in our conceptualization of the emerging megalopolitan character, not only of North Carolina's Main Street, but more importantly as the metro that connects an equally vibrant South Carolina portion of the gradual merging of urban spaces across a Carolina Piedmont.

The dynamic growth core of Metrolina is Charlotte (CP 12.27 - 12.31). With two of the nation's largest banks, and a traditional concentration of wholesaling, warehousing and redistri-

bution (Chapter 6), the "Queen City" is the state's leading merchant city, and a leading entrepreneurial center in the southeast of the United States. Its location in the central Piedmont between Washington D.C. and Atlanta, is favored by excellent land and air transportation access and services. It is a location that benefits from being in the center of the nation's most rapidly growing manufacturing corridor, I-85 from Atlanta to Richmond. While the nation's manufacturing employment increased by only 1.2 percent from 1991 to early 1998, the increase was 5.5 percent along I-85, and the vast majority of this increase was along North Carolina's Main Street (Price 1998). Clearly this represents a symbiotic relationship with Charlotte's emergence as the nation's second leading center of finance. Further aiding the city's locational advantage has been the persistent increase in passenger and goods traffic through the Charlotte/Douglas International Airport (CDIA). With a 7.8 percent increase, CDIA was 21st in the country in passenger traffic and second in passenger growth during 2000, following only Las Vegas McCarran International among the 25 leading airports in the country. CDIA is the major hub of US Airways, which controls about 90 percent of the traffic. (Reed 2001).

The Metrolina State Geographic Region includes nine counties (Figure 12.21). To the Census Bureau defined metropolitan statistical area of Charlotte-Gastonia-Rock Hill we have added Anson, Stanly, and Iredell counties to the Metrolina SGR, and taken away York County, South Carolina. Metrolina SGR with its 2000 Census population of 1.5 million is by far the largest of the 13 North Carolina SGRs, but ranks second to the Piedmont Triangle SGR in its rate of population growth (Figure 9.2). Color Plate 12.32 shows the development core of Metrolina, with Charlotte's urbanization spilling into adjacent counties. Six of Metrolina's counties have over 100,000 people, and although Charlotte's county, Mecklenburg, grew at the astonishing rate of 36 percent during the 1990s, two of its adjacent suburban counties, Union

(46.9 percent) and Cabarrus (43.5 percent), were literally exploding, with no signs of slowing down (Table 12.4). Under the best of circumstances it is impossible to plan infrastructural development to meet the needs of an almost 50 percent increase in users and consumers at the county level. Earlier we discussed the difficulties experienced by these counties; their sprawl problems will intensify with the completion in a few years of the new Outer Beltway.

As in all of the large metro SGRs, there are considerable differences among the member counties in matters of population size, rate of growth, and the range of socio-economic conditions identified in Figure 12.21. Anson, Stanly, and Lincoln counties have the fewest people, but where Anson and Stanly (CP12.33 and 12.34) are disadvantaged by being two counties away from Mecklenburg County, as well as off Main Street, Lincoln County touches the corner of Mecklenburg, while having a significant share of the rapidly developing Lake Norman shoreline. A comparison of the population structures of these smaller counties

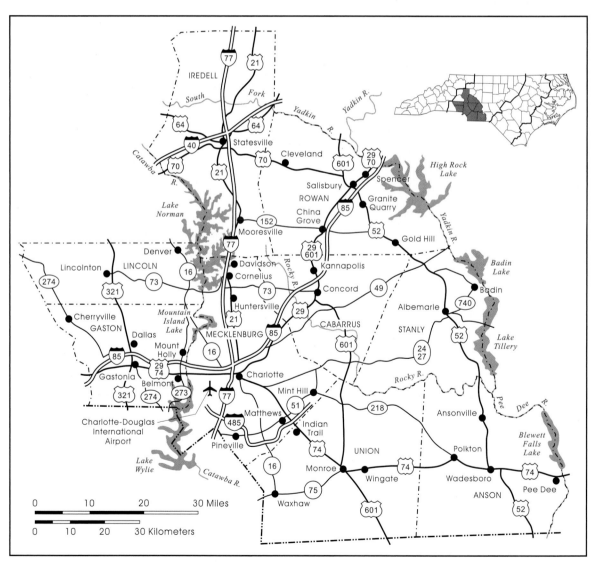

**Figure 12.21:** Metrolina State Geographic Region.

504

**Photo 12.30:** Charlotte rises on its Piedmont hill in the center of the Metrolina State Geographic Region. From Wilkinson Boulevard, a major transportation artery leading west out of town, and an early strip development focus, the view of the city is perhaps not the most enticing, however it does dramatize the "uptown" character quite well.

provides a good indication of what it means to be within which portion of the metropolitan umbrella. Lincoln County's population diagram (Figure 12.22e) shows the effects of incoming middle age households with children in the 5 to 14 age cohorts. Lincolnton City's 45.5 percent growth during the 1990s, complemented by the persistent suburban community spillover along Lake Norman, suggests that the trend has accelerated. On the other hand, Anson County illustrates the population structure conditioned by years of out-migrating youth (Figure 12.22a). Higher than average birth rates in this rural county of mostly minority and poor households insure a continuing higher proportion of the younger cohorts (5-19); the absence of opportunities throw young people into the labor market of other counties. A higher than norm older population (65+ cohorts) completes the picture of a rural county lagging in economic development. Stanly County has a somewhat stronger economic position, and its population structure indicates a similar but less severe condition (Figure 12.22h).

Iredell and Rowan counties are traditional industry dependent counties that happen to be in key locations vis a vis Main

Street. Earlier in history, Rowan benefited by Salisbury's growing significance as North Carolina's "western capital", and as a major node on the North Carolina Railroad (Figure 12.6; CP 12.4 and 12.8). To its immediate north, in Spencer, spread the switching yards and train repair depot of Southern Railways (Photo 12.10). With the demise of railroads as the major provider of goods and people transport, Interstate 85 was built to pass Salisbury's front door. Even so, Salisbury was unable to extract much advantage from its position and yielded to Statesville, its traditional competitor and county seat of Iredell County, in growth momentum. In 1990 Rowan and Iredell counties exhibited population structures that were remarkably similar (Figures 12.22d and g). However, Iredell took off with a population growth of 31.6 percent during the 1990s, while Rowan lagged the state average with 17.8 percent. Statesville, with its 2000 population of 23,320 and a 1990s growth rate of 32.7 percent, outgained Salisbury (26,462; 14.6 percent). Statesville's advantage, now rapidly being built on, is its location at the juncture of I-40 and I-77. Trucking, warehousing and redistribution facilities are now finding this city to have locational advantages even over Charlotte, one of

| METROLINA | Land Area in sq. km | Pop. 1990 | Pop. sq.km. 2000 | Pop. 2000 | 1990s % Pop. Change | % White 2000 | Median Age in 2000 | % Fam. Below Poverty | Annual Average Infant Mortality Rate 1994-98 | % High School Grads'90 | % Coll. Grads. 1990 | Fem. Fam. Head of Hshld'90 | NC Enterprise Tiers'97 |
|---|---|---|---|---|---|---|---|---|---|---|---|---|---|
| Anson | 1,377 | 23,474 | 18.4 | 25,275 | 7.7 | 49.5 | 38.0 | 13.4 | 11.4 | 60.8 | 7.7 | 17.3 | 1 |
| Cabarrus | 944 | 98,935 | 138.8 | 131,063 | 43.5 | 83.4 | 37.2 | 6.0 | 5.4 | 67.4 | 12.3 | 10.6 | 5 |
| Gaston | 923 | 174,769 | 206.2 | 190,365 | 8.9 | 83 | 36.0 | 8.2 | 9 | 60.9 | 10.4 | 12.9 | 3 |
| Iredell | 1,488 | 93,205 | 82.4 | 122,660 | 31.6 | 82.2 | 37.7 | 7.0 | 9.4 | 66.5 | 11.8 | 11.3 | 5 |
| Lincoln | 774 | 50,319 | 82.4 | 63,780 | 26.8 | 90.2 | 36.6 | 7.3 | 7.3 | 62.0 | 10.5 | 9.7 | 4 |
| Mecklenburg | 1,366 | 511,211 | 509.1 | 695,454 | 36 | 64 | 34.3 | 7.2 | 7.1 | 81.6 | 28.3 | 12.5 | 5 |
| Rowan | 1,325 | 110,605 | 98.4 | 130,340 | 17.8 | 80.0 | 37.6 | 6.8 | 9.3 | 66.0 | 11.7 | 10.9 | 4 |
| Stanley | 1,023 | 51,765 | 56.8 | 58,100 | 12.2 | 84.7 | 36.9 | 7.9 | 9.1 | 62.1 | 9.4 | 10.0 | 3 |
| Union | 1,651 | 84,210 | 74.9 | 123,677 | 46.9 | 82.8 | 34.6 | 6.2 | 8.2 | 69.0 | 13.2 | 10.5 | 5 |
| **Region Totals** | **10,871** | **1,198,493** | **141.7** | **1,540,714** | **28.6** | **73.9** | **36.4** | **7.8** | **8.5** | **66.3** | **12.8** | **11.7** | **3.9** |

**Table 12.4:** Metrolina State Geographic Region.
**Source:** U. S. Bureau of the Census, 2000; North Carolina State Planning Office, various years.

505

the country's leaders in wholesaling and redistribution. Between 1989 and 1999, more than 100 companies opened new facilities or expanded existing facilities in the Statesville area. Jeff McKay, director of economic development of the Greater Statesville Development Corporation, commented appropriately on the critical advantage of Statesville's location of two major north-south and east-west interstates, "We like to say that you can get on an interstate in Statesville and not hit another red light until you get to Barstow, California," (as quoted in Fischer 2000, 31).

Cabarrus and Union counties are prototypes of suburban development. Similar to Rowan and Iredell in size, these two counties suffer from the problems of urban overspill from Mecklenburg County and from their own inexpert attempt to funnel development in their direction without appropriately planning the needed infrastructure. In 1990 Union County exhibited the suburban impact in its population structure, with its middle aged households (40-54 cohorts) and dependent children (5-19 cohorts) clearly outdistancing the state averages for these age groups (Figure 12.22i). Cabarrus is in the same league, but a step behind (Figure 12.22b). The heyday of textiles pumped Kannapolis into prominence (Chapter 6). Although Kannapolis exceeded the state average 1990 by expanding at a rate of 31 percent, reaching 27,890 in 2000, its rate of growth is only one-third of that experienced by its next door neighbor of Concord, also the county seat in Cabarrus. Concord expanded its town limits into the hornet's nest of development at the Mecklenburg County border (University City; CP 12.10 and 12.11), and in the process increased its population to 55,977 by 2000, a 104 percent growth during the 1990s. Mill villages, with their low salaried workers, have been pushed aside by large scaled employment centers such as Philip Morris, the newly constructed Corning Inc. optical fiber plant, and the "shoppertainment" empire of Concord Mills (Martin 1999). The population structure for the Union and Cabarrus counties are expected to be even more similar in 2000, with suburban pressures continuing.

Gaston County distances itself from any of the other Metrolina SGR counties. As the traditional center of North Carolina's textile and apparel industry, the county has been troubled by this industry's consolidation and restructuring process, including the gradual relocating of its plants to offshore locations (Chapter 6; CP12.35). With a labor force dominated by blue color manufacturing industries that have generally not been hiring younger replacement workers for several decades, Gaston County in 1990 showed all the signs of a gradually aging population structure (Figure 12.22c). In comparing the set of Metrolina counties' population diagrams, only Gaston's is moving toward an increasingly equal distribution among the different age cohorts. During the 1990s, the county also grew at a slower rate than any other Metrolina county, with the exception of rural Anson. Gastonia, the county seat, exceeded the state average growth rate for the 1990s with 28.8 percent, and continues as one of the larger mid-sized cities (66,277) in the state, mostly through the annexation of adjacent territory. With a large number of initially single industry towns in Gastonia's immediate vicinity, it takes a

major multi-municipality effort to coordinate infrastructure development. Among the county's eleven other municipalities only three, Cramerton, Mount Holly, and Ranlo, exceeded the state's population growth rate for the 1990s, while population declines were recorded by Lowell, McAdenville, and Spencer Mountain (Photos 1.2 and 1.3).

The main economic engine of Metrolina SGR, Mecklenburg, is the most populated county in the state and one of the fastest growing (Table 12.4). Charlotte's own population increase for the 1990s, approaching 150,000, was only in part gained by expansion of its territorial limits. Mecklenburg County experienced an estimated 130,000 net in-migrants during the decade, most of whom settled into a city that now covers over 50 percent of the county's land area. In the process Charlotte has become the only major city in the country whose population is growing faster than that of its suburbs. The reason is that the city is able to expand as the county urbanizes. Since 1990 the city annexed 60 square miles and nearly 70,000 people (Dodd 2000). For the smaller municipalities in the county, growth is even more feverish. Almost the only space remaining for urban growth in the county is in its northern portion. Here Huntersville exploded with its increase from 3,023 people in 1990 to 24,960 in 2000, while Cornelius expanded by 383 percent to 11,969. Gamely trying to stall the inevitable, Davidson, home of the nationally prominent private Davidson College and a human-scaled downtown of estimable personality, gained only 76 percent to its 2000 population of 7,139. Also in the northern part of Mecklenburg, and reaching across the boundary into Cabarrus County, is University City. This is not an incorporated entity, rather an urbanizing landscape focused in its center on UNC Charlotte, the commercial center of University Place. Here also if the University Hospital, and the University Research Park covering 3,400 acres with 43 corporations. The latter include large tenants such as IBM (2,300 workers), the new Wachovia Bank (10,000+), and incoming TIAA/CREF, the world's largest pension fund which is expected to eventually employ 10,000 people in its Park facilities. It is thought that by 2005, University Research Park, almost absent in research facilities, will have 40,000 employees (Smith 2000). Though envisioned as a "new town" when first contemplated in the 1970s, the evolving version of University City is now one of North Carolina's preeminent examples of urban sprawl (CP 12.10 and 12.11). Its commercial center still harbors the image of small, human scale ambience, but it was early in its development strangled by a distinctively pedestrian unfriendly highway system, and then by acre upon acre of behemoth box retailers. The potential for a humanized urban landscape has long since passed. Contiguous to this older core is Lowe's Motor Speedway, Blockbuster Pavilion, Philip Morris Tobacco factory with 3,000 plus employees, and most significantly in its future urban sprawl generating context, Concord Mills with its 220 stores and restaurants (Chapter 6). In the current version of unincorporated University City there is now a population of over 100,000, sprawling in mostly isolated but culturally diverse residential communities over some 36 square miles of territory. University City has an active Area Cham-

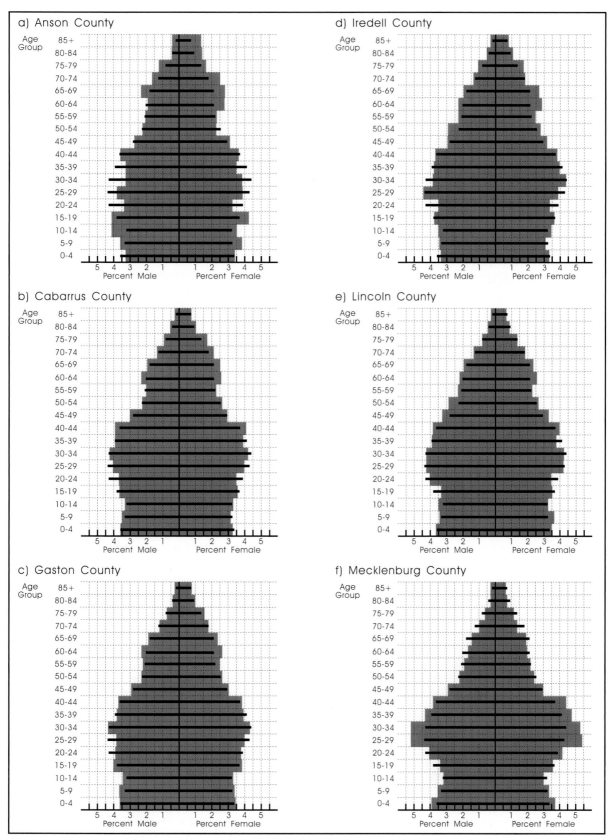

**Figure 12.22 a-f:** Metrolina Population Diagrams. Solid black lines represent state averages.
**Source:** U. S. Bureau of the Census, 1990.

507

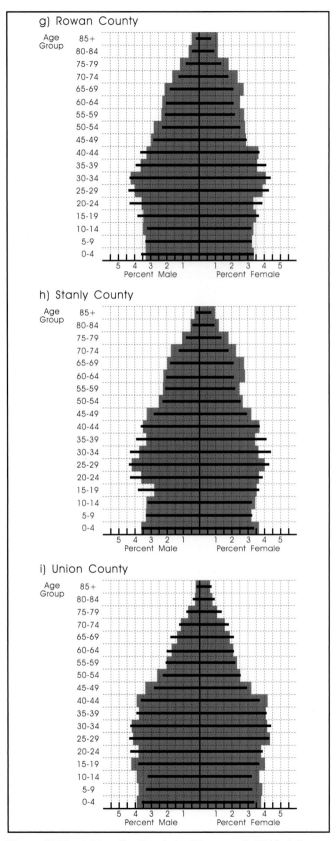

**Figure 12.22 g-i:** Metrolina Population Diagrams. Solid black lines represent state averages.
**Source:** U. S. Bureau of the Census, 1990.

ber of Commerce, much agitated over the prospects of future growth seemingly guaranteed by the planned east-west I-485 beltway (Markoe 2001).

University City Area Chamber of Commerce could learn from Pineville, to the south of Charlotte, what it means to be at the receiving end of an Interstate intersection. This is a cautionary tale for all small towns that expect wealth to pour down the access ramp from the freeway. Within a few years of its connection to the first I-485 off-ramp, Pineville's land was gobbled up by shopping centers, motels, and restaurants, with no room remaining for housing. Commercial development ran amok, anchored by the Carolina Place super regional mall and loads of big box retailers. Planning was clearly in the hands of developers, with the result of increasing the tax base from $160 million to $570 million over the same decade that the town increased its population from 2,970 to 3,449, while tripling its police force to handle traffic control and business protection (Chapman 1999). Roads leading in all directions pump in tens of thousands of shoppers daily, with an anguishing, almost constant, traffic congestion for the town's residents, who find themselves wishing for clean air and a more humane existence.

Other southern tiered suburban municipalities in Mecklenburg County were shadowed in their more marginal, though still impressive, population growth, with Matthews expanding 62 percent during the 1990s to 22,137 people, and Mint Hill growing 28.5 percent to a population of 14,922 in 2000. Mecklenburg County exudes the vitality of youthful maturity. Figure 12.22f exemplifies this kind of population structure, dominated as it is by 25-44 aged cohorts with a significant tilt toward the female gender.

### Western Piedmont

In Chapter 6 we defined the Western Piedmont SGR as North Carolina's Western Manufacturing District, an area steeped in traditional industry, mostly labor intensive and low wage textiles and apparel manufacturing. Figure 12.23 and Color Plate 12.36 identify the major land use features of this region to be two largely parallel running systems of small towns. In the north, Hickory, Morganton, and Marion are positioned east-west along US Highway 70, and, subsequently I-40; the "Furniture Highway" (U.S. 321) branches off from Hickory to Lenoir (Chapter 6 and Photo 12.31). In the southern part of Western Piedmont development is along US Highway 74, with closely spaced towns from Kings Mountain in the east to Rutherfordton in the west. Between the two parallel stretches of development core is located the South Mountains, traversed by U.S. 221 and 64, and N.C. 18, and other predominantly rural stretches with many options for recreational activity (Photo 12.32). Administratively and functionally, most of the northern section of the SGR, comprised of Alexander, Catawba, Caldwell and Burke counties, is much better integrated than is the southern section, and the two sections are functionally not well linked (Photo 12.33). Hickory is the lead city in a region that has benefited from the regional integration effort of the Region B Council of Governments, the so-called

**Photo 12.31:** Valdese (Burke County) is one of many small Western Piedmont industrial towns. Valdese was settled initially by Waldensians from Central Europe in the 19th Century.

**Photo 12.32:** Lake Tahoma, west of Marion (McDowell County), is a private lake. The privilages of private ownership are clearly evident.

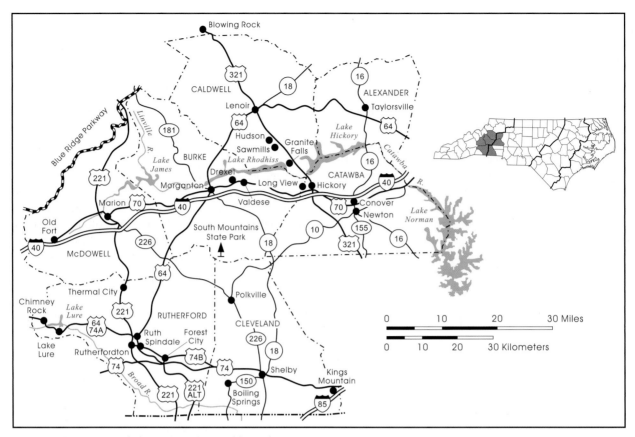

**Figure 12.23:** Western Piedmont State Geographic Region.

Unifour Regional Council. At the same time commercial development has concentrated between Hickory and Newton-Conover on U.S. 70, paralleling I-40.

In comparing state geographic regions, the Western Piedmont places itself in the middle ranks among the 13 SGRs on most accounts from physical and population size to median age (Table 9.2). Yet, there is an interesting and not normally expected correlation between economic well being and levels of education. Indices normally indicating lower quality of life conditions for the Western Piedmont, such as high percentages of families below

the poverty level, annual average infant mortality rate, and percent female head of households, are among the lowest in the state. Almost universally, low rates on these indices as well as high levels of educational attainment, are interpreted as equating to high levels of quality of life. This does not all come together for the Western Piedmont. Here high school graduation rates and the percent who completed college are significantly below state averages. In this SGR people on the average survive better economically and have better than average health and social environments, although they are not as well educated; this is a

**Photo 12.33:** Alexander County is famous for its gold and gem mines. Here visitors can pan gold at the Hiddenite Gold Mine.

510

hallmark of traditional blue color manufacturing communities in North Carolina. As an aside it should be noted that this is one of four state geographic regions without a major state university. Western Piedmont has one relatively small, private four year institution of higher education, Lenoir Rhyne, in Hickory. The generally positive economic conditions has allowed the state to rate the region high on the N.C. Enterprise Tiers (Chapter 9).

Population change during the 1990s have varied among the counties of the Western Piedmont SGR (Table 12.5). Alexander County (CP 12.31), which has benefited from a Hickory area urban overspill, gained 22 percent, the most in a region of population increases ranking well below state norms. With younger families now moving into the county from the south Alexander's population structure will be even more youthful in 2000 than in the diagram shown in Figure 12.24a. In most of the Western Piedmont counties population in the 45 and over cohorts exceed the state averages. This again is a characteristic of predominantly blue color manufacturing economies where economic restructuring has left fewer opportunities for permanent employment for younger age groups. Employees here tend to age in place. Another interesting characteristic involves the higher than norm percentages allocated to young men in the 15-19 age group. A much lower female percentage in this age category suggests that low wage, labor intensive work is available in these counties for males, but less so for females. This 'excess' of males turns into a 'deficiency' when compared to state averages for the subsequent two age cohorts (20-29 years). Note especially the population diagrams for Burke, Cleveland, McDowell and Rutherford counties (Figures 12.24b, e, f, and g). These counties have the "blue color" labor look of their population profiles; note especially Rutherford County, which comes closets to attaining an equal distribution among all age cohorts (Photo 12.34). Caldwell and Catawba counties appear to have a population structure more like the average for Piedmont counties (Figures 12.24c and d) with the exception of the 20-24 young adult population, who may be off to college, may be in the military, or may have acquired jobs in the more economically diversified nearby Piedmont counties.

## SUMMARY

Main Street dominates the human geography of the North Carolina Piedmont, as it dominates the state and much of the southeast of the United States. However, much of its growth over the past three decades was due to 30-35% traditional cost advantage in business locations over northern and mid-western regions. This advantage has now narrowed to less than ten percent, and future growth is likely to be stimulated to a much greater degree by the present complex of "new line" growth industries functioning on a global scale of managerial efficiency and productive competitiveness, as well as on the evolution of a regional commitment to ensure the maintenance of a high quality living environment. Capitalizing on the interlocking interdependence of its "city states" and the complexities of their economic engines, Main Street will avoid getting left behind in the expanding global marketplace of ideas, polity, and economy. Simultaneously, there is scant evidence that the overall quality of life, which should include an environment substantially free of odiferous and noxious air, polluted water, and overcrowded and deteriorating green space, will soon see a major improvement. Critical to long term quality of life conditions is the necessity to

**Photo 12.34:** County fairs are among the most popular family affairs in North Carolina. At the Cleveland County Fair tradition rules, from the judging of farm crops and animals to the entertainment, food, and noise of the Midway.

| WESTERN PIEDMONT | Land Area in sq. km | Pop. 1990 | Pop. sq.km. 2000 | Pop. 2000 | 1990s % Pop. Change | % White 2000 | Median Age in 2000 | % Fam. Below Poverty | Annual Average Infant Mortality Rate 1994-98 | % High School Grads'90 | % Coll. Grads. 1990 | Fem. Fam. Head of Hshld'90 | NC Enterprise Tiers'97 |
|---|---|---|---|---|---|---|---|---|---|---|---|---|---|
| Alexander | 674 | 27,544 | 49.9 | 33,603 | 22 | 92 | 37.3 | 7.3 | 10 | 59.0 | 7.9 | 9.2 | 4 |
| Burke | 1312 | 75,740 | 68 | 89,148 | 17.7 | 86 | 38.2 | 7.7 | 10 | 60.1 | 10.6 | 10.8 | 4 |
| Caldwell | 1222 | 70,709 | 63.4 | 77,415 | 9.5 | 91.8 | 38.1 | 8.2 | 8.6 | 56.8 | 8.9 | 10.8 | 4 |
| Catawba | 1036 | 118,412 | 136.8 | 141,685 | 19.7 | 85 | 37.2 | 4.8 | 6.2 | 66.7 | 14.2 | 10.6 | 4 |
| Cleveland | 1203 | 84,958 | 80 | 96,287 | 13.3 | 76.8 | 38.0 | 8.4 | 8.9 | 63.5 | 11.1 | 13.1 | 3 |
| Mc Dowell | 1144 | 35,681 | 36 | 42,151 | 18.1 | 92.2 | 39.7 | 8.4 | 9.7 | 58.5 | 8.1 | 10.0 | 2 |
| Rutherford | 1461 | 56,956 | 43.1 | 62,899 | 10.4 | 86.8 | 37.9 | 9.0 | 7.8 | 59.4 | 9.8 | 11.5 | 3 |
| **Region Totals** | **8052** | **470,000** | **67.5** | **543,188** | **15.6** | **85.9** | **38.1** | **7.7** | **8.7** | **60.6** | **10.1** | **10.8** | **3.4** |

**Figure 12.5:** Western Piedmont State Geographic Region.
**Source:** U. S. Bureau of the Census, 2000; North Carolina State Planning Office, various years.

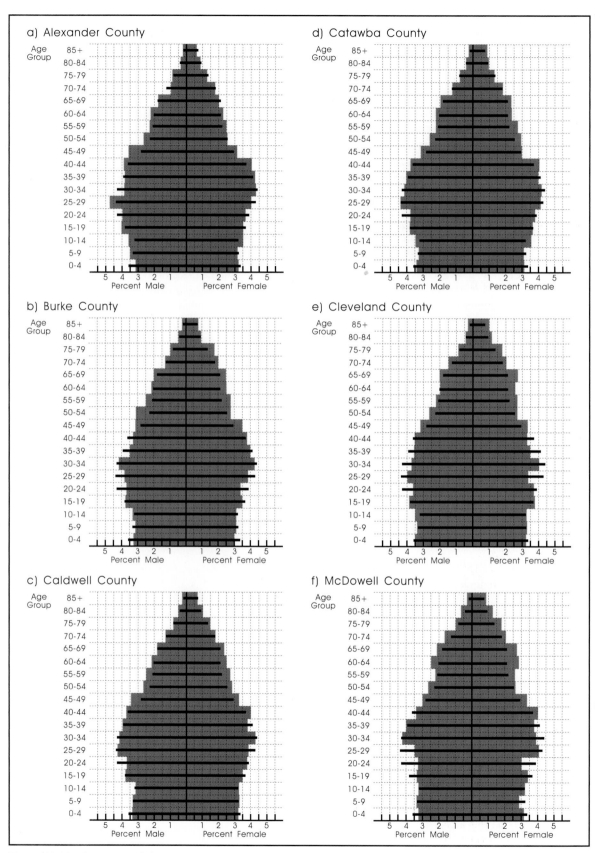

**Figure 12.24 a-f:** Western Piedmont Population Diagrams. Solid black lines represent state averages.
**Source:** U. S. Bureau of the Census, 1990.

512

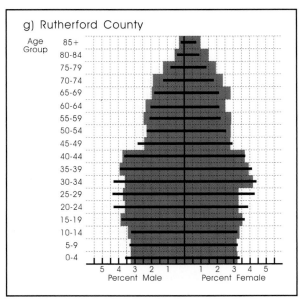

**Figure 12.24 g:** Western Piedmont Population Diagrams. Solid black lines represent state averages.
**Source:** U. S. Bureau of the Census, 1990.

harness urban sprawl before its all devouring tentacles reach deep into the remaining open, green spaces of the region's Green Heart. Continued inattention to these critical regional problems may ensure the killing of the golden goose image that has provided the stimulus for recent economic growth. Smart growth options are only just beginning to appear as appropriately marketable to land speculators and developers. Sincere statewide efforts at coming to an understanding of the nature of the problem, including a recent (January, 2001) final report by the N.C. Smart Growth Commission, flounder at the gates of the Governor's Mansion and the Legislature. Here political pressures define an uncertainty and a reluctance to provide the leadership necessary to invoke statewide laws aimed at controlling sprawl and actively supporting smart growth strategies. The land is still waiting for the nickel to drop. As Pogo was seen to exclaim in his comic strip many decades ago, "we have seen the enemy, and they are us!"

## END NOTES

1) Though the concept of Main Street has been commonly used to designate the main shopping street for individual cities, the term has also gained favor at a larger scale in describing the main artery(ies) linking closely spaced cities. One prominent example is I-5 linking Portland, Oregon; Seattle, Washington; and Vancouver, British Columbia; here the reference is to the Cascade Main Street. Equally we could refer to North Carolina's Main Street as the Piedmont Main Street, but find this a bit cumbersome. Given the absence of any competing urban form within hundreds of miles, we find this moniker perfectly adequate for describing our North Carolina urban phenomenon.

# Mountain Region

## INTRODUCTION

A mountainous landscape dominates the fourth primary region of North Carolina. Westward from Winston-Salem and Charlotte the mountains rise in as they climb along the Brevard fault, marking the beginning of the Blue Ridge, the most prominent landscape feature in this section of the Appalachian Region. A comparison of Figure 13.1 with the geomorphic and elevation maps in Chapter 1 (Figures 1.5 and 1.6; CPs 1.9 and 1.10) will aid in establishing the physical geographic dimensions of this region. The Mountain Region includes counties whose topography defines the change in elevation from Piedmont surfaces, through the foothills area, to the mountains proper (impressively presented to the traveler driving along Interstate 77 through Surry County north into Virginia). The physiographically transitional counties have strong local relief, in some cases marked not only by the physical dominance of the Blue Ridge Escarpment, but also by outlying mountain ridges and complexes of erosion resistant granites, such as Pilot Mountain (Surry County; Photo 1.4), the Brushy Mountains (Wilkes, Alexander, and Caldwell counties; CP 5.3c), and the South Mountains (Burke, Mc Dowell, and Rutherford counties). The many landform configurations and elevation differences influence regional climate, natural vegetation, and human activity. However, while the Mountain Region is fairly easily defined in its physical geography, the human geography and local government administration demand a different approach when these counties are defined at the State Geographic Region (SGR) scale. For reasons explored in Chapter 12, five counties (Alexander, Caldwell, Burke, McDowell and Rutherford) from the Mountain State Primary Region are included within the Western Piedmont State Geographic Region, which is discussed as a SGR in the Piedmont Region chapter. The remaining Mountain Region counties are grouped into three State Geographic Regions: Northern Mountains SGR, Asheville Basin SGR, and Southwest Mountains SGR. The regional landscape characteristics are well illustrated on the state land cover map (CP 1.14) where the greens of the forest dominate and the colors defining development are channeled by rock structures and valley passages. These relationships are illustrated in greater detail on the SGR land cover maps (CP 13.9, CP 13.11, and CP 13.13).

Dominated by ancient rock materials, the Mountain Region was covered by virgin forests prior to European settlement, which began in a pioneering fashion in the 18th century (Photo 13.1). Deciduous hardwoods, pines, and mixed forests, the second most complex forest mix on the continent of North America, covered the lower elevations while spruce-fir forests emerged in the rugged terrain of the higher mountains (CP 13.1). Exposed to the exploitative behavior of waves of settlers and loggers, the virgin forests gave way to managed land use with agriculture prevailing in the northern mountains and forestry dominating in the southern portions. Small villages and towns now compose a settlement pattern spread through valleys that are more readily accessible than steep slopes and ridge tops for transportation and building. Only Asheville provides a metropolitan setting (CP 13.7). In the face of large scale land clearance, most notably the comprehensive and environmentally devastating logging practices of the early 20th century (Chapter 5), and then the much more recent conversion of high slope and ridge country into second home developments and resorts (Photo 13.2), it is remarkable that stands of old growth forests remain in the region. These forest stands are scattered in the least accessible terrain of the national forests. Despite the spread of settlement, forests still comprise the major land cover in most counties of the Mountain Region, especially in the Southwest Mountain State Geographic Region (CP 13.1b and CP 13.4).

Differences in land ownership patterns, with the federal government heavily vested in the southern mountains, tend to highlight differences among the state geographic regions within the Mountain Region. An example is the extensive acreage of the two National Forests, Pisgah and Nantahala, in the Mountain Region (Table 13.1). More than 50 percent of the designated national forest acreage is still held in private ownership, mostly as infill parcels. As indicated in Figure 13.2 and Table 13.2, counties in the Southwestern Mountain State Geographic Region have large percentages of their lands taken up by the Forest Service. For some counties, additional land is taken up by other federal ownership, as in Swain County with the Great Smoky National Park, or by state forests. For some of these counties, precious

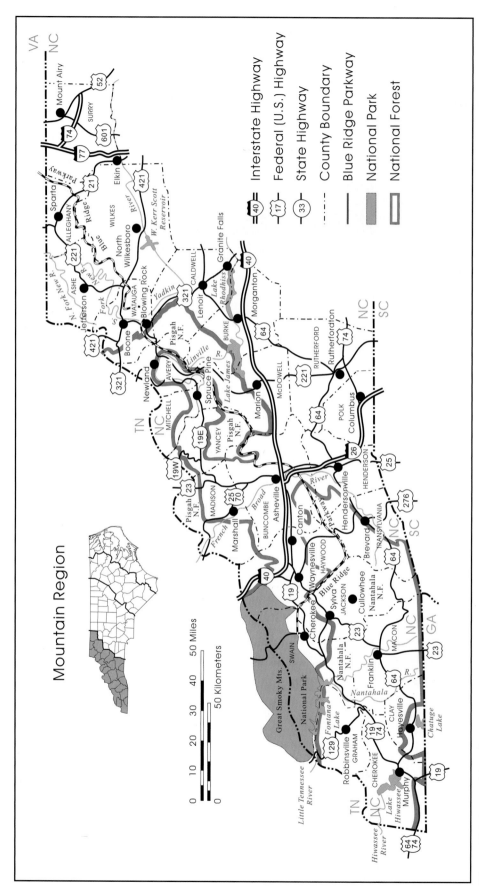

**Figure 13.1:** Mountain Region General Location Map.

516

**Photo 13.1:** The overshot waterwheel from an old grist mill near Alexander Mill, Rutherford County, has been refurbished and erected next to a traditional styled mountain vacation cabin.

little private land is available for property taxes. On the other hand, some northern counties are entirely without federal lands, except for that narrow ribbon of the Blue Ridge Parkway (Photo 13.3).

A major influence on this highland region is elevation and slope. The foothills to the east of the Blue Ridge are marked by a much higher population density resulting from better and more widespread agricultural lands, better sites for industrial development, and much better access to the economic heart of the state, the booming Piedmont Region. To the west, land transportation continues to be handicapped by the difficulty and costs of mountain road construction. Frequently, travel from the northern mountain counties to the southwest is facilitated by getting "off the mountain," (i.e., driving the foothills roads that parallel the Blue Ridge) and then getting back "up the mountain." The many ridges running parallel to the northeast-southwest trending Blue Ridge,

Great Smoky Mountains, and Unakas, handicap intermountain transportation. For example, traveling by auto from Asheville one can drive the intermountain route (US highways 19, 19E and 221 - very little of which is four-lane) and reach Sparta (Alleghany County) 146 miles and four hours later; the alternative route is I-40, I-77 and US 21, a distance of 164 miles, but only two and a half hours, away. On the other hand, when traveling by auto from Asheville to Murphy in Cherokee County there are no advantages in getting "off the mountain," as no facilitating interstate highway crosses the "mountain wall" overlying the border of North Carolina with South Carolina and Georgia. Intermountain travel in this direction has seen much recent improvement with the partial four-laning of US 19, 21, and 441. Asheville itself, of course, is very well connected by freeway systems. These will radiate to the four corners of the country with the expected 2002 completion of the Appalachian Highway (19W) across the moun-

**Photo 13.2:** This vacation home is located some 500 feet below the Blue Ridge Parkway in the upper reaches of the Elk Creek watershed. Near Triplett (Watauga County) the home is within the 7,500 acre Heavenly Mountain Resort. The 1,500 planned single-family homes, condominiums, Transcendental Mediation spiritual center, and educational and golf course facilities, are examples of the pressures on mountain land that is now bringing development to the steep escarpment. (Photo: http://www.elkvalley.com)

517

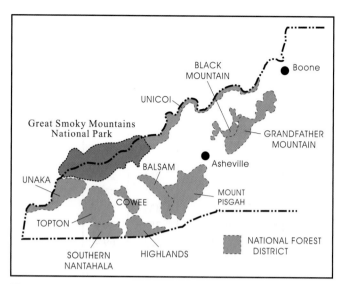

**Figure 13.2:** Old Growth Forest Locations, 2000.
**Source:** Henderson, 2000.

|  | Gross Acerage | NFS Acreage | Other Acreage |
|---|---|---|---|
| Nantahala NF | 1,349,000 | 527,709 | 821,291 |
| Pisgah NF | 1,076,511 | 505,420 | 571,091 |
| **National Forests Total** | **2,425,511** | **1,033,129** | **1,392,382** |

**Table13.1:** National Forests of the Mountain Region.
**Source:** www.fs.fed.us.

tains to Johnson City and points northwest (Photo 13.4). Incidentally, the "mountain wall" defined by the southern face of the Blue Ridge is the feature that gave rise to the name Appalachian Mountains. As an imposing physical rise from the northern Georgia Piedmont, it was noted on a 1565 map, "The Province of Florida in America" as "Montes Apalatchi," by the French artist, Jacques LeMoyne (Davis 2000). Undoubtedly derived from a grouping of Appalachee villages in North Florida, the name eventually became permanently ascribed to the extensive mountain system some distance to the north.

Variations in Mountain Region characteristics spill over into its human geography. A comparison of the state geographic regions, shown in Table 9.2, demonstrates that the Mountain Region has lower population densities than average for the state, lesser population growth, generally more poverty, but, in an interesting contrast, better health conditions, as indicated by the lowest infant mortality rates. Among the Mountain SRGs, the Asheville Basin, with its more urban and older populations, tends to differ itself from the other SRGs in significant ways, especially in educational attainment and population density. As is true for all the state primary regions, when it comes to county level comparisons, the variations among mountain counties can be extraordinary (Tables 13.3, 13.4, and 13.5). In the index of relative poverty by county (the NC Enterprise Tiers) a number of mountain counties are lagging in economic development and find themselves in the poorest category. However, as people elsewhere have been seeing an increase in their expendable income, in their vacation time, and in their ability to access remote places, the North Carolina Mountain Region has seen an incredible increase in tourism, open space recreational activities, and seasonal homes. The impact on land and life is palpable. Even as some mountain communities continue to whither away, most are experiencing minor booms as investments of vacation dollar stimulate local economies; often there is a toll on the landscape.

As is the case for the Tidewater Region, the Mountain Region has attracted considerable interest from regional researchers and authors fostering a rich literature of history, culture, and natural environment. (note, for example the history contributions of the van Noppens (1973), Blackmun (1977), and Bishir, Southern and Martin (2000); the natural environment work by Brown (2000) and Davis (2000b) and the massive compilation of the

**Photo 13.3:** The Grandfather Mountain Viaduct on the Blue Ridge Parkway is an outstanding example of highway construction in a fragile mountain environment. This has become a popular setting for the filming of automobile commercials. (Photo by North Carolina Division of Tourism)

| SGR | County | Pisgah National Forest Acres | Nantahala National Forest Acres | Total (sq. km.) | Percent of Area |
|---|---|---|---|---|---|
| Northern Mountains | Avery | 28,327 | | 131 | 20.5 |
| | Mitchell | 18,615 | | 86 | 15.0 |
| | Watauga | 393 | | 2 | 0.2 |
| | Yancey | 38,230 | | 177 | 21.9 |
| Asheville Basin | Buncombe | 31,464 | | 150 | 8.8 |
| | Haywood | 68,281 | | 317 | 22.1 |
| | Henderson | | 17,295 | 80 | 8.3 |
| | Madison | 55,217 | | 256 | 22.0 |
| | Transylvania | 82,154 | 4,380 | 401 | 40.9 |
| Southwest Mountains | Cherokee | | 93,173 | 432 | 36.6 |
| | Clay | | 64,979 | 301 | 54.1 |
| | Graham | | 113,251 | 525 | 69.4 |
| | Jackson | | 76,930 | 357 | 28.1 |
| | Macon | | 152,700 | 708 | 52.9 |
| | Swain | | 22,296 | 103 | 7.5 |
| Western Piedmont | Burke | 47,946 | | 222 | |
| | Caldwell | 49,391 | | 229 | |
| | Mc Dowell | 68,107 | | 316 | |
| **Total** | | **488,125** | **545004** | **4,792** | |

**Table 13.2:** National Forest Acreage by County, 1999.
**Source:** www.fs.fed.us.

Southern Appalachian Assessment, United States Department of Agriculture (1996). The reader may wish to look at the publications of the Appalachian Consortium Press and the Appalachian Regional Commission for a more extensive listing of current and relevant work on the Mountain Region.

**Photo 13.4:** Linking the Asheville Basin to the Ridge and Valley Province has been accomplished toward the southwest by I-40 to Knoxville Tennessee. A link is being completed to the northwest through the limited access, and very costly, highway U.S. 19W, connecting the Johnson City, Tennessee-Bristol, Virginia area to Asheville. The terrain difficulties of these highways are illustrated in Photo 8.5.

# THE NATURAL LANDSCAPE

## *A Majestic Landscape*

From the Appalachian foothills, ranging from 1,000 to 2,000 feet in elevation, to the Blue Ridge Mountains, ranging from 2,000 to over 6,000 feet, the Mountain Region provides a splendid array of complex topography. Of course, the Blue Ridge is but one of several distinguishable physiographic provinces within the larger Appalachian Mountain System, which reaches from the St Lawrence River to the coastal plain in Alabama and Mississippi. First defined definitively by the geographer Arnold Guyot in 1861 (Wall 1977), and then in greater detail by Nevin Fenneman in his *Physiography of Eastern United States* (1938), the Appalachian Mountain System is not a unified whole, rather it comprises six unique provinces: New England, Adirondacks, Appalachian Plateaus, Ridge and Valley, Blue Ridge, and Piedmont. Among the six provinces, the Blue Ridge and the Piedmont are the only ones present in North Carolina. Yet, for people living in the Mountain Region, adjacent regions take on significance because of their proximity and their varying influences on local life.

Geologically, the Appalachians are a very old mountain system. In the geology time scale (see Figure 1.8) the oldest rocks in North Carolina are dated to 1.8 billion b.p. (before present). Mountain building movements in the earth's crust, orogenies involving folding, faulting, and vulcanism, created a mountain system that reached its greatest heights and complexities in North Carolina. Using Figure 1.8, it is possible to recount briefly the more critical events in the evolution of the Blue Ridge, and adjacent Appalachian physiographic provinces. Major uplifts occurred during the Paleozoic (570 to 290 million years b.p.). These orogenies upthrusted and folded extensive depths of sedimentary materials deposited in a vast sea existing both prior to the initial uplift and between the orogenic periods. Layers of sandstone, limestone, and especially the coal-bearing strata of the Pennsylvanian Period became important to not only understanding the present lay of the land but also the economic wealth that came from the land. Most directly affected by the orogenies was the Blue Ridge Province, which was extensively underlain by Proterozoic (Precambrian) crystalline metamorphic materials, such as schists, gneisses, and slates, with intrusions of igneous granites. The heights achieved by this geology resulted in part from the hardness of the materials to erosional forces that include precipitation, frost heave, solar radiation, landslides, wind, and vegetation root development, and the much more recent human activities of mining, road cutting and construction. Recent geologic evidence suggests that the North American tectonic plate continues to exert westward pressure on a very stable part in its more central portion, the northeast-southwest trending New York-Alabama Lineament. Persistent crustal pressures against the stable Lineament are resulting in continued upward movement of the Blue Ridge Mountains. To some geologists, this explains why the Blue Ridge has not eroded down in eleva-

tion to the level of the Piedmont. In fact, the hypothesis fuels the idea that the Appalachians actually eroded down to an almost level peneplain; then 140 million years b.p. the uplift began and continues to the present (Horan 2001). Of course, this indicates that the Blue Ridge is orogenically a relatively young mountain system, though the earth materials being exposed continue to be among the oldest, geologically speaking.

Comprised almost entirely of metamorphic and igneous rock, the Blue Ridge contains a variety of metallic and nonmetallic deposits, but is devoid of the fuel resources found as coal or hydrocarbons (natural gas and oil) in the Appalachian Plateau Province. Place names such as Micaville, Saphire Valley, Gneiss, Marble, Granite Falls, Hiddenite, like many others in the Mountain Region, attest to the importance of rocks, minerals, and mining, both in the past and currently.

Although some iron was mined during the colonial days, the first major mining activity in the United States started in 1799 with the discovery of gold at the Piedmont Region is Reed Gold mine (Cabarrus County). By 1828 gold had been located in the South Mountains of Burke County. Mining activity became well established in the Mountain Region by the late 1860's with the large-scale extraction of mica. Even today the Yancey-Mitchell-Avery county area leads the nation in mica production. Some high-grade sheet mica is still used for insulation but most is in the form of fine powder used in cement, paint, roofing and rubber manufacture. The Spruce Pine area in Mitchell County has mined feldspar since 1911 and still leads all areas in North America. Feldspar is used in the manufacture of glass and porcelain.

Widely dispersed mining activity of crushed stone occurs in all mountain counties except Caldwell, Graham, and Clay counties. The principal use is for road construction. Asbestos and olivine are usually found in similar rock formations and are mined in Yancey and Jackson counties. Olivine serves as a flux-enhancer in blast furnaces.

Gemstones have long been collected in the Mountain Region, especially in Jackson and Mitchell counties. The first diamond discovered in the state came from the Brindle Town Creek area in Burke County in 1843. There are over two-dozen commercial sites of digging and panning for sapphires, rubies, and garnet; the Franklin-Sylva area is best known for this activity. Uranium oxide occurs in the Avery-Caldwell-Burke county area and there has been interest to prospect for other deposits.

The Blue Ridge Plateau lies between the Blue Ridge Mountains, marking the eastern terminus of the province and the Eastern Continental Divide, and the western ranges of the Unicoi, Great Smoky Mountains, Bald Mountains and the Unaka Mountains. Narrowing to 50 miles in the north, the plateau widens to 100 miles as it reaches the South Carolina and Georgia borders. Traverse ridges and mountain ranges multiply toward the southern portions of this plateau; the more prominent ranges include the Black (with the highest peak in eastern United States—Mt Mitchell at 6,684 feet), Newfound, Balsam, Cowee, Nantahala, Tusquitee, and Snowbird mountains. While providing boundaries between river basins, the ridgelines of these ranges also provide many miles of county boundaries.

### A Four Season Environment

The entire Mountain Region lies within the warm and humid southeast. This subtropical climate is modified at higher elevations that cool average temperatures providing pleasant summer conditions for recreational activities, and possibilities for snowfall and a ski industry in the late winter (Chapter 2 provides considerable detail on weather and climate conditions of the Mountain Region.) Tourism promoters for the various sub-regions of the mountains waste no time in informing prospective visitors of the four season qualities of the mountain environment (Robinson 1996). In the summer a ten-degree average temperature difference frequently exists between the Piedmont heat and the cool of mountain valleys. At higher elevations, as along the Blue Ridge Parkway on the crest of the Balsam Mountains, temperatures will be cooler still (Photo 13.5). A generally dry fall shows off spectacular tree color. Winter generally is cool enough to produce snowfall and to maintain adequate depths of manufactured snow for the largest concentration of ski resorts in the southeast of the country (Photo 13.6). Spring is a time of new growth and wildly rushing streams; a time for waterfall watching and river rafting.

In fact, one of the more appealing outcomes of topographic abruptness and large amounts of precipitation is the frequency of spectacular waterfalls. Among the region's estimated 500 waterfalls are some of the highest in the eastern part of the country. The Southwest Mountains State Geographic Region is the wettest region in the country outside of the state of Washington's Olympic Peninsula. A coincidence of complex physiography, striking local elevation differences, high annual average precipitation totals, and generally small drainage basins have created many small rivers with waterfalls and rapids that extend for miles, as along the Nantahala and the Cheowee rivers. The rivers also provided a large number of possibilities for hydroelectric development. This potential has now been nearly exhausted by the Tennessee Valley Authority, which began developing hydro dams in the 1930's along rivers tributary to the Tennessee River. The Southwest Mountains SGR has a great density of lakes, and therefore many opportunities for recreational activities and vacation home locations in striking natural environments. Less attention had been paid to the smaller area of hydroelectric/ recreational development potential in the Southwest Mountains SGR that was outside the bounds of the Tennessee River Basin. A number of swift flowing, full volume rivers flow from the "mountain wall" to South Carolina and Georgia. Although they all are dammed in those states, upstream the rivers had been largely left alone, until the mid-1980s, when a California group proposed building a dam on the Horsepasture River in Transylvania County, a river legendary for its remarkable waterfalls. The resulting controversy led to the declaration of the Horsepasture River as a Wild and Scenic River, with no future option for hydro or other development.

Elsewhere in the Mountain Region, especially outside the Asheville Basin, the landscape offers fewer opportunities for such water resource development. In the Northern Mountain SGR there is the narrowing of the Blue Ridge Plateau, and a corresponding decrease in the Tennessee River Basin's reach into the state. Attempts at damming rivers have come at a time

**Photo 13.5:** The Wilson Ridge Overlook is illustrative of the many opportunities afforded the visitor traveling the Blue Ridge Parkway. The location is on the east slope of Grandfather Mountain, with a steep drop of over 1,000 feet into the recently designated Wilson Creek Wilderness.

521

**Photo 13.6a:** A popular recreational attraction to the Mountain Region during the winter is skiing. This area provides the southern-most skiing on the east coast and as such attracts people from all over the southeastern United States. **b:** Recently, snowboarding has become popular among the younger enthusiasts as they seek the 'extreme' sports. (Photos: North Carolina Division of Tourism).

when locals have had a greater influence in the decision making process. Such was the case of the New River, where the Appalachian Power Company in the 1960s proposed two hydroelectric dams that would back up water in lakes reaching into Alleghany and Ashe counties. Facing the loss of several existing communities, including 15 churches, many farms, and much agricultural land, local communities and an array of non-governmental organizations cooperated in influencing the North Carolina Assembly to declare the New River a State Wild and Scenic River, and later to have an even larger portion of the river declared a National Wild and Scenic River. Like many newly protected natural treasures in the state, the New River now finds itself well watched over by it own locally derived and based support group - in this case, the National Committee for the New River (Photo 13.7).

### Complex Plant Communities

The Mountain Region has a wide range of vegetative ecosystems, including some that are seriously endangered. The environmental complexes come about naturally with the range in elevation from 1,000 to over 6,000 feet, variations in slope orientation and steepness, and differences in precipitation and hydrology. At the highest elevations, typically above 5,500 feet, a mist shrouded collection of needle-leaved bearing evergreen trees, mostly firs (locally: she-balsams) and spruce (he-balsams), with a ground cover of mosses and lichens (pot scrapings) dominates. On well rounded peaks, at least 4,900 feet in elevation, the Scots-Irish settlers used seasonal grazing, or transhumance, practices carried with them from their homeland, for the feeding of farm animals, mostly cattle and sheep. The well-known mountain bald ecosystem resulted from this. Clearly this is a vegetative ecosystem influenced by human use over time. While the grazing animals kept down the brush, the bald was invaded by non-

native species, such as English Plantain, dandelion, and white clover (Brown 2000). The mountain cove forests are at lower elevations, in valleys protected from easy access logging, with many sites still having "old growth forest" (Chapter 5). In an earlier day, a climax forest of chestnut (before a blight killed nearly every chestnut tree in the country in the early part of 20th century), red oak, chestnut oak, white oak, and tulip poplar covered the mountains from elevations of 1,500 to 4,500 feet. In the southern parts of the Blue Ridge locust, maples, hickories, buckeye, beech, and birch, at the higher elevations, complemented these species.

Wilma Dykeman, a noted author of Appalachian history, captured well an important attribute of vegetation complexes in Western North Carolina, as quoted in Early (1993, 15):

Twenty-five thousand years ago, as a great icecap formed over Labrador and pushed slowly out across North America, animal and plant life fled before its crushing destruction. Seeds were distributed by wind, animals and insects in front of the creeping glacier, until at last all of the northern United States was buried under ice, and trees and plants once native to Canada made their last stand on the heights of the Southern Appalachians.

Natural forests of the southern Appalachian Region during the Pleistocene epoch (Figure 1.8) were dominated by conifers and inhabited by tapirs, mammoth, and bison. Even with the melt-back of continental glaciation, (which, incidentally, did not affect directly any of the Mountain Region) the spruce-fir forests of the higher elevation survived the warming of the climate as an unlikely situated subarctic ecosystem. Native Americans, who have been archeologically proven to have lived in the region

**Photo 13.7:** The New River in Ashe County flows leisurely through meadows and forests of the Blue Ridge Plateau. Not noted for rapids and waterfalls, it is all the more attractive for family activities like canoeing and tubing. As a nationally designated Wild and Scenic River, it is monitored by local watershed defined interest groups coordinated by the National Committee for the New River; a genuine bottom-up approach to enhancing the community and environment welfare of the Mountain Region.

some 12,000 to 15,000 years ago, hunted pleistocene animal life. Only the bison remained to historic times.

Vast expanses of virgin forest, intricately dissected slopes and narrow flood plains restrained development for over a century. Then, over a number of decades leading into the 20th century, powerful denuding forces of the logging companies moved in, mowed down the forest, and built a rail net to move out the tree wealth. Much of the accessible areas still in forest are well along in the "third forest" management period (Chapter 5 and CPs 5.13 to 5.15). Even today, forest cover dominates the landscape in many of the region's more isolated areas. Still virtually undeveloped in the Mountain Region are the Brevard fault escarpment and the Blue Ridge escarpment north of the Asheville Basin. The steep slopes and rugged terrain have created an unlikely scenario for development. Pressures of development are encroaching on the ridges of the escarpment and in some mid-slope areas that have been opened by road access. These areas were untouched just a few short decades ago, but the increased pressures of development have encouraged the disruption of the traditional vegetative cover.

*Biological Hot Spots*

The intersect of elevation, slope steepness and orientation, geologic character, hydrology, and microclimate factors insures a vegetation environment that is rich in species, which otherwise find their individual niches from the subarctic to the subtropical. In fact, new and unusual species continue to be discovered by botanical inventories. A study presently underway in the Great Smoky Mountains National Park, the All Taxa Biodiversity Inventory, has thus far uncovered 67 species of life previously unknown to science, as well as 195 species not before known to have inhabited the Park (Fordney 2000). Another such study is being undertaken in the Jocassee Gorge (CP 1.19), on the Transylvania County border with South Carolina, where the state for the first time decided to instigate a species inventory as part of the overall process of preparing its newest state park for visitors. Funded by the N. C. Heritage Trust Fund the objective is to identify areas of rare species populations, and while some of these are intended for educational purposes, the intent is primarily to divert visitors away from most concentrations, so as to protect the species. Nearly 400 rare species call the western North Carolina Mountains home. We now know that the area harbors the widest diversity of amphibians and snails in North America, and the continent's second largest variety of hardwood and evergreen trees. An earlier Nature Conservancy study reported that North Carolina has a total of 3,658 species in the state. From this we can gather that over ten percent of the extant species are rare and endangered.

The Southern Appalachian Forest Coalition and the Nature Conservancy are collaborating on what has been named the Blue Ridge Project. While the Coalition focuses on public lands, the Conservancy works with private landowners to designate and conserve areas where there are know quantities of rare species populations, so-called "biological hot spots." The central idea is to focus on hot spots where rare species thrive, and then work to preserve enough habitat in the vicinity to boost the rare species' chance of survival (Henderson 2000a).

Developers often clear land for construction without understanding the available alternatives for species preservation. "These folks are losing thousands of dollars worth of landscape stock, then turning around and buying plants from nurseries at high cost," maintains one botanical consultant. Soils and plants already on site are naturally adapted to that area, with built-in tolerance to the vagaries of weather and requiring of no extraneous life support, other than to be left alone; as opposed to the extensive care and nurturing needed by exotic plant life that new residents may introduce to their property. In Transylvania County, one major development, Sapphire Ridge, is utilizing a clearly defined ecological approach to the siting and sizing of property, homes and road access. Of 452 acres in the development, 24 mini-estates at ten acres each are being sold with ecological restrictions, leaving the remaining 212 acres in a conservation easement (Appalachian Voice 2000).

Locating rare species is important to their preservation, but protecting rare species against development and poaching is quite another matter. Public land designation, like national forests, does not necessarily protect rare species. National forests allow logging, mining, and recreation that can disrupt and cause decline in some plant and animal species (CP 13.3). Logging and road building are permanently prohibited only in wilderness areas of the forests (Henderson, 2000a). As detailed in Chapter 5, there is a growing industry for Appalachian herbs and wooded plants. Having perceived medicinal values ranging from the curing of headaches and other pain ailments to a failing libido makes certain species sought after by poachers. A demand also exists for ornamentals, such as galax and Fraser fir. Poaching has resulted in the near eradication of ginseng, goldenseal root, black cohosh root, and other species. The impact of poaching has resulted in a major state effort to save the endangered species. Clever ways are being used to mark plants so they can later, for example at a farmer's market, be identified as stolen property. Some plants are being marked in the field with something akin to grocery store bar codes, while others are dusted with fluorescent powder. Poaching is now punished with up to a six-month prison sentence for a second offense (Suchetka 1999).

*Old Growth Forests*

Contrary to old assumptions that barely an acre of the states forests escaped loggers, recent surveys describe 77,000 acres of cove or old growth forests in the million acre Pisgah and Nantahala national forests (CP 13.4a and b; CP 5.24 and 5.25), with another 125,000 in the Great Smoky Mountain National Park (Figure 13.2). Trees over 150 years old dominate nearly half of that acreage, with few signs that humans ever intruded. One 450 year-old white oak was located, with an additional 19 trees more than 300 years old. Old growth refers to forests stands that have never been cut or have recovered from human intrusion. They are critical in building soils, filtering water, and providing shelter for wildlife, especially deep-woods migratory birds (Henderson, 2000b). In isolated valleys, remnant moist cove forests lose about one percent of their canopy trees each year due to natural causes. This averages out to a one hundred year life cycle before trees become vulnerable to wind blow, age, or disease; however, as indicated, some trees may last 200 to 300 years. The inherent wetness of these areas insure that forest fires are infrequent. Notable and reasonably accessible mountain cove forests are found in the Great Smoky National Park, Graham County's Joyce Kilmer Memorial Forest, (especially trails in the Santeetlah Creek watershed), and Ashe County's Bluff Mountain Preserve (CP 5.24 and 5.25). These forests were protected by steep slopes and roadless terrain, which made them simply too hard to reach.

An example of the U. S. Forest Service approach to national forest management that includes protection of cove for-

ests is provided in Box 5A. The area depicted on the Land and Resources Management Plan is at the intersection of three counties (Clay, Macon, and Cherokee) in the upper reaches of the Nantahala River. Note the location of the Nantahala Lake and Dam; water is released on schedule to allow downstream river rafting and canoeing. Two areas shown on this management map include fairly extensive old growth forest. One is situated between Hickory Knob and Junaluska Creek, in the northwestern quadrant of the map. This area is in Management Area 4C, where the forest is to be left alone, with no timber management, and closed to motorized traffic. The other area is found in Clay County just overlapping into Macon County, in the southwestern quadrant of the map. Here the management designation is Area 5, indicating a large block of backwoods country with little evidence of human activity, that is slated to be left alone.

About 21 percent of the old growth in the Pisgah and Nantahala national forests is permanently protected as wilderness. A ban on road construction in roadless areas would increase the area protected to about 58 percent. Most of the land not currently listed as wilderness is not indicated in forest plans as loggable land, but the land is not permanently protected (Henderson, 2000b). Forest Service policy can change with changing federal administration, but wilderness law has permanence. However, large old growth trees in secluded mountain cove forests are valuable enough to harvest selectively by the most recent tool in logging technology, the helicopter.

*Mountain Bogs*

Estimates indicate that about half of North Carolina's wetlands have been destroyed since European settlement. Carolina bays have been ditched and drained for agriculture, saltwater marshes drained for coastal development, bottomland hardwood forests drained for crops and pine plantations, and pocosins have been converted to large farms, as related in earlier chapters.

Mountain bogs are quite different from the other wetland areas of the state. These bogs are often smaller in size than their counterparts in the vast wetlands of the Tidewater and Coastal Plain regions. Mountain bogs tend to emerge where excess water enters an area, with beavers often credited for either developing these circumstances or helping maintain them. Typically they are supported by groundwater seepage, but in some cases surface waters feed them from higher elevations. In the latter case, they are referred to as fens. Mountain bogs are usually unprotected because their small size makes them difficult to identify, locate, and map without extensive fieldwork. They can be only yards across in size and most are less than five acres in area. Additionally, terrain and accessibility are limiting factors to appropriate identification and inclusion on the National Wetlands Inventory (NWI). It is difficult to know if development may be destroying valuable wetland habitat when they are not identified and not part of the NWI database.

Figure 13.3 illustrates the vegetative communities common to mountain bogs. In addition to the plant life indicated in this sketch, mountain bogs may include such rare and showy species

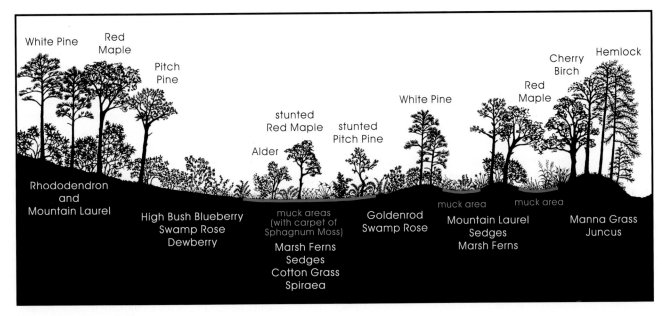

**Figure 13.3:** Mountain Bog.
**Source:** Venters (1995); illustration by Anne Runyon, by permission.

as Gray's Lily and several types of wild orchids. While bogs may act as filters by absorbing pollutants from run-off, this is not a frequent situation for the small mountain bog. Rather its importance derives from its role as a habitat for a variety of plant and animal life. Mountain bogs appear as shallow, waterlogged depressions, and are easily overlooked as a wetland area by loggers and developers. Protection of these bogs is difficult, but necessary, because mountain bogs provide critical habitat and a unique ecosystem for many endangered species.

*National Parks and Blue Ridge Parkway*

Providing public access to the fragile natural environments of the Appalachian Mountain System has been a major challenge that the national and state governments have met with great success in North Carolina. With the creation of the National Park Service in 1924, some 20 choices emerged as competitive for national park development. The Great Smoky Mountain National Park and the Shenandoah National Park were chosen. In 1909, Benton McKaye, visionary geographer and public servant, proposed the building of a great carriage way to crown the Blue Ridge and to make its splendors available to all. Expressed as an important environmental engineering project of great significance to several states, the idea found fertile ground several decades later in the depression years and the era of the New Deal. The National Industrial Recovery Act of 1933 authorized the project, and in the process provided work to thousands of unemployed workers. Principally Spanish and Italian masons did its dominating rock masonry work, while Waldensian stonecutters from Valdese (Burke County) quarried stone into handsome facings for the arched tunnels and bridges (Bishir, Southern and Martin 1999).

The Blue Ridge Parkway is a uniquely shaped National Park whose character and reputation depend upon maintaining picturesque views for visitors. The scenic corridor connects the Shenandoah N.P. with the Great Smoky Mountains N. P., traversing some 470 miles and generally following the crest of the Blue Ridge (Figure 13.1). An important aspect of the Parkway's charm lies in successfully incorporating a diversity of mountain environments in its traverse. It was recognized by the chief architect, Stanley W. Abbott, "that too little variation, even in majestic scenery, could be monotonous, so he sought and achieved modulation and contrast in roadway placement" (Bishir, Southern and Martin 1999, 86). Vistas compete with quiet glens, pasture lands, and forest, with an occasional interlude of special parks and historic culture centers. The Parkway corridor is approximately 400 yards at the narrowest section to over 8,000 yards (4.5 miles) where larger island parks (CP 5.25) are incorporated. The Parkway attracts more than 30 million travelers each year. Following years of disagreements with landowner Hugh Morton about siting appropriateness and landscape disruption of the road around Grandfather Mountain, the Parkway saw completion in 1987 with the Linn Cove viaduct traversing the rugged slopes of Grandfather Mountain (Photo 13.3 and 13.5). Linn Cove is a 1,243 foot, double s-shaped concrete ribbon viaduct, comprising 153 pre-cast segments and supported by reinforced steel concrete pylons that minimize cutting into the mountain (Photo 13.3). The linear shape of the Parkway makes management difficult and encroachment from development is increasing pressures on the visual quality along the parkway. Preservation of the rural landscape and the natural scenery visible from the Parkway became the charge of the Conservation Trust for North Carolina during 1995, the governor's "Year of the Mountains." Passing through a much more rugged terrain with a greater domination by national forests, the 252 miles of Parkway in North Carolina have not been as pressured by adjacent development as had been the case for the 217 miles of its passage through Virginia. Where the Parkway now is passing through countryside in the proximity of urban places, such as Roanoke in Virginia, and Boone and Asheville in North Carolina, land values have skyrocketed, up to $40,000 per acre for lots that have the advantage of overlooking the nation's most popular scenic highway (Quillin 2000). Driving the Parkway for the privilege of looking at private homes detracts from the expectation of a bucolic experience. A related problem is that people are now increasingly using the Parkway for commuting to work and other activities. Easements or purchase by the Conservation Trust of North Carolina, the Coalition for the Blue Ridge Parkway, and other land preservation groups, have protected more than 18,000 acres along the parkway since 1996; most of it was a single easement protecting Asheville's watershed (Henderson 1999). The efforts are not always successful, as in the case of the Balsam area south of Asheville, in the proximity of the highest point (6,047 feet) on the Parkway. In October, a tapestry of red, yellow, and orange leaves carpets the steep slopes, but a disharmonious blend of rooflines and sundecks of varying and jarring colors now interrupt the view. Most people who buy property near the Parkway do tend to be responsive to the pleas of preservationists, but the dichotomy of behavior is nonetheless striking. As we endeavor to protect our natural resources while providing access for their enjoyment, that very act elevates our desire to possess adjacent lands now having a certified beauty, and increases the marketing value of the land, with the eventual result of destroying our natural environment.

## PATTERNS OF HUMAN SETTLEMENT

### A Cherokee Saga

Some five hundred years ago, an agricultural people whom we know of today as the Cherokee lived in what is now parts of Tennessee, North Carolina, South Carolina, and Georgia. Descendants of an Iroquian language group that migrated south about 3,500 years ago, the Cherokees apparently were residing in this southeastern, mostly mountainous region, for 1,000 to 2,000 years prior to European contact. Ancestors of the Cherokees constructed their temples (or other prominent buildings) on mounds that rose ten to twenty feet from the valley floors. The practice of mound building, typical of Mississippian culture, ended by the 17th century and existing mounds continued to have some usage (Figure 13.4). Owning their land collectively, Cherokees farmed the valleys and hunted the forests while living in compact villages and small towns (Bishir et al. 1999). Spanish conquistadors, led by Hernando de Soto, Juan Pardo, and Tristan de Luna, arrived during the 16th century, bringing with them European trading practices, plants, and human diseases. The Cherokee response was to increase economic activities in goods favored by the traders, causing the disappearance of elk

and bison. They expanded their cultivated fields with peaches, watermelon, pears, and cow peas, began herding cattle and building houses using traditional European log construction methods (Brown 2000, 6).

William Bartram was a Quaker naturalist who traveled through northern Georgia and western North Carolina in 1776. He visited 39 Cherokee villages and described their habit of clearing forest spaces for agriculture, wood needs, and defense. He observed a landscape already affected by European encroachment through the hunting and subsequent decimation of beaver and otter (for skins) and deer (for meat). Bartram also found a population depleted by disease and the recent war with the British (the Cherokee War of 1760-61), which the Indians fought toward the end of the French and Indian Wars. Disagreement exists among scientists as to whether the grassy plains and open savanna lands described by Bartram were natural or were caused by controlled fires set by the Indians. Although this observation might fuel the issue of the Piedmont open savanna grasslands discussed in Chapter 12, for the Cherokees it had become a mute question, as they lost vast amounts of their traditional lands following the Revolutionary War. The Cherokees were unwise enough to side with the British during the war and again suffered defeat, the burning of crops and villages, and the death of a significant percentage of their population. Their lands were mostly granted to soldiers of the victorious armies, such as Robert Love who received a land grant covering most of present Haywood County. Other families squatted on Indian lands and, in so doing, eventually were granted preemptive rights for the building of mills, smithies, and other businesses, as well as for fertile valley bottom lands. Promises and treaties guaranteeing the Cherokee continuing property right were constantly broken as white settlers moved into Indian Territory. In the 1760s, one Indian grieved about, "the number of families that have come from North Carolina and Virginia and settled upon a great deal of our land, . . . are circumstances very alarming to us . . . we were promised quiet possession of our lands and redress for our grievances" (DeVorsey 1966, as quoted in Davis 2000b, 95-96). A statement on the quotation wall of the North Carolina State Museum of Art provides apt testimony to the universality of this treatment of the Native Americans (Photo 13.8).

Conditions for the Cherokees took a turn for the worse with the election of Andrew Jackson in 1828. He brought into being his promised Indian Removal Act (1830), which forced the Cherokee Nation onto the "Trail of Tears" to Oklahoma Territory, with the loss of an estimated four thousand lives. However, not all Cherokees were forced to relocate. A group of Indians had settled along an isolated stretch of the Oconaluftee River. Separated from the remainder of the Cherokees, this group declared themselves citizens of North Carolina and, as the Eastern Band of Cherokees, eventually achieved recognition by state government as having the right to remain on lands that subsequently became part of the Qualla Boundary (Figure 13.4). These rights were firmed up by the corporate charter granted the Cherokee Nation by the North Carolina General Assembly in 1883. Incor-

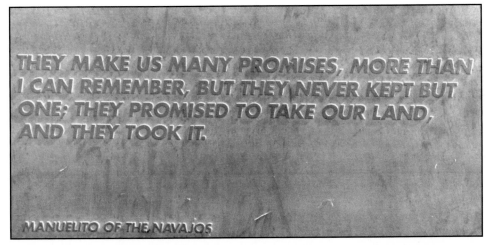

poration makes it possible for the Nation to enter into contracts, to own and manage property, and to sue and be sued (Jones 1996). It laid the foundation for the tourist economy, that began replacing agriculture in the 1940s and led to the present gambling casino (CP 13.2e, CP 13.8). Even so, there continues to be disagreements between the Cherokee Nation and the federal, state, and local governments on property rights and related taxation. At times the state has shown an active interest in the exploitation of Qualla Boundary natural resources, only to be rebuffed by the courts. At other times, moves have been made by counties to assess property taxes against Boundary property, only to lose in state court. In 1980, the court ruled that while the state could not tax earnings derived from work on the Reservation, neither could local government tax its property (Jones 1996). Other current issues regarding Cherokee land use are discussed in the section on the Southwest Mountain State Geographic Region.

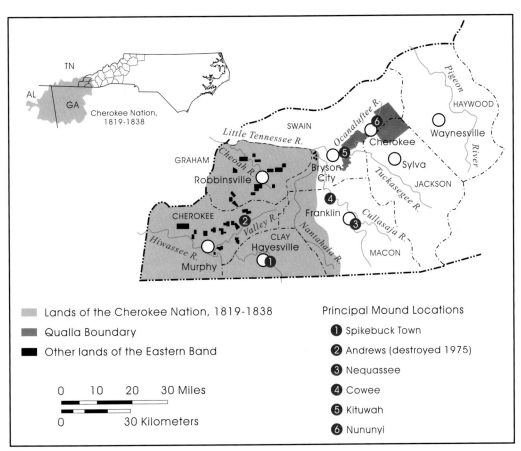

**Figure 13.4:** Cherokee Lands and Sites in Western North Carolina.
**Source:** Bishir, Southern and Martin 1999, 13.

527

## The Settlement Process to the Present

Following the Revolutionary War the great wave of white western migration went over the mountains into Tennessee and Kentucky. When Scotch-Irish and German settlers ventured west into the North Carolina Mountains, they followed the major rivers, such as the Yadkin and Catawba, or the Cherokee Indian trails. The sequent occupance of settlers followed a typical pattern: "long knives" (hunters and trappers) were followed by traders and cattlemen, and finally by merchants and agriculturalists. Valleys of the Blue Ridge Plateau, with their alluvial, fertile, and easily cultivable soils, were first settled (CP 5.3a). Families able to gradually control significant acreage in such favored agricultural environments tended over time to branch off into commercial activity and professional service, and to emerge as local and regional leaders. Eventually slave holding supported their increasing wealth. Latecomers settled in less favorable terrain. In the late 1700s, permanent white settlement reached the eastern divide and had moved into the western-most counties (Cherokee and Graham) by 1820. Western Piedmont regions filled quickly, and new counties were created to accommodate the growing population: Burke and Wilkes counties were formed in 1777, and Rutherford County in 1779.

Settlers ventured more slowly into the deep valleys of the mountains, where wilderness was still perceived as threatening and forests were full of wolves, bears, and panthers. Small and rugged farmstead sites were carved out in narrow valleys and on steep slopes - "up the hollow," as the locals still call it (CP 7.1a). Farmsteads were laboriously carved out of the forest cover, frequently by "deadenings." Settlers cleared and burned acres of underbrush and larger trees were girdled by removing a wide strip of bark at their base to prevent the sap rising. Indian corn was the most successful early crop for the "deadenings," because it could be planted in soil filled with roots and stumps. Other crops, especially wheat, barley, rye and oats, were planted as row crops in the more accessible bottomlands, or awaited the clearing out of the deadwood. Fruit crops, especially apples, were longer in arriving, but eventually assumed considerable importance (Photo 3.4). Stone or wood rail fences were used to prevent crop browsing by forest animals or the farm's domesticated animals. Farmers favored hogs that from the earliest day were found very useful in their ability to fatten by scouring the mast of the forest. Hogs had great utility for the subsistent household; hogs provided not only meat, but also lard for cooking and greasing of weapons and implements, and hides for leather. Hunting was especially important in the earlier years of settlement, because it took some time before crop agriculture and animal husbandry could become the mainstays of the household economy. Elk, bear, deer, and smaller animals, such as turkey, rabbits, squirrels, pigeons and migratory birds, were all-important, but most significant were the buffalo (CP 5.19). The buffalo was a source of meat, hide, and tallow, all products that came to figure prominently in early trade and the developing cash economy. Wholesale harvesting of animals moving in herds was indiscriminate and caused the disappearance of elk and buffalo by the latter decades of the 18th century. Cattle also assumed a prominent place for the mountain farmer, although cattle figured more prominently in ranching in the Ridge and Valley and Piedmont provinces, with drovers herding the cattle to the mountains for grazing in the summer (Davis 2000a). Many place names have been derived from the various practices and sense of space of the hill farmers. Meat Camp in Watauga County, for example, comes from the "camping" of beef cattle during the warm season. Similarly, connecting Meat Camp to the Valley and to the Piedmont was the Buffalo Trail, one of several prominent cross-mountain routes (Photo 3.5 and CP 5.36). In addition, Elk frequently occurs among mountain place names.

The backbone of the economy, until the logging boom of the late 19th century, was the farm household, a largely self-sufficient, economic unit, dependent on the land and the energy of its members in providing food, clothing, shelter, and other necessities of life. Small towns grew where favored by road access and established trade routes; many became county seats as new counties west of the Blue Ridge began forming into the 19th century. When Buncombe County was carved out of the western portion of Rutherford and Burke counties, in 1791, it comprised over one third of the Appalachian Mountain Region. The county seat of Asheville was incorporated in 1798, although the town had only a couple of hundred people. Buncombe County was gradually divided into ten smaller counties.

National economic prosperity accelerated the exploitation of Appalachian natural resources, especially coal and wood at the turn of the 20th century. Private companies acquired either large acreages for their needs, or they purchased mining and/or logging rights from owners. Heavy logging reduced the forest cover in the Blue Ridge from 1900 to the 1920s. Sawmills proliferated and were served by narrow gauge railroads, pushed into the Mountain Region from adjacent states or the North Carolina Piedmont. The Piedmont was evolving into a major market for hardwoods for its expanding furniture industry (Chapter 6). The Western North Carolina Railroad, an offshoot of the state owned railway system, extended to Morganton in 1861 (Figure 13.5). The railway continued toward Asheville, but it was not until 1879 that the Blue Ridge was first scaled, with the laying of rail over the Eastern Divide near Ridgecrest. A little later that same year the Asheville and Spartanburg Railroad completed its famous Saluda grade to the Blue Ridge Plateau in Polk County (Photo 13.9). Rail reached Murphy (Cherokee County) from Georgia in 1888 and from Asheville in 1891. With logging rails coming to the county from all directions, the argument might be made that Cherokee County has not been as well connected since that time. It needs noting that logging rails were narrow gauge (three feet apart), as compared to the standard 5 feet, 8 1/2 inches. The northern Blue Ridge counties saw their connections come only from Tennessee and Virginia, with the "Virginia Creeper" (VC) reaching Todd (Ashe-Watauga County border) as late as 1916. (The VC is now a favorite bike trail.) New villages and towns emerged because of

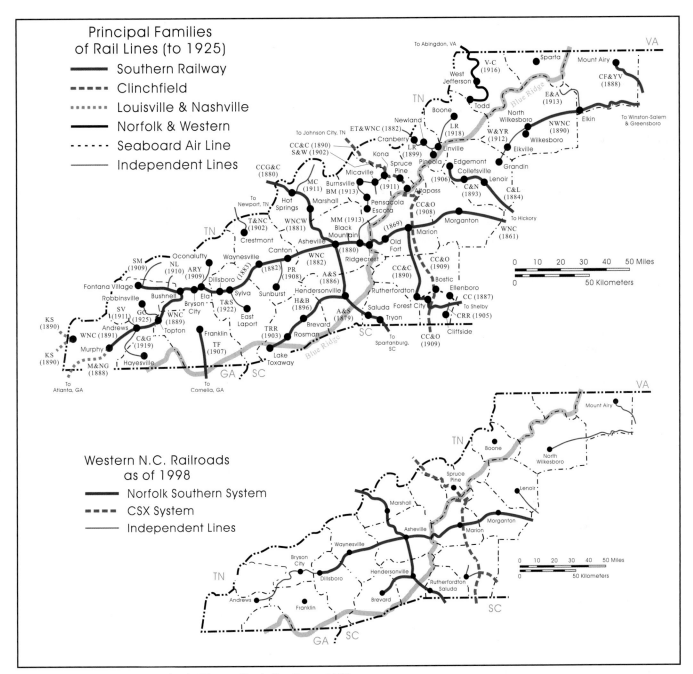

**Figure 13.5:** Railroad Construction in Western North Carolina to 1925.
**Source:** Bishir, Southern and Martin 2000, 34.

their favorable position in logging and mineral extraction. Some of these towns were able to continue growing based on other locational advantages when the mining/logging boom dissipated. Examples include, Spruce Pine (Mitchell County), Burnsville (Yancey County), Black Mountain (Buncombe County), Canton (Haywood County), and Murphy. Other towns declined swiftly following the demise of the extractive industries, as, for example, Todd, Edgemont (Caldwell County), Cranberry and Plumtree (Avery County), Kona (Mitchell County), Crestmont (Haywood County), Oconalufty (Swain County), and Apalachia (Cherokee

County), which was drowned with the filling of Lake Apalachia by the Tennessee Valley Authority. Many of these latter settlements are now ghost towns, as exemplified by Plumtree (CP 13.6d). Others have magically bounced back due to a favorable tourism location, such as Saluda in Polk County (Photos 6.4a and b), or because of an enhanced proximity to a growth center, such as Todd's location relative to Boone in Watauga County (CP 5.14). Some rail lines connected points of increasing attractiveness to tourists. In this way visitors were able to come very near the top of Mt. Mitchell by 1910. However, with the massive logging came

major problems of soil leaching, erosion, flooding, and forest fires. The 1941 "flood of the century" washed away many a rail lines that were never rebuilt. Comparing the 1925 rail transport map with the 1998 map reveals the changing fortunes of rail in the Mountain Region, a reflection of what has been happening across the country. Log transport, for example, is now almost entirely by truck (CP 5.23). What is not shown in Figure 13.5 is that all existing rail is goods transport, with the exception of the Dillsboro (Jackson County) to Andrews (Cherokee County) line that serves the seasonal tourists (Photo 13.10).

Until the 1940's, this region was still one of the most isolated sections of Eastern America. Subsequently, the arrival of industrialization, tourism, and the growth of institutions of higher education have replaced isolation with development and traffic. Now there is concern for the quality of natural environments once associated with isolation. Old growth or virgin forests have been bulldozed and replaced with tourist and second home developments, condominiums, golf courses, ski resorts, Christmas tree farming, and the new civilization of fast food, stores, and mini-mart gas stations. Popularity and access has caused land prices to soar. The once exquisite Maggie Valley, west of Asheville, is now full of snake farms and other tourist attractions (North Carolina Focus 1996). Control over the land has traditionally been left to the owners, as zoning has been slow to catch on and be implemented.

### Contemporary Land Ownership and Use

The Weeks Act of 1911 authorized the purchase of land for the National Forest System (Chapter 5). The move toward federal land management was especially strong in the southwestern counties, resulting in their proportionally greater share of public lands.

Today, these same areas have great value for recreation, timber production, and watershed protection. Recently, changes in agricultural land use and ownership have become a source of concern for many. Fewer farms and less crop acreage reflect a national trend, but probably of greater significance to mountain communities is the increase in non-local and out-of-state ownership.

Private land accounts for about two-thirds of the Mountain Region. Much of this is in small, isolated tracts (under 100 acres), which may foster environmental deterioration. Poorly graded access roads, private dumping, and water pollution resulting from inappropriate septic and wastewater disposal are common environmental issues. There has been a trend for large companies to buy up and consolidate holdings for subdivision and resort development. This has resulted in less farmland, as well as a change in occupation from farming to service industries.

### Mountain Agriculture

Family farms have been reduced in numbers over the past several decades. Those that remain are predominantly small land holdings. Agricultural crops include corn, wheat, soybeans, burley tobacco, Irish potatoes, cabbage, green beans, tomatoes, strawberries (Photo 3.3), and blueberries. An assessment of the state county agricultural production maps (Figures 5.1-5.17) indicates that the Mountain Region is marginal in agricultural production. In the northernmost counties (Ashe, Alleghany, Surry, and Wilkes), there is still substantial crop production, but the strength here is in broilers, beef, and dairying. There is still much agricultural land that supports hay and permanent pasture, a production condition that minimizes soil erosion and stream sedimentation (Chapter 8). Row crops have been largely confined to terraces along river courses or to relatively flat interfluves (CP 5.3a). In the Asheville Basin, tree crops such as apples (Photo 3.4 and CP 5.3c) and peaches often occupy sloping terrain where cold air drainage minimizes damage from late spring freezes (Chapter 2). Once an economic mainstay, the family farm often is used as a second source of income. Many farmers now seek work in the more developed rural centers or commute to the manufacturing industries in larger cities. It is not uncommon for commutes of an hour to and from work. Farming's outlook is slowly changing in the mountains as traditional crops give way to new farming economies

What remains of land in agricultural production in the Blue Ridge Province is devoted largely to specialized cash crops, although the chicken broiler, tobacco, and apple growing industries have suffered considerably in recent years (Photo 3.11). Vineyards have flourished for decades in the Waldensian settlements of Burke County, and they are now taking hold on a much larger scale in Polk, Buncombe, and Surry counties. The Biltmore Estate Winery was developed largely as an afterthought to support the tourism functions of the Biltmore House, but is emerging as one of the larger vineries on the east coast (Photo 3.12). Shelton Vineyards near Dobson in Surry County, one of eight new wineries coming on line in 2000-2001, have aspirations rivaling those of Biltmore. Boutique wineries, the smaller producers such as Rockhouse Vineyards (located in Polk County), are emerging across the foothills to find a niche increasingly given space by the emerging positive image of the North Carolina wine industry. This image is sparked by the state sponsored North Carolina Grape Council's education, research and promotional efforts, to cultivate interest in the production of *vitis vinefera* as a substi-

tute for the declining tobacco production. The positive image is further supported by early innovators, such as the Biltmore Estate (Photo 13.13) and Westbend Vineyards in Lewisville, Yadkin County (Tracy 2001).

*Horticulture and Ornamentals*

White fir, white spruce, Norway spruce, Colorado blue spruce, Leyland cypress, Canaan fir and Fraser fir are the varieties of Christmas trees grown in the Mountain Region. Of these species, Fraser firs account for 96 percent of the Christmas trees grown in the high country; 88 percent of those trees come from Ashe, Avery, Alleghany, Watauga, and Jackson counties (Photo 13.14). The Fraser fir has a limited native geographical habitat range that extends through southwest Virginia, western North Carolina, and eastern Tennessee, and is found at elevations exceeding 4,500 feet. This species was also known as the balsam fir and was named for the Scottish botanist-explorer John Fraser, who frequented these mountains in the late seventeen hundreds (Jakobsen 2000). Christmas tree farming has not always been as commercialized as it is today (Photo 13.15). Gerry Moody, the Avery County Extension agent, said, "until the late 1940's and early 1950's, most Fraser firs were cut from forests on Roan Mountain to be sold as Christmas trees. When people began growing the trees, they collected seed cones from two sites, Roan Mountain and Mt. Rogers. Most of the Fraser firs in plantations today come from these sources" (Jakobsen 2000).

With annual revenues exceding 100 million dollars, Christmas tree farming is an economically viable operation. This is a very labor intensive industry that has about 30,000 acres spread over 2,000 farms. North Carolina is second only to Oregon in Christmas tree production and is first in dollars per tree, accord-

**Photo 13.10:** Carrying tourists from May through October, along a right-of-way dating to 1884, the Great Smoky Mountain Railway connects Bryson City to the popular white water rafting sites of the Nantahala Gorge. Each year the Nantahala Outdoor Center attracts 200,000 visitors to rivers that vary in their degree of challenge from the family focused Nantahala and French Broad rivers to the wild and rambunctious Nolichucky and Ocoee rivers.

**Photo 13.11:** Burley tobacco is staked and drying in the field (Madison County). Scenes like this have become rare, as tobacco consumption, government subsidies, and producer purchasing policies have changed to lower the demand for this traditional mountain cash crop.

**Photo 13.12:** Vineyards cascade to the French Broad River on the grounds of the premier French styled chateau in North America, the Biltmore House. Inspecting a vineyard, among the first planted in the early 1980s, is a Geography of Viticulture class from Appalachian State University. William Cecil, owner of the Biltmore Estate, has succeeded in complementing the image of the Loire Valley chateau milieu desired by his ancestor, George W. Vanderbilt.

ing to the N.C. Department of Agriculture's Marketing Division (Jakobsen 2000). The growth of this industry during the past forty years has mirrored that of the growing population in the High Country. Concern for people and the environment has focused mainly on the use of pesticides. Use of most pesticides is by permit. Moody said, "pesticides are an important and necessary tool in producing healthy, quality trees and are used responsibly in programs like IPM" (Integrated Pest Management). IPM was implemented in the early 1990s to help develop alternatives to pesticide use, which has dropped twenty percent since initiating this program.

*Explosion of Craft Industries*

In 1930, leaders of major arts and crafts studios, such as the John C. Campbell School (Clay County), Biltmore Industries (Buncombe County), and the Penland School of Crafts (Mitchell County), came together to form an organization to promote and market mountain crafts (CP 13.10). The Southern Highlands Handicraft Guild was a cooperative of artisans and craftspeople whose work further stimulated an already active, though unorganized, region-wide crafts movement. Appalachian crafts were dominated earlier by folk toys, such as panty-hose dolls, gee-haw whimmy diddles, and dancing figures on wood paddles, but an increasing sophistication in artistic expression was promulgated by craft schools and by study centers attached to universities and community colleges (Bellebuono 2001). Hundreds of studios and galleries where crafts are sold, generally through consignments of local artists, are scattered from Alleghany to Cherokee counties. Most are members of cooperative groups and promulgate their own businesses through printed brochures, web pages, and toll free numbers. Many are members of the Southern Highland's Craft Guild, whose headquarters is located at the Folk Art Center on the Blue Ridge Parkway near Asheville. The Folk Art Center is a public/private partnership built by the National

Park Service, The Appalachian Regional Commission, and the Guild. The Guild's mission includes marketing, preservation of mountain crafts, sharing resources and education. Its 700 members come from nine different states. The Folk Art Center's special events and educational days highlight the great variety of goods now being produced in the Southern Highlands (fiber and linen work, ceramics, furniture and other wood products, painting and metal work). Complementing the Folk Art Center's Allanstand Craft Shop is the Parkway Craft Center at Moses Cone Manor on the Blue Ridge Parkway near Blowing Rock (Watauga County). It is difficult to assess the overall economic impact of this industry, as there is no federal tracking of sales. A study by Dave and Michaels (2001) compares their findings of the national craft market revenues to those of other related industries, for which data is readily available: fine crafts market, $29.9 billion; retail floral market, $16 billion; organic foods market, $4 billion; and the toy industry, $29.9 billion.

### Growth and Development

Avery County had a property tax base of $8 million in 1963; that has grown to more than $1.4 billion in 2000 (Avery County Tax Assessor 2000). This increase is significant and it has had profound impacts on the environment. Throughout the Mountain Region, this trend holds true. Watauga, Buncombe, Cherokee and other counties have experienced similar growth and have seen land costs and tax bases steadily rising. Many of the now landowners are from out of region, with a significant number being out of state, particularly Florida and Georgia.

Ownership of land in the Mountain Region is changing at a pace not seen before; the rate of change varies, depending upon location and available amenities. Counties containing recreation areas for skiing, golf, and fine restaurants that cater to the vacationers are finding an exploding population of second homes and land that is no longer locally owned. In a recent comparison

**Photo 13.15:** A magnificent view of the Biltmore estate in Asheville (Buncombe County), home to the Biltmore Forest and fine wines from their vineyard (See Figure 13.12). (Photo by North Carolina Division of Tourism)

**Photo 13.14:** Both Ashe and Avery counties claim to be the Christmas tree capital of the world. Local boosterism aside, these large-scale producers compete with counties of the Blue Ridge Province in Pennsylvania and elsewhere.

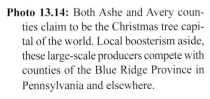

**Photo 13.15:** Christmas trees have become the new cash crop of the northern Mountain Region. Fraser firs favor elevations over 4,000 feet on the mid-slopes of the mountains. Tree cutting, heavily dependent on a Hispanic labor force, begins in October for delivery to distant markets and weekend packages are available for those who wish the adventure and tradition of cutting their own Christmas tree. (Photo by North Carolina Division of Tourism)

between Avery and Ashe counties, residents owned only 35 percent of the homes in Avery County, whereas Ashe County showed 77 percent ownership by residents. The remaining ownership of Avery's homes are from North Carolinians who are not residents (some 26 percent); an additional 24 percent are owned by Florida residents, with residents of South Carolina, Tennessee, Georgia, Virginia and other states owning the remaining 15 percent. The result has been skyrocketing land prices that the local residents cannot afford when competing with their counterparts in the "gated" communities (Photos 13.1 and 13.2). Ashe County may only be in the beginning stages of this boom, as only 16 percent of homes are owned by North Carolinians outside the county, with out-of-state owners comprising the remaining 7 percent. There has been increasing activity in this county from "outside" interests. Jefferson Landing, a golf course oriented community, has located in Jefferson, the largest town in Ashe. The stereotype of the poverty of Appalachia may still hold true, but in many areas of the Mountain Region a transformation is in progress (Winsor and Mann, 2001).

## THREE STATE GEOGRAPHIC REGIONS

### *Introduction*

We earlier alluded to the harmonious natural qualities of the Mountain Region, and to the generally uniform patterns of culture and settlement. These characteristics are central to our defining this as a state primary region. Movement into and through the mountains was limited and the Mountain Region provided a transportation barrier to the west of the country. It was well into the 19th century before isolated mountain communities began seeing signs of economic interest from the outside; the Mountain Region became more integrated into the state economy as transportation access improved. This interest was

largely fuelled by the wealth of the region's natural resources, particularly the forests. Rail lines were built to aid in extracting the timber, although passenger traffic was developed simultaneously. In the process, the northern mountain communities became well connected to southern Virginia and eastern Tennessee, while the southwestern mountain communities became actively integrated into the economies of Chattanooga, Tennessee, and Atlanta, Georgia. For a period of time, even Asheville and Hendersonville were better connected to Spartanburg, South Carolina, than to the North Carolina Piedmont. With the exhaustion of the logging resources, the railroads were largely discontinued and their role providing vital access to the outside quickly dissipated. In the case of the Northern Mountains Region, no major road system displaced the rail connection for many decades. Eventually, the region's attractiveness encouraged interest from people residing in the western Piedmont and the region was reconnected to the state at large. In the process, the connection between the Northern Mountains and the remainder of the Mountain Region remained very poor. The Asheville Basin received much more attention in the development of a contemporary transportation network. The Asheville Basin now functions as a major communication and transportation node, a facilitator of goods and services needing transport over the mountains between the North Carolina, South Carolina, Tennessee, and points beyond. Although the Southwestern Mountains lost its excellent rail connections following the resource extraction period, the region has maintained its interstate links; inhabitants of this region are more apt to be involved with matters of concern to southeastern Tennessee and northern Georgia, than with those of North Carolina. For example, out-of-state newspapers are popular in places such as Andrews, Hayesville, and Franklin. It is this connection to the outside, as well as the inadequate links between places within the Mountain Region, that help define the three discrete state geographic regions (SGR): Northern Moun-

**C.P. 13.1a:** Appalachian State University students take a break following an arduous spring climb to the top of Grandfather Mountain at 5,326 feet. Part of the Blue Ridge in the northern mountains, Grandfather (along with the Linville Gorge) was to be part of a proposed national park prior to the designation of the Great Smoky Mountains National Park. In the mid-1980s during a breezy, cool and clear day, you could seemingly see forever.

**C.P. 13.1b:** This scene shows a quiet, summer afternoon in a secluded valley of the Nantahala Mountains along the border of Clay and Macon counties. At an elevation of 3,500 feet, natural vegetation is a mix of deciduous trees. The open land has recently been purchased for a vacation home and construction has begun, evident in the lower part of the open field.

*Photo by Ole Gade.*

**Color Plate 13.1:** Mountain environments vary considerably by sub-region, elevation, and season.

**C.P. 13.2a:** The four seasons are foci of the tourist literature. While summers still provide the heaviest tourist flow, fall images (such as this spot in the heart of the Appalachian State University campus) are enticing many visitors to view the vivid mountain colors of October.

*Photo by Ole Gade.*

**C.P. 13.2b:** Winter months, especially from late December to late February, are the favorite time for snow enthusiasts. Aside from the skiing and snowboarding at major resorts such as Beech Mountain, Hawksnest, Sugar Mountain, and Appalachian Ski Mountain, there is normally a week or so during the season when enough natural snow falls to suit the cross country skier. The Moses Cone Estate's 25 miles of carriage trails off the Blue Ridge Parkway provide the needed terrain.

*Photo by Ole Gade.*

**Color Plate 13.2:** Many activity choices are available in the mountains for vacationers. Outdoor opportunities vary by season, landform, natural vegetation, wildlife, and water resources. Outdoor activities are complemented by an array of cultural opportunities, including: craft fairs; shops and museums; outdoor theater; festivals of local color, music, art, and drama; and the more traditional commercial entertainment and sightseeing nodes.

*Photo by Ole Gade.*

**C.P. 13.2c:** Water sports and activities are largely a summer affair. The southwestern mountains have many opportunities, as exemplified by the Horsepasture River in the Jocassee Gorge of Macon County.

*Photo by Ole Gade.*

**C.P. 13.2d:** Rugged and scenic terrain at high elevation has spurred considerable interest in hiking, shown here by an access sign to the Appalachian Trail. Following the crest of the Appalachians, the 2,137 mile trail connects Springer Mountain in Georgia with Mount Katahdin in Maine.

**C.P. 13.2e:** The casino owned by the Eastern Band of the Cherokee and managed by Harrah's Entertainment entered the tourist activity scene in 1997. Located on the Cherokee Indian Reservation, the casino already is the most popular tourist attraction in the state, with 3.2 million visitors in 1999. The casino is now the anchor for major investments in hotels, restaurants, and other tourist attractions in this otherwise very rural and low income area of the state.

*Photo by Ole Gade.*

**Color Plate 13.2:** Recreation activities in the Mountain Region.

**C.P. 13.3a:** Asheville, in its confining physiographic basin, increasingly suffers the effects of smog and airborne toxins. At times (this photo was taken during the summer of 2000), it is impossible to see the nearby surrounding mountains and it becomes necessary for many people to stay indoors to ward off negative health effects.

*Photo by Ole Gade.*

*Photo by Ole Gade.*

**C.P. 13.3b:** The reasons for Asheville's traditional attraction to tuberculosis sanatoriums, exclusive hotels, retirees, and tourists are more readily apparent from this photo taken in November of 1970. Healthy and restorative air and water built the city's image one hundred years ago. Asheville now is known as a "New Age Mecca" and the "City of Lights."

**C.P. 13.3c:** Excess acidity in the air contributes to a weakening of Spruce and Balsam trees, increasing their vulnerability to attacks of the woolly aphids. Throughout North Carolina's Mountain region there is evidence of the results of this devastating combination, but none more damaging than in the Black Mountains where Mount Mitchell stands nearly naked of its traditional tree cover.

*Photo by Ole Gade.*

**Color Plate 13.3:** A major environmental disaster is in the process of enveloping the North Carolina Mountain Region. Atmospheric pollution emanating from the region of Tennessee coal fired steam plants, from manufacturing industries of the Upper Midwest, and from local industries and automotive exhaust is having a devastating impact on communities and land.

**C.P. 13.4a:** Scattered through the million acres of the Nantahala and Pisgah national forests are some 77,000 acres of old growth forest, where dominant tree growth exceeds 150 years of age. Although much of this acreage awaits protection from logging, in the Joyce Kilmer Memorial Forest a visitor still has an opportunity to gaze at the tall trees.

*Photo courtesy of the North Carolina Division of Tourism.*

*Photo by Chris Wilson.*

**C.P. 13.4b:** The Green Salamander (*Aneides aeneus*) is listed as endangered in North Carolina. Populations of the Green salamander declined 98 percent between 1970 and 2000. Many other salamander species of the Mountain Region have experienced similar population declines.

*Photo by Maria Mayerhofer.*

**C.P. 13.4c:** The *Liatris helleri*, an endangered plant species, is becoming scarcer as hikers wandering off marked trails trample the plant and the soil, creating a difficult road to recovery for this lovely small flower.

**C.P. 13.4d:** On Grandfather Mountain, Hugh Morton has created a habitat attractive to certain endangered species, including eagles.

**Color Plate 13.4:** In the wake of the massive human encroachment on mountain ecologies, endangered environments and species have been the focus of conservation activity in recent years.

*Photo by Ole Gade.*

**C.P. 13.5a:** A top-of-the-hill view is an attraction along the Blue Ridge escarpment, where slopes drop 1,500 feet to the foothills. Seasonal homes came early to Blowing Rock (Watauga County), with some homes dating to the early 20th century.

**C.P. 13.5b:** The importance of a grand, mountain top view persisted until the construction of a ten-story condominium on the very top of Little Sugar Mountain (Avery County). This kind of development excess has now been curbed through legislative enactment of the Mountain Ridge Law.

*Photo by Robert E. Reiman.*

**Color Plate 13.5:** Mountain environments are very vulnerable to development. High elevations and a scenic, rugged terrain cut by steeply sloped and narrow valleys with slender floodplains make the area attractive to visitors and developers. As mountaineers are wont to say, "Tell the flatlander that hit comes with a pretty view," and the land is quickly sold.

*Photo by Ole Gade.*

**C.P. 13.5c:** Building extravagant seasonal homes on steep mountain slopes continues in the absence of environmental laws protecting against cut-and-fill excavations, severe soil erosion, and stream sedimentation. Development continues without the reasonable expectation of community water and sewer systems. With leaves gone in the fall, slopes take on an eerie resemblance to a strip mined landscape in parts of Watauga County and elsewhere.

**C.P. 13.5d:** Well-planned developments come with underground power lines, community water and sewer, and view lots in excess of $100,000. A development at the top of Blackburn Knob (3,800 feet elevation) overlooks Boone Valley (Watauga County), with 'Tater Hill and Snake Mountain in the distance.

*Photo by Ole Gade.*

**Color Plate 13.5:** Mountain Region development.

**C.P. 13.6a:** An abandoned mill stands forlornly by the remnants of its dam on the North Toe River in Mitchell County.

**C.P. 13.6b:** The decline of general farming in the mountains has meant the gradual abandonment of homes and farm buildings, with many cultural relicts disappearing in the process. In only a few cases have properties been restored to their former glory, as is the case of this "painted Victorian lady" in the Watauga River valley west of Boone.

**Color Plate 13.6:** "Diamonds in the rough" is an apt description of many historic properties in the Mountain Region. Recently, considerable work has been completed in identifying and describing historic properties, but little is done to renovate and preserve the properties for future generations.

**C.P. 13.6c:** In the mid 1970s, a "for sale" sign hung over the doorway of the Mast Store in Valle Crucis (Watauga County). The "Vale of the Crosses" was settled in the 1770s, with a healthy farming community developing over the next hundred years. The Mast family began building the community store and post office in the latter part of the 19th century. Suffering from competition with nearby large retail centers, the store was closed. However, the store sold quickly and major renovations were completed as the property was added to the National Register of Historic Properties.

**C.P. 13.6d:** Mining and forestry exploitation brought short-lived success to many mountain communities in the early part of the 20th century. Ghost towns now exist in a number of locations, as is the case of Plumtree on U.S. Highway 19E in Avery County. Only the Presbyterian Church remains in use.

**Color Plate 13.6:** Historic preservation in the Mountain Region.

**C.P. 13.7a:** Pack Square was the early Asheville crossroads, the site of courthouses, inns, and mercantile places in a succession of change and style. Interesting contrasts in architecture developed as the Jackson Building appeared in a turn-of-the-century Commercial Victorian style, followed by a commercial building and the public library built in an Italianate style. In the distance is the pink roofed City Hall, built in 1926 in an extravagant Art Deco style, with the new county court house next door, built two years later in a very austere Federal style.

*Photo by Ole Gade.*

**C.P. 13.7b:** Wall Street has been renovated to reflect its 1920s shopping street glory. The current Wall Street is an eclectic mix of architecture containing art galleries, esoteric shops, and restaurants. The ambiance is amplified by an attractive redeveloped streetscape.

*Photo by Ole Gade.*

**Color Plate 13.7:** After two decades of a difficult restoration process, downtown Asheville has emerged as the historic architectural pearl of North Carolina. Block by block, the chrome and steel facades of the 1950s were removed from retail buildings, storefronts were reconstructed to their original design, and upper stories were converted to residences. With architectural treasures from the Federal and Victorian periods (beginning in the 1880s) to the Art Deco of the 1920s and 1930s, Asheville exemplifies the best of the current civic movement toward the redevelopment and preservation of the state's urban architectural heritage.

544

**C.P. 13.7c:** The S&W Cafeteria, the premier downtown dining destination from the 1930s through the 1960s, was built at the height of the Art Deco revolution. It is now renovated and benefitting from the newfound interest in the downtown.

**C.P. 13.7d:** With historic preservation proceeding from east to west, the Grove Arcade is the last leg of a successful downtown renovation. Tennessee millionaire E.W. Grove built the structure in 1920, following his hiatus to Asheville seeking the mountain cure. A monument to early 20th century indoor shopping malls, the Arcade is now being restored to accommodate some 70 merchants of fresh local foods and crafts. In the background is the Battery Park Hotel, built in 1924. It has been converted to apartments.

**Color Plate 13.7:** Restoration of downtown Asheville.

**C.P. 13.8a:** For decades, individuals dressed as Plains Indians pandered to the prevailing image of the Cherokee Indian. A picture with the "Indian Chief" could be had for a dollar. Also enhancing the average tourist's simplistic sense of American Indian culture are the shops on the main street of Cherokee where tom-tom drums, tomahawks (made in the Philippines), moccasins (mass produced in Taiwan), and pseudo leather apparel with bangles and beads are overflowing the counters.

*Photo by Ole Gade.*

*Photo by Ole Gade.*

**C.P. 13.8b:** Along U.S. 441 toward Newfound Gap, visitors may experience the more traditional and genuine Cherokee culture and its history at the Museum of the Cherokee Indian. The outdoor drama *Onto These Hills* tells the story of the Cherokee from the early 1500s through the tragic Trail of Tears.

**C.P. 13.8c:** Wearing traditional clothing, Cherokees at the Oconaluftee Indian Village demonstrate arts and crafts, reenact typical community activities, and engage visitors in discussions of life and values within Cherokee society. The possible impacts of the gaming casino on the Cherokee lifestyle are not yet known.

**Color Plate 13.8:** Regenerating the image and the economy of the Eastern Band of the Cherokee Nation.

*Photo by Ole Gade.*

# Northern Mountains Region

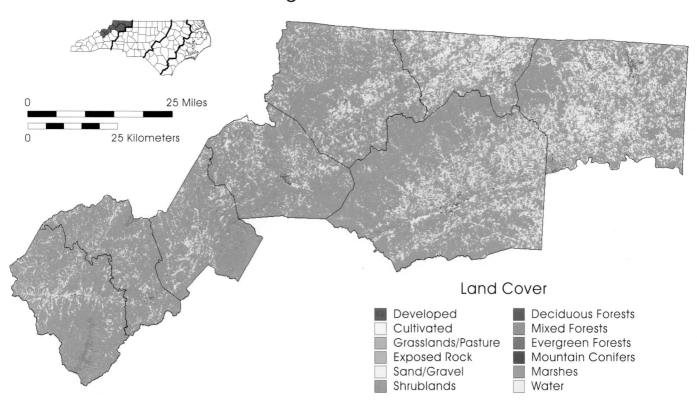

## Land Cover

- ■ Developed
- □ Cultivated
- ■ Grasslands/Pasture
- ■ Exposed Rock
- □ Sand/Gravel
- ■ Shrublands

- ■ Deciduous Forests
- ■ Mixed Forests
- ■ Evergreen Forests
- ■ Mountain Conifers
- ■ Marshes
- □ Water

0 ——— 25 Miles

0 ——— 25 Kilometers

**Color Plate. 13.9:** Northern Mountains State Geographic Region Land Cover, 1998.
**Source:** Modified from the North Carolina Center for Geographic Information and Analysis, 1998.

*Photo by Ole Gade.*

**Color Plate. 13.10:** The Local Color Weaving Studio in Burnsville (Yancy County) exemplifies the arts and crafts entrepreneurial activities that have become very important to mountain communities during the past several decades.

547

# Southwest Mountains Region

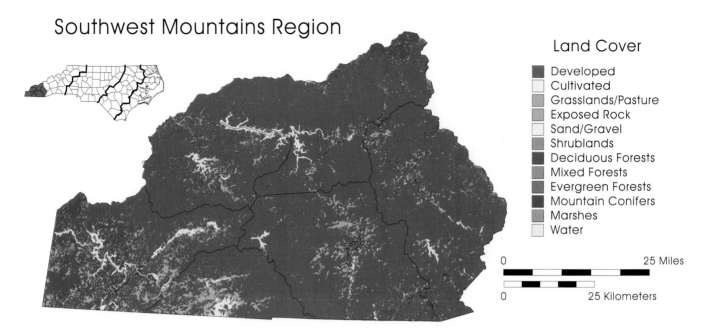

Land Cover

- ◼ Developed
- ◻ Cultivated
- ◼ Grasslands/Pasture
- ◼ Exposed Rock
- ◻ Sand/Gravel
- ◼ Shrublands
- ◼ Deciduous Forests
- ◼ Mixed Forests
- ◼ Evergreen Forests
- ◼ Mountain Conifers
- ◼ Marshes
- ◻ Water

0              25 Miles

0              25 Kilometers

**Color Plate. 13.11:** Southwest Mountains State Geographic Region Land Cover, 1998.
**Source:** Modified from the North Carolina Center for Geographic Information and Analysis, 1998.

*Photo by Ole Gade.*

**Color Plate. 13.12:** The John C. Campbell Folk School fall festival poster for 1997 identifies some of the activities the school offers its students. Located in Brasstown (Clay County), the school draws students from throughout the country. The John C. Campbell Folk School is fashioned on the principles of the Danish Folk High School.

# Asheville Basin Region

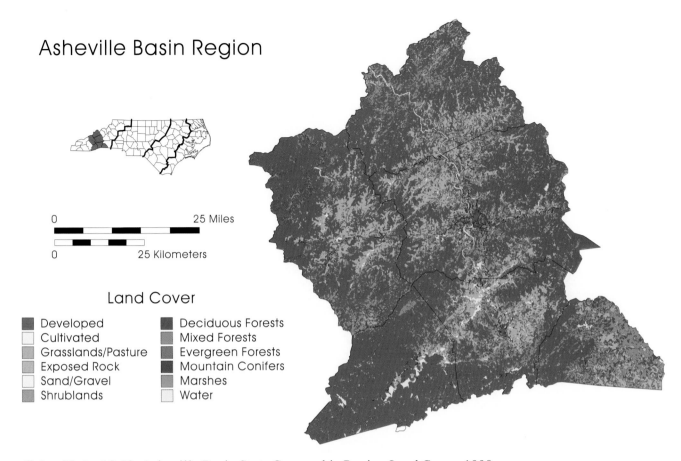

0                 25 Miles

0               25 Kilometers

## Land Cover

- Developed
- Cultivated
- Grasslands/Pasture
- Exposed Rock
- Sand/Gravel
- Shrublands
- Deciduous Forests
- Mixed Forests
- Evergreen Forests
- Mountain Conifers
- Marshes
- Water

**Color Plate. 13.13:** Asheville Basin State Geographic Region Land Cover, 1998.
**Source:** Modified from the North Carolina Center for Geographic Information and Analysis, 1998.

*Photo by Ole Gade.*

**Color Plate. 13.14:** Hendersonville (Henderson County) figures prominently among the many Asheville Region communities benefitting from retirement settlement and seasonal tourism. It also is the center of the state's apple growing industry.

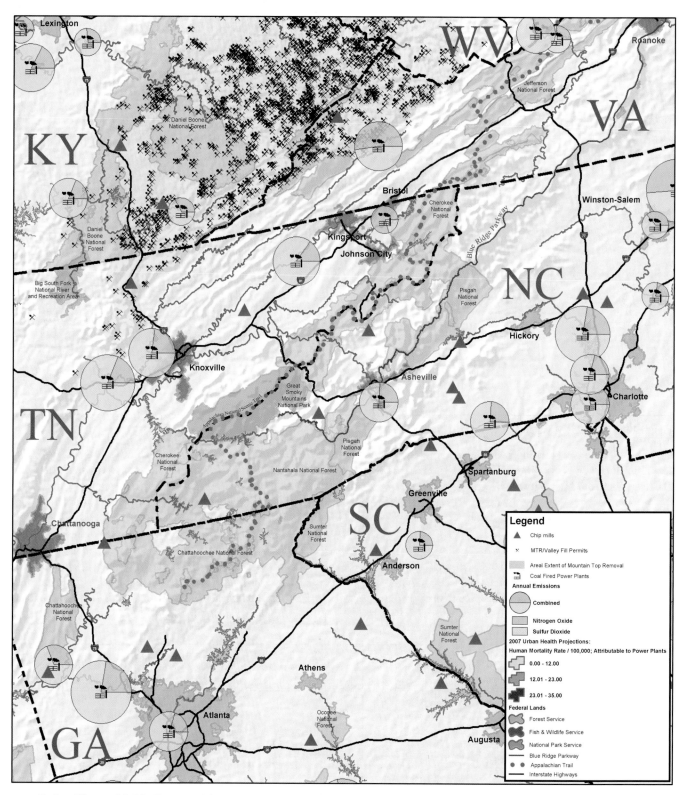

**Color Plate. 13.15:** Encroaching Environmental Threats on the Mountain Region.
**Source:** Appalachian Voices and Project for Appalachian Community and Environment (PACE), 2001.

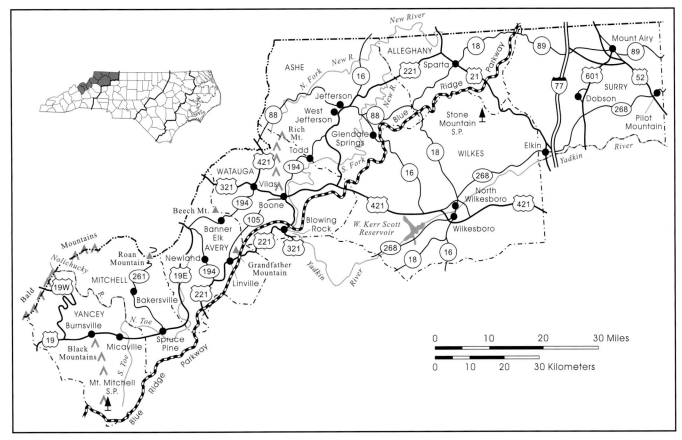

**Figure 13.6:** Northern Mountains State Geographic Region.

tains, Asheville Basin, and Southwest Mountains. Differences in the basic characteristics of these SGR's are shown in Table 9.2. For the reader who desires more specific information about individual counties, a large array of data on diverse topics is presented in the initial nine chapters of this text.

### Northern Mountains

The Northern Mountains State Geographic Region is a southeast-northwest, elongated area bordering Tennessee and Virginia (Figure 13.6). Within this SGR are eight counties that include some of the smallest in physical size in the state (Alleghany, Avery, and Mitchell), and one (Wilkes) that is among

the largest in the state (Table 13.3). In the aggregate, this SGR is one of the states smallest in population size. It also is characterized by a very slow population growth, by state standards (Table 9.2), and by having an older population with a smaller percentage of individuals having achieved either high school or college degrees. Cultural traditions, as well as the age factor, influenced the lower than state average infant mortality rate and the percent of households having a female head. Due to a greater percentage of incomes derived from primary economic activities and prevailingly low salaries, the SGR has one of the highest levels of state support for industrial investment.

| NORTHERN MOUNTAINS | Land Area in sq. km | Pop. 1990 | Pop. sq.km. 2000 | Pop. 2000 | 1990s % Pop. Change | % White 2000 | Median Age in 2000 | % Fam. Below Poverty | Annual Average Infant Mortality Rate 1994-98 | % High School Grads'90 | % Coll. Grads. 1990 | Fem. Fam. Head of Hshld'90 | NC Enterprise Tiers'97 |
|---|---|---|---|---|---|---|---|---|---|---|---|---|---|
| Alleghany | 608 | 9,590 | 17.6 | 10,677 | 11.3 | 95.7 | 44.0 | 15.4 | 2.1 | 52.6 | 9.0 | 7.8 | 1 |
| Ashe | 1,104 | 22,209 | 22.1 | 24,384 | 9.8 | 97.2 | 43.4 | 15.3 | 11.6 | 55.6 | 8.1 | 9.2 | 2 |
| Avery | 640 | 14,867 | 26.8 | 17,167 | 15.5 | 94 | 39.3 | 10.2 | 12.4 | 62.2 | 12.4 | 8.7 | 3 |
| Mitchell | 574 | 14,433 | 27.3 | 15,687 | 8.7 | 97.9 | 43.2 | 12.9 | 7.7 | 55.3 | 9.2 | 8.3 | 1 |
| Surry | 1,391 | 61,704 | 51.2 | 71,219 | 15,4 | 90 | 39.5 | 8.5 | 7.7 | 57.3 | 9.4 | 9.7 | 4 |
| Watauga | 810 | 36,952 | 53 | 42,695 | 15.5 | 96.5 | 31.1 | 10.1 | 9 | 72.0 | 27.4 | 7.1 | 4 |
| Wilkes | 1,961 | 59,393 | 33.5 | 65,632 | 10.5 | 93 | 39.2 | 10.7 | 8.3 | 54.1 | 8.8 | 9.9 | 3 |
| Yancey | 809 | 15,419 | 22 | 17,774 | 15.3 | 98 | 42.0 | 14.8 | 4.6 | 60.7 | 10.0 | 8.3 | 2 |
| **Region Totals** | **7,897** | **234,567** | **33.6** | **265,235** | **13.1** | **97.4** | **40.2** | **12.2** | **7.9** | **58.7** | **11.8** | **8.6** | **2.5** |

**Table 13.3:** Northern Mountains State Geographic Region, 1990-2000.
**Sources:** U.S. Bureau of the Census, 1990, 2000; North Carolina State Planning Office, 1997-2000.

As is typical for the state geographic regions there is considerable divergence from average conditions when individual counties are considered. Population size, for example, ranges from 10,677 in Alleghany County to 71,219 in Surry County, a county that is benefiting from its foothills location and improved access via I-77. Wilkes also has a more sizeable population (65,632) due to an accommodating environment for agriculture and excellent connections to the Piedmont population centers. Among the six counties of the Blue Ridge, Watauga County is the largest in population with 42,595 people. During the 1990s, Avery, Surry, Watauga and Yancey counties all experienced population growth at a steady 1.5 percent per year; this rate was the highest in the SGR, but still much below the state average. The three mountain counties, especially Watauga and Avery, have seen much residential construction over that decade, but most of this was for seasonal homes. These are occupied by people who are not included in the census counts, and therefore do not factor into population data. For the Blue Ridge Province counties, the second home construction and seasonal occupancy influence land values, commercial retail investment, service employment and related low wages, and local politics, while also dramatizing the visible contrasts in poverty and wealth. As elaborated in Chapter 7, Watauga County is specially favored in economic diversity and stability due to the existence of Appalachian State University in Boone. This county also is benefiting more than most by recent transportation improvements, which will connect Boone to four-lane highways from Winston-Salem (via U.S. 421) and from Charlotte (via U.S. 321). Considerable controversy surrounds the designation of the routes, especially in the Blowing Rock area. For the other mountain counties, conditions are much more dependent on the vagaries of tourism and vacation travel (CP 13.1a and 13.2). Yet, there are critical differences throughout the region. It is possible to draw a rough east-west line through Watauga County north of Boone and discover that the landscape to the north of this line still is barely impacted by tourism, vacation homes, and mountain resort development. Traditional agricultural landscapes still flourish; Sugar Grove, Bethel, Mabel, and Meat Camp, in northern Watauga County are all maintaining a pleasant and easy flowing historic mountain community milieu, relatively unbothered by the land disturbing activities and hectic seasonal tourism of the Boone-Blowing Rock-Foscoe-Valley Crucis-Vilas ring in the southern part of the county (CP 13.5a-c). Alleghany and Ashe counties are much like northern Watauga County. However, these counties are now receiving much interest from speculative developers since the granting of National Wild and Scenic River status to the New River. Avery and Yancey counties are more like southern Watauga County in land use development. Mitchell County continues to have more difficult access and is viewed as generally less desirable due to its strip-mined environment near Spruce Pine. Color Plate 13.9 illustrates the differences between the tourism/recreation development and the more traditional land cover of the Northern Mountains SGR. The Blue Ridge Escarpment is easy to see by the broad green space angling northeast-southwest between the more heavily populated foothills portions of Wilkes and Surry counties and the Blue Ridge Plateau counties (Alleghany to Yancey), which demonstrate a much lower population density; the breaks in this forest expanse occur where agriculture is dominant, as in Alleghany and Ashe counties.

Demographically the Northern Mountains SGR reflects the nature of population growth and economic activities very well (Figures 13.7a-h). Alleghany, Ashe, Mitchel and Yancey counties all show their Blue Ridge Province locations by having above average percentages of people aged 50 and older. These clearly are counties of aging populations, having experienced net outmigration of younger people over the past half century, a condition not offset by the scale of investment in recreational and scenic resources. As a result, these are counties devoid of maturing young people with families and children. In a curious way, Watauga County is in a very similar situation, in spite of its overwhelmingly youthful population. If the college-aged cohorts were removed from this county's population profile, the remainder would look a lot like the general Blue Ridge Province profile. Surry and Wilkes counties are fairly close in population structure to counties with traditional manufacturing industries of the Piedmont Region (for example, Gaston, Iredell, and Caldwell counties).

Urban development and growth is limited in the Northern Mountains SGR. The Wilkes urban agglomeration is made up of two towns: Wilkesboro, the traditional county seat, and North Wilkesboro, the commercial and manufacturing center. The Wilkes urban agglomeration had about 35,000 people in 2000. This is by far the largest urban concentration in the Northern Mountains SGR. Boone (Watauga County), with Appalachian State University, is actually the largest town with 13,472 residents in 2000. Throughout the Mountain Region, there is a great reluctance to incorporate areas of urban growth outside of municipal boundaries. Despite urban growth, many of the incorporated towns are seeing only small increases. Only Mount Airy (8,484 people) and Elkin (4,036) in Surry County are the other incorporated places with over 2,000 people, in all of the Northern Mountains SGR. In the near future, the counties of this SGR are not likely to see much of an expansion of present population growth levels.

### Southwest Mountains

There is much physical environmental and human settlement similarity between the Northern Mountains SGR and the Southwest Mountains SGR (Figure 13.4). Even so, the Southwest Mountains has the smallest SGR population in the state; the region comprises only six counties that are of average or smaller physical size (Figure 13.8). There is an aging population with generally low levels of educational attainment. There also is great wealth amidst poverty, a condition generated by the same forces as exist in the Northern Mountains SGR. On the other hand, population growth is about at the state average and health conditions appear above average (Table 13.4; see also Chapter 7). The six counties included in the Southwest Mountains are all border counties. Jackson County shares a border with South

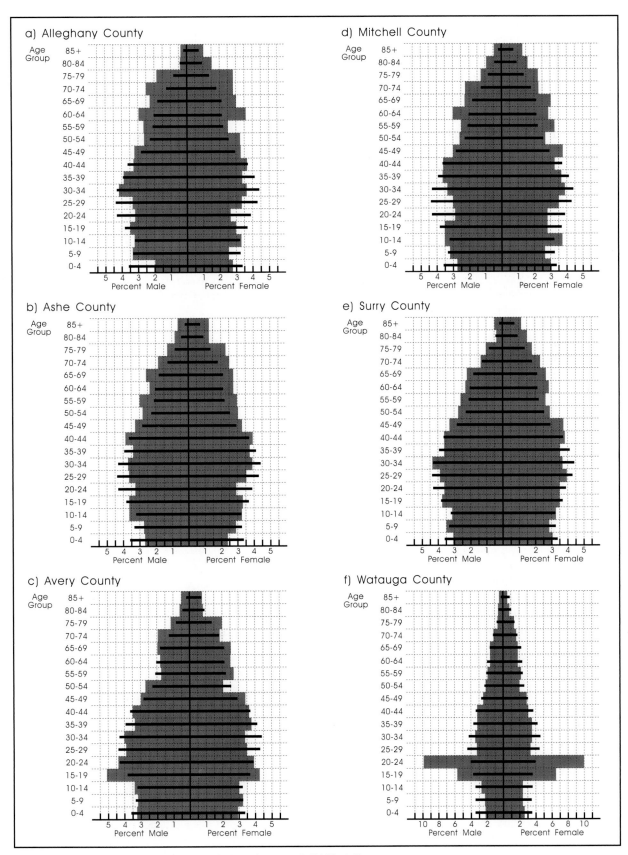

**Figure 13.7 a-f:** Northern Mountains Population Diagrams. Solid black lines represent state averages.
**Source:** U.S. Bureau of the Census, 1990.

553

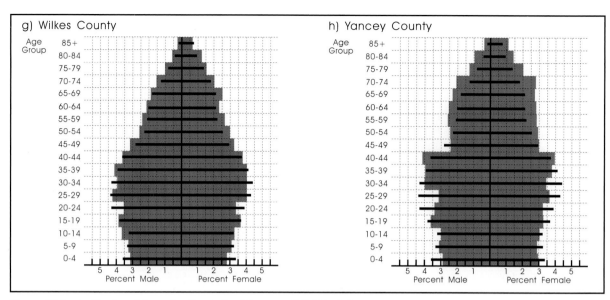

**Figure 13.7 g-h:** Northern Mountains Population Diagrams. Solid black lines represent state averages.

**Source:** U.S. Bureau of the Census, 1990.

Carolina; Macon, Clay, and Cherokee counties share one with Georgia; and Cherokee, Graham and Swain counties border Tennessee (Figures 13.1 and 13.8). All six counties are very mountainous with most of the land in federal forest or parkland (Great Smoky Mountains National Park), and an additional large acreage is Cherokee Indian Reservation land in the Qualla Boundary (CP 13.8). This aspect of landownership is clearly reflected in CP 13.11, the land cover map for the SGR. Forests overwhelmingly

dominate this region. Population density for the SGR is the lowest in the state.

As indicated in early chapters, this is the region of high elevations, copious precipitation, and a largesse of imposing waterfalls amidst a bounty of natural plant and animal life (CP 13.1b; 13.2c; 13.4a). Therefore, there exists a deepening concern over the preservation of remaining wilderness areas. All six counties are developing tourism and recreation opportunities. Visi-

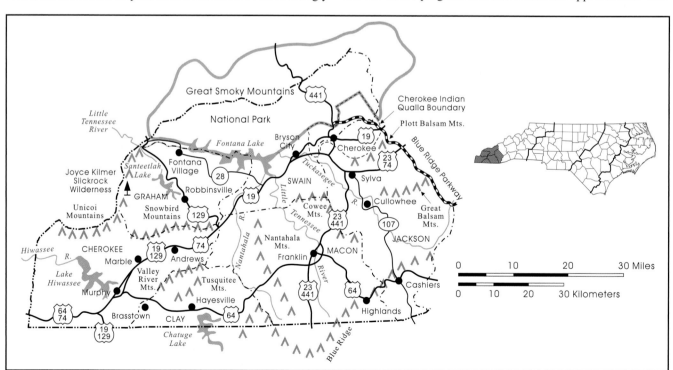

**Figure 13.8:** Southwest Mountains State Geographic Region.

554

| SOUTHWEST MOUNTAINS | Land Area in sq. km | Pop. 1990 | Pop. sq.km. 2000 | Pop. 2000 | 1990s % Pop. Change | % White 2000 | Median Age in 2000 | % Fam. Below Poverty | Annual Average Infant Mortality Rate 1994-98 | % High School Grads'90 | % Coll. Grads. 1990 | Fem. Fam. Head of Hshld'90 | NC Enterprise Tiers'97 |
|---|---|---|---|---|---|---|---|---|---|---|---|---|---|
| Cherokee | 1,179 | 20,170 | 20.6 | 24,298 | 20.5 | 94.8 | 43.0 | 15.3 | 11.2 | 59.9 | 8.0 | 9.6 | 2 |
| Clay | 556 | 7,155 | 15.8 | 8,775 | 22.6 | 98 | 45.4 | 14.4 | 8.9 | 62.9 | 12.6 | 6.9 | 3 |
| Graham | 756 | 7,196 | 10.6 | 7,993 | 11.1 | 91.9 | 41.6 | 22.7 | 2.1 | 56.9 | 10.0 | 8.9 | 1 |
| Jackson | 1,271 | 26,835 | 26.1 | 33,121 | 23.4 | 85.7 | 37.9 | 11.7 | 8.9 | 68.7 | 19.7 | 10.1 | 3 |
| Macon | 1,338 | 23,504 | 22.3 | 29,811 | 26.8 | 97.2 | 46.9 | 12.0 | 7.9 | 66.7 | 13.2 | 7.9 | 4 |
| Swain | 1,368 | 11,268 | 9.5 | 12,968 | 15.1 | 66.3 | 39.4 | 21.5 | 6 | 59.0 | 9.9 | 13.2 | 1 |
| **Region Totals** | **6,468** | **96,128** | **18.1** | **116,966** | **21.7** | **89.7** | **42.4** | **16.3** | **7.5** | **62.4** | **12.2** | **9.4** | **2.3** |

**Table 13.4:** Southern Mountains State Geographic Region, 1990-2000.
**Sources:** U.S. Bureau of the Census, 1990, 2000; North Carolina State Planning Office, 1997-2000.

tors are responding by flocking to a richness of managed natural resources, including the Blue Ridge Parkway, the Great Smoky Mountains National Park, the Appalachian Trail, and an almost infinite number of rushing rivers and tranquil lakes. Hill tracts offer opportunities for hunting wild boar, deer, and bear, for mountain biking and for contemplating in wilderness and old growth forests (such as John Muir Woods). Perhaps the most unexpected recreational opportunity is the modern, large-scale Harrah's Casino in Cherokee, Swain County (CP 13.2e). A final characteristic of the region is the access and distance factor to the region relative to anywhere with urban ambience. As one resident of Andrews (Cherokee County) has it, "We're an hour and 45 minutes from elsewhere – Atlanta, Chattanooga, the Knoxville area, Asheville" (as quoted in Gregutt 1998b, 26).

Comparatively speaking, these counties are on the smaller end of the size spectrum in most categories. Only the most populated county (Jackson), with Western Carolina University located in Cullowhee, stands out as markedly different (Table 13.4). The counties bordering Georgia are experiencing population increases that are near or higher than average for the state. The demographic composition of the population by county does show some interesting variations (Figure 13.11a-f). Most unique is Jackson County, which readily displays the significance of its student population. Clay, Cherokee, and Macon are three of the counties with the most rapidly aging populations in the state, with Graham County not far behind. Although students are counted in the census, seasonal residents and visitors are not (CP 13.12). Swain County stands out with a higher share in child cohorts because of the higher fertility rate of its Cherokee population, but young adults are abandoning this county about as vigorously as Macon and Cherokee counties.

These are rural counties par excellence. The town of Franklin in Macon County is the largest in the Southwest Mountains, with 3,490 people in 2000; Andrews and Murphy (Cherokee County) had 1,602 and 1,568, respectively. Bryson City (Swain County) was the only other town with over 1,000 residents (1,411 people in 2000). Residents here are as querulous about their municipalities expanding through annexation, as are people in the Northern Mountains Region. Andrews had to de-annex some 40 percent of its population in the early 1990s due to protests against earlier expansion of its territorial limits.

### Asheville Basin

The Asheville Basin State Geographic Region is similar to the other two Mountain Region SGRs in physical size, but here ends the major similarities. With all of its six counties within the Blue Ridge Province, the SGR still has a population as large as the other two SGRs combined. One reason for the greater concentration of people and economic activity in the SGR is clearly the extent of the Asheville Basin itself, its eminent centrality with respect to the natural resources of the Mountain Region, and its role as an intermediary node for cross mountain transportation routes. The early benefits accrued to Asheville and then subsequently influenced development in adjacent Haywood and Henderson counties. Note the concentrations of land use and development on the region's land cover map (CP 13.13). The star shaped axes of development focused on Asheville are readily identifiable. Like awkwardly radiating spokes on a wheel, the development axes extend to Waynesville in Haywood County, Brevard in Transylvania County, Mars Hill in Madison County, and Hendersonville in Henderson County (Figure 13.10). Traffic is fed along interstates (I-40 and I-26) and the Appalachian Highway (19W). In the process, Asheville has placed itself in a very tight transportation noose, with very little development maneuverability. The city, however, has been well endowed with architectural riches adorning its central area (CP 13.7), and, in part due to its ease of access to the Blue Ridge Parkway and the Smokies, a persistence in popularity for tourists and vacationers that belies its deteriorating physical environment (CP 13.3 and 13.7).

In comparing the counties of the Asheville Basin, the expected variations quickly appear. Buncombe County, for example, is nearly three times the size of Polk County (Table 13.5). Overall, the Asheville Basin SGR is increasing its population at a rate lower than the state average. However, Polk and Henderson counties have above average growth, a rate almost twice that of distant Transylvania County and the much more manufacturing focused Haywood County. Madison County appears as something of an aberration in this collection of fairly wealthy counties (Chapter 7). Madison had a comparatively low rate of population increase for the 1990s, and has a more youthful population, (in what is the SGR with the oldest average population in the state). The county also has an extraordinarily high percentage of families with below poverty level incomes, and the lowest percentage of adults with a high school diploma.

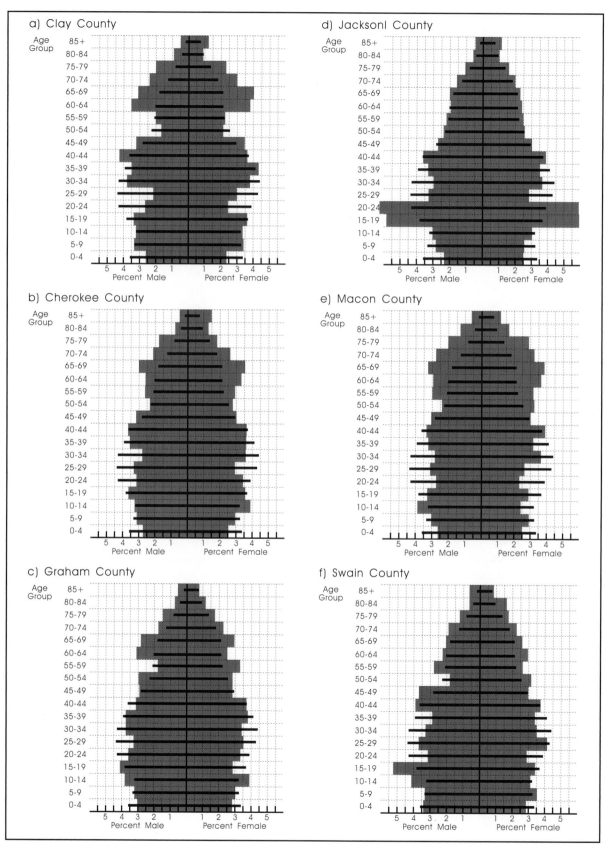

**Figure 13.9 a-f:** Southwest Mountains Population Diagrams. Solid black lines represent state averages.
**Source:** U.S. Bureau of the Census, 1990.

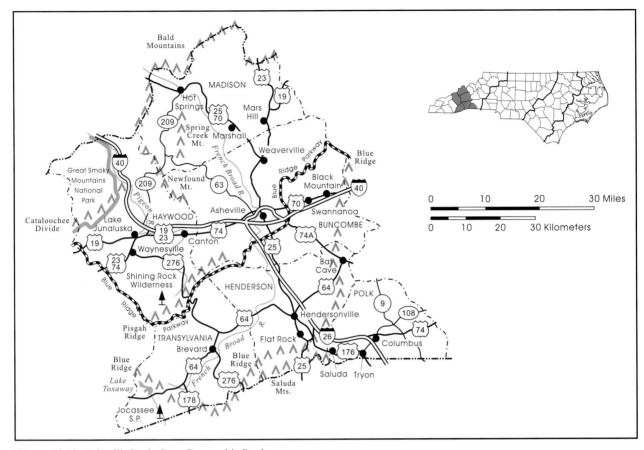

**Figure 13.10:** Asheville Basin State Geographic Region.

In the set of demographic profiles characterizing the Asheville Basin's population structure, it is possible to suggest that all counties are in a race to see which one will have the best example of a graying population (Figure 13.11a-f). Buncombe County is by far the most youthful looking, even though its population is an average 3.7 years older than that of the state average. For a hundred years, Asheville has been looked upon as a retirement center, but Henderson, Polk, and Haywood counties are now leading the way. The latter is more of a blue color labor county and may see its aging population more as the result of an aging-in-place process, as opposed to the weight of inmigrating elderly that tilts both Henderson and Polk toward a graying of their population.

| ASHEVILLE BASIN | Land Area in sq. km | Pop. 1990 | Pop. sq.km. 2000 | Pop. 2000 | 1990s % Pop. Change | % White 2000 | Median Age in 2000 | % Fam. Below Poverty | Average Annual Infant Mortality Rate 1994-98 | % High School Grads'90 | % Coll. Grads. 1990 | Fem. Fam. Head of Hshld'90 | NC Enterprise Tiers'97 |
|---|---|---|---|---|---|---|---|---|---|---|---|---|---|
| Buncombe | 1,700 | 174,357 | 121.4 | 206,330 | 18,3 | 89.1 | 39.8 | 8.2 | 7.9 | 74.5 | 19.1 | 10.9 | 5 |
| Haywood | 1,435 | 46,948 | 37.7 | 54,033 | 15.1 | 96.8 | 44.2 | 9.5 | 9 | 68.0 | 12.8 | 9.2 | 3 |
| Henderson | 968 | 69,747 | 92.1 | 89,173 | 27.9 | 92.5 | 44.5 | 7.5 | 9.9 | 76.2 | 19.5 | 8.2 | 5 |
| Madison | 1,164 | 16,953 | 16.9 | 19,635 | 15.8 | 97.6 | 40.6 | 15.5 | 10.2 | 66.7 | 13.2 | 8.0 | 3 |
| Polk | 616 | 14,458 | 29.7 | 18,324 | 26.7 | 92.3 | 46.5 | 6.9 | 16 | 71.0 | 21.9 | 8.4 | 5 |
| Transylvania | 980 | 25,520 | 29.9 | 29,334 | 14.9 | 93.7 | 43.0 | 9.7 | 13.6 | 72.1 | 17.9 | 8.0 | 4 |
| **Region Totals** | **6,863** | **347,983** | **60.7** | **416,829** | **19.8** | **91.7** | **43.1** | **9.6** | **11.1** | **71.4** | **17.4** | **8.8** | **4.2** |

**Table 13.5:** Asheville Basin State Geographic Region, 1990-2000.
**Sources:** U.S. Bureau of the Census, 1990, 2000; North Carolina State Planning Office, 1997-2000.

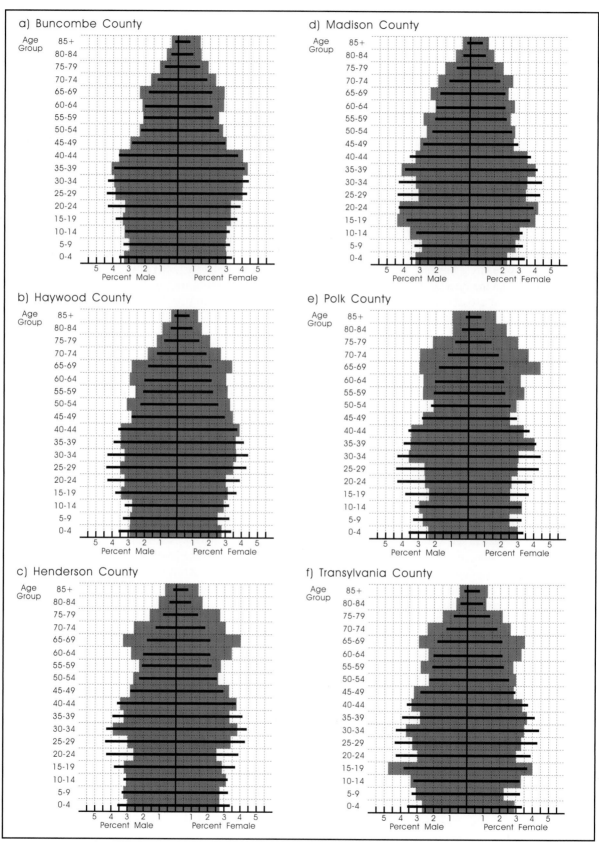

**Figure 13.11 a-f:** Asheville Basin Population Diagrams. Solid black lines represent state averages.
**Source:** U.S. Bureau of the Census, 1990.

# SUMMARY

All in all, the Mountain Region will continue to face numerous challenges. The many areas of the region that exhibit superior natural environmental qualities, and that are not yet preserved in their condition for perpetuity, are threatened by engulfing developmental investment interests. Land in the mountains may not immediately show the visible signs, but this land is among the most contested in the state. Commercial interests tend to rule in an environment whose population is more apt to be laissez faire about land ownership and environmental protection due to a deep-seated sense of independence. The Mountain Area Management Act was introduced in the General Assembly in early to mid-1970s. It was defeated twice by a coalition of the development lobby and local landowners, who were "just not about to let Raleigh tell them what to do with their land." Proponents of the measure were environmental interests from everywhere and legislators from the Piedmont, where justifiable concern was raised about the prospects of an early death of the goose that lays the golden egg. At the present, only a couple of counties exercise countywide land use controls. It is truly a buyer beware situation for the thousands who trek to the mountains for a vacation or permanent home location. A deteriorating natural environment too frequently enshrouded in acid fog is one of the penalties that inaction has brought. Couple this with inappropriate construction approaches in a fragile environment, and haphazard location of asphalt plants, landfills, and other noxious land uses, and the result is an endangered Mountain Region landscape. Much as is the case with the coastal environment of the Tidewater Region, in the Mountain Region there is a premium on commercial development of the most fragile natural landscapes. The fault, however, does not lie primarily with the development community. It belongs to a public that selfishly want their own property in the very midst of the wildest and most scenic landscape, and is willing to elevate the commercial value of our most fragile natural environments.

# Appendices

## Appendix A: Metric/English Conversions

| *Metric* | *English* | *Conversions* |
|---|---|---|

### Linear Measure

| | | |
|---|---|---|
| centimeter (cm) | inch (in) | 1 cm = 0.3937 in |
| | | 1 in = 2.54 cm |
| meter (m) | foot (ft) | 1 m = 3.28 ft |
| | | 1 ft = 0.305 m |
| kilometer (km) | mile (mi) | 1 km = 0.621 mi |
| | | 1 mi = 1.61 km |

### Area Measure

| | | |
|---|---|---|
| square centimeter (cm$^2$) | square inch (sq in) | 1 cm$^2$ = 0.155 sq in |
| | | 1 sq in = 6.4516 cm$^2$ |
| square meter (m$^2$) | square foot (sq ft) | 1 m$^2$ = 10.764 sq ft |
| | | 1 sq ft = 0.0929 m$^2$ |
| square kilometer (km$^2$) | square mile (sq mi) | 1 km$^2$ = 0.3861 sq mi |
| | | 1 sq mi = 2.59 km$^2$ |
| hectare (ha) | acre | 1 ha = 10,000 m$^2$ = 2.471 acres |
| | | 1 acre = 43,560 sq ft = 0.4047 ha |

### Volume Measure

| | | |
|---|---|---|
| cubic centimeter (cm$^3$) | cubic inch (cu in) | 1 cm$^3$ = 0.061 cu in |
| | | 1 cu in = 16.387 cm$^3$ |
| cubic meter (m$^3$) | cubic foot (cu ft) | 1 m$^3$ = 35.315 cu ft |
| | | 1 cu ft = 0.02832 m$^3$ |
| liter (l) | gallon (gl) | 1 l = 1,000 cm$^3$ = 0.264 gl |
| | | 1 gl = 231 cm$^3$ = 3.7853 l |

### Mass

| | | |
|---|---|---|
| gram (g) | ounce (oz) | 1 g = 0.0353 oz |
| | | 1 oz = 28.35 g |
| kilogram (kg) | pound (lb) | 1 kg = 2.205 lbs |
| | | 1 lb = 0.454 kg |
| metric ton (m ton) | short ton | 1 m ton = 10$^3$ kg = 1.102 short ton |
| | | 1 short ton = 2,000 lbs = 0.907 m tons |

### Temperature

| | | |
|---|---|---|
| Celsius degrees (C$^o$) | Fahrenheit degree (F$^o$) | 1 C$^o$ = 1.8 F$^o$ |
| | | 1 F$^o$ = 5/9 C$^o$ |

### Temperature Scales

$$^oC = 5/9 \, (^oF - 32)$$
$$^oF = 9/5 \, (^oC) + 32$$

# Appendix B. Scientific Names of Vegetation

| Common Name | Scientific Name | Common Name | Scientific Name |
|---|---|---|---|
| ***Mountain Region*** | | shortleaf pine | Pinus echinata |
| American chestnut | Castanea dentata | sourwood | Oxydendrum arboreum |
| beech | Fagus grandifolia | southern red oak | Quercus falcata |
| black locust | Robinia pseudoacacia | sweet gum | Liquidambar styraciflua |
| blueberry | Vaccinium spp. | sycamore | Plantanus occidentalis |
| chestnut oak | Quercus prinus | Virginia pine | Pinus virginiana |
| cucumber tree | Magnolia acuminata | | |
| fire cherry | Prunus pennsylvanica | ***Coastal Plain and Tidewater Regions*** | |
| Fraser fir | Abies fraseri | American beach grass | Ammophila breviligulata |
| hemlock | Tsuga canadensis | bald cypress | Taxodium distichum |
| mountain-ash | Sorbus americana | broomsedge | Andropogon spp. |
| mountain-laurel | Kalmia latifolia | bulrush | Scripus spp. |
| northen red oak | Quercus ruba | cattail | Typha spp. |
| red spruce | Picea rubens | cordgrass | Spartina spp. |
| rosebay rhododendron | Rhododendrum maximum | croton | Croton punctatus |
| sugar maple | Acer saccharum | dune elder | Iva imbricata |
| tulip poplar | Liriodendron tulipifera | live oak | Quercus virginiana |
| white oak | Quercus alba | longleaf pine | Pinus palustris |
| white pine | Pinus strobus | needlerush | Juncus spp. |
| yellow birch | Betula lutea | pond pine | Pinus serotina |
| yellow buckeye | Aesculus octandra | primrose | Oenothera humifusa |
| | | red cedar | Juniperus virginiana |
| ***Piedmont Region*** | | saw grass | Cladium spp. |
| ash | Fraxinus spp. | sea oats | Uniola paniculata |
| dogwood | Cornus florida | spurge | Euphorbia polygomifolia |
| elm | Ulmus spp. | swamp gum | Nyssa sylvatica |
| loblolly pine | Pinus taeda | tupelo gum | Nyssa aquatica |
| mockernut hickory | Carya tomentosa | Venus' flytrap | Dionaeu muscipula |
| post oak | Quercus stellata | water oak | Quercus nigra |
| redbud | Cercis canadensis | wax myrtle | Myrica cerifera |
| river birch | Betula nigra | wire grass | Cynodon dactylon |
| scarlet oak | Quercus coccinea | yaupon | Illex vomitoria |
| shagbark hickory | Carya ovata | | |

# Appendix C: Population Calculations

## Population

$$\text{Percentage of N.C. population residing in area} = \frac{\text{Population of area}}{\text{Population of North Carolina}} \times 100$$

$$\text{Percentage male population in area} = \frac{\text{Male population of area}}{\text{Total population of area}} \times 100$$

$$\text{Percentage female population in area} = \frac{\text{Female population of area}}{\text{Total population of area}} \times 100$$

## Natural Increase

$$\text{Rate of natural increase} = \frac{\text{Number of live births minus number of deaths}}{\text{Population of area}} \times 1{,}000$$

## Live Births

$$\text{Birth rate} = \frac{\text{Number of live births}}{\text{Population of area}} \times 1{,}000$$

$$\text{Male birth rate} = \frac{\text{Number of male live births}}{\text{Population of area}} \times 1{,}000$$

$$\text{Female birth rate} = \frac{\text{Number of female live births}}{\text{Population of area}} \times 1{,}000$$

## Infant Deaths

$$\text{Infant mortality rate} = \frac{\text{Number of infant deaths}}{\text{Number of live births}} \times 1{,}000$$

## Deaths

$$\text{Death rate} = \frac{\text{Number of deaths}}{\text{Population of area}} \times 1{,}000$$

$$\text{Age-specific death rate} = \frac{\text{Number of deaths in age group}}{\text{Population in age group}} \times 1{,}000$$

## Migration

$$\text{Immigration rate} = \frac{\text{Number of immigrants}}{\text{Total destination population}} \times 1{,}000$$

$$\text{Emigration rate} = \frac{\text{Number of emigrants}}{\text{Total destination population}} \times 1{,}000$$

$$\text{Net migration rate} = \frac{\text{Number of immigrants - Number of emigrants}}{\text{Total population}} \times 1{,}000$$

### Residual Method of Migration Estimation

$$\text{Net migration} = (P_2 - P_1) - (B - D)$$

$P_1$: Population at the second census
$P_2$: Population at the first census
B: Number of births
D: Number of deaths

### Distance Decay

$$M_{ij} = \frac{P_i P_j}{d_{ij}}$$

$M_{ij}$: Gross migration between places i and j
$P_{ij}$: Population of places i and j
$d_{ij}$: Distance between places i and j

# Author Index

# People, Agencies and Organizations Index

# Place Index

577

# Subject Index

# Bibliography

Adams, D. A. et al (1994). *Status and Trends Report of the Albemarle-Pamlico Estuarine Study*. Raleigh: North Carolina Department of Health, Environment and Natural Resources (Revised and updated Critical Areas section, covered by memo dated August 12).

Ahrens, C. D. (1991). *Meteorology Today: An Introduction to Weather, Climate, and the Environment (4th Edition)*. St. Paul, MN: West Publishing Co.

Alexander, A. and P. Kelley (2001), "Hidden Ills Plague New Luxury Care," *The Raleigh News and Observer*, July 29.

*A Profession in Jeopardy: Why Teachers Leave and What We Can Do About It* (1996). Raleigh NC: Public School Forum of North Carolina.

Algeo, K. (1997), "The Rise of Tobacco as a Southern Appalachian Stable: Madison County, North Carolina", *Southeastern Geographer*, 37:1, 46-60.

Allegood, J. (1997), "Salvage Efforts to Take Years," *Raleigh News and Observer*, November 3.

Allegood, J. (1997), "Virginians Toast Gaston Pipeline," *Raleigh News and Observer*, November 8.

Allan, C. J. (1993), "Coweeta Hydrologic Laboratory and Tallulah Gorge," in D. G. Bennett (ed.) *Snapshots of the Carolinas: Landscapes and Cultures*. Washington, D.C.: Association of American Geographers, 239-242.

Anderson, W. H. (1991), "What Goes Around, Comes Around," *Business, North Carolina*, July, 44-50.

Arthur, B. (1995), "Poetic Geography," *The State*, September 14.

Ashcraft, C. L. (1992), "Catfish Fever," *The State*, 61:3.

Associated Press. (1998), "Four Hurricanes Roil the Atlantic," *The New York Times*, September 26, http://www.nytimes.com/aponline/a/AP-Four-Hurricanes.html.

Averitt, D. L. (1994). *In Search of Common Ground; A Briefing Paper on School Reform and the Religious Right*. Raleigh NC: Public School Forum of North Carolina.

Avery, S. (2000), "State Report Finds More Doctors, Fewer Dentists," *The Raleigh News and Observer*, November 18.

Ayres, H., J. Hager, and C. E. Little (eds.) (1998). *An Appalachian Tragedy: Air Pollution and Tree Death in the Eastern Forests of North America*. San Francisco CA: Sierra Club Books.

Baker, S. (1982). *Storms, People, and Property in Coastal North Carolina*. Raleigh: University of North Carolina Sea Grant College Program.

Ball, J. (1999). From an interview conducted in Soul City on November 4.

Barefoot, D. W. (1995). *Touring North Carolina's Lower Coast*. Winston-Salem: John F. Blair, Publisher.

Barnes, J. (1998). *North Carolina's Hurricane History* (Rev. and Updated ed.). Chapel Hill, NC: The University of North Carolina Press.

Barnes, K. (1994), "N.C. Towns Have Lots to Chair About: Furniture Discounts Building up National Reputation," *Advertising Age*, October 10, 1-2.

Barrett, B. (2000), "Meager Yield in Farm Preservation," *Raleigh News & Observer*, September 22.

Barrett, B. (2001), "Indirect Approach Works in Durham: Developers Using Annexation Ploy," *Raleigh News and Observer*, January 26.

Barnett, C. W. (1993). *The Impact of Historic Preservation on New Bern, North Carolina*. Winston-Salem: Bandit Books.

Barrentine, Richard, Executive Director, International Home Furnishings Market, High Point (personal interview, March and April, 1995).

Barringer, J. (1995), "A Fish Tale," *Salisbury Post*, June 24.

Barry, R. G. (1992). *Mountain Weather and Climate* (2nd ed.). New York, NY: Routeledge.

Bascom, J., K. Carey and L. Zonn (1996), "Riding the Fifth Wave: Building a Global Transpark in Rural North Carolina," in D. G. Bennett (ed.) *Snapshots of the Carolinas*. Washington DC: Association of American Geographers, 203-208.

Bass, G. (1994), "The Sun Also Rises," *North Carolina*, August, 44-51.

Beimfohr, O. W. (1953), "Some Factors in the Industrial Potential of Southeastern Illinois," *Transactions of the Illinois State Academy of Science*, 46, 97-103.

Bell, A., J. Morrill, and T. Mellnik (2001), "Racial Gap in Voting Still Prevails," *Charlotte Observer*, June 18.

Bennett, D. G. (1992), "The Impact of Retirement Migration on Carteret and Brunswick Counties, N.C." *The North Carolina Geographer*, 1, 25-38.

Berry, B. J. and J. B. Parr (1988). *Market Centers and Retail Location: Theory and Applications*. Englewood Cliffs, N. J.: Prentice Hall

Berry, B. J. L., E. C. Conkling, and D. M. Ray (1997). *The Global Economy in Transition* (2nd ed.). Upper Saddle River NJ: Prentice Hall.

Betts, J. (1996a), "A Short History of Corrections," in M. R. Whitman and R. Coble (eds.) *North Carolina FOCUS: An Anthology on State Government, Politics, and Policy*. Raleigh NC: North Carolina Center for Public Policy Research, 695-698.

Betts, J. (1996b), "Work Force Preparedness; Training 21st Century Workers," in M. R. Whitman and R. Coble (eds.) *North Carolina FOCUS: An Anthology on State Government, Politics, and Policy*. Raleigh NC: North Carolina Center for Public Policy Research, 491-497.

Betts, J. (1998), "The Lake That Wouldn't Drain," *Charlotte Observer*, January 16.

Betts, J. (1998), "High Risks on the Outer Banks," *Charlotte Observer*, November 2.

Betts, J. (1999), "Are Jobs Always the Trump Card When Environmental Questions Arise?" *Charlotte Observer*, April 25.

Betts, J. (2000), "Bowles Campaigns, But He Is Not Running for Any Public Office," *Charlotte Observer*, March 5.

Beyle, T. (ed.) (2000), "Historical Issues on NC Politics," *North Carolina DataNet*, 25, 3.

Bingham, L. (1997), "Mill Workers Lament Plant Closing", *Fayetteville Observer-Times*, February 2.

Birdsall, S. S. (2001), "Tobacco Farmers and Landscape Change in North Carolina's Old Belt Region," *Southeastern Geographer*, 41, 1, 65-73.

Bishir, C. W. and M. T. Southern (1996). *A Guide to the Historic Architecture of Eastern North Carolina*. Chapel Hill: University of North Carolina Press.

Bishir, C. W., M. T. Southern and J. F. Martin (1999). *A Guide to the Historic Architecture of Western North Carolina*. Chapel Hill: The University of North Carolina Press.

Bishir, C. W. (1990). *North Carolina Architecture*. Chapel Hill: University of North Carolina Press.

Bivins, L. (2000), "Smoother Sailing," *North Carolina*, 58, 7, 14-19.

Blackman, O. (1977). *Western North Carolina: It's Mountains and Its People to 1880*. Boone, N. C.: Appalachian Consortium Press.

*Blowing Rocket, The* (1993), "Blowing Rock Battles Blizzard With Big Blitz," March 19.

Blum, B. A. (1996), "Research Challenges Created by the New Federalism," *Focus* (University of Wisconsin-Madison, Institute for Research on Poverty), 17, 1, 2.

Bolton, C. and J. Warren (2001), "The Fight Isn't Over at Shearon Harris," *Raleigh News and Observer*, January 4.

Boraks, D. (1999), "Fiber-Optic Giant in Cabarrus," *Charlotte Observer*, October 3.

Bourne, L. S. (1991), "Recycling Urban Systems and Metropolitan Areas: A Geographical Agenda for the 1990s and Beyond," *Economic Geography*, 67, 3, 185-209.

Boushey, H. (2001), "Reform Welfare Reform," *Charlotte Observer*, August 28.

Bradbury, T. (1994), "Glocalization," *The Charlotte Observer* (editorial), October 15, 18A.

Breisach, G. (1988), "North Carolina Regions," *The Charlotte Observer* (editorial cartoon).

Brewer, M. (1981), "The Changing U. S. Farmland Scene," *Population Bullitin*, 36, 5, 1-40.

Brookings Institution, Center on Urban and Metropolitan Policy (2000). *Adding It Up: Growth Trends and Policies in North Carolina*. A Report Prepared for the Z. Smith Reynolds Foundation.

Brown, M. L. (2000). *The Wild East: A Biography of the Great Smoky Mountains*. Gainesville FL: University of Florida Press.

Brundtland Commission (1987). *Our Common Future*. (For the World Commission on Environment and Development). Oxford, England: Oxford University Press.

Burgess, C. (1999), "North Carolina's Endangered Species Safari," *Friend of Wildlife*, 46, 3, 2-6.

Burgin, W. G. (1992), "A Peach of a State," *The State*, 60:2, 26-29.

Burke, P. (2001), "Affordable Homes," *Charlotte Observer*, July 27.

Burton, I. (1963), "A Restatement of the Dispersed City Hypothesis," *Annals of the Association of American Geographers*, 53, 3, 285-289.

Buscher, P. (1998). *Age-Adjusted Death Rates*. Statistical Primer (State Center for Health Statistics), No 13. (Reprinted in *North Carolina Leading Causes of Death, Vital Statistics–Volume 2, 1998*. Raleigh NC: North Carolina Department of Health and Human Services, Division of Public Health., State Center for Health Statistics, 158-168.)

Cabe, S. and R. Reiman (1996), "Sandhills of the Carolinas," in G. G. Bennett (ed.) *Snapshots of the Carolinas*. Washington DC: Association of American Geographers, 83-86.

Cadwallader, M. (1996). *Urban Geography: An Analytical Approach*. Upper Saddle River NJ: Prentice-Hall, Inc.

Castle, E. N. (1981), "Is There a Farmland Crisis," *Christian Science Monitor*, August 31, 23.

Cecchi, S. (1999). *Balancing Ecology and Economics in the "Heart Region" of North Carolina*. Boone NC: Unpublished Monograph.

Cenziper, D. (1999), "Disparities Persist as Schools Struggle for Racial Balance," *Charlotte Observer*, February 28.

Cenziper, D. and T. Mellnik (1999), "Schools Again at Brink of Change," *Charlotte Observer*, January 10.

Chang, J., O. Gade, and J. Jones (1991), "The Intermediate Socioeconomic Zone: A North Carolina Case Study," in O. Gade, V. P. Miller, Jr., and L. M. Sommers (eds.) *Planning Issues in Marginal Areas*. Boone NC: Appalachian State University, Department of Geography and Planning, Occasional Papers in Geography and Planning, Vol. 3, 149-165.

Chapman, D. (1999), "Pineville Pays for Growth Run Amok," *Charlotte Observer*, August 4.

Chapman, D. (1999), "Success Is All In the Details," *Charlotte Observer*, June 16.

Chapman, D. and C. D. Leonnig (1999), "Squeezing Out the Poor," *Charlotte Observer*, June 13, 1999.

Chase, R. (2000), "Turkey Restoration a Wild Success," *Charlotte Observer*, March 19.

Chase, R. (1998), "Farmers to Till Truffles Instead of Tobacco?" *Charlotte Observer*, July 26.

Cheney, D. W. and R E. Morrison. (1985), "Summary of Field Briefing on the Carolina Tornadoes of March 28, 1984," in *Field Briefing on Tornado Prediction in the Carolinas During the Severe Weather of March 28, 1984*. Washington, D.C.: U.S. Government Printing Office.

Chestang, E. (1996), "The Great Cotton Explosion," in D. G. Bennett (ed) *Snapshots of the Carolinas: Landscapes and Cultures.* Washington, DC: Association of American Geographers, 175-177.

Cimino, K. (2001), "Commissioners to Drop Merger Fight," *Charlotte Observer*, August 7.

Civilian Labor Force Estimates for North Carolina, 1985-1997. (1997). Raleigh: Employment Security Commission of North Carolina.

Clabby, C. (2000), "Proposal Would Move Dix," *The Raleigh News and Observer*, April 16.

Clabby, C. and L. Bonner (2000), "A Case of Benign Neglect," *The Raleigh News and Observer*, March 26.

Clay, James W., D. M. Orr, Jr., and A. W. Stuart, editors, (1975) *North Carolina Atlas.* Chapel Hill: The University of North Carolina Press.

Clay, J. W., D. M. Orr, Jr., and A. W. Stuart (1982). *The Metrolina Urban Region: An Economic Atlas.* Charlotte: University of North Carolina at Charlotte Urban Institute.

Cook, P. (1992), "Triangle East Retools Its Marketing Message," *North Carolina Business*, February, 22-25.

Cooper, G. V. (1998). *A Central Park for North Carolina, Possibility-thinking Workshop.* Document Presented at Workshop, Asheboro NC, July.

Corbett, T. (1996), "The New Federalism: Monitoring Consequences", *Focus* (University of Wisconsin-Madison, Institute for Research on Poverty), 17, 1, 3-6.

Cromartie, J., and C. B. Stack (1989), "Reinterpretation of Black Return and Nonreturn Migration to the South, 1975-1980," *Geographical Review*, 79, 297-330.

Crouch, M. (2000), "N. C. Community College Teachers' Pay 48th In U.S.," *Charlotte Observer*, November 1.

Dadres, S. and D. K. Ginther (2001), "Regional Research and Development Intensity and Earnings Inequality," *Economic Review* (Federal Reserve Bank of Atlanta), 2nd Quarter, 13-26.

Dave, D., M. S. Dotson, and R. Kirkpatrick (1999). *The Economic Impact of Appalachian State University on Watauga County, North Carolina.* Boone NC: Appalachian State University Center for Business Research.

Davis, L. (1991), "High Water Marks: At Badin Lake, Alcoa Has Shown That Industry Can Use—and Not Abuse—a River," *Business North Carolina*, April, 56-60.

Department of Corrections (2001). *Annual Statistical Report, Fiscal Year 1999-2000.* Raleigh NC: Office of Research and Planning, North Carolina Department of Corrections.

Diamant, J. (1998), "Here Are N.C. Counties Where You Are More Likely to Get Pulled Over," *Charlotte Observer*, February 8.

Dicken, P. (1992). *Global Shift: The Internationalization of Economic Activity* (2nd Ed.) New York: Guilford Press.

*Directory of North Carolina Manufacturing Firms*, 1992-93.

Dodd, S. (1999), "New Road Cut Through Watershed," *Charlotte Observer*, August 22.

Dodd, S. (2000), "Charlotte Outgrowing Its Suburbs, U.S. Study Says," *Charlotte Observer*, June 29.

Dodd, S. (2001), "What Follows the Big Store?" *Charlotte Observer*, March 9.

Dodd, S. (2001), "Boom Bypasses Carolina's Poverty," *Charlotte Observer*, July.

Dolan, R. and Lins, H. (1986). *The Outer Banks of North Carolina.* U.S. Geological Survey Professional Paper 1177-B, U.S. Government Printing Office.

Dudley, J. (1993). *Carteret Waterfowl Heritage.* Harker's Island: Core Sound Waterfowl Museum.

Dunbar, G. S. (1958). *Historical Geography of the North Carolina Outer Banks.* Baton Rouge: Louisian State University Press.

Dyer, L. (1996), "Residents in Shadow of City Seek Protection," *Charlotte Observer*, September 24.

Dyer, L. (1999), "Concealed-Gun Laws' Impact Unclear," *Charlotte Observer*, March 23.

Dykeman, W. and J. Stokel (1995), "The People and the Land," *Appalachia*, 28, 1&2, 1-11.

Eagleman, J. R. (1990). *Severe and Unusual Weather* (2nd ed.). Lenexa, KS: Trimedia Publishing Company.

Early, L. S., ed. (1993) *North Carolina Wild Places, A Closer Look.* North Carolina Wildlife Resources Commission, Raleigh, North Carolina.

Early, L. S. (1996), "Safe Harbor in the Sandhills," *Wildlife in North Carolina*, 60, 10, 10-15.

Edmondson, B. (1996), "When Boomers Retire," *American Demographics*, (June), 60.

Elmore, K. (2000), "AIDS Among Women in North Carolina," *The North Carolina Geographer*, 8, 41-54.

Employment Security Commission (1998). *North Carolina's Largest Manufacturing and Nonmanufacturing Employers.* Raleigh: Department of Labor, Labor Market Information Office.

Epperson, D. L., G. L. Johnson, J. M. Davis, and P. J. Robinson. (1988). *Weather and Climate in North Carolina.* Raleigh, NC: Agricultural Extension Service, North Carolina State University.

Escott, P. D. (1991), "The Capital's Gains," *North Carolina Business*, December, 33-39.

Evinger, S. (1996), "How to Record Race," *American Demographics*, (May), 36.

Farm Labor Organizing Committee (1999). (www.iupui.edu/-floc/nc.htm)

Fender, R. (1991), "A Regional Approach to the Administration of Rural Small Community Planning and Development," In *Planning Issues in Marginal Areas*, O. Gade, V. P. Miller Jr., and L. M. Sommers (eds.) Boone, NC: Appalachian State University, Department of Geography and Planning, Occasional Papers in Geography and Planning, 3, 93-100.

Finger, B. (1996), "Making the Transition to the Mixed Economy," in M. R. Whitman and R. Coble (eds.) *North Carolina Focus: An Anthology on State Government, Politics, and Policy.* Raleigh NC: North Carolina Center for Public Policy, 45-56.

Fischer, S. (2000), "We're No. 1!" *North Carolina*, April, 27-38.

Flono, F. (1999), "N. C. School Boards Face a Taxing Question," *Charlotte Observer*, October 29.

Flono, F. (2001), "Universal Education Praised But Resisted," *Charlotte Observer*, September 7.

Frankenberg, D. (1997). *North Carolina's Southern Coast: Barrier Islands, Coastal Waters, and Wetlands*. Chapel Hill: The University of North Carolina Press.

Franklin, S. (1999), "Easing On-the-Job Pain," *Charlotte Observer*, August 7.

Frey, W. H. (1996), "Immigrant and Native Migrant Magnets," *American Demographics* (November), 36-40, 53.

Frey, W. H. and A. Spear, Jr. (1992), "The Revival of Metropolitan Population Growth," *Population and Development Review*, 18:1 (March), 129-146.

Frome, C. (1962*). Whose Woods Are These: The Story of the National Forests*. Garden City NY: Doubleday & Company, Inc.

Fullwood, N. (2000), "Let's Declare a Humanitarian Emergency," *The Raleigh News and Observer*, March 26.

Furuseth, O. (1997), "Restructuring of Hog Farming in North Carolina: Explosion and Implosion," *The Professional Geographer*, 49:4, 391-403.

Furuseth, O. J. (2001), "Hog Farming in Eastern North Carolina," *Southeastern Geographer*, 41, 1, 53-64.

Gade, O. (1989), "Regional Development in a Southern State: The North Carolina Experience, 1970-1988," In *Development in Marginal Areas*, G. Gustafsson (ed.) Karlstad, Sweden: Karlstad University Research Report 89:3, 37-46.

Gade, O. (1991), "Dealing With Disparities in Regional Development–The Intermediate Socioeconomic Region," In *Planning Issues in Marginal Areas*, O. Gade, V. P. Miller Jr., and L. M. Sommers (eds.) Boone, NC: Appalachian State University, Department of Geography and Planning, Occasional Papers in Geography and Planning 3, 19-30.

Gade, O. (1995), "Who is Being Served? North Carolina Regions in a New Age," *The North Carolina Geographer*, 4, 15-29.

Gade, O. (1996), "Furniture in North Carolina," in Bennett, G. D. (ed.) *Snapshots of the Carolinas: Landscapes and Cultures*. Washington DC: Association of American Geographers, 165-170.

Gade, O. (1988), "Regional Development in a Southern State: The North Carolina Experience, 1970-1988," in G. Gustafsson (ed) *Development in Marginal Areas*. Karlstad, Sweden: University of Karlstad, Research Report 89:3.

Gade, O. (forthcoming), "The Evolving Urban and Economic Structure Since 1900," in Bennett, G. D. (ed.) *The Geography of the Carolinas*. Baltimore: Johns Hopkins University Press.

Gade and D. Cui (1994), "Whither Rural Development? North Carolina in the 1980s," In *Marginal Areas in Developed Countries*, U. Wiberg (ed.) Umeå, Sweden: Umeå University Center for Regional Science, 25-44.

Gade, O., D. Stillwell and A. Rex (1986). *North Carolina: People and Environments*. Boone, N. C.: GEOAPP.

Gade, O. and J. Young (1996), "North Carolina's Piedmont Urban Crescent: A Field Guide," in Bennett, G. D. (ed*.) Snapshots of the Carolinas: Landscapes and Cultures*. Washington DC: Association of American Geographers, 251-255.

Garcia, L. (ed.) (1991). *Rural America at the Crossroads: Networking for the Future*. Washington DC: Congress of the United States, Office of Technology Assessment.

Gares, P. A. (1999), "Climatology and Hydrology of Eastern North Carolina and Their Effects on Creating the Flood of the Century," *The North Carolina Geographer*, 7, 3-11.

Garloch, K. and J. Horan. (1989), "Hugo Was Really Storm Of 2 Centuries," *Charlotte Observer*, September 29.

Geary, B. (1997), "Raleigh's Best Hope," *The Independent*, November 12-18, 13-17.

Geary, B. (1999), "Triangle2K: Deliver Us From Sprawl," *The Independent*, December 1-7.

Gilmor, S. (1996), "End of the Road," *Winston-Salem Journal*, February 23.

Glass, B. (1992). *The Textile Industry in North Carolina, A History*. Raleigh: North Carolina Division of Archives and History.

Generalized Geologic Map of North Carolina (1991). North Carolina Geologic Survey.

Glascock, N. and C. Whitlock (1998), "Law vs. Reality," *The Raleigh News and Observer*, November 30.

Godschalk, D (ed.) (1998). *Coastal Hazards Mitigation: Public Notification, Expenditure Limitations, and Hazard Areas Acquisition*. Chapel Hill: University of North Carolina, Center for Urban and Regional Studies.

Goldberg, J. (2000), "Dearth of Dentists Hits Rural Counties," *Charlotte Observer*, November 28.

Goldberg, J. (2001), "Third of N.C. Households Can't Pay Basic Bills, Advocacy Groups Say," *Charlotte Observer*, January 10.

Gomez, J. (1999), "Urban Renewal, One House at the Time," *The Raleigh News and Observer*, October 17.

Goodge, G. and G. Hammer. (1993), "Special Weather Summary," in *Climatological Data, North Carolina: March 1993*. Asheville, NC: National Climatic Data Center.

Government Performance Audit Committee (1992). *Our State, Our Future: Economic Development* (Issue Papers, North Carolina General Assembly). Raleigh NC: KPMG Peat Marwick, Government Services Management Consultants.

Gray, W. M. and J. D. Sheaffer. (1991), "El Niño and QBO influences on tropical cyclone activity," in M. H. Glantz, R. W. Katz, and N. Nicholls (eds.) *Teleconnections Linking Worldwide Climate Anomalies: Scientific Basis and Societal Impact*. Cambridge, United Kingdom: Press Syndicate, 257-284.

Gregutt, P. (1998), "Moving Mountains," *North Carolina*, February, 21-32.

Griffin, A. (1998), ""Norman: A Gold Coast," *Charlotte Observer*, April 5.

Griffin, A. (2000), "Billions Sought for Rural N.C." *Charlotte Observer*, February 22.

Grosvenor, H. (1996), "Earle Village: A Community in Transition," *Urban Land*, January, 50-54.

Grove, J. M. (1988). *The Little Ice Age.* New York, NY: Methuen & Co. Ltd.

Hackett, T. (1999), "Risking the Future of Our Cities," *Ford Foundation Report*, 30, 3, 4-7.

Hackney, B. (1992), "Golf Drives Moore on Course to Diversity," *North Carolina*, November, 16-22.

Haider, D. (1992), "Place Wars: New Realities of the 1990s," *Economic Development Quarterly*, 6, 127-34.

Hall, C. B. (2000),"Rural Areas Struggle as Boom Fades," *The Raleigh News and Observer*.

Hammer, Siler, George Associates (1999). *The Research Triangle Park: The First Forty Years.* Silver Springs MD.

Hammersley, L. (1983), "N. C. Infant Mortality Rate Rises," *Charlotte Observer*, June 20.

Haney, D. Q. (2001),"At 20 Years, AIDS Fight Not Over, Victory Not Assured," *Charlotte Observer*, June 3.

Hansen, N. (1994), "The Strategic Role of Producer Services in Regional Development," *International Regional Science Review*, 16, 1 & 2, 187-195.

Hardie, A. V. (1960), "Special Weather Summary," in *Climatological Data, North Carolina: March 1960.* Asheville, NC: National Climatic Data Center.

Hart, J. F. (1996), "Tobacco in North Carolina," in D. G. Bennett (ed) *Snapshots of the Carolinas: Landscapes and Cultures.* Washington, DC: Association of American Geographers, 179-182.

Hart, J. F. and E. L. Chestang (1990), "Vertical Integration and Confinement Production of Broilers, Turkeys, and Hogs," in D. G. Bennett (ed) *Snapshots of the Carolinas: Landscapes and Cultures.* Washington, DC: Association of American Geographers, 183-187.

Hart, J. F. and E. L. Chestang (1996), "Turmoil in Tobaccoland," *Geographical Review*, 86:4, 550-572.

Hart, J. F. and C. Mayda (1998), "The Industrialization of Livestock Production in the United States," *Southeastern Geographer*, 38, 1, 58-78.

Hayes, C. R. (1976). *The Dispersed City: The Case of Piedmont, North Carolina.* Chicago: The University of Chicago, Department of Geography Research Paper No. 173.

Henderson, B. (2001c), "Custodians of Catawba Work on Collaboration Throughout Basin," *Charlotte Observer*, March 3.

Henderson, B. (2000), "Rare Species Feel at Home in the Blue Ridge," *Charlotte Observer*, April 7.

Henderson, B. (2000), "Survey Sports Old-Growth Bonanza," *Charlotte Observer*, June 21.

Henderson, B. (2001b), "Cluster of Easements Will Protect 531 Acres," *Charlotte Observer*, January 20.

Henderson, B. (2001a), "Duke's Plan for Shoreline Criticized," *Charlotte Observer*, January 16.

Henderson, B. (2000b), "The Catawba River: Under Siege," *Charlotte Observer*, September 3 and 4.

Henderson, B. (2000a), "Navigating Dams' Destiny," *Charlotte Observer*, August 27.

Henderson, B. (2000b), "Carolinas Oozing Ingredients for Smog", *Charlotte Observer*, July 20.

Henderson, B. (2000c), "Burgeoning Buffers Face Foes," *Charlotte Observer*, February 25.

Henderson, B (1998), "Plant Raises Worries in Fragile Land," *Charlotte Observer*, 15 August.

Henderson, B. (1989), "War of the Woods," *Charlotte Observer*, February 18.

Henderson, B. (1998), "Summit Seeks to Point to New Path," *Charlotte Observer*, November 7.

Henderson, B. (1998), "Poor County Bets Ecology can Rescue Its Economy," *Charlotte Observer*, August 9.

Henderson, B. (1997), "Chip Mills Gobble Forests, Jobs, Foes Say," *Charlotte Observer*, August 24.

Henderson, B. (1997a), "Does *Pfiesteria* Attack People?" *Charlotte Observer*, November 13.

Henderson, B. (1997b), "Microbe *Vibrio* is Proven Killer for Humans," *Charlotte Observer*, November 13.

Henderson, B. (1997), "Trouble for Timber?" *Charlotte Observer*, August 27.

Henderson, B. (1997), "Homeowners Near N.C. Surf File Suit to Limit Beach Access," *Charlotte Observer*.

Hensley, B. F. (1995), "Harvesting Nature's Pharmacy," *North Carolina*, 53:9, 12-14.

Heppen, J. (2000), "The 2000 Presidential Election in the Many Souths of North Carolina," *The North Carolina Geographer*, 8, 64-66.

Herbert, G. R. and S. Johnston (1979), "Urban Social and Economic Conditions in North Carolina," in W. J. Wicker (ed.) *Urban Growth and Urban Life.* Chapel Hill, N. C.: The University of North Carolina Press, 1-9.

Hidore, J. J. (1993), "North Carolina Nor'easters and Their Related Storm Hazards," *The North Carolina Geographer*, 2:3, 32-44.

Hidore, J. J. and J. C. Patton (1993), "North Carolina Hurricanes," in D. G. Bennett (ed.) *Snapshots of the Carolinas: Landscapes and Cultures.* Washington, D.C.: Association of American Geographers, 69-72.

*Highlights of the Land and Resources Management Plan: Amendment 5*(1994). Asheville NC: United States Department of Agriculture, Forest Service Southern Region.

Hinesley, E. (1996), "The Pocosin Project," *Friend of Wildlife*, 44, 2, 16.

*Historical News, The*(1988) Volume 18 Number 66-NC, September.

Hodge, A. (1993), "Pint-Sized Paradise," *The State*, September, 34-36.

Holmes, S. A. (1996), "Income Gap Between Rich, Others Greatest Since '40s," *New York Times*, June 19.

Hopkins, S. M. (1996a), "Whole New Herd," *Charlotte Observer*, November 3.

Hopkins, S. M. (1996b), "Out to Pasture; Carolinas Dairy Farmers Struggle to Stay in Business," *Charlotte Observer*, August 25.

Hopkins, S. M. (1996c), "Cotton's Comeback," *Charlotte Observer*, October 20.

Hopkins, S. M. (1997), "Turkey Production Sees 'Rough' 2 Years," *Charlotte Observer*, November 7.

Hopkins, S. M. (1996), "High-Tech Silver Lining," *Charlotte Observer*, November 17.

Hopkins, S. M. (1997a), "Why Can't We Move This Stuff," *Charlotte Observer*, August 17.

Hopkins, S. M. (1997b), "Textiles' Dark Legacy," *Charlotte Observer*, November 24.

Hopkins, S. M. (1997c), "Wringing Profits From Textiles," *Charlotte Observer*, December 27.

Hopkins, S. M. (1998), "Asia's Storm Washes Over Carolinas," *Charlotte Observer*, January 23.

Hopkins, S. M. and A. Y. Williams (1998), "Freightliner to Add 1,095 Jobs", *Charlotte Observer*, March 12.

Horan, J. (1999), "Pasture or Populated Subdivision?" *Charlotte Observer*, October 3.

Horan, J. (1994), "Our Disappearing Fish'" *Charlotte Observer*, August 28.

Horan, J. (1994), "Preserving Coast: More to be Done," *Charlotte Observer*, September 4.

Horan, J. (1995), "Bracing for the Winds," *Charlotte Observer*, September 8.

Housing Assistance Council (2001). *Why Homes Matters: HACs 2000 Report on the State of the Nation's Rural Housing.* Washington DC: Home Assistance Council. (http://www.ruralhome.org/pubs/HACAnnual2000.pdf).

Hower, W. (1998), "Developers, Cities See a Green Future in 'Brownfields'", *Raleigh News and Observer*, November 1.

Hui, T. K. and S. Ebbs (2001), "Charter Schools See Gains," *The Raleigh News and Observer*, June 11.

IFC Consulting (1999). *Assessment of State Incentives to Promote Redevelopment of Brownfields* Prepared by ICF Consulting, Fairfax VA and the E.P Systems Group, Inc., Louisville KY for the U.S. Department of Housing and Urban Development: Office of Policy Development and Research (HC #5966, Task Order 13).

Jakobsen, L. M. (2000), "Western North Carolina's Christmas Trees: Growers' Hard Work Produces Yuletide Beauty," *Carolina Mountain*, December/January.

Johnson, J. H. and D. M. Grant (1997), "Post-80 Black Population Redistribution Trends in the United States," *Southeastern Geographer*, 37:1, 1-19.

Johnson, M. (1997), "To Restructure or Not to Restructure: Contemplations on Postwar Industrial Geography in the U.S. South," *Southeastern Geographer*, 37, 2, 162-192.

Johnson, M. (2001), "Justices Uphold N. C. 12th," *Charlotte Observer*, April 19.

Johnson-Webb, K. D. and J. H. Johnson (1996), "North Carolina Communities in Transition: An Overview of Hispanic In-Migration," *The North Carolina Geographer*, 5, 21-40.

Jones, D. (1997). *The Central Park Concept—A Business Plan.* In a letter to Dr. Kenneth E. Peacock, Dean, Appalachian State University School of Business, dated November 3.

Jones, M. S. (1996) "The Cherokee Reservation," in D. G. Bennett (ed.) *Snapshots of the Carolinas: Landscapes and Cultures.* Washington DC: Association of American Geographers, 33-36.

Jones, S. (1998), "Towns Fight Group Homes With Zoning, Lawsuits," *Charlotte Observer*, August 19.

Kane, D. and J. Wagner (2000), "Grades Mixed on Higher Education," *The Raleigh News and Observer*, December 1.

Kasarda, J. D. (1995), "Transportation Infrastructure for Competitive Success in the Fast Century," *Transportation Quarterly* (in press).

Kelly, R. and B. Kelly (1993). *The Carolina Watermen: Bug Hunters and Boatbuilders.* Winston-Salem: John F. Blair, Publisher.

Kelly, S. R. (1982), "U.S. Tobacco Program May Face Radical Reform," *Charlotte Observer*, July 4, 1B, 4B.

Kincaid, R. (2001), "Development Restrictions Best for Davidson," *Charlotte Observer*, May 1.

Klein, L. (2000), "Migrant Workers Not Allowed Visitors," *Charlotte Observer*, 4 February.

Knox, P. L. (1991), "The Restless Urban Landscape: Economic and Sociocultural Change and the Transformation of Washington, DC," *Annals, Association of American Geographers*, 81, 2, 181-209.

Krueger, B. and M. McLaughlin (1996), "North Carolina's State Parks: Finding a Dedicated Source of Funding," in M. R. Whitman and R. Coble (eds.) *North Carolina FOCUS: An Anthology on State Government, Politics, and Policy.* Raleigh NC: North Carolina Center for Public Policy Research, 681-691.

Lail, Leroy, Executive Director, Furniture Mart, Hickory (personal interview, March, 1995).

Lally, K. A. and T. Johnson (1994). *The History and Architecture of Wake County, North Carolina From British and African Settlement to 1941.* Raleigh NC: Wake County Government.

Lambrew, J. M. and J. Betts (1996), "Rural Health Care in North Carolina: Unmet Needs, Unanswered Questions," in M. R. Whitman and R. Coble (eds.) *North Carolina FOCUS: An Anthology on State Government, Politics, and Policy.* Raleigh NC: North Carolina Center for Public Policy Research, 581-589.

Landau, R. (1995), "Hollywood of the East?" *The State*, 63, 2, 21-30.

Laws, G. (1994), "Implications for Demographic Change for Urban Policy and Planning," *Urban Geography*, 15 (1), 90-100.

Leatherman, Stephen P. (1988). *Barrier Island Handbook.* Coastal Publication Series, The University of Maryland, College Park, Maryland, 1988.

Leavenworth, S. and J. E. Shiffer (1998), "Airborne Menace," *Raleigh News and Observer*, July 5.

Leland, E. (1992), "Down East" *Charlotte Observer*, 8 November.

Leland, E. (1996), "Private Prisons: Businesses Want a Piece of the Rock," in M. R. Whitman and R. Coble (eds.) *North Carolina FOCUS: An Anthology on State Government, Politics, and Policy*. Raleigh NC: North Carolina Center for Public Policy Research, 707-709.

Leland, E. (1999), "Coming Home," *Charlotte Observer*, March 14.

*Lenoir News-Topic*, January 5, 1991.

Leonnig, C. D. (1999), "Success With Bricks, But Not With Earle Village's People," *Charlotte Observer*, June 14.

Lineback, N., Miller, L., Bice, D. (1987) *Horizons of North Carolina*. Walsworth Publishing.

Longman, P. L. (1998), "Who Pays for Sprawl?" *Charlotte Observer*, May 10.

Lord, D. (1971), "The Growth and Location of the United States Broiler Chicken Industry," *Southeastern Geographer*, 11, 29-42.

Lord, D. (1996), "The New Geography of Cotton Production in North Carolina," *Southeastern Geographer*, 36:2, 93-112.

Lord, J. D. (1987), "Banking Across State Lines," *Focus*, 34, 1, 10-15.

Lord, J. D. (1996), "Charlotte's Role as a Major Banking Center," in Bennett, G. D. (ed.) *Snapshots of the Carolinas: Landscapes and Cultures*. Washington DC: Association of American Geographers, 209-213.

Lubitz, R. L. (1996), "Structured Sentencing in North Carolina," in M. R. Whitman and R. Coble (eds.) *North Carolina FOCUS: An Anthology on State Government, Politics, and Policy*. Raleigh NC: North Carolina Center for Public Policy Research, 699-704.

*Making North Carolina A High Performance State.* (1994). Raleigh: North Carolina Department of Commerce (The Comprehensive Strategic Economic Development Plan of the North Carolina Economic Development Board).

*Making Strategic Choices to Become First in America: An Examination of the Unfinished Business of School Improvement in North Carolina* (2001). Raleigh NC: The Public School Forum of North Carolina.

Malveaux, J. (1999), "Compensation for Farmers Too Little Too Late," *Charlotte Observer*, January 21.

Manuel, J. (2000), "Timber Tantrums," *Friend of Wildlife*, 48, 2, 2-7.

Manuel, J. (1998), "Chip Mills in North Carolina," *Friend of Wildlife*, 45, 1, 2-5.

Manuel, J. (1998), "North Carolina Wildlife Gamelands", *Friend of Wildlife*, 44, 4, 305.

Manuel, J. (1992), "Every Breath We Take," *Park Guide* (The 1992 Guide to Research Triangle Park), 26-31.

Markoe, L (2001), "Reaching for Respect," *Charlotte Observer*, April 23.

Martin, E. (2000), "Sweet & Sour," *North Carolina*, 58, 2, 12-13.

Martin, E. (1999), "Looms to Lasers," *North Carolina*, September, 33-48.

Martin, E. (1999), "Rising to the Top," *North Carolina*, 57, 1, 20-29.

Martin, E. (1996), "Lee's Changing Landscape," *North Carolina*, 54, 7.

Martin, E. (1999), "The College Countdown," *North Carolina*, 57, 8, 52-74.

Martin, E. (2000), "Low Wealth Schools Marks Sixth Year in Court," *North Carolina*, 56, 9, 76-78.

Matthews, E. (ed.) (1999). *Choices for a New Century*. Raleigh NC: N.C. Rural Economic Development Center, Inc.

Mayer, H. M. (1969). *The Spatial Expression of Urban Growth*. Commission on College Geography Resource Paper No. 7. Washington DC: Association of American Geographers.

Mayer, H. M. and C. R. Hayes (1983). *Land Uses in American Cities*. Champaign ILL: Park Press.

Mayfield, M. W. and J. DeHart (1966), "Carolina Whitewater," in Bennett, D. G. (ed.) *Snapshots of the Carolinas*. Washington DC: Association of American Geographers, 91-94.

McDonald, T. (2000), "Housing Disparity Still Lives in the Triangle," *The Raleigh News and Observer*, September 7.

McDowell, R. W. (1990), "Escaping the Prison Cap," *North Carolina*, 46, 10, 62-63..

McKnight, T. L. (2000). *Physical Geography: A Landscape Appreciation (6th ed.)* Upper Saddle River, NJ: Prentice Hall.

McLaughlin, M. (1996), "The Health of Minority Citizens in North Carolina," in M. R. Whitman and R. Coble (eds.) *North Carolina FOCUS: An Anthology on State Government, Politics, and Policy*. Raleigh NC: North Carolina Center for Public Policy Research, 543-568.

McLaughlin, M. and B. Skinner (1997), "Can We Brighten the Future for North Carolina," *North Carolina Insight*, 17, 2-3, 100-120.

Minor, J. (1960), "Watauga in Disaster Area: Red Cross, Guard Units Act to Aid Snow Victims," *Watauga Democrat*, March 17.

Moorhead, K. (1995), "Wetland Conversions: Counting the Losses," *Wildlife in North Carolina*, 59, 3, 26-31.

Morrill, J. (1999), "Slim Budgets, County Growth Lead to School Inequities," *Charlotte Observer*, March 1.

Morrill, J. and T. Mellnik (1996), "Tobacco PACs Pay to be Heard," *Charlotte Observer*, September.

Morris, G. (1993), "The Phantom Fayetteville," *The State*, January, 25-29.

Morris, G. (1998). *North Carolina Beaches*. Chapel Hill: The University of North Carolina Press.

Musante, G. (1997), "Angier, Rooted But Branching Out," *Raleigh News and Observer*, June 29.

National Oceanic and Atmospheric Administration (NOAA). (1998*). Ongoing La Niña Conditions in the Tropical Pacific Ocean are Expected to Increase Atlantic Hurricane Activity*. http://www.publicaffairs.noaa.gov/stories/sir12.html.

National Oceanic and Atmospheric Administration (NOAA). (1989). *Hurricane Hugo (1989).* http://wchs.csc.noaa.gov/images/hugopath.gif.

National Research Council. (1994). *Hurricane Hugo: Puerto Rico, The Virgin Islands, and Charleston, South Carolina.* Washington, D.C.: National Academy of Sciences.

National Geographic Magazine Special Edition (1993). *Water: The Power, Promise, and Turmoil of North America's Fresh Water.* National Geographic Society, Volume 184, No. 5A.

Neff, J. (2000), "Legislation Gives Power to Railroad," *The Raleigh News and Observer,* June 27.

Nelson, C. H. (1996), "Hosiery Makers Study Italian Concept of Industry Alliances," *North Carolina,* 54, 7, 53.

*New York Times Almanac 2001* (2000). New York NY: Penguin Putnam Inc.

Newbold, K. B. (1997), "Race and Primary, Return, and Onward Interstate Migration,*" Professional Geographer,* 49:1, 1-14.

Newman, C. (1995), "North Carolina's Piedmont: On a Fast Break," *National Geographic Magazine,* 187, 3, 114-138.

Newsom, M (1999), "The Prairie School," *Charlotte Observer,* July 19.

Newsom, M. (1998), "Don't Want Sprawl? Then Change the Rules," *Charlotte Observer,* May 10.

Nichols, J. (1995), "Marine Panel Wades in," *Raleigh News and Observer,* April 10.

*North Carolina's Environment* (1991). Raleigh, N.C.: Department of Natural Resources and Community Development.

*North Carolina's Environment* (1981). Raleigh, N.C.: Department of Natural Resources and Community Development.

North Carolina Geographic Alliance (1994). *North Carolina Water: Can We Keep It Fit for Life?*

*North Carolina Leading Causes of Death, Vital Statistics–Volume 2, 1998.* Raleigh NC: North Carolina Department of Health and Human Services, Division of Public Health., State Center for Health Statistics.

*North Carolina Municipal Population, 1993* (1994). Raleigh: Office of State Planning.

Office of State Planning (1996). *North Carolina Municipal Population '95.* Raleigh: North Carolina, Office of the Governor.

Office of State Planning (1997). *State Demographics* (a series of continually updated state demographic data on the municipal and county level, compiled by T. William Tillman, Jr., State Demographer, and available on the Web Page, http://www.ospl.state.nc.us/demog/

Oliver, R. (1992), "Selling Convertible Sofas in Convertible Currencies," *North Carolina Business,* April, 14-16.

Oliver, R. and L. H. Towle (1993), "Collecting the Peace Dividend," *North Carolina,* March, 18-40.

Orr, D. M. and A. W. Stuart (eds.) (2000) *The North Carolina Atlas: Portrait for a New Century.* Chapel Hill NC: The University of North Carolina Press.

Otterbourg, K. (1996), "How Healthy is North Carolina's Population," in M. R. Whitman and R. Coble (eds.) *North Carolina FOCUS: An Anthology on State Government, Politics, and Policy.* Raleigh NC: North Carolina Center for Public Policy Research, 529-542. (Reprinted from *North Carolina Insight,* May 1992, 2-19).

Otterbourg, K. and M. McLaughlin (1993), "North Carolina's Demographic Destiny: The Policy Implications of the 1990 Census," *North Carolina Insight,* (August), 2-65.

Owenby, J. R. and D.S. Ezell. (1992). *Monthly Station Normals of Temperature, Precipitation, and Heating and Cooling Degree Days 1961-1990: North Carolina.* Asheville, NC: National Climatic Data Center.

Owens, D. W. (1985), "Coastal Management in North Carolina," *Journal of the American Planning Association,* 51, 3, 322-329.

Paik, A. (1998), "Group Urges Farm Workers to Fight Back," *Raleigh News and Observer,* July 5.

Palmquist, R. B., F. M. Roka, and T. Vukina (1997), "Hog Operations, Environmental Effects, and Residence Property Value," *Land Economics,* 73:1 114-124.

Patterson, D. (1996), "Turkey Has Turkey Day, of Course, But the Menu is Strictly Barbecue," *Charlotte Observer,* November 26.

Peek, C. (1993), "Looking Up Down East," *North Carolina,* February, 36-45.

Perez, L. (2000), "Some in Wake County Not Prospering From Growth," *Raleigh News and Observer,* March 15.

Perlmutt, D. and F. Rhee (1998), "Coast's Bill for Rebuilding Keeps Going to Taxpayers," *Charlotte Observer,* August 30.

Persson, L. O. and U. Wiberg (1995). *Microregional Fragmentation: Contrasts Between a Welfare State and a Market Economy.* Heidelberg, Germany: Physica-Verlag.

Peters, S. F. (1995), "Keeper of the Neuse," *Wildlife in North Carolina,* 59, 4, 2-9.

Philander, S. G. (1990). *El Niño, La Niña, and the Southern Oscillation.* San Diego, CA: Academic Press, Inc.

Phillips, C. T. (1955), "North Carolina's Rich Crescent," *Journal of Geography,* 55, 4, 182-187.

Phillips, J. D. (1994), "The Forgotten Hardwoods of the Coastal Plain," *The Geographical Review,* 84, 162-171.

Phillips, J. D. (1997), "A Short History of a Flat Place: Three Centuries of Geomorphic Change in the Croatan National Forest," *Annals of the Association of American Geographers,* 87:2, 197-216.

Pierce, N. and C. Johnson (1995). Pierce Report: Recommendations for Our Region's Future. Charlotte, N. C.: Charlotte City Council.

Pierce, N. (2001), " 'Carfree Cities': Exploring How Cars Drive Us," *Charlotte Observer,* March.

Pilkey, O. H., et al (1978). *From Currituck to Calabash: Living With North Carolina's Barrier Islands.* Research Triangle Park: North Carolina Science and Research Technology Center.

Pilkey, O. H. and K. L. Dixon (1996). *The Corps and the Shore.* Washington D.C.: Island Press.

Pilkey, O. H., et al (1998). *The North Carolina Shoreline and Its Barrier Islands: Restless Ribbons of Sand.* Durham: Duke University Press.

Postman, L. (1999), "The World of Shoppertainment", *Charlotte Observer*, July 12.

Poteat, J. and L. Giannusa (2000). *Local School Finance 2000.* Raleigh NC: Public School Forum of North Carolina.

Powell, C. (1999), "Marine Fisheries as a Crossroads," *Wildlife in North Carolina*, March, 4-17.

*Public Policy and Charter Schools* (2000). Raleigh NC: Public School Forum of North Carolina.

Pugh, T. (1997), "Welfare Reform Revisited: What Happens When the Checks Stop?" *Charlotte Observer.*

Purvis, K. (1996), "N.C. Ostrich en Route to Beefless Britain," *Charlotte Observer*, April 9.

Pyle, G. (1996), "AIDS Comes to the Carolinas–And Stays," in G. G. Bennett (ed.) *Snapshots of the Carolinas: Landscapes and Cultures.* Washington DC: Association of American Geographers, 141-145.

Pyle, G. F. and O. J. Furuseth (1992), "The Diffusion of AIDS and Social Deprivation in North Carolina," *The North Carolina Geographer*, 1, 1-12.

Raleigh News and Observer, (1996a), "Elements bludgeon Triangle: Recovery will be slow, difficult," *The News and Observer*, September 7.

Raleigh News and Observer. (1996b), "The Storm and the Aftermath," *The News & Observer*, September 7.

Randall, D. P. (1968), "Wilmington, North Carolina: The Historical Development of a Port City," *Annals of the Association of American Geographers*, 58, 3, 441-451.

Ratzan, S. C., G. L. Filerman, and J. W. Lesar (2000). *Attaining Global Health: Challenges and Opportunities.* Washington DC: Population Reference Bureau (Population Bulletin, 55, 1).

Rawlins, W. (1996), "Water-Users Starting to Recycle Treated Sewage for Irrigation," *Raleigh News and Observer*, June 20.

Rawlins, W. (1995), "Wake Buys 82.9 Acres for Reservoir," *Raleigh News and Observer*, April 10

Reed, T. (2001), "Charlotte Tops in On-time Arrivals," *Charlotte Observer*, April 26.

*Regionalism in North Carolina.* (1980). Raleigh: North Carolina Department of Natural Resources and Community Development.

Rhee, F. (1995), "Declaring a State Vegetable," *Charlotte Observer*, March 10.

Rhee, F. (1998), "Medical Firm Gets Big Fine," *Charlotte Observer.*

Robinson, P. J. (1996), "A View of North Carolina's Climate," *The North Carolina Geographer*, 5:1, 11-20.

Robinson, P. J. (1993), "The Spatial Scale of Daily Precipitation in North Carolina," *The North Carolina Geographer*, 2:3, 21-31.

Rochman, B. (2000), "Wake Jails Battle Syphilis," *The Raleigh News and Observer*, April 11.

Rochman, B. (2000), "Fight Against STDs, Dogged But Delicate," *The Raleigh News and Observer*, December 30.

Roe, C. E. (2000), "Private Land Trusts: Partners for Community Conservation," *Popular Government*, Fall, 42-45.

Ross, T. E. (1992), "Aquaculture and Economic Development: Potentials in Southeastern North Carolina," *The North Carolina Geographer*, 1, 55-61.

Ross, T. E. (1994). *Atlas of Robeson County* (2nd ed.) Southern Pines: Karo Hollow Press.

Ross, T. E. (1996). *Atlas of Moore County, North Carolina: Portrait of an Eclectic Southern County.* Southern Pines: Karo Hollow Press.

Ross, T. E. (1996), "Carolina Bays: Coastal Plain Enigma," in D. G. Bennett (ed.) *Snapshots of the Carolinas.* Washington DC: Association of American Geographers, 83-86.

Ross, T. E. (1995), "The Lumbees: A Study of Population Growth in a Non-Reservation Indian Tribe," in T. E. Ross, T. G. Moore, and L. A. King (eds.) *American Indians: A Cultural Geography* (2nd. ed.) Southern Pines NC: Karo Hollow Press, 279-290.

Ross, T. E. (1999). *American Indians in North Carolina: A Geographic Interpretation.* Southern Pines NC: Karo Hollow Press.

Rothenberg, Daniel (1998). *With These Hands: The Hidden World of Migrant Farmworkers Today.* New York: Harcourt Brace and Company.

*Rural Prosperity Task Force Report* (2000) (http://ruraltaskforce.state.nc.us/).

Sample, H. A. (1998), "Undercounted, Overlooked," *The Raleigh News and Observer*, May 24.

"Saving Our Babies," (2000), Editorial, *Charlotte Observer*, August 14.

Schmidt, S. K. and D. Gerlach (2001). *Working Hard Is Not Enough.* Raleigh NC: North Carolina Justice and Community Development Center and NC Equity.

Schoenbaum, T. J. (1992). *Islands, Capes, and Sounds: The North Carolina Coast.* Winston-Salem: John F. Blair, Publisher.

Scholz, J. K. and K. Levine (2000), "The Evolution of Income Support Policy in Recent Decades," *Focus* (University of Wisconsin-Madison, Institute for Research on Poverty), 21, 2, 9-15.

*Securing the Future: Rural Development Strategies for the 1990s* (1991) Raleigh NC: The North Carolina Rural Economic Development Center.

Selby, E. F. (1999), "The Transformation of Labor Geographies in the Crab Processing Industry of Eastern North Carolina," The North Carolina Geographer, 7, 47-55.

Sharer, J. (1999), "Hispanic/Latino Health in North Carolina: Failure to Communicate?" *North Carolina Insight*, 18, 2-3, 2-13.

Shiffer, J. E. (1996), "Lazy River" *Raleigh News and Observer*, June 30.

Shiffer, J. E. (1997), "Welfare's Stubborn Resistance," *The Raleigh News and Observer*, May 27.

Shiffer, J. E. (1998), "The River Chronicles," *The Raleigh News and Observer*, August 9, 12, 19, 22, 26, 30.

Shiffer, J. E. (1998), "Chipping Away at N.C.'s Forests," *The Raleigh News and Observer*, November 27.

Shiffer, J. E. (2000), "State Agency Puts Cap on Eastern Well Water," *The Raleigh News and Observer*, December 15.

Shuford, Harley 'Buck' Jr., President, Century Furniture Company, Hickory, and President of the Furniture Manufacturers Association of America, High Point (personal interview, March, 1995).

Shumway, J. M. and R. D. Jackson (1995), "Native American Population Patterns," *Geographical Review*, 85:2, 185-201.

Silberman, T. (2000), "In Search of Certified Teachers," *The Raleigh News and Observer*, August 13.

Silberman, T. and J. C. Bradbury (1997), "Year-Round Schools: North Carolina School Systems Test the Waters," *North Carolina Insight*, 17, 1, 2-29.

Simmons, T. (1999), "Lower Expectations Limit Blacks' Potential," *The Raleigh News and Observer*, November 22.

Simmons, T. (2000), "Mission Accomplished: Historically Black Colleges and Universities," *The Raleigh News and Observer*, February 27.

Simmons, T. and S. Ebbs (2001), "Separate and Unequal Again," *The Raleigh News and Observer*, February 18.

Simpson, B. and A. C. Simpson (1997). *Into the Sound Country*. Chapel Hill: The University of North Carolina Press.

Simpson. B. (1990). *The Great Dismal: A Carolina's Swamp Memoir*. Chapel Hill: The University of North Carolina Press.

Smith, D. (2000), "Research Park Tops All Hopes," *Charlotte Observer*, July 30.

Smith, P. M. and C. D. West (1994), "The Globalization of Furniture Industries/ Markets," *Journal of Global Marketing*, 7, 3, 103-131.

Smith, S. (1996), "Carolina Beach," *The State*, 63, 9, 10.

Snyder, B. (1973), "Edubygodcation," *Antipode*, 5, 1, 2-5.

*Southern Appalachian Man and the Biosphere* (1996). The Southern Appalachian Assessment Reports, vol. 1-5. Atlanta GA: U. S. Department of Agriculture, Forest Service, Southern Region.

*South's Fourth Forest: Alternatives for the Future* (1988). Washington DC: United States Department of Agriculture, Forest Resource Report No. 24.

Spaid, E. L. (1991), "Fighting the Development Tide," *The Christian Science Monitor*, February 27.

Speizer, I. (1996), "The New Work Forces," *The Raleigh News and Observer*, July 21.

Speizer, I. (2000), "Hamlet Fire's Ultimate Scar," *The Raleigh News and Observer*, February 15.

Stack, C. (1996). *Call to Home: African-Americans Reclaim the Rural South*. New York: Basic Books.

Stackhouse, S. (1994), "Business and Academia: The R&D Connection," *Area Development*, 29, 5, 38-40.

Stancil, J. (1996), "Experts Say U. S. Must Discuss How 'Safety Net' is Rewoven," *The Raleigh News and Observer*, September 29.

Stancil, N. (1999), "Living in the Nuclear Shadow," *Charlotte Observer*, October 10-12.

Stancil, N. (1997), "Carolinas Flavor Moves Overseas," *Charlotte Observer*, October 19.

Stanley, D. W. (1992). *Historical Trends: Water Quality and Fisheries, Albemarle-Pamlico Sounds*. Greenville NC: East Carolina University, Institute for Coastal and Marine Resources.

Starr, G. E. (1994). *The Lumbee Indians: An Annotated Bibliography, With Chronology and Index*. Jefferson NC: McFarland & Co.

State Center for Health Statistics (1996). *North Carolina Vital Statistics*, Volume I-1995. Raleigh: N.C. Department of Environment, Health and Natural Resources.

*State of the South, The* (2000). Chapel Hill NC: MDC, Inc.

Steel, J. (1991). *Albemarle-Pamlico Estuarine System: Technical Analysis of Status and Trends*. Raleigh: North Carolina Department of Environment, Health and Natural Resources.

Stick, D. (ed.) (1998). *An Outer Banks Reader*. Chapel Hill: The University of North Carolina Press.

Stillwell, H. D. and E. P. Leahy (1970). *Navigable Waterways of North Carolina*. Greenville: East Carolina University, Regional Development Institute.

Stonich, S. C. (1998), "Information Technologies, Advocacy, and Development: Resistance and Backlash to Industrial Shrimp Farming," *Cartography and Geographic Information Systems*, 25:2, 113-122.

Stradling, R. (2001), "Farmers Unite to Conserve Land," *Raleigh News and Observer*, January.

Stradling, R. (2001), "Smart-Growth Ideas Abound," *Raleigh News and Observer*, January 20.

Stradling, R. (2000), "Polluted-Properties Law Fails to Fulfill High Expectations," *Raleigh News and Observer*, March 12.

Strahler, A. H., Strahler A. N. (1987) *Modern Physical Geography* (3rd ed.) Wiley and Sons.

Strahler, A. H., Strahler A. N. (1998) *Introducing Physical Geography* (2nd ed.) Wiley and Sons.

Storpe, M. (2001), "N.C. Ranks 5th in U.S. in Prescription Use," *Charlotte Observer*, June 20.

Stuart, B. (1979). *Making North Carolina Prosper: A Critique of Balanced Growth and Regional Planning*. Raleigh: North Carolina Center for Public Policy Research, Inc.

Stuckey, Jasper L. (1965) *North Carolina, It's Geology and Mineral Resources*. Raleigh: N.C. Department of Conservation and Development.

*Things That Matter: Guiding Principles for Strengthening the System of Funding North Carolina's Public Schools* (1999). Raleigh NC: Public School Forum of North Carolina.

Thompkins, D. A. (1889) *Cotton Mill: Commercial Features*. Charlotte: Observer Printing House.

*Wachovia North Carolina World Index*, 1994.

Towle, L. H. (1994), "Doing Business High on the Hog," *North Carolina*, 52:7, 48-58.

Trenberth, K. E. (1991), "General characteristics of El Niño-Southern Oscillation," in M. H. Glantz, R. W. Katz, and N. Nicholls (eds.) *Teleconnections Linking Worldwide Climate Anomalies: Scientific Basis and Societal Impact*. Cambridge, United Kingdom: Press Syndicate, 13-42.

Trevor, G. and J. Morrill (1993), "The Redistricting Game," *Charlotte Observer*, July 18.

Turnage, S. (1995), "Anything But Dismal," *The State*, 63, 5, 24-28.

Tursi, F. (2000), "Unfit to Breathe," *Winston-Salem Journal*, February 6.

Tuttle, S. (2000), "DENR's Ozone Report Spells Trouble for State's Urban Counties," *North Carolina*, 58, 8, 31.

Tuttle, S. (1995), "Smiling Through the Pain," *North Carolina Business*, August, 14-18.

Tuttle, S. (1994), "Regionalism is the Way," *North Carolina Business*, June, 4.

Ukes, F. M. (1995), "Lean and Mean: US Meat-Packing in an Era of Agro-Industrial Restructuring," *Environment and Planning D: Society and Space*, 13, 683-705.

U. S. Bureau of the Census (1980). *Census of Population and Housing: North Carolina*. Washington DC: U.S. Government Printing Office.

U. S. Bureau of the Census (1990). *Census of Population and Housing: North Carolina*. Washington DC: U.S. Government Printing Office.

U.S. Department of Agriculture (1969). *A Forest Atlas of the South*. Asheville: U.S. Forest Service, Southeastern Forest Experiment Station.

U.S. Department of Commerce (1984). *Climatological Data Annual Summary, North Carolina*. Asheville, N.C.: National Climatic Data Center.

Van Hoppen, I. W. and J. J. Van Hoppen (1973). Western North Carolina Since the Civil War. Boone, N. C.: Appalachian Consortium Press.

Venters, V. (1995), "From Worthless to Wonderful," *Wildlife in North Carolina*, 59, 6, 4-21.

Waggoner, M. (2000), "Families Hold Several Jobs, Still Can't Make It," *Charlotte Observer*, May 6.

Waggoner, M. (2001), "Out With Outhouses Is Easier Said Than Done, Agencies Find," *Charlotte Observer*, August 27.

Wagner, J. (1997), "Clock Starts Ticking Today for Many of State's Welfare Families," *The Raleigh News and Observer*, July 1.

Wagner, J. and J. E. Shiffer (1997), "Welfare Reform Affects Us All," *The Raleigh News and Observer*, March 16.

Warf, B. and J. Grimes (1997), "Southern Services in the Late Twentieth Century," *Southeastern Geographer*, 37, 2, 251-267.

Warrick, J. and P. Stith (1995),"Corporate Takeovers," *News and Observer*, Raleigh, February 21.

*Watauga Democrat* (1960), "Watauga Digging Out Of Mountainous Snowfall: Crews Work Round Clock to Open Roads," March 10.

Watson, B. (1993), "New Respect for Nor'easters," *Weatherwise*, 6, 18-23.

Weber, A. L. (1981), "City Space: Environmental Psychological Perspectives on Urban Revitalization," in W. J. Wicker (ed.) *Urban Growth and Urban Life*. Chapel Hill NC: The University of North Carolina Press, 134-155.

Weeks, L. (1995), "Shielded Woodpeckers Add Extra Challenge for Military," Fayetteville Observer-Times, April 9.

Whisnant, R. (1999), "Brownfields in a Green State," *Popular Government*, Winter.

Whitacre, D. (2001), "Backers Push Fast Trains as Boon for Southeast," *Charlotte Observer*, March 20.

White, G. F. et al (1976). *Natural Hazard Management in Coastal Areas*. Washington: NOAA, Office of Coastal Management.

Whitfield, P. (1993), "Turkey Time in Raeford," *The State*, September, 30-32.

Whitman, M. R. (1996), "The Right to Education and the Financing of Equal Educational Opportunities in North Carolina's Public Schools," in M. R. Whitman and R. Coble (eds.) *North Carolina FOCUS: An Anthology on State Government, Politics, and Policy*. Raleigh NC: North Carolina Center for Public Policy Research, 121-141.

Whitmore, T. (2000), "Area Without a Name: Will Charlotte Do?" *Charlotte Observer*, August 27.

Whittington, D. (1993), "The Selling of an Industry," *North Carolina Business*, November, 112-16.

Whittington, D. (1995), "Big Wheels," *North Carolina*, 53, 11, 18-25.

Wildman, D. (2001), "College Faculty Leaving Because Salaries Too Low," *Charlotte Observer*, August 7.

Williams, A. Y. and A. Veverka (2001), "First Union to Buy Rival; Its New Name: Wachovia," *The Charlotte Observer*, April 17.

Williams, B. (1997), "Bootleg Cigarettes Linked to N.C." *The News and Observer*, Raleigh, June 1.

Williams, T. (1996). What Good is a Wetland? *Audubon*, November-December, pp 43-53.

Wilson, T. (2000a), "Infant Death Rate Stumps State," *Charlotte Observer*, June 4.

Wilson, T. (2000b), "Rest Homes Resisting New Rules," Charlotte Observer, March 28.

Wilson, T. (2000c), "State Funding Key to Keeping Health Plan," *Charlotte Observer*, December 21.

Winsberg, M. (1997), "The Great Southern Agricultural Transformation and Its Social Consequences," *Southeastern Geographer*, 37:2, 193-213.

Winberry, J. J. (1996), "Kudzu: The Vine That Almost Ate the South," in Bennett, D. G. (ed.) *Snapshots of the Carolinas*. Washington DC: Association of American Geographers, 99-102.

Winsor, R., and S. Mann (2001). *Vacation Homes and Gentrification*. Boone NC: Appalachian State University, Department of Geography and Planning. Unpublished Manuscript.

*Winston-Salem Journal.* (1960), "Northwest Gets Snow for Third Wednesday; Mountains Hardest Hit," March 17.

Wrinn, J. (1999), "Saving the Farm: Easement Shields Iredell Plantation," *Charlotte Observer*, March 2.

Woodbury, P. (1999), "The Moving of Hatteras," *Our State*, 66, 12, 40-41.

*World Almanac and Book of Facts 2000* (1999). Mahwah NJ: Premedia Reference, Inc.

Wright, G. L. (2001), "As Prison Population Snowballs, N. C. Debates a Building Program," *Charlotte Observer*, July 7.

Wright, G. L., E. Frazier, and T. Mellnik (2001), "Blacks Key to Rising N. C. Prison Population," *Charlotte Observer*, July 15.

Yarger, L. (1998), "Slippery Standards," *The Independent Weekly*, March 18-24.

Yeager, N. and J. Betts (1996), "Health Care Cost Containment: Does Anything Work," in M. R. Whitman and R. Coble (eds.) *North Carolina FOCUS: An Anthology on State Government, Politics, and Policy.* Raleigh NC: North Carolina Center for Public Policy Research, 591-600.

Young, W. (1995), "Ostrich Farmers Seek Rowan Land," *Salisbury Post*, September 26.

Zaldivar, R. A. (1998), "Nursing Homes' Woes Targeted," *Charlotte Observer*, July 22.